WORSHIP AND THEOLOGY
IN ENGLAND

WORSHIP AND THEOLOGY IN ENGLAND

WORSHIP AND THEOLOGY IN ENGLAND

I. *From Cranmer to Hooker,*
1534–1603

II. *From Andrewes to Baxter and Fox,*
1603–1690

HORTON DAVIES

WILLIAM B. EERDMANS PUBLISHING COMPANY
GRAND RAPIDS, MICHIGAN / CAMBRIDGE, U.K.

WORSHIP AND THEOLOGY IN ENGLAND
First published in 5 volumes by Princeton University Press:
I. *From Cranmer to Hooker, 1534–1603* (1970)
II. *From Andrewes to Baxter and Fox, 1603–1690* (1975)
III. *From Watts and Wesley to Maurice, 1690–1850* (1961)
IV. *From Newman to Martineau, 1850–1900* (1962)
V. *The Ecumenical Century, 1900–1965* (1965)

VI. *Crisis and Creativity, 1965–Present*
published 1996 by Wm. B. Eerdmans Publishing Co.

From Cranmer to Hooker, 1534–1603
© 1970 Princeton University Press
From Andrewes to Baxter and Fox, 1603–1690
© 1975 Princeton University Press

Combined edition published 1996 by
Wm. B. Eerdmans Publishing Co.
255 Jefferson Ave. S.E., Grand Rapids, Michigan 49503 /
P.O. Box 163, Cambridge CB3 9PU U.K.
All rights reserved

Printed in the United States of America

02 01 00 99 98 97 96   7 6 5 4 3 2 1

Library of Congress Cataloging-in-Publication Data
Davies, Horton.
Worship and theology in England / Horton Davies.
p.   cm.
Includes bibliographical references and index.
Contents: v. 1, [pt. 1.] From Cranmer to Hooker, 1534-1603;
[pt. 2.] From Andrewes to Baxter and Fox, 1603-1690 —
v. 2, [pt. 1.] From Watts and Wesley to Maurice, 1690-1850;
[pt. 2.] From Newman to Martineau, 1850-1900 —
v. 3, [pt. 1.] The ecumenical century, 1900-1965;
[pt. 2.] Crisis and creativity, 1965-present.
ISBN 0-8028-0891-3 (v. 1: pbk.: alk. paper). —
ISBN 0-8028-0892-1 (v. 2: pbk.: alk. paper). —
ISBN 0-8028-0893-X (v. 3: pbk.: alk. paper)
1. England — Church history — Modern period, 1485-
2. Public worship — History. 3. Theology — England — History.
4. Theology, Doctrinal — History — England. I. Title.
BR755.D35   1996
274.2 — dc20   95-4514
                                        CIP

OUTLINE

VOLUME I
FROM CRANMER TO HOOKER

PART ONE: HISTORICAL AND THEOLOGICAL

PART TWO: THE LITURGICAL ALTERNATIVES

PART THREE: LITURGICAL ARTS AND AIDS

VOLUME II
FROM ANDREWES TO BAXTER AND FOX

PART ONE: THE CONTEXT OF WORSHIP

WORSHIP
AND THEOLOGY
IN ENGLAND

I. *From Cranmer to Hooker,*
1534–1603

CONTENTS

ix

CONTENTS

PART TWO: THE LITURGICAL ALTERNATIVES

CONTENTS

PART THREE: LITURGICAL ARTS AND AIDS

ACKNOWLEDGMENTS

A scholar's literary indebtedness is properly acknowledged in the Bibliography. The other debts that he has incurred should not be recorded so impersonally. It is a great pleasure to thank Dr. James Thorpe, the Director, and the Trustees of the Huntington Library and Museum for the award of a grant-in-aid which enabled me to spend the spring of 1968 in the most congenial setting of San Marino, California. I am also grateful to Mrs. Noelle Jackson of the same city for the care with which she typed my manuscript. It is also my privilege to thank the members of the Princeton University Research Committee on the Humanities and Social Sciences for two summer travel grants that made it possible for me to research in the British Museum and the Bodleian Library.

It is with pride that I thank my son, Hugh Marlais Davies of the class of 1970 at Princeton University, for his help in drawing up the Bibliography and the three Indices, and for the understanding of art and architecture that went into chapter X of this volume. I cannot begin to thank my wife, Brenda, for all her concern and encouragement.

H. D.
Christmas, 1969

INTRODUCTION

THE AIM of this series of five volumes, *Worship and Theology in England*, is to give an account of two aspects of the Christian life, worship and the theology that undergirds it, from the Reformation to the present. Worship, however, is understood in no narrow or rubrical sense, but as the corporate offering of thought, emotion, and decision-making as a response of the Christian churches to the divine saga of Christ and His followers throughout history. This series, then, is a study of the art of Christian adoration as expressed through the ritual and ceremonial of the major Christian denominations in England in the past 400 years. It is an adoration expressed in prayers and preaching, in sermons as in sacraments, in religious architecture and sacred music, in devotion and in duty. I have concentrated particularly on three traditions: the oldest, the Roman Catholic; the new Anglican; and the newest, the Puritan, the two latter originating in the sixteenth century.

This volume bears the subtitle *From Cranmer to Hooker, 1534-1603*, thereby indicating that the lion's share of the interest is devoted to the origin and early development of worship of the Church of England, which remarkably combines the characters of Catholic and Protestant worship. The first name in the subtitle is that of the virtual founder of the Church of England, Thomas Cranmer, the first non-Catholic Archbishop of Canterbury. He is—like Calvin—a scholar who was reluctantly pulled into the maelstrom of a religio-political revolution. Though not so great a theologian, his liturgical work, the Book of Common Prayer, has endured longer and become the chief channel of the doctrine and devotion of the Anglican Communion for four centuries. The second name in the title is that of Richard Hooker, notable defender of the Church of England against the attacks of the Puritans, as his mentor, Bishop Jewel, had been of the same church against the attacks of the Roman Catholic controversialists. Hooker gloried in a church freed of the superstition of Rome and the scrupulosity and intensity of Geneva, affirming that Anglicanism's first loyalty was to Scripture, its second to the pure traditions of the primitive and undivided church, and its third to reason. The opening date of this volume is that of the breaking away of the English church from the international Roman Catholic church affirming allegiance to the Pope, into an autonomous national religious community. The closing date, three years after the death of Richard Hooker, is that of Queen Elizabeth's death, and is intended to recall that she, the "Supreme Governor" of the Church of England had been the stabilizer of both church and nation during her long rule. Without her there could have been no "Elizabethan Settlement."

The organisation of this volume reflects in the first part, which is concerned with the history and theology of the period, the impassioned partisanship of the period. This was a time when a man gave no quarter in upholding his particular form of Christian allegiance, unless, of course, he tamely submitted to the principle of *cuius regio eius religio* and adopted the religious tenets of his prince. But with the rapid shifts of religion dependent on each successive change of sovereign in England, not only a time-serving parson but even a moderately cautious minister had to become a veritable Vicar of Bray. In Tudor England conscience could cost a man his consciousness.

Thus the first three chapters demonstrate that it was a continuing struggle to affirm Anglican doctrine against the contentions of the Catholics on the right and those of the Puritans on the left.

Chapter I shows the struggle between the Catholic theologians who affirmed the adamantine strength of a tradition of faith that was a thousand years old in England against a puny upstart babe, while they accused the *nouveaux pauvres* Anglicans of heresy in doctrine and schism in organization. On the other side, the Anglican theologians, under the leadership of Bishop John Jewel of Salisbury, retorted that it was not Rome but Canterbury which had refused to depart from the norms of the Bible and of the Primitive church; hence Catholics were the horrid innovators.

Chapter II reviews the various facets of the Puritan argument that the Church of England was a miserable compromise, "a leaden mean," a mere halfway house from Rome, in retaining so many vestiges of an idolatrous church in its ritual and ceremonial, as well as in its discipline and polity, and in demanding that Canterbury become as Protestant in its devotions as it was in its doctrine. The Puritan apologetic is traced from the Vestiarian to the Admonitions Controversies, with its unwearying demand for the purgation of impure practices.

Chapter III, on the Eucharistic Controversy closes Part One. I attempt to show that the apparent triviality of the acrimonious discussion of the mode of Christ's presence in the sacrament of Holy Communion did in fact lead to a significant watershed of opinion, not only between Catholic and Protestant, but among Protestants. One is indeed tempted to agree with the position of A. L. Rowse, that "No one who does not know the literature of the time would believe the whole libraries written for and against Transubstantiation, for and against the presence of Christ in the sacrament of the Eucharist, the precise nature of the presence, whether a sacrifice, or merely commemorative, or not."[1] Yet however much one may lament the bitterness of the disputants, he cannot dismiss it as a superficial and unremunerative waste of intellectual energy. In the nature of things it makes a vast difference to one's faith and practice whether he believes Transubstantiation to be the explanation of an amazing miracle or the crassest of crude superstitions masked by scholasticism. It will also have many practical consequences, including the relative strengths of faith and reason, the importance of Communion compared with the Sermon, and the relative significance of the priestly compared with the prophetic role of the ministry. Nor should it be forgotten, as Luther's *Table Talk* so often reminds us, that Luther believed that the Gospel he had rediscovered had overthrown the Papacy, Monasticism, and the Mass in the Reformation.[2] It is only the humanist or the sceptic who dismisses the Eucharistic Controversy in the sixteenth century as a semantic squabble, much as Gibbon derided the debate in the Council of Nicea as an argument over a diphthong! We are concerned in this chapter to show that philosophical differences underlay eucharistic theories, that there were four intelligible theories of the presence, and that these theories led to differences of spiritual formation and outlook.

Part Two describes, from the original documents and wherever possible in the original spelling, the four alternative types of Christian worship available in Tudor England, under the heading "Liturgical Alternatives."

In Chapter iv I review Roman Catholic worship from two perspectives. The first considers the weaknesses of Catholic worship at the end of the Middle Ages and of attempts made to rectify and standardise it during the sessions of the Council of Trent, and rescues from undeserved oblivion the contribution made by the Theatine Bishop of Asaph, Thomas Goldwell. The second perspective gives a view of the desperate difficulties of the Recusants who

---

1 *The England of Elizabeth*, p. 434.
2 Luther, *Works, Table Talk*, ed. and tr. Theodore G. Tappert, p. 134.

after the Bull of 1570 were forced to choose between Catholicism and patriotism and between celebrating clandestine masses in remote country houses in England in ever present fear of the agents of the king, or go into exile. There are fascinating glimpses of the stratagems of a spiritual resistance movement.

Chapters v and vi review the development, respectively, of Anglican worship and preaching, although Anglican sacramental thought and practice receives attention in Chapter iii. Chapter iv concentrates on the novelty and the character of the successive revisions of the English Book of Common Prayer, especially those in 1549 and 1552. Considerable attention is devoted to the Prayer Book of 1549 to determine whether its theology is crypto-Catholic, Lutheran, Calvinist, or Zwinglian in tinge; an assessment is made of the strengths of the worship of the "bridge-Church," which has had so profound an impact on the worship of English-speaking countries and even beyond the Anglican Communion. This vernacular, participatory, responsive, Biblical, and sacramental liturgy, has also given a significant place to the proclamation of the oracles of God in preaching. This is assayed in Chapter vi, which deals chiefly with a comparison of the pulpit contributions of the racy, humorous, and popular Latimer with those of the meditative and oratorical Hooker.

Chapters vii and viii are the complement of the Anglican chapters. They are devoted, respectively, to the worship and preaching of the Puritans. In Chapter vii I discuss the Puritan critique of the Book of Common Prayer, the long controversy over whether the most sincere and Spirit-led prayer uses or rejects prayer-books, and considers the major Puritan ordinances of worship. Chapter viii elucidates the distinctive Puritan development of the sermon according to the structure of doctrine, reason, and use, and discusses the characteristic Puritan concern for developing a psychology of spirituality.

Chapter ix presents the most radical, iconoclastic, and charismatic alternative of worship, that of the various groups of Separatists, whether Barrowist, Brownist, or Anabaptist, the forebears of the later Free church tradition in worship in England.

Chapters iv-ix attempt to provide a full and objective descriptive and evaluative account of four of the major liturgical options open to Englishmen in the sixteenth century.

Chapters x-xii form Part Three, "Liturgical Arts and Aides." Chapter x concentrates on religious architecture and art, showing the Anglican preference for Gothic as illustrating its intention to give a sense of continuity from the old Catholic to the new Anglican Church in England, while demonstrating significant adaptations of its inherited fanes for a worship that used the eye less and the ear more than Catholic worship had, which was yet more intellectual and more congregational in character. Nonetheless it seems and is symbolically more bare and austere than Catholic worship. An important question propounded in this and the following chapter is: how far has Anglican church art moved in a secular direction? The elaboration of the tombs of the small gentry in the parish churches as status symbols and the reduced role of the choirs in Anglican parish churches might suggest that secularism had moved far. But then, as Chapter XI on religious music reminds us, this was the great age of English composers, when Tallis and Byrd were at their zenith, and also when metrical psalmody ran through the masses like a musical measles, so contagious was its popularity.

Chapter XII is a kind of summary and climax of this book. It takes the shape of a comparative analysis of the forms of spirituality approved and used by Catholicism, Anglicanism, and Puritan-Protestantism. It aims to show how the different theological emphases and modes of the formation of the spiritual life led to varied types of spirituality which, however much they had in common, were distinctive and authentic. I argue that the Catholic type of spirituality was essentially a spirituality for the "religious," the professionals, whereas Protestant spirituality was characteristically that of the laity in their "callings" in the secular world. It is also argued that Catholic spirituality concentrates on imitating the imitators of God—the saints—while Protestant spirituality concentrated less on the interior reproduction of the historic "Christ-event" in the individual than on the responsive love of neighbour for Christ's sake. In a word, it is the devotional as ethical. Unquestionably each type of spirituality, however different its rationale (and sixteenth-century Anglicanism is closer to Protestant than to Catholic piety, although seventeenth-century Anglican piety in Lancelot Andrewes, Laud, and Cosin approximates Catholicism), produces saints remarkably alike, whether we think of Sir Thomas More or of a Protestant martyr like John Bradford, both of whom left behind them noble prayers on their journey to God.

PART ONE

HISTORICAL AND THEOLOGICAL

CHAPTER I

CATHOLICS AND PROTESTANTS
IN CONTROVERSY (1534-1568)

IN THE COURSE of the sixteenth-century Christians in England experienced the confusion of five different changes of the established religion, all (to be sure) versions of the Christian faith and life, but each dissimilar and each demanding an absolute obedience to the royal change of faith.[1] In the early years of Henry VIII's reign Henry was an orthodox Catholic, proudly rejoicing in the title of *Fidei Defensor* bestowed on him by a grateful Pope for his defense of the seven Catholic sacraments[2] against Luther's iconoclastic reduction of them to three (subsequently to two). England at the time was as Catholic as France or Spain.

Once Henry found the Pope unwilling to declare his marriage with Catherine of Aragon null and void so that he might produce a male heir from another wife, and declared himself to be "Supreme Head" of the Church in England, England's faith changed. This non-Papal and nationalistic Catholicism veered from a humanistic and liberal (even Erasmian) form to the rigid conservative mode of the religion of "The Six Articles." From the Roman Catholic standpoint England was in schism. But apart from the denial of the Papal supremacy there was no trace of heresy, and the doctrine and ceremonies of England were much nearer to Catholicism than to the detested Lutheranism.

The third change came with the accession of the adolescent Edward VI who was surrounded by Protestant protectors, Somerset and then Northumberland. The religious thrust of the reign was increasingly Protestant. This can be seen in the more radical character of the 1552 Book of Common Prayer compared with the first version of 1549, in the profusion of Scripture translations, in the virtualist or memorialist doctrines of the Holy Communion current in this period, in the official encouragement of the proclamation of Protestant doctrine from the pulpits and in the Articles, and

---

[1] Sir Maurice Powicke writes: "The one definite thing which can be said about the Reformation in England is that it was an act of State." *The Reformation in England*, p. 1.

[2] *Assertio Septem Sacramentorum Adversus Martin. Lutherum.* Henry was probably assisted by Fisher, More, and Lee. Cf. E. G. Rupp, *Studies in the Making of the English Protestant Tradition*, p. 90.

in the permissions for ministers to marry. Never had England been more Protestant, whether in ceremonies, its admiration and delight in preaching, or its Communion doctrine. Certainly no one had ever scrupled the pomp and circumstance of episcopal dress more than John Hooper, bishop-designate of Gloucester who was sent to prison to cool off because he protested that he would not make his oath of allegiance in episcopal vestments. No greater exemplar of Protestant preaching on the bench of bishops than Latimer could be found, and it was Nicholas Ridley, Bishop of London, who insisted that in his diocese all altars had to be replaced with tables, because for him the Communion was the commemoration of a sacrifice, not its re-presentation in the Mass.

The fourth "about turn" came with the accession of Catherine of Aragon's daughter, the sanguinary Mary, who tried to turn the clock back to pre-Reformation times with the full restoration of orthodox Papal Catholicism.

The fifth and most enduring change came with the accession of Elizabeth in 1558, and brought an attempt to make the Church of England as comprehensive as possible. This form of Protestantism, combined Calvinistic doctrine with a modified Catholicism in worship and in church order. It was quite deliberately a *via media*, hoping to gain the allegiance of Englishmen, neither stiffly Papistical nor incorrigibly Puritan.

These five changes in the established religion of England offered, on one hand, either a Catholicism of the conservative (Marian) or liberal (Henrician) kind, or, on the other, Protestantism of the conservative (Elizabethan) or liberal (Edwardian) kind.

In the sixteenth century there were two major religious debates and controversies. The first, to which this chapter is devoted, was between the Catholics and the Protestants. The second, to which the energies of men in Elizabeth's reign were devoted, was between Anglicans and Puritans. Later still, there will be brief consideration of the debate between the patient Puritans and the impatient Puritans (or Separatists). In the present chapter the concern is exclusively with the grand debate between the English Catholics and Protestants as they developed their apologetic and their distinctive theologies, searching desperately for decisive authorities in doctrine and ethics. It was these theologies in controversy that would ultimately be the determinants of their differing forms of worship, which, in turn, through capturing the affections and

4

aspirations of the people would determine their religious ideals and their moral actions.

There is one great obstacle to defining the differences between Catholic and Protestant theologies in England, as distinguished from attempting the same task on the European Continent. It is that the earliest shapers of English Protestantism were surreptitious proclaimers of the truths they affirmed in closed gatherings of friends and supporters or through the medium of illicit books; for, with the exception of Edward VI, the Tudor sovereigns were most reluctant Protestants. Indeed, it has been wittily said that in England the most distinctively Protestant doctrine was that of the divine right of kings! Certainly there were no great theological reformers in England of the stature of Luther or Calvin or Zwingli, even though in Edward's time Bucer ornamented the University of Cambridge and Peter Martyr Vermigli the University of Oxford; but both were imports, while both Luther and Zwingli were German and Swiss, respectively. Protestantism, except for the brief reign of Edward VI, was a *religio illicita* in England until 1558, as Christianity was for so many centuries in the Roman empire. It has had its translators of the Bible, notably Tyndale and Coverdale, and its martyrs for the faith to whom Foxe's *Book of Martyrs* bore valiant testimony for many generations. But its theologians were rather apologists for the religion of an establishment than the constructors of theological systems, which, like Luther's, were hammered out through courageous experience, or like Calvin's, through a reconstruction of the testimonies of the Bible with an admirably clear and cogent architectonic. John Jewel was a good and Hooker an excellent apologist, but neither was an original or creative theologian, though I will make considerable use of the writings of each. Erastianism discourages originality, particularly so ferocious and dangerous a form of it as Henry's.[3]

1. *Pope or Prince:*
Which Was to be the Church's earthly ruler?

The very first issue to be raised was a largely political and practical one: was the Pope, as faithful Catholics maintained, or the Christian prince, as the Protestants affirmed, to be the head of the church? If the church was thought of as an international

[3] See A. G. Dickens, *The English Reformation*, p. 184: "If this curious situation tended to prohibit constructive thought, it did not prevent the promulgation of a series of commonsense, practical reforms."

body, transcending the continents and the centuries, then unquestionably in the medieval West the Pope was the rightful head. If there was, with growing nationalism, a desire to conceive of national churches in the plural, then ancient precedents might be found in the Israelite people of God ruled by their godly sovereigns or in the autocephalous and national orthodox churches of the East. The separation of the English church from the spiritual dominion of the Papacy was essentially a political act of the sovereign; there was hardly a less religiously motivated Reformation than Henry VIII's English one, even if the German Reformation was also partly motivated by politics as Luther's shrewd tract, *An den christlichen Adel deutscher Nation* of 1520, demonstrates.

Luther, with insight, had seen in this "Appeal to the Christian Nobility of the German Nation" that the Papal tyranny was buttressed by three Papal claims: that spiritual power was superior to temporal power; that the Pope alone could interpret Scripture; and that he alone had the right to convene a general council of the church. These were the three walls that effectively prevented reformation of the Church of God. The first claim negated the right of the Christian magistracy to effect reformation either in his country or by means of calling a general council, as Constantine had done in convening the great Christological Council of Nicaea. The second prevented any appeal to the Scripture, so that all claims that the church of the present might be renovated by a return to the apostolic and primitive pattern, unless seconded by the Pope himself, were immediately declared to be heresy. Luther might well have preferred to control the rate of the Reformation in Germany through a council of bishops, but so few of them turned to the Reformed faith that the only alternative was to turn to the lay political leaders, the dukes. This appeal Luther made to the magistrates in virtue of the priesthood of all believers. It was the only way to break the tyranny of the Papacy and the clericalism of the Roman Catholic church, even if there was always the possibility that the temporal sovereign might be a worse tyrant than the Pope.

It would be entirely wrong to suggest that the Reformation in England was, as Hilaire Belloc has termed it, the 'English Accident.' For apart from the king's interest in securing his second-generation throne by male issue and his rapacity for the property of the church as was evident in the dissolution of the monasteries, there were two forces moving towards reformation, or at least spiritual renovation, in England. One was the secret brotherhood of Lollards[4] who longed to see the "dominion of grace" overwhelming the legal, institutional, and all too wordly external carapace of the church, of whom, since they were covert companies, we know very little. The other force was the band of Cambridge scholars who gathered from time to time in the White Horse Inn and who must have included Erasmians as well as Lutherans; from them the greatest Protestant episcopal leadership was to come in King Edward's reign. The outright supporters of Reformation were forced, like Tyndale, Coverdale, Joye and Roy, to live on the Continent and to propagate their views in writing, publishing them often on secret presses and having them smuggled into England from about 1520 to 1535.[5] If the Protestants espoused their doctrines in England more openly or more carelessly than that, they were burned at the stake.[6] Unquestionably, however, there were Protestants in England committed to a national Reformation while the king was still a "defender of the faith" of Rome, and for whom his later turning from Rome was not quick or thoroughgoing enough.

Clearly the first task on the Protestant side was to establish the right of the Christian prince to act in the Pope's stead. Tyndale, the great translator, produced *The Obedience of a Christian Man* in 1527. There was in the back of his mind the common Catholic accusation that one recent effect of the preaching of the gospel was the sheer anarchy of the Peasants' Revolt in Germany in 1525. It was therefore a rather stiff dose of political authoritarianism that he prescribed. "The King is in the room of God," he wrote, "and his law is God's law, and nothing but the law of nature and natural equity which God graved in the hearts of men."[7] The King's power was so absolute, according to Tyndale, that governors of nations "are even the gift of God, whether they be good or bad. And whatsoever is done to us by them, that doth God, be it good or bad."[8]

---

[4] A. G. Dickens, *Lollards and Protestants in the Diocese of York, 1509-1558*, pp. 243-46; and J. E. Oxley, *The Reformation in Essex to the death of Mary*, pp. 3-15.

[5] William A. Clebsch, *England's Earliest Protestants*, pp. 10f., writes of 1520-1535 as, "that initial and most difficult time," when "the fountain of faith was a banned Bible, and when the gospel rediscovered by Luther rallied Englishmen to martyrdom."

[6] Rupp, *English Protestant Tradition*, pp. 196f.

[7] *Doctrinal Treatises*, p. 240.

[8] Such a doctrine hardly served the needs of the Protestants under Catholic Queen Mary; Ponet's treatise *Of Politick Power* recognized the possibility of temporal as well as spiritual tyranny and its right to be overthrown. See Winthrop S. Hudson, *John Ponet (1516?-1556), advocate of limited Monarchy*.

In the early days there was hardly time to formulate (even if the king had allowed it) a doctrine of the powers and duties of the Christian prince. There was, instead, an assertion of the king's right to wield ecclesiastical power than any statement of his duty to lead the church toward a spiritual reformation. In the expression of the divine right of the sovereign there was nothing to choose between the "Henricians," whether they were Foxe and Cranmer on one side or Tunstal and Gardiner on the other. Indeed, all would have subscribed to the strong defense of the royal supremacy given in Gardiner's classic, *De Vera Obedientia* (1536). Gardiner saw the king as the head of a Christian nation and inevitably and naturally as the head of the Christian church within that kingdom: "Seinge the churche of Englande consisteth of the same sortes of people at this daye, that are comprised in this worde realme of whom the kinge his [*sic*] called the headde, shall he not being called the headde of the realme of Englande be also the headde of the same men when they are named the churche of Englande. . . . They [*sic*] kinge (saye they [the Catholics]) is the headde of the realme but not of the churche: whereas notwithstonding ye churche of Englāde is nothing elles but ye cōgregatiō of men and women of the clergie and of the laytie in Christe's profession, that is to say, it is justly to be called the churche because it is a communion of Christen people."[9] The finest expression of the interdependence of ruler and people in a Christian commonwealth is to be found in the opening paragraph of the *Homily of Obedience*, prescribed for the Edwardian Church in 1547 and republished in Elizabeth's reign: "Almighty God hath created and appointed all things in heaven and earth and water in a most excellent and perfect order. In heaven he hath appointed distinct and several orders of archangels and angels. In earth he hath assigned kings, princes, and other governors, under them in all good and necessary order . . . every degree of people in their vocation, calling and office . . . [and] hath appointed unto them their duty and order: some are in high degree, some in low, some kings and princes, some inferiors and subjects, priests and laymen, masters and servants, fathers and children, husbands and wives, rich and poor: and every one hath need of other: so that in all things is to be lauded and praised the

---

[9] Sigs. D verso—Dii recto et verso. Bishop Gardiner was a great supporter of the King's spiritual rights in Henry VIII's reign, but when the political tables were turned under Elizabeth, his chaplain, Thomas Harding, was bitterly critical of a temporal prince's usurpation of the spiritual role of Pope or bishop. See *A Confutation of a Booke intituled An Apologie of the Church of England*, pp. 317 recto, 320 recto, 299 verso.

goodly order of God without which no house, no city, no common-wealth can endure or last."[10] From this excerpt it can be seen that the whole interdependence of society was thought to depend on the subordination of the people to the prince, both politically and religiously. Moreover, in a society still predominantly Christian (unlike the secular world of the present day), it could be assumed that the king would act upon Christian motives (or, at least, motives mixed with Christianity) and according to Christian doctrinal, liturgical, and ethical standards. The sovereign was seen as the protector of the social order, a dike against the chaos that would ensue if "degree" and "dependency" were overthrown.

Two complementary concepts controlled the political thinking of the Erastian Henricians; both were due to the Erastian tradition and to the renewed interest in legal studies that had "brought Constantine and Byzantine notions of the powers of Christian princes and the claim of civil law"[11] to their attention. The first concept was that the Christian prince has sacred obligations, since he rules by the providence and under the law of God, with responsibility for God's people. The counterpart of this concept was that the Christian prince has Christian subjects, pledged to honor the authority of God in their prince. Thus a claim of law becomes an interior claim of conscience, because the "Powers that be are ordained of God."[12]

Assuming that there was a general agreement among those who had broken with the Papacy, that a Christian prince was the appropriate instrument to undertake the reformation of the church, there was an equally strong negative conviction that the Popes had so far departed from their evangelical office as not to be in any true sense the successors of Peter. Such was the continuing jeremiad of the Protestant pamphleteers. This contention in the controversy with Rome was effectively if crudely propagated with woodcuts or etchings contrasting the meek Christ riding on a lowly ass into Jerusalem with the proud and pompous Pope donning his triple crown as he was carried in state in the gestatorial chair borne by Italian noblemen.

This view is set forth at length, but in a much more dignified fashion, by John Jewel, Elizabethan bishop of Salisbury and author of *An Apology or Answer in Defence of the Church of England* (1564). Here is Jewel in his most ironical vein, asking:

---

10 Certain Sermons . . . [Homilies], ed. Corrie, p. 104.
11 P. M. Dawley, *John Whitgift and the English Reformation*, p. 18.
12 Rom. 13:1.

9

What one thing (tell me) had Peter ever like unto the Pope, or the Pope like unto Peter? Except peradventure they will say thus: that Peter, when he was at Rome never taught the Gospel, never fed the flock, took away the keys of the kingdom of heaven, hid the treasures of his Lord, sat him down only in his castle in St. John Lateran and pointed out with his finger all the places of purgatory and kinds of punishments, committing some poor souls to be tormented and other some again suddenly releasing thence at his own pleasure, taking money for so doing; or that he gave order to say private Masses in every corner; or that he mumbled up the holy service with a low voice and in an unknown language; or that he hanged up the sacrament in every temple and on every altar and carried the same about before him, whithersoever he went, upon an ambling jennet, with lights and bells; or that, he consecrated with his holy breath oil, wax, wool, bells, chalices, churches, and altars; or that he sold jubilees, graces, liberties, advowsons, preventions, first fruits, palls, the wearing of palls, bulls, indulgences, and pardons; or that he calleth himself by the name of the head of the church, the highest bishop, bishop of bishops, alone most holy; or that by usurping he took upon himself the right and authority over other folk's churches; or that he exempted himself from the power of any civil government; or that he maintained wars, set princes together at variance, or that he, sitting in his chair, with his triple crown, full of labels, with sumptuous and Persian-like gorgeousness, with his royal scepter, with his diadem of gold, and glittering with stones, was carried about, not upon palfrey, but upon the shoulders of noblemen.[13]

Then Jewel argues that the true Petrine succession would be seen if the Pope went from country to country and from house to house preaching the Gospel, if he proved to be "the watchman of the house of Israel," and if he "doth not feed his own self, but the flock." Furthermore, Jewel wanted to see Peter's authority as ministerial, not judicial, and his acts on an equality with those of all other bishops instead of lording it over them. But the onus of the accusation was the departure from the simplicity and spirituality of a preeminent servant of God by one who, amid the panoply and

[13] Jewel, *An Apology of the Church of England*, ed. John E. Booty, pp. 130-31. See also Booty's *John Jewel as Apologist of the Church of England*; and W. M. Southgate, *John Jewel and the Problem of Doctrinal Authority*.

10

sheer worldliness of Renaissance Rome, could call himself *servus servorum Dei* only in the bitterest irony. Rather was he *princeps principorum*, as if he had claimed the very throne of Christ as *rex regum*, who was supposed to be only his vicar.

2. *Scripture as the Primary Category for Doctrinal Authority*

It was settled, then, that the Christian prince, presumably advised by his theologians, was the true instrument for the reformation and disciplining of the national church. But a larger question remained: Which criteria should the reformers use as their patterns for the renovation of the church? Were they to follow Scripture, or tradition, or reason, or the guidance of the Holy Spirit? Were they to follow one or more of these criteria, and which, in case several were to be used, was to have priority? Difficult as the question of criteria was, it would be even more difficult if one questioned these weasel words. Since "Scripture" contained two testaments and could be found in several, often tendentious, translations, and according to some Christians included the Apocrypha as a secondary authority; since there were different levels of authority in Scripture; and further, since theologians might and did use a different controlling concept or congeries of concepts in interpreting Scripture, it was hard to judge what was meant by accepting the primary authority of Scripture. "Tradition" was also a very elastic concept, because there were believed to be unwritten traditions that Christ had passed on secretly to his apostles between his resurrection and ascension, and Western Roman Catholics and Eastern Orthodox, while agreeing substantially on the authority of the Ecumenical Councils, accepted other councils or refused to accept them. The Anglicans appealed to the undivided and primitive church, and specifically to the *traditio quinquesecularis*, that is, to the tradition of the first five centuries of the church. In the eyes of the Roman Catholics, as the Council of Trent formulated the dogma, Scripture and tradition were to have coordinate authority; but for the Anglicans, Scripture had absolute primacy. When it came to the Puritans, Scripture was the almost exclusive criterion, not only of faith but of worship, church government, and ethics; the only meaning they could give to tradition, apart from apostasy, was the pure and primitive tradition of the apostolic church as reflected in the pages of the New Testament. Reason, which played a large part in the Anglican apologetics of Hooker and his successors, was to have little importance for Puritanism.

11

The Puritans were to give an absolute and almost exclusive role to the Scriptures, but there was a subordinate stress on the role of the Holy Spirit as providing the *testimonium internum*, or inner witness, to the truth of Christ. With the Society of Friends the Spirit was to become primary and the Scriptures merely a check on the integrity and authenticity of Christian experience. In moving from the settled Catholic recognition of the coordinate authority of Scripture and tradition, and the placement of ultimate power in the hands of the Pope in disputed issues, Protestants were opening a Pandora's box.

In the early decades of the sixteenth century, however, it was clear that opinion was that only the authority of the word of God in the Holy Scriptures was sufficient for the reform and rebuilding of the church. There was a constant appeal to the word of God as the only standard authoritative enough to purge the corruptions of the church. This had been inherent in the appeal of Erasmus to the newly translated New Testament. It was not until 1535 that Coverdale published the first complete translation of the Scriptures in English, which was published not in England but on the Continent. Moreover, the translation appeared 19 long years after Erasmus had finished work on his translation in England. The adoption of the Bible as the instrument and criterion of the Reformation in England was slow. Even though the Convocation petitioned Henry VIII in 1534 that the entire Bible be translated into English, it was only in 1537 that a revised English translation, known as Matthew's Bible, appeared; a generally approved translation, heavily dependent on Coverdale, though not mentioning his name, appeared in 1539 and, with a preface by Thomas Cranmer, in 1540. The latter was "the Bible with the largest volume in English," which the Injunctions of 1538 had ordered to be set up in every church in England.

Cranmer's typically vivid, clear, and modest preface revealed his deep appreciation for the Bible "in the vulgar tongue." He warned those who would refuse it (presumably the conservative Catholics) and those who would abuse it by disputatiousness (presumably the argumentative, radical Protestants). How new a vernacular translation was in England can be seen by the curiously medieval comparison Cranmer used to indicate the surpassing value of the Bible, for he described it as "the worde of God, the moost preciouse Juell and moost holy relyque that remayneth upon earth."[14] He

[14] Preface to *The Great Bible* (1540), p. 4.

further claimed that "yt is as necessary for the lyfe of mans soule, as for the body to breath."[15] Cranmer was constantly aware that the purpose of studying the Bible was not for men to gain a reputation for learning and become masters of theology, but for God to master them. He therefore concluded that every man who comes to read the Bible should bring with him the fear of God, "and then next a fyrme and stable purpose to refourme his owne selfe," and to be a good example to others by his life, "whych is sure the moost lyvelye and effecteous fourme and maner of teachynge."[16]

It would have been impossible to have attacked the international power and authority of the Roman Catholic church, with its immense prestige and immemorial traditions, unless it was believed that the Scriptures were the very word and expression of the will of God. It should not be forgotten that the Reformation in every land was a Reformation, "according to the pure Word of God" to give its full title as its rationale; the "purity" of the Word of God was always contrasted with the impurity of the traditions of men. Cranmer would not have dared to affirm the doctrines of the reformed faith on his own authority as a scholar. The ultimate authority was his own careful reflection on Scripture, as he indicates in his controversy with Stephen Gardiner on the mode of Christ's presence in the Holy Communion: "I, having exercised myself in the study of Scripture and divinity from my youth (whereof I give most hearty lauds and thanks to God), have learned now to go alone. . . ."[17] Archbishop Cranmer was almost certainly the author of the preface to the first prayer-book of Edward VI (1549), which declared that the lections were so arranged, "that all the whole Bible (or the greatest parte thereof) should be read over once in the year, intendyng thereby, that the Cleargie, and specially suche as were Ministers of the congregacion, should (by often readyng and meditacion of Gods worde) be stirred up to godlines themselfes, and be more able also to exhorte other by wholsome doctrine, and to confute them that were adversaries to the trueth."[18] There was another aim in this order, namely, "that the people (by daily hearyng of holy scripture read in the Churche) should continuallye profite more and more in the

[15] *Ibid.*, p. 5.
[16] *Ibid.*, pp. 6-7.
[17] *Works of Thomas Cranmer*, 2 vols., I, 224.
[18] Cranmer, *The First and Second Prayer Books of Edward VI*, ed. E.C.S. Gibson, p. 3.

knowledge of God, and bee the more inflamed with the love of his true religion."[19]

Bishop Jewel, the first Elizabethan apologist, placed great stress on the primacy of God's Word in Scripture as the basic criterion for doctrine and life. The Scriptures of the Old and New Testaments were for him, "the heavenly voices whereby God hath opened unto us his will"; they alone quieted the otherwise restless heart of man, and they contained all that was necessary for salvation. However, their supreme value for him as an apologist of the Church of England was "that they be the foundations of the prophets and apostles whereon is built the church of God; that they be the very sure and infallible rule whereby may be tried whether the church doth stagger and err and whereunto all ecclesiastical doctrines ought to be called to account; and that against these Scriptures neither law, nor ordinance, nor any custom ought to be heard; no, though Paul himself, nor an angel from heaven, should come and teach the contrary."[20] Jewel had sounded the authentic Protestant note of the absolute primacy of Scripture.

It is only when this is understood that we can sympathise with the vast endeavours in the Protestant fold to train ministers to expound the Scriptures in the original languages of Hebrew and Greek, with the assistance of the learned commentaries both patristic and contemporary, and, above all, the unwearying insistence from Latimer onwards that the soul of man would perish without the bread of the word of God delivered in preaching—for, in Cranmer's words, "in the Scryptures be the fatte pastures of the soule."[21] Even the very sacraments were meaningless unless the people learned what promises God had attached to these signs of the Gospel.[22]

Latimer, the greatest popular preacher of the age, declared, "this office of preaching is the only ordinary way that God hath appointed to save us all thereby."[23] Moreover, his memorable sermon "Of the Plough" was a brilliant application of the Parable of the Sower, with its theme of God's Word as the seed, the congregation the field, and the preacher the ploughman: "He hath first a busy work to bring his parishioners to be a right faith . . . and then to confirm them in the same faith; now casting them down with the law and with threatenings of God for sin; now ridging

19 *Ibid.*, p. 3. 20 Jewel, *Apology*, p. 30.
21 Preface to *The Great Bible*, p. 3. 22 See Tyndale, *Works*, I, pp. 274f.
23 Latimer, *Works*, I, p. 306. The sermon was preached in London on January 18, 1548.

them up again with the Gospel and with the promises of God's favour; now weeding them by telling them their faults and making them forsake sin; now clotting them by breaking their stony hearts and by making them supple-hearted, and making them to have hearts of flesh, that is, soft hearts and apt for doctrine to enter in; now teaching . . . now exhorting . . . so that they have a continual work to do."[24]

Edmund Grindal, Parker's successor as Elizabeth's Archbishop of Canterbury, was planted firmly in the same tradition. He faced the wrath of Elizabeth and subsequent sequestration rather than fulfill her command to prohibit "prophesyings" or gatherings at which local ministers could improve the exposition and application of Scripture by conference. In his defense of the refusal he told the queen that homilies were no substitute for preaching: "The godly preacher is termed in the Gospel *fidelis servus et prudens, qui novit famulitio Domini cibum demensum dare in tempore*, who can apply his speech according to the diversity of the times, places and hearers, which cannot be done in homilies; exhortations, reprehensions, and persuasions are uttered with more affection, to the moving of the hearers, in sermons than in homilies."[25]

In the task of reforming the Church of England it was agreed that it was the task of the Christian prince to undertake the reforming, and that the standard should be according to the Scriptures, the Pure Word of God which alone had sufficient authority, as the expression of the divine will, to destroy the vain traditions of men.

3. The Primitive Church as an Important Secondary Norm

But were all the traditions of the early church during the period when it was most pure and primitive to be jettisoned and abandoned? By no means, was the answer of the Anglican divines, as from Cranmer on there emerged a singularly fine tradition of patristic scholarship, itself fed by the conviction that the Tudor church had much to learn from the first six centuries of Christian history before the establishment of the Roman primacy of the medieval type. There seem to have been two basic reasons for the acceptance of the early church's guidance as an authority second only to Scripture. Since a private man might read his idiosyncrasies into Scripture and use a text as a pretext, there was a need for a rule where the Scripture was obscure or did not speak with unam-

---

[24] *Ibid.*, pp. 59ff.
[25] Edmund Grindal, *Remains*, ed. W. Nicholson, pp. 382f. The letter is dated December 20, 1576.

biguous voice. This very point was at the heart of the Catholic polemic urging the dangerous subjectivity to which the church was prone by the publication of the Scriptures in the vernacular. John Jewel expresses this argument for the Catholics as he reports it. The Catholics had called the Scriptures "a bare letter, uncertain, unprofitable, dumb, killing, and dead"; they added "a similitude not very agreeable, how the Scriptures be like to a nose of wax or a shipman's hose; how they may be fashioned and plied all manner of ways and serve all men's turns."[26] The second ground for seeking the approval of the apostles and fathers of the early church was the desire to return beyond corruption to the first five centuries of Christian history, where the foundation of the primitive church was in the Scriptures, and its explication in the four general councils and the writings of the early Church Fathers.

This linking of Scripture and the primitive church was central to the establishment of religion in England. The chime rang as clearly in the apologists as it did in the official theological formulas and liturgies of the Anglican church. It is reechoed in Jewel's *Apology* at the outset, where he observes what his strategy in controversy will be: "Further, if we do show it plain that God's Holy Gospel, the ancient bishops, and the primitive church do make on our side, and that we have not without just cause left these men [the Roman Catholics], and rather have returned to the apostles and old catholic fathers."[27] When he reached the conclusion, Jewel argued that the Church of England was no innovator, but a renovator, "and we are come, as near as we possibly could, to the church of the apostles and of the old catholic bishops and fathers, which church we know hath hitherto been sound and perfect and, Tertullian termeth it, a pure virgin, spotted as yet with no idolatry nor with any foul or shameful fault; and have directed according to their customs and ordinances not only our doctrine but also the sacraments and the form of common prayer."[28] Similarly the preface to the first Book of Common Prayer appeals to the "auncient fathers" whose order it is attempting to restore; even when Cranmer seems most to be moving away from tradition, as in the publication of the Great Bible in English, he is careful to insist that the Saxon forefathers of the English had their Saxon translations, and his very motives and considerations for reading the vernacular Scriptures are drawn from John Chrysostom and Gregory Nazian-

26 Jewel, *Apology*, p. 77.   27 *Ibid.*, p. 17.
28 *Ibid.*, pp. 120-21.

zus. Not only was there useful guidance to be obtained from the undivided church of the first five or six centuries, but the more attentive to its teaching the Church of England was, the less could it be accused of what was the most original form of original sin for the traditionalists, namely, the sin and scandal of innovation. The study of the Fathers was a proof that her firm intention was *renovation*.

Cranmer, Jewel, and Whitgift exemplify the great patristic erudition of the leaders of the Anglican church in Tudor times.[29] Even so, it was neither a blind nor servile deference to the authority of the Fathers. Latimer, for instance, while respecting the judgment of the Fathers, refused to enslave himself to them: "These doctors, we have great cause to thank God for them, but I would not have them always to be allowed. They have handled many points of our faith very gladly, and we have a great stay in them in many things; we might not well lack them; but yet I would not have men sworn to them, and so addict as to take hand over head whatsoever they say."[30] The vigorous and independent Thomas Becon, Cranmer's chaplain, was of a similar opinion. If the Fathers swerved from the doctrine of Christ, he did not in the least care how venerable, ancient, or saintly they might be. "When Christ saith in the gospel, 'I am the truth,' He said not, 'I am the custom.' "[31] In short, the Anglican theologians were true to the Fathers as long as the latter followed Scripture as their primary authority. Through their patristic scholarship Anglicans claimed to show that what Rome regarded as Anglican heresies were in reality primitive orthodoxies.

4. *Justification by Faith Alone, and its Consequences*

It was clear that the Church of England, in separating from the great and historic Roman Catholic church, would have to articulate its own ecclesiology and provide its own definitions of the scope and authority of the ministry and the nature of the sacraments. These will be considered shortly. But it was in their understanding of soteriology and, in particular, the mode of the appropriation of salvation that Anglicans differed the most from Catholicism. It was the doctrine of Justification by Faith, especially in

---

[29] Cranmer, *Remains*, pp. 77-78; and H. F. Woodhouse, *The Doctrine of the Church in Anglican Theology (1547-1603)*, p. 22.

[30] Latimer, *Sermons*, 2 vols., I, 218.

[31] T. Becon, *Prayers and Other Pieces*, p. 390.

its Lutheran form of *sola fide* (by faith alone) that challenged the entire Catholic system.

This was the primary doctrine the great German Reformer had learned from the Epistles of St. Paul to the Romans and the Galatians, a doctrine that was essential to his rediscovery of the Gospel. The Henrician formularies[32] show a slow change from a combination of justification by faith combined with the predispositions of contrition and charity[33] toward a closer approximation to Luther's doctrine in the fourth part of *The Institution of a Christian Man*.[34] The most unqualified expressions of the doctrine, however, are to be found in those writers who had renewed the experience of Luther, who knew both the imponderable gravity of sin and the extreme costliness of grace, and who were appalled by the "cheap grace"[35] which the Roman Catholic church was then offering through such indulgence hucksters as Tetzel, or through the much more respectable austerities by which it was thought possible to purchase at least part of one's own salvation on the installment plan. The word of liberation, as it came to Luther and those like him, was that salvation had already been won by Christ; it had only to be accepted in faith, it had no longer to be achieved. Such a Protestant saw, as Gordon Rupp has aptly summed it up, "that the relation between God and Man in Jesus Christ, of which the divine side is Grace and the human Faith, was the ground of Christian experience from beginning to end."[36] With such a conviction he was delivered from the bondage of guilt and anxiety, condemnation and fear, and translated from the kingdom of darkness into the light, love, and liberty of the sons of God. Rome thought such a salvation was too easily and conveniently obtained, and suspected, quite understandably, that the doctrine of justification by faith alone masked an invitation to Anti-nomianism. The Roman church also saw its sacramental system, especially the sacrament of penance; its doctrines about the future life, especially

[32] Conveniently collected in Charles Lloyd, ed., *Formularies of Faith* (Oxford, 1825).

[33] *Ibid.*, pp. xvi-xxvii, 16.

[34] *Ibid.*, pp. 209f.: "Item, that sinners attain this justification by contrition and faith, joined with charity, after such sort and manner as is before mentioned and declared in the sacrament of penance. Not as though our contrition or faith, or any works proceeding thereof, can worthily merit or deserve to attain the said justification. For the only mercy and grace of the Father, promised freely unto us for his Son's sake Jesu Christ, and the merits of his blood and passion, be the only sufficient and worthy causes thereof."

[35] A modern phrase of Dietrich Bonhoeffer's for a phenomenon as old as man.

[36] Rupp, *English Protestant Tradition*, p. 164.

purgatory; its carefully articulated canon law; its judicious balance of the threatenings of law with the promises of the Gospel; and its whole system of spirituality in the monasteries and its casuistical ethics threatened by the rude hands of iconoclasts who would tear down in a few weeks the work of dedicated men through a millennium. Justification by faith was indeed an article for the standing or falling of the church.[37]

It is not always easy to recognise this fact because of the apparent similarity of the terminology of the disputants on each side. It is essential, however, to recognise that the Continental Reformers and the English Protestants after them made a fundamental distinction between Justification as God's forgiving acquittal of sinful man, for which they reserved the term, and Sanctification which is its consequence, by which they intended the inner regeneration of the Holy Spirit; for the latter the Catholics reserved the term Justification. The Protestant doctrine of Justification "by faith alone" depends on the distinction that it makes between Justification and Sanctification in order to safeguard the fact that its Gospel is all the operation of God's free and unearned grace. Otherwise, it was felt that man will attempt to argue that his own works or predispositions are preconditions for the reception of grace. One of the earliest English Protestants and martyrs, Barnes, affirms both objectively, that justification is the work of God in Christ on the cross, and subjectively, that it is appropriated by faith: "The Scripture doth say that Faith alone justifieth because that it is that alonely whereby I do hang of Christ, and by faith alonely am I partaker of the merits and mercy purchased by Christ's blood."[38] There was no Anti-nomianism in Barnes' exposition of the doctrine, for he saw its true consequence as, "finally of a fleshly beast it maketh me a spiritual man: of a damnable child it maketh me a heavenly son; of a servant of the devil it maketh me a free man of God."[39]

One of the clearest expressions of the doctrine is found in Cranmer's *Homily of Salvation*, in which he describes Justification as a triple work: "Upon God's part, his great mercy and grace:

---

[37] The Catholic teaching is aptly stated by Edmund Campion (see [A. Nowell], *A true report of the Disputation or rather private Conference had in the Tower of London, with Ed. Campion Iesuite, the last of August, 1581 . . . Whereunto is ioyned also a true report of the other three dayes conference had there with the same Iesuit* . . . published 1583, sig. F.f.1.): "Fayth onely as it is a good worke, ioyned with hope and charitie, doeth iustifie."

[38] Barnes, *Works*, ed. Foxe, p. 241, cited in Rupp, *English Protestant Tradition*, p. 167.

[39] Barnes, *Works*, p. 235.

upon Christ's part, justice, that is the satisfaction of God's justice or price of our redemption, by the offering of his body and shedding of his blood in the fulfilling of the law perfectly and thoroughly: and upon our part, true and lively faith in the merits of Jesus Christ, which is not yet ours, but God's working in us."[40] Cranmer had clearly appropriated Luther's distinction between faith as an intellectual assent to doctrine, and as *fiducia*, or staking one's whole life in trust. This is what he meant by "lively faith," which he defined as "a sure trust and confidence of the mercy of God through our Lord Jesus Christ and a steadfast hope of all good things to be received at God's hand."[41]

While a man's salvation owed everything to Christ, yet he was afterwards expected to live as a sanctified being. It was not that good works justified a man before God, but rather that the justified man did good works because he was justified. Tyndale insisted, "Faith only maketh a man safe, good and righteous and the friend of God, yea and the son and heir of God and of all his goodness, and possesseth us with the Spirit of God."[42]

One of the most radical conclusions derived from the acceptance of the sole mediatorship of Christ the Justifier and Redeemer was the great reduction in the status and role of the Virgin Mary and the saints. The diminution of the invocation of the saints in Henry VIII's reign can be charted with almost mathematical precision. The traditional list of saints' names in the Litany of the Sarum use included 58 saints. When Bishop Hilsey published his *Manual of Prayers or the Prymer in English and Laten* in 1539 the number was reduced to 38, while Cranmer's English Litany[43] of May 27, 1544 abandoned the long catalogue of saints formerly invoked, replacing it with a comprehensive petition addressed to patriarchs, prophets, apostles, martyrs, confessors, virgins, and all the company of heaven.

Becon poked fun at the numerous mediators of the Catholic church who virtually reduced the humble laymen to living as practicing polytheists. He imagined them as saying: "If we fast the

[40] Cranmer, *Works*, II, p. 129.

[41] Cranmer, *Remains*, p. 135. See also Tyndale's distinction between a "historical" and a "lively" faith in *The Exposition of the Fyrste Epistle of Seynt Jhon* (1531), cap. II, verse 2, in *English Reformers*, Library of Christian Classics, ed. T.H.L. Parker, p. 113.

[42] *Wicked Mammon*, from *Doctrinal Treatises*, p. 50. See also Hooper, *Early Works*, p. 50.

[43] Its full title is *An exhortation unto prayer, thoughte mete by the Kynges maiestie and his clergy, to be read to the people in every church afore processyons. Also a Letanie with suffrages to be said or song in tyme of the said processyons.*

blessed saints' evens and worship them with a *Paternoster, Ave* and *Creed*, they will do for us whatever we ask. St. George will defend us in battle against our enemies. St. Barbara will keep us from thundering and lightning. St. Agasse [Agatha] will save our house from burning. St. Anthony will keep our swine. St. Luke will save our ox. St. Job will defend us from the pox. St. Gertrude will keep our house from mice and rats. St. Nicholas will preserve us from drowning. St. Loye will cure our horse. St. Dorothy will save our herbs and flowers. St. Sith [Osyth] will bring again whatever we lose. St. Apolline will heal the pain of our teeth. St. Sweetlad and St. Agnes will send us maids good husbands. St. Peter will let us in at heaven-gates—with a thousand such-like."[44]

Unquestionably the banning of the invocation of the saints in Reformed worship and the inevitable iconoclasm of requiring the images and shrines of the Virgin and the saints to be removed from all the churches must have left many vacant spaces in the affections of the simple believers, as if they had lost their friends, for God was the distant and awesome Creator and Christ was the Judge of Doomsday. Some echo of this loss undoubtedly lay behind various Catholic uprisings, from the Pilgrimage of Grace to the revolt of the Western counties. An echo of it remains even in the Homily prepared to discredit this lingering affection, that entitled *Against Peril of Idolatry*, which contrasts the pure Anglican worship and the more exciting Roman Catholic worship and reports: ". . . a women said to her neighbour, 'Alas, gossip, what shall we now do at church, since all the saints are taken away, since all the goodly sights we were wont to have are gone, since we cannot hear the like piping, singing, chanting, and playing upon the organs, that we could before?' "[45]

All this wealth of piety was condemned as superstition; the rich

[44] Becon, *Works*, 3 vols., II, 536. With this may be compared the following words of Jewel in his *Apology*, ed. Booty: "Neither have we any other mediator or intercessor, by whom we may have access to God the Father, than Jesus Christ, in whose name all things are obtained at his Father's hand. But it is a shameful part, and full of infidelity, that we see everywhere used in the churches of our adversaries, not only in that they will have innumerable sorts of mediators . . . so that, as Jeremiah saith, the saints be now 'as many in number, or rather above the number of the cities'; and poor men cannot tell to which saint it were best to turn them first; and though there be so many as cannot be told, yet every one of them hath his peculiar duty and office assigned unto him of these folks, what thing they ought to ask, what to give, and what to bring to pass. But besides this also, in that they do not only wickedly but also shamelessly, call upon the Blessed Virgin, Christ's mother, to have her remember that she is a mother and to command her Son and to use a mother's authority over him." p. 38.

[45] Gardiner, *Certain Sermons*, p. 351.

art associated with it had to go. The reason was not that the Protestants despised art but that they loved religion more. The gravamen of their objection to the prayers and devotions addressed to the Virgin Mary and the saints was that these derogated from the sole mediatorship of Christ.

There were, of course, strong Catholic counterarguments. Catholics insisted that there was no worship of the saints, only the paying of homage to the saint and not to the image. The Protestant reply was that the saints would refuse to accept honour which was defrauding God of his due. If the Catholics argued that tradition gave the approval to bedecking the images of the saints as eminent servants of God, the Anglican reply was that the true honouring of the saints was to live in charity, giving generously and living in simplicity as they did. "No service of God, or service acceptable to him can be in honouring of dead images, but in succouring of the poor, the lively images of God."[46]

If the first consequence of the emphasis on Justification by faith alone in Christ reduced the status and importance of the Virgin and the saints, a second equally radical consequence was the downgrading of the importance of good works based on an emphasis that they played no part in the gaining of salvation. If Pelagianism was the danger into which Catholicism could easily fall with its emphasis on good works, the peril confronting Protestantism was Antinomianism. The former attributed too much to man and too little to God; the latter gave God all the glory in the initiation and accomplishment of salvation at the risk of making man too passive a recipient of God's gifts. The extraordinary paradox at the heart of Protestantism was that predestinarians should have been so ethically active. It was because no Protestant was to presume upon his election, and also because with the Reformation there came a new sense of vocation which Max Weber aptly called an intra-mundane asceticism. Previously the "religious" in the great medieval Catholic church were those who tried to obey the counsels of perfection and by withdrawal from the world into monasteries became the athletes of spirituality seeking perfection through chastity, poverty, and perfection.[47] Those who lived in the workaday world were

---

[46] *Ibid.*, Homily "Of Alms Deeds," p. 269. Is any significance to be read into the fact that, on the dissolution of the monasteries which had provided many alms freely for the poor and with the new doctrine of justification by faith and not by good works, it was necessary to provide a three-part homily, "Of Alms Deeds," extending to 104 large pages in a modern edition?

[47] See the Anglican critique in the third part of the Homily, "Of Good Works," Gardiner, *Certain Sermons*, pp. 56-58.

doomed to live a second-class Christian life. With the onset of the Reformation, however, Luther had insisted that God could be served through one's secular vocation as farmer, teacher, house-wife, mother.[48] In fact, Luther had even insisted that the Christian's sense of indebtedness could never be paid directly to God, but could be paid only by regarding the neighbour as Christ. It was this double safeguard of living to serve God in the world through one's daily calling and by treating one's neighbour as a Christ, that prevented the main body of Protestants from falling into any pits of Anti-nomianism or passivity.[49]

The Church of England was careful in defining the relationship of faith to good works in order to safeguard the primacy of the former without minimizing the latter. The 11th of the 39 Articles insisted that the meritorious cause of Justification is the atoning work of Christ: "We are accounted righteous before God only for the merits of our Lord and Saviour Jesus Christ . . . and not for our own works." The instrumental cause of Justification was asserted in the same article to be faith: "We are accounted righteous . . . by faith. . . . Wherefore that we are justified by faith alone is a most wholesome doctrine, and very full of comfort."[50] It is significant that Article 11, "Of Good Works," was one of the four new articles added by Parker and that there was nothing corresponding to it in earlier versions of Anglican Articles. It states: "Albeit that good works, which are the fruits of faith, and follow after justification, cannot put away our sins, and endure the severity of God's judgment: yet are they pleasing and acceptable to God in Christ, and do spring out necessarily of a true and lively faith, in so much that by them, a lively faith may be as evidently known, as a tree discerned by the fruit." It is but another example of the balance that characterised the Elizabethan *via media*.

This radical doctrine of Justification by faith alone, the central theological tenet of the Reformation, discovered (or, as he believed, rediscovered in St. Paul) by Luther, was recovered by the English Protestants. It changed, as I have hinted, the very style of religious life in England in the most profound ways—theologically, liturgically, ethically, and aesthetically. It removed much anxious

48 C. S. Lewis once remarked that the Reformation lowered the honors standard of the degree in spirituality and raised the passing level.

49 See Luther's *Von der Freiheit eines Christenmenschen* (1520); and Karl Holl, *The Cultural Significance of the Reformation* (New York, 1959).

50 The New Testament sources for the doctrine of justification are: Romans 3:28-30, 4:2-5, and Galatians 2:16, 3:5ff. But the Epistle of James 2:14-26 denies that man is justified by faith alone without good works.

scrupulosity, banishing, as it were, all thermometers for fevered hypochondriacs. Although a sinner, man was assured of his salvation by faith; *simul justus et peccator*. Out with *angst*. Man did not have to calculate his salvation and wonder how many more good deeds might ease his way through purgatory or would tip the scales of divine justice in his favour on the Day of Judgment. So the demand for more masses, more pilgrimages, more scourgings, more fastings, more penances, and more indulgences came to an abrupt end. The concentration on the victory of salvation achieved on the cross by Christ as the sole mediator between God and man reduced the role of all the other mediators from the Blessed Virgin to the great company of the saints, and banished most of them and their shrines from the churches and ultimately from the consciousness of the worshippers. Here too there would be a sense of relief, for how could one be sure in the older dispensation if one's prayers had been addressed to the correct celestial postal box number? Now it was enough to trust the overruling providence of God in the assurance that Christ, who had worn the vesture of humanity, thoroughly understood the human plight and was the incarnation of the love of God. (There would also be a deep sense of loss, for some of the local or national saints seemed closer to the devout, less awesome than the greater dignitaries of heaven.[51] There would certainly be a grievous aesthetic loss as the rood-screens with their representations of the crucified Savior and the watching Mother and St. John were pulled down together with all the images in stone and carved wood, or the representations of divine persons in the stained-glass windows.) The respect for the "second-milers"— the ascetical and mystical athletes—the monks and nuns and the celibate priesthood, and, indeed, for the entire hierarchical conception of the church, would be greatly reduced; and a married clergy would bring the parson and people closer in their understanding of family problems. The sacraments would be reduced in number (from seven to two) and in significance, and the pulpit would come into greater prominence, as would the role of teaching the common people the meaning of faith, requiring more schools and

[51] *The Bishops' Book*, which is "Henrician Catholic" in character, still preserves the sense of the saints all assisting the humble believer in his pilgrimage, as the following passage shows: "And I believe, that I being united and corporated as a living member into this catholic church . . . not only Christ himself, being head of this body, and the infinite treasure of all goodness, and all the holy saints and members of the same body, do and shall necessarily help me, love me, pray for me, care for me, weigh on my side, comfort me, and assist me in all my necessities here in this world." Charles Lloyd, ed., *Formularies of the Faith*, p. 58.

schoolmasters, and forcing the parish minister to catechise every Sunday afternoon. The liturgy would be radically revised so that nothing forbidden in the Bible would find a place in the worship; moreover, the biblical material would oust many of the saints' legends. As we shall see, even the shapes of the chalices would change. But the biggest change of all would come with the sense that the laity were not second-class citizens, spectators at the Mass, but participants in worship who by their daily conversation and callings were God's servants in the world; the godly father now became at family prayers in his home a father-in-God. This Protestant faith was simpler and more austere than Catholicism, but it was exciting for those who desired more responsibility in religion.

5. The Redefinition of the Church

England's severing of the bonds that linked it to the international Roman Catholic church required a radical revision of the doctrine of the church, as also of the dependent doctrines of the ministry and the sacraments. The Roman Catholic church defined itself in terms of institutional continuity, to distinguish itself from heretical and schismatical groups. St. Augustine, for example, stressed the institutional continuity and geographical spread of the church, as two of its marks, its apostolicity and catholicity, to distinguish Catholic Christians from the Donatist dissidents in North Africa. In doing so he was moving away from his earlier stress on the church as constituted by grace and faith. Now the Reformers returned to the earlier Augustine who had defined the church as the *coetus electorum*, the congregation or community of the elect, who had saving faith in Christ.[52] This was a mystical rather than an institutional doctrine of the church, stressing that divine initiation in salvation which was the primary concern of reformers all too conscious of the weaknesses where faith was too anthropocentric.

The great strength of the Catholic church had been its insistence on unity, for it was a unity achieved by charity that was the unmistakable sign of the authenticity of the church. The Protestants, however, believed that the Catholic church in the West had forfeited both its apostolicity and its holiness and that it had been invaded by worldliness. The Catholic church might, indeed, claim that it was the largest church and possibly the historically longest church, but the Protestants replied to the charge that they were schismatics and breakers of the unity of the church by stressing

[52] Woodhouse, *Doctrine*, p. 57.

that this was the only way to return the church (or their part of the church) to holiness and to apostolic ways, that truth mattered more than tradition, and that charity could dwindle into indifference. Thus of the four traditional marks of the church—unity, holiness, apostolicity, and catholicity—it might be said that the Catholics stressed the first and fourth and the Protestants the second and third. The Catholic church denied that the Church of England was a true church, but the Anglicans admitted that the Catholic church was a true church.[53]

The Bishops' Book (1537) begins the interpretation of the ninth article of the Apostles' Creed by asserting that there is among the saints in heaven and the faithful people of God on earth "a company of the elect" which is the church and "mystical body of Christ" who is its "only head and governoor." The source of its holiness is the Holy Spirit, though it is a mixed community consisting of true wheat mingled with chaff. It affirms a belief that "particular churches, in what place of the world soever they be congregated, be the very parts, portions, or members of this catholic and universal church."[54] In obvious reference to the Roman church it is denied that "any one of them is head or sovereign over the other," while it is insisted that "the church of Rome is not, nor can worthily be called, the catholic church, but only a particular member thereof. . . ."[55] The "King's Book" (the popular name for the *Necessary Doctrine and Erudition for any Christian Man*) of 1543, defined "catholic" as "not being limited to any place or region of the world," because "God of his goodness calleth people, as afore, without exception of persons or privilege or place."[56] It affirms that all these differently governed churches are together "one holy catholic church." The unity of this church "is not conserved by the Bishop of Rome's authority or doctrine; but the unity of the catholic church, which all Christian men in this article do profess, is conserved and kept by the help and assistance of the Holy Spirit of God, in retaining and maintaining of such doctrine and profession of Christian faith, and true observance of the same, as is taught by the scripture and the doctrine apostolic."[57] The over-

---

[53] Richard Hooker affirmed in his sermon on *Justification*: "The best learned in our profession are of this judgment, that all the corruptions of the Church of Rome do not prove her to deny the Foundation directly; if they did, they should grant her simply to be no Christian Church." B. Hanbury, ed., *The Ecclesiastical Polity and other Works of Richard Hooker*, III, 409.

[54] Lloyd, *Formularies*, p. 55.   [55] *Ibid.*

[56] *Ibid.*, p. 246.   [57] *Ibid.*, p. 247.

riding concern expressed in this ecclesiology is to affirm that there is a spiritual unity of all Christians and that "this unity of the holy church of Christ is not divided by distance of place nor by diversity of traditions, diversely observed in divers churches, for good order of the same."[58] Clearly the Reformation had shattered the external framework of unity; all that could be gathered from the ruins was the assertion of a spiritual unity between national churches.

Following the examples of Wittenberg, Zurich, and Geneva, the more Protestant *Forty-Two Articles* had a functional definition of the Church: "The visible Churche of Christ is a congregation of faiethfull Menne, in the whiche the pure worde of God is preached, and the sacraments be duelie ministred, according to Christes ordinaunce, in all those thinges that of necessitie are requisite to the same."[59] This article remained unchanged in the Elizabethan *Thirty-Nine Articles*, probably because it was borrowed from the corresponding article in the Augsburg Confession.[60] The ensuing Elizabethan article—that is, the 20th—declares that the church has power "to decree Rites or Ceremonies, and authority in controversies of faith"[61] yet this is qualified by the flat declaration that the church may not "ordain anything that is contrary to God's word written," nor should it to enforce any unscriptural doctrines "to be believed for necessity of salvation." In 1563 a significant clause was added to Article 34, "Of the Traditions of the Church," which read: "Every particular or national Church hath authority to ordain, change, and abolish ceremonies or rites of the Church ordained only by man's authority, so that all things be done to edifying."

It was left to Hooker to develop the most impressive apologia for the Elizabethan Settlement. He argued that the powers of church and state were coordinate. This was stated in the famous definition: "We hold, that seeing there is not any man of the Church of England but the same man is also a member of the commonwealth; nor any man a member of the commonwealth, which is not also of the Church of England . . . so with us, that no person appertaining to the one can be denied to be also of the

---

[58] *Ibid.*, p. 246.
[59] Article XX; the *Forty-Two Articles* of 1553 are reprinted in Latin and English on pp. 70-89 of E.C.S. Gibson, *The Thirty-Nine Articles of the Church of England* (1898).
[60] This reads: "Est autem ecclesia congregatio sanctorum, in qua evangelium recte docetur, et recte administrantur sacramenta."
[61] This clause was added in 1563.

other."[62] These are not independent but interdependent societies ruled by one head, the Christian ruler of the realm. Indeed, Hooker maintained that they were two aspects of *one* society, "being termed a Commonweal as it liveth under whatsoever Form of secular Law and Regiment, a Church as it liveth under the spiritual Law of Christ."[63] In theory this is admirable; as we saw earlier, the insistence on the divine right of the king made for a great sense of national security under the Christian prince. But the king who controlled the church could also crush tender consciences and all but the most courageous prophets. What was civilly advantageous might be spiritually weakening. Thus it was that during Elizabeth's reign many who cared most about religion, the Catholic Recusants and the Puritans, were almost equally abhorrent to the equable and compliant Erastianism of the middle way.

In addition to the discussion of the marks of the church, which occupied so much of the time of the controversialists and which inevitably concentrated on the legal, institutional, and exterior fabric of the church, there was a recognition of its deeper aspects, namely, its personal and interpersonal dimensions. Anglican teaching on the church's nature neglected neither the Biblical nor the patristic understanding of the relationship of the church to Christ and of Christians to each other. Woodhouse has characterized this aspect of Anglican ecclesiology as "summed up in four words— incorporation, dependence, obedience, and representation."[64] Christ is the head and the church is his body; by this Pauline metaphor it was understood that the direction of the Christians is under the rule of Christ, and that the unity of the members of the church inheres in him. The members of the church further depend wholly for their lives on him, a teaching that is expressed in the Johannine metaphor of Christ as the vine and the members as the branches. The obedience required of Christians is that of servants to their divine master, or of soldiers to the captain of their salvation, the "obedience of faith." The church also consists of Christ's representatives, those who through their commitment are his witnesses or ambassadors, to use two other familiar New Testament metaphors. Enough has been said by now to show that the Anglican understanding of the church had devotional depth which prevented it from being merely a rationalisation of the political domination of a spiritual society. For the church was seen most profoundly as

---

[62] *Ecclesiastical Polity*, Book VIII, i, 2.
[63] *Ibid.*   [64] *Ibid.*, p. 31.

that organism through which Christ, by means of the Holy Spirit, perpetuated his work in England.

The claims of the nascent Church of England did not go unchallenged. The Roman Catholic apologists hammered away at what they considered to be the four weaknesses in the Anglican position: schism, heresy, divisiveness, and immorality.[65] Anglicans had fractured the unity of Christendom and lacked the charity that is the essential bond of Christians. Thomas Harding, the able Recusant controversialist, challenged Jewel with these words: "Ye have divided the Church of God, ye have rent our Lordes nette, ye have cut his wholewoven cote, which the wicked souldiers that crucified him, could not finde in their hartes to do."[66]

Even worse, from the Catholic standpoint the Anglicans had fallen away from the foundation of apostolic and Catholic doctrine, and were teaching heresy, such as the denial of the primacy of the Pope and of the doctrine of transubstantiation. The Jesuit Robert Persons gives as the first reason why orthodox Catholics might not attend Anglican worship: "because I perswading my selfe their doctrine to be false DOCTRINE, and consequently to be venomous doctrine, I may not venture my soule to bee infected with the same."[67]

The Catholic propagandists skillfully used the charge that Protestantism was a destructive and revolutionary force that divided kingdoms, freed men of their oaths of loyalty, and was followed by all who were lax and lewd. Persons, in his subtle Epistle Dedicatory to Queen Elizabeth, while affirming Catholic loyalty, contrived to show that she should be suspicious of the loyalty of her Protestant subjects, for it was Luther's teachings that had ignited the Peasants' Revolt of 1525; he glossed Calvin (in the *Institutes* III:9), as exempting the consciences of the faithful from the power of all men by reason of their liberty in Christ.[68]

The fourth charge was that Protestantism was an easy, convenient faith that attracted the immoral. All the pretence to return to

[65] See Booty, *Jewel*, p. xvii.

[66] *A Confutation of a Booke intituled An Apologie of the Churche of England*, p. 262 recto. See also Robert Persons, *A brief discourse containing certain reasons Why Catholikes refuse to goe to Church* (Douai, 1601), sigs. C8 verso, C11 recto.

[67] *Ibid.*, sig. B12 recto. See also Harding, *A Confutation of a Booke intituled An Apologie of the Church of England*. Harding compares the fountain of the water of life of Catholicism with the Anglican "leaking pittes, which holde no pure and holesome water, but myre and puddles, with the corruption whereof ye have poysoned many soules." See also pp. 7, 24 verso, 25 verso, 132, 133 verso.

[68] *Ibid.*, sigs. A8 recto and verso.

Biblical simplicity was only an excuse of libidinous libertarians to throw off the healthful discipline of the church, to neglect the grace of the sacraments, and to throw off those Christian standards which had been maintained for a millennium, to serve their own rapacity and lust. Harding posed the alternative ethical demands of Anglicanism and Protestantism: "Let any man of reason iudge, whether he that maketh his belly his God would not holde with that gospell which mainteineth only faith to iustifie, the keping of the commaundementes to be impossible, confession of sins not to be necessarie, stedfast trust in Christes passion to be the only sufficient waye to save al men, lyve they never so loosly and disorderly: rather then with the gospell, which preacheth no salvation to be without keping the whole lawe (so farre as man may kepe it), or rising again from synne by penaunce, that only faith to iustifie which worketh by charitie, that all mortal synnes under paine of damnation must be confessed to a priest if occasion suffer, that Christes passion is applied by meanes of the sacraments unto us, and not by confidence of our own phansies. . . ."[69]

The Anglicans were no less confident of their own superiority to the Roman Catholic church; their general charges against Rome were as vitriolic as Rome's against Anglicanism. They accused Catholics of diminishing the gravity of sin and therefore depreciating the glory of God and the generosity of divine grace, as well as overestimating the power of man's free will by their stress on good works. Their teaching of the Mass, which they regarded as a renewal of the sacrifice of the cross, was a denial of the original sufficiency of Christ's sacrifice, and their doctrine of Transubstantiation was a fable contrary to Scripture and common sense alike. The Church of Rome, from the Pope and Cardinals down, sought its own glory. Its doctrinal faults were as nothing compared to its glaring moral evils, which only proved that far from being the only true church of Christ, it was disobedient to the voice of Christ.[70]

6. Church Order and the Sacraments

In church order there seemed to be a close approximation between Rome and Canterbury, for the Church of England retained the threefold historic ministry of bishop, priest, and deacon, and the leaders of the church even inherited some of their former

[69] *Ibid.*, pp. 301 recto and verso. The charge is repeated on pp. 8, 34, 253 verso.
[70] Woodhouse, *Doctrine*, pp. 137-38.

political duties as the ecclesiastical agents of royalty. The same traditional character of the ministry was to be seen also in the retention of a liturgy, instead of giving the ministers the right to frame their own prayers within a set of general directions, as was the case in the Reformed churches of Switzerland.

Nonetheless, the difference between the respective understandings of the status and the functions of the sacred ministry was great. The Anglican ministers of the word and sacraments were not as hierarchically raised above the laity as their Roman Catholic counterparts, nor, of course, were they required to be celibates. Permission for ministers to marry meant that they shared to a considerable extent the same problems as the laity and that their rectories and vicarages became centers of hospitality and understanding. Furthermore, faced (at first in Elizabethan times) with an intransigent Presbyterian claim that the Genevan Church Order alone was the true Biblical pattern of church order, the Anglicans modestly affirmed that episcopacy was of the *bene esse* but not of the *esse* of the church. While they could have made strong historic claims for episcopacy, they did not presume to unchurch other Protestants because they lacked this form of the ministry. Nor did the Church of England in our period assert that the validity of the sacraments depended on the Apostolical succession of bishops. Norman Sykes has rightly observed that "the absence of any statement concerning the doctrinal significance of episcopacy is noteworthy."[71] The concept of Apostolicity in early Anglican theology was no "pipe-line" theory of the transmission of episcopal power and authority, but rather the concern to safeguard the fidelity of teaching in line with that of the apostles as recorded in the New Testament. The bishops were indeed regarded as the successors of the Apostles, but it was never affirmed that they held the powers of the apostles or that the church was as dependent on the bishops in the way it was dependent on the Apostles. Anglicanism in this age was content to stress the fact that Christ had given authority to the church and that the importance of the bishops was in maintaining order, charity, and true doctrine in the church, as well as officiating as Christ's representatives at ordinations and confirmations. Not until the last years of Elizabeth's reign was there an insistence that new ordinations must be at the hands of a bishop of the Church of England, and not until 1662 were all ministers

---

71 *The Church of England and Non-Episcopal Churches in the Sixteenth and Seventeenth Centuries*, p. 7.

of the Church of England required to be episcopally ordained.[72] In short, Apostolic faith alone was essential, but a particular type of church government was secondary to the faith; indeed, it existed to safeguard the faith. Quite typical in its alegalistic attitude was Hooker's affirmation, in relation to the two sacraments of baptism and the Lord's Supper, that Christ gave gifts to his church, but that what he did was far more important than how he did it.[73]

The primary tasks of the ministers of the Church of England were to preach the word and administer the sacraments.[74] As the new primary authority of the Anglican church was the Scriptures; as its concern was to reform both faith and morals by the Word of God, the preacher of that word had a very important role. While it would be simplistic to state that the Protestant word replaced the Catholic sacraments in the Church of England, because its genius was to combine Reformed and Catholic elements, there was a new interest in and concern for the fuller and more frequent proclamation of the word. Latimer was no exception in affirming, "the true ladder to bring a man to heaven is the knowledge and following of the scripture," rather than the Mass.[75] The high emphasis given to sermons by Anglicans and Puritans was, according to Christopher Hill, part of the Protestant intellectual concern, "to elevate teaching, discussion, the rational element in religion, generally, against the sacramental and memorial aspects."[76] Since all were required to attend the sermon and the service of worship, preaching became a major educational instrument from the time of Elizabeth on. Louis B. Wright has emphasized that this was a means of entertainment as well as an intellectual exercise. It was understood that the master of every household would catechise his children and servants about the sermon; several would be seen taking notes during the sermon. The most noteworthy sayings of the minister would be dutifully recorded in commonplace books for further consideration.[77] Unquestionably the spiritual formation of the Elizabethan people depended more on preaching and teaching than on the sacraments.

The number of the sacraments was reduced from seven to two,

[72] Woodhouse, *Doctrine*, p. 101. Cf. Hooker, *Ecclesiastical Polity*, III, ii, 2.
[73] *Ibid.*, v, lxvii, 3.
[74] Themes which will be treated fully in succeeding chapters, but which are briefly outlined here.
[75] Hugh Latimer, *Sermons*, p. 97.
[76] Christopher Hill, *Society and Puritanism*, p. 55.
[77] *Middle-Class Culture in Elizabethan England*, pp. 277-78. This also accounts for the many family and private devotional books published in this period.

though what the Catholics termed sacraments were often retained in modified form as rites, services, or ordinances. For example, Holy Orders was a Catholic sacrament, but Ordination was an important ceremony for the setting apart and authorising of the Anglican ministry. Confirmation was an important service, but was not defined as a sacrament; the same was true of Holy Matrimony. Even Extreme Unction was retained in the form of Communion of the Sick. For Penance alone there is no equivalent, except the shadow of it in the general Absolution in the prayer-book given after the General Confession of sins by the minister in Christ's name. The two major Gospel sacraments were retained—Baptism, the sacrament of initiation, and Holy Communion, or the Lord's Supper, the sacrament of spiritual nourishment.

Anglicans differed greatly from Catholics in their interpretation of the meaning of the Eucharist, and in the manner in which they celebrated it. The Anglican objections to the Roman Mass were comprehensively and tersely listed by John Jewel in his notable "Challenge Sermon," preached at St. Paul's Cross November 26, 1559 and again on March 31, 1560, which had been repeated at Court exactly a fortnight earlier. Jewel criticised: using Latin and not the vernacular, Communion in one kind, the teaching in the Canon on sacrifice, the adoration of the Sacrament, and private celebration.[78] Anglicans were eager to assert the "Real Presence" of Christ in the Eucharist, which conveyed the grace of God that it represented, but the *mode* of the presence is not contended for as being both too common a matter of disputation and too high a mystery for human intelligence.[79]

[78] *Works*, I, 9-16. For more scurrilous criticism see Bridges on transubstantiation in *A Sermon preached at Paules Crosse*, in which he affirms that the Catholics "turned Chryst out of his owne likenesse, and made him looke lyke a rounde cake, nothyng lyke to Iesus Christe, no more than an apple is lyke an oyster, nor so mutche, for there appereth neyther armes nor handes, feete nor legges, back nor belly, heade nor body of Chryst: but all is visoured and disguysed under the fourme of a wafer, as lyghte as a feather, as thinne as a paper, as whyte as a kerchiefe, as round as a trenchour, as flat as a pancake, as smal as a shilling, as tender as the Priestes lemman that made it, as muche taste as a stycke, and as deade as a dore nayle to looke upon. O blessed God, dare they thus disfigure our Lord and Saviour Iesus Christ?" (1571), p. 125.

For a fuller treatment of Catholic and Anglican Eucharistic doctrine see Chap. III.

[79] See Hooker, *Ecclesiastical Polity*, v, lxvii, 6: ". . . why do we vainly trouble ourselves with so fierce contentions, whether by consubstantiation or else by transubstantiation the sacrament be first possessed with Christ or no? — a thing which no way can either further or hinder us however it stand, because our participation of Christ in this sacrament dependeth on the co-operation of His omnipotent power which maketh it His body and blood to us, whether with change or without alteration of the elements such as they imagine, we need not greatly to care or inquire."

Only Baptism and Holy Communion are appointed by Christ as sacraments of his Gospel, with the appropriate sign of water for the cleansing of Baptism, and the appropriate signs of bread and wine for the body and blood of Christ in the Lord's Supper. Bradford declared: "There are two Sacraments in Christ's Church: one of initiation, that is, wherewith we be enrolled, as it were, into the household and family of God, which sacrament we call Baptism; the other wherewith we be conserved, fed, kept, and nourished to continue in the same family, which is called the Lord's Supper, or the body and blood of our Saviour Jesus Christ, broken for our sins and shed for our transgressions."[80] These are, however, in no sense bare signs, but communicating and "effectual signs of grace and God's will towards us, by the which he doth work invisibly in us," as the 25th of the 39 Articles said. As noted by Philip Edgcumbe Hughes, the efficacy has a double reference, both to the promise of the Gospel and to the faith of the believers who are the recipients of the sacrament.[81] Cranmer affirmed that the sacraments were not *signa nuda*, empty signs: "As the washing outwardly in water is not a vain token, but teacheth such a washing as God worketh inwardly in them that duly receive the same, so likewise is not the bread a vain token, but showeth and teacheth the godly receiver what God worketh in him by His almighty power secretly and invisibly. And therefore as the bread is outwardly eaten indeed in the Lord's Supper, so is the very body of Christ inwardly by faith eaten of all them that come thereto in such sort as they ought to do, which eating nourisheth them unto everlasting life."[82]

What seemed the greatest novelty was the mode of the celebration of Holy Communion. The service was in English, and the communicants received consecrated bread and wine. Former spectators at a mystery were conscious of participating in the Lord's Banquet. Some of the mystery may have been dissipated, along with the gain of intelligibility, simplicity, and sharing for the people.

7. The Liturgical Consequences of Theological Change

There remains only to be considered in outline the consequences of theological change on the nature of Anglican worship, taking

[80] John Bradford, *Works*, 2 vols., I, 82.
[81] See Hughes, *The Theology of the English Reformers*, an admirably systematic doctrinal anthology with careful critical introductions, pp. 158f.
[82] *Works*, I, 17.

the First Prayer Book of Edward VI as the norm.[83] There is little evidence that the king had replaced the Pope as the earthly head of the Church in England, except for the requirement that the second in the series of collects at Communion is one of two alternatives for the king, and that he is briefly mentioned in the Suffrages for matins and evensong. The most prominent anti-Papal utterance was the round condemnation in the Litany: "From all sedicion and privye conspiracie, from the tyrannye of the bishop of Rome, and his detestable enormities . . . Good lorde, deliver us."[84] The Erastianism of the prayer-book is also possibly reflected in the collect for peace which emphasizes twice a day that God is "author of peace and lover of concord."

There is, however, abundant evidence of the seriousness with which the primacy of the Scriptures was reflected in Anglican worship. It is most prominent in the elimination of non-Biblical lections and in the arrangement for the reading of the Old Testament through once a year as the first lesson at both matins and evensong, while the New Testament is appointed for the second lesson at matins and evensong, "and shal be red over orderly every yere thrise, besides the Epistles and Gospelles: except the Apocalips, out of the whiche there be onely certain Lessons appoynted upon diverse proper feastes." The Psalms were, of course, a very important feature of Anglican worship. The other place where the Scripture's importance was plainly evident was in the requirement at every Communion service for a sermon to be preached or a homily read. Since the people possessed copies of the prayer-books in which they could follow the services and anticipate each lesson, prayer, and ceremony, the very unpredictability of a sermon, as contrasted with a homily, must have made this the most exciting part of worship.

Justification by faith found its place among the homilies and in the Pauline epistles, all of which were included three times a year as lessons. The influence of the doctrine was, however, clear in the modifications introduced into Roman collects to make them Reformed in character. The standard ending for a collect was,

[83] While the First Prayer Book of Edward VI (1549) lasted for only three years, it yet had a profound influence on subsequent Anglicanism. The Second Prayer Book of Edward VI (1552) lasted for only a year, and was extremely Protestant in character.

[84] This and all subsequent citations in this chapter will be to the Edward Whitechurche (March 1549) edition in the Huntington Library copy. References will also be given, for convenience, to the Everyman edition, introduced by Bishop E.C.S. Gibson. The reference here is to p. 232.

"Through Jesus Christ Our Lord," thus stressing the mediatorship of Christ. Clearly a collect for a saint's day was composed to suggest that he be imitated in his dependence on God's grace or in the following of Christ. In no case was there an invocation of the saint. The denial of the merits of the saints and the affirmation of faith in the sole merit and mediatorship of Christ can be seen plainly in the collect for Saint Mary Magdalene's Day: "MERCY-FUL father, geve us grace, that we never presume to synne thorough the example of any creature; but if it shall chaunce us at any time to offende thy divine maiestie; that then we may truely repent, and lament the same, after the example of Mary Magdalene, and by lyvely faith obtaine remission of all our sinnes; through the onely merites of thy sonne our saviour Christ."[85] Moreover, there was a considerable reduction in the number of saints' days; almost all of those retained had some connection with the earthly life or Gospel of Christ. The emphasis was more on the Christological than the sanctoral cycle in the Anglican prayer-book.

The same desire to instruct the people in the Christian faith and give the Gospel of Christ priority, is certainly responsible for the prayer-book's being prepared in English, as was the notable Anglican invention of providing in a single volume a book that priest and people could share. The Preface, almost certainly the work of Cranmer, shows how deliberately these features were considered; so that, "is ordeyned nothyng to be read, but the very pure worde of God, the holy scriptures, or that whiche is evidently grounded upon the same;[86] and that in suche a language and ordre, as is most easy and plain for the understandyng, bothe of the readers and hearers."[87]

This concern for edification (a Pauline term for building up in the faith),[88] combined with giving a greater responsibility to the laity because they were recognised as being an important part of the people of God and not merely those who were not the "religious," must also account for the expectation that the laity would model their devotions on the prayer-book and that heads of house-

[85] P. 198.

[86] This evidently refers to the Biblically-based doctrines propounded in the various exhortations in the prayer-book, as, for example, in the office for holy communion.

[87] Particular exception is taken to the fact that, "the service in this Churche of England (these many yeares) hath been read in Latin to the people, whiche they understood not; so that they heard with theyr eares onely; and their hartes, spirite, and minde, have not been edified thereby." Cf. Article XXIV.

[88] The main references are: I Corinthians 14:5, 12, 26 and Ephesians 4:12, 16, 19.

holds would lead the devotions in their own homes and test their children and servants on how well they had understood and remembered the sermons preached in church. All this may have reflected a growing sense of "the priesthood of all believers"; it certainly reflected an understanding of the church that was less hierarchical than the Catholic and that made much less rigid the difference between the clergy and the laity. It should also be noted that in 1549, when Cranmer was replying to the West Country rebels who wanted among other things the restoration of the Latin rite, he wrote that "worship should be the act of the people and pertain to the people, as well as to the priest: And it standeth with reason that the priest should speak for you and in your name, and you answer him again in your own person, and yet you understand never a word, neither what he saith nor what you say yourselves."[89]

The spirit of simplicity, of reverence for God and respect for men, orderliness, and dignity so typical of Anglicanism, is finely expressed in two homilies. The first, "Of the Right Use of the Church," states that: ". . . the material church or temple is a place appointed . . . for the people of God to resort together unto; there to hear God's holy word, to call upon his holy name, to give thanks for his innumerable benefits bestowed upon us, and duly and truly to celebrate his holy Sacraments. . . ."[90] The second, "Of the Time and Place of Prayer," stresses the Anglican ethical emphasis in worship: ". . . Churches were made . . . to resort thither, and to serve God truly; there to learn his blessed will; there to call upon his mighty name; there to use the holy Sacraments; there to travail how to be in charity with thy neighbour; there to have thy poor and needy neighbour in remembrance; from thence to depart better and more godly than thou camest thither."[91]

The veil is removed from the sensitive and reserved spirit of Anglicanism only once and that is in the Prayer of Humble Access that cries, "down peacock feathers" to all human pretensions, and, characteristically combines a Protestant beginning with a Catholic ending. The rubric introducing it goes: *Then shall the priest turning him to gods boorde, knele down, and say in the name of all them that receyve the Communion, this prayer following.* "We do not presume to come to this thy table (o mercifull lord) trusting

---

[89] *Works*, III, 169f. See also A. L. Rowse, *Tudor Cornwall*, pp. 262ff.; and *Troubles connected with the Prayer Book of 1549*, ed. Nicholas Pocock, n.s., 37, pp. 148f.

[90] *Certain Sermons*, p. 156.   [91] *Ibid.*, p. 350.

in our owne righteousness, but in thy manifold and great mercies: we be not woorthie so much as to gather up the cromes under thy table: but thou art the same lorde whose propertie is alwayes to have mercie: Graunt us therefore (gracious lorde) so to eate the fleshe of thy dere sonne Jesus Christ, and to drynke his bloud in these holy Misteries, that we may continuallye dwell in hym, and he in us, that our synfull bodyes may bee made cleane by his body, and our soules washed through hys most precious bloud. Amen."[92]

Perhaps the single most impressive characteristic of the Anglican revision of worship was its deep simplicity. Instead of many diverse "Uses" of various cathedrals in the realm of England, there was now one uniform order of *Common* Prayer. Instead of four principal service books,[93] and three supplementary ones[94] being necessary for the conduct of divine worship, as had been the case for Roman Catholic celebrants of worship, the single Book of Common Prayer served alike for bishops, the lesser clergy and the part of the laity. Instead of an unintelligible service in Latin there was now an easily understood service in English. Instead of many burdensome and mystifying as well as elaborate ceremonies, as in the Roman rites and ceremonies, these had been reduced to a few simple and significant signs. Instead of the lustrations, prostrations, and frequent crossings, the deeply significant signs were those given in the Gospel itself, such as the affusion of water in Baptism, and the fraction of the bread and libation of wine in the Holy Communion, and a few simple and time-honoured customs such as bowing in prayer and at the reception of Holy Communion, signing with the cross in Baptism, and the use of the ring in marriage. The ornaments, too, were greatly simplified, whether reference was made to the surplice as the usual vestment for matins and evensong, with the alb, tunicle, and cope for the celebration of Communion, or to the decoration of the churches, which were to lose the holy figures on the Roodlofts, or the stone or glass images of Christ, the Virgin, or the saints. Similarly the subtle polyphonic Gregorian chanting was to be substituted for the

92 P. 225 of the Everyman edition of *The First and Second Prayer Books of King Edward VI.*

93 The four principal service books were: the Missal or Mass book, the Breviary or Book containing the seven daily Offices, the Manual with the occasional rites as Baptism or Burial, and the Pontifical containing such rites as Ordination which required the presence of a bishop.

94 The supplementary books consisted of: the Lectionary (with the lessons needed at Mass), the Gradual with the musical portions of the Mass, and the Antiphoner with the musical portions of the Breviary Office.

English mode of chanting (one syllable to a note). In short, simplicity, order, intelligibility, and fidelity to the Bible were to replace the riches of tradition and an impressive mystery and pageantry. Spectators became participants and ethics were preferred to aesthetics. It was felt, rightly or wrongly, to be a return to the simplicity of Christ and to the purity of the primitive church.

CHAPTER II

ANGLICANS AND PURITANS
IN CONTROVERSY (1564-1603)

CANTERBURY fought with Rome in the days of Henry VIII and Edward VI and with Geneva in the days of Elizabeth. The first Anglican apologetic in the writings of Jewel produced a polemic against Catholicism. The second Anglican apologetic in the hands of Whitgift, Bancroft and especially Hooker, produced an armoury against the slings and arrows of Puritanism. What made the second battle so acrimonious was that it was between foes in the same Protestant household.

As early as 1529 there were signs of a rift in Protestant solidarity, the harshest evidence of which was in the inability of the Saxon and Swiss Reformers at the Colloquy of Marburg to produce a unifying interpretation of the Eucharist that would satisfy Luther's demand for the 'real presence' and Zwingli's allegorical and memorial requirements. Even more ominous for the future unity of Protestants in England was the war between the "Coxians" and the "Knoxians" among the Marian exiles in Frankfurt which foreshadowed the controversy over liturgy between Anglicans and Puritans as it would break out with the "Admonitioners" in the early 1570s.[1] Significantly the "Coxians" desired to maintain their loyalty to the second prayer-book of Edward VI of 1552, for the defence of the doctrines of which Cranmer, Ridley, and Latimer had been burned at Oxford. The "Knoxians" fought for a form of worship modelled on Calvin's Genevan Order, which, in their judgment, was more in accordance with the model of Scripture and the custom of the earliest church, the very criteria the Puritans were to apply in their criticisms of the Book of Common Prayer in Elizabeth's reign. Even the beginning of the controversy could be seen

---

[1] For the importance of the influence of the exiles see Christina H. Garrett, *The Marian Exiles* (Cambridge, 1938). Miss Garrett shows that in the eight communities of the exile (Emden, Aarau, Wesel, Zurich, Strassburg, Frankfort, Basel, and Geneva), there were about 788 exiles, among whom were 67 clergymen and 117 theological students. Of the 788, two became Privy Councillors of Queen Elizabeth, 16 became bishops (and three archbishops), and three were printers and publishers who became "ardent servants of the Elizabethan Reformation." For the genesis and development of the liturgical squabble see my *Worship of the English Puritans*, pp. 27-34. For a relatively accessible edition of the source see Edward Arber's 1908 edition of *A Brief Discourse of the Troubles begun at Frankfort in the year 1554 about the Book of Common Prayer and Ceremonies.*

in advance in Edward VI's reign with Hooper's great reluctance to wear episcopal robes which seemed to him to symbolize the Lord Bishop rather than the Father in God or chief pastor of the diocese. For it was the "Vestiarian Controversy"[2] in 1566 that began to divide Elizabethan Protestants into two camps.

1. *The Puritans*

The term "Puritan" came into use during the Vestiarian Controversy late in 1567 according to Stow, who, however, says that it was used by Anabaptists to refer to themselves as being Puritans or "unspotted Lambs of the Lord."[3] It is much likelier that the term was used by less iconoclastic Protestants who wanted to "reform the reformation" or by those who criticised the pretensions of such purists or precisionists. Unquestionably the entire movement was characterised by a concern that the Reformation should proceed according to the norm of the "pure" word of God further than it had already done in England; the impurity of the Church of England was seen in its retention of the vestments of Catholicism along with some Catholic ceremonies. The movement was also notable for an admiring adherence to Geneva (or Zurich) for its theology, its Presbyterian church order of ministers, teachers, elders, and deacons, its Genevan service book or liturgy, and its Genevan translation of the Bible. In the seventeenth century Puritanism included Calvinistic Anglicans, Presbyterians, and Independents, together with several smaller sectarian groupings in the days of the Commonwealth.

Perhaps the two most important components in the term were the implicit seriousness and intensity of this uncompromisingly Biblical faith and the way that it is supposed by the more compliant to be shot through with superiority and hypocrisy. Both shades of meaning are suggested by Shakespeare's taunt at the vain, cross-gartered Malvolio in *Twelfth Night*, where the Puritan is challenged: "Dost thou think because thou art virtuous there

---

[2] See J. H. Primus, *The Vestments Controversy, An Historical Study of the Earliest Tensions within the Church of England in the reigns of Edward VI and Elizabeth*, p. 71: "The Marian exiles' first-hand experience of the methods of 'the best reformed churches' on the continent was largely responsible for various religious tensions in the years of Elizabeth's reign, not least of all, for the tensions regarding the use of vestments." See also Powel Mills Dawley, *John Whitgift and the English Reformation* (New York, 1954), pp. 69f.

[3] See "Puritan" in the *New English Dictionary*. William Haller, *The Rise of Puritanism*, p. 8, insists that Puritanism was generated by the shock of disappointment that Queen "Elizabeth did not reform the church but only swept the rubbish behind the door." See also H. M. Knappen's *Tudor Puritanism*, Appendix 2: Terminology.

shall be no more cakes and ale?"[4] The intensity and strictness is suggested by naming one offensively Puritan character in Ben Jonson's play, *Bartholomew Fair*, "Mr. Zeal-of-the-land Busy." These are, however, more caricature than character sketch, and it will do no harm if we are reminded that Edmund Spenser and John Milton were proud to be designated Puritans, combining seriousness in religion with courtesy and learning.

"Puritan" was a handy smear term for the opponents of further reformation in Elizabeth's reign. Field and Wilcox, authors of the *First Admonition to Parliament*, complained that the term was applied to poor simple people who were serious about their religion and who were thus charged as heretics, "calling them Puritanes, worse than the Donatists."[5] In his reply Whitgift made matters worse by stating that the term aptly recalled the *Cathari*, not because they were purer than others but only because they claimed to be, and "separate themselves from other churches and congregations as spotted and defyled."[6] As Knappen points out,[7] it took the Puritan apologists 20 years to accept the designation for themselves, after vainly trying to show its inapplicability to themselves or its greater suitability for the Anglicans who, by their strictness over vestments and ceremonial which should be *adiaphora*, were creating new schisms. It was a term used several times by the critics of Anglicanism in the bitingly shrewd and scurrilous *Marprelate Tracts*.[8] In the end their successors were to speak warmly of the "good old Puritans," and Puritans themselves were to bear the designation as a mark of pride, as a scar in spiritual warfare. The Puritans, as the Quakers and Methodists later did, turned a sarcastic nomenclature invented by their enemies into a badge of courage and fidelity.

Because of the flexibility of the term "Puritan," it is best not to circumscribe it too narrowly. Certainly it cannot be equated with English Presbyterianism, for the Puritans included in their camp those who disagreed on church government. We shall find Anglican (that is, Episcopalian) Puritans, Presbyterian Puritans, and Independent Puritans. Nor can Puritanism be the name for English Calvinists, since that archenemy of Puritanism, Archbishop Whitgift, was a Calvinist in doctrine, and the sources of English Puri-

---

4 Act II, scene iii, line 123.
5 Field and Wilcox, *First Admonition*, sig. A 1 b.
6 *Answer to the Admonition*, p. 18.
7 *Tudor Puritanism*, p. 488.
8 The Marprelate Tracts, ed. Pierce, pp. 22, 242, 245, 257.

tanism, especially in the reign of Elizabeth, flowed almost as much from Zurich as from Calvin's Geneva, and Wittenberg and Strassburg were not without their mediating influence.

What is clear is that Puritanism was marked by the desire, as expressed by the admonitioners, for the "restitution of true religion and the reformation of the church of God"[9] according to the scriptural norm in all things, doctrine, worship, and ecclesiastical government. Perhaps the most objective account of the origin of the nickname, given by one of the sternest critics of Puritanism, appears under the caption "Anno Reg. 7" in Heylyn's *Ecclesia Restaurata*, or *History of the Reformation*: "This year the *Zuinglian*, or *Calvinian* Faction began to be first known by the name of *Puritans*, which name hath ever since been appropriated to them, because of their pretending to a greater Purity in the Service of God, than was *held forth* unto them (as they gave it out)' in the *Common-Prayer* Book; and to a greater opposition to the Rites and Usages of the Church of Rome, than was agreeable to the Constitution of the Church of *England*."[10] The aptness of this description lies in its suggestion that the Swiss Reformers were the mentors of the Puritans, and that the Puritans wished to make worship and ceremonies conform more closely to the Biblical pattern and the norm of the Continental Reformed churches.

Is it possible to interpret Puritanism more strictly without losing the spirit and ethos of the movement? William Haller sees its essence as a vital form of English Calvinism centered on "the dynamic Pauline doctrine of faith, with its insistence on the overruling power of God, on the equality of men before God, and on the immanence of God in the individual soul"[11] which was lucidly and trenchantly formulated in Calvin's theology and strikingly exemplified in the city of God in Geneva. The steel in the Puritan soul was the conviction of the truth of the doctrine of predestination with all the ringing assurance of St. Paul's battle-cry: "If God be for us, who can be against us?"[12] H. M. Knappen follows G. M. Trevelyan in using the term "Puritanism" to mean "the religion of all those who wished either to 'purify' the usage of the established church from the taint of popery or to worship separately by forms

[9] *The First Admonition to Parliament*, in *Puritan Manifestoes*, ed. W. H. Frere and C. E. Douglas, p. 8.

[10] *Ibid.*, edition of 1661, p. 172.

[11] *Ibid.*, p. 8.

[12] Rom. 8:31. For the thrust of predestination in Paul's thought see Rom. 8:28-35.

so 'purified.' "[13] The dominating characteristics of the Puritans, in his view, were bibliolatry, a tendency toward individualistic interpretation of their authority, a seriousness that made them wary of gaiety, a passionate love for civic freedom, and a moral earnestness.[14]

My own view is that the flexibility and unity of Puritanism are best preserved if I describe their subdivisions as conforming or nonconforming Puritans, or even better, as patient and impatient Puritans. In the first category I include all who desired further reformation according to the Word of God and following the examples of the best Reformed churches, but who saw this happening in the context of the nation; these were the Anglican and Presbyterian Puritans. In the second category we see those Puritans who, like Robert Browne, wanted a "Reformation without tarrying for anie," and who instead adopted the "gathered church" concept of ecclesiology. The church was then to consist not of the "mixed multitude" but only of committed and covenanted Christians, living like island colonies in the midst of a sea of half-Christians or nominal Christians.[15] This second group, or series of groups, organised themselves independently of the national church. Imprecise as this inclusive use of the term may prove to be, it at least avoids the awkwardness of other alternatives such as "Separatist" and "Semi-separatist," which deny the fundamental unity in the desire to build a Biblical theocracy in England, which was shared by all the groups.

2. The Strategies of Puritanism

Protestantism seemed to be united in the first years of the reign of Elizabeth by a sense of the importance of maintaining a common front against the inflexible Catholicism they had so recently experienced under Mary. That Catholicism was steeling itself to win back the provinces lost to Protestantism by the Council of Trent and by the creation of Ignatius Loyola's new Order, the Society of Jesus, sworn to a "cadaveric" obedience in defense of the Pope and of the church, and with its priests superbly trained in will and imagination through the *Exercitia Spiritualia*. The patience of the established church and of the Puritans gave away after the defeat

[13] *Tudor Puritanism*, p. 488. Trevelyan's proposal was made in *England under the Stuarts*, pp. 60-71.

[14] Haller, *Rise of Puritanism*, p. 489.

[15] Browne, the founder of the Independent (or later, Congregational) ecclesiology, expounded his views in *A Treatise of Reformation without tarrying for anie* (1582).

of the armada in 1588 had ensured the relative safety of England from foreign and Papist attack, and there was little need to maintain a common Protestant front.

However much they might hope that the Elizabethan Settlement would rid itself increasingly of the vestiges of Catholic vestments and ceremonies, the Puritans at the beginning of Elizabeth's reign kept themselves in patience through hope. The advanced wing of Edwardian Reformers had gone into exile in Emden, Wesel, Zurich, Strassburg, Frankfurt, Basel, Geneva, and Aarau, where they had become familiar with the customs in worship and church government of the Reformed churches of Germany and Switzerland, as well as with their leading ministers and theologians. No less than 67 clergy and 117 theological students, with the backing of William Cecil and several merchants, were preparing to be the Protestant vanguard in England when the tide should turn against Marian Catholicism. They were sustained by the superb examples of the Marian martyrs such as Latimer, Ridley, and Cranmer who at the end of Edward VI's reign were preparing further steps to bring England closer to the Continental Reformation. Naturally, since 16 of the exiles became bishops and three archbishops, not to mention those who gained professorships, prebendaries, and canonries in the Church of England, there was every reason to hope that the exiles would take over the Church of England.

There were, however, three forces working against such a result. There was the queen herself, who desired that the externals in religion should remain much the same, because this might quiet her more conservative subjects belonging to the old faith and because it pleased her love of pageantry. She also disliked the egalitarianism of Presbyterianism, and even more, its spokesman John Knox, who had condemned women rulers in his tactless *The First Blast of the Trumpet against the Monstrous Regiment of Women*. It is true that this was directed against Elizabeth's sister, Mary, but might not a second blast be directed at her by this courageous and uncompromising Scot in whom the iron of the French galleys had entered? Elizabeth was determined to control both church and state, which she did with a firm hand as Archbishop Grindal, the Marian exile, was to know to his regret, through four years of suspension although he was Primate of All England. The second obstacle was the division between the conservative and the radical exiles, corresponding to the "Coxians," who followed the example of Cox, the avaricious Bishop of Ely, in making the best of both worlds,

45

and the "Knoxians" like Humphrey, Sampson, and Whittingham who had to be content with deaneries which they forfeited rather than wear the "idolatrous gear" prescribed by Archbishop Parker's "Advertisements" in 1566. The third and saddest obstacle was the tendency of youthful reformers to become middle-aged conservatives, to lose their own fire as they basked in the rays of court preferment. The Elizabethan bishops, from Jewel to Parkhurst, from Aylmer to Horne, soon developed a fatty degeneration of the conscience as they became religious civil servants charged with creating a religiously compliant people for their sovereign. Only the stoutest hearts resisted the blandishments of the balmy breezes of flattery and the sunshine of promotion.

The Puritans' first strategy was developed only after their initial disappointment during the Vestiarian Controversy. Indeed, no Puritan protest was necessary at first because Puritan-minded ministers took matters much into their own hands, often in iconoclastic ways. The disorder in worship in the realm was complete.

Archbishop Parker was requested by the queen to provide diocesan certificates describing the "varieties and disorders" existing in the ceremonies of the church. The results showed that some ministers said the service in the chancel, others in the nave; some led worship from the pulpit, others from a chancel seat. Some kept the order of the Book of Common Prayer, others "intermeddled" metrical Psalms; some read the service in a surplice, others without one. The Communion table was variously placed, either "altar-like distant from the wall a yard" or facing north and south in the midst of the chancel, or even in the nave of the church. Sometimes it was a trestle with a table top, usually it was a table. Occasionally it had a carpet on it, often it bore none. Communion was administered by some clergy with a surplice and cope, by some with only a surplice, by others wearing neither vestment. Some clergy used a Catholic chalice, others an Anglican communion cup, and yet others merely a common cup. Some clergy used unleavened, and other leavened, bread. There was equal variety in the postures for the reception of Communion—some knelt, some sat, some stood. As for the Sacrament of Baptism some ministers administered it with surplice, some without; some used a font, others used a basin; and some used the signation with the cross, while other refused to use it.[16]

[16] Lansdowne MSS, viii, 7, cited vol. 1, pp. civ-cv of W.P.M. Kennedy, *Elizabethan Episcopal Administration*, 3 vols.

Clearly some order was desirable. It was Parker's unhappy duty to require all the clergy to accept his "Advertisements."[17] The first vestiarian troubles had broken out as early as 1563. It seems Archbishop Parker drew up the "Advertisements" in 1564 and submitted them, unsuccessfully, to Cecil for the royal signature of authority on two separate occasions. The queen presumably refused to bear the odium caused by this demand for uniformity. They were finally issued in 1566 under the signatures of the archbishop and bishops as commissioners in causes ecclesiastical. The principal minister in cathedral and collegiate celebrations of Holy Communion was to use a cope, while the celebrant in a parish church "shall wear a comely surplice with sleeves."[18] All communicants were to receive kneeling. Each man in holy orders was to promise to preach only if he had the license of the bishop, to read the service prescribed in the Book of Common Prayer, to wear the appointed apparel in church and the appropriate clerical garb when travelling, to accept no secular employments, to read a chapter in both Testaments daily, and to give several unimportant assurances in addition.[19]

The leaders of the Anglican church could urge that it was a church aiming at the greatest comprehensiveness in its demand for uniformity, and that it was avoiding the Scylla of Rome and the Charybdis of Geneva on its middle course; but the true friends of Reformation considered the Anglican establishment to be less a golden mean and more of a "leaden mediocrity."[20] And Elizabeth, in the words of John Knox, was "neather gude Protestant nor yit resolute Papist."[21] This did not satisfy the firm Calvinists who had been temporary sojourners in the city of Geneva during their exile, such as Thomas Sampson, Laurence Humphrey, William Whittingham, Anthony Gilby, and Thomas Lever.[22] Dean William Whittingham argued that there were four grounds on which something indifferent in the church (that is, neither approved nor prohibited by Scripture) might be used: it must contribute to God's glory, consent with His word, edify His church, and display Chris-

[17] H. Gee and W. J. Hardy, *Documents illustrative of English Church History*, pp. 467-75.

[18] *Ibid.*, p. 471.　　　　　　　　　　[19] *Ibid.*, p. 475.

[20] *Zurich Letters*, 2 vols., I, 23.

[21] Knox, *Works*, ed. David Laing, II, 174.

[22] It is noteworthy that only three of the exiles who later accepted bishoprics—Pilkington, Bentham, and Scory—had been to Geneva, and of these, Pilkington was tender to those clergymen in his diocese who had Vestiarian scruples. See J. H. Primus, *The Vestiarian Controversy*, p. 74.

tian liberty. When applied to the vestments, he found the first three principles absent by reason of Papal and superstitious origin and use, and the last broken by the demand for absolute conformity.[23] Alexander Nowell, also a Marian exile, and the dean of St. Paul's cathedral, produced an eirenicon urging disputants to accept the magisterial authority to prescribe vestments, while petitioning for their removal on the grounds that they were subject to abuse, as a public testimony to the rejection of superstitions, as a profession of Christian liberty, and a removal of a cause of dissension among brethren in the same household of faith.[24] The importance of the Vestiarian Controversy was that it polarised Puritan and anti-Puritan opinion and once and for all put the Puritans on notice that they could expect no further moves on the part of the queen in a more Reformed church direction.

Though the queen was an obstacle, Parliament might not be. The Puritans remembered happily their near victory in 1563. In the Convocation of that year there were both radical and moderate reform proposals put forward to ease consciences on the matters of the vestments and ceremonies. The radical proposals would have eliminated all the ancient vestments. The moderate proposals would have required the surplice alone for all services, with the provision that no minister should officiate except in "a comely garment or habit," a deliberately vague term to allow for the substitution of the black Genevan gown.[25] The proposals included the omission of crossing in Baptism, making kneeling at the reception of Holy Communion optional, with the abolition of organs and saints' days. This was the "moderate policy of the exilic party";[26] it was defeated by only one vote in the lower house.[27]

The result of this narrow defeat was to alert the leaders of Puritanism to the necessity for a protracted literary and political warfare. The Vestiarian Controversy had touched only the periphery of the zone of battle. Now the Puritans would concentrate on the centre. From this time on the Anglican Book of Common Prayer and the ecclesiastical government by bishops become the chief objects of Puritan attack, always with the presumption that the Genevan Service Book and the Presbyterian form of church

23 *Ibid.*, p. 88.
24 *Ibid.*, p. 93.
25 D. Wilkins, *Concilia Magnae Britanniae* (1737), 4 vols., IV, 237-40.
26 A phrase of W. H. Frere and C. E. Douglas, *Puritan Manifestoes*, p. ix.
27 J. Strype, *Annals of the Reformation*, 4 vols., II, 335; also H. Gee, *The Elizabethan Prayer Book*, p. 164.

order were to be preferred for their Biblical basis. The focal point of the Puritan attack changed from Convocation to Parliament.

The new strategy was quite successful at first. In 1566 a group of Puritans in the House of Commons initiated the first ecclesiastical bill of an uncontentious nature, in fact to give civil standing to the Articles of Religion. It had passed the three readings in the lower house and one reading in the House of Lords when it was stopped at the special command of the queen who disliked this attempt to interfere with her ecclesiastical prerogatives.[28]

Before the next Parliament met in 1571 the Puritans organised for the attack. Cartwright had already attacked the organisation of the English church and its worship on the pretext of lecturing in Cambridge University on the Acts of the Apostles. He was to be followed rapidly by the authors of *The First Admonition to Parliament*, whose aim was "to proffere to your godly considerations, a true platforme of a church reformed, to the end that it being layd before your eyes, to beholde the great unlikenes betwixt it & this our english church. . . ."[29] In their eyes the Book of Common Prayer was "an imperfect booke, culled & picked out of that popishe dunghill, the Masse book full of all abhominations."[30] *The Second Admonition to Parliament* has been attributed to Cartwright; but whether Cartwright or another Puritan was the author, he was entirely out of patience with the bishops: "What talke they of their being beyond the seas in quene mariee's days because of the persecution, when they in queene Elizabethes dayes are come home to raise a persecution?"[31] From this time on there was a growing body of dissident Puritan literature, both scholarly and scurrilous, from Cartwright and Travers to the anonymous author of the *Marprelate Tracts*, which, as their name implies, were merciless in their attacks on the bishops.

From then on the Puritans would use every means at their disposal to disseminate their views. They would publish tracts, pamphlets, and broadsides from underground presses in England and overseas. They would use the great medium of the pulpit. They would found a college like Emmanuel in Cambridge especially to train a Puritan ministry and godly laity through the munificence of Sir Walter Mildmay, who had previously given generously to

28 Parker, *Correspondence*, ep. ccxxiv, p. 291, ccxxv, p. 293.
29 *Puritan Manifestoes*, p. 8.
30 *Ibid.*, p. 21.
31 *Puritan Manifestoes*, p. 112. For the question of authorship see A. F. Scott Pearson, *Thomas Cartwright and Elizabethan Puritanism*, p. 74.

another Puritan centre in the same university, Christ's College.[32] They would endow scholarships to maintain the supply of trained Puritan ministers from the universities. They would endow lectureships in the greater towns to ensure that the country people flocking to the markets there would hear sound preaching leading to the practise of piety. They would arrange to supplement theological training with conferences, or "prophesyings,"[33] gatherings in which ministers would discuss the import of Scripture passages, translating them from the original languages and applying them to the needs of the contemporary situation—and incidentally providing a superb channel for Puritan propaganda. Beginning in 1564 these became spread all over England within the next decade and were only halted temporarily by the queen's suspension of Grindal, her Archbishop of Canterbury, because he countenanced such means of more rapidly educating ministers and responsible laity in theology.[34] Puritans published primers and books of devotion[35] for families and private persons through such printers as John Day, which supplemented the Puritan interpretation of the Bible as found in the marginal annotations to the Geneva Bible, or the Puritan interpretation of history as found in the superb aide-mémoire, Foxe's *Acts and Monuments of matters happening in the Church*.[36] The Puritans set up a complete Presbyterian system of church organisation in the Channel Islands (an English possession a few miles from the coast of France), and a presbytery

[32] Fuller, in *The Worthies of England*, ed. J. Freeman, p. 177, tells of Mildmay, Elizabeth's Chancellor of the Exchequer, "coming to court after he had founded his College, the Queen told him, 'Sir Walter, I hear you have erected a puritan foundation.' 'No, Madam,' saith he, 'far be it from me to countenance anything contrary to your established laws; but I have set an acorn, which when it becomes an oak, God alone knows what will be the fruit thereof.' "

[33] See Leonard J. Trinterud, "The Origins of Puritanism," in *Church History*, xx, i, 46, who shows that these seminars for Biblical exposition were frequently organised by the Swiss and Rhineland cities where they would have become familiar to the Marian exiles. For a contemporary English account see *Harrison's Description of England in Shakespeare's Youth*, ed. F. J. Furnivall, 2 vols., I, 18-19.

[34] Archbishop Grindal sent his famous letter in defence of "prophesying" to Queen Elizabeth on December 20, 1576. It is to be found in Strype's *The History of the Life and Acts of Edmund Grindal*, pp. 578ff. On May 7, 1577 the queen, ignoring her primate, sent letters to all the bishops commanding the suppression of "prophesyings" in their dioceses; Grindal was sequestered by the royal order and confined to his palace in Lambeth for six months. Since Grindal remained impenitent, his suspension was never fully removed in the ensuing six years until his death in 1583, despite appeals made to the queen by bishops and the Convocation.

[35] Puritan, Anglican, and Catholic devotional manuals will be considered in the final chapter.

[36] Commonly known as "Foxe's Book of Martyrs," it appeared in Latin in Strassburg in 1544 and was published in an enlarged English edition in 1563.

in Wandsworth in 1572, the very year the Admonitioners were pressing their propaganda on Parliament.[37] When all else failed, the persistent Puritans would establish their colonies in exile in Holland and eventually found theocracies in the New World in the Plimouth Plantation and the Bible Commonwealth of Massachusetts. Such was the assiduity of these predestinarians, and such was the variety of their strategies for creating the kingdom of God on earth.

We now turn to the theological differences between official Anglicanism and the Puritans during the reign of Elizabeth, and to a consideration of the liturgical consequences of these differences.

3. Anglican and Puritan Concepts of Scripture

The Puritans believed that the Church of England had accepted the primacy of the Scriptures in its doctrinal statements (certainly the Thirty-Nine Articles of 1571 were as Calvinistic a summary of Pauline doctrines as could be wished), but that it had not followed the Scriptures either in its form of church order or in its worship, both of which retained too much of the false traditions and accretions of Roman Catholicism. Their very position indicated that the Puritans believed the Scriptures to be an authority for more than doctrine and ethics, whereas the Anglicans restricted the authority of Scripture to belief and behavior. In brief, the Anglicans, following the example of the conservative Luther, argued that whatever traditions of the ancient church were not forbidden by Scripture might be retained by a Protestant national church; whereas the Puritans argued that the Scriptures were a pattern and model for worship and the form of church government very much in the spirit of John Calvin. For Luther and the Anglicans the Scriptures were a *Trostbuch*, a book eliciting faith. For Calvin and the Puritans, however, the Bible was *la saincte parole et loi de Dieu*; its teaching was to cover all aspects of life and especially to direct life within the church, both liturgical and administrative. To ignore its teaching was merely to prove that one was not yet freed from the absurd pride and interior darkness which was the legacy of original sin and of unredeemed nature.

Cartwright insisted that "the word of God contains the direction of all things pertaining to the church, yea, of whatsoever things

---

[37] Knappen, *Tudor Puritanism*, p. 304; Pearson, *Cartwright*, pp. 74ff., 157-66; Richard Bancroft, *Daungerous Positions and Proceedings* (1593), p. 43.

can fall into any part of man's life."[38] Should any questions of ceremonies still remain obscure, he had four infallible Pauline tests which he would put to them. First, do they offend any, especially the Church of God? His authority here was I Corinthians 10:32. Second, is all done in order and comeliness? Here his authority was I Corinthians 14:40. Third, is all done for edifying, building up in the faith? The authority now is I Corinthians 14:26. Fourth, is all done to the glory of God? This authority, Romans 14:6-7.

It was left to a later Puritan theologian to express with greater precision the Puritan concept of Biblical authority. This was the learned William Ames, whose *Medulla theologica*[39] was translated as the *Marrow of Sacred Divinity* and had a great success as a classic of Reformed theology and piety. Ames affirms that "All things necessary to salvation are contained in the Scriptures and also those things necessary for the instruction and edification of the church," and draws the conclusion: "Therefore, Scripture is not a partial but a perfect rule of faith and morals. And no observance can be continually and everywhere necessary in the church of God, on the basis of any tradition or other authority, unless it is contained in the Scriptures."[40]

On the Anglican side, Whitgift answers Cartwright's assertion of the comprehensive applicability of the authority of Scripture by agreeing that "nothing ought to be tolerated in the Church as necessary unto salvation, or as an article of faith, except it be expressly contained in the Word of God, or may manifestly thereof be gathered";[41] but he also draw the corollary, "Yet do I deny that the Scriptures do express particularly everything that is to be done in the church."[42] He goes on to show that while the Scriptures urge the necessity of Baptism they do not prescribe its mode; whether "in fonts, basins, or rivers, openly or privately, at home or in the church, every day in the week or the sabbath day only" was left to the church to determine.[43]

The best expositor of the Anglican understanding of the author-

---

[38] Whitgift, *Works*, 3 vols., I, 190.
[39] The *Medulla theologica*, published in Amsterdam in 1623, was the fruit of Ames's lectures to the sons of Leyden merchants. It was followed by 12 Latin printings; three printings of an English translation appeared between 1638 and 1643. The best modern English translation with historical introduction is by John D. Eusden, *The Marrow of Theology, William Ames, 1576-1633.*
[40] Ames, *Marrow*, p. 189.   [41] Whitgift, *Works*, I, 180.
[42] *Ibid.*, p. 191.   [43] *Ibid.*, p. 201.

ity of Scripture was Hooker, the greatest apologist of the Elizabethan age. For him the Bible was the revelation of the nature of God and His purposes for mankind, but God had not intended his Word to prescribe the detailed ordering of worship, the method of church government, or the details of conduct. All these he left to the discretion of men. Such matters were to be determined by the use of reason; reason would take into account propriety, decency, proportion, according to the circumstances of the case. The Bible gives man such information only as he cannot obtain by his reason. Otherwise, if the Bible were the only and exclusive criterion, the law of reason and the law of nature, which both reflect their Creator, would be wholly abrogated by the Scriptures. Hooker spoke directly to the contentions of the Puritans in the following passage: "Let them with whom we have hitherto disputed consider well, how it can stand with reason to make the bare mandate of sacred Scripture the only rule of all good and evil in the actions of mortal men. The testimonies of God are true, the testimonies of God are perfect, the testimonies of God are all sufficient unto that end for which they were given. Therefore accordingly we do receive them, we do not think that in them God hath omitted anything needful unto his purpose, and left his intent to be accomplished by our devisings."[44] Thus for Hooker and Anglicanism the Bible was authoritative in doctrine, and prescribed the outstanding ordinances in worship, such as prayer, praise, preaching, and the two sacraments of Baptism and Holy Communion, but it was never intended to be authoritative in the determination of the details of worship. Times, circumstances, and ceremonies are properly to be decided by the church rulers in accordance with the guidance of antiquity and the imperatives of right reason.

The Puritan replied, in effect, that the Anglican accepted the authority of the Bible in theory but not in practise. It was inconsistent of the Anglican, he charged, to accept the biblical authority for doctrine but not for ecclesiastical government or worship. The Anglican seemed to set aside any parts of the Bible that seemed to go against the contemporary usages of the Anglican church by dismissing them as appropriate only for the times of their origins and therefore no part of the eternal law of the Christian religion. It was too convenient to be true.

By contrast, the Puritan held that the Bible was the revealed will of God from end to end, through and through. He believed it

44 *Ecclesiastical Polity*, II, viii, 5.

53

to be authoritative not only for doctrine and ethics, but also for every aspect of ecclesiastical and even human life. It was an absolute code. It was the expression of the Divine will in matters theological, moral, judicial, political, military, economic, ecclesiastical, and even sartorial. Therefore it was necessary to look to its pages not only for general laws or pointers but for detailed guidance.[45]

4. Theories of Human Nature

Both Anglicans and Puritans accepted the doctrine of original sin, but they estimated differently the seriousness of the effects of man's wound. Anglicans found man to be deficient in spiritual capacity; his other powers were weakened, but not desperately wounded and in need of redemptive blood transfusions, as the Puritans claimed. Man's reason was, for the Anglicans, unimpaired; it had a natural capacity to distinguish between good and evil in a moral order. Cranmer assumed, for example, that men could choose the good without the help of sanctifying grace.[46] Jewel affirmed that, "Natural reason holden within her bonds is not the enemy, but the daughter of God's truth."[47] Donne held that reason must be employed when the meaning of Scripture is unclear, but, "Though our supreme court . . . for the last appeal be Faith, yet Reason is her delegate."[48]

In contradistinction the Puritans interpreted the Fall, with Calvin, as resulting in a total interior perversion of man's perspective and powers. Some remnants of man's intelligence remain in matters not connected with his salvation, such as in liberal studies, mechanical arts, jurisprudence, and architecture. Had Calvin known Freud he would have agreed with his diagnosis of man's psyche as being given to both wishful thinking and deep rationalizations. "We are," he complained, "so utterly mastered under the power of sin that our whole mind, heart, and all our actions bend

---

[45] Peter Bayne, in *Puritan Documents*, p. 10, observes: "in considering that urgency of appeal to Scripture and Scripture alone, which throughout its whole history was made by English Puritanism, an appeal which with our modern prepossessions, may seem to us to be a wilful searing of the eye-balls of reason and conscience, it is essential to recollect that it was against the authority of Rome that Calvin and his followers asserted the supremacy of God's written Word."

[46] *Works of Thomas Cranmer*, 2 vols., II, 143.

[47] Jewel, *Works*, 4 vols., I, 501.

[48] Donne, *Essays in Divinity*, ed. E. M. Simpson, pp. 114-16, cited by John H. A. New, *Anglican and Puritan, The Basis of their Opposition, 1558-1640*, p. 8, to which this chapter owes much, even though I take issue with New on several points.

towards sin."[49] In brief, as St. Augustine had seen, man is hopelessly crippled, being *incurvatus in se*, twisted in on himself.

William Perkins, the popular Puritan theologian of Cambridge, claimed that "Original sin is nothing else but a disorder of evil disposition in all the faculties and inclinations of men, whereby they are all carried inordinately against the law of God." Its location is not a part, but rather the whole of man, body, and soul. In the first place, the very appetites are greatly corrupted, as are the outward senses. Even the very understanding of man, according to the Spirit of God, "is only evil continually: so we are not able of ourselves to think a good thought."[50] Perhaps the clearest statement of the difference between Anglican and Puritan estimates of human nature was that of John H. A. New, to the effect that the Puritans did not deny that man had a true knowledge of good and evil, but rather, "they asserted a total inability in man to desire and to choose rightly, and in that lay their alienation from Anglicanism."[51] It was further explained by the Puritans that man's inability to choose aright was because he was blinded by pride and disordered in his appetites. To trust in reason was to trust in a constant temptation to pride and therefore away from the humility and tractability that true repentance brings.

Though the Puritans depreciated the role of unredeemed reason in religion, it would be an egregious error to conclude that they were despisers of human learning, whether theological or humanistic. They shared with their opponents the rich cultural legacy of the Renaissance. Their leaders were almost all men of learning, many of whom had held high positions at Oxford and Cambridge. Cartwright was Lady Margaret Professor of Divinity in the University of Cambridge, which was a hive of Puritan activity.[52] In New England they were apostles of religion and learning. Perry Miller pays them this tribute: "The greatness of the Puritans is not so much that they conquered a wilderness, or that they carried a religion into it, but that they carried a religion which, narrow and starved though it may have been in some aspects, deficient

---

[49] Calvin's *Letters*, ed. Jules Bonnet, II, 189. This information is contained in a letter to the Protector Somerset, 22 October 1548. Other pertinent Calvin references are to the *Institutes*, II, ii, 13-14; II, iii, 1; IV, xv, 10; and the Commentary on Romans, at Romans 7:14.

[50] Perkins, *The Works of that Famous and Worthy Minister of Christ in the University of Cambridge*, 3 vols., I, 165.

[51] New, *Anglican and Puritan*, p. 10.

[52] For a lively and comprehensive account of Cambridge Puritanism see Harry C. Porter, *Reformation and Reaction in Tudor Cambridge*.

in sensuous richness or brilliant color, was nevertheless, indissolubly bound up with an ideal of culture and learning. In contrast to all other pioneers, they made no concessions to the forest, but in the midst of frontier conditions, in the very throes of clearing the land and erecting shelters, they maintained schools and a college, a standard of scholarship and competent writing, a class of men devoted entirely to the life of the mind and of the soul."[53] Harvard College was founded by the Puritans in 1636, only seven years after they had reached Boston and its environs. The Puritan was a true son of Jerusalem, but he paid frequent visits to Athens.

If the Anglican apologist claimed that all God reveals must be comprehended by human reason, because the author of both revelation and reason is God, the Puritan replied that this was to make reason a judge over revelation, and man an arbiter of God. Had the Anglican replied that there could be no discrepancy between what is rational and what is revealed, the Puritan would have retorted that human reason is unfitted for the task of comprehending the majesty and mystery of God's ways. The Puritan would have pointed to the perverseness of human nature, and to history's confirmation of the wickedness of men. You may give men (we may suppose him to argue) an education in the wisdom of antiquity and in modern skills, but they will continue to be mean and cruel, selfish and carnal. The galleon of human nature, richly laden with the treasures of antiquity, and steered by the natural reason of man, is bound to shipwreck on the rock of human perversity.

The twofold legacy of Calvin found secure lodging in the Puritan safes: the all-sufficiency of Scripture and a radical restatement of original sin to make clearer not only the utter inadequacy of man, but the creating, providing, and directing omnipotent adequacy of God.

5. Predestination: God's Rule and the Triumph of the Elect

Predestination is not an Anglican, Puritan, or even a Protestant doctrine; it is a Christian doctrine. But Calvinism (I refer to the later rather than the earlier Calvin) made much of it. It appears as the 17th of the Thirty-Nine Articles of the Church of England, formulated in 1563. The first paragraph reads: "Predestination to life, is the everlasting purpose of God, whereby (before the foundations of the world were laid) He hath constantly decreed by His

[53] Perry Miller and T. H. Johnson, *The Puritans*, pp. 11f.

56

counsel secret to us, to deliver from curse and damnation, those whom He hath chosen in Christ out of mankind, and to bring them by Christ to everlasting salvation, as vessels made to honour. Wherefore they which be endued with so excellent a benefit of God, be called according to God's purpose by His Spirit working in due season: they through grace obey the calling: they be justified freely: they be made sons of God by adoption: they be made like the image of His only-begotten Son Jesus Christ: they walk religiously in good works, and at length by God's mercy, they attain to everlasting felicity."[54]

Essentially the doctrine was an extension of justification by faith, a reasseveration that salvation is wholly the work of God, "before the foundations of the world," so that man cannot take any credit for his salvation. Even though it seems, especially in the explicit form of 'double predestination,' to accuse God of arbitrariness in making a few elect and a multitude reprobate, regardless of their response to His mercy, for those who have been chosen or elected it is a doctrine of great comfort, in that it assures them that however great temptation or suffering may be, they cannot lose their salvation because God has predestined them to salvation. It is a doctrine that offers a strong consolation where the faithful are conscious of being God's resistance movement, as, for example in Catholic France, where the Huguenots defined their Protestant community as an anvil which has worn out many hammers.

This sense of the strengthening or comfort[55] to be derived from the doctrine is to be found in the second paragraph of the same article: "As the godly consideration of predestination, and our election in Christ, is full of sweet, pleasant, and unspeakable comfort to godly persons, and such as feel in themselves the working of the Spirit of Christ, mortifying the works of the flesh, and their earthly members, and drawing up their mind to high and heavenly things, as well because it doth greatly establish and confirm their faith of eternal salvation to be enjoyed through Christ, as because it doth fervently kindle their love towards God: so, for curious and carnal persons, lacking the Spirit of Christ, to have continually before their eyes the sentence of God's predestination, is a most dangerous downfall, whereby the devil doth thrust them either into

---

[54] See E.G.S. Gibson, *The Thirty-Nine Articles of the Church of England*, pp. 459-92, for an account of the history of the interpretation of the 17th article.

[55] Modern usage has weakened the original force of "comfort" (derived from the Latin *fortis*), which in Elizabethan times meant to strengthen or invigorate rather than to console.

desperation, or into wretchedness of most unclean living, no less perilous than desperation."

Calvin recognized that this was a *decretum horribile* and cautioned that people should not delve into the hidden counsels of God precisely because of the dangers of despair or anti-nomianism.[56] Yet despite the weaknesses of the doctrine, either in the dark shadow that it throws on the grace of God or in its denial of human freedom and responsibility that are supposedly the prerequisites of moral life and accountability, it was a conviction that God could give man "new dignity for old degeneracy,"[57] an ineluctable assurance.

The Puritan recognized that his confidence came from the immutability and omnipotence of God, and from the firm grasp of Christ on the elect soul (rather than from its feeble and wavering hold on Christ). Cartwright had a succinct confirmation: "We learn that they that are truly reconciled and called shall abide for ever. This is a true doctrine, a saint once, a saint forever. It is impossible that they which believe should perish."[58] Predestination leads inevitably to the doctrine of the perseverance of the saints.

Both Anglicans and Puritans accepted predestination, but the Puritans held more vigorously to both consequences of the doctrine, positive and negative. Anglicans *implied* the negative consequence, namely, reprobation. Some Anglicans even went so far as to dilute the doctrine of predestination with the cold water of God's indiscriminate charity. The eternal damnation of the reprobate was qualified by the belief that the wicked, by their obstinate refusing of the repeatedly proffered grace, were to blame, rather than God; this was where the wedge of Arminianism slightly opened the closed door of reprobation. By the same token, the sovereignty of God was weakened as His mercy widened, and the mystery of God diminished as His will for all humanity appeared more rational, and the power of God was demeaned as man's freedom and power were elevated.[59] Officially, however, Anglicanism,

---

[56] There is good reason to believe that while Elizabethan Puritanism stressed the doctrine of predestination, as in the writings of William Perkins, yet his great pupil William Ames gave the doctrine less prominence in his theological system, and, by stressing the covenant aspect of the dealings of God with men, lessened their arbitrariness. See Ames, *Marrow of Theology*, pp. 27-28. See also Norman Pettit, *The Heart Prepared: Grace and Conversion in Puritan Spiritual Life.*

[57] New, *Anglican and Puritan*, p. 20.

[58] Thomas Cartwright, *A Commentary upon the Epistle of St. Paul written to the Colossians* (1612), expounding Colossians 1:23-29.

[59] Two Anglican Arminians in the last decade of the sixteenth century were

which had sent representatives to the Synod of Dort in 1618 to maintain predestination against the Arminian inroads of the Remonstrants, was orthodoxly predestinarian.

William Haller has seen a further strength of Puritanism in its full acceptance of the doctrine of predestination—that is, an implicit egalitarianism in the acceptance of the will of God who is no respecter of persons, and who, in casting down the mighty from their seats and raising the humble and meek, is the great revolutionary, as the Magnificat shows.[60] There is no more democratic doctrine than the universal depravity posited by the doctrine of original sin, and no more aristocratic doctrine than the doctrine of election, by which God chooses the godly select. The last in the world's estimation are to be first in the kingdom of God in the most radical transvaluation. The conviction that this was the Puritan's august destiny as a "saint" may also be the source of his ethical dynamism and ceaseless energy, which contrasted so vigorously with the compliance, not to say docility, inculcated so frequently by Erastian Anglicanism.

6. Understandings of the Church

Anglican and Presbyterian Puritan alike believed in the necessity of a Protestant national church in England. The Anglican theory was that church and state were coterminous, and that as one was born an Englishman so was he christened a member of the Church of Christ. "There is not," said Hooker, "any man of the Church of England but the same is also a member of the Commonwealth, nor any man a member of the Commonwealth, which is not also of the Church of England."[61]

To a considerable extent the same was true for Presbyterian Puritans, with the exception that they believed that, although each parish comprised a 'mixed multitude' of the elect wheat and reprobate tares or weeds which had to be allowed to grow up together until the harvest of the day of judgment, yet it was the duty of the parish minister, assisted by his godly churchwardens (when godly elders were not yet openly allowed in England), to discipline

---

Peter Baro and William Barrett, but they were rapped over the knuckles for their beliefs. In the 1630s and 1640s Richard Montagu, John Cosin, and William Laud belonged to the influential group of Anglican Arminians. See Charles and Katherine George, *The Protestant Mind of the English Reformation* (Princeton, 1961), pp. 67-68.

60 *Rise of Puritanism*, pp. 89ff. It is Peter who confesses (in Acts 10:34): "I perceive God is no respecter of persons."

61 *Ecclesiastical Polity*, VIII, i, 2.

evildoers and keep them away from the celebrations of Holy Communion until they amended their lives.

The third ecclesiology was that proposed by Robert Browne, the father of the 'gathered church' idea, and practiced by Separatist Puritans such as Barrowe, Penry, and Greenwood. They believed that the local congregation should consist only of committed Christians, or "visible saints"—a doctrine to gain its strongest following with the rise of the Independents to power and influence in the days of the Commonwealth and Protectorate.[62] The Anglican and Separatist positions were consistent; that of the Presbyterian or "Consistorial" Puritans was inconsistent in trying to combine a parochial congregation of "all comers," which was indiscriminate in character, with a disciplined nucleus (or "gathered church" group) within each parish.[63]

The most decisive differences between Anglican and Presbyterian Puritan concepts of the church concerned the pattern of church order or government, and the relation of the church to the state. In the matter of ecclesiastical government Anglicans kept the threefold ministry of bishop, priest, and deacon, hallowed by centuries of tradition. The Genevan order was much more to the liking of the Presbyterian Puritans, with its provision for pastors, doctors (teachers), elders, and deacons. The first two categories were ordained clergy, but the third consisted of ordained laymen who were charged with sharing the spiritual overseeing of the flock's faith and morals with the clergy, and who had the privilege of distributing the sacred elements to the members in the Lord's Supper. It was a remarkable attempt to express in the very structure of church order the priesthood of all believers. In this respect the followers of Geneva thought they were recovering the pattern of the Apostolic church. This they intended to introduce in their "Discipline." It was an attempt to maintain the purity of the members of the church of Christ, a matter of the greatest concern to Puritans as a group who were impatient with a merely nominal or superficial Christian witness.

The claim that the Presbyterian church order was restoring the pattern of the apostolic and primitive church was not conceded

[62] For the full development of the Independent ecclesiology see Geoffrey E. Nuttall, *Visible Saints: The Congregational Way, 1640-1660.* The writings of Barrowe, Greenwood, and Penry have been edited by Leland H. Carlson in the "Elizabethan Nonconformist Texts" series.

[63] "Consistorial" is a term applied to Cartwright, Travers, Field, Fenner, Gilby, and other leading Genevan Puritans by Richard Bancroft in *A Survey of the Pretended Holy Discipline* and *Daungerous Positions and Proceedings*, both of which appeared in 1593.

by the Anglican apologists. Whitgift, for example, said that the form of the church depends on time and place. Indeed, he insisted that the Apostolic Church cannot be taken in all respects as a model for later churches because there was a total absence of Christian magistrates. In Christianity's early days of persecution Whitgift granted there might well have been the need for seniors (or elders) to assist in setting up the organization of the congregations, as well as for deacons to look after the needs of the poor, but that in more enlightened Elizabethan days such offices were not necessary. The coming of the Christian state made any distinction between church and state a mere anachronism. Cartwright rebutted this argument by stating that there was greater need for elders in the present because ministers needed greater assistance than when there was a more plentiful effusion of the gifts of the spirit. But church government, Cartwright insisted, cannot be decided, as Whitgift had suggested, by considerations of utility or efficiency or convenience, but only by obedience to the pattern plainly shown in God's Word, and God "will plane the ways be they never so rough."[64]

On the issue of the proper relationship of church and state, both Anglicans and Presbyterian Puritans asserted the importance of joint responsibilities; yet the Presbyterians believed in a "two-kingdom" doctrine. The Anglican church is ultimately subsumed under the English state, and this is fittingly expressed in the acknowledgment of the queen as the 'supreme Governor' of the Church of England. The Presbyterian theory, however, refused to place the church under the state, for the princes or magistrates were subject to the sovereignty of God and needed the guidance of the Word of God as preached. Thomas Cartwright clearly envisioned the primacy and priority of the claim of the church: "As the hangings are made fit for the house, so the Commonwealth must be made to agree with the Church, and the government thereof with her government. For, as the house is before the hangings, and therefore the hangings which come after must be framed to the house which was before, so the Church before there was any Commonwealth and the Commonwealth coming after, must be fashioned and made suitable unto the Church."[65] The church must lead the state in the theocracy envisioned by Cart-

---

[64] The debate on ecclesiology between Whitgift and Cartwright is summarised in A. F. Scott Pearson, *Church & State: Political Aspects of Sixteenth Century Puritanism*, pp. 120f.
[65] Cited in Whitgift, *Works*, III, 189.

wright, which would turn England into a second and larger city of God, like Geneva. In short, the Anglicans with a one-kingdom theory, leaned toward secularising the church as the state's department of religious affairs, while the Puritan two-kingdom theory looked in the direction of spiritualising the state.

7. *Views of the Sacraments*

Anglicans and Puritans were agreed in much of their understanding of the nature of the sacraments. They denied Transubstantiation, Consubstantiation, and a naked Memorialism (the latter is often wrongly attributed to Zwingli). Both Anglicans and Puritans insisted that Communion was the commemoration (not the repetition) of Christ's sacrifice, and that it was a means of grace, as also that it must be received in faith.[66] The sacraments, in short, commemorate but also communicate the grace of God.[67] Anglicans and Puritans reduced the number of sacraments from the traditional seven of the Catholic church and the Orthodox churches to two—Baptism and Holy Communion—believing that these two were Sacraments of the Gospel. That is, they believed that the two sacraments represented the forgiveness and new life which were the chief gifts of Christ's death and resurrection, and were given in ordinances for which there were a Dominical warrant and example.

There were, of course, differences of emphasis in the understanding of Baptism and Communion. For Anglicans the sacraments were the chief means of grace, whereas for Puritans, in the tradition of Calvin the sacraments were seals of grace, confirmations of a prevenient grace already received, proofs that the divine promises of the Gospel are fulfilled. Cartwright defined a sacrament: "a signe & seale of the covenant of grace, or an action of the Church, wherein by outward things done according to the ordinance of God, inward things being betokened, Christ and his benefits are offered to all, and exhibited to the faithfull,

[66] Hooker declared: "The real presence of Christ's most blessed body and blood is not therefore to be sought for in the sacrament, but in the worthy receiver of the sacrament." *Ecclesiastical Polity*, v, vi, 67.

[67] New's *Anglican and Puritan* is accurate in stating (p. 62) that for both the Sacraments were "commemorations and participations in grace with a living Christ," but no Puritan would have agreed with the conclusion of the same sentence "by virtue of His real spiritual presence in the consecrated elements." The Puritans did not reserve the Sacrament, as would have been appropriate if they were conscious of a presence in the consecrated elements; rather, they insisted that Christ was present in the action in general, in fulfillment of His promise, and in the hearts of His faithful people.

for the strengthening of their faith in the eternall Covenant."[68] The Anglican did not feel it necessary to have a sermon preached at a Holy Communion service,[69] but the Puritan did, so that the sign would 'speak'—that is, that the meaning of the affusion of water in Baptism and of the bread broken and the wine poured out in the Lord's Supper should be proclaimed in the preaching.

The Anglicans were frequently told that the Eucharist was the sacrament of incorporation into the body of Christ, but there was little in the arrangement of the service to suggest this, for the participants received the consecrated elements singly and successively. On the other hand, the Puritans tried to recapture the banquet aspect of the Last Supper in their Lord's Supper, and were acutely conscious of being guests at Christ's table; they received the sacred elements as a group, not as individuals. Their emphasis on the importance of the Communion as a testimony or badge of Christian commitment also stressed the corporate aspect of the Communion service.

John New was probably right in seeing Anglicanism's appreciation of the sacraments as implying a more dynamic view than the more static view of the Puritans.[70] Surely Anglicanism's keeping of marriage as "holy matrimony," of confirmation and burial as *sacramentalia* or quasi-sacramental rites, pointed in this direction. Puritans, on the other hand, found no need for confirmation; they regarded marriage as a civil ordinance on which it was appropriate to seek the divine blessing, and burial as the termination of a life, at which prayer was appropriate. In no case did they think these occasions marked stages where divine grace was appropriately given for strengthening.

As I will have fuller opportunity to point out later,[71] there was a different order of priorities in the Christian life for Anglicans and Puritans. Anglicans give the primacy to sacraments, and Puritans to sermons, as channels of the knowledge and the grace of

---

[68] *A Treatise of Christian Religion or The Whole Bodie and substance of Divinitie* (1616), published posthumously, p. 212. William Ames wrote in *The Marrow of Theology*, p. 197, that "the special application of God's favour and grace which arises from true faith is very much confirmed and furthered by the sacraments."

[69] However, it should be remembered that the only place where a sermon was called for in the Prayer Book was at Holy Communion. Presbyterians had infrequent Communions preceded by a preparatory sermon and followed by a thanksgiving sermon on each occasion, as is attested by Robert Baillie, *A Dissuasive from the Errours of the Time* (1645), p. 29.

[70] *Ibid.*, p. 76.

[71] In separate chapters on the Eucharist and on preaching I will discuss these differences in much greater detail.

God. The supreme moment for the Anglican in worship was when, on his knees before the altar, he received the sacramental symbols of the sacrifice of his Savior. The supreme moment for him was when the preacher, ascending like a Moses to his Sinai, revealed the oracles of God and the internal testimony of the Holy Spirit assured him inwardly of its truth and transforming power.

This differing evaluation of sacraments and sermons led to functional differences between the Anglican priest and the Puritan minister. The Anglican clergyman needed to spend less time in preparing sermons and so could concentrate on spiritual contemplation and on the tasks of administration and visitation. The Puritan minister, on the other hand, spent long hours in his study, preceded and succeeded by prayer, reading the Scriptures in their original languages and conning every reputable Scripture commentary he could lay his hands on. In other words, for the Anglican the sacramental was the primary mode of Christ's presence, but for the Puritan the primary mode of Christ's presence was kerygmatic.

8. Concepts of Ethics and Eschatology

The softening or weakening of the negative aspect of the doctrine of predestination in the interests of God's universal charity led to a weakening of the presentation of the two eschatological alternatives, heaven or hell, in Anglican thought. Less the sovereignty than the benevolence of God was stressed; the strong implication was that the truest service of God was the service of the neighbour. For the Puritans, however, living "in my Great Taskmaster's eye" (as Milton was to phrase it[72]), actions had abiding consequences; the sovereign God could never be interpreted as our Grandfather who art in heaven. God's sovereignty involved his severity, so although the elect would be saved they still had to undergo the severity of the day of judgment. In their diaries (which were their spiritual accounting books) Puritans often anticipated the great assize in their imaginations.

Both Anglicans and Puritans insisted that good works were incapable of contributing to a man's salvation, that they were the harvest of the indwelling of the Holy Spirit and a necessary proof that the redeemed man was also the sanctified man.

Anglican ethics tended to be more perfectionist and Puritan ethics more pragmatic, in keeping with the Anglican presupposi-

[72] "On his having arrived at the age of twenty-three."

tion inherited from the Middle Ages, that grace completes nature,[73] and in contrast with the Puritan disjunction between the natural and the spiritual man. Also, as we have seen, the Puritan took more seriously the disruptive force of original sin and the stain and corruption it spread in persons and institutions. This was a strong countervailing force against any tendency toward sentimental utopianism (which arose in Commonwealth Puritanism under strong eschatological pressures, coupled with an overwhelming conviction of the possession of the saints by the Holy Spirit; but the Presbyterians were never intoxicated by such theological drink). Furthermore, the ethics of Puritanism were forged in a world of everyday work and politics, and the attempt to subordinate politics and economics to the way of righteousness was a very disenchanting occupation.

By contrast, Anglican ethics (in the one-kingdom concept of the state-church entity) tended to support the status quo, to sanctify what *was* rather than what *should be*. There were remarkable examples of individual Anglican generosity to the poor that deserve to be called sacrificial generosity. The spirituality that fed the ethics of Anglicanism was too other-worldly to produce a transforming ethic. (We may suppose that for one George Herbert there were hundreds of Robert Herricks in the rectories of England.)

The Puritan's conception of "calling" leads us into the fullest appreciation of his understanding of human life and destiny. The reference is not to the general calling to faith and obedience in the Gospel, but to the particular vocation—which, in the thought of Perkins, can be subdivided into the familial obligations imposed by one's position in a household (father and husband and master of servants) and the obligations imposed by one's profession or trade and one's role as citizen.[74] In this calling a man had to have the necessary gifts from God and the approbation and confirmation of men (exactly, it should be noted, the requirements before a man can be ordained in the Puritan ministry).[75] Robert Bolton insisted a Christian's first duties were fruitful performance of holy tasks, but that his second duty was to decline idleness, "the very rust and canker of the soule," and "be diligent with conscience and faithfulnesse in some lawfull, honest particular Calling . . . not so much to gather gold . . . as for necessary and moderate provi-

---

[73] St. Thomas Aquinas wrote: "Grace completes rather than destroys nature."
[74] "A Treatise of Vocations," in *Works*, I.
[75] *Ibid.*, p. 760.

sion for family and posteritie: and in conscience and obedience to that common charge, laid upon all the sonnes and daughters of Adam to the worlds end."[76] But what was supremely important was that God was served in the secular calling: "whatsoever our callings be, we serve the Lord Jesus Christ in them," John Dod said, and he added the consoling thought for the underdog: "Though your worke be base, yet it is not a base thing to serve such a master in it."[77]

This then was an intramundane asceticism to which Puritans were called. Perhaps here we can see most clearly the difference between Anglican and Puritan ethics. In Anglicanism there was a sense that the true following of God is to be found in the self-deprivation and restraint of nature that were inherent elements of the monastic emphasis on evangelical poverty and chastity—this was completely lacking in Puritanism. But even in Anglicanism it was temporary, seasonal, Lenten. The Puritan ethic was totally integrated with general and secular callings. Anglican writers such as Hall and Sanderson were far from oblivious to instruction on callings, but they did not as strikingly insist that all callings are equal in God's sight and make no difference in terms of man's ultimate destiny. The Anglican was too clearly aware of the differences of degree in society and of the existing social hierarchy to be able to say with Perkins: "the action of a sheepheard in keeping sheep, performed as I have said, in his kind, is as good a worke before God, as is the action of a Judge, in giving sentence, or of a Magistrate in ruling, or a Minister in preaching."[78]

In comparison with Puritanism, Anglican ethics seem static. Puritanism was a spiritual dynamo, charged with the responsibility of creating New Jerusalems in England, after the Biblical pattern renewed in Geneva. Anglican thought was too paralysed by rational hesitations and compromises, by the smoothing away of the rough edges of severity in the interests of Divine charity, and by a greater tolerance. The result was seen in an imprecision and vagueness of attitude, all tending to elasticities of conscience in the half-light of uncertainty. The narrow but absolute certainties of the Puritan provided infinitely greater drive and impetus in ethics. The certainty of man's depravity, the absolute trustworthiness of God combined with his sovereign power to effect

---

[76] *Works*, 4 vols., IV, 66-67.
[77] John Dod and Robert Cleaver, *Ten Sermons . . . of the Lord's Supper* (1609), p. 82.
[78] *Works*, I, 758.

His will against all obstacles, the unmistakable oblig
commandments, the certainty and clarity of the patteri
pose for all aspects of human life in the world of S
drove the Puritan toward an ethics of challenge, not
ance, toward fight rather than flight. Only 50 yea.. aiter tne
period under study the meaning of human life would be expressed
in sublime epitome at the Westminster Assembly of Divines, of
both Presbyterian and Independent wings of Puritanism, as follows: "man's true end is to glorify God and to enjoy him for
ever."[79]

9. Two Christian Styles

We have yet to try to discover the heart of Anglican and Puritan piety and where their distinctive styles of Christian devotion
and life are to be found.

At the heart of Anglican piety there was the awed wonder at
the condescension of the God-man, sheer adoring amazement at
the humility of the Incarnation. The greatest Anglican sermons,
such as those of Andrewes,[80] Donne,[81] or, for that matter, Newman[82] before 1845, took as their starting point the paradox of
Bethlehem, where the Divine Son stoops to conquer and is most
compelling in His weakness. They seemed to be happiest when
they narrated the chief events of the Gospel from the Gospels,
beginning with the Virgin Birth, where the second Eve recovers
what the first Eve lost, and provides through her Son the Savior

[79] The Westminster Shorter Catechism.

[80] In Andrewes' *Ninety-Six Sermons*, 5 vols., there are 17 on the Nativity, three
on the Passion, 18 on the Resurrection, 15 on Pentecost (Whitsunday), seven on
Christ's Temptations, and 15 on the Lord's Prayer—a total of 60 "Christological"
sermons.

[81] "Donne preached at St. Paul's his great series of Easter Sermons, which,
together with his series of Christmas Sermons, may be held perhaps to represent
his finest achievement as a preacher." (*The Sermons of John Donne*, ed. G. R.
Potter and E. M. Simpson, 10 vols., IV, 6.) A sample of the paradoxes of the
Incarnate Christ and the tenderness such contemplation inspires is the following
excerpt from a sermon on the Crucifixion in Donne's *LXXX Sermons* (1640), p.
401: ". . . I see those hands stretched out, that stretched out the heavens, and
those feet racked, to which they that racked them are foot-stooles; I heare him,
from whom his nearest friends fled, pray for his enemies, and him whom his father
forsooke, not forsake his brethren; I see him that cloathes this body with his
creatures, or else it would wither, and cloathes this soule with his Righteousnesse,
or else it would perish, hang naked upon the Crosse; And him that hath, him that
is, *the Fountain of the Water of Life*, cry out, He thirsts. . . ."

[82] Newman's great Incarnational sermons, "Christ the Son of God made man"
and "The Incarnate Son a Sufferer and a Sacrifice," are found in Vol. 5 of his
Parochial and Plain Sermons, 8 vols. (1868); they were preached during his
Anglican days. The finest of all on the same theme is, however, his Catholic
sermon, "Omnipotence in Bonds," from *Sermons preached on Various Occasions*.

a second chance for humanity, on through the agony and bitter sweat of the Passion to the miracle of the Resurrection, where God tolls a bell for the beginning of a new eternal life for redeemed man. For the Anglican, then, the heart of piety was devout meditation and adoration evoked by contemplation on the mysteries of the Divine revelation concentrated in the saga of Christ's life. It became the Sacrament of the love of God, from the Nativity to the Passion to the Resurrection. This single, richly meaningful event was like a diamond presenting a different facet at every festival in the round of the Christian Year, inviting the Christian to imitation. In this meditation Christ was seen as the supreme revelation of the nature of God and of the possibilities open to man; the response evoked was always a gratitude of tenderness. It seems to be the continuation of the mysticism of medieval England.

English Puritanism, however, did not lose itself in the mystery of the Incarnation, which it regarded as a subject for theological explanation rather than meditation. It had little interest in the retrospective gaze and little incentive, since it had rejected the Christian Year because of the multitude of saints' days, which hid the solitary splendor of the king of saints, Christ. Its center of interest was not in the incidents of the Gospels, but in the Epistles of St. Paul and in the Acts of the Apostles, for it was absorbed in trying to live in the Spirit. Puritanism's point of departure was not the Nativity, the Passion, or the Resurrection, but the Ascension of Christ and the descent of the Holy Spirit. The Puritans were interested in the glorification of Christ at His ascension rather than in His humiliation at Bethlehem or Calvary. They had little interest in the historic drama of the past, only with the civil war of the soul in the present, in which Christ fought with Satan for possession. Theirs was not so much an imitation of Christ, as Anglican piety was, but a recapitulation in themselves of the story of Everyman Adam, from temptation and fall, through reconciliation, restoration, and renewal. They were interested in the stages of the redeemed soul's progress: election, vocation, justification, sanctification, glorification. "Here," said Haller, "was the perfect formula explaining what happened to every human soul born to be saved."[83]

The Puritan was not oblivious to the major events in the life of Christ, but the birth he cared for was the rebirth of the soul, his own regeneration. The crucifixion he bothered about was the crucifixion of the old Adam in him by the power of the new Adam,

[83] *Rise of Puritanism*, p. 90.

Christ. The Christian life was not for him the recapitulation of the main events in the life of Christ as it was for Anglican piety, so that in him the Biblical promise, "if we suffer with Him, we shall reign with Him"[84] is fulfilled. Rather, for the Puritan, life was a struggle against the forces of Satan under the orders of Christ the Captain of salvation, together with Christ's elect. It was a warfare from which there was no release, but the tired troops were encouraged by the assurance that the victory of Christ and His saints on earth was sure and would be the prelude to the triumphant return of Christ with all His saints to heaven. Ultimately the difference of style between the Anglican and the Puritan was the difference between life as a pilgrimage toward the shining towers of heaven glimpsed mystically as the clouds part, and life as a fighting the good fight of faith, with the courage of obedience, empowered by the sword of the Spirit.[85]

10. *Theology's Consequences for Worship*

The theological differences between Anglicanism and Puritanism inevitably led to differences in the practice of worship. The chief differences were the following: First, Anglicans were free to use the customs of the ancient church, provided Scripture did not veto them, whereas the Puritans demanded a positive warrant in Scripture for all their ordinances and even for the details of their organisation. Second, the chief means of grace for the Anglicans were the sacraments, especially Holy Communion, while for the Puritans it was unquestionably the lively oracles of God in preaching (though it should be recalled that there was an admirable tradition of preaching in the Church of England, especially in cathedral and university pulpits, and that there was a strong tradition of eager and reverent attendance at the Lord's Supper on the part of Puritans). This Anglican emphasis on the primary role of the sacraments was partly responsible for the ever-present dangers in the Church of England of sacerdotalism and the "sacristy mind," or of a play-acting in the form of ritualism. On the other hand, the Puritan mania for sermons often brought its revenge in a dreary and desiccated didacticism in devotions in the Puritan tradition of worship. The third consequence of the different theological outlooks was a deep loyalty to liturgical worship in Anglicanism and

84 2 Timothy 2:12.
85 For an excellent study of Puritan thought on the holy spirit see Geoffrey F. Nuttall, *The Holy Spirit in Puritan Faith and Experience.*

more than a little suspicion of its formality in the Puritan tradition. Puritanism, however, was not cut all of one cloth; the Presbyterians preferred a national liturgy with some variety and freedom of words in the pastoral prayer, while the Separatists and the Independents appreciated more impromptu praying by the minister. In the fourth place, Anglicans kept such ancient vestments as the surplice and the cope, and such time-honoured ceremonies as kneeling for the reception of Holy Communion, the signing of the Cross in Baptism, and the use of the ring in marriage. All these vestments and ceremonies were rejected by the Puritan iconoclasts as the remnants of Romish superstition. Fifth and finally, the Christian calendar, celebrating the chief events in the life of the Incarnate Son of God and commemorating the Virgin and the leading saints, was retained in streamlined form by the Church of England, but was discarded by the Puritans, although they had their own special days such as the weekly sabbath and special days of humiliation and thanksgiving, by which they marked the judgments and the providences of God as related to the nation or the family. These five major differences of interest and emphasis must be examined in greater detail.

The Puritans, as just mentioned, were fully committed to the acceptance of the Holy Scriptures as the supreme liturgical criterion and canon. This was made plain by William Bradshaw, a friend of William Ames, in his *English Puritanisme* (1605), who asserts at the outset: "IMPRIMIS they hould and maintaine that the word of God contained in the writings of the Prophets and Apostles, is of absolute perfection, given by Christ the Head of the Churche, to bee unto the same, the sole Canon and rule of all matters of Religion, and the worship and service of God whatsoever. And that whatsoever done in the same service and worship cannot bee iustified by the said word, is unlawfull."[86]

In trying to reproduce the worship of the Apostolic church of the New Testament the Puritans discovered six perpetually binding ordinances: Prayer, Praise, the proclamation of the Word, the administration of the sacraments of Baptism and the Lord's Supper, Catechising, and the exercise of Discipline. They sought for the types of prayer and the matter of suitable prayers in the New Testament, as well as for the varieties of approved praise. They even sought for the details of their ordinances in the Scriptures. They found the authority for holding two services on a Sunday

[86] *Ibid.*, p. 1.

from the requirement of a double burnt offering recorded in Numbers 28:9, and the sanction for introducing the Lord's Supper with a sermon in Acts 20:27.

Biblical fidelity could all too easily degenerate into Bibliomania in the more extreme forms of text-hunting and strained interpretation. Perhaps the most extreme example was arguing that God abhorred the responses in the Litany of the Book of Common Prayer from the prohibition of cuckoo's meat to the Jews in Leviticus.[87] Disregarding such special pleading and hair-splitting interpretation as mere eisegesis, it must still be recognized that the value of providing a Biblical warrant for all the ordinances of Puritan worship was that each was directly related to the divine will, and that this gave these ordinances an august authority for those who used them, as the Puritans did, in the obedience of faith. By contrast, the Anglican was free to use all decent, edifying, and comely ceremonies not prohibited by the Scriptures, and the church had the right, in his view, to arrange the details of worship as suited its convenience and traditions.

The excitement the Anglican kept for the sacrament, the Puritan exhibited over the sermon. The "sacramental principle," itself based on the supremely sacramental encounter of God with man in the Incarnation, enabled the Anglican in Platonist fashion to see in all the beauties of earth shadows of the more glorious realities in heaven by an analogy of ascent, for there was no fundamental dichotomy for him between nature and grace. He believed that the sacraments conveyed grace to fortify his soul; as bread and wine formed the staple diet of his earthly body, so the grace of the sacrament strengthened his spirit. The mystical approach to the sacrament elated Hooker with an almost Baroque ecstasy: "The very letter of the Word of Christ giveth plain security, that these mysteries do, as nails, fasten us to his very Cross, that by them we draw out, as touching efficacy, force, and virtue, even the blood of his gored side; in the wounds of our Redeemer we there dip our tongues, we are dyed red both within and without, our hunger is satisfied, and our thirst for ever quenched; they are things wonderful which he feeleth, great which he seeth, and unheard of which he uttereth, whose soul is possest of this Paschal Lamb, and made

---

[87] The author owes this example of overingenious biblical interpretation to a suggestion by the Rev. Dr. William McMillan, author of *The Worship of the Scottish Reformed Church 1550-1638*, in a book review of *The Worship of the English Puritans* in the *Dunfermline and West of Fife Advertiser*, issue of 24 July 1948. Unfortunately Dr. McMillan gave no Puritan bibliographical source.

joyful in the strength of this new Wine; this Bread hath in it more than the substance which our eyes behold; this Cup hallowed with solemn benediction availeth to the endless life and welfare both of soul and body, in that it serveth as well for a medicine to heal our infirmities and purge our sins, as for a sacrifice of thanksgiving; with touching it sanctifieth, it enlighteneth with belief, it truly conformeth us unto the image of Jesus Christ."[88]

The Puritan preacher made exactly the same claim for the proclamation of the word of God. The minister was, in the Pauline phrase, Christ's ambassador, and his Master's messages were delivered from the pulpit with the authority of a royal representative. It is surely a means of grace which could transform and convert the stony heart into a sensitive and charitable spirit, or supply new motives for living, or expel fears and anxieties, or create a divine dissatisfaction with the world as it is and a desire to rebuild it, or make it possible to bear suffering without bitterness—and these were all the triumphs of the Holy Spirit won from the pulpit. As that great Puritan author of *The Arte of Prophecying*, William Perkins, wrote: "Preaching of the word is Prophecying in the name and roome of Christ whereby men are called to the state of Grace, and conserved in it."[89] The sacrament had the advantage that its objectivity was guaranteed by the operation of God, although even it could be taken for granted and become too familiar. Preaching had the advantage of variety but the disadvantage of subjectivity.

It was only in the later development of Puritanism that there was a clear-cut opposition to all set forms of prayer and liturgies, as "stinting" the Spirit. Cartwright, for example, disliked the Book of Common Prayer, he was looking for another national formulary of prayer to replace it with. In general, he approved of liturgies: "First, for testifying the consent of all true Churches, in the things that concerne the worship and service of God, which may appeare by such bookes. Secondly, for direction of the Ministers to keepe in their administration (for substance) like soundnesse in doctrine and prayer. Thirdly, to helpe the weaker and ruder sort of people especially; and yet so, as the set forme make not men sluggish in stirring up the gift of prayer in themselves, according to divers

[88] *Ecclesiastical Polity*, v, 67.
[89] The full title is *The Arte of Prophecying, Or, a Treatise Concerning the Sacred and Onely True Manner and Methode of Preaching*, and is to be found in Vol. II of the three-volume edition of the *Works* of Perkins issued posthumously in 1613. It had first appeared in Latin in 1592. The quotation is II, 646.

occurents."[90] However, William Perkins, in his important *Cases of Conscience*, in answer to the question, Is a set form of prayer lawful? replied, "it is not a sinne," because the Psalms of David are in a form and most of them are prayers. Still he seemed to think prayer in the Holy Spirit was preferable since it required great gifts which many lack and therefore fall back on forms of prayer. His words were: "Secondly, to conceive a forme of prayer requires gifts of memorie, knowledge, utterance, and the gifts of grace. Now every child and servant of God, though he have an honest heart, yet hath he not all these gifts; and therfore in the want of them may lawfully use a set forme of prayer, as a man that hath a weake backe, or a lame legge, may lean upon a crutch."[91] The Anglicans had no alternative but to approve of the liturgy since it was one of the requisite modes for establishing an uniformity in religion. It is significant, however, that the Book of Common Prayer was defended, not only on the grounds of convenience and utility, but on the strongest historic grounds that all liturgies came from one common mould and that the churches of the past had always worshipped God in this way.[92]

This consideration of the Vestiarian Controversy has shown how unwilling the Puritan ministers were to accept the garments they considered hopelessly polluted by Roman Catholic use and association. I have not, however, shown with sufficient force how radical Anglican opinion detested the piling up of ceremony on ceremony and considered it as characteristically Roman Catholic. One of the most amusing castigations of excessive ceremonialism comes from the pen of the martyrologist, John Foxe: "What Democritus or Calphurnius could abstaine from laughter, beholding only the fashion of their masse, from the beginninge to the latter end, wyth suche turning, returning, halfe turning and hole turning, such kissinge, blessing, crowching, becking, crossing, knocking, ducking, wasshing, rinsing, lyfting, touching, fingring, whispering, stoping, dipping, bowinge, licking, wiping, sleping, shifting with

[90] *Treatise*, p. 256.
[91] *Works*, II, p. 67.
[92] Hooker writes (*Ecclesiastical Polity*, v, 26): "No doubt from God it hath proceeded, and by us it must be acknowledged a work of his singular care and providence, that the Church hath evermore held a prescript Form of Common Prayer, although not in all things everywhere the same, yet for the most part retaining the same analogy. So that, if the Liturgies of all ancient Churches throughout the world be compared among themselves, it may be easily perceived that they had all one original mould, and that the public Prayers of the people of God in Churches throughly settled, did never use to be voluntary dictates proceeding from any man's extemporal wit."

a hundreth thinges mo. What wise man, I saye, seing such toyish gaudes can keepe from laughter?"[93] In utter contrast, the Puritans aimed at the simplest celebration of the Lord's Supper. The whole thrust of their worship, with the requirement of family preparation at home, and the need for children to recall the main points of the sermon to the satisfaction of their parents, was less on the external and legal requirements of worship than on the spiritual and interior demands it made. Significantly Perkins distinguished between outward and inward worship. The outward worship was the use of the ordinances, but only for the purpose of inward worship. Inward worship consisted of adoration of God and cleaving to Him. The adoration of God was expressed through the cultivation of four virtues: Fear, Obedience, Patience, and Thankfulness. Cleaving to God was possible through the cultivation of faith, hope, love and inward invocation.[94]

It is to be noted in the fifth and final place that the Anglicans kept the structure of the Christian calendar, while the Puritans utterly rejected it. The advantage of the structure of the Christian Year was that it led to that annual remembrance of the chief events of the Christian saga, so that it was another *itinerarium in mentis Deum*, and required its minister to preach on the Gospel or the epistle chosen for the day. Its other advantage was that it kept alive, through its reduced sanctoral cycle and the commemoration of certain saints, the sense of the communion of saints and of the unity of the church triumphant in heaven with the church militant on earth. Puritanism, in concentrating on the spiritual meaning of the Scriptures for the present, was to take a more instrumentalist view of Christ, leaving to Anglicanism a more contemplative view. Puritanism was afraid of being stranded on the shores of the Palestine, and of not making England the holy land and the English people the holy nation. But as a result, relevance was often found at the cost of highly tendentious and idiosyncratic exegesis, because the ark of the church, having cut the painter that bound it to history, was free to move with the winds of the Holy Spirit or as led on by the will-of-the-wisp of private fantasy. The great Anglican preachers found the historic Christian doctrines of the Incarnation, Reconciliation and Resurrection to be no more burdensome than sails are to a boat. Puritan freedom could very easily degenerate into license, as Anglican circumscription could easily

---

[93] *Acts and Monuments* (1563), sig. EEEeb. A similar list, with better rhythm and cadence, can be found in Thomas Becon's *The Jewel of Joy* (1560), folio xxx.
[94] *Cases of Conscience*, in *Works*, II, 62-63.

degenerate into a set of clichés. Both form and freedom had their rights and their representatives, but—what was not apparent in this controversy—they were complementary, not alternative needs. Form needs freedom to keep it fresh, and freedom needs form to prevent it from turning to irresponsible chaos.

In the last analysis there was a difference of spirit between the Anglican and Puritan ways of worship. On one side were the Anglicans whose historic and aesthetic bent found delight in the continuity of the church from Apostolic times, and rejoiced to read in the Fathers the testimony of a far-off witness to the same God and Father of Christ, and was encouraged by the examples of the saints. The Anglicans found joy in the symbolism that spoke to the eye as the sermon and organ music to the ear. They were happy that the architecture reflected the crucifixion in its very shape of nave and chancel crossed by transepts, and in the furnishings which praised God through the crafts of men in carved wood and stone, as in painted window and curiously wrought metal.

On the other side were the Puritans who are too readily dismissed as color-blind and tone-deaf Philistines in church. Yet for them all these Anglican delights were compromises with Roman Catholicism, debilitating distractions from the true service of God and man, outward shows as pretty and irrelevant as carousels, the otiose gilding of the lily and the varnishing of sunlight. The Puritans believed that worship was essentially the turning of the heart in reverent gratitude to God, and the slow shaping of the will by long discipline until it is the responsive instrument for the Spirit's bidding. When they came to build their own meetinghouses, the houses were scrubbed, white, bare, as austerely naked as the soul should be in the sight of God, stripped of all its disguises and pretensions.

The ultimate contrast, though never absolute, seemed to be between the Anglican's sense of the beauty of holiness combined with the holiness of beauty, sacramentally understood and perfectly mirrored in the poems of George Herbert, rector of Bemerton, and the Puritan's sense of the primacy of the Holy Spirit introspectively understood moving reluctant man through the stages of spiritual growth and disciplined training. The Anglican was a pilgrim and the Puritan a soldier; the former's piety was solitary or familial, the latter's was as a member of God's elect, one of the predestined and invincible ironsides of God. A pilgrim might go alone; but a soldier fights most effectively as a part of a disciplined regiment.

CHAPTER III

THE EUCHARISTIC CONTROVERSY[1]

THE EXAMPLES of the Christian humanists like Erasmus and Colet, the labours of Tyndale and Coverdale as translators of the Bible into English, and the conviction of all the Reformers, that the Gospel alone had the power to overthrow the old strongholds of corruption and superstition, combined to give a primary place to teaching and preaching from the pulpit in the sixteenth century. By contrast, nowhere was disagreement greater than in the interpretation of the meaning of the Catholic Mass, Lutheran or Anglican Holy Communion, or Reformed Lord's Supper. This disagreement was dramatically exposed at the Colloquy of Marburg in 1529. The Colloquy had been convened by Philip of Hesse to unite the forces of the Saxon and Swiss Reformers, but it only revealed the depths of the yawning chasm between Lutheran and Zwinglian interpretations of the Eucharist.[2] It is interesting that the English divines, both Catholic and Protestant, devoted a vast amount of attention to this theme, particularly from 1540 to 1560, when political changes forced them to take cognizance of religious change. The Anglican church, proud of its patristic heritage from the time of Cranmer, followed the early fathers in their devotion to Christ inspired by the chief sacrament, without depreciating the role of preaching.[3]

From the moment King Henry VIII entered the lists against Luther with his *Assertio Septem Sacramentorum* in 1521, up to the publication of the fifth book of Hooker's *Treatise of the Laws*

---

[1] The only modern scholarly histories of Anglican Eucharistic interpretation are two studies by C. W. Dugmore, *Eucharistic Doctrine in England from Hooker to Waterland* and *The Mass and the English Reformers*. The second deals with the period under study here, and is valuable in its fairness to Cranmer; but it underestimates the impact on Cranmer of the Continental Reformers and the Continental exiles in England. Gregory Dix's *The Shape of the Liturgy* also is least satisfactory in its treatment of the Continental Reformers.

[2] The Reformers had agreed on the first 14 articles, disagreeing only on the 15th. Cf. the "Relatio Rodolphi Collini de Colloquio Marburgensi," in *Zwinglii Opera*, ed. M. Schuler and J. Schulthess, IV, 173-82. Most of it is given in B. J. Kidd, *Documents illustrative of the Continental Reformation*, pp. 247-54; W. Köhler, *Das Marburger Religions-Gespräch: Versuch einer Rekonstruktion*, Schriften des Verein für Reformationsgeschichte, no. 148.

[3] Paradoxically the Oxford Movement of the nineteenth century, which owed as much to Newman's preaching as to the 90 "Tracts," tended to depreciate sermons and sermon-tasters. See W. D. White's dissertation, "John Henry Newman, Anglican Preacher," Princeton University, 1968.

of Ecclesiastical Polity written against the Puritans in 1597, there was a continuing controversy about the Eucharist, and especially about the mode of Christ's presence in the sacrament. This may seem to have been a very narrow theological issue at the outset, but as the debate developed and the issues proliferated, it became a crucial issue of faith and life as well as liturgy; one's eucharistic beliefs were in many of the Tudor years literally a matter of life or death.

The importance of the matter may be seen in a listing of some of the questions raised in the controversy. What were the chief Scriptural sources for the institution and meaning of the Eucharist? Did not John 6 and I Corinthians 11 give radically different interpretations? How were the Dominical words *Hoc est corpus meum* ("This is my body") to be interpreted—literally or figuratively? Did "body" refer to Christ's historical body, His resurrected body, or the church as His extension or "Body?" If a literal interpretation was preferred, was "Transubstantiation" or "Consubstantiation" the better interpretation of Christ's presence, following Scripture and the Fathers? Or was it even better to affirm this as a supreme and transcendent mystery? Where is the "body" of Christ located: on the altar, in heaven, or in the hearts of the faithful? If it is on the altar, is the body "in" or "under" the bread and wine, and at what point in the Liturgy does consecration take place? Is the Eucharist a propitiatory sacrifice for the living and the dead? But if Christ's sacrifice was complete on the Cross, what need was there for repetition? Or was the Eucharist a memorial banquet? Or was it the oblation of the church with thanksgiving? What were the eschatological dimensions of the Eucharist? Is consecration effected by Christ the Word made flesh as the priest uses His words of institution, as was commonly held in the West, or was it, as in the East, effected by the agency of the re-creating Holy Spirit? Was faith essential to the reception of the Eucharist, or would a wicked man really be partaking of the body of Christ? Who were the chief exponents of the various interpretations of the modality of Christ's sacramental presence, and were their philosophical presuppositions nominalist or idealist? Was there a direct ratio between the more conservative the doctrine of the Eucharist and its more frequent reception? To be precise, did a transubstantiatory interpretation lead to more frequent reception of the Holy Communion than a Zwinglian or Memorialist interpretation of the

Lord's Supper? These were some of the major theological issues raised by the Eucharistic controversy.

It should not be forgotten, however, that in the midst of the prolonged and bitter struggle the contending parties were not merely discussing doctrines. They were fighting for a way of religion as life. Complete tolerance arose only in a state of utter indifference to the issues. It was not a matter of intellectual tastes or traditions; it was one of arriving at and defending the *truth*, and it was often the disillusioned Catholic who was the most vigorous Protestant, as in the case of the former Cistercian Hooper who became a convinced supporter of Swiss theological views when in Zurich from 1547 to 1549. Unquestionably though Gardiner was Bishop of Winchester in the same Church of England in which Hooper was Bishop of Gloucester, Gardiner's meat was Hooper's poison. Bishop Gardiner was a loyal Erastian, but not a rigid and inflexible antiquarian theologian. He acknowledged that there was a time when the Catholic church had not tied the doctrine of the Real Presence to the essential explanation of Transubstantiation. Yet for him to deny the reality of the miraculous presence of Christ in the mutation of the bread and wine into the very body and blood of Christ was to deny the omnipotence of God,[4] to refuse the most straightforward explanation of Christ's words at the Last Supper, and to reject the marvellous consolation the faithful had received for more than a millennium. Hooper's explanation of the meaning of the Sacrament as a picture of the Divine benevolence, as proof of God's promises, and as a sign of Christian allegiance, must have seemed the sorry reduction of the chief sacrament to a sermon illustration. Yet that high Transubstantiatory evaluation of the Mass seemed to John Hooper the rankest idolatry and a superstition only explicable in terms of priestcraft exploiting the credulity of simple people.[5]

---

[4] Gardiner, in replying to Cranmer, stated that a miracle had been flattened to a mere memento in Cranmer's Eucharistic doctrine, and presented the latter's reductionistic view ironically: "So as in the ordinance of this Supper after this [Cranmer's] understanding, Christ shewed not his omnipotency, but only that he loved us, and would be remembered of us." From *Writings and Disputations of Thomas Cranmer . . . relative to the Sacrament of the Lord's Supper*, ed. J. E. Cox (Parker Society, Cambridge, 1844), p. 16. Henceforth this will be referred to as Cranmer's *Lord's Supper*.

[5] The vehement Hooper, who in Zurich had become the friend of Bullinger, Zwingli's successor, was irrational on the subject of transubstantiation, which he believed was sheer idolatry. This explains, if it does not condone, the offensiveness of his writing, as follows: "The mother of this idolatry was Rome, and the father unknown. A bastard is this transubstantiation doubtless. Lanfrancus [Archbishop of Canterbury in 1020] that enemy of truth and true religion . . . with others begat this wicked woman transubstantiation." *The Early Writings of John Hooper*, ed. Samuel Carr (Parker Society, Cambridge, 1843), pp. 117-18.

It was the same exhilarating sense of deliverance, of recognition that iconoclasm is God's demand for cleansing the temple of superstition, that was so admirably illustrated in the engraving John Day added to the heading of the chapter on the reign of Edward VI in the expanded folio edition of John Foxe's *The Acts and Monuments of Martyrs* (1583).[6] For Hooper it was the cleansing of the temple to root out the Mass books, monstrances, chalices, hosts, all the vestments, and the stone altars. For Gardiner it was to remove the only justification for having a temple; for what was a temple without an altar of sacrifice, an empty shell from which religion had vanished? So soul-deep were the differences revealed in the Eucharistic controversy.

The study of the Eucharistic controversy will, of course, center on England and the theologians of the Church of England. It will also involve several forays to the continent of Europe, to consider the Eucharistic thought of Luther,[7] Zwingli,[8] and Calvin,[9] as well as Oecolampadius.[10] It is equally important to examine the sacramental views of three men whom Archbishop Cranmer invited to England to advise him in furthering the reformation of the English church: Martin Bucer,[11] a former Dominican and influential mediating theologian who was appointed regius professor of Divinity at Cambridge in 1549; Peter Martyr Vermigli,[12] formerly abbot of the Augustinians at Spoleto and regius professor of Divinity at Oxford; and John à Lasco,[13] Polish nobleman, former Catholic bishop, the friend of Hooper, who after visiting England at Cran-

---

6 *Acts and Monuments*, p. 1294. See also the reproduction in this book.

7 See Luther, *Werke* (Weimar, 1883ff., ed. J.C.F. Knaake and others), Vols. 6 and 8; Yngve Brilioth, *Eucharistic Faith and Practice* (1956); Leonhard Fendt, *Der Lutherische Gottesdienst der 16 Jahrhundert* (Munich, 1923); J. J. Pelikan, "Luther and the Liturgy" in *More about Luther: Martin Luther Lectures*, Vol. 2 (Decorah, Iowa, 1958); Vilmos Vajta, *Luther on Worship* (Philadelphia, 1958).

8 *Huldreich Zwinglis samtliche Werke: Corpus Reformatorum*, ed. E. Egli and G. Finsler, 13 vols., IV; Brilioth, *Eucharistic Faith*; C. C. Richardson, *Zwingli and Cranmer on the Eucharist*; F. Schmidt-Clausing, *Zwingli als Liturgiker*.

9 The standard edition of Calvin's *Opera*, in 59 volumes, is Baum, Cunitz, Reuss, Lobstein, and Erichson, *Corpus Reformatorum*; see vols. 29-77. See also E. Doumergue, *Jean Calvin*, II; and Ronald S. Wallace, *Calvin's Doctrine of the Word and Sacrament*.

10 See E. Staehelin, *Das theologische Lebenswerk Johannes Oekolampads*, Quellen und Forschunger zur Reformationsgeschichte, vol. XXI; *Die evangelischen deutschen Messen bis zu Luthers Deutscher Messe*, ed. Julius Smend, pp. 213-19, for Oecolampadius' *Form und Gestalt das Herren Nachtmal*, tr. and ed. Bard Thompson, *Liturgies of the Western Church*, pp. 211-15.

11 See G. J. Van de Poll, *Martin Bucer's Liturgical Ideas*.

12 See Joseph C. McLelland, *The Visible Words of God; An Exposition of the Sacramental Theology of Peter Martyr Vermigli, A.D. 1500-1562*.

13 See K.A.R. Kruscke, *Johannes à Lasco und der Sacramentsstreit*, Studien zur Geschichte der Theologie und der Kirche, vol. VII; John à Lasco, *Works*, ed. A. Kuyper, 2 vols.

mer's request returned in 1550 to be the superintendent of the foreign Protestant congregations in England. Furthermore, it will be impossible to understand the development of Anglican Eucharistic thought unless it is contrasted with the Catholic understanding of the Mass as expounded by St. John Fisher, the martyred bishop of Rochester and friend of Sir Thomas More, and the two bishops, Stephen Gardiner and Cuthbert Tunstall, with whom Cranmer was engaged in a literary duel. As we look for the sources of Ridley's influence on Cranmer, it will be necessary to review the thought of Ratramnus of Corbie, to whom, incidentally, both Gardiner and Ridley appealed as they produced different interpretations of his famous treatise, *De Corpore et Sanguine*.[14] Nor must the sacramental writings of the earliest English Reformers be forgotten, especially those of John Frith and William Tyndale.[15]

1. *Four Eucharistic Theories*

Before entering the thicket of details about the Eucharistic controversy, it may prove helpful to survey the landscape, recognising that the English divines had a choice of four alternative explanations of the presence of Christ in the Eucharist. These may be labelled in the most general fashion as: Transubstantiation; the Real Presence (sometimes affirmed as Consubstantiation, but occasionally without any theory, merely affirming the mystery of Christ's corporal presence as an inexplicable mystery); Virtualism; and Memorialism.

Since the year 1215 Catholics have described their explanation of the mysterious presence of Christ in the Eucharist by the term "Transubstantiation." This scholastic explanation makes a distinction between the underlying "substance," or essence, of every material object, and its "accidents," or superficial, sensible qualities. It is asserted that at the moment of consecration the substances of the bread and wine change into the body and blood of Christ, but that the accidents remain unaltered. Since substance is imperceptible, the change is apprehended by faith, and is, in the strictest sense, as the Mass says, a *mysterium fidei*; it is effected by the omnipotence of God. Because the accidents do not change, the

---

[14] Ratramnus, *Opera*, vol. CXXI, 11-346, *Patrologia Latina*, ed. J. P. Migne. Ratramnus was opposed to the carnal view of the Eucharist held by Paschasius Radbertus.

[15] Cf. *The Whole Workes of W. Tyndall, John Frith, and Doct. Barnes, three worthy Martyrs, and principall teachers of this Churche of England* (1572); William Clebsch, *England's Earliest Protestants, 1520-1535*, pp. 88f., 109ff., 126ff., 133ff.

senses cannot detect any difference after the mutation. We may note that Cranmer had two difficulties with this theory. As a nominalist he found it impossible to think of the accidents of any material object existing apart from its substance. Thus to be told this was the real miracle denied that it was any explanation at all.[16] Furthermore, Cranmer found it difficult to accept the view that a body may exist simultaneously in many places, as is required by the view that there is the body and blood of Christ on every Catholic altar, for this was contradictory to empirical knowledge of the nature of bodies and to Scripture and the Apostles' Creed which located Christ's body in heaven.

Luther's highly original Eucharistic doctrine tries to preserve the strength of the Catholic position without its weaknesses. Often termed "Consubstantiation" because of its partial indebtedness to William of Occam's formulation, it yet moved beyond Occam's formulation of an *esse definitive* to affirm an *esse repletive*, totally rejecting an *esse circumscriptive*. Luther affirmed the identity of Christ's body in heaven with that in the sacrament, through his doctrine of the ubiquity of Christ's body which fills all things. According to Luther, at the consecration the minister did not make something present which was not there before (which was the Nominalist view). Rather, he only made manifest what in all other cases is hidden. The differences between Catholic, Lutheran, and other Protestant views are clear in the following statement of Cyril Richardson: "Where in Catholicism the body is a substance separate from other substances and made accessible in a sacrament; and while in much Protestantism the "body" is an inaccessible object, irrelevant at once to faith and to this world, so that to "eat it" means only to have faith in the Passion, in Luther it is that which underlies all reality, gives it its being, and supports it as the creation of God."[17] According to Luther, then, Christ is present in the Sacrament substantially and in His human nature. For a while Cranmer's "Commonplace Book" found this view attractive, but in time he came to deny any substantial or corporeal unity, and this doctrine of Luther's failed to meet the second of Cranmer's difficulties on the subject of ubiquitarianism. The result was that Luther's

16 Cranmer's *Lord's Supper*, p. 45: "And although all the accidents, both of the bread and wine remaine still, yet, say they, the same accidents be in no manner of thing, but hang alone in the air, without anything to stay them upon."

17 See Richardson's review of C. W. Dugmore's *The Mass and the English Reformers*, in *Journal of Theological Studies*, New Series, vol. XVI, pt. 2 (October 1965), 436.

explanation in the long run seemed to make the mystery even more baffling.[18]

The third account of the meaning of Holy Communion was Zwingli's, commonly known as Memorialism, a view more often caricatured than expounded. It was quite Protestant in considering the body of Christ to be located and circumscribed in heaven and in affirming that it is by His divinity and not in His humanity that Christ is present in the Lord's Supper. In no sense can Christ be substantially present in the consecrated elements. On the contrary, he can be known only by the mind or consciousness or faith of the participants in Holy Communion. The result was that there is in Zwingli no distinctive *Eucharistic* presence of Jesus Christ. Therefore, in substance the value of the Supper is that it helps to communicate faith, as does preaching. According to Cyril Richardson, "The elements" were, for Zwingli, "the reminders of a past redemption, not vehicles of a present grace."[19] There were three essential components of Zwingli's teaching: (1) the Lord's Supper is an *eucharistia*—an act of thanksgiving for the sacrificial act of Christ on the Cross here remembered; (2) it is a *synaxis*—a gathering together on the part of the church as the body of Christ to express the unity of the Christian community and its loyalty, of which the Lord's Supper is the badge; and (3) it is a prop or aid to faith.

Two lesser points in Zwingli's thinking should also be mentioned. *Hoc est corpus meum* means *hoc significat corpus meum*, on the analogy of Exodus 12:11, where the paschal lamb is eaten as a Passover, but is not itself a Passover. Second, Chapter 6 of St. John's Gospel was interpreted as the eating of Christ's flesh to be understood always as believing in Christ's Passion. The usual criticism of the Zwinglian idea is to call it, with Dom Gregory Dix, the doctrine of the "Real Absence"; that is, to argue that for Zwingli the Communion is a historical tribute and that its accent is on the past not the present. This, however, is to do less than justice to Zwingli's recognition that Christ is made contemporary by a rich doctrine of faith, not as consciousness of Christ, so much as a being grasped by God through the Holy Spirit. It is the overly subjective, even solipsistic interpretation of faith in Zwingli that

[18] It was similar considerations that caused some Anglican theologians (of whom Queen Elizabeth was possibly first) to affirm the "Real Presence" as an ultimately inexplicable mystery; the Benedictine theologians of Maria Laach Abbey have made the same point in the present century. For the latter see Horton Davies, *Worship and Theology in England*: Vol. 5: *The Ecumenical Century, 1900-1965*, Chap. 1, esp. pp. 26-31.

[19] C. C. Richardson, *Cranmer and Zwingli on the Eucharist*, p. 19.

makes his doctrine seem so thin. On the other hand, the truth in the criticism is that for Zwingli the Sacraments were not *signa exhibitiva*, signs that exhibit and communicate what is present, but *signa representativa*, signs that represent, symbolise, or commemorate what is absent.[20]

The fourth theory was what has been called, a little inadequately, "Virtualism," that is, the belief that while the bread and wine continue to exist unchanged after the Consecration, yet the faithful communicant receives together with the elements the virtue or power of the body and blood of Christ.[21] This was an attempt to preserve the positive values of Transubstantiation and of the doctrine of the "Real Presence," without metaphysical explanations that baffle the intelligence, on the one hand, and to avoid the reductionism of the Zwinglian Memorialist views on the other. It was espoused by Bucer and by Calvin, both of whom tried to produce in this way a halfway point between Luther and Zwingli; it was believed that this was in fact achieved in the Sacramental articles of the *Consensus Tigurinus* of 1549, in which Bullinger, Zwingli's successor, joined with Calvin. Calvin's *De Coena Domini*, written in 1540, was translated into English by Coverdale;[22] it showed that Calvin was much nearer to Luther's views than to Zwingli's on the significance of the Eucharist. This view was popularised in the Church of England by Hooker in his *Laws of Ecclesiastical Polity*.

Calvin defined a sacrament as "an external sign, by which the Lord seals on our consciences His promises of goodwill towards us in order to sustain the weakness of our faith, and we in our turn testify our piety towards Him, both before Himself and before angels as well as men."[23] The sacraments are seals of the word, confirmations of the Divine promises, and signs of union with the body of Christ.[24] Calvin, says Ronald S. Wallace, "cannot get away

20 C. H. Smyth, *Cranmer and the Reformation under Edward VI*, p. 20, draws attention to the fact that the Reformed Church in Zurich came under the guiding influence of such distinguished Hebraists as Leo Jud, Pellican, and Bibliander, who were deeply impressed by the correspondence between the Old Testament signs and the New Testament sacraments, particularly the links between circumcision and baptism, and between the Passover and the Lord's Supper. Curiously, however, in regard to the latter, they did not stress the element of sacrifice common to both the Passover and the Lord's Supper, but did emphasize unduly the commemorative aspect also common to both.

21 *The Oxford Dictionary of the Christian Church*, ed. F. L. Cross, p. 1,425.

22 Coverdale's translation of Calvin was entitled *A fayth ful and most godly treatise concernynye [sic] the sacrament*, which Pollard and Redgrave's *Short Title Catalogue* lists as being published probably in 1549 by Day.

23 *Institutes* IV:14:i.   24 *Ibid.*, 17:i.

from the fact that our bodies as well as our souls are involved in this union, and that the sacrament of the Lord's Supper especially testifies that the flesh of Christ, the body in which He lived and died is also involved."[25] The point to be emphasized is that Calvin believed Christ does not merely give us the benefits of His death and resurrection, but the very body in which He suffered and rose again.[26] How does the body of Christ located at the right hand of God become our food in the Eucharist here on earth? The answer is: "Though it seems an incredible thing that the flesh of Christ, while at such a distance from us in respect of space, should be food for us, let us recall how far the secret virtue [*virtus arcana*] of the Holy Spirit surpasses all our conceptions and how foolish it is to desire to measure its immensity by our feeble capacity. Therefore what our mind does not comprehend, let faith conceive, viz. that the Spirit really unites things separated by grace."[27] Calvin rejected the Catholic and Lutheran views of the presence of Christ because they would not allow the signs to be true signs or the promises to be true promises, for, to him, Transubstantiation and Consubstantiation turn the signs of the body and blood of Christ, the bread and wine, into the body and blood of Christ. He also rejected the opposite view, that to eat is only to have faith, because this endangers the reality of the presence of Christ and thus denies the fulfillment of God's promise that the signs are not empty but show forth the promises. Calvin, without doubt, believed that it was the powerful activity of the Holy Spirit that made possible the participation of the flesh of Christ in the Supper.[28] Finally, Calvin never let it be forgotten that the mystery of our union with Christ is an eschatological reality to be completed fully in the life beyond death for our flesh as well as our spirits.[29] The defect of this theory is that it also posits a miracle to cross the abyss between two incompatible statements.

It will be apparent in our consideration of the Eucharistic controversy that a central figure such as Cranmer will, on growing dis-

[25] Ronald S. Wallace, *Calvin's Doctrine of the Word and Sacraments*, p. 151.

[26] Cf. Calvin's *Commentary* on I Corinthians 11:24, *Corpus Reformatorum* edition, vol. 39, p. 487; and Wallace, *Calvin's Doctrine*.

[27] *Institutes* IV:17:x.

[28] François Wendel, *Calvin*, pp. 350ff., says that Calvin's two statements that seemingly cannot be reconciled, namely the presence of the flesh of Christ in the sacrament and the location of Christ's body in heaven, are in fact compatible; it is the Holy Spirit that makes possible the participation in the body of Christ without its being enclosed in the elements.

[29] See Wallace, *Calvin's Doctrine*, chap. 13, for a full explanation of Calvin's teaching, notable for both fidelity and clarity.

illusioned with the Catholic theory, appear to turn to the Lutheran view first and thereafter to the Calvinist or Zwinglian views, which of the two latter being a point of contention between interpreters. Also, it seems clear that there was a danger that a Virtualist theory would fall into a Memorialist theory, because of the greater ease of defending the latter on empirical and rational grounds, even if it seems to do less than justice to tradition and Christian experience.

It may, however, be convenient at this point in the discussion, to list the important affirmations commonly made by mediating and radical Protestant theologies. Firstly, all agreed in their opposition to the Catholic doctrine of Transubstantiation and the corporeal presence of Christ in the Eucharist as being contrary to the nature of sacraments as signs (rather than the things signified), and contrary to Scripture. Secondly, all stressed that Christ is made present by the action of the Holy Spirit. Thirdly, all asserted that the communion of the faithful is confirmed and strengthened by sharing in the Lord's Supper. Fourthly, the sacrament is in a primary sense the memorial of Christ's death and resurrection. Fifthly, there was agreement that the elements are powerful signs eliciting from the faithful the remembrance of Christ's work and consequently a confession of the forgiveness of sins through Christ's Passion. Sixthly, all affirmed that the sacrament is received by faith in the heart or conscience of the believer. Finally, some Protestants would emphasize that the presence of Christ is not limited to the sacraments, and that it is through the moving of the mind to recall the work of Christ that a sharing in Christ is effectual.[30]

2. The Catholic Case: Fisher, Tunstall, and Gardiner

Henry VIII's *Assertio Septem Sacramentorum*, written against Luther's reduction of the seven Catholic sacraments to three (Penance,[31] Baptism and the Eucharist) in *The Babylonian Captivity of the Church* (1520) won for the king the title of *Fidei Defensor*[32] (Defender of the Faith) from a grateful Pope, a title

---

[30] This perceptive summary appears on p. 36 of Gordon E. Pruett, "Thomas Cranmer and the Eucharistic Controversy in the Reformation," unpub. Ph.D. thesis, which I had the privilege of directing and to which I am much indebted in this chapter.

[31] Luther initially accepted Penance as a sacrament, because of his conviction that the forgiveness of sins was the first gift of the Gospel, but later gave it up because it did not conform to his threefold requirement that a Sacrament of the Gospel must be (1) clearly instituted by Christ; (2) have a divine promise attached to it; and (3) have a confirmatory sign. Only Baptism and the Eucharist met these triple requirements.

[32] Leo X gave the title on October 11, 1521.

which continued incongruously to appear obscurely abbreviated as "Fid. Def." above the heads of sovereigns on English coinage within recent memory. The work is, however, more of chronological than of intrinsic importance. The Eucharistic treatise of John Fisher, friend of Erasmus, Chancellor of the University of Cambridge, Bishop of Rochester, and Catholic martyr, is of far greater importance.[33] In this work entitled, *De Veritate Corporis et Sanguinis Christi in Eucharistia*, published in 1527, Fisher defended the Catholic doctrine against the criticism of Oecolampadius.[34]

According to the most recent biographer of John Fisher, *De Veritate* is his "theological masterpiece."[35] It is in the prefaces to each of the five books that Fisher's freshness may be found. In the books themselves there is the usual catena of citations from the Church Fathers. The first preface attempts to prove the Real Presence from the unanimity of the Catholics as contrasted with the disagreements of their adversaries, as can be seen in the mutual slaughter of the Lutherans in the Peasants' Revolt and in the pride in the minds of Luther and Oecolampadius which has caused their disagreements. In the second preface Fisher demonstrates the values of the Sacrifice of the Mass from the varying names given to it, such as The Sacrament of the Lord's Body and Blood, the Mysteries, the Synaxis or Communion, the Eucharist or Thanksgiving, the Sacrifice, the Bread, the Lord's Food, the Viaticum, the Mystical Blessing, the Banquet, and the Exemplar or Antitype. These names show the wealth of the meanings of this sacrament and the folly of conceiving it as consisting of bread and wine only, as well as the sense in calling it a figure, for the bread and wine were signs of the realities, the real body and real blood of Christ. The third preface tries to confirm the faith of readers by enumerating 14 points of corroboration:

> The reality of Christ's Body in the Eucharist is proved by the most clear words of the same Christ. 2. The reality is supported by the immensity of Christ's love. 3. The same is

[33] Henry VIII had John Fisher executed on June 22, 1535, while his friend, Sir Thomas More, suffered a similar fate on July 6, 1535. Both were canonised by Pope Pius XI.

[34] Oecolampadius (1482-1531), the German Reformer, first introduced Reformed principles to Basel in 1522. At Marburg in 1529 he defended the Eucharistic doctrine of Zwingli, but in his more developed thought on the sacrament he anticipated Calvin. His sacramental theology will be considered in the thought of John Frith, his English disciple, in the next section of this chapter.

[35] Edward Surtz, S.J., *The Works and Days of John Fisher*, p. 337.

corroborated by the consent of the Fathers. 4. It is confirmed by Christ's promises. 5. It is established by many Councils. 6. It is demonstrated by innumerable miracles. 7. It is defended by revelations most worthy of credence. 8. Christ's protection against heresies has never been wanting. 9. Persons who frequently receive the Sacrament advance in every virtue. 10. Persons who have idle opinions about it meet with ill fortune. 11. Enemies of this Sacrament have no clear Scripture on their side. 12. They produce the solid testimony of no orthodox writer. 13. They can present no miracles and no revelations. 14. Dissenters from the common belief of the Church mutually cut one another's throat.[36]

The cumulative effect of these considerations is great, except, of course, that arguments 9 to 14 merely state negatively what arguments 1 and 3-7 state positively.

The fourth preface argues for a belief in the "Real Presence" on the basis of the consent of the Fathers during 15 centuries. The fifth preface shows Fisher bending all his energies to prove that the sixth chapter of St. John's Gospel refers to the Eucharist, from the unanimous testimony of the Fathers for such an interpretation, the necessity for bodily eating (*corporalis esus*) as well as for faith, and from the words of Christ Himself seen in their scriptural contexts.

Fisher, in fact, had a formidable array of weapons; the strongest was the inherent improbability of any teaching at variance with tradition, with 1,500 years to support it, being right or of the central tradition of the church having been in error for so long. He was also astute in seeing where the argument of Oecolampadius was weakest, namely in his assertion that the New Testament promises eternal life to the man "who eats my body" and to the man "who believes in Me," and that therefore there is no need for the Sacrament on the part of the man who has faith. Fisher replied that no general faith is adequate, but a special one which believes what is proposed to it and also does what is commanded. Further, not only simple faith but the sacraments are essential to the Christian life, because this is the unanimous patristic testimony, because faith dissolves unless strengthened by the sacraments, and because without receiving the sacraments, there can be no certainty about the possession of a living faith.

[36] Tr. Edward Surtz, S.J., in *ibid.*, p. 341.

The second Catholic treatise to be considered was written by Bishop Cuthbert Tunstall of Durham, a Henrician who had sympathised with Catherine of Aragon but whose position became impossible under Edward VI. Tunstall was eventually imprisoned in his house in London, where in 1551 he wrote *De Corporis et Sanguinis Domini in Eucharistia*. The manuscript was taken by his great-nephew Bernard Gilpin to Paris where it was published in 1554 by Michael Vascosanus. Gilpin's biographer recounts several incidents purporting to show that Tunstall disliked too rigid a definition of the mode of Christ's presence in the Eucharist, regarding this as a mystery that transcended human language. He reports Gilpin as saying of Tunstall: "I remember that Bishop *Tonstall* often tolde me that Pope *Innocent* the third had done very unadvisedly, in that he made the opinion of Transubstantiation an Article of faith: seeing that in former times it was free to holde or refuse that opinion. . . . Moreover the Bishop tolde me that he did not doubt but that himselfe, if he had beene in that Councell, could have prevailed with the Pope to have let that businesse alone."[37]

As one might expect, this treatise affirms the corporeal presence as the plain intention of Scripture and as the consentient tradition of the church—the two main arguments of Catholic apologists during the period.[38] The first deals with the three explanations:[39]

> But how the bread, which before the consecration was common bread, by the ineffable sanctification of the Spirit passed into His Body, the most learned of the ancients regarded as something inscrutable. . . . Moreover, before Innocent III, Bishop of Rome, who presided at the Lateran Council, it seemed to those scrutinising more curiously that it could be brought about in three ways: Some thinking that together with the bread, or in the bread, the body of Christ is present, as fire in a mass of iron, which mode Luther seems to have followed: Others that the bread is reduced to nothing or corrupted: Others that the substance of bread is trans-

[37] George Carleton, *Life of Bernard Gilpin*, p. 42.

[38] C. W. Dugmore, *The Mass and the English Reformers*, p. 152. However, the treatise contains two books: the first sets forth the Scriptural evidence for the Real Presence; it attempts to answer the Protestant criticisms against the Catholic sacramental doctrine; the second consists largely of an armory of patristic proof texts to support the orthodox interpretation of the Eucharist.

[39] Here the careful translation of Fr. Edward Quinn has been used. It will be found for these central passages in his article on "Bishop Tunstall's Treatise on the Holy Eucharist," in *The Downside Review*, vol. 51, no. 148 (October 1933), 674ff.

muted into the substance of Christ's body: which mode Innocent followed, and rejected the other views at that Council, although to those investigating more curiously not fewer but rather more miracles seem to arise than in the modes rejected by him. But it seemed to those who were present with Innocent at that Council that all miracles give way before the omnipotence of God, to which nothing is impossible, because this mode seemed to them most in agreement with these words of Christ, 'This is my body, this is my blood.' For John Scotus in the fourth book of Sentences, the eleventh distinction, the third question, citing Innocent, says there were three opinions: One that the bread remains, and yet together with it is truly the body of Christ: Another that the bread does not remain, and yet it is not converted, but ceases to be, either through annihilation, or through resolution into matter, or through corruption into some other thing: A third, that bread is transubstantiated into the body and wine into the blood. But each of these opinions sought to maintain in common that one thing, that there truly is the body of Christ, because to deny that is clearly against faith.[40]

Tunstall asks whether it was right of the church to choose one of these three explanations as most in accordance with the institution of the Eucharist by Christ, and to reject the other two. His conclusion is that the church wisely decided to affirm Transubstantiation: "I think it right on a matter of this kind, because the Church is the pillar of truth, that her firm judgment should be

[40] The original reads: "Caeterum quo modo panis qui ante consecrationem erat communis, ineffabili spiritus sanctificatione transiret in corpus ejus, veterum doctissimi quique inscrutabile existimaverunt. . . . Porro ante Innocentium tertium Romanum episcopum, qui in Lateranensi concilio praesedit, tribus modis id posse fieri curiosius scrutantibus visum est: Aliis existimantibus una cum pane, vel in pane Christi corpus adesse, veluti ignem in ferri massa, quem modum Lutherus secutus videtur: Aliis panem in nihilum redigi, vel corrumpi: Aliis substantiam panis transmutari in substantiam corporis Christi: quem modum secutus Innocentius, reliquos modos in eo concilio reiecit, quanvis miracula non pauciora, imo vero plura quam in reliquis reiectis ab eo modis, oriri curiosius investigantibus videantur. Sed Dei omnipotentiae, cui nihil est impossibile, miracula cuncta cedere, his qui cum Innocentio in eo consilio interfuerunt visum esse, quod is modus maxime cum verbis hisce Christi. Hoc est corpus meum, hic est sanguis meus, congruere illis visus est. Nam Joanne Scotus libro quarto Sententiarum, distinctione undecima, quaestione tertia, recitando Innocentium, ait tres fuisse opiniones: Una, quod panis manet, & tamen cum ipso vere est corpus Christi: Alia, quod panis non manet, & tamen non convertitur, sed desinit esse, vel per annihilationem, vel per resolutionem in materiam, vel per corruptionem in aliud: Tertia, quod panis transubstantiatur in corpus, et vinum in sanguinem. Quaelibet autem istarum voluit istud commune salvare, quod ibi vere est corpus Christi, quia negare est plane contra fidem."

observed. Moreover, those who publicly contend that this mode of Transubstantiation is to be entirely rejected because the word 'Transubstantiation' is not in Scripture show themselves to be too prejudiced in their judgment. As if Christ could not effect in that way what He wills, from whose omnipotence and the operations of the Holy Spirit they seem totally to detract by their assertion. And they themselves fall into a much greater sin of audacity than that which they bring up against the Lateran Council. Since indeed if we believe them, neither Christ nor the Holy Spirit could bring it about that the bread should pass into the substance of the body of Christ."[41] The weakest point of the argument is to accuse the Protestants of lacking faith in the omnipotence of God. They did not deny that God could perform a Eucharistic miracle; they asked whether it was consonant with the revelation of God given by Christ in the wilderness when He refused to win men by miracles and when He taught that even if a man came back from the dead to warn Dives's relations, still they would not believe. Nevertheless, Tunstall by his tender devotion to the person of Christ[42] and by his long view of history, is an attractive apologist, and not least so in his lack of rigidity.

If Fisher was the most learned writer in Tudor Catholic sacramental theology, and Tunstall the most open-minded, Gardiner is the shrewdest controversialist. The chief purpose of his *Explication and Assertion of the true Catholic Faith, touching the most blessed Sacrament of the Altar with confutation of a booke written agaynst the same* (1551), as the latter part of the title obscurely indicates, was to confute Cranmer's recent treatise which, though claiming to be orthodox, was actually heterodox.

---

[41] The original reads: "Iustum existimo ut de eiusmodi, quia ecclesia columna est veritatis, firmum eius observeretur iudicium. Caeterum qui palam contendunt illum modum transubstantionis reiiciendum penitus esse, quod vocabulum transubstantionis in spiritus in scripturis non reperiatur, nimis praefacti iudicii sese ostendunt. Quasi vero Christus eo modo, illus quod vult efficere non posset: cuius omnipotentiae & spiritus sancti operationi, in totum detrahere sua assertione videntur. Et in multo maius audaciae crimen incidunt ipsi, quam quod Lateranensi concilio obiicunt; quando quidem si illis credimus, nec Christus, nec spiritus sanctus id efficere possit ut panis in corporis Christi substantiam transeat." The passages in notes 40 and 41 are taken from *De Veritate Corporis et Sanguinis Domini in Eucharistia*, fols. 45-47.

[42] This is finely expressed in the words in which the help of Christ is sought in writing this treatise: "Tuo igitur Christo auxilio freti obsecramus, ut luminae gratiae tuae nos illustres, et rem destinatam tuto sine formidine aggrediemur ut corporis et sanguinis tui veritatem in eucharistia esse, ex ipsis tuis verbis evincamus, atque huic veritati adversantium perversa dogmata, e fidelium circum ventorum mentibus te favente, sine quo nihil possumus, eradicere concemur. Vale." His unusual qualities are also seen in his *Certain Godly and Devout Prayers*, an example of which is cited in the next chapter, on Catholic worship.

Gardiner shrewdly points out, as I will emphasize in Chapter V on the Anglican Prayer Books, that there were five places in the 1549 Prayer Book that Cranmer took the chief responsibility for, which imply a Catholic doctrine of the Eucharist. Yet Cranmer contradicted this earlier teaching in his treatise, *A Defence of the True and Catholic Doctrine of the Sacrament of the Body and Blood of our Saviour Christ* (1550).

Gardiner begins by demonstrating how heterodox Cranmer is in denying the doctrine of the Real Presence of Christ, not only Transubstantiation, and by denying that wicked men eat and drink the body and blood of Christ. He points out that Luther, Bucer, and Melancthon accepted the doctrine of the Real Presence and berated Oecolampadius for denying it.[43] Gardiner then turns to consider the statement of Cranmer, that Christ's risen body is in heaven and cannot be on the altar. Gardiner agrees with the former part of the statement but cannot accept the consequence Cranmer draws from it. Gardiner affirms that the church acknowledges Christ's body in heaven and also in the sacrament, "not by shifting of place but by the determination of his will."[44]

Gardiner admits that there is an ambiguity in speaking of the "corporal" presence of Christ in the Sacrament. It can indeed be said that Christ is corporally present in the Sacrament, but if the term "corporally" referred to the manner of the presence, "then we should say Christes body were present after a corporall maner, which we say not, but in a spirituall maner, and therefore not locally, nor by maner of quantitie, but in such a maner as God only knoweth. . . ."[45]

The next issue Gardiner dealt with was Cranmer's contention that Christ intended the words "This is my body" to be figuratively and not literally understood. Gardiner replies that Christ made bread his body by calling it so, just as he made water wine by calling it so at Cana of Galilee. He answers the argument that when Augustine and other Fathers of the church use some passages referring to the literal presence and other passages that are clearly figurative in their reference to the presence, the latter usage is to conceal the mystery from the profane.[46] In fact, only six persons have held the figurative doctrine of the presence in the Eucharist (which Cranmer calls Catholic): Ratramnus, Beren-

---

[43] *De Veritate Corporis*, sig. 6-6v.
[44] *Ibid.*, sig. 20.
[45] *Ibid.*, sig. 38 v. See also J. A. Muller, *Stephen Gardiner and the Tudor Reaction*, pp. 210-12.
[46] *Ibid.*, sig. 41 v.-42.

garius, Wycliff, Oecolampadius, Swinglius, and Vadianus. Gardiner rather contemptuously refused to include Peter Martyr in the list since he was not learned, or Cranmer since Cranmer followed Peter Martyr.[47] The remainder of the third book of this treatise is spent hunting through the fathers in whom Cranmer found a metaphorical meaning in regard to Christ's sacramental presence, to insist that its natural meaning in each context is a literal one.

In Book Five Gardiner scores a clever debating point. He says that Cranmer has been greatly concerned with the eating and drinking of Christ's body and blood, and has been attempting to prove that the evil do not receive the body and blood of Christ. But if this is only a metaphorical eating, why waste so much useless energy on the matter?

In Book Five Gardiner defends Transubstantiation as the true doctrine of Christ's mysteries. He accuses Cranmer of error in asserting that faith is to be confirmed by reason, because it transcends reason and "natural operation," being the gift of God and the operation of the omnipotent God.[48] Nor can he accept Cranmer's argument against Transubstantiation on the grounds that there cannot be a change in the substance without a change in the accidents, for there is in all objects an inwardness. It is not, says Gardiner, by the evidence of our senses that we affirm the resurrection of the body, but only by faith.[49] Gardiner argues that as the divinity of Christ who was both God and man operates invisibly in his soul, so the invisible "soul" of the bread and wine operates through their bodily elements and thus "this Sacrament [is] the image of the principall mystery of Christes person."[50]

Gardiner observes that the Fathers used many equivalents for Transubstantiation, including "transition," "mutation," "transelementation," and "conversion."[51] Yet this parallel between the two natures in Christ's person and in the Sacrament cannot be pressed too far, for in the two natures of Christ there was not mutation but only assumption of the human nature into the divine nature.

Gardiner's biggest guns are trained on the six major criticisms Cranmer makes of the Catholic doctrine; it is here that his ingenuity is impressive. Cranmer argued that the Catholics, when asked what is eaten in the Sacrament, have to assert that this refers only

---

[47] Ibid., sig. 74 r and v.
[49] Ibid., sig. 105.
[51] Ibid., sig. 113.

[48] Ibid., sig. 97 v.-98.
[50] Ibid., sig. 122.

to the accidents and that these have been "broken, eaten, dronken, chawed and swalowed without any substaunce at all."[52] He anticipates every logical objection that Cranmer can raise in his answer: "But where this auctor [Gardiner always refers in this indirect way to Cranmer] saith that nothyng can be answered to be brokē but the accidētes: yes verely, for in tyme of contēciō, as this is to him that would aske, What is brokē, I would in other termes answere thus, That thou seest is broken. And thē if he would aske further, What that is, I would tell him the visible matter of the Sacrament, under whiche, is present Invisibly the substance of the most precious body of Christ, if he will aske yet further, Is that bodye of Christ broken, I will say no. For I am lerned in fayth, that that glorious body nowe impassible can not be broken, or divided, and therefore it is holy in every parte of that is broken."[53] To Cranmer's second criticism, that Transubstantiation is contrary to all experience in asserting that accidents persist although the substance has changed, Gardiner replies that faith believes in the almighty power of God and that this is a mystery transcending human comprehension.[54] Cranmer's third criticism, that the Papists make substance without accidents and accidents without substance, is rather weakly rebutted by accusing Cranmer of jesting about serious matters.[55]

Cranmer's fourth empirical criticism of the metaphysics of Transubstantiation is that the Catholics assert that there is a vacuum where substances of the bread and wine were, but it is known that nature abhors a vacuum. Gardiner replies that it is quantity not substance that fills space. Here Gardiner scores a debating point, but he follows it up by admitting that ordinarily there is no quantity without substance, but that this is extraordinary because of a divine miracle.[56] Cranmer's next objection is that Catholics are not ashamed to admit that the substance is made of accidents when bread moulders or becomes worm-ridden, or wine sours. Gardiner speculates that the corruption of accidents may create new accidents, but affirms that the *prima materia* (common to both wine and vinegar) does not change.[57] Cranmer's last argument is to ridicule the Catholics for affirming that "substance is nourished without substance by accidentes onely, if it chaūce any catt, mouse, dogge, or any other thinge to eat the

52 *Ibid.*, sig. 133.
54 *Ibid.*, sig. 135 v.-136.
56 *Ibid.*, sig. 136 v.-137.

53 *Ibid.*, sig. 134 v.
55 *Ibid.*, sig. 136 r. and v.
57 *Ibid.*, sig. 138.

Sacramentall bread or drink the Sacramentall wyne."[58] Gardiner denies that vermin devouring any hosts do in fact violate Christ's precious body. He retorts in some heat that Cranmer's doctrine is an absurdity in declaring that Christ's body is actually only in heaven, that the bread only remains bread, and yet the figure should be called by the name of the reality.

It is in his criticism and attempted confutation of Cranmer's fifth book that the profoundest issue was raised: How can the all-sufficient oblation of Christ for the sins of the world made on Calvary be repeated, as Catholics claim it is, on their altars, without derogating from its sufficiency and finality? Here Gardiner replies that Scripture, while asserting that the work of Christ on the Cross was perfect, yet asserts that it is often to be remembered in the church and exhibited in such a way that it may be fed upon, this sacrifice is a propitiation for the sins of the world, as the Council of Nicea, the teachings of St. John Chrysostom, and the exposition of Peter Lombard testify.

In the course of this debate with Cranmer, Gardiner made some good points, but he fell back all too frequently for good dialectics on the mystery of the sacrament, the omnipotence of God, and the relatively unanimous consent of tradition. These were all good churchly arguments, but since the first was not denied by Protestants it might seem irrelevant to them to insist on mystery when the issue was: which is the best explanation of the mystery available? Nor did Protestants deny the omnipotence of God; they questioned whether this was His method in the Sacrament. Third, since tradition may consist of human inventions and corruptions, Protestants could not see that tradition settled anything. It is interesting, however, that so great was the fear of change in this era of intellectual and religious revolution, that even the Protestants had to appeal in their arguments to the "pure" and "primitive" church—in short, to an earlier, uncorrupted "tradition." Perhaps the best tributes to the effectiveness of Gardiner's arguments were two. The first was that Cranmer reissued his original treatise with changes to attempt to meet Gardiner's charges under the revealing title, *An Answer to a Crafty and Sophistical Cavillation devised by Stephen Gardiner*. The second was the radical reorganization of the doctrine and the words of the revised Anglican Prayer Book of 1552, in which every passage smacking of a Catholic interpretation—at the five points at which Gardiner discovered orthodox Catholicism—was wholly excised.[59]

---

[58] *Ibid.*, sig. 138 r. and v.
[59] For convenience the five places where Gardiner found Catholic doctrine in the

3. *The Teaching of the Early English Reformers*

The contrast between the sacramental theology of the Catholics and that of the early English Reformers is striking. If the Catholics believed in the corporal presence, the Protestants rejected it outright as idolatry and superstition, and tended to follow the example of Zwingli or Oecolampadius in their Memorialism. They were sacramental radicals. This section is given over to John Frith, William Tyndale, John Hooper, and Thomas Becon, all of whom endured exile and imprisonment for their beliefs, and the first three of whom were martyred for their convictions.

John Frith (1503-1533) was imprisoned for heresy in 1528, but escaped to Marburg where he assisted Tyndale in his translation of the Pentateuch and Jonah into English. Returning to England in 1532 he was arrested after a book he had prepared for a friend, and not for publication, got into the hands of Thomas More, and he was condemned to death for denying purgatory and transubstantiation.[60] *A booke made by Iohn Frith prisoner in the tower of London* (1533)[61] reads freshly; while it expounds the views of Oecolampadius,[62] it does so with dialectical brilliance and verve.

His principal contention was that the Eucharist involves "the spirituall and necessarie eating of his body & bloud, which is not received with the teth and bellye, but with the cares and faith."[63] He offered two 'proofs' that it is not an essential article of faith to believe in the presence of the natural body of Christ in the Sacrament. Many did, in fact, receive it and believe it to their damnation. By contrast, says Frith, "it is not his presence in the bread that can save me, but his presence in my hart through faith in his blood, which hath washed out my sinnes and pacified ye fathers wrath toward me."[64] His second argument was that the same faith will save his contemporaries as saved the patriarchs before Christ's incarnation, but they were not bound under pain of damnation to

---

First Prayer Book of Edward VI were: (1) in the words of administration; (2) in a post-communion rubric; (3) in the commemoration of the dead in the intercessions; (4) in the prayer of consecration and particularly in the invocation of the Holy Spirit (*epiklesis*); and (5) in the rubric requiring kneeling while saying the prayer of humble access. Each of these claims is examined in detail in Chap. V.

[60] There is a sympathetic account of Frith in Clebsch, *England's Earliest Protestants*, who claims that "Frith displayed the finest mind, the most winsome wit, and the boldest spirit among the men who wrote theology in English between 1520 and 1535" (p. 78).

[61] It was published as part of *Workes of Tyndall*.

[62] Frith borrowed from two works of Oecolampadius: *De Genuina verborum domini, Hoc est corpus meum, iuxta vetustissimos authores, expositione liber* (1525) and *Quid veteres senserint de Sacramento eucharistiae* (1530).

[63] *Ibid.*, p. 107 v.   [64] *Ibid.*, p. 108.

believe this, nor were his contemporaries.[65] The manna and water given to Moses and the Israelites are the same as the bread and wine are to those in the Christian dispensation.[66] If, however, faith is enough, then it could be objected, why institute a sacrament?

Frith maintained that there are three reasons for instituting the sacraments. The first is a sociological consideration: to be "knit in fellowship" it is essential to have visible tokens of sacraments or signs or badges of belonging. "And there is no difference betweene a signe or a badge and a Sacrament, but that the Sacrament figureth a holy thyng, and a signe or a badge doth signifie a worldly thing."[67] Second, there is a pedagogical foundation for the sacraments: "that they may be a meane to bryng us unto faythe, and to imprint it the deeper in us, for it doth customably the more move a man to believe, when he perceiveth the thyng expressed to diverse senses at once."[68] The third reason for the institution of sacraments was that "they that have received these blessed tydinges and worde of health, do love to publishe this felicitie unto other men."[69] Apart from the Gospel to which the sign testifies, the Sacrament is meaningless. For, "if a man wot not what it meaneth, and seeketh the health in the sacrament and outward signe, thē may he wel be likened unto a fond fellow, which when he is very drye, and an honest man, shew him an alepole and tell him that there is good ale inough, would go and sucke the alepole, trusting to get drinke out of it, and so to quench his thyrste."[70]

Frith continues by denying a mutation in the bread by the testimony of Scripture (especially I Corinthians 10 and 11, Acts 2, and Luke 22) by the evidence of experience since mouldering of bread proves that bread remains after the prayer of consecration, and by the witness of such doctors of the church as Gelasius, Origen, Nestorius, Bede, and Augustine.[71] His fourth argument for denying the corporal presence of Christ in the Eucharist was that Christ's body according to his manhood must be "in one place, heaven, and so not in the Sacrament."[72]

Frith then brings forward six considerations to convince his readers that the doctrine of the corporal presence in the Eucharist is unreasonable. Each sacrament is, in the first place, a sign of a holy reality, and so cannot be the holy thing itself. Therefore

[65] Ibid., p. 109.
[67] Ibid., p. 112.
[69] Ibid.
[71] Ibid., pp. 117-25.

[66] Ibid., p. 109 v. in the margin.
[68] Ibid., p. 112 v.
[70] Ibid., p. 112 v.-p. 113.
[72] Ibid., p. 140.

the Sacrament is the representation of the bodily presence of Christ, not the corporal presence itself.[73] Second, it is not necessary for the flesh of Christ to be in the Sacrament if it is the remembrance, not the flesh, that profits the Christian.[74] Third, if the end is superior to the cause, and the end of the Sacrament is the remembrance of Christ's body, and if the Sacrament is his natural body, then the remembrance is better than the body itself.[75] Fourth, if the soul eats what the angels in heaven eat, and the angels' meat is "the joy and delectation they have of God and his glory," so the soul similarly eats through faith the body of Christ which is in heaven, and this is a spiritual not a corporal manducation. In the fifth place, just as the bread is Christ's body, so it is claimed, so the breaking of Christ's body would be his death; but on Maundy Thursday the breaking of the bread at the Last Supper was not the breaking of his body, but only a representation of it, and so with the Sacrament.[76] The sixth rather recondite argument from silence allows Frith to argue that since the apostles were Jews, to whom it was forbidden to eat or drink human or animal blood, any doctrine of the corporal presence of Christ in the Apostolic church would have been such an affront as to have excluded all Jews from the Christian faith.[77] His conclusion, on the nature of consecration, was: "And so I say that it is ever cōsecrated in hys hart that beleveth, though the Priest consecrate it not. . . . For except thou know what is meant therby and beleve, gevyng thankes for hys body breakyng & bloudshedyng, it can not profite thee."[78] Frith ended as he began, by insisting that it is the spirituality of the rite that matters, not the external sign, he was utterly opposed to the notion that grace is quantifiable.

The value of Frith's teaching was that it stressed the importance of the divine promise of grace and reinterpreted the meaning of grace. Like Luther, Frith understands grace to be the benevolence and mercy of God. He did not, with the scholastics, think of it as a quasi-physical essence that is infused into the soul of the recipient. This conception of grace was capable of revolutionising the role of the sacraments and the power of the church, but Frith did not draw the political and social implications of a concept which would reduce the power of the priesthood and take the sting out of

[73] *Ibid.*, p. 143.
[74] *Ibid.*
[75] *Ibid.*
[76] *Ibid.*, p. 143 r. and v.
[77] *Ibid.*, p. 143 v.
[78] *Ibid.*, p. 153.

the interdict.[79] Frith did, however, criticise the *ex opere operato* conveyance of grace. It is infrequently realised by Protestant critics of this concept that the Catholic church had two strong pastoral reasons for affirming this concept, namely, that it stressed the objectivity of grace which was entirely appropriate if the omnipotence of God was being considered, and it reassured the faithful that unworthy priests did not obstruct the passage of grace. Frith felt that it was not the omnipotence but the generous mercy of God which was His outstanding characteristic as revealed in the Gospel, the graciousness, rather than the justice of God. He thought the church was acting as if it had a corner on the power of God, and was behaving as if it had control over grace and could almost automate it.[80]

William Tyndale's contribution to the debate was *A brief declaration of the Sacraments*.[81] He conceived of the sacraments as seals of the divine covenant made with men, so that circumcision foreshadows Baptism, and the Passover the Lord's Supper. He was chiefly aware of the pedagogical value of the sacraments, "And

[79] William Clebsch visualises dramatically (*England's Earliest Protestants*, pp. 128-29) the socio-political effects of the changed conception of grace as applied to the sacraments: "To portray sacramental grace as issuing from God's favour to the believer's faith, rather than from the empowered priesthood, to the sacramental stuff, undermined the whole religious system by which Latin Christianity had extended its influence over the common and public life of Western Europe. Without an *ex opere operato* Sacrament of Baptism the whole ideal of Christendom as a social unity, entered by being engrafted into a uniform religion, would inevitably erode. If the visible Church was not identifiable with God's elect, the weapon of excommunication would lose its power to produce conformity in religion, society, and politics. If the power to transmute bread and wine into the veritable food and drink of salvation were stripped from the Church, it must forfeit the power of the interdict and of the ban which held the temporal sword in bondage to the spiritual." The fragmentation into competing nationalisms had begun long before the Reformation, the Renaissance had a further disruptive effect, and, Canossa, at which the spiritual claims to dominate the temporal were dramatically proved, was 500 years in the past. For these reasons I believe the claims for the changed concept of grace, though important, are exaggerated.

[80] Foxe seemed to think that Frith influenced the development of Cranmer's Eucharistic thought directly, and helped to lead Cranmer to the views that were expressed in the prayer-book of 1552. This is, however, highly improbable for two reasons. The first is that in 1533 Cranmer was a believer in the corporal presence in the Eucharist. Also, it is likelier that Cranmer read Oecolampadius than Frith because of the wide reputation of the scholarly Reformer of Basel. Secondly, Cranmer could have found the emphases and interpretations he was seeking in the Eucharistic thought of Ridley and of the Ratramnus which both Frith and Ridley claimed as the partial progenitor of their thoughts. Frith refers to Bertram, i.e. Ratramnus, in *Workes of Tyndall, Frith and Barnes* (1572), p. 141 r. and v.

[81] It can be found in *Workes of Tyndall*, pp. 436-52; and in *Doctrinal Treatises and Introductions to different portions of the Holy Scriptures by William Tyndall, Martyr 1536*, ed. Henry Walter, pp. 345-89. References are to the former volume, except in note 86, where the reference is to the second volume.

hereof ye see, that our sacraments are bodies of stories only; and that there is none other virtue in them than to testify and exhibit to the senses and understanding the covenants and promises made in Christ's blood."[82] Tyndale says there are three contemporary explanations of the *Hoc est corpus meum*. The Romanists, he insists, "compel us to believe, under pain of damnation, that the bread and wine are changed into the very body and blood of Christ really: as the water at Cana Galilee was turned into very wine."[83] The Lutherans said: "We be not bound to believe that bread and wine are changed: but only that his body and blood are there presently."[84] The Reformed churches said: "We be bound by these words only to believe that Christ's body was broken, and his blood shed for the remission of our sins; and that there is no other satisfaction for sin than the death and passion of Christ."[85] Tyndale recognized that the Lord's Supper had, besides a pedagogical, a sociological value. His own view was strictly Memorialist.

How simple Tyndale's notion of the early Eucharist was may be seen in the manner in which he sets forth his detailed proposal for the restoration of the Lord's Supper. He pictured a minister gathering his flock together for a service in which the didactic interest was so dominant that it almost drove devotion away. Apart from a lengthy explanatory sermon on the doctrine of the atonement and on the meaning of the sacramental signs, there are several exhortations, and few prayers. Tyndale saw forgiveness of sins as the primary gift of the Gospel, and insisted that the congregation approach the holy table with genuine forgiveness in their hearts and a determination to follow Christ in love. The readings were to include I Corinthians 11 and John 6. The rest can be told in Tyndale's own words:

> These with such lyke preparations and exhortations had, I would every man present should professe the Articles of our fayth openly in our mother toung, and confesse his sinnes secretly unto God, praying intierly that hee would now vouchsafe to have mercy upon hym, receive his prayer, glewe hys hart unto hym by fayth and love, encrease hys fayth, geve hym grace to forgyve and to love hys neighbour as him selfe, to garnish hys lyfe with purenes and innocency, and to confirme hym in all goodnes and vertue. Then againe it behoveth the curate to warne and exhorte every man deepely

82 *Doctrinal Treatises*, p. 358.   83 *Ibid.*, p. 366.
84 *Ibid.*, p. 367.   85 *Ibid.*

to consider and expende with hym selfe, the signification & substaūce of this Sacrament, so that he sit not down an hipocrite and a dissembler, sith God is searcher of harte and raines, thoughtes and affectes: and see that he come not to the holy table of the Lorde without that fayth whiche he professed at hys Baptisme, and also that love which the Sacrament preacheth and testifieth unto hys hart, lest hee now found guilty of the body and bloud of the Lord . . . receive his own damnation. And here let every man fall downe uppon hys knees saying secretly with all devotion their *pater noster* in English, theyr curate as example kneelyng downe before them, which done let hym take the bread and eft the wyne in the sight of the people hearing him with a loude voyce with gravitie, and after a Christen religious reverence rehearsing distinctly ye wordes of the Lordes Supper in the mother toung. And thē distribute it to the ministers, which taking the bread with great reverence, will devide it to the congregation every man breakyng and reaching it forth to his next neighbour and member of the mistike body of Christ, other ministers folowyng with the cuppes powring forth & dealing them the wyne, all together thus beyng now partakers of one bread and one cuppe, the thyng therby signified and preached printed fast in their hartes.[86]

Ultimately the Eucharist was for Tyndale the most vivid of all visual aids for the mental communication of the Gospel, through which the costliness of redemption and its chief benefit, forgiveness of sins, and the unity of love which should characterise the Christian community were most dramatically exhibited.

John Hooper was another Zwinglian among the early English Reformers, which is not surprising since he had spent from 1547 to 1549 in Zwingli's city of Zurich as a young man. He refused to believe that man is saved by sacraments, for this "doth derogate the mercy of God, as though His holy Spirit could not be carried by faith into the sorrowful and penitent conscience except it rid always in a chariot and external sacrament."[87] His succinct definition of the Lord's Supper was: "It is a ceremony instituted by Christ, to confirm and manifest our society and communion in his

[86] *Workes of Tyndall*, pp. 477 v.-478, which is a separate statement of Tyndale's, not in his treatise on the Sacrament, on *The Restorying of the Lordes Supper*.
[87] *The Early Writings of John Hooper*, ed. Samuel Carr, p. 131.

body and blood, until he come to judgment."[88] Sacraments, for Hooper, do not convey grace not otherwise obtainable; they proclaim the Gospel visually: "The sacraments be as visible words offered unto the eyes and other senses, as the sweet sound of the word to the ear, and the Holy Ghost to the heart." Each of the two sacraments "teach and confirm none other thing than that the mercy of God saveth the faithful and believers." In short, the sacraments were "seals of God's promises in Christ."[89] In another place Hooper confirmed this definition, but went on to say that the sacraments were not *signa nuda*, empty signs, which is precisely what opponents of the Zwinglian doctrine had always maintained them to be. Hooper's fullest statement was: "I believe also the holy sacraments (which are the second mark or badge of the true church) to be the signs of reconciliation and great atonement made between God and us through Jesus Christ. They are seals of the Lord's promises, and are outward and visible pledges and gages of inward faith, and are in number only twain, that is to say, baptism and the holy supper of the Lord. The two which are not void and empty signs, but full; that is to say, they are not only signs whereby something is signified, but also they are such signs as do exhibit and give the thing that they signify indeed, as by God's help we will declare hereafter."[90] However much Bishop Hooper protested that the sacraments, in his interpretation, were channels of grace, yet so strong was his Memorialism that it is difficult to accept the statement. With characteristic clarity he asserted, "I believe that the holy supper of the Lord is not a sacrifice, but only a remembrance and commemoration of this holy sacrifice of Jesus Christ. . . ."[91]

Hooper was highly critical of the idea that there could be any spiritual benefit from the corporeal presence of Christ in the Eucharist, since Christ had taught his disciples, as recorded in John 6, that "the flesh profiteth nothing," and had assured them, regarding his forthcoming return to God the Father: "It is expedient that I go away." Hooper's inevitable conclusion was: "We must therefore lift up our minds to heaven [where Christ's ascended body now is] when we feel ourselves oppressed with the burden of sin,

---

88 *Ibid.*, p. 175.

89 *Ibid.*, p. 513.

90 *Later Writings of Bishop Hooper, together with his Letters and other Pieces,* ed. Charles Nevinson, p. 45.

91 *Ibid.*, p. 32. Characteristically the next sentence asserts that the Mass is an invention of man, a sacrifice of Anti-Christ, and "a stinking and infected sepulchre."

and there by faith apprehend and receive the body of Christ slain and killed, and his precious blood shed, for our offences: and so by faith apply the virtue, efficacy, and strength of the merit of Christ to our souls, and by that means quit ourselves from the danger, damnation, and curse of God." He adduced a powerful citation in confirmation of this interpretation: "And St. Augustine saith, *Ut quid paras dentem et ventrem? Crede et manducasti*: 'Why preparest thou the teeth and belly? Believe and thou hast eaten.' "[92] So convinced was he of the fact that the assertion of the corporal presence of Christ in the Sacrament is idolatry, that in a sermon preached at the court of King Edward VI he urged the magistrates to require all communicants to receive standing or sitting, but not kneeling. He preferred the posture of sitting, for it expressed the fact that Christ had come, "that should quiet and put at rest both body and soul."[93] Hooper was insensitive in ridiculing the convictions of others with which he disagreed.[94] Yet he was the most vigorous exponent of Memorialism in England on both biblical and rational grounds; he was, apparently, without a trace of mysticism.

The last of the present group of early English reformers also occasionally confused sacredness with insensitivity and truth with tactlessness. The opinions of Thomas Becon are of unusual interest because Cranmer chose him to be his chaplain. Becon's *Catechism*[95] provides a full treatment of the Protestant understanding of the Lord's Supper and an extensive critique of the Catholic Mass. The dominant emphasis was on the Lord's Supper as a banquet, a spiritual food in which "Christ Jesus the Son of God witnesseth that he is the living bread, wherewith our souls are fed unto everlasting life."[96] The Lord's Supper was instituted as a remembrance of Christ's death, as a sign of the unity and concord among Christians,

[92] *Early Writings*, p. 530.

[93] *Ibid.*, p. 537. This anticipated the protest Knox would make against kneeling for the reception of holy communion before the same august auditory, and which would result in the hurried inclusion of the "black rubric" in the prayerbook of 1552.

[94] See his satirical remark that the consecration in the Mass is achieved at the final syllable -*um* in the recital of the words, *Hic est corpus meum* (*Early Writings*, p. 525). In this respect he was no better than the presumably Protestant persons who gave a dead cat a monk's tonsure and put a white disc in his mouth, resembling a host, which was later hung on the pulpit at St. Paul's Cross, or Weston, Catholic Dean of Westminster, who referred to the Protestant communion table as "an oyster-board." See Millar MacLure, *The Paul's Cross Sermons, 1534-1632*, p. 51.

[95] References are to the Parker Society edition of Becon's *Catechism*, ed. J. Ayre.

[96] *Ibid.*, p. 229.

as a means of confirming and strengthening faith, as a proclamation that Christ's body and blood are the true nourishment of the faithful soul, and to move Christians to be thankful for the death of Christ and for its benefits and fruits.[97]

Becon discovered 11 "errors" in the Roman Catholic Mass. It is a private banquet, not a common meal.[98] It is a communion in one kind, not two.[99] It changes a commemorative into a propitiatory sacrifice.[100] The sacrament which should be a meal is reserved in boxes and pixes.[101] There is idolatry in turning the sacrament into a "gazing stock."[102] The service is not in the vernacular, but in Latin.[103] The Romanists allow noncommunicants to be present as spectators.[104] Celebrations are rare, usually once a year.[105] The 9th, 10th, and 11th errors in the Mass are doctrinal in character, consisting of Transubstantiation, the corporal presence, and the assertion that the ungodly and the wicked, not only the godly and faithful, consume the body and blood of Christ in the Sacrament.[106]

Clearly the early English reformers were much more acute in their criticisms of the Catholic Mass in doctrine and practice than they were successful in elaborating a Protestant understanding of Holy Communion which was not a reductionistic Memorialism. It was to take considerable time before there would be developed a third alternative to the corporal presence affirmed by Catholics and Lutherans, on the one hand, and the failure within Zwinglian terms to define a presence of Christ in the Sacrament any different from its modality in the preaching of the word, on the other. Unquestionably this is what not only Cranmer, but Bucer and Calvin, were groping for in the 1540s and 1550s. In this search the researches of Nicholas Ridley, Bonner's successor as bishop of London, are important in their own right, as well as in their impact on the development of Archbishop Cranmer's thought.[107]

4. The Sacramental Theology of Cranmer's Advisors

It appears that it was in 1545 that Ridley read Ratramnus's *On the Body and Blood of the Lord* which held that the Sacrament

97 *Ibid.*, pp. 231-32. 98 *Ibid.*, pp. 238-40.
99 *Ibid.*, pp. 240-45. 100 *Ibid.*, pp. 245-51.
101 *Ibid.*, pp. 251-53. 102 *Ibid.*, p. 253.
103 *Ibid.*, pp. 253-55. 104 *Ibid.*, pp. 255-57.
105 *Ibid.*, pp. 257-60. 106 *Ibid.*, pp. 260-97.
107 Brooks, the Marian Bishop of Gloucester, said, when speaking to Ridley at Ridley's trial in Oxford in 1554: "Latimer leaneth to Cranmer, Cranmer to Ridley, and Ridley to his own wit." Cf. Ridley's, *A Brief Declaration of the Lord's Supper* (written while he was imprisoned in 1544), ed. H.G.C. Moule, p. ix.

was a figure of the body and blood rather than the veritable body and blood of Christ after the consecration. Ridley was relieved that a ninth-century monk could hold such a view without any official condemnation during his lifetime. Ratramnus's treatise was reprinted in Cologne in 1531 by Johann Präl at the instigation of Oecolampadius, and Leo Jud translated it into German. Ridley himself had referred to Ratramnus as "Bertram" in the Debate in the House of Lords in 1548, as well as in the Oxford Disputation of 1554. "This Bertram," said Ridley, "was the first that pulled me by the ear and that brought me from the common error of the Romish church and caused me to search more diligently and exactly both the Scriptures and the writings of the old ecclesiastical fathers in this matter."[108]

After Ridley has set forth the accounts of the Last Supper in the three synoptic Gospels and in the Pauline account in I Corinthians 11, he says that those who accuse him of making the Sacrament only "a bare signe or figure" which represents Christ "none otherwise than the Ivy Bush doth represent the wine in a tavern, or as a vile person gorgeously apparelled may represent a king or a prince in a play,"[109] seriously misinterpret his teaching.

The central issue in the controversy was: "As, whether there be any Transubstantiation of the bread, or no: any corporal and carnal presence of Christ's substance, or no. Whether adoration (due only unto God) is to be done unto the Sacrament, or no? and whether Christ's body be there offered in deed unto the heavenly Father by the priest or no: and whether the evil man receiveth the natural body of Christ or no." But, as Ridley was careful to show, all five questions depended on one question, "which is, What is the matter of the Sacrament: Whether is it the natural substance of bread, or the natural substance of Christ's own body?"[110] If the answer to the second part of the question is in the affirmative, then Transubstantiation must be affirmed, the Sacrament may rightly be adored, the priest does indeed offer up Christ's body to the Father, and both good and evil alike receive, with different effects, the veritable body and blood of Christ. But if it were found that the natural substance of bread is the material substance (for there cannot be two substances occupying one space) in the Sacrament, then it must follow there is no such thing as Transubstantiation and the natural substance of Christ's human nature which he took

108 *Ibid.*, p. 200.   109 *Ibid.*, p. 104.
100 *Ibid.*, p. 106.

of the Virgin Mary is in heaven where He now reigns in glory, and is not here enclosed under the form of bread.[111] Thus were the logical alternatives posed with a clarity rare in so complex and obscure a controversy.

What was the mode of Christ's presence in the Eucharist in Ridley's thought? Briefly, he denied the presence of Christ's body in the natural substance of his human and assumed nature, but granted the presence of the same by grace. He affirmed that "the substance of the natural body and blood of Christ is only remaining in heaven and so shall be" until the Day of Judgment. He also affirmed that because the human nature of Christ is joined with the divine nature in Christ, the second person of the Trinity, therefore "it hath not only life in itself, but is also able to give and doth believe on his name. . . ." This happens "By grace (I say) that is, by the gift of this life . . . and the properties of the same, meet for our pilgrimage here upon earth, the same body of Christ is here present with us."[112] He clarified the concept with the analogy of the sun, which is in heaven, yet is present on earth by "his beams, light and natural influence, where it shineth upon the earth. For God's Word and his Sacraments be, as it were, the beams of Christ, which is *Sol iustitiae*, the Sun of righteousness."[113]

Ridley went on to support his arguments with scriptural and patristic evidence, as all the other controversialists did. We need not follow him, especially in the drearier part of his pilgrimage. He did, however, make some shrewd points. One was the assertion that he could find another Transubstantiation if that is what is wanted, and he discovered it in the statement of Christ: "This cup is the New Testament in my blood." If "This cup" is a figure of speech, so is "This is my body." Another telling point was that in the Gospels of Matthew and Mark, Christ speaks of the fruit of the vine as his cup, and quite plainly so. Thus the natural substance of the wine remains still, which ought not to be the case if Transubstantiation is to be believed.[114] Transubstantiation destroys the nature of the Sacrament by denying the sign. Furthermore, it denies the truth of the human nature of Christ, making those who assert it into Monophysite heretics, a thrust he must particularly have enjoyed, being so often at the other end of that particular sword. The positive values of the Lord's Supper were three, according to the statement of Ridley in the Cambridge Debate of 1549:

111 *Ibid.*, pp. 106-108.   112 *Ibid.*, pp. 110-11.
113 *Ibid.*, p. 111.   114 *Ibid.*, pp. 126-27.

unity, nutrition, and conversion.[115] The first two are easily explained. The unity is the unity of the mystical body of Christ, his people, which is sealed and expressed in the Lord's Supper. The nutrition is the spiritual feeding of the soul by the spiritual body of Christ apprehended by faith. The conversion is not any substantial change in the nature of the bread and wine, but only in the use to which they are put, which is a sacred and not a common use. The conversion of use was what Cranmer and Peter Martyr termed a "sacramental mutation," a disturbingly ambiguous phrase.

This is the best-argued treatise on the Eucharist from the Protestant side in sixteenth-century England. It is notable for the logical presentation of the two major explanations and of their consequences. The writing is always pellucid, the illustrations both pertinent and illuminating. One can imagine how very attractive Cranmer found Ridley's clear explanations of complex issues and his presentation of a Eucharistic theory which attempted to be a true middle way between Transubstantiation and Memorialism. Not less impressive was Ridley's determination to put his convictions into practice however strong the conservative opposition might be. He was the first Protestant bishop in England to insist that all altars in his diocese of London be replaced by Communion tables. We can hear through the arches of the long years the clarity and firmness of his voice as he explains his reasons: "For the use of an altar is to make sacrifice upon it; the use of a table is to serve for men to eat upon. Now, when we come to the Lord's board, what do we come for? to sacrifice Christ again, and to crucify him again, or to feed upon him that was once only crucified and offered up for us? If we come to feed upon him, spiritually to eat his body, and spiritually to eat his blood (which is the true use of the Lord's Supper), then no man can deny but the form of a table is more meet for the Lord's board, than the form of an altar."[116]

Cranmer was anxious to get the best Protestant scholars in Europe to advise him, and a succession of them found haven in England. In 1547 Peter Martyr, Tremellius, and Ochino reached England. The next year John à Lasco, Martin Bucer, and Paul Fagius came. Others were Utenhove of Ghent, Dryander from

[115] For an account of this important debate see Jasper Ridley, *Nicholas Ridley: A Biography*, pp. 179-80.

[116] *The Works of Nicholas Ridley, D.D. Sometime Lord Bishop of London, Martyr, 1555*, ed. Henry Christmas, p. 322.

Spain, Micronius from Switzerland, Valerandus from the Netherlands, and Alexander and Veron from France. Cranmer found
positions for all of them, but he made particular friends of Bucer,
Peter Martyr, and John à Lasco, each of whom had decided views
on the Eucharist.

Bucer[117] seems to have had the greatest influence on Cranmer,
but after Bucer's death on February 28, 1551, Martyr and à Lasco
came into their own. Bucer's influence was to be expected, since
he had not only advised Archbishop Hermann Wied on the reformation of the archdiocese of Cologne, but, after the death of
Zwingli in 1531, he was the leader of the Reformed Churches in
Switzerland and southern Germany. His greatest strength was his
persistently irenic concern to unite the parties within Protestantism, but which carried with it the weakness of seeming to make
too many diplomatic concessions.[118] For example, he was not content to let the chasm between the Saxons and the Swiss that had
opened at Marburg in 1529 remain open. In gaining from the
obdurate Luther the Wittenberg Concord of 1536,[119] which
accepted Consubstantiation but conceded that while the unworthy
did receive the body of Christ yet the unholy did not, he found
that the Swiss refused the Concord. Since Cranmer's hope was
exactly the same—getting the maximum of concord among Anglicans—Bucer's stay in England was a source of great satisfaction
to Cranmer. Moreover, his influence was to continue in those Cambridge theologians who were proud to be his friends and attend
his immensely popular lectures, such as Parker, Sandys, and
Grindal, the great statesmen-prelates of the Elizabethan church.[120]

What, then, was Bucer's Eucharistic theology? If we are to take
the Strassburg Liturgy in 1539 as the standard of his practice
(which, incidentally, shows an increasing conservatism as contrasted with his earlier sacramental theology in the *Grund und
Ursach* of 1524[121]), then Bucer held a doctrine of the spiritual real
presence of Christ in the Eucharist. Whenever Holy Communion

---

117 See *Opera*, ed. R. Stupperich, *Scripta Anglicana fere omnia a C. Huberto
collecta*, esp. the *Censura*; A. E. Harvey, *Martin Bucer in England*; W. Pauck,
Das Reich Gottes auf Erden. Eine Untersuchung zu Butzers De Regno Christi;
C. Hopf, *Martin Bucer and the English Reformation*; and G. J. Van de Poll,
Martin Bucer's Liturgical Ideas.
118 C. H. Smyth, *Cranmer and the Reformation under Edward VI*, p. 153, calls
Bucer, "the Trimmer of Protestantism."
119 *The New Schaff-Herzog Encyclopedia of Religious Knowledge*, vol. II, 323a.
120 Smyth, *Cranmer and Reformation*, p. 173.
121 See Bard Thompson's introduction to Bucer's Strassburg Liturgy in *Liturgies of the Western Church*, pp. 161-66.

was scheduled the minister was required to append to his sermon an exhortation which set forth in the simplest terms Bucer's doctrine, including the words: "The Lord truly offers and gives His holy and sanctifying body and blood to us in the Holy Supper, with the visible things of bread and wine, through the ministry of the church."[122] The rite has three alternative Great Prayers, replacing the Roman Canon; the emphasis in each of them was on the consecration of the persons, not the elements, that by the power of the Holy Spirit they might receive Christ, the true nourishment of the soul in the sacrament. The first prayer contained the following petition: "And grant us, O Lord and Father, that with true faith we may keep this Supper of they dear Son, our Lord Jesus, as he hath ordained it, so that we verily receive and enjoy the true communion of His body and blood, of our Saviour Himself, who is the only saving bread of heaven. In this holy sacrament, He wishes to offer and give Himself so that He may live in us, and we in Him, being members of His body and serving thee fruitfully in every way to the common edification of thy Church. . . ."[123] The second prayer included the petition ". . . grant that we may now accept with entire longing and devotion His goodness and gift, and with right faith receive and enjoy His true body and true blood, yea, Himself our Saviour, true God and man, the only true bread of heaven: That we may live no more our sinful and depraved life, but that He in us and we in Him may live His holy, blessed and eternal life, being verily the partakers of the true and eternal testament, the covenant of grace. . . ."[124] Here we can discern the distinction between the Bucerian and Zwinglian doctrines of the Lord's Supper. Bucer believed that as the body eats the bread and drinks the wine, so does the soul eat the spiritual body of Christ, the soul's true bread, and that this spiritual presence of Christ is vivifying and hallowing, to eternal life. Zwingli, on the other hand, held that bread and wine are only figures or metaphors for the body of Christ now in heaven. Sacraments for Zwingli are *signa nuda*, but for Bucer *signa exhibitiva*, conveying what they represent. Bucer's doctrine is most clearly seen in Cranmer's disputation at Oxford in 1555, when the beleaguered archbishop claimed Tertullian's statement that: *Nutritur corpus pane symbolico, anima corpore Christi*: that is, 'Our flesh is nourished by symbolical or sacramental bread, but our soul is nourished with

---

[122] *Ibid.*, p. 165. [123] *Ibid.*, p. 173.
[124] *Ibid.*, pp. 176-77.

the body of Christ.' "[125] A moment later Cranmer expounded his own view: "The body is nourished both with the sacrament and with the body of Christ: with the sacrament to a temporal life; with the body of Christ to eternal life."[126] It was clearly the doctrine that underlay the Holy Communion rite in the 1549 prayer-book.[127]

Peter Martyr was the great friend of Bucer, for whom Bucer had obtained the chair of theology at Strassburg. The clearest brief statement of his belief in the spiritual presence and in spiritual manducation in the Eucharist is that which was made in a speech during the Cambridge Disputation in May 1549:

> D. Martyr. I answer: when we receive the sacrament faithfullie, two kinds of eatings are there, and also two sorts of bread. For the receiving of the bodie of Christ, which we have by faith, is called a metaphoricall eating: even as the bodie of Christ which we receive, is a metaphoricall bread. There also have we an eating of the sacramentall signes; the which is a proper eating; and true bread was given for a signe: and so in sixt of *Iohn*, there is mention onlie of metaphoricall eating, and of metaphoricall bread: but in the supper of the Lord, wherein he communicated with his apostles, there was had a proper eating; and true bread was given for a signe; and so in the supper was given both sorts of bread, even naturall and metaphoricall: and both sorts of eating is performed; to wit, both a naturall eating in signes, and also a metaphoricall, as touching the bodie of Christ, which we receive by faith. . . . But as for the words; *Take ye, and eate ye,* I saie, that they must thus be understood: As ye receive this bread, and eat it with your bodie; so receive ye my bodie by faith, and with the mind, that ye may be strengthened thereby in stead of meate.[128]

The fullest statement of Peter Martyr's doctrine is found in Udall's translation of the detailed report of the Oxford Debate, entitled *A discourse or traictise of Petur Martyr Vermilla Florētine, the*

---

[125] *Writings and Disputations of Thomas Cranmer*, ed. J. E. Cox, p. 420. There is only one difference between Bucer and Cranmer. Bucer maintained that the body of Christ is spiritually present in the Eucharist and is spiritually received by the souls of worthy believers. Cranmer, however, taught that Christ's body is not present in the substance of the sacraments, but in the action of administration.

[126] *Ibid.*, pp. 420-21.

[127] This is more fully treated in Chap. v, with reference to Bucer's criticisms in the *Censura* of the 1549 prayer-book.

[128] Cited in Smyth, *Cranmer and Reformation*, p. 129.

publyque reader of divinitee in the Universitee of Oxford, wherein he openly declareth his whole and determinate iudgemente concernygne the Sacramente of the Lordes Supper in the sayde Universitee. It is mainly concerned with finding 49 arguments against Transubstantiation, and much less so in providing clear explanations of the meaning of 'spiritual eating.' It has one concluding statement on the matter: "For we have saied and doe confirme that these materiall sygnes dooe moste truely sygnyfye, represente, and exhibite unto us the bodye of Chryste, to bee eaten: howbeit it is spiritually, that is, wyth the mouth of the solle to bee eaten, and not of the bodye."[129] His most original contribution was his interpretation of Paul's doctrine of incorporation in Christ in Ephesians. This incorporation takes place in communicating in the sacrament, and by faith, but we become part, not of the incarnate body of Christ, but are conjoined with the flesh of the risen Christ.[130]

What is of chief importance, however, are those four features of sacramental doctrine common to Martyr and Bucer and which provide the lineaments of Cranmer's doctrine of the Eucharist: The first is the assertion that Christ's body and blood are in some sense in the Sacrament and not merely in a metaphorical or figurative manner. Secondly, that presence is apprehended only by those who have faith. It is the sanctifying and revivifying power of the Holy Spirit who stirs up such faith. The same Holy Spirit, in the fourth place, effects the conjunction between the believers and the body of Christ, transforming the elements from common into sacramental usage and bringing about the realities of which the bread and wine are signs. Only on the fifth point is there disagreement, concerning the consecration. Martyr joins the action of the Holy Spirit in effecting the "sacramental mutation" with the words of consecration; Bucer believes increasingly that it is people, not things that are consecrated. So (as his *Censura* on the 1549 prayerbook indicates), he wished to avoid a technical consecratory formula in the Holy Communion.

The third member of Cranmer's foreign advisers in England was John à Lasco.[131] It is just possible that his influence may have turned Bucer as well as Martyr toward a more radically Memorialist doctrine of the sacrament which found expression in the Sec-

---

129 Fol. cix.
130 *Ibid.*, fol. cviii v.-cix.
131 See John à Lasco, *Brevis ac dilucida de sacramentis ecclesiae Christi tractatio* (1552).

ond Prayer Book of 1552.[132] It is not necessary to rehearse the Memorialist type of sacramental doctrine, but only to recall that à Lasco reemphasizes that the Eucharist is a present reminder of a past redemption, a visual aid to the preaching of the Gospel, a badge of the loyalty of Christians gathered in community, and a confirmation and pledge of the reliability of God's promises. It is a figure or representation of the historic crucifixion, not a communication of the body of Christ. Above all, the metaphor of "eating" at the Lord's Supper is consistently interpreted as believing in the passion of Christ. His Nominalism rejected the connections the realist can see between universals in the mind and in the object considered and so makes a corporal identification with Christ impossible. On the contrary, since mind and body were a dichotomy for à Lasco, faith has to be concentrated in the mind and consciousness, however objective it may be in character. John à Lasco had nothing new to say, but what he said he said with vigor and clarity; a reductionist position is always more impressive in attack than in exposition. But by the same token, it seems to make short work of any mediating viewpoint, such as was held by Bucer and Cranmer in the 1549 prayer-book.

5. *Cranmer's Eucharistic Theology*

The development of Cranmer's thought as seen in the Eucharistic rites of the 1549 and the 1552 prayer-books will be considered later.[133] My immediate purpose is to illuminate its facets by two approaches: through the pen war with Gardiner and by comparing it with the teaching of Zwingli and Calvin, with whom, in its last stage, it had the closest affinities.

Cranmer will remain a mysterious figure and his teaching unclear, partly because his Erastianism, with its conviction of the divine right of kings caused him to try to meet the differing needs of two successive monarchs and their changing moods, partly because his work being incorporated in two prayer-books and a book of homilies is anonymous, and partly because he was surrounded by advisers with differing theological viewpoints. It is, however, probable that in his tenure of the Archbishopric of Canterbury he held three different views of the modality of Christ's presence in the Eucharist. The first was Transubstantiation, which

132 The probable influence of à Lasco on the 1552 prayer-book is examined in Chap. V.
133 See Chap. V.

he began to question in 1538.[134] The second was a doctrine of the
Real Presence which was close to Lutheran views.[135] The third—
which he came to accept under the influence of Ridley in 1546
and to which he had openly committed himself by the time the
third edition of the translation he had made of the catechism of
Justas Jonas appeared—was a more radical doctrine. It is not yet
wholly clear *how* radical this doctrine was, whether sacramentarian like the Lollards and Zwingli, or virtualist like Calvin.[136]
Cyril Richardson holds the former, and Peter Brooks and C. W.
Dugmore the latter view.[137]

Cranmer wrote his own full exposition of Eucharistic doctrine
in the *Defence of the True and Catholic Doctrine of the Sacrament
of the Body and Blood of Our Saviour Christ* in 1550.[138] This pro-
voked Stephen Gardiner's rejoinder, already considered, namely,
*An Explication of the True Catholic Faith touching the Most
Blessed Sacrament of the Altar* (1551), and a rebuttal from
Cranmer—*A Crafty and Sophistical Cavillation devised by M.
Stephen Gardiner . . . against the True and Godly Doctrine of the
Most Holy Sacrament . . . with an Answer unto the same . . .*
(1551). Cranmer's first full-length treatise on the Eucharist, in

[134] In a letter of August 15, 1538 Cranmer wrote to Cromwell about Adam
Damplip of Calais, accused of denying transubstantiation while affirming the real
presence, that, "herein I think he taught the truth." Cranmer, *Miscellaneous
Writings and Letters*, ed. J. E. Cox, p. 375.

[135] It is difficult to evaluate Cranmer's Commonplace Book in which citations
from different authors are given over a period of time. It does seem important,
however, to mention two excerpts from an anti-Zwinglian tract of 1527 by Luther,
entitled, *Das dies Wort Christi noch fest stehen Widder die Schwermgeister*
included in the Commonplace Book and given in Peter Brooks, *Thomas Cranmer's
Doctrine of the Eucharist*, pp. 30-35; and the fact that there are no citations from
the sacramentarians. From this one might hazard two highly tentative conclusions.
The first is, Cranmer was more anxious to refute than to espouse sacramentarian-
ism, the second, that he had felt the sting of some of the Zwinglian criticisms of
the doctrine of the Real Presence and was eager to have these doubts removed.

[136] Jasper Ridley, *Thomas Cranmer*, p. 256, inclines to the opinion that it was
neither Ridley nor à Lasco who converted Cranmer to a new Eucharistic doctrine,
but that "perhaps he was really converted by Henry and the times." This could
mean that Henry's death in 1547 and Somerset's Protectorship over the young
Edward VI encouraged Cranmer to develop or divulge an already developed Protestant direction, yet with characteristic caution. D. G. Selwyn, in "A Neglected
Edition of Cranmer's Catechism," *Journal of Theological Studies*, New Series, XV
(April 1964), 84, believes that Cranmer had three different doctrines of the
Eucharist.

[137] Richardson's views are expounded in *Zwingli and Cranmer; Anglican Theo-
logical Review*, vol. 47, no. 3 (1965), 308-13; and *Journal of Theological Studies*,
New Series, XVI, pt. 2 (October 1965), 421-37. Brooks' views appear in *Thomas
Cranmer's Doctrine of the Eucharist*; and Dugmore, *Mass and English Reformers*.

[138] See *The Remains of Thomas Cranmer*, ed. H. Jenkyns, vol. 2, for the text
of the *Defence of the True and Catholic Doctrine of the Body and Blood of Our
Saviour Christ*. The first reference is to p. 297.

five parts and almost 200 pages long, had as its aim to show how and why the Eucharist was instituted from Scripture and the church Fathers and to confute the four major "errors" of the Catholic interpretation. The first part, sadly recalling that the sacrament which was ordained to create concord was the occasion of variance and discord, declared that the Eucharist is the spiritual food of the soul, was ordained to confirm faith, expresses the unity of Christ's mystical body, and is spiritually eaten with the heart, not the teeth. It concluded by enumerating the "four principal errors of the Papists."[139] The first was Transubstantiation; the second was the corporal presence of Christ in the Sacrament; the third was the assertion that evil men drink the very body and blood of Christ as do godly men; and the fourth was the claim that the priests "offer Christ every day for remission of sin, and distribute by their masses the merits of Christ's passion."[140] The remaining four parts of the book consist of the attempt to refute these four "errors" from Scripture and the Fathers; in it the positive teaching of Cranmer is also to be found.

Transubstantiation was "against the word of God, against nature, against reason, and against all our senses" as also "against the faith and doctrine of the old authors of Christ's Church. . . ."[141] Cranmer's nominalism[142] becomes apparent in his argument that Transubstantiation is against reason, for the Nominalists insisted that what gives being to an entity is its individual characteristics, so that if the accidents of a substance are negated then its being is also. "And most of all," wrote Cranmer, "it is against the nature of accidents to be in nothing. For the definition of accidents is to be in some substance, so that if they be, they must needs be in something. And if they be in nothing, then they be not."[143] Thus the assertion that the accidents of bread and wine remain after the consecration, but that the substance changes to the body and blood of Christ, as Transubstantiation maintains, was plainly unacceptable to any Nominalist.

Cranmer found equally unacceptable (in part three) the assertion that there is a corporal presence of Christ in the Eucharist. He referred to Christ's words in John 6: "It is the spirit that giveth

139 *Ibid.*, marginal gloss, p. 308.
140 *Ibid.*, pp. 308-12.
141 *Ibid.*, p. 320.
142 For Cranmer's philosophical presuppositions see the debate between E. G. McGee, who thinks of Cranmer as a nominalist, and W. J. Courtenay who denies it, in the *Harvard Theological Review*, vol. 57 (July and October 1964).
143 *Remains of Cranmer*, II, 318.

life, the flesh availeth nothing. The words which I spake unto you, be spirit and life." These, he says are not to be understood, "that we shall eat Christ with our teeth grossly and carnally, but that we shall spiritually and ghostly with our faith eat him, being carnally absent from us in heaven; and in such wise as Abraham and other holy fathers did eat him, many years before he was incarnate and born."[144] The Dominical words, "This is my body" are to be interpreted figuratively.[145] At this point it is worth citing an earlier explanation of what Cranmer means by spiritual feeding on Christ: "And the true eating and drinking of the said body and blood of Christ, is with a constant and lively faith to believe, that Christ gave his body and shed his blood upon the cross for us, and that he doth so join and incorporate himself to us, that he is our head, and we his members, and flesh of his flesh, and bone of his bones, having him dwelling in us, and we in him. And herein standeth the whole effect and strength of this sacrament. And this faith God worketh inwardly in our hearts by his Holy Spirit, and confirmeth the same outwardly to our ears by the hearing of his word, and to our other senses by eating and drinking of the sacramental bread and wine in his holy Supper."[146] This is the central thrust of the latest development in Cranmer's teaching. It is important to recognise that while Cranmer denied the corporal presence of Christ, since his risen body is in heaven, he affirmed the spiritual eating of the body and blood of Christ as conveying all the benefits of Christ's death and resurrection to the soul; this is the objective work of the Holy Spirit, who through the preaching of the word as well as in the sacraments creates faith and revivifies the Christian and the church.

In the fourth part of the treatise Cranmer insists that only godly persons eat the spiritual food of the sacrament, since faith must be the mouth of the soul. "For unto the faithful, Christ is at his own holy table present with his mighty Spirit and grace, and is of them more fruitfully received, than if corporally they should receive him bodily present."[147] He cites St. Augustine to prove that the unworthy do not eat the true bread of Christ.

In Part 5 Cranmer denies that the priests offer Christ anew on their altars. His first reason is that the sacrifice on the Cross was once and for all times sufficient to make satisfaction for the sins of the past and of the future. To argue that the Mass is a sacrifice

---

[144] *Ibid.*, p. 378.   [145] *Ibid.*, p. 381.
[146] *Ibid.*, p. 306.   [147] *Ibid.*, pp. 437-38.

propitiatory is to say "that Christ's sacrifice were not sufficient for the remission of our sins; or else that his sacrifice should hang upon the sacrifice of a priest."[148] Thus the true nature of the sacrifice in the Lord's Supper is that this is the grateful remembrance of Christ's sacrifice. It is also a sacrifice of praise, made by the people themselves. "But the humble confession of all penitent hearts, their knowledging of Christ's benefits, their thanksgiving for the same, their faith and consolation in Christ, their humble submission and obedience to God's will and commandments, is a sacrifice of laud and praise, accepted and allowed of God no less than the sacrifice of the priest."[149]

Leaving Cranmer's treatise, we may now consider his cluster of Eucharistic concepts. On the primary issue of the character of Christ's body there was no question to him but that this is an empirical object, circumscribed and located in heaven and therefore absent from this world, the sacrament, and the participants in the sacrament.

As a strictly logical consequence of the denial of any link between Christ's body in heaven and the Eucharistic elements, Christ can only be present in the Eucharist by the power of His divinity and must be absent in His flesh or humanity. Clearly Cranmer rejected any possibility of developing a doctrine through which the Body of Christ could have empirical and mystical qualities, thus conjoining a location in heaven and a pervasive, substantial presence on earth. The Occamist and Lutheran possibilities were thereby rejected.

With equal rigor Cranmer insisted that the bread and wine were and are only bread and wine. They are not in essence converted into the body and blood of Christ, as in Transubstantiation, nor do they accompany the body and blood, as in Consubstantiation. The bread and wine as self-enclosed, impermeable objects of the Nominalist tradition, they are incapable of receiving sanctification and so cannot be vehicles of grace. The elements are, of course, instruments of God's working and "promise, signify, and exhibit" the grace of the Sacrament. Yet what is accomplished, is done in us and not in the sacraments. As Richardson correctly remarks: "Nature is split from categories of consciousness and personality and cannot participate in the holy," and so, "the whole fluid, mystical, substantial way of thinking whereby the divine can impregnate the natural is overthrown in the interests of emphasis

---

[148] *Ibid.*, p. 452.   [149] *Ibid.*, p. 459.

on conscious faith and of relations between God and man in terms of personal encounter."[150]

The manducation of Christ's body must be a figure, a metaphor, for Cranmer. He freely acknowledged that the patriarchs of the Old Testament spiritually fed on Christ before He had a human body at all, and that it is possible to eat Christ's body spiritually after He has gone to heaven. Thus eating the body is possible without any reference to the Body at all. Preaching and mediation on the Passion are equally effective ways of eating Christ's body spiritually. Clearly, then, what happens in the Sacrament is altogether of the same character as what happens in preaching and meditation. The only difference is that the Sacrament provides visible signs to remind Christians of their duty. Spiritual feasting is then believing, exercising faith in the Passion of Christ.

The difficulty in explaining Cranmer with any certainty is caused by the residual ambiguities in his expressions of his Eucharistic doctrine. One mystery in Cranmer is that although he had by his denial of corporal presence reduced manducation of Christ's body to the act of believing, yet he insisted that Christ truly, substantially, and naturally dwells in the communicants and they in Christ. Thus we have the paradox that Cranmer often spoke of the double indwelling, yet at the same time insisted on the absence of Christ's body. Perhaps what we have here, as Richardson suggests, is an unresolved tension between Realist and Nominalist notions in Cranmer.[151]

For Cranmer, "incorporation" of the believers with Christ meant having faith in Christ's Passion, the presence of Christ in His divinity, and the virtue or grace that comes from Christ to us in our believing. Here Cranmer's teaching diverged considerably from Bucer's. Bucer regarded the virtue of the body as substantially identical with it. Cranmer repudiated such a view in the words: "Doth not all men know, that of everything the virtue is one and the substance another?" The unreformed Nominalist in Cranmer made him insist that the beams of the sun were not of the same substance as the sun itself. He failed to see that a true incorporation into the humanity of Christ, and not a mere metaphor, requires considerable modifications of the concept of the nature of the body of Christ. It can no longer be conceived of as merely an absent object; it must be thought of in dynamic terms, as a mystical

---

[150] *Journal of Theological Studies*, XVII, pt. 2, p. 427.
[151] *Ibid.*, p. 429.

substance which is accessible to the believer. This was the core of both Patristic and Scholastic thinking on the issue. Cranmer was inconsistent, not only in trying to unite Nominalist and Realist notions of the body of Christ, but also in allowing that through the Incarnation and Atonement there was a participation of the believer in Christ's flesh and that this was taught by the Sacrament but not effected by it.

There are strengths and weaknesses in Cranmer's Eucharistic doctrine. The strengths are chiefly the Biblical insights and recoveries: the recognition that sacraments are signs, seals of the divine promises; the importance of the interiority of faith; and the link between Christ and the application of His benefits to the believers is the power of the Holy Spirit, the giver of new life. As we have seen, Cranmer's basic weakness was his circumscribed notion of "Body" and his overcorrective stress on "spiritual eating" by faith. It was partly his unwillingness to admit, "that Christ can be present in fact by the Spirit and the sacrament, and not merely by figure, when there is no faithful reception."[152] Bromiley, while making such a criticism, was careful to point out that Cranmer was more than a Memorialist or a supporter of the view that the Sacrament is merely a symbolical reenactment of the crucifixion. The unity of Christians is with the crucified and risen Christ by the power of the Holy Spirit, but it is not a natural or organic unity. It is the Holy Spirit who creates faith, so that the presence of Christ in the signs is appropriated by faith, but never created by faith, as some critics of his subjectivity suppose it to be. It must be remembered that the term "spiritual" in Cranmer's writing and thought is not a vague noun: it has the vigor and precision of the New Testament concept of life in the Spirit as contrasted with the dying life of the world. Thus Cranmer's phrase "spiritual eating" was no equivalent for figurative eating, but for the nourishment of the soul to a life beyond life, in short, a life with new dimensions of quality as well as of extension, eternal life.

If at this stage one were asked whether Cranmer was more of a Zwinglian than a Calvinist, then he might point to the fact that the 42 Articles of the Church of England were in the process of being formulated concurrently with the preparation of the prayer-book of 1552, and that they spoke of the sacraments as "effectual signs," which convey what they signify. This would make the Eucharistic doctrine more Calvinist than Zwinglian, which, after all, is what

---

152 G. W. Bromiley, *Thomas Cranmer, Theologian*, p. 75.

should be expected 21 years after the death of Zwingli and two years after the *Consensus Tigurinus*.

The problem may, however, be more fully resolved after a comparison of Cranmer's teaching with that of Zwingli and Calvin. Rightly or wrongly Cranmer has been assumed to be "Zwinglian" or "sacramentarian" in the last phase of his development by such scholars as C. H. Smyth and Gregory Dix, so the assertion must be examined. Undoubtedly there is close agreement between Cranmer and Zwingli. Both denied that the Eucharist is a participation in the substance of the body of Christ.[153] Both asserted that persons and not the elements participate in the Holy.[154] Christ is present in the Eucharist by his divine, not his human, nature.[155] Christ's body is in one place, not ubiquitous, and that one place is heaven. Moreover, even if it were naturally present in the Eucharist, it would be of no avail since the flesh profits nothing, according to a Johannine logion of Jesus.[156] The distinction, if not dichotomy, between flesh and spirit, as between mind and body, is strongly stressed; this can readily be seen in the fact that Cranmer put the text, John 6:13 on the title page of the *Defence*, and "the flesh profiteth nothing" was Zwingli's favorite motto. Cranmer identified "eating the body" with believing in the Passion of Christ as effecting atonement, and so did Zwingli. Because both Cranmer and Zwingli are Nominalists, they are eager to attack Transubstantiation and to deny the abstract possibility of any participation in the concept of substance, and this causes the abyss between spirit and flesh in their sacramental thought. Quite inconsistently, however, Cranmer affirmed a substantial unity between Christ and human nature in the Incarnation, while denying it in the Eucharist.

There are, however, important differences between the thought of Cranmer and Zwingli. Both had been Catholic priests, but Cranmer had a higher evaluation of the Eucharist, since he desired a weekly Communion, for the Eucharist was the pledge of the presence of Christ. For Zwingli it was sufficient to have a quarterly Communion. Also, Cranmer interpreted the Eucharist as a *sigillum Verbi*, a seal of the Word of God and His promise to men. Zwingli

---

[153] Cf. Cranmer, *Writings and Disputations*, pp. 96, 186; and Richardson, *Zwingli and Cranmer on the Eucharist*, pp. 20-21.

[154] Cf. Cranmer, *Writings and Disputations*, p. 11 and *Miscellaneous Writings and Letters*, 413ff.; and Zwingli, in Richardson, *Zwingli and Cranmer* (1949).

[155] Cf. Cranmer, *Writings and Disputations*, p. 186; and Zwingli, in Richardson, *Zwingli and Cranmer*.

[156] Cranmer, *Writings and Disputations*, pp. 363, 416; and Zwingli, in Richardson, *Zwingli and Cranmer*.

held the same view, but was more impressed by the fact that the Eucharist was the public pledge of Christians, their avowal of their determination to live in the obedience of faith that should characterise disciples.[157] Moreover, Cranmer gives the elements and the act of eating greater importance than Zwingli does. The question then arises: was Cranmer willing to affirm that the "signs" in the Sacrament actually confer what they signify? In short, was Cranmer a virtualist or dynamic receptionist, with closer affinities to Calvin or Bucer than to Zwingli?

Cranmer undoubtedly would have agreed with Calvin that in the sacrament God seals his love to men through the recalling of Christ's sacrifice and that men testify their piety toward God in their participation in the sacrament. He would also share Calvin's view that Transubstantiation and Consubstantiation are to be rejected because they turn the signs into the realities and therefore cease to be true sacraments. Furthermore, he would see that the faith by which the sacrament is appropriated is objective as well as subjective and that the Holy Spirit of God is the link between Christ and His people.

There are passages of Cranmer where he sounds very like Calvin: ". . . although Christ in his human nature, substantially, really, corporally, naturally, and sensibly be present with his Father in heaven, yet sacramentally and spiritually he is here present."[158] Yet if we analyse that very sentence, the second part is Calvinist, but the first part is not. Calvin believed that the flesh of Christ,[159] as well as His divine power, and our bodies and spirits are mysteriously united in the Eucharist. Cranmer did not hold the latter view. More characteristic of Cranmer is the following citation: "I say (according to God's word and the doctrine of the old writers) that Christ is present in the sacrament, as they teach also, that he is present in his word, when he worketh mightily in the hearts of the hearers."[160] As Gordon Pruett has suggested, in the light of this citation, we are justified only in speaking of "Cranmer's doctrine of the presence in the Christian life." This, of course, includes Christ's presence in the Lord's Supper. This diffused rather than focussed or concentrated presence of Christ in the Christian life was, for Cranmer, a consequence of the theologian's belief that

---

[157] Cranmer, *Writings and Disputations*, p. 398; and Zwingli, in Richardson, *Zwingli and Cranmer*, p. 21.

[158] *Writings and Disputations*, p. 47.

[159] Calvin, *Institutes* 4:17:32; see also note 25 above.

[160] *Writings and Disputations*, p. 11; and Bromiley, *Cranmer*, p. 72.

Christ is influential through his divine, and not his human, nature. Yet when one is ready to conclude that for the latest expression of Cranmer's thought all thought of the sense of Christ being present in his humanity, flesh, or *body*, is ruled out, one recalls these words: "And therefore in the book of the holy communion we do not pray that the creatures of bread and wine may be the body and blood of Christ; but that they may be unto us the body and blood of Christ; that is to say, that we may so eat them, and drink them, that we may be partakers of his body crucified, and of his blood shed for our redemption."[161] This is much more than Zwingli would have said. We know that Cranmer frequently and quite explicitly rejected the notion that the sacraments are bare signs. Yet it is less than Calvin had affirmed. On the other hand, the acceptance of the "black rubric" in the Prayer Book of 1552 is more consonant with a Zwinglian than a Calvinist interpretation.

Disappointing as this conclusion may be, after following the winding trail of Cranmer's thought, it is appropriate to recall that Cranmer did more than write a treatise on the Eucharist. He left the Church of England with a copy of the Great Bible in every parish and copies of the Book of Common Prayer in almost every pew. F. E. Hutchinson's tribute to Cranmer is just: "*lex orandi*, the regulation of public worship together with a wide circulation of the Bible, would do more to affect the character of the religion of English people for years to come than definitions of doctrine reflecting the controversies of the time. Here Cranmer was at his best and rendered his greatest service to the Church of England."[162]

6. Eucharistic Doctrine after Cranmer

Cranmer's influence, both in its affirmations and negations, lived on. In the 42 Articles of 1553, the negation was foremost: "a faithful man ought not to believe . . . the real and bodily presence (as they term it) of Christ's flesh and blood." By 1563 the 28th of the 39 Articles declared more positively: "The body of Christ is given, taken, and eaten in the Supper only after an heavenly and spiritual manner. And the mean whereby the body of Christ is received and eaten in the Supper is faith."

Jewel followed Cranmer in his assertions that there are three distinctions between Anglican and Catholic doctrine: "first, that we put a difference between the sign and the thing itself that is

[161] *Writings and Disputations*, p. 271.
[162] *Cranmer and the English Reformation*, p. 104.

signified. Secondly, that we seek Christ above in heaven, and imagine not him to be bodily on earth. Thirdly, that the body of Christ is to be eaten with faith only, and none other wise."[163] Cranmer would have been delighted with Jewel's explanation that the sacrament was eaten "with the mouth of faith" and equally with his denial of any corporal presence of Christ because Christ's body was in heaven: "the sacrament-bread is bread, it is not the body of Christ: the body of Christ is flesh, it is no bread. The bread is beneath: the body is above. The bread is on the table: the body is in heaven. The bread is in the mouth: the body in the heart. The bread feedeth the outward man: the body feedeth the inward man. . . . Such a difference is there between the bread, which is a sacrament of the body, and the body of Christ itself."[164] With Cyprian, Jewel affirmed that the sacramental food is *cibus mentis, non ventris*.[165] The same distinction between the sacrament and the thing signified by it was made succinctly two decades later by Edmund Grindal: "Christ did eat the sacrament with the apostles: ergo, the sacrament is not Christ."[166]

Edwin Sandys, who became Archbishop of York in 1576, wrote of a spiritual eating, as contrasted with the physical eating, which Transubstantiation presupposes: "In this sacrament there are two things, a visible sign and an invisible grace: there is a visible sacramental sign of bread and wine, and there is the thing and matter signified, namely the body and blood of Christ. . . . Thy teeth shall not do him violence, neither thy stomach contain his glorious body. Thy faith must reach up into heaven. By faith he is seen, by faith he is touched, by faith he is digested. Spiritually by faith we feed upon Christ, when we steadfastly believe that his body was broken and his blood shed for us upon the cross; by which sacrifice, offerred once for all, as sufficient for all, our sins were freely remitted, blotted out, and washed away. This is our heavenly bread, our spiritual food. This doth strengthen our souls and cheer our hearts."[167]

The fullest and freshest treatment of the Eucharist in the Eliza-

---

[163] Jewel was answering the criticism of the Catholic writer, Harding, that what is given in the Eucharist must exist in the Eucharist to be given, and cannot, therefore, reside exclusively in heaven. See Jewel, *Works*, I, 449.

[164] Jewel, *Works*, II, 1,121; also see I, 9, 12.

[165] *Ibid.*, II, 1,121.

[166] *The Remains of Edmund Grindal, D.D.*, ed. William Nicholson, p. 43, cited in C. W. Dugmore, *Eucharistic Theology in England from Hooker to Waterland*, pp. 9-10.

[167] Sandys, *Sermons*, ed. J. Ayre, 2 vols., I, 88-89.

bethan age was that of Richard Hooker, though he too moved in the tracks laid down by Thomas Cranmer. Although he acknowledged that "the fruit of the Eucharist is the participation of the body and blood of Christ," he rejected Transubstantiation and Consubstantiation with the statement: "there is no sentence of Holy Scripture which saith that we cannot by this sacrament be made partakers of his body and blood except they be first contained in the sacrament, or the sacrament converted into them."[168] Hooker was plainly tired of unprofitable and "fierce contentions" on the explanations of the Eucharist, and insisted that they were irrelevant from a practical standpoint, "because our participation of Christ in this sacrament dependeth on the co-operation of his omnipotent power which maketh it his body and blood to us, whether with change or without alteration of the element. . . ."[169] Hooker expounded his own theory of instrumentality as if interpreted by Christ, thus: *"this hallowed food, through concurrence of divine power, is in verity and truth, unto faithful receivers, instrumentally a cause of that mystical participation, whereby as I make myself wholly theirs, so I give them in hand an actual possession of all such saving grace as my sacrificed body can yield, and as their souls do presently need, this is to them and in them my body."*[170] The real presence of Christ is to be sought, according to Hooker, not in things but in persons, not in consecrated elements but in consecrated persons receiving grace through faith.[171]

I may appropriately end this chapter, which has asked so many questions and dealt with so many differences where there may not always have appeared to be distinctions, with the positive appraisal of Hooker, ecstatically speaking of the communicant's experience of the Eucharist: "They are things wonderful which he feeleth, great which he seeth and unheard of which he uttereth, whose soul is possessed of this Paschal Lamb and made joyful in the strength of this new wine, this bread hath in it more than the substance which our eyes behold, this cup hallowed with solemn benediction availeth to the endless life and welfare both of soul and body, in that it serveth as well for a medicine to heal our infirmities and purge our sins as for a sacrifice of thanksgiving; with touching it sanctifieth, it enlighteneth with belief, it truly conformeth us unto the image of Jesus Christ; what these elements are in them-

---

[168] *Ecclesiastical Polity*, ed. Keble, v, lxvii, 6, p. 353.
[169] *Ibid.* [170] *Ibid.*, v, lxvii, 12, p. 359.
[171] *Ibid.*, v, lxviii, 1, p. 363.

selves it skilleth not, it is enough that to me which take them they are the body and blood of Christ, his promise in witness hereof sufficeth, his word he knoweth which way to accomplish; why should any cogitation possess the mind of a faithful communicant but this, O my God thou art true, O my Soul thou art happy!"[172]

[172] Three criticisms may be offered of Hooker's Eucharistic thought: piety is no substitute for theological clarity; he had an inadequate doctrine of sacrifice; and Hooker, like Cranmer, did not draw the Eucharistic implications of his admirable doctrine of the Incarnation. It has been stated best by L. S. Thornton in *Richard Hooker, a Study of his Theology*, pp. 87-88: "The principle of the Incarnation is that things Divine and heavenly are actually embodied in things earthly and visible in such sense that they are no longer two entities but one; that one entity however has two aspects and belongs to two orders, the heavenly and the earthly. This is the truth both as regard to the Church and the Eucharist which Hooker missed because he had another presupposition in his mind."

PART TWO:
THE LITURGICAL ALTERNATIVES

CHAPTER IV

CATHOLIC WORSHIP

To RECOUNT the history of sixteenth-century Catholic worship in England is to walk along a heavily shadowed path on which the gleams of light are few, and those are of a wintry and ominous glint. Henry VIII might keep up the outward panoply of worship, as he insisted on the overdone royal pageantry of the Field of the Cloth of Gold. It became an increasingly hollow ceremonialism, however, for the dissolution of the monasteries was bringing to an end the great traditions of spirituality fostered by the monks, friars, and nuns, and the all too common "bare, ruined choirs" of the religious houses were mute testimony to a new secularity.

A new spring (though short-lived, as it turned out) seemed possible to faithful Catholics when Reginald Pole, Cardinal and kinsman of Henry VIII, was appointed one of the three presidents of the Council of Trent in 1545, and four years later was almost elected Pope. Another sign of the same hope was the important role in the Council played by Thomas Goldwell, bishop of St. Asaph, a Theatine who had experienced in this revolutionary group the disciplined fervour of the counterreformation, and who was the protagonist of a renovated liturgy and disciplined spirituality. The hope was, in fact, achieved with the accession of Mary to the throne of England and the submission of England to the spiritual authority of the Papacy in December 1554. But Mary and Pole, then the Archbishop of Canterbury, died on the same day four years later to the great relief of Protestants and most of England. The last desperate rays of the sun setting on a dominant English Catholicism were seen in the brilliant and doomed gallantry of the Jesuit priests, like Campion, who invaded England in 1580 and after, and by their agonies and dying testimonies encouraged vacillating Recusants (those who refused to worship according to the Book of Common Prayer) to stand firm in the faith. The story falls into three major parts: pre-Elizabethan Catholic worship; the Tridentine revaluation of worship and the part played in it by Englishmen; and the largely secret and wholly valiant worship of the Elizabethan Recusants.

127

1. *On the Eve of the Reformation*

Despite the Lollard insistence on simplicity in religion and worship, and the Erasmian criticisms of the superstition of the people and the avarice of the clergy, yet the Latin Mass, according to the Salisbury Use, especially when celebrated on a great festival in a medieval cathedral or by the entire community of a prestigious abbey, was an impressive act of corporate adoration of the living God. It is almost impossible to describe what the loss of such a liturgy must have meant to a nation that had accepted for a thousand years its reinforcement of faith and spirituality. It is easier to appreciate the visible aesthetic than the invisible spiritual loss. The austere sublimity of the Gregorian chanting, the sunlight fractured through the rose window or dyed by the lights of the vast West window, the images, all testified to a faith that made wayfaring men the companions of the saints, and provided a fit context of *son et lumière* for the miracle by which the God of the Incarnation made a new epiphany in the Mass, to provide iron rations for the warrior-pilgrims of the church militant. How splendidly did the church through the sacraments, despite the worldliness of its prelates and the somnolence of its priests, surround the main stages of the life of the plain man and woman with glimpses of transcendental glory that transfigured their dull diurnal routine! How unimaginably bleak and bare and colour-blind must the simple and didactic services of incipient Protestantism have seemed to the same Darby and Joan, when the iconoclastic excitements of sermons, which appealed to brain but not to heart or imagination, had worn off! Sacramentals abolished; sacraments reduced from seven to two and these explained so as to lose their sense of the numinous. Images in glass and stone smashed and replaced by the ubiquitous royal coat of arms. Ceremonies such as lustrations, elevations, prostrations, and the like, as well as exorcisms and dirges and tolling of bells, were prohibited as superstitious. Vestments were radically reduced in numbers and ornateness. The magic and mystery, as well as the majesty of worship had been dissipated. What was left must have seemed vacuous and uninspired, mere penny-plain, whitewashed religion.

It is only too easy, in the tradition of Pugin and Ruskin, to re-create a sentimentalised, rose-coloured Middle Ages in which donors are always godly and artists are inspired allegorists.[1] G. G.

[1] One is reminded of Dean Inge's remark about Ruskin, that he knew about everything in the medieval cathedral except the altar.

Coulton has rightly questioned whether many of the donors were not trying to bribe their way into heaven, and making a good end to what had been a wicked life, and whether the designers were not repeating superstitious legends in place of the authentic narratives of the Gospel.[2] A. G. Dickens asks similar questions: "Where lay communities genuinely supplied the means, did they not pay more regard to pretty fictions about the saints than to the searching demands of Pauline theology? When actually Christocentric, did not popular art concentrate unduly upon such favourite themes as the Passion and the Nativity, to the neglect of a fuller and more balanced presentation of Christ's life and teaching?"[3] When allowance is made for mixed motives, one can only regret the greedy iconoclasm which led to the loss of so many medieval art treasures through the melting down of reliquaries, images, and metal-encrusted Gospel covers. The lost of monastic libraries was also a cultural and spiritual deprivation. Some gains to education resulted from the spoliation of the monasteries, through the foundation or reendowment of grammar schools in the cathedral cities and the establishment of Christ Church in Oxford and Trinity in Cambridge, which dwarfed the older foundations, and the creation of new chairs in both universities.[4] The vast number of empty ecclesiastical buildings in London testified to the disappearance of a way of life; the new architectural landscape was secular. There were no new foundations to train men in the culture and discipline of the spiritual life,[5] nor any hospices for the poor. In this spiritual drought the twin streams of spirituality and hospitality had almost dried up.

While there must have been immorality in the monasteries, it was to Cromwell's advantage to exaggerate this to provide an excuse for pillaging them. If God made the country and man made the town, as Cowper believed, and a succession of prophets like Amos anticipated him in this judgment, then it is in the country that we would expect the familiar piety of Catholicism to linger longest, undisturbed by the new learning and newer ambition of

2 *Art and the Reformation*, chaps. 19, 20.

3 *The English Reformation*, p. 10.

4 *Ibid.*, p. 150. At Cambridge in 1540 and Oxford in 1546, Henry VIII established regius professorship in divinity, medicine, law, Hebrew, and Greek.

5 One must not forget Archbishop David Mathew's warning that "the state of the monasteries during their last years was less encouraging than is suggested by the Gasquettinted sunset. In country parishes however there were in many cases a deep constant attachment between the parishioners and their priests. . . . The Christian ages and the sacramental life were behind them constantly supporting." *Catholicism in England*, p. 2.

the cities and towns. Countrymen awaited with faith the regularity of God's blessing on the seasons; for them religion was as inevitable as the march of the seasons. It is not surprising that it was the areas farthest from London that proved truest to Catholicism, both in the Pilgrimage of Grace of 1536 which protested against the dissolution of the monasteries and the Western Uprising of 1549 which protested against the abolition of the Latin Mass with the demand that all the people use the First English Prayer Book of 1549. Church and state were interlocked; there was no reason to think that the anti-Lutheran Henry VIII would bring the great house of Catholicism tumbling down merely to secure his throne and line by the hope of an heir from another wife and to fill his depleted coffers with the proceeds from the deprived monasteries. Wittenberg and its rebellious priests seemed as remote as Doomsday.

Yet in 1534 England passed the Act of Supremacy which cut England off from the Pope and Western Catholic Christendom, and which declared: "Be it enacted by the authority of the present Parliament that the King our sovereign Lord, his heirs and successors, Kings of this realm, shall be taken, accepted, and reputed the only Supreme Head in earth of the Church of England, called *Ecclesia Anglicana*."[6] The following summer there were the martyrdoms of John Fisher, Bishop of Rochester, and of Thomas More.

The proof of the discontent among the common people was their dissatisfaction with the new English prayer book. The people's deep sense of loss in being prevented from using the Catholic ritual and ceremonial was evident in the Western Uprising. The uprising began when the parishioners of Sampford Courtenay in Devon succeeded in persuading their priest to say the Mass publicly and in Latin in open defiance of the law, to the great approbation of the common people in the neighbourhood. There was a suspicion of the rich who stood to benefit most from Protestantism. An old lady, forbidden to say her beads in public in the village of St. Mary's Clyst, informed the other villagers: "Ye needs must leave beads now; no more holy bread for ye, nor holy water. It is all gone from us or to go, or the gentlemen will burn your houses over your heads."[7] Whether or not the discontent was fomented by dis-

[6] Henry Gee and W. J. Hardy, *Documents Illustrative of English Church History*, pp. 243-44.
[7] Mathew, *Catholicism in England*, p. 13.

possessed priests, as seems likely, the nature of the protest could plainly be seen in the articles put forward by the Devon and Cornwall men, all wanting to turn the clock back. The conservatism of these countrymen was untouched by the influence of the counterreformation, for their third request was: "We will have the Mass in Latin as was before and celebrated by the priest without any man or woman communicating with him." They also desired to adore the Reserved Sacrament; wanted the Communion, as far as partaking of the consecrated wafer was concerned, only once a year, at Easter; desired to have Baptism administered on weekdays as well as Sundays; and obviously missed the Catholic ceremonies, as the 7th article indicates: "we will have holy bread and holy water made every Sunday, palms and ashes at the times appointed and accustomed, images to be set up again in every church, and all other ancient ceremonies used by our mother the Church." They found the new liturgy impersonal and deficient in the sense of the Communion of the Saints, hence they begged: "we will have every preacher in his sermon and every priest at his Mass pray specially by name for the souls in purgatory as our forefathers did." Perhaps the most naive of all the articles was the 10th, which offered a left-handed compliment to Protestants as "men of the Book." It read: "we will have the Bible and all other books of Scripture in English to be called in again; for we be informed that otherwise the clergy shall not of long time confound the heretics." The entire document was the touching manifestation of a spiritual vacuum in the English countryside.[8]

2. Piety in Mary's Reign

The tragedy of Queen Mary's reign is that she is "Bloody Mary" to all Protestants because her burning of heretics in Smithfield scorched itself into the English memory through the work of the great martyrologist, Foxe. To Catholics she was "Good Queen Marye," as in the long and undistinguished, but devout, daily prayer she composed and was retained in the Bedingfield Papers in the "Sydenham Prayer Book." This prolix prayer breathes the spirit of an utter dedication to God, narrow and proper rather than deep, legalistic rather than lyrical; it evinces a total commitment to the ways of the Catholic church.[9]

[8] *Troubles connected with the Prayer Book of 1549*, ed. Nicholas Pocock, New Series, xxxvii, pp. 148f.
[9] Catholic Record Society Publication No. 7, entitled, *Miscellanea, VI, Bedingfield Papers, etc.*, pp. 23-27.

What a deep and genuine Catholic piety was like in Queen Mary's days may be ascertained from the account of the life of Magdalen Dacre, who was a maid of honour at Mary's court and later married the Viscount Montague. Her father was a man of wit and daring. When Henry VIII told Lord Dacre that Parliament had given consent for the king to become head of the English church, and sought his opinion, Magdalen's father replied, "Hereafter, then, when your Majesty offendeth, you may absolve yourself."[10] It is related in her biography that the court of England was then "a school of virtue, a nursery of purity, a mansion of piety," and that "the Queen herself did shine as the moon in all kinds of virtue, whose praises all histories do record."[11] Magdalen Dacre used to spend several hours in devout meditation before the crucifix in the chapel either before others had risen from their beds or long after they had gone to bed, so sincere was her devotion to God. Even in the reign of Protestant Elizabeth, Magdalen had Mass said twice a week for the repose of her husband's soul, and she herself said the Office of the Dead for him. She maintained three priests in her household and often had as many as 80 persons dependent on her for sustenance.[12] She visited the poor in their cottages and sent them medicines, food, wood, or money.[13] The strict regimen of her spiritual life in the time of the Renaissance deserves to be recorded, for it was unaccompanied by any Pharisaic superiority or censoriousness.

For the most part she did every day hear three masses, and more would willingly have heard if she might, and such was her affection to this divine sacrifice that, when upon any occasion in the winter it was said before day, she in that cold and unseasonable time could not contain herself in her bed, but rising endured not to be absent from that heavenly sacrifice.

In her private devotions she did every day say three offices, that is of the Blessed Virgin, of the Holy Ghost, and of the Holy Cross, whereto she added at least three rosaries, the Jesus Psalter, the fifteen prayers of St. Brigit, which because they began with O are commonly called her fifteen Oes, and the common litanies, and, finally, sometimes the Office of the

---

[10] A. C. Southern, ed., *An Elizabethan Recusant House, comprising the Life of the Lady Magdalen, Viscountess Montague*, p. 7.
[11] *Ibid.*, p. 12.   [12] *Ibid.*, p. 39.
[13] *Ibid.*, p. 40.

Dead. Which prayers, when in her infirmity she could not say herself, she procured to be said by others, distributing to every one a part.[14]

If such is the private image of Marian piety, what was the public view of the restoration of the Catholic faith and worship in Queen Mary's reign? The first Parliament in the new reign abolished the second Edwardian Prayer Book of 1552, reestablished the Mass, the Catholic ordination service, and the remainder of the Catholic sacramental ritual. Laws abolishing certain holy days and days of fasting and a law for putting away images and certain books were repealed, but only after eight days of stormy debate and by a vote of 270 votes to 80 on the third reading in the House of Commons.[15] The episcopate was purged of married and heretical bishops, and the old Henricians and the new appointees proceeded to dismiss about one-eighth of the clergy who had married and would not give up their wives.[16] The most difficult task was to persuade Parliament to acknowledge the spiritual supremacy of the Apostolic See and the abolition of the spiritual jurisdiction of the sovereign over the English Church. This delicate matter was accomplished early in 1554 in the long Second Act of Repeal, which begins by acknowledging that England had "swerved from the obedience of the Apostolic See, and declined from the unity of Christ's church," and which restored the ecclesiastical status quo of 1529. Insofar as Parliament could legislate the return of England to the Catholic faith, it had been accomplished, but a series of factors made a complete return impossible.

The new nobility and gentry were dependent on the Henrician dissolution of the monasteries, and would not think of giving up their lands to the church, nor, indeed, was the queen prepared to endanger her throne by asking for their return. Thus it was a church shorn of most of its temporalities that returned to power. Furthermore, the effect of a monarch as head of the Church of England had been to diminish the power of the archbishops and bishops, not to mention the clergy, almost all of whom had shown themselves to be compliant to the monarch's demands and in no

14 *Ibid.*, p. 47.
15 Philip Hughes, *Rome and the Counter-Reformation in England*, p. 67. For the Act of Repeal see Gee and Hardy, *Documents of English Church History*, pp. 377-80.
16 W. H. Frere, *The Marian Reaction*, chap. 3, where it is claimed that 1,057 deprivations of the clergy for marriage out of approximately 8,000 incumbents can be traced in the documents.

sense the successors of Thomas à Becket. The queen seemed to be more Spanish than English in her style of life, and her consort was, of course, an unpopular Spaniard. Her chief spiritual advisor, Cardinal Pole, the Archbishop of Canterbury, was a man of great spirituality and scholarship, but of little diplomatic ability. It was excessively myopic of Mary to revive the hated statute *De Heretico Comburendo* in 1554, for the English were a tolerant people and would not forgive her the deaths of so many valiant men of another faith in so short a reign.[17] Whatever the reasons, Mary had time to make enemies, and she lacked the popularity and the length of reign to make friends on the grand scale. It would have been wiser if she had vowed, like her sister and successor Elizabeth, "not to make windows in men's minds."

The new liturgical requirements were made clear in the instructions Mary issued to the archbishops and bishops on March 4, 1554.[18] The traditional procession before the High Mass on Sundays and festival days was to be restored, and the old Litany of the Saints in Latin was to displace the new Litany of the Book of Common Prayer in English. The days of fasting and the holy days abolished in the reign of Edward VI were reinstituted, together with the ancient ceremonies associated with Ash Wednesday, Palm Sunday, and the last three days of Holy Week. The Catholic rite alone was to be used for Baptism and Confirmation.

The rest of the intentions for Marian liturgical practice can be derived from a consideration of the remarkably careful articles and injunctions prepared for Bishop Bonner's prolonged visitation of the diocese of London in the autumn of 1554.[19] His aim was to restore in all their plenitude the old religious customs as well as the full Catholic liturgy. Detailed directions were given for the replacement of service books, vestments, and church furniture presumably destroyed by the iconoclasts of the prior reign. The previously unemployed craftsmen must have been working overtime in

[17] The situation was well characterised by the Venetian ambassador, *Venetian Calendar*, VI, 1,074-75: "With the exception of a few very pious Catholics, none of whom, however, are under thirty-five years of age, all the rest make this show of recantation, yet do not effectually resume the Catholic faith, and on the first opportunity would be more than ever ready and determined to the unrestrained life previously led by them. . . . They discharge their duty as subject to their prince by living as he lives, believing what he believes, and in short doing whatever he commands, making use of it for external show to avoid incurring his displeasure rather than from any internal zeal; for they would do the like by the Mahometan or Jewish creed."

[18] Printed in Gee and Hardy, *Documents of English Church History*, pp. 380-83.

[19] See W. H. Frere and W. M. Kennedy, *Visitation Articles and Injunctions of the Period of the Reformation*, Alcuin Club Collections XV, vol. 2, pp. 331-72.

the first years of Mary's reign as they provided stone altars for wooden Communion tables, carved the calvaries for rood-lofts and statues, and made pyxes. A Catholic handbook of doctrine and piety for the least instructed of his clergy was prepared by Bonner under the title, *A profitable and necessary doctrine with certain homilies adjoined thereto.* In the simplest terms it explained the Creed, Sacraments, Commandments, *Our Father, Hail Mary,* seven capital sins, and Beatitudes.

There is one interesting sidelight on both the infrequency with which the chief Sacrament of the Eucharist was celebrated, and on the conservative way in which it was administered. It shows that the new insights of the Council of Trent had not yet reached the Bishop of London, who, during the sequestration of Cranmer, was virtually the Archbishop of Canterbury. He did not think it proper to exhort the priests to invite the people to communicate at Mass more frequently. Indeed, he implied that this is the less necessary precisely because bread is blessed at the Mass and given to the people as a sacramental. It was ironical that he mentioned that the bread was a reminder of unity, and "that all Christian people be one mystical body of Christ, like as the bread is made of many grains, and yet but one loaf," when it is the sacrament of incorporation which best testifies to that unity. Almost incidentally he suggested that "the said holy bread is to put us also in remembrance of the housel, and the receiving of the most Blessed Body and Blood of our Saviour Jesus Christ, which the people in the beginning of Christ's church did oftener receive than they do use now in these days to do."[20]

How conservative and insulated England had become through being cut off from the revivifying counterreformation piety of the Council of Trent can be seen by comparing Bonner's attitude to the Sacrament, with the statement of the Fathers at Trent, made only three years earlier: "This holy synod, with fatherly concern, warns, exhorts, begs, and beseeches by the loving heart of our God, that all and singular, who count themselves of the Christian name, come together in harmony now at any rate, in this sign of unity, this bond of love, this symbol of agreement, and that, mindful of the great majesty and understanding love of Our Lord Jesus Christ who gave His beloved life as the price of our salvation, and His flesh for our eating, all Christians will believe and reverence

---

20 Philip Hughes, *The Reformation in England,* III, 75, comments on Bonner's merely historic interest in days when Holy Communion was received frequently.

these sacred mysteries of His body and blood with a faith so constant and so firm, with such devoutness of spirit, with such dutiful worship, that they may be able frequently to receive this supersubstantial bread, and that it may truly be to them the life of their soul, and an everlasting health of mind, made strong by whose strength they may be qualified to arrive, from the journeying of this woeful pilgrimage, at our fatherland which is heaven."[21]

Pole's reforming concern is seen in the plans for a restored Catholicism in England. It is visible in the decisions of the great national council he summoned and over which, as Papal legate, he presided during the winter of 1555-1556. Every anniversary of St. Andrew's Day 1554, the memory of the day of England's reconciliation with Rome, was to be gratefully recalled at a special celebration with a solemn procession and a sermon explaining the reason for the festival. Pole's hand can be seen in the decree against absentee bishops and in another, insisting that it was the personal responsibility of the bishop to preach and catechise. The spirit of the counterreformation and of Pole is also seen in the bishops' requirement to erect diocesan seminaries to train candidates for the priesthood and to provide (until a preaching priesthood was trained) bands of itinerant preachers to tour the dioceses. In four years the death of the queen and the cardinal ruined the entire plan. Pole's wider influence was felt through the work of the Council of Trent.

3. *Englishmen and the Counterreformation*

The two most eminent Englishmen at the Council of Trent were the Cardinal President, Reginald Pole, and the Theatine, Thomas Goldwell, who was bishop of St. Asaph; Goldwell was very interested in the reform of the liturgy.

Pole was Cardinal Deacon with the title of Santa Maria in Cosmedin. His mother was niece to Edward IV, reigning at the time of her birth, first cousin to his successor, Edward V, niece to Richard III, and first cousin to Elizabeth, the consort of Henry VII, as well as dear friend of Catherine of Aragon. He was schooled by the Carthusian monks at Sheen, and went on to Magdalen College, Oxford, for six years, which was still in the fervour of its founding by William Waynefleet. In 1519 Pole went to the University of Padua where he became adept in Renaissance learning. Even

---

[21] October 11, 1551; Session XIII; Decretum, c. viii, De usu admirabilis huius sacramenti.

Bembo praised him in 1522 as "perhaps the most virtuous, erudite
. . . grave young man in Italy at the present time."[22] Many years
as a diplomat for the Pope, combined with an unassailable purity
of life and modesty of manner and an eagerness for the reform of
the church, excellently equipped him to be one of the three presidents of the Council of Trent when it resumed in 1545. When the
canon of Sacred Scripture was under preliminary consideration, as
a proponent of reform, it was Pole who argued that the Council
should examine the claims of each separate book for inclusion in
the Canon, for the Lutherans had argued that the Catholics were
afraid to look too closely into their origins. When the discussion
moved to the adoption of an official version of the Bible, Pole made
the interesting suggestion that the Hebrew and Greek texts be
added to the Vulgate lest the Catholic church should seem to be
limited to the Latin culture.[23] If a man is known by his friends,
then we may judge that Pole's great friend Cardinal Contarini
spoke for him when attempting to construct a theory of justification that would provide a way of moving closer to Lutheran views.[24]
Pole and Contarini were later accused of heresy by the inquisitorial
Pope, Paul IV, a charge that shadowed Pole's last years. The last
irony was that he, who had such good reason to fear the machinations of the politicians because of the way his ancestors and near
relations had been slaughtered because of their closeness to an
insecure throne and who had therefore been inclined to put his
complete trust in God, should find God's man, the Pope, treach-
erous, too.

Goldwell, the other Englishman at Trent, was the last survivor
of the ancient English hierarchy, who lived to be 84. This bishop
of St. Asaph in remote Wales went abroad during the first months
of Henry VIII's anti-Catholic measures and met Pole, with whom
he was thereafter to be closely associated, in Padua in 1532. From
1538 to 1547 Goldwell was in charge of the hospice for English
pilgrims in Rome. In 1547 he joined the new reformist order of
the Theatines, one of the greatest of the new counterreformation
orders (like the Jesuits), founded in 1524. Aiming to combat
the worldliness and general laxity of the clergy, the Theatines
demanded an oath of poverty to apply communally as well as personally. Its members went to work among the poor in the great

22 Cited Hughes, *Reformation in England*, p. 32.
23 *Ibid.*, pp. 41-42.
24 See the article on Pole by Herbert Thurston, S.J., in *Catholic Encyclopedia*,
v, 335-37.

cities and were dependent on the providence of God as they went about preaching, catechising, and administering the sacraments. Their founders were Count Gaetano da Tiene (St. Cajetan) and Gian Pietro Carafa, bishop of Chieti and the future Paul IV. They revolutionised the image of the clergy and the church in the areas where they worked, but their numbers were select and small. Their own lives were austere, but their churches were splendid tributes to the Divine Majesty. Goldwell joined them when he was about 47, a remarkable tribute to his willpower and dedication.[25]

From time to time Goldwell would leave his pastoral duties for other tasks, as when he was given leave in 1549-1550 to attend Cardinal Pole at the conclave to elect a successor to Paul III. When he had the great privilege of conducting the Vespers of the Council of Trent on June 25, 1561, the vigil of St. Vigilius,[26] the protector of the Council, his great friend Pole had been dead for three years. Since the Theatines were greatly concerned with the improvement of the Breviary and the Missal, having been encouraged by Pope Clement VII in 1529 to devote their energies to the task, and as Paul IV was also a Theatine, Goldwell was greatly concerned with liturgical renewal. Paul IV granted permission to the Theatines to adopt certain minor alterations in worship, but he did not believe that these matters had been sufficiently discussed by the representatives of the entire Catholic church to make them universally binding on the faithful. When the Council of Trent met anew under Pope Pius IV, the matter was referred by His Holiness to the fathers of the Council. At their request he sent them the annotations made by Paul IV and preserved in the Theatine archives. The Council entrusted the work of revision to a Commission, of which Goldwell, being a Theatine, was appointed a member. The Council of Trent did not have time to complete its liturgical work. The Pontiff then appointed a special Congregation at Rome, of which Goldwell was a member, to continue the work of revision;[27] the work was concluded on July 9, 1568 with the provision for a uniform Roman Missal and Breviary which became the undeviating standard of Catholic worship throughout the world until the second Vatican Council initiated the far-reaching changes of the present day.

Goldwell received many honours, including the presidency of

[25] T. E. Bridgett and T. F. Knox, *The True Story of the Catholic Hierarchy deposed by Queen Elizabeth with fuller memoirs of its last two survivors*, pp. 214-15.

[26] *Ibid.*, p. 226.   [27] *Ibid.*, pp. 238-39.

the General Chapter of the Order of Theatines in 1566, 1567, and 1572. St. Pius V appointed him to the office of Vicar (or representative of the Cardinal Archpriest) in the St. John Lateran Church in Rome; and in 1574 Cardinal Savelli made him his suffragan, or vicegerent. Among Goldwell's duties was the responsibility for administering the sacrament of Holy Orders to the many persons from many lands who desired to be ordained priests in Rome. The *Pontifical* Goldwell used has several corrections and annotations in his own handwriting. After his death the Congregation of Rites made considerable use of it in the correction of the old Roman *Pontifical*, and many emendations were adopted to conform with Goldwell's wishes. This was his final liturgical legacy to the Catholic church, in whose renewal he had shared.[28] The Catholics of England could take great pride in the contributions of Pole and Goldwell to the renewed spirituality and worship of the international Roman Catholic church.

4. The Case for Catholic Liturgical Reform

Having observed, however briefly, the two major English representatives among the fathers of the Council of Trent, it is important to consider the overall liturgical work of the Council, as it was to determine the pattern of English Catholic worship for four centuries to come.[29]

It is impossible to understand the reasons for the Tridentine reforms of the liturgy apart from some minimal knowledge of the morphology of the medieval Mass. It is now customary for liturgiologists to describe the medieval Mass as the "allegorical" or "dramatic" mass, by which is intended the view that the holy banquet had been turned into a mysterious spectacle, the chief moment of which was the elevation of the Host by the celebrating priest. As Latin became increasingly unfamiliar to the humble believers who assisted at the Mass, they came to believe that the

---

[28] *Ibid.*, pp. 247-48.

[29] The major volumes consulted for this and the following section in this chapter are: *Concilium Tridentinum. Diariorum, Actorum, Epistolarum, Tractatuum,* henceforth *Conc. Trid. Nova collectio edidit Societas Goerresiana;* Hermanus A. P. Schmidt, *Introductio in Liturgiam Occidentalem;* Joseph A. Jungmann, *Missarum Sollemnia; eine genetische Erklärung der römischen Messe;* and the English edition, *The Mass of the Roman Rite: Its Origins and Development (Missarum Sollemnia),* tr. Francis A. Brunner, 2 vols. I have also had the benefit of the advice of a learned monk and friend, Father Reinhold Theisen, O.S.B., the author of *Mass Liturgy and the Council of Trent,* which has proved invaluable. An authoritative article is H. Jedin's "Das Konzil von Trient und die Reform des Romischen Messbuches," *Liturgisches Leben,* VI, 30-66.

Mass could be interpreted as a complete representation of the Passion of Christ, so that the arrival of the priest at the altar symbolized the capture of Christ, the *Confiteor* the standing before Annas and Caiaphas, etc., or, that the whole life of Christ was figuratively represented in the mass and hence was to be understood as divided into the 40 works of Christ's life or the 33 years of his life.[30] Like human nature, the liturgy could not leave well enough alone, so imagination went to work during the long spells of unintelligibility to create elaborate and unhistorical fancies.[31] Popular devotion was no longer concentrated on incorporation into the body of Christ or on fellowship with Christ and His church. As the immensely popular legend of the Middle Ages, the Holy Grail, makes clear, the people's desire was to glimpse the celestial mystery of the miracle. To see the sacred Host became the principal, if not the exclusive, concern of worshippers in the High Middle Ages. In the cities the people ran from one church to another in the hope of witnessing the miracle often. In England it was not enough for the priest to elevate the Host, for the people cried, "Higher, Sir John, higher!"[32] They insisted on glass chalices[33] in order to have ocular demonstration of the miracle effected by consecration. They believed that a glimpse of the Host would spare them from blindness, or poverty, or death on that day on which they had seen it. In all these ways, the total action of the Eucharist was sacrificed to a single moment of epiphany; the sense of the community created by the Holy Communion was sacrificed to an individual egotism. The result was that all sense of the Mass as a *sacrifice* for the living and the dead, as a *communion* with God and His people, or as a *banquet* was lost. Clearly some reinterpretation was necessary, not to mention changes in the mode of celebration.

Another valid reason for reconsideration was the trenchant criticism of the Mass made by the Protestant Reformers. These were contained in Luther's *Von der Winkelmesse und Pfaffenweihe* and

---

[30] Schmidt, *Introductio*, p. 367.

[31] *Ibid.* "Fine Medii Aevi allegoria Missae irretitur suis propriis imaginationibus et pervenit usque ad insolitissimas inventiones, ne dicamus ad stultitias."

[32] *Ibid.*, p. 269. "In Anglia eveniebat, quod sacerdoti qui S. Hostiam non satis alte elevebat, acclamabatur: 'Altius, Domine Joannes, altius.'" See also E. Dumoutet, *Le désir de voir l'Hostie*, for the growing importance of the "elevation" for the people. So great had the mania for miracles become, and so deep was the conviction of the "instant" benefits available from the Mass, that there was an enormous growth of "altarists" whose only duty it was to celebrate the Mass and say the Office. In 1521, for example, Strassburg had 120 Mass foundations, and in England Henry VIII suppressed 2,374 chantries just before his death. Jungmann, *Missarum Sollemnia*, I, 130.

[33] Schmidt, *Introductio*, p. 269.

Calvin's *Petit Traicté de la Saincte Cène*. The Reformers had three main objections to the private Mass.[34] They objected to its sacrificial character. Luther, for example, argued that the Mass was not a *sacrificium*, but a *beneficium*—not a sacrifice renewed by men but the thankful recognition by men of a gift of God. They particularly criticised the failure to administer Communion to the laity, when the priest receives alone, as a departure from the example and institution of Christ and a denial of the fellowship of Christ of which this sacrament is the renewal of incorporation. They believed that the Mass is essentially a Communion service and that where there is no reception by the faithful there is no Communion. They insisted that the custom of the private Mass lacked apostolic authority and was introduced by Gregory the Great. The Council eventually limited the conditions on which the private Mass was permitted.

In other matters there was considerable agreement between Protestants and Catholics, such as on the need for a simplification of ceremonies and for greater intelligibility in worship with vernacular preaching (the Protestants would also have said a vernacular rite was necessary), and a necessity for greater lay participation in worship. These criticisms, whether accepted or rejected, required the attention of the fathers at Trent.

A third reason for liturgical revision at the Council of Trent was the prevalence of abuses in the celebration of the Mass. An objective survey of such abuses in contemporary practice was ordered on 20 July, 1562.[35] The seven members appointed prepared their work, but because the fathers were growing increasingly weary of the Council it was only summarized instead of being presented in full. Several canons were proposed for the correction of the abuses,[36] and, of course, there was a definitive decree "On what must be observed and avoided in the celebration of the Mass." The decree exhorted the bishops to eliminate avarice, irreverence, and superstition as they might find them in the celebration of Mass

[34] See Theisen, *Mass Liturgy*, p. 76. The most recent treatment of Calvin's sacramental teaching is Kilian McDonnell, O.S.B., *John Calvin, the Church, and the Eucharist*, which is invaluable in showing that Calvin's teaching was elaborated in contradistinction to that of the Roman Catholic Church at every point. Calvin declared in the *Petit Traicté de la Saincte Cène* (*Opera Selecta*, I, 519f.): "wherever there is no breaking of bread for the communion of the faithful, it is only a false and deceitful imitation of the Lord's Supper."

[35] *Conc. Trid.*, VIII, 721.

[36] Schmidt, *Introductio*, p. 370. Schmidt prints a list of the abuses (pp. 371-77), of the corrective canons (pp. 378-80), and the decretum (pp. 380-81).

in their own dioceses. In this compendious fashion the commission summarised the three major abuses they found.

Avarice is present whenever the Mass is sold for a price or celebrated only for the sake of profit. Bishop Perez de Ayala, for example, believed that the offering of Masses for many intentions gained more money for the celebrants but rendered Masses less efficacious in the popular mind. On another occasion de Ayala insisted, "the sacrifice of the Mass is offered for sins and for the appeasement of God's anger; not for human affairs such as a successful business deal, fertility, good sailing or the recovery of stolen goods."[37]

Irreverence was common, and could be attributed to celebrations by ignorant and unlettered priests. The Council fathers observed that sincerity was of great importance, and in an earlier draft had criticised those who pronounced the sacred words like actors on a stage; it was recommended that celebrants speak gravely and clearly.[38] They also condemned excessive slowness and celerity in speech. Others behaved more like amateur actors, gesticulating inappropriately, as by moving their heads in the shape of a cross, bowing so low in their veneration of the sacred species that their hair becomes enveloped in it, or exaggeratedly striking their breasts at the *Agnus Dei* or at the *Lord, I am not Worthy*.[39]

The third abuse was superstition. This was particularly attendant on the celebration of series of Masses which led to foolish expectations of material benefits. Erasmus had criticised it in his *Liber de sarcienda ecclesiae*[40] and Luther in his *De captivitate babylonica*.[41] They particularly objected to the idea that the material benefits desired, such as good hunting or good business, could be guaranteed by a multiplicity of Masses. Another superstition took the form of celebrating with a predetermined number of candles, such as 12 for the apostles or 7 for the Mass of the Holy Spirit, because they were believed to render the votive Masses more efficacious. The Council criticised the abuses, along with the "dry Mass"—that is, a rite in which the consecration and communion were missing, but in which the blessed Sacrament reserved in a ciborium is exhibited to the people for adoration.[42] Although the Commission proposed the abolition of the dry Mass, 12 fathers

[37] Theisen, "Reform of the Mass Liturgy and the Council of Trent," in *Worship*, vol. 40 (1966), no. 9, pp. 565-83; this particular reference is to p. 569.
[38] *Conc. Trid.*, VIII, 919, 10-13.
[39] *Ibid.*, pp. 14-27.
[40] Theisen, "Reform of Mass Liturgy," p. 572.
[41] Luther, *Werke*, vol. 6, p. 519.
[42] Theisen, "Reform of Mass Liturgy," pp. 573f.

spoke against it as a useful means of stimulating the devotion of priests, so the matter was shelved.

A final reason for the reconsideration of worship at the Council of Trent was the need for greater uniformity of celebrations of worship and for less corrupt texts. Nicholas of Cusa, bishop of Brixen, provided a practical example of reform by requiring in 1453 and 1455 that all the Mass books in his diocese should be assembled at certain centres and corrected from one perfect example.[43] The truth was, the Mass books had in many ways become a "tangled jungle."[44] This could easily happen, as Theisen explains, because in the Middle Ages all types of votive Masses, sequences, prefaces, and Mass series came to be included in the "Missals," as new formularies and texts were composed to suit the needs of the people. It was easy for this to take place; the Missals were copied by hand, with no supervision by ecclesiastical authority.[45] It was, in fact, Thomas Campeggio, bishop of Feltria, who was the first of the Tridentine fathers to recommend the provision of an authorised uniform Missal. In 1546 he urged that a purged Missal be prepared that would be identical for all churches.[46] If there was chaos in the late medieval period, there was more in the Reformation because many priests had taken the law into their own hands and abbreviated or added as they saw fit. In Austria some priests omitted even the Canon of the Mass.[47]

On the matter of purged texts, one of the most far-reaching proposals came from the progressive leader of the Augustinians, Jerome Seripando, who suggested that only the words of holy Scripture should be used in the Missal and Breviary.[48] He was apparently anxious to eliminate the apocryphal and poorly devised sequences and prefaces, and to remove the legendary accounts of some of the saints. The commission on worship was also concerned that the Council should consider some unauthorized accretions to the Canon of the Mass including such expressions as *Hostia immaculata, calix salutaris* at the Offertory and the prayers added at the commingling.[49] There was the further complication, that different dioceses had their own patron saints and appropriate

[43] Jungmann, *Missarum Sollemnia*, I, 131-32.
[44] *Ibid.*, p. 133.
[45] Theisen, "Reform of Mass Liturgy," p. 577. See also Jungmann, *Missarum Sollemnia*, I, 133.
[46] *Conc. Trid.*, V, 25, 8-10.
[47] Jungmann, *Missarum Sollemnia*, I, 134.
[48] *Conc. Trid.*, V, 26, 42-43.
[49] Jungmann, *Missarum Sollemnia*, I, 134.

Masses. In short, there was a desperate need for consistency in the celebration of the Mass, the lack of which was bewildering to the priests and the people.

These four factors—the Gothic transmutation of the Mass and its continuing influence on the sixteenth century; the Protestant criticisms; the necessity to avoid the abuses of avarice, irreverence, and superstition in the celebration of the Mass; and the demand for the unification of rites and texts—cumulatively accounted for the attention paid by the Tridentine fathers to the reform of the liturgy.

5. The Character and Consequences of Trent's Liturgical Reforms

If the Gothic Mass can be characterised as "dramatic" or "allegorical," the Mass that was finally made uniform by the fathers at Trent may be termed the "rubrical" Mass.[50] The term rightly suggests the end of individualism, eccentricity, and arbitrary variety, and the arrival of the codification of the liturgy. Such a description of the liturgy codified in 1570 indicates that the primary concern of the fathers at the Council of Trent was protective rather than creative.

Certainly in regard to the Canon of the Mass, the Mass ceremonies, and the acceptance of the private Mass (within certain carefully stated conditions), the work of the Council was defensive. Theisen has described its work as "defensive, on the one hand, purifying and immobilizing on the other."[51] It was in the most literal sense distinguished by an attitude of anti-Protestantism or counterreformation. Individual reformists such as Seripando were too far ahead of their times, in suggesting that a Biblical norm would purify the worship of the church and remove the reasons for the defection to Protestantism, and it was not likely that an Augustinian, even the general of the Order, could convince conservatives who would not forget that Luther himself had been an Augustinian monk.

The Council was aware of the defects in the celebration of the liturgy. Jedin has referred to the report of the commission of seven bishops appointed in the later sessions to provide a survey of current practise as "the most comprehensive accumulation of reform ideas."[52] The fathers were even made aware of some defects

50 Schmidt, *Introductio*, p. 382: "Nunc rubricistae, h.e.iuris liturgici periti, primas partes habent. Nunc semper quaestio est de codificatione liturgicae."
51 Theisen, *Mass Liturgy*, p. 111.
52 Jedin, "Das Konzil," VI, 34-35.

in the Canon of the Mass during this time. There was, for example, the omission of the words *quod pro vobis tradetur* (I Corinthians 11:24) and *quod pro vobis datur* (Luke 22:19) in the consecration of the bread. There was also the insertion of the words *mysterium fidei* in the words of consecration over the chalice. There were severe grammatical difficulties in the prayer *Communicantes*. Similarly the recitation of the Canon and of the consecratory formulas aloud, instead of secretly, were demanded by many.[53] The Council also considered the many ceremonies that might be thought of as cluttering the essential simplicity of the rite, as its members had criticised, and condemned such abuses as avarice, superstition, and irreverence in celebrating the Mass.

Why, then, did the Council not incorporate these changes by revising the ceremonies and the Canon? Why was a great opportunity missed? First, the Council saw, as its chief task, the defense and preservation of the liturgy as the supreme channel of the sanctification of the church, a church severely challenged by the Protestants who had particularly directed their criticisms at the Canon.[54] To have changed the liturgy would have amounted to admitting serious error on the part of the church.[55] The Protestants were cast in the role of innovators, the Catholics as conservers. Since many of the significant reforms had been first suggested by the Protestants, it seemed like a confirmation of heresy to agree to them.

A second and important reason for conservatism was that historical studies of the liturgy were only at their very beginnings at this time. It was, says Theisen, the common opinion of the time that St. Peter had instituted the way of celebrating Mass and that St. James had set this down in writing.[56] The intervening centuries have added greatly to the store of early liturgical texts, which were

---

[53] Theisen, *Mass Liturgy*, pp. 111-12.

[54] Luther was vitriolic in speaking of the Canon in the preface to his *Formula Missae et Communionis pro Ecclesia Wittembergensis*: ". . . the Canon, that mangled and abominable thing gathered from much filth and scum. Then the Mass began to be a sacrifice; the Offertories and paid-for prayers were added; then Sequences and Proses were inserted in the *Sanctus* and the *Gloria in excelsis*. Then the Mass began to be a priestly monopoly, exhausting the wealth of the whole world, deluging the whole earth like a vast desert with rich, lazy, powerful celibates. Then came Masses for the dead, for travellers, for riches, and who can name the titles alone for which the Mass was made a sacrifice?" (Bard Thompson, *Liturgies of the Western Church*, p. 108.) Luther's anger caused him to mix his metaphors badly!

[55] Bishop Frederick Nausea of Vienna (as Theisen points out in *Mass Liturgy*, p. 112) admitted as much in a speech before the Council in January 1552. See *Conc. Trid.*, VII, 48ff.

[56] *Mass Liturgy*, p. 39.

unavailable in the sixteenth century, and historical method has determined the histories of various families of liturgies in East and West which were not even divined by Protestant or Catholic scholars in the controversial period under study here. Whatever the reasons, however, the Tridentine attitude to liturgy was essentially protective and defensive.

As for the liturgical achievements of the Council, although there was a strong demand for it in the Council, the Council only provided the impetus for an unified and purified Missal. But many proposals and ideas of reform suggested by the Council fathers were acknowledged by the post-Tridentine Commission that prepared the Missal of Pope Pius V, published in 1570. Unquestionably the Council provided the momentum that resulted in the production of major authorized liturgical texts in the years immediately following the conclusion of the Council of Trent in 1563: the *Breviarium Romanum* (1568) and the *Missale Romanum* (1570). In 1596 the *Pontificale Romanum* came out, the *Ceremoniale Episcoporum* in 1600, and in 1614 the *Rituale Romanum*. Second only to the publication of the first two of these volumes was the establishment of a new Congregation of Rites in 1588, to which disputed questions could be referred, and whose usual reply, it has been said was: Observe the rubrics![57]

The Council itself did not undertake the task of reforming the Missal. By a decree of the 25th session, the task of reforming Breviary and Missal was left to the Pope. In 1564 Pius IV created a commission for this purpose which was enlarged by his successor, Pius V. There are no official reports of the Commission available, but its major achievement was the *Missale Romanum ex decreto ss. Concilii Tridentini restitutum, Pii V. Pont. Max. iussu editum*, which was made binding on almost the entire Catholic church by a bull of July 14, 1570. The ideal of the Commission was to return "to the liturgy of the city of Rome, and indeed, the liturgy of that city as it was in former times."[58] The bull indicates that the scholars of the Commission had consulted the oldest and most uncorrupt texts available and that they believed they had brought the Missal to the pristine norm of the rite of the holy Fathers.[59] They had cleared away several accretions, but had not produced a rite of any patristic norm—assuming there was such

---

[57] Jungmann, *Missarum Sollemnia*, I, 140.
[58] *Ibid.*, p. 136.
[59] The exact wording of the bull is "ad pristinam sanctorum Patrum normam ac ritum."

a single rite. Nor had they produced an early Roman rite, for that was not marked by ceremonial elaboration or diffuseness of ritual, since "the genius of the Roman rite is marked by simplicity, practicality, a great sobriety and self-control, gravity and dignity."[60]

What were the characteristics of the new Roman Missal? The most important fact was that a uniform Mass rite was now imposed on the whole church. There were Council fathers who had wanted each bishop to have the liberty to allow variations, but they were greatly outnumbered by those who felt that the primary need was for order in the contemporary chaos.[61] There is plenty of evidence of pruning. The later Middle Ages had greatly cluttered the church year with saints' feasts. These were so reduced in the new Missal that there were only about 150 days, excluding octaves, free of feasts. Only those feasts were retained which were kept in Rome itself up to the end of the eleventh century.[62] The innumerable later feasts introduced chiefly under Franciscan influence from the thirteenth century on were nearly all eliminated; and there were few saints of countries other than Italy still commemorated in the Missal. On the other hand, memorial days for the Greek Fathers were introduced into the Missal, indicating the newer appreciation of the church fathers. This was later to be expressed in Bernini's *Cathedra Petri* in St. Peter's, which depicts Saints Athanasius and Chrysostom, together with two Latin bishops, as supporters of the Petrine throne and of the implied infallibility of the teaching office of the Pope, under the guidance of the Holy Spirit, symbolised by the dove in effulgent rays.

Pruning was also evident in the ruthless excision of sequences which had flourished in other Mass books. The sequences were a luxuriant modern growth that had never taken hold in Italy. The sentimental Marian insertions in the *Gloria in excelsis*, then widely accepted, were deleted.

A decided innovation lay in the fact that the same commission had prepared both the Breviary and the Missal. There was now agreement between the two basic books of the Catholic church's worship as to the calendar and the choice of collects and Gospels for each Mass.

[60] See Edmund Bishop's superb essay on the early Roman Mass, "The Genius of the Roman Rite," in *Liturgica Historica, Papers on the Liturgy and Religious Life of the Western Church*, p. 12.

[61] Schmidt, *Introductio*, I, 380, states that the Spanish and Portuguese bishops sponsored a uniform rite, while the French bishops argued for diocesan variety.

[62] Jungmann, *Missarum Sollemnia*, I, 136.

Furthermore, the rubrics were unified and codified and printed in the preface of the new Missal. Nearly all of them were lifted bodily from the *Ordo Missae* of John Burchard of Strassburg, a papal master of ceremonies; the book had appeared in 1502 and had circulated widely since that time. The codification of rubrics, coupled with the work of the Congregation of Rites, greatly reduced the opportunities for irreverence or idiosyncrasy.

Happily, the Council and the church, despite some conservative criticism, did not curb the rich polyphonic music that originated during this period. Palestrina was working closely with the influential Theatines, and the compositions of the Fleming, Jacques de Kerle, which were sung at the last sessions of the Council of Trent, seem to have convinced the wavering that the new music could be used to glorify God.[63] The road to the future was left open for great masterpieces of music in this mode.

The chief advantage of the new Missal, then, was its almost universal prescription, which thus enabled it to be increasingly the organ of the unity of the church's teaching on faith, morals, and devotion. Deviations by addition or omission were henceforth severely dealt with; the only rites allowed to vary from the new Roman Missal were those of churches which could prove a tradition of 200 years for their own use. The dioceses that took advantage of the permission included Milan, Toledo, Trier, Cologne, Liège, Braga, and Lyons.[64]

Obviously it was a great advantage to the church to have greater uniformity in the celebration of the Roman Rite, for the new rite would reflect the order, clarity, and stability of the Catholic church, menaced alike by the passionate subjectivity of Gothic and Protestant minds. Exaggerations and arbitrarinesses, squalor and irreverence, were now excluded. Concern for a better form for the liturgy, more elegantly expressed than hitherto and controlled by the Congregation of Rites, was an admirable ideal. There was, however, one grave defect in the entire conception of fixation: it excluded the development which is natural to the life of the Catholic church. If, as Jungmann suggests, the advantage was that "all arbitrary meandering to one side or another was cut off, all

[63] Schmidt, *Introductio*, p. 382: ". . . quia in ipso Concilio patres pluries musicam polyphonicam audierant, ad conclusionem pervenerant, artem polyphonicam esse aedificantem, devotam ac convenientem, ergo non improbandam, dummodo omne lascivum ac impurum excluderetur."

[64] Jungmann, *Missarum Sollemnia*, I, 138.

floods prevented, and a safe, regular and useful flow assured," yet the price to be paid was "that the beautiful river valley now lay barren and the forces of further evolution were often channelled into the narrow bed of a very inadequate devotional life, instead of gathering strength for new forms of liturgical expression."[65]

The Baroque culture might give the Roman Rite glorious polyphonic music, and the Mass could be celebrated in churches the architecture of which tried to bring heaven down to earth with *trompe l'oeil* painted domes with phalanxes of angels providing a new Jacob's ladder of worship, and there could be censings to delight the nose and candles to please the eye, and sermons to fascinate the ear—but all this was merely external. The radical failure, the legacy of which has lasted to our own day, was the inability to give the people a sense of participating in worship. The repudiation of the vernacular translations of the Roman Rite and the insistence on a *Roman* rite without diocesan variations, and the legalism that ensued in this "rubrical" Mass, created an abyss between priests and people. The result was that while the aesthetically splended Mass went on, the people were occupying themselves with devotional exercises that were not based on the liturgical texts, for these were not translated for the common people; in a very short time the devotion of the masses was not based on the Mass at all, but became extraliturgical. It was an ironical consequence of a reform of the Liturgy designed to avoid deviations, that it should have encouraged unliturgical devotions in reaction to the externality of a fixed and inalterable liturgy, artificially made interesting as a theatrical spectacle by Baroque adventitious aids. No amount of pomp and circumstance could disguise the seriousness of the alienation of the people from participation in the Messianic banquet of their Lord.[66] Happily the Second Vatican Council has opened the dam, and the waters of liturgical freedom now flow again.

Having looked at the international movement in Catholic worship (and the contribution of two Englishmen to it before and during Queen Mary's reign), we are now ready to survey the worship of English Catholics during the long reign of Queen Elizabeth, from 1558 to 1603.

[65] *Ibid.*, pp. 140-41.
[66] Father Louis Bouyer, a French oratorian and former Protestant minister, presents a devastating critique of Baroque liturgy in his *Life and Liturgy.*

6. *Elizabethan Recusant Worship*

The worship of the Catholics in Elizabethan England reflected the propitiousness or hostility of the government toward them. From 1559 to 1573 they did not find it unduly difficult to exercise their faith or to worship. The situation deteriorated in 1570 when the bull, *Regnans in Excelsis*, which excommunicated Queen Elizabeth, forced her Catholic subjects to choose between their religion and their country. From 1574 to 1583 there was a serious attempt to revive English Catholic life with the training of Jesuits for the English Mission in Douai, which had been opened as a seminary for English priests in 1568. After 1584 there was an acceptance of the decline of Catholicism into a cultured and quiescent minority, with the occasional raising of false hopes by political plots, from the Gunpowder Plot to the final disillusionment brought on by the failure of the Pretender. This, the third phase, was to be a long one in Catholic life, lasting from 1584 until 1829, when the Catholic Emancipation Act gave Catholics the same political and religious rights as all other denominations of Christians in England.[67]

Some indication of the disadvantages Catholics were under in the second half of the sixteenth century may be gained from the consideration of the penal ecclesiastical legislation passed by the Parliaments of Elizabeth. The Act of Uniformity of 1559 made illegal in the churches of England the use of any service book other than the Book of Common Prayer; it required every person to attend his parish church on Sundays and holy days, "upon pain of punishment by the censures of the Church, and also upon pain that every person so offending shall forfeit for every such offence twelve pence, to be levied . . . to the use of the poor in the same parish. . . ."[68] In 1585, however, it was found necessary to enact legislation against Jesuits and Seminarists. The Act[69] declared that any Jesuit or Catholic seminarist who came to England was to be considered guilty of high treason, and anyone helping such persons shall be "adjudged a felon, without benefit of clergy, and suffer death, lose, and forfeit, as in the case of one attainted of felony."[70] The same act made it a crime to send any child overseas for edu-

---

[67] This division of the reign of Elizabeth into three periods corresponding to the varying character of Catholic activities and attitudes is suggested by W. R. Trimble, *The Catholic Laity in Elizabethan England.*

[68] Gee and Hardy, *Documents of Church History,* p. 403.

[69] 27 Elizabeth, Cap. 2. *Ibid.,* pp. 485-92.

[70] *Ibid.,* p. 487.

cation, without permission, and £100 had to be paid in each case.[71] Even to withhold information about a Jesuit in the realm was punishable by a fine of 200 marks.[72] Finally—and this is an unintended testimony to the astonishing endurance of Catholics in the old faith—the Act Against Recusants was passed in 1593. Its provisions included the demand that every person over 16 and a Roman Catholic ("popish recusant" is the term in the Act) convicted of not attending a place of common prayer to hear divine service there, should stay in his home and not move outside a radius of five miles from it, and "shall lose and forfeit all his and their goods and chattels, and shall also forfeit to the queen's majesty all the lands, tenements, and hereditaments, and all the rents and annuities of every such person so doing or offending, during the life of the same offender."[73] The laws became increasingly severe against the Catholics until they were financially crippling for the nobility and gentry and mortally dangerous for the daring Jesuits and secular priests who ministered to them. Evelyn Waugh's novel *Edmund Campion* gives a poignant account of the furtive priests living in the shadows continual fear of the queen's pursuivants during the latter part of the Elizabethan period.

It is perhaps easier to criticise than to understand the motives of those Catholics who in the early years of Elizabeth's reign apparently attended Anglican worship without affronting their consciences. J. H. Pollen may well be right in suggesting that many of them were simply "waiting for another change of the royal whim, of which they had experienced so many. Three creed-compelling sovereigns had died in 11 years, and the reigning queen was far from enjoying strong popular support. Or again, she might marry a Catholic, for there was as yet no Protestant prince who was her peer."[74] On the other hand, Elizabeth's was a forced Catholicism in the reign of Mary, her sister; she could not have forgotten how her people hated the Catholic *autos-da-fé* at which the Protestants were burned in Smithfield, nor was she unaware of the fact that to the Pope her father's marriage to Anne Boleyn, her mother, was illicit, and therefore she was illegitimate. Quite apart from the fines which must have made the Laodicean and lukewarm Catholics frequent Anglican sanctuaries, the more committed Catholics could have argued truly enough that attendance at morning and evening prayer according to the Book of Common Prayer was

[71] *Ibid.*, p. 488.   [72] *Ibid.*, p. 491.   [73] *Ibid.*, p. 501.
[74] Pollen, *The English Catholics in the Reign of Queen Elizabeth*, p. 94.

not attending Mass (for they recognised a doctrinal world of difference between the Roman Mass and the English Communion service), although the prayers were for the most part a translation from the Breviary and the Missal.

Whatever the reasons or excuses, Catholics seem to have attended Anglican services at least minimally. What is of greater interest, however, is the information that certain Catholic priests found it possible to square their consciences to permit them to celebrate Anglican Communions and Roman Masses in succession. This may be called the period of convenient Catholic compliance, and those who took advantage of these arrangements might be termed Anglican papists! Nicholas Sanders in *The Rise and Growth of the Anglican Schism*, first published in 1585, gives the facts: "At the same time they had Mass secretly in their own houses by those very priests who in church publicly celebrated the spurious liturgy, and sometimes by others who had not defiled themselves with heresy; and very often in those disastrous times they were on one and the same day partakers . . . of the Blessed Eucharist and the Calvinistic supper. . . . Yea, what is still more marvellous and more sad, sometimes the Priest saying Mass at home for the sake of those Catholics whom he knew to be desirous of them, carried about his Hosts consecrated according to the rite of the church, with which he communicated them at the very time in which he was giving to other Catholics more careless about the faith, the bread prepared for them, according to the heretical rite."[75] Allen, a future cardinal, also attests to the truth of this practise, of which he was a witness and which he condemned, since it involved Catholics becoming "partakers often on the same day (oh! horrible impiety) of the chalice of the Lord and the chalice of devils."[76]

In London in the earlier years of Elizabeth's reign many Catholics attended Mass at the Spanish embassy chapel. In December 1567 some Englishmen who had heard Mass at the chapel were questioned by the government and a few were imprisoned. As a result of severe remonstrations the ambassador, Don Guzman de Silva, agreed to exclude Englishmen from his chapel in the future.[77] Two years earlier the ambassador had stated that the authorities

[75] The quotation is from the 1877 edition, with introduction and notes by D. Lewis, pp. 266-67.

[76] *Douay Diaries*, p. xxii, cited p. xxx of T. Law's introduction to Laurence Vaux, *A Catechisme or Christian Doctrine*.

[77] *Calendar, State Papers, Spanish*, I, 686.

were so confused by the chaos of the differing liturgical practises in the Anglican churches (mirrored by the Vestiarian Controversy) that Catholics could celebrate their own form of worship with less danger; consequently "Mass is much celebrated in secret, and many people confess and communicate most devoutly [even in London], which is quite common in other parts of the country."[78]

It appears that during the first decade of Elizabeth's reign the ecclesiastical penal laws were not strictly applied. The laxity would account for the varying degrees of nonconformity. The result was that "some failed to come to church; some, it would seem, worshipped according to the prescribed rites, but absented themselves from the sermon; others did not receive Communion."[79]

The slackness in prosecution of the Catholics, especially where they were numerous and of good social position, must also account for the persistence of Catholic religious customs in an officially Protestant England, which were so frequently reported to the bishops and as frequently warned against in their visitation articles and injunctions.

[78] *Ibid.*, I, 418.

[79] Trimble, *Catholic Laity*, p. 14. There was even a fourth alternative—to say Catholic prayers during the Anglican service. "There be many in the Diocese of Chichester, which bring to the church with them the popish Latin primers and use to pray upon them all the time when the Lessons be a reading and in the time of the Litany. . . ." *Disorders in the Diocese of Chichester Contrary to the Queen's Majesty's Injunctions*, P.R.O., S.P., 12, vol. 60, no. 71, cited in Hughes, *Reformation in England*, III, 248.

A fifth ruse was employed by lords of the manor—to allow their church to go to ruin; thus there would be no church from the worship of which they could dissent and be delated as Recusants. Augustus Jessopp, *One Generation of a Norfolk House*, p. 205, describes the method: "It was easy to reduce the fabric to a ruinous condition in any out-of-the-way village where the lord of the manor was all but supreme, where he was resident and the parson was not; accordingly a systematic destruction of the churches in Norfolk commenced and went on to an extent that may well amaze us; foremost among these was the church at Bowthorpe. It was convenient to have a clergyman of the new school coming and using the new Prayer-Book, and reporting absences at the bishop's visitation, therefore Mr. Yaxley, the lord of the manor, 'converted [the church] to a barne, and the steeple to a dove house,' and Mr. Waldegrave could no more be returned as 'not keeping his church.' It could hardly be expected, however, that the family would live like heathens, and it was in houses of this kind that the Missionaries [Jesuit priests] found an eager welcome."

Finally, a common trick was to refuse attendance at Anglican communions by pretending to be out of charity with one's neighbors or with the parson. Christopher Boreman of South Newington declared in 1584, "that he is not in love and charity with his neighbours"; Philip Wakeridge of Newton Valence in Hampshire, who absented himself from communion for a year, declared in court that the incumbent "Mr. Stanlie . . . is his adversary." Some were successful in their recusancy, notably John Downes of Babingley, of whom it was reported in 1597: "He is a notorious recusant and obstinately refuseth to be partaker with the Church of England. He hath not repayred to church this xx years." A Tindal Hart, *The Man in the Pew, 1558-1660*, pp. 181-82.

All of these Catholic customs were forbidden in Elizabeth's Injunctions of 1559 in which the clergy were instructed as to the subjects of their sermons, including what to approve and what to condemn. The third injunction forbade such "works devised by man's fantasies," as "wandering to pilgrimages, setting up of candles [presumably before images or relics], praying upon beads or such like superstition."[80] The 23rd injunction required the removal and destruction of "all shrines, coverings of shrines, all tables, candlesticks, trindals, and rolls of wax, pictures, paintings, and all other monuments of feigned miracles, pilgrimages, idolatry, and superstition, so that there remain no memory of the same in walls, glass windows, or elsewhere within their churches and houses."[81] Against the background of the determination of the queen and her bishops to extirpate Catholic customs, their survival was remarkable.

Bells were still rung on All Saints' day and on All Souls' day in honour of the saints and to remind parishioners of their duty to pray for their holy dead. Bell-ringing on these two days was prohibited in Norfolk in 1569, "as a superstitious ceremony used to the maintenance of popery, or praying for the dead."[82] The sacring bell continued to be sounded in the Midland counties and in the north.[83] The bringing of candles to church on Candlemass day so that they might be blessed and carried in procession was a custom maintained in the Catholic north well into Elizabeth's reign[84] As late as 1584 parishioners of Churchill in Oxfordshire were presented for keeping copes and relics. The indictment was: "there was abowt a vi or vii yeares agoe in the custodie of one Wm Kerrie three copes or vestments, one of velvit and ii of silke and two crosses, of wch they tooke one of the crosses and put it to the belfounders in Oxford to make there saucebell withall, wch said reliques have remaynid in the custodie of this respondent ever synce undefaced untill they by chaunce came to light of late."[85]

A persistent use of the Rosary must have continued among the country people in remote places for many years, both because England's devotion to the Virgin Mary was renowned in Catholic days when every large church had a chapel in her honor and the

[80] Gee and Hardy, *Documents of Church History*, pp. 419-20.
[81] *Ibid.*, p. 428.
[82] W.P.M. Kennedy, *Parish Life under Queen Elizabeth*, p. 117.
[83] *State Papers, Domestic*, vol. 36, 41 (21).
[84] Kennedy, *Parish Life*, p. 118.
[85] *The Archdeacon's Court, 1584*, ed. E. R. Brinkworth, 2 vols., II, 200, 201, 205, cited in A. Tindal Hart, *The Country Clergy in Elizabethan and Stuart Times*, p. 36.

Rosary was one of the most common forms of devotion. Also, as late as 1571 all the clergy and churchwardens of the northern counties are requested to see that none of their parishioners used or had beads. At the same time the people were forbidden "superstitiously to make upon themselves the *sign of the cross* when they first enter into any church to pray."[86] The tenaciously held religious customs of many generations are not easily uprooted.

Yorkshire had many faithful Catholics as well as "loyal Lancashire." The Visitation returns of 1567 indicted clergy for many forbidden practises such as making wafers for Holy Communion with the impression of the crucifixion on them, retaining holy water stoops, or keeping images and tabernacles. The Rector of Roos, Nicholas Coke, even managed to preserve his rood-loft intact with all its images of the crucified Christ, the weeping Virgin Mother, and St. John.[87] Prohibited as these devout customs were, the faith had been too dearly purchased by the lives of Catholic saints and martyrs from Saints Thomas More and John Fisher up to the sacrifices of Edmund Campion and Robert Southwell, for it to be easily extinguished by government decree. But as government pressure increased and its agents grew more persistent, Catholics had to celebrate more and more secret Masses.

7. *Clandestine Masses*

From 1570 on, Recusants, if discovered at a Catholic Mass, were heavily fined; their priests were imprisoned and often hung, drawn, and quartered at Tyburn. The wonder is not that many conformed to Anglicanism, but that so many priests and laity remained committed and courageous Catholics.

The stiffening of Catholic resistance was undoubtedly aided by the example of the Elizabethan martyrs. There were 189 priests and layfolk, men and women, put to death for their faith between January 4, 1570 and February 17, 1603. Of the 189, 126 were priests, 111 of them secular clergy, one Benedictine, one Dominican, two Franciscans, and 11 Jesuits.[88] Their spirit was eloquently expressed in the challenge of the Jesuit Campion to the Privy Council: "Many innocent hands are lifted up to heaven for you daily by those English students, whose posterity shall never die, which beyond seas, gathering virtue and sufficient knowledge for

---

[86] Kennedy, *Parish Life*, p. 118.
[87] J. S. Purvis, ed., *Tudor Parish Documents of the Diocese of York*, p. 31; see also pp. 152, 162 for further evidence of the continuation of Catholic customs.
[88] Philip Hughes, *Rome and the Counter-Reformation in England*, p. 240.

the purpose, are determined never to give you over, but either to win you heaven, or to die upon your pikes."[89] Campion reminded his judges in his statement before receiving the sentence of death that he and martyrs like him were no treasonable foreigners, but inheritors of a proud English traditon: "In condemning us, you condemn all your own ancestors—all the ancient priests, bishops and kings—all that was once the glory of England, the island of saints, and the most devoted child of the see of Peter. . . . To be condemned with these lights—not of England only, but of the world—by their degenerate ancestors, is both gladness and glory to us."[90]

The Catholic apologists found it necessary, especially after 1570, to try to persuade the government that Catholics were recusants or emigrants into the Low Countries for spiritual and not political reasons. At the same time, they hoped that such writings would reinforce wavering Catholics in their determination not to bow the knee in the House of Rimmon in England. William Allen's reasons for recusancy or emigration in 1581 are as follows:

> The universal lacke then of the soveraine Sacraments cath-
> olikely, ministred, without which the soule of man dieth, as
> body doth without corporal foode: this cōstrainte to the con-
> trarie services, whereby men perish everlastingly: this intol-
> erable othe repugnāt to God, the Church, her Ma.ties hon-
> our, and al mens cōsciences: and the daily dangers, dis-
> graces, vexations, feares, imprisonments, empoverishments,
> despites, which they must suffer: and the railings and blas-
> phemies against Gods Sacraments, Saincts, Ministers, and al
> holies, which they are forced to heare in our Countrie: are
> the only causes, most deere Sirs, or (if we may be so bold
> and if our Lord permitte this declaration to come to her
> M.ties reading) most gratious Soveraine, why so many of us
> are departed out of our natural Countrie, and so absent our
> selves so long from that place where we had our being, birth,
> and bringing up through God, and which we desire to serve
> with al the offices of our life and death: onely craving corre-
> spondence of the same, as true and natural children of their
> parents.[91]

[89] Philip Caraman, *The Other Face, Catholic Life under Elizabeth*, p. 117.
[90] *Ibid.*, p. 227.
[91] *An Apologie and true declaration of the institution and endevours of the two English Colleges* (1581), sig. B3v.-5r.

In 1601 the Jesuit leader Robert Persons wrote *A brief Discourse containing certain reasons why Catholikes refuse to go to Church*. The main reasons were: the pollution of heresy; the scandal or stumbling-block this was to true believers; the fact that going or not going to church "is made a signe now in *England* distinctive between religion and religion, that is, betwixte a Catholike and a Schismatike";[92] and because it encouraged schism. Because such risks were taken to celebrate and assist at the clandestine Masses, they were marked by great fervor. Father Robert Persons reported, "No one is to be found in these parts to complain that services last too long. Nay, if at any time Mass fails, to last nearly a whole hour, this is not much to the taste of many of them. If six, eight, or even more services are held on the same day and in the same place, which happens not infrequently when priests are holding meetings among themselves, the same congregation will be present at all of them."[93] The letters of Father Persons provide the fullest account of how the Douai-trained priests were welcomed by Catholics, the secret places in which they celebrated worship, the ruses used to put government agents off the trail, the thoroughness and relentlessness of the government's search for the recusants' gatherings for worship, and the effects the martyrdoms had on the constancy of Catholics' commitment. His letters, in short, give the most complete, vivid, and accurate account of what the religious life of the Recusants, a *gens lucifuga*,[94] as Newman was to call them, was like in those days. For this reason, I will make full use of them.

In 1580 Persons and other members of the English Mission passed through most of the counties of England, preaching and administering the sacraments, "in almost every gentleman and nobleman's house that we passed by, whether he himself was a Catholic or no, if he had any Catholics in the house." They would enter as acquaintances of relations of some person in the house or as friends of some gentleman accompanying them. After the usual greetings they were shown to their quarters which were always in a retired part of the house. There they "put on priestly dress, conferred secretly and generally late at night with the Cath-

---

[92] *Ibid.*, sig. C8v. See the similar views expressed in Thomas Stapleton's *Apologia pro rege Catholico Philippo II* (1592).

[93] Letter of August 1581, in *Letters and Memorials of Father Persons, S.J.*, no. 39, vol. I, ed. L. Hicks, p. 46.

[94] This crepuscular term was used by Newman in his sermon, "The Second Spring," in *Sermons preached on various occasions*.

olics of the household and those who would come from outside, and heard their Confessions. Next morning Mass was said, followed by a Sermon or Exhortation."[95]

The fear in which the Recusants and their fugitive priests lived is conveyed in a letter describing the ruses that were resorted to for the avoidance of the pursuivants: "It is the custom of the Catholics themselves [Persons wrote] to take to the woods and thickets, to ditches and holes even, for concealment, when their houses are broken into at night. Sometimes when we are sitting at table quite cheerfully, conversing familiarly about matters of faith and piety . . . if it happens that someone rings at the front door a little insistently, so that he can be put down as an official, immediately, like deer that have heard the voice of hunters and prick their ears and become alert, all stand to attention, stop eating, and commend themselves to God in the briefest of prayers. . . . It can truly be said of them that they carry their lives always in their hands."[96] Father Robert Southwell gave an equally vivid description of the searches of the pursuivants for their human prey: "Their serches are very many and severe. Their serve God, as on Sondaies, holy daies, Easter, Christmas, Whitsontide [Pentecost] and such very great feastes. They come ether in the night or early in the morning, or much about dinner time; and ever seeke their opportunities when Catholikes are or would be best occupied or are likely to be worst provided, or looke for nothing. Their manner of searching is to come with a troupe of men to the house as though they come to fight a field. They beset the house on every side, then they rush in and ransacke every corner—even women's beds and bosomes—with such insolent behaviour that their villanies in this kind are half a martyrdome."[97]

---

[95] *Letters and Memorials*, p. xxiii.

[96] *Ibid.*, p. 86, letter of August 1581.

[97] *The Letters and Despatches of Richard Verstegan*, ed. A. G. Petti, no. 52 (1959), 7. The letter is probably the work of Southwell, the Jesuit priest and poet, author of the nativity poem, "The Burning Babe." It was written in December 1591. Southwell lived hourly with the thought of death, and his poem, "I dye alive," ends with the quatrain:

> Not where I breath, but where I love, I live;
> Not where I love, but where I am, I die;
> The life I wish, must future glory give,
> The death I feele in present daungers lye.

(Christobel M. Hood, *The Book of Robert Southwell*, p. 116.) For an account of pursuivants hammering at the door at 5 a.m. on a day in October 1591 while Father Southwell was celebrating Mass and Friars Garnet, Gerard, and Oldcorne

To these general accounts may be contrasted a description of the "Little Rome" which Lady Magdalen, Viscountess Montague, maintained in Elizabeth's reign at her country house. Her biographer states: "She built a chapel in her house (which in such a persecution was to be admired) and there placed a very fair altar of stone, whereto she made an ascent with steps and enclosed it with rails, and, to have everything comfortable, she built a choir for singers and set up a pulpit for the priests, which perhaps is not seen in all England besides. Here almost every week was a sermon made, and on solemn feasts the sacrifice of the Mass was celebrated with singing and musical instruments, and sometimes also with deacon and subdeacon. And such was the concourse and resort of Catholics, that sometimes there were 120 together, and 60 communicants at a time had the benefit of the Blessed Sacrament. And such was the number of Catholics resident in her house and the multitude and note of such as repaired thither, that even the heretics, to the eternal glory of the name of the Lady Magdalen, gave it the title 'Little Rome.' "[98]

To have been apprehended as a priest, even in the early days of the reign before the screw of torture was fully turned, must have been an ignominious and horrifying experience. Stow reports such an incident on September 8, 1562, when a priest was seized while saying Mass at Lady Cary's house in Fetter Lane, London. His captors were the Bishop of Ely's men, by whom the "priest was violently taken and led, as ten times worse than a traitor, through Holborn, Newgate market and Cheapside to the Counter at the stocks called the Poultry, with all his ornaments on him as he was ravished from Mass, with his Mass-book and his porttoys [Breviary] borne before him, and the chalice with the pax[99] and all other things, as much as might make rude people to wonder upon him. And the number of people was exceeding great that followed him, mocking, deriding, cursing, and wishing evil to him, as some to have set him on the pillory, some to have him hanged, some hanged and quartered, some to have him burnt, some to have

---

were in the same house, see *John Gerard, the Autobiography of an Elizabethan*, pp. 41-42.

The contribution of Nicholas Owen, a renowned Jesuit, who is said to have helped Gerard escape, should not be forgotten. He designed famous "priests holes," or hiding places, for recusant priests at Hindlip Hall. *D.N.B.*, XLII, 433.

[98] *An Elizabethan Recusant House, comprising the Life of the Lady Magdalen, Viscountess Montague (1538-1608)*, ed. A. C. Southern, p. 43.

[99] A pax was a tablet with a representation of the crucifixion, which was kissed by the officiating priest and the people at Mass.

him torn in pieces and all his favourers, with as much violence as the devil could write. . . ."[100]

In the midst of Persons' anguish in having to report to the Superior of the English College in Rome the death of other members of the Jesuit Order, he rejoiced that the martyrdoms were strengthening the Catholic faith. "Finally, it cannot be told," he writes, "and far less believed, unless we saw it with our own eyes, how much good their death has brought about. All with one voice, our enemies as well as ourselves, declare that if their lives had been prolonged to their hundredth year they could not have benefited their cause as much as has their short life[101] but glorious death."[102] The result was that Masses were being celebrated in London with greater frequency than for many years and were better attended and listened to than ever. So loyal were the Catholic recusants that when they were chased out of one house, they celebrated Mass in another; "when they are dragged to the prisons, they find a way to perform the holy sacrifice there also."[103] The supreme consolation for those being put to death for their faith— despite public abuse, private torture, and horrible consummation of their witness on earth—was the assurance of wearing the crown of martyrdom which the risen Christ himself would place upon their victorious brows. This is the only explanation of the following record of the reaction of Catholics who watched the martyrdom of Thomas Maxfield: "Whilst all these things were in acting [Maxfield was being hung. drawn and quartered before their eyes] wee Catholikes, who had before implored for him the divine assistance, did now beseech him, as being arived [sic] at the haven of glorie, to render by his prayers the eternal Maiestie propicius."[104] It was a practical response, which in its sheer matter-of-factness witnessed profoundly to the Catholic belief in the Communion of Saints. Martyrdom is the ultimate and climactic gift of adoration and worship of the living God. It was given unstintingly by the Catholics of Elizabethan England.

8. *The Faithful Remnant Prepared for Endurance*

Tempting as it is to conclude this chapter at the high point of martyrdom, the sad truth is that those responsible for the spiritual

[100] *Stow Memoranda*, p. 121, cited in Caraman, *The Other Face*, p. 42.

[101] Hughes, p. 242, points out that 85 of the 126 priest martyrs had not been ordained more than five years before their martyrdom and that 28 had been ordained less than two years.

[102] *Letters and Memorials*, p. 133; letter of March 1, 1582.

[103] *Ibid.*

[104] *Miscellanea*, III, no. 3 (1906), 46.

welfare of English Catholics knew that martyrdom was impossible for all except the choicest few. Preparation had to be made for the long-term future, which did not realistically include the dream of England as a nation restored to obedience to Rome. Rather it envisioned a faithful remnant who had to be prepared for endurance in a climate at worst of hostility, at best of indifference.

Harding, one of the ablest English Catholic apologists, saw that the situation had gone beyond the hope of convincing Englishmen through polemical writing. He believed the time had come to try to make converts through devotional books. Richard Hopkins, in his *Of Prayer and Meditation*, claimed that it was Harding who "perswaded me earnestlie to translate some of those Spanishe bookes into our Englishe tounge, affirming that more spirituall profite wolde undoubtedlie ensewe thereby to the gayning of Christian sowles [since they were much more successful in disposing] the common peoples myndes to the feare, love, and service of almightie God."[105] Hopkins took Harding's advice, to the great advantage of English spirituality. *Of Prayer and Meditation* is a translation of Luis de Granada's *Libro de la Oracion y Meditacion* (1554); Hopkins also translated de Granada's *Memorial de la Vida Christiana* in 1586. Both were highly successful and may well have inspired the religious poetry of Crashaw and Vaughan in the next century.[106] The fiery, intense mysticism of de Granada, now available for the first time in English, seemed most suitable for English Catholics suffering from persecution.

If Harding was disillusioned by crabbed controversialism, so was Persons by the linking of recusancy with political plotting. As he was about to leave Rheims with Edmund Campion for England, Allen, the leader of the English Mission in Rome, informed them of the papal expedition to Ireland of 1580, which was ultimately directed against England. Persons said: "We were heartily sorry. . . . As we could not remedy the matter, and as our consciences were clear, we resolved, through evil report or good report, to go on with the purely spiritual action we had in hand; and if God destined any of us to suffer under a wrong title [that is, as political traitors] it was only what He had done and would be no loss to us, but rather gain in God's eyes who knew the truth, and for whose sake alone we had undertaken this enterprise."[107] Since both

---

[105] *Of Prayer, and Meditation* (1582), sig. A6v, cited in A. C. Southern, *Elizabethan Recusant Prose, 1559-1582*, p. 181.
[106] An opinion of E. Allison Peers, *Spanish Mysticism*, p. 20.
[107] Richard Simpson, *Life of Edmund Campion*, p. 146.

controversial and political approaches were dubious, it was better to concentrate on spiritual means of witnessing.

Hotheads would continue to believe in political action even after the crushing of the Spanish Armada had doomed any hope of Catholic Spain's conversion of England by the sword. Wiser heads, however, realised that Catholics were too few to have prevented the disestablishment of Catholicism at the beginning of the reign, and powerless in the cities, where middle-class mercantile interests were Protestant, as were the majority of the nobles and the higher gentry. In addition, the most influential force for conformity was the almost sacrosanct respect of all classes for the crown, so that the upper classes "by training, and intellectual formation and self-interest obeyed the royal will, and the lower classes by long conditioning followed the leadership of those above them.[108]

In reading Laurence Vaux's *A Catechisme or Christian Doctrine* (and *The Use and Meaning of the Holy Ceremonies of Gods Church* that appears with it in all English editions) one has the sense that this exiled English priest was providing his minute account of Catholic ritual and ceremonial because it was in danger of being forgotten, and it might keep alive hope in the minds of the recusants. It went through eight editions from 1567 to 1605, and was the manual of the English exiles in Louvain. It is probably because a full ritual and ceremonial of Catholic worship in England had virtually disappeared in Elizabeth's reign that we have this marvellously detailed description of worship as the recusants would have celebrated divine worship had they been allowed to do so. Baptism's ceremonies are detailed. They include exorcism, the signation of the Cross, the placing of salt in the child's mouth, the putting of spittle in the child's ears and nose, the anointing the child's breast and back with oil, the pouring of holy chrism on the head, and the use of the candle. The meaning of each is given in Vaux. The explanation for the anointing with oil is: "The childe is anoynted upon the breast with holy Oyle, to signifie: that the holy Ghoste should alwaies dwell in that harte and breast by faith and charitie," and, "The child is anoynted upon the backe with holy Oyle, to signifie the yoke of our Lord, which is sweete and light."[109] Holy Orders and Extreme Unction are similarly described in great detail.

[108] Trimble, *Catholic Laity*, p. 266.
[109] *A Catechisme or Christian Doctrine*, ed. Thomas G. Law, n.s., vol. IV (reprint of the 1583 edition), pp. 55-56.

The fullest and longest description is of the celebration of the Mass, or Sacrament of the Altar. There is a rather fanciful allegorical interpretation of the celebrant's vestments, which is of interest. The amice signifies the cloth on Christ's face when he was buffeted by the Jews, the alb the white cloak which Christ wore when Herod returned him to Pilate, the girdle represents the scourge, the "Favell" on the left arm the cord with which Christ was bound, and the stole stands for the other ropes. The upper vestment represents the derisive purple garment put upon Christ as a king.[110] The various actions of the priest are heavily allegorised as representations of various incidents in the narrative of the passion and death of Christ. The preparation of the elements is symbolically interpreted, too: "Bread & wine are then brought to the Priest at the Altar, to the ende he may do with thē as Christ in his last supper did, when he was now going to his deth. The Chalice betokeneth the grave: the white corporace betokenethe the white sheete, wherein Ioseph did fold Christes body, whē it was layed into the grave: & the paten representeth the stone wherewith the grave was covered."[111] After explanations of the priest's secret prayer and the salutations at the beginning of the great prayer of intercession, Vaux reaches the act of consecration, described and explained thus: "[he] cometh at the laste to take Christes person upon him, saying in his name and power over the breade. This is my body and over the wine. This is my bloude &c. By whiche wordes no faithfull man doubteth, but that Christes body and bloud are made really present under the forme of bread and wine, In token of which beleefe the priest lyfteth up the holy Sacrament, to put us in remembrance, how Christ was exalted upon the Crosse for us, and the people adore with godly honor the selfe body and bloud, which dyed, and was shed for us. And the in wordes also the Priest beseecheth, the said body and bloud of Christe being most acceptable to God, in his owne nature, to be accepted also of God in respect of the Church, which being yet sinfull, adventureth to handell and to offer suche preciouse giftes. And anone the faithfull soules are comēnded also unto God, to the end no members of the Churche may be omitted of the Churche in the comōn sacrifice which toucheth the whole body of the Churche."[112]

The Mass concludes with the Lord's Prayer (curiously this usage is allegorised as a prayer of seven petitions calling to mind the seven "words" of Christ on the Cross), the kiss of peace, and if

---

[110] *Ibid.*, pp. 89-90. [111] *Ibid.*, p. 91. [112] *Ibid.*, p. 92.

the priest communicates alone, "if none other be prepared there unto (as Christ upon the Crosse ended his owne Sacrifice alone) or if other be ready, they receave also with the priest even as Christ at his Supper gave his Sacrament to others also."[113] The persistence of the allegorical interpretation of the Mass (the pedigree is by Durandus out of Dionysius) is striking at this late date. While there is some recovery of the Tridentine insistence on the centrality of the sacrifice offered by Christ, together with the whole church, (the head with the members), there is more of the Gothic allegorical than of the Tridentine rubrical Mass in Vaux's interpretation.

What is unmistakable is that the Mass was the chief means of grace for recusant Priest and people alike. It enabled them to enter deeply into the sufferings of Christ and so bear their own burdens with less complaint; and it offered them the medicine of immortality. For John Rastell, writing in 1564, there was a deep spiritual consolation in the sacrament, which was not to be interpreted in a grossly carnal manner, for Christ is now at the right hand of God the Father. He advised his readers not to let their thoughts and desires rest in Christ's flesh only, but "goe hyer by your faith, and cōsider that blessed sowle of his, so chast, patient, wise, charitable, bright, glorious, and yet hyer and hyer, in to the heavens, and above all heavens, beholding and wondering, how the maker of them all, whom thowsand thowsandes, and ten hundred thousand thousands do wayte upon: ys present here for us, to be receaved of us, and to incorporate us in to hym selve."[114]

[113] *Ibid.*, p. 93.
[114] *A Confutation of a Sermon* (1564), sig. LI, cited in Southern, *Elizabethan Recusant Prose*, p. 87.

CHAPTER V

ANGLICAN WORSHIP:
THE PRAYER-BOOKS

As CATHOLIC worship is mediated by the Missal and the Breviary, so is Anglican worship maintained and renewed by the Book of Common Prayer. The Roman rite, at least until the Second Vatican Council, was an international liturgy magisterially celebrated in the Latin tongue; the Anglican rite, which has great affinities with the Roman rite, has always been celebrated in the English vernacular, and with the spread of English colonists in the Western world it has become an international liturgy. On all hands it is acknowledged as the only surviving sixteenth-century liturgy in continuous use, and as the bond of union of the Anglican communion. According to Gregory Dix, the various Anglican rites in their diverse forms probably serve some 20 million people,[1] and may well have influenced some of the 150 million of the different Protestant churches of the world in their ordering of worship.[2] The Book of Common Prayer is the book of both priest and people, uniquely so, and has continued to be an impressive handbook of devotion and discipleship for four centuries. Within its wide and charitable bounds High Churchman, Broad Churchman, and Low Churchman or Evangelical have found ample freedom and adequate spiritual nourishment. It is a book which has raided the devotions of Judaism as well as Christianity, and is a treasury that borrows from Eastern Orthodoxy as well as from Western Catholicism (Roman and Gallican), and from German and Swiss, as well as indigenously English, Protestantism. Its dignity, sobriety, compactness, and practicality make it a peculiarly English vehicle of devotion. To understand something of its history is an introduction to the spirit of the Church of England. If Protestantism is best understood in its Confessions such as the Heidelberg (or Puritanism in the Shorter Westminster Confession) and in the vigorous application of the Word of God to the contemporary situation in the pulpit, Anglicanism is only imperfectly understood in the Books of Homilies or in the Thirty-

[1] *The Shape of the Liturgy*, p. 613.
[2] For Anglican liturgical influence on Protestant forms of worship see W. D. Maxwell, *The Book of Common Prayer and the Worship of Non-Anglican Churches.*

Nine Articles, but supremely in the Book of Common Prayer and in the celebration of Holy Communion. It is for this reason that the chapters on Anglican worship concentrate on the successive revisions of the Book of Common Prayer in 1549, 1552, and 1559 and on the immense importance of Holy Communion and the prolonged controversies as to the mode of Christ's presence in that central Sacrament, while not ignoring the pulpit.

1. The Preparation for Liturgical Reform

The great achievement of Anglicanism is, of course, the First Prayer Book of King Edward VI of 1549. This was no sudden achievement of Archbishop Cranmer and his advisers, but the slow growth of various earlier experiments in England and overseas, and notably issuing in the production of an English *Litany* and of an English *Communion Order* before the publication of the climactic *Book of Common Prayer*.

Thomas Cranmer, whose name will always be associated with the first English Prayer Books, achieved fame as the supporter of Henry VIII's claim to the right to divorce his Spanish queen in 1529, and was employed by the monarch as his ambassador in Germany in 1532, where Cranmer first made contact with the Protestant vernacular rites of Lutheranism in Nuremberg and other centres.[3] The next year he was made Archbishop of Canterbury, but, although Germany had apparently convinced him of the importance of vernacular services, he had to wait 12 years before he could put these convictions into practice, with the publication of the Litany in English.

With so arbitrary a master as Henry VIII, Cranmer had to walk warily during this reign and to conceal his embryonic Protestantism. Some slight indications of his future reformist attitude can be gleaned from certain changes made in the church services during Henry's reign. There was a significant reduction between 1536 and 1541 in the number of holy days to be observed. A "Sarum" Breviary was issued which omitted the title of the Pope and was to that minimal extent "reformed." In the Convocation on February 21, 1543 Cranmer announced there would be a sweeping reform of all the service books; on the same day there was intro-

[3] Cranmer married Margaret, the niece of the German Reformer, Osiander. He was largely responsible for drafting the Brandenburg-Nuremberg Church Order of 1533, the prototype of the famous Church Order of Cologne, which influenced the First Book of Common Prayer of 1549 and *The Order of the Communion* of the previous year.

duced an English reading from the Bible at both matins and vespers on every Sunday and holy day in every church. All this was but the tip of the iceberg. Below an even more fundamental revolution was being evolved in the scholarly mind of the archbishop, in his plan to reduce the Breviary to two hours only.

Cranmer's first revolutionary achievement in the reign of Henry VIII was the issue of an English Litany on June 18, 1544 under the unwieldy title, *An Exhortacion unto prayer, thoughte mete by the Kinges maiestie, and his clergy, to be read to the people in euery church afore processyons. Also a Letanie with suffrages to be said or song in the tyme of the said processyons.*[4] In 1544 Henry VIII was at war with Scotland and France. On June 11, 1544 he wrote to Cranmer declaring his determination to have "general processions in all cities, towns, churches, and parishes of this realm, said and sung with such reverence and devotion as appertaineth, forasmuch as heretofore the people, partly for lack of good instruction and calling, partly for that they understood no part of such prayers and suffrages as were used to be sung and said, have used to come very slackly to the procession . . . we have set forth certain godly prayers or suffrages in our native English tongue."[5]

It appears that Cranmer took a patriotic opportunity, as the king conceived it, for some moderate measure of Reformation. Its importance was that it became soon afterwards the sole authorized form of service for processions; it is the oldest single part of the Book of Common Prayer.[6] It was derived from many sources, including the Sarum Litanies, Luther's Litany in its Roman form, the York Litany, possibly the Litany of Brixen, and certainly the Liturgy of Constantinople, from which is derived St. Chrysostom's prayer.[7] It could hardly be more critical of the Papacy than it is, with the scurrilously honest petition for delivery "from the tyranny of the bishop of Rome, and all his detestable enormities."[8] Its dominating characteristic is a concentration on the mediatorial power of the Holy Trinity and a diminished emphasis on the mediation of the

---

[4] It is conveniently reprinted as an appendix (pp. 564ff.) to *Private Prayers put forth by authority during the reign of Queen Elizabeth,* ed. W. K. Clay; or in F. E. Brightman, *The English Rite,* 2 vols., I, 174-90.

[5] Cranmer, *Miscellaneous Writings and Letters,* ed. J. E. Cox, p. 494.

[6] See Brightman, *English Rite,* I, lviii-lxviii.

[7] The "Prayer of Chrysostom" is an English version of the Latin translation of the Orthodox Liturgy, namely, the *D. Liturgia S. Ioannis Chrysostomi* (Venice, 1528). See Dowden, *The Workmanship of the Prayer Book,* pp. 227ff.

[8] *Private Prayers set forth by authority during the reign of Queen Elizabeth,* p. 572.

saints, though the Virgin Mary is mentioned by name and there is a general reference to saints, angels, and patriarchs. It was probably as close an approach to Protestantism as Cranmer dared make at the time.[9]

The accession of the boy King Edward VI on January 28, 1547 gave Cranmer the opportunity for religious reformation. Somerset, the Lord Protector of the realm, was a convinced Protestant. The Protector and the archbishop issued a series of *Royal Injunctions* to be administered in a general visitation of all the dioceses by 30 visitors. The *Injunctions* made a series of minor but important changes in the church service. Injunction 22 required that in addition to the existing English lesson at matins and evensong, the Epistle and Gospel at parish high Mass were also to be read in the vernacular. The 24th Injunction insisted that the Litany was in the future to be sung kneeling and not in procession so that the veneration of shrines on the way might be prohibited. Provision was also made for a *Book of Homilies* to be distributed by the visitors to each church, which were to be read each Sunday. The *Homilies*, according to T. M. Parker, "expounded a moderate version of justification by faith only and tacitly ignored such subjects as the Eucharist and other Sacraments, while attacking in strong terms popular Catholic customs regarded by the Reformers as superstitious."[10] On the 27th of January 1548 the Council ordered the abolition of the proper ceremonies for Candlemas, Ash Wednesday, and Palm Sunday. Those special to Good Friday were soon abolished, as well as the use of holy water and holy bread. While this was happening it seems that there was official encouragement of the wholesale smashing of images that took place. All foreshadowed the future simplification of the English liturgy and its total rendering into English.

Furthermore, there were several experimental services in the vernacular during the first two years of Edward VI's reign.[11] The first experiment took place on East Monday, April 11, 1547, when Compline in English was sung in the Royal Chapel.[12] The

---

[9] Brightman, *English Rite*, I, lxvii, observes, rightly that "the Litany is enough to prove he [Cranmer] had an extraordinary power of absorbing and improving other people's work."

[10] *The English Reformation to 1558*, p. 125.

[11] Fully described from the relevant manuscript evidence in the British Museum and the Bodleian Library in "Edwardine Vernacular Services before the First Prayer Book," in Walter Howard Frere, *A Collection of Papers on Liturgical and Historical Subjects*, ed. J. H. Arnold and E.G.P. Wyatt, Alcuin Club Collections, no. 35 (1940), pp. 5-21.

[12] F. A. Gasquet and E. Bishop, *Edward VI and the Book of Common Prayer*, p. 58.

service already existed in several versions, as in Bishop Hilsey's *Manual*, Henry VIII's Primer, and in the older primers. The significance in 1547 was its use in the Royal Chapel, which in Edward VI's reign was something of a national liturgical laboratory. A second important experiment took place on November 4, 1547, at the opening Mass of Parliament and Convocation, when the *Gloria in excelsis*, *Credo*, and *Agnus Dei* were sung in English. Six months later, according to Wriothesley, "Poule's quire with divers other parishes in London sung all the service in English, both Mattens, Masse & Evensonge"; on May 12, 1548, on the anniversary of the death of Henry VII, which was kept at Westminster Abbey, the Mass was "song all in English with the consecration of the Sacrament also spoken in English."[13] On September 4, 1548 Somerset sent a letter to the authorities of the University of Cambridge, ordering them "in their colleges, chapels, or other churches to use one uniform order, rite and ceremonies in the Mass, Matins, and Evensong, and all divine service in the same to be said or sung such as is presently used in the King's Majesty's Chapel" pending further changes.[14] On September 9 Robert Ferrar was consecrated Bishop of St. David's; at the Eucharist both the administration and the consecration of the Sacrament were in English. Nor should it be forgotten that the *Litany* had been available since 1544 in English; its use was required by the *Royal Injunctions*. In these ways the English vernacular was making liturgical inroads. The final barriers seemed to be yielding when even the Eucharist was celebrated in English, though admittedly the consecration of a bishop was a special and far from regular occasion. As Cranmer's *Litany* had been the first step in the vernacular walk, so *The Order of the Communion*[15] was the penultimate step in the same path.

On December 17, 1547 an act was passed in Parliament, "Against such as unreverently speak against the Sacrament of the Altar, and of the receiving thereof under two kinds." As a directory for the priest *The Order of the Communion* was issued on March 8, 1547-48. It comprised the English devotions, provided solely for communicants, which were to be interpolated in the middle of the Latin Mass, which now had the lessons in English. The time was almost ripe for the provision of the Canon of the Mass in

[13] Charles Wriothesley, *A Chronicle of England*, ed. W. D. Hamilton, 2 vols., new series, xi, pts. i and ii, 1875-77), II, 2.
[14] Gasquet and Bishop, *Edward VI*, p. 147.
[15] Printed as a facsimile of the British Museum copy, C.25, f.15, in H. A. Wilson, *The Order of Communion, 1548*, Henry Bradshaw Society, vol. 34, 1908.

English, and last of all for the formula of Consecration in English. These were the last bastions of the Latin rite, the retention of which seemed synonymous with the maintenance of mystery and the unity of all Catholic worshippers. Thus the English *Order of the Communion* provided the communicant with the intelligibility necessary to full sharing in the rite, while reserving to the celebrant the privilege of conducting the worship in the venerable ecclesiastical language. The authorship of the *Order*, as of the First Book of Common Prayer which followed a year later, remains obscure. The letter of the Council addressed to the bishops hardly lifts the veil in affirming that the book was compiled by "sundry of his majesty's most grave and well learned prelates and other learned men in the Scripture."[16] Like the *Litany*, the *Order* shares the distinction of being subsequently incorporated into the Book of Common Prayer. This was Cranmer's most ambitious liturgical project hitherto.

The *Order* was the form of administration to be used in the Mass, immediately following the celebrant's Communion, and was inserted in the traditional Latin Mass. It included an exhortation to the communicants, with a warning and an invitation, and followed with confession, absolution, and the "comfortable words," together with a prayer before Communion, the words of administration, and a Blessing.

Its major sources are the Holy Scriptures, the Greek rite, the medieval commonplaces, the traditional Roman rite, and the *Pia Deliberatio*, or Church Order, of Cologne, prepared for Hermann von Wied, Prince-Archbishop of Cologne, by Martin Bucer; it in turn, as I have indicated, was based on the work of Osiander in the Brandenburg-Nuremberg Church Order. The *Pia Deliberatio*, a distinctively Lutheran Church Order, influenced the *Order of the Communion* in providing suggestions for the exhortation, the confession (in part), the "comfortable words," and the clauses added to the end of the formula of absolution and to the form of administration.[17] In view of the importance of the words of administration it is interesting to learn that they were adapted from the Sarum form of Communion for the Sick, which is: *Corpus domini nostri iesu christi custodiat corpus tuum et animam tuam in vitam aeternam.* This form is partly reduplicated and partly redistributed

[16] Edward Cardwell, *Documentary Annals of the Reformed Church of England*, 2 vols., I, 61.
[17] Brightman, *English Rite*, I, lxxiii.

so that "body" may answer to "corpus" and "soul" to "sanguis," and is expanded with "which was geven for thee" and "which was shed for thee." The relevant rubrics and words of administration read:

> And when he doth deliuer the Sacrament of the body of Christe, he shall say to euery one, these wordes followyng.
> The bodye of oure Lorde Jesus Christ, which was geuen for the, preserue thy body unto euerlastyng life.
> And the priest deliuering the Sacrament of the bloud, and geuing euery one to drinke once and nomore, shal saye.
> The blud of oure Lorde Jesus Christ, which was shed for the, preserue thy soule unto euerlastyng life.[18]

These words are typical in their conflation of Scripture, the Sarum Use of the Mass, and the German Lutheran church orders of Brandenburg-Nuremberg of 1533 and Cologne of 1543.[19]

The Sarum Use and the orders were a series of open experiments in liturgy from the *Litany* of 1544 to the *Order of the Communion* of 1548. In his study and in his mind, however, Archbishop Cranmer was conducting other liturgical experiments.[20] The experiments were entirely concerned with the simplification of the Daily Office, and almost certainly never went beyond Cranmer's study or their ideas beyond the minds of his confidants and fellow-liturgists in Henrician and Edwardine days. Frere believes the experiments "belong to the earlier stages of development, the first probably being anterior to the accession of Edward VI, and the second not long subsequent to it."[21] Brightman, on the other hand, believes that the first literary experiment belongs to the last years of Henry VIII, and the second one probably from 1547.[22] The manuscript itself introduces a complication, since it places the earlier draft

18 Wilson, *Order of Communion*, sig. C.j. verso.

19 The general theological character of the *Order* is described by W. Jardine Grisbrooke as follows: "It contains little positively offensive to the upholders of the old faith, but is clearly a product of the new. . . ." *Studia Liturgica*, Vol. I, No. 3, p. 150.

20 See Cranmer's *Liturgical Projects*, ed. J. Wickham Legg, Henry Bradshaw Society, vol. 50, 1915. These volumes were brought to public notice by Gasquet and Bishop after they had evaluated MS. Reg. 7 B iv. in the British Museum in their book, *Edward VI and the Book of Common Prayer*. The manuscript is discussed in Appendix i, its chief contents described and summarised in Appendices ii-iv, and the character of the experiments considered in Chaps. 2 and 4. Legg, *Edward VI*, p. ix, assigns the second draft to about 1543-47.

21 *Papers*, p. 5.

22 *English Rite*, I, lxxviii. Brightman appears to follow Legg's dating.

second. More important, however, than the dates are the contents of the two experiments.

The first includes all the canonical hours from matins to compline, derives its material almost wholly from the Sarum Breviary, and yet follows very closely the structure of the second recension of Cardinal Francisco Quiñones' revised *Breviarium Romanum* which was first published by Paul III in 1535, the second recension following a year later.[23] It reduced the readings from the lives of the saints to a bare minimum, so that the entire Psalter might be read in a week and nearly all the Bible in a year. Furthermore, the different Hours were made almost equal in length. In addition, the Breviary was made more compact by eliminating the antiphons, versicles, and responses. This immensely popular work of reconstruction went through a hundred editions before it was proscribed by Pope Paul IV in 1558.

The second literary experiment is even more interesting, because here the Hours were reduced to two, matins and evensong. The reduction was due in part, according to the explanation, because the existing arrangement required far to much unnecessary repetition, and partly because the ancient distribution of the Hours of the day had become obsolete; in practice the services were accumulated or concentrated at two hours in the day. The schema is introduced by a preface which is reproduced in the main from the first recension of Quiñones. This particular experiment foreshadowed Cranmer's work in the First and Second Prayer Books, where Sunday worship consisted of matins and evensong (which the minister was also to say daily in his parish church) with the Order for Holy Communion.

Both Offices begin with the Lord's Prayer in English, followed by *Domine labia* at matins and *Deus in adiutorium* at evensong, with the ensuing *Gloria Patri*, etc. Then follows the Hymn and three Psalms, then the Lord's Prayer in English. At matins there were three lessons (at evensong, two), followed by *Te Deum* at matins and *Magnificat* at evensong. A fourth lesson was to be read at matins on Sundays, great festivals and saints' days, and lessons were always to be read in English and from the pulpit, that they might be audible and intelligible. After *Benedictus* at matins and *Magnificat* at evensong there followed *Dominus vobiscum*, the

23 Quiñones' breviary of 1535 was reprinted by J. Wickham Legg, and the second recension of 1536, also edited by Legg, appeared in two volumes, as Henry Bradshaw Society publications in 1908 and 1912.

collect of the day, and *Benedicamus Domino*, to which the response was *Laudemus et superexaltemus nomen eius in saecula. Amen.*

In both public experiments in worship, from the *Litany* to the *Order of the Communion*, as in the special services in the Royal Chapel and in St. Paul's Cathedral in London and at Westminster Abbey, as well as in the literary experiments in his study, Cranmer had been preparing the Church of England to take the momentous step of relinquishing the Roman Liturgy, which had sustained the devotion of English Christians for almost 10 centuries. It had been the exclusive medium and channel of the nation's worship from the last decade of the sixth century—when Augustine of Canterbury (as he was to be known) and his monks landed on the island of Thanet and thence came to the shores of Kent, where their singing of the Gregorian chant charmed the ancient English and made them anxious to glorify God in the Latin Liturgy—down to the sixteenth century. No wonder that the step to give it up was taken warily, that its abandonment was the cause of riots, that the interruption of their liturgical habits[24] made the English, who were renowned for their devoutness in the fifteenth century, antipathetic to a coerced national form of worship, which excluded the most conscientious Christians, whether Roman Catholic recusants or Puritan pietists.

2. The First English Prayer Book (1549)

It is curious that the First Prayer Book, which along with the King James translation of the Bible is one of the great religious landmarks of the English spirit, has resisted the most assiduous efforts of scholars to penetrate the obscurity of its joint authorship. It is well known that its chief author was Cranmer, impelled thereto as much by duty as studious inclination. But it is not known who his fellow compilers were, though there are some likely candidates. It is known that in September 1548 a group of bishops and divines were assembled in Chertsey and (probably during the king's stay on September 22-23) at Windsor, in order to settle

---

24 Dix, *Shape of Liturgy*, pp. 686-87, writes: "With an inexcusable suddenness, between a Saturday night and a Monday morning at Pentecost 1549, the English liturgical tradition of nearly a thousand years was altogether overturned. Churchgoing never really recovered from that shock. Measures of compulsion kept the churches reasonably full in the reign of Edward VI and the earlier half of Elizabeth's. But voluntary, and above all weekday, churchgoing—on the popularity of which most fifteenth century travellers had remarked—virtually disappeared." See also Ridley, *Works*, p. 60, for a reluctant confirmation that Catholic was much higher than Protestant church attendance.

outstanding liturgical questions and provide "a uniform order of prayer."[25] It is also known that five bishops and four divines took part in the consecration of Ferrar to the see of St. David's on September 9, 1548. It is a natural supposition that those who took part in the consecration were those who were conveniently near because they were the same group who were concerned with the reform of the Liturgy. If this supposition is correct, their names are: Archbishop Cranmer, Bishops Ridley of Rochester, Holbeach of Lincoln, Thirlby of Westminster, and Goodrich of Ely, together with Drs. May, Dean of St. Paul's, Haynes, Dean of Exeter, Robertson, afterwards Dean of Durham, and Redman, Master of Trinity College, Cambridge. An additional piece of evidence is that at the service the consecration and administration of Holy Communion was performed in English.[26] The first Edwardine Act of Uniformity, passed January 21, 1549, states that the king, on the advice of the Lord Protector and his council, "has appointed the Archbishop of Canterbury, and certain of the most learned and discreet bishops, and other learned men of the realm" on the basis of Scripture and the usages of the primitive church to "draw and make one convenient and meet order, rite, and fashion of common and open prayer and administration."[27]

What were the purposes of the new Book of Common Prayer as defined in the first Act of Uniformity of Edward VI and in the preface of the Prayer Book itself?[28] The Act suggests that a primary consideration was the general confusion in the kingdom over the use of different forms of Roman rite, namely, "the Use of Sarum, of York, of Bangor, and of Lincoln" and of more recent varieties of "forms and fashions."[29] From the Council's standpoint it is most desirable, the Act goes on to maintain, that "a uniform quiet and godly order should be had."[30] The preface to the First Prayer Book also holds, though only as the fourth reason, that

25 *Grey Friars of London Chronicle*, ed. J. G. Nichols, Camden Society, vol. liii, p. 56.

26 Proctor and Frere, *A New History of the Book of Common Prayer*, pp. 44-45. See also British Museum *Catalogue of an Exhibition commemorating the four hundredth anniversary of the introduction of the Book of Common Prayer*, pp. 19f.

27 Gee and Hardy, *Documents illustrative of English Church History*, p. 359.

28 Further insight into the intentions of Cranmer and the other compilers of the First English Prayer Book of 1549 is provided by the proclamation prefixed to the *Order of the Communion* of the previous year. It expressed a determination, "to trauell for the reformation & setting furthe of suche godly orders as maye bee moste to godes glory, the edifying of our subiectes, and for the advauncemente of true religion," so that, "a uniform quiet and godly order should be had. . . ."

29 Gee and Hardy, *Documents*, p. 358.

30 *Ibid.*, p. 359.

unity will come from a uniformly prescribed liturgy: "And where heretofore, there hath been great diuersitie in saying and synging in churches within this realme: some folowyng Salsbury use, some Herford use, some the use of Bangor, some of Yorke, and some of Lincolne: Now from hēcefurthe, all the whole realme shall haue but one use."[31]

Unquestionably the notion that the "Uses" of the medieval cathedrals had created the confusion is greatly exaggerated, though the innovators were the likelier culprits. In fact, the medieval "Uses" were not alternatives to the Roman rite, but minor alterations and adaptations of the same rite in accordance with the usages of the great cathedral churches, such as York, Hereford and Salisbury. The employment of the "Uses" was not necessarily rigid; there was some variety in ceremonial details, and some difference with reference to lessons or Psalms, even sometimes with regard to collects and antiphons. "English worship in the pre-Reformation period nevertheless exhibited a general unity of pattern so that the habitual attendant at the services of Salisbury cathedral was entirely at home in the services of York minster."[32] The great "inconveniences" claimed to result from a diversity of medieval "Uses" had in fact been seriously mitigated by a previous decision at the Convocation of Canterbury in 1542 to prohibit the use of any but the Salisbury Breviary in the Southern Province.

The first reason given in the preface to the First Prayer Book—and it is a substantial one—for the issuance of the Book of Common Prayer was that a Scriptural and primitive form of worship should be available in the vernacular English. The Latin service was not understood by the people, and thus contradicted St. Paul's demand that worship should be with the spirit and with the understanding. As a result, "the seruice in this Churche of England (these many yeares) hath been read in Latin to the people, whiche they understoode not; so that they haue heard with theyr eares onely; and their hartes, spirite, and minde, haue not been edified thereby."[33] The sincerity of this motive is hardly subject to question when considering the slow and steady experiments that we have seen Cranmer engaging in with this paramount aim in mind.

---

[31] All references to the 1549 prayer-book will be to the Page Collection copy in the Henry E. Huntington Library, which was printed by Edward Whitechurche in May. This reference is to Aiiv.

[32] *The book of common prayer of the Churche of Englande: its making and revisions M.D.xlix—M.D.clxi. set forth in eighty illustrations, with Introduction and Notes*, ed. E. C. Ratcliff, p. 9.

[33] Aii.

Cranmer and his advisors were equally concerned with providing a rite that was Biblical in inspiration and content, uncluttered by saints' lives and legends, and in which the arrangement of the lections was such that it enabled the books of the Bible to be read consecutively. In this revision they claimed they were returning to patristic use: "But these many yeares passed this Godly and decent ordre of the auncient fathers, hath bee so altered, broken, and neglected, by planting in uncertein stories, Legēdes, Respondes, Verses, vaine repeticions, Commemoracions, and Synodalles, that commonly when any boke of the Bible was begon: before three or foure Chapiters were read out, all the rest were unread."[34] In consequence, now "is ordeyned nothyng to be read, but the very pure worde of God, the holy scriptures, or that which is euidently grounded upon the same,[35] and that in suche a language and ordre, as is moste easy and plain for the understandyng, bothe of the readers and hearers."[36]

A third consideration was that of convenience. It is almost impossible to imagine what a revolution it was to provide a single service book that was adequate for all regular occasions and many special occasions. Previously the parish had had to provide a considerable number of service books for the use of the priest. First, he needed the *Ordinal* or *Pica* or *Pie*, from which he would discover what service he should recite in the Canonical Office on any given day. The preface to the first Book of Common Prayer refers to "the nōbre and hardnes of the rules called the pie, and the manifolde chaunginges of the seruice, was the cause, it to turne the boke onely, was so hard and intricate a matter, that many times, there was more busines to fynd out what should be read, then to read it when it was founde out."[37] In addition to the *Ordinal* the priest needed a *Missal* or Mass-book. A *Processional* was also required, this being a collection of psalms, anthems, litanies, and prayers which were appointed to be sung or said in processions before the celebration of the principal Mass of the day on Sundays and holy days. For the occasional rites such as Baptism, Matrimony, Churchings of Women, Visitation of the Sick, Burials, and Blessings over food, the priest needed a *Manual*. For his own Canonical Office, he required a *Breviary*. Churches with choirs of singers needed at least one *Graduale* (in English "Grayle") containing the

---

[34] *Ibid.*

[35] Presumably this means exhortations based on doctrine derived from the Bible.

[36] Aii v.   [37] *Ibid.*

musical portions of the Mass and an *Antiphonary* for the musical parts of the Breviary. Furthermore, a bishop needed a *Pontifical* for ordaining priests and deacons, confirming children, and consecrating a church, although this was his personal book. Thus the parishioners were responsible for providing a minimum of six and a maximum of eight or nine service books for their priest. The inconvenience of using so many books must have been irritating in the extreme and disruptive of dignity and reverence in worship.

There was another great convenience that the single vernacular, Biblically-based, uniform Book of Common Prayer brought. It is that for the first time in the history of a nation a vernacular prayer book was made available with traditional and contemporary resources which was both the priest's and the people's common book. In the four centuries in which it has been used, it has served as a resource for family and private prayers as well as for public and corporate worship, and has stimulated a splendid and singular lay devotion of which some outstanding examples are the Ferrars of Little Gidding in the seventeenth century and Susannah Wesley in the eighteenth. Another of its by-products may well be the lack of any serious anti-clericalism in English history, because the married English clergyman in his rectory or vicarage was closely in touch with the life of his parishioners; he could never be thought of as celebrating a mysterious and magical rite in a foreign tongue which gave him social distance and distrust; he was freed from the temptation of any sacerdotal airs and graces. Debatable as the latter is, however, the main point is that the Book of *Common* Prayer was a form of devotion which bound clergy and congregation together because priest and people alike shared it and had their copies of it, because the responses were a kind of "conversation" between them in worship, and because both parties shared a common appreciation for a rite that spread a Biblical faith that attempted to be intelligible in its expression, was rationally organised in its structure, and one that linked the Jewish and Christian centuries in felicitous phraseology and musical cadence.

In sum, then, we can see in the first English prayer-book three distinguishing characteristics that made it unique. It was a vernacular rite aimed at edification and presupposing good order and intelligibility. It was a single book to be used by priest and people alike. It was a uniform rite aimed at the religious unification of the English people. Furthermore, it was imposed by the political power of England, with inhibitory penalties. The Act of Uniformity required the use of *The Booke of the Common Prayer and Administracion of the Sacramentes and Other Rites and Ceremonies of the Churche, after the Use of the Churche of England* on and after Whitsunday, June 9, 1549.

The 1549 prayer-book is divided into 14 sections. First comes the Preface with the reasons for introducing the Prayer Book in English. There follows a Calendar for Psalms and Lessons. Then comes the Order for matins and evensong throughout the year. The next and most substantial section of the book (amounting to two-thirds of it) contains the Introits, Collects, Epistles, and Gospels to be used at the celebration of Holy Communion throughout the year, with proper Psalms and lessons for various feasts and days. The fifth section provides the Order for "The Supper of the Lorde and holy Communion, commonly called the Masse." The following sections contain the services of Baptism (public and private), Confirmation (including a catechism for children), Matrimony, for the Visitation of the Sick and Communion of the Sick. The 10th section provides a burial service and the 11th a form for the Purification of Women after childbirth. The 12th part contains Scripture and prayers suitable for Ash Wednesday. The 13th and 14th sections are practically extended rubrics, the former dealing with Ceremonies omitted and retained, and the final section providing notes "for the more plain explicaciō, and decent ministracion of thinges cōteined in this boke." The First Prayer Book provided a comprehensive, condensed, pruned and purified as well as primitive, liturgy for England.

3. A Predominantly Catholic or Protestant Rite?

Opinions differ as to how conservative or radical a revision of Catholic worship the 1549 prayer-book was, as can be seen from the carefully expressed opinions of three Anglicans. Bishop Gibson maintained that "it was an honest attempt to get rid of mediaeval corruptions and to go back to what was primitive and Catholic."[38] To Dom Gregory Dix, Cranmer's aim, more ambiguously and subtly in 1549 and more openly in 1552, was to replace the Catholic understanding of the sacrifice of the Mass with a commemoration of Calvary not distinguishable from Zwinglian "Memorialism," and therefore a radical Protestantism.[39] E. C. Ratcliff asserts that

[38] *The First and Second Prayer Books of King Edward VI*, ed. E.C.S. Gibson, Introduction, p. x.
[39] Dix, *Shape of the Liturgy*, pp. 656f., 670f.

"Cranmer in 1546 at Ridley's persuasion abandoned the Catholic belief that by consecration the eucharistic bread and wine become the Body and Blood of Christ."[40] What is clear in this crepuscular situation is that the government wanted to give the impression that this was a simplified and purified version of the Roman Rite in English dress. So much at least can be gathered from the reply given to the Western rebels who had called the new Prayer Book Service a "Christmas game" and wanted their old Mass back. They were, in effect, told that they were receiving the Mass. The government's words were: "It seemeth to you a new service, and indeed it is none other but the old: the selfsame words in English which were in Latin, saving a few things taken out."[41]

Some clue and answer to the question of the theological conservatism or radicalism of the 1549 prayer-book may be provided by a consideration of the sources Cranmer and his advisers drew on. The single greatest source for the new rite was the Holy Scriptures; it is interesting that the Psalms, all Lessons, including the Gospels (with a single exception),[42] and the Epistles are taken from the "Great Bible" which was issued in 1539 and revised in 1540 and is a composite Tyndale-Coverdale version. That, of itself, would indicate a strong Protestant bias in the rite, as also would the preference for the vernacular. On the other hand, there are strongly traditional Catholic sources that went into its making. The Latin rite, according to the Use of Sarum,[43] had a considerable influence also. It provided the structure of the different offices and (with the exception of the Lessons) suggested the various passages of Scripture to be used in the services. It also supplied most of the rest of the content of the services, with the important exceptions of the didactic and hortatory materials.

If we look at the latter element, which is strong, then the scales are tipped on the Protestant side, for this type of contemporary material comes almost exclusively from the Lutheran *Kirchenordnungen*, though it is difficult to pinpoint an exact source in many cases.[44] The Church Orders showing the clearest influence on the

---

40 *First and Second Prayer Books*, p. 10.
41 *The Acts and Monuments of John Foxe*, ed. George Townsend, 8 vols., v, p. 734.
42 The Gospel at baptism.
43 See *The Use of Sarum*, ed. W. H. Frere, 2 vols. and *The Sarum Missal*, ed. J. Wickham Legg.
44 Brightman, *English Rite*, I, lxxx, warns that the contributions of the Lutheran Church Orders are considerable but not strictly measurable, "since similarity between the books apart from actual quotation does not of necessity imply—and

prayer-book are those of Electoral Brandenburg of 1540 (largely the work of Osiander) and Cologne of 1543 (largely the work of Bucer). The ideas of the didactic and hortatory passages in the prayer-book were borrowed from these two Orders, and occasionally the very words either in the Latin or, in the case of the latter, in the English translations that appeared conveniently in 1547 and 1548. There was also an influence in practice from the same Lutheran sources, particularly when this involved a modification of the traditional customs in worship. It can be seen in providing a direction for worshippers to offer money at the celebration of Mass or Holy Communion, in the prayers to be offered at the holy table in a dry Mass (*missa sicca*),[45] in the way in which declarations are made in marriages, in the use of Mark 10:13ff. as a Baptismal lection, and in the recognition of private houses, in some conditions, as a suitable locale for Baptisms. The same influence is evident in the adoption of new customs, such as the separating of communicants from the general congregation at Mass, the use of the litany throughout the year and not only at special seasons like Lent and Rogationtide, and the communicating of the sick directly from the altar.[46] Here again the preponderance of Protestant and therefore of radical influence seems to be definitely decided.

Nonetheless, other and more traditional sources for the first prayer-book can be found. The influence of Eastern Orthodoxy can be found in two spots: in the inclusion of an invocation of the Holy Spirit, or an *epiklesis*, in the prayer preceding the recital of the Institution narrative, and in the Prayer of St. Chrysostom. There is also a probable influence from the Mozarabic rite. Traditional influence can also be seen in certain Continental Catholic revisionary documents. The first and second recensions of the Breviary of Cardinal Quiñones left their mark on Cranmer's simplification and purification of the Offices of matins and evensong and on the Lectionary and Calendar as a whole. The *Encheiridion* and the *Antididagma*, both coming from the Catholic party in the reforming diocese of Cologne, also had an impact.[47]

---

where the similarity is one of omission there is no means of knowing—that the one has borrowed from the other."

[45] See J. Dowden, *Further Studies in the Prayer Book*, pp. 186ff.

[46] These are detailed in Brightman, *English Rite*, I, lxxx-lxxxi. The claims of German Lutheran influence on the Book of Common Prayer, although exaggerated, are set forth in H. E. Jacobs, *The Lutheran Movement in England*, Chaps. 17-23.

[47] These influences are shown in detail in Brightman, *English Rite*, II, 690, 692, 694, 734, 778.

Finally, it should be remembered that the first Book of Common Prayer incorporated the *Litany* of 1544 and *The Order of the Communion* of 1548. The former was derived from Catholic and Lutheran sources, as well as from Eastern Orthodoxy; the latter derived from the same sources, although its dependence was greatest on the *Simplex ac Pia Deliberatio*—the Cologne Church Order.

My conclusion, in reference to the sources used by Cranmer and his advisors, is deliberately inconclusive. That is, I still see a considerable and wary conservatism, bent on preserving all that could be preserved from tradition that was consonant with Biblical directives and the customs of the primitive church. At the same time I observe an increasing trend toward the vernacular and an approximation to Lutheran *Kirchenordnungen*.[48] This doubtful conclusion leads to another inquiry, and that is, was the language of the First English Prayer Book *deliberately* and consciously ambiguous in the hope of placating Catholics, while pleasing more radical Protestants?

Are we to place any credence in the charge that the traditional language of the 1549 prayer-book was a deliberate equivocation, as is suggested by E. C. Ratcliff,[49] Jardine Grisbrook,[50] and T. M. Parker?[51] Was the traditional language employed for the purpose of creating a comprehensive rite wide enough to include both Catholics and Protestants? Or was it a camouflage for a liturgical revolution, that without it might have led to widespread civil war? Intriguing as these suggestions are, it is improbable that such a wary scholar as Cranmer would plot a theological or liturgical revolution, so different is this from all the previous evidence we have for his methods. Furthermore, it is extremely unlikely that a radical Communion doctrine would be introduced into a uniform liturgy intended to produce—as the Act of Uniformity insists—

---

48 Jardine Grisbrook, *Studia Liturgica*, affirms that many Anglicans tended to maintain the Catholic character of the first prayer-book only by comparison with the more radical nature of the second, but that they forgot (a) what was omitted from the Catholic rite in the 1549 formulary and (b) were ignorant of what was common to the 1549 rite and the Continental Lutheran Church Orders. Gasquet and Bishop (*Edward VI*, p. 184), make a similar observation.

49 Ratcliff, *Book Common Prayer*, p. 15, refers to "the large equivocal element in the Book of 1549."

50 Grisbrook, *Studia Liturgica*, p. 158, suggests that Cranmer disguised a novel Eucharistic doctrine in traditional language to avoid the probability of widespread civil war.

51 Parker, *English Reformation*, p. 130, insists that the conservatism of the Eucharistic doctrine is more apparent than real, arguing that "this is an ingenious essay in ambiguity," since, while the prayers do not deny Catholic doctrine, yet a careful use of the words "would enable a Protestant to use the service with a good conscience."

"so godly order and quiet in this realm."[52] The suggestion seems to me to be too sinister to comport what is known of Cranmer's character.

On what, then is the charge of deliberate equivocation based? Ratcliff rightly points out that contemporaries interpreted the doctrinal trend of the 1549 book differently. To the radical Bishop Hooper of Gloucester and Worcester it was so redolent of Sarum as to be "very defective . . . and in some respects indeed manifestly impious."[53] On the other hand, the immovably Catholic Princess Mary would not admit the rite into her chapel so convinced was she of its departure from the Catholic norm. It is significant, however, that the Henrician Catholic, Stephen Gardiner, found it to be so traditional in its phraseology that he believed it was compatible with a Catholic interpretation. In fact, Gardiner maintained that there were five places in the Communion Order where he detected Catholic Eucharistic doctrine: (1) the words of administration and the use of the terms 'body' and 'blood'; (2) the rubric which requires the bread to be broken into at least two pieces, and comments, "menne muste not thynke lesse to be receyued in parte then in the whole, but in eache of them the whole body of our sauiour Jesu Christ";[54] (3) the *epiklesis* implies a mutation of the elements; (4) the Prayer for the Church[55] and especially the commendation of the dead presupposes a "Mass propitiatory"; and (5) the central petition of the Prayer of Humble Access, which begs: "Graunt us therefore (gracious lorde) so to eate the fleshe of thy dere sonne Jesus Christ, and to drynke his bloud in these holy Misteries, that wee maye continually dwell in hym and he in us, that our synful bodyes may bee made cleane by his body, and our soules washed through his most precious bloud."[56]

Gardiner, a former Master of Trinity College, Cambridge and a devotee of the New Learning, had for a time believed it was not necessary to tie the doctrine of the corporal Presence of Christ in the Sacrament to the Aristotelian metaphysics with which it was defended and explained in the theory of Transubstantiation. It

[52] Gee and Hardy, *Documents*, p. 360.

[53] *Original Letters relative to the English Reformation*, ed. Hastings Robinson, I, 79.

[54] For his life see J. A. Muller, *Stephen Gardiner and the Tudor Reaction*. Gardiner's Eucharistic views are contained in the *Explication and Assertion of the True and Catholic Faith of the Blessed Sacrament of the Altar*, which, together with Cranmer's response to it, *Answer unto a Crafty and Sophisticall Cavillation devised by Stephen Gardiner*, are to be found in Cranmer, *Works*, I, 10-365.

[55] The Book of Common Prayer (1549), fol. cxxi.

[56] *Ibid.*, fol. cxviii.

is not generally known that Cranmer for a while accepted a similar belief or that he constantly repudiated the charge that he taught a nude Memorialism (such as Zwingli is charged with upholding),[57] and that he was firmly convinced of the real and spiritual presence of Christ in the Eucharist. Cranmer denied the *inclusio localis* because it was contrary to the evidence of the senses, destroyed the nature of the sign in the sacrament by the mutation of bread, and contradicted the assertion of the Scriptures and the Apostles' Creed that the body of Christ was in heaven. At the same time he believed Christ was spiritually present, objectively so, because it was the power of the Holy Spirit that conveyed the benefits of His Cross and Resurrection to the believer, who received Christ in the heart by faith.

It has been a common mistake to assume that there was no fourth alternative open to Cranmer besides the Catholic, Lutheran, and Zwinglian. There was, in fact, a fourth available possibility in Virtualism, the Eucharistic doctrine according to which, while the bread and wine remain unchanged after the consecration, the faithful communicants receive with the elements the *virtue* or power of the Body and Blood of Christ. This was the view of the Eucharist affirmed by Martin Bucer, Henry Bullinger, Peter Martyr, and John Calvin. It has been argued at length by C. W. Dugmore in *The Mass and the English Reformers* and more recently by Peter Brooks in *Thomas Cranmer's Doctrine of the Eucharist*, that Cranmer's was a high Calvinist doctrine.

Cranmer shared with Calvin several negative and positive points of Eucharistic doctrine. Both denied that the Eucharist is in the medieval sense a propitiatory sacrifice. Both denied Transubstantiation for the same reasons that it is destructive of the "sign" in the Sacrament and contrary to empirical experience. Both affirmed that the body of Christ is located in heaven and only in heaven. Both had what Brooks calls a "sursum corda" approach; they asserted that the hearts of the believers have to be lifted to heaven there to feed on Christ spiritually. Such participation was declared possible through the power of the Holy Spirit. Both affirmed fur-

---

[57] The late Dom Gregory Dix, that learned and witty liturgiologist, has widely spread the notion that Cranmer's was a Eucharistic doctrine of the "Real Absence," and reiterates the view in his *Shape of the Liturgy* (pp. 656, 659) that Cranmer taught a Zwinglian doctrine. He is, however, unjust to Zwingli in accusing him of teaching subjectivity. As Cyril Richardson rightly insists, for Zwingli "the objectivity is not understood in substantial categories but in mental and personal ones." *Journal of Theological Studies*, New Series, vol. 16, pt. 2 (October 1965), 436.

ther that the "signs" in the Lord's Supper are neither empty nor nude, but deliver what God has promised to attach to them. Calvin and Cranmer denied that there is any feeding of the ungodly in the Eucharist (*manducatio impiorum*) since the Sacrament works from faith to faith. Calvin would also have agreed with Cranmer's claim that as the bread and wine feed the body of the believer, so does the spiritual presence of Christ feed the soul of the believer.

In these ways Cranmer's doctrine seemed closer to Calvin's than Zwingli's. My own judgment is that Dugmore and Brooks have made a convincing case, particularly in the light of three considerations: (1) If Cranmer was a Zwinglian, why didn't he more patently and unambiguously use Zwinglian language instead of the conservative language he does? I reject the thesis that accuses him of using ambiguous language for political purposes. (2) In 1548 and 1552 the Eucharistic debate and issues had long since passed the positions affirmed by Zwingli, who had died in 1531; it seems therefore anachronistic to call Cranmer's views Zwinglian 17 or 20 years after Zwingli's death. This is particularly so when Bullinger, Zwingli's successor in Zurich, had helped make the Eucharistic doctrine of Zurich agree more closely with that of Calvin in the *Consensus Tigurinus* of 1549. (3) Calvin provides in his doctrine of the Holy Spirit an admirable account of the dynamics of the Eucharist in a way that preserves its objectivity.

Yet as Cyril Richardson has shown,[58] there were still two obstacles in the path of easy acceptance of Cranmer's doctrine as unequivocally Calvinist. The first was that Calvin uses substantialist language in speaking of manducation frequently and apparently deliberately, whereas there is only one clear case of such usage in Cranmer. Calvin intended us to understand that there is in the Sacrament a true participation in Christ's flesh or human nature. This Cranmer denies; he affirmed that the participation is through the divine nature and power, mediated through the Holy Spirit. Cranmer, therefore, stands with Zwingli in drawing a strict line between spirit and substance. The second difficulty in seeing Cranmer as a consistent Calvinist in Eucharistic doctrine derived from his agreement to accept the "black rubric" in the Second Prayer Book, which utterly excluded "anye reall and essencial

---

[58] Cyril Richardson's powerful statement of the view that Cranmer's Eucharistic doctrine is Zwinglian was first stated in *Zwingli and Cranmer on the Eucharist*; it has recently been elaborated over against the views of Dugmore in *The Journal of Theological Studies*, New Series, vol. 16, pt. 2 (October 1965), 421-37; and against the views of Brooks in *The Anglican Theological Review*, vol. 47, no. 3 (1965), 308-13.

presence there beeyng of Christ's naturall fleshe and bloude." This would appear to be conclusive proof of his Zwinglianism but for two other considerations. Since this was apparently foisted on Cranmer at the last minute when the Second Prayer Book was already coming off the printing presses and at the royal request, after the beseeching of King Edward by his chaplain, John Knox, it can hardly be regarded as the free expression of Cranmer's Eucharistic teaching. Nor, unless Knox deviated in his Eucharistic beliefs from Calvin (an unlikely supposition of one who was so close a disciple), can we regard this doctrine as un-Calvinist.

Furthermore, however close to Calvin or Zwingli Cranmer's Eucharistic beliefs were, it must be noted that Cranmer and Zwingli differed in their evaluation of the importance of the Eucharist. Cranmer, like Calvin, desired a weekly Eucharist, whereas Zwingli settled for a quarterly Eucharist. On balance, then, I think Cranmer moved from a Catholic through a Lutheran to a Calvinist or Virtualist doctrine of the Eucharist, and that the final stage was accompanied by the strong influence on him of Nicholas Ridley, relying on the Nominalism he found in Radbertus. Cranmer, it must be insisted, affirmed that by the power of the Holy Spirit, the true consecratory agent in the sacrament, Christ with all the benefits of his passion and resurrection was spiritually present at the Lord's Table, and that this was known in the hearts of believers by the interior testimony of faith. Faith did not create the presence —that would be blasphemy. Rather it confirmed the presence through the power of the Holy Spirit. Cranmer would undoubtedly have agreed with the statement made by his mentor, Ridley, in the Cambridge Debate of 1549. There Ridley stated that the three practical benefits of the Eucharist were unity, nutrition, and conversion.

If this view of Cranmer's Eucharistic teaching is accepted, then, there is no need to describe Cranmer as a crypto-Zwinglian hiding behind a quasi-Catholic mask of language, for his was a mediating, not an iconoclastic, position. Possibly Cranmer was inconsistent, even confused. It may be that he was groping toward a clearer expression of his sacramental theology. He may even have been adumbrating a mediating position which tried to conserve the Catholic value of the Eucharist, while abandoning its anachronistic metaphysical underpinnings. But he was assuredly not an éminence grise, nor was he an archiepiscopal Rasputin at Edward's court, however intriguing such a hypothesis may be.

There is, however, one further argument to be considered, which seems to shadow Cranmer's integrity by those who use it. It is the claim of Ratcliff[59] and Dix[60] that the rite of 1549 was merely a trial balloon, an experiment that could be revised at the first opportunity. It was conceived as a kind of liturgical litmus paper to test exactly how much Protestant acidity Englishmen could stomach, with the intention of giving them a larger dose next time. This view is bolstered by the evidence in a letter written by Martin Bucer and Paul Fagius on April 26, 1549 to the ministers of Strassburg, reporting on a visit they had paid the previous day to the Archbishop of Canterbury. Referring to the proposed prayer-book, presumably then in the process of being printed since it was to be introduced at Pentecost that year, they wrote: "We hear that some concesions have been made both to a respect for antiquity, and to the infirmity of the present age; such, for instance, as the vestments commonly used in the sacrament of the eucharist, and the use of candles: so also in regard to the commemoration of the dead, and the use of chrism; for we know not to what extent or in what sort it prevails. They affirm that there is no superstition in these things, and that they are only to be retained for a time, lest the people, not having yet learned Christ, should be deterred by too extensive innovations from embracing his religion, and that rather they may be won over."[61]

As a comment on this excerpt, it can be said that Cranmer's welcome to the strangers of distinction may have led them to believe that he was more firmly of their opinion than was in fact the case. But, at all events, it is notable that the reasons given for the conservative nature of the revision, were two and not merely one. There was the typically English desire to keep the tradition of the past, as far as possible; and there was the sensible idea that reform should be undertaken slowly, so that, using the scriptural analogy, babes in the new faith should be given milk before they are ready for the strong meat of the Gospel. Moreover, Bucer and Fagius called for no changes in the actions, words, or theology of the first Prayer Book, but only in the ceremonial with which it was celebrated, which they thought might be changed. Furthermore, they explicitly stated that the leaders of the English church "affirm that there is

[59] *Ibid.*, p. 15.
[60] *Ibid.*, p. 658. Dix, however, relies on F. M. Powicke, *The Reformation in England*, pp. 89f.
[61] *Original Letters relative to the English Reformation*, ed. Hastings Robinson, 2 vols., II, 535-36.

no superstition in these things." My conclusion is that there is no indication here of a proposal for a revised Prayer Book to follow the Book of 1549, only for a possible future modification of ceremonial. I find no evidence of any equivocation by Cranmer.

In short, I attribute the apparent confusion in the rite which has caused Catholics and Protestants to interpret it diversely, as due to several possible causes in combination, none of them amounting to the sinister purpose of saying one thing and meaning another. First, it should be remembered that, however important Cranmer was, he was working with a committee, and further that there was a considerable disagreement between the similar Cranmerian and Ridleian views and those of highly placed Bishops Bonner, Gardiner, Tunstall, Day, Thirlby, and others.[62] Next, Cranmer had not fully clarified his own views, which appeared to have moved from a Lutheran to a Calvinist direction and which were intermediate between Transubstantiation and Memorialism. Third, since the aim of producing this uniform rite was to end the innovations of the ultra-Protestants and to prevent the recrudescence of the more crassly magical popular Catholic view of the Mass, its intention clearly was mediatorial and not iconoclastic. Finally, *festina lente* was precisely the imperative of gradualism that Cranmer had followed throughout his career, of which the First Prayer Book was the continuance of a policy that had produced the ever-increasing Protestantism of the *Litany* followed by *The Order of the Communion*, and the further stage of which would be the prayer-book of 1552. It was not a radical or Zwinglian type of Protestantism, but a more conservative or mediating Protestant doctrine of the Eucharist that was expressed clearly or darkly in the Communion order of the first Prayer Book.

After these preliminary discussions we are in a position now to estimate how Protestant the 1549 prayer-book was by comparing the Communion rite in it with the Roman Catholic Mass in the

---

[62] The lack of agreement of the bishops in their interpretation is carefully analysed in Gasquet and Bishop, *Edward VI*, pp. 129-39. This is also the theme of the letter written by Peter Martyr to Bucer, dated from Oxford, December 26, 1548: "The other matter which distresses me not a little is this, that there is so much contention among our people about the Eucharist that every corner is full of it. And even in the supreme council of the state in which matters relating to religion are daily brought forward, there is so much disrupting of the bishops among themselves and with others, as I think was never heard before." There is also a later, interesting reference to the new respect that Cranmer had won as a theologian, who had hitherto been regarded as an administrator, but had now "shewn himself so mighty a theologian against them [the 'popish party'] as they would rather not have proof of, and they are compelled . . . to acknowledge his learning and power and dexterity in debate." *Ibid.*, pp. 469-70.

Sarum Use. In this comparison I will be concerned not only with words but also significant actions, whether included or omitted.

The first half of the Communion service of 1549 closely followed the medieval rite; Introit, *Kyrie*, *Gloria*, collects, Epistle, Gospel, and Creed were retained in the same order as in the Catholic Mass. The preparatory prayers were fewer, however, and an Erastian flavor appears in the following of the collect for the day with the collect for the king. The Gradual, which in the Sarum rite was accompanied by the priest's ceremonial preparation of the chalice and paten, was entirely omitted. Notice that the term "Mass" is the third alternative permissible title after "Lord's Supper" and "Holy Communion" and that it will disappear altogether in 1552, also that the fourth rubric in the introduction to the service allows the ceremonial cope to be substituted for the sacrificial chasuble, which Grisbrook described as "a discreet but powerful blow at the old sacrificial doctrine at the very outset."[63]

The most notable deviations from the Sarum Rite come after the Creed and sermon, or homily, for the character of the immediately following Offertory was greatly altered. In the ancient and medieval liturgy the bread and wine were offered to God as gifts of the people in readiness for the sacrifice. But in the 1549 rite there was only an offering of alms at this point, and they were not placed on the altar but in the "poor mennes box." The offertory sentences had no Eucharistic reference; the preparation of the elements takes place without any ceremony. One can only conclude that Cranmer, like Luther, wished to rid his rite of any suggestion of oblation or sacrifice.[64]

If the character of the Offertory was changed, the Canon of the Mass was so altered as to be wholly unrecognisable, after the *Sursum corda*, the Preface, and the *Sanctus*. It consisted of eight parts.[65] The first was a long intercession for the church, king, ministers of state, clergy, those in adversity, and, after a short thanksgiving, for the example of the saints and for the dead. If the commemoration of the dead and mention of the saints is a Catholic item, it is important to notice the omission of any pleading of the sacrifice or of the resurrection of Christ in connection with the intercession. The second section includes a commemoration of the

[63] Grisbrooke, *Studia Liturgica*, p. 154.

[64] Gasquet and Bishop do not overstate the case (*Edward VI*, p. 196): "It will therefore appear that the ancient ritual oblation with the whole of which the idea of sacrifice was so intimately associated, was swept away."

[65] The entire Canon can be found in fols. cxv-cxvii.

death of Christ and of the institution of the Last Supper, but it excludes any pleading of the sacrifice of Christ in the Eucharist. The third section is a petition for the consecration of the elements: "with thy holy spirite and worde, vouchsafe to blesse and sanctifie these thy gyftes, and creatures of bread and wyne, that they maie be unto us the bodye and bloude of thy moste derely beloued sonne Jesus Christe." Here we have an interesting combination of Eastern and Western consecratory forms, since the Eastern *epiklesis* regards the Holy Spirit as the agent of consecration, while the Western formula regards Christ the word of God as consecrating through the repetition of his words in the Institution narrative. Even if there is a strong stress on the subjective, "that they may be unto us,"[66] there is a strong stress on the objective power of God the Holy Spirit and God the Son, which seems to be wholly orthodox, though perhaps unduly anxious in providing a double insurance in a hybrid Eastern-Western formula of consecration.

The fourth section of the Canon is the Narrative of Institution from I Corinthians 11, which is common to Catholic and Protestant Communions, but with the significant rubric: *These wordes before rehersed are to be saied, turning still to the Altar, without any eleuacion, or shewing the Sacrament to the people.*[67] What Cranmer gave with one hand—the affirmation of the corporal presence in the consecratory formula—he seemed immediately to take away with the other by the abolition of the ceremony of elevation. The fifth section is the *anamnesis*, "the memoryall whyche thy sonne hath wylled us to make, hauyng in remembraunce his blessed passion, mightie resurreccyon, and gloryous ascencion," which seems to be so worded as to avoid any reference to any offering or sacrifice of the body and blood of Christ or of the bread and wine as people's oblations. The sixth part of the Canon is a petition for the acceptance of "this our Sacrifice of praise and thankes geuing." The seventh part is an offering of "our selfe [*sic*], oure soules, and bodies, to be a reasonable, holy, and liuely sacrifice unto thee," that the communicants may be incorporated into Christ. The eighth and final section of the Canon is the petition that the "bounden duetie and seruice" of those present may be accepted and that their prayers may be brought up to the Divine Majesty.

---

[66] Day, bishop of Chichester, refused his assent to the book because, among other reasons, the words immediately following the *epiklesis*, "that they maie be unto us," were not changed to read "that they maie be *made* unto us the bodye and bloude of . . . Jesus Christe." See Gasquet and Bishop, *Edward VI*, pp. 131-32.

[67] *Ibid.*, fol. cxvi.

The Canon, or Prayer of Consecration, concluded, there follow the Lord's Prayer and the *Pax Domini*. From there the deviation from the Sarum Rite is almost total. Although the *Agnus Dei* is retained it is removed until the people's Communion. After a reminder that Christ the Paschal Lamb is offered up, there is an exhortation to repentence and charity, and an invitation to partake of the Sacrament after making a general confession. The absolution follows, then the "Comfortable Words" of Christ and the "Prayer of Humble Access." The Communion is delivered in the following words: "The Body of oure Lorde Jesus Christe which was geuen for thee, preserue thy bodye and soule unto euerlasting lyfe," and "The bloud of our Lorde Jesus Christ which was shed for thee preserue thy bodye and soule unto euerlastyng lyfe."[68] As was mentioned, the *Agnus Dei* in English is sung while the people communicate. The Communion Order approaches the end with a section known as the "Post-Communion," which includes sentences of Scripture stressing the ethical duties of Christians, since sanctification is the proper expression of gratitude for redemption, a prayer of thanksgiving for "the spirituall foode of the most precious body and bloud of thy sonne, our saviour Jesus Christ" and the concluding Blessing.

What conclusion are we, at last, to draw from this Communion Rite which is an amalgam of ancient Catholic and modern Lutheran forms, with an Eastern *epiklesis* added for good measure? It is clear that in the absence of the elements of oblation and of sacrifice and with the obvious intention to do away with any occasion of adoration of the elements (explicitly denied in the rubric forbidding elevation) that the corporal presence is denied. Even the force of the *epiklesis* tending in the direction of a corporal presence is weakened if not nullified by two considerations. The first is the strongly subjective modification introduced by the phrase "be unto us," which was seen by the conservative bishop Thirlby of Westminster and which he proposed to rectify by changing the phrase to read "be made unto us," which was hotly rejected by Cranmer and his associates. The second consideration is that the emphasis on a "spiritual presence," dear to Cranmer's heart since 1546, would be strengthened by an *epiklesis* invoking the power of the Holy Spirit, and the final prayer of thanksgiving reinforces this view with its gratitude for "*spirituall* foode." If it can be established as at least probable that no corporal presence is intended, then this

[68] *Ibid.*, fol. cxviii v.

cannot be considered a Catholic rite, however much its structure, order, and terminology recall a partially Catholic model. Nor, since the German Lutherans of the north in this period believed in the corporal presence, though not in Transubstantiation (a belief sometimes unhappily termed "Consubstantiation"), can this Order be considered a Lutheran Rite, despite its indebtedness in so many details to various German *kirchenordnungen*, and despite the fact that Gasquet and Bishop, who have made the most thoroughgoing comparative analysis of the rite, considered it to be Lutheran.[69] The only alternative left is to call it a Reformed rite, even if its phraseology and contents show an immediately greater indebtedness to Roman and Lutheran than to Reformed sources. But to which section of the Reformed church does its theology of the Eucharist belong? Is it Zwinglian and Memorialist, as Gregory Dix believed?[70] It is impossible to accept this view, because Zwingli had been dead 18 years and his successor Bullinger had helped frame a more mediating doctrine of the Eucharist. It was this view that was held, with only minor variations, by Bucer, Peter Martyr, Pullain, à Lasco (all foreigners befriended by Cranmer and living in England), and the greatest Reformed theologian of them all—Calvin—whose sacramental views had been fully formulated as early as 1540, four years after the publication of the first edition of his *Institutio Christianae Religionis*. It was a Eucharistic doctrine that affirmed that *in the sacramental action* Christ was present to grant forgiveness and eternal life through His humanity and that, although the body of Christ was in heaven, by the power of the Holy Spirit He was present through transformation, and in the sacrament united His elect to one another.[71]

69 *Ibid.*, p. 195: "And even if it were not an ascertained fact that, during the years when it was in preparation, Cranmer was under the influence of his Lutheran friends, the testimony of the book itself would be sufficient to prove beyond a doubt that it was conceived and drawn up after the Lutheran pattern."

70 *Op. cit.*, pp. 656, 659.

71 The best recent treatments of Calvin's sacramental teaching are Ronald S. Wallace, *Calvin's Doctrine of the Word and Sacraments*; and Kilian McDonnell, *Calvin, the Church, and the Eucharist*. Calvin's *Petit Traicté de la cène*, first appearing in 1540, was translated into English by Miles Coverdale and published probably in 1549 (according to the *Short Title Catalogue*, item 4412.1) as *A Faythful and moste Godly treatyse concernynge the most Sacred Sacrament of the blessed body and bloude of our sauior Christ*, compiled by John Caluine; it was reprinted in *Writings and Translations of Myles Coverdale, Bishop of Exeter*, ed. G. Pearson, pp. 434-66. Calvin's doctrine in its distinctive emphasis may be gathered from two brief citations from this treatise. First he writes: "The bread is not unworthily called the body; forasmuch as it doth not only represent it unto us, but also bring unto us the same thing . . ." (p. 440). Second, he approves Zwingli and Oecolampadius for having criticised a gross carnal presence of Christ

Much has been said about the indebtedness of Cranmer and his associates to many and varied sources, but what of the values of this rite? Was it no improvement over the ancient Roman rite? One improvement it clearly had, apart from the other advantages of a vernacular liturgy and of a book which is equally for the use of priest and people: the Roman Canon, unlike the liturgies of the East, were insufficient in intercessory prayers. This was remedied in 1549 by the comprehensive intercessions of the Prayer, "for the whole estate of Christ's Church," which follows the singing of the *Sanctus*. Furthermore, while early liturgies were called "Eucharists" in token of the large element of thanksgiving in them, this was not prominent in the Latin Canon. The defect was rectified in the 1549 book, both in the Prayer of Consecration and in the noble post-Communion Prayer of Thanksgiving. Furthermore, the emphasis is strong on the need for the offering of "ourselfe, our soules, and bodies" in union with Christ's supreme offering now being commemorated. Perhaps one can even mark as the distinctive characteristic of the Anglican rite the sobering demand that devotion should lead to the duty to serve the community. It seems as if Anglicanism was from the first afraid of that romanticism which could so easily drown ethics in aesthetics; so at the conclusion of the service of Holy Communion there is the disenchanting series of Scriptural reminders that the service of God must issue in the service of men.

Moving from content to style, it is widely recognised that Cranmer was not only a highly skilful editor who could meld the most heterogeneous sources into a polished literary product, but that he

---

in the sacrament, but condemns them for having "omitted to declare what presence of Christ in the supper we ought to believe, and what communion of his body and blood is there received: insomuch that Luther supposed them willing to leave nought else but the bare signs, void of the spiritual substance" (pp. 463-64). Calvin's point is that to the seals of God's promises, which the sacramental signs are, the verity is also added. Also see Wallace, *Calvin's Doctrine*, pp. 151-53; and Calvin's *Institutes* IV:17:iii-x.

If the question is asked, how did Cranmer have access to Calvin's thought? it can be answered that John Knox was a minister at Berwick-on-Tweed during Edward VI's reign, that by 1549 the great *Institutio* was 13 years old, and that Coverdale had already published an English translation of Calvin's *Short Treatise on the Sacrament*, together with a Calvinist Church Order for Denmark and parts of Germany, and, most important, à Lasco and Pullain were using Calvinist orders of worship for the churches of the strangers of which they were superintendent ministers in England. In fact, there is clear verbal dependence on Pullain's Order of worship in the third collect in the Communion Order of 1549 which is to be used after the Offertory when there is no Communion to follow; it is possible that there are verbal echoes of the three prayers of thanksgiving after Communion in the Calvinist Danish order, already referred to, in the post-Communion Prayer of Thanksgiving, since all four are concerned with spiritual eating and drinking.

could write with an ear sensitive to the cadences of the English language. Sometimes he even improved on the lapidary elegance of the Roman collects he was translating. For example, the second collect (for Peace) which is used at matins, renders the Sarum original which begins "Deus auctor pacis et amator, quem nosse vivere, cui servire, regnare est . . ." as "O God, which art the author of peace and louer of concorde, in knowledge of whom standeth oure eternall life, whose seruice is perfect fredome. . . ." Another example of a happy translation from an equally felicitous Latin original can be found in the first collect after the offertory, to be used when Communion was not celebrated. The Latin phrase *inter omnes vias et vitae huius varietatis* is rendered as "emonge all the chaunges and chaunces of this mortall life."[72] These are freer but far more felicitous translations than more exact ones would have been. The fact is that Cranmer was much more than a facile manipulator of scissors and paste; he was, in several instances, a creator.[73] His were the then new collects for Eastertide and those for several of the evangelists, as well as the admirable prayer of thanksgiving after Communion, which is an excellent summary of the varied meanings of Holy Communion, as thanksgiving, mystery, grace, incorporation with Christ, fellowship in the Church, or anticipation of the Kingdom of God. The prayer is, in addition, most happy in making the transition from the mystery of the sanctuary to the morality of "good works" in the workaday world. Another masterly prayer of Cranmer's was the famous "Prayer of Humble Access" which combines reverence and tenderness in the approach to God, with sense and without sentimentality.[74]

Unquestionably the literary quality of the First Book of Common Prayer is high. But while the language of the time was vigorous and rich, there was also a tendency toward prolixity and vaguely worded sentences, along with a Latinity that could easily become cumbersome if not firmly controlled. As it was, Cranmer may be said to have created a superb vehicle of liturgical prose, which

---

[72] Book of Common Prayer, fol. iiii and cxx.

[73] Another example of Cranmer's improving on a collect in the original Latin is that for the Fourth Sunday after Easter. But in justice, it must be admitted that Cranmer on the rare occasion could perpetrate an unhappy construction, as in the confusion of the following petition in the second collect at evensong (the offending words are italicised): "Geue unto thy servauntes that peace which the world cannot geue; *that both* our hartes may be sette to obey thy commaundementes, *and also that by thee we* being defended from the feare of our enemies, may passe our time in rest and quietnesse."

[74] See the comments of Massey H. Shepherd, Jr. on these two major prayers in *The Oxford American Prayer Book Commentary*, pp. 82-84.

met simultaneously, as Stella Brook has defined them, "the workaday but important requirements of ease of articulation, and the need to create aural effects of sonority and dignity and rhythmic balance."[75] In addition, the language gave shape to profound thought and aspiration.

In concluding my consideration of the contents and style of the 1549 prayer-book, I may have left the impression that in structure, diction, and sources used the volume was fairly conservative; that view may be reinforced as we consider its successor, the more radical prayer-book of 1552. In fact, however, as the revision of other services in the 1549 book show, it was a volume more distinguished by innovation than conservatism. In the two daily offices of matins and evensong all invocations of the saints and all allusions to their merits and intercession were excised; also, the Calendar removed the names of all but a few "scriptural" saints. In the office of Baptism the impressive secondary ceremonies such as the use of salt, spittle, oil and candle are done away with, with the exception of the exorcism before and the signation of the cross and the anointing with chrism after Baptism. The new rite of Confirmation removed the anointing with chrism which all previous rites in Christendom had considered essential. Further, there are whole areas of life untouched by the new book, such as the lack of any formulas for the blessing of sanctuaries or of their contents. Nor was there any form for the commendation of the dying to God, which must have been a grievous loss to an elderly person who might have received great comfort from the rich medieval rite. After all, the central rite of Mass or Holy Communion had been changed from the offering of a sacrifice for the living and the dead to a commemoration of the sacrifice of Christ offered on the cross for the world and a renewal of spiritual fellowship with Him and with living Christians. Change, to mid-sixteenth-century worshippers, was more obvious than continuity.[76] That was clearly shown by the popular reaction to the introduction of the Book of Common Prayer of 1549.

4. *The Reception of the 1549 Prayer-book*

The publication of the First English Book of Common Prayer generated three responses, varying from acceptance through tem-

[75] *The Language of the Book of Common Prayer*, p. 122.

[76] On this issue I find the summary judgment of F. E. Brightman (*English Rite*, I, lxxxii), that "Rite and Ceremony are simplified," inadequate. W. Jardine

porary acquiescence to dissatisfaction. Since the book was introduced by an Act of Uniformity which carried heavy fines for noncompliance, it had to be accepted willy-nilly by most of the country. In some cases it may even have been warmly accepted. This is the impression given by Dryander in a letter of June 5, 1549 to Bullinger in Strassburg: "A book has now been published a month or two back, which the English churches received with the greatest satisfaction." Whatever reservations Dryander thought Bullinger may have had about some ceremonies retained in the book, he was anxious that Bullinger realize what an advance it represented, so he added: "Meanwhile this reformation must not be counted lightly of; in this kingdom especially, where there existed heretofore in the public formularies of doctrine true popery without the name."[77]

There is more evidence that the Continental divines who had recently been invited to England by Cranmer and certain Englishmen in the Reformed cities of Strassburg or Zurich were acquiescent, and not enthusiastic about the Prayer Book of 1549. Their attitude was that this was only the important first instalment of a reformation of worship that must proceed further. For them the 1549 book was important only as an interim rite.[78] John Butler, writing on February 16, 1550 to Thomas Blaurer, obviously considered the prayer-book a halfway house: "The affairs of religion are now, through the mercy of God, in a more favourable position, considering the state of infancy and rudeness of our nation. Baptism, for instance, and the Lord's Supper, are celebrated with sufficient propriety, only that some blemishes in respect to certain ceremonies, such for instance as the splendour of the vestments, have not yet been done away with."[79] Richard Hilles, writing to Bullinger on June 4, 1549, gave the impression that Cranmer is more anxious to please the German than the Swiss divines, and that Bucer, who had recently come to Cambridge, might keep him conservative. "Thus," he wrote, "our bishops and governors seem, for the present at least, to be acting rightly; while, for the preservation of the public peace, they afford no cause of offence to the

---

Grisbrook's statement, pp. 152-53, is more convincing when he affirms that "the majority of the ceremonies with which the Englishman approached his Maker were not simplified at all—they were abolished."

[77] *Original Letters*, ed. Hastings Robinson, 2 vols., I, 350-51.

[78] This is clear in a joint letter from Martin Bucer and Paul Fagius to the Strassburg ministers, April 26, 1549. *Original Letters*, II, 534-37.

[79] *Ibid.*, p. 635.

Lutherans, pay attention to your very learned German divines, submit their judgment to them, and also retain some popish ceremonies."[80] Thus the opinion of Protestant scholars in England seemed to be acceptance for lack of anything better.

But it was Bucer, whom Hilles had thought to be in the conservative school, who had written the fullest and most careful evaluation of the 1549 book in the *Censura Martini Buceri super libro sacrorum, seu ordinationis Ecclesiae atque ministerii ecclesiasticii in regno Angliae.*[81] His most serious criticism was a dislike for the very concept of the consecration of things, including the water in Baptism and the bread and wine in the Communion service. He believed the signs of the sacraments were potent only while in sacramental use.[82] He would abolish in the Communion Order the invocation of the Holy Spirit, the manual acts accompanying the recital of the Institution narrative, and the sign of the cross in Baptism. He would also abolish the exorcism and chrism in Baptism and the oil for the sick. Bucer was highly critical of mass vestments and of ceremonial signs without Biblical warrant. He argued the need of many more homilies to be written for the instruction of clergy and people, and rejected several traditional customs, among them the use of the choir for divine service as perpetuating an unfortunate distinction between ministers and laity and because it was difficult to hear the minister leading worship from the choir. He disliked the use of wafer bread instead of ordinary bread for the Eucharist, condemned the placing of the sacrament in the mouths rather than in the hands of communicants, and would abolish as superstitious all prayers for the dead.[83] Hooper was the most critical of the Protestants: "I am so much offended with that book, and that not without abundant reason, that if it be not corrected, I neither can nor will communicate with the church in the administration of the supper."[84]

A serious Catholic criticism was that of the deposed Bishop of

[80] *Ibid.,* I, 266.

[81] This comprises pp. 456ff. of *Scripta Anglicana,* published in Basel in 1577. For the liturgical work of Bucer see Jan van de Poll, *Martin Bucer's Liturgical Ideas.*

[82] "Nonnulli eam sibi fingunt superstitionem, ut existiment nephas esse, si quid ex pane et vino communicationis ea peracta supersit, pati id in usum venire vulgarem; quasi pani huic et vino insit per se aliquid nominis aut sancti etiam extra communicationis usum." *Ibid.,* p. 464.

[83] These were, of course, only the major negative criticisms in a book of 28 chapters, which was laudatory of many of Cranmer's innovations. The main points are summarised in Proctor and Frere, *New History,* pp. 73ff.

[84] Letter of March 27, 1550, *Original Letters,* I, 79.

Winchester, Stephen Gardiner. Gardiner accused Cranmer of believing a radical Eucharistic doctrine which Cranmer had concealed in the 1549 Prayer Book. Gardiner, tongue in cheek, took great delight in interpreting the doctrine in the most Catholic way possible.[85] Indeed, if one wished to find the most compelling reason for revising the 1549 book soon after it appeared, it would be to silence Gardiner's criticism of inconsistency on the part of Cranmer. The criticism appeared in *The Explication of the True and Catholic Faith of the Blessed Sacrament of the Altar*, summarised earlier in this chapter. The contention was that in five separate places in the Communion Order a Catholic interpretation could be put on the words and actions. Gardiner strongly believed that the Dominical words, "This is my Body" should be accepted by the faithful as literal truth, and if Christ be the eternal Son of God, the miracle is not only possible it is probable. If the corporal Presence transcends man's wit, then reason must bow to the superiority of faith which transcends it. "I know by faith Christ to be present but the particularity how he is present, more than I am assured he is truly present, and therefore in substance present, I cannot tell. . . ."[86] Holding such views, it was inevitable that Gardiner would either retain the 1549 rite in order to prevent matters becoming worse or hope for a return to the Sarum Use, possibly in a vernacular rite.

The most vehement critics of the 1549 book were the Cornish and Devonian rebels who revolted in the Western Uprising of 1549, and who were finally put down by soldiers. They had been clearly instructed by priests, as was evident in their demands, but the statement of the demands was a significant pointer to what they felt was lacking in the first prayer book. There were 16 demands. Four were crucial—the 4th, 7th, the 9th (which marked their acute sense of loss), and the 8th, which expressed an acute dislike for the new Prayer Book. They missed the adoration of the reserved Sacrament: "(4) Item, we will have the Sacrament hang over the high altar and there to be worshipped as it was wont to be, and they which will not consent we will have them die like heretics against the holy Catholic faith." They missed the colorful ceremonies and images of the familiar medieval rite: "(7) Item,

---

[85] As an exercise in Catholic ingenuity it foreshadowed Newman's interpretation of the Thirty-Nine Articles in Tract 90.

[86] Muller, p. 210. Gardiner held that the 1549 book "is well termed not distant from the Catholic faith." *Writings and Disputations of Thomas Cranmer relative to the Lord's Supper*, p. 92.

we will have holy bread and holy water made every Sunday, palms and ashes at the times appointed and accustomed, images to be set up again in every church and all other ancient, old ceremonies used heretofore by our mother the holy Church." They particularly missed a sense of unity with their recent ancestors, for the repose of whose souls Masses and prayers might be said: "(9) Item, we will have every preacher in his sermon and every priest at his Mass pray specially by name for the souls in purgatory as our forefathers did." All of this was a protest against the barrenness and impersonality of the new Anglican rite, and the sheer didacticism which reached the top of the mind, but did not penetrate through the senses, as ancient rites and profound symbolism had. The rebels felt the new prayer book was only a shadow, or a mimicry, of the ancient Mass, and they said so: "(8) Item, we will not receive the new service because it is like a Christmas game, but we will have our old service of matins, mass, evensong, and procession [the Litany] in Latin, not in English, as it was before. And so we, Cornishmen (whereof certen of us understand no English) utterly refuse this new English."[87] Elsewhere the dissatisfaction among adherents of the older faith was deep, though less articulate.

Some indications of the difficulty the government had in forcing the people to accept the new prayer-book can be seen in the extraordinary measures that were taken to make the prayer-books acceptable, for example, to the universities. Early in May 1549 Ridley was an official visitor to the University of Cambridge, where he led an inquisition into the religious life and services in the colleges. On Sunday, May 26, he ordered six altars to be removed from the chapel,[88] and presided over a public disputation in which two propositions were to be affirmed. The first was that Transubstantiation could not be confirmed by the Scriptures or the writings of the first 10 centuries; the second was that the only oblation in the Lord's Supper was the giving of thanks and commemoration of Christ's death.[89] The purge was effective only for a short time, since during Pentecost in 1550 Bucer wrote to Calvin: "by far the greater number of the Cambridge fellows are either the most bitter papists or profligate epicureans"; many parochial clergy recited the service so "that the people have no more understanding of the mystery of Christ than if the Latin instead of the vulgar tongue

[87] *Troubles connected with the Prayer Book of 1549*, ed. N. Pocock, New Series, 37, pp. 148f.
[88] Charles Henry Cooper, *Annals of Cambridge*, 3 vols., II, 28.
[89] Proctor and Frere, *New History*, pp. 212-13.

were still in use."[90] Nor was the success of the visitor to Oxford, Holbeach, bishop of Lincoln, any greater. Bucer was distressed by the account he read of the Acts of the Disputation at Oxford, which he had received from Peter Martyr. He felt that most people reading the report, "will be entirely of the opinion that you assert that Christ is altogether absent from the Supper and that the only presence is that of his power and spirit."[91] Oxford seemed to be slipping back into the old faith more rapidly than Cambridge. John Stumphius, a disciple of Bullinger, informed him by letter on February 28, 1550 that, "those cruel beasts the Romanists, with which Oxford abounds, are now beginning to triumph over the downfall of our duke [Somerset], the overthrow of our gospel at its last gasp, and the restoration of their darling the mass, as though they had already obtained a complete victory."[92] Stumphius informed Bullinger on November 12, 1550 that, "the Oxford men, who have been hitherto accustomed to do so, are still pertinaciously sticking in the mud of popery."[93] Even the cruelest measures had failed to achieve loyalty to the prayer-book in Oxford. John ab Ulmis reported from Oxford on August 7, 1549 that there had been a rebellion in Oxfordshire; "the Oxfordshire papists are at last reduced to order, many of them having been apprehended, and some gibbeted, and their heads fastened to the walls."[94]

The most dramatic exhibition of the division of conviction that the introduction of the new prayer-book had created was in St. Paul's cathedral in London, where Bishop Edmund Bonner, who disliked the book, postponed celebrating worship according to its requirements in ritual and ceremonial as long as possible. His Dean, William May, however, introduced the new book before he was legally required to do so,[95] and rejoiced in the iconoclasm it encouraged. On March 17, 1549, the second Sunday in Lent, following a sermon by Coverdale, the Dean "commanded the Sacrament at the high altar to be pulled down."[96] Although all chantry

90 *Original Letters*, II, 546-47.
91 *Scripta Anglicana*, p. 549. So alarmed was Bucer that he urged Peter Martyr, if his conscience permitted, to secure a chance to alter the report to affirm the reality of Christ's presence in the sacrament.
92 *Original Letters*, II, 464.
93 *Ibid.*, II, 467-68.
94 *Ibid.*, 391. These riots, as well as being occasioned in part by religious reaction, were partly caused by dissatisfaction with the enclosures of formerly monastic lands.
95 Wriothesley, *Chronicle of England*, II, 9, states that "Paul's choir and divers parishes in London began the use after the new books in the beginning of Lent."
96 *Grey Friars of London Chronicle*, p. 58.

priests had been dismissed, Mass continued to be said in St. Paul's in private chapels; on June 24 the Council, considering it unsuitable that the cathedrals of St. Paul's and St. Peter's, Westminster, should continue to disregard the Act of Uniformity, wrote letters to both Bonner and Thirlby commanding them to discontinue the deviations from the new book.[97] Meanwhile Cranmer entered the fray, and on Sunday, July 21, 1549, set an example of the new simplicity; he "did the office himself in a cope and no vestment, nor mitre, nor cross, but a cross staff was borne afore him, with two priests of Paul's for deacon and subdeacon with albs and tunicles, the dean of Paul's following him in his surplice."[98] Wriothesley records that the archbishop, wearing a silk cap instead of a mitre, "gave the communion himself unto eight persons of the said church."[99] Again, on Saturday, August 10, 1549, Cranmer went to St. Paul's and preached on the Western Uprising, accusing Popish priests of fomenting the revolt. On the same day Bonner was summoned before the Council; injunctions were delivered which accused him of celebrating Mass in the old days in person, but now of seldom or never celebrating Communion according to the new order.[100] The Council compelled Bonner to celebrate the Communion in his cathedral in mid-August, where he "did the office at Paul's both at the procession and the communion, discreetly and sadly."[101] He was also required to preach to a vast auditory at Paul's Cross, where he maintained with all his might the corporeal presence in the Lord's Supper."[102] A doomed man, he made a final public protest on his last free Sunday, October 15, when the preacher at St. Paul's vehemently criticized the doctrines of Transubstantiation and corporal presence, by leaving the church before the sermon was over to show his abhorrence of such heretical doctrines. He was committed to the Marshalsea prison on September 20 and deprived of his bishopric on October 1, 1549.

Considerable opposition to the Prayer Book must have been expected from the beginning. How otherwise could it be undergirded by an Act of Uniformity *insisting* that the new rite be used, with penalties for a failure to use it? Indeed, the prescience of the Council is seen in their prohibition in the Act of "any interludes, plays, songs, rhymes or by other open words in derogation, deprav-

[97] Strype, *Ecclesiastical Memorials*, 3 vols., II, 210-11.
[98] *Grey Friars of London Chronicle*, p. 60.
[99] *Ibid.*, II, 16.   [100] Foxe, *op. cit.*, V, 762.
[101] *Grey Friars of London Chronicle*, p. 62.
[102] Foxe, *Acts and Monuments*, V, 750.

ing or displaying of the same book; or of anything contained therein."[103] It is unfortunate that their collective wisdom did not enable them to see that a compromise book that was neither truly Catholic nor consistently Protestant, instead of pleasing both religious persuasions, would alienate both. The general unpopularity of the prayer-book ensured that its life would be a brief one—only three years.[104]

5. The Second Prayer Book of Edward VI

There were three reasons for the Second Prayer Book of 1552. First, Cranmer had been accused of duplicity (or inconsistency) by Gardiner for holding a more radical doctrine of the Eucharist in his *Defence of the True and Catholick Doctrine of the Sacrament* (1550) than he had dared to express in the First Prayer Book. Cranmer's honour was impugned, and the implication of Gardiner's accusation was obvious: if rite and theology were indeed at odds, let Cranmer create a new rite which would be a clearer mirror of his Eucharistic theology than the vague rite of 1549 was, which, in its obscurity, could still be interpreted in a Catholic way. It is significant that when the 1549 Book came to be revised, at every point where Gardiner had detected residual Catholicism the words were expunged; even the Canon itself was so rearranged as to exclude the remotest possibility of its being interpreted as a propitiatory sacrifice for the living and the dead.

Second, there were several who were urging Cranmer to proceed to produce a genuinely reformed formulary of worship. Peter Martyr's brief, and Martin Bucer's exhaustive, criticisms—as well as the examples of the liturgies devised on the model of Geneva by the superintendents of the "churches of the strangers," John à Lasco and Valérand Pullain, not to mention the urgent appeals of Nicholas Ridley—were pushing Cranmer in the direction of the Swiss.

Third, the more precipitate English members of the Reforming

---

[103] Gee and Hardy, *Documents*, p. 362.

[104] Yet its usefulness was much greater than might be supposed. It lived on partly in the revised rite of 1552 and in its reappropriation in 1559. It was regarded as a Eucharistic norm by English and Scottish High Churchmen. The Scots produced the mislabeled "Laudian Liturgy" of 1637 (cf. Gordon Donaldson, *The Making of the Scottish Prayer Book of 1637*), and were influenced by the 1549 prayer-book, as was the English revision of 1661 and as were the Non-Jurors from 1688. The Scottish Episcopal Church bishops consecrated Samuel Seabury the first bishop of the Protestant Episcopal Church of the United States on the condition that the American church would use the Scottish Communion Order, which owed more to the Prayer Book of 1549 than to its successor of 1552.

party, notably Ridley who moved from Rochester to London in April 1550, and Hooper who was consecrated bishop of Gloucester on March 8, 1551 after scrupling the vestments, were wholly dissatisfied with the rubrics of the 1549 book. Ridley, first on his own authority and later with the backing of the Council, had demanded that all altars be removed in the churches of his diocese, insisting that altars were appropriate only for the renewal of a sacrifice, whereas holy tables befitted the celebration of the reformed rite of the Lord's Supper. Hooper was also eager to sweep away the "altars of Baal," along with all vestments and ceremonies associated with the old sacrificing priests. There were also great practical difficulties involved in these ceremonial changes, for which the old rubrics were unable to provide any guidance. The people were used to kneeling before the altar at Communion, but what was the appropriate posture in front of a holy table? The priest had previously been told to stand before the middle of the altar fixed at the east end of the choir, but where should he stand at a movable table placed either at the entrance to the chancel or even in the nave of the church?[105] To compound the rubrical problems, it was well known that conservative priests had continued to offer what was in effect an English Mass by retaining the old ceremonial, including many signs and gestures not comprehensively excluded by the rubrics of 1549.[106] Cumulatively these considerations built up a head of reforming pressure which was finally released in 1552. Also, the political fall of Somerset and his replacement by the radical Protestant Northumberland, a man of violence, facilitated the changes.

Now the only difficulty remaining was the government's need to explain its about-face and how a good rite it had authorised was being abolished after only three years' use. In fact, the First Prayer Book was eulogised in the opening paragraph of the second Act of Uniformity, but it was added that the sensuality and ignorance of God on the part of so many who refused to attend parochial worship made a second reformation necessary, a revision of the First Prayer Book to make it, "more earnest and fit to stir Christian people to the true honouring of Almighty God."[107] To this end the

---

[105] Proctor and Frere, *New History*, pp. 69-70.

[106] *Ibid.*, p. 64. Bucer early in 1551 wrote: "Some turn the prescribed form of service into a mere papistical abuse." Cited Gasquet and Bishop, *Edward VI*, p. 269.

[107] Gee and Hardy, *Documents*, pp. 370-71. These reasons do not square with the eulogy of the First Prayer Book in the opening paragraph of the Act, which

First Prayer Book was perused, explained, and perfected in the Second Prayer Book, and an Ordinal was added.

Differences between the two books will be examined first in the Occasional Offices, then in the two Daily Offices, and, finally, in the Communion Order. Almost all that survived from the ancient baptismal office in the 1549 order was abandoned; the exorcism, the white vesture put on the child as a token of innocency after baptism, the anointing, and the triple renunciation and profession were reduced to a single renunciation and profession, while the sign of the cross was made on the child's forehead but no longer also on its breast. The service of Confirmation in 1552 eliminated the bishop's signing each child on the forehead with the cross (which was appropriately foreshadowed by the signation of the cross at baptism, retained in the 1552 order of Baptism and inconsistently excluded from the Order of Confirmation), but keeps, as it must, his laying his hand upon the head of each child. However, an excellent, brief new prayer was introduced: "Defende, O lord, this child with thy heauenly grace, that he may continue thine for euer, and dayly encrease in thy holy spirite more and more, until he come unto thy euerlastyng kyngdom."[108] In the burial service of 1549 allowance was made for "the celebration of Holy Communion when there is a burial of the dead." This was eliminated from the Burial Order of the 1552 book. References to an intermediate state are removed and a lengthy service is reduced without any theological loss. One prayer, thanking God for the deliverance of the deceased person from this world, ends much more felicitously in the revised version: "beseching thee, that it maye please thee of thy gracious goodnesse, shortely to accomplyssh the noumbre of thyne electe, and to hasten thy kingdome, that we with this our brother, and al other departed in the true faith of thy holy name, maye haue our perfect consummacion and blisse, both in body and soule, in thy eternal and euerlastyng glory." The main differences are the elimination of Catholic vestiges in doctrine or practice, the reduction of ceremonies, the abbreviation of unduly long forms, and the improvement of language for the sake of clarity. The additions are generally of a didactic or hortatory character.

---

speaks of it as "a very godly order" in the vernacular, "agreeable to the word of God and the primitive Church, very comfortable to all good people desiring to live in Christian conversation . . ." (ibid., p. 369). If it was so admirable what was the need of revision?

108 All references to the 1552 prayer-book are to the Grafton impression of August 1552 (S.T.C. 16283) in the Huntington Library. This reference is to fol. 112.

Matins and evensong were retitled "morning prayer" and "evening prayer." Each of the Daily Offices had a lengthy introduction of a pentitential character prefixed to it, that consisted of a selection of 12 scriptural sentences, a short exhortation to the confession of sins, which gave an admirable summary of the reasons for worship,[109] after which followed the general confession and absolution. While it might be argued that the introduction to the Daily Offices was excessively introspective, especially when some of the exaggerated affirmations of the General Confession are remembered, and too pentitential for all times and seasons. Nonetheless, it served as a useful preparation for worship and as a transition from the street to the sanctuary.

The most radical revision and reconstruction was undertaken on the Order for the "Lordes Supper or Holye Communion." It is noted that there was a change in the title and that "commonly called the Masse" was eliminated. The term "offertory" was removed, and the terms "table" and "Lord's table" were substituted for "altar." The rubrics were radically changed. The curious and complicated rubric referring to the provision of bread and wine by families, together with a communicant from each family in turn, was eliminated. No direction was given as to the time when the bread and wine should be placed on the table. Ordinary bread was to be used instead of the unleavened bread. The rubric directing the minister to take sufficient bread and wine for the number of communicants disappeared. Bucer had called attention to the way many priests inclined their heads over the bread and wine during the prayer of consecration as if they longed for a mutation of them, and particularly asked "that the little black crosses and the rubric about taking the bread and wine into the hands should be removed from the book as well as the prayer for the blessing and sanctifying the bread and wine."[110] All these requests were fulfilled. The previous provision that a priest in a cope should on Wednesdays and Fridays say the first part of the Communion office was abolished. It was now directed that the table for the Communion stand in the body of the church and that the minister place himself at the north end of the table. Finally, a long rubric on kneeling, thereafter commonly called the "black rubric," was issued as a royal proclamation through the insistence of John Knox after some copies of the

---

[109] These were: "humbly to knowledge our synnes before God," "to rendre thanckes . . . ," "to sette furth hys moste worthie praise, to heare his mose holy worde, and to aske those thynges whiche be requisite and necessarie, as wel for the bodye as the soule." 1552 Prayer Book, fol. 1 verso.

[110] *Censura*, p. 472.

revised book had already been printed.[111] The rubric denied that kneeling at the Sacrament was not to be interpreted as if "any adoracion is doone, or oughte to bee doone, eyther unto the Sacramentall bread or wyne there bodily receyued, or unto anye reall and essencial presence there beeyng of Christ's naturall fleshe and bloude."[112] All vestments were abolished except for the episcopal rochet and surplice.

It should also be noted that "low Mass" became the norm in the revision, as singing was discouraged. The Introit, the response to the Announcement of the Gospel, the *Osanna* and *Benedictus,* the "Peace of the Lord" and "Christ our Paschal Lamb," the *Agnus Dei,* and the "Postcommunion" were omitted. All that was left that was required to be sung was the Epistle, Gospel, and *Gloria in excelsis.* Proof that "low Mass" was the new model can be seen in the fact that the Epistle and Gospel were assigned to the priest alone.

The most significant changes in the Communion rite, however, were changes in the order of the items, as may be seen in the diagram on Communion order, which compares the orders of 1549 and 1552. Items whose order was changed are italicised.

Communion Order

1549	1552
Sermon	Sermon
	Offertory
	Intercession for living
Exhortation	Exhortation
	Penitential preparation
Offertory	
Preface and Sanctus	Preface and Sanctus
	Prayer of Humble Access
Intercession for living	
Consecration	Consecration
	Communion
Oblation	
Lord's Prayer	Lord's Prayer
Penitential preparation	
Prayer of Humble Access	
Communion	
Thanksgiving	*Oblation,* or Thanksgiving

[111] For its history see R. W. Dixon, *History of the Church of England,* 6 vols., III, 475ff.

[112] 1552 Prayer Book, fol. 102.

In comparing the first with the second Communion office it is quite obvious that the order of 1549 fairly closely resembled the shape and order of the Sarum Use of the medieval Mass, while the 1552 order was so altered as to bear no shadow of a semblance with the order of the Mass. It seems as if Cranmer was determined to eliminate all those parts of the 1549 rite that Gardiner had claimed were patently orthodox Catholic. The intercession was removed from any connection with the Consecration, and the Prayer for the Dead was omitted; no one could argue this was intended as a propitiatory sacrifice for the living and the dead.

The prayer for the sanctification of the elements, which Gardiner had approved as orthodox, was replaced by a form designed, as Bucer wished, to avoid the supposedly superstitious notion of consecration. But in the attempt to avoid Romanism it had unwittingly become more Romanist than ever, for it was perpetuating the medieval scholastic belief that consecration came through the repetition of the Dominical words in the Institution narrative! The Prayer of Humble Access ("We do not presume to come to this thy table"), which previously came immediately before the Consecration (though the term was not used in 1549 or 1552), where it could not be referred to the Eucharistic elements and from the phrase "in these holy misteries," was expunged. The *Benedictus* was deleted from the *Sanctus* presumably because it might imply the most realistic corporal descent into the elements. The very brief *anamnesis* of 1549 was entirely abolished, and sadly abbreviated remnants at the end of the 1549 Canon were reworded and made an alternative to the prayer of thanksgiving which was also revised slightly. Even the Lord's Prayer was placed after the Communion, possibly lest no one should misinterpret the petition for daily bread as having any Eucharistic reference. The last criticism of Gardiner was met with the formulas of administration, which were highly subjective and strongly Memorialist. The words at the delivery of the wine, for example, were: "Drynke this in remembraunce that Christes bloude was shedde for the, and be thankful."[113] There was no direction for the preparation of the elements, presumably because this might lead to the reintroduction of the old conception of offertory which Cranmer was eager to eliminate from the rite. Even more disturbing was the absence of directions for fraction and libation. Indeed, the fear of superstition had itself become a superstition with Cranmer, so that almost every

---

[113] *Ibid.*, fol. 100.

element of the numinous was excluded from the rite. Typical, for instance, was the insistence that ordinary bread rather than wafers was to be used for the Communion, and that the minister might take home whatever was left over.

It is easier to criticise this rite than to defend it. It was anathema to High Churchmen, while it was perhaps excessively eulogised by Low Churchmen and ultra-Protestant evangelicals in the Anglican fold. The rite tried to model itself more on the New Testament account of the Last Supper than on ancient traditions. Also, what is often called an iconoclastic oddity, its transference of the *Gloria in excelsis* as a climactic post-Communion thanksgiving may have been a stroke of genius.[114] Since in a true Eucharist in which the people of God really participate in the eschatological banquet, the act of communion is the climax; all that usually follows afterwards is necessarily an anti-climax. Cranmer, however, prevented such a lowering of the spirits by this lyrical act of superabundant praise. Finally, if Cranmer's theological outlook, with its increasing Protestantism, is accepted, the Prayer Book of 1552 may indeed be—in words of Gregory Dix—"not a disordered attempt at a catholic rite, but the only effective attempt ever made to give liturgical expression to the doctrine of 'justification by faith alone.' "[115] Cranmer had in fact restructured the Offertory to conform with his view that, "the humble confession of all penitent hearts, their knowledging of Christ's benefits, their thanksgiving for the same, their faith and consolation in Christ, their humble submission . . . to God's will and commandments, is a sacrifice of laud and praise."[116] This is, however, far from being a typical assessment of the 1552 rite. More common is the view of Proctor and Frere, that it was an "illstarred book" and that with it "English religion reached its low water mark."[117]

Some light is thrown on the character of the 1552 Book of Common Prayer by a consideration of the sources Cranmer and his unknown collaborators used. Since the book was a revision, naturally enough the First Prayer Book was the primary source. Bucer's careful and detailed *Censura* was another important source; while his conservative theological ideas proved unacceptable, about two-

[114] See *Walter Howard Frere: A Collection of his papers on Liturgical and Historical Subjects*, ed. J. H. Arnold and E.G.P. Wyatt, Alcuin Club Collections, no. 35, p. 193.

[115] *Shape of Liturgy*, p. 672.

[116] *Defence of the True and Catholick Doctrine of the Sacrament*, in *The Remains of Thomas Cranmer*, ed. Henry Jenkyns, 4 vols., II, 459.

[117] *New History*, p. 85.

thirds of his objections were satisfied.[118] His friend, Peter Martyr, a former Augustinian canon and Regius Professor of Divinity at Oxford, made an independent critique of the 1549 book on the basis of a partial translation of it into Latin by Cheke; but when he saw the fuller work of Bucer he concurred with all of Bucer's criticism. He did, however, object to the rubric permitting the reservation of the Sacrament for communicating the sick.[119] All Gardiner's commendations of places in the rite where a Catholic interpretation of the 1549 rite was possible were taken as criticisms, and, as we have seen, were entirely altered by rephrasing or repositioning.

Another possible source of influence must be considered, where influence is hard to detect. This influence, if proven, demonstrates that Calvinist rather than Lutheran rites were looked to for models of the 1552 book. The first was the *Liturgia Sacra seu Ritus Ministerii in ecclesia peregrinorum profugorum propter Euangelium Christi Argentinae. Adiecta est ad finem breuis Apologia pro hac Liturgia per Valerandum Pollanum Flandrum*, published in London on February 23, 1551. This is the liturgy that was used by the French and Flemish congregation which had migrated from Strassburg and had been given the use of the buildings of Glastonbury Abbey by the Protector, Somerset. The interest of the liturgy is that it had connections with both Bucer and Calvin. Pullain had, in fact, succeeded Calvin as the minister (with one intervening link) of the *ecclesiola gallicana*, and Calvin had translated and paraphrased for the French reformed congregation in Strassburg the service which Bucer had developed for the German Reformed congregation in Strassburg.[120] Considering that the Archbishop of Canterbury had to oversee the "churches of the strangers" in the realm and that he was deeply involved in liturgical revision, it would be surprising if Cranmer had not scrutinised the liturgy more out of delight than from a sense of duty.

Proctor and Frere conclude that the similarity between the 1552 Prayer Book and the *Liturgia Sacra* (and also à Lasco's *Forma ac Ratio tota ecclesiastici Ministerii in peregrinorum, potissimum uero Germanorum Ecclesia*, a rite prepared for the Emden refugees worshipping in Austin Friars in London, and which originated

118 Brightman, *English Rite*, book I, p. cxlv.
119 *Ibid.*, p. cxliv.
120 For the history of this rite see A. Erichson, *Die Calvinische und die Altstrassburgische Gottesdienstordnung*; and E. Doumergue, *Jean Calvin*, 7 vols., II, 494f.

with Farel, the first Genevan reformer and colleague of Calvin)[121] is collateral, not lineal.[122] But this assessment is difficult to maintain if one examines the Latin of Pullain and the English of Cranmer side by side in additions that were made for the first time in the rite of 1552.

The real novelty in the Daily Offices was the penitential introduction that was added. It is precisely in the general confession and in the following absolution that the interdependence of ideas and words can be shown. Pullain's *tuas leges sanctissimas assidue transgredimur* was exactly paralleled by "we haue offended against thy holy lawes"; Pullain's *agnoscimus . . . peccatores esse nos miseros* becomes "us miserable offendours." Furthermore, it may well be that the inclusion of the recitation by the minister of the Decalogue in the Communion Office, to which the people made a response, originated in Pullain's *Liturgia Sacra*, or in another Swiss Church Order of Calvinist provenance through the example of Bishop Hooper of Gloucester and Worcester. What *is* clear is that the final petition of the people, which includes the *Kyrie* and reads, "Lorde, haue mercye upō us, & write al these thy lawes in our hartes, we beseche the," could easily have come from Pullain's *dignare cordibus nostris eam ito tuo spirito inscribere*.[123] It is possible that the words in the absolution in the Daily Offices, referring to God—"whiche desireth not the deathe of a synner, but rather that he maye tourne from his wickednesse, and liue"—find their origin in à Lasco's *Forma ac Ratio*, where there appears *neque amplius velis mortem peccatoris sed potius convertatur et vivat*.[124] *The Pious Consultation* of Archbishop Hermann von Wied of Cologne also continued to influence the revision.

If the major influences on the 1549 rite were Roman and Lutheran, the chief impact on the 1552 rites was Reformed. This is not a revolutionary conclusion, because the iconoclastic nature of the revision is evident. What is not commonly understood, however, is that the Eucharistic theology that dominates the revised rite may well be not low Zwingli but high Calvin.[125] If the Eastern

---

121 The Farel directory is reprinted in J. G. Baum, *Première Liturgie des églises reformées de France de l'an 1533*.

122 Proctor and Frere, *New History*, p. 90.

123 *Ibid.*, pp. 86-88, where the relevant passages from the rite of Pullain are cited.

124 *Ibid.*, pp. 89-90, where the relevant material from the à Lasco rite can be found.

125 Among Anglicans C. W. Dugmore, *The Mass and the English Reformers*, and Peter Brooks, *Thomas Cranmer's Doctrine of the Eucharist*, are the only historians known to me who stress that Cranmer's doctrine of the Eucharist was a

invocation of the Holy Spirit was formally excluded—because Gardiner had argued that this clearly implied a mutation of the elements—it was clearly understood that the Holy Spirit made the spiritual presence of Christ in the sacrament possible, with all His benefits. It was equally understood that the same Holy Spirit created and maintained the gift of faith and united in the *vinculum caritatis* the Head and the members of the church. With such an august belief, the ceremonial could afford, like the rite itself, to be simple. It is only simple for those who have interpreted it through a reductionistic Memorialism, in which Christ is remembered as a martyr, not as the living and transforming Lord. We do well to remember that Cranmer died for an affirmation, not a negation. Although his rite of 1552 was only to endure for a year before the Marian Reaction swept it away, it was revived in 1559 by Queen Elizabeth. It, or its predecessor, has remained the sum and substance of Anglican worship ever since.

6. *The Elizabethan Prayer Book of 1559*

The third and least creative of the Tudor Books of Common Prayer was the Elizabethan Prayer Book of 1559, yet it was the one that lasted the longest. In fact, it was only modified in the most minimal way until the revision at the Restoration in 1661. It is in the Elizabethan setting that we have the best opportunity to see its long-term qualities and its inherent weaknesses.

On the accession of Elizabeth November 17, 1558, the people were readier to accept Protestantism than they had been in the days of Henry VIII or Edward VI. It was expected that the prayer-book would be restored and the Sarum Use under Mary set aside. On December 27 the queen issued a proclamation prohibiting any change in the existing order, "until consultation may be had by Parliament." As an interim arrangement an exception was made for reading the Gospel and the Epistle of the day in English, and for the recitation of the English Litany (the only vernacular form of worship permitted under Queen Mary) as said in the Queen's Chapel. The clause for deliverance, "from the tyranny of the bishop of Rome and his detestable enormities," was omitted from the printed edition of the Litany issued January 1, 1559. According

high Reformed doctrine, rather than a low Reformed one. These views, however, have been challenged by T. M. Parker in the *Journal of Theological Studies*, vol. 12, pt. 1 (1961) and C. C. Richardson in the same journal, vol. 16, pt. 2 (1965).

to E. C. Ratcliff,[126] there is some reason to think that two proposals were made for appropriate rites, the first for the restoration of the rite of 1549, and the second for the one similar to that used by the congregation of English emigrants in Frankfort, where a famous liturgical war[127] had broken out among the Marian exiles between the Coxians, who supported the 1552 prayer-book, and the Knoxians, who wanted a more Genevan form.

The prayer-book eventually established by the Elizabethan Act of Uniformity of April 1559 was the Second Prayer Book of 1552, but with three specific important changes. An additional table of lessons for Sundays, festivals, and holy days was provided. In the Eucharist an attempt at comprehension and inclusion of the differing viewpoints was made, which might be confusing theologically, but which was admirable in its sense of charity. The objective and subjective emphases of the Communion were combined by amalgamating the forms of administration of 1549 and 1552 so that at the delivery of the consecrated bread the words are: "The body of our Lord Jesus Christ which was geuen for thee, preserue thy body and soule into euerlasting life: and take and eate this, in remembraunce that Christ died for thee, and feede on hym in thy hearte by fayth, wyth thankes geuynge." The Litany's form was not that of 1552, but was the form used in the Royal Chapel, in which the anti-Papal clause was removed. The infamous black rubric was excised, and, although this had not been hinted at in the Act of Uniformity when the 1559 book appeared, it contained a new rubric ordering the use of the vesture worn in "the seconde yeare of the reyne of King Edward the VI." This was intended to cover the use of the Mass vestments. In practice, however, the usual vesture was the surplice, over which was worn a cope in the Queen's Chapel and in some cathedral and collegiate churches, in accordance with the rubric of 1549.

Several unauthorised changes in worship were made during Elizabeth's reign.[128] There was no uniform text of the Book of

---

126 The booke of common prayer of the Churche of England: its making and versions, p. 19.

127 A Brief Discourse of the Troubles at Frankfort, 1554-1558, ed. E. Arber.

128 There was an inconsistency in requirements. The queen's Injunctions demanded the use of wafer bread at the Communion, "of the same fineness and fashion round, though somewhat bigger in compass and thickness, as the usual bread and wafer, heretofore named singing cakes which served for the use of the private Mass." (Frere and Kennedy, Visitation Articles, III, 28.) On the other hand, the prayer-book directed the use of "bread such as is usual to be eaten." Liturgies and Occasional Forms of Prayer set forth in the Reign of Queen Elizabeth, ed. W. K. Clay, p. 198.

Common Prayer issued. The texts printed by Jugge and Cawood, on the one hand, and Grafton, on the other, were not themselves uniform, nor were they consistent with each other. One major unauthorised change was made in the collect for St. Mark's Day (involving an inversion of the order). The new ritual "settlement" combined the Act of Uniformity, the new prayer-book, and the Royal *Injunctions* of 1559 (which repeated 26 of the 38 Injunctions of 1547, together with 29 new ones). But even these regulations were insufficient to bring order to the general ceremonial chaos, so that Archbishop Parker's *Advertisements* were issued for his own province without the formal royal consent.[129] The queen, only 18 months after coming to the throne, ordered Parker and his advisors to prepare a new table of lessons and Kalendar. In 1563 the Convocation of Canterbury sanctioned the production of a further Book of Homilies which included 20 sermons, to which another was added in 1571 by Convocation, entitled "Against Disobedience and wilful Rebellion." The latter was occasioned by the uprising in the north in November-December 1569. Haphazard as the arrangement may seem, Elizabeth, in fact, jealously preserved her prerogatives as "Supreme Governor" of the Church of England and used her bishops not only as licensers of all books printed but also to keep a tight rein on their clergy. The clergy were expected to be the maintainers of loyalty to the throne, the makers of morale, and the upholders of "degree" and stability in society as much as judges were. Although there was a shortage of preachers for the first 20 years of her reign, those who preached were carefully licensed, and muzzled if they dared to speak out of turn.[130] The

[129] The precise authority for the Ornaments Rubric and its relation to the "Advertisements" of 1566 is still a controversial question. The rubric is the ruling placed in the 1559 prayer-book at the beginning of the Order for Morning and Evening Prayer, which requires that the Ornaments of the Church and Ministers shall be those in use "by the authority of the Parliament in the second year of the reign of King Edward VI." The Act of Uniformity of 1559, however, to which the prayer-book was attached, added the qualification that such use should continue "until other order shall be therein taken by the authority of the Queen's Majesty with the advice of her Commissioners appointed and authorized under the great seal of England for causes ecclesiastical, or of the Metropolitan of this realm." The only explicit statement about the ornaments is in the Prayer Book of 1549, but it was produced in the third (not the second) year of Edward VI. The Judicial Committee of the Privy Council have on two occasions ruled that Parker's "Advertisements" were the "other order" foreshadowed in the Act. This ruling has been widely disputed because the "Advertisements" had not statutory authority and because they could not be regarded as overriding the later reenactment of the rubric by Parliament in 1604 and 1662. See J. T. Micklethwaite, *The Ornaments of the Rubric*.

[130] W.P.M. Kennedy, in *Elizabethan Episcopal Administration*, 3 vols., I, cvi, defines preaching as "a ministerial activity which was the most uniformly controlled of all, as it was made the active handmaiden of Elizabethan state-craft."

Liturgy was for Queen Elizabeth the way to maintain religious uniformity in her realm, a political mechanism for the manufacturing of loyalty. But she was pitiless toward those who marched to the beat of a different drummer, or those whose consciences would not allow them to worship according to the Book of Common Prayer, whether Catholic or Puritan.[131]

When the novelty of a vernacular rite had worn off, and the reading of printed homilies rather than the preaching of unpredictable sermons was the order on Sunday (as it was for the first 20 years of Elizabeth's reign), and now that the Anglican services were set off by so little ceremony and symbolism, church attendance must have been excessively dull, especially with the lack of other interesting activities on Sundays. It should be remembered that a large number of people were there by compulsion, not by choice, that the services were long and routine, and that most churches were crowded. In such circumstances it is not surprising that many should find the worship boring, or that misbehaviour and shouting, not to mention scuffling, were frequent interruptions of the service. Men talked, laughed, cleared their throats, slept and snored, and refused to stand up for the Creed or the Gospel, to turn to the East or to bow at the name of Jesus. The accusation against William Hills of the parish of Holton St. Mary in Suffolk, that he "used in tyme of devine service open and lowde speeches to the disturbance of the minister"[132] seems characteristic of the time.

Females were equally adept at interrupting worship, whether it was Mary Knights of Bythburgh in Suffolk, who "do bring maistifs to church into the stoole with her wherebie the parishioners cannot haue their seats," or Jane Buckenham, who entered church one Sunday and abused the parson, "calling him blacke sutty mowthed knave, to the greate disgrace of his callinge."[133] There is one recorded case in which two women brawled in church over their right to sit in a certain seat. The Southwell Act Books recorded for February 16, 1587 that a woman of Nottinghamshire, Joan Halome, had alleged, "that the . . . said Luce Wentworth did give the occasion of making the disturbance in the churches, for that she would not kepe her place, where she was first sett; but came ouer her backe and marred her apparel in the stall, where she was

---

131 E. C. Ratcliff, Book of Common Prayer, p. 19: "The Elizabethan Prayer Book was equally obnoxious to Papists and to Puritans."
132 A. Tindal Hart, *The Man in the Pew, 1558-1660*, p. 130.
133 *Ibid.*

sett. Wherappon the saide Johanne Halome did pricke the said Lucie with a pynne."[134]

We can only suppose that it was sheer monotony that drove some of the less patient members of the captive congregations to high jinks, such as those described in the visitation articles of the Elizabethan bishops. W.P.M. Kennedy does not exaggerate when he says, from a thorough examination of episcopal injunctions and visitation articles of the Elizabethan period, that "there was a disposition . . . to treat the Sunday services as fit subject for merriment, and to turn the parish church into either a parochial club, or a controversial meeting."[135] In the parishes of the huge diocese of Coventry and Lichfield the churchwardens, along with the clergy, were instructed to choose four to eight well-built men in each parish who would take an oath to maintain order during the services. These "orderlies" paced the aisles during services with a monitory white wand in their hands. If the misbehaving were impenitent or refractory, the "two honestest" of the orderlies frogmarched them to the chancel door and made them stand facing the people for 15 minutes.[136]

It doesn't seem to fit the romantic picture of "Good Queen Bess" and her golden days, but the village churches, as is apparent from the numerous visitation returns from the countryside, were in a ruinous condition. As a consequence of destruction and neglect, the churches had "damp green walls, rotting earth floors, and gaping windows."[137] The country people, always conservative, were tired of the disruptive religious changes; their spirits had been shaken by the iconoclasm of the returning Genevan exiles, the lack of energy or money on the part of clergy and churchwardens, and the sheer greed or indifference of the lay impropriators and farmers of the rectory. One did not expect color or pageantry in Elizabethan Anglicanism, for, as William Harrison wrote, "all images, shrines, tabernacles, roodlofts, and monuments of idolatrie are removed, taken down and defaced; onelie the stories in glasse windowes excepted, which for want of sufficient store of new stuffe . . . are not altogither abolished in most places at once, but by little and little suffered to decaie, that white glasse may be provided and set

---

[134] *Ibid.*, p. 131.
[135] *English Life under Queen Elizabeth*, p. 128.
[136] *Calendar of State Papers, Domestic*, XXXVI, 41 (13).
[137] A. Tindal Hart, *The Country Clergy in Elizabethan and Stuart Times, 1558-1660*, p. 40.

up in their roomes."[138] It soon reached the point where one expected a bare simplicity but was grateful to find that the church walls were newly whitewashed and that the earth floor had recently been covered with straw or rushes to make kneeling easier.

An interesting description of English religion in general and worship in particular is given in Harrison's *Description of England*, written from the standpoint of a loyal Anglican with some Puritan, but no Separatist, tendencies. Acknowledging that there was a substantial lack of pastors, so that every parish could not have one, there was also, he affirmed, a dearth of preaching, so that besides the four sermons per annum there were homilies read in church, "by the curate of meane vnderstanding."[139] His account of Sunday worship (daily offices and Communion) is worth citing in its entirety:

> And after a certeine number of psalmes read, which are limited according to the dates of the month, for morning and euening praier, we haue two lessons, wherof the first is taken out of the old testament, the second out of the new; and of these latter, that in the morning is out of the gospels, the other in the after-noone, out of some of the epistles. After morning praier also we haue the letanie and suffrages, an inuocation in mine opinion not deuised without the great assistance of the spirit of God, although manie curious min-sicke persons vtterlie condemne it as superstitious, and sauor-ing of coniuration and sorcerie.
>
> This being doone, we proceed vnto the communion, if anie communicants be to receiue the eucharist; if not we read the decalog, epistle and gospell, with the Nicene creed (of some in derision called the drie communion), and then proceed vnto an homilie or sermon, which hath a psalme before and after it, and finallie vnto the baptisme of such infants as on euerie sabaoth daye (if occasion so require) are brought vnto the churches; and thus is the forenoone bestowed. In the after-noone likewise we meet againe, and after the psalmes and lessons ended, we haue commonlie a sermon, or at the least-wise our youth catechised by the space of an houre. And thus do we spend the sabaoth daie in good and godlie exercises,

---

[138] *Harrison's Description of England in Shakespere's Youth*, ed. F. J. Furnivall, 2 vols., I, 32.
[139] *Ibid.*, p. 28.

all doone in the vulgar tong, that each one present may heare and vnderstand the same. . . .[140]

This picture of Elizabethan worship in 1577 can be filled out from the information in the rubrics of the 1559 prayer-book and the norm that is suggested by consideration of the deviations from it recorded in episcopal visitations and injunctions. Harrison only hinted at two of the defects in the worship of his time.

The clergy were under a daily obligation to say the services of morning and evening prayer, "in a loud voice" and "in the accustomed place of the church, chapel, or chauncel, except it be otherwise determined by the ordinary of the place." When the services were public the clergyman was to ring a bell to give the well-disposed good warning. The Litany was to be said on Sundays, Wednesdays, and Fridays. Those who intended to communicate at the Lord's Supper or Holy Communion were requested to give their names to the curate, whose duty it was to warn notoriously wicked persons and forbid them to approach the Lord's table until they had openly declared their repentance and amendment, and to reject those unreconciled in a quarrel until penitent and prepared to return to amity.

The Lord's table, covered with a white linen cloth at times of Communion, was "to stand in the body of the church, or in the chancel where morning and evening prayer be appointed to be said." The "priest standing on the north side" was to begin the rite. After the offertory it was the duty of the churchwardens to gather "the devotion of the people and put the same into the poor men's box." On the offering days—Christmas, Easter, St. John the Baptist, and St. Michael—every man and woman was ordered to pay the accustomed dues. After the Nicene Creed the priest announced the holy days and fasting days of the ensuing week. On holy days, when there was no Communion, the "ante-communion" service, with the reading of a homily, was prescribed. No celebration of Holy Communion was to take place "except there be a good number to communicate with the priest according to his discretion." His discretion was restricted by the rubric "and if there be not above twenty persons in the parish of discretion to receive the Communion, yet there shall be no Communion except four, or three at the least communicate with the priest." In cathedrals or collegiate churches weekly Communion was the minimum laid down for priests and

[140] *Ibid.*, pp. 29-30.

deacons. The bread had to be "such as is usual to be eaten at table with other meats, but the best and purest white bread that conveniently may be gotten." The bread and wine were to be paid for by the parish through the churchwardens. As Communion attendance became larger the old chalices (in which it was usual for only the priest to communicate) were ordered to be melted down to produce Communion cups with wider and deeper bowls, looking like inverted bells.[141] Communicants knelt to receive at the holy table or altar, and every parishioner was ordered to receive Communion at least three times a year, of which Easter was one.

Baptism was to be administered on Sundays and holy days, immediately following the last lesson at morning or evening prayer. Provision was to be made for godfathers and godmothers. The child was to be dipped in the font (or, if it were weak, water was to be poured on it[142]) and the forehead was to be signed with the sign of the cross. In special cases private Baptism could be arranged.

Confirmation according to the approved rite was to be administered to those who could repeat in English the Creed, the Lord's Prayer, and the Ten Commandments, and who knew the short Catechism which was printed with the Order for Confirmation in the Elizabethan Prayer Book.

Banns were to be published on three consecutive Sundays or holy days; provision was made for Communion at a marriage. An order was provided for the visitation of the sick, with an opportunity for private Confession and Absolution. Further, if opportunity and the condition of the sick person allowed, and there were sufficient friends and neighbours to join in, a private celebration of Holy Communion was possible. A burial service (in which, it may be noted, it became increasingly common to include a sermon,[143] and not only for distinguished deceased persons), a form for the Churching of Women, and a Commination against Sinners (to be used at different times of the year) concluded the

141 The contrast of the old and the new is perfectly exemplified in the marginal illustration to *A Booke of Christian Prayers*, printed by John Day in 1578 (see illustrations, Pl. 11). Note at the bottom of the picture the deep, bell-shaped Protestant communion cup and the "idolatrous" Catholic chalice depicted in the lefthand margin, along with rosary beads, candlestick, monstrance, episcopal rochet and crucifix.

142 Another illustration reproduced from *A Booke of Christian Prayers* depicts an Elizabethan baptismal ceremony. The child, wrapped in swaddling bands, is presumably weak, since the clergyman appears to have poured water over it, rather than dipped it.

143 A. F. Herr, *The Elizabethan Sermon, A Survey and Bibliography*, p. 46.

different public services of the Church of England in Elizabethan days.[144]

Harrison's description and its amplification fail, however, to do more than mention two problems of Elizabethan worship. The first was insufficient amount of preaching. Many country parishes must have gone month after month hearing only a homily; four sermons a year, often the maximum, was a spare diet of the word of God. As Elizabeth's reign went into its third decade the number of preachers increased considerably, until by the end of the reign there were many good preachers and two outstanding ones—the brilliant Lancelot Andrewes and the popular Henry Smith. The increase in the number of sermons was undoubtedly stimulated by Puritan criticism of nonpreaching parsons as no more than "dumbe dogges," the admirable examples Puritan ministers provided of faithful expository preaching, and the excellent Puritan training schools for preaching ("prophesyings"[145]).

If there ever was an ideal of a weekly Communion, it soon lapsed. The second weakness of Anglican worship during this period was infrequent celebration of Communion. The most frequent directive from the bishops is that there must be "sufficient number of celebrations for the parishioners to receive three times in the year at the least—Easter being one."[146] In larger city or county town parishes the ideal seems to have been that of a monthly communion.[147] But there was a great abyss between the ideal and the real.

We have seen that there was a Puritan supplementation of Anglican worship by further religious exercises such as "prophesyings." Similarly there was an undoubted Catholic supplementation of worship, either by priests with strong inclinations toward older ways or by pious laity who had not ceased to believe in the religious practices of their youth. The clergy must frequently have aided their parishioners in maintaining the old devotional practises.

[144] For much of the material of the summary of worship according to the Book of Common Prayer in the previous five paragraphs, I am indebted to Kennedy, *Elizabethan Episcopal Administration*, I, xxxviii-xl.

[145] "Prophesyings" were meetings of ministers for the study, discussion, and exposition of scripture. The meetings served as a means of educating the clergy homiletically and for disseminating Puritan views. They originated in the Swiss and Rhenish cities (where the Marian Exiles learned their value). (See Leonard J. Trinterud, "The Origins of Puritanism," in *Church History*, XX [1951], no. 1, p. 46. They were held in England as early as 1564 and became very popular in the next decade.

[146] See Frere and Kennedy, *Visitation Articles and Injunctions*, III, 275, 307, 337.

[147] *Ibid.*, III, 167.

Some priests paid the holy table the same respect as they had the older altar, elevated the Host at the sacrament, and rang the passing bell more than was permitted. They would also be the priests who affected not to notice parishioners praying in the Lady Chapel, and who readily offered absolution to people whose consciences were not stilled by the all-too-convenient General Confession they were taught to repeat in the Book of Common Prayer.

The episcopal articles and presentment lists give us a glimpse of countrymen who hoarded the old vessels, images, and vestments in their cottages when the parish authorities wished to dispose of them, because they evoked precious memories and might even be needed again.[148] There was a deep, innate conservatism that attached people to religious objects and holy associations which could not be erased by official Protestant decree. P. M. Dawley has described these survivals: "People stole into the churches at night to pray, occasionally burning a candle stub on the feasts of Our Lady and the saints; they paused before the ruined churchyard crosses to utter the familiar intercessions. During the services they fingered their beads and could not keep their hands from the sign of the cross or penitent 'knockings' upon the breast. Through many a darkened village on the eve of All Souls' the bells of the parish tolled the forbidden remembrances of the departed, and by the time the churchwardens arrived at the church they found either the belfry ropes stilled, or a group gathered there too formidable to restrain."[149]

7. An Evaluation of Anglican Worship

There is much to criticise and admire in the Book of Common Prayer, though many of the criticisms are directed less to the book itself than the circumstances of its introduction.

The three Tudor Books of Common Prayer were a coerced formulary of worship intended for "soul control"—that is, to force the parson and people in a direction predetermined by their sovereign and Council. The blasphemous fact is (and it held wherever the doctrine of *cuius regio, ejus religio* was accepted) that Almighty God was to be honoured by a form of worship reinforced by the strongest temporal penalties. Every minister declining to use the

---

148 One Christopher Smyth of Pateley Bridge in Yorkshire was ordered to make a declaration penance for selling a New Testament in the Tyndale translation for 10 shillings, to be paid "whan masse shalbe said within this realme." *Tudor Parish Documents of the Diocese of York*, ed. J. S. Purvis, p. 150.
149 *John Whitgift and the English Reformation*, p. 119.

Prayer Book or using other forms of worship was subject to an ascending series of punishments, ending, for the third offense, in deprivation and life imprisonment. Any lay person depraving the book or obstructing the use of it was subject to heavy penalties. Absence from church on Sundays or holy days was punishable by a fine of 12 pence for each offense, the sum to be levied by the churchwardens for the use of the poor of the parish. The later Elizabethan Acts against Recusants and Puritans contained even stiffer penalties, including imprisonment and in extreme cases, death. Among those who used the Book of Common Prayer we are then to assume in every last parish a number of liturgical prisoners to whom the Prayer Book was anathema, either because its doctrine and ceremonies were insufficiently Catholic, or, in the case of the Puritans, for whom it was still too Catholic in retaining certain ceremonies and vestments. The Catholics believed that a memorial to Christ had replaced a sacrifice of His Body for the living and the dead, hence that the Anglican Eucharist was but the shadow of a shade. The Puritans deplored the retention in the prayer-book of such Catholic ceremonies as the signing of the cross in Baptism, the bowing at the name of Jesus, the turning to the East for the Creed, the kneeling for Communion, and the use of the ring in marriage. They also found the vestments as well as the retention of the episcopal form of government, supported by ecclesiastical courts, too great a deviation from primitive Christianity as they understood it. Moreover, Puritans and Separatists abhorred the very notion of a set form of liturgy as a "quenching of the Spirit," a denial of the Spirit-induced spontaneity of the New Covenant. Catholics and Puritans sensed in Anglican worship a lack of intensity and deep conviction. Neither group could think of bishops as *pastores pastorum*, but only as ecclesiastical superintendents of police, as the *Marprelate Tracts* so clearly show.[150] Compliant worshippers used the Book of Common Prayer; the conscientious worshippers of Roman or Puritan allegiance preferred their own more committed communities and ways of worship, but still had to attend the parish churches of the Church of England.

The English people greatly admired the mettle of Elizabeth, but found it difficult to determine her religious convictions as, at the beginning of her reign, she swayed between Catholicism and Protestantism. Jewel complained of the royal prevarication to Peter

---

[150] See William Pierce, *An historical introduction to the Marprelate Tracts; a chapter in the evolution of religious and civil liberty in England.*

Martyr in Zurich in a letter of April 2, 1559: "If the Queen would but banish it [the Mass] from her private chapel, the whole thing might be easily got rid of. Of such importance among us are the examples of princes."[151] Sampson, another former exile in Marian days, also wrote to Peter Martyr in 1560 of his disappointment that three recently consecrated bishops were to celebrate the Lord's Supper without a preparatory sermon, and "before the image of a crucifix, or at least not far from it, with candles, and habited in the golden vestments of the papacy. . . ."[152] Although she was "Supreme Governor" of the Church of England, Elizabeth left her Archbishop of Canterbury to undertake unpopular tasks such as enforcing Parker to issue the *Advertisements* to unify the use of vestments and ceremonial in the current rubrical anti-Nomianism. Yet in her high-handed way she had no qualms in sequestering Archbishop Grindal when he had the courage to refuse to suppress the "prophesyings" in 1577 at her behest. Since religion was essentially a matter of political expedience with the queen, it was no wonder that the bishops found it difficult to enforce her Prayer Book, especially as men and women of conscience so often turned out to be Recusants or Puritans.

In the 1559 prayer-book there was what political realists would have called "compromise" and what theologians, Catholic or Reformed, would have considered only confused thinking. The most notable liturgical example was the juxtaposition of a Catholic sentence (implying Christ's corporal presence in the Eucharist) with another (implying a doctrine of Memorialism) in the words of Administration, thus combining the 1549 and the 1552 formulas. Perhaps Jewel, the first apologist for the Church of England, was not far from the truth in seeing the "Elizabethan Settlement" as less a golden mean than a leaden mediocrity. After all, could Catholic church order be readily joined to Calvinist Articles of Faith, and a liturgy combining Catholic, Reformed, and Lutheran elements? The English Reformation, more the work of sovereigns and statesmen than of heroic reformers like Luther, Zwingli, and Calvin, has been a profound enigma to Catholics and Protestants alike: the Elizabethan Prayer Book, too, has a sphinx-like character for those who like theology and liturgy clear and consistent.

As I concluded earlier, worship according to the Book of Com-

---

[151] *Zurich Letters*, ed. Hastings Robinson, pp. 28-29.
[152] *Zurich Letters, 1558-1579*, ed. Hastings Robinson, pp. 63-64.

mon Prayer must often have seemed exceedingly boring. The disappearance of so much ceremonial splendor was an affront to the eyes and a deadening of the pictorial imagination. Strict instructions were given that "all shrines, covering of shrines, all tables, candlesticks, trindals, rolls of wax, pictures, paintings, and all other monuments of feigned miracles, pilgrimages, idolatry, and superstition" were to be completely destroyed, "so that there remain no memory of the same in walls, glasses, windows, or elsewhere, or repairing both the walls and the glasses."[153] Thus the medieval *biblia pauperum* were rudely snatched away from the illiterate, and even the literate are often grateful for "illustrations" of doctrine or duty. With these representations of divine persons or events also went many of the symbolical ceremonies which had made the ancient rites of baptism, ordination, and burial so memorable. The substitutes for these acts of aesthetic iconoclasm were the royal arms painted on boards, in which an improbably quiescent greyhound faces an incredibly tame lion as supporters, the monitory Decalogue painted on two wooden tablets, and the carved and painted tombs which the more successful Elizabethans built for the ancestor worship of the future, and which ironically were the liveliest artistic objects in the church. Nor were the popular metrical psalms which were introduced in the hobbling metre of Sternhold the musical equivalent of the Gregorian chanting, so austere in its solemnity and so apt to induce reverence. The irreverence at so many Elizabethan services is one indication of their dullness, a dullness compounded by aesthetic colour-blindness and cacophony.

A more serious and allied criticism of worship according to the prayer-book is that it was impersonal, formal, and artificial. The sense of the church as a great family divided by the narrow stream of death disappeared between the 1549 and the 1552 Prayer Books. While in the 1549 book there was a prayer for the whole state of Christ's church, in the 1552 book the prayer was restricted to the whole state of Christ's church militant here on earth; thus the sense of the communion of saints was weakened and hardly kept alive by the greatly reduced festivals of the "scriptural" saints, who, after all, had lived long ago. Nor did Anglicanism compensate for this loss, as Puritanism did, by stressing the intimate communion of the covenanted members of Christ's church, for the national church was a "mixed multitude," not a community of

[153] Kennedy, *Elizabethan Episcopal Administration*, I, 44.

"visible saints" to use a favourite, though later, Puritan term.[154] The doctrine of the church as consociation of the elect gave support and warmth to Puritan gatherings for worship.

The Puritans were conscious of an excess of decorum, dignity, and formality—not to mention legalism—in the Anglican services. They sensed a chilling social distance which, they were sure, conflicted with Christian cordiality and community. That is why the author of the *Second Admonition to Parliament* attacks the impersonality and artificiality of the Elizabethan Book of Common Prayer in 1572: "The Book is such a piece of work as it is strange we will use it, besides I cannot account it praying, as they use it commonly, but only reading or saying of prayers, even as a child that learned to read, if his lesson be a prayer, even so it is commonly a saying and reading prayers, and not praying. . . . For though they have many guises, now to kneel and now to stand, these be matters of course, and not any prick of conscience, or piercing of the heart. . . . One he kneeleth on his knees, and this way he looketh and that way he looketh, another he kneeleth himself fast asleep, another he kneeleth with such devotion, that is so far in talk, that he forgetteth to rise till his knees ache, or his talk endeth, or the service is done! And why is all this? But that there is no such praying as should touch the heart."[155]

Finally, on the negative side, there was a spirit of dignity and decorum, a sense of good order and good taste, but there was neither the lyricism that is appropriate to souls committed to the high ventures of faith in the power of the resurrection (such as inspired most of the prayers of the Eastern Orthodox rites), nor was there that massive historic sense of the world being an amphitheatre in which the saints watching in the stands encourage the earthly runner, though weary, to run the straight race (which the sanctoral cycle of the Roman rite expressed). The spirit of Anglican liturgy was rather one of reverent humility and submission than of triumphant rejoicing. It was too often introspective and penitential; its dignity was in danger of being a Laodicean substitute for enthusiastic commitment. By the same token it was a suitable form of worship for sober, pragmatic, prudent, and rational members of the social establishment, which was presumably why it has been described historically—but there are too many excep-

---

154 J.H.A. New, *Anglican and Puritan, the Basis of their Opposition, 1558-1640*, pp. 40-41.
155 *Puritan Manifestoes*, ed. W. H. Frere and C. E. Douglas, p. 115.

tions for the *mot* to be *juste*—as the formulary of the Tory party on its knees.

This has been a formidable series of negative criticisms against the Book of Common Prayer. It has been criticised as the instrument of religious control as put forward by the authority of a queen who equivocated in matters of faith, as a document marred by theological confusion, as the medium of a repetitive and dull form of worship, as a formulary of devotion likely to lead to a sense of impersonality in worship, and, finally, as a book spiritually tepid and admirably suited to the "top people." Yet this cannot be the last word on a historic, influential, and well-loved book of corporate devotions, for if that is all there is to be said about it, it would never have survived its detractors. It alone has survived in continuous use amid the plethora of evanescent new liturgies of the sixteenth century; those who use it today are found in many countries and they worship through it in many languages. What, then, are the qualities of the Book of Common Prayer that have given it enduring value?

First, it is salutary to recall that what can be conceived politically as a "great compromise" may be conceived liturgically as the "great comprehension." P. M. Dawley has written of the combination of the "Catholic" (1549) and "Protestant" (1552) words of the administration in the Elizabethan rite of Holy Communion, that "no single action was more important in ensuring a wide acceptance of the religious settlement."[156] In this ecumenical age, we are able to realise what an immense and honourable task was attempted by Cranmer and his associates in trying to span the Catholic and Protestant chasm with the bridge of liturgy (as also in church order by preserving the historic forms of the ministry). For our present consideration it does not matter that Catholics and Separatists excluded themselves from the Anglican Settlement, but only that the experiment of inclusiveness was made and that the Prayer Book of 1559 was its liturgical laboratory. So, in fact, although it was the national formulary of English worship, it preserved an international heritage. The Book of Common Prayer enabled Englishmen to worship God with the voices of the past and the present conjoined. As Jews had worshipped God in the Temple and Synagogue in the Psalter, as citizens of the Roman empire had worshipped Him in lapidary collects and in the Order of the Mass, as members of the Eastern Orthodox Church did in the

---

[156] *John Whitgift and the English Reformation*, p. 58.

prayer of St. John Chrysostom or as in the climactic moment of "invocation" in the prayer of Consecration in the 1549 rite, as the German Lutherans did in the penitential introductions to the Daily Offices, as Calvinists did in the metrical psalmody and in parts of the prayer of confession, so did English worshippers make these experiences their own through the Book of Common Prayer. The comprehensive and compassionate spirit of Cranmer—a reserved, reverent, scholarly, and tentative spirit—breathes through its entirety, and made it possible through his researches and superb editing and writing. Many countries, many centuries, march through the Book of Common Prayer to the present.

Second, the Book of Common Prayer has become the bond of unity of the Anglican communion through its many provinces throughout the world. It has managed to satisfy the spiritual needs of high churchman, broad churchman, and low churchman. They appear to have found ample sustenance and variety in this treasury of devotions and guide to spirituality. (The tragedy is that an act of Parliament is needed in England to add to it the splendid prayers that have been composed since the last legally authorised revision of over 300 years ago).

Third, the Book of Common Prayer is unique in being the first Book of *Common* Prayer, in that it has always been used both by priest and people, whereas previously priests had a different set of prayer books and the people had none, unless they were Latin scholars. Such a book has kept minister and people close in English life. It has encouraged the growth of a lay spirituality of depth. In yet another sense, the prayers of the Prayer Book are *common*— that is, they have a richly responsive construction and character, whether in the Litany, or in the versicles and responses of the Suffrages, or in the general confessions, and elsewhere. This means that there has always been in Anglican worship a continuing dialogue between priest and people, an ongoing liturgical "conversation." This can be contrasted with the tyranny of the ministerial voice in Reformed worship, for the minister's is often the only voice heard in prayer, and the congregation is mute, and often says the permitted "Amen" with little conviction. As Hooker was to point out to the Puritans, these "arrow prayers" are likelier to provoke the people to devotion than the long pastoral prayers of the Reformed Churches which are likelier to turn the church militant into the church somnolent. Not only praises, but prayers are shared in the Anglican (as in the Roman and Orthodox) rites.

The Book of Common Prayer gave a sense of the priority of prayers and sacraments over preaching, sometimes to the detriment of preaching, though there was a great post-Elizabethan Anglican tradition of preaching. But prayer was given the primacy of consideration in the Book of Common Prayer, in accordance with its title, and this is its great glory that through this model of devout spirituality it has, under God, helped to train prophets like F. D. Maurice and William Temple and saints like George Herbert and Nicholas Ferrar, William Law, and John Wesley, as well as John Henry Newman. It has also raised many men and women from the mire to the mountains of aspiration.

CHAPTER VI

ANGLICAN PREACHING

THE LITURGY has nearly always taken precedence over the sermon in the esteem of the Church of England, yet the new church slowly established an important preaching tradition which reached its zenith in the golden sermons of Andrewes and Donne early in the next century. The assigning of an important role to preaching was greatly accelerated by the Christian Humanists of Catholicism and by the Protestant Reformers on the Continent and in England.

The friends of the new learning were also the friends of preaching. John Fisher, the Catholic bishop of Rochester and vice-chancellor (from 1501) and chancellor of the University of Cambridge (from 1504), was himself a great oratorical preacher who was selected to preach the funeral sermons of Henry VII and Lady Margaret, the great benefactress of the university. Lady Margaret, probably on the advice of her confessor, John Fisher, established a preachership at Cambridge in 1504. The preacher, a resident Cambridge fellow without cure of souls, was to preach once every two years in each of 12 parishes in the dioceses of London, Ely, and Lincoln. Fisher also advised Erasmus to write his treatise on preaching, *Ecclesiastes, sive concionator Evangelicus*, and recommended that the Lady Margaret Readers should give attention to preaching. John Colet, the friend of Erasmus and More and a distinguished Greek scholar, lectured at Oxford University on the meaning of the Pauline Epistles with great critical insight and the plea for a return to the discipline of the early Church. In 1505 he became dean of St. Paul's cathedral in London, where he preached expository sermons at every festival. The same innovation was introduced by Ralph Collingwood, dean of Lichfield, who preached a weekly sermon in his cathedral.[1] Richard Fox, the bishop of Winchester, founded Corpus Christi College, Oxford in 1516 and a Readership in Greek to promote the study of the Scriptures in the original languages. In line with the same emphasis and concern was the establishment of Regius Professorships of Greek and

---

[1] F. E. Hutchinson, "The English Pulpit from Fisher to Donne," in A. W. Ward and A. R. Waller, eds., *The Cambridge History of English Literature*, vol. 4, p. 224. For Colet see E. H. Harbison, *The Christian Scholar in the Age of the Reformation*, pp. 56-67.

Hebrew at Cambridge in 1540 and at Oxford in 1546. The Reformation increased the momentum started by the Renaissance.

To the Reformation is owed the great drive toward set preaching instead of largely informal instruction. The Reformation's impact took three forms. First, in the first generation of Protestantism no man could be born a Protestant—he was *made* one. He had to be convinced of the truth of the Protestant position, which was based largely on a knowledge of the Scriptures, which was expounded in sermons, rather than on entrenched traditional Catholicism. Protestants were convinced that every man must make up his mind about his religion for himself under the eyes of his Maker. This conviction urged them to preach the word of God and instruct men in the truth. Finally, the substitution of English for Latin in the worship of the church was itself a stimulus to preaching.[2]

Anglican preaching in Tudor England moves from Latimer to Hooker through two quite different periods, the Edwardian and the Elizabethan. In the reign of Edward VI, which marked a radical Protestant change from the conservative, non-Papal Catholicism of Henry's final years, there were few preachers who appeared in the public forum; but all who did were strong personalities. They zestfully proclaimed the dominance of Scripture over tradition, and were prophetic Reformers, applying the Biblical criterion to the overthrowing of false doctrine and social injustice. Such were Latimer, England's most popular sixteenth-century preacher and a friend of the poor, and the inflexible, Savonarola-like John Hooper, imprisoned for his Vestiarian views, then freed and, like Latimer, a Protestant martyr in Mary's reign. With them should be numbered the significant, but less dominant, Lever and Bradford whose preaching was delivered with an urgent simplicity appropriate to the early days of open Protestantism in English history. Lever's and Bradford's preaching was, inevitably, iconoclastic, and therefore produced much excitement especially in court circles. Latimer and Hooper preached memorable series of sermons. Their second-generation Elizabethan successors seem, perhaps unfairly, smaller and more inhibited figures in "tuned" pulpits.

1. Homilies

Apart from the individual sermons of Latimer and Hooper, a new simple style of thematic preaching was being forged in Henry's

---

[2] Arthur Pollard, *English Sermons*, p. 8.

reign, and became public in Edward's reign in the form of model sermons, or official "homilies." The plan to issue prescribed homilies for the use of illiterate or discontented clergy was first agreed to at a convocation early in 1542, and was duly prepared within the next 12 months. The collection of 12 homilies was not, however, issued until early in the reign of Edward VI. They appeared July 31, 1547, with the authority of the council. A second book, containing another 21 homilies, was issued in 1571 under Queen Elizabeth, although it was probably completed by 1563.[3]

Bishop Ridley asserts that the *Homilies* of 1547 were so designed that some were "in commendation of the principal virtues which are commended in Scripture," and "other against the most pernicious and capital vices that useth (alas!) to reign in this realm of England."[4] In its approach the plan seemed, therefore, medieval rather than Protestant. Its Henrician context is suggested by the preponderance of ethical over theological themes.

It is generally agreed that of the 12 homilies in the first book, Cranmer wrote 5: A fruitful Exhortation to the Reading of Holy Scripture; Of the Salvation of all Mankind; Of the true and lively Faith; Of Good Works; and, probably, An Exhortation against the Fear of Death. Bishop Bonner is the reputed author of the homily, Of Christian Love and Charity, while Archdeacon John Harpsfield is believed to have written the homily, Of the Misery of all Mankind. With less confidence the homilies, Against Whoredom and Adultery, and Against Swearing and Perjury, have been attributed to Cranmer's chaplain, Thomas Becon.[5]

In these homilies there is evidence of nostalgia for the simple Christian way of life depicted in the New Testament, and of a protest against the legalities and complexities of a tradition-bound church, which A. G. Dickens has characterised as the motive power of English Protestantism.[6] It can be found in the words of Cranmer,

---

[3] The two books of homilies were reproduced as *Certain Sermons appointed by the Queen's Majesty to be declared and read by all Parsons, Vicars, and Curates, every Sunday and Holiday in their Churches, and by Her Grace's Advice perused and overseen for the better understanding of the Simple People.* The second edition of 1574 is the basis of G. E. Corrie's edition of the homilies, entitled, *Certain Sermons,* which appeared in Cambridge in 1850, and to which all references hereafter will be made. The 21 Elizabethan homilies were largely the work of Jewel, although Grindal wrote number 5, and probably Parker, number 17.

[4] *Works,* ed. H. Christmas, p. 400.

[5] See J. T. Tomlinson, *The Prayer Book, Articles, and Homilies,* pp. 232-35. The three other homilies were: Of the Declining from God; An Exhortation to Obedience; and Against Strife and Contention.

[6] *The English Reformation,* p. 138. "In the Bible, in the notion of a return to the original spirit of Christianity, in the rebirth of a fragment of the ancient

where the nostalgia becomes also an impatient iconoclasm; Cranmer was trying to tear down superstition and replace it with a supposedly more authentic, because more Biblical and simpler, faith:

> What man, having any judgment or learning, joined with a true zeal unto God, doth not see and lament to have entered into Christ's religion such false doctrine, superstition, idolatry, hypocrisy, and other enormities and abuses; so as by little and little, through the sour leaven thereof, the sweet bread of God's holy word hath been much hindered and laid apart? Never had the Jews, in their most blindness, so many pilgrimages unto images, nor used so much kneeling, kissing, and censing of them, as hath been used in our time. . . . Which sects and religions had so many hypocritical and feigned works in their state of religion, as they arrogantly named it, that their lamps, as they said, ran always over: able to satisfy not only for their own sins, but also for all other their benefactors, brothers and sisters of religion, as most ungodly and craftily they had persuaded the multitude of ignorant people: keeping in divers places, as it were marts or markets of merits; being full of their holy relics, images, shrines, and works of overflowing abundance ready to be sold. And all things which they had were called holy, — holy cowls, holy girdles, holy pardons, beads, holy shoes, holy rules, and all full of holiness.[7]

Even the willingness to accept the Bible as the criterion for criticism of the corrupt accretions of tradition could not be assumed. So the first homily, A fruitful exhortation to the Reading of Holy Scripture, had to refute the common notion that only the learned

---

world so infinitely more precious to Christians than the glories of Greece and the grandeurs of Rome, here lay the true strength of the Reformation. One who has never felt this nostalgia, this desire to sweep away the accretions, to cross the centuries to the homeland, can understand little of the compulsive attraction of the New Testament, even less of the limited but real successes of Protestantism, successes which cannot, any more than those of the Counter Reformation be explained away by reference to ambitious kings and greedy nobles."

[7] *Certain Sermons*, pp. 55-56. Later in the same Homily of Good Works annexed unto Faith, Cranmer denounced the superstition of the life of the "religious" with their three-fold vows, and many "papistical" superstitions and abuses, from beads, rosaries, stations, and jubilees, to fastings, indulgences, and masses satisfactory. The gravamen of his criticism is that they "were so esteemed and abused to the great prejudice of God's glory and commandments, that they were made most high and most holy things, whereby to attain to the everlasting life, or remission of sins" (p. 58).

were trained to expound its teachings: "Unto a Christian man, there can be nothing either more necessary or profitable than the knowledge of holy Scripture; forasmuch as in it is contained God's true word, setting forth his glory, and also man's duty. And there is no truth nor doctrine, necessary for our justification and everlasting salvation, but that is, or may be drawn out of that fountain or well of truth. . . . These books, therefore, ought to be much in our hands, in our eyes, in our ears, in our mouths, but most of all in our hearts. For the Scripture of God is the heavenly meat for our souls, the hearing and keeping of it maketh us blessed, sanctifieth us, and maketh us holy; it turneth our souls; it is a lantern to our feet; it is a sure, steadfast, and everlasting instrument of salvation; it giveth wisdom to the humble and holy hearts, it comforteth, maketh glad, cheereth, and cherisheth our conscience; it is a more excellent jewel, or treasure than any gold or precious stone; it is more sweet than honey or honeycomb; it is called *the best part* which Mary did choose, for it hath in it everlasting comfort."[8]

2. *Edwardian and Elizabethan Sermons Compared*

With the conviction and recommendation indicated in the foregoing, it would be astonishing if the leading Edwardian preachers were not primarily expositors of the Scripture. It is important that the first book of homilies was itself so full of the content of the Scriptures, and that it used the topical approach with simplicity. The excitement was in the novelty of scriptural teaching in the vernacular, its controversy with the old faith, and the stripping away of the accumulation of superstitious and idolatrous beliefs and practises.

The first book of homilies was issued as a standard of Biblical doctrine and preaching for the nation. It fulfilled a need, since there were few Reformed ministers with the requisite background, training, and conviction. Their numbers did not grow appreciably in Mary's reign, during which the more convinced members of the Reformed faith went to the stake or into exile. The same situation at the beginning of Elizabeth's reign made it necessary to continue to use the first book of homilies and, later, to produce a second. This time, however, as the universities turned out more and more clergymen for the (Reformed) Church of England, the books of homilies became less an incentive for preachers than a theological

8 *Ibid.*, pp. 1-3.

straitjacket, which the Puritans, along with enlightened prelates, such as Grindal, and other former Marian exiles, felt inhibited the encouragement of imaginative application of Biblical exposition.

In due course there appeared on the Elizabethan scene, not the towering prophetic figures of Edward VI's days but a large number of competent and devoted preachers, some of whom, like Henry Smith,[9] Richard Hooker, and the early Lancelot Andrewes,[10] were admirable orators of the English pulpit. The opportunities for preaching had increased considerably since Edward.

St. Paul's Cathedral provided lectures every day, and sermons on Sunday, from its large staff comprising a dean, chancellor, treasurer, five archdeacons and 30 Prebendaries. London boasted 123 parish churches.[11] Several clergymen drew large and growing congregations with their preaching ability. Stephen Egerton, of St. Anne's, Blackfriars, had many female admirers in his congregation. Richard Bancroft, later Archbishop, preached to large congregations at St. Andrew's, Holborn, where he was succeeded by the popular Dr. John King. The brilliant preacher at St. Giles, Cripplegate was Lancelot Andrewes. At Christ Church, Newgate, the Puritan minister Richard Greenham gathered crowds; Henry Smith, another Puritan, was more popular than any preceding preacher as he preached in St. Clement Dane's.[12] Such enthusiastic listeners did not always mean that the people craved the bread of life (though they often did); it meant they also delighted in the rich fruitcake which some Christian cooks provided. The unquestioned fact is that Elizabethans not only listened to sermons but increasingly read them for their pleasure and edification.[13]

The Elizabethans, like St. Paul's Athenians, were eager to hear "some new thing." It was not always soundness of doctrine or sincerity of manner that drew them, but humour, wit, even sensationalism. Controversy was sure to attract them. Indeed, the more thoughtful prelates were disturbed about the criteria by which the populace judged sermons. Archbishop Sandys referred to the popular view in one of his sermons: "The preacher is gladly heard of

---

[9] Smith is considered in Chap. VIII.

[10] Andrewes' important contributions to worship, spirituality, and preaching will be considered in the forthcoming vol. II of this series.

[11] Stow, *Survey of London*, ed. C. L. Kingsford, vol. 2, p. 143.

[12] See Alan F. Herr, *The Elizabethan Sermon, A Survey and Bibliography*, p. 27; and John Bruce, ed., *The Diary of John Manningham*, p. 75.

[13] Herr, *Elizabethan Sermon*, p. 27, affirms that the number of sermons published in each decade increased from nine in 1560-1570 to 69 in 1570-1580, to 113 in 1580-1590, to 140 in 1590-1600.

the people that can carp the magistrates, cut up the ministers, cry out against all order, and set all at liberty. But if he shall reprove their insolency, pride, and vanity, their monstrous apparel, their excessive feasting, their greedy covetousness, their biting usury, their halting hearts, their muttering minds, their friendly words and malicious deeds, they will fall from him then. He is a railer, he doteth, he wanteth discretion."[14] Jewel was of much the same opinion, but he said the generally poor (in his opinion) response to preaching was due to a contempt for the role of the preacher.[15] At the turn of the century both Hooker and Andrewes complained that their congregations were full of persons with itching ears. Hooker remarked that in the day when religion flourished, most men, "in the practice of their religion wearied chiefly their knees and hands, we especially our ears and tongues." Lancelot Andrewes, preaching on the text, "Be ye doers of the words and not hearers only,"[16] claimed that the teaching of St. James was particularly urgent in an age "when hearing of the Word is growen into such request, that it hath got the start of all the rest of the parts of Gods service," so that "Sermon-hearing is the *Consummatum est* of all Christianitie."[17]

The competitive pressure to interest the congregations and even more the readers of sermons can be seen in the attempt to produce intriguing sermon titles. The genesis of one such title was provided by the author in the dedication of his volume of sermons. John Stockwood of Tunbridge was ready to publish a treatise on August 20, 1589, when he recalled that August 24 would be St. Bartholomew's Day and that the famous London Fair would closely follow. Hence he wrote: "the time falling out so fitlie with the finishing of this worke, and the publishing of the same, I have geven unto it the name of a *Bartholmew Fayring*, the rather by the noveltie of the title to drawe on the multitude of people that nowe out of all places of our county repaire unto to the citie, to the better beholding and consideration of the matter cotained in the treatise."[18]

To assume that Elizabethan sermons consisted only of Christian doctrine, Christian standards of behaviour (though this was an elastic category), and the requirements of Christian piety would be inaccurate. There was a great deal of what would today be

---

[14] *Works* (chiefly sermons with miscellaneous pieces), ed. J. Ayre, Sermon 14.
[15] *Works*, 4 vols., II, 1,014.   [16] James 1:22.
[17] Both citations are given by F. E. Hutchinson in *Cambridge History of English Literature*, vol. 4, chap. 12.
[18] *Bartholmew Fayring*, sig. A3 r.

regarded as secular matters in the scope of the Elizabethan sermon, which helped to account for the growing interest of congregations in the final decades of the century. Local and international politics, the question of the royal succession, the social and economic problems of the poor, the ravages of plagues or catastrophic fires, the inconsistency of the weather, and facts every pregnant woman should know[19] were all included in sermons of the period. Such scope not only allowed for a great variety of treatment and originality in sermons, but also gave them a direct relevance to the issues of the day.

Perhaps the greatest distinction between Edwardian and Elizabethan sermons was mood and manner. The typical, early vernacular sermons had been those of the harangue, in which Becon and Latimer specialized. During Elizabeth's reign the controversial sermon had moved "from the hustings to the lecture room."[20] A new generation had arisen since the advent of the Reformation, which was used to theological controversy and interested in its technicalities. As a result, the sermons of Jewel and Hooker appealed to the intelligence in addition to the emotions of their hearers. Appeals to antiquity, supported by citations from the Fathers and Doctors of the church, take the place of appeals to prejudice.

3. Biblical Interpretation[21]

In the sixteenth century medieval exegesis had appealed to the literal, tropological, allegorical, and anagogical senses of Scripture, an approach which led to a great deal of ingenuity and hunting for hidden meanings, and which made possible the explanation of what on a consistently literal basis looked like contradictions in Scripture. Its defect was both the subjectivity it encouraged and the departure from the historical sense which stimulated the acceptance of fables in lieu of facts.

Inevitably Protestantism preferred a literal or historical to an allegorical interpretation of Scripture, except when the intention was clearly metaphorical, as when Jesus declared that he was the true vine or the door. While Protestants were as anxious as Catholics to preserve the primacy of faith, though interpreting the term differently, they also paid a long-needed tribute to reason as they

19 See Christopher Hooke, *The Child-birth or Woman's Lecture* (1590), referred to in Herr, *Elizabethan Sermon*, p. 29.
20 Hutchinson, "English Pulpit."
21 Further consideration is given to this theme in chap. VIII.

expounded the historical contexts in which the servants of God spoke or acted in their own times and for the benefit of the future. J. W. Blench notes that the early English Reformers discontinued the allegorising of the figurative expressions of the poetic and prophetic books of the Old Testament favoured by the exponents of the old learning, that instead they were fond of the historical books of the Old Testament. Blench also observes that the same preachers were anxious to provide the original meaning of Biblical expressions, according to the original languages in which the Bible was written.[22] In this the English reformers were aided by the exemplars of the new learning such as Colet, Erasmus, and Stafford.[23] Latimer, for example, protested against Cardinal Pole's exegesis as being too farfetched; he argued that no preeminence for Peter is intended in Luke 5: 1-7, in which Christ selected Peter's boat rather than another's as the pulpit from which He addressed the people, and from which He commanded the nets to be lowered with the resulting miraculous catch of fish. Latimer refuted the argument from common sense experience, asserting that a wherryman at Westminster bridge could tell the cardinal the natural meaning of the passage. It was obvious that Christ "knoweth that one man is able to shove the boat, but one man was not able to cast out the nets; and therefore he said in the plural number, *Laxate retia*, 'Loose your nets'; and he said in the singular number to Peter, 'Launch out the boat.' Why? Because he was able to do it. But he spake the other in the plural number, because he was not able to convey the boat, and cast out the nets too; one man could not do it. This would the wherryman say, and with better reason, than to make such a mystery of it, as no man can spy but they."[24]

The English reformers, however critical they were of Catholic allegoric glosses did not themselves always abide by the literal sense without making any accommodations to their own times or to their audiences. Hooper's series of sermons on the Book of Jonah

---

[22] *Preaching in England in the late Fifteenth and Sixteenth Centuries: A Study of English Sermons, 1450—c. 1600*, pp. 39-40. This erudite volume is indispensable.

[23] Thomas Becon said it was a common saying that "When Master Stafford read, and Master Latimer preached, then was Cambridge blessed." He added that it might be doubted whether Stafford owed more to Paul, "or that Paul, which before had so many years been foiled with the foolish fantasies and elvish expositions of certain doting doctors . . . was rather bound unto him, seeing that by his industry, labour, pain, and diligence, he seemeth of a dead man to make him alive again. . . ." (*The Jewel of Joy*, in Thomas Becon, *The Catechism*, ed. J. Ayre, p. 426.) Stafford was expert in Hebrew, Greek and Latin; he brought not only the Pauline Epistles but also the Gospels to life.

[24] *Sermons*, ed. G. E. Corrie, pp. 205-206.

are a case in point. For example, it is very doubtful if a strictly historical interpretation would draw a trite moral lesson from the sleep of Jonah, "that when we think ourselves most at rest, then we be most in danger."[25] Further, Jonah emerges from the whale and the waters strikingly like a newly baptized Lutheran theologian. Latimer, too, was hardly consistent in the same way as Hooper. Quite unhistorically Latimer asserted that those labourers who criticised the Lord of the vineyard because labourers hired late in the day received the same pay as themselves, despite their longer hours, are "merit-mongers, which esteem their own work so much, that they think heaven scant sufficient to recompense their good deeds; namely for putting themselves to pain with saying of our lady's psalter, and gadding on pilgrimage and such-like trifles."[26] There was considerable flexibility in showing the relevance of the Biblical teaching to the contemporary situation of the hearers. In its way, this meant making a wax nose of Scripture, as the Catholics so often accused the Protestants of doing, if not in the interpretation, then in the application.

Anglican preachers in Elizabeth's reign, such as the Calvinist William Whitaker, the Puritans Deringe and Perkins, and Thomas Drant and John Chardon, were extremely critical of the Catholic fourfold sense of Scripture. Yet they did employ typology to some extent, particularly in their use of Old Testament figures. For example, John Foxe affirmed that Samson, in defeating the Philistines, was Christ victorious over the powers of darkness.[27] Bishop John Jewel of Salisbury used the traditional types and anti-types in seeing the water that Moses struck from the rock as a figure of the blood of Christ, the miraculous manna as a foreshadowing of the body of Christ, and the brazen serpent of Numbers 21:9 as the type, or foreshadowing of the crucifixion of Christ. In most cases, however, they are referred to as such in Scripture.[28]

But other Elizabethan preachers, particularly the witty and florid Thomas Playfere or the erudite and subtle Lancelot Andrewes, refused to be restricted by the literal sense. Playfere delighted in allegorising poetical expressions from the Psalms or the Song of Songs. A simile from the latter—"Thy two breasts are like two

[25] Hooper, *Early Writings*, ed. S. Carr, p. 454.

[26] *Remains*, ed. G. E. Corrie, p. 220. This instance of inconsistency is taken from Blench, *Preaching in England*, p. 47.

[27] *A Sermon of Christ crucified preached at Paules Crosse the Friday before Easter, commonly called Goodfryday* (1570), fol. 41 recto. See also Blench, *Preaching in England*, p. 61.

[28] See *Works*, ed. J. Ayre, 4 vols., vol. 2, 968-70.

young roes that are twins, which feed among the lilies" (4:5) — he interpreted as the two Testaments that feed the church with the pure milk of God's word.[29] Andrewes, following the example of such a distinguished Latin expositor as St. Jerome, used the allegorical method to extract "spiritual" meanings from refractory texts with great ingenuity. On the whole, however, most Elizabethan preachers insisted on the primacy of the historical meaning of Scripture in its context.

4. Sermon Topics

The single most decisive change in interest, as one moves from Catholic to early Protestant sermons, was from the other-worldly to the this-worldly, though the distinction was not absolute, since Catholic sermons were also concerned with current duty and Protestant sermons with future reward. Nonetheless, the change of emphasis is striking.

Some important Catholic themes were either ignored or were treated infrequently or incidentally, such as the shadowy transience and mutability of this world contrasted with the substantial and enduring joys of eternity or the morbid meditation on skulls, skeletons, and advancing decrepitude. It was a serious loss that the loving contemplation of the Passion of Christ also virtually disappeared.[30]

Edwardian preachers warmed to the immediate and urgent task of Reformation in church and state, according to the divine plan revealed in the Scriptures. They demanded that the old strongholds of superstitious doctrines and idolatrous practices be torn down; there is the intoxication of iconoclasm in their sermons. The really courageous critics of Catholicism in Henry's reign, like "little" Bilney who so impressed Latimer and Barnes, paid the supreme penalty. Latimer himself waited until the time of Edward VI before attacking Catholic doctrine directly; prior to this, he delivered attacks on the abuses of neglecting the poor in favour of giving opulent vestments to a church, or decorating images when the true image of God was to be seen in the face of a poor man. Even in 1537 Latimer in his forthright Convocation sermon harshly criticised contemporary teachings on purgatory, with their assertion

---

[29] *The whole Sermons of That Eloquent Divine of Famous Memory: Thomas Playfere, Doctor in Divinitie* (1623), p. 230. See Blench, *Preaching in England*, pp. 64-65.

[30] In Chap. XII I suggest that this is because Protestants are less interested in the *person* than in the *work* of Christ, and concentrate more on the Atonement than on the Incarnation.

that imprisoned souls are utterly dependent on the assistance of the living. He insisted that such teaching was purely speculative, that it denied the mercy of the living God, and that it was founded on the greed of the "purgatory pick-purse."[31]

In Edward's reign Latimer and Hooper assaulted Catholic doctrines with vigour. Both struck out at the doctrine of the sacrifice of the Mass, which Latimer accused of evacuating the fulness and finality of Christ's offering on the cross, and which Hooper echoed by declaring that the historic crucifixion is the only propitiatory sacrifice necessary.[32] Their style was often mocking and railing, which must have been highly offensive to good Catholics, although Catholics, in turn, were equally insensitive to tender Protestant consciences. Hooper ridiculed the legalism of a formula of consecration in the Mass (as contrasted with the sovereign action of the Holy Spirit): "After this their wicked and idolatrical doctrine, this syllable (um) in this oration, Hoc est corpus meum, to say, 'This is my body,' hath all the strength and virtue to change and deify the bread! But I pray you, what syllable is it that changeth and deifieth the wine?"[33] While intellectually superior, it was not morally superior to the Protestants who referred to the Mass as a "Jacke of the boxe"[34] or who hung on Paul's Cross a dead cat with shaven crown and a white disc in its mouth.[35] If such insensitivity ruled, the Marian dean of Westminster, Hugh Weston, could hardly be blamed for describing the Protestant Communion tables set up by Bishop Ridley of London as oyster boards!

It was also interesting that Bishops Latimer and Hooper were linked in the public mind as defenders of and liberal donors to the poor. Both were critical of the corruption of judges and magistrates who took bribes. What differentiated their sermons from those of their Catholic predecessors was that their charges were uncomfortably precise and particular.[36] Latimer spoke like a sixteenth-

---

[31] Sermons, p. 50. For other abuses Latimer criticised see ibid., pp. 38-55.
[32] See Latimer's Sermons, pp. 72-73; and Hooper's Early Writings, p. 500.
[33] Hooper, Early Writings, p. 523.
[34] Chronicle of the Grey Friars of London, ed. J. G. Nichols, p. 55.
[35] Millar Maclure, The Paul's Cross Sermons, 1534-1642, p. 51.
[36] See Latimer, Sermons, pp. 128, 190; and Hooper, Early Writings, pp. 482-83. Latimer, in his second sermon before Edward VI, appealed to the young king to hear himself the suits of the poor: "I must desire my Lord Protector's grace to hear me in this matter, that your Grace would hear poor men's suits yourself. Put them to none other to hear, let them not be delayed. The saying is now, that money is heard everywhere; if he be rich, he shall soon have an end of this matter. Others are fain to go home with weeping tears, for any help they can obtain at any judge's hand. Hear men's suits yourself, I require you in God's behalf, and put it not to the hearing of these velvet coats, these upskips" (p. 127).

century Amos at court in the name of a mightier sovereign—God. The calling of a prophet was a dangerous one, especially in Henry VIII's time. In fact, Latimer reported that he was once accused of preaching seditious doctrine in the king's presence, a charge Henry asked him to reply to. After facing his accuser Latimer ended his words to the king by saying: "But if your Grace allow me for a preacher, I would desire your grace to give me leave to discharge my conscience: give me leave to frame my doctrine according to mine audience: I had been a very dolt to have preached so at the borders of your realm, as I preach before your Grace."[37] The answer was a tribute to Latimer's honesty and courage, but its shrewd prudence contained a whiff of the danger he was in. Latimer told Henry's successor: "The poorest ploughman is in Christ equal with the greatest prince there is. Let them therefore, have sufficient to maintain them, and to find their necessaries."[38]

In Elizabeth's reign it was the Puritan Deringe alone who in 1569 dared to criticise the queen to her face. Deringe was prohibited for a time from preaching because he had told Elizabeth to take away her authority from the bishops because they would not ordain preaching ministers and tolerated pluralities and non-residence.[39] Other preachers before less august persons were, however, ready to continue the diatribe against greedy, lazy, illiterate, and incompetent parsons. This kind of jeremiad runs through the Elizabethan age, whether the critic in the pulpit was a prelate like Jewel[40] or a minister such as Pagit[41] or Bush.[42] Some plain speaking took place during the Vestiarian and Disciplinarian controversies. The sermons of Sampson and Humphrey at Paul's Cross[43] and Fulke at Great St. Mary's, Cambridge,[44] against the vestments, and the sermon of Robert Beaumont[45] for compliance with the ecclesiastical law, show that few holds were barred in the homiletical warfare. The "disciplinarians" who supported Cartwright were equally forthright in their demands and accusations. William

---

[37] *Sermons*, p. 135.

[38] *Ibid.*, p. 249; this citation was part of a plea to stop enclosures of common land.

[39] See J. W. Blench, *Preaching in England*, pp. 300-301. The offending sermon and its consequences are described in the article on Blench in the *Dictionary of National Biography*, XIV, 393.

[40] *Works*, vol. II, 999, 1,011.

[41] Eusebius Pagit, *A Godly Sermon preached at Detford* (1586), sig. A vi v.

[42] Bush, *A Sermon preached at St. Paules Crosse on Trinity Sunday 1571*, sig. F ii r.

[43] Maclure, *Paul's Cross Sermons*, p. 205.

[44] H. B. Porter, *Reformation and Reaction in Tudor Cambridge*, p. 121.

[45] *Ibid.*

Charke, in demanding a Presbyterian parity of ministerial status from the pulpit of Great St. Mary's, Cambridge, asserted that archbishops and bishops were introduced into the church by the devil.[46] Less than a year later, Richard Crick argued for an equality in the ministry from St. Paul's Cross,[47] where Thomas Cooper,[48] bishop of Lincoln and later a butt of "Marprelate," had preached a sermon in June 1572 in reply to the *Admonition to Parliament*. While the timid or the office-seekers tuned their pulpits to the prevailing doctrine, there was some independence of judgment and freedom in its expression in the Elizabethan pulpit. That is, indeed, why Archbishop Whitgift discouraged frequent preaching: "But, if any hath said that some of those which use to preach often, by their loose, negligent, verbal and unlearned sermons, have brought the word of God into contempt, or that four godly, learned, pithy, diligent, and discreet preachers might do more good in London than forty contentious, unlearned, verbal and rash preachers, they have truly said, and their saying might well be justified."[49]

In addition to airing internal controversies from the pulpits, there were anti-Catholic polemics which continued into Elizabeth's reign. Happily the spirit in which it was conducted was generally more scholarly and less vindictive than it was under Edward. The new tone was set by Jewel's famous Challenge Sermon which he preached at Paul's Cross on November 26, 1559 and March 31, 1560, as well as at court. Jewel provided a historical and rational basis for his attack on the Catholic Mass—for the use of Latin in the Mass, its giving communion in one kind, the teaching on sacrifice, the encouragement of adoration of the sacrament, and private celebrations. After 1570, when Pope Gregory XIII issued the bull *Regnans in Excelsis* absolving Catholics from loyalty to Queen Elizabeth, and with the surreptitious introduction of seminarists into England, Protestant-Catholic relations worsened. The situation was reflected in the mocking manner of Tyrer's and Bridges' sermons which condemned Roman Catholicism as a superstitious religion of externals, for its postponement of salvation through the teaching of purgatory, and for an evasive scholastic subtlety.[50]

The Elizabethan preachers did, however, find new subjects for

---

[46] *Ibid.*, p. 141.
[47] Maclure, *Paul's Cross Sermons*, pp. 208-209.
[48] *Ibid.*, p. 308.
[49] *Defence of the Answer to the Admonition*, tractate XI, sec. 3.
[50] Ralph Tyrer's criticisms are contained in *Five godlie sermons* . . . (1602), pp. 302-304, while Bridges' are in *A Sermon preached at Paules Cross* (1571), p. 125.

their critical powers. There was a complaint that the indifference of the people had led to decay of the furnishings in the churches. In his Homily for Repairing and keeping clean of Churches, Bishop Jewel exhorted many congregations: ". . . forasmuch as your churches are scoured and swept from the sinful and superstitious filthiness, wherewith they were defiled and disfigured, do ye your parts, good people, to keep your churches comely and clean; suffer them not to be defiled with rain and weather, with dung of doves and owls, stares and choughs, and other filthiness, as it is foul and lamentable to behold in many places of this country."[51] Another theme for denunciation was the new paganism emerging through classical learning, which, it was claimed, was replacing Christianity. This occupied the attention of Bishops Curteys and Cooper. Curteys charged: "Wee buylde Castles and toures in the ayre to get us a name. So many heads, so many wittes, so many common wealths. Plato his Idaea [sic], Aristotle's felicitie, and Pythagoras numbers, trouble most men's brayns."[52] Bishop Cooper inveighed against the new "Heathenish Gentilitie, which raigneth in the hartes of godlesse persons, Atheistes, and Epicures. . . ."[53] Closely allied to the criticism—and a particular aversion of the Puritans[54] —was the disapprobation of stage plays, popular romances, and translations of novellas about love.

On the positive side, Elizabethan Anglicans found much to praise. The "Gloriana" of the poets found clerical panegyrists on "Queen's day" each November 17th, and thanked God that "the Supreme Governor of this realm . . . as well in all spiritual things and causes as temporal"[55] had maintained the peace and unity of church and state, preserving them from the perils of religious wars abroad and civil war at home.

The Church of England itself was praised in sermons of Richard Bancroft, future Archbishop of Canterbury, Richard Hooker, who wrote the finest apologia of the *via media* between Papal and Puritanical extremes that had appeared. Bancroft saw the Anglican church as the middle ground between authoritarianism and libertin-

51 *Certain Sermons appointed by the Queen's Majesty*, ed. Corrie, p. 278.

52 *A sermon preached before the Queens Maiestie at Grenewiche*, sig. Civ verso, cited in Blench, *Preaching in England*, p. 305.

53 *Certain Sermons wherein is contained the Defense of the Gospell now preached, against such Cavils and false accusations, as are objected against the Doctrine it selfe and the Preachers . . . by the friendes . . . of the Church of Rome* (1580), p. 189, cited in Blench, *Preaching in England*, p. 305.

54 These are considered in Chap. VIII.

55 An important phrase in the oath of Supremacy: Elizabeth wisely avoided calling herself "Supreme Head of the Church," as her brother and father had done.

ism in the Christian religion,[56] which was a church that combined scriptural authority with decent custom. Hooker desired to move from theory to facts, to ask whether the Church of England's ministry of the word and sacraments had not nourished its children in spirituality and the love of God, in a moving appeal: "I appeal to the conscience of every soul, that hath been truly converted by us, whether his heart were never raised up to God by our preaching; whether the words of our exhortation never wrung any tear of a penitent heart from his eyes; whether his soul never reaped any joy, any comfort, any consolation in Christ Jesus, by our sacraments, and prayers, and psalms, and thanksgiving; whether he were never bettered, but always worsed by us."[57] Hooker's strength was not only in his recognition of the rule of law and the force of custom in human societies, but in the judicious reasonableness and quiet dignity of his own spirit. In an age of contention his fairness in presenting the positions of his opponents was refreshing.

Perhaps the most important contribution Anglican preachers made during the century was the "new wholesomeness of tone" and "peculiarly fragrant spirituality" in the preaching of Hooker and Andrewes.[58] For ultimately it was recognised that the Christian gospel was not a matter of theological contention but of the application of the transforming love of God to the souls that were battered by sin, beaten by suffering, and terrified by the approach of death. This spirituality of forgiveness, the courage of faith, and the hope of the life everlasting was central to the preaching of Hooker and Andrewes, and, one might add, to the gospel of Puritanism, where the disputatiousness was more evident.

5. Sermon Structure

In the Middle Ages there were two forms of sermon construction, "ancient" and "modern." The ancient, copied from the homilies of the Church Fathers, either expounded and applied a passage of Scripture according to the order of the text or a thematic treatment of any subject according to Scripture and sense. The modern construction was more elaborate; it usually consisted of the Theme (a Scriptural text), the Exordium (which was a subordinate element

---

[56] *A Sermon preached at Paules Crosse . . . Anno 1588*, pp. 89-90.

[57] *Works*, vol. III, 679-80.

[58] Blench, *Preaching in England*, p. 319. The Puritan divines were greatly concerned with manners and ethics, which did not greatly concern Hooker and Andrewes. But they are equally interested in providing Christian palliatives for bruised consciences. See Chap. VIII.

of the theme), the Bidding Prayer, the Introduction of the Theme, the Division (with or without subdivisions of the topic), and finally, the Discussion. Dean Colet, Richard Taverner's *Postils* and Longland's sermons on the Penitential Psalms all favoured the ancient form. It was, however, chiefly on important public occasions such as the funeral of a prince, a confutation of heresy (e.g. Fisher's Sermon against Luther in 1521[59]), or in addresses to the clergy that the modern form was used by the early sixteenth-century Catholics.

By contrast the early Reformers discarded the modern form entirely in favour of various simpler ones. These might be topical, as the official *Book of Homilies* was, or they might be a simple exposition and application of the text, as in the sermons of John Bradford. Subtlety and erudition were avoided in the interests of making a simple and direct exposition of Christian truth. Hooper's sermons on the Book of Jonah are particularly interesting because in their use of lessons ("Doctrines") and moral applications ("Uses") from each verse, they anticipated the structure of the favourite Puritan preachers' sermons in Elizabeth's time.

Elizabethan sermons used a great variety of constructions. Perhaps most used a simplified version of the modern style, which almost reverted to the classical form. The classical was recommended by Reuchlin's *Liber Congestorum de arte praedicendi* (1503) and Erasmus's *Ecclesiastes* (1535); the form came to Elizabethan preachers by way of the treatise of Hyperius of Marburg, which was translated into English by John Ludham in 1577 as *The Practice of Preaching*. According to the treatise the essential parts of a sermon were: (a) reading of the sacred Scripture, (b) invocation, (c) exordium, (d) proposition, or division, (e) confirmation, (f) confutation, and (g) conclusion.[60]

The ancient sermon form is found in Becon's *Postils* (which are like Taverner's in expounding and applying the meaning of a summary of the Gospels and Epistles of the church's lectionary). Abbott's and King's sermons on Jonah, Deringe's on Hebrews, and Rainolds's on Obadiah and Haggai were constructed on this model.

The new Reformed method, of which Bishop Hooper's Jonah sermons were the first examples in England, was particularly

---

[59] See the analysis of this sermon's structure in Edward Surtz, *The Works and Days of John Fisher (1469-1535)*, pp. 302-306.
[60] See Blench, *Preaching in England*, p. 102.

approved by the Puritans and was "canonised" by the recommendation of William Perkins in his *Art of Prophecying*.[61]

6. *Sermon Styles*

Generally there was a great contrast between the styles of Edwardian and Elizabethan preachers. Like the Gospel, it was commending, Edwardian preaching was plain and direct. Particularly in Latimer, and a few others, it was also a racily colloquial style. The first *Book of Homilies* shares the simplicity and directness, but only occasionally the colloquialism.

Style among the Elizabethan preachers varied more widely. There was a great difference in pulpit style between the Ciceronian eloquence of Richard Hooker and the studied simplicity and concentrated directness of Walter Travers, a Puritan divine, both of whom preached at the Temple. Thomas Fuller says, "Here the pulpit spake pure Canterbury in the morning, and Geneva in the afternoon."[62] Travers expressed his views about the purposes of preaching and the imperative necessity for plainness of style forthrightly: ". . . the holie scriptures are to be expounded simplie and sincerely, and uttered with reverence. For some to shew themselves to the people to be lerned, stuffe ther sermons with divers sentences out of Philosophers, Poets, Orators, and Scholemen, and of the auncient fathers, Augustine, Hierome and others, and thos often times rehersed in greek or latin; by which pieces, sometime illfavoredly patched togither, they seeke and hunt for commendation, and to be esteemed lerned of the people, which also some doe that are unlerned."[63]

Travers was a learned man who hid his learning in his sermons. He was a senior fellow of Trinity College, Cambridge, a friend of Calvin's successor, Beza, and in 1595 he became provost of Trinity College, Dublin. William Holbrooke would have agreed with him when Travers observed: "The pulpit is not a place for a man to shewe his wit and reading in, but for plainnesse and evidence of the spirit."[64]

---

[61] The influence of Perkins is considered in Chap. VIII.

[62] *The Worthies of England*, ed. John Freeman, p. 133. Walter Travers, Cecil's candidate for the Mastership of the Temple, had been passed over in favour of Hooker. Their dignified dispute about the nature of a reformed national church was the crucible out of which the fifth book of Hooker's *Ecclesiastical Polity* came.

[63] *A full and plaine declaration of Ecclesiastical Discipline*, p. 104.

[64] Maclure, *Paul's Cross Sermons*, p. 147. Most preachers at Paul's Cross, Maclure notes, condemned the witty and extemporary extremes of preaching, preferring the plain, though carefully prepared, style (p. 146).

While English literature was delighting in euphuism, the sheer love of language for its own sake, and the brilliant joining of spiritual and sensual experience in the metaphysical love poems of John Donne, it would have been surprising if there were no preachers who revelled in wordplay and wit. Such preachers were Thomas Playfere, Lady Margaret Professor of Divinity at Cambridge, who used subtle reasoning and minute analysis and quoted from the Church Fathers and from classical poets; and John Carpenter, rector of Northleigh in Devon, who was fond of puns and heaping up similes. Two examples must suffice for a style which was in the reign of James I to achieve the acme of popularity, and which was peculiarly suitable for dazzling courtiers, as used by Lancelot Andrewes and John Donne. Typical was Playfere's: "Nay our very reason is treason, and our best affection is no better than an infection."[65] This is very like the wit in the early Shakespearian comedies, as in *Love's Labour's Lost* or in some of the passionate exaggerations in the hero's amorous protestations in *Romeo and Juliet*. Carpenter's examples boggled the imagination by leaving a confused, ornate impression, as when he said: "The polluted vessel is with water washed, the raw flesh is seasoned with salt, the dropping vine must bee pruned with a knife: the weake stomackes must have bitter wormewood; the slow Asse a whip, the heavie Oxe the goade, the idle scholler correction, and the fleshly Christian sower affliction."[66]

One could say of the varieties of Elizabethan preaching what Dryden said about Chaucer's *Canterbury Tales*—"Here is God's plenty." A contemporary preacher at Paul's Cross afforded the following description of their differences: "Some would have long texts: some short textes. Some would have Doctours, Fathers, and Councels: some call yt mans doctrine. Some would have it ordered by Logicke: some terme that mans wisdome. Some would have it polished by Rhetoricke: some call yt persuasibleness of wordes. And agayne in Rhetoricke some would have it holy eloquence, liable to the Ebrue & Greeke phrase: Some would have it proper and fittyng to the English capacitie. Some love study and learnyng in Sermons: Some allow onely a sudaine motion of the spirite. Some

---

[65] *The Meane in Mourning* (originally preached in 1595), printed 1623, p. 55, cited in A. F. Herr, *The Elizabethan Sermon*, p. 102.

[66] *Remember Lots Wife* (1588), sig. C8 r., cited in Herr, *Elizabethan Sermon*, p. 102. Carpenter was also addicted to puns, as when he said, "From Lots wife is learned the lot of the wicked in this world, with a terror unto all backsliders and wicked Apostates" (sig. E1 v.).

would have all said by heart: some would have oft recourse made to the booke. Some love gestures: some no gestures. Some love long Sermons: some short Sermons. Some are coy, and can broke no Sermons at all."[67]

7. *Representative Preachers: Latimer and Hooker*

After a quick survey of the sermons, rather than the preachers, of the Edwardian and Elizabethan periods, a corrective can be provided by two portraits of preachers contrasting in style and approach yet complementary, namely those of Latimer and Hooker.

Latimer was the originator of popular preaching. There would be no one like him until George Whitefield or John Wesley in the eighteenth century and Charles Haddon Spurgeon in the nineteenth. He exemplified Phillips Brooks' definition of preaching, "truth through personality." Not a great scholar, in his earlier years he was an opponent of the new learning, yet he was marvellously compounded of courage and compassion. He not only produced a series of sermons on the Card; he was himself a card and character.[68] He had a great gift for vivid narration and used an incisive vocabulary, replete with colloquialisms and proverbs.

Latimer had a whimsical and kindly sense of humour, which was occasionally ironical and mordant. Himself a preaching prelate (he was consecrated Bishop of Worcester in 1535), he denounced unpreaching prelates with an arsenical application of alliteration: "But now for the fault of unpreaching prelates, methink I could guess what might be said for excusing of them. They are so troubled with lordly living, they be so placed in palaces, couched in courts, ruffling in their tents, dancing in their dominions, burdened with ambassages, pampering of their paunches, like a monk that maketh his jubilee; munching in their mangers, and moiling in their gay manors and mansions, and so troubled with loitering in their

[67] John Dyos, *A Sermon preached at Paules Crosse* (1579), sig. F3 r., cited in Maclure, *Paul's Cross Sermons*, p. 146.

[68] He introduced his listeners to a game much like whist, known as "triumph": "I will, as I said, declare unto you Christ's rule, but that shall be in Christ's cards. And whereas you are wont to celebrate Christmas in playing at cards, I intend, by God's grace, to deal unto you Christ's cards, wherein you shall perceive Christ's rule. The game we shall play at shall be called the triumph, which if it be played at, he that dealeth shall win; the players likewise shall win; and the standers and lookers upon shall do the same; insomuch that there is no man that is willing to play at this triumph with these cards, but they shall all be winners, and no losers." The ingenuity of the man, his ability to catch common interest, and the looseness and naturalness of the style, with its digressions and repetitions and grammatical imprecision, are all to be found in this excerpt from the *Sermons*, ed. Corrie, p. 8.

lordships, that they cannot attend it."[69] But irony more often yielded to anecdote, as when in his third sermon before Edward VI he told the following story: "A good fellow on a time bade another of his friends to a breakfast and said, 'If you will come, you shall be welcome; but I tell you aforehand, you shall have but slender fare: one dish and that is all.' 'What is that?' said he. 'A pudding and nothing else.' 'Marry,' said he, 'you can draw me round about the town with a pudding. These bribing magistrates and judges follow gifts faster than the fellow would follow a pudding."[70]

Latimer's humour expressed his empathy with the common people when he said: "I had rather ye should come of a naughty mind to hear the word of God for novelty, or for curiosity to hear some pastime, than to be away. I had rather ye should come as the tale is told by the gentlewoman of London: one of her neighbours met her in the street, and said, 'Mistress, whither go ye?' 'Marry,' said she, 'I am going to St. Thomas of Acres to the sermon; I could not sleep all this last night, and I am going now thither; I never failed of a good nap there.'" It was a story Latimer could tell without fear of it rebounding on him, for no one surely ever fell asleep at his lively sermons, which had the character of conversations with the congregation, often divagatory, but always lively.

For his iconoclastic utterances Latimer had developed a vocabulary as inventive in abuse as Skelton's, with some unforgettable minting of words: "flattering clawbacks," "merit-mongers," "pot-gospellers," "mingle-mangle" (compromise), "these bladder-puffed up," "wily men," "flibbergibs," "upskips," "ye brain-sick fools, ye hoddy-pecks, ye doddy-pols, ye huddes." Latimer represented the Pharisees as saying to Christ: "Master, we know that thou art Tom Truth."[71] He succeeded in holding the easily straying attention of courtiers and the interest of a royal boy of 11 years in "a nipping sermon, a rough sermon and a sharp, biting sermon."[72]

Latimer comes more alive in his sermons than any preacher in Tudor England, not only because of his impressive individuality and deep humanity, but also because of the many autobiographical references in his sermons. Some of his finest passages of illustration are drawn from his memories of early life as a yeoman's son and country boy,[73] how he was taught to shoot the bow,[74] or his con-

---

[69] *Sermons*, p. 67. [70] *Ibid.*, p. 140.
[71] *Ibid.*, p. 201.
[72] Most of Latimer's phrases in this paragraph were collected by Hutchinson, *Cranmer and English Reformation*.
[73] *Sermons*, pp. 24, 101. [74] *Ibid.*, pp. 197-98.

version through Bilney, with whom he would visit prisoners in the castle.[75] He is never better able to use his countryman's knowledge than in the famous sermon, "Of the Plough."[76] He was equally moving when he spoke of the perils of a court preacher[77] or of the confusion and fear in Bilney's mind as he bore his faggot to the stake (incidentally an anticipation of Latimer's own martyrdom in 1555).[78]

For all its strength, it was not flawless preaching. Latimer was a people's preacher, not a preacher's preacher; he was certainly not a scholar's preacher, for he was critical of theological subtleties.[79] His sermons lacked the imaginative power of Fisher, and there was no poetry in them. They lacked clear structure; Latimer wandered all over the place as the fancy or the interested (or bored) look of the congregation dictated.[80]

Latimer's sermons and life show that he had two overriding concerns: to proclaim the word of God without fear or favour and to be the champion of the poor and the oppressed. As early as 1522 Cambridge University recognized his zeal in reforming ecclesiastical and social abuses by licensing him as one of only 12 preachers commissioned to preach anywhere in England. Even after he became Bishop of Worcester he continued to denounce evils in church and state. Latimer's Protestantism brought him first in Henry's time to resign his see of Worcester because his views conflicted with his sovereign's, and to the Tower in 1546; he was liberated after the accession of Edward VI and reached his zenith of popularity as court preacher. Mary's reign brought him to the Bocardo prison, with Ridley as his companion and his friend Cranmer as the silent and distant observer. Latimer's preaching was too courageous, too direct, and too compassionate ever to be mistaken for demagoguery. It was, whether in denunciation, retelling a Biblical narrative, or in exposition, despite all its delightful divagations, prophetic and popular preaching at its best. Latimer was even capable of writing a good Communion meditation, perhaps the last task one would have laid on his charitable shoulders. Here,

---

[75] Ibid., pp. 334-45.
[76] Ibid., pp. 59-78.
[77] Ibid., pp. 134-35.
[78] Ibid., p. 222.
[79] He dismissed "school-doctors and such fooleries" after his meeting with Bilney, and characterised the spinners of theological subtleties with the words, "as for curiouse braynes nothinge can content them."
[80] Latimer does not worry about being discursive ("I will tell you a pretty story of a friar to refresh you withal") or to make a good point even if it is out of order ("peradventure it myght come here after in better place, but yet I wyll take it, whiles it commeth to my mind.")

too, his understanding of the Gospel's relevance to the hardships of life was as practiced as ever, as when he was expounding the Lord's Supper as a Great Banquet where Christ is *epulum et hospes*: "But now ye know that where there be great dishes and delicate fare, there be commonly prepared certain sauces, which shall give men a lust to their meats: as mustard, vinegar, and such like sauces. So this feast, this costly dish, hath its sauces: but what be they? Marry, the cross, affliction, tribulation, persecution, and all manner of miseries: for, like as sauces make lusty the stomach to receive meat, so affliction stirreth up in us a desire to Christ. For when we be in quietness, we are not hungry, we care not for Christ: but when we be in tribulation, and cast in prison, then we have a desire to him; then we learn to call upon him. . . ."[81] Latimer was in the unfamiliar role of priest; he was better as a prophet.

Hooker, though lacking the immediate empathy, the capacity to project his personality, the humour, and the prophetic zeal of Latimer, was able to plumb a spirituality of greater profundity. Latimer certainly believed in the doctrine of the cross; his life was its scarlet seal. Yet he lacked the theological subtlety, the command of style, and the imagination to express it as Hooker or Andrewes could. Latimer was incapable of the concentration of thought and expression of the doctrine of the cross, in order to be able to say, as Hooker did: "Affliction is both a medicine if we sin, and a preservative that we do not."[82] Hooker shone best as a priest, as the apologist of the church and the representative of the people before God.

Hooker's sermons read better today than Latimer's, though they were preached in a very indifferent manner. Fuller said of his delivery: "He may be said to have made good music with his fiddle and stick alone, without any rosin, having neither pronunciation nor gesture to grace his matter."[83] Izaak Walton confirmed the impression: ". . . his sermons were neither long nor earnest, but uttered with a grave zeal, and an humble voice; his eyes always fixt on one place to prevent his imagination from wandering, insomuch that he seemed to study as he spake. . . ."[84] They read well because they are meaty and the skilful use of rhetoric was largely con-

81 *Sermons*, pp. 463-64.
82 *Works*, III, 636. See also the fourth paragraph of the sermon, "A Remedy against Sorrow and Fear," for a fuller statement of the grounds for patience in troubles.
83 Fuller, *Worthies of England*, p. 264.
84 Walton's *Life of Hooker*, in *Works*, ed. Keble, I, 79.

cealed. Walton rightly emphasized the reasonableness of his approach—he did "rather convince and persuade, than frighten men into piety"—and the modesty which sought for neither amusement nor self-glorification in sermons. But it is difficult to believe that his "unlearned hearers" were edified by sermons demanding such concentration. Certainly his sermons that have survived seem rather to have been prepared for the lawyers of the Temple than for the parishioners of Drayton Beauchamp, Boscombe, or Bishopsbourne churches, of which Hooker was successively rector. The clarity of his definitions, the building up of his "cases," the confirmation of his doctrines with Biblical and Patristic examples, and the rationality of his approach, confirm the impression.

It is only a *felix error* (Walton's phrase) that Hooker's sermons survived at all. It was the opposition of "Geneva" Travers (afternoon Reader at the Temple Church) that made Hooker write out for private circulation some of the sermons to which Travers had made objections. Samuel Taylor Coleridge wrote of the sermon, "The Certainty and Perpetuity of Faith in the Elect": "I can remember no other discourse that sinks into and draws up comfort from the depths of our being, below our own distinct, with the clearness and godly loving kindness of this truly evangelical and God-to-be-thanked-for-sermon."[85] Canon F. E. Hutchinson was of the opinion that Hooker's sermons on the certainty of faith, justification, and the nature of pride had "more permanent value than any sermons of the reign."[86] The historian of preaching, J. W. Blench, sees Hooker's great mission as that of "bringing peace to the bruised conscience; instead of excoriating the wounds of the soul, he brings precious unguents to soothe and heal them."[87] This was high praise, especially when it is recalled that only a fraction of Hooker's sermons have survived.

Hooker's themes were central and practical. He was the great preacher of faith—faith as the power to trust in God's promises because of the memory of His past mercies;[88] the invincibility of the faith of the elect;[89] the primacy of justification by faith, with works as consequences, not preconditions;[90] contagious faith as it

[85] See S. T. Coleridge, *Notes on English Divines*, in *Works*, IV, ed. H. N. Coleridge, *ad. loc.*

[86] "The English Pulpit from Fisher to Donne," *The Cambridge History of English Literature*, IV, chap. 12, p. 236.

[87] *Preaching in England in the late fifteenth and sixteenth centuries*, p. 319.

[88] See "The Certainty and Perpetuity of Faith in the Elect," esp. in sec. 7.

[89] *Ibid.*, sec. 6.

[90] See "A Discourse of Justification, Works, and how the Foundation of Faith is overthrown."

works through love;[91] faith's necessary edification, especially against mockers;[92] and faith strengthened by the Lord's Supper.[93] How practical and judicious he could be is evident in his consideration of whether God's elect can ever find their faith utterly to fail. "The question," he said, "is of moment; the repose and tranquillity of infinite souls doth depend on it."[94] Equally practical was his advice to the despondent in the same sermon: "of us, who is here which cannot very soberly advise his brother? Sir, you must learn to strengthen your Faith by that experience which heretofore you have had of God's great goodness to you, *Per ea quae agnoscas praestita, discas sperare promissa*, By those things which you have known performed, learn to hope for those things which are promised."[95]

Faith, though central, was not the only theme of Hooker's sermons. He preached on "The Nature of Pride" (a sermon title), and had an impressive funeral sermon called "A Remedy for Sorrow and Fear." He was always impressed by the generosity of grace, and ended a sermon on Matthew 7:7, 8 ("Ask and it shall be given you; seek and ye shall find; knock, and it shall be opened unto you") by asking his hearers to act as if they believed "it is the glory to God to give": "Let there be on our part, be no stop, and the bounty of God we know is such, that he granteth over and above our desires. Saul sought an ass, and found a Kingdom. Solomon named wisdom, and God gave Solomon wealth also, by way of surpassing. 'Thou has prevented thy servant with blessings,' saith the Prophet David. 'He asked life, and thou gavest him long life, even for ever and ever.' God a giver; 'He giveth liberally, and upraideth none in any wise': and therefore he better knoweth than we the best times, and the best means, and the best things, wherein the good of our souls consisteth."

[91] See the second Sermon on Jude, para. 32 and 33: "If there be any feeling of Christ, any drop of heavenly dew, or any spark of God's good Spirit within you, stir it up, be careful to stir it up, be careful to build and edify, first yourselves, and then your flocks, in this most holy Faith. 33. I say, first, yourselves; for he, which will set the hearts of other men with the love of Christ, must himself burn with love."

[92] See the first sermon on Jude.

[93] See the second sermon on Jude, para. 11: ". . . is not all other wine like the water of Marah, being compared to the cup which we bless? . . . Doth not he which drinketh behold plainly in this cup, that his soul is bathed in the blood of the Lamb? O beloved in our Lord and Saviour Jesus Christ, if ye will taste how sweet the Lord is, if ye will receive the King of Glory, build yourselfes." It should be noted that Hooker, advocate of reason as he is, shows his affectionate pastoral concern here and particularly in paragraph 12 of this sermon.

[94] "The Certainty and Perpetuity of Faith in the Elect," para. 6.

[95] *Ibid.*, para. 7.

Among the qualities of Hooker's sermons were the capacity to develop a central and practical theme with many Biblical illustrations and an occasional patristic citation,[96] the appeal to reason and experience,[97] the use of careful definitions,[98] his charitable tolerance,[99] and his quiet and uncontentious spirit. Allied to these was his mastery of the art of persuasion and his use of various literary devices to attain his ends.[100]

Hooker was a master of the balanced sentence. The following is an example of his architectonics, and typical in its robust common sense: "The light would never be so acceptable, were it not for that usual intercourse of darkness. Too much honey doth turn to gall; and too much joy, even spiritual, would make us wantons. Happier a great deal is that man's case, whose soul by inward desolation is humbled, than he whose heart is through abundance of spiritual delight lifted up and exalted beyond measure. Better is it sometimes to go down into the pit with him, who, beholding darkness, and bewailing the loss of inward joy and consolation, crieth from the bottom of the lowest hell, 'My God, my God, why hast thou forsaken me?' than continually to walk arm in arm with Angels, to sit as it were in Abraham's bosom, and to have no thought, no cogitation, but 'I thank my God it is not with me as it is with other men.' No, God will have them that shall walk in light to feel now and then what it is to sit in the shadow of death. A grieved spirit is therefore no argument of a faithless mind."[101] How majestically the magisterial conclusion is arrived at, yet how inevitable!

Hooker also knew how to begin and end sermons. Perhaps the best examples of each can be drawn from the sermon, "The Nature of Pride." It begins: "The nature of man, being much more delighted to be led than drawn, doth many times stubbornly resist authority, when to persuasion it easily yieldeth." It concludes by

---

[96] "The Certainty and Perpetuity of Faith in the Elect" is full of such instances, including Abraham, Job, Habakkuk, Peter, John, Paul, Nathanael; and there is a reference to Sallust.

[97] The first sermon on Jude, para. 15.

[98] "A Remedy against Sorrow and Fear," para. 6, has this definition of fear: ". . . fear is nothing else but a perturbation of the mind, through an opinion of some imminent evil, threatening the destruction or great annoyance of our nature, which to shun it doth contract and deject itself." See also his statement of the cause of superstition in "A Discourse of Justification," sec. 23.

[99] "A Discourse of Justification," sec. 27 and 39, where he argued that the Church of Rome, even in its insistence on works, did not deny the foundation of Christianity.

[100] See Fritz Pützer, *Prediger des englischen Barok*, pp. 36f.

[101] "The Certainty and Perpetuity of Faith in the Elect," para. 6.

agreeing, with St. Augustine, that God helps the conceited soul by withdrawing his grace and so establishes it later the more surely on Him: "Ask the very soul of Peter," demands Hooker, "and it shall undoubtedly make you itself this answer: My eager protestations, made in the glory of my ghostly strength, I am ashamed of; but those crystal tears, wherewith my sin and weakness was bewailed, have procured my endless joy; my strength hath been my ruin, and my fall my stay." These concluding paradoxes, which anticipate both Donne and Andrewes, are also reminiscent of El Greco's *St. Peter's Repentance*,[102] with its great luminous eyes, washed with "crystal tears."

Hooker, too, could create memorable similes and metaphors to fasten his lessons on the memory of his congregations. "As a loose tooth is a grief to him that eateth, so doth a wavering and unstable word in speech, that tendeth to instruction, offend."[103] This is in itself the perfect lapidary comment on Eliphaz's query: "Shall a wise man speak words of the wind?"[104] Equally apt was his vivid description of the bewilderment fear throws Christians into: "But because we are in danger, like chased birds, like doves, that seek and cannot see the resting holes that are right before them: therefore our Saviour giveth his Disciples these encouragements beforehand, that fear might never so amaze them. . . ."[105]

Not all excellences are to be found even in Hooker. The vigour of Latimer and his attack are replaced by a peace that sometimes is indistinguishable from a euphoric blandness. The brilliant surprises sprung by Donne and Andrewes are missing in him. There is probably far too much solid meat in every one of his sermons to be easily digestible by his listeners. His delivery might do for the law court, but it was extremely dull for the pulpit. His strengths were the deep respect he had for the church, the adoration and reverence for Christ and His ordinances, and the dignity he kept even in controversy, and the compassion for humanity, which, though less obtrusive, might be as real as Latimer's.

The first generation of the English reformers needed a prophet such as Latimer, with his thundering demand for obedience to the Gospel, his brusque way with opposition, his denunciation of social injustice, his racy colloquialisms, and his courage and compassion.

---

102 This painting is to be found in the Putnam Gallery of the Art Museum of San Diego.

103 "A Discourse of Justification," sec. 39.

104 Job 15:2.

105 "A Remedy against Sorrow and Fair," last para.

The second generation of Anglicans needed the balance, the attachment to the Church of England, and the sweet reasonableness and deep devotion of Hooker. The first generation needed prophetic courage to begin the task of reformation, the second, saintly sagacity for the task of consolidation. The contribution of Latimer and Hooker were therefore complementary.

CHAPTER VII

PURITAN WORSHIP[1]

THE SCOPE of Anglican worship was firmly defined by the official prayer-books of the Church of England. Puritan worship is a much more amorphous term, partly because of the various groups included within Puritanism, partly because of the change in the interests of Puritans from one decade to another.

Puritanism included loyal Anglicans using the prayer-book, yet hoping for an improved formulary of worship less open to ceremonial or Vestiarian criticism and encouraging a greater use of expository preaching. The term embraced embryonic Presbyterians—known as "Disciplinarians"—who regarded *John Knox's Genevan Service Book*[2] or its revisions prepared by English Puritans[3] as more truly patterned on God's word and the usage of the primitive church. Third, Puritanism included the semi-Separatists, like the Leyden minister of the Pilgrim fathers, John Robinson, and the proto-Independents such as the Brownists and Barrowists who desired to establish a more charismatic worship, with full opportunity for extemporary, Spirit-inspired prayers. All three forms were used by Puritans.

Furthermore, the interest of Puritanism differed, even in liturgical matters, in three different decades. In the 1560s Puritanism centred on trivial sartorial and ceremonial issues. Could a sincerely Protestant minister wear the surplice, a garment worn by the sacrificing priests of the Roman Catholic church, without compromising his faith? Could he legitimately take part in an Anglican liturgy that required him to bow at the reception of the consecrated species in Holy Communion, and thus commit the idolatry of worshipping the created instead of the Creator, to say nothing of seem-

---

[1] My *The Worship of the English Puritans* (1948) is an extensive treatment of the theme from approximately 1550 to 1750, with full documentation. The present chapter reconsiders the issues only in the sixteenth century, and uses supplementary research materials.

[2] See William D. Maxwell, *John Knox's Genevan Service Book 1556.*

[3] The so-called Waldegrave and Middleburg editions. The former is entitled, "A booke of the forme of common prayers, administration of the Sacraments: &c. agreeable to Gods Worde and the use of the reformed Churches," and was probably printed in 1584 or 1585. There is a reprint of it in Peter Hall, *Fragmenta Liturgica*, I. The Middleburg edition was printed by Schilders of that city in 1586, 1587, and 1602. It is reprinted in Peter Hall, *Reliquiae Liturgicae*, I. The originals are in the British Museum. See British Museum Catalogue, vol. L 50, pp. 711-12.

ing to condone the rejected Roman doctrine of Transubstantiation? Could he decently make the sign of the cross in administering Baptism, since this was to introduce a sacramental sign, if not a new sacrament, without explicit sanction from the Bible? Could he insist on the wearing of rings in the service of Holy Matrimony when there was no authority for it in God's word? Small as the issues were, they raised the fundamental question of authority for worship—the Bible or tradition? As was seen before,[4] the bishops claimed that where the Scriptures were silent, the church could act, while the Puritans insisted on an explicitly Biblical sanction for every ordinance of worship and almost every detail of worship.

When, however, the battle for a more truly Reformed type of worship moved into the seventies, with the Admonition controversy, there was a far more radical criticism of the Book of Common Prayer, and a dissatisfaction with episcopacy (especially as prelatically involved in demanding obedience through the mechanisms of High Commission and Star Chamber) and with the ecclesiology of the Church of England since it lacked provision for disciplining and purifying the church membership. It was in this period, under the guidance of Cartwright, Travers, and Fenner, as well as Field and Wilcox, that the Genevan pattern in worship, church order, and government, and discipline was openly espoused.

In the 1580s, however, the difference between the patient and impatient Puritans widened. Robert Browne, a leader of the impatient Puritans, became a Puritan Separatist and established independent congregations in Norwich and elsewhere. After his release from prison, to which he was condemned for an act of schism, he and his congregation emigrated to Holland. In Middleburg in 1582 he published a call for creative impatience in *A Book which sheweth the Life and Manners of all true Christians*, and in *A Treatise of Reformation without tarrying for any and of the Wickedness of those Preachers which will not reform till the Magistrate command or compel them*. His conviction was that reformation "was not to be begun by whole parishes, but rather of the worthiest, were they never so few." He insisted that such "gathered Churches,"[5]

---

[4] See Chap. II.

[5] It is pertinent to cite Browne's definition of a "gathered" church: "The Church planted or gathered [from out of the world] is a company or number of Christians or believers, which, by a willing covenant made with their God, are under the government of God and Christ, and keep his laws in one holy communion: because Christ hath redeemed them unto holiness and happiness for ever, from which they were fallen by the sin of Adam." (From *A Booke which sheweth the Life and Manners of all true Christians* (Middleburg, 1582), C3 r.; also ed.

bound under God by covenant were to be independent of the state and to be self-governing. Barrow, Greenwood, and Penry were the martyrs of the new *ecclesiolae*, protesting in the name of the freedom of the gospel; but Browne recanted and received episcopal ordination in 1591, and was rector of Achurch, Northants until his death in 1633.[6] In 1588 and 1589 the *Marprelate Tracts* voiced the growing bitterness of the Puritans against the entrenched episcopal establishment.

More positively during the same period, Puritan ministers were giving an example of the godliness and learning that was at the heart of Puritanism. Richard Greenham fulfilled an exemplary pastorate at Dry Drayton, Cambridgeshire from 1570 to 1591, where he also taught pastors, including the brilliant Puritan preacher, Henry Smith, lecturer at St. Clement Danes from 1587, and his son-in-law, the long-lived John Dod, whose kindly witticisms were widely quoted.[7] William Perkins, fellow of Christ's College, Cambridge, had a great influence as a teacher and preacher. He was the most influential of all the early Puritan moral theologians;[8] his *Arte of Prophesying* was the major manual of Puritan preaching. Perkins died in 1602, and his mantle fell on his successors, Paul Baynes and the great theological casuist, William Ames.

It is necessary to look back at Puritanism with the eyes of John Geree, writing in 1646, in *The Character of an old English Puritane or Nonconformist* to find the essential spirit of Puritanism, especially as it relates to worship:

> The Old English Puritane was such an one that honoured God above all, and under God gave every one his due. His first care was to serve God, and therein he did not what was good in his own, but in God's sight, making the word of God the rule of his worship. He highly esteemed order in the house

---

A. Peel and L. H. Carlson, *The Writings of Robert Harrison and Robert Browne*, p. 253. The Church is to consist only of Christians, all members are to share the privileges and responsibilities of its government; and the Church is to be free of episcopal and royal interference.

6 Browne, however, died in Northampton gaol, where he was incarcerated for assaulting a policeman. It is understandable why Independents (later Congregationalists) disliked being called "Brownists."

7 He would, for example, inform friends who had come into money that although they had transferred from a boat to a ship, they were still at sea. Cf. Gordon S. Wakefield, *Puritan Devotion*, pp. 7-8.

8 In the seventeenth century he was considered the equal of Hooker and almost the equal of Calvin.

of God: but would not under colour of that submit to superstitious rites, which are superfluous and perish in their use.
. . . He made conscience of all God's ordinances, though some
he esteemed of more consequence. He was much in praier;
with it he began and closed the day. In it he was exercised in
his closet, family and publike assembly. He esteemed that
manner of praier best, where by the gift of God, expressions
were varied according to present wants and occasions; Yet he
did not account set forms unlawful. Therefore in that circumstance of the Church he did not wholly reject the liturgy but
the corruption of it. He esteemed reading an ordinance of God
both in private and publike; but he did not account reading to
be preaching. . . . The Sacrament of Baptism he received in
Infancy, which he looked back to in his age, to answer his
ingagements, and claim his priviledges. The Lord's Supper
he accounted part of his soul's food: to which he laboured to
keep an appetite. He esteemed it an ordinance of nearest communion with Christ, so requiring most exact preparation.[9]

Here was the absolute primacy of the Biblical criterion in Puritan
worship—"to serve God . . . making the word of God the rule of
his worship," the preference for extemporary prayer without denying the value of set forms, the importance of preaching as of meditation on God's word, and the centrality of the Lord's Supper, "an
ordinance of nearest communion with Christ." In all of it there was
the profound sincerity and inwardness, as well as intensity, of
Puritan worship. Geree's final words in the characterization of an
old Puritan are: "his whole life he counted a warfare, wherein
Christ was his captain, his arms, praiers, and tears. The Crosse
his Banner and his word *Vincit qui patitur*."[10]

1. SOLA SCRIPTURA *as Liturgical Criterion*

The main principle of the absolute authority of God's word in
the Scriptures for faith, ethics, and worship was expressed by all
Puritans. To depart from this is the utmost human impertinence
and pretentiousness, for it implies that one knows God's will better
than He does, or that the inherent weakness of original sin does not
blind one's judgment through egocentricity. God's word is a full,
not a partial revelation of the divine purpose for humanity. Con-

[9] Cited by Wakefield, *Puritan Devotion*, p. xxii. Incidentally, the second chapter
is an excellent study of Puritan interpretation of Scripture.
[10] *Ibid.*

siderations of tradition or aesthetics are, therefore, strictly irrelevant once the Biblical criterion for worship has been accepted. Even when there are cases not mentioned in the Scriptures, St. Paul has provided four secondary criteria for testing for all orders and ceremonies of the church.[11]

On this basis of the binding authority of Scripture the Puritans established that the worship of the Apostolic Church was characterised by six ordinances—prayer, praise, the reading and preaching of the word, the administration of the sacraments of Baptism and the Lord's Supper, catechising, and the exercise of discipline. The *locus classicus* for Apostolic worship was Acts 2:41-42: "Then they that glady received his worde were baptized; and the same day there were added to the Church about thre thousand soules. And they continued in the Apostles doctrine and felowship, and breaking of bread, and prayers."[12] The types of prayer, supplications, intercessions, thanksgivings, were derived from I Timothy 2:1ff. and invocation or adoration and confession were derived from the example of the Lord's Prayer. For praise, they turned to Ephesians 5:19, with its reference to "psalmes, and hymnes and spiritual songs, singing and making melodie to the Lord in your hearts."[13] The proclamation of the Gospel became the central feature of Puritan worship, its importance attested to by the entire corpus of the Scriptures, which provided a saving knowledge of God, but especially in II Corinthians 1:12 and Romans 10:14-15. Their authority for the "Gospel Sacraments" was Matthew 28:19-20 and I Corinthians 11:23-26, among other texts. Puritans had to look hard to find a text to justify their using a set form of words for catechism when they tended to reject both set sermons (read homilies) and set forms of prayer (a liturgy). II Timothy 1:13 provided the required proof-text: "Kepe the true paterne of the wholsome wordes which ye has heard of me in faith and love which is in Christ Iesus."[14] Finally, the demand for purity in the church to be protected by the exercise of ecclesiastical censures was sanctioned by Matthew 18:15-18 and 18:2; I Corinthians 5:3-5, and the Third Epistle of John 10, which also provided the complete procedure for admonishment, excommunication, and readmission of penitent offenders.

---

[11] See Chap. II for the four Pauline epistolary references for the secondary criteria of worship.
[12] The Genevan version of the Bible, 1560.
[13] *Ibid.*   [14] *Ibid.*

The Scriptures also provided the Puritans with the authority for their occasional ordinances. Prophesyings, gatherings for expounding the Scriptures and for answering questions due to difficulties in comprehending their meaning, were sanctioned by I Corinthians 14:1 and 31. If a day of humiliation was held for the corporate expression of the people's penitence following a great natural, political, or military calamity, the invariable order was fasting, prayer, and sermon, as in Acts 13:1-3 and 14:23. When the exiled Puritans in Arnhem anointed their sick with oil and prayed for their recovery, it was strictly according to the model supplied by James 5:14-15.

Even such details as the frequency of divine services were sought in the Scriptures. The double burnt offering in Numbers 28:9 sanctioned two services on the Lord's Day; even the necessity for the Lord's Supper being preceded by a sermon was supplied by the precedent of Acts 20:27. Acts 4:36 and I Corinthians 16:2 enabled the Puritans to determine who should collect the offertory and at what point in the service it should be presented. Text scrutinizing went to ludicrous extremes on occasion, however. It was argued that marriage, not being a sacrament, did not require the services of a minister for its solemnisation, since it was not included in the list of pastoral duties in II Timothy 4:2ff. A text became a pretext when Matthew 11:28, "Come unto me, all ye that are wearie & laden, and I will ease you," was taken as proof that the only appropriate posture at the Lord's table was sitting, as witnessing to the rest that Christ promised to his disciples. Of equal perversity and ingenuity was Cartwright's argument for stability of position in worship (over against the mobility of the one presiding over Anglican worship who moves from prayer desk to lectern to pulpit to altar) drawn from Acts 1:15: "Peter stood up in the midst of the disciples." The most extreme example was the denial of the right to have responses in public prayers because the flesh of the repetitive cuckoo was forbidden in Leviticus.[15]

While the Puritans in their controversy with the Anglicans were not above straining the natural meaning of texts to yield significances unintended by the writers of the Biblical books, yet normally they were far from being legalists. It was they who disapproved of burdensome ceremonies, citing Acts 15:28 as their warrant for

[15] This example is given without bibliographical reference by the distinguished Scottish liturgiologist, the Rev. Dr. William McMillan, author of *The Worship of the Scottish Reformed Church 1550-1638*, in a book review in *The Dunfermline Press and West of Fife Advertiser* (24 July, 1948).

Christian freedom. Again it was not the Puritans but the Anglican bishops who were trying to impose vestments, which seems Aaronical rather than Christian, and became a stumbling block to the weaker brethren. It was in the strength of their conviction of the Scripture as the sole criterion for determining the ordinances and the details of worship that they went on to attack the Book of Common Prayer.

2. The Puritan Critique of the Prayer-book

Hooker provided a fair summary of the Puritan critique of the Book of Common Prayer, because it had

> too great affinity with the Form of the Church of Rome; it differeth too much from that which Churches elsewhere reformed allow and observe; our attire disgraceth it; it is not orderly read, nor gestured as beseemeth; it requireth nothing to be done which a child may not lawfully do; it hath a number of short cuts or shreddings, which may be better called wishes than Prayers; it intermingleth prayings and readings in such manner, as if suppliants should use in proposing their suits unto mortal Princes, all the world would judge them mad; it is too long, and by that mean abridgeth Preaching; it appointeth the people to say after the Minister; it spendeth time in singing and in reading the Psalms by course, from side to side; it useth the Lord's Prayer too oft; the Songs of *Magnificat*, *Benedictus* and *Nunc Dimittis*, it might very well spare; it hath the Litany, the Creed of Athanasius, and *Gloria Patri*, which are superfluous; it craveth earthly things too much; for deliverance from those evils against which we pray it giveth no thanks; some things it asketh unseasonably, when they need not be prayed for, as deliverance from thunder and tempest, when no danger nigh; some in too abject and diffident manner, as that God would give us that which we for our unworthiness dare not ask; some which ought not to be desired, as the deliverance from sudden death, riddance from all adversity, and the extent of saving mercy towards all men. These and such like are the imperfections whereby our form of Common Prayer is thought to swerve from the Word of God.[16]

[16] *Ecclesiastical Polity*, Book v, chap. xxvii, sec. 1.

Within its brief scope this was a remarkable summary of the many incisive criticisms of the Prayer Book of the Church of England by the Puritan writers. While the Second Prayer Book of Edward VI required a priest or deacon only to wear a surplice, in 1559 Queen Elizabeth reinstated the ornaments rubric of the second year of King Edward VI's reign, requiring alb and vestment or cope. No amount of episcopal insistence that the vestments were to be worn for the sake of decency, comeliness, and good order blinded the Puritans to the fact that the vestments, theoretically *adiaphora* and of their nature indifferent, were made essential requisites of Anglican worship. Puritans argued that the requesting of the vestments was an infringement of the crown rights of Christ the Redeemer, who had freed Christians from the bondage of the ceremonial law of the Old Covenant which was now being reintroduced by Archbishop Matthew Parker in his *Advertisements*.[17] Other Puritan arguments used against the vestments were their association with the now discredited Roman Catholic faith, that they were garments of priests who believed in the sacrifice of the Mass and in Transubstantiation, and not at all suitable for a faith which asserted the doctrine of the priesthood of all believers, and that they were symbols of pomp and grandeur wholly unsuitable for the disciples of a humble Christ. Furthermore, they were out of step with the Continental Reformed churches in the matter of vestments.

The three "noxious" ceremonies were discarded as having no Biblical authority. *A Survey of the Booke of Common Prayer by way of 197 Queres grounded upon 58 places*[18] argued that kneeling at the Communion was un-Apostolic, unprimitive, unreformed, and utterly unsuitable for those who wished to avoid the appearance of evil. The same was true of the other two ceremonies, namely the crossing of the child in Baptism and the use of the ring in marriage, which were considered by Puritans to be unwarrantable human additions to the Dominical institutions as recorded in Scripture, and therefore arrogantly presumptuous. Query 95 of the *Survey* asked:

---

[17] *A Parte of a Register* (c. 1590, MS in the Dr. Williams' Library, Gordon Square, London), p. 41, states: "if it be abolished and *Christ* bee come in steede, then a great iniurie is done to Christ for manie causes. The one is, that those ceremonies which Christ by his passion did abolishe should in contempte of him and his passion be taken agayne." The interpretation of the Ornaments Rubric and the relative authority of Parker's *Advertisements* are controversial issues. For a brief note, with suggested further reading, see the *Oxford Dictionary of Church History*, ed. F. L. Cross, p. 995b.

[18] It is to be found in W. H. Frere and C. E. Douglas, *Puritan Manifestoes*, reissued with a preface by Norman Sykes, 1954.

"Whither the childe be not received againe by and with Crossing, and so may seeme to be a sacrament as well as Baptism for that cause . . . as if regeneration were by baptisme, and incorporation by crossing?"[19] Robert Johnson of Northampton asked where was the consistency, why the shaven crown was rejected but not the square cap, why the tippet was commanded and the stole forbidden, and "Wee would knowe why you do reiect *hallowed beades*, and yet receyve *hallowed ringes*. . . . ?"[20] His conclusion was: "And of these things I say we would have and heare some reason taken and gathered out of the word of God, which if we shall heare, we shall be gladde to learn. . . . If the conscience be perswaded, the hande shall straightway subscribe." If God did not ordain these ceremonies, how can they either please Him or build up his people in the faith?

Puritans were also greatly concerned that officially prescribed homilies, produced during a shortage of educated Protestant clergy, would oust sermons. This was why they berated the clergy of the Church of England as "dumb dogs" who could read the Book of Common Prayer and the homilies, but who could not or would not preach. The Puritans argued that while the word was all one, whether read or preached, nonetheless the preached word was more effective when it was applied to the minds and hearts of the congregation, whether for information, consolation, or rebuke. The point was, "As the fire stirred giveth more heat, so the Word, as it were, blown by preaching, flameth more in the hearers than when it is read."[21]

Archbishop Grindal, in his historic letter to the queen, stated the Puritan position strongly in his defence of "Prophesyings": "The Godly Preacher is termed in the Gospel a Faithful Servant, who knoweth how to give his Lord's family their appointed food in season; who can apply his speech to the diversity of times, places and hearers; which cannot be done in Homilies: exhortations, reprehensions, and persuasions, are uttered with more affection, to the moving of the Hearers, in Sermons than in Homilies."[22] Hooker himself grudgingly admitted the power of Puritan sermons as "the art which our adversaries use for the credit of their Sermons," and acknowledged the "especial advantages which Sermons naturally

19 *Ibid.*, p. 90.
20 *A Parte of a Register*, p. 104.
21 Hooker's *Ecclesiastical Polity*, ed. Hanbury, vol. ii, p. 76n.
22 See John Strype, *The History of the Life and Acts of Edmund Grindal*, p. 595.

have to procure attention, both in that they always come new, and because by the hearer it is still presumed, that if they be let slip for the present, what good soever they contain is lost, and that without all hope of recovery."[23]

The Puritans objected also to the lections in the Book of Common Prayer. They took exception to the number of readings from the Apocrypha as implying a slight on the sufficiency of the canonical Scriptures,[24] and to the fragmentation of Scripture in the epistles and gospels.[25] Chillingworth would later affirm that the Bible was the religion of Protestants. The Bible, the whole Bible, and nothing but the Bible, is the whole religion of Puritans.

The prayers of the prayer-book were also heavily criticised. The collects were, in their view, as Hooker suggested, "wishes" rather than prayers, mere "short-cuts" to prayer, as contrasted with the longer prayers of the primitive and Reformed churches.[26] Their brevity was distracting for the Puritans, but for Hooker they had the advantage of keeping the worshipper awake by a "piercing kind of brevity."[27] The accuracy of collects for celebrated anniversaries was also questioned[28] and the stylized endings were considered "vain repetitions." The Litany was thought to be something of an anachronism, since its petitions were unrealistic and inappropriate to the condition of most who used it. The people's responses were stigmatised as "vain repetitions" and a mere tossing to and fro of tennis balls. The latter was a common derisive metaphor employed by the Puritans for responses which they considered were forbidden by St. Paul's words in I Corinthians 14:6, requiring only one person to speak at once, and approving *Amen* as the only word of corporate response permitted.[29]

Not only the types of prayer were criticised, but also the content. It was asserted that the prayer-book craved too many material blessings. For example, the author of *The Second Admonition*

---

[23] *Ecclesiastical Polity*, Book v, chap. xxii, sec. 20.

[24] *A Survey of the Booke of Common Prayer* complains: "In place of 182 chapters canonical left unread, there be 132 out of the Apocrypha appointed by the Calendar to be read:" Frere and Douglas, *Puritan Manifestoes*, p. 26.

[25] Query 44 of *A Survey* asks: "Whither the reading of these Epistles and Gospels (so called) be not the same fault which is blamed as unorderly in the preface of the Communion Book, *viz.* a breaking of one peece of Scripture from another?"

[26] See *The Second Admonition*, i, 138; iii, 210ff.

[27] *Ecclesiastical Polity*, Book v, chap. xxxiii.

[28] For example, the Collect for the Sunday after Christmas reads: "Almighty God who hast given us thy only begotten Sonne to take our nature upon him and *this day* to be borne of a pure Virgine, &c." See Frere and Douglas, *Puritan Manifestoes*, p. 57.

[29] *Ibid.*, p. 49.

believed that more than a third of the prayers, excluding psalms and Scriptural citations, were "spent in praying for and praying against the (commodities and) incommodities of this life, which is contrary to all the arguments or contents of the Prayers of the Church set down in Scripture, and especially of our Saviour Christ's Prayer, by the which ours ought to be directed."[30] Two petitions in the collects were criticised for smacking more of Popish fear than Christian confidence.[31] Finally, the criticisms of the prayers revealed a fundamental difference of attitude between the Anglicans and the Puritans on the repetition of the Lord's Prayer. For some Puritans the Lord's Prayer was a pattern for prayer to be imitated; for all Anglicans it was a set prayer to be repeated.

The Puritans also had criticisms to offer of the orders for the celebration of the sacraments in the prayer-book. In baptism the Puritans took exception to the ceremony of the signing with the cross, private Baptisms, Baptism by women, the interrogatories put to the child, and the custom of godparents acting as sponsors of the child. These practises were all contrary to the Reformed doctrine of Baptism as expounded, for example, in Calvin's *Institutio Christianae Religionis*.[32] The practices denied the fact that God's promises are sealed in the presence of the Christian community, not in the corner of a house. Women were forbidden by St. Paul to speak in the church; if they baptised they usurped the pastor's responsibility. Children inherited the promises made to the faithful and their seed in virtue of the election to grace of their parents, and it was parents who must stand as sponsors for their children, not godparents. The interrogations addressed to children were criticised as simply irrational.[33]

Puritan objections to the Anglican way of celebrating Holy Communion were many. The mode of individual delivery, *seriatim*, was thought to contradict the simultaneous corporate reception envisaged by Christ whose words were in the plural number.[34] They

30 *Second Admonition*, i, 136.

31 The Collect for the twelfth Sunday after Trinity contains the clause, "and giving unto us that that our prayer dare not ask" and the post-offertory prayer in the Communion Office with the clause, "and those things which for our unworthiness we dare not . . . ask." Frere and Douglas, *Puritan Manifestoes*, sec. vii, "The Humble Petition of 22 Preachers."

32 *Ecclesiastical Polity*, Book iv, chap. xvi.

33 The Puritan baptismal criticisms are detailed in the first *Admonition to Parliament* as found in Frere and Douglas, *Puritan Manifestoes*, p. 14; and in *A Parte of a Register*, pp. 55ff.

34 Query 62 of *A Survey of the Booke of Common Prayer* asks: "Whither the delivery of the Communion into the hands of the communicants be according to

also disapproved of substituting for the Scriptural words of delivery others neither scriptural nor evidently grounded in Scripture.[35] Even greater was the Puritan deprecation of the cheapening of the Holy Communion by admitting the unworthy to it without any examination of the quality of their life.[36] Criticism was also voiced at the requirement of a thrice-a-year minimal attendance at the Lord's table.

An admirable summary of Puritan criticisms of the Anglican Communion was made by the authors of *An Admonition to Parliament*, by means of contrasting the primitive order of Communion with the prayer-book order:

> They had no introite . . . but we have borrowed a piece of one out of the masse booke. They read no fragments of the Epistle and Gospell: we use both. The Nicene Crede was not read in their Communion we have it in oures . . . (examination of communicants then, not now). Then they ministred the Sacrament with common and usual bread; now with wafer cakes. . . . They received it sitting; we kneeling, according to Honorius decree. Then it was delivered generally and indefinitely, Take ye and eat ye: we particularly and singulerly, Take thou and eat thou. They used no other wordes but such as Chryste left: we borrow from Papistes The body of our Lorde Iesus Chryste which was geven for thee,&c. They had no Gloria in excelsis in the ministerie of the Sacrament then, for it was put to afterward. We have now. They took it with conscience. We with custume. They thrust men by reason of their sinnes from the Lords Supper. We thrust them in their sinne to the Lordes Supper. They ministred the Sacrament plainely. We pompously, with singing, pyping, surplesse and cope wearyng. They simply as they receeved it from the Lorde. We, sinfullye, mixed with mannes inventions and devises.[37]

Here we may pause to recognize the strength of the characteristic Puritan pleas for simplicity, for fidelity to God's Word and the example of the primitive Church, for the sacredness of God's ordinances, and for a high seriousness and sincerity in worship.

Christ, his institution. Seeing he said, and in the plural number said, Take ye, eate ye, drink ye all, &c."

[35] This objection is found in the second part of the 62nd Query of *A Survey of the Booke of Common Prayer*.

[36] Frere and Douglas, *Puritan Manifestoes*, p. 13.

[37] *Ibid.*, p. 134.

The Puritans did not spare the other occasional orders of worship in the prayer-book from criticism. Marriages and burials were considered essentially civil, not religious. Exception in the marriage order was taken to the words, "With my body I thee worship," as a derogation of the recognition that worship is alone due to God and not to his creatures, however lovely or distracting. In the burial service exception was taken to the indiscriminate, euphoric, and universalistic words: "We commit his body to the ground in sure and certain hope of the resurrection to eternal life."[38] The order for "The Churching of Women" was approved as a thanksgiving for safe delivery of a mother from childbirth, but in its form it was criticised as resembling too much the Jewish service of purification, and confusing ritual impurity with ethical sin.[39] The Puritans objected to Confirmation as virtually the creation of a third sacrament, which since it required a bishop for its administration, seemed to reduce the significance of the other two sacraments which required no bishop for their administration. It was also felt that the Lord's Supper added the grace of confirmation of Baptism and that a separate service of Confirmation was therefore otiose. In the third place, the Puritans objected to the laying on of hands in a manner that was un-Apostolic while claiming to follow the model of the apostles. The Puritans, with their Genevan view that bishops or ministers (apart from apostles and prophets) were the sole order of the ministry, recognised in the Church of New Testament days, while elders and deacons, who were lay officials, found the Ordinal unacceptable. They also vigorously attacked the presumption of the presiding bishop being required to say, while laying hands on the ordinand, "Receive ye the Holy Ghost," interpreting, instead, the mood of the verb as imperative instead of optative. Therefore it seemed blasphemous to them to imply that the Holy Spirit was in episcopal captivity.

Finally, the Puritan, while rejoicing that so many saints' days had been removed from the calendar of the Church of England, still believed that there was only one festival of the church, and that was a weekly one—the Lord's Day, commemorating the Lord's resurrection from the dead, the new exodus of the New Covenant. On this day every week he rehearsed the mighty saga of God in

[38] *Ibid.*, p. 144. Query 173 of *A Survey.*

[39] Query 179 of *A Survey* asks: "Whither weake and superstitious womē may not be occasioned to thinke this Service rather a Purification (which were Iewish) than Thankes-giving . . . as if women were by childbirth uncleane, and therefore unfit to go about their business, until they are purified." Frere and Douglas, *Puritan Manifestoes.*

the creation, redemption, and sanctification of man through the celebration of the incarnation, life, atonement, and resurrection of Christ. Thus the entire drama of salvation was to be recalled each Lord's Day. There was, therefore, no need for separate festivals, which would only fragment God's self-revelation in the continuing deed of Christ. Saints' days were also regarded as a denial of the sole mediatorial role of Christ, as well as diminishing the glory due to God alone. Puritans had special Fast Days and Thanksgiving Days in which they reflected on particular manifestations, respectively, of God's judgment and mercy. However, Thanksgiving Days were occasional and rare, and were no more than the foothills of their corporate devotion. The Lord's Day services were the peaks of their life of public worship.

3. Prayer-books or Prayers without a Book?

One major issue for the Puritans in our period was whether corporate worship should be according to the book or the spirit. At issue was whether God was best worshipped through a liturgy (and one which was more fully based on the word of God than the Book of Common Prayer), or through extemporary prayer more fully responsive to the particular needs of a given congregation than a liturgy could be and which trusted the guidance of the Holy Spirit in the leading of worship. It seems, on the face of it, as if the Presbyterian Puritans preferred a liturgy like Calvin's Englished by John Knox, which also allowed a very restricted area of freedom for the minister in the words he might use in the prayer of illumination before the sermon, and that the non-Presbyterian Puritans considered a liturgy allowable but extemporary prayer by the minister as preferable. Both viewpoints were held by Puritans until the Westminster Assembly approved a compromise which allowed for order and liberty, by providing a manual with some set prayers and alternatives, as well as suggested topics for prayer and a theological structure and order of items. But that came a generation and a half after the period under study here.

The Puritans ransacked the Scriptures for light on the debate. Their search was inconclusive, however; for although the Old Testament yielded set forms of praise, as in the Psalms (many of which were equally prayers) and the Aaronic blessing (Numbers 6:24ff), these were given under the Old Dispensation and were not necessarily to be imitated by Christians. The New Testament was equally inconclusive, for Anglicans could argue that the Lord's

Prayer was intended to be repeated (as the Presbyterians did), while the semi-Separatist Puritans such as John Robinson insisted that it was a model of prayer on which the pastor was to create his own prayers. Furthermore, the non-Presbyterian Puritans, who might be denominated proto-Independents, insisted that responsive prayers were vetoed by the insistence in I Corinthians 14:14 and 16 that only the minister's voice was to be heard in prayer, except for the concurrence of the congregation in uttering "Amen," and that the use of read prayers would seem to be a "quenching of the Spirit," for "the Spirit helpeth, our infirmities for we know not to pray for as we ought."[40] Robinson's comment on this text ironically suggests that the Anglicans considered their prayer-book superior to the inspiration of the spirit: "Yes, Paul, with your leave, right well; for we have in our prayer-book what we ought to pray, word for word, whether the Spirit be present or not."[41]

The Brownists, the Barrowists, and the earliest Independents were decidedly against the repetition of the Lord's Prayer. The Brownists in their Confession of 1596 complained that "we are much slandered, if we denyed or misliked that forme of prayer commonly called the Lord's Prayer"[42] because they did not use it in public worship. John Penry, the Barrowist leader, denied that Christ's wish was, "that the disciples or others should be tyed to use these very wordes, but that in prayer and geving of thankes they should follow his direction and patterne which he had geven them, that they might know to whom, with what affeccion and to what end to pray. . . ."[43] John Robinson, Leyden pastor of the Pilgrim fathers, decided, among other considerations, that the different Matthaean and Lucan forms of the Lord's Prayer indicated that the Lord's Prayer was not intended to be repeated word for word; the absence of apostolic testimony to the use of this prayer demanded that it be regarded as a model for prayer rather than as a prescribed prayer.[44] Though the Puritans acknowledged Scripture as sole authority for doctrine and practice, they would for argument's sake turn to tradition occasionally as a support. For example, Robinson produced Tertullian as a witness from the early Church for the practice of *ex tempore* prayer, citing the *Adversus*

[40] This key Puritan proof text comes from Romans 8:26.
[41] *A just and necessary Apology* in *Works*, ed. Robert Ashton, 3 vols., III, 21ff.
[42] Williston Walker, *The Creeds and Platforms of Congregationalism*, p. 61.
[43] Champlin Burrage, *The Early English Dissenters in the light of recent Research*, 2 vols., I, 56.
[44] *Works*, vol. 1, p. 23.

Gentes: "We pray, saith he, without any to prompt us, because we pray from the heart."[45]

In making the case for free prayer as against liturgical forms the Puritans combined theological and practical objections. In the first place, prayers that were read implied the self-sufficiency of man and denied the effects of original sin in him as well as the conviction that God must be served as his word dictates, and his word dictates a dependence on the holy spirit. It was also felt increasingly that if ministers did not exercise the gift of free prayer the talent would atrophy in them. Another consideration was that set prayers had insufficient flexibility to meet the changes of providence in the life of the nation or the individuals making it up. Yet another reason for desiring to use free prayer was the conviction that it might be thought to be the only way to worship God if set prayers in a liturgy were made legally binding. The Puritans were careful in distinguishing the demands of God from the preferences of men; they considered the demands of God to be prayer; the preference of men in the Established church was for liturgy with unchanging formulas. Finally, the imposition of set liturgies brought persecution in its wake.

In the last analysis the two types of prayer, liturgical and free, represented two differing conceptions of the nature of the church. The Book of Common Prayer and all liturgies stressed the corporate nature of the church, while free prayer emphasized the need of individuals in a family church. If liturgical prayer reflects what is held in common in its creeds, confession, and abstract collects praying for the graces of the Christian life needed by all Christians, then free prayers made room for the distinctiveness of the individuals in the gathered church. Liturgical prayer did not require that the minister know all the members of his congregation. Free prayer, on the contrary, presupposed as its context a compact community, all of whom were known by the minister and who could voice their aspirations and needs in prayer. The two kinds of prayer seemed to bear out Ernst Troeltsch's demarcation between "Church" and "Sect" types of the Christian life. Liturgical prayer required a parish as a background, with the nation as the wider horizon; free prayer suggested not Israel but the holy remnant, a committed and closely knit family for whom the charismatic, intimate, and informal ways of free prayer were congenial.

---

[45] The relevant part of the Latin original is: *sine monitore, quia de pectore*, citation from Robinson, *Works*, III, 28.

Each type of worship had the defects of its own qualities. Precisely because the Book of Common Prayer envisioned the English nation on its knees before God, its prayers had to be general, "common" prayers, and therefore impersonal ones. This was where the author of the Second Admonition found the greatest weakness in the Book of Common Prayer: "there is no such praying as should touch the hearte."[46] Because free prayer thinks in terms of the "gathered" church its characteristic is a sincere and informal simplicity as between friends; its almost intrinsic defect is disorder.

Anglican critics, of course, stressed the weaknesses of free prayer as strongly as the Puritans did those of the Anglican liturgy. They claimed that free prayer might be no more than the result of mental laziness, could tend to ostentation or vulgarity, and wrongly presupposed that all ministers could express themselves fluently and felicitously in public, or that the people could give their assent on the first hearing of a prayer with deep meaning. The criticisms were put comprehensively by Hooker:

> To him that considereth the grievous and scandalous inconveniences whereunto they make themselves daily subject, with whom any blind and secret corner is judged a fit house of Common Prayer; the manifold confusions they fall into, where every man's private spirit and gift (as they term it) is the only Bishop that ordaineth him to this ministry; the irksome deformities whereby, through endless and senseless effusions of indigested Prayers, they oftentimes disgrace in most insufferable manner the worthiest part of Christian duty towards God, who herein are subject to no certain order, but pray both what and how they list; to him, I say, which weigheth duly all these things, the reasons cannot be obscure why God doth in public Prayer so much respect the solemnity of places where, the authority and calling of persons by whom, and the precise appointment even with what words or sentences his name should be called on amongst his people.[47]

In considering such a citation, one is inclined to wonder whether there was a different theology, as well as ecclesiology, differentiat-

---

[46] Frere and Douglas, *Puritan Manifestoes*, p. 115. The quotation continues: "And therfore another hath so little feeling of the common prayer that he bringeth a booke of his owne, and though he sitte when they sitte, stand when they stande, kneele when they kneele, he may pause sometime also, but most of all he intendeth his owne booke, is this praying?"

[47] *Ecclesiastical Polity*, Book v, chap. xxv, sec. 5.

ing Anglican and from Puritan worship. Hooker, at the end of the citation above, seems to imply that worship is court etiquette, an approach to the King of kings, where awe dominates over affection, whereas however strong their sense of holiness in approaching God the Puritans did not forget that it was holy *love* to which they responded when they cried, "*Abba*, Father" in their simple and often spontaneous confessions and petitions.

There was, I must again insist, a difference of opinion among the Puritans on the question of set and free prayers. There was agreement that the Book of Common Prayer was unacceptable as the permanent liturgy of Protestant England. Objection to this particular liturgy was before too many decades to lead to a radical rejection of all liturgies. Cartwright, the first leader of the English Presbyterians, who was well acquainted with the practice of the Continental Reformed churches in spells of involuntary exile, strongly favoured a set form of prayer as a medium for expressing the unity of Reformed churches, as a direction of ministers in sound doctrine and prayer, and as a means of assisting the weaker brethren—"and yet so, as the set forme make not men sluggish in stirring up the gift of prayer in themselves, according to divers occurents; it being incident to the children of God in some measure."[48] William Perkins fully allowed that a set form of prayer might be used, but only because, "to conceive a forme of prayer requires gifts of memorie, knowledge, utterance, and the gifts of grace," and not every child of God had these gifts, though he might have an honest heart. Hence, "in the want of them [such] may lawfully use a set forme of prayer, as a man that hath a weake backe, or a lame legge, may lean upon a crutch."[49] Perkins even met the objection that set forms of prayer "limit and binde the Holy Ghost" with the answer: "If we had a perfect measure of grace, it were somewhat, but the graces of God are weak and finall in us. This is no binding of the Holy Ghost, but a helping of the Holy Spirit, which is weake in us by a crutch to leane upon: therefore a man may with good conscience, upon defect of memory and utterance &c. use a set forme of prayer."[50] The implication was, of course, that the spiritual athlete will dispense with crutches.

Richard Rogers, on the other hand, denied that only *ex tempore* prayers were acceptable worship, because all Reformed churches

---

[48] *A Treatise of Christian Religion or The Whole Bodie and substance of Divinitie* (posthumously published in 1616), p. 256.
[49] *The Whole Treatise of the Cases of Conscience* (1608), Book II, p. 77.
[50] *Ibid.*, pp. 77-78.

had a "prescript forme of prayer."[51] It would have been astonishing if Puritans who acknowledged their Genevan ancestry had not approved of a Reformed liturgy, bearing in mind that both in Strassburg and Geneva Calvin had used one during his ministry, even if he also recognised the right of the ministers to frame their own prayers from time to time.

4. Puritan Prayer-books

The Puritans had two examples of Protestant liturgies in English to consider adopting or modifying. One was the most Protestant of the Anglican liturgies, that of 1552, which, as we have seen, was unacceptable, despite the fact that it had won Knox's approval[52] after the inclusion of the black rubric and the qualified approval of John Calvin himself.[53]

The other liturgy was William Huycke's English translation of Calvin's *La Forme des Prières* which appeared in 1550 and may have been taken from Calvin's 1542 or 1547 edition.[54] For the learned there was available the longer Strassburg form of Calvin's liturgy which Poullain or Pollanus had translated from French into Latin in 1551 and which was entitled, *Liturgia sacra, seu Ritus ministerii in Ecclesia peregrinorum, profugorum propter Euangelium Christi Argentinae.* This form in particular owed much to the influence of the Reformer Martin Bucer,[55] as Calvin acknowledged.

The most important of the prayer-books used by the Puritans was almost certainly the Calvin-inspired volume, known popularly as "John Knox's Genevan Service Book," the correct title of which was *The Forme of Prayers and Ministrations of the Sacraments, etc., used in the English Congregation at Geneva: and approved by the famous and godly learned man, Iohn Calvyn. Imprinted at Geneva by Iohn Crespin. MDLVI.* This was drawn up by the Presbyterian-Puritan party of "Knoxians" at Frankfort-am-Main, consisting of Knox himself, Whittingham, Gilby, Foxe and Cole,

51 *Seven Treatises* (1603), Book II, chap. 4, p. 224.

52 Laing (editor of Knox's *Works*, 1855), in vol. 4, pp. 43-44, states that despite Knox's former "good opinion of the Book [of Common Prayer], he discovered in the English Book . . . things superstitious, impure, unclean, and unperfect."

53 Calvin's letter in the original Latin (with the deprecatory phrase, *multas tolerabiles ineptias*) will be found in Laing's edition of Knox's *Works*, vol. 4, p. 51. An English translation is in *A Brief Discourse of the Troubles at Frankfort* (1846 edn.), pp. xxxiv-xxxvi.

54 See W. D. Maxwell, *John Knox's Genevan Service Book, 1556,* p. 71.

55 See the statement by James Hastings Nichols, in *Corporate Worship in the Reformed Tradition,* p. 57: "Consequently Martin Bucer must be given credit as the chief architect of the Calvinist form of worship."

all Marian exiles. In addition to being originally written for Englishmen who wished to reform the Reformation, it came to be used widely in Scotland until the *Book of Common Order* (as it was retitled when it became, with some modifications and additions, the official service book of the Scottish Kirk) was ousted first by the "Laud's Liturgy" and shortly afterward by the *Westminster Directory* in 1644.

A Brief Discourse of the Troubles begun at Frankfort in the year 1554 about the Book of Common Prayer and Ceremonies is probably Whittingham's account of four attempts to meet the liturgical demands of the "Coxian" Anglican and "Knoxian" Presbyterian-Puritan parties, none of which was successful. When the "Knoxians" regathered in Geneva in 1556 they revived the work of the Calvinist committee which had begun its task in January 1555. Their Genevan Service Book was used with little adaptation by the English exiles for their worship in the church of Marie la Nove, which was in Maxwell's words, "the cradle of Puritanism."[56] Here, with a congregation of 186 members, tranquillity reigned, so much so that Knox wrote in December 1556 of the place as "the maist perfyt schoole of Chryst that ever was in the erth since the dayis of the Apostillis. In other places, I confess Chryst to be trewlie preachit; but maneris and religioun so sinceirlie reformat, I have not yit sene in any uther place."[57]

The Sunday morning service consisted of: a Confession of sins; a Prayer for pardon; a metrical Psalm; a Prayer for illumination; scripture reading; sermon; baptisms and publication of banns of marriage; long prayer (of intercessions and petitions) and Lord's Prayer; Apostles' Creed (recited by the Minister); a metrical Psalm; and the blessing (Aaronic or Apostolic). Three characteristics of the service were unmistakably Calvinist. It was Biblical, didactic, and congregational. Its Biblical basis is seen in the Confessional prayer based largely on the ninth chapter of Daniel, in the use of metrical Psalms, and in the preference for Biblical blessings compared with the Anglican blessing ("The peace of God"), which was used in the original interim order of Frankfort. It was didactic in that the climax of the service was approached by a prayer that the preacher may be illuminated by the Holy Spirit to declare God's word and the congregation to receive the seed of God's word in the sermon, which was an exposition of the lesson read; the climax of the worship and the summary of the historic

---

[56] *Ibid.*, p. 7.   [57] Knox, *Works*, vol. 4, p. 240.

faith, the Apostles' Creed, preceded the closing acts of worship. The congregational and participatory character of the service was in the provision of easily memorized metrical psalms. Perhaps the clearest indication of Calvinism was the statement of the doctrine of original sin so dominant in the opening prayers of confession, particularly in the alternative form.[58]

The order for the Lord's Supper was: The Words of Institution and Exhortation; The Eucharistic Prayer (including Adoration, Thanksgiving for Creation and Redemption, Anamnesis, Doxology); Fraction; Delivery; People's Communion while Scripture was read; Post-Communion Thanksgiving; Psalm 103 in metre; Blessing (Aaronic or Apostolic).

The Lord's Supper was to be celebrated monthly. The service was remarkable in four ways. It rightly gave a large element in the Eucharistic prayer to thanksgiving for creation as well as redemption. It warned against the cheapening of grace by "fencing the tables" against scandalous recipients, while at the same time insisting in the exhortation that "this sacrament is a singuler medicine for all poor sicke creatures, a comfortable helpe to weake soules, and that our lord requireth no other worthines on our parte, but that we unfaynedly acknowledge our noghtines, and imperfection."[59] It had an implicit *Sursum corda* in the end of the exhortation, "to lift up our mindes by fayth above all thinges worldlye and sensible, and therby to entre into heaven, that we may finde, and receive Christ, where he dwelleth undoubtedlye verie God, and verie man, in the incomprehensible glorie of his father, to whom be all praise, honor and glorye now and ever. Amen."[60] It lacked an *epiklesis*,[61] or explicit invocation of the Holy Spirit on the elements and the people of God, but this may have been thought unnecessary, since Calvin had a strong sense of the Holy Spirit as effective in all services in the reading and preaching of the word of God, as well as the sacraments, in taking the things of Christ and applying them to the faithful. Once again, there was the concern to be faithful to the Biblical authority in the recital of the Institution narrative as a warrant for the ordinance.

Strype, the ecclesiastical historian, reports that John Knox's

---

[58] ". . . we are miserable synners, conceyved and borne in synne and iniquitie, so that in us there is no goodnes." Maxwell, *Book of Common Prayer*, p. 87.

[59] *Ibid.*, p. 124.

[60] *Ibid.*

[61] This lacuna was filled by later Puritans, both in the Order for the Lord's Supper in the Westminster *Directory* and in Baxter's *Reformed Liturgy*.

Genevan Service Book was being used as early as 1567 in England. After mentioning the moderate Puritans who remained "in the Communion of the Church" of England, he continues: "But another sort there was, that disliked the whole constitution of the Church lately reformed; charging upon it many gross remainders of Popery; and that it was still full of corruptions not to be borne with, and Anti-Christian; and especially the habits the clergy were enjoined to use in their ministration and conversation. Insomuch that the latter separated themselves into private assemblies, meeting together not in Churches, but in private houses, where they had ministers of their prayer, they used a Book of Prayers framed at Geneva, for the congregation of English exiles lately sojourning there. Which book had been overseen and allowed by Calvin and the rest of his divines there, and indeed was for the most part taken out of the Genevan form."[62] There is confirmation of Strype's assertion in the reprint of "The examination of Certain Londoners before the Ecclesiastical Commissioners June 20, 1567."[63] In his answer to the Bishop of London (Grindal), the Puritan Smith admitted that the cause of attending private assemblies was the displacing of good preachers, and continued: "and then were we troubled and commanded to your courts from day to day, for not coming to our parish churches: —then we bethought us what were best to do; and we remembered that there was a congregation of us in this city in Queen Mary's days; and a congregation at Geneva, which used a book and order of preaching, ministering of the sacraments and discipline, most agreeable to the word of God; which book is allowed by that godly and well-learned man, Master Calvin, and the preachers there; which book and order we now hold." It is significant that the description of the *Forme of Prayers* and particularly the terms in which Calvin is referred to almost exactly correspond with the Crespin edition of 1556.

Strype has two more references to the use of a Genevan book by English Puritans. In 1571 the Puritans "did still in their own or other churches, or in private houses, read different from the established office of Common Prayer: using the Genevan form or mangling the English book, and preached without licenses."[64] He also reports that in 1584 there was a petition to Parliament for which the Puritans "had compiled and got in readiness a new platform of

[62] John Strype, *The History of the Life and Acts of Edmund Grindal*, pp. 168f.
[63] *The Remains of Edmund Grindal*, ed. W. Nicholson, pp. 203f.
[64] *The Life and Acts of Matthew Parker*, 3 vols., II, 65.

ecclesiastical government, agreeable to that of Geneva, and another form of prayer prescribed therein, in room of the old one, for the use of this Church."[65] These instances made it clear that the *Forme of Prayers* had an important clandestine existence in England to complement its open acceptance and use in Scotland, and that it served as a model for the worship of the proto-Presbyterian[66] Puritans in England.

It is also important to note that there were two adaptations of the John Knox's Genevan Service Book current among English Puritan congregations, the first of which was used in England, and the second by the Puritan exiles in Middleburg. The first was printed by Waldegrave and entitled, *A booke of the forme of common prayers, administration of the Sacraments, &c. agreeable to Gods Worde, and the use of the reformed Churches.*[67] It was probably printed in 1584 or 1585, almost certainly in the earlier year in support of the petition to Parliament for the Genevan discipline and Genevan prayer-book. Both Bancroft and Hooker referred to this or to one of the further editions printed for the English Puritans in 1586, 1587, and 1602. From Bancroft it is learned that prior to its introduction into the Low Countries in 1587, it was used possibly exclusively in Northamptonshire under the direction of a notable Puritan, Edmund Snape, an associate of Cartwright. Bancroft alluded to the formulary to substantiate his claim that the Puritans who claimed liberty to worship God according to their consciences and the Word of God, yet proposed, with Parliamentary sanction, to impose this book exclusively in corporate worship.[68]

Hooker also referred to the Waldegrave Liturgy in the fifth book of *The Laws of Ecclesiastical Polity* under the engaging title "Of them who allowing a set Form of Prayer allow not ours." He claimed that the Puritans changed from supporting free prayers to demanding a set formulary: "Now, albeit the Admonitioners did seem at the first to allow no prescript form of Prayer at all, but thought it best that their Minister should always be left at liberty to pray as his own discretion did serve; yet because this opinion on better advice they afterwards retracted, their defender and his

---

[65] *The Life and Acts of John Whitgift*, 3 vols., I, 348.

[66] A term coined to designate would-be Presbyterians who were unable in an Anglican state church to establish the full Presbyterian discipline and government with classes, synods, and a general assembly.

[67] Reprinted in Peter Hall's *Fragmenta Liturgica*, 7 vols., I, 1f.

[68] Richard Bancroft, *Dangerous Positions and Proceedings* . . . (1593), Book III, x.

associates have sithence proposed to the world a form such as themselves like."[69]

Bancroft's evidence, corroborated by Hooker, includes two interesting suppositions. The first is that the Puritans moved from free prayer to set forms; their alarm at the freedom of the prayers of more radical Puritans such as the Brownists may have encouraged them to follow Knox rather than Barrowe. Second, it was believed that the "Admonitioners" were behind the publication of the Waldegrave Liturgy, along with the Middleburg Liturgy. Cartwright had ministered to the English congregation there, and his friend Dudley Fenner was in Middleburg in 1586. Unquestionably Waldegrave was the printer for the Puritans. Since he had issued in 1584 the "Brief and Plain Declaration concerning the Desires of all those Faithful Ministers that have and do seek for the Discipline and Reformation of the Church of England," it would be a natural sequel to publish in the same or following year the formulary of worship appropriate for a Reformed Church of England. The Star Chamber in June 1586 restricted Puritan printing, at which time the Waldegrave Liturgy was taken to Middleburg to be republished by Richard Schilders in 1586.

The Waldegrave and Middleburg Liturgies were firmly based on Knox's Genevan service book, with a few significant variations. Their Puritan character is evident from the marginal Scriptural references and warrants for each liturgical action and for the content of the prayers. The first rubric of the Middleburg Liturgy prescribed a "Reader's Service,"[70] which was to take place before the entire congregation gathered to begin the liturgy proper. It was to be led by "one appointed by the Eldership [who] shall reade some Chapters of the Canonicall bookes of Scripture, singing Psalmes between at his discretion: and this reading to bee in order as the bookes and Chapters followe, that so from time to time the holy Scriptures may bee readde throughout."[71] This was the Puritan answer to Anglican shredding the Scripture in "pistling" and "gospelling."

When the minister arrived, the liturgy began with solemn confession of man's insufficiency and the affirmation of God's suffi-

---

[69] *Ecclesiastical Polity*, Book v, chap. xxvii, sec. 1.

[70] The Reader's Service was introduced into Scotland in 1560. See Maxwell, *Book of Common Prayer*, pp. 177-79, for a description.

[71] The title is *A Booke of the Forme of Common Prayers, Administration of the Sacraments, &c. agreeable to Gods Worde and the Use of the Reformed Churches* (Middleburg, 1586). It is reprinted in Hall's *Reliquiae Liturgicae*, vol. 1; and Bard Thompson's *Liturgies of the Western Church*.

ciency as Creator: "Our helpe be in thee name of the Lorde, who hath made both Heaven and Earth." So had Calvin's own service began, yet this opening sentence of Scripture was omitted in the Knox book.

There were other significant changes. The first alternative form of confession in Knox's book was omitted, leaving the Bucer-Calvin prayer of confession, to which Knox and his associates had added a petition for pardon. Three alternatives were provided for the prayer of intercession, instead of one in Knox; both Knox and the Puritan liturgies permitted the minister to substitute his own prayer of intercession. The third alternative prayer of intercession was heavily penitential in character. One has the impression that it may well have been used by Puritans for additional services on "days of humiliation."

The Waldegrave Liturgy added to the recitation of the Apostles' Creed required in the Knox book that of the Decalogue; while the Middleburg Liturgy omitted both (this, incidentally, is the only significant difference between the two Puritan liturgies of Waldegrave and Middleburg). In fact, with the exceptions already noted, there is a remarkable unity in word and action between Knox's "Genevan Service Book" and the Waldegrave and Middleburg Liturgies. All three agree in their orders for Baptism and the Lord's Supper and for the Marriage service. The Waldegrave and Middleburg orders make no provision for burials, while the Knox book reduces the burial service to its barest essentials.

The spirit of the three liturgies is well expressed in the appended comment in all three to the order for the Lord's Supper, to the effect that their aim had been, "that Christ might witness to our faith, as it were with his own mouth . . . so that, without his word and warrant, there is nothing in this holy action attempted."[72] In ethos, structure, and words the three liturgies agree. The few unimportant changes in wording made in the Waldegrave and Middleburg order were for clarity and solemnity. Knox's archaism, "the Sacrament is a *singuler* medicine for all poor sick creatures," was changed to "*excellent* medicine." The Knoxian order for the Lord's Supper in fencing the tables against persons of evil life says that if we are unworthy receivers "we kindle God's wrath against us," which the Puritan liturgies qualified as "*heavy* wrath." The list of those anathematized was lengthened in the Waldegrave and

[72] Maxwell, *Book of Common Prayer*, p. 128; Waldegrave: Hall, *Fragmenta Liturgica*, vol. i, p. 68; Middleburg: Hall, *Reliquiae Liturgicae*, vol. i, p. 61; and Thompson, *Liturgies*, p. 340.

Middleburg Liturgies to include the man who committed the chief liturgical sin for Puritans, "a mainteyner of Images, or mannes inventions in the service of GOD."[73] Once again we see in Puritan worship and life the vivid understanding of the obedience of faith and the solemn demand for sanctification. This worship may seem aesthetically bleak, but it was, above all, theologically vertebral and ethically vigorous. The Puritan liturgies also show that at least the Cartwrightian Puritans, while allowing a subordinate place for free prayer, never gave up the idea of a liturgy for the unity, discipline, and common instruction of congregations of the Reformed church.

5. The Gospel Sacraments[74]

According to Puritan thought the possibility of communion with God was established when God comes to his elect in the form of the "word," and the "word" is a term combining the meanings of first, Jesus Christ the Incarnate Word, second, the scriptures, and third, the proclamation of the gospel in preaching and in the sacraments. Perkins defined a sacrament as "A Signe to represent, a seale to confirme, an instrument to conveye Christ and all his benefits to them that doe beleeve in him."[75] The holy spirit used the senses to convey the benefits of Christ to men, "because wee are like *Thomas*, wee will not beleeve till wee feele them in some measure in our hearts."[76] There were only two sacraments of the gospel for the Puritans—Baptism, the sacrament of admission or initiation into the church of God, and the Lord's Supper, the sacrament of nourishment and preservation in the church. If we could have asked Perkins what is done in Baptism, he would have a ready, concise reply: "In the assemblie of the Church, the covenant of grace betweene God and the partie baptised is solemnly confirmed and sealed."[77] In the Lord's Supper the former covenant "solemnly ratified in Baptisme, is renewed in the Lord's Supper, between the Lord himselfe and the receiver."[78] What is the meaning of the eating of the bread and the drinking of the wine in the Lord's Supper? Perkins insisted that the outward actions "are a second seale, set by the Lords owne hand unto his covenant. And they do give every

---

[73] Middleburg: Thompson, *Liturgies*, p. 335.

[74] See also Chap. II for a comparison of Anglican and Puritan interpretations of the sacraments.

[75] *The Foundation of the Christian Religion gathered into sixe principles* (1595), sig. C4 v.

[76] *Ibid.*   [77] *Ibid.*   [78] *Ibid.*, D i recto.

receiver to understand, that as God doth blesse the bread and wine to preserve and strengthen the bodie of the receiver: so Christ apprehended and received by faith, shal nourish him, and preserve both bodie and soule unto eternall life."[79]

In the divine economy and ordering, sacraments fulfilled five important functions. They were instruments of signification, showing the cleansing and renewing power of God's pardoning and empowering grace. They were also confirmatory of faith; that is, they pointed to God's fulfillment of his promises, which encourages the wavering and unsteady of purpose. Third, the sacraments are not only witnesses to God's generous love but also witnesses to the believer's inner commitment to Christ. They are, as it were, badges of membership of the church, signs of the identification with the company of God's people. Finally, sacraments foster the brotherly love that there should be between members of Christ's church: they express and extend the reconciling love of Christ which is in the brethren to the neighbour.[80]

Puritans insisted that infant Baptism was appropriate because the sacrament does not declare our faith but testifies to the initiative of God's grace in Christ for man's salvation. Children, as the seed of covenanted members of the body of Christ, are entitled to the fruits of the divine promises.[81] God both seals his promise and also the means by which He fulfills His promise, that is, incorporation into Christ. Since this was clearly a sacrament of the church for admission into the church, it should be performed publicly before the gathered congregation and not privately in a home. Since it was an ecclesial act it should be performed by an ordained minister, without allowing laymen or women to perform it in exceptional circumstances.[82] Furthermore, no one could take away the responsibility of parents to bring up their children in the knowledge and love of God and in the ways of His ordaining; for this reason

---

[79] *Ibid.*

[80] The points made in this paragraph can be verified in Perkins, *Works*, I, 73; II, 92; Cartwright, *A Treatise of the Christian Religion* (1616), pp. 219-29; and Richard Rogers, *Seven Treatises* (1603), pp. 217f.

[81] Perkins, in *Works*, I, 129, argued that it is the faith of parents that gives their child "a title or interest in the covenant of grace."

[82] John Knox's *Forme of Prayers* begins the Order of Baptism with the following ominous rubric: "First note, that for asmooche as it is not permitted by Godswoord that wemen should preache or minister the sacramentes: and it is evident, that the sacramentes are not ordeined of God to be used in privat corners, as charmes or sorceries, but left to the congregation, and necessarily annexed to Gods woord, as seales of the same: therfore the enfant which is to be baptised shalbe broght to the churche on the day appointed to comen prayer and preaching. . . ." Maxwell, *Book of Common Prayer*, p. 105.

godmothers were unknown at Puritan baptismal ceremonies.[83] Nor, of course, was there any signing of the cross, for this was a human addition to God's appointment as described in the New Testament.

The order for Baptism in the Puritan liturgies (Waldegrave and Middleburg) has an identical structure consisting of six items: (1) The Interrogation (immediately following the Sermon); (2) A lengthy Exhortation and Explanation of the purpose of Baptism; (3) Recitation of the Apostles' Creed by the father (or by a surety in his unavoidable absence); (4) Prayer for grace and for the reception of the child into Christ's kingdom, completed by the Lord's Prayer; (5) The act of Baptism in the Triune Name; (6) Concluding Thanksgiving. The exhortation made it clear that all who received baptism need not "have the use of understanding and faythe, but chiefelye that they be conteyned under the name of gods people," so that children "wythout iniurie . . . can not be debarred from the common signe of Gods children." Still the lack of the outward action was not prejudicial to their salvation, should they die before being presented to the church.[84] Further, there was no magic in the water; it is the Holy Spirit that works regeneration in the heart of the elect.[85]

The demand made of the father of the child was to provide that his children shall be taught, "in all doctrine necessary for a true Christian: chiefely that they be taught to rest upon the justice of Christ Iesus alone, and to abhorre and flee all superstition, papistrie, and idolatrie."[86] The father, as proof of his consent to the performance of these duties, or in his absence the surety, was then required to recite the Apostles' Creed. Theological clarity and fidelity are not incompatible with human tenderness, as can be seen in the moving prayer preceding the act of Baptism: "ALMIGHTIE and everlasting God, which of thy infinite mercie and goodnes, hast promised unto us, that thow wilt not only be our God, but also the God and father of our children: we beseche thee that as thou hast vouchesaved to call us to be partakers of this thy great mercie in the felowshipe of faithe: so it may please thee to sanctifie with thy sprite, and to receive in to the number of thy children this infant, whom we shall baptise according to thy woord, to the end that he comming to perfite age, may confesse thee onely the true God and whom thow hast sent Iesus Christ: and so serve him, and be profit-

[83] Both Calvin and Pullain allowed godfathers as alternatives, but never godmothers; in this they were followed by the Presbyterian type of Puritans. The Independent Puritans, however, utterly rejected male and female godparents.
[84] *Ibid.*, p. 106.　　　[85] *Ibid.*, p. 107.　　　[86] *Ibid.*, p. 109.

able unto his churche, in the whole course of his lyfe: that after this life be ended, he may be broght as a lyvely member of his body unto the full fruition of thy ioyes in the heavens, where thy sonne our Christ raigneth world wyth out end."[87] The service is simple, solemn, sincere, and a clear testimony to the covenant conception that dominated Puritan thinking and living with God, with the family, and with the households of faith, and which made of the sacraments of Baptism and the Lord's Supper the seals of God's covenant—grace.[88]

Perkins was the clearest and most popular of the early Puritan theologians; his teaching on the theology of the Lord's Supper is typical. Applying his general definition of sacraments to the sacrament of the Eucharist, it should be noted that it is a sign representative of the reconciling sacrifice of Christ on the Cross anticipated at the Last Supper, a seal confirming God's holy covenant of love with His people, and an instrument conveying Christ and all his benefits, chiefly pardon and eternal life, to the faithful. Their meaning is summed up in his catechetical answer to the question, "What meaneth the bread and wine, the eating of the bread and drinking of the wine?" The answer he gave: "These outward actions are a second seale, set by the Lords owne hand unto his covenant. And they doe give every receiver to understand, that as God doth blesse the bread and wine, to preserve and strengthen the bodie of the receiver: so Christ apprehended and received by faith, shal nourish him, and preserve both bodie and soule unto eternall life."[89]

I have already referred to the earliest of the English Puritan liturgies, the Order for the Communion,[90] and to some of its leading characteristics, particularly the inclusion of thanksgiving for creation as well as redemption in the Eucharistic prayer, the implicit *Sursum corda* in the exhortation, and the lack of an explicit *epiklesis*. It is now appropriate to consider the rationale for this important service as contained in a concluding paragraph addressed

---

[87] *Ibid.*, p. 110.

[88] The significance of the sacraments as seals of the covenant of grace in its practical implications is well brought out by Walter Travers, in *A full and plaine declaration of Ecclesiasticall Discipline owt off the word off God and off the churche off England from the same* (published probably in Zurich, 1574), p. 24: "So that seing the lorde to have sete his sygnet to the confyrming of our Salvacion and to have sealed yt up, we might the more quietlie rest and acquiete our selves in his faith and custodie."

[89] Perkins, *The Foundation of the Christian Religion gathered into six principles* (1595), sig. D i r.

[90] This was considered in the previous section of this chapter.

"To the reader." The primary intent was to renounce the error of the Papists by denying Transubstantiation, which in the Reformed view overthrew the nature of a sacrament since it confused the sign with the reality signified. Other aims in arranging the order were to "restore unto the sacramentes theyr owne substaunce, and to Christe his proper place." This place is thought to be usurped by the Catholic priests as though "the intent of the sacrificer should make the sacrament." The words of institution were read not as a consecratory formula but "to teache us how to behave in our selves in the action, and that Christ might witnes unto our faith as it were with his owne mowthe, that he hath ordeined these signes for our spiritual use and comforte."

After the warrant for the action had been read, "wee do first therefore examyne owr selves, accordyng to saint Pauls rule, and prepare our myndes that we may be worthie partakers of so high mysteries." Then followed in full fidelity to the Pauline record the fourfold action: "Then takyng bread wee geve thankes, breake, and distribute it, as Christ our Saviour hath taught us. Fynally, the ministration ended, we gyve thankes agayne accordyng to his example. So that without his woorde, and warrant, there is nothynge in this holy action attempted."[91]

Most impressive are the strong sense of obeying the divine commands in worship, the vivid dramatic power of the prophetic symbolism of breaking bread and pouring wine, as well as the strong sense of sharing in a banquet and holy supper with Christ and His friends. The memorial aspect, as those also of mystery and thanksgiving, are strong. The complementary dimensions of the eschatological banquet and the sense of the communion of saints, as well as the reinvigoration of the Christian hope through Christ's resurrection, are weaker in this rite. Little is said of the sacrifice of the church linked with Christ's sacrifice. The concept of sacrifice dominates the Roman Catholic Mass, and the sense of the rehearsal of the mystery of our redemption and of incorruption in eternal life controls the Orthodox Eucharist. The Anglican Holy Communion, as its name implies, is suffused with a sense of the great privilege of the meeting of God with men, and men with men, in their coinherence with Christ. In Puritanism it was the holy banquet of God's elect that was the uppermost thought. Such a concept drew greatly on the example of the Last Supper, and had an appeal as strong as it was simple.

[91] Maxwell, *Book of Common Prayer*, pp. 127-28.

6. A Critique

Puritanism was a new and vigorous movement of protest against the dead hand of tradition, against the idolatry that worships man's works instead of yielding first to the behests of the living God, and against the superstition that tries to dominate and domesticate deity. It was a movement of the "learned godly," the religious intellectuals of the day, a movement that found its strongest support in university circles, especially the University of Cambridge.[92]

What was the novelty of Puritanism? It was, in the first place, a new criterion of Scriptural authority that it offered, or at least the return to a criterion of the early church which cut away the massive tangle of encumbrances which had grown over the central oak of Scripture. With a rude hand it scraped away the parasitical ivy and mistletoe, however aesthetic, so that the Scripture might stand out in its splendid solitude. Or, to use a more apt metaphor, it allowed the voice of Scripture to speak the divine promises and commandments in the power of the Holy Spirit without the seductive sounds of the carousel of church tradition to interrupt it. This strong, simple Biblical authority seemed a liberation to those who were appalled by the somnolence, the superstition, and the sheer accommodation of the church to the worldliness of the Renaissance, though in its concern to return to the original texts of Christianity, as the Renaissance scholars returned to the original texts of the classical world of Greece and Rome, there was gain as well as loss. This digging down to the bedrock of Scripture, even when it led to bibliolatry, as we have seen, and even to deep disagreements between private interpretations, was an immense gain in simplicity for the learned and the unlettered. In worship it gave a sense of direct Biblical (and therefore divine) authority for every ordinance practised by the Puritans, from preaching to the celebration of the sacraments, from the types and order of the prayers to the form of praise (Psalms but not hymns). Hence the emphatic rejection within Puritanism of "men's inventions," or "will-worship," and the overpowering sense that God's elect were worshipping God in His own way as demanded and as exemplified in His word. No other conclusion could be drawn from the use of the lengthy readings from the Scriptures, entire chapters at a time, the baptismal formula used in the sacrament of Initiation, and the Warrant for

[92] This has been admirably demonstrated by Harry C. Porter in his *Reformation and Reaction in Tudor Cambridge*.

the Lord's Supper in the reading of the Pauline words of institution, and the use of the Biblical words at the delivery of the holy
bread and wine to the people, the careful way the sermon eluci-
dated the Scriptures, and the metrical versions of the Psalms used
in praise. Each of these elements in Puritan worship contributed
to the impression of the utmost fidelity on the part of minister,
office-bearers, and congregation to God's holy word and law, the
Bible.

The second impression Puritan worship made on those accustomed to the Roman Catholic or Anglican traditions was its extreme
simplicity. It was decidedly a simple, unornate type of worship,
which suitably met in white-walled churches with only tables of
the commandments for instruction rather than adornment, and
which despised, as distracting, "storied windows richly dight casting a dim, religious light" and allowed windows to cast the natural
light of the sun as the worship gives place to the interior illumination of the Holy Spirit. So strong was the sense of the numinous
in the approach of God in word and sacrament that any symbolism
or decoration is felt to be utterly adventitious, not a gilding the lily,
but a varnishing of sunlight. It was, to change the metaphor, a
bare stage—like the Elizabethan theatre—so that the provocative
images of Scripture could make their own impact on the *tabula rasa*
of the sensitive imagination without tinsel trappings, or merely
distracting stage decor. This is why the only ceremonies permitted
were sacramental signs, such as the affusion of water in Baptism
and the breaking of bread and pouring of wine in the Lord's
Supper.

The third impression which Puritan worship made, especially
in the Independent-Puritan rather than in the Presbyterian-Puritan
circles, was of an affirmation of the dynamic role of the Holy Spirit.
This was clearly allowed for in Presbyterianism in the proclamation of the word, as the preceding prayer of illumination makes
clear. It was always theoretically possible for the Presbyterian minister to provide his own words in the prayers of intercession, but
(watched by the eagle eye of the session and warned by the presbytery and the classis of the dangerous freedom of the semi-Separatists and the Anabaptists) he usually chose not to exercise that
liberty. In fact, however, it was the proto-Independents who took
with the utmost seriousness the Pauline conviction that the Holy
Spirit would be the guide in extemporary prayers, and gave up
prayer-books of every kind.

Puritanism was responsible for the insistence on the interiority of worship, for it is the Spirit of God that searches the heart. The same concern made Puritan fathers prepare for Sunday worship in the congregation by daily family worship in the home.[93] It was the Spirit that motivated Richard Rogers to assert that public worship without private help was cold: "for hearing of the word read and preached, doth little profit where it is not ioyned with preparation to heare reverently and attentively, and where it is not mused on after, yea and as occasion shall offer, conferred on also. . . ."[94] The very intensity of Puritan worship and life, with its deep seriousness so amusingly criticised by the Elizabethan and Jacobean dramatists, springs from the overriding concern for sincerity before God. In an emphasis that looked forward to the Quakers, Perkins gave priority to inward worship, consisting of the adoration of God and cleaving to Him, over outward worship. Adoration comprised four virtues—fear, obedience, patience, and thankfulness, while cleaving to God was possible through faith, hope, love, and inward invocation.[95]

The doctrine of the Holy Spirit in Puritanism is also seen in the demand for integrity of life. The fruits of righteousness, the harvest of the Holy Spirit, are the evidences of sanctification and proofs of the calling of the elect. This was manifested externally in the insistence that the holy table at Communion be fenced against all who lived scandalously. It was all the more honoured among Presbyterian Puritans because Farel and Calvin were expelled from Geneva for maintaining the purity of the Genevan church in precisely this manner. "Holy Discipline" was regarded as the third distinguishing mark of the true church by all Puritans, the other two being the preaching of the word of God and the true and due administration of the Gospel sacraments. So seriously was the duty of disciplining the faithful taken that they appointed officers whose task it was to rebuke the members who did not live according to their Christian profession, and to bring them to the parting of the ways at which they either confessed their sorrow before the congregation and produced fruits worthy of repentance and were restored to the communion of the local church, or, if they persisted in their course of scandalous conduct, they were solemnly excommunicated as "limbs of Satan."[96]

[93] See Chap. XII for Puritan spirituality.
[94] *Seven Treatises*, p. 225.   [95] *Works*, 3 vols. (1613), II, 62-63.
[96] See my *Worship of the English Puritans*, chap. 14, for a description of procedures for excommunication and restoration.

The overwhelming concern to prevent worship becoming stereotyped and stale is seen not only in creative prayers (instead of set prayers) and original sermons (instead of official homilies), but also in an innovation within Puritanism of days of thanksgiving and humiliation. This practise appears to have derived directly from the observation of Old Testament practise, and seems not to have been used elsewhere corporately and consistently in the history of Christianity. It was not so much that the Puritans rejected the Church Year or even that they telescoped it so that each Sunday celebrated the mighty acts of God from Creation to Incarnation, and from the first to the second Advent.[97] Rather it was the recognition that history is the acting out of the divine providence and that God continues to reveal Himself in judgment and mercy many times in the life of a nation and of a family. The appropriate response to these acts of judgment was a Day of Fasting and Humiliation. The appropriate response to the acts of mercy or deliverance was a Day of Thanksgiving. Each was kept by fasting and prayer, whether the act of judgment was national or family calamity and whether the act of mercy was the deliverance of the nation from the hands of its enemies or the deliverance of a mother from childbirth. But it was this recognition of the continuing guidance of God in special providence, as recorded in the private spiritual diaries of the Puritans or referred to in the sermons of their ministers, which gave a sense of the immediacy of the Holy Spirit in their lives. It is well known that the entire army of Cromwell gathered for fasting and prayer to seek the divine will. It is less well known that this was a feature of the earliest Elizabethan Puritanism to mark the understanding of the ways of divine providence by days of fasting and prayer, set apart for that purpose.

William Perkins said there were two just occasions for religious fasting: "The first is, when some iudgement of God hangs over our heads, whether it be publike, as Famine, Pestilence, the Sword, destruction, &c. or private. The second cause of fasting is, when wee are to sue, and seeke by prayer to God for some speciall blessing, or for the supply of some great want."[98] As an example of the latter, Perkins listed Christ fasting and spending the whole night in prayer before choosing His 12 disciples. Perkins insisted that

---

[97] A. G. Matthews, in *Christian Worship*, ed. Nathaniel Micklem, p. 173: "The Sabbath retained its lonely splendour as the sole red-letter day of the Puritan Calendar."

[98] *Works* (1613 edn.), II, *Cases of Conscience*, p. 102.

the true way to keep a fast was to abstain from meat, drink, and all delights that "may cheare and refresh nature"; by such abstinence as will afflict the body, and subdue the flesh to the "will and word of God," we stir our devotion to God, lead to contrition or inward sorrow, and admonish us of guiltiness before God. All this may seem masochistic to modern ears, though to the sixteenth century Catholic or Protestant it was recognised that the refractory and rebellious will of man is not easily brought into the captivity of Christ. It is all the more interesting to read of the rapture with which these exercises of fasting and prayer were entered into by the Puritans, as in the case of one John Lister (b. 1627) who testified in his autobiography how his spirituality was formed by memorising the sermons and lectures he heard at monthly preaching marathons, at funerals, and at Sunday worship. He vividly recalled the days of fasting: "O what fasting and praying, publicly and privately, what wrestling with God was there day and night? Many of those weeping, praying and wrestling seasons, both day and night, were kept in my dear mother's house, and the feasts were kept with great strictness and severity; not many of us, old or young, eating so much as a morsel of bread for twenty-four hours together; this was a great weariness for men. . . ."[99] For those who believed they were wresting a great blessing from God the experience would be one of exhilaration, not exhaustion. Puritans made few concessions to children, and this may account for Lister's memory of his own childhood boredom, but also of the intense interest that the "weeping, wrestling, and praying seasons" had for the adults. Here, again, is evidence of the intensity of the interior civil war of the Spirit in which all Puritans were engaged.

The fourth quality of Puritan worship was its deep concern that the people of God should not be spectators or listeners, but sharers in the worship, a feeling that arose from a profound conviction of the solidarity of God's chosen people. At first glance, it might seem that Anglican worship, with its responses in the versicles and the litany, gave a larger place to the laity than Puritanism did, for the latter required the minister's voice alone to be heard in prayer, except for the concluding amen, which indicated the congregation's concurrence with the minister. In fact, however, in gatherings of Puritans for worship, there were several points at which the congregation played a significant part. Even where they were theo-

99 *The Autobiography of Joseph Lister*, ed. T. Wright, pp. 5-6, cited in Ronald A. Marchant, *The Puritans and the Church Courts in the Diocese of York, 1540-1642*, p. 115.

retically passive, as in listening to the preaching, a high degree of silent cooperation was expected, as they "mused" on God's word and its relevance to their lives. The metrical Psalms were popular in worship, not only because of the attractive tunes to which they were set, but also because, being so often in common metre and rhymed, they were easily memorised. They provided a more democratic vehicle for praise than the intricate chants that required trained choirs to sing them in the Roman Catholic and Anglican cathedrals and town churches of note. Furthermore, there was no division in Puritan meetinghouses between the sacred space of the sanctuary or chancel[100] and the secular space of the nave. Puritan elders (if Presbyterian) and deacons (if Independent) served the congregation with the sacred elements of bread and wine, which all members received. There was every incentive for members of the congregation to listen attentively to the sermon, not only because the exposition of the oracles of God was the climax of the service, but also because children and servants knew that it was the duty of the heads of Puritan households to test how carefully they had remembered the main "heads" of the sermon. Indeed, it was often noted that eager Puritan church members assisted their memories with notebooks and recalled the "doctrines" and "uses" of the sermons in their Sunday evening private devotions. Also, many unscrupulous printers published pirated sermons of famous preachers.[101] The Puritans never forgot, whether in church, home, or the marketplace, that there was never a holiday from God for His elect. Their worship was a shared commitment.

Was this solemn, simple, Biblical, shared worship without defects? It was only to be expected that Sunday services which aimed to make every gathering of worship a renewed Pentecost should occasionally become merely a "Low Sunday." Extemporaneous prayer could be sadly abused, by prolixity,[102] sensationalism, rambling thought or speech, and spiritual superficiality.

It can be, and was, argued that Puritan worship made too great demands on the spiritual and intellectual capacities of both minis-

---

[100] Cartwright criticises the Anglican minister because "in saying morning and evening prayer [he] sitteth in the chancel with his back to the people as though he had some secret talk with God which the people might not hear." Cited in Whitgift, *Works*, II, pp. 487f.

[101] See Alan F. Herr, *The Elizabethan Sermon, A Survey and Bibliography.*

[102] Bishop Aylmer of London is accused by "Marprelate" (*The Marprelate Tracts*, ed. William Pierce, p. 187) of saying that long Puritan prayers before and after sermon are nothing else but "beeble-babble, beeble-babble." See also Benjamin Brook, *Lives of the Puritans*, 3 vols., I, 433.

ters and congregations. Hooker thought Puritan prayers presumed an attention span greater than it was reasonable to expect of congregations, and defended collects and responses on the ground that they would more easily retain the interest of congregations. He made a plea for an aspect almost forgotten in Puritan worship with the reminder that "in public Prayer we are not only to consider what is needful in respect of God, but there is also in men that which we must regard."[103] Concentrated Calvinism may overwind the human mechanism, as the cases of Jonathan Edwards' Uncle Hawley and of the gentle castaway from grace, the poet Cowper, remind us by their tragic suicides. Some who found Puritanism too demanding must have slipped with relief back into the comfortable compliance of the Church of England—understandably so, whether ministers or church members. It cannot have been easy for ministers to produce two new sermons for each Lord's Day, as well as a frequent weekday lecture, with the high level of godly learning their congregations had a right to expect. Every public prayer they offered was expected to be extemporaneous. They had responsibilities to take their part in "prophesyings" and in days of humiliation and thanksgiving. They had to visit their congregations so as to bear in mind the special needs of the poor, the sick, the infirm, the old, and especially those who were distressed in conscience. Ministers were expected to keep abreast of the latest casuistry and to keep up to date in Biblical knowledge by reading some of the vast commentaries on books of the Bible which proliferated in the sixteenth and seventeenth centuries. In addition to all this, they had to conduct their own household prayers and private meditations, and keep a spiritual diary. The Puritan ministry was a zestful, but highly strenuous calling, testing the powers of mind, heart, and will to the utmost.

Given this expectation, one can hardly wonder that Puritan sermons and the whole ethos of the services of the Puritans were excessively didactic. This was, of course, merely the defect of a good quality, the application of the mind to the understanding of faith. Yet, granting the primacy of the theological task in an era of profound change and transition such as the sixteenth century was, there came a time when criticism must yield to the "obedience of faith" and the critical intellect seemed unwilling to give way to devotional "musings" and meditation in worship. There was a serenity, at least quietness, of spirit in Roman Catholic and Angli-

[103] *Ecclesiastical Polity*, Book v, chap. xxxii, sec. 2.

can worship, as there was also in the worship of the Religious Society of Friends, but this is not to be found in the agitated worship of the Puritans and their successors. E. C. Ratcliff saw that the prophetic protest would have to stabilise and become sacerdotal: "In general, Independent worship has tended to place too great a burden on the minister, and to leave the congregation too much to the minister's direction, with the result that a ministry and worship designed to be prophetic have not infrequently developed features reminiscent of the 'sacerdotalism' against which the Independents made their earnest protest."[104]

The fear of Catholicism became itself a superstition among the Puritans. They did not give sufficient heed to the customs of the primitive Church and were even neglectful of the traditions of the Reformed Churches in Europe. It must, however, be acknowledged that very little was known at the time about the early families of Christian liturgies; the Puritans were not in any case likely to look to those quarters where liturgical lore was to be found, however meagre. The result was that Puritan worship, for all its strengths, was also controlled by a naive primitivism which relegated all centuries between the first and the sixteenth to the discard. Its determination that the ethical was a primary category had the consequence of suspecting and distrusting the aesthetic, except in the realm of music. Bunyan might recall in the images of his allegory, that "the famous town of Mansoul had five gates . . . Ear-gate, Eye-gate, Mouth-gate, Nose-gate, and Feel-gate." Puritans, for all practical purposes, were so conscious of the dangers of absolutising the finite or confusing an image with the reality which it reveals and also hides that they were blind in their worship, or at least colour blind. Their simple worship and dignified meetinghouses had the beauty of etchings, with the result that the painter or sculptor must find his spiritual home in the Catholic, Orthodox, or Anglican traditions, not in Puritanism. It also meant that Puritans are starved of the glory of the Creation in their worship.

Finally, authoritative and august as the Biblical criterion was in Puritan worship, demanding and eliciting a splendid loyalty, it was too rigidly applied. For every detail of worship a Biblical sanction, or at the very least, a Biblical silence, was required. This legalistic application of Scripture can be illustrated from Cartwright who argued from the single case of John the Baptist

---

[104] *The Study of Theology*, ed. K. E. Kirk, p. 474.

preaching a sermon before his baptising that all Baptisms must be preceded by preaching.[105]

The worship of the Puritans was characterised by fidelity, simplicity, spontaneity and spirituality, as well as relevance. From the perspective of history it can be recognised for what it was— a singularly effective, prophetic protest against formalism. But institutional forms need to be revitalised, not jettisoned; even spontaneity runs into a stereotype, and supposedly aliturgical worship has its own awkward structure that makes it a liturgy. The spirit without the forms of worship was only a ghost whispering through the individual keyhole. The forms without the spirit were merely puppetry. The choice was no longer liturgical or charismatic worship, but a structure with possibilities for freedom, treasuring the past but open to the present and the future, in short, a liturgy with liberty. This the Puritans did not discover until 1644, and then not fully.

[105] Cited in D. J. McGinn, *The Admonition Controversy*, p. 101.

CHAPTER VIII

PURITAN PREACHING

THE PURITANS were not the only group in England who emphasised the central importance of preaching. But no others—not even such eminent exponents of the art of commending the Gospel as Richard Hooker or Lancelot Andrewes—elevated the proclamation of the Word of God as highly.[1] For the Puritan it was the climax of divine service; for the Anglican it was "so worthy a part of divine service." Hooker admitted it to be "the blessed ordinance of God, Sermons as the keys to the Kingdom of Heaven, as wings to the Soul, as spurs to the good affections of man, unto the sound and healthy as food, as physic unto diseased minds."[2] This evaluation is hardly to be distinguished from that of the "silver-tongued" Elizabethan Puritan preacher, Henry Smith, who had spoken of the Word of God as "the *Star* which shuld lead us to Christ, the *Ladder* which shuld mount us to heaven, the *Water* that shuld clense our leprosie, the *Manna* that shuld refresh our hunger, & the *booke* that we shuld meditate on day & night."[3]

1. *The Primacy of Preaching*

There was, however, a difference. For Smith the proclamation of the Gospel was "the one thing necessary," the listening to the words of Christ which the Master had commended in Mary as contrasted with the Martha who was "busied with many things." Whereas for Hooker, himself a preacher whose matter was as solid as Andrewes' sermons, but much less animatedly delivered, the Gospel was equally conveyed in the reading of the lessons from the Gospel and the Epistle in the liturgy, and in the dramatic reenactment of the same Gospel through the sacraments of Baptism and Holy Communion.[4] For the Puritan the proclamation of

[1] For the Puritans the Sacraments were "seals" of the Word (*sigilla Verbi*), that is, confirmations of God's promises in the Gospel. For the Anglicans, however, the sacraments were means of grace, at least as important as preaching.

[2] *Treatise on the Laws of Ecclesiastical Polity*, book v, sec. 22.

[3] *The Sermons of Maister Henrie Smith gathered into one volume* (Richard Field for Thomas Man, 1593), from "The Arte of Hearing in two Sermons," p. 646.

[4] In *Ecclesiastical Polity*, book v, sec. 21, Hooker argued that one can come to a saving knowledge of God through "conversation in the bosom of the Church," through "religious education," by "the reading of learned men's books," as well

294

the Gospel through preaching brought men to the existential cross-roads, where the way led either to life everlasting or to destruction, and the aim of his preaching was to convert his hearers from worldliness to godliness. He wished to transform, not merely to inform.

William Bradshaw rightly insisted that the Puritans gave the primacy in worship to preaching: "They hould that the highest and supreame office and authoritie of the Pastor, is to preach the gospell solemnly and publickly to the Congregation, by interpreting the written word of God, and applying the same by exhortation and reproof unto them. They hould that this was the greatest worke that Christ & His Apostles did."[5] No Puritan preacher ever forgot that St. Paul had spoken of preaching as "the power of God unto salvation."[6] Preaching was, in short, the declaration of the transforming revelation of the living God confirmed in the hearts of the believers by the interior witness of the Holy Spirit.

I have already indicated that the high evaluation of preaching by the Puritans was due to their conviction that this was God's primary way of winning men to His allegiance, hence it was the most important task of the first apostles and of all subsequent witnesses. In addition, there was a series of confirming considerations, all of which reinforced this evaluation.

Among the additional incentives was the recognition of the great dearth of preaching in Reformed England, itself a paradox for reformation was accomplished only "according to the Word of God." The "apostle of the North," Bernard Gilpin, had apprised the young King Edward VI of this desperate lack of preachers in 1552. He declared of Christ's Gospel: "But yet, it is not heard of all Your people, a thousand pulpits in *England* are covered with dust, some have not had foure Sermons these fifteene or sixteene

---

as by lections of the scriptures and by homilies. He excoriated the Puritan claims, "how Christ is by Sermons lifted up higher, and made more apparent to the eye of faith; how the Savour of the Word is made more sweet, being brayed, and more able to nourish, being divided, by Preaching." (Book v, sec. 22, p. 12.) Fuller said: "Mr. Hooker's voice was low, stature little, gesture none at all. . . ." *The Church History of Britain*, edn. of 1837, III, 128.

5 *English Puritanisme, containing the maine opinions of the rigidest sort of those that are called Puritanes in the realm of England* (1605), p. 17. See also Christopher Hill, *Puritanism and Revolution*, pp. 269-71; and Stuart Barton Babbage, *Puritanism and Richard Bancroft*, p. 372: "The Puritans magnified the office of preaching and it was through preaching that they exercised their greatest influence."

6 Romans 1:15-16. See also Romans 10:13-15, I Corinthians 1:21, and Ephesians 1:13. John Penry cited the last three references before the High Commission. Cf. *The Marprelate Tracts*, ed. William Pierce (1589), pp. 64-65.

years, since Friers left their limitations and a few of those were worthy the name of Sermon."[7] The Catholic reign of Mary worsened the situation for Protestants, and Elizabeth and her Council clearly preferred to restrict the issuing of the episcopal licenses to preachers who were compliant and not potential troublemakers. Muzzled, if not mute, many of Elizabeth's ministers of religion became minions of state. Hungry parishioners were fed the driest form of homilies. If they were so fortunate as to have a preaching rector or vicar and lived near a fair-sized town, they could count on good sermons four times a year.[8] As Millar Maclure has characterised the situation, "The drone of the homilies replaced the mutter of the Mass."[9] In these circumstances, the Puritan preachers were indeed pastors, that is, shepherds, sustaining the sheep with solid provender, high in theological vitamins, often indigestibly so, but a great strengthening after the starvation diet they were used to.

The second ground for Puritan insistence on preaching was the complete inadequacy of the alternative—the reading of approved homilies. It was not only that a sermon was unpredictable and therefore provided an element of novelty in a prescribed service; it was the applicability of a good sermon to the conditions of the congregation. Cartwright, or the author of the *Second Replie* (in the "Admonition Controversy") put his finger on the weak point of homilies: "For where the preacher is able according to the manifold windings and turnings of sin to wind and turn in with it to the end he may strike it, the homilies are not able to turn neither off the right nor off the left, but to what quarter soever the enemies are retired it must keep the train wherein it was set of the maker."[10] These printed homilies, while their doctrine was admirable (often they had been prepared by the leading divines), nevertheless were cold rations and no adequate substitute for the "living oracles" of God spoken with conviction and sincerity, illus-

---

[7] *A Sermon preached in the Court at Greenwitch, before King Edward the Sixth, the first Sonday after the Epiphany, Anno Domini, 1552* (1630), p. 25. Gilpin observed on p. 23 that at Oxford and Cambridge "the decay of students is so great, there are scarse left of every thousand, an hundred."

[8] From Bishop Cox's interpretation of the Royal Injunctions of 1560, the regulation went as follows: "If the person be able, he shall preach in his own person every month; or else preach by another, so that his absence be approved by the ordinary of the diocese in respect of sickness, service, or study at the universities. Nevertheless, for the want of able preachers and parsons, to tolerate them without penalty, so they preach in their own persons, or by a learned substitute, once in every three months of the year." Strype, *Annals of the Reformation,* I, 318.

[9] *Paul's Cross Sermons,* p. 54.

[10] D. J. McGinn, *The Admonition Controversy,* p. 395.

trated from the pursuits and interests of the parish, and applied to the needs of people who were if not the friends of the minister, at least well-known acquaintances, and, above all, his spiritual responsibility. The Puritans raised an outcry against both "dumbe dogges" (unpreaching parsons) and ersatz sermons such as these homilies were, which were spoiling the taste for real preaching. Henry Smith asserts, "And the droane never studieth to preach for hee saith, then an Homelie is better liked of than a Sermon."[11] Learned preachers often poked fun at the homilies, calling them "Homelies," and "humbles."

Furthermore, sermons could penetrate to the hearts of the congregation in a manner impossible for prescribed homilies. Cartwright made the point: "As the fire stirred giveth more heat, so the Word, as it were, blown by preaching, flameth more in the hearers, than when it is read."[12] Topsell indicated that a true listening to preaching is one that expects not only the light of information but the warmth of affection: "Let us therefore so sorte our selves in the congregation, where our eares may be beaten with an understanding sounde, and our hearts bee touched with a heavenly power, that the coales of zeale may be enflamed, and the light of knowledge may be kindeled."[13] Even Hooker grudgingly admitted that sermons were more popular than homilies, due, he suggested, to the exaggerated claims Puritans made for sermons, but also to more sensible considerations. The first was that men knew they could always read over a homily another time if they did not give it their full attention the first time, whereas the sermon was unrecoverable; the second was that sermons "come always new."[14]

A combination of the circumstances just mentioned, including the tight control of preachers by the bishops, the dearth of preaching, and the substitution of printed homilies for sermons, led the Puritans to try to make good the defect by the introduction of "Prophesyings," which constituted a kind of extramural theological course on homiletics organised by ministers with Puritan sympathies in the larger towns to train their younger colleagues in the art and craft of expounding and applying the Gospel. These meetings began as early as 1564, and flourished in the following

---

11 *Ibid.*, pp. 309-10. A satirical name for "homilies" in a sermon of Thomas Lever is cited in *The Cambridge History of English Literature*, IV, 233.

12 *Ecclesiastical Polity*, vol. 2, p. 76, cites the Cartwright observation.

13 *Times Lamentation* (1599), p. 303.

14 Hooker's *Ecclesiastical Polity*, Book v, sec. 22, p. 20.

decade. Writing in 1577, Harrison gave a careful account of the procedure at a "prophesie or conference." The exercises took place weekly at some places, fortnightly at others, monthly in some places, and elsewhere twice a year. It was "a notable spurre unto all the ministers, thereby to applie their bookes, which otherwise (as in times past) would give themselves to hawking, hunting, tables, cards, dice, tipling at the alehouse, shooting and other like vanities, nothing commendable in such as should be godlie and zealous stewards of the good gifts of God, faithfull distributors of his word unto the people, and diligent pastors according to their calling."[15] According to Harrison, "such is the thirstie desire of the people in these daies to heare the word of God, that [the laity] also have as it were with zealous violence intruded themselves among" the ministers, though only as hearers.[16] The method was:

> Herein also (for the most part) two of the yoonger sort of ministers doo expound, ech after other, some peece of the scriptures ordinarilie appointed unto them in their courses (wherein they orderlie go through with some one of the evangelists, or of the epistles, as it pleaseth the whole assemblie to choose at the first in everie of these conferences); and when they have spent an houre or a little more betweene them, then commeth one of the better learned sort, who . . . supplieth the roome of a moderator, making first a brief rehearsall of their discourses, and then adding what him thinketh good of his owne knowledge, wherby two houres are thus commonlie spent at this most profitable meeting. When all is doone, if the first speakers have showed anie peece of diligence, they are commended for their travell, and incouraged to go forward. If they have beene found to be slacke, their negligence is openlie reprooved before all their brethren, who go aside of purpose from the laitie, after the exercise ended, to iudge of these matters, and consult of the next speakers and quantitie of the text to be handled in that place.[17]

The new scene of Puritan activity in England originated in the Swiss and Rhenish cities, where the Marian exiles had undoubt-

---

[15] *Harrison's Description of England in Shakespere's Youth*, ed. F. J. Furnivall, pp. 18-19.

[16] *Ibid.*, p. 18.

[17] It should be noted that Thomas Fuller's account of prophesying, in *The Church History of Britain*, ed. J. S. Brown, III, 6-7, is substantially the same, except that Fuller asserts that after the first young divine has preached "five or six more observing their seniority, successfully dilated on the same text."

edly come across them and been impressed by them, and introduced them into England.[18] It was an excellent device for improving the education of the clergy, for keeping them in a state of
holy emulation, for raising the standard of Biblical studies (and
the use of good commentaries) as well as preaching. Notably the
young ministers were taught to expound successive passages of
Scripture, not to take texts as mere pretexts to illustrate topics.
They were, moreover, encouraged to read whole chapters of the
Bible, which was to account in part for their dislike of Anglican
shredding of the Scripture lessons as mere "pistling and gospling."
The example set by the older men—with their knowledge of the
Biblical languages in many cases, the disciplining of their minds
to the Word of God, and the fervency of their preaching—must
have been profoundly influential.

In time the exercises became not only miniature theological
colleges for continuing ministerial education (and, as was typical
of the Puritan movement, a means of further theological education for laymen), but they also became centres of Puritan propaganda for the "Discipline," and as such provided the framework
of the later classes and presbyteries.[19]

Queen Elizabeth felt they were a threat to the established
Church, and instructed Archbishop Grindal to request his brother
bishops to forbid all "prophesyings" in their dioceses. On December 20, 1576 Grindal sent his famous letter to Queen Elizabeth
in defence of prophesyings: "I am forced with all humility and
yet plainly to profess that I cannot with safe conscience and without the offense of the Majesty of God, give my consent to the suppressing of the said exercises; much less can I send out my injunction for the utter and universal subversion of the same. . . ."[20]
Ignoring her archbishop the queen on May 7, 1577 issued instructions directly to the bishops, commanding suppression. Grindal
was sequestered by the royal orders and confined for six months
to his palace in Lambeth. Because he remained obdurate his suspension was never fully removed, despite frequent appeals made
on his behalf to the queen by his bishops and by the House of
Clergy. This single event shows that even if the queen did not
like to make windows in men's souls, she was not adverse to
restricting their views. It also indicates how desperate the need

18 See Leonard J. Trinterud, "The Origins of Puritanism," in *Church History
of Britain*, vol. 20, no. 1, pp. 46f. *Prophezei* were organized by Zwingli in Zurich
in 1525 and in England in John à Lasco's Church of the Strangers.

19 P. M. Dawley, *John Whitgift and the English Reformation*, p. 146.

20 The letter is reproduced in Strype, *The History of the Life and Acts of
Edmund Grindal*, pp. 578-79.

was for the Puritan protest for more preaching, that it was supported by the Primate of All England at the cost of his authority. Now the only way open to the Puritans to supply the lack of preachers was to get well-trained Puritan ministers appointed as lecturers in a given parish, their stipends being provided by men of substance and most often in London. A preeminent example was Henry Smith, an immensely popular lecturer at St. Clement Dane's Church in the Strand from 1587 to 1590, whom Bishop Aylmer tried to remove from this position but who was reinstated almost certainly by the influence of his stepmother's brother, Lord Burghley, to whom he dedicated the collected edition of his *Sermons* in 1593. Less conspicuously there were secret gatherings of Puritan ministers to continue these exercises.

Important as the role of preaching was in the Puritan discipline and culture of the spiritual life,[21] it must be remembered that it was reinforced by a cluster of ancillary practises, all dependent on the recognition of the primacy of the Bible as containing the will of God. Psalm-singing might be contemptuously termed "Genevan jigs" by Elizabeth, but these religious songs confirmed the lessons of obedience to God's law, the privileges of the people of God, and men's security in the providential rule of the Shepherd God. Fast-days and conferences were the Puritan substitutes for Catholic pilgrimages, as sermons on "cases of conscience" and Puritan diary-keeping was the substitute for the Catholic confessional.[22] Private prayer in the language of the heart was another exercise, along with private Bible-reading, that made men and women eager to respond to the marching orders of the living God. The sermons themselves were to be summarised carefully from notes taken during the service so that the heads of households could be sure their children had heeded the Word of God preached from the pulpit. As Marshall Knappen has observed of these mutually reinforcing spiritual techniques: "These called for more intelligence and more concentration than any of the Catholic techniques." Yet one may dissent from his conclusion, at least as applied to the great Catholic mystics, like St. Teresa of Avila or St. John of the Cross, that "doubtless, if used properly, they were capable of

---

21 The culture of the spiritual life of Catholics and Anglicans, as well as Puritans, is treated in detail in a later chapter.

22 The Puritan preachers provided a whole genre of sermons denominated "cases of conscience." To take only two examples among hundreds, Richard Greenham, the teacher of Henry Smith, produced *Godly instructions for the due examination and direction of all men* (1599) and William Perkins, *The whole treatise of the cases of conscience* (1604).

putting a finer edge on the spiritual life also."[23] Puritan spirituality was certainly admirably adapted for the thoughtful laymen of the age; it was a Bible-centred spirituality.

It may well have been Hooker's practise of reading his heavily freighted sermons that blinded him to the importance of a face-to-face confrontation with his congregation, and accounted for the strange observation: "Men speak not with the instruments of writing, neither write with the instruments of speech; and yet things recorded with the one, and uttered with the other, may be preached well enough with both."[24] The point was that a man could address other men directly from the pulpit, whereas the most eloquent writing was indirect speech. Preaching was a striking on the soul, as Miles Mosse, a preacher at Paul's Cross, well knew, when he said: "*Vox est ictus animi*: passing through the eare, and braine, and blood, it smiteth (as it were) and giveth a stroke upon the verie soule, and so with a kind of Violence doth deeply affect it. . . . But yet further, besides all the worke of Nature, there is in Preaching a speciall gift of grace: which enableth a man to speak with such evidence of the Spirit, & with such power to the Conscience, as no pen of man by writing can expresse: whereof Preaching is the most likely, and effectuall instrument of salvation and so to be respected."[25]

For these reasons, then, the Puritans believed that preaching was the means chosen by God for illuminating the minds, mollifying the hearts, sensitising the consciences, strengthening the faith, quelling the doubts, and saving the souls of mankind. To that end the Puritan brethren dedicated their chief energies to preaching clearly, faithfully, sincerely, and movingly, trusting that the Holy Spirit would take their human words and make them the "lively oracles of God" to their congregations.

2. *Biblical Interpretation*

The Puritans were not the first Protestants. It is therefore not surprising that in their Biblical interpretation they adopted many of the early Protestant principles. Perhaps the most distinctive Protestant principle for the interpretation of Scripture was the determination to use as the primary meaning the literal or historical sense of the texts, as contrasted with the medieval allegorical inter-

---

[23] *Tudor Puritanism; A Chapter in the History of Idealism*, p. 399.
[24] *Ecclesiastical Polity*, book v, sec. 21.
[25] *Justifying and Saving Faith* (1614), sig. gg2, cited in Maclure, *St. Paul's Cross Sermons*, p. 145.

pretation. Tyndale referred to the Catholic fourfold mode of scriptural interpretation, for contrast: "They divide Scripture into four senses the literal, tropological, allegorical, and anagogical. The literal sense is become nothing at all: for the Pope hath taken it clean away. . . . The tropological sense pertaineth to good manners (say they), and teacheth what we ought to do. The allegory is appropriate to faith; and the anagogical to hope, and things above."[26] This led to a great deal of ingenious subjectivity in the interpretation of Scripture. But it also had the advantage of providing intelligibility when there were contradictions or obscurities. It also had some practical purposes in mind, for the tropological meaning provided ethical guidance, the allegorical meaning gave spiritual assistance, and the anagogical sense kept the eschatological dimension of Scripture vivid. Protestantism was also interested in the same guidance, but it was content to try and find it by exegesis rather than by eisegesis, however brilliant the latter might be.

Tyndale, the great English translator, stands with all Protestants on the primacy of the literal sense. "Thou shalt understand," he writes, "that the scripture hath but one sense, which is the literal sense. And that literal sense is the root and ground of all, and the anchor that never faileth, whereunto if thou cleave, thou canst never err or go out of the way. Nevertheless, the scripture useth proverbs, similitudes, riddles or allegories, as all other speeches do: but that which the proverb, riddle, or allegory signifieth, is ever the literal sense, which thou must seek out diligently: as in English we borrow words and sentences of one thing, and apply them to another and give them new significations."[27]

It is clear that the older Henrician divines like St. John Fisher, an accomplished preacher of ornate sermons in the older mould, preferred the allegorical approach. Fisher would, for example, interpret the four rivers of paradise referred to in Genesis 2: 10-14

[26] From "The Obedience of a Christian Man," *Doctrinal Treatises*, ed. H. Walter, p. 303.

[27] *Ibid.*, p. 304. William Whitaker, the Calvinist Master of St. John's College, Cambridge, was more guarded in his qualified rejection of the nonliteral senses of scripture: "These things we do not wholly reject: we concede such things as allegory, anagoge, and tropology in Scripture; but meanwhile we deny that there are many and various senses. We affirm that there is but one true, proper, and genuine sense of Scripture arising from the words rightly understood, which we call the literal: and we contend that allegories, tropologies, and anagoges are not various senses, but various collections from one sense, or various applications and accommodations of that one meaning." *A Disputation on Holy Scripture against the Papists, especially Bellarmine and Stapledon*, tr. and ed. W. Fitzgerald, p. 403.

as symbolising the four cardinal virtues,[28] and use Sinai as symbolising a Jewish synagogue and Sion the Christian church.[29] This was the very characteristic that the racy Latimer criticised in Catholic exegesis, so that the Catholics were inclined to see subtleties where none existed. For example, Latimer argued that when Christ chose the boat of Peter, it was misinterpreted by Catholics as teaching the primacy of Peter among the apostles.[30] While the Catholics were attracted to the poetical and prophetical books of the Bible for their texts and expositions, the Protestants were rediscovering the historical books of the Old Testament.[31] Latimer was a master at retelling the narrative portions of the Old Testament and applying them to current situations. He expounded the first two chapters of the first book of the Kings in order to apply the usurpation of Adonijah to the overweening ambition of Lord Seymour, at the time imprisoned in the Tower of London.[32] Equally, Latimer was glad to preach one of his "nipping, rough, and hard biting" sermons against bribery and unpreaching prelates as he related the story of the sons of Eli from the second and third chapters of the first book of Samuel. Similarly, the most popular of Elizabethan Puritan preachers, Henry Smith, had three sermons on King Nebuchadnessar, as a type of pride.

A second characteristic of Protestant Biblical interpretation, as contrasted with medieval Catholic exegesis, was a deep concern to discover the native meaning of Biblical expressions and derive them from the original languages. John Bradford, chaplain to Nicholas Ridley, was not unusual in emphasising that μετάνοια, the Greek word for "repentance," means a "forethinking" and has no reference to the developed Catholic sacrament of Penance. This emphasis on Biblical and Patristic learning reached its climax in

[28] *The English Works of John Fisher*, part I, ed. J.E.B. Mayor, 2nd edn., E.E.T.S., e.s. xxvii, 1935, pp. 24-25.

[29] *Ibid.*, p. 167.

[30] *Sermons by Hugh Latimer, sometime Bishop of Worcester, Martyr, 1555*, ed. G. E. Corrie, pp. 205-206.

[31] The contrast between Catholic and Protestant exegesis of the scriptures must not be too rigidly drawn, however, for several English Catholic preachers imbued with the "New Learning" emphasised the literal sense, such as Colet, Stafford, and Taverner. Moreover, even Latimer and Hooper were prepared to accommodate historical narrative to the current political situation in the search for monitory lessons for their contemporaries.

[32] Seymour had aspired to marry the widow of Henry VIII, Queen Catherine Parr, as Adonijah aimed to marry Queen Abishag on the death of King David. The names of the living aristocrats are not once mentioned, but the implications are clear. Cf. F. E. Hutchinson's "The English Pulpit from Fisher to Donne," vol. 4, *Cambridge History of English Literature*.

the Jacobean erudition (if not occasional pedantry) of the sermons of Bishop Lancelot Andrewes, but it was often used by Protestants in the interpretation of such disputed texts as the Vulgate, *Hoc est corpus meum.*

Since only the Bible, as the divinely inspired Word or message of God, was able to serve as the standard by which a corrupt church could be corrected, it was of crucial significance that it be expounded literally for Protestants. For them it was the standard of doctrine—of information, as well as of correction—of reformation. For the Puritans, however, it was not only a standard of faith and morals, but it served as the only authoritative criterion for the ordinances and the details of worship and of ecclesiastical government. There were Puritans (like Cartwright) who would have curbed the magistrates with a theological whip in a theocracy and applied the regulations of *Leviticus* to Leviathan, as Hobbes was to name the state. To the reflective mind of Hooker, this was bibliolatrous, but the very excess of respect given to the Bible rather than to the Christ, who was its climax and criterion, helps us to understand the energy and intellectual zest that was given to the study of the Scriptures and the application of its lessons for the people from the pulpits of the Puritan preachers.

3. *The Structure of the Sermon*

If the primary purpose of preaching is to present the claims of God on man through the criticism and comfort of the Gospel, the structure of the Puritan sermon had to be simple, memorable, and practical. As such, it aimed to produce light and heat, illumination of the mind and warming of the affections.

The structure of the Puritan sermon was anticipated by Bishop Hooper, who in this respect, as in his objections to ornate vestments,[33] deserves the title, "the father of Nonconformity." It was exemplified in his series of sermons on Jonah preached at the court of King Edward VI. The structure took the form of the exposition of a passage of Scripture *secundem ordinem textus*, by collecting lessons (or "doctrines") from each verse and adding the moral applications (or "uses") of them.[34] The outstanding Puritan

---

[33] See J. H. Primus, *The Vestments Controversy.* See also Geoffrey F. Nuttall and Owen Chadwick, *From Uniformity to Unity, 1662-1962*, p. 162; and W.M.S. West, "John Hooper and the Origins of Puritanism," *Baptist Quarterly* (October 1954-April 1955).

[34] See J. W. Blench's *Preaching in England in the late fifteenth and sixteenth centuries*, pp. 94, 101-102, to which I owe much in this chapter. Blench has

lecturers used the same method as Hooper, which had been made widely known through the Latin commentaries of Musculus.

It was outlined with characteristic clarity in the famous *Art of Prophesying* of William Perkins, lecturer at St. Andrew's Church, Cambridge, the most eminent Puritan scholar of Elizabethan times, and an admirable preacher. The preacher's task was: (1) "to reade the Text distinctly out of the Canonicall Scriptures"; (2) "to give the sense and understanding of it being read, by the Scripture it selfe"; (3) "to collect a few and profitable points of doctrine out of the naturall sense"; (4) "to apply (if he have the gifte) these doctrines rightly collected to the life and manners of men in a simple and plaine speech."[35]

What was perhaps most interesting about the structure of the Puritan sermon was that it was streamlined in the direction of changing man's mind with a view to improving his behaviour. There was little interest in speculative thought or even speculative divinity. Of paramount concern was that godliness which desires to know the will of God in order to follow it. Puritan theology was, as Perkins described it, "the science of living blessedly for ever."[36] If the form of the Puritan sermon was indeed so functional, was there a place for the imagination? The answer was that metaphors, similes, and *exempla* provided the illustrations that were the windows of the sermon, illuminating the doctrine while sustaining the interest of the auditors, and possibly even nerving their wills to action.

For an example of the typical structure of a Puritan sermon one could turn to the sermons of Thomas Cartwright, which were constructed in the approved Swiss manner, and which were dutiful and dull, or to the livelier sermons of Edward Topsell, the author of two sets of Old Testament sermons, the first on the book of Ruth, entitled *The Reward of Religion*,[37] and the second on the

---

shed almost as much light on Renaissance preaching in England as Owst did on medieval English preaching.

35 *Works*, vol. 2, p. 673.

36 "Perkins," *Dictionary of National Biography*, vol. 45. The exact source of the definition is Perkins' *A Golden Chaine* (1600), p. 1. It is interesting to note that Perkins, the teacher of William Ames, was said to have preached so that "his sermons were not so plain but that the piously learned did admire them, nor so learned but that the plain did understand them." Thomas Fuller, *The Holy State* (1648), p. 81.

37 *The Reward of Religion. Delivered in sundry Lectures upon the Booke of Ruth, wherein the godly may see their dayly both inward & outward trials, with the presence of God to assist them, & his mercies to recompense them* (1597, first published 1596).

book of Joel, called *Times Lamentation*.[38] The more interesting alternative has been selected; the 16th of the 17 sermons on Ruth will be analysed.

The text is Ruth 4:16-17: "And Naomi took the child and laid it in her lappe, & became nurse unto it. And the women her neighbours gave it a name, saying, there is a child borne to Naomi and called the name thereof Obed; the same was the father of Ishai the father of David."

Topsell, after reading out the text, put it in its historical context and observed what comfort the birth of this son of Boaz brought to his grandmother Naomi, how she helped her daughter nurse him, and how the women of Bethlehem helped Naomi. Topsell derived four practical lessons from verse 16 and one from verse 17. His structure consisted of providing five doctrines and applying them.

(1) The first doctrine is that just as previously miseries were heaped on Naomi, now she knows the multiplied mercies of God in the birth of this boy. The application, or "use," is: "Thus we see it is a righteous thing with God, first to wound and then to heale, first to strike and then to stroke."[39] Then examples of a similar experience are given from the lives of Job, Joseph, and David. (2) The second doctrine from the same verse is that here is an example of a worthy grandmother who, out of gratitude to God, love of her grandson, and a desire to help her daughter, helped in the nursing of the child. The use of this doctrine is that it reminds aged parents who live to see their children's children that they have a duty to care for them. (3) Since Naomi is said here to be nurse of the child of Ruth, it is appropriate to raise a question with two parts. Is it lawful (A) to put children out to nurse from their own mother? Is it lawful (B) to commit their tuition to others? "Unto the first question I aunswere, that every woman being of health of body and minde, is bound by the worde of God to nurse her owne children. . . ."[40] This is confirmed by the examples of Sarah, Manoah's wife, Bathsheba, Elizabeth the wife of Zachariah, and the Virgin Mary who suckled the Saviour. To have the child nursed by some woman who is not its mother is a sign that its parents lack natural affection. Moreover, it is unnatural for a child to be nursed by a woman who did not bear

[38] The full title is *Times Lamentation, or an exposition of the prophet Joel in sundry sermons or meditations* (1599). It was reissued in 1601 and 1613.
[39] *The Reward of Religion*, pp. 285-86.
[40] *Ibid.*, p. 288.

him, "for the same body whereof he had his being is most fitte for his feeding."[41] The second part of the question must now be answered: is it right for parents to entrust their children to others for their upbringing? "I aunswere that every man and woman are bounde to see their childrens first instruction, that is, if it be possible to have them in their keeping at their first entrance to knowledge, and when they are first capable of any goodnesse."[42] Biblical examples are given in the instances of Isaac remaining with Abraham and little Benjamin with old Jacob. (4) After the important double question has been answered Topsell returns to the normal structure of the sermon. The fourth doctrine and use is the recognition of how important is the bringing up of children.

Topsell finally devotes his attention to the seventeenth verse. He reiterates that the child was named Obed, which signifies serving, or a servant, showing how he should serve for the comfort of Naomi, Boaz and Ruth. The women of Bethlehem proved to be good neighbours of Naomi. So the final doctrine (5) is to point out "the duty of the faithfull to be helpers one to another in the service of God, and admonition of their dueties."[43] The preacher concludes by giving the examples of the ruler of the temple who went to Jesus to seek help for his ailing child, the four friends who carried the palsied man to Christ for healing, and the friends of Dorcas who sought the aid of Peter to restore her to life.

The Puritan sermon structure was simple because it drew its lessons as the narrative proceeded. It was amply illustrated by godly examples drawn from other parts of the Bible to supplement the text. It was easily remembered, because to reread the texts at home was to recall the preacher's commentary and application of the passage. It did not provide a vehicle for the richer resources of rhetoric, with set pieces of sustained eloquence, grandiose comparisons and contrasts, tirades, apostrophe, and so forth, such as can be found in the Catholic sermons of St. John Fisher or of Hugh Weston, the Marian Dean of Westminster. Nor did the sermon form lend itself to the brilliant word analysis, patristic erudition, metaphysical and far-fetched conceits, and sheer sparkle of Lancelot Andrewes. Such elaborate rhetoric, "taffeta terms," and ornate diction, were suitable for sermons on state occasions, but it meant that the Word of God, which is sharper than any sword, and which could pierce to the quick of the conscience, remained sheathed in a

---

[41] *Ibid.*, p. 290. [42] *Ibid.*, p. 291. [43] *Ibid.*, p. 293.

jewelled scabbard. The Puritan sermon was no ceremonial sword; least of all was it like the painted, wooden sword of a homily officially prescribed. It was a lithe, lean, sharp instrument, poised to strike the soul.

Thus a simple, straightforward form for the sermon was felt to be appropriate to the Gospel itself, a reminder that the preachers were after all clay vessels, yet containers of the Gospel, that the greatest preacher of Christ the world had seen, St. Paul, had insisted that the Gospel was to be preached not by words of eloquence but by the integrity of conviction.

Great ingenuity was required of the preacher, not so much in providing the doctrines of the scripture, nor even in the illustrations from literature and life, but chiefly in the application of the lessons to the variety of persons and conditions in his congregation, especially in a city church. Perkins defined application as "that, whereby the doctrine rightly collected, is diversely fitted according as time, place, and person doe require."[44] He even categorised seven types of application, referring specifically to their conditions in relation to salvation. (Other preachers would of course apply lessons to the age, sex, and callings of the persons represented in their congregations.) But Perkins' sevenfold application is interesting. It includes: "unbeleevers, who are both ignorant and unteachable"; some who "are teachable, but yet ignorant"; some who "have knowledge but are not as yet humbled"; those who are humbled; some who believe; some who "are fallen"; and, finally, "there is a mingled people."[45] The requirement that every doctrine have a use is the proof of the practical nature of Puritan preaching, being directed to the conversion of the will and the betterment of behaviour.

4. Sermon Style

While one can refer to a Puritan sermon structure, there was no single Puritan style of sermon. J. W. Blench, in his analysis of the style of Elizabethan preachers, maintains that there were three major styles—plain, colloquial, and fully ornate—but he finds it necessary to subdivide the first category, to which most Puritan sermons belong, into three parts: the first, bare and austere; the

---

44 *The Arte of Prophesying, Or, a Treatise concerning the sacred and onely true Manner and Methode of Preaching*, included in *The Workes of that famous and worthy Minister of Christ in the University of Cambridge, M. William Perkins* (1613), 3 vols. This treatise was first issued in Latin, as the preface to the three-volume edition of his works indicates. The citation reference is to vol. 2, p. 664.
45 *Ibid.*, pp. 665-68.

second, less colourless, employing tropes but not schemata; and the third, moderately decorated, using tropes but rarely using schemata.[46]

The silver-tongued Henry Smith used the fully ornate style, as did the Calvinist and future Archbishop George Abbott. Abbott defended this, a little self-consciously, in asserting that ministers of the Gospel have liberty "not only nakedly to lay open the truth, but to use helps of wit, of invention and art (which are the good gifts of God), so to remove away all disdain and loathing of the word from the full hearts of the auditory—similitudes and comparisons, allusions, applications, yea parables and proverbs which may tend to edification and illustrating the word; for they have to do with weak ones as well as with the strong—with some of queasy stomachs, with some who must be enticed and allured with a bait of industry and eloquence, of pretty and witty sentences."[47] Smith and Abbott were exceptions, for the vast majority of those with Puritan leanings used the first or second, or in rare cases, like Richard Greenham (tutor of Perkins), the third variation of the plain style.

Perkins, Laurence Chaderton (first Master of Emmanuel College, Cambridge), Fulke, Gifford and Thomas White, preferred the austerely plain style, considering the use of even the simplest rhetorical devices or of classical learning as a distraction and a drawing of attention to the preacher rather than his message. Perkins, for example, insisted that "*humane wisedome* must be concealed, whether it be in the matter of the sermon, or in the setting forth of the words," because the preaching is the proclamation of the wisdom of Christ and not of human skill, and because the hearers must ascribe their faith to divine, not human agency. At the same time, he would not allow the same argument to be made in justification of barbarism and Philistinism in the pulpits. The minister "may, yea and must privately use at his libertie the arts, Philosophy and variety of reading, whilest he is framing his sermon: but he ought in publike to conceal all these from the people, and not to make the least ostentation. *Artis etiam est celare artem: it is also a point of art to conceal art.*"[48] Perkins contended that this principle ruled out the use of Greek or Latin phrases, for they disturb the mind of the auditors, "that they cannot fit those

[46] *Ibid.*, p. 163.
[47] *An Exposition of the Prophet Jonah*, II, 331, cited in Blench, *Preaching in England*, p. 182.
[48] Perkins, *Works*, II, 670.

things which went afore with those that follow," strange words prevent the understanding of what is spoken, thus there is great distraction.[49] Perkins also condemned telling stories and all profane and ridiculous speeches. The most appropriate style for a preacher, in Perkins' view, was "a speech both simple and perspicuous, fit both for the people's understanding, and to expresse the Maiestie of the Spirit."[50]

Unquestionably Bartimaeus Andrewes would have agreed with him, for this Andrewes believed that the use of rhetorical devices and citations from the Fathers and classical authors was a departure from the simplicity of the Gospel. With irony he said: ". . . there are some who thinke Christe too base to be preached simply in him selfe, and therfore mingle with him too much the wisdom of mans eloquence and thinke that Christ commeth nakedly, unlesse cloathed with vaine ostentation of wordes. Others esteem him too homely, simple and unlearned, unlesse he bee beautified and blazed over with store of Greeke or Latin sentences in the pulpits; some reckon of him as solitarie, or as a private person without honour and pompe, unlesse he bee brought foorth of them very solemnly, accompanied and countenaunced, with the auncient Garde of the fathers and Doctors of the Churches to speake for him: or els he must be glossed out and painted with the frooth of Philosophie, Poetry, or such like."[51] Yet while one sees the point of this diatribe, one must also recognise that if Lancelot Andrewes had taken the advice of Bartimaeus Andrewes, this great star would have been eclipsed in the homiletical firmament.

There were, however, eminent Puritan preachers who denied that preaching should be devoid of illustrations. They recognised

---

[49] *Ibid.*, pp. 671-72. With this view, however, should be contrasted the words of Henry Smith which he states here (*Sermons*, collected edn. of 1593, pp. 311-12) and repeats (*ibid.*, p. 662): "There is a kinde of Preachers risen up but of late, which shrowde and cover everie rusticall and unsaverie, and childish and absurd sermon, under the name of the simple kind of teaching, like the Popish Priestes, which make ignorance the mother of devotion, but indeede to preach simplie is not to preach rudely, nor unlearnedly, nor confusedly, but to preach plainly, and perspicuously, that the simplest man may understand what is taught as if he did heare his name." An early supporter of the plain Puritan preaching was Edward Dering, who challenged, "Let the sinner come forth, that hath been converted by hearing stories or fables of poets, I am sure there is none: for faith is onely by the worde of God: or let the preacher come forth that useth such things, and doth it not either to please men, or to boast of his learning." *XXVII Lectures or Readings upon part of the Epistle written to the Hebrues* (1576), no. 20.

[50] *A Dilucidation or Exposition of the Apostle St. Paul to the Colossians*, ed. A. B. Grosart, p. 6.

[51] *Certaine verie godlie and profitable Sermons upon the fifth Chapiter of the Songe of Solomon* (1583), p. 26.

that illustrations, and even divagations from the theme of too intense an exposition and application of Biblical doctrine, provided a welcome relief for the congregation and might even drive the lessons home. Such were preachers like Anthony Anderson or Thomas Cartwright, the father of Presbyterian Puritanism in England. Cartwright pointed out that a lie might seem more credible than the truth, when he employed the simile: "as the fruit that groweth now in Sodom hath a more excellent show than other fruit; and yet, come to feel it, it goeth to froth and wind, and that loathsome." Other preachers were more inventive. "In our daies," says Edward Topsell, "men quake in the congregation like steeples in the sea."[52] The same Puritan preacher wished to illustrate the problem of King Claudius in *Hamlet*—namely the dryness of the spiritual life—and said of those with cold affections in worship, that "their voices in prayer are like unborne children, crie they cannot, much lesse speak anything, not so much as to say *Amen*."[53] Topsell could provide a series of metaphors that had a fine cumulative effect, as when he was describing the importance and effect of unity in worship: "Agreement in battle getteth victorie; content in a common weale maketh peace; unitie in musicke maketh harmonie; and the fellowship in praier conquereth the divell; getteth peace of conscience, and soundeth sweetely in the eares of God."[54] It may well have been, as Perry Miller has suggested,[55] that the modification of the bare and austere Puritan style of preaching to include tropes is due to the influence of the Ramist *Rhetorica* of Talon and to the feeling that clarity justified their use, whereas the schemata introduced ostentation and artificiality.

There was also a group of Puritan preachers that used not only tropes but some of the rhetorical schemata. Among them were Richard Greenham, as well as Arthur Dent, Stephen Gosson, and the most popular and skilled Puritan preacher of them all—Henry Smith. Topsell would also be in this category; that is, his style was relatively simple, and he used rhetorical devices moderately.

A lengthy excerpt will show the architectonic that lay behind the directness of Henry Smith, as he illustrated the different kinds of hearing which are given to a sermon:

> As ye come with divers motiōs, so ye heare in divers manners: one is like an *Athenian* and he hearkeneth after newes:

52 *Times Lamentation* (1599), p. 212.
53 *Ibid.*, p. 201.   54 *Ibid.*, p. 303.
55 See *The New England Mind: The Seventeenth Century*, pp. 355-57.

if the Preacher say any thing of our Armies beyond sea, or Counsell at home, or matters of Court, that is his lure: another is like the Pharisie, and he watcheth if anything bee sayd that may bee wrested to be spoken against persons in high place, that he may play the divell in accusing of his brethren, let him write that in his tables too: another smackes of eloquence, and hee gapes for a phrase, that when he commeth to his ordinarie, he may have one figure more to grace and worship his tale: another is male-content, and he never pricketh up his eares till the Preacher come to gird agaynst some whom he spiteth, and when the Sermon is done, he remembreth nothing which was sayd to him, but that which was spoken agaynst other: another commeth to gaze about the Church, he hath an evill eye, which is still looking upon that from which Iob did avert his eye: another commeth to muze, so soone as hee is set, hee falleth into a browne studie, sometimes his minde runnes on his market, sometimes of his iourney, sometimes of his suite, sometimes of his dinner, sometimes of his sport after dinner, and Sermon is done before the man thinke where he is: another commeth to heare, but so soone as the Preacher hath sayd his prayer, he falles fast asleepe, as though he had been brought in for a corps, & the preacher should preach at his funerall.[56]

Only a master of the pulpit would have used so sinister a final simile and so ghoulish a reminder that the sleep of negligence is an image of the sleep of death, and yet done it so slyly. Similarly, we see a complex sentence structure yielding great clarity of meaning when Smith was arguing for simplicity in hearing the Word of God in the sermon: "As the little birds pirk up their heads when their damme comes with meat, and prepare their beaks to take it, striving who shall catch most (now this looks to be served, now that looks for a bit, and every mouth is open until it bee filled): so you are here like birds, and we the damme, the word the food; therefore you must prepare a mouth to take it."[57]

Another requirement that encouraged simplicity was the expectation that the sermon would be delivered without a manuscript. Perkins made this clear in his *Arte of Prophesying* by writing that something must be said about the training of the memory, "because

[56] "The Arte of Hearing, in two sermons," included in *The Sermons of Maister Henrie Smith gathered into one Volume* (1593), Richard Field for Thomas Man), pp. 642-43.

[57] Perkins, *Works*, II, p. 670.

it is the received custom for preachers to speake *by heart* before the people."[58] So excellent were the memories of the Puritan preachers, in fact, that it would not have been difficult for them to have preached extemporaneously, as one of the most famous, "Father Dod," was once required to do. The story goes that he had once preached in Cambridge against the drunkenness of the university students, which greatly enraged them. One day a group of them encountered Dod walking in a wood. They took him captive and held him in a hollow tree, promising to release him only on condition that he preach a sermon on a text they chose. They gave him the word "malt" for a text, and on this he expatiated, beginning: "Beloved, I am a little man, come at a short warning, to deliver a brief discourse, upon a small subject, to a thin congregation and from an unworthy pulpit," and taking each letter as a division of his sermon.[59]

Memorising of sermons gave the Puritan preachers a firm structure, a clear progression, and all the advantages of order, with the advantages of flexibility, so that as they watched the congregation they could explain further if there was incomprehension or add additional illustrations as needed. Also, the artificiality of reading from a manuscript was avoided.

It is interesting to consider the advice Perkins gave to would-be ministers in his influential treatise, particularly on matters of voice and gesture. The voice, he advised, should be moderate when inculcating the doctrine, but in the exhortation "more fervent and vehement."[60] The general rule for gestures was that they should be grave so that the body may grace the messenger of God. "It is fit therefore," Perkins wrote, "that the trunk or stalke of the bodie being erect and quiet, all the other parts, as the arme, the hand, the face and eyes, have such motions as may expresse and (as it were) utter the godly affections of the heart. The lifting up of the eye and the hand signifieth confidence. 2 Chron. 6. 13-14 . . . Acts, 7. 55 . . . the casting downe of the eyes signifieth sorrow and heaviness. Luk. 18.13."[61]

The impression has rightly been given that the Puritan preacher regarded his calling with the utmost seriousness and took great

---

[58] *Ibid.*, II, 672. Beside the words "*by heart*," there appears in the margin the word "memoriter."

[59] *Dictionary of National Biography*, vol. 15, p. 145b. This courageous minister, in a sermon preached in court, told Queen Elizabeth that the negligence of the general run of ministers was partly her fault, for she allowed it to go unchecked because it was of no particular political importance.

[60] Perkins, *Works*, II, 672. [61] *Ibid.*

pains over it. It does not mean, however, that his preaching lacked humour. It almost entirely lacked the witty conceits of the metaphysical preachers like Lancelot Andrewes and John Donne, and it rarely emulated Latimer's raciness, but it did not disdain the whimsical or mocking strains. The former may be illustrated by the immensely popular Henry Smith in "The Affinitie of the Faithfull," where he remarked: "The Divell is afrayde that one Sermon will convert us, and we are not moved with twentie: so the divell thinketh better of us than we are."[62] The mocking mood was well expressed by Topsell:

> Surely I beleeve *Paul* was deceived when he said, *Faith came by hearing and hearing by the word of God.* What an impudent blasphemie were this, to say that Ladies and gentlewomen, on whose faces the sunne is not good inough to looke, whose legges must not walke on the ground, but either keep aloft in their bowers, or take the ayer in their coaches, whose hands must touch nothing but either chaines of pearle, cloathe of gold embrodered, and fine needle wrought garments; that these beautiful stars (I say) should come downe from their nicenes and learn faith at the mouth of preachers? Yet further, must our gallant youthes and proper servingmen, whose heads are hanged with haire as if they would fright away both Christ and his ministers from the place where they stand, come frō the taverns, from gaming houses, from the playhouses, frō the ale-houses, from the whoore-houses, and from all their disports, to be ratled up for their follies by preaching, & forsake the fashions of the world to be new fashioned in their minds, that in stead of infidelities (wherewith the most of that crew are infected) they may have faith engraffed in them by hearing the Gospell, least as they consume their purses, they condemne their soules, neither can robbe for more soules, as they do for more purses?[63]

The Puritans had one rare preacher, however, who was capable of producing conceits of the type that Andrewes and Donne delighted in. He was, of course, Henry Smith. Speaking of prayer, he said that it was "such a strong thing that it overcommeth God, which overcommeth all."[64] He was witty even in his prayers, for one petition went: "Teach us to remember our sinnes, that Thou

---

[62] Smith's *Sermons* (1593 edn.), p. 255.
[63] *Times Lamentation* (1599), p. 26.   [64] *Sermons* (1593), p. 878.

maiest forget them."[65] Referring to Satan, Smith says: "as a compasse hath no end, so he makes no end of compassing."[66] Though the Puritan sermons were very serious, they were not innocent of whimsicality, irony, or wit; these, like lightning flashes, lit up the terrain of preaching all the more dramatically because of their rarity.

How long was the Puritan sermon? Cartwright wished the unduly prolix preacher to be curbed: "Let there be, if it may be every sabbath-day, two sermons, and let them that preach always endeavour to keep themselves within one hour, especially on the week-days."[67] Knappen claims that there are records of two- and three-hour sermons.[68] It is difficult to tell from the written sermons how long the originals were, because they were so often greatly expanded in the writing out. Furthermore, speed of delivery varied. One incident, thought to be remarkable enough to record, would seem to indicate that a two-hour sermon was not a great rarity. Fuller tells that Laurence Chaderton, the first Master of Emmanuel College, Cambridge, who was brought up a Catholic under Vaux, the celebrated author of the *Catechisme*, and became a Puritan at that famous nursery of the "Brethren," Christ's College, was once visiting his native Lancashire. Probably because there was a dearth of Protestant preaching in this loyal Catholic shire, Chaderton's "plain but effectual way of preaching" was greatly appreciated. He was about to conclude "his sermon which was of two hours' continuance at least, with words to this effect, 'that he would no longer trespass upon their patience.' Whereupon all the auditory cried out (wonder not if hungry people craved more meat), 'For God's sake, sir, go on, go on.' Hereat Mr. Chaderton was surprised into a longer discourse, beyond his expectation, in satisfaction of their importunity. . . ."[69] Regular attenders at city congregations, who could count on getting two sermons each Sunday as well as a weekday lecture, would not require the gargantuan meal Chaderton gave while, as it were, on a "mission tour." One firm limitation was the impatience of his patron. Anderson referred to this so bitterly as to suggest that he or a friend had suffered such an indignity: "his service and Homilyes he must cut short, and measure them by the Cookes readynesse, and dynner dressing; the roste

[65] *Ibid.*, pp. 3-4. [66] *Ibid.*, p. 1,066.
[67] D. Neal, *The History of the Puritans*, 5 vols., vol. 5, appendix 4, p. xv.
[68] M. M. Knappen, *Tudor Puritanism*, p. 390.
[69] Thomas Fuller, *The Worthies of England*, ed. J. Freeman, p. 301.

neare ready, the kitchin boye is sent to master Parson to bydde him make haste, the meate is readye, and hys mayster cals for dynner; he commeth at a becke, not daring to denye or make longer staye, least his delaye might cause the cook to burne the meate, and he be called of mayster and men, Syr John burne Goose. . . ."[70]

5. Favourite Topics

The Puritan preacher was never at a loss for a sermon topic. There were plenty in the Bible: history, prophecy, poetry, proverbs, parables, allegories, apocalypses. Puritan themes were as many and varied as those of the Bible itself. That this is hardly an exaggeration can be seen from the fact that Topsell can make an ingenious sermon from a genealogy.[71] But there were favourite themes peculiarly relevant to the Elizabethan situation to which the Puritans addressed themselves.

They were not particularly enamoured of Queen Elizabeth. For Spenser she might be "Gloriana," but to Knox she would only have been one other of the "monstrous regiment of women." The queen, of course, thought the Puritans a troublesome group, and frequently tried to tame them. Nor was another common topic of loyal Anglicans a favourite in Puritan pulpits, a eulogy of the Church of England, because the Puritan ministers wished to reform the Reformation of the Church.

In fact, criticism of the Church of England was frequently heard. It began with the controversies in which the Puritans crossed swords with the bishops—in the Vestiarian and Presbyterian or Admonitions controversies of the 1560s and 70s. It caused a furore in 1565 when Thomas Sampson, Laurence Humphrey, and William Fulke preached against the surplice, and eight years later at Paul's Cross, Richard Crick dared to plead for Cartwright's presbyterian principles. Throughout the reign the Puritan divines are highly critical of ignorant, unpreaching, negligent, and compliant parsons in the Church of England. Among many who employed this theme were Edward Topsell,[72] Edward Dering,[73]

[70] Anthony Anderson, *The Sheild of our Safetie set foorth* (1581), sig. T iv verso-V i recto.

[71] The reference is to the eighteenth and last sermon of his series on the Book of Ruth, in *The Reward of Religion* (1597).

[72] *Times Lamentation* (1599), p. 20.

[73] *A Sermon preached before the Quenes maiestie . . . the 25 day of February, Anno 1569*, sig. E iv verso-F i verso.

Bartimaeus Andrewes,[74] and Eusebius Paget.[75] In the criticisms of Roman Catholicism there was, of course, little to distinguish Anglican from Puritan preaching, so that Anthony Anderson, in contrasting the great uncertainties of a belief in purgatory with the assurance that justification by faith brings, was making a Protestant, rather than an Anglican or Puritan point.[76]

Many of the old secular topics were revived by the Elizabethan Puritans. Knewstub and Smith condemned covetousness in the usury of the day and the enclosing of common lands.[77] Henry Smith excoriated extravagant apparel. Adam and Eve may have covered themselves with leaves, but the women "[now] cover themselves with pride, like Satan which is fallen down before the like lightening: ruffe upon ruffe, lace upon lace, cut upon cut, four and twenty orders, until the woman be not so precious as her apparel."[78] Thomas White[79] criticised fastidious and delicate feeding, while Anthony Anderson ridiculed late rising.[80] Stockwood[81] and White[82] denounced the misuse of Sunday. Proof of the presence of continuity in preaching was the theme and the manner of Henry Smith's "set piece" on mutability and transience, which might have been preached as naturally by St. John Fisher: ". . . our life is but a shorte life: as many little sculs are in Golgotha as great sculs; for one apple that falleth from the tree, ten are pulled before they are ripe; and parents mourn for the death of their children, as often the children for the decease of their parents. This is our *April* and *May* wherein we flourish; our *June* and *July* are next when we shall be cut down. What a change is this, that within fourscore years not one of this assembly shall be

74 *Certaine verie godly and profitable Sermons upon the fifth Chapiter of the Songs of Solomon* (1595), p. 121.

75 *A godly Sermon preached at Detford* (1586), sig. A vi verso.

76 *The Sheild of our Safetie set foorth* (1581), sig. G i verso. One must observe, however, that the great space given in works of spiritual direction to such issues as, how one may be assured of election by God, would imply that in some Protestants at least this supposed certainty of election was a whistling in the dark. For two examples of many, see John Downame, *The Christian Warfare* (1604), book II, chap. 9, "Of the meanes whereby we may be assured of our election," and the first of Richard Rogers' *Seven Treatises* (1603), which demonstrated "who are the true children of God."

77 *The Lectures of John Knewstub on the twentieth chapter of Exodus and certaine other places of Scripture* (1579), p. 145.

78 From "Two Sermons on Usurie," Smith, *Sermons*, pp. 160-62.

79 *A Sermon preached at Pawles Crosse on Sunday the thirde of November, 1577*, p. 64.

80 *The Sheild of our Safetie set foorth*, sig. T iv v.

81 *A Sermon preached at Paules Crosse on Barthelmew Day* (1578), p. 50.

82 White, *Sermon at Pawles Crosse*.

left alive? but another Preacher, and other hearers shall fill these rooms, and tread upon us where our feet tread now."[83]

What then, were the new topics of the Puritan preachers? According to J. W. Blench,[84] the expert on preaching in the sixteenth century, the Puritans found only two new topics, a criticism of romances and stage plays and of the principle of *realpolitik* in the Elizabethan form of Machiavellianism, a very practical form of atheism. Stockwood considered the popular romances to be only pornography; there was an element of professional jealousy of the popularity of the plays when he asked: "Will not a fylthye playe wyth the blast of a Trumpette, sooner call thyther a thousands, than an houres tolling of a Bell, bring to the Sermon a hundred?" It would be two centuries before an English preacher would transform audiences into congregations by dramatic preaching that emptied the theatres. The playwrights would then retaliate by ridiculing the Rev. George Whitefield in their plays as "the Reverend Dr. Squintum."[85]

Interestingly enough, we have to wait for the advent of Puritanism before there was a pulpit celebration of the joys of marriage as companionship; this, from the mouth of Henry Smith, was the homiletical equivalent of Shakespeare's great sonnet: "Let me not to the marriage of true minds admit impediments." The novelty of this approach had to wait, one can only suppose, until divines needed no longer to be celibates. It is instructive to compare the attitudes of St. John Fisher and Henry Smith to marriage as exhibited in their sermons. In Fisher's exposition of the parable of the sower, which was allegorically interpreted, the ground which brings forth spiritual food a hundredfold, and therefore most abundantly, is virginity. The soil that produces sixtyfold is widowhood, where there are some seeds of carnality; but the soil which only produces thirtyfold is marriage, in which the weeds are more successful than the corn.[86] With this must be contrasted Smith's *epithalamium*. A good wife, he insisted, is "such a gift as we should account from God alone, accept it as if he should send us a present from heaven, with this name written on it, *The gift of God*."[87] Recognising procreation of children and the avoidance of fornication as two of the causes of marriage, Smith stressed

---

[83] *Sermons*, p. 274. See also p. 348 for another typically medieval example.
[84] *Preaching in England in the late fifteenth and sixteenth centuries*, p. 305.
[85] See Horton Davies, *Worship and Theology in England*: vol. 3: *From Watts and Wesley to Maurice, 1690-1850*, pp. 176-79.
[86] *English Works of John Fisher*, ed. Mayor, pp. 235-36.
[87] Smith, *Sermons*, p. 8.

the importance of the third cause—"to avoyd the inconvenience of solitarinesse signified in these words, *It is not good for man to be alone,* as though he had said: this life would be miserable and irksome, and unpleasant to man, if the Lord had not given him a wife to companie his troubles."[88] Man, without a wife, is "like a Turtle, which hath lost his mate, like one legge when the other is cutte off, like one wing when the other is clipte, so had the man bene if the woman had not bene ioyned to him: therefore for mutuall societie God coupled two together, that the infinite troubles which lie uppon us in this world, might be eased with the comfort and help one of another, and that the poore in the worlde might have some comfort as well as the rich. . . ."[89] This tender preacher reminded every husband that his wife's "cheekes are made for thy lippes, and not for thy fists."[90] He also had a fascinating part of a sermon in which he advised what "signes of fitness" are to be looked for in choosing a wife or husband.[91]

The most distinctive and the profoundest of the Puritan sermons were those that offered spiritual direction. To a modern reader they would most readily be categorised as religious psychology, but to the Elizabethan world they were psychiatry—quite literally the healing of the soul. It is significant that Ezekiel Culverwell, in his introduction to the collection of Richard Rogers, *Seven Treatises . . . leading and guiding to true happiness both in this life and in the life to come* (1603), suggested that this work should in one respect be called "the Anatomie of the soule, wherein not only the great and principall parts are laid open, but every veine and little nerve are so discovered, that wee may as it were with the eye behold, as the right constitution of the whole and every part of a true Christian." It also deserved, Culverwell said, in another respect to be called "the physicke of the soule," because it supplies most of the "approved remedies for the curing of all spirituall diseases, with like preservatives to maintaine our health, in such sorte as may be enjoyed in this contagious ayre. . . ." This was one common image for the application of the transforming Gospel to the troubled consciences of men.

Another equally common metaphor was taken from military life. It presupposed that the life of the Christian is like that of the knight in Dürer's etching, determinedly going his solitary way through the pitfalls prepared by hideous death and monstrous

88 *Ibid.*, p. 15. 89 *Ibid.*, p. 16.
90 *Ibid.*, p. 44. 91 *Ibid.*, p. 22.

devil, maintained by the courage of faith. The spiritual life was then interpreted on the analogy of continuing combat against the stratagems of Satan; considerable use was made of the sixth chapter of St. Paul's Epistle to the Ephesians, where the armour of salvation is described in detail. One of the most popular Puritan accounts of the spiritual life as an interior civil war was John Downame's *The Christian Warfare*, which first appeared in 1604.[92] Its lengthy subtitle provides an excellent summary of the author's intentions: *wherein is generally shewed the malice, power and politike stratagems of the spirituall enemies of our salvation, Satan and his assistants the world and the flesh; with the meanes also whereby the Christian may withstand and defeate them.*[93] It was a kind of Protestant counterpart to the famous *Spiritual Exercises* of St. Ignatius Loyola, the founder of the Jesuits, and aimed to train the will to the obedience of faith. It could not sustain the comparison, not only because Downame lacked Ignatius' power to grip the imagination, but also because it lacked rules within it for "thinking with the Church." However, the prevalence of such series of sermons, later made into handbooks for devotional direction, suggests that the Puritan ministers were filling a great gap left by the proscription of Catholicism in England. The third most common image for the Christian life, the pilgrimage, was medieval in origin. It would come into its own in Puritan thought in the next century with the sailing of the "Pilgrim Fathers" in 1620, and, supremely, in the creation of the classical Puritan prose epic, Bunyan's *Pilgrim's Progress*. A fourth image, the ship or the Ark of Salvation, was of course a popular medieval concept of the Christian life, but its stress on the corporate character of Christianity as the religion of *the Church*, made it generally unattractive to Puritans, for whom Christianity was the religion of the *elect*.

What is particularly interesting as well as impressive in this genre of Puritan sermons, was the almost scientific nature of the study of the soul, and the great practicality of the advice the Puritan brethren offered the members of their congregations in these

---

[92] By 1634 it had gone into a fourth edition. Another briefer example of the same approach was William Perkins, *The combat between Christ and the Divell displayed* (1606).

[93] The rest of the subtitle reads: "And afterwards more speciallie their particular temptations against the severall causes and meanes of our salvation, whereby on the one side they allure to securitie and presumption, and on the other side, drawing us to doubting and desperation, are expressed and answered. Written especially for their sakes who are exercised in the spirituall conflict of temptations and are afflicted in conscience in the sight and sense of their sinnes."

series of lectures. An elementary introduction to this "science of the soul" may be found in William Perkins' *The Foundation of the Christian Religion gathered into sixe Principles*,[94] which is in the form of a catechism. To the question: "How doth God bring men truely to beleeve in Christ?" the answer is: "First he prepareth their hearts, that they might be capable of faith: and then he worketh faith in them." But, the questioner persists, How does God prepare men's hearts? The answer is: "By bruising them, as if one would break an hard stone to powder: and this done by humbling them." But how does God humble a man? Answer: "By working in him a sight of his sinnes, and a sorrow for them."[95] Then Perkins shows that God proceeds to graft faith onto the heart, and he lists three "seeds" of faith. The first is a profound sense of humility when a man acknowledges the burden of his sins and feels that "he stands in great need of Christ."[96] The second is "an hungring desire and longing to be made partakers of Christ and all his merits," and the third is "a flying to the throne of grace from the sentence of the lawe, pricking the conscience."[97] What then follows? It is then that God, "according to his merciful promise, lets the poor sinner feele the assurance of his love wherewith he loveth him in Christ, which assurance is a lively faith."[98]

The practical question is then asked, as to what benefits a man receives from his faith in Christ. The summary answer, inevitable in a brief catechism, is justification and sanctification; other treatises give a fuller account of the stages in the economy of salvation. But how is a man to know that he is sanctified? What graces of the spirit will his life show? One undoubted sign will be repentance, "which is a setled purpose in the hart, with a carefull indevour to leave all his sinnes, and to live a Christian life according to all God's commandments."[99] A second sign of true repentance is a "continuall fighting and struggling against the assaults of a mans owne flesh, against the motion of the divell, and the enticements of the world."[100] So far so good. But what follows after a man wins victory over temptation or affliction? The answer is: "Experience of God's love in Christ, and so increase of peace of conscience and ioy in the holy Ghost."[101] What follows

---

94 This first appeared in 1590. All references are, however, to the three-volume edition of the *Works* of 1608. The same stages are shown in chap. 4 of the first of *Seven Treatises* of Richard Rogers.

95 Perkins, *Works*, sig. C i v.   96 *Ibid.*, sig. C i r.
97 *Ibid.*, sig. C ii v.   98 *Ibid.*
99 *Ibid.*, sig. C iii v.   100 *Ibid.*
101 *Ibid.*

if he should be defeated in a temptation? The answer is equally explicit: "After a while there will arise a godly sorrow, which is, when a man is grieved for no other cause in the world but this onely, that by his sinne he hath displeased God, who hath bene unto him a most mercifull and loving Father."[102] Every man had to reenact the drama of the fall and the restoration and redemption in his own soul; Perkins and other leading Puritan divines and preachers provided a prompter's copy of the part from the pulpit, or, to change the metaphor, the preacher provided a strategy for winning the interior civil war between the forces of light and darkness in his own soul. This was, however, elementary strategy that Perkins offered in this case.

The more detailed advice would be offered in a series of week-day lectures, offering a fuller anatomy and physic of the soul with Rogers, or more detailed plan of attack against the demonic strategy of the Evil One, in the case of Downame. A few citations from each will make clear the truth of William Haller's claim that "the formulas of Paul and Calvin, it seemed, offered the key to the problem of government not alone in church and state but also in man's inner life"[103] and of his other assertion of election, vocation, justification, sanctification, and glorification, that "here was the perfect formula explaining what happens to every human soul born to be saved."[104]

Rogers told his hearers what benefits they were to expect from hearing the Word preached; this was itself an indication of the high hopes of Puritan preachers evaluating their tasks. Rogers sees six firm benefits coming to attentive listeners: "Therefore, if he may by the preaching of the Word ordinarily *be led into all truth* necessarie for him to know, and be delivered from errour in religion and manners; *if he may be established and confirmed in the knowledge of the will of God*; if he may be reformed in his affections and life daily, more and more encreasing therin, and overcomming himselfe better thereby; if hee may both be brought to bestow some time of his life (as his calling will permit) in reading, and so as that he may profit thereby; and finally if he may *become an example* in time unto others, I may boldly affirme and conclude, that the ordinarie preaching of the word is a singular meanes whereby God hath provided that his people should grow and increase in a godly life."[105]

---

[102] *Ibid.*
[104] *Ibid.*, p. 90.

[103] *The Rise of Puritanism*, p. 35.
[105] *Seven Treatises* (1603), pp. 215-16.

Another example of the practicality and prudence of his spiritual direction can be seen in the fifth treatise, in which Rogers considers the "lets which hinder the sincere course of the Christian life" and which he interprets as diabolical tricks. One is to keep the believer in a wandering and unsettled course;[106] a second, by the leaving of one's first love;[107] a third, the lack of preaching.[108] Another group of Satan's stratagems are concerned with attacking the believer in his unmortified affections: first, the fear that he will not persevere and pride in his gifts;[109] second, of other unruly affections such as touchiness and peevishness;[110] third, worldly lusts.[111] In case the would-be Christian is discouraged by this time, the sixth treatise follows with the listing of the 10 privileges that belong to every true Christian.

A similar kind of book was *The whole treatise of the Cases of Conscience . . .* by William Perkins, which he gave as a series of weekday lectures which were collected and printed after his death. The aim of the book was "to discover the cure of the dangerousest sore that can be, *the wound of the Spirit.*"[112] It covered the entire range of problems that would be raised by sensitive souls in matters of the spiritual or the ethical life, from "How a man being in distress of minde may be comforted"[113] to "Whether there be any difference between the trouble of Conscience and Melancholy?"[114] or, "How are we to use Recreations?"[115] We have here a complete spiritual and ethical directory for living the theocratic life impressive in its combination of Biblical guidance and sheer common sense. Again it should be noted that the Puritans had no interest in speculative theology or mysticism, but only in practical theology and ethics.

As a final example of the distinctive contribution of English Puritanism in the pulpit of this period, John Downame's *Christian Warfare* will be considered, especially as it enumerates the signs by which the elect soul may know that it has, in fact, been chosen and predestined to eternal salvation by God, so that it may con-

---

[106] *Ibid.*, p. 425.   [107] *Ibid.*, p. 432.   [108] *Ibid.*, p. 437.
[109] *Ibid.*, p. 441.   [110] *Ibid.*, p. 447.   [111] *Ibid.*, p. 451.
[112] Perkins, *Works*, from prefatory letter of Thomas Pickering of Emmanuel College, Cambridge.
[113] *Ibid.*, pp. 88f.   [114] *Ibid.*, pp. 194f.
[115] *Ibid.*, pp. 121f. The answer to the third question, in part, is: "Againe, the Bayting of the Beare, and Cockefights are no meete recreations. The baiting of the Bull hath his use and therefore it is commanded by civill authority, and so have not these . . . Games may be devided into three sorts. Games of wit and industry, games of hazzard, and a mixture of both." Athletic sports, chess, and draughts were approved, but games of "hazzard" were not.

fidently walk the razor edge between presumption and despair. Downame offered 10 "signes and infallible notes of our election." The first was "an earnest desire after the meanes of our salvation"; the second, the use of "the spirit of supplication"; the third, a mind on "heavenlie things" after it is weaned from the world; the fourth "the sight of sin and sorrow for it"; and the fifth, "an hungering desire after Christ's righteousnesse."[116] The sixth sign was the vigour of the "inward fight between the flesh and the spirit"; the seventh, a new obedience; the eighth, our "love of the brethren"; the ninth, the love of God's ministers; and the tenth and last, "an earnest desire of Christs comming to iudgement."[117]

With few exceptions Puritan preachers deliberately avoided rhetorical devices and stylistic graces that would have made their sermons more interesting. They were exceedingly sparing of humour; they did not show even in their hunt for similes and metaphor, which were permitted to illustrate their doctrines provided they did not distract the hearers, that imaginative fertility that distinguished Lancelot Andrewes and John Donne, who were the glories of the Jacobean age. Their qualities were Biblical fidelity and a profound conviction that will not be trivial about the majestic claims of God or toy with the plight of men. Their originality consisted in the assiduity and penetration with which they described the psychology of salvation and consoled distressed consciences.

[116] The "signs" will be found, respectively, on pp. 235, 236 *bis*, 237, and 239 of *Christian Warfare*.

[117] The sixth to tenth "signs" will be found, respectively, in *ibid.*, pp. 239, 240, 243, 245, 247.

CHAPTER IX
THE WORSHIP OF
THE SEPARATISTS

THE RADICAL DIFFERENCE between Puritans and Separatists was in their relation to the state church. The Puritans worked, however reluctantly, within the structure of the establishment, improving it and supplementing it whenever possible. The Separatists wished, in the words of Browne, for "Reformation without tarrying for any." Their patience with conformity and compromise was at an end. They claimed the text for their act of shaking the dust off their feet was the command of God, "Come ye out from among them and separate yourselves, saith the Lord."[1] The earliest Separatists may have believed that their self-exclusion from the national church would accelerate the process of reformation in the church which they had left. But as it hardened, Separatism became more rigid and regarded the parent religious community as a "false" church. Except for the difference in the attitude toward the established church, the Separatists were largely in agreement with the Puritans.

This was particularly the case in worship, because both groups took as their criterion the authority of the Scriptures as the Word of God. If the Independent Puritan, Henry Jacob, could say: "For as much as wee are in conscience throughly perswaded, that Gods most holy word in the New Testament is absolutely perfect, for delivering the whole manner of Gods worship . . . ,"[2] his thoughts were anticipated by Richard Fitz, the minister of the "Privye Churche" in London, a Separatist who wrote of his conventicle members, as "the myndes of them that . . . have set their hands and hartes, to the pure unmingled and sincere worshippinge of God, according to his blessed and glorious worde in al things, onely abolishing all tradicions and inventions of men. . . ."[3] Both parties insisted that only such ordinances as were warranted by the Word of God were to be permitted in divine worship. Every tradition, other than that of the primitive apostles, was written off as a "human devyce."

Apart from the intrinsic interest in watching a deeply dedicated

---

[1] II Corinthians 6:17.
[2] Champlin Burrage, *The Early English Dissenters*, 2 vols., II, 162.
[3] *The Trewe Markes of Christes Churches*, in *ibid.*, II, 13.

group of Christians experimenting in freedom, there was a historical significance in Separatist worship out of proportion to its small numbers. The Separatists provided the Puritans with practical illustrations of a worship modelled, as they believed, on the usage of the New Testament. While the Puritans denounced the idolatries and impurities of Anglican worship as then established, the Separatists provided the living remedy. There was, it is true, little community of sympathy between the Puritans and Separatists. Puritans considered Separatists schismatics, and Separatists thought Puritans timeservers. It was unlikely that there was much direct influence on the Puritans by the Separatists, so much were they at loggerheads. Yet there was some contact; this can be seen in persons who crossed the frontier between Puritans and Separatists. In the case of Francis Johnson, the conclusion might well be that Separatism was the left wing of Puritanism; for the successor of Travers and Cartwright as Puritan Minister to the Church of the Merchant Adventurers in Holland became an outstanding Barrowist minister. On the other hand, Puritanism seemed to the right wing of Separatism in the case of John Robinson, who began as a Brownist; and under the influence of Henry Jacob and William Ames became an Independent Puritan. Puritanism and Separatism aimed at the same end—a Church of England fully reformed in worship, discipline, and church government, as well as in doctrine. They differed only in their estimate of the capacities of the national church for improvement.

It will be assumed, with only a minimum of argument, that the term "Separatists" cannot legitimately be applied to the Independents, but that it is more properly reserved for the Barrowists, the Brownists, and the Anabaptists.[4] It is also assumed, since all parties, including the moderate Separatists, agreed in denouncing the obscure and eccentric sects such as the Family of Love, that their influence on Puritan or Separatist worship was negligible. The first assumption, that the Independents were not Separatists, can be shown to be reasonable by a brief examination of the writings of two of their earliest leaders, Henry Jacob and John Robinson. Jacob was the pastor of the first English congregation of Independents, founded in 1616. Among his papers was discovered a copy of "A third humble Supplication" of the Puritans addressed to the king in 1605 and corrected in Jacob's handwrit-

[4] Nor is this statement intended to imply that the Independents had no antecedents among the Barrowists or that there was no connection between early Anabaptists and the later Baptists.

ing. He was representing the views of the Puritans who at that time had asked for toleration and permission "to Assemble togeather somwhere publikly to the Service & Worship of God, to use and enioye peacably among our selves alone the wholl exercyse of Gods worship and of Church Government . . . without any tradicion of men whatsoever, according only to the specification of Gods written word and no otherwise, which hitherto as yet in this our present State we could never enjoye."[5] Jacob and his fellow Puritans appended a guarantee that if this was allowed them, they would "before a Iustice of peace first take the oath of your Maiesties supremacy and royall authority as the Lawes of the Land at this present do set forth the same," and promised to keep communion with other churches, to pay all ecclesiastical dues, and to submit themselves, in any case of trespass, to the civil magistrate. Jacob was no Separatist; Robinson began as a Separatist and later became a Puritan.[6] Independents are, therefore, considered as Puritans, not Separatists.

1. The Barrowists

The worship of the Barrowist Separatists claims attention, first because it was established in England before that of the Brownists, with which it has affinities. The Barrowists flourished from 1587 to 1593. Their leaders, Barrow himself, Greenwood, and Penry, all died as martyrs to the cause of Separatism.

What were the reasons for their separation from the Church of England? Henry Barrow addressed himself to the question, providing four reasons related to worship, the character of church membership, the quality of the ministers, and type of church government. Anglicans worshipped God falsely, "their worship being

---

[5] Burrage, *English Dissenters*, I, 286.

[6] Robinson had penned *A Iustification of Separation from the Church of England* in 1610, but the following passage by the same hand shows his attitude after his conversion to charity by Jacob and his kindlier view of Puritanism: "To conclude, For my selve, thus I beleeve with my heart before God, and professe with my tongue, and have before the world, that I have one and the same faith, hope, spirit, baptism, and Lord which I had in the Church of England and none other: that I esteem so many in that Church, of what state or order, soever, as are truly partakers of that faith (as I account many thousand to be) for my Christian brethren: and my selfe a fellow-member with them of one misticall body of Christ. . . ." (*A Treatise of the Lawfulness of Hearing of Ministers* [1634], pp. 63f.) This is very like the spirit of the Puritans who sailed to Boston in 1629 and 1630 and of whom Cotton Mather wrote in the preface to his *Magnalia Christi Americana* (1702), to the effect that England's daughter New England was "by some of her *Angry* Brethren . . . forced to make a *Local Secession*, yet not a *Separation*, but hath always retained a Dutiful Respect unto the *Church of God in England*" (p. viii).

made of the invention of man, even of that man of sinne, erronious [sic], and imposed upon them."[7] Then, the "prophane multitude" receive all the privileges of membership of the Church of England without professing purity of doctrine or of life. Third, the ministry was "false" and "antichristian" and was imposed on the people as well as maintained by them. Fourth, "that their churches are ruled by and remaine in sujection unto an antichristian and ungodly government, cleane contrary to the institution of our Saviour Christ." These criticisms were curtly phrased, but not very illuminating because of the imprecise nature of their charges.

It is interesting that Barrow, when examined by Bishop Aylmer and Lord Burghley on March 18th, 1588/9, was specifically asked what he found idolatrous about the worship of the Church of England; Barrow replied that it was entirely idolatrous. Then he mentioned that the commemoration of the saints violated the first commandment, that the observations of fasts was idolatrous, and that the same was true of naming days after saints. Asked for his criticism of the Book of Common Prayer, he replied that prayers should not "be stereotyped and stinted, nor should they be tied to place manner, time, nor form."[8]

Barrow's criticism of set prayers or stinted forms was particularly severe. He had a superb definition of prayer, against which to test all read prayers. "Praier," he wrote, "I take to be a confident demanding which faith maketh thorow the Holy Ghost, according to the wil of God, for their present wantes, estate, *etc.*"[9] He viewed read prayers as leading to the utter extinction of the Spirit of God and a denial of the sincere spontaneity that should characterise prayer: "How now? Can any read, prescript, stinted leitourgie, which was penned many yeares or daies before, be said a powring forth of the heart unto the Lord? . . . Is not this (if they wil have their written stuffe to to be held and used as praier) to bind the Holy Ghost to the froth and leaven of their lips as if it were to the holy word of God? Is it not utterly to quench and extinguish the Spirit of God, both in the ministerie and the people, while they tye both them and God to their stinted numbred praiers?"[10] Barrow further felt that the content of the Book of Common Prayer was borrowed too much from Roman Catholicism and that it tended to

[7] *The Writings of Henry Barrow, 1587-1590*, ed. Leland H. Carlson, p. 8.
[8] *Ibid.*, p. 16.
[9] *A Briefe Discoverie of the False Church* (1590/1, Dordrecht), pp. 64-65 and reprinted in Carlson, *Writings of Barrow*, p. 365.
[10] *Ibid.*, p. 65.

encourage a ministry that would not preach or pray in words of their own: "Is this the unitie and uniformitie that ought to be in al churches? And is amongst al Christe's servantes, to make them agree in a stinking patcherie devised apocrypha leiturgie, good for nothing but for cushsions and pillowes for the idle priestes, and profane carnal atheistes to rock them a sleepe and keep them in securitie, wherby the conscience is no way either touched, edified or bettered?"[11] What is perhaps most astonishing to learn is that the Barrowists rejected the repetition of the Lord's Prayer. Many Puritans repeated it as the Dominical warrant and model, but the Separatists regarded it as part of the Sermon on the Mount and as an illustration of the kind of prayer they should aim at, but not apishly imitate.[12]

The fullest statement of the radical position on the Lord's Prayer is expressed by John Penry, also a Barrowist martyr:

> We answer first that the scrypture yt selfe sheweth his meaning herein to be, not that the disciples or others should be tyed to use these very wordes, but that in prayer and geving of thankes they should followe his direction and patterne which he had geven them, that they might know to whom, with what affeccion and to what end to pray as yt is expresslie sett downe in these wordes. After this manner therfore pray ye, and not as men will now have us: Say over these very wordes. Secondly we doubt not but that we may use anie of these wordes as others applying them to our severall necessyties as we see Christ himselfe did when he prayed. O my father yf this cupp cannot pass from me but that I must drinke yt, thy will be done where yt is plaine that Christ himselfe who gave the rule doth shew us how to use yt, to weet . . . in praying according as our specyall necessyties shalbe, whether we use any of these wordes or other, or pray with sighes & groanes that cannot be expressed.[13]

11 *Ibid.*, pp. 65-66.

12 See Leland Carlson's comprehensive summary of Barrow's objections to the Book of Common Prayer, in *The Writings of Henry Barrow, 1590-1591*, p. 6. Barrow, says Carlson, asserts that Anglican worship is too Roman, uses lections from the Apocrypha and others from the Bible that are arbitrarily selected, prayers are prescribed and are mechanical and second-hand, and are delivered in a superstitious and unscriptural manner. See also *ibid.*, pp. 100-101. It should also be noted that the Separatist Greenwood gave nine reasons against the use of set prayers in church, though he was willing for them to serve as the basis of meditation. See Leland H. Carlson, ed., *The Writings of John Greenwood, 1587-1590*, pp. 17-19.

13 The evidence for the Barrowist refusal to repeat the Lord's Prayer can be

Turning from theory to practice, there is a comprehensive and vivid account of the Barrowist gatherings for worship: "In the somer tyme they mett together in the feilds a mile or more about London, there they sitt downe uppon A Banke & divers of them expound out of the bible as long as they are there assembled."[14] It appears that they would arrange in advance where their next Sunday's meeting was to be held and there they would assemble at the selected rendezvous as early as five o'clock in the morning. There they might well remain for the entire day, kept there partly by the prolixity of their Biblical "exercises" and partly for fear of detection if they should stir while it was still daylight. There ". . . they contynewe in there kinde of praier and exposicion of Scriptures all that daie. They dyne together, After dinner make collection to paie for there diet & what mony is left some one of them carrieth it to the prisons where any of there sect be committed."[15] The kind of prayer they used was extemporaneous: simple, impassioned, sincere, and moving. It was the distinctive contribution of the Separatists to worship. The Independents and Baptists were to follow the example of the Separatists, and in time the Independents would persuade the English Presbyterians of the Westminster Assembly to adopt the expedient of a manual of worship, suggesting the order and the topics of the prayers but not the words themselves. It was, therefore, an influential precedent that the Separatists set in their insistence on "free prayer," for it had great strengths, as in simplicity, intimacy appropriate to those who cry "Abba, Father" in their approach to the august yet loving Creator, and directness, and great weaknesses, as when it was prolix, disordered, and a chain reaction of endless cliches.

At the beginning the Barrowists apparently used neither psalms nor hymns, unlike the Puritans, who were fond of psalm-singing at church and at home. The documents do not mention singing at all. Henoch Clapham, however, states that the Barrowists were first persuaded to sing in their assemblies by a man who urged its necessity, namely Francis Johnson, Barrowist pastor of the congregation in Kampen and Naarden: "*Franc-Iohnson* (being advised

---

found in Carlson, *Writings of John Greenwood*, pp. 261-62, where Greenwood tells Bishop Cooper that to repeat the Lord's Prayer is "popish doctrine, and such praier were superstitious babling." See also Burrage, *English Dissenters*, II, 56. It should be noted that the final phrase of the citation in Burrage, II, 74f., echoes Romans 8:17, which was the *locus classicus* of the authority for a pneumatic-charismatic type of prayer.

[14] Burrage, *English Dissenters*, I, 26.
[15] *Ibid.*

by one that talked with him thereabouts in the *Clinke* at London) did presse the use of our singing Psalmes (neglected before of his people for Apocrypha;) whereupon his Congregation publikely in their meetings used them, till they could have them translated into verse, by some of their Teachers. . . ."[16]

The Barrowists administered the sacraments of Baptism and the Lord's Supper. But, in the case of children, they held it to be unlawful to baptise children in the churches of the establishment, preferring to let them go unbaptised until a satisfactory Baptism could be administered by a true preacher of the Gospel; in this they resembled the Donatists of fourth-century Africa. The method of administering Baptism among them was described in the deposition of one Daniel Bucke. He reported that Johnson baptised seven children in 1592, as follows: "they [the congregation] had neither god fathers nor godmothers, and he tooke water and washed the faces of them that were baptised: the Children that were there baptised were the Children of Mr. Studley Mr. Lee with others beings of severall yeres of age, sayinge onely in the administracion of this sacrament I doe Baptise thee in the name of the father of the sonne and of the holy gost withoute usinge any other cerimony therein and is now usually observed accordinge to the booke of Common praier. . . ."[17] The same witness described the Barrowist administration of the Lord's Supper: "Beinge further demaunded the manner of the lordes supper administred amongst them he said that fyve whight loves [*loaves*] or more were sett uppon the table and that the Pastor did breake the bread and then delivered to the rest some of the congregacion sittinge and some standinge aboute the table, and that the Pastor delivered the Cupp unto one and he to an other, and soe from one to an other till they had all dronken usinge the words at the deliverye thereof accordinge as it is sett downe in the eleventh of the Corinthes the xxiiijth verse."[18] It is to be noted that the Lord's Supper as celebrated by the Barrowists was characterised by simplicity and fidelity to the New Testament narrative. In particular, the prophetic symbolism of Christ in breaking the bread and pouring out the wine, as representations of His body about to be broken and His blood about to be shed, was repeated with great solemnity. This fidelity to the words and

[16] *A Chronological Discourse* (1609), p. 36.

[17] British Museum, Harleian MS 6849, folio 216 v., reproduced in Burrage, *English Dissenters*, I, 142f.

[18] British Museum, folio 217 v., reproduced in Burrage, *English Dissenters*, I, 143.

331

actions of Christ in the institution of the sacrament was later to be a feature of both Presbyterian and Independent celebrations of Communion.

Another important ordinance of the Barrowists was the use of ecclesiastical "discipline" for the maintenance of the relative purity of the Church. It could in severe cases of dishonouring the name and fame of Christ lead to excommunication, or, to use the more sinister and also Biblical name, the "handing over to Satan." Where due regret had been expressed, and retribution made where necessary, the sinner was welcomed back into the fold publicly in the rite of "Restoration." The Barrowist excommunication against two offenders, Robert Stokes and George Collier, is described by Robert Aburne: "He saieth that they did use to excommunicate amongst them, and that one Robert Stokes, and one George Collier, and one or twoe more whose names he Remembreth not, wear excommunicated, and that the said Iohnson thelder did denounce thexcommunication against them, and concernynge the manner of proceadinges to excommunication he saieth, that they the said Stokes and the Rest beynge privatelye admonished their pretended errors, and not conforming themselves, and by Witnes produced to their congregacion, then the said Iohnson, with the Consent of the whole Congregacion, did denounce the excommunication, and that sithence they weare excommunicated which was a halfe yere and somewhat more sithence, they wear not admitted to their Churche."[19]

The Separatists provided the Puritans with an example of rigid discipline. Both parties insisted on the retention of the purity of the Church in doctrine and in life. Both Puritans and Separatists pleaded for a threefold reformation—Gospel-doctrine, Gospel-government, and Gospel-discipline. The doctrine of the "gathered church" and of the "visible saints," which played so large a part in Puritan theory and practice, was presupposed by the Barrowist discipline.

Since the Barrowists held that marriage was essentially a civil ceremony, there was no need for minister or church. Christopher Bowman, a deacon of the church of which Francis Johnson was the minister, declared: ". . . Mariage in a howse without a Mynister by Consent of the parties and frends is sufficient."[20] The Angli-

---

[19] British Museum, Harleian MS 6848, folio 41 v., cited by Burrage, *English Dissenters*, I, 143.

[20] British Museum, Harleian MS 6848, folio v., cited by Burrage, *English Dissenters*, I, 144.

can marriage ceremony was scrupled by the Separatists, not only because it required the use of the ring, a ceremony for which there was no warrant in the Word of God, but also because the New Testament was able to supply no example of a marriage service being performed by Christ or the apostles.

Burials were also considered to be civil rather than religious. In *A Briefe Discoverie of the False Church*, Barrow gave the subject more than cursory treatment. He found no authority "in the booke of God, that it belonged to the ministers office to burie the dead. It was a pollution to the Leviticall priesthood to touch a carcase or anything about it."[21] Barrow objected to the trappings of mourning gowns and the exorbitant costs of funerals for the families of poor men. He particularly excoriated encomia (laudatory sermons) for the dead because of their usual insincerity: "To conclude, after al their praiers, preachment, where (I trow) the priest bestoweth some figures in his commendations (though he be with the glutton in the gulfe of hell) to make him by his rhetorick a better Christian in his grave than he was ever in his life, or else he yerneth his money ill. After al is done in church, then are they all gathered together to a costly and sumptuous banquet. Is not this jolly Christian mourning?"[22]

Hitherto Barrow had criticised the insincerity of formal burial services. He must have been thinking of the common Puritan criticism of the Office in the Book of Common Prayer which assures the mourners that everyone is buried "in sure and certain hope of the Resurrection to eternal life" regardless of their faith or ethics. He went on to show the medieval fascination and fear of death and the Elizabethan's sense of being mocked by mutability, which finds the making of exquisite monuments a gilding of the skull. In the ensuing passage Barrow is pointing to a fact, namely that the Elizabethans developed a monumental art in their tombs which enabled the newly rich as the newly dead to dominate the parish church.[23] "Neither will I trouble them to shew warrant by the Word, for the exquisite sculpture and garnishing of their toombes, with engraving their armes and atcheavements, moulding their

---

[21] Barrow, *Briefe Discoverie*, p. 126; cited in L. H. Carlson's edition of *The Writings of Henry Barrow, 1587-1590*, p. 459.

[22] Barrow, *Briefe Discoverie*, p. 127.

[23] A notable example of early seventeenth-century tombs in the parish church is that of the Fettiplace family at Swinbrook, near Burford in Oxfordshire. The phenomenal increase in Elizabethan funerary carving as status symbols for newly rich families will be considered more fully later in Chap. X.

images and pictures, and to set these up as monuments in their church: which church must also (upon the day of such burials) be solemnly arrayed and hanged with blacks, that even the verie stones may mourne also for companie. Is not this christian mourning, thinke you?"[24] The one recorded funeral of a Separatist known to me is that of Eaton. The account of it asserts that his many followers marched in procession behind the body to the graveside and without prayers or commendations or a sermon thrust it into the grave and stamped earth on it. This seemed more like good riddance than a good burial, but it was entirely in keeping with the Separatist conviction that it was a civil matter.

Separatists appear to have had no formal ordination to their church offices. Clapham informs us that Johnson and Greenwood were chosen as pastor and teacher, respectively, "Without any *Imposition of hands*." If they had already received the charismatic endowment of the Holy Spirit, there was apparently no need for the formal recognition of this on the part of a closely knit congregation. It seems, however, that Francis Johnson, when he came to Amsterdam a few years later, had a ceremony of the imposition of hands, and that this was performed by lay members of his congregation.[25] The same reporter gives us an amusing account of the way in which the offertory was taken at the Barrowist meetings:

And hereupon it was, that the *Separatists* did at first in their Conventicles, appoynt their Deacons to stand at the Chamber dore, at the people's outgate, with their Hats in hand (much like after the fashion of a Playhouse) into the which they put their voluntary. But comming beyonde seas, where a man might have seaven Doyts for a penny, it fell out, howsoever their voluntary (at the casting in) did make a great clangour, the *Summa totalis* overseene, the maisters of Play came to have but a few pence to their share. Whereupon, a broad Dish (reasonable flat) was placed in the middest of their convention, but when the voluntarie was cast in, others might observe the quantitie. But this way served not the turne, for a few doyts rushing in upon the soddaine, could not easily be observed, of what quantity it might be. Upon this, the Pastor gave out, that if (besides giftes from others abroad) they

[24] Barrow, *Briefe Discoverie*, p. 127.
[25] Henoch Clapham, *A Chronological Discourse* (1609), p. 31.

would not make him *Tenne pounds* yearely at least, he would leave them, as unworthy the Gospel.[26]

Barrowist sermons were all of an expository character; they must have been delivered in a homely, possibly rough-hewn manner. Clapham styled these preachers "Syncerians" and complained that they had spoiled preaching by "holding every howers talke, A Sermon: Insomuch as a number would not goe to meate (if a few were present of their faction) but there must be a kind of Sermon."[27] Barrow himself, again according to Clapham, disliked too casual and unpolished preaching, "saying of that, and of some Pinsellers and Pedlers that then were put to preach in their Thursedayes Prophecie, that it would bring the Scriptures into mightie contempt."[28] It is to be observed that the Separatists joined hands with the Puritans in regarding "Prophesying" as a valuable means of inculcating scriptural doctrine, and also as a way of training preachers.

Yet another parallel between Barrowists and Puritans was their invariable custom of founding a church on a covenant subscribed by officers and members. For instance, Abraham Pulberry in 1592 admitted upon examination that "hee hath made a promise to the Lord in the presence of his Congregacion when hee entred thereunto that hee would walke with them as they would walke with the Lorde."[29] In similar words, another declared, "as longe as they did walke in the lawes of God hee would forsake all other assemblies and onely followe them."[30]

As we look back on the worship of the Barrowists we can see that it was marked by a determined fidelity to worship God only as He had commanded in His holy Word, by a search for simplicity as well as sincerity, and by an intimacy characteristic of a small community. Above all, one recognises in these Separatists gatherings the intensity and dedication of a faith that would not only remove mountains but endure prisons and martyrdom. As ceremony was a vain show, so was the repetition of formal prayers like the collects of the Book of Common Prayer; mere "mumbling," and creeds that might be recited parrot fashion off the top of the mind were replaced with covenants which come from the warmth of the heart and were bound with the steel of a will converted and conformed to God. It was a narrow worship, but it ran deep. It

26 *Ibid.*, p. vi.
28 *Ibid.*
30 *Ibid.*, p. 45; see also p. 60.

27 *Ibid.*, p. vii.
29 Barrow, *Briefe Discoverie*, II, 34.

was critical of the Church of England, and risked Pharisaic contempt. But it was a way of life that was deeply compassionate to its own at the risk of martyrdom.

2. *The Brownists*

Browne's company achieved a complete separation from the Church of England in 1581 in Norwich. Though emerging a few years earlier than the Barrowists, their future was sought in Holland because Browne and his followers moved there in 1581 or 1582 to avoid persecution. The Barrowists made Separatism more widely known in practise than the Brownists, though Browne's writings gained a wide notoriety in England.[31] In fact, their ecclesiology and worship were very much like that of the Barrowists, and both were probably the parents of Independency.

The following description of the meetings of the Brownists for worship is given in *The Brownists Synagogue*:

> In that house where they intend to meet, there is one appointed to keepe the doore, for the intent, to give notice if there should be any insurrection, warning may be given them. They doe not flocke all together, but come 2 or 3 in a company, any man may be admitted thither, and all being gathered together, the man appointed to teach, stands in the midst of the Roome, and his audience gather about him. He prayeth about the space of halfe an houre, and part of his prayer is, that those which come thither to scoffe and laugh, God would be pleased to turne their hearts, by which meanes they thinke to escape undiscovered. His Sermon is about the space of an houre, and then doth another stand up to make the text more plaine, and at the latter end, he intreates them all to goe home severally, least the next meeting they be interrupted by those which are of the opinion of the wicked, they seeme very stedfast in their opinions, and say rather then they will turne, they will burne.[32]

Browne himself was the authority for an account of the service in Middleburg: "Likewise an order was agreed on ffor their meetinges together, ffor their exercises therein, as for praier, thanckes giving, reading of the scriptures, for exhortation and edifiing, ether by all men which had the guift, or by those which had a speciall

---

[31] Robert Browne's *A Booke which sheweth the life and manners of all true Christians*, published in 1582 in Middleburgh, was one of the more famous.
[32] (1641), pp. 5f.

charge before others. And for the lawefulness of putting forth questions, to learne the trueth, as iff anie thing seemed doubtful &
hard, to require some to shewe it more plainly, or for anie to shewe
it him selfe & to cause the rest to understand it."[33] This report
reveals that "prophesying" occupied a central part in the Brownist
gatherings, with opportunity to question the preacher. The distinction between "praier" and "thanckes giving" may mean no more
than that prayers of petition and thanksgiving were offered. It
might also mean that Browne was referring to special days of
thanksgiving on which some signal mercy of Divine providence
might be commemorated. Such days were not infrequently held,
as were days of humiliation, during the Commonwealth and Protectorate. Since the Brownists had a set of officers named "receev-
ers," it may be assumed that they took up collections from their
church members.[34] Discipline was enforced along Puritan lines.
This may be inferred from Browne's reference to "separating
cleane from uncleane."[35] An autobiographical reference leads one
to assume that Browne regarded marriage as a civil custom requiring no ecclesiastical solemnisation.[36]

For other ordinances practised by the Brownists we have no
direct evidence. Since Browne and his friends, previously Puritans,
aimed at setting up congregations as near as possible to the New
Testament model, it is most probable that the sacrament of Baptism and the Lord's Supper were administered by them. There is,
further, no reason to suppose that there was any liturgical difference between the Brownists and the Barrowists; the latter certainly
celebrated both sacraments. Browne's innovations were in the
sphere of church government and not, it would seem, in church
worship. Like the Barrowists, the Brownists founded a church on
a covenant. As Browne's writings appeared five years before the
rise of the Barrowists, it is likely that they were indebted to him,
as the Puritans were to both sets of Separatists.

3. The Anabaptists

As the relationship of the Brownists to the Independents is
obscure, so is that of the Anabaptists to the Baptists. The Anabaptists seem to have had no organised existence in England before
1612. In the latter years of the short reign of Edward VI several

33 *A True and Short Declaration* (1582), pp. 19f.
34 *Ibid.*, p. 20.
35 *A Booke which sheweth the life and manners of all true Christians* (1582),
sig. K 2v.
36 *Ibid.*

publications appeared, criticising the "pestilent" opinions of the continental Anabaptists. In 1560 there was issued "A Proclamation for the banishment of Anabaptistes that refused to be reconciled, 22 Septembris."[37] Throughout the country Anabaptists were encountered, not in organised societies, but as families or as individuals. After 1589 on there was a 20-year silence about them. It was broken only when William Sayer was imprisoned as an Anabaptist in the Norfolk county gaol in 1612. Hence Elizabethan Separatism was almost exclusively the contribution of the Barrowists and the Brownists. But the origin of English Anabaptism is to be found in Holland, that great asylum for religious refugees. Francis Johnson, the Barrowist minister, stated that there were "divers" Anabaptists in his congregation who were eventually excommunicated. The first Baptist congregation to be settled in England was that over which Thomas Helwys, who anticipated Roger Williams in his plea for religious toleration, presided, along with Thomas Murton. This group withdrew from John Smyth's congregation in Amsterdam and returned to England about 1612.

The characteristic difference between the Anabaptists and the other Separatists concerned the subjects and the mode of administering Baptism. Helwys made believer's Baptism, by sprinkling or pouring, a necessity for salvation. So dogmatic was he on this point that he insisted that the contrary practice of infant Baptism was sufficient to warrant the penalty of eternal damnation being inflicted on those who held it: ". . . if you had no other sin amongst you al, but this, you perish everie man off you from the highest to the lowest, iff you repent not."[38]

There is a comprehensive description of public worship in the Amsterdam congregation:

> The order of the worshippe and government of our church is 1. we begynne with a prayer, after reade some one or tow chapters of the bible gyve the sence thereof, and confer upon the same, that done we lay aside our bookes, and after a solemne prayer made by the 1. speaker, he propoundeth some text out of the Scripture, and prophecieth owt of the same, by the space of one hower, or thre Quarters of an hower. After him standeth up a 2. speaker and prophecieth owt of the said text the like time and space, some tyme more some tyme lesse. After him the 3. the 4. the 5. &c as the tyme will

[37] Burrage, *Briefe Discoverie*, I, 62.
[38] *Ibid.*, p. 253.

geve leave, Then the 1. speaker concludeth with prayer as he began wth prayer, wth an exhortation to contribution to the poore, wch collection being made is also concluded wth prayer. This morning exercise begynes at eight of the clock and continueth unto twelve of the clocke the like course of exercise is observed in the aftnwne from 2. of the clocke unto 5. or 6. of the Clocke. last of all the execution of the government of the church is handled.[39]

This description of Anabaptist worship in Amsterdam, where the Mennonites were prominent, demonstrates how opposed they were to the use of set forms in worship. They were logical enough in their attempt to gain a spirit-led worship to put away the Bible in their service, as a form of words. The second unusual feature of this worship was the special offertory prayer.

The minister of the Amsterdam Anabaptist congregation was John Smyth, who began as a Puritan within the Church of England. His famous treatise on the Lord's Prayer, *A Patterne of true Prayer*, is one of the fairest considerations of the claims of liturgical prayer ever made. His conclusion in 1605 about the legitimacy of repeating the Lord's Prayer was that ". . . Christ leaveth it arbitrie unto us, as a thing indifferent when we pray to say this prayer, or not to say it, so be that we say it in faith and feeling; or if wee say it not, yet to pray according unto it."[40] Three years later he decided to forego all set forms, as the initiator and defender of the most extreme form of pneumatic worship. In *The Differences of the Churches of the Separation* (1608) he declared: "Wee hould that the worship of the new testament properly so called is spirituall proceeding originally from the hart: & that reading out of a booke (though a lawfull ecclesiastical action) is no part of spirituall worship, but rather the invention of the man of synne it being substituted for a part of spirituall worship; therefore in time of prophesjng it is unlawfull to have the booke as a helpe before the eye wee hould that seeing singinging [*sic*] a psalme is a parte of spirituall worship therefore it is unlawfull to have the booke before the eye in time of singinge a psalme."[41]

The rejection of forms in worship was so complete that it almost approached Quakerism 40 or 50 years before it originated. This

---

[39] British Museum, Harleian MS 360, folio 71; Letter of the Bromheeds to Sir William Hammerton.
[40] *The Works of John Smyth*, ed. W. T. Whitley, I, 81.
[41] *Ibid.*, p. v.

"spiritual worship" while it does not altogether do away with books, regards the part of worship in which they are used as the mere preparation for the pure worship which proceeds without them. This interpretation of radical spiritual worship is confirmed by the words of Helwys, when contrasting the worship of his community with that of the Johnsonians, also in the city of Amsterdam. Helwys explained: "They as partes or meanes of worship read Chapters, Textes to preache on & Psalmes out of the translacion, we alreddy as in prayinge, so in prophesiinge & singinge Psalmes lay aside the translacion, & we suppose yt will prove the truth, that All bookes even the originalles themselves must be layed aside in the tyme of spirituall worshipp, yet still retayninge the readinge & interpretinge of the Scriptures in the Churche for the preparinge to worshipp, Iudginge of doctrine, decidinge of Controversies as the grounde of or faithe & of or whole profession."[42]

Singing in unison was not a feature of early Anabaptist or Baptist praise. The precedent of solo singing was so rigidly followed by succeeding Baptist congregations that as late as 1690 that great innovator, Benjamin Keach, had difficulty in persuading his own congregation to sing in unison.

The sermons, it can be surmised from the importance of "prophesying" in worship, were long expositions of Scripture, rarely lasting less than an hour.

Little is known about the administration of the two "Gospel Sacraments," as they were called in this period in these circles. Baptism was, as we have seen, dispensed only to believers, to those "which heere, beleeve and with penitent hartes receave ye doctrine of ye holy gospell: for such hath ye Lord Iesus commaunded to be baptized, and no un-speaking children."[43] Helwys did not insist on sprinkling or dipping as the mode of Baptism; immersion was insisted on by the London Baptists of 1633. This church, under the leadership of Jessey and Blunt, used immersion as the only legitimate mode of administering the scrament, "being convinced of Baptism, yt also it ought to be by diping ye Body into ye Water, resembling Burial & riseing again."[44]

There are no accounts of early Baptist celebrations of the Lord's Supper. Yet since their sacramental doctrine was so clearly Zwinglian or Calvinist, it is probable that their service resembled that of the other Separatists in its simplicity, its fidelity to the

[42] Letter of Sept. 20, 1608, cited by Burrage, *Briefe Discoverie*, II, 166.
[43] *Ibid.*, p. 196.   [44] Cf. *ibid.*, p. 303.

account of the Dominical institution in the First Epistle of Paul to the Corinthians, Chapter XI, verses 23ff. Most likely it repeated not only Christ's words of delivery but also his manual actions of fraction and libation.[45] The ordinance of the Lord's Supper was almost certainly kept every Lord's day. In this respect the Barrowists in Amsterdam were in agreement with the English Anabaptist congregation there. Johnson asked, "Whether it be not best to celebrate the Lords supper where it can be every Lords day; this the Apostles used to do; by so doing we shall return to the intire practise of the Churches in former ages."[46] The Anabaptist Confession of faith insisted that they dare not omit it on the Lord's day: "Oblata iusta occasione impedimenti, affirmamus coenam dominicam omitti posse donec tollantur impedimenta: aut aliter non audemus omittere quoque die sabbati quum convenimus and praestandum caetera Dei publici Ministerii. . . ."[47] The same Confession forbade laymen to celebrate the sacraments, because the privilege was in inseparably linked to the office of the minister of the Word of God.[48] In this matter they concurred with the other Separatists. John Robinson, for instance, was unwilling to allow his godly ruling elder, Brewster, to celebrate the Lord's Supper aboard the *Mayflower*, though no clergyman would accompany them on the perilous voyage to Plimouth Plantation.

Marriage was sanctioned by the Anabaptists only if both contracting parties belonged to their own communion, a most restrictive device in the early days of a new movement. If this rule was broken it was often accompanied by ecclesiastical censure, sometimes leading to excommunication. The *Short Confession of Faith* declared: "Wee permitt none of our communion to marry godles, unbeleeving, fleshly persons out of ye church, but wee censure such (as other synnes) according to the disposition & desert of ye cause."[49] The practice was enforced in Baptist and Independent congregations until the end of the seventeenth century.[50]

It is probable that the Anabaptists held love-feasts. This was certainly a feature of the church life of the early Separatists. In 1568, we are informed, "About a week ago they discovered here

[45] *Ibid.*, p. 106.   [46] *Ibid.*, p. 293.   [47] *Ibid.*, p. 235.
[48] Ministrationem sanctorum sacramentorum inseparatim cum ministerio verbi, coniunctam esse agnoscimus et cuique membro corporis administrare sacramenta non licere. *Ibid.*, p. 235.
[49] *Ibid.*, pp. 198f.
[50] For the Baptist practice see the *Fenstanton, Warboys and Hexham Records*, ed. E. B. Underhill; for the Congregational practice see Norman Glass, *The Early History of the Independent Church at Rothwell*, pp. 75f.

a newly invented sect, called by those who belong to it 'the pure or stainless religion'; they met to the number of 150 in a house where their preacher used half of a tub for a pulpit, and was girded with a white cloth. Each one brought with him whatever food he had to eat, and the leaders divided money amongst those who were poorer, saying that they imitated the life of the apostles and refused to enter the temples to partake of the Lord's supper, as it was a papistical ceremony.[51] It is unlikely that they were Baptists, because the latter did practise the Lord's Supper. These sectarians may have been the "Family of Love" about whom little is known. On the other hand, there is evidence that love-feasts were held by the English Baptists as a general feature of their church life, but never as a substitute for the Lord's Supper. The church record of the Warboys congregation has this entry for 1655: "The order of love-feast agreed upon, to be before the Lord's Supper; because the ancient churches did practise it, and for unity with other churches near to us."[52] Another ordinance that appears to have been used exclusively in England by the Baptists was feet-washing. Their warrant for it was Christ's humility in performing this menial service for His disciples.[53] The Assembly of the General Baptists "had long agreed that the practice of washing the feet of the saints, urged in Lincolnshire by Robert Wright in 1653, and in Kent by William Jeffrey in 1659, should be left optional as not specified in Hebrews VI."[54]

Three distinctive contributions were made by the Anabaptists or Baptists to English Separatist worship. Their most distinctive custom was, of course, that they practised believers' Baptism by immersion. Second, in their opposition to set forms of worship they went further than the other Separatists. This position was radically expressed by John Smyth: "That the reading out of a Book is no part of spiritual worship, but the invention of the man of sin; that Books and writings are in the nature of Pictures and Images; that it is unlawful to have the Book before the eyes in singing of a Psalm."[55] The third influence exerted by the Baptists was the method of running exposition of the Bible or interpolated com-

---

[51] *A Calendar of Letters and State Papers relating to English Affairs, preserved principally in the Archives of Simancos*, II, 7.

[52] *Fenstanton*, ed. Underhill, p. 272.

[53] John 13:5.

[54] "Original Sin, Feet-Washing and the New Connexion," *Transactions of the Baptist Historical Society*, vol. 1 (1908-1909), 129f.

[55] This is a summary of Smyth's views as abstracted from his *The Differences of the Churches of the Separation* by Robert Baillie, in *A Dissuasive from the Errours of the Time* (1645), p. 29n.

ment during the public reading of the Scriptures. This was the practice of the General Baptists, as is demonstrated by Grantham's survey of their church life made in 1678; it was the method used by the New England Puritans. John Smyth seems to have been the initiator of this trend of teaching.[56]

4. *Other Underground Congregations*

It now remains to consider other influences on Separatist congregations, which derive from certain obscure congregations in England and on the Continent. As their relation to the established Church was questionable, they were not considered as Separatist. Although their worship was like that of the Separatists, their form of church government was not. The first in point of time and in importance as a precedent was the "Privye Churche" that met in London during the reign of Queen Mary.[57] Its importance lay in the fact that it was organised for worship under persecution, providing later Separatists with a precedent for gathering secretly to worship, in defiance of the laws of the land, according to their own conscience.

A similar underground church was the Plumber's Hall congregation. They were of the lineage of the Marian secret church, as they proudly claimed, "we bethought us what were best to doe, and we remembered that there was a congregation of us in this Citie in Queene Maries dayes: And a congregation at *Geneva*, which used a booke and order of preaching, ministring of the Sacraments and Discipline, most agreeable to the worde of God: which booke is alowed by that godly & well learned man, Maister *Calvin*, and the preachers there, which booke and order we now holde."[58] This congregation was Puritan rather than Separatist, and had the clearest affinities with Presbyterianism, except that it was pre-Presbyterian and pre-Puritan. The congregation was discovered in 1567.

A congregation similar to the Plumber's Hall was known as the "Privye Churche" of Richard Fitz, which the London authorities also discovered in 1567. Their minister made the three Puritan demands: "trewe markes of Christs churche" consist in "Fyrste and formoste, the Glorious worde and Evangell preached, not in bondage and subjection, but freely, and purely. Secondly to have the Sacraments mynistred purely, onely and all together accord-

---

[56] *Works*, I, lxxxvii f.
[57] For the details see Foxe's *Acts and Monuments*, VIII, 485f., 558f.
[58] Cited in Albert Peel, *The First Congregational Churches*, p. 7.

inge to the institution and good worde of the Lord Jesus, without any tradicion or invention of man. And laste of all, to have, not the fylthye Cannon lawe, but dissiplyne onelye, and all together agreable to the same heavenlye and almighty worde of oure good Lorde, Jesus Chryste."[59] The discipline so strongly insisted upon was practised, not after the second diet of worship on the Lord's day, as was the Baptist custom, but "on the fourth day in the weke we meet and cum together weekely to use prayer & exercyse disciplyne on them whiche do deserve it, by the strength and sure warrant of the lordes good word as in Mt. xviii. 15-18 and I Cor.v."[60]

The close affinities of this congregation with the later phenomenon of Independency are seen, not only in modes of worship, but in the adoption of a covenant. On this account Albert Peel argued that "there is no valid reason for moderns to deny to Fitz's congregation, and probably to others contemporary with it, the title of 'the first Congregational Churches.' " In my view, however, since Robert Browne had not yet written his justification for the autonomy of each local congregation, so that it might the better serve Christ, without interference from bishops or magistrates, it is premature to title this congregation "Congregational." Furthermore, by its attachment to Geneva it was proto-Presbyterian rather than proto-Congregational.

Two conclusions follow from this study of Separatist worship. The first is that the Separatists put into practice a "Reformation without tarrying for any," while the Puritans resolved to attain the liturgical achievements of the Separatists within the established Church. Some were immediately attainable as supplements, such as the "prophecyings," additional free prayers which could be added to the forms of prayer in the Book of Common Prayer, and the singing of psalms. It was particularly in the field of extemporaneous prayer that the Separatists were innovators. Other features of Separatist worship such as the founding of churches on covenants, if imitated, could have led to splits in the parish churches between the covenanted and the uncovenanted. Nor was it possible to celebrate worship in the parish churches without using the three "noxious ceremonies," the ring in marriage, the signing of the cross in Baptism, and kneeling to receive Holy Communion. It was also necessary to wear the Anglican vestments. But all these matters being of the *esse*, not the *bene esse* of true

[59] *Ibid.*, p. 32.   [60] *Ibid.*, p. 33.

344

churchmanship, could wait for a monarch or parliament more propitious to the Puritan demands in the future.

The truly decisive influence of the Separatists was in their radical opposition to any set forms of prayer, including the Lord's Prayer. It is worth recalling the irony of Barrow's attack on set prayers (as in the Prayer Book), to make his plea for free prayer ring with conviction in our ears: "Shall we think that God hath any time left these his servants so singularly furnished and destitute of his grace, that they cannot find words according to their necessities and faith, to expresse their wantes and desires, but need thus to be taught line unto line, as children new weaned from the brestes, what and when to say, how much to say, and when to make an end; to say this collect at the beginning, that at the end, that before the tother after, this in the morning, that at after noone, *etc.*"[61] This fine conception of liberty in prayer, with great possibilities of achievement, as also of bathos, was the heritage that Separatism transmitted to Independency and through Independency to the English Presbyterians at the Westminster Assembly of Divines, and thence through the Pilgrims and Puritans to the new world. It was a noble heritage; it was this influence of Separatism which probably accounts for the departure of Puritanism from some of the liturgical customs of the European Reformed churches. Unquestionably it brought fervour, freedom, intimacy, and sincerity into worship, though sometimes at the cost of order and dignity. Often its freshness was a tonic for those who had developed the familiarity that breeds contempt for set forms, even for the richest and most felicitously phrased of literary forms such as the Book of Common Prayer was and is.

[61] *Briefe Discoverie*, p. 74.

PART THREE

LITURGICAL ARTS AND AIDS

CHAPTER X

RELIGIOUS ARCHITECTURE
AND ART

DID PROTESTANTISM kill, secularise, or simplify religious architecture and art in England? This is almost as controversial and intriguing an issue as the much debated question whether Protestantism originated or abetted capitalism.

It has been fashionable for historians to deplore the aesthetic losses caused by the Reformation. They can be seen plainly in the contrast between the richness of the architectural setting of Catholic worship and the austerity of the context within which Protestant worship is celebrated. With typical vigour and a preference for the inanimate over the living, A. L. Rowse insists that "the saddest thing about the Reformation, sadder perhaps than the loss of lives, was the enormous loss in things of beauty, for they were in no way responsible for the fate that befell them."[1] G. G. Coulton,[2] that stern mentor among the medievalists, challenged the Puginesque contrast between the "ages of faith" with all their variegated splendour of stone, wood, metal, and glass in cathedrals and monasteries, and the industrial ugliness of Victorianism, as a piece of romantic sentimentality. The balance seems to have been struck by A. G. Dickens.[3] He acknowledges that one of the most impressive features of medieval religion was its ability to inspire "lively art and craftsmanship" and observes that some of the most splendid Gothic edifices (churches and palaces) continued to be built in the reigns of Henry VII and Henry VIII. Yet he also remarks that much glass-making had become a wearying stereotype and that sacred statues were crudely mass-produced. Furthermore, he even raises again some of the ethical questions that Coulton had about the much vaunted "religious" achievements of the medieval artists. Was there no fear in the faith that built the cathedrals? Were the pious donors never expiating their sins with conscience money? Did not the Church itself use indulgences to raise its fanes? Did not its theologians and architects from the Abbot Suger on allow the central events of Christian history to be overlaid with super-

[1] *The England of Elizabeth*, p. 465.
[2] See G. G. Coulton's *Art and the Reformation*, chaps. 19, 20.
[3] *The English Reformation*, pp. 9-10.

stition and almost incredible legends? Also, what of the vaunted anonymity of the medieval artist who is supposed not to have wanted his right hand to know what the left hand was doing? There is, of course, no question about the splendour of medieval art, even if there is a questioning of some of the naïveté in the rose-window-tinted view of medieval piety. Moreover, one is not likely to aggrandise the lowly status of Reformed architecture and art by the process of minimising the greatness of medieval Catholic art. The question remains: did Protestantism produce an authentic religious architecture and art in sixteenth-century England?[4]

1. *Iconoclasts and Iconophiles*

Unquestionably there was a strongly iconoclastic element in English Protestantism, which was actively fought by the English Catholics of the time. The views of Bishop John Hooper of Gloucester, in Edward's reign, and of William Burton, a Bristol preacher in Elizabeth's reign, were typical of the iconoclasts who desired to do away with all images of the Holy Trinity, the Incarnate Son of God, and the saints, as a breaking of the Second Commandment against "graven images."

Hooper had fled England in 1539 to avoid persecution for his extreme Protestant views, and had lived from 1547 to 1549 in Zurich, perhaps the most radical of the Reformed centres, where he was greatly influenced by John à Lasco. He returned to England in 1549 and became a prominent opponent of Bonner, a Henrician Catholic who was Bishop of London. A critic of priestly vestments, transubstantiatory doctrine, and devotion to the saints, he inevitably desired to remove all traces of "idolatry," which he interpreted images of God and the saints to be. These views were reflected in his injunctions for the Dioceses of Gloucester and Worcester, especially referring to images in windows:

---

[4] If the question had not been limited to England, it might in one way have been easier to answer because the impact of Lutheranism, especially in the Scandinavian countries, was not as iconoclastic as Calvinism; yet Calvinism produced some interesting variations in church shapes among the Huguenots (see Paul de Félice, *Les Protestants D'Autrefois*, 4 vols., I, chap. 1). It is, however, significant that Karl Holl, in *Die Kultur bedeuting der Reformation*, tr. as *The Cultural Significance of the Reformation*, claims that Protestantism contributed significantly to politics, economic life, education, and the understanding of history, philosophy, poetry, and music, yet the only first-rate painter to be claimed for Protestantism is Rembrandt, who was active a century after the Reformation and whose church affiliation (Mennonite or Dutch Reformed?) is uncertain, even if his work is thoroughly Biblical in its inspiration. See the fascinating work of W. A. Visser T'Hooft, *Rembrandt and the Gospel*.

Item, that when any glass windows within any of the churches shall from henceforth be repaired, or new made, that you do not permit to be painted or portrayed therein the image or picture of any saints; but if they will have anything painted, that it be either branches, flowers or posies [mottoes], taken out of Holy Scripture. And that ye cause to be defaced all such images as yet do remain painted upon the walls of your churches, and that from henceforth there be no more such.[5]

William Burton, a Puritan preacher of the Church of England, denounced the stained glass at St. Thomas's Church in Bristol:

It likewise appeareth what dishonour and disgrace have been offered by gross idolaters which would take upon them to paint and picture out the invisible and incomprehensible majesty of the Almighty like a man whose breath is in his nostrils, whose being is not of himself, whose years are but a span long, and in his best estate is altogether vanity. Whatsoever ye do, saith the Scripture, do all to the glory of God. That is, strive to do it so, as God may get the most glory by it. Are such representations of God to the advancing of his glory? What do they show and teach us that we might give Him everlasting praise for? He is painted as a man as you see in yonder story of creation in yonder window in a dozen places together. What may we learn by them? A man hath his being from another. If God be as he is painted forth, he hath so too, which to say is blasphemy.[6]

The two charges of Protestantism against the representation of God and the saints thus were blasphemy and idolatry. It allegedly was blasphemy to represent God anthropomorphically, though it could very well be argued that since in the Incarnation God had become man here was the true icon of the invisible God[7] and a perfect justification for the making of copies of a true image. This, in fact, was the heart of the Catholic contention. The charge of idolatry seemed more appropriate to the reverence for the saints,

5 *Visitation Articles and Injunctions*, eds. W. H. Frere and W. M. Kennedy, ii, 289.
6 *David's Evidence* (1596), pp. 140-41. A marginal note indicates that he is pointing to windows in St. Thomas's Church, Bristol. The D.N.B. says he preached at Bristol in 1590.
7 Colossians 1:15 is usually translated in the West as "the image of the invisible God." Yet the Greek original, rendered "image," is actually ἐικὼν.

who are, after all, created beings, lacking aseity, which was Hooper's main point. The Catholic defence of reproductions of the saints was that these imitators of God were reminders of the potentialities of men and women responsive to the endowments of divine grace. It is of course arguable that poor representations of divine beings are worse than none.

The Catholic view of images may be illustrated from the defence of them in "The King's Book," and in Harding's controversy with Jewel. *A Necessary Doctrine* of 1534 provides an exposition of the Second Commandment, which interpreted the veto against graven images as applying not to their creation but to their extreme veneration. Their positive purpose was "that we (in beholding and loking upon them . . .) may call to remembraunce the manifolde examples of vertues, which were in the sainctes, whom they do represent. And so maye they rather be provoked, kendled, and styred, to yelde thankes to our lorde and to praise him and his sayde saintes, and to remembre and lamente our synnes and offences, and to praye God, that we may have grace to folowe their goodnes & holy lyvyng."[8] As an illustration, it was said that the image of Christ on the rood, or the depiction of the crucifixion on walls or windows, was made so that the beholder might learn Christ's virtues, remember his "paynefull and cruel passion," and "condemne and abhorre our synne, which was the cause of his so cruell death."[9] There were two caveats, however, against a misuse of images. Those who would trust more in one image than in another were in error, as were those who spent money on bedecking images rather than helping "poor christen people, the quicke and lyvinge images of god, which is the necessary worke of charitie commanded by god."[10]

Harding adduced three arguments for making and using images. The first was that images are the theological instructors of "the

[8] *A Necessary Doctrine and erudition for any chrysten man, set furth by the Kynges maiesty of Englande &c.* (1534), commonly known as the "King's Book," sigs. L recto and verso.

[9] *Ibid.*, L verso.

[10] *Ibid.*, L iii recto. It is also worth citing Sir Thomas More's view of the value of images: "Albeit that every good Christian hath a remembrance of Christ's passion in mind, and conceiveth by devout meditation a form and fashion thereof in his heart, yet is there no man I ween so good nor so well learned, nor in meditation so well accustomed, but that he findeth himself more moved to pity and compassion, upon beholding of the holy crucifix, than when he lacketh it." (*Dialogue against Tyndale* in *The English Works*, reproduced in facsimile from William Rastell's edition of 1557 and edited with a modern version by W. E. Campbell, II, 15-16.) See also Johan Huizinga, *The Waning of the Middle Ages*, chap. 12.

simple and unlearned people, which be utterly ignorant of letters [who] in pictures doo as it were reade and see nolesse then others doo in bookes, the mysteries of christen Religion, the actes and worthy dedes of Christ and of his Sainctes."[11] The second argument was that images are vivid reminders to sluggish souls of their indebtedness to Christ and the saints, and are encouragements "to the like will of doing and suffering, and to all endeavour of holy and vertuose life."[12] The third argument was in fact an extension of the second, to the effect that images are reminders of all things necessary to salvation. In recalling the benefits and merits of Christ and the virtuous examples of the saints, Harding said: "that if we bee such as they were, we may by Gods grace through Christ atteine the blysse they be in, and with them enioye lyfe everlasting."[13]

The Anglican rebuttal of the chief arguments for the use of images in worship was contained in the homily, "Against Peril of Idolatry." It was addressed particularly to the claim that arguments against idolatry do not apply to the images of the true God, Christ and the saints, that images of Christ may be made although He was God, because He took human flesh and became a man. The reply was: "For Christ is God and man: seeing therefore that of the Godhead, which is the most excellent part, no image can be made, it is falsely called the image of Christ. . . . Furthermore, no true image can be made of Christ's body, for it is unknown now of what form and countenance he was."[14] Two other arguments for images were rebutted. One was that it is not the image that is honoured but the saint whose image it is; the other was that tradition approves of creating saints' images. The reply was that honouring of saints by such was to dishonour them by despoiling God of honour; the true honouring of the saints is to live in charity, giving generously and living simply as they did, since the true service of God is in helping the poor, the living images of God, not in honouring dead simulacre of the saints.[15]

The importance of the arguments is that they had some reason

---

[11] Thomas Harding, *An Answer to Maister Iuelles Chalenge* (1565), p. 189 verso.

[12] *Ibid.*, p. 190 recto. [13] *Ibid.*, p. 191 recto.

[14] *Certain Sermons* (1574 version, reprinted and edited by G. E. Corrie), p. 217. It should be noted that the outline of this homily is contained in Bishop Ridley's "Treatise on the Worship of Images," yet the contents are almost entirely a literal translation of Bullinger's treatise, *De origine cultus Divorum et simulacrorum erronea*.

[15] *Certain Sermons*, ed. Corrie, p. 269.

on their side in their desire to protect men from false notions of God. However psychologically weak the understanding of iconoclasts was, they were not colour-blind Philistines utterly insensitive to aesthetic values.

In some measure in Anglican worship, and altogether in Puritan worship, the iconoclasts won the arguments with the iconophiles. The result was the almost complete smashing of the figures on the roodscreen and the ending of the making of religious sculptures in wood, as well as the almost total elimination of painting on walls or windows of churches. The monastic churches, except when they were kept as parish churches, must have suffered the greatest despoiling, for their windows no longer needed to be glazed. Many must have soon been emptied of windows for the lead.[16]

The melancholy story is told in part in the 28th Article of the Royal Injunctions of 1547: "Also, that they shall take away utterly extinct and destroy all shrines, covering of shrines, all tables, candlesticks, trindles or rolls of wax, pictures, paintings, and all other monuments of feigned miracles, pilgrimages, idolatry, and superstition: so that there remain no memory of the same in walls, glass-windows, or elsewhere within their churches or houses. And they shall exhort all their parishioners to do the like within their several houses."[17] Thirty years later William Harrison wrote of the imageless Anglican churches: "Churches themselves, belles and times of morning & evening praier remain as in time past, saving that all images, shrines, tabernacles, rood loftes & monuments of idolatrie are removed, taken down & defaced: Onlie the stories in glasse windowes excepted, which, for want of sufficient store of new stuffe, & by reason of extreame charge that should grow by the alteration of the same into white panes, throughoute the realme, are not altogether abolished in most places at once, but by little and little suffered to decaie that white glass may be set up in their roomes."[18]

Goldsmiths, silversmiths, glaziers, painters, and carvers must immediately have turned from ecclesiastical to secular work. Painters of glass turned to heraldry.[19] It is equally meaningful that

---

[16] Christopher Woodforde, *English Stained and Painted Glass*, p. 38.

[17] Eds. W. H. Frere and W. M. Kennedy, *Visitation Articles and Injunctions*, II, 126.

[18] *Harrison's Description of England in Shakspere's Youth*, 2 vols., ed. F. J. Furnivall, I, 18f.

[19] Woodforde, *English Glass*, p. 33.

painters in oils turned away from religious paintings for churches (which were forbidden them) and found secular inspiration in portraits and miniatures,[20] thus exhibiting that growing individualism which was the legacy of the Renaissance and Reformation. Eric Mercer may indeed be right in distinguishing Renaissance from Reformation individualism by regarding the former as celebrating the exceptional and the latter as recognising the importance of the common man.[21] In this sense the Reformation may have assisted in the process of the secularisation of art and in moving it from the church to the home, although this does not necessarily mean that all its sacred quality has been lost, since man is made in the image of God.

Did the advent of English Protestantism bring any relief to a cluttered, complicated, and overdecorated worship? The various uprisings, from the Pilgrimage of Grace to the Western Rebellion in Cornwall and Devon, showed that the Catholics were conscious of an impoverishment in worship. Yet Protestants rejoiced in a simplification of worship and a functionalism which austerity in aesthetics aided. This is plainly to be seen in the significant illustration in Foxe's *Acts and Monuments* in the folio edition of 1573,[22] which symbolises the religious meaning of the reign of the young Protestant, Edward VI. It depicts a simple Renaissance temple in the foreground, at which an attentive congregation is listening to the preaching of the Gospel, while on a platform a table replaces an altar and on it is a loaf and a large communion cup from which all will partake, while the sacrament of Baptism is being celebrated by a minister and an eager family gathered around the font at the entrance of the church. In the upper left of the woodcut, there is the porch of a Gothic church from which Roman Catholics are emerging in haste, each with a sack or luggage on his shoulder, as he rushes toward the "Ship of the Roman Church" bearing the emblem of the five wounds of Christ. The legend says: "The Papistes packing away their Paltry." What they are removing is heavy service books (such as missals, sacramentaries, pontificals, and breviaries), and with them vestments, tabernacles, croziers, candlesticks, censers, bells, monstrances, and

20 See Ellis Waterhouse's *Painting in Britain, 1530-1790*, p. 19, for the judgment: "Alone of painters in Elizabeth's reign, Hilliard and his rival, Isaac Oliver, are worthy to be named as contributors to the age of Shakespeare." Both were "limners," or miniaturists in portraits.
21 *English Art, 1553-1625*, p. 6.
22 II, 1,294, which is included in the illustrations to the present volume.

crucifixes, while behind there is a conflagration of images. Another legend reads: "Ship over your trinkets and be packing you Papistes." This is all very crude, but also telling. There is no mistaking the fact that for Protestants these pieces of liturgical paraphernalia were "paltry," mere trinkets.

The relief Protestants felt in the newly found simplicity of their worship is admirably expressed by Bernard Gilpin in a sermon preached before the court in 1552. He contrasted Catholic with Protestant worship: "They [Catholics] come to the Church to feede their eyes, and not their soules; they are not taught, that no visible thing is to be worshipped. And for because they see not in the church the shining pompe and pleasant variety (as they thought it) of painted clothes, candlesticks, images, altars, lampes, tapers, they say, as good to goe into a Barne; nothing esteeming Christ which speaketh to them in his holy Word, neither his holy Sacrament reduced to the first institution."[23] That kind of streamlining of worship, and simplicity of style, seemed to Protestants to comport more naturally with the worship of the New Testament as it had been recovered in the vernacular Bibles of the era for the benefit of the common man.

I have already mentioned the iconoclasm that destroyed so much medieval art, and the simplification of Anglican worship through the removal of so much priestly paraphernalia from the celebration of the liturgy, along with the secularization of painting and much architecture. Are we then to assume that Anglicans and Puritans merely adapted Catholic churches for their own worship, and that they made no architectural nor artistic contributions of their own? Such would be an oversimplification of an intricate question.

2. Anglican Architecture

The style of ecclesiastical architecture does not usually differ markedly from the leading domestic architecture of the age, particularly in a time of increasing secularity. It is therefore important at least to glimpse the character of Tudor architecture in general, as a preliminary to studying Anglican ecclesiastical architecture.

There appear to be three styles of Tudor architecture, corresponding roughly to three successive periods.[24] First, there was

[23] *A Sermon preached in the Court at Greenwitch, before King Edward the Sixth, the first Sonday after the Epiphany, Anno Domini 1552* (1630), sig. C3 recto and verso; also pp. 21-22.

[24] John Harvey, *Tudor Architecture*, pp. 12-13.

the rich, ornate work inspired by the ostentatious Edward IV, of which the most notable examples are St. George's Chapel, Windsor (1474-1500); Magdalen College, Oxford (1474-1490); and the central tower of Canterbury Cathedral (1490-1497). The succeeding style is simpler and more austere, and is expressed in expanses of plain brick walls, with cuspless arches and tracery. Typical of this style are Corpus Christi College, Oxford (1512-1518), and Wolsey's Hampton Court (1515-1525). The third mongrel style, mixing Gothic and Classical, can be seen in Henry VIII's Hampton Court (1531-1536), Titchfield Place (1537-1540), and Cowdray (1537-1548). The native Gothic, whether elaborate or simple, was mingled unnaturally with the new French and Italian influences. Gothic art was inspired by the horizontal and dynamic line, while Roman art stressed the horizontal and static. The demand for classical details and even for classical elevations ended in almost total dislocation.[25]

But before the Gothic died it had a glorious swansong in the designs of Robert and William Vertue in Henry VII's Chapel in Westminster Abbey. Begun in 1503 and practically completed in 1519 by William Vertue after Robert's death in 1506, this is the most opulent and splendid of all English royal chapels. The richness of the detail is prevented from being fussy or cloying because of the sureness of the structure and the lines of the design. This is a most attractive example of fan-vaulting, with pendants and eastern corona. As Harvey says, "Here all is airiness and grace, and it is as though the stone pendants were themselves borne up by a floating lacework of gossamer traceries."[26]

Perhaps the most remarkable fact about Anglican Church architecture is not the Gothic revival which flourished in the nineteenth century, but the Gothic *survival* which continued from 1558 to 1662.[27] It is most significant that Gothic survived longer in England, and was less altered from its medieval precedents, than

[25] *Ibid.*, pp. 38-39.   [26] *Ibid.*, p. 27.

[27] This thesis has been argued with a plethora of supporting evidence in John M. Schnorrenberg's "Early Anglican Architecture, 1558-1662: Its Theological Implications and Its Relation to the Continental Background," unpub. Ph.D. thesis, Princeton University, 1964. It is a view also put forward by Eric Mercer in *English Art, 1553-1625*, Oxford History of English Art, pp. 85-87, who claims that there were three reasons for continuing to use Gothic styles in architecture, of which the first was the strongest. "This appreciation of the aesthetic appeal of Gothic was the basis of its deliberate use, and the intention was either to advertise the religious functions of the building, or to give it an archaic air, or to emphasize a particular feature by the contrast of its ornament with the classical character of all the rest" (p. 85).

among the Lutherans of Germany and Sweden. The use of this style fully or partly Gothic in England seems increasingly a deliberate attempt to maintain the continuity of the medieval with the reformed Church of England; in this respect it is of a piece with English life in general. Outward forms are maintained even if their contents are transformed. A ruling monarchy becomes in time a mere figurehead of a sovereign. A religious primer looks like the old primers, but it has increasingly Protestant contents. So it was with ecclesiastical architecture: the old forms were maintained and repaired, and even the additions are not often unGothic, despite the fact that the worship was no longer a dramatic spectacle, but equally intended to be heard until Christopher Wren, a century after the beginning of Elizabeth's reign, designed definitely "auditory" and, therefore, Protestant churches. Even when this Gothic survival became a deliberate revival, as during the Commonwealth period, it was still used as an expression of loyalty to a persecuted Church.

It could, of course, be argued that in the sixteenth and early seventeenth centuries in England, no style other than Gothic was possible for the buildings of the Church of England. Had the Church of England so wished, however, it could have followed the Renaissance styles already being used in secular architecture in order to indicate its break with the older religion of Roman Catholicism. Anglican church-building could even have followed the example of the French Calvinists, the Huguenots, with their plans for single-roomed structures shaped as squares, circles, polygons, and ovals, and built in the classical style.[28] That this possibility was not taken seems a proof that the national church sought to affirm continuity rather than discontinuity in its architecture. The taste continued to be firmly Gothic, especially when the theology was conservatively orthodox, as, for example, that of Archbishop Laud. He favoured Gothic buildings, with occasional classical details, even though the most outstanding architect and designer of his time was the classicist, Inigo Jones. The classical style was not to triumph in Anglicanism until 1663, when Wren designed the first of his churches, Pembroke College Chapel, Oxford, in a classic style. Until then Gothic reigned supreme.

Nineteen churches or chapels were built or rebuilt during the reign of Elizabeth. Several of them were enlarged by the adding of

<hr>

[28] de Félice, *Les Protestants D'Autrefois*, I, 11.

a tower, an aisle, a porch, a chapel, or combination of some of these features. Five have been destroyed, three remodelled, and the rest enlarged and altered.[29] In these circumstances generalisations have to be more tentative than usual. The number of churches involved seems small, which was due to lack of funds in the impoverished churches. The reforms of Henry VIII and Edward VI gave the sovereign as supreme "head," or "governor," of the Church of England a vast patronage of "livings," the tax on their first fruits, and on the presentation to bishoprics. Also, several sees were left vacant for long periods, enabling the queen to pocket the revenues.[30]

The few new churches were built in the traditional Gothic style —St. Peter's, Brooke, Rutlandshire in 1579, and St. Nicholas, Bedfordshire about the same year. The most elaborate, and largest, Elizabethan church surviving is St. Wilfred, Standish, Lancashire, which was rebuilt probably between 1582 and 1584, the largest donor being the rector, Richard Moody. It is of the standard Gothic plan and elevation, with an arch inside and two exterior turrets to mark the distinction between chancel and nave. The church of St. Michael, Woodham Walter of 1563-1564, is an early example of Gothic survival in Essex, and interesting because it is built of brick, and has stepped gables, and square-headed windows filled with tracery. Interestingly the donor, Thomas Radcliffe, the third Earl of Sussex, was thought to have strong Protestant leanings, yet he had the church consecrated and at the direction of the Calvinist Bishop Grindal.

With one exception the additions made to existing churches were Gothic added to Gothic. The exception was the unique seven-sided porch built by Bishop Jewel for St. Leonard's Church, Sunningwell, Berkshire, about 1562. Although it has flat-headed Tudor windows, the porch has Ionic pillars on pedestals with entablature *en ressant.*[31] It is possible that Jewel, as Bishop of Salisbury and a decided Protestant, recalled the Renaissance neo-classical architecture he had seen in his years of exile in Frankfort, Strassburg, or Zurich.

---

[29] Schnorrenberg, "Early Anglican Architecture," pp. 46f. In the appendix (p. 279) it is pointed out that about 152 Anglican churches were built or rebuilt between 1558 and 1662.

[30] Ely was without a bishop from 1581 to 1600, Norwich from 1578 to 1585, and Oxford from 1558 to 1567, 1568 to 1589, and 1590 to 1603.

[31] See Basil Clarke and John Betjeman, *English Churches*, illustration no. 129.

3. *The Elizabethan Conception of the Church*

Catholicism, with its realistic doctrine of the Eucharist, conceived of the church in the most literal sense as the house of God, since the tabernacle housed God and the church housed the tabernacle. Calvinists, however, believed that the church was the house of prayer and preaching—the assembling place of the people of God—and Puritans believed that the saints, that is, God's people in the process of being sanctified, were the temples of the Holy Spirit and that churches were meetinghouses. The Elizabethan Anglican view of the church seems to have been midway between the Roman Catholic and Calvinist concepts, insofar as it can be determined from the pertinent homilies dealing with this theme (Nos. 1, 2, 3, and 8 in the edition of 1563), from the writings of Hooker, and in comparison with the Lutheran and Calvinist views of the function and purpose of a church edifice.

The homilies present two views of the Church. In one, it was viewed as the earthly shadow of the heavenly mansion;[32] the building mediated numinosity. In the other, it was affirmed that its holiness was not of itself, "but because God's people resorting thereunto are holy, and exercise themselves in holy and heavenly things."[33] The former view was Catholic and the latter, Calvinist. The Anglicans combined both numinous and functional concepts of the religious sanctuary.

Richard Hooker typified these views in his *Ecclesiastical Polity*, for the edifice as well as the people are holy, dedicated to God. In a famous citation Hooker claimed that although worship is acceptable to God wherever it is offered, "the very majesty and holiness of the place where God is worshipped, hath *in regard of us* great virtue, force, and efficacy, for that it serveth as a sensible help to stir up devotion, and in that respect no doubt bettereth even our holiest and best actions in this kind."[34] Furthermore, he affirmed that the gravest of the Fathers had claimed that "the house of prayer is a Court beautified with the presence of the celestial powers; that there we stand, we pray, we sound forth hymns to God, having his Angels intermingled as our associates," hence, "how can we come to the house of prayer and not be moved with the very glory of the place itself so to frame our affections praying, as doth beseem them, whose suits the Almighty doth

[32] *The Two Books of Homilies*, ed. J. Griffiths, p. 166.
[33] *Ibid.*, p. 275.
[34] *Ecclesiastical Polity*, Book v, chap. 16, para. 2.

there sit to hear, and his Angels attend to further?"[35] We have only to substitute "saints" for "angels" to realize how medieval this appeal was. Yet Hooker could also insist on the functional importance of the church, without an addiction to "stiffness": "It cannot be laid to any man's charge at this day living, either that they have been so curious as to trouble bishops with placing the first stone in the churches they built, or so scrupulous, as after the erection of them to make any great ado for their dedication. In which kind notwithstanding as we do neither allow unmeet nor purpose the stiff defence of any unnecessary custom heretofore received; so we know no reason wherefore churches should be the worse, if at the first erecting of them; at the making of them public, at the time when they are delivered as it were into God's own possession, and the use whereunto they shall ever serve is established, ceremonies fit to betoken such interests and to accompany such actions be usual, as in the purest times they have been."[36]

Hooker's views were not exclusively Calvinist, for they did not heed the caveat of Calvin: ". . . there is great need of caution, lest we either consider them as the proper habitations of the Deity, where he may be nearer to us to hear our prayers—an idea which has begun to be prevalent for several ages—or ascribe to them I know not what mysterious sanctity, which might be supposed to render our devotions more holy in the Divine view."[37] The first Hooker citation above directly contradicts the second part of the Calvin citation. Nor did Luther support to any extent the views of Hooker, since he had an intense dislike for all ecclesiastical triumphalism—"all the high, big and beautiful churches, towers and bells in existence." Luther wrote: "For indeed, the Christian Church on earth has no greater power or work than common prayer against everything that may oppose it. This the evil spirit knows well, and therefore he does all he can to prevent such prayer. Gleefully he lets us go on building monastic houses, making music, reading, singing, observing many masses, and multiplying ceremonies beyond measure. . . . But if he noticed that we wished to practise this prayer, even if it were under a straw roof or in a pig-sty, he would indeed not endure it, but would fear such a pig-sty far more than all the high, big and beautiful churches, towers and bells in existence, if such prayer be not in them. It is indeed not a question of the places and buildings in which we assemble, but

---

[35] *Ibid.*, chap. 25, para. 2.   [36] *Ibid.*, chap. 12, para. 1.
[37] *Institutes* III: xxx.

only of this unconquerable prayer, that we pray it, and bring it before God as a truly common prayer."[38]

The conclusion must be that while Edwardian Anglicanism was strongly iconoclastic and functional in its conception of the church building, Elizabethan Anglicanism combined the functional approach of the house of prayer with a recognition that churches themselves were capable of stirring up feelings of holiness and numinosity, a view closer to Catholicism than to Protestantism, as expressed at any rate by Luther or Calvin.

4. *The Adaptation of Churches for Anglican Worship*

There is no need to deal further with the iconoclasm that changed the churches from "tuppenny coloured" to "penny plain" in the days of Edward VI, nor even with the positive sense of the simplification and uncluttering of worship which ensued. My present concern is rather with first the Edwardian and then the Elizabethan rearrangements that were made for participation in a new vernacular liturgy and to make the edification of the people more feasible.

Hooper, Bucer, and Ridley were convinced that the medieval two-roomed church (with nave separated from chancel by rood-screen and arch, as well as by steps) was fundamentally unsuited to Reformed worship. The Church of England had inherited such buildings, yet it was convinced that the true liturgical unit was not the clergy, with the laity as onlookers, but the whole body of the faithful gathered at worship. Even the larger parish churches had insufficient space for vast gatherings of the people, since much of the space was taken up by chantry chapels, and the choir intervened between the nave and the altar; where there was a tympanum over the roodloft there was little chance of glimpsing the altar, and only the elevation of the Host in the Eucharist was visible.

The most radical solution to the problem was Hooper's suggestion that all chancels be closed off and only the naves used. The advantages were that the people would better understand what the minister was reading and the communicants would be able plainly to see and understand what was happening at the altar in Holy Communion. Moreover, the minister, being close to the people, would then be able to tell whether his reading was being under-

[38] "The Treatise of Good Works" (1520), tr. W. A. Lambert, in Luther's *Works*, I, 235.

stood or not.[39] Hooper was unsuccessful in his advocacy, but in his own dioceses of Gloucester and Worcester, as his injunctions of 1551-1552 show, he was able to enforce his own intense dislike of the screens that separated clergy from the people and which symbolised for him the veil of the Temple in the Old Dispensation which had been done away in Christ, thus making screens unnecessary in a Christian church.

Bucer, in his *Censura* of 1551, was strongly critical of the rubric before Matins in the First Prayer Book of Edward VI, which read, "The priest being in the quire shall begin with a loud voice . . ." because a minister in a returned stall in the chapel with his back to the congregation could not be heard clearly in a large church even if he raised his voice. Furthermore, Bucer objected that a special place for the clergy, such as the chancel was, gave the laity the impression that the ministry were nearer God than the laity and that the liturgy was the special prerogative of the clergy. He believed that the round, single-room churches of antiquity, with the priest surrounded by the congregation so that they might easily hear and see, was the most desirable church architecture. In the Reformed church at Strassburg, Bucer had put his liturgical ideas into practice. For the vernacular Communion on Sunday mornings the altar was moved to the western side of the chancel. The minister probably stood behind it, facing the people. Because of acoustic difficulties in huge medieval churches it became customary to pull the altars into the nave near the pulpit, and the service, apart from the actual Communion, was conducted from the pulpit. The baptismal font was placed near the altar and pulpit so Baptism could be administered in front of the entire congregation.[40]

The most striking event in Edward VI's reign from a liturgical standpoint was the movement officially led by Ridley, and suggested originally by Hooper, to abolish high altars of stone and replace them with wooden communion tables. Altars in chantry chapels had already been removed by the order for the dissolution of the chantries in 1548. Individual iconoclasts, without legal authority, had virtually been incited to take the law into their

---

[39] Hooper, *The Early Writings of John Hooper*, ed. S. Carr, pp. 491-92.

[40] This paragraph conflates material drawn from G.W.O. Addleshaw and Frederick Etchells, *The Architectural Setting of Anglican Worship*, pp. 23-24; and W. D. Maxwell, *John Knox's Genevan Service Book, 1556*, pp. 36-39, 46-47, 115-16.

own hands following Hooper's Lenten sermon before the court in 1550, during which he had hoped that the magistrates would be pleased "to turn the altars into tables, according to the first institution of Christ."[41] Bishop Ridley, in the injunctions for the diocese of London put out in the summer of 1550, exhorted curates, churchwardens, and others in authority "to erect and set up the Lord's Board, after the form of an honest table, decently covered."[42] Ridley argued that altars were appropriate for the Jewish sacrifices of the Old Testament, but as they had been brought to an end by Christ's one all-sufficient sacrifice on the cross, so also should altars cease to be used; in their places should be tables suitable for celebrating the Lord's Supper in which Christians spiritually feed on Christ. Ridley believed that the table agreed with Christ's institution of the sacrament and the practice of the apostles and the primitive Church.[43]

Addleshaw and Etchells, however, pointed out that the communion table had one great practical advantage over an altar: its mobility.[44] It could be placed in that part of the church where the communicants could best see and hear, and the most "convenient" place from 1550 to 1553 for the position of the communion table was the choir or chancel. Furthermore, Addleshaw and Etchells observe that the rubric in the First Prayer Book, which ordered the communicants to move into the chancel at the Offertory and to stay there until the rest of the service was still obeyed, but "instead of kneeling with their faces toward the Lord's board fixed in the form of an altar against the east wall, they now knelt all around it set in the form of a table in the middle of the chancel."[45]

The more radical Communion arrangements of the Edwardian reformers were not retained in the relatively conservative Elizabethan settlement of religion. The two-room medieval plan of architecture and worship was retained. Although at the beginning of Elizabeth's reign the great rood and its figures were taken down and the doom painted on the tympanum was whitewashed over, where they had survived or been restored, the chancel screens were not destroyed, thus indicating that there was to be a partition between chancel and nave. The communion tables were to remain as substitutes for stone altars and were to be covered with "a fair linen cloth" reaching to the ground on all four sides. The Royal

---

[41] Hooper, *Early Writings*, p. 488.
[42] *Visitation Articles*, ed. Frere and Kennedy, ii, 242-44.
[43] Nicholas Ridley, *Works*, ed. H. Christmas, pp. 322-23.
[44] *Ibid.*, p. 27.   [45] *Ibid.*, p. 28.

Injunctions of 1559 indicate that the table was to remain where the altar had hitherto stood, "saving when the Communion of the Sacrament is to be distributed," and on that occasion was to be put "in good sort within the chancel, as whereby the minister may be more conveniently heard of the communicants in his prayer and ministration, and the communicants also more conveniently, and in more number communicate with the said minister."[46] The Interpretations of the Bishops of 1560-1561 specified that the communion table was to be moved into the nave in front of the chancel door, "where either the choir seemeth to be too little or at great feasts of receivings."[47]

The whole process of adapting medieval churches for Anglican worship is admirably summarised in the words of Addleshaw and Etchells: "The process by which medieval churches were adapted for Prayer Book worship might be summed up as one of taking the communicants into the chancel for the Eucharist, so that they can be within sight and hearing of the priest at the altar; and of bringing down the priest from the chancel into the nave so that he could be amongst his people for Morning and Evening Prayer."[48] Though the one-room plan of an "auditory" church, which Wren was to use for his churches a century later, was more logical for Anglican worship, the Elizabethan arrangement had two advantages, quite apart from the continuity of using a Gothic building for Anglican worship. The first was that moving to the chancel for the Communion service seemd to give the Sacrament a special sacredness, which has been strongly emphasised through most of Anglican history; the chancel screen helped to separate the liturgy of the catechumens from the liturgy of the faithful, thus imparting to the climax of worship a sense of deep mystery.

5. Communion Plate

With the disappearance of shrines, crucifixes, reliquaries, ornate candlesticks, and elaborately chased chalices, the goldsmiths and silversmiths could hardly have made a living if they had depended solely on ecclesiastical patrons. The silversmiths, at least, were to spend a considerable part of their time in changing Roman Catholic chalices into ampler Anglican communion cups. Though there was no prescribed pattern for Edwardian commun-

---

[46] Gee and Hardy, *Documents illustrative of English Church History*, pp. 439-41.
[47] *Visitation Articles*, III, 62.
[48] Addleshaw and Etchells, *Architectural Setting*, p. 45.

ion cups, it is interesting that seven examples that survive are virtually identical in shape, having a bell-shaped bowl, a spool-shaped stem with a moulded rib round the waist, and a moulded base.[49] An excellent example of this type of communion cup is to be found in St. Mary's Church, Beddington.[50] Of even greater importance is the 1549 St. Mary Aldermary communion cup on loan to the Victoria and Albert Museum in Kensington, which originally was probably made for the Royal Chapel, since it bears Edward VI's royal arms.[51] Its great importance is that it has a cover which, when reversed, becomes a paten. The paten cover was to become a leading characteristic of Anglican communion plate for a century and a half after the creation of this the first surviving example.

The typical Elizabethan communion cup does not, however, have the shape of an inverted bell for its bowl, but the shape of a beaker. Its stem is spool-shaped, usually with a moulding round the middle, and it has a stepped and moulded base. The slightly domed cover that usually accompanied it had a flat knob which served as a foot when used as a paten.

The most significant fact about both Edwardian and Elizabethan communion cups, however, is their size as compared with the Roman Catholic chalices which they replaced and which often were smelted down to help make communion cups. The reason for this is that communicants at the Catholic Mass received the Host in the form of consecrated wafers, but not the consecrated wine, with the exception of the celebrating priest, for whom a small chalice was sufficient. Anglican Communions were, however, in both kinds,[52] and it was necessary to have a communion cup large enough to enable all communicants to partake, as well as a paten on which the consecrated wafers would stand. But when bread replaced wafers, larger patens became necessary.[53]

The decision that every English church had to have its chalice converted into a communion cup appears to have been Archbishop

---

[49] See Charles Oman, *English Church Plate, 1597-1830*, p. 192.

[50] The Beddington communion cup and paten of 1551 are illustrated in plate 49 of Oman's volume.

[51] Oman, *English Church Plate*, plate 50, illustrates the cup and paten-cover. The earliest surviving Edwardian cup is that of the church of St. Lawrence Jewry of 1548, which is shown on plate 52A in Oman's book.

[52] As from May 1, 1548.

[53] The Puritans insisted on household bread instead of wafer bread, and eventually their view prevailed. For the controversy see Archbishop Matthew Parker's *Correspondence*, eds. J. Bruce, T. T. Perowne, p. 478; and *Zurich Letters*, ed. Hastings Robinson, I, 248.

Parker's, with the probable assistance of Grindal. It seems rather strange that so tolerant a Primate should have taken so decidedly Protestant a step. Charles Oman makes the interesting suggestion that this decision was a means and not an end, a means to force ambivalent clergy to decide between Catholicism and Anglicanism. "It was," he says, "notorious that in the early years of this reign there were many clergy who were prepared not only to celebrate the Communion at the parish church but also to say Mass up at the manor for those who preferred the old service. The conversion of the parish chalice into a communion cup would help to curb the activities of these unreliable individuals."[54] In spite of this ingenious hypothesis it should be pointed out that the number of ambivalent priests was never large. Besides, there were other ways of curbing them; and after the Second Prayer Book of 1552 there was little possibility of mistaking Anglican Communion doctrine for Transubstantiation. But it is quite clear that the use of cups instead of chalices, combined with the vernacular liturgy and the Communion in both kinds, meant that Holy Communion was plainly distinguishable from the Mass.

Edmund Guest, the Bishop of Rochester, provided the earliest diocesan injunctions for the conversion of chalices into cups in 1565:

> Item, that the chalice of every parish church be altered into a decent cup therewith to minister the Holy Communion, taking away no more thereof but only so much as shall pay for the altering of the same into a cup. And the said cup to be provided in every parish within my said diocese by or on this side of the feast of Saint Michael the Archangel next coming after the date thereof.[55]

The symbolism on the silver communion cups was of the simplest character, especially when compared with the rich variety of medieval designs on chalices. On Edwardian and Elizabethan church plate we find only the sacred monogram, usually depicted with the letters I H S with a cross above and three nails below. On Recusant plate there was a growing tendency to add a heart beneath the nails.[56]

With this Anglican simplicity should be compared the splendid

54 *English Church Plate*, p. 135.
55 Frere and Kennedy, *Visitation Articles*, III, 162.
56 Oman, *English Church Plate*, p. 225.

liturgical equipment used by the Catholic Recusants, as reported in John Gerard's autobiography. After listing vestments, Gerard continues: "Six massive silver candlesticks stood on the altar, and two smaller ones at the side for the elevation. The cruets, the lavabo bowl, the bell and thurible were all of silver work; the lamps hung from silver chains, and a silver crucifix stood on the altar. For the great feasts we had a golden crucifix a foot high. It had a carved pelican at the top, and on the right arm an eagle with outstretched wings, carrying on its back its little ones, who were learning to fly; and on the left arm a phoenix expiring in flames so that it might leave behind an offspring; and at the foot was a hen gathering her chickens under her wings. The whole was worked in gold by a skilled artist."[57] The Anglican church would not know such splendour until the influence of Bishop Lancelot Andrewes was felt through Archbishop Laud and others in the nascent High Church tradition early in the next century.

6. Church Furniture

Anglicans would probably have made do with the medieval arrangements of their churches had they not been provoked to consider change by the Puritans. We have seen that larger patens became necessary parts of communion plate because the Puritans insisted on the use of household bread instead of the wafers which could conveniently be contained in a cover-paten. Anglican priests might have been content with their fonts at the west end of their churches, fittingly symbolising the entry by Baptism into the Christian church.[58] The Puritans, however, objected because the congregation could not as a whole see and hear the service of Baptism, which was particularly important to them as signalising the covenant of God with His people and their children; they did not allow godparents to take away from the congregation its rights as cosponsors of the child with the parents. Even on grounds of convenience the Puritans had a point, especially when the Baptism took place in a crowded nave after the second lesson at matins or evensong, for only those in the immediate vicinity of the font could see and hear the Sacrament. The Puritan demand was not,

[57] John Gerard, *The Autobiography of an Elizabethan*, tr. from the Latin by Philip Caraman, pp. 195f.

[58] Bishop Richard Montagu, appointed to Norwich in 1638, is credited with the statement that the font should be placed in the West end of the church, "in order to signify our entrance into God's church by baptism" (*First Report of the Royal Commission on Ritual* (1867), p. 580b, cited by Addleshaw and Etchells, *Architectural Setting*, p. 65).

however, met by the Church of England; it was only in their own meetinghouses that they were able to use their portable fonts, which were attached to pulpits when needed or set permanently near the pulpit or communion table in accordance with the customs of the Reformed churches in Scotland and on the Continent.

The reading desk became an important article of furniture in the Church of England, primarily because on most Sunday mornings the entire service was conducted from it and the pulpit, except on Communion Sundays. It therefore had to be in a central position in the church where the priest could be heard best. Sometimes the desk stood alone. Sometimes it had the clerk's seat in front of it. Sometimes it was combined with the pulpit and clerk's seat to make a single piece of furniture. A combination of reading pew and pulpit became a pulpit with two storeys, of which there are extant examples in Halston Chapel, Shropshire and St. Ninian's, Brougham, Westmorland. When the clerk's seat, the reading desk, and the pulpit were combined, the "three-decker" was produced, of which there are extant examples in the churches of Parracombe, Devon; Kedington, Suffolk; and Coxwold, Yorkshire.[59] When the reading pew was a separate piece of furniture its position was on one side of the screen or chancel arch, or in a vast nave, where it might be placed against the first pillar; opposite it was the pulpit.

The desks had candlesticks attached to them. Pulpits often had an hourglass and at the back a wooden peg on which hung the parson's black gown which he wore while preaching. The clerk's seat occasionally had a music stand, since in parishes without any official choir he led the singing himself with a pitch pipe. There might also be a psalm-board attached to the pulpit.

The pews, of two types, were arranged about the pulpit and reading desk. The most common were the low-backed straight pews, or benches, many of which, especially in the west country, had carved ends. There are particularly fine examples of Renaissance heads in the carved benchends in Talland Church, Cornwall (c. 1537-1547),[60] and of Elizabethan roses and profiles in Milverton church, Somerset. The other type of pew developed in and popularised in the seventeenth century was the "box pew." It contained a small rectangular enclosure, with a seat on three sides and an opening on the fourth, with high sides and backs which permitted only the heads of the occupants to be seen. It has been

59 *Ibid.*, p. 75n.
60 Basil Clarke and John Betjeman, *English Churches*, plate 107.

369

said that their introduction was due to the desire of the Puritans to avoid such "high" liturgical gestures as bowing at the *Gloria* and at the name of Jesus, or turning to the east for the Gospel and the Apostles' Creed, without being detected by Laudian spies. The real reason was probably the purely functional one of enabling the pew's occupants to avoid draughts. Such distinctive and comfortable pews may also have carried a certain social cachet for their occupants, especially when the affluent were able to afford adding rails with curtains along the tops of these boxed pews for greater protection against draughts.

7. Anglican Adornment of Churches

It will come as no surprise that the adornment of Anglican churches was simple, even austere. Such one would expect from the iconoclasm of Edwardian days, but one might not have anticipated the erosion of neglect under Elizabeth. The neglect may even have been encouraged by the Puritan dislike of all aestheticism, which was guilty of association with Roman Catholicism. That, at least, was the implication of John Howson, chaplain to Queen Elizabeth and future Bishop of Oxford, in a sermon from Paul's Cross in 1598. Howson charged that covetous country gentry conveniently object to "idolatry" as a mask for their depredations. The result was, he complained, that "in Countrey Villages . . . the Churches are almost become . . . little better than hogstyes; for the best preparation at any high feast is a little fresh straw under their feete, the ordinary allowance for swine in their stye . . . and in cities and boroughes they are not like the Palaces of Princes as they were in the primitive church, but like a countrey hall, faire white limed, or a citizens parlour, at the best wainscotted; as though we were rather Platonists then Christians, who would neither have gold nor silver in their churches because it was *individiosa res*, and gave occasion to sacriledge."[61] These "irreligious Julianists" make a slender allowance to God, "like a Stoicks dinner, or Philosophers breakfast," consisting only of bare walls and roof to keep out the rain. Ironically, he observed, "Neither is it lawful to add any ornament . . . except perchance a cushion and a wainscot seate, for ones owne ease and credite."

Whatever the reasons—including iconoclasm, neglect, and con-

---

[61] *A Second Sermon preached at Pauls Crosse the 21. of May, 1598* (1598), sig. D3, cited in Millar Maclure, *The St. Paul's Cross Sermons, 1534-1642*, p. 133.

venience—the fact remains that Elizabethan churches were simple and bare compared with their appearance in the Middle Ages. The stained glass windows had not entirely disappeared, although the representations of the Deity and the saints had been removed, and increasingly clear glass was replacing coloured panes. The rood-lofts, with their carved and painted figures of the Christ, the Virgin and St. John, had been pulled down, and the painting of the doom on the tympanum had been whitewashed over. So also were all of the wall paintings of scenes in the life of the Virgin, or of St. Christopher bearing the Christ child. The pillars of the nave had had wooden or stone brackets with saints standing in the niches; all were torn out.

What was to replace all this aesthetic richness? Undoubtedly the two Gospel sacraments, with the affusion of water and the breaking of the bread and the libation of the wine, would stand out in solitary glory and not be lost in the fussy sacramentalia of medievalism. But were there no additions to the equipment of churches, apart from the utilitarian cover-patens and large communion cups, by the Tudor Church of England?

There were two: painted wooden boards bearing the Royal Arms, the Lord's Prayer, the Creed, and the Tables of the Ten Commandments, affixed by royal commandment, and the sculptured tombs placed there by rising families. The royal arms were generally set up on the tympanum where the rood had formerly stood, a most unfortunate position, since it implied that the worship of the sovereign had replaced the worship of Christ, a point not lost to Catholic critics of the Church of England such as Harding, and used in his controversy with Jewel. It was believed that the painted wooden boards gave a good indication of the ways of the Church of England, whose supreme governor was the sovereign, and which regarded the Lord's Prayer as a summary of devotion, the Decalogue as a summary of behaviour, and the Apostles' Creed as a summary of belief.

The Royal Arms, with their exotic animal supporters, the golden lion and silver greyhound, added a greatly needed touch of colour to the nave. In fact, although it accented the Erastianism of the Church of England, it was quite common in other Reformed and un-Reformed churches on the Continent to include the arms of monarchs or of local nobles in the churches.

The painted boards served a triple function. They demonstrated that the building was a church and was to be used for sacred pur-

371

poses; they informed the worshippers about the essentials of the Christian way of life; and they provided attractive decoration.[62]

The provision of sculptured tombs in churches had a much more secular intention, and was a particularly interesting Elizabethan phenomenon. Sculptors found a livelihood in fashioning the representations of the saints in medieval churches, and even of the tombs of monarchs, queens, prelates, and nobles and their ladies. With the advent of the Reformation, however, the wealth and iconographical possibilities of the old faith largely disappeared from England. The newly wealthy classes could not express their religious feeling in the old manner by the erecting or adornment of churches; they expressed it in terms of ancestor worship, itself an index of their own wealth and worth. They had to be large to be impressive, for the tomb-makers of the period were mainly uninspired. It was only in size, material, and richness of decoration that tombs could be distinctive, not in design or quality of carving. "By about 1600," writes Eric Mercer, "it was almost *de rigueur* for a landed family to have a series of magnificent tombs in the local church."[63]

So important was the concept of tombs as family properties by the middle of the sixteenth century, that the government could not enforce their desire for religious uniformity in reference to mortuary sculpture and its type of decoration. In Sussex there is a series of tombs with representations of religious scenes and themes abhorrent to the Reformers; they extend in date from the dissolution of the monasteries to the accession of Elizabeth. In old Selsey church there are representations of St. George and the Dragon and of the martyrdom of St. Agatha on the tomb of John Lews, who died in 1537, and his wife, Agas. Richard Sackville's monument, c. 1540, in West Hampnett, depicts the Trinity with the naked Son reclining lifeless in the arms of the Father, while John Gounter's monument of about 1557 at Racton shows the risen Christ.[64]

Medieval tombs often showed cadavers in shrouds, to remind the beholder that the body is only the fragile and corruptible prison of the soul. The medieval tomb with its plea for a prayer for the soul of the departed was much humbler than the inscription on the Elizabethan tombs, reciting the deceased's ancestry and achieve-

[62] See Edward Cardwell, *Documentary Annals of the Church of England*, 2 vols., I, 262; a royal letter of 1560 states the triple purpose of the required tables of the commandments to be set up in the east end of churches.

[63] *English Art, 1553-1625*, p. 218.

[64] These examples are provided by Mercer, *English Art*, pp. 219f.

ments. The medieval *Orate pro anima* was changed to *Memoriae sacrum*.[65] Elizabethans had dismissed the Catholic doctrine of purgatory as unscriptural, and prayers for the dead were thought to be superstitious; so the spectator was not to think of the deceased as he now is, but as he was in the prime of life. This the effigy portrait helped him to do. These Renaissance men and women are shown at the crest of the wave of life. The man is depicted in his robes of office and the woman in her matronly dignity. As the fashions changed they were to be shown, not lying down with their hands folded in prayer and pious resignation, but very much alive —kneeling with their progeny in prayer or even sitting as if in conversation in parallel niches. They were painted richly and gilded, to give them verisimilitude. Furthermore, by heraldry and inscriptions there was an endeavour to stress less the death of an individual than the survival of the family.[66]

It is also interesting that although prayers were no longer to be offered for the dead in the Elizabethan Church of England, the tombs of the dead continued to bear the shape of altars at which such prayers could be offered. The most popular design showed husband and wife facing each other across a prayer desk on their knees, with their sons and daughters behind or below them. Other figures on the tombs turned toward the visitor in the church, which seemed, at least to the dramatist Webster, unseemly and irreverent, as he records in *The Duchess of Malfi*:

> Princes' images on their tombs
> Do not lie, as they were wont, seeming to pray
> Up to heaven, but with their hands under their cheeks
> As if they died of the toothache; they are not carved
> With their eyes fixed upon the stars, but as
> Their minds were wholly bent upon the world,
> The self-same way they seem to turn their faces.[67]

Here, clearly, Elizabethan sacred art had become secular.

8. *Religious Influences on Domestic Art*

In the change in the character and inscriptions of tombs we have seen one example of the influence of religion—the negative influence of Protestantism causing disbelief in purgatory and of the utility of praying for the dead. Are there others, comparable

---

65 John Buxton, *Elizabethan Taste*, p. 136.
66 *Ibid.*, p. 142.   67 Act IV, scene ii, ll. 165-70.

to the restrictions imposed by Byzantine religion on art, forbidding sculpture because of its three dimensionality, banning all drama except that of the Liturgy itself, and prohibiting instrumental music, yet inspiring icons, mosaics, murals, and miniature ivory carvings?[68]

Certainly another negative influence was that of forbidding the painting on walls or windows of churches of representations of the Trinity and the saints, and of any incidents involving them. It helped to produce two positive effects, insofar as the Renaissance and the Reformation went together a considerable way. One positive effect was to drive painters to concentrate on portraits of the living with all the distinctive traits of an unique personality. While the Renaissance celebrated the man of distinction, the Reformation stressed the calling, significance, and dignity of every man as a cooperator with God. It is probably not without significance that the most private form of portrait painting, aiming at catching the secret, intimate, and personal life of the sitter so disregarded in the official oil paintings, was the miniature, or that Nicholas Hilliard, England's greatest miniaturist was a Protestant of the Protestants who had been a Marian exile.

A second influence Protestantism had on the development of art in England was to give a preference in domestic paintings, frescoes and tapestries, less for the pagan themes of a neoclassical art than for Biblical subjects. Moreover, with the growing ethical impact of Protestantism, and its delivery of individuals from a dependence on the mediation of the saints or on the priesthood in their approach to God, art turned from portraying the Madonna and the saints to the Biblical exemplars of faith.

Mural paintings are rare, because frescoes did not fare well in the damp English climate, and because there was probably a preference for either the cheaper painted cloths or the warmer tapestries on the walls. There are, however, in Queen Hoo Hall in Hertfordshire wall paintings of King Solomon worshipping false gods, and at Harvington Hall in Worcestershire can be detected the faint remains of battle scenes from the Old Testament.[69]

At the turn of the century and from 1600 to 1620, interior decoration of halls and houses was concentrated on the classics, on scientific interests, or on religious themes.[70] There were several

[68] Ernst Benz, *The Eastern Orthodox Church, Its thought and life*, tr. Richard and Clara Winston, from *Geist und Leben der Ostkirche*, p. 1.
[69] Buxton, *Elizabethan Taste*, p. 93. [70] Mercer, *English Art*, p. 124.

causes, including the continuity of religious themes from the Middle Ages to the end of the Tudor age. Such are to be seen in a plaster ceiling with a tree of Jesse found in a house in the Butterwalk at Dartmouth, or a scene reminiscent of the Last Judgment on the chimney piece in the Hall at Burton Agnes.[71] Protestantism brought the vernacular Bible into wide use, which was another important cause for the increasing fondness for Biblical decoration. There were favourite scenes from the Old and New Testaments incorporated in domestic decoration, such as Daniel in the den of lions at Stockton House, Wiltshire, or Samson and the gates of Gaza at the Old House in Sandwich. At this time, although politics were no longer shaped by religious criteria, ethics were still based on the appeal to Christianity, another reason for the popularity of religious themes in decor. New Testament themes were late on the scene. When they did come, they had a strong moral didacticism inherent in the selection of the theme. For example, the most popular themes were Dives and Lazarus, the Return of the Prodigal Son, the Good and the Bad Steward. It is the same ethical impulse that was responsible for the innumerable emblematic figures, especially of the virtues, which were displayed on ceilings, friezes, and overmantels. It is interesting that halls and mansions of any pretension which had mural decoration were almost always classical in theme, but that such small houses as Knightsland Farm at South Mimms (c. 1590), and the Swan Inn at Stratford (c. 1580) used Biblical and moral subjects.[72] The implication is that the gentry and merchants preferred Biblical and moral subjects for the decoration of their homes, while the courtiers were equally interested in the classics and the Bible.[73] One may suppose that some of the gentry and merchants were Puritans, who might find such representation distracting in church but didactic at home.

Such a supposition seems less wide of the mark when it is recalled that the leader of the Elizabethan Puritan party, the Earl of Leicester, had a notable collection of paintings at Leicester House in London, including about 50 portraits, a group of historical paintings, and several religious paintings. The later group included a *Nativity* ("Christ how he was born in an ox-stall"), a *St. John the Baptist preaching in the Wilderness*, a *Persecution of Saul* [is a *Conversion* of Saul intended, at the time of which the risen Christ is reported to have said, Saul, Saul, why persecutest thou me?], a *Mary Magdalene*, and such Old Testament scenes as

[71] *Ibid.* [72] *Ibid.*, p. 128. [73] *Ibid.*, p. 126.

Elijah taken up in the Fiery Chariot and *Noah and the Flood*. In other houses Leicester also had a *St. Jerome*, a *Deposition* from the cross, and a *St. John the Baptist* beheaded.[74] It is tantalising that we do not known who the Italian and Dutch painters of the works were. It is even more tantalising that we know so little of what other art collectors had gathered. But it is enough to show that although England had no artists of the highest quality in the visual arts, with the possible exception of Hilliard, her poets and dramatists were able to show that her imagination was not fettered by Protestantism, and, indeed, found the struggle between the old and the new faith, as between faith and science, issues worthy of the plays of Shakespeare and of the poems of Donne in which agape and eros fight over again the drama of religions and the Renaissance.

The chapter opened with a question which can now be answered, however tentatively. In matters of religious architecture English Protestantism was exceedingly conservative, building, rebuilding and adding exclusively in the Gothic style, but also adapting the Gothic interiors to the vernacular worship and without radical transformations. In liturgical furnishings there was a new functionalism and simplicity, and even a utilitarianism. In ecclesiastical decoration there was iconoclasm and almost total colour blindness, the carving of Tudor benches and choir stalls being the only general exception. In the matter of tombs secularity prevailed. The total effect was of the simplification of religious worship and instruction in an appropriately simplified church interior. The austerity was partly a conviction and partly the result of neglect. Surprisingly, while religious art was banished from the church, it made its way into the homes of the people who had the taste for it and who could afford it.

In the succeeding age High Anglicans would be the perceptive patrons of a richer ecclesiastical architecture and art, which is proof that Elizabethan religious art was not dead, but, like the daughter of Jairus, only sleeping.

74 Buxton, *Elizabethan Taste*, p. 100.

CHAPTER XI

CHURCH MUSIC

TWO STATEMENTS about sixteenth-century church music, itself a controversial subject, can be made. The first is that there was a great need for choral reform because of the chaos in musical practice. This was as readily agreed to by Roman Catholics as by Anglicans, Lutherans, and Calvinists. Second, there was disagreement about the best way to reform musical practice. Lutheran hymns and chorales, Anglican anthems and chants, and Calvinist psalmody were three different ways of meeting the need for change.

The early sixteenth-century situation in choral composition and singing is described by Stanford and Forsyth in writing of the time when unrelated themes were intermixed in the counterpoint in church music: "When the world turned topsy-turvy, and people first realized that music was not carpentering in 3-inch lengths, a sort of licentious orgy of music set in. It is difficult to explain with reverence just what happened. And if you want a modern analogy with the state of church music at that time, you may imagine one of our composers taking as his base an Anglican chant, and spreading it out so that each note occupied three or four bars; then for his treble using 'Take a pair of sparkling eyes' (*allegro con molto*), and for his alto part fitting in as much as he could of 'Tipperary' or 'Onward Christian Soldiers,' or both. . . . It has been described by contemporary sufferers, and if half what they say is true, it must have been like rag-time gone mad."[1] Further evidence of the seriousness of the situation is seen in the fact that the Council of Trent, in its meeting between 1545 and 1547, was disposed for a time to exclude music altogether from the service of the Roman Catholic church.[2] This drastic step was not taken, partly because of the worshipful and aesthetic music being produced for the Church by such Catholic musicians as Palestrina (himself one of the great figures of the Counter-Reformation), Orlando di Lasso, and Vittoria, and partly also because the Roman church refused to employ the Protestant remedy of vernacular hymns. In regard to the latter, however, it is interesting to recall that at the Council

1 Charles V. Stanford and Cecil Forsyth, *The History of Music*, p. 138.
2 Millar Patrick, *Four Centuries of Scottish Psalmody*, p. xxi.

of Trent the Emperor Ferdinand sought permission for the use of German hymns, as Cardinal Lorraine did for French hymns, but the Papacy used all its authority to suppress vernacular hymnody.

1. *Reformation Remedies*

It is, of course, impossible to understand Reformation remedies for the people's praise without first considering the diagnoses of the ills put forward by the leading Reformers, Luther[3] and Calvin.[4]

Luther had a great love of music, believing it to be a direct gift of God. He defended it against the iconoclasts, whose hatred of the Roman Catholic Mass was so unreasonable that they would have suppressed hymn-singing and organ-playing in religious services. Luther wrote in the preface to Walther's first collection of hymns in 1524: "I am not of the opinion that all the arts should be stricken down by the Gospel and disappear, as certain zealots would have it; on the contrary, I would see all the arts, and particularly music, at the service of Him who created them and gave them to us."[5] Luther's aim was not to suppress the Mass but to bring it within the spirit and scope of the gospel as he understood it. He wished it to be translated from Latin into German so the entire congregation would understand the words that priests and choristers were singing. As early as 1523 Luther wrote in the preface of the *Formula Missae et Communionis pro Ecclesia Wittembergensis*: "I also wish as many of the songs as possible to be in the vernacular, which the people should sing during Mass either immediately after the *Gradual*, and immediately after the *Sanctus* and *Agnus Dei*. For who doubts that once upon a time all the people sang these, which now only the choir sings or responds when the bishop is consecrating? But these songs may be ordered by the bishops in this manner, they may be sung either right after the Latin songs, or on alternate days, now Latin, now the vernacular, until the entire

---

[3] The following works are selected as introductions to the subject of Lutheran music: Christhard Mahrenholz, *Das evangelische Kirkengesangbuch. Ein Bericht uber seine Vorgeschichte*; Mahrenholz's *Luther und die Kirchenmusik*; Paul Nettl, *Luther and Music*; and Basil Smallman, *The Background of Passion Music*. See particularly the introduction to Luther's hymnody in vol. 35 of the Weimar *Ausgabe*.

[4] For Calvinistic music, which had a greater influence on English congregational music, see the following sources: Pierre Pidoux, *Le Psautier huguenot du 16e siècle*, 2 vols.; R. R. Terry, *Calvin's First Psalter* (1539); interpretations: O. Douen, *Clément Marot et le psautier huguenot*, 2 vols.; Charles Garside, Jr., *Zwingli and the Arts*; and Percy A. Scholes, *The Puritans and Music in England and New England*.

[5] Cited in Théodore Gérold's "Protestant Music on the Continent," The New Oxford History of Music, vol. 4: *The Age of Humanism 1540-1630*, ed. Gerald Abraham, p. 419.

Mass shall be made vernacular. But poets are wanting among us, — or they are not known as yet, — who can put together pleasingly pious and spiritual songs, as Paul calls them, which are worthy to be used by all the people in the Church of God."[6]

Luther made three striking contributions to the reform of worship: the recovery of the sermon (his own were marked by Biblical fidelity, a profound understanding of faith, vivid illustrations drawn from the observation of common life, and a marvellously racy and idiomatic German speech); the restoration of Communion to the people; and the introduction of German hymns, some of them written by him and set to Luther's own music.[7] An interesting development of the hymn was the chorale, in which portions of Scripture (especially narratives of the Passion of Christ) were sung with different voices representing the narrator (or evangelist), the principal characters, and the people's response. This particular development is to be found in embryo in Luther's *Deudsche Messe und Ordnung Gottis Diensts*[8] of 1526.

Luther's reforms were based on four principles. Worship was to be ruled by the shape and spirit of the gospel of Christ; its primary purpose is to create faith; it must be intelligible to produce the maximum participation of the people; and no liturgy was to be a law and hindrance to Christian freedom.[9]

Calvin, also, saw the need to deliver the common people from the two languages unintelligible to them—Latin and polyphony—and the need for two media which had to be found or created by those insistent on reform. What was necessary, in short, was "words which the people could understand, cast in a form in which they could without undue difficulty read or memorise them; and . . . music, of a type which they would be able to sing."[10] The major Protestant churches solved the double problem in the same way; they used versified texts set to simple melodies. The difference between Luther and Reformed church music depended, however, on two factors. The first was that the models for spiritual songs were different in each case. Luther used the customary verse forms,

---

6 See *Liturgies of the Western Church*, selected and ed. Bard Thompson, p. 119.
7 Gérold, "Protestant Music," pp. 422-23, lists five hymns (including the great "Ein feste burg is unser Gott"), the melodies and words of which were by Luther.
8 *Liturgies*, p. 132.
9 The dimension of Christian freedom in Luther, expressed in his wishing to prevent any Wittemburg liturgy from becoming a new liturgical law, and the primacy of faith, are finely brought out in Vilmos Vajta's interpretation, *Luther on Worship*, pp. 174f.
10 Millar Patrick, *Four Centuries of Scottish Psalmody*, p. 3.

stanzaic in form, which the German people were familiar with in the Latin hymns and in the vernacular songs of the day, both secular and sacred, permitting a succession of verses to be sung to the same melody. Second, while Calvin restricted the subject matter to the Psalms, Luther also used New Testament material and started the churches following his leadership on the path to Christian hymnody.

In 1537 Calvin and Farel, the reformers of the Genevan church, designed a scheme for introducing singing into worship, but before the plan took effect they were expelled from Geneva. While spending four years as pastor to the French Protestant church in Strassburg, Calvin's convictions about the importance of the people's praise were reinforced by the admirable congregational singing in the Lutheran churches in Strassburg, where the practice was then a decade old. Consequently he published a small volume of four sheets of 16 pages each, with the title *Aulcuns Pseaulmes et Cantiques / mys en chant. A Strasburg 1539.* This historic volume contained 17 Psalms in metre, five of which Calvin is believed to have composed;[11] the remaining 12 were the work of Clément Marot. Calvin persuaded Théodore Beza to complete the work, and the entire Huguenot Psalter was published in 1562. Its brilliance is not only in the literary quality, especially of Marot's religious verse, but also in its unique "ingenuity in using every kind of structural device to render impossible the monotony so characteristic of the Psalters used in England, Scotland, and America."[12] Calvin argued that the Psalter was also the book of Christian, as well as Jewish, praise, inspired by the Holy Spirit; to depart from it in themes as well as words, except insofar as the exigencies of rhyme and metre dictated, was presumptuous. Thus the Calvinist influence restricted both style and content in Christian praise much more than the Catholic or Lutheran influences and examples did. On the other hand, the solemnity of some English versions of the Psalms, sung to the melodies of Louis Bourgeois, were incomparable in their devotional depth and expression of the majesty of God and the humility of man *coram Dei.* Others were merely jogging doggerel.

---

[11] Psalms 25, 36, 46, 91, 138 and the additional versions of the Song of Simeon and the versified Decalogue, according to Douen, *Clément Marot.*

[12] Patrick, *Scottish Psalmody,* p. 19; see also Waldo S. Pratt, *The Music of the French Psalter of 1562: A Historical Survey and Analysis.*

2. Luther's Influence on English Worship and Praise

Luther's chief influence was in the gradual acceptance of the vernacular in English worship. The acceptance was so gradual that the English Litany of 1544 used for processions was the only form of service in the vernacular to be approved during the 38 years of Henry VIII's reign. Henry wished to use it to inspire patriotism in his wars with France and Scotland. This was not possible if the people did not understand and share in the worship, "forasmuch as heretofore the people, partly for lack of good instruction and calling, partly for that they understood no part of such prayers or suffrages as were used to be sung and said, have used to come very slackly to the Procession."[13] When the English Protestants got the opportunity to introduce changes in worship during the reign of the young Edward VI, they set to work immediately to produce a vernacular liturgy, which appeared two years after Edward VI succeeded. The Protector, Somerset, however, sent visitors within six months of the coronation to end all Popish practices and ceremonies in the cathedrals and churches. Their instructions reveal a great concern for intelligibility in worship, as also for simplicity, as they insisted on informed teaching and preaching, the reduction of candles and bell-ringings at Mass, and the use of English processions and Litany instead of the Latin.

The specific directions given at particular cathedrals further reinforced the desire for a comprehensible and uncomplicated liturgical style. At Winchester the singing of sequences was forbidden, and before Mass and evensong each day chapters from the Old and New Testaments were to be read to the choristers. At Canterbury sung Lady Mass was abolished on holy days so that a sermon or reading from the homilies could be substituted. At York the choir was forbidden to sing more than one Mass per day or to sing responds. It was instructed to replace Latin anthems or responds with English substitutes; it was also recommended that the services of the lesser hours, dirges, and "commendations" be ended.

The more iconoclastic Anglican Edwardian clergy such as Cranmer's chaplain, Thomas Becon, criticised at once the unintelligibility, oversubtlety, and expensiveness of Catholic music: "There

---

13 Cited in F. E. Brightman, *The English Rite*, 2 vols., I, lix. During the outgoing procession the Litany was sung, as also the Our Father, versicle, response and collect; during the returning procession there was sung the Anthem ("O Lord, arise . . ."), and before the choir steps the versicle, response, collects, which were followed by the Mass.

have been . . . which have not spared to spend much riches in nourishing many idle singing men to bleat in their chapels, thinking so to do God on high sacrifice . . . but they have not spent any part of their substance to find a learned man in their houses, to preach the word of God, to haste them to virtue, and to dissuade them from vice. . . . A Christian man's melody, after St. Paul's mind, consisteth in heart, while we recite psalms, hymns and spiritual songs, and sing to the Lord in our hearts. All other outward melody is vain and transitory, and passeth away and cometh to nought. . . . So ye perceive that music is not so excellent a thing, that a Christian ought earnestly to rejoice in it."[14] In fact, the Edwardian order of the day was the requirement for virtue rather than musical competence, as the 30th Article of the Royal Injunctions for St. George's Chapel, Windsor (February 8, 1550) clearly demonstrated:

Also, whereas heretofore when descant, prick-song, and organs were too much used . . . in the church, great search was made for cunning men in that faculty, among whom there were many that had joined with such cunning evil conditions, as pride, contention, railing, drunkenness, contempt of their superiors, or such-like vice, we intending to have Almighty God praised with gentle and sober quiet minds, and with honest hearts, and also the commonwealth served with convenient ministers, do enjoin from henceforth, when the room of any of the clerks shall be void, the Dean and prebendaries of this church shall make search for honest and quiet men, learned in the Latin tongue, which have competent voices and can sing, apt to study, and willing to increase in learning: so that they may be first deacons and afterwards admitted priests; having always more regard to their virtue and learning than to excellency in music. . . .[15]

The great simplification in church music that had come about in Edward VI's reign was indirectly an expression of Luther's concerns in worship. It is most conveniently seen in the difference between the 1549 and the 1552 prayer-books. The first Book of

[14] In Becon's *Jewel of Joy*, in *The seconde parte of the bokes which Thomas Beacon hath made* (1560), vol. 2, part 2, folio xiii. In the *Catechism of Thomas Becon*, ed. J. Ayre, p. 429, Becon stated: "To say the trueth, musycke is a more vayne and triefelynge science than it becommeth a man borne and appoynted to matters of gravitye, to spēde muche tyme about it."

[15] Frere and Kennedy, *Visitation Articles*, II, 775-76.

Common Prayer required in the Liturgy the following eight items to be sung: the Introit, the Kyrie (optional), Gloria in Excelsis, the Creed, the Offertory, the Sanctus, O Lamb of God, and Post-Communion. The second prayer-book required only a sung Gloria in Excelsis. The intensification of anti-Marian feeling during the reign of King Edward meant also that the Tudor composers lost "one of their most characteristically intimate forms of devotion—the motet in honour of the Blessed Virgin."[16] Even John Marbeck's *Book of Common Praier Noted* (1550) was unable to rouse any great enthusiasm, although its "quasi-mensural notion of unison chant should have satisfied the most ardent among the reformers."[17] It certainly attempted to put into practice Cranmer's desire for a simplicity that would take the form of a note to a syllable. Moreover, even in the reign of Elizabeth the general church music seemed to be characterised by "drabness,"[18] compared to the brilliant poetry of the age and the rich quality of the secular madrigals.

Clearly the chief influence of Luther was early and indirect, since it came through Martin Bucer and Peter Martyr, Regius Professors respectively in Cambridge and Oxford in Edward's time, in their help in the provision of the first English vernacular prayer-book. Neither they nor their sponsors in England followed Luther's explicit recommendation that choral music, together with the new congregational music, should be cultivated in the reformed churches and schools. Consequently (apart from the late Elizabethan cultivation of anthems and services, both developed in cathedrals and collegiate chapels, and not in parish churches), the congregational music of the English Reformed church followed the Calvinist rather than the Lutheran model.[19] The Elizabethan development of verse anthems can hardly be regarded as due to Lutheran influence, since it came so late (some 40 years after Luther's death. In any case they were limited to cathedral and collegiate churches; there was no provision for congregational participation. For the praise in parish churches the Calvinist impact was paramount.

16 Denis W. Stevens, *Tudor Church Music*, p. 19.
17 *Ibid.*, p. 55.
18 This term is used by Frank L. Harrison in "Church Music in England," *The New Oxford History of Music*, vol. 4: *The Age of Humanism, 1540-1630*, ed. Gerald Abraham, p. 470, to characterise all Elizabethan parish church music, except the music in cathedrals, collegiate churches, and a few schools such as Eton.
19 *Ibid.*, p. 465.

3. Calvin's Influence on English Praise

Although the decisive influence leading the directors of parish praise to accept metrical psalmody was Genevan, the initial impact in England was Lutheran. About 1539 there first appeared Myles Coverdale's *The Goostly psalmes and spirituall songs drawen out of the holy Scripture, for the conforte and consolacyon of soch as love to rejoyse in God and his worde.* It had a Lutheran character, not only because Coverdale and Luther had been Augustinian monks, but because it drew heavily on the Lutheran originals for title, introduction, words, and music. It contained 13 metrical psalms, together with metrical versions of the Magnificat, the Nunc Dimittis, Lord's Prayer, Creed, Decalogue, and over a dozen German and Latin hymns. None of the settings was harmonised. These metrical psalms were intended to be sung by the "lovers of Gods worde" at their homes or at their work, instead of "balettes of fylthynenes," and by children "in godly sports to passe theyr tyme." Coverdale wrote: "Yee [a] wolde God that our mynstrels had none other thynge to playe upon, neither our carters and plowmen other thynge to whistle upon, save Psalmes, hymnes, and soch godly songes as David is occupied with all. And yf women syttinge at theyr rockes [distaffs] or spynninge at the wheles, had none other songes to passe theyr tyme withall, than soch as Moses sister, Elchanas wife, Debbora, and Mary the mother of Christ have song before them, they shulde be better occupied, than with hey nony nony, hey troly loly, & soch lyke fantasies."[20]

The origin of the influential Huguenot Psalter, to which English and Continental congregational praise owed so much, is paradoxical. Sir Richard Terry observed that there was no more ironic historical development than "the chain of circumstances which led to metrical psalmody beginning as the favourite recreation of a gay Catholic court and ending as the exclusive 'hall-mark' of the severest form of Protestantism."[21]

It was the great and growing popularity of metrical psalmody that matters for our purposes, rather than its secular origins. Still, as R. E. Prothero recounts the story,[22] when Marot's *Psalms* first appeared, they were sung to the popular airs of the day by Catholics and Calvinists. The Dauphin (the future Henry II) loved the

---

[20] Cited by Morrison Comegys Boyd, *Elizabethan Music and Musical Criticism,* pp. 39-40.

[21] *Calvin's First Psalter* (1539), ed. R. R. Terry, p. iii.

[22] *The Psalms in Human Life,* p. 137.

sanctes chansonnettes, singing them, setting them to music, encouraging the adoption of a particular psalm as a motto for each leading courtier. Henry sang Psalm 42 (Like as the hart desireth the water-brooks; *Sicut cervus . . .*) as he hunted the stag in the forest of Fontainebleau, riding by the side of his favourite, Diane of Poitiers, for the motto of whose portrait as a huntress he selected the first verse of his favourite psalm. In France, says Prothero, "the metrical version of the Psalter, in the vulgar tongue, was one of the principal instruments in the success of the Reformed church."[23] So much was this so, where the children were taught to learn the metrical psalms by heart, that to chant psalms meant in popular parlance to turn Protestant. They fired Huguenot soldiers, as later they were to encourage Cromwellian troops in battle; they were equally potent sources of spiritual strength in defeat or in humiliation. It is to Calvin's credit that he edited the first printed edition of metrical psalms for church worship. Through this influence metrical psalmody became the people's praise par excellence, not only in the parish churches of England, but also in their open-air demonstrations and in their homes.

Calvin's attitude toward the metrical psalms was best expressed in his preface to the Genevan edition of Marot's Fifty Psalms, together with a liturgy and catechism, in June 10, 1543, where he said: "Nous ne trouvons meilleurs chansons ne plus propres pur ce faire, que les pseaumes de David, lesquels le sainct Esprit luy a dictez et faits."[24] The French Psalter contained great poetry, sublime music by Bourgeois, Greiter, and Franc, for which Goudimel made four-part settings.[25] Bourgeois was also fond of singing in parts, which Calvin resisted, partly because of the printing expenses involved, and probably also because harmonic practice was then in a state of flux.[26] It may be guessed that it was the music that carried the Calvinistic theology into the hearts of the people through the powerful sense of faith and utter trust in God as expressed so personally in the metrical psalmody. This view led Robert Bridges to write: "Historians who wish to give a true philosophical account of Calvin's influence at Geneva ought probably to refer a great part of it to the enthusiasm attendant on the singing of Bourgeois's melodies."[27]

The English success of the metrical psalms, both in the eager-

[23] *Ibid.*, p. 138. [24] *Ibid.*, pp. 140-41.
[25] Gérold, "Protestant Music," p. 443. [26] Patrick, *Scottish Psalmody*, p. 19.
[27] Cited in Percy Dearmer, *Songs of Praise Discussed*, p. 391.

ness with which versions poured out of the presses and in the use made of them, was comparable to the Genevan. John Jewel's testimony to their popularity in a letter to Peter Martyr sent from London on March 5, 1560 is impressive: "Religion is now somewhat more established than it was. The people are everywhere exceedingly inclined to the better part. The practice of joining in church music [the psalms] has very much helped us. For as soon as they had once begun singing in public, in only one little church in London, immediately not only the churches in the neighbourhood, but even in the towns far distant began to vie with each other in the same practice. You may sometimes see at St. Paul's Cross, after the service, six thousand persons, old and young, of both sexes, all singing together and praising God. This sadly annoys the Mass priests and the devil. For they perceive by these means the sacred discourses sink more deeply into the minds of men, and that their kingdom is weakened and shaken up at almost every note. . . ."[28]

Further evidence of the popularity of the metrical psalms was the many editions published during the Elizabethan period. Between 1560 and 1579 at least 20 different editions of Sternhold and Hopkins came out, while between 1580 and 1599 there were 45.[29]

4. Sternhold and Hopkins—The "Old Version"

Pre-Sternholdian psalmody is of little significance. Coverdale was too dependent on German sources and too Lutheran in doctrine to suit Henrician church needs, while the more academic experiments of the poets Surrey and Wyatt were no more suitable for common worship than the later versions of Spenser. It was Sternhold's version, completed by Hopkins, that best supplied the need for church and domestic psalmody in metre.

Sternhold produced his first edition, with 19 metrical psalms, probably in 1548, as a minor courtier. The third edition of 1551 contained 37 psalms of his and seven by Hopkins, the schoolmaster who supplemented his work. It was not until 1562, however, that John Daye published *The Whole Booke of Psalmes collected into Englysh metre, by T. Starnhold, I. Hopkins, and others*. Thereafter the ensuing editions of the Old Version were the composite

---

[28] *Zurich Letters*, II, 71. See a slightly different version of the letter in Jewel's *Works*, ed. Ayre, IV, 1,231.

[29] The figures are taken from E. B. Schnapper, *The British Union Catalogue of Early Music printed before 1801*.

work of Sternhold, Hopkins, Whittingham, Wisedome, William Kethe, and John Craig. They remained in vogue until the "New Version" of Tate and Brady supplanted them in 1698.

Influential as the compilation was, it was, alas, often no more than divinity couched in the sorriest doggerel. The droll Fuller rightly estimated that the versifiers had drunk more of Jordan than of Helicon, adding that two hammerers on a smith's anvil would have made better music.[30] Queen Elizabeth disliked the new "Genevan jigs," as did the poets. Edward Phillips, Milton's nephew and himself a minor poet and Cavalier, described someone as singing with a "wofull noise":

> Like a crack'd saints' bell jarring in the steeple
> Tom Sternhold's wretched prick-song for the people.

The witty and dissolute Earl of Rochester had little time for the Puritans or their psalmody, as the following squib suggests, when he heard a clerk lining out a psalm:

> Sternhold and Hopkins had great Qualms,
> When they translated David's Psalms,
>   To make the heart full glad:
> But had it been poor David's fate
> To hear thee sing and them translate,
>   By God 'twould have made him mad![31]

How poor, in fact, was the work of Sternhold and Hopkins? It was awkward and obvious, but at times capable of a sustained dignity, as in Psalm I, verses 3 and 4, which celebrate the righteous man:

> He shall be lyke the tree that groweth
>   fast by the river side:
> Which bringeth forth most pleasant frute
>   in her due tyme and tyde.
> Whose leaf shall never fade nor fall,
>   but florish still and stand:
> Even so all thinges shall prosper well
>   that this man takes in hand.

The inspired Pegasus is often hobbled, as in Psalm XVI, in a complaint against idolaters:

[30] Thomas Fuller, *The Church History of Britain* (1655), IV, 73.
[31] Both versified comments on Sternhold and Hopkins were derived from R. E. Prothero's *The Psalms in Human Life*, p. 113.

> They shall heape sorrows on their heads,
>   which runne as they were mad:
> To offer to the Idols gods
>   alas it is too bad.

Perhaps the greatest achievement was Sternhold's version of the "Old Hundredth," which begins: "All people that on earth do dwell." Hopkins reaches the greatest heights in Psalm XVIII:

> The Lord descended from above
>   and bowd the heavens hie;
> And underneath his feete hee cast
>   the darkness of the skie.
> On Cherubs and on Cherubins
>   full royally he rode
> And on the winges of all the windes
>   came flying all abrode.

These are lines worthy of being illustrated by William Blake.

Despite the frequency of Double Common Metre, the inversions, the very obviousness of the plain rhymes, they were easily memorised and fitted to simple tunes for ordinary worshipers. They were, in fact, used with great delight in church and at home and entirely fulfilled the hopes of the subtitle of the 1566 edition: "allowed to be soong of the people together, in churches, before and after morning and evening prayer: as also before and after the Sermon, and moreover in private houses, for their godly solace and comfort, laying apart all ungodly songes and ballades, which tend only to the nourishing of vice, and corrupting of youth."

Unfortunately the old modal tunes and most of those originating from Geneva, which had been conserved in the Anglo-Genevan Psalter of 1566, 1568, and 1560, were increasingly dropped from the successive editions of Sternhold and Hopkins. The return to a heavy style was due in all probability to the demand of the Reformers for a style of music encouraging distinct articulation of the words, with one note to a syllable, and also to Cranmer's requirement that the harmonising should be note against note—that is, in plain chords.[32] The greatest criticism that can be made of the English metrical psalmody, both words and music, was the monotony it induced. As W. H. Frere remarked: "The English tradition

---

[32] Patrick, *Scottish Psalmody*, pp. 39-40.

hardly ever got away from the jog-trot of D. C. M."[33] Its chief advantage was that it provided for the people of the average parish church an easily memorised set of rhymes and tunes, thus returning to the common people the privileges snatched from them by professional choirs singing complex polyphonic motets and anthems.

Sternhold and Hopkins did not have the field of metrical psalmody to themselves by any means. But no other compilation matched theirs in popularity. Robert Crowley's *Psalter of David newly translated into Englysh metre* (1549) was the first complete English metrical Psalter, and the first to contain harmonised music, although it was restricted to a single chant-like tune. The first Sternhold and Hopkins with music was published in Geneva in 1556 as *One and Fiftie Psalmes of David*. In later editions of this Anglo-Genevan Psalter (so-called because it was prepared for the use of English Protestant refugees in Geneva under the joint ministry of Goodman and Whittingham, also the editor of the Geneva Bible), Whittingham and Kethe broke away from standard common and double metre and thus broke some of the monotony. In 1567 Archbishop Parker issued his psalter privately. In the preface he explained that friends had persuaded him to publish it along with the tunes Thomas Tallis had composed to go with it. Parker urged that a sad tune accompany a sad psalm and a joyful tune a joyful psalm. He then provided a versified reaction to Tallis's tunes:

> The first is meek, devout to see,
> The second, sad, in majesty,
> The third doth rage, and roughly brayeth,
> The fourth doth fawn, and flattery playeth,
> The fifth delighteth, and laugheth the more,
> The sixth bewaileth, it weepeth full sore,
> The seventh tradeth stout, in forward race,
> The eighth goeth mild, in modest pace.

Tallis's brilliant and imaginative pupil, William Byrd, also produced several psalm tunes of great delight. In 1588 he published *Psalmes, Sonets and songs of sadness and pietie*, which included 10 metrical psalms, 7 devotional songs, and 16 secular compositions. A year later there appeared his *Songs of sundrie natures*, including three-part settings of the penitential psalms, and 8

---

33 In the introduction to the historical edition of *Hymns Ancient and Modern*. "D.C.M." is Double Common Metre.

anthems (3 of which were in verse form). The psalms were appropriately set in the minor modes. In 1611 Byrd published *Psalms Songs and Sonnets*, which included 2 fine verse anthems, "O God that guides" and the penitential prayer, "Have mercy upon me," as well as further psalm tunes of great richness and solemnity.[34]

The psalm tunes were the work not only of the masters such as Tallis and Byrd, but also of many minor composers of the day, who also paid tribute to the popularity of this simple musical genre. Among those who produced collections of psalm tunes were Cosyn (1585), Daman (1591), East (1592, which contained settings by Farmer, Kirkby, Allison, Farnaby, Dowland, Cobbold, Johnson, and Cavendish), and Barley (1599).[35] There was no lack of metrical psalmody or tunes for psalms.

One question remains: why was popular praise limited to metrical psalmody? Why were there so few hymns produced in the Tudor age in England and those not of a popular character? Certainly it was not for lack of archiepiscopal support. For a letter of Cranmer's, written on October 7, 1544 or 1545, to King Henry VIII shows that he had translated the Latin hymn *Salva festa dies* into English and expected the king to appoint a better translator.[36] Yet in the successive editions of the Book of Common Prayer the only hymns included were translations of the *Veni Creator* in the Ordinal. Translations of ancient hymns were no new phenomena, either. Rough translations of Latin hymns were frequent in the pre-Reformation Sarum primers; they were to be found in the primers of Henry VIII, which were scrutinised by Cranmer.

Did the growing influence of Calvinism repress the production of hymns?[37] This is a strong possibility, considering the influence of the returning exiles from Geneva and other Reformed centres at the crucial beginning of Elizabeth's reign, or the importance of Puritanism during the last three decades of her reign. What is indubitable is that the Sternhold and Hopkins Old Version quickly acquired an almost canonical authority, and dominated the field to the virtual exclusion of experiments on the Lutheran or Latin models, which had seemed promising only two decades before. Not only did the metrical psalms lie to hand, but it was only too

[34] Peter Le Huray, *Music and the Reformation in England, 1549-1660*, pp. 371ff.

[35] Percy Young, *A History of British Music*, p. 152.

[36] Cranmer, *Works*, ed. Jenkyns, II, 412.

[37] This is the view of C. S. Phillips, in *Hymnody Past and Present*, p. 153; and H.A.L. Jefferson, in *Hymns in Christian Worship*, p. 32.

easy to find tunes for common metre verses. Perhaps the decisive reason for the failure of hymns to develop was the strong sixteenth-century sense in nascent Protestantism of "the Bible and the Bible only" as the liturgical, doctrinal and moral criterion. To develop original hymns of Christian experience would have seemed a human impertinence when God had already provided approved forms of praise in the Psalms. If it were argued that the New Testament Canticles were also approved sources of hymnody, some Protestants would have answered that our circumstances do not match those of the Blessed Virgin in the *Magnificat* nor of Simeon in the *Nunc Dimittis*, so these songs are not suitable for repetition.[38] Even if the point were conceded, it could yet be argued that it gave Elizabethans no authority for making their own transcripts of Christian experience into parts of public worship.

The only traces of Tudor hymnody left in modern English hymnbooks are poems recently made to serve the purpose of common praise for which their high individual lyrical or meditative quality made them unsuitable. "Most glorious Lord of life" is a Spenserian sonnet which now appears as No. 283 in the *English Hymnal*, while Shakespeare's "Poor soul, the centre of my sinful earth" appears inappropriately in *Songs of Praise* (No. 622). Edmund Campion's moving song, "Never weather-beaten sail," is also included in *Songs of Praise* (No. 587). Three other poems, however, are included in *Songs of Praise* which seem more suitable as hymns—Campion's "Sing a song of joy" (No. 639); Thomas Gascoigne's "You that have spent the silent night" (No. 38); and Sir Henry Wotton's "How happy is he born and taught" (No. 524).[39]

For the best English Church music in Elizabethan times one had to go to the cathedrals, the collegiate churches, and the Queen's Chapel. There one could find music fit to match the brilliance of the poetry of the period.

5. Music in the Great Churches

Although great music was composed for the Church of England in Elizabethan and Stuart times, the Church played only a minor role in the general musical life of the country. Madrigals and masques were greatly preferred to motets. The choral music of

---

[38] This was, in fact, a point of the polemic of the Puritans against the use of the Canticles of the New Testament.

[39] Sir Philip Sidney's exquisite "Lord in me there lieth naught" is a paraphrase of Psalm 139 rather than a hymn. It appears in *Songs of Praise* (no. 605).

Elizabethan England was cultivated mainly by professional musicians in cathedrals and in a few other endowed churches.[40] As Walter Woodfill observed, "However much psalms were sung in the parish churches, the fine religious choral music of the age was virtually the monopoly of some two dozen cathedrals, royal peculiars such as Westminster, the principal colleges of Oxford and Cambridge, and schools such as Eton."[41]

It was in the cathedrals and abbeys of the old faith that the most glorious choral music was to be heard. Oddly enough, it was a loyal Catholic, William Byrd, who composed the best church music in Elizabethan days, who had protested in his will that he hoped "to live and dye a true and p[er]fect member of his holy Catholycke Church wthout wch I beeleve theire is no Salvation."[42] For a time it looked as if the rich and ancient tradition of choral singing might die out. Peter Le Huray, for example, thought the Protestant iconoclasts of Edward VI's reign might have swept it away, had not the Catholic Mary rescued it by her accession. "Is it," he asked, "too fanciful to see in the accession of a Catholic monarch, its ultimate salvation?"[43]

Several divines were anxious to revise the Book of Common Prayer in a more Protestant direction, especially Archbishop Holgate of York, Bishop Ridley of London, and Bishop Hooper of Gloucester. Their view was that choral and instrumental music was of little value in worship, and they reduced it where they could. The Royal Injunctions for St. George's Chapel, Windsor (February 8, 1550), were straws in the wind of iconoclasm:

> Article 27: Also, because the great number of ceremonies in the church are now put away by the King's Majesty's authority and act of Parliament, so that fewer choristers be requisite, and the College is now otherwise more changed than it hath been, we enjoin from henceforth there shall be found in this College only ten choristers. . . .[44]

This was, in fact, extending the process of reducing the choral establishments which had begun with the spoliation of the monasteries and continued with the abolition of the chantries.

---

[40] Woodfill, *Musicians in English Society from Elizabeth to Charles I*, p. 153. See also the authoritative monograph by Edmund H. Fellowes, *English Cathedral Music from Edward VI to Edward VII.*

[41] Woodfill, *Musicians*, p. 156.

[42] Cited in Young, *British Music*, p. 144.

[43] Le Huray, *Music and the Reformation*, p. 29.

[44] Frere and Kennedy, *Visitation Articles*, II, 224.

Unquestionably the Catholic services had given the composer greater and more frequent opportunities for choral compositions than the Protestant composer ever had. The imposing ceremonial of High Mass in the Sarum Use demanded music of great dignity and rich complexity. Every third day was a festal occasion, and every day the Daily Office (especially matins and vespers) generated a need for solemn settings for antiphons, hymns, responsories, and canticles. Choirs were now smaller than in pre-Reformation days, partly because of the royal confiscation of ecclesiastical lands and revenues and partly because of inflation. Even so, the great churches often retained a choir of 20 voices; where they were thinner, they were helped by organs, lutes, and hautboys. In a pinch the choirmaster could manage with 16 voices, because the norm of later Tudor texture was to require five-voice parts.[45]

The basic question is, how much of the venerable choral tradition inherited from Catholicism, which had been repudiated so decisively in the parish churches by the satisfaction with psalmody of a metrical kind, survived in the great churches in the reigns of Edward and Elizabeth? It must be made clear at the outset that there were large problems to be faced, even supposing there had been the financial and musical resources necessary to maintain the tradition. It was difficult, though not impossible, to fit English texts to music previously composed for Latin texts, for English is a stress language and Latin a quantitative language. The difficulty had, indeed, been surmounted in paraliturgical ways by the provision of vernacular carols for Christmas and Easter and other festivals.[46] It was even popular to mix Latin and the vernacular since the days of the macaronic songs of the Goliards.

A second problem was to fit English choral music into Cranmer's "contortions," that is, his demand that each syllable of a word should be represented by a musical note. According to Denis Stevens, Cranmer confused the musico-liturgical functions of homophony and polyphony.[47] Cranmer had prescribed that the new

---

[45] Stevens, *Tudor Church Music*, p. 13. Fayrfax, the famous composer who died in 1521, and had been associated with the Abbey of St. Albans, wrote music in five parts. On the other hand, a Scottish priest and contemporary, Robert Carver, composed a motet, *O bone Jesu*, with 19 voice parts in the acclamations.

[46] This problem was not, however, an entirely new one, nor insuperable, for the paraliturgical forms such as carols for Christmas and Easter had been closely bound up with the vernacular since the mid-fifteenth century; it was fashionable to mix Latin and vernacular texts as in the macaronic songs.

[47] Stevens, *Tudor Church Music*, p. 18.

style of church music was not to be "full of notes [i.e. melismatic] but, as near as may be, for every syllable a note."[48] In making this suggestion Cranmer was proposing music for a processional litany, for which it was appropriate. But for nonprocessional choral pieces it was wholly unsuitable. Furthermore, since processions in Edward's time were thought to be either superstitious or unnecessary by the reforming party, the projected English version of the Sarum *Processionale* came to nothing.[49]

Yet Cranmer's influence was not inoperative. Two of the Wanley part-books[50] contain 10 communion services dating from the last decade of Henry VIII's reign, but only two attempted to follow Cranmer's directions. The chief monument to Cranmer's ideals of music is, of course, Merbecke's *The Book of Common Praier Noted* (1550).

This work helped to resolve some of the difficulties of Anglican musicians. It was the work of a composer of decided Protestant leanings, who, in fact, in Henry's reign had only been reprieved from the stake at the last minute for publishing Protestant writings and for preparing a concordance of the Bible. By the same token, he was *persona gratissima* to Northumberland and Cranmer in Edward VI's reign; his book was published by Richard Grafton, printer to the King's Majesty. From the year of his escape from death in 1543 until his death in 1585, he remained a member of the musical staff at St. George's, Windsor. Like the Prayer-Book, Merbecke's music was intended to be used by congregations. Its best quality was that the music for the Mass and the Divine Office was "singable and never difficult."[51] A typical English compromise, it was reminiscent of plainsong, but of a gambolling Gregorian, with all the rhythmic mannerisms of the period.[52]

The duration of the prayer-book was brief, and not only because of difficulty in singing it.[53] It was unfortunate that Merbecke had prepared his music for what turned out to be only an interim rite. Two years later the text of the second prayer-book was modified

---

[48] Cited E. H. Fellowes, *English Cathedral Music*, p. 25.

[49] *Ibid.*, p. 18.

[50] In the Bodleian Library, Oxford (MS Mus. Sch. E 420-422).

[51] C. Henry Phillips, *The Singing Church*, p. 61.

[52] For example, if a long note is surrounded by shorter notes, it requires the accent, and a high note is accented if placed in the midst of low notes and vice versa.

[53] Phillips, *Singing Church*, p. 62, says: "a modern performance shows it can easily be sung by the uninitiated."

too greatly to permit Merbecke's music to be retained. The swift onset of Mary's reign a year after the second Book of Common Prayer left the composer with insufficient time or spirit for revision, even if he had intended such. The appropriate eulogy was provided by C. Henry Phillips: "The failure of the book to be retained as a singers' handbook was a blow to congregational worship and so also to the intention of the reformers to create a congregational service. From now on only the service without the music can be described as congregational."[54]

If the prospect for the great choral tradition in ecclesiastical music was bleak in Edward's reign, was it better in Elizabeth's? While the Elizabethan prayer-book was practically a reprinting of the austere book of 1552, its ceremonial was a return to the 1549 book with its more 'Catholic' ornaments. The removal of the "black rubric" offered no consolation for either extreme Protestants or incipient Puritans. Indeed, the criticisms of the returning Protestant exiles were anticipated in the following Royal Injunction of 1559 concerning music:

49. *Item*, because in divers Collegiate and also some parish Churches, heretofore there have been livings appointed for the maintenance of men and children to use singing in the church, by means whereof the laudable science of music has been had in estimation, and preserved in knowledge: the Queen's Majesty, neither meaning in any wise the decay of anything that might conveniently tend to the use and continuance of the said science, neither to have the same so abused in the church, that thereby the common prayer should be the worse understood of the hearers, willeth and commandeth, first that no alterations be made of such assignments of living, as heretofore hath been appointed to the use of singing or music in the Church, but that the same so remain. And that there be a modest distinct song, so used in all parts of the common prayers in the Church, that the same may be as plainly understood, as if it were read without singing, and yet nevertheless, for the comforting of such that delight in music, it may be permitted that in the beginning, or in the end of common prayers, either at morning or evening, there may be sung an Hymn, or such like song, to the praise of Almighty God, in the best sort of melody and music that may be con-

54 *Ibid.*

395

veniently devised, having respect that the sentence of the Hymn may be understood and perceived. . . .[55]

It should be noted that the emphasis on hearing and understanding the words met the Puritan concern, and that the proponents of metrical psalmody interpreted the latter as falling within the definition of a "hymn." Otherwise, the entire, widespread practice of singing metrical psalms was unauthorised. Certainly Puritanism may have been partly responsible for the depreciation of choral music, but hardly for the despising of church music. Bishop Robert Horne of Winchester (a Marian exile) prepared an injunction in 1571 that smacked of Puritanism:

> 6. *Item*, that in the choir no more shall be used in song that shall drown any word or syllable, or draw out in length or shorten any word or syllable, otherwise than by the nature of the word it is pronounced in common speech, whereby the sentence cannot be well perceived by the hearers. And also the often reports or repeating of notes with words or sentences, whereby the sense may be hindered in the hearer, shall not be used.[56]

As a result of the research of Percy A. Scholes, it is now recognised that the Puritans have been greatly maligned as haters of music.[57] They believed in congregational music but not in elaborate and costly polyphonic music sung by choirs filching the rights of the congregation.

Whatever the reasons—musical or financial poverty, inflation, or a narrow Biblicism that restricted popular praise to psalmody—the result in the early years of Elizabeth's reign has been described as a "decline in musical standards,"[58] or as "drabness."[59] The marvel is that the situation should have improved so markedly later in the reign.

Some idea of the standards of music in the Royal Chapels may be guessed from the following account of St. George's Chapel, Windsor in 1575, when the queen was in residence, by the secretary of the visiting Duke of Württemberg: "The castle stands upon a knoll or hill. In the outer court is a very beautiful and spacious church, with a low flat roof covered with lead, as is

[55] Frere and Kennedy, *Visitation Articles*, III, 22-23.
[56] *Ibid.*, III, 319.
[57] In his *The Puritans and Music in England and New England*; and in his edition of *The Oxford Companion to Music*, pp. 756-68.
[58] Le Huray, *Music and the Reformation*, p. 39.
[59] See note 18 above.

common with all churches in England. In this church his highness listened for more than an hour to the beautiful music, the usual ceremonies, and the English sermon. The music, and especially the organ, was exquisite. At times could be heard cornets, then flutes, then recorders, and other instruments. And there was a little boy who sang so sweetly, and lent such charm to the music with his little tongue, that it was really wonderful to listen to him. Their ceremonies indeed are very similar to those of the papists, with singing and so on. After the music, which lasted a long time, a minister or preacher ascended the pulpit for the sermon, and soon afterwards, it being noon, his highness went to dinner. . . ."[60] Further evidence for the improved attitude to music as the reign developed is to be found in Richard Hooker's paean to music. Music is apt, he averred, for all occasions—"as seasonable in grief as in joy; . . . as decent, being added unto actions of the greatest weight and solemnity, as being used when men most sequester themselves from action . . . a thing which all Christian Churches in the world have received, a thing which so many ages have held, . . . a thing which always heretofore the best men and wisest governors of God's people did think they never could commend enough. . . ." Hooker questioned whether "there is more cause to fear lest the want thereof be a maim, than the use a blemish, to the service of God."[61]

The queen would have agreed with Hooker that music was never to be commended enough by the "wisest governors of God's people," among whom she counted herself. Her love of music was intelligent and informed. John Buxton was right in thinking that, "in her judgment the music which was composed for her Chapel Royal or for private enjoyment was a greater glory to her realm than the poetry written for her court, or the plays written for the London theatres."[62] The queen had 60 musicians in her service, both singers in the Chapel Royal and instrumentalists. The Chapel Royal counted among its musicians such distinguished composers as Tallis and Tye (the founders of English cathedral music), Mundy, Byrd, Morley, Bull, Tomkins and Orlando Gibbons. As a mark of her favour, Queen Elizabeth gave the exclusive right to print musical scores jointly to Tallis and Byrd, and later to Morley. Similarly King Henry VIII had arranged at the dissolu-

60 Le Huray, *Music and the Reformation*, pp. 80-81, using as his source, W. B. Rye, *England as seen by Foreigners*.
61 *Ecclesiastical Polity*, Book v, secs. 38-39.
62 Buxton, *Elizabethan Taste*, p. 173.

tion of Waltham Abbey in 1540 for Tallis to be taken into the Chapel Royal, as he had recognised the ability of Christopher Tye. Royal musical patronage showed a considerable insight into musicians and interest in church music.

6. The Leading Composers

Literature is a national, music an international, art. It is a pity that the fame of poets and dramatists such as Shakespeare and Marlowe, Ben Jonson and Webster, has eclipsed the international fame of such composers as William Byrd and Thomas Morley. For example, in 1583 the madrigalist Filippo di Monte sent Byrd a setting for eight voices for the opening of the 137th Psalm, *Super flumina*, to which compliment Byrd replied by sending his own setting of *Quomodo cantabimus* from the same psalm.[63] A few years later Morley's work was published in Germany soon after it had been issued in England, and Dowland was for several years lutenist to King Christian IV of Denmark.

One of the interesting facts about the greatest Elizabethan composers is that several of them were Catholics, including Tallis,[64] Byrd, and Morley. Yet they held office in the Chapel Royal of a Protestant queen. As Tallis was Byrd's teacher, so Byrd was Morley's teacher. As long as they fulfilled their musical duties with satisfaction the queen allowed them to think and compose as they pleased. They were able to fulfill their duties with comparative ease. In the Anglican communion service they had to provide music for the *Kyrie* and *Creed* only. For morning and evening prayer the canticles to be set to music were the *Venite*, the *Te Deum*, *Benedictus* (or *Jubilate*), the *Magnificat* and *Nunc Dimittis*. There was ample time, if the spirit was willing, in which to compose hymns or to adapt Latin motets to English texts.

Thomas Tallis (c. 1505-1585), the teacher of Byrd, was second only to his pupil in fame in sixteenth-century England. Today he is remembered chiefly as the composer of the simple harmonisations of the responses in the prayer-books of the Anglican church. Little is known about his life. He was organist of Waltham Abbey when Henry VIII decided to transfer him to the Royal Chapel, and his music reflected its pre-Reformation inspiration in many Latin motets, its post-Reformation utility in the form

---

[63] *Ibid.*, p. 171.

[64] Tallis is generally thought of as a Catholic (e.g. Stevens, *Tudor Church Music*, p. 22), but I owe to Dr. A. L. Rowse the suggestion that the form of Tallis's will indicates that he died a Protestant.

of English anthems. Tallis's five-part *Salvator mundi* and short anthem, "Hear the voice and prayer," have been revived with great acceptance in our own day. The former manages to be nobly serene and moving at the same time. His ingenious and varied output of high quality included five English anthems published in Daye's *Certain Notes* (1560-1563), a few Latin Services, about 50 motets, some of which were published in a joint work with Byrd in 1575, entitled, *Cantiones Sacrae*. Perhaps his most amazing composition was a motet in 40 parts, which ended with the words, *respice humilitatem nostram*, and was an astonishing musical contradiction of the theme of humility. It has been described by Sir Henry Hadow as "an ocean of moving and voluminous sound."[65]

William Byrd (1543-1623) was the most renowned composer of his day. He was, by common consent, the most distinguished musician from the Reformation to the Restoration. Born probably in Lincolnshire, Byrd was organist of Lincoln cathedral at the age of 20 and joint organist with Tallis of the Royal Chapel after 1569. He was the founder of the rich English madrigal tradition; as a liturgical composer he was thought to be the equal of Palestrina and Lassus.[66] An excellent teacher, his pupils included Thomas Morley, Orlando Gibbons, and John Bull.

Byrd was the first famous English composer to have his works published to any extent in his own time, though those published were a fraction of the whole. The joint work with Tallis was the *Cantiones quae ab argumento Sacrae vocantur*, which was dedicated to the queen. But in 1589 and 1591 Byrd published two volumes of his *Cantiones Sacrae* alone. In 1588 the *Psalmes, Sonets, and Songs of Sadnes and Pietie* appeared, with a dedication to Sir Christopher Hatton. Byrd's *Songs of Sundrie Natures* was printed in 1589, and the *Liber Primus Sacrarum Cantionum quinque vocum*, followed by its successor of sacred songs for five voices, in 1591. A volume including three undated masses appeared about 1603. Two books of *Gradualia* came out in 1607, and in 1611 there appeared the *Psalms, Songs, and Sonnets*.

In addition to church music this fertile and profound composer wrote string music, keyboard music, and secular choral

---

65 *English Music*, pp. 3f.

66 See the evaluations of Byrd recorded by Percy A. Scholes in *The Oxford Companion to Music*, p. 128b. Morrison Comegys Boyd, in *Elizabethan Music and Musical Criticism*, p. 80, claims that "Byrd's church music rivals that of Palestrina in contrapuntal skill and beauty, and surpasses it in expressiveness."

music, almost all of high quality. His religious music, like that of his mentor Tallis, has great nobility and sometimes attains sublimity. Also, like Tallis, Byrd was able to produce with equal facility services for the Latin and English rites. His technique is brilliant and warm, especially when fitting music to vernacular texts with action in them. In this his work contrasts with the cold perfection of Tallis's Latin works or the simpler earnestness of Tye.[67] It was a style combining dignity with pathos, plumbing the spiritual depths of the sacred texts he set to music. "He believed," says C. Henry Phillips, "in his heart as well as in his mind the dogmas of his faith . . . and could in addition carry over into his music his strong emotional conviction."[68]

Byrd was also an important experimenter. He was able to achieve beauty in the Short Services even when required to compose according to the Cranmerian restriction of a syllable to a note, so pure were his verbal rhythms. In his Second Evening Service he developed a novel idea which would revolutionise English sacred music. He composed certain verses for solo voices with an independent organ accompaniment. For about 50 years afterwards Short Services, alternating solo or duet passages with the music of the whole choir, were composed with great musical and devotional satisfaction.[69]

Byrd's most outstanding religious works are his three masses,[70] his *Gradualia* or Latin motets for the Catholic Daily Offices, and his music for Anglican services. Less consistently good are the early motets of 1575 and the English anthems, though some are outstanding. Byrd and his pupil Gibbons were pioneers in the composition of verse anthems. They often scored the music for viols to accompany the solo passages.[71] His greatest Anglican anthems include "How long shall mine enemies triumph," "O Lord, make thy servant Elizabeth," "Prevent us, O Lord," and "Arise, O Lord!" He also composed special psalms in an elaborate chant style of which the most notable is "O clap your hands." Byrd's work, whether in the form of motet or madrigal, was the glory of Tudor musical accomplishment. E. H. Fellowes believed

---

[67] See Phillips, *Singing Church*, p. 67.

[68] *Ibid.*, p. 93.

[69] Winfred Douglas, *Church Music in History and Practice*, rev. Leonard Ellinwood, pp. 117-18.

[70] Young, *British Music*, p. 153, writes of Byrd's development of a "sense of the interdependence of liturgical thought, verbal meanings, and rhythm and overtone, and musical techniques" as being "evident throughout the Masses."

[71] Woodfill, *Musicians in English Society*, p. 150.

that few short choruses for four boys' or women's voices could be found in all music to compare with the brilliance of "Rejoice, rejoice" and the chorus of "From the Virgin's womb."[72]

Thomas Morley (1557-1604?) became organist of St. Paul's cathedral in 1591. In 1592 he was appointed a Gentleman of the Royal Chapel. He wrote a famous primer in the form of a dialogue which was being studied 200 years after its initial publication— *A Plaine and Easie Introduction to Practicall Musicke* (1597).[73] The composer of at least two of the settings to Shakespeare's songs, Morley was an expert writer of madrigals when the genre was at its peak. Possibly at no other period was there such harmony between poets and musicians or such willingness to make music the servant of the word. A typical excerpt from Morley's primer makes this clear: "Now having discoursed unto you the composition of three, four, five and six parts with these few ways of canons and catches, it followeth to show you how to dispose your music according to the nature of the words which you are therein to express, as whatsoever matter it be which you have in hand, such a music must you frame to it. You must therefore, if you have a grave matter, apply a grave kind of music to it; if a merry subject, you must make your music also merry, for it will be a great absurdity to use a sad harmony to a merry matter, or a merry harmony to a sad, lamentable, or tragical ditty."[74] The greatest achievements of the age were in vocal music.

Morley's great reputation as a madrigalist may well have overshadowed his achievement as a church musician. The fact that little of his church music was published also helps to account for its inadequate recognition. In the undated *Whole Booke of Psalmes*, printed by W. Barley, "the assigne of T. Morley," there are four settings of tunes by Morley, two of which, together with a previously unpublished third, appeared in Ravenscroft's Psalter of 1621. Barnard also published a Morning and Evening Service of four and five parts, respectively; an Evening Service of five parts; and a verse anthem, "Out of the Deep." His renowned Burial Service was published by Boyce. There are, however, 10 unpublished motets and several anthems, preces and psalms, responses, and other services yet unpublished.[75]

---

[72] *English Cathedral Music from Edward VI to Edward VII*, p. 81.

[73] Morley's *Plaine and Easie Introduction to Practicall Musicke*, ed. R. A. Harman.

[74] *Ibid.*, p. 290.

[75] From *Grove's Dictionary of Music and Musicians*, ed. H. C. Colles, III, 519a-521a.

Morley's achievement is all the greater, considering that he died at the age of 45. Few of his English anthems have survived. One full anthem begins with the Latin words *Nolo mortem peccatoris*, then breaks into English, "Father, I am thine only Son." This penitential composition was the most suitable for Good Friday. "Out of the deep," with its alternate verses for solo and chorus is also poignant. In the first of his four Services Morley demonstrated an experimental advance even on Byrd, for in addition to solo song with organ accompaniment, he used passages for duet, trio, and quartet of solo voices. His was the earliest setting of the Burial Service in the English prayer-book; it was widely used in the seventeenth and eighteenth centuries. It is a complete setting, including "I am the Resurrection and the Life," "Man that is born of woman," "Thou knowest, Lord," and "I heard a voice from heaven." It is sensitive and beautiful. Morley's prestige in his own time was second only to that of his master, Byrd.[76] In 1614, a decade after Morley's death, Thomas Ravenscroft said of him: "he did shine as the Sun in the Firmament of our Art."[77]

These planets in the firmament of English music, were, it should be remembered, surrounded by a galaxy of stars. Their contemporaries included Tye, cofounder with Tallis of English cathedral music, Whyte, Weelkes, Tompkins, Dowland, Bull, Wilbye, and Orlando Gibbons, although the last came to full maturity in the Jacobean age. This was a golden age for English composers, for in the closing years of Elizabeth's reign, Gloriana had 30 or 40 composers worthy of remembrance, of whom only the most outstanding have been mentioned. They represented "the fine flower of the polyphonic style of composition."[78]

7. Gains and Losses

In considering the impact of the Reformation on English music there are to be seen clear gains and clear losses. On the negative side, there was the loss of much of the sonority and richness, subtlety and intricacy of medieval Catholic polyphonic music. The number and size of choirs in churches were reduced. The significance of the liturgical composer was lessened in Anglicanism, since the Mass required more settings (not forgetting the major Daily Offices) than the Anglican services. He thereupon found

[76] From Fellowes, *English Cathedral Music*, pp. 83-87.
[77] In Ravenscroft's *Brief Discourse* (1614).
[78] Fellowes, *English Cathedral Music*, p. 68.

other outlets for his inventive powers, as in madrigals, as he was in the next century to do in opera. The quality of the music of parish churches was poorer, as metrical psalms were substituted for motets. In brief, as the movement away from purely liturgical music gained momentum, music became increasingly secular in an age of expanding humanism.[79] But before the Tudor period was over Byrd had produced matchless Masses, which were not only the best of his work, but outstanding in the entire range of English music.

There were, however, gains in the influence of the Reformation on music, as on worship. The emphasis on the vernacular led not only to a far greater understanding, but inevitably to an increased popular participation in worship. One immediate advantage was the gain in the simplicity and directness of musical techniques, and the consigning of musical extravagances, such as allowing 15 bars for one syllable, to utter oblivion. The argument for the need to reduce overcomplex and overflorid music to simpler dimensions was so overwhelmingly cogent that it produced not only the Calvinist metrical psalm, the Lutheran chorale, and the Anglican Service, anthem, and psalm tune, but even the model *Missa brevis* of Palestrina. All these were creative responses to new conditions and new demands.

The greatest of the contributions to the popular praise of England and Scotland was metrical psalmody, which dominated the hearts of the people and therefore the parish churches and their homes. These were set to memorable tunes, in which admittedly the French combination of Marot's words to Bourgeois' tunes was never reached in English. Where England did, however, make a significant and original contribution to church music was in the anthem, especially as composed by Byrd and Gibbons.[80] This was a development Purcell would exploit almost a century later.

This transformation of the motet into the anthem, and its development in a responsive direction, occurred almost concurrently with the development of the madrigal. It provided a great opportunity for expression in music. Indeed, it may well be that the primary emphasis on the "Word" in Protestantism (supremely exemplified in the importance of preaching) and the insistence on

[79] Young, *British Music*, p. 151.

[80] William Byrd wrote 17 verse anthems and about 60 full anthems, while Orlando Gibbons wrote 24 verse anthems and 10 full anthems. The most prolific composer in this genre was Thomas Tomkins, another of Byrd's pupils, who composed 50 verse anthems and about 41 full anthems. Le Huray, *Music and Reformation*, p. 224.

the vernacular, led to the great concentration on making choral music the expression or representation of the words of the text in verse anthem and madrigal.[81] When settings were made for verse anthems, which allowed for verses to be sung partly in solo or duet and partly in chorus, Byrd had invented a fertile new vehicle of praise, with the accompaniment of cornets and sackbuts, recorders and viols, or of organs. Richard Farrant and William Mundy also favoured verse anthems. The new style became immensely popular, and immediately so, because there were good, practical reasons for it. The task of performance was placed on the ablest singers (now increasingly difficult to get), and the solo voices stood out against the musical accompaniment.

How colourful and enchanting the new style of anthems was can be appreciated from the impressions of a seventeenth-century listener, who summed up his delight when hearing a solemn anthem, "Wherein a sweet melodious treble or countertenor singeth single and a full choir answereth, much more when two such single voices interchangeably reply to one another, and, at the last, close all together. . . ."[82] This expression of joy in church music is excelled only by John Milton, the son of an Elizabethan and Jacobean composer of motets and madrigals, whose desire was:

> There let the pealing organ blow,
> To the full-voiced quire below,
> In service high and anthems clear,
> As may, with sweetness, through mine ear,
> Dissolve me into ecstasies,
> And bring all heaven before mine eyes.[83]   20

[81] This is well argued in chap. 5 of Stevens, *Music and Poetry in the early Tudor Court,* and partly rebutted by Le Huray in *Music and Reformation,* pp. 135-36. Le Huray points out that at this time the "simultaneous," or horizontal (as contrasted with the "successive" or vertical), technique of writing music, by which all the parts were developed together, also aided expressiveness in music, as shown, for example, in the famous motets of Josquin des Prez, *Absolon fili mi* and *Planxit autem David.* The issue, then, is whether the change in technique followed or preceded the search for expressiveness.

[82] Charles Butler, *The Principles of Musick* (1636), p. 41, cited in Le Huray, *Music and Reformation,* p. 225.

[83] *Il Penseroso,* ll. 153-58.

CHAPTER XII

SPIRITUALITY: CATHOLIC, ANGLICAN, PURITAN

CHRISTIAN public worship was undergirded and supplemented by spirituality. The external observance of the liturgy was merely a mechanical ritualism, a lifeless puppet articulated by rubrical strings, apart from the culture and discipline of the spiritual life. Thus spirit-inspired devotion was the life and power of the liturgy.

It was the spirituality of an age, reflected in Roman Catholic, Anglican, and Puritan primers and books of devotion, that pointed to the highest ideals and deepest motivations of conduct in Tudor England. C. J. Stranks has rightly argued that a study of the spiritual training reflected in prayer books can provide "if not a history, then a pointer to the history of those ideas which determined the day to day conduct of each man with his neighbour."[1]

In addition, while the liturgy was the medium of official, clerically-conceived piety, popular books of private and family devotions, especially when the contents were selected by laymen, were better indications of lay predilections and concerns in prayer. Books of personal and familial prayers were reinforcements of the Christian life corporately mediated by the liturgy. They also supplied new concerns which seemed to be lacking or were not emphasised in the public forms of worship. These new concerns were in the forefront in Protestant books of prayer, because the Reformation gave a great impetus to new forms suitable for family prayers, since these were naturally of greater interest to the married Protestant clergyman than to the ascetical priest or monk of the old faith.

There were, however, unexpected continuities between medieval and renaissance themes and types of prayer, thus linking Catholic and Protestant devotions. In several cases Catholic prayers, slightly or severely doctored, were incorporated into Protestant books of prayer. Unsuspecting fathers of Protestant households were approaching God in the accents of the great Catholic humanist, Erasmus, or of the Spaniard Vives, or even of the English Jesuit, Robert Persons. The most notable case of

---

[1] C. J. Stranks, *Anglican Devotion: Studies in the Spiritual Life of the Church of England between the Reformation and the Oxford Movement*, p. 9.

Catholic devotional influence on a Protestant was that of Persons via Bunny on Baxter. The Jesuit's *First Booke of the Christian Exercise, appertayning to resolution* appeared in 1582 with the avowed aim of convincing the unconverted by stressing those considerations of his own sinfulness and its reward, and God's grace and generosity, with the utmost vividness. This Ignatian type of treatise was bowdlerized by Edmund Bunny, the Puritan minister of Bolton Percy in 1584. He impertinently introduced his purified Persons thus: "I perceived that the booke insuing was willingly read by divers, for the persuasion that it hath to godliness of life, which notwithstanding in manie points was corruptly set downe: I thought good in the end to get the same published againe in better manner. . . ."[2] Persons, improbably purged in the "Bunny Club" edition, went through nine issues in 16 years. Richard Baxter, one of the most attractive Puritan saints of the seventeenth century, was converted to Christianity by reading Bunny's version of Persons. Baxter records that: "a poor Day-Labourer in the Town . . . had an old torn book which he lent my Father, which was called Bunny's Resolution (being written by Parson's the Jesuit, and corrected by Edm. Bunny. . . . And in the reading of this Book (when I was about Fifteen years of Age) it pleased God to awaken my Soul, and shew me the folly of Sinning and the misery of the Wicked, and the unexpressible weight of things Eternal, and the necessity of resolving on a Holy Life, more than I was ever acquainted with before. The same things which I knew before came now in another manner, with Light, and Sense, and Seriousness to my Heart."[3]

There was another reason for studying private and family devotions. It was that here if anywhere sincere religion was likely to be found, despite the notable dissent of Samuel Butler in his novel satirising Victorian hypocrisy, *The Way of All Flesh*. At least, it was likelier to be found in the silence of solitude or in small groups. Certainly, it was only the households prepared at home in prayer that were able genuinely to share in the gatherings of public worship. Mere spectators at public worship were formalists; they had already travelled halfway to hypocrisy. If private and familial piety was strong, so would public worship be vigorous.

---

[2] Bunny's version (1584), sig. 2, as cited in A. C. Southern, *Elizabethan Recusant Prose, 1559-1582*, p. 185. Augustus Jessopp, in his *One Generation of a Norfolk House, a Contribution to Elizabethan History*, p. 90, drew attention to the influence of Persons on Baxter in 1879.

[3] *Reliquiae Baxterianae* (1696), p. 3.

If personal and family prayer was rare or sporadic, then worship would be perfunctorily celebrated and sparsely attended. Happily, in the Elizabethan age the printing (and presumably the use) of supplementary books of prayer, combining instruction in the art of prayer with examples of prayer for different persons and situations, was prolific.

1. The Popularity of Devotional Books

H. S. Bennett has described the demand for religious books in sixteenth-century England as "insatiable."[4] Louis B. Wright points out that 60 percent of the breviaries, books of hours (or primers), and manuals printed in the first half of the century came from overseas, despite the intermittent restrictions on the importing of books.[5] Two examples of many that might be chosen to illustrate the voracity of the public appetite for books of devotions were those issued by F. G. (especially *A Manual of Prayers*, which went into 15 editions between 1583 and 1613) and Edward Dering, a famous Puritan minister, whose *Godly Private Prayers* was issued in over 20 editions between 1576 and 1626.[6] It is known that more than 80 different collections of private devotions were printed during the reign of Elizabeth I.[7]

Why was the demand so great? Even after allowing for the excitement over the relatively recent invention of printing, and the widespread Renaissance conviction of the efficacy of book learning, in both of which religion shared, the predominance of this particular genre of religious literature has still to be explained. The truth seems to be, as Helen White has suggested, that the greatest controversy in sixteenth-century England was over the issue of religious allegiance. The effect of the controversy was to place a heavier responsibility on the individual for the conduct of his own private religious life.[8] The Protestant principle of the priesthood of all believers was taken in its fullest implications by the Puritan merchants of the middle classes. These, as Wright has shown, except in the most affluent households, lacked the chaplains considered indispensable in aristocratic households. Laymen

---

4 *English Books and Readers, 1475-1557*, p. 65.
5 *Middle-Class Culture in Elizabethan England*, p. 228. On p. 24 Wright claims: "Of all the works that poured from the press in the sixteenth and seventeenth centuries, these [devotional books] had the widest circulation and remained popular longest."
6 See Faye L. Kelly, *Prayer in Seventeenth-Century England*.
7 *Christian Prayers and Meditations*, preface, p. 14.
8 Helen C. White, *Tudor Books of Private Devotion*, pp. 149, 150, 174.

had to act as their own curates, as priests in their own households. The moderate Puritans who were the authors of the majority of English manuals of devotion, "unaware of what they were doing . . . were undermining the future authority of the Church."[9] They taught the London citizen to claim the promises of God in Holy Scripture, to model his prayers on the simple and profound petitions of the Psalmist and on the comprehensive concerns expressed in the Lord's Prayer; if he lacked the gift of extemporaneous utterance, they provided samples and directions for prayer. The heads of middle class households assumed the responsibility for teaching their children, apprentices, and maidservants, the essentials of religious belief, duty, and devotion. The less learned and dedicated his neighbouring clergyman was, the more concerned was the Puritan citizen to be independent of him.

Nor should it be overlooked that the manuals of devotion inculcated important ethical ideals directly or indirectly. They instructed all the members of the household in their social duties and obligations, laying before them the virtues appropriate to their callings in the household, the town, and the state, affirming the duty to be generous toward the poor and handicapped, to overcome abrasive anger with the lenitives of patience and forgiveness, and to cultivate the prudential virtues of honesty, industry, and thrift. They confirmed the oncoming generation in respect for the constituted authority of the queen and her magistrates, if not always for her bishops. The most popular books of devotion were, however, completely uncontroversial.

An example of the compassion taught in the manuals of devotion is selected from one of the most popular manuals of the age, *A Booke of Christian Prayers, collected out of the aunciēt writers and best learned in our tyme, worthy to be read with an earnest mynde of all Christians, in these daungerous and troublesome dayes, that God for Christes sake will yet still be mercyfull unto us.* Issued by the printer John Daye, this volume contains wide marginal illustrations on each page. For example, "A prayer for them that be in povertie" is illustrated with woodcuts of "Charity" feeding the hungry, giving drink to the thirsty, harbouring strangers, clothing the naked, and visiting the sick and prisoners, with the appropriate Biblical references to these Dominical commendations. The prayer itself, though wordy and confusing in combining a meditation and a series of petitions, is moving:

[9] Wright, *Middle-Class Culture*, p. 240.

They that are snarled and intangled in ye extreme penury of things needfull for the body, cannot set theyr myndes upō thee O Lord, as they ought to doe: but when they be disapoynted of the thynges which they doe so mightely desire, their hartes are cast downe, and quayle for excesse of grief. Have pitie upon them therfore O mercyfull Father, and releeve their misery through thine incredible riches, that by thy remouvyng of their urgent necessitie, they may rise up unto thee in mynde. Thou O Lord providest inough for all men with thy most liberall and bountyfull hand: but whereas thy giftes are, in respect of thy goodnesse and free favour, made common to all men, we (through our naughtynesse, nigard-shyp, and distrust,) doe make them private and peculiar. Correct thou the thyng whiche our iniquitie hath put out of order: let thy goodnesse supply that which our niggardly-nesse hath plucked away. Geve thou meate to the hungry, and drinke to the thirsty: Comfort thou the sorrowfull: Cheare thou up the dismayde: Strengthen thou the weake: Deliver thou them that are prisoners: and geve thou hope and courage to them that out of hart.

O Father of all mercy have compassion of so great misery. O Fountaine of all good thynges, and of all blessednesse, washe thou away these so sundry, so manifold and so great miseries of ours, with one drop of the water of thy mercy, for thyne onely Sonne our Lord & Saviour Jesus Christes sake. Amen.[10]

2. Catholic and Royal Primers

English Catholicism had inherited a great tradition of spirituality,[11] which had blossomed richly in the fourteenth-century mystics, including Richard Rolle of Hampole, the Benedictine Monk of Farne, the anonymous author of *The Cloud of Unknowing*, Walter Hilton, the Lady Julian of Norwich, and Margery Kempe, as well as the unknown visionary who wrote *Piers Plowman*. In addition to nourishing these exponents of high mysticism (some of them monks, some hermits, and some anchoresses), the Catholic

10 Edition of 1581, pp. 53-54.
11 For an introduction to this tradition see *Pre-Reformation English Spirituality*, ed. James Walsh, which contains biographical essays on English writers on spirituality from Bede to Augustine Baker, with a notable chapter on Thomas More. See also *English Spiritual Writers*, ed. Charles Davis; and David Knowles, *The English Mystical Tradition*.

Church also made provision for the "lower" mysticism of those who wished to love God and serve men in the world. This spiritual food continued to be supplied in the turbulent sixteenth century.

The Catholic devotional books for the laity were usually known as "primers."[12] They had been the most popular medieval manuals of devotion, consisting of brief handbooks of prayer and basic religious instruction. The earliest contained the Psalter and the Litany, and often the Vigils of the Dead were added. By the end of the thirteenth century, while the Litany and the Vigils of the Dead were retained, the Psalter had been reduced to the Seven Penitential Psalms and the important addition was made of the Hours of the Blessed Virgin. These had started as a monastic devotion in Lent and Advent, supplementary to the Day Hours, but they proved so attractive that the lay folk desired to have them at all seasons, especially since special prayers were added which carried indulgences. Much legendary material, some dubious and much unedifying, was included in these prayers. Yet the material provided a tender Marian devotion through which it was hoped that adoration of the infant Saviour might grow, but which also might be stifled by sentimentality.[13]

The standard, or model, primer developed the following features, according to Helen C. White, at the end of the fifteenth century: the Hours of the Blessed Virgin, the Seven Penitential Psalms, the Fifteen Gradual Psalms, the Litany, the Office for the Dead and the Commendations or prayers following that Office.[14] Most primers of the period also included prayers for special occasions and needs; some provided an extensive selection of prayers for private or corporate use, covering many applications. It was in these additions that Protestant editors of prayers were to find attractive possibilities for their own adaptation and invention. Monarchs with an interest in modifying or reforming the country's religion also found primers to be potent instruments of change, until, with the provision of a liturgy in English (as with the Book of Common Prayer of 1549), there was no longer any need for a person to carry a primer to church in order to take an intelligent

[12] For two texts see *The Prymer or Lay Folk's Prayer Book*, ed. Henry Littlehales; and *Horae B.V.M. or, Sarum and York Primers, with Kindred Books of the Reformed Roman Use*, ed. E. Hoskyns; see also C. C. Butterworth, *The English Primers, 1529-1545*.

[13] Stranks, *Anglican Devotion*, p. 15.

[14] "Sixteenth Century English Devotional Literature," in Joseph Quincy Adams Memorial Studies, ed. J. G. McManaway, G. E. Dawson, and E. E. Willoughby, pp. 439-46.

part in the worship, which up to that year had been largely in Latin. The first Anglican prayer-book was made available for use at home as well as for public worship. Thus the disuse of English primers was directly related to the disuse of Latin in the liturgy.[15] The primer lived on usefully in the educational field, for prayers were composed and included in the major pedagogical handbooks of the period, even in the instructions issued by military commanders. The queen herself was reputed to compose private prayers.

Even though the provision of an official vernacular prayer-book for use in churches and homes rendered primers eventually unnecessary, yet while religion was in the process of change, royal primers performed a useful state function and served as intriguing reflectors of royal religious policy.[16] Henry VIII's primer, or "boke of ordinarie prayers," appeared in 1545, six years after the unofficial but important experimental primer of Bishop Hilsey of Rochester. The royal book kept the traditional title and the opening Office of *Dirige*, though the latter was reduced by two-thirds. Psalms of thanksgiving and praise replaced the previous psalms of penance and mercy. The Prayers of the Passion were altered so as to emphasise the practical lessons to be drawn from contemplating the sufferings of Christ, rather than providing a medium for imaginative and emotional unity with the Crucified. The hymns in the Little Hours were changed from the praise of the Virgin Mary to the praise of Christ. The Litany was rewritten so as to lessen the honouring of the saints.

The Primer of Edward VI (1553) was a combination of the Book of Common Prayer and a primer. Those parts of it which provided private devotions showed a transition from the liturgical and universal to the practical and occasional. Here first appeared in an official publication in England the start of the change, "from the general spiritual provision for all sorts of men in one situation to the special prayers for particular classes and conditions of men," which was to dominate the prayers of the later sixteenth and early seventeenth centuries.[17] The chief Protestant writers of prayers

15 See Kelly, *Prayer.*
16 Hilsey's Primer (1539) was used as a means of religious change chiefly through its unqualified Erastianism and its assertion of the eucharistic doctrine of the Real Presence against the sacramentarians.
17 See White, *Tudor Books of Private Devotion,* chaps. 6, 7. Chap. 6 deals chiefly with the reign of Henry VIII, and chap. 7 with the reign of Elizabeth. The convenience of the Primer as an instrument of religious change was that its editors could provide alternative selections of Scripture to mark theological changes, and

during this reign (excluding Archbishop Thomas Cranmer) were Thomas Becon (Cranmer's chaplain) and Bishop Hilsey.

It is interesting that in the rapidly improvised primer of Queen Mary's reign (1555), the Marian prayers and the prayers invoking the saints were only partly restored. The Henrician Primer's borrowings from Vives, and even the compositions of Becon, were rather surprisingly retained.

The Elizabethan Primer of 1559 owed more to the Henrician book of 1545 than to the Edwardian book of 1553. The Marian elements were further reduced, however, and there were changes in the liturgical sections, but the book was substantially that of Elizabeth's father rather than that of her brother.

Since the primers supplied the needs of the lay Catholics there was little incentive to produce supplementary prayers for Catholics until the Holy Communion service in English supplanted the Latin Mass. Apart from one significant exception, almost all the important Catholic works on prayer in English appeared during the reign of Queen Elizabeth, and at a time when it became clear that England's faith and worship were likely to remain Protestant for decades to come.

The exception was the remarkable collection of *Certain Devout and Godly Prayers made in Latin by the Reverend Father in God Cuthbert Tunstall* (1558), which was translated and printed by Thomas Paynell in 1558. A Catholic in doctrine and religious practice, holding a high sacramental doctrine, he was a reluctant Erastian under Henry VIII who had him appointed to the sees successively of London and Durham.[18] He was imprisoned in Edward VI's reign for his opposition to the official religious policy. In 1547 he had voted against the abolition of the chantries, and in 1549 against the Act of Uniformity and the legislative enactments that permitted priests to marry. In 1552 Tunstall was tried for high treason and deprived of his bishopric. Queen Mary reinstated him, but he refused the Oath of Supremacy on the accession of Queen Elizabeth. Here, when it was dangerous, was a man of conscience. His refusal to countenance persecution of Protestants in Queen Mary's reign shows that he was a man of compassion. These qualities are evident in his book of prayers. The most notable

---

alternative special prayers for the same purpose, while retaining the title and format of the volume, so as to give the impression that nothing of any consequence was changed.

[18] For a biography see Charles Sturge, *Cuthbert Tunstall, Churchman, Scholar, Statesman, Administrator.*

expression of them was his "Prayer unto God for the Dead which have no man that prayeth for them," which recalled the suppression of the chantries. It deserves citation in full:

> Have mercy, we beseche the O Lorde god have mercy, for the precyous death sake of thy onelye sonne our Lorde Jesu Chryst, of those soules ye which have no intercessors that remember thē, or that doth put the in remembraunce of them, nor no consolation, nor hope in there [sic] torments, but onelye that they are created and made lyke unto thy similitude and Image, and markyd wt the signacle of thy faith, the whiche other thrugh the negligence of those whiche are alyve, or of the slydynge course of tyme are cleane forgotten of theyr frendes, and posteritie. Spare them o Lord, and defende thy workmanship in them, nor despise not the work of thy handes, but putte forthe thy hande unto them, and beynge delyvered frō the tormente of paynes, brynge them through thy great mercies, the whych are celebratyd and estemyd above all thy workes, to the felowshyp of the hevenly citezins, which livest and reigneste God, through all worldes. So be it.[19]

A. C. Southern divides the recusant books of spirituality produced during Elizabeth's reign into four main categories: general spiritual directories, books on penance, books on the Rosary, and Psalters and Hours. Since the three last categories were traditional, it is in the first category that originality is to be sought. Of the general directories of spirituality, six seem to Southern to merit mention, and only three of these display creativity. They are the previously mentioned Persons, *The First Booke of the Christian Exercise, appertayning to Resolution* (1582), Hide's *Consolatorie Epistle to the afflicted Catholikes* (1580), and the anonymous *Certayne devout Meditations* (1576).

Of these the most impressive is the work of Persons. His mystical aspiration has nothing in common with the desire to be alone with the Alone. At its most lyrical and inspired it is still an ecclesial consummation that is sought—a communion with God in the communion of the saints—as the soul ascends:

> Imagine, besides all this, what a ioye it shall be vnto thy soule at that daye, to meet with all her godlie freendes in heauen, with father, with mother, with brothers, with sisters:

[19] *Certain Devout*, sig. D iii v.-D iv.

with wyfe, with husband, with maister, with scholares: with neyghboures, with familiares, with kynred, with acquayntance: the welcomes, the myrthe, the sweet embracementes that shall be there, the ioye whereof (as noteth S. Cyprian) shalbe vnspeakable. Add to this, the dalye feasting and inestimable triumphe, whiche shalbe there, at the arriuall of new bretheren and sisters coming thither from time to time with the spoyles of their enemies, conquered and vanquyshed in this world. O what a cōfortable sight will it be to see those seates of Angells fallen, filled vpp agayne with men & wemen from day to day? to see the crownes of glorie sett vpon their heades, and that in varietie, according to the varietie of their cōquestes. One for martyrdome, or confession against the persecutor: an other for virginitie or chastitie against the flesh. . . .[20]

Within the same mystical tradition, but derivative as even a good translation must still be, was Richard Hopkins' *Of Prayer and Meditation*, which made available in English the admirably lucid and simple introduction to the spiritual life and the 14 meditations for the mornings and evenings of one week on the major mysteries of the Catholic faith composed by Fray Luis de Granada, the Spanish Dominican who became Provincial of his Order in Portugal.[21] This important book, the *Libro de la Oración*, of 1553, stressed the significance of the prepared heart for meditation. It had a strong influence on St. Francis de Sales in the writing of his *Introduction to the Devout Life*.

In 1575 *Certaine devout and Godly petitions, commonly called Iesus Psalter* appeared. The book consists of 150 petitions, which are divided into 15 decades for the 15 chief petitions, are further divided into three series according to the three stages of the mystical life—purgation, illumination, and union. Attributed to Richard Whytford, a member of the Brigittine Order, they maintain the ascetical tradition of spirituality, even if the arrangement is contrived.

Important as was the work of Fr. Persons in mediating the Ignatian tradition of the sons of Loyola and the work of Hopkins in making available the work of the Spanish mystic, Luis de Granada, they were only a trickle of the flood of Counter-Reforma-

[20] *Ibid.*, sig. 14.
[21] The only English account of Fray Luis de Granada's mysticism is in E. Allison Peers, *Studies in the Spanish Mystics*, vol. 1, pp. 33-76.

tion spirituality that irrigated a desiccated Europe. For the most part, English Catholics in a newly Protestant country were insulated from the new spirituality. For most of the laity the old, worn, dogeared primers had to suffice as guides to spirituality unless they had access to the clandestine Jesuits or to the chaplains of aristocratic families who could be their spiritual directors.

3. *Protestant Manuals of Devotion*

The Protestant books of devotion can be characterised as a supplement to public worship consisting of directions on the values and methods of prayer, with an anthology of prayers suitable for private and household use.

Both Catholic humanists and Protestant reformers encouraged the study of the Scriptures. The new scripturalism found expression in the publication of prayer manuals consisting largely of selections of Scriptures, with indications of how they were helpful in particular situations, such as a Psalm to encourage one in despair to renewed hope in God. The Catholic primers had made good use of the Psalms, and now so did the Protestant manuals. New translations of them appeared, annotated in such a manner as to claim their confirmation of Reformed doctrines; even the "cursing" psalms seemed fitting expression for maledictions of those who clung to superstition and idolatry instead of embracing the true faith. The partisanship of the Psalmist appealed to the partisanship of the Protestant. Thomas Sternhold provided a popular versified English translation of the Psalms, the first edition of which, with 19 Psalms, appeared in 1547, and the second, with 37, in 1549, the year of his death. In 1557 a third edition was issued which included seven more Psalms, the work of John Hopkins. The complete edition of 1562, issued by John Daye, the Marian exile and printer, shaped the public as well as the private piety of Elizabethan England, for it was often included with the Book of Common Prayer. Sternhold was unwilling that the Devil should have the catchiest metres and the most cheerful tunes, so he wrote nine of his psalms in the ballad metre of Chevy Chase. Their appeal, even if the verse was often jogging, was nationwide, so much so that a Roman Catholic author grudgingly paid them this tribute: "There is nothing that hath drawne multitudes to be of their Sects so much, as the singing of their psalmes, in such variable and delightful tunes. These the souldier singeth in warre, the artizans at their worke, wenches spinning and serving, apprentices in their shoppes, and wayfaring men in their travaile, little knowing (God wotte) what a serpent lieth under these sweet flowers."[22]

Clement Marot anticipated Sternhold in 1533 in France by using metres and tunes associated with the boudoir and the ballade. He won the Dauphin's admiration for *ces sanctes chansonettes.*[23] The age produced more elegant English versions of the Psalms, such as those of Philip Sidney or Edmund Spenser,[24] but none so suitable for common praises as the mediocre verse of Sternhold and Hopkins.

Yet another consequence of the Biblicism of the time was the production of anthologies of prayers and spiritual directions, which consisted of Scripture prayers from the Old and New Testaments, or recommendations to prayer drawn from holy writ. One popular book, among many of the same type, was Richard Grafton's *Praiers of the Holi Fathers,* issued about 1540.

It also became popular to include in collections of prayers those which had been composed or used by Protestant reformers or martyrs, or even brief summaries of Christian doctrine composed by such men. For example, Henry Bull's *Christian Praiers and Holie Meditations*[25] in the 1578 edition contains three works of John Bradford, the Protestant martyr, two on prayer and the third a summary of doctrine as well as his last prayer at Smithfield. Furthermore, John Daye's *A Booke of Christian Prayers,*[26] appearing in the same year, has two prayers by Calvin, and one each by Bradford, Knox, and John Foxe.

In due time manuals of devotion of a more specific character were prepared, which had in mind the needs of persons in particular callings, or suffering particular kinds of distress. Such were collections of prayers for the poor or for those about to die. In 1585 William Perkins issued his *A Salve for a Sicke Man, or, A Treatise containing the nature, differences, and kindes of death; as also the right manner of dying well.* The rest of the subtitle indicates how useful Perkins intended his prayers to be: *And It may serve for spirituall instruction to 1. Mariners when they goe*

---

[22] Thomas Harrap, *Tessaradelphus,* cited in White, *Tudor Books of Private Devotion,* p. 44; and in Stranks, *Anglican Devotion,* pp. 14-15.

[23] R. E. Prothero, *The Psalms in Human Life,* p. 51.

[24] Spenser's *Seven Penitential Psalms* are excellent poetry.

[25] All references are to the Henry E. Huntington Library copy of the edition of 1578, although the less comprehensive, first edition is of 1566.

[26] When Bull's and Daye's collections of prayer are examined in detail they will be found to have preserved many Catholic prayers also, both traditional and contemporary.

to sea. 2. Souldiers when they goe to battell. 3. Women when they travell of child. Particularly at the end of the century, with the raging of the plague, uncertainty over Elizabeth's successor, and general disillusionment, the demand for palliatives for the fear of death became widespread; it is noteworthy that the book went through six editions by 1632. Christopher Sutton's *Disce Mori. Learne to Die* (1600) met the same *fin de siècle* need, which is mirrored so hauntingly in the plays of Webster, particularly in the macabre parts of *The Duchess of Malfi.* To come to a good end was almost as important as living a good life; in this concern Renaissance bravado conspired with Christian fortitude, as one realises by reading accounts of the death of a martyr or the end of a magnifico. In each case, "ripeness is all."

Prayers for the poorer people were the special concern of Thomas Tymme and Thomas Dekker, the poet-playwright. Tymme produced in 1598 a handbook of prayers for the lower classes, entitled *The Poor Mans Pater noster, with a preparative to praier: Wherto are annexed divers godly Psalmes and Meditations.* Dekker's *Foure Birds of Noahs Ark* (1609) provides prayers for schoolboys, apprentices, servingmen, servinggirls, seamen, colliers, and even galley slaves. As remarkable as its compassion is the book's application of the Protestant principle of the priesthood of all believers, the conviction that God can be served faithfully and fully outside a monastery while discharging one's calling and duty in the secular world. The most popular of all the books aiming at the common people was Arthur Dent's *The Plain Mans Path-way to Heaven,* which was arranged "Dialogue wise for the better understanding of the simple." Issued first in 1601, it reached 25 editions by 1640.[27]

Part of the Protestant contribution to devotion was the composition of books on the culture and practice of the spiritual life, some of which were very successful. One memorable guide to prayer was Abraham Fleming's *The Diamond of Devotion,* which appeared in 1581. Another was John Norden's *The Pensive Mans Practise* (1584), which went to 40 editions. It contains "very devout and

---

[27] Some indications of the practical Puritan ethos may be divined from the nine signs of damnation as delineated by Dent. They are pride, whoredom, covetousness, contempt of the Gospel, swearing, lying, drunkenness, idleness, and oppression. Four of the seven deadly sins of the medieval Church have been retained, but the extra five have been recruited from the Old Testament, from mercantile prudence, and one—contempt of the Gospel—sums up the rejection of the New Covenant, and under it may be subsumed the other eight vices.

necessary prayers for sundry godly purposes, with requisite per-swasions before every Prayer."

However, the most characteristic and influential Protestant devotional manuals combined examples of prayer with directions on the methods, motives, and ends of prayer. They were thus both directories of prayers and collections of prayers. New as they seemed, they were, in a sense, merely the Protestant continuation of the functions of the Catholic and Royal primers. Their novelty was in their strong Biblicism and their concern for the different callings and conditions of men. The pioneer English Protestant work in collecting prayers for many occasions and for various call-ings was Thomas Becon's *A Pomaunder*[28] *of Prayer* of 1558.[29] It did not, however, contain directions on prayer. The quality of the distinctive Protestant directory and anthology combined can be discerned most readily by a survey of the contents of three most influential books of this type.

The first of them is *A Godly Meditation*, which was issued first in 1559 by the printer William Copland and which reappeared successively under the imprints of Rowland Hall (1562), William Seres (1564), John Allde (1578), and Elizabeth Allde in 1604, 1607, 1614, and 1632. To this volume were added John Brad-ford's *Private Prayers and Meditations with other Exercises*. Many of the devotions were in fact Bradford's translations of the *Excita-tiones Animi in Deum* of the Spanish Catholic humanist, Ludovicus Vives (1492-1540). A brief meditation is followed by a short prayer appropriate to the events of an ordinary day. Waking is to recall that God intends to awaken the soul from the sleep of sin and death, and the act of rising is to be a memento of Adam's fall and "the great benefit of Christ by whose help we do daily arise from our falling." Meals are to be occasions on which our depend-ence on God is recalled and also when it is remembered that the food of the soul is Christ's body broken and his blood shed. Most similar reflections were the thoughts of Vives, but there were char-acteristic additions or modifications of John Bradford, the Protes-tant martyr. For example, while with Vives the safe return home at night from a journey led to thoughts of gratitude for the safety and quiet which a house affords and the joys of our eternal home,

---

[28] A pomander is a sweet-smelling ball of spices carried as a preservative against infection, and hence metaphorically a handbook of fragrant and protective prayers. See D. S. Bailey, *Thomas Becon and the Reformation of the Church in England.*

[29] Becon also wrote *The Sick Man's Salve* in 1561, which ran to 17 editions by 1632.

for Bradford imprisoned for the faith, the occasion suggested the darkness of the religious situation under Queen Mary's reign: "So long as the sun is up, wild beasts keep their dens, foxes their burrows, owls their holes, etc., but when the sun is down then come they abroad: so wicked men and hypocrites keep their dens in the Gospel; but, it being taken away, then swarm they out of their holes like bees, as this day doth teach."[30] The last thought for the day is a reflection on sleep: "Think that, as this troublesome day is now past, and night come, and so rest, bed, and pleasant sleep, which maketh most excellent princes and most poor peasants alike; even so after the tumults, troubles, temptations, and tempests of this life, they that believe in Christ have prepared for them an haven and rest most pleasant and joyful. As you are not afraid to enter into your bed, and to dispose yourself to sleep, so be not afraid to die, but rather prepare yourself to it; think that now you are nearer your end by one day's journey, than you are in the morning."[31]

The scheme, whereby the events of each day suggested thoughts which directed the soul to God and the meaning of life, was a good one, even if the reflections themselves tended to be dutiful rather than delightful and often commonplace rather than striking or profound. The judgment of Stranks on this book is sound: "The habit of moralising common incidents and common things, which grew wearisome when carried to excess by later writers, helped to bring the highest thoughts into day to day affairs and emphasises that pathways to God lie all around us."[32] Its most happy fruitage in Anglicanism would be in the poems and devotional works of George Herbert in the following century.

The second volume of great popularity and influence (which also shows the impact of Vives and Bradford) was that published by Henrie Bull, *Christian Praiers and Holie Meditations*, about 1566. No copy of the first edition is known to exist, but the editors of the Parker Society edition issued in 1842 reprinted an edition earlier than 1570. The original compiler of the book was a Fellow of Magdalen College, Oxford, during the reign of Edward VI, who sought refuge on the Continent during Queen Mary's reign and returned during Elizabeth's. His book has the Vives-Bradford structure, but he also drew on the works of reformers other than Bradford and from the primers of Edward VI and Henry VIII.

30 Ed. A. Townshend, *The Writings of John Bradford*, 2 vols., vol. 2, p. 239.
31 *Ibid.*, p. 241.
32 *Anglican Devotion*, p. 25.

The 1578 edition of the same work begins with a lengthy introduction on the benefits, preparation for, and the parts of prayer. "By the benifite of prayer," Bull wrote, "therefore we attaine to those riches which God hath laide up in store for us: for thereby we have familiar accesse to God, and boldlie entering into the sanctuarie of heaven, we put him in mind of his promises: so that now by experience we feele and finde that to be true in deede, which by the worde we did before, but onely beleeve: now we injoy those treasures by prayer, which by faith wee did before but onely beholde in the Gospell of our Lorde Iesus."[33] Then follow two of John Bradford's meditations, the first on prayer in general, and the second on the Lord's Prayer. These provide instruction on how to pray, to whom to pray, and what to pray for, and stress the Divine invitations in Holy Scripture, through which God "allureth us with manie sweet promises to call upon Him."[34] Prayer is of two kinds, petition and thanksgiving. In petitions, requests for spiritual benefits were to take precedence over pleas for corporal benefits. Three reasons of Bradford's are given for asking for corporal benefits, which are almost a theology of Protestant prayer: to acknowledge God as author and giver; to understand that the Divine providence is bountiful; and "that our faith of reconciliation and forgiveness of sins should be exercised through asking of these corporal things."[35] The introduction and Bradford meditations comprise a third of the compilation.

The main part of the book consists of prayers. First there are 14 private prayers of the Vives kind related to the events of the day.[36] Then follows a group of 50 prayers[37] and meditations suitable for use either in families or in public assemblies. These include confessions of sin and many meditations on such themes as the presence of God, the Divine providence, the power, goodness, beauty and other attributes of God, and meditations on the Passion, Resurrection and Glorification of Christ. Some of the prayers are for improvement in the Christian life, as in petitions for true repentance, for increase of faith, for "the true sense and feeling of God's favour and mercy in Christ," and for present help in temptation. Yet other prayers are for particular classes of people: for those persecuted for their faith, for the sick, for those about to die, and for women in childbirth. There are still other prayers to be

---

[33] Bull, *Christian Praiers*, using the 1578 edition.
[34] *Ibid.*, p. 35.   [35] *Ibid.*, p. 59.
[36] *Ibid.*, pp. 132-34.   [37] *Ibid.*, pp. 165-346.

said before and after the preaching of God's Word, and before and after receiving Holy Communion.

The third part[38] consists of psalms and graces before and after a meal. Then follows an amorphous collection of prayers "commonly called Lidley's,"[39] which include petitions for forgiveness, for understanding God's Word, for the leading of a godly life, and the prayer "which Master John Bradford said a little before his death in Smithfeelde." The Litany ensues, including 15 prayers. The book concludes with "A Godly Instruction, conteining the Summe of all the Divinitie necessary for a Christian Conscience," also the work of the Protestant martyr, Bradford.

There is little that is original in this volume. But what is impressive is its comprehensiveness, its possibly unconscious transconfessional borrowings, and the practicality of the instruction of the laity in the spiritual life. These prayers and meditations have a moving simplicity and brevity which verge on the concentrated concision of Roman collects. Here, for example, is the private prayer to be offered before going to bed: "O Lord Jesus Christ, my watchman and keeper, take me into thy protection. Graunt that my body sleeping, my minde may watch for thee, and be made merrie by some sight of that celestiall and heavenly life, wherein thou art the king and prince, together with the father and the holie Ghost, where the angels and holy soules be most happy citizens. Oh purifie my soule, keepe cleane my bodie, that in both I may please thee, sleeping and waking forever. Amen."[40] Echoes of Compline still sound through these words, like a Catholic angelus heard in a Protestant harvest field.

The third volume of wide popularity and influence was John Daye's *A Booke of Christian Prayers and Meditations in English, French, Italian, Spanish, Greek, and Latin,* issued in 1569. The edition of 1581,[41] less cosmopolitan and scholarly and more national and popular in appeal, was entitled *A Booke of Christian Prayers, collected out of the aunciēt writers, and best learned in our tyme, worthy to be read with an earnest mynde of all Christians, in this daungerous and troublesome dayes, that God for Christes sake will yet still be mercyfull unto us.* The title is an interesting product of piety and mercantile prudence. The page opposite the title page illustrates the same spirit with a portrait of Queen Elizabeth at prayer. An attractive feature of this edition is

---

38 *Ibid.,* pp. 347-62.   39 *Ibid.,* pp. 362, 408.   40 *Ibid.,* p. 164.
41 All succeeding references are to this edition.

that it has marginal illustrations of the Christian virtues and of the various ranks in the social hierarchy, from emperors to peasants, suggesting that their secular callings are potentially sacred.

The work consists of 122 prayers. Their subjects and the order in which they are arranged are similar to the work of Henry Bull examined earlier. It is therefore only worth commenting on its distinctive contribution. It lacks the treatises on spirituality and doctrine that Bull's work has, providing a prefatory note of only a single page on private prayer. It does, however, have three prayers for the universal Church, and three for the queen, as well as 15 for the remission of sins, 14 against despair, four prayers to be said before the receiving of Communion, and four prayers to be said at the visitation of the sick. The Vives-Bradford influence is strong in the opening part of the work, and four prayers are acknowledged to be after St. Augustine.[42] The most pronounced characteristic of the work, apart from the marginal illustrations, is its strongly pragmatic bent, as seen in the number of petitionary prayers, seeking cleanness of heart, faith, love towards Christ, true mortification, "continuance in seeking after Christ,"[43] and "for Christ's direction and success in all our doings."[44] The intercessory element is admirable, as already seen in its fine prayer, "for them that be in povertie," but which is also found in three prayers for love towards our neighbour,[45] a prayer of children for parents,[46] and prayers for the persecuted,[47] for such as are in adversity,[48] and two prayers for our "evilwillers."[49]

4. Catholic and Protestant Spirituality Compared

The most striking difference between Catholic spirituality and Protestant devotions is in the locus and ethos of their spiritual training. For the Catholic it was the monastery or the convent in which the life of perfection was sought. For the sixteenth-century Protestant it was in the family that Christian nurture begins and

---

[42] Sister Marian Leona, a scholar working at the Huntington Library in San Marino, has been kind enough to let me read her manuscript, as yet unpublished: "Renaissance Prayers: A Sixteenth Century Ecumenical Encounter." She carefully documents the borrowings of the prayers of Juan Luis Vives, or Lodovicus, by Protestant compilers of prayers. His first prayers were published in Bruges in 1535 and appeared in England included in *Preces Privatae* of 1539, and next in the Royal Primer of 1545, which prints seven of them. They appeared in English Protestant manuals of devotion as late as the Elizabeth Allde edition of *A Godly Meditation* of 1633.

[43] Leona, "Renaissance Prayers," p. 103.

[44] *Ibid.*, p. 114. [45] *Ibid.*, p. 50. [46] *Ibid.*, p. 49.

[47] *Ibid.*, p. 51. [48] *Ibid.*, p. 52. [49] *Ibid.*, p. 54.

matures. For both, of course, the Christian life was nourished in the larger public gatherings for worship, whether at Mass or the elevation of the Word. But the primary foundation of training was different.

The ethos of Catholic and Protestant spirituality was also different. For Catholicism the end of the spiritual life was unity with God, along the arduous path of mysticism. It was, to adapt St. Bonaventura's daring book title, an *itinerarium cordis ac mentis in Deum per ardua*. It involved great sacrifices of earthly love for the Divine love who is also lightning. It meant a perpetual striving for purity, for the will ductile to God's every leading, and an unregretted abandonment of the world. It meant listening to the Dominical counsels of perfection with attentive ear and heart. All of this was easier for Protestants to criticise than to comprehend, for it was a lifelong habit of discipline. For the contemplative man's true end is the vision of God, glimpsed mystically here and now as the mists divide about the towers of felicity's home, but hereafter Jerusalem with all its lights ablaze and God face to face. This was a concept several high Anglicans had cherished; but it did not attract many Protestants. It would rarely occur to a Protestant to define prayer as the means to unity with God as St. John Fisher did so eloquently: "Prayer is like a certeine golden rope or chaine lett downe from heaven, by which we endeavour to draw God to us whereas we are more truly drawne to him. . . . This rope or golden Chaine holy S. Dionisius calleth prayer, which truly is let downe to us from heaven and by God himselfe fastened to our hearts. . . . Lastly, what other thing doth it, but elevates the mind above all things created, soe that att last it is made one spirit with God, fast bound unto him with the Golden line or Chaine of Prayer."[50]

For the much less contemplative and more active Protestant the true end of man was to do the will of God. His end was ethically and, to a lesser extent, mystically conceived. His love for God was proved by obedience. He believed that the true test of Christian discipleship was not to use the adoring titles in approaching Christ, but to do his will. It is significant that the Protestant used the word "service" equally to refer to divine worship and to giving human help. He believed that he should love the brother he had seen rather than be content with adoring the invisible God whose ikon

[50] *A Treatise of Prayer and the Fruits and Manner of Prayer* (1640), pp. 19, 20, 22, cited by Kelly, *Prayer in Sixteenth-century England*, p. 29.

was Christ. Such love for Christ as he felt must issue in action for the brethren for whom Christ died. It is, however, to press the contrast between Catholic and Protestant concepts of prayer too far to claim, as Faye Kelly does by implication, that while Fisher never used prayer as a means of obtaining personal favours, "never a means of improving one's self except in the sense of drawing closer to God,"[51] Protestants have no such scruples, since the bulk of prayers for them took the petitionary form. One has only to refer to William Perkins, the greatest of the sixteenth-century Puritan theologians, with his insistence that all prayer is to be grounded on God's word and a seeking of His will,[52] to refute the imputation that Protestant prayers were personal whims. Protestant pragmatism never ceased to be amazed by the grace of God offered to the undeserving, but it was not "lost in wonder, love, and praise" of God; it sought to get on with God's work. No one familiar with the works of charity and mercy undertaken for so many centuries by the Catholic church will lightly accuse that great Church of ethical escapism, but he might consider that some forms of spirituality cultivated by the more exalted monks and hermits, such as the Carthusians and the Calmaldolese, were obsessively and exclusively other-worldly. While never denying the primacy of the love of God as the motivation for all human concern, the Protestants believed that God was best loved in his children, especially the neediest.

Another difference between Catholic and Protestant pieties was dependent on the time when salvation was believed to be complete. For the Protestant, salvation was the accomplished work of Christ.[53] The elect soul was saved when it was called, being predestined to salvation. Acts of sanctification by that soul were then merely the proofs of the "calling," or election. For the Catholic, salvation was complete only when the purified soul emerges into heaven from purgatorial cleansing. Prayers for the dead were therefore a significant part of Catholic piety. They play no part at all

---

[51] *Ibid.* With this should be compared the view of Gordon Wakefield, *Puritan Devotion*, p. 33: "The Puritans have as much to say about Mystical Union, as about Divine Election in their doctrine of the Church." See also T. F. Torrance, *Kingdom and Church*, pp. 100ff.

[52] Perkins, *Cases of Conscience*, as republished in the posthumous folio edition of the *Works* (1611), vol. 2, pp. 63-64.

[53] One example is John Owen's Eucharistic doctrine of the finished work of Christ for men: "He [Christ] does not tender himself as one that *can* do these things . . . nor does he tender himself as one that *will* do these things upon any conditions as shall be prescribed unto us; but he tenders himself unto our faith as one that *hath* done these things. *Works*, ed. Goold, vol. 9, p. 565.

in Protestant piety. Furthermore, Catholics naturally invoked the prayers of the saints, particularly of the Blessed Virgin, for themselves and for their beloved dead. The intercession of the Mother of Christ or of the saints played no role in Protestant piety. The books of personal and familial prayers mirror these important differences of belief and practice.

Catholics were sufficiently realistic about human nature to know that only a few elect souls have the gifts and the opportunity to become saints and preeminent pointers to God. Protestants, to use C. S. Lewis's metaphor, dropped the honours degree in spirituality for the passing degree a much larger number of students were able to attain. The result was that Protestants did not seek a "religious" vocation. They desired, instead, to be religious in their family life and secular vocations. This is clearly indicated in the multitude of prayers for persons in different callings in the Protestant manuals of devotion. Thomas Becon, for example, in *The flower of godlye praiers* (1561), specified the relationship of the different groups of vocations to their masters, to their work, and to God. Landlords pray, for instance, to God that they may "remember themselves as tennauntes and not racke and strech our rentes" and recalled that they were "straungers and pilgrimes in this world having here no dwelling place, but seking one to come."[54] Becon proposes that merchants pray that they may "so occupye theyr marchaundise without fraude, gile, or deceite, that the common weale may prospere and floryshe with the abundance of worldly things through theyr godly and righteous travailes, unto the glory of thy name."[55]

Catholics and Protestants appear to have intended different purposes for a manual of devotion. To a Catholic a book of devotion meant an account of his duties as a member of the Church, which would spur him to accept its doctrine with firmer faith, provide him with officially approved devotions, as well as kindle his love for Christ and the saints. It might even encourage him to seek mystical experience. For the Protestant, it was thought of as a work in elementary theology, including clear instruction on the nature of prayer, which would enable him to form his own petitions in his own words. For this reason the manual would also include specimen prayers and directions for his public and private duties.

[54] Folio 39 verso.
[55] *Ibid.*, folio 40. See also Thomas Dekker, *Foure Birds of Noahs Arke*, ed. F. P. Wilson, pp. 36-39, for an excellent prayer intended for the use of merchants.

The Protestant believed that "there was no need of ecstasies, trances, visions, in order to lay hold of God. The act of understanding was of itself an act of union."[56] Thus it is not unfair to say that Catholic devotions were churchly in character while Protestant devotions were inclined to encourage independence of ecclesiastical authority and greater dependence on the Bible and the thoughtfulness of the individual.

It may well be true that Catholic and Protestant devotions, while Christ-centred, concentrated on different aspects of the Christian's role. So much of Catholic devotion seems to have been Incarnation-centred, so much of Protestant devotion Cross-centred. Or to put it in another way, the Catholic lovingly concentrated on the human aspects of God the Son: his relationship to his Mother, and his example in defeating temptations in the wilderness, in teaching, healing, praying, and loving; while the Protestant concentrated on Christ's redemptive function, as Mediator of forgiveness, as pioneer and perfector of faith, as well as giver of eternal life to the faithful. It seems as if the Catholic concentrated on the benefactor and the Protestant on the benefits; that would be one reading of the pragmatism of Protestant lay prayers and the preponderance of petitions over thanksgiving and even over intercession. Another interpretation would, as indicated before, stress the contemplative aspect of Catholic and the practical aspects of Protestant piety.

On the whole, it seems true that the Catholics emphasized the human aspects of Christ, while the Protestants concerned themselves with the divine power and gifts of the Saviour and Redeemer who delivered men from sin, suffering, and death. Yet even when this difference has been stressed, it cannot be made absolute. The ever-present crucifixes in Catholic churches, quite apart from the annual renewal of the climactic events of Holy Week, were a reminder that the image of the Virgin Mother with the Holy Infant in her arms, whether hieratically depicted as the throne of wisdom in Romanesque art or as the sublimest evocation of maternal tenderness, as in Gothic art, was, while dominant, far from being the only image of Christ in historic Catholicism. One recalls that certain humanistic and rationalistic forms of Protestantism have seen the role of Christ less as saviour than as teacher and exemplar. The difference is rather a difference of interest, or in the words of

---

[56] The citation comes from Stranks, *Anglican Devotion*, pp. 246-47; the entire paragraph is dependent on this source of information.

Helen C. White, the expert on Tudor devotional life, "this shift in the attitude towards Christ's life on earth is probably the key to the most significant difference between English devotion in the fifteenth century and the seventeenth."[57]

There were other, minor, differences. One notes, for example, the decidedly national character of Protestant prayers, as contrasted with the typically international Catholic devotions. This was often more than the fulfillment of the Biblical injunction to pray for all in authority; it frequently led to "political" prayers practically indistinguishable from royalist propaganda. Through the various royal primers and the required prayers in the Book of Common Prayer, as well as in the approved Protestant manuals (which required episcopal approval before being given a license for publication), there was a sense of the sacredness of the sovereign, as if he or she were the eye of God. The handbooks implied in their prayers for the queen and the magistrates that the maintenance of religion, the present civil authority, and the social order itself were interdependent. As Faye Kelly so justly remarks: "It is not always easy to be quite sure whether religion is being used to defend the power of the state or whether the power of the state is being marshalled to defend the existing religious order."[58]

Another difference was the Protestant preference for Biblical phraseology, as well as doctrine, wherever and whenever possible, as if it were a talisman against superstition and corrupt tradition. The intention was expressed by Thomas Becon in *The flower of godlye praiers*: "I have travailed to the uttermost of my power to use in these prayers as few words of my own as I could, and to glean out of the fruitful field of the sacred scriptures whatsoever I found meet for every prayer that I made, that when it is prayed, not man, but the Holy Ghost may seem to speak."[59]

The most surprising characteristic in an acrimonious and controversial age was the phenomenon I referred to earlier—the retention by Protestants of the prayers of Catholics, such as those of St. Augustine or the contemporary Erasmus and Juan Luis Vives. St. Augustine's *Confessions* had been a classic of spirituality for a thousand years, and their author seems today to be the foster par-

---

[57] *Tudor Books of Private Devotion*, pp. 246-47.

[58] Kelley, *Prayer in Sixteenth Century England*, p. 63.

[59] *Works*, vol. 3, pp. 12-13. A further consequence of the Biblicism for Protestants and especially for Puritans is that the latter substituted the patriarchs and the prophets for the Catholic saints as exemplars and companions of the godly way. See Wakefield, *Puritan Devotion*, p. 27.

ent of both Catholic and Protestant Christianity, so that his inclusion is less surprising than that of contemporaries. Erasmus had remarkably put his finger on the pulse of the times; his streamlined Catholicism proved very attractive to Luther and other first-generation Protestants. To cite the prayer of his most commonly used by Protestants is to understand why he spoke to their condition, as in this "Prayer for Peace in the Church" in an age of turbulence and confusion: "Thou seest (O good shepherd) what sundry sortes of wolves have broken into thy shepecotes, of whom every one crieth, Here is Christ, here is Christ, so that if it were possible the very perfecte persons should be brought into errour. Thou seest with what wyndes, with what waves thy sely shyp is tossed, thy ship wherein thi litle flock is in peril to be drouned. And what is nowe lefte, but that it utterly synke and we al perish."[60] What, however, was the secret of the attraction for Vives? It was more than the fact that he had been brought over to England from Bruges to help tutor Princess Mary, the elder daughter of Henry VIII and Catherine of Aragon, and that he had been a lecturer at Oxford, residing at Corpus Christi College. The fact that he was imprisoned by Henry VIII for taking Catherine's side in the "King's Matter" might have endeared him to later Protestants, were it not for the fact that he recanted to gain his freedom. His attraction lay in the informality and naturalness of the prayers, their intensely personal character, and their practicality being so directly related to the everyday experience of every man. Finally, it was a simple matter to adapt his prayers for Protestant use. Whatever the reasons, the phenomenon of prayers that crossed the vast religious divide of the sixteenth century is an intriguing and important one, and a promise and presage for the future.

5. Puritan Spirituality

At the outset Puritan spirituality would seem to be no more than a profoundly Biblical form of devotion lived in deep intensity and seriousness. Apart from such depth of commitment it was undistinguishable from Tudor Anglican spirituality. This is a true, but not wholly true, view. Anglican spirituality approximated that of Puritanism, but it also had a continuing link with Catholicism in Lancelot Andrewes and his successors. Protestantism had its

[60] *The Primer in Englishe and Latin set foorth by the Kinges Maiestie and his Clergie*, sig. R5-R5verso.

Lutheran, Calvinist, and Free church traditions; Puritanism's affinity was not with Lutheranism, but it *was* an English form of Calvinism with great variations which have later been developed into what is now known as the Free church tradition.

The first characteristic of Puritan spirituality was that it flourished best in the life of the family. The Puritan household was a little church, with the father as its father-in-God. His duty was to conduct the weekday prayers both morning and evening for his wife, the children, the servants, and possibly any apprentices. On Sunday, after returning from worship, it was his task to rehearse the children in their catechism and to check whether they had properly memorised and understood the main points of the sermon, and to arrange for reading aloud from the Bible or some other godly books, whether from the sermons of an approved minister or from the Protestant classic, Foxe's *Book of Martyrs*.[61] In these duties he was aided by the Bible, along with the manuals of devotion and prayers, which even provided him with the words of appropriate graces before and after meals. Serious, stringent, inflexibly disciplined as it may seem to later generations, this spirituality was mingled with the joy of psalm-singing[62] to catchy tunes and motivated by the sense that this is exactly how God's elect must live in a world of snares and traps laid by the ungodly, until they gain the reward of joining the everlasting community of the friends of Christ. This was the life of sanctification; this was how "saints" were matured. But they were saints who rejoiced in their marriages and in their children. Theirs was an intramundane asceticism for an extramundane reward. The monastery was the training ground of Catholic spirituality; the family was the seedplot of Puritan Christian life.

The location of Puritan spirituality in the family was aided by two powerful factors. The first was the fact that religion was not associated with a sacred building for them, as it was for Catholics or for High Church Anglicans. When they eventually separated from the Church of England and erected their own buildings for worship, they called them "meeting-houses," not "churches." For them the word "church" referred exclusively to the company of

---

[61] Lady Margaret Hoby records in her diary that she listened one Lord's day to someone reading from the Book of Martyrs, and on a weekday heard her minister read from the sermons of Richard Greenham. *The Diary of Lady Margaret Hoby*, ed. Dorothy M. Meads, pp. 75, 86.

[62] Knappen, in *Tudor Puritanism*, pp. 388-89, calls such "rouse-ments," that is, "emotional trimmings to reach the affections as well as the mind."

God's faithful people, the *communio electorum*, gathered to hear the reading and exposition of the oracles of God. Thus they could by the easiest of transitions conceive of the "church in the house" on the analogy of the gatherings of persecuted Christians of the primitive church, or use the even earlier precedent of the house meetings of the Apostolic church.

The second factor was the new significance given family life by the Reformers. God's covenant, invariably read at Baptismal services, was "to you and your children." This recognition helped weld family life into an enduring solidarity in Christ. The head of the family, who had promised at the Baptism of his children (Puritans did not approve of sponsors taking the vows instead of parents) to supervise their Christian nurture, was duty bound to teach his children the Scriptures and to make sure they understood the main points of Christian doctrine, behaviour, and worship. His promises at Baptism, his commitment in the covenant of church membership, the examples of the godly in the Scriptures which he read as God's marching orders, and the responsibility for which he must account to God at the Great Assize on the Day of Judgment, all confirmed him in the duty of being a prophet and priest to his own household. As J. Mayne wrote in *The English Explained*: "The parents and masters of families are in God's stead to their children and servants . . . every chief householder hath . . . the charge of the souls of his family."[63] The Puritan head of the household was truly fulfilling the role of the priesthood of all believers while conducting family prayers.

All forms of Christian spirituality claim to be Biblical, but each is dependent on a different selection from the Scripture; the proof passages are often taken from the same book of the Bible. Catholic sacramentalism made considerable use of the Fourth Gospel, and especially of the Prologue affirming that Christ, the Word became flesh. This was the foundation of the sacramental principle. Yet the Society of Friends used the same Gospel to affirm the priority and sovereign freedom of the Holy Spirit which, like the wind, blows where it pleases, and to claim that the inner light is the illumination of every man by Christ—assertions which challenge institutional ecclesiasticism to the full. Similarly, the most iconoclastic of the sacramentarian Protestants, the followers of Zwingli the Reformer of Zurich, turned to the sixth chapter of the same

[63] Cited by Hart, *Country Clergy*, p. 200.

Gospel[64] for support for their Memorialist doctrine of the Lord's Supper. Puritan theology and spirituality was predominantly Pauline, rather than Johannine, although the Puritans made good use of Augustine and Calvin as his interpreters.

With Paul, they saw the Christian life in terms of a historic recapitulation which is reenacted in the soul of every man. The second Adam, Christ, undoes the evil effected by the first Adam, and leads the bewildered and frightened soul from paradise lost to paradise regained. He is, in the military metaphor so appropriate for these spiritual men of steel, the captain of their salvation. The Scripture, in which the external Word of God is attested to by the *testimonium internum Spiritus Sancti*, is their iron ration: they would have no truck with tradition. Neither Popes nor bishops, but the Holy Spirit, would be their teacher, with occasional assistance from the Fathers or their own contemporary theologians, all of whom claimed to be following the guidance of the Holy Spirit. They took seriously the words of the Word of God when tempted in the wilderness: "Man shall not live by bread alone, but by every word which proceeds from the mouth of God." Their weapons were, as recorded in Ephesians,[65] the sword of the spirit which is the Word of God, and the shield of faith which extinguishes the flaming darts of the Evil One. Their armour included the helmet of salvation, the breastplate of righteousness. Their protection was integrity and their sandals were the preparation of the pacifying gospel. Their lifelong concern was to fight the good fight of faith; to this end they prayed incessantly, watched the progress of their souls in diaries which recorded their fears, failures, and solaces, sang psalms, and held private sessions of fasting when under the judgments of God, and of thanksgiving at some family occasion for joy. Godly reading, private and family prayers, making and renewing churchly and personal covenants, and diligence in their daily calling and active sharing in worship, together with earnest and active prosecution of the duties of charity, were their way of living the Christian life.

The Puritans had two immense sources of comfort and encouragement. One was their belief on predestination. Its premise—universal depravity—"by levelling all superiority not of the Spirit, enormously enhanced the self-respect of the ordinary man."[66] The

---

[64] See John 6:67 as a support of Zwinglian doctrine, while 6:49-51 supports Catholic sacramentalism.

[65] Ephesians 6:10-17.

[66] William Haller, *The Rise of Puritanism*, pp. 90f.

only true aristocracy was created by God, not by blood or inheritance. It was an aristocracy of the spirit and character. The triumph
of God's elect was foreordained: "If God be for us, who can be
against us?"[67] The work of salvation, being wholly God's, could
not fail. The second source was that Paul had provided a chart of
the stages in the progress of the Christian soul on pilgrimage. It
was to move from election, through vocation, justification, and
sanctification, to glorification. The Puritans *knew* this was the sure
path through the vale of tears to eternity. Their ministers encouraged the laity to develop introspection and thus enable them to
travel hopefully. As I have mentioned, one popular guide of this
type was the work of the moderate Puritan, Arthur Dent, appropriately titled *The Plain Mans Pathway to Heaven.* If the military
metaphor be preferred, and the struggle for spirituality was seen
as an interior civil war of the spirit against the flesh, then the
equivalent book, also of great popularity, was John Downame's
The Christian Warfare.[68] Then there was always Foxe's *Book of
Martyrs* to stir up their latent heroism.

The Puritan spiritual life has been criticised as too intense and
rigid. Its introspection has been considered as spiritual valetudi-
narianism. From a modern standpoint it has seemed not only too
inhibited, but also a dull routine. This judgment, however, is
caused by a failure to recognise that even if the Puritan was rarely
jocular, he had deep springs of joy. Richard Rogers wrote in his
diary: "But we must finde that our harty imbracing of the doctrine
of god and love of it and labouring after a good consc[ience] to
find ioy in Christes redeeming us is that which maketh our lives
ioiful, for this cannot by any malice of man nor devil, be taken
from us. I had exper[ience] of this of lat."[69] Moreover, on another
occasion, he indicated how singing psalms and other activities had
cheered him: "my mind hath veary heavenly been exercised in
considering, both by med[itation], singing ps. 119: 14, 15, 16,
and confer[ence], of godes goodnes in cheering our hartes with
the bottomless and unexpressable treasur of his word, and feling
of his favour, and inioying of his benef[its]. . . ."[70]

The Puritan spiritual life was earnest, intense, and well-disci-

[67] Romans 8:32.
[68] This book, originally a group of sermons, is described and evaluated in
detail in Chap. VII. It is worth recalling that *The Christian Warfare* (pp. 235-
47) enumerates 10 "signes and infallible notes of our election."
[69] *Two Elizabethan Puritan Diaries by Richard Rogers and Samuel Ward*, ed.
M. M. Knappen, p. 73.
[70] *Ibid.*, p. 99.

plined. It seems rigid, inflexible, and sour to its critics. To Shakespeare, satirising it in the character of Malvolio in *Twelfth Night*, it smacked too much of preciousness and complacency. To Ben Jonson it was a dreadfully boring regimen. In *The Silent Woman* Truewit tells Morose that if he marry one who is "precise" ("Puritan" and "Precisian" were interchangeable terms), he will have to listen to "long-winded exercises, singings, and catechisings." Jonson is even more scathing of Puritan prolixity, pretentiousness, and arguments over predestination in *Bartholomew Fair*, as he describes a rich old Puritan widow seen through the eyes of Quarlous, who says to his friend:

> Dost thou ever think to bring thine ears or stomach to the patience of a dry grace as long as thy table-cloth; and droned out by thy son here . . . till all the meat on thy board has forgot it was that day in the kitchen? or to brook the noise made in a question of predestination, by the good labourers and painful eaters assembled together, put to them by the matron your spouse; who moderates with a cup of wine, ever and anon, and a sentence out of Knox between? Or the perpetual spitting before and after a sober-drawn exhortation of six hours, whose better part was the hum-ha-hum? or to hear prayers groaned out over thy iron chests, as if they were charms to break them? And all this for the hope of two apostle-spoons, to suffer! and a cup to eat a caudle in! for that will be thy legacy. She'll have conveyed her state safe enough from thee, and she be a right widow.

6. *The Products of Piety*

We have seen how different the Catholic and Protestant forms of devotion were. It will be interesting to observe that there were few marked differences between the products of these pieties. For that reason I will compare a Catholic and a Puritan noblewoman, a Catholic and a Protestant martyr, an Anglican bishop and a Puritan minister. Also, I will consider the spirituality of an Anglican squire and an Anglican minister of state.

Lady Magdalen Montague was a notable chatelaine and a Catholic.[71] Hers was an unobtrusive spirituality, so her chaplain informs us, even when she was a young maid of honour at Queen Mary's Court:

[71] See Chap. IV for further information on the Lady Magdalen, Viscountess Montague and her spiritual regimen.

she accustomed to rise from her bed very early, and attiring herself with all possible speed hastened to the chapel, where, kneeling against a wall and the other part of her face covered with her head attire, she accustomed to spend certain hours in devout prayer and to shed abundance of tears before Almighty God. And yet withal would she not be any time from any office of piety prescribed to her and her companions. Neither was she content in this sort to spend the day, but arose from her bed in the night, and prostrate on the ground applied herself to prayer a good part of the night. Which when the Lady Magdalen [her mother] had once perceived, she finding her devotion to be discovered, no otherwise than if she had been apprehended in some notorious lewd fault, falling on her knees, with many tears, she besought her for the honour of God that she would not bewray her secret exercise of piety to any creature while she lived.[72]

As a widow she was deeply concerned for her husband's soul, "for whom she twice every week caused mass to be said, and herself said the office of the dead."[73] Every year she commemorated the anniversary of his death, and thanked God at almost every meal for the bounty that came to her through her husband. At "Little Rome," in one of her country homes, though a Recusant she caused impressive celebrations of the Mass to take place on all the most solemn festivals; each week a sermon was preached in her chapel. Hers was almost a monastic piety, for she heard three Masses each day and read three Offices. Most impressive was her large liberality to the eighty persons or more whom she supported financially to help to maintain their Catholicism in days of persecution:

She maintained three priests in her house, and gave entertainment to all that repaired to her, and very seldom dismissed any without the gift of an angel. She redeemed two out of prison at her own cost, and attempted the like for others, and gave money to other Catholics both in common and particular. Her alms, distributed every second day at her gates to the poor, were plentiful and such as some of the richer Protestants did calumniate that they augmented the number of beggars and nourished their idleness. When she desisted from her prayers, she accustomed to spend much time in sewing shirts

[72] An Elizabethan Recusant House, comprising the Life of the Lady Magdalen, Viscountess Montague (1538-1608), ed. A. C. Southern, pp. 12-13.
[73] Ibid., p. 23.

or smocks for poor men and women, in which exercise she seemed to take much pleasure; sometimes, also, when she had leisure, she visited the poor in their own houses and sent them either medicines or meat or wood or money, as she perceived their need. . . .[74]

She was no cardboard saint, too good to be true. She was attractive enough to appeal to the wandering eyes of a prince, and brave enough to slap down his intruding hand. Though spiritual, she was also a woman of spirit.

Her Puritan counterpart was Lady Margaret Hoby, who lived at Hackness in Yorkshire and seems to have been almost equally devout, using all opportunities for worship and instruction in the Christian life with great assiduity. She was a notable benefactor of the local Anglican parish church, but her resources (though perhaps not her concern for her neighbours) were considerably less than those of Viscountess Montague, so that we read little about her charities. A typical weekday was spent thus: "After privat praiers I did read of the bible, then I went to publeck [worship?], after to work, then to breakfast: and so about the house: after, to dinner: after dinner I did see Lightes made allmost all the after none, and then I took a Lector, then to supper: after, I hard Mr. Rhodes Read of Grenhame [Greenham the Puritan divine], and then I praied and so went to bed. . . ."[75] The red letter day of the Puritan calendar was the Lord's Day. This is how Lady Hoby spent one: "After privat praier I went to church wher I hard the word preached, and received the sacramentes to my Comfort: after I had given thankes and dined, I walked a whill, and then went to church, whence, after I had hard Catcizising and sarmon, I returned home and wret notes in my bible, and talked of the sarmon and good thinges with Mrs. Ormston: then went to praier, after to supper, then to repetecion of the wholl daies exersice and praiers, hard one of the men reade of the book of marters, and so went to bed."[76]

Both women attended public worship, both took part in private and household prayers; both were obviously helped by the chief sacrament, and enjoyed sermons. The difference between them was that the devotions of Lady Montague are more objective and structured, while those of Lady Hoby are as varied as sermons, extemporaneous prayers, and Biblical note-taking can be, with the

[74] *Ibid.*, p. 40.
[76] *Ibid.*

[75] *Diary of Lady Margaret Hoby*, p. 86.

exception of the catechising, which must have had a formal structure. One doubts whether there was much difference in the time they spent at their devotions or their secular duties, or in the dedication with which they were performed.

Next we compare a Catholic and a Protestant martyr, Thomas More (1478-1535) and John Bradford (c. 1510-1555), each of whom paid the supreme tribute of loyalty unto death. Thomas More was, of course, a famous humanist and friend of Erasmus and Holbein. He was the author of *Utopia* and a legal luminary, who was the first lay Lord Chancellor of England under Henry VIII; he was a man of wit, wisdom, and courage. When he was about 21 he thought seriously about adopting the ascetic life. Taking a lodging at the Charterhouse, he submitted himself to the discipline of a Carthusian monk. From 1499 to 1503 he wore a hairshirt next to his skin, scourged himself every Friday and other fast day, allowed himself only four or five hours sleep each night, lying on the bare ground and using a log for a pillow. Though he abandoned the idea of relinquishing the world, he continued for the rest of his life to be scrupulous in fulfilling his religious duties. Twice married and an exemplary husband and father, he was particularly close to his learned daughter Margaret, whose husband, William Roper, wrote the earliest biography, entitled *The Mirror of Vertue in Worldly Greatness; or, the Life of Syr Thomas More*, during Mary's reign in manuscript form, which was printed in Paris in 1626. His own testament of devotion, intended chiefly for his family, was printed by William Rastell in 1533, as *A Dyaloge of Comfort against Tribulacion*. It was here in prison, like his friend, Bishop John Fisher, that his deep faith and spiritual life were really put to the test as he faced the imminence of death. That harsh, horrific, yet holy event, took place on July 7, 1535. Four centuries later More was canonized by Pope Pius XI.

As a layman More knew that the greatest danger to the spiritual life is an inability to detach oneself from the entanglements of the world. It is for this reason, he believed, that God sends tribulation, a subject which More treated more exhaustively than anyone else before or since, mainly in the three books of his *Dialogue*. Our temptations are our severest test as Christians. Here we do battle with a formidable adversary, the devil, who is both stronger and more brilliant than we are. Should he win, our fate is death, which does not only separate body from soul, but "the whol entire man . . . from the fruition of the very fountain of life, Almighty Glorious

God."[77] Yet there is no reason to be terrified by Satan, for though he can defeat us, God is more than a match for him. Our shield is God's truth, and we cling to God by faith, for which we must continually pray, saying with the apostles, "Lord increase our faith," or with the father of the dumb child, "I believe, good Lord, but help thou the lack of my belief!"[78]

As Germain Marc'hadour pointed out,[79] the Christendom into which More had been born had lost its militant spirit and the decay of chivalry was symptomatic of the softening of the soul's fibre. Erasmus, influenced by Colet as was More, was critical of the passive, compliant, sentimental and fugitive spirituality then dominant. He published his *Enchiridion*, a "handbook" or "hand-dagger" for the Christian knight's daily warfare. More embodied this new type of Christian man, informed and energetic, ready for attack as well as defence. Although he believed that the roles of leadership in the Church were reserved for the priests and bishops who were the salt of the earth spoken of in the Sermon on the Mount, he could not agree that the Church was to be equated with the clergy. He believed that "God hath given everyman cure and charge of his neighbour."[80] He implied that others should share with him the duty of confuting Protestant pamphleteers, but to do that properly meant that they must better understand the faith. There might be a danger in intellectual pride, but the greater danger lay in intellectual laziness. His mind was fully in accord with the principle of Anselm, *fides quaerens intellectum*. More was convinced that less time should be devoted to logic and more to the divine revelation in Holy Scripture. In More's *Life of Pico* there is an appendix in which is found Pico's advice to his nephew, with which More cordially agreed. It reads, in part: "Thou mayst do nothing more pleasant to God, nothing more profitable to thyself, then if thine hand cease not day nor night to turn and read the volume of Holy Scripture. There lieth privily in them a certain heavily strength, quick and effectual, which with a marvellous power transformeth and changeth the reader's mind into the love of God."[81]

Since this marvellous spiritual bread of God's Word is meant

---

[77] *The Worke of Sir Thomas More Knyght* (1557), ed. William Rastell, p. 1,286. This is the first English edition of the *Works*.

[78] *Ibid.*, p. 1,143.

[79] The essay on the spirituality of Sir Thomas More by Germain Marc'hadour, in *Pre-Reformation English Spirituality*, pp. 224-40, has proved invaluable both for its thoughts and citations in the ensuing five paragraphs.

[80] Rastell, ed., *Worke of Knyght*, pp. 143, 279.

[81] Cited by Marc 'hadour in *English Spirituality*, p. 228, p. 13.

for all men, More made it clear that he fully approved the production of an English translation.[82] The truth of the Scriptures may be misinterpreted by heretics, because they ignore or defy the Catholic church, which was the "perpetual apostle" of Christ.[83] More's spirituality was Christo-centric and Church-centred at the same time. He believed that the fullest life is to be found in Christ; after His glorification, Christ is present chiefly through the word of the Scriptures and through the Blessed Sacrament. Perhaps it was this sacramental element in the piety which distinguished More from the Protestant martyr most clearly. For More the essence of the Eucharist was the communion with God and men that it created and sustained. He wrote: "The *thing* of the Blessed Sacrament is the unity and society of all good folk in the mystical body of Christ. . . . Our Saviour is the worker of this communion: in giving his own very body into the body of every Christian man, he doth in a certain manner incorporate all Christian folk and his own body in one corporation mystical."[84] More was fully convinced of the importance of human solidarity and of the profounder solidarity of souls in the Church, of the Church militant on earth united with the Church triumphant in heaven, and the souls being purified in purgatory. Heaven, indeed, was for More the jubilant society where God's folk are merry together with "the Trinity in his high marvellous majesty, our Savior in his glorious manhood sitting on his throne with his immaculate Mother and all that glorious company."[85]

Marc'hadour suggests that the secret of the exhilaration in More's spirituality was not jocosity, but its ability to teach us "the art of transmuting everything—the drab, the tedious, the tragic—into gladness, through 'clearness of conscience' and the conviction that the Almighty is also the All-loving."[86] This is the meaning of More's own *riddle*: "Though I might have pain, I could not have harm. . . . In such a case a man may lose his head and suffer no harm."[87] The malice of others cannot defeat God. With the Psalmist, More was convinced that underneath are the everlasting arms of God and that death is a rebirth to eternal life.

There were two spurs to send him up to the high country of spirituality if life seemed dull and stale. One was the spur of fear, fear of his own death; the other was the spur of love, of recalling

---

[82] Rastell, ed., *Worke of Knyght*, pp. 240-47.
[83] *Ibid.*, p. 458.
[84] *Ibid.*, pp. 1,336, 1,347.
[85] *Ibid.*, p. 1,261.
[86] *English Spirituality*, p. 234.
[87] See More's *Letters*, nos. 210, 216.

the death of the Son of God for him. Let them, said More, "spur forth thine horse through the short way of this momentary life to the reward of eternal felicity."[88] More wrote two unfinished treatises on the Passion. He clearly held the truth of the Carthusian motto: *Stat crux dum volvitur orbis*. Christ's Passion was the unmoving, still centre of divine love in the world's whirligig. For More the world was always a prison, but a happy prison if one knows that God is the chief gaoler, and that at death he throws the prison gates wide open for the liberated soul. That was the faith of a great Catholic martyr.

The Protestant martyr, John Bradford, was a much less colourful figure. It seems that he was a native of Manchester and served for some years as secretary to Sir John Harrington, the paymaster of the English forces in France. He then decided on a legal career and is said to have been converted by a sermon of Latimer's so that he was moved to restore monies he had embezzled. He read theology at St. Catharine's Hall, Cambridge, where he took a master's degree and was elected into a fellowship at Pembroke College in the same university. He was appointed chaplain to the sturdy Protestant Bishop Ridley of London. On the accession of Queen Mary in 1553 he was imprisoned for alleged sedition. For a year and a half, while incarcerated, he wrote letters of spiritual advice to many correspondents, also the polemical work, *The Hurt of Hearing Mass*. His prayers, as we have seen, became the current coin of Protestant devotions, because of their sincerity, moving eloquence, and profound convictions, and because his Christian witness was sealed with the blood of martyrdom. He died at Smithfield "where he was led with a great company of weaponed men to conduct him thither,"[89] so that the huge crowd of sympathisers would not attempt to rescue him.

Such a martyrdom had been prepared for by a life of deep consecration. It was reported of him while at St. Catharine's Hall that: "He used in the morning to go to the common prayer in the college where he was, and after that he used to make some prayer with his pupils in his chambers; but not content with this he then repaired to his own secret prayer and exercise in prayer by himself, as one that had not yet prayed to his own mind; for he was wont to say to his familiars, 'I have prayed with my pupils, but I have not yet prayed with myself.' "[90]

[88] *Worke of Knyght*, p. 13.
[89] *Writings of Bradford*, ed. Townshend, vol. 1, p. xi.
[90] *Ibid.*, p. xix.

The life of the Tudor laity was so encircled by prayer that it is no surprise to learn of William Cecil, Lord Burghley, Queen Elizabeth's chief minister of state and the busiest man in England, that he was not too busy to attend prayers. According to the report printed in Francis Peck's *Desiderata Curiosa*,[91] Burghley always attended morning and evening prayer, and never missed a sermon on Sunday or failed to attend Holy Communion on the first Sunday of the month. Late in his life, particularly, in addition to all his other alms-givings, he gave his chaplain 20 shillings for the poor when at a sermon.

An equally devout Anglican layman was Squire Bruen of Bruen Stapleford in Cheshire, who succeeded to the family estates in 1587. His special care was to conduct the family prayers, that he considered "the very goads and spurs unto godliness, the life and sinews of grace and religion." Rising at 3 or 4 a.m. in summer and 5 a.m. in winter, he prayed in private, read and meditated on some portion of Scripture, and composed a fair copy of "some part of such sermons as he had by a running hand taken from the mouth of the preacher." Then he summoned his household to prayers, which comprised an introductory prayer imploring divine blessing on their exercises of devotion, the singing of psalms, the reading and exposition of Scripture, ending with a prayer of thanksgiving. Similar prayers were offered in the evening. Each Sunday the squire walked to Tarvin church, a distance of about a mile, "calling all his family about him, leaving neither cook nor butler behind him, nor any of his servants, but two or three to make the doores and tend the horse untill their returne." On his journey, he collected as many tenants and neighbours as possible, marching at the head of his Christian company with a joyous heart, and leading them in the singing of psalms.

Such was his reputation for holiness that a number of the gentry in the neighbourhood entrusted their children to his care and direction. Besides his own family and servants, he once had as many as 21 boarders in his home. He was a man of liberal bounty. Every week the poor people of Chester and surroundings, in addition to his own parishioners, flocked to the gates of Stapleford House to receive of his generosity.[92] The picture is idyllic, and

[91] The work was published in London in 1732, over a century after Burghley's death. The reference is to p. 45, the information from which is summarised by Stranks, *Anglican Devotion*, p. 26.

[92] The information on Squire Bruen is derived from Hart, *Man in the Pew, 1558-1660*, pp. 193-94.

perhaps far from typical, but it is a vignette of Anglican piety to set beside those of George Herbert as Rector of Bemerton or the Ferrar family at Little Gidding in the next, turbulent, century.

My final comparison is of a dedicated Puritan minister, Richard Rogers, and a gifted Anglican Bishop, Nicholas Ridley of London. Rogers is already familiar as the writer of practical theological treatises on the Christian life, which were an impressive psychology of prayer in themselves.[93] It is fortunate that his private diary[94] has survived and that it is so informative on the subject of his spiritual methods for maintaining the vigour of the Christian life. It appears that Rogers had a programme of meditation on such themes as humility, the forgiveness of sins, the preparation for the seeking of God, and peace with God. In addition, however, he set up regular times for study of the Bible, for private prayer and for family prayers.[95] Other forms of disciplining the spiritual life included keeping the diary itself as both an outlining of the goal, and a record of failure and of determination to overcome failure and the preparation of sermons for weekly occasions. An important Puritan custom that he used was the making of a covenant or solemn vow. As Haller rightly insists, "instead of promising to go on a pilgrimage or to make gifts to a shrine, the Puritan in time of stress, would vow to keep a better course, or even to cause others to do so. . . ."[96] Other forms of spiritual stimulus were psalm-singing, conferences with fellow Christians on spiritual matters, and attendance at public worship and the Lord's Supper. Not least in the Puritan's calendar were occasions of fasting. Of one such occasion, Rogers wrote interestingly that it provoked him to write his own *Seven Treatises* which ran to five editions before being abridged. Here is his account: "The 6 of this month we fasted betwixt our selves min[isters] to the stirring upp of ourselves to greater godlines. Veary good thinges we gathered to this purpose, ef[esians] 1:1-2, and then we determined to bring into writinge a direction for our lives, which might be both for ourselves and others."[97] It is not by the originality of his spiritual discipline that the Puritan is known, but rather the assiduity, endurance, and intensity of his spirituality which made the minimal concessions to the natural man. Like Jesuit spirituality, it was intended for vertebrate Christians.

[93] See Chap. VII.
[94] See M. M. Knappen, *Two Elizabethan Puritan Diaries by Richard Rogers and Samuel Ward.*
[95] *Ibid.,* pp. 65, 96.   [96] *Ibid.,* p. 8.   [97] *Ibid.,* p. 69.

I conclude with an account of the prayer and study schedule of an exemplary Edwardian Bishop, Nicholas Ridley of London. This is how he maintained the culture of the spiritual life in Fulham Palace, as recorded by Foxe the martyrologist: "Duly every morning, as soon as his apparel was done upon him, he went forthwith to his bedchamber, and there upon his knees prayed the space of half an hour; which being done, immediately he went to his study (if there came no other business to interrupt him) where he continued till ten of the clock, and then came to the common prayer, daily used in his house. The prayers being done, he went to dinner where he used little talk, except otherwise occasion by some had been ministered, and then it was sober, discreet and wise, and sometimes merry, as cause required."[98]

Piety and humour have not always been conjoined and it is intriguing that the Catholic martyr More and the Protestant martyr Ridley combined holiness with hilarity. Like so many good men in this century of divided religious allegiances, they were forced to become Catholic or Protestant instead of remaining merely Christian. Though tragically divided in life, in their deaths they were undivided, and share, so one may hope, an equal eschatology.

From the vertiginous standpoint of the present, the differences of spirituality between Catholic, Anglican, and Puritan in the Tudor age seem small. In fact, the difference between Anglican and Puritan spirituality of equal fervour was negligible, so much so that the label "Protestant" adequately covers both before the advent of the Caroline divines. All three forms of Christian spirituality rely on the inspiration of the purifying and empowering Holy Spirit. All three acknowledge that they are constrained and motivated by the love of Christ for the undeserving. All three produce the same effects: the security of faith, the serenity of hope, the peace and joy of believing, and the compassionate charity that seeks the good of others. Finally, all three pieties are the iron rations of pilgrims seeking the same goal—the shining citadels of the communion (and community) of saints.

[98] *The Acts and Monuments of John Foxe*, ed. S. R. Cattley and G. Townsend, 8 vols., VII, 408.

BIBLIOGRAPHY

1. Liturgical Texts
2. Periodicals
3. Sources in English Literature
4. Books

1. SELECTED LITURGICAL TEXTS

(Arranged Chronologically by Denomination)

ANGLICAN

Cranmer's Liturgical Projects. Ed. J. Wickham Legg. Henry Bradshaw Society, vol. 50, 1915.

The Order of Communion, 1548. Ed. H. A. Wilson. Henry Bradshaw Society, vol. 34, 1908.

First Prayer Book of Edward VI, 1549. Ed. Vernon Staley. 1903.

The First and Second Prayer Books of King Edward VI. Ed. E.C.S. Gibson. Everyman edition, 1910.

The Liturgies of 1549 and 1552 with other Documents set forth in the Reign of Edward VI. Ed. J. Ketley. Cambridge: Parker Society, 1844.

John Marbeck. *The Book of Common Praier Noted.* 1550.

Liturgies and Occasional Forms of Prayer set forth in the Reign of Queen Elizabeth. Ed. W. K. Clay. Cambridge: Parker Society, 1851.

Private Prayers put forth by authority during the Reign of Queen Elizabeth. Ed. W. K. Clay. Cambridge: Parker Society, 1851.

Thomas Sternhold and John Hopkins. *The Whole Book of Psalmes collected into Englysh metre.* 1562.

[Homilies]. *Certain Sermons appointed by the Queen's Majesty* . . . 1574. Reprinted and ed. G. E. Corrie. Cambridge, 1850.

PURITAN

John Knox's Genevan Service Book, 1556. Ed. William D. Maxwell. Edinburgh, 1931.

A Booke of the Forme of Common Prayers, Administration of the Sacraments, &c. agreable to Gods Worde, and the Use of the Reformed Churches. Published in 1584 and 1586, respectively, as the Waldegrave and Middelburg Puritan Liturgies; reissued, ed. Peter Hall. *Fragmenta Liturgica,* vol. 1, Bath, 1848, *Reliquiae Liturgicae,* vol. 1, Bath, 1847.

REFORMED

Richter, A. L., ed. *Die evangelischen Kirchenordnungen d. sechszehnten Jahrhunderts.* 2 vols. Weimar, 1846.

443

Smend, Julius. *Die evangelischen deutschen Messen bis zu Luthers Deutscher Messe.* Göttingen, 1896.

Terry, Richard R. *Calvin's First Psalter* (1539). Facsimile edition, 1932.

Thompson, Bard, ed. and intro. *Liturgies of the Western Church.* Cleveland and New York, 1962. This is a wide selection of Catholic, Lutheran, and a variety of Reformed Rites.

ROMAN CATHOLIC

The Prymer or Lay Folk's Prayer Book. Ed. Henry Littlehales. Early English Text Society, 1897.

The Sarum Missal in English. Tr. F. E. Warren. 2 vols. 1911.

The Use of Sarum. Ed. W. H. Frere. 2 vols. Cambridge, 1898-1901.

The Sarum Missal. Ed. J. Wickham Legg. Oxford, 1916.

Breviarium Romanum Quignonianum. Ed. J. Wickham Legg. Cambridge, 1888.

The Second Recension of the Quignon Breviary. Ed. J. Wickham Legg. 2 vols. Henry Bradshaw Society, 1908-1912.

2. PERIODICALS

DENOMINATIONAL

ANGLICAN
Theology

BAPTIST
Transactions of the Baptist Historical Society

CONGREGATIONALIST
Transactions of the Congregational Historical Society

ROMAN CATHOLIC

The Downside Review, Benedictine Abbey of Downside, near Bath, England.

Worship, St. John's Benedictine Abbey, Collegeville, Minnesota.

INTERDENOMINATIONAL

Church History, Chicago.
Journal of Ecclesiastical History, London.
Journal of Theological Studies, Oxford.
Studia Liturgica, Rotterdam, Holland.

3. SOURCES IN ENGLISH LITERATURE

Incidental use was made of Sir Thomas Wyatt and Edmund Spenser as writers of psalms more suitable for private meditation than for public praise. Passing mention was also made of Thomas Dekker's remarkable prayers for artisans.

It was noted that the three major competing religious traditions, Catholic, Anglican, and Puritan, had their own poets. In Ben Jonson the Catholics had a major dramatist and poet, and a superb lyricist in the Jesuit, Robert Southwell.

The Anglicans could boast of John Donne, writer of sensual love poems and profoundly spiritual poems, in whom erudition and wit were commingled, and who—as Dean of St. Paul's cathedral, London —was a great pulpit luminary.

The Puritans counted the gentle allegorist, Edmund Spenser in their number, partly because of his championship of Archbishop Grindal (as "Algrind" in *The Shepherd's Calendar*), who refused to put down the Puritan "prophesyings" even at royal command. But their greatest poet, Milton, was not born until the next century.

Both Anglicans and Catholics were intensely critical of the Puritans, for their intensity of religion outraged the moderation and easygoing ways of Erastian Anglicanism. Their Biblicism posed a threat to Catholicism's appeal to tradition. Thus it was that Shakespeare and Ben Jonson helped to create the stereotype of the Puritan as one who was a hypocrite in faith and a blue-nosed busybody who hated others to be happy. Shakespeare's caricature is Malvolio in *Twelfth Night* and Jonson's is Mr. Zeal-of-the-land-Busy in *Bartholomew Fair*.

Both Webster and Donne are referred to for their expression of a Jacobean *fin de siècle* preoccupation with death and disintegration, which finds expression alike in the divine and amatory poems and sermons of Donne and in *The Duchess of Malfi* of Webster. The latter's *White Devil* was used for an interesting quotation which satirized the growing Jacobean use of tomb hatchments in church as status symbols.

4. BOOKS

(Except where otherwise indicated, all books were published in London)

Abraham, Gerald, ed. *The Age of Humanism, 1540-1630.* The New Oxford History of Music, vol. 4. 1968.

Addison, W. *The English Country Parson.* 1948.

———. *Worthy Dr. Fuller.* 1951.

Addleshaw, G.W.O. and F. Etchells. *The Architectural Setting of Anglican Worship.* 1948.

Allen, William. *An Apologie and true declaration of the institution and endevours of the two English Colleges.* 1581.

Anderson, Anthony. *The Sheild of our Safetie set foorth.* 1581.

Anderson, M. D. *The Imagery of British Churches.* 1955.

Andrewes, Bartimaeus. *Certaine verie godlie and profitable Sermons upon the fifth chapiter of the Songe of Solomon.* 1595.

Andrewes, Lancelot. *Ninety-Six Sermons.* 5 vols. Oxford, 1850-1856.

[Anglican homilies]. *Certain Sermons appointed by the Queen's Majesty.* . . . [1574]. Reprinted and ed. by G. E. Corrie. Cambridge, 1850.

[Anglican homilies]. *The Two Books of Homilies.* Ed. J. Griffiths. Oxford, 1859.

Arber, Edward, ed. *A Brief Discussion of the Troubles begun at*

Frankfort in the year 1554 about the Book of Common Prayer and Ceremonies. 1908.

Babbage, Stuart B. *Puritanism and Richard Bancroft.* 1962.

Baillie, Robert. *A Dissuasive from the Errours of the Time.* . . . 1645.

Bancroft, Richard. *Dangerous Positions and Proceedings . . . under pretence of Reformation and for the Presbiteriall Discipline.* 1593.

————. *A Sermon preached at Paules Crosse . . . Anno 1588.*

Barnes, Robert. *Works.* Ed. Foxe, 1573.

Barrow, Henry. *The Writings of Henry Barrow, 1587-1590.* Ed. Leland H. Carlson. 1962.

————. *The Writings of Henry Barrow, 1590-1591.* Ed. Leland H. Carlson. 1964.

Baskerville, G. *English Monks and the Suppression of the Monasteries.* 1937.

Baum, J. G. *Première Liturgie des églises reformées de France de l'an 1533.* Strassburg, 1859.

[Baxter, Richard]. *Reliquiae Baxterianae.* 1696.

Bayne, Peter, ed. *Puritan Documents.* 1862.

Becon, Thomas. *The Catechism of Thomas Becon.* Ed. J. Ayre. Cambridge: Parker Society, 1844.

————. *The Jewel of Joy.* 1560.

Betjeman, John, ed. *Collins Guide to English Parish Churches.* Rev. edn. 1959.

Bennett, H. S. *English Books and Readers, 1475-1557.* Cambridge, 1952.

Benz, Ernst. *The Eastern Orthodox Church, Its Thought and Life.* Tr. by Richard and Clara Winston from *Geist und Leben der Ostkirche.* Hamburg, 1957. New York, 1963.

Birt, H. N. *The Elizabethan Religious Settlement.* 1907.

Bishop, Edmund. *Liturgia Historica, Papers on the Liturgy and Religious Life of the Western Church.* Oxford, 1918.

Black, J. B. *The Reign of Elizabeth, 1558-1603.* 2nd edn., 1959.

Blench, J. W. *Preaching in England in the Late Fifteenth and Sixteenth Centuries.* Oxford, 1964.

Blomfield, Reginald. *A History of Renaissance Architecture in England, 1500-1800.* 2 vols. 1897.

Bolton, Robert. *Works.* 4 vols. 1631-1641.

Bond, F. *An Introduction to English Church Architecture from the 11th to the 16th Century.* 2 vols. 1913.

Bonnet, Jules, ed. *Calvin's Letters.* London and Edinburgh, 2 vols., 1855-1857.

Booty, John E., ed. *An Apology of the Church of England by John Jewel.* Ithaca, N.Y., 1963.

————. *John Jewel as Apologist of the Church of England.* 1963.

Bouyer, Louis. *Life and Liturgy.* South Bend, Ind., 1956.

Boyd, Morrison Comegys. *Elizabethan Music and Musical Criticism.* 2nd edn. Philadelphia, 1962.

Bradford, John. *Works.* Ed. A. Townshend. 2 vols. Cambridge: Parker Society, 1848, 1853.

Bradshaw, William. *English Puritanisme, containing the maine opin-*

ions of the rigidest sort of those that are called Puritanes in the realm of England. 1605.

Bridgett, T. E. and T. F. Knox. *The True Story of the Catholic Hierarchy deposed by Queen Elizabeth with fuller memoirs of its last two survivors*. 1889.

Brightman, F. E. *The English Rite*. 2 vols. 1915.

Brinkworth, E. R., ed. *The Archdeacon's Court, 1584*. 2 vols. Oxfordshire Record Society, 1942, 1946.

Brilioth, Yngve. *Eucharistic Faith and Practice, Evangelical and Catholic*. 1930.

Bromiley, G. W. *Thomas Cranmer, Theologian*. 1956.

Brook, Benjamin. *The Lives of the Puritans*. 3 vols. 1813.

Brook, Stella. *The Language of the Book of Common Prayer*. 1965.

Brook, V.J.K. *A Life of Archbishop Cranmer*. 1962.

Brooks, Peter. *Thomas Cranmer's Doctrine of the Eucharist*. 1965.

Browne, Robert. *A Booke which sheweth the life and manners of all true Christians*. Middelburg, Holland, 1582.

———. *A Treatise of Reformation without tarrying for anie*. Middelburg, 1582.

———. *A True and Short Declaration*. . . . Middelburg, Holland, 1582.

———. *The Writings of Robert Harrison and Robert Browne*. Ed. A. Peel and L. H. Carlson, 1953.

Buchberger, M., ed. *Lexikon für Theologie*. 10 vols. 1930-1938.

Bukofzer, Manfred E. *Music in the Baroque Era from Monteverdi to Bach*. New York, 1947.

Bull, Henry. *Christian Praiers and Holie Meditations*. 1578.

Burrage, Champlin. *The Early English Dissenters in the light of recent research*. 2 vols. Cambridge.

Burton, William. *Davids Evidence*. 1596.

Butler, Charles. *The Principles of Musick*. 1636.

Butterworth, C. C. *The English Primers, 1529-1545*. Philadelphia, 1953.

Buxton, John. *Elizabethan Taste*. 1963.

Calendar of State Papers, Domestic Series, of the Reigns of Edward VI, Mary and Elizabeth. Ed. R. Lemon, 1856.

Calendar of State Papers, Domestic Series, of the Reign of Elizabeth. Ed. M.A.E. Green, 1872.

Calvin, John. *Commentary on I Corinthians. Corpus Reformatorum*. 101 vols. vol. 49.

———. *Letters*. Ed. Jules Bonnet. 2 vols. London and Edinburgh, 1855-1857.

———. *Institutes of the Christian Religion*. Tr. Thomas Norton, 1599.

Cambridge History of English Literature. Ed. A. W. Ward and A. R. Waller. 15 vols. Cambridge, 1907-1932.

[Campion, Edmund]. Richard Simpson, *Life of Edmund Campion*. 1896.

Caraman, Philip, ed. *The Other Face, Catholic Life under Elizabeth I*. 1950.

Cardwell, Edward. *Documentary Annals of the Reformed Church of England*. 2 vols. Oxford, 1844.

———. *History of Conferences and other Proceedings connected with the Revision of the Book of Common Prayer, 1558-1690*. Oxford, 1840.

———. *Synodalia*. 2 vols. Oxford, 1842.

Carleton, George. *Life of Bernard Gilpin*. 1629.

Carlson, Leland H., ed. *The Writings of Henry Barrow, 1587-1590*. 1962.

———. *The Writings of Henry Barrow, 1590-1591*. 1964.

———. *The Writings of John Greenwood, 1587-1590*. 1962.

Carpenter, S. C. *The Church in England, 1597-1688*. 1954.

Cartwright, Thomas. *A Commentary on the Epistle of St. Paul written to the Colossians*. 1612.

———. *A Treatise of the Christian Religion*. 1616.

[Catholic Record Society]. *Miscellanea*. vol. 3, no. 3, Catholic Record Society, 1906.

[Catholic Record Society]. *Miscellanea. Bedingfield Papers, etc*. no. 7, 1909.

Chester, Allan G. *Hugh Latimer, Apostle to the English*. Philadelphia, 1954.

Clapham, Henock. *A Chronological Discourse*. 1609.

Clark, Francis. *Eucharistic Sacrifice and the Reformation*. 1960.

Clark, W. K. Lowther, ed. *Liturgy and Worship*. 1932.

Clarke, Basil and John Betjeman. *English Churches*. 1964.

Clay, W. K., ed. *Liturgies and Occasional Forms of Prayer set forth in the Reign of Queen Elizabeth*. Cambridge: Parker Society, 1847.

———. *Private Prayers put forth by authority during the Reign of Queen Elizabeth*. Cambridge: Parker Society, 1851.

Clebsch, William. *England's Earliest Protestants, 1520-1535*. New Haven, 1964.

Coleridge, S. T. *Notes on English Divines*. Works, vol. 4. Ed. H. M. Coleridge, 1853.

Collins, A. Jefferies, ed. *Manuale ad usum percelebris ecclesie Sarisburiensis*. vol. 91. Henry Bradshaw Society, 1960.

Collinson, Patrick. *The Elizabethan Puritan Movement*. Berkeley, Calif., 1967.

Concilium Tridentinum Diariorum, Actorum, Epistolarum, Tractatuum. Nova Collectio edidit Societas Goerresiana. Fribourg and Barcelona, 1919.

Cooper, Thomas. *An Admonition to the People of England*. 1589.

Coulton, G. G. *Art and the Reformation*. Oxford, 1928, 2nd edn., 1953.

Coverdale, Myles. *The Goostly psalmes and spirituall songs drawen out of the holy scripture*. . . . c. 1539.

———. *A faythful and most godly treatise concernynge the sacrament*. Trans. of Calvin's *De Coena Domini*. c. 1549.

———. *Writings and Translations of Myles Coverdale, Bishop of Exeter*. Ed. G. Pearson, Cambridge: Parker Society, 1844.

Cox, J. C. *English Church Fittings, Furniture and Accessories*. 1923.

———— and C. B. Ford. *The Parish Churches of England*. 7th edn., 1954.

Cranmer, Thomas. *Cranmer's Liturgical Projects*. Ed. H. Wickham Legg, vol. 1. Henry Bradshaw Society, 1915.

————. *Miscellaneous Writings and Letters*. Ed. J. E. Cox, Cambridge: Parker Society, 1846.

————. *The Remains of Thomas Cranmer*. Ed. H. Jenkyns. 4 vols. Oxford, 1833.

————. *Writings and Disputations . . . Relative to the Sacrament of the Lord's Supper*. Ed. J. E. Cox, Cambridge: Parker Society, 1844.

Cross, F. L., ed. *The Oxford Dictionary of Church History*. Corrected impression of 1963.

Curtis, Mark H. *Oxford and Cambridge in Transition, 1558-1642*. Oxford, 1959.

Darby, Harold S. *Hugh Latimer*. 1953.

Davies, Horton. *The Worship of the English Puritans*. 1948.

————. *From Watts and Wesley to Maurice, 1690-1850, From Newman to Martineau, 1850-1900, The Ecumenical Century, 1900-1965. Worship and Theology in England*, vols. 3-5. Princeton, 1961-1965.

Davis, Charles, ed. *English Spiritual Writers*. 1961.

Dawley, Powell M. *John Whitgift and the English Reformation*. New York, 1954.

Daye, John, ed. *A Book of Christian Prayers, collected out of the auncient writers and best learned in our tyme. . . .* 1578.

Dearmer, Percy. *Songs of Praise Discussed*. 1933.

de Félice, Paul. *Les Protestants D'Autrefois*. 4 vols., 2nd edn. Paris, 1897-1902.

Dekker, Thomas. *Foure Birds of Noahs Ark*. 1609.

Dent, Arthur. *The Plain Mans Path-way to Heaven*. 1601.

Dering, Edward. *A Sermon preached before the Quenes maiestie . . . the 25 day of February, Anno 1569*.

————. *Godly Private Prayers*. 1576.

Devlin, Christopher. *The Life of Robert Southwell, Poet and Martyr*. 1956.

D'Ewes, Simonds, ed. *Journals of all the Parliaments during the reign of Queen Elizabeth*. 1862.

Dickens, A. G. *The English Reformation*. 1964.

————. *Lollards and Protestants in the Diocese of York, 1509-1558*. 1959.

Dickinson, F. H., ed. *Missale ad usum insignis et praeclarae ecclesiae Sarum*. Burntisland, 1861-1883.

Dictionary of National Biography. Ed. Leslie Stephen and Sidney Lee. 63 vols. 1885-1900.

Dix, Gregory. *The Shape of the Liturgy*. 1945.

Dixon, R. W. *History of the Church of England*. 6 vols. 1891-1902.

Dod, John and Robert Cleaver. *Ten Sermons . . . of the Lords Supper*. 1609.

Donaldson, Gordon. *The Making of the Scottish Prayer Book of 1637*. Edinburgh, 1954.

Donne, John. *Essays in Divinity*. Ed. E. M. Simpson. Oxford, 1952.

Douen, O. *Clement Marot et le psautier huguenot*. 2 vols. Paris, 1878-1879.

Douglas, Winfred. *Church Music in History and Practice*. Rev. and ed. L. Ellinwood, 1963.

Doumergue, E. *Jean Calvin*. 7 vols. Lausanne, 1899-1927.

Dowden, John. *Further Studies in the Prayer Book*. 1908.

———. *The Workmanship of the Prayer Book in its Literary and Liturgical Aspects*. 1899.

Downame, John. *The Christian Warfare*. 1604.

Drysdale, A. H. *History of the Presbyterians in England, their Rise, Decline and Revival*. 1889.

Dugmore, C. W. *Eucharistic Doctrine in England from Hooker to Waterland*. 1942.

———. *The Mass and the English Reformers*. 1958.

Dumoutet, E. *Le désir de voir l'Hostie*. Paris, 1926.

Egli, E. and G. Finster, eds. *Huldreich Zwinglis Sämtliche Werke*. Corpus Reformatorum, 13 vols. Leipzig, 1905-1935.

Elton, G. R. "The Reformation in England." In *The New Cambridge Modern History*, vol. 2. 1958.

———. *England Under the Tudors*. 1955.

———. *The Tudor Revolution in Government*. 1953.

Erichson, A. *Die Calvinische und die Altstrassburgische Gottesdienst ordnung*. Strassburg, 1894.

Eusden, John D., ed. *The Marrow of Theology, William Ames, 1576-1663*. Boston and Philadelphia, 1968.

Farner, Oskar. *Hulrych Zwingli*. 3 vols. Zurich, 1943-1954.

Fellowes, Edmund H. *English Cathedral Music from Edward VI to Edward VII*. 3rd edn., 1946.

Fendt, Leonhard. *Die Lutherische Gottesdienst des 16. Jahrhunderts*. Munich, 1921.

Field, J. E. *English Liturgies of 1549 and 1661*. 1930.

Fisher, John. *The English Works of John Fisher*. Ed. J.E.B. Mayor. 1935.

———. *A Treatise of Prayer and the Fruits and Manner of Prayer*. Paris, 1640.

Fleming, Abraham. *The Diamond of Devotion*. 1581.

Fitzgerald, W., tr. and ed. *A Disputation on Holy Scripture against the Papists, especially Bellarmine and Stapledon*. Cambridge: Parker Society, 1849.

Foxe, John. *Acts and Monuments*. Ed. S. R. Cattley and G. Townsend. 8 vols. 1837-1841.

———. *A Sermon of Christ crucified preached at Paules Crosse the Friday before Easter, commonly called, Goodfryday*. 1570.

Frere, Walter Howard. *A Collection of His Papers on Liturgical and Historical Subjects*. Eds. J. H. Arnold and E.G.P. Wyatt. Alcuin Club Collections, no. 35, 1940.

———. *The English Church in the Reigns of Elizabeth and James*. 1904.

————. *The Marian Reaction in its relation to the English clergy.* 1896.

————. *The Use of Sarum.* 2 vols. Cambridge, 1898-1901.

———— and C. E. Douglas. *Puritan Manifestos.* 1954. 2nd edn. N. Sykes.

———— and W. M. Kennedy. *Visitation Articles and Injunctions.* 3 vols. 1910.

Frith, John. *A booke made by Iohn Frith prisoner in the tower of London.* 1533.

Fuller, Thomas. *The Church History of Britain.* Ed. J. S. Brewer. 6 vols. Oxford, 1845.

————. *The Holy State.* Edn. of 1698.

————. *The Worthies of England.* Ed. J. Freeman, 1952.

G. F. *A Manual of Prayers.* 1583.

Gairdner, James. *The English Church in the Sixteenth Century.* 1902.

Garrett, C. H. *The Marian Exiles.* Cambridge, 1938.

Garside, Charles. *Zwingli and the Arts.* New Haven, Conn., 1966.

Gasquet, F. A. and E. Bishop. *Edward VI and the Book of Common Prayer.* 1891, 3rd edn., 1928.

Gee, Henry. *The Elizabethan Clergy and the Settlement of Religion, 1558-1564.* Oxford, 1898.

————. *The Elizabethan Prayer-Book and Ornaments.* 1920.

———— and W. J. Hardy. *Documents illustrative of English Church History.* 1896 and 1921.

George, Katherine and Charles. *The Protestant Mind of the English Reformation.* Princeton, N.J., 1961.

Gerard, John. *John Gerard. The Autobiography of an Elizabethan.* Tr. from the Latin by Philip Caraman, intro. by Graham Greene. 1951.

Geree, John. *The Character of an old English Puritane or Nonconformist.* 1646.

Gibson, E.C.S., ed. *The First and Second Prayer Books of King Edward VI.* Everyman edn., 1910.

————. *The Thirty-Nine Articles of the Church of England.* 1898.

Gilpin, Bernard. *A Sermon preached in the Court at Greenwitch before King Edward the Sixth, the first Sonday after the Epiphany, Anno Domini 1552.* Reissued 1630.

Glass, Norman. *The Early History of the Independent Church at Rothwell.* 1871.

Greenham, Richard. *Godly instructions for the due examinations and directions of all men.* 1599.

Greenslade, S. L. *The Work of William Tyndale.* 1938.

Greenwood, John. *The Writings of John Greenwood, 1587-1590.* Ed. Leland H. Carlson. 1962.

[Grey Friars]. *Grey Friars of London Chronicle.* Ed. J. G. Nichols. vol. 53. Camden Society, 1852.

Griffiths, John, ed. *The Two Books of Homilies Appointed to be Read in Churches.* Oxford, 1859.

Griffiths, Olive M. *Religion and Learning: A Study of English Presbyterian Thought.* 1935.

Grindal, Edmund. *The Remains of Archbishop Grindal.* Ed. W. Nicholson. Cambridge: Parker Society, 1843.

————. *The History of the Life and Acts of Edmund Grindal.* Ed. J. Strype. Oxford, 1821.

Grove's Dictionary of Music and Musicians. Ed. H. C. Colles. 3rd edn. New York, 1927.

Hadow, Sir Henry. *English Music.* 1931.

Hall, Peter, ed. *Fragmenta Liturgica.* 7 vols. Bath, 1848.

————. *Reliquiae Liturgicae.* 5 vols. Bath, 1847.

Haller, William. *Foxe's Book of Martyrs and the Elect Nation.* New York, 1963.

————. *Liberty and Reformation in the Puritan Revolution.* New York, 1955.

————. *The Rise of Puritanism, 1570-1643.* New York, 1938.

Harbison, E. Harris. *The Christian Scholar in the Age of the Reformation.* New York, 1956.

Harding, Thomas. *An Answer to Maister Iuelles Chalenge.* Antwerp, 1565.

————. *A Confutation of a Booke intituled An Apologie of the Church of England.* Antwerp, 1565.

Harrison. *Harrison's Description of England in Shakspere's Youth.* Ed. F. J. Furnivall. 2 vols. 1877.

Harrison, Robert and Robert Browne. *The Writings of Robert Harrison and Robert Browne.* Ed. A. Peel and Leland H. Carlson. 1953.

Hart, A. Tindal. *The Country Clergy in Elizabethan and Stuart Times, 1558-1660.* 1958.

————. *The Man in the Pew, 1558-1660.* 1966.

Harvey, A. E. *Martin Bucer in England.* Marburg, 1906.

Harvey, John. *Tudor Architecture.* 1949.

Hautecour, Louis. *Histoire de l'architecture classique en France.* vol. 1. Paris, 1943.

Hay, George. *The Architecture of Scottish Post-Reformation Churches, 1560-1843.* Oxford, 1947.

Herr, Alan Fager. *The Elizabethan Sermon, A Survey and Bibliography.* Philadelphia, 1940.

Heylyn, P. *Ecclesia Restaurata, the History of the Reformation of the Church of England.* 1661.

Higham, Florence. *Catholic and Reformed: A study of the Anglican Church, 1559-1662.* 1962.

Hill, Christopher. *Puritanism and Revolution.* 1958.

————. *Society and Puritanism.* 1964.

Hillerdal, Gunnar. *Reason and Revelation in Richard Hooker.* Lund, 1962.

Hoby, Lady Margaret. *The Diary of Lady Margaret Hoby.* Ed. Dorothy M. Meads. 1933.

Holl, Karl. *The Cultural Significance of the Reformation.* Trans. of *Die Kultur bedeuting der Reformation,* 1911, revised 1948, Tübingen. New York, 1959.

Hooker, Richard. *The Ecclesiastical Polity and other Works of Richard Hooker.* Ed. Benjamin Hanbury. 3 vols. 1830.

Hooper, John. *The Early Writings of John Hooper*. Ed. S. Carr. Cambridge: Parker Society, 1843.
————. *The Later Writings of Bishop Hooper*. Ed. C. Nevinson. Cambridge: Parker Society, 1852.
Hopf, C. *Martin Bucer and the English Reformation*. Oxford, 1946.
Hoskyns, E. *Horae B. V. M. or Sarum and York Primers, with Kindred Books of the Reformed Roman Use*. 1901.
Howell, Wilbur Samuel. *Logic and Rhetoric in England, 1500-1700*. Princeton, N.J., 1956.
Hudson, W. S. *John Ponet, Advocate of Limited Monarchy*. Chicago, 1942.
Hughes, Philip. *The Reformation in England*. 3 vols. 1950-1954.
————. *Rome and the Counter-Reformation in England*. 1944.
Hughes, Philip Edgcumbe. *The Theology of the English Reformers*. 1965.
Hutchinson, F. E. *Cranmer and the English Reformation*. Reissued 1951.
Jackson, S. M. *Huldreich Zwingli*. New York, 1901.
Jacobs, H. E. *The Lutheran Movement in England*. 1892.
Jefferson, H.A.L. *Hymns in Christian Worship*. 1950.
Jenkyns, Henry, ed. *The Remains of Thomas Cranmer*. 4 vols. Oxford, 1833.
Jessopp, Augustus. *One Generation of a Norfolk House, A Contribution to Elizabethan History*. 1879.
Jewel, John. *An Apology of the Church of England*. Ed. J. E. Booty. Ithaca, N.Y., 1963.
————. *The Works of John Jewel, Bishop of Salisbury*. Ed. J. Ayre. 4 vols. Cambridge: Parker Society, 1845-1850.
Jones, Rufus M. *Spiritual Reformers in the Sixteenth and Seventeenth Centuries*. 1914.
Jungmann, Josef A. *Missarum Sollemnia; eine genetische Erklarung der römischen Messe*. 2 vols. Wien, 1948-1949. Trans. into English by Francis A. Brunner as *The Mass of the Roman Rite; Its Origins and Development (Missarum Sollemnia)*. 2 vols. 2nd edn. of 1949. New York, 1951-1955.
Kelly, Faye L. *Prayer in Seventeenth-century England*. Gainesville, Fla., 1966.
Kennedy, W. M. *Elizabethan Episcopal Administration*. 3 vols. Alcuin Club Collections, 1924.
Kennedy, W.P.M. *Parish Life under Queen Elizabeth*. 1914.
Kidd, B. J., ed. *Documents illustrative of the Continental Reformation*. Oxford, 1911.
["King's Book," i.e. Henry VIII's]. *A Necessary Doctrine and erudition for any chrysten man, set furth by the Kynges maiesty of Englande &c.* 1534.
Kirk, Kenneth E. *The Study of Theology*. 1939.
Knappen, Marshall M. *Tudor Puritanism; A Chapter in the History of Idealism*. Chicago, 1939.
————. ed. *Two Elizabethan Puritan Diaries by Richard Rogers and Samuel Ward*. 1930.

Knewstub, John. *The Lectures of John Knewstub on the Twentieth chapter of Exodus and certaine other places of Scripture.* 1579.

Knowles, David. *The English Mystical Tradition.* 1961.

Knox, D. B. *The Doctrine of Faith in the Reign of Henry VIII.* 1961.

Knox, John. *Works.* Ed. David Laing. 6 vols. Edinburgh, 1895.

Knox, S. J. *Walter Travers: Paragon of Elizabethan Puritanism.* 1962.

Kramm, H. H. *The Theology of Martin Luther.* 1947.

Lasco, John à. *Works.* Ed. A. Kuyper. 2 vols. Amsterdam, 1866.

Latimer, Hugh. *Sermons and Remains.* Ed. G. E. Corrie. 2 vols. Cambridge: Parker Society, 1844-1845.

Leatherbarrow, J. S. *The Lancashire Elizabethan Recusants.* N.s., vol. 110. Manchester: Chetham Society, 1947.

Legg, J. Wickham, ed. *Breviarium Romanum Quignonianum.* Cambridge, 1888.

————. *The Sarum Missal.* 1916.

————. *The Second Recension of the Quignon Breviary.* 2 vols. Henry Bradshaw Society, 1908-1912.

————. *Some Principles and Services of the Prayer Book historically considered.* 1899.

Le Huray, Peter. *Music and the Reformation in England, 1549-1660.* London and New York, 1967.

Leys, M.D.R. *The Catholics in England: 1559-1829, A Social History.* 1961.

Lister, Joseph. *The Autobiography of Joseph Lister.* Ed. T. Wright, 1842.

Littlehales, Henry, ed. *The Prymer or Lay Folk's Prayer Book.* Early English Text Society, 1897.

Lloyd, Charles. *Formularies of Faith.* Oxford, 1825.

Luther, Martin. *Werke.* 58 vols. Weimar, 1883-1963.

————. *Works* in English translation. Ed. A. Spaeth and H. E. Jacobs. 6 vols. Philadelphia, 1915-1932.

————. *Works* in English translation. Ed. J. Pelikan and H. T. Lehmann. 54 vols. St. Louis and Philadelphia, 1955-1968.

Mackerness, E. D. *A Social History of English Music.* 1964.

Mackie, J. D. *The Early Tudors, 1485-1558.* 1952.

Maclure, Millar. *The St. Paul's Cross Sermons, 1534-1642.* Toronto, 1958.

Magee, Brian. *The English Recusants: A Study of the Post-Reformation Catholic Survival and the Operation of the Recusancy Laws.* 1938.

Mahrenholz, Chrishard. *Das evangelische Kirchengesangbuch. Ein Bericht über seine Vorgeschichte.* Kassel and Basle, 1950.

————. *Luther und die Kirchenmusik.* Kassel, 1937.

Manningham, John. *The Diary of John Manningham.* Ed. John Bruce. Camden Society, 1868.

Marbeck, John. *The Book of Common Praier Noted.* 1550.

Marchant, Ronald A. *The Puritans and the Church Courts in the Diocese of York, 1560-1642.* 1960.

Marsden, J. B. *History of the Early Puritans to 1642.* 1850.

Marshall, John S. *Hooker and Anglican Tradition*. Sewanee, Tenn., 1963.

Martz, Louis L. *The Poetry of Meditation*. 1954.

Mather, Cotton. *Magnalia Christi Americana*. 1702.

Mathew, David. *Catholicism in England*. 1936.

Maxwell, William D. *The Book of Common Prayer and the Worship of Non-Anglican Churches*. 1950.

————. *John Knox's Genevan Service Book, 1556*. Edinburgh, 1931.

Mayor, J.E.B., ed. *The English Works of John Fisher*. 2nd edn. Early English Text Society, extra series xxvii, 1935.

McDonnell, Kilian. *John Calvin, the Church, and the Eucharist*. Princeton, N.J., 1967.

McGinn, D. J. *The Admonitions Controversy*. New Brunswick, N.J., 1949.

McGrath, Patrick. *Papists and Puritans Under Elizabeth I*. 1967.

McLelland, J. C. *The Visible Words of God; An Exposition of the Sacramental Theology of Peter Martyr Vermigli, A.D. 1500-1562*. Grand Rapids, Mich., 1957.

McManaway, J. G., G. E. Dawson, and E. E. Willoughby, eds. *Joseph Quincy Adams Memorial Studies*. Washington, D.C., 1948.

McMillan, William. *The Worship of the Scottish Reformed Church, 1550-1638*. 1931.

Mercer, Eric. *English Art, 1553-1625*. Oxford History of English Art, vol. 7. Oxford, 1962.

Meyer, Arnold Oskar. *England and the Catholic Church under Queen Elizabeth*. Trans. from the German by J. R. McKee. 1916.

Meyer, Carl S., ed. *Cranmer's Selected Writings*. 1961.

————. *Elizabeth I and the Religious Settlement of 1559*. 1960.

Michell, G. A. *Landmarks in Liturgy*. 1961.

Micklem, Nathaniel, ed. *Christian Worship*. Oxford, 1936.

Miller, Perry. *The New England Mind: The Seventeenth Century*. New York, 1939.

Miller, Perry and T. H. Johnson. *The Puritans*. New York, 1938.

Moorman, J.R.H. *History of the Church in England*. 1953.

More, Sir Thomas. *Letters*. Ed. E. E. Rogers. Princeton, N.J., 1947.

————. *The Worke of Sir Thomas More Knyght*. Ed. William Rastell, 1557; also a modern facsimile ed. W. E. Campbell, 1931.

Morison, Stanley. *English Prayer Books, An Introduction to the Literature of Christian Public Worship*. Cambridge, 1943.

Morley, Thomas. *A Plaine and Easie Introduction to Practicall Musicke* [1597]. Ed. R. A. Harman. 1952.

Morris, Christopher. *Political Thought in England: Tyndale to Hooker*. 1953.

Muller, J. A. *Stephen Gardiner and the Tudor Reaction*. New York, 1926.

Neal, Daniel. *The History of the Puritans*. 5 vols. 1822.

Neale, J. E. *Elizabeth I and Her Parliaments, 1559-1581*. 2 vols. 1953.

————. *Elizabeth I and Her Parliaments, 1581-1601*. 1958.

————. *The Elizabethan House of Commons*. 1950.

Neale, J. E. *England's Elizabeth*. 1958.

Nettl, Paul. *Luther and Music*. Philadelphia, 1948.

New, John H. A. *Anglican and Puritan, the Basis of their Opposition, 1558-1640*. Palo Alto, Calif., 1964.

New Catholic Encyclopedia. 15 vols. New York, 1967.

New Schaff-Herzog Encyclopedia of Religious Knowledge. 2 supplementary vols. Ed. Lefferts A. Loetscher. Grand Rapids, Mich., 1955.

Newman, John Henry. *Parochial and Plain Sermons*. 8 vols. 1868.

————. *Sermons preached on Various Occasions*. 1857.

Nichols, J. G., ed. *Chronicle of the Grey Friars of London*. 1852.

Nichols, James Hastings. *Corporate Worship in the Reformed Tradition*. Philadelphia, 1968.

Nicholson, William, ed. *The Remains of Edmund Grindal*. Cambridge: Parker Society, 1843.

Norden, John. *The Pensive Mans Practise*. 1584.

Nowell, A. *A True report of the Disputation or rather private conference etc.* [concerning Edmund Campion]. 1583.

Nuttall, Geoffrey F. *The Holy Spirit in Puritan Faith and Experience*. Oxford, 1946.

————. *Visible Saints: The Congregational Way, 1640-1660*. Oxford, 1957.

Nuttall, Geoffrey F. and Owen Chadwick. *From Uniformity to Unity, 1662-1962*. 1962.

Oman, Charles. *English Church Plate, 1597-1830*. 1957.

Original Letters relative to the English Reformation. Ed. Hastings Robinson. 2 vols. Cambridge: Parker Society, 1846-1847.

Owen, John. *Works*. Ed. W. H. Goold. 16 vols. Edinburgh, 1850-1853.

Owst, G. R. *Literature and Pulpi⟨t⟩ in Mediaeval England*. 2nd edn. Oxford, 1961.

————. *Preaching in Mediaeval England*. Cambridge, 1926.

Oxley, J. E. *The Reformation in Essex to the Death of Mary*. Manchester, 1965.

Ozinga, Murk D. *De Protestantische Kerkengebouw in Nederland*. Amsterdam, 1929.

Paget, Eusebius. *A godly Sermon preached at Detford*. 1586.

Parker, Matthew. *The Life and Acts of Matthew Parker*. Ed. J. Strype. 3 vols. Oxford, 1821.

————. *Correspondence from 1535 to 1575*. Ed. J. Bruce and T. T. Perowne. Cambridge: Parker Society, 1853.

Parker, T.H.L., ed. *The English Reformers*. 1966.

————. *The Oracles of God: An Introduction to the Preaching of John Calvin*. 1947.

Parker, T. M. *The English Reformation to 1558*. 1950.

Patrick, Millar. *Four Centuries of Scottish Psalmody*. London and New York, 1949.

Pauck, Wilhelm. *Das Reich Gottes Auf Erden*. Berlin and Leipzig, 1928.

Peacham, Henry. *The Complete Gentleman, The Truth of our Times, and The Art of Living in London.* Ed. Virgil B. Heltzel. Ithaca, N.Y., 1962.

Pearson, A. F. Scott. *Church and State: Political Aspects of Sixteenth Century Puritanism.* Cambridge, 1928.

———. *Thomas Cartwright and Elizabethan Puritanism.* Cambridge, 1925.

Peel, Albert. *The First Congregational Churches.* Cambridge, 1920.

———, ed. *The Notebook of John Penry.* Camden Society, 1944.

———. *The Seconde Parte of a Register.* vol. 1. Cambridge, 1915.

——— and Leland H. Carlson, eds. *Cartwrightiana.* 1951.

———. *The Writings of Robert Harrison and Robert Browne.* 1953.

Peers, E. Allison. *Spanish Mysticism.* 1924.

———. *Studies in the Spanish Mystics.* 2 vols. 1927.

Pelikan, Jaroslav J. "Luther and the Liturgy." In *More About Luther.* Martin Luther Lectures. vol. 2. Decorah, Iowa, 1958.

Perkins, William. *The Combat between Christ and the Devil.* 2nd edn. 1606.

———. *The Foundation of the Christian Religion gathered into six principles.* 1595.

———. *A Golden Chaine.* . . . 1600.

———. *A Salve for a Sicke Man.* 1595.

———. *The whole treatise of the cases of conscience.* 1604.

———. *The Workes of that Famous and Worthy Minister of Christ in the University of Cambridge, M. William Perkins.* 3 vols. Cambridge, 1613.

Persons, Robert. *A brief discourse containing certain reasons Why Catholikes refuse to goe to Church.* Douai, 1601.

———. *Letters and Memorials of Father Robert Persons, S.J.* Ed. L. Hicks. no. 37, Catholic Record Society, 1942.

Pettit, Norman. *The Heart Prepared: Grace and Conversion in Puritan Spiritual Life.* New Haven, Conn. and London, 1966.

Pevsner, N. *The Englishness of English Art.* 1956.

Pidoux, Pierre. *Le Psautier huguenot du 16ᵉ siècle.* 2 vols. Kassel and Basle, 1962.

Phillips, C. Henry. *The Singing Church.* 1945.

Phillips, C. S. *Hymnody Past and Present.* London and New York, 1937.

Pierce, William. *An Historical Introduction to the Marprelate Tracts.* 1908.

Pierce, William, ed. *The Marprelate Tracts, 1588, 1589.* 1911.

Playfere, Thomas. *The Whole Sermons of that Eloquent Divine of Famous Memory: Thomas Playfere, Doctor of Divinitie.* 1625.

Pocock, Nicholas, ed. *Troubles connected with the Prayer Book of 1549.* Camden Society, N.S., xxxvii, 1884.

Pollard, A. F. *The History of England from the Accession of Edward VI to the Death of Elizabeth (1547-1603).* 1910.

———. *Thomas Cranmer and the English Reformation, 1489-1556.* 1904.

Pollard, Arthur. *English Sermons.* 1963.

Pollen, J. H. *The English Catholics in the Reign of Queen Elizabeth.* 1920.

Porter, H. C. *Reformation and Reaction in Tudor Cambridge.* Cambridge, 1958.

Potter, G. R. and E. M. Simpson, eds. *The Sermons of John Donne.* 10 vols. Berkeley, Calif., 1953-1962.

Powicke, F. M. *The Reformation in England.* 1941.

Pratt, Waldo S. *The Music of the French Psalter of 1562: A Historical Survey and Analysis.* New York, 1939.

Primus, John H. *The Vestments Controversy.* Kampen, 1960.

Proctor, F. and W. H. Frere. *A New History of the Book of Common Prayer.* 1920.

Prothero, R. E. *The Psalms in Human Life.* 1903.

Pruett, Gordon E. "Thomas Cranmer and the Eucharistic Controversy in the Reformation." Unpublished Ph.D. thesis. Princeton University, 1968.

Purvis, J. S., ed. *Tudor Parish Documents of the Diocese of York.* Cambridge, 1948.

Pützer, Fritz. *Prediger des englischen Barok.* Bonn, 1929.

[Quinones, Francisco]. *The Second Recension of the Quignon Breviary.* Ed. J. W. Legg. 2 vols. Henry Bradshaw Society, 1908-1912.

Ratcliff, Edward C. *The booke of common prayer of the Churche of England: its making and revisions MDXLIX—MDCLIX set forth in eighty illustrations with Introduction and Notes.* 1949.

Ratramnus of Corbie. *Opera.* In *Patrologia Latina.* Ed. J. P. Migne. Paris, 1852. vol. 121.

Ravenscroft, Thomas. *A Brief Discourse. . . .* 1614.

———. *The Whole Book of Psalms.* 1621.

Read, Conyers. *The Tudors.* 1936.

Reed, Luther D. *The Lutheran Liturgy.* Philadelphia, 1947.

Richardson, Cyril C. *Zwingli and Cranmer on the Eucharist: Cranmer dixit et contradixit.* Evanston, Ill., 1949.

Richter, A. L. *Die evangelischen Kirchenordnungen d. sechszehnten Jahrhunderts.* 2 vols. Weimar, 1846.

Ridley, Jasper. *Nicholas Ridley: A Biography.* 1957.

———. *Thomas Cranmer.* 1962.

Ridley, Nicholas. *A Brief Declaration of the Lord's Supper.* Ed. H.G.C. Moule, 1895.

———. *Works.* Ed. H. Christmas. Cambridge: Parker Society, 1841.

Robinson, H., ed. *Original Letters Relative to the English Reformation.* 2 vols. Cambridge: Parker Society, 1846-1847.

———. *Zurich Letters.* 2 vols. Cambridge: Parker Society, 1842-1845.

Robinson, John. *A Iustification of Separation from the Church of England.* 1610.

———. *A Treatise of the Lawfulness of Hearing of Ministers.* 1634.

———. *Works.* Ed. Robert Ashton. 3 vols. 1852.

Rogers, Richard. *Seven Treatises . . . leading and guiding to true happiness both in this life and in the life to come.* 1603.

Rowse, A. L. *The England of Elizabeth.* 1953.

———. *Tudor Cornwall.* 1941.

Rupp, E. Gordon. *Six Makers of English Religion, 1500-1700.* 1957.
———. *Studies in the Making of the English Protestant Tradition.* Cambridge, 1949.
Rye, W. B. *England as seen by Foreigners.* 1865.
Sanders, Nicholas. *The Rise and Growth of the Anglican Schism* [1585]. Ed. D. Lewis. 1877.
Sandys, Edwin. *The Sermons of Edwin Sandys, D.D.* Ed. John Ayre. 2 vols. Cambridge: Parker Society, 1841-1842.
Schmidt, Hermanus A. P. *Introductio in Liturgiam Occidentalem.* Rome, Freiburg, Barcelona, 1960.
Schmidt-Clausing, F. *Zwingli als Liturgiker.* Göttingen, 1952.
Schnapper, E. B. *The British Union-Catalogue of Early Music printed before the year 1801.* 2 vols. 1957.
Schnorrenberg, John M. "Early Anglican Architecture, 1558-1662: Its Theological Implications and Its Relation to the Continental Background." Unpublished Ph.D. thesis, Princeton University, 1964.
Scholes, Percy A., ed. *The Oxford Companion to Music.* 1938.
———. *The Puritans and Music in England and New England.* London, 1934, 2nd edn., New York, 1966.
Schuler, M. and J. Schulthess, eds. *Zwinglii Opera.* vol. 4. Zurich, 1841.
Seebohm, F. *The Oxford Reformers, Colet, Erasmus, and More.* 2nd edn., 1869.
Shepherd, Massey H., Jr. *The Oxford American Prayer Book Commentary.* New York, 1951.
Shirley, J. *Richard Hooker and Contemporary Political Ideas.* 1949.
Simpson, Alan. *Puritanism in Old and New England.* Chicago, 1955.
Simpson, E. M., ed. John Donne. *Essays in Divinity.* Oxford, 1952.
Sisson, C. J. *The Judicious Marriage of Mr Hooker and the Birth of the Laws of Ecclesiastical Polity.* 1940.
Smallman, Basil. *The Background of Passion Music.* 1957.
Smend, Julius. *Die evangelischen deutschen Messen bis zu Luthers Deutscher Messe.* Göttingen, 1896.
Smith, Henry. *The Sermons of Maister Henrie Smith gathered into one Volume.* 1593.
Smith, H. Maynard. *Henry VIII and the Reformation.* 1948.
Smith, L. C. *Tudor Prelates and Politics, 1536-1558.* Princeton, N.J., 1953.
Smithen, F. J. *Continental Protestantism and the English Reformation.* 1928.
Smyth, C. H. *Cranmer and the Reformation under Edward VI.* Cambridge, 1926.
Smyth, John. *The Differences of the Churches of the Separation.* 1608.
———. *The Works of John Smyth.* Ed. W. T. Whitley. Cambridge, 1915.
Southern, A. C., ed. *An Elizabethan Recusant House, comprising the Life of the Lady Magdalen, Viscountess Montague (1538-1608).* 1950.
———. *Elizabethan Recusant Prose, a Historical and Critical Account*

of the Books of the Catholic Refugees printed and published abroad and at secret presses in England. 1955.

Southgate, W. M. *John Jewel and the Problem of Doctrinal Authority.* Cambridge, Mass., 1962.

Southwell, Robert. Christopher Devlin. *The Life of Robert Southwell Poet and Martyr.* 1956.

———. *The Book of Robert Southwell.* Ed. Isabel M. Hood. Oxford, 1926.

Staley, Vernon, ed. *First Prayer Book of Edward VI, 1549.* 1903.

Stanford, Charles V. and Cecil Forsyth. *The History of Music.* 1916.

Stephens, W.R.W. and W. Hunt. *History of the English Church.* 9 vols. 1899-1912.

Sternhold, Thomas and John Hopkins. *The Whole Booke of Psalmes collected into Englysh metre.* 1562.

Stevens, Denis W. *Tudor Church Music.* New York, 1955, London, 1961.

Stevens, J. *Music and Poetry in the Early Tudor Court.* 1961.

Stockwood, John. *A Sermon Preached at Paules Crosse on Barthelmew Day.* 1578.

Stow, John. *Survey of London.* Ed. C. L. Kingsford. 2 vols. Oxford, 1908.

Stranks, C. J. *Anglican Devotion: Studies in the Spiritual Life of the Church of England between the Reformation and the Oxford Movement.* 1961.

Strype, J. *Annals of the Reformation.* 4 vols. Oxford, 1824.

———. *Ecclesiastical Memorials.* 3 vols. Oxford, 1824.

———. *The History of the Life and the Acts of Edmund Grindal.* Oxford, 1821.

———. *The Life and Acts of John Whitgift.* 3 vols. Oxford, 1827.

———. *The Life and Acts of Matthew Parker.* 3 vols. Oxford, 1821.

———. *Memorials of Thomas Cranmer.* 3 vols. in 4. Oxford, 1848-1854.

Sturge, Charles. *Cuthbert Tunstall, Churchman, Scholar, Statesman, Administrator.* 1938.

Summerson, John. *Architecture in Britain, 1530 to 1830.* The Pelican History of Art. Harmondsworth and Baltimore, 1954.

Surtz, Edward. *The Works and Days of John Fisher.* Cambridge, Mass., 1967.

Sutton, Christopher. *Disce Mori. Learne to Die.* 1600.

Swete, H. B. *Church Services and Service-Books before the Reformation.* Rev. edn. by A. J. MacLean. 1930.

Sykes, Norman. *The Church of England and Non-Episcopal Churches in the Sixteenth and Seventeenth Centuries.* 1948.

Terry, Richard R. *Calvin's First Psalter* [1539]. Facsimile edn. 1932.

Thompson, Bard, ed. and selection. *Liturgies of the Western Church.* Cleveland and New York, 1962.

Theisen, Reinhold. *Mass Liturgy and the Council of Trent.* Collegeville, Minn., 1965.

T'Hooft, W. A. Visser. *Rembrandt and the Gospel.* New York and Cleveland, 1960.

Thornton, L. S. *Richard Hooker, A Study of His Theology.* 1924.

Tillyard, E.M.W. *The Elizabethan World Picture.* 1945.

Tomlinson, J. T. *The Prayer Book, Articles, and Homilies.* 1897.

Topsell, Edward. *Times Lamentation, or an exposition of the prophet Joel in sundry sermons or meditations.* 1599.

————. *The Reward of Religion. Delivered in sundry Lectures upon the Booke of Ruth, wherein the godly may see their dayly both inward and outward trials, with the presence of God to assist them, and his mercies to recompense them.* 1597.

Torbet, R. G. *The History of the Baptists.* Philadelphia, 1950.

Torrance, Thomas F. *Kingdom and Church.* Edinburgh, 1956.

Travers, Walter. *A full and plaine declaration of Ecclesiastical Discipline.* Zurich, 1574.

Trevelyan, George M. *England under the Stuarts.* 1933.

Trimble, W. R. *The Catholic Laity in Elizabethan England.* Cambridge, Mass., 1954.

Tunstall, Cuthbert. *De Corporis et Sanguinis Domini in Eucharistia.* Paris, 1554.

Tyndale, William. *Doctrinal Treatises.* Ed. H. Walter. Cambridge: Parker Society, 1848.

————. *The Whole Workes of W. Tyndall, John Frith, and Doct. Barnes, three worthy Martyrs, and principall teachers of the Churche of England. . . .* 1572.

Tyrer, Ralph. *Five godlie sermons. . . .* 1602.

Underhill, E. B., ed. *Fenstanton, Warboys and Hexham Records.* 1847.

Usher, R. G. *The Reconstruction of the English Church.* 2 vols. New York, 1910.

————. *The Presbyterian Movement . . . illustrated by the minute book of the Dedham Classis.* Camden Society, 1905.

Vajta, Vilmos. *Luther on Worship.* Philadelphia, 1958.

Van de Poll, G. J. *Martin Bucer's Liturgical Ideas.* Assen, 1954.

Vaux, Laurence. *A Catechisme or Christian Doctrine.* Manchester: Chetham Society, 1885.

Verstegan, Richard. *The Letters and Despatches of Richard Verstegan.* Ed. A. G. Petti. no. 52. Catholic Record Society, 1959.

Wakefield, Gordon A. *Puritan Devotion, Its place in the Development of Christian Piety.* 1957.

Walker, Williston. *The Creeds and Platforms of Congregationalism.* New York, 1893.

Wallace, Ronald S. *Calvin's Doctrine of the Word and Sacraments.* Edinburgh, 1953.

Walsh, James, ed. *Pre-Reformation English Spirituality.* New York, 1965.

Walton, Izaak. *Life of Hooker.* In Hooker, *Works.* Ed. J. Keble. Oxford, 1836.

Waterhouse, Ellis. *Painting in Britain, 1530-1790.* Pelican History of Art. London and Baltimore, 1953.

Welsby, P. A. *George Abbott: The unwanted Archbishop.* 1962.

Wendel, François. *Calvin.* 1963.

West, W.M.S. "John Hooper and the Origins of Puritanism." A summary of an unpublished doctoral dissertation submitted to the Faculty of Theology of the University of Zurich; printed for private circulation in 1955; which appeared in *The Baptist Quarterly*, London, Oct. 1954 to April 1955.

White, Helen C. *The Tudor Books of Private Devotion.* Madison, Wis., 1951.

———. *Tudor Books of Saints and Martyrs.* Madison, Wis., 1963.

White, Thomas. *A Sermon preached at Pawles Crosse on Sunday the thirde of November, 1577.* 1577.

White, W. D. "John Henry Newman, Anglican Preacher." Unpublished Ph.D. thesis, Princeton University, 1968.

Whitgift, John. *Works.* Ed. J. Ayre. 3 vols. Cambridge: Parker Society, 1851-1853.

———. *The Life and Acts of John Whitgift.* Ed. J. Strype. 3 vols. Oxford, 1822.

Wilkins, D. *Concilia Magnae Britanniae. . . .* 4 vols. 1737.

Williams, George Hunston. *The Radical Reformation.* Philadelphia, 1962.

Wilson, H. A., ed. *The Order of Communion, 1548.* Henry Bradshaw Society. vol. 34. 1908.

Woodfill, Walter. *Musicians in English Society from Elizabeth to Charles I.* Princeton, N.J., 1953.

Woodforde, Christopher. *English Stained and Painted Glass.* Oxford, 1954.

Woodhouse, H. F. *The Doctrine of the Church in Anglican Theology, 1547-1603.* 1945.

Wright, Louis B. *Middle-Class Culture in Elizabethan England.* Chapel Hill, N.C., 1935.

Wriothesley, Charles. *A Chronicle of England.* Ed. W. D. Hamilton. 2 vols. N.S., XI, parts i and ii. 1875-1877.

Young, Percy. *A History of British Music.* 1967.

[Zurich]. *The Zurich Letters.* Ed. H. Robinson. Cambridge: Parker Society, 1846.

———. *The Zurich Letters, 1558-1579,* ed. H. Robinson, Parker Society, Cambridge, 1842.

INDEX

I. Index of Persons

Abbott, Abp. George, 243, 309
Abraham, Gerald, 378n., 383n.
Ab Ulmis, John, 199
Aburne, Robert, 332
Adams, J. Q., 410n.
Addleshaw, G.W.O., 363n., 364, 365, 368n.
Agatha, St., 21, 372
Agnes, St., 21
A Lasco, John, 79n., 106f., 110-112n., 191, 192n., 201, 204f., 299n., 350
Alexander, 107
Allde, Elizabeth, 418
Allde, Richard, 418
Allen, Cardinal, 152, 156
Allison, 390
Ames, William, 52, 58n., 63n., 257, 305n., 326
Amos, 239
Anderson, Anthony, 311, 316n., 317
Andrewes, Bartimaeus, 310, 317
Andrewes, Bp. Lancelot, xix, 67, 218, 227, 232f., 236, 242, 253, 294, 304, 307, 310, 314, 324, 368, 428
Annas, 146
Anselm, St., 437
Anthony, St., 21
Apolline, St., 21
Aquinas, St. Thomas, 65n.
Arber, Edward, 40n., 211n.
Arnold, J. H., 168n., 207n.
Ashton, Robert, 269n.
Athanasius, St., 147
Augustine, St., of Canterbury, 173
Augustine, St., of Hippo, 25, 55, 91, 96, 102, 114, 244, 253, 422, 427, 431
Aylmer, Bp. John, 46, 290n., 300, 328
Ayre, J., 102n., 121n., 233n., 235n., 236n., 382n.

Babbage, Stuart B., 295n.
Bailey, D. S., 418n.
Baillie, Robert, 63n., 432n.
Baker, Augustine, 409n.
Bancroft, Abp., 40, 51n., 60n., 232, 241, 277f., 295
Barbara, St., 21
Barnard, 401
Barley, W., 401
Barnes, Robert, 19n., 80n., 237
Baro, Peter, 59n.
Barrett, William, 59n.
Barrow, Henry, 60, 257f., 327-329, 333f.

Baum, J. G., 79n., 209n.
Baxter, Richard, 275n., 406
Bayne, Peter, 54n.
Baynes, Paul, 257
Beaumont, Robert, 239, 241n.
Becon, Thomas, 17, 20, 21n., 102f., 229, 234f., 243, 381f., 412, 418, 425, 427
Becket, Abp. Thomas à, 134
Bede, the Venerable, 46, 409n.
Belloc, Hilaire, 6
Bembo, Cardinal, 137
Bennett, H. S., 407
Bentham, Bp. Thomas, 47n.
Benz, Ernst, 374n.
Berengarius, 91
Bernini, 147
Betjeman, John, 359, 368n., 369n.
Beza, Theodore, 244, 380
Bibliander, 83n.
Bilney, T., 237, 248
Bishop, Edmund, 147, 168n., 169n., 187n., 188n., 191, 202n.
Blake, William, 388
Blaurer, Thomas, 195
Blench, J. W., 235, 237, 239n., 250, 304n., 305n., 309, 318
Blunt, 341
Boleyn, Queen Anne, 151
Bolton, Robert, 65
Bonaventura, St., 423
Bonhoeffer, Dietrich, 18n.
Bonner, Bp. Edmund, 103, 134f., 187, 199f., 229, 350
Bonnet, Jules, 55n.
Booty, John E., 10n., 21n., 29n.
Boreman, Christopher, 153n.
Bourgeois, Louis, 380, 385, 403
Bouyer, Louis, 149n.
Boyce, 401
Boyd, Morrison C., 384n., 399n.
Bradford, John, xix, 34n., 228, 243, 303, 416, 418, 419, 420-422, 436, 439
Bradshaw, William, 70, 295
Brady, Nicholas, 387
Brewster, William, 341
Bridges, John, 33n., 240n.
Bridgett, T. E., 138n.
Brightman, F. E., 167n., 168n., 170n., 179n., 180n., 194n., 208n., 381n.
Brigit, St., 132
Brilioth, Abp. Yngve, 79n.
Bromiley, G. W., 117n.
Brook, Benjamin, 290n.

463

INDEX

Fuller, Thomas, 50n., 244, 249, 295n.,
298n., 305n., 315, 387
Furnivall, F. J., 50n, 215n., 298n.,
354n.

Gardiner, Bp. Stephen, 8, 13, 21n.,
78f., 85f., 90-94, 111f., 182, 187,
197, 201, 206, 208, 210
Garnet, Henry, 158n.
Garret, C. H., 40n.
Garside, Charles, 378n.
Gascoigne, Thomas, 391
Gasquet, Cardinal F. A., 168n., 169n.,
187f., 191, 202n.
Gee, Henry, 47n., 130n., 133f., 150n.,
174n., 182n., 201f., 365n.
Gelasius, 96
George, C. and K., 59n.
George, St., 20, 372
Gerard, John, 158n., 159n., 368
Geree, John, 257, 258
Gérold, Théodore, 378n., 379n.
Gertrude, St., 20
Gibbon, Edward, xvii
Gibbons, Orlando, 397, 399, 402f.
Gibson, Bp. E.G.S., 13n., 27, 35n.,
57n., 178
Gifford, 309
Gilby, Anthony, 47, 60n., 273
Gilpin, Bernard, 88, 295, 296n., 356
Glass, Norman, 341n.
Goldwell, Bp. Thomas, xvii, 127,
136-138
Goodman, Christopher, 389
Goodrich, Bp. Thomas, 174
Goold, 424n.
Gosson, Stephen, 311
Goudimel, 385
Gounters, John, 372
Grafton, Richard, 212, 394, 416
Granada, Fray Luis de, 161, 414
Grantham, Thomas, 343
Greenham, Richard, 232, 257, 300n.,
309, 311, 429n., 435
Greenwood, John, 60, 257, 327, 329n.,
330n., 334
Gregory XIII, 240
Gregory Nazianzus, 16
Greiter, 385
Griffiths, J., 360n.
Grindal, Abp. Edmund, 15, 45, 50,
107, 121, 221, 229, 232, 263, 276,
299, 367
Grisbrooke, W. J., 171n., 181, 188,
195n.
Grosart, A. B., 310n.
Grove, 401
Guest, Bp. Edmund, 367

Hadow, Sir Henry, 399
Hall, Bp. Joseph, 66
Hall, Peter, 255n, 277n., 278n., 279n.

Hall, Rowland, 418
Haller, William, 41n., 59, 68, 322,
431n., 441
Halome, Joan, 213f.
Hamilton, W. D., 169n.
Hammerton, William, 339n.
Hanbury, Benjamin, 26n., 263
Harbison, E. H., 227n.
Harding, Thomas, 8n., 29f., 121n.,
161, 352f., 371
Hardy, W. J., 47n., 130n., 133f., 150n.,
174n., 182n., 201f., 365n.
Harman, R. A., 401n.
Harpsfield, John, 229
Harrap, Thomas, 416n.
Harrington, Sir John, 439
Harrison, F. L., 383n.
Harrison, William, 50n., 214f., 218,
298, 354
Hart, A. Tindal, 153n., 213f., 430n.,
440n.
Harvey, A. E., 107n.
Harvey, John, 356n., 357
Hatton, Sir Christopher, 399
Haynes, Dean, 175
Helioys, Thomas, 338, 340
Henry II, King of France, 384f.
Henry VII, King, 136, 349
Henry VIII, King, 3, 5f., 20, 40, 76,
85f., 127, 129f., 137, 140n., 166f.,
169, 171, 210, 239, 303n., 349, 352,
381, 390, 394, 397, 411f., 419,
428, 436
Herbert, George, 65, 75, 226, 441
Herod, King, 163
Herr, A. F., 217n., 232n.,
245n., 290n.
Herrick, Robert, 65
Heylyn, Peter, 43
Hicks, L., 157n.
Hide, 413
Hill, Christopher, 32, 295n.
Hilles, Richard, 195f.
Hilliard, Nicholas, 355n., 374, 376
Hills, William, 213
Hilsey, Bp., 20, 169, 411f.
Hilton, Walter, 409
Hobbes, Thomas, 304
Hoby, Lady Margaret, 429n., 435
Holbeach, Bp. Henry, 174, 199
Holbein, 436
Holbrooke, William, 244
Holgate, Abp. of York, 392
Holl, Karl, 23n., 350n.
Honorius, 266
Hood, Christobel M., 158n.
Hooke, Christopher, 234n.
Hooker, Richard, xv, 5, 11, 26n., 27f.,
32f., 53, 59, 62, 71, 73n., 76, 83,
122f., 225, 228, 232f., 241f.,
249-255, 257n., 261, 263f., 271f.,
291, 294f., 297, 301, 360f., 397

466

Maclure, Millar, 102n., 238n., 239n.,
244n., 246n., 296n., 301n., 370n.
Mahrenholz, Christhard, 378n.
Manningham, John, 232n.
Marbeck, John, 383, 394, 395
Marc'hadour, Germain, 437, 438
Marchant, Ronald A., 289n.
Marlowe, 398
Marot, Clément, 378n., 380, 384f.,
403, 416
Martyr, Peter, 5, 79, 92, 106f., 109f.,
183, 187n., 191, 199, 201, 208,
221, 383, 386
Mary Magdalene, St., 37
Mary, Queen of England, 4, 44, 45,
127, 131f., 149, 151, 182, 210,
228, 248, 276, 296, 343, 374, 392,
395, 412, 419, 428, 433, 436, 439
Mather, Cotton, 327n.
Mathew, Abp. David, 129n., 130n.
Matthews, A. G., 288n.
Maurice, F. D., 226
Maxfield, Thomas, 160
Maxwell, W. D., 165n., 255n., 273n.,
274, 278n., 279n., 281n., 284, 363n.
May, William, 174, 199
Mayne, J., 430
Mayor, J.E.B., 303n.
McDonnell, Kilian, 141n., 191n.
McGee, E. G., 113
McGinn, D. J., 296n.
McLelland, J. C., 79n.
McManaway, J. G., 410n.
McMillan, William, 71n., 260n.
Meads, Dorothy M., 429n.
Melancthon, 91
Mercer, Eric, 355, 357n., 372,
374n., 375n.
Micklem, Nathaniel, 288n.
Micklethwaite, J. T., 212n.
Migne, J. P., 80n.
Mildmay, Sir Walter, 49, 50n.
Miller, Perry, 55, 56n., 311
Milton, John, 42, 64, 387, 404
Monk, the, of Farne, 409
Montagu, Bp. Richard, 59n., 368n.
Montague, Viscount, 132
Moody, Richard, 359
More, St. Thomas, xix, 80, 86n., 95,
130, 155, 227, 352n., 436-439, 442
Morley, Thomas, 397, 398, 399,
400, 402
Moses, 96
Mosse, Miles, 301
Moule, H.G.C., 103n.
Muller, J. A., 91n, 182, 197n.
Mundy, William, 397, 404
Murton, Thomas, 338
Musculus, 305

Nausea, Bp. Frederick, 145n.
Neal, Daniel, 315n.

Nestorius, 96
Nettl, Paul, 378n.
New, J.H.A., 54n., 55, 58n., 62, 223n.
Newman, Cardinal J. H., 67, 76n.,
157, 197n., 226
Nevinson, Charles, 101n.
Nicholas, St., 20
Nichols, J. G., 174n., 238n.
Nichols, J. H., 273n.
Nicholson, W., 15n., 121n., 276n.
Norden, John, 417
Northumberland, Lord Protector, 3,
202, 394
Nowell, Alexander, 19n., 48
Nuttall, Geoffrey F., 60n., 69n., 304n.

Occam, 81, 115
Ochino, 106
Oecolampadius, 79, 86, 87, 91, 92,
95, 98n., 104, 191n.
Oldcorne, Edward, 158n.
Olivier, Isaac, 355n.
Oman, Charles, 366n., 367
Origen, 96
Ormston, Mrs., 435
Osiander, 166n., 170, 180
Osyth, St., 21
Owen, John, 424n.
Owen, Nicholas, 159n.
Owst, G. R., 305n.
Oxley, J. E., 7n.

Paget, Eusebius, 239, 317
Palestrina, 148, 377, 399, 403
Parker, Abp. Matthew, 15, 23, 46f.,
107, 212, 221, 229n., 262, 276n.,
367, 389
Parker, T.H.L., 20n.
Parker, T. M., 168, 181, 210n.
Parkhurst, Bp. John, 46
Patrick, Millar, 377n., 379n., 380n.,
385n., 388n.
Pauck, Wilhelm, 107n.
Paul III, 138, 172
Paul IV, 137, 138, 172
Paul, St., 18, 23, 28, 43, 110, 232,
235n., 259, 264f., 269, 284, 308,
320, 322, 341, 375, 379, 382, 431
Pearson, A. F. Scott, 49n., 51n., 61n.
Pearson, G., 191n.
Peel, Albert, 257n., 343n., 344
Peers, E. Allison, 161n., 414n.
Pelikan, J. J., 79n.
Pellican, 83n.
Penry, John, 60, 257, 269, 327, 329
Perez, de Ayala, Bp., 142
Perkins, William, 55, 58n., 65f., 72f.,
236, 244, 257, 272, 280, 283, 287f.,
300n., 305, 308-310, 312f., 320f.,
416, 424
Perowne, T. T., 366n.
Persons, Robert, 29, 157f., 160f.

II. Index of Places (and Churches)

(Churches are assumed to be Anglican except when otherwise indicated)

472

III. Index of Topics

WORSHIP
AND THEOLOGY
IN ENGLAND

II. *From Andrewes to Baxter and Fox,*
1603–1690

CONTENTS

xi

PART THREE: THE HISTORY AND FORMS OF WORSHIP

ACKNOWLEDGMENTS

IT WOULD HAVE BEEN impossible to complete these five volumes and over fifteen years of research in the libraries of Britain and the United States without the help of several institutions and persons to whom I tender my thanks: to Princeton University for leaves of absence, and to its Committee for Research in the Humanities and Social Sciences for grants for summer travel and support as well as for typing; to the John S. Guggenheim Memorial Foundation of New York City for two Fellowships; to the Henry E. Huntington Library and Art Gallery of San Marino, California, for a Grant-in-aid; to the Princeton University Press, its Director, Herbert S. Bailey, Jr., and to several of its editors; and to my colleagues past and present of the Department of Religion at Princeton University for their encouragements, despite their ironical references to my "pentateuch."

The Bibliography owes much to the help I received from David Moessner of the Class of 1971 at Princeton, now reading theology at Mansfield College, Oxford. My companion and helper in so much of this research, which delayed her own research into the English Renaissance, is my wife, Marie-Hélène, to whom I owe more than words can convey. Other expressions of my indebtedness will be found in footnotes, in the List of Illustrations, and, of course, in the Bibliography.

HORTON DAVIES

INTRODUCTION

THIS VOLUME concludes my study of the history and theology of Christian worship in England from the Reformation and Counter-Reformation until the present. I began liturgical research as a graduate student in the University of Oxford thirty-five years ago and thirty-three hundred miles away from Princeton University where I have the honour to teach amid Neo-Gothic buildings with all modern conveniences. The present series of five volumes has used up almost all of my spare time for thirteen years. My greatest regret is that it is so long, especially as I detest prolixity. It seems supremely ironical that an account of Christian worship in a single nation should be longer than the Old and New Testaments combined. It would be some mitigation if this introduction were to prove the briefest I have written.

My sub-title bears three symbolic names: *From Andrewes to Baxter and Fox: 1603-1690.* They direct attention to the fact that the most creative religious thinking and living in the seventeenth century was the achievement of the Anglican Caroline divines, the Puritan pastors, and the new Religious Society of Friends, or Quakers.

Lancelot Andrewes, who had twice turned down Queen Elizabeth's proposals to make him a Bishop, was Dean of Westminster Abbey when our history begins. He fathered an important tradition of Biblical and Patristic scholarship, a knowledge of and fondness for liturgiology, a love of the Eucharist and of appropriately high ceremonial. He was a brilliant "Metaphysical preacher," a distinguished apologist of the Church of England, as well as the author of *Preces Privatae* which raided the liturgies of the East and West as a monarch, and demonstrated his own reverence for God and sensitivity to human needs. This remarkable Father-in-God (who died as Bishop of Winchester) gave Anglicanism its direction for at least a century to come, as it distinguished itself from both Rome and Geneva. He let Anglicans see that their church was firmly built upon the traditions of the primitive church of the first five centuries. He was followed by Cosin, Wren, Hammond, Bramhall, and Laud, as well as by many others. His authorities were, so he stated, "one canon, reduced to writing by God himself, two testaments, three creeds, four general councils, and the series of Fathers of that period—the centuries, that is, before Constantine and two after—determine the boundary of our faith."

Baxter, the second name, who, like Fox, died at the end of our period, symbolizes the Puritans at their least political and most spiritual. The author of the classic concept of the Reformed ministry, *Gildas Salvianus, the Reformed Pastor*, as of the Reformed liturgy, he was the leader of the "Presbyterian" divines at the Savoy Conference with the Anglicans in 1661, who had written a sensitive treatise on the cultivation of the spiritual life, *The Saints Everlasting Rest*, an incisive autobiography, and a comprehensive textbook on casuistry, *The Christian Directory*. Not a university man, he was one of the most learned men of his time, and he possessed a spirit that admirably reflected his highest loyalties.

The third name is, of course, that of the century's most persistent quester for religious truth, George Fox, who finally created his own religious burrow. After trying both conventional and unconventional forms of Christianity in the fantastic Commonwealth laboratory of experimental sectarianism, he founded, what the Quaker apologist, Barclay, called a third type of Christianity. This denied all external formal religion, repudiated the sacraments and sacerdotalism, that all Fox's friends might be ministers and receive the inner illumination and warmth of the Holy Spirit.

Theologically, the three names and the traditions for which they stand, represent three different understandings of religious authority. Andrewes stands for the triple cord of Scripture, the Catholic heritage of the first five centuries in doctrine, polity, and liturgy, as well as reason. Baxter, as a Puritan, though with Arminian leanings, stands for the supremacy and sole domination of sacred Scripture, with an experimental emphasis on the empowering of the Holy Spirit which illuminates Scripture. Fox represents the primacy of the Holy Spirit in the hearts of men and women, with Scripture as a subordinate check on experience. Their names are an indication of the importance and variety of the major traditions of belief, behaviour, and worship in England.

This particular volume is planned differently from the others. In the first place, instead of providing separate studies of Anglican, Roman Catholic, and Dissenting theologies, as I did in Volume I, I have given up this idea. One reason was that there is little basic theological change between the sixteenth and the seventeenth centuries, apart from the growing Arminianism and pragmatism of the Church of England[1] and among the General or Non-Calvinist

---

[1] Furthermore, the main task has already been undertaken by others. These include H. R. McAdoo in *The Spirit of Anglicanism*, J.H.A. New in *Anglican*

Baptists. A more compelling reason was that it might prove more intriguing to derive the theology from the architecture which was its outward and visible expression. Hence Part One, "The Context of Worship," begins with Chapter I: "Church Architecture: Its Theology." This considers the differing nature of the holy communities worshipping in Anglican, Roman, Puritan, and Quaker churches, chapels, or meeting-houses. It also asks how important the following factors were in determining church architecture: symbolism, functionalism, social prestige, and economics.

After the theological and theoretical considerations, it seemed desirable to see what in fact had been built, so Chapter II was inevitably styled, "Church Architecture: Achievements." It documents the "Gothic survival" type of architecture in Anglicanism before the Great Fire and the "Wrenaissance" that followed it, and the domestic simplicity of the first Puritan meeting-houses and the domestic elegance of the later ones.

While still considering the background of worship, it is clear that the patterns of private and family devotion or spirituality are of great importance. Public worship is likely to be no more than a formal nod to God unless it is engaged in by praying households of faith, whether these be monasteries and convents or families about the domestic hearth. Chapter III is entitled, "Spirituality: Preparation for Public Worship." It examines the brilliant spirituality of the Counter-Reformation in Spain, Italy, and France, as these manuals filtered through in the English translations to the many religious houses of English exiles in the Low Countries and to the Recusants in England. It also glimpses the household altars of Anglicans, Puritans, and Quakers.

The fourth and last chapter of the first part deals with preaching. The seventeenth century was the golden age of preaching in England, with Andrewes, Donne, Jeremy Taylor, Bunyan and Baxter, to mention only the brightest luminaries in a great galaxy. What George Herbert said (and exemplified) of the country parson could be said of almost every preacher of this century, that he "preacheth constantly, the pulpit is his joy and throne." This was the case even when the congregation wished he would abdicate, as

---

and Puritan, the Basis of Their Opposition, 1558-1640; and Gerald Cragg in Puritanism in the Period of the Great Persecution and in The Church and the Age of Reason, 1648-1789. However, a synoptic and detailed account of the institutional and intellectual developments of Roman Catholicism in seventeenth century England is needed to fill out David Mathew's Catholicism in England which was published in 1936.

probably the Presbyterian hearers of Dr. Manton did when he preached the 190th successive sermon on a single Psalm. The title of Chapter IV is self-explanatory: "Preaching: Stimulus and Supplement to Worship."

Part Two, "Cultic Controversies," mirrors the extraordinary theological wrangling that riddled the seventeenth century. It is reflected in the bitter but often ingenious titles of lengthy pamphlets like William Prynne's *A Brief Survay and Censure of Mr. Cozens His Couzening Devotions* (1628), and more seriously and tragically in the Civil War that tore England asunder and deserves, at least in some respects, Trevelyan's title for it, the "Metaphysical War." The four chapters in this section deal with four major and continuing problems in worship. Chapter V treats the question of the most appropriate "Style in Worship: Prestigious or Plain?" It is concerned with whether prayer, vestments, and ceremonial should be highly stylized or austerely simple. Chapter VI contrasts the Roman Catholic and Anglican retrospective Calendar of Christological and Sanctoral Days, with the contemporary Puritan Calendar of Sabbaths and Days of Thanksgiving and Humiliation. Its title over-simplifies the issue as that of "Calendary Conflict: Holy Days or Holidays?" The truth in it is that Puritans wanted a weekly holy day, the Sabbath, while the Anglicans wanted an element of festivity and holiday hilarity. They and the Roman Catholics would have agreed more readily with Herrick, vicar, poet, and propagandist for the jollity of Church feasts:

> For Sports for Pagentrie and Playes,
> Thou hast thy Eves and Holydayes . . .
> Thy Wakes, thy Quintels, here thou hast,
> Thy May-poles too with Garlands grac't:
> Thy Morris-dance; thy Whitsun-ale;
> Thy Sheering-feast, which never faile.
> Thy Harvest home; thy Wassaile bowle,
> That's tost up after Fox i' th'Hole;
> Thy Mummeries: thy Twelfe-tide Kings
> And Queenes; thy Christmas revellings.

Chapter VII, entitled "Sacred Music: Splendid or Scriptural?" reviews the issues raised in Chapter IV in a different context. Here Anglicans insist that in cathedrals and other great churches

there is value in offering chants, verse anthems sung by professional choirs, and organ music and string symphonies or interludes, as men's best music to God. The Puritans stake the claim
of metrical psalmody as an apter expression of the priesthood of
all believers with rhymed and easily memorable jingles to easy
tunes, so that even the illiterate can join in God's praise.

The last Chapter in Part Two is Chapter VIII. It describes and
analyses the different theories of the presence of Christ: corporal
presence, real spiritual presence, or memorialism in the Mass, Holy
Communion, or Lord's Supper. It also asks which religious group
values the Eucharist most. Its title is: "The Chief Sacrament:
Means of Grace or Mnemonic?"

Part Three deals with "The History and Forms of Worship,"
and it requires less explanation than the other two parts.

Chapters IX and X tell the story of the ups and downs of the
Anglican Prayer Book. It was loved by the Caroline divines,
loathed as an instrument of tyranny by the Puritans and proscribed
by them, secretly used during the Commonwealth and Protectorate,
restored with the king in 1660, and revised conservatively in 1662
and very slightly later. Chapter IX is titled, "The Anglican Prayer
Book Admired and Rejected: 1603-1659," and Chapter X is
styled, "The Prayer Book Restored and Revised: 1660-1689."

The next two chapters deal respectively with Puritan and Nonconformist Worship. Chapter XI, "Puritan Prayer Books," concentrates on the Westminster or Parliamentary Directory of 1644
and on Baxter's Savoy or Reformed Liturgy of 1661. Both are
viewed in the light (or dark) of the criticisms of their contemporaries. Chapter XII, "Nonconformist Worship: Presbyterians and
Independents, 1662-1690," deals with their worship chiefly during the shadows of persecution.

Chapter XIII moves away from the Anglican-Puritan struggle
which dominated the century to consider the secret and forbidden
worship of the English Roman Catholics or their rare open worship
in the chapels of embassies in London or in the royal chapels of
Catholic queens in England.

Chapter XIV goes in the opposite direction to consider "Radical
Worship: The Baptists and Quakers."

The final Chapter XV, a summation of the entire book is entitled, "A Concluding Survey and Critique."

In this acrimoniously partisan century one is grateful that on both the Anglican and Puritan sides there were ecumenical spirits. The Puritan Baxter was happy to call himself a "meer Catholick" regarding party labels as mere libels. The droll Anglican church historian, Dr. Thomas Fuller, wrote: "For those who endeavour to make the way to heaven narrower than God hath made it, by prohibiting what he permits, do in event make the way to hell wider, occasioning the committing of such sins, which God hath forbidden." One's sympathies are entirely with Jeremy Taylor when he complained: "How many volumes have been writ about angels, about immaculate conception, about original sin, when all that is solid reason or clear revelation in all these three articles may be reasonably enough comprised in forty lines? And in these trifles and impertinences men are curiously busy, while they neglect those glorious precepts of Christianity and holy life which are the glories of our religion, and would enable us to a happy eternity."

This is a century of apparently implacable hostility, of fratricide between Christians, of almost unbearable prolixity in pen and pulpit, of deliberate misrepresentation of one's theological opponents, of damnable dogmatism even in speculative matters, and of hideous intolerance. It is, at the same time, like lilies growing in manure, an era which produced the brilliant sermons of Andrewes and Donne, those exemplary and complementary pastors Herbert and Baxter, the two religious epics of the Biblical visions and musings of Milton and Bunyan, and the greatest constellation of religious poets England has ever seen. The same century saw the beginnings of distinguished Patristic scholarship, a sense of social justice as the correlate of the Christian faith, and in the Society of Friends the tiny embodiment of that reconciliation which the era needed on a vaster scale. To have lived in that time must have led men and women to dream wild dreams and to waken to the wilder nightmares of reality. But the seeds of hope were already planted even in the cracked earth of disillusionment. They would eventually blossom into toleration, a reasoned faith, and that charity which leads to ecumenical appreciation. Even if one would not wish to have lived in their century, one cannot withhold admiration for their faith, their zest, and their endurance. The famous and the humble invite us to make the seventeenth century pilgrimage; to steal quietly inside their churches or meeting-houses or homes, to join in the liturgy or to listen to extemporary prayers, to sing their metrical psalmody, to hear and take notes of their sacred oratory, and to share, above all, their ornate Eucharist or simple Lord's Supper. In all these experiences, the curtain of the centuries is pulled back, and Christ encounters his elect, whether Roman Catholic, Anglican, Puritan, Baptist, or Quaker. The spectrum of their many-coloured worship refracts the white radiance of eternity.

PART ONE

THE CONTEXT OF WORSHIP

CHAPTER I

CHURCH ARCHITECTURE:
ITS THEOLOGY

GEORGE HERBERT, the poetical rector of Bemerton, celebrated the Church of England as the happy medium between the splendour of Roman Catholicism and the squalour of Puritanism, and succeeded in being unfair to all three traditions. Counter-Reformation church architecture in England was, with the exception of the royal chapels of Stuart queens and of King James II, and certain foreign embassy chapels in London, exceedingly restrained. Puritan architecture had its theological reasons, irrespective of its aesthetic tastes, for its simplicity which was far from squalour. And Anglican architecture itself was demonstrating an intriguingly distinctive quality of "Gothic survival" almost until the time of Wren. Most serious, however, was the assumption by Herbert that architecture, ceremonial, and fittings of churches are matters of subjective choice between aesthetic richness or imaginative poverty. His spurious and simplistic conclusion is, therefore, inevitably:

> A fine aspect in fit array,
> Neither too mean, nor yet too gay,
> Shows who is best.[1]

The aim of this chapter is to show that the selection of church architecture and fittings is a complex of at least five interrelated

---

[1] "The British Church," *The Works of George Herbert* (ed. F. E. Hutchinson, Oxford, 1941), p. 109. Archbishop William Laud expressed the median position of the Church of England with felicity. "Truth usually lies," he averred, "between two extremes and is beaten by both, as the poor Church of England is at this day by the Papist and the Separatist." (Cited in E.C.E. Bourne, *The Anglicanism of William Laud* [1947], p. 79.) John Donne, a former Roman Catholic, is deeply concerned by the problem of the intermediate role of the Church of England. It is anguished in the sonnet which begs:

> Show me, dear Christ, thy spouse, so bright and clear.
> What! is it She, which on the other shore
> Goes richly painted? or which rob'd and tore
> laments and mourns in Germany and here?

In *Satire* III Donne shows Mirreus seeking true religion at Rome, "because hee doth know/ That shee was there a thousand yeares agoe,/ He loves her ragges so." The rags are the unhappy additions to Rome's pristine purity. In reaction Crantz goes to the opposite extreme, following what "at Geneva is call'd/ Religion, plaine, simple, sullen, yong,/ Contemptuous, yet unhansome."

factors, which help to account for the differences (and partial similarities) in the four traditions under consideration. That is, these factors have helped to make Anglican, Roman Catholic, Puritan, and Quaker sacred buildings what they are.

One basic factor is the nature of the holy community envisaged by the worshippers of the church, chapel, or meeting-house. A second is where the dominant foci of worship are: on sacraments or on sermons, on praises or prayers, or on a combination of each? A third determinant of architecture and fittings is whether the sacred space is planned functionally or with a view to its numinous or symbolic quality? A fourth is socio-political. Is the church or meeting-house built to show by its external impressiveness and its interior richness the social prestige of the donors or worshippers, or by its simplicity their sense of the irrelevance of such considerations? And are churches or meeting-houses in England (and Europe) in the politically polarized seventeenth century a reflection of the views of its strongest supporters, whether the absolutism associated with ecclesiastical Baroque architecture or the simpler republicanism or democracy of the meeting-house? A fifth is the closely related economic consideration in architecture. What resources are available to the architect in finance and materials? How significant in the motivation of his patrons is the desire for grandeur, or the love of simplicity? Or, how far is sheer economic necessity responsible for design?

Furthermore, all these factors involved in ecclesiastical architecture and furnishings will also reflect the way the architect or builder and his patrons or customers understand the nature of God and the ceremonial style appropriate for the approach to the Divine.

1. *The Nature of the Holy Community*

For the Anglican worshippers the Church expresses the deep sense of the English nation on its knees, united by its Prayer Book and linked with its cousins across the Atlantic in Virginia, or gathering in English embassies in European capitals, owing allegiance to their sovereign who is both king and supreme governor of the church. Church and nation were coextensive for the Anglican, despite the fact that Recusant Catholics and dissenting Puritans denied the Erastian equation. This link was clearly expressed verbally in the Prayer for the King, and visually in the royal arms that so often replaced the figures of the rood in the days of Catholicism. It was the constant and not always convincing argument of the Anglican apologists that the Anglican church rightly held on to the fanes of the medieval church because they had been built and served by Englishmen, irrespective of the change of religious allegiance. To make that claim to continuity visible it was necessary that Anglican architecture should be "Gothic *survival*," rather than revival. And the liturgical changes that came about made little modification in the architecture, except for the removal of some statuary and stained-glass that naively represented God or the Holy Trinity, or proclaimed too obviously the intercession of the saints.[2] On the other hand, the dedication of the parish churches to particular saints, and the retention in the Anglican calendar of the major festivals of Christ, of the Virgin and the apostles, as also of other New Testament saints, and their representation in the stained-glass or on the choir stalls, kept a sense of the communion of saints alive in the Anglican Communion. In a more restricted sense also, the tombs and gravestones of the ancestors in the nave or in the graveyard kept alive a sense of continuity of Christians through the generations.

The union of throne and altar was vigorously propounded by John Bede in 1612: "Of all the creatures of the Universe, none draweth nearer to the Creator than man; neither any degree of men, so much as doth the King. . . . As the face of Moses descending the Mount from God, shone bright and glorious: so the Maiesticke looke of a King (reflecting divine beames, received from the King of Kings) daunteth the most proud and savage hearts of inferiors."[3] Thus the dominant conception of the church held by Anglicans was that of the subjects of the heavenly and earthly Kings united in prayer and sacrament, a "mixed multitude" to their Puritan detractors, but to them a devout nation.

For the Roman Catholics the holy community was the international body of Christians owing allegiance to the Pope in the Petrine succession and outnumbering all others through the centuries (voting, as G. K. Chesterton said in our own century, by tombstones). The church militant on earth was united with the church triumphant in heaven, and the experience, concern, and intercession of the great saints of the past were available for the

---

2 The sixteenth-century modifications are described in Horton Davies, *Worship and Theology in England* (Princeton, N.J., 1970), Vol. I, pp. 356-65.

3 *The Right and Prerogative of Kings, Against Cardinal Bellarmine and Other Jesuits* (1612), p. 1. I owe this reference to the kindness of the Rev. Belden C. Lane of Princeton Theological Seminary, as also those in footnotes 4 and 9.

spiritual strengthening of the faithful of the present. All representations of that mystical unity were not only lawful but encouraged in Roman Catholic chapels, and the relics of a saint were included in every altar, and each day in the Catholic calendar honoured the memory of some distinguished imitator of God, while statuary, woodcarvings, and glass were aids to the memory of the pious. On the roods that survived, the central crucifix spoke eloquently of the suffering and sacrifice of the Saviour, between the grieving Virgin Mother and the beloved disciple John. The greatest contemporary theologian the Catholics had was Cardinal Bellarmine (1542-1621), whose books were translated into English and secretly read by the Recusants. He defined the church as comprising "a convocation or congregation of men which are baptized and make profession of the faith and law of Christ under the obedience of the chief Bishope of Rome."[4]

For the Puritans the holy community was conceived as the covenanted fellowship of the households of faith, the saints (in the sense of those in the process of being sanctified), the local outcropping of the hidden *coetus electorum*, the members of which were only known to God. Yet for practical purposes, those who owned the covenant acknowledged its obligations to walk in all the ways God in Christ had made known to them and who lived in ethical conformity with such expectations, were acknowledged as "visible saints." As Perry Miller has shown, the very idea of covenant meant not only that the "saint" had bound himself to God, but that God had also bound himself to be his God. The fundamental point, so he insists, is that the undertaking had a voluntaristic basis. "Where two parties do stand mutually obliged one to another in a voluntary Agreement, there is a Covenant."[5] Involved in this covenant on the part of men and women chosen by God was the responsibility for fellowship and mutual encouragement and oversight (or discipline).[6] The same emphasis on expressing outward-

---

[4] *An ample declaration of the Christian Doctrine* (English trans., 1604), p. 65. It was a frequently reprinted exposition of the Creed, Lord's Prayer and Decalogue.

[5] *The New England Mind: The Seventeenth Century* (Boston, 1961), p. 375. It should be noted that the unmodified Calvinist position insisted on the unconditonal sovereignty and freedom of God, without contractual obligations, on God's mysterious unpredictability in election, and, consequently on the impossibility of any human, linear tradition of succession. For a study of the origins of the Puritan covenant idea in the Rhineland and its exponents, including Oecolampadius and Bucer, as well as William Tyndale in England, see Leonard J. Trinterud, "The Origins of Puritanism" (*Church History*, XX, 1951, pp. 37-57).

[6] These aspects of the covenanted life are admirably analysed and illustrated in Geoffrey F. Nuttall's *Visible Saints* (Oxford, 1957), pp. 74ff. John Owen's *Eschol, or Rules of Direction* (1648) affirms that true Christians are to exhibit

ly the inner light, the illumination and grace of the Holy Spirit, marked the tightly knit, deeply committed, suffering and witnessing early Quaker communities that sprang up in the days of Commonwealth turbulence to give their testimony for peace. They, too, though without taking a formal covenant, were bound to God and to one another in loving fellowship, but they were a potentially universalistic communities in the way that Puritans were not, for while the Calvinist doctrine of providence was retained by them, they abhorred and rejected the doctrine of double predestination and reprobation. But the meeting-houses of both Puritans and Quakers are testimonies to simplicity, the fear of the idolatrous eye, and to the nature of "gathered churches" out of the world. But chiefly, these meeting-houses are, as their very titles indicate, *domestic*. They are homes for the people of God to meet in,[7] not houses of God. The true altar for the Puritan as for the Quaker is the prepared human heart, where the Holy Spirit dwells, and so all places are sacred, and therefore special places are only conveniences not necessities.

Thus the nature of the holy community, whether international as in Roman Catholicism, national as in Anglicanism of this period, or local, is reflected in the character of the architecture appropriate to express these ecclesiologies.

2. *Foci in Worship as Functional Factors in Architecture*

If ecclesiastical architecture is partly determined by the nature of the holy community, it is even more strongly influenced by the community's understanding of the high points of its worship, its foci of major interest. This is as basic as it is obvious, for whatever else a church or meeting-house may be used for, its primary function is liturgical.

At first glance, it is clear that the church will eloquently, if silently, express the character of the worship (and the worship-

---

"affectionate sincere love" and "vigilant watchfulness over each others conversation" [latter term means "way of life" in seventeenth-century and Biblical usage]. (Cited by Nuttall, *op. cit.*, p. 74.) The purpose of this intensity and exclusiveness was to try to preserve the purity of church membership. John Robinson, pastor of the Pilgrims in Holland, claimed that "only saints, that is, a people forsaking all known sin of which they may be convinced, doing all the known will of God, increasing and abiding ever therein . . . Of such only, externally, and so far as man can judge, the true church is gathered." (*A Justification of Separation from the Church of England*, 1610, *The Works of John Robinson*, ed. J. Ashton, II, p. 10.)

7 George Fox's *Journal*, I, 8 states: "The Lord showed me clearly that he did not dwell in these temples which men had commanded and set up, but in people's hearts."

7

pers) from its exterior and its interior. Its exterior will indicate whether it is world-affirming in its splendour and triumphalism or world-denying in its simplicity and even its fugacity, as in the days of persecution, for Huguenots in France and Nonconformists in England after 1662. Its interior, too, if it is formal, grand, ornate, will bespeak the use of a liturgy, or if it is domestic the appropriateness of the spontaneity and directness of free prayer in the family.

Such general considerations apart, church architecture will be largely determined by the worshipping community's priorities in worship. In the Church of England, the holy table (if one were of Puritan or Latitudinarian leanings) or the altar (if one were a high churchman of the Laudian or Non-Juror tradition) predominated. Not only was it the centre—to which the aisles and the steps of the chancel (and the central opening of the screen in some cases) directed one's gaze and feet, but it was railed by Laudian fiat to mark its great sacredness and dignity. If the chancel were more sacred than the nave, the most sacred part of the chancel was the altar. But there were also other liturgical foci, marking the great, if subordinate, importance of the pulpit, and the prayer-desk, as well as the font. George Herbert, as Izaak Walton reminds us, determined in the rebuilding of Leighton Bromsgrove, a project shared with the neighbouring Ferrar family, on two pulpits of equal height so that "they should neither have a precedency or priority of the other; but that prayer and preaching, being equally useful, might agree like brethren, and have an equal honour and estimation."[8]

The Caroline divines certainly stressed the primacy of the church as a place of devotion,[9] and Herbert is typical in this respect. His *Country Parson* shows the parson entering the church and "humbly adoring, and worshipping the invisible majesty and presence of Almighty God." In his other book, *The Temple*, a poem entitled "The Church Porch" endorses the view:

[8] It should be noted, however, that Herbert was more of a liturgical and architectural innovator than is commonly recognised, and so this view of the equal importance of prayer and preaching may be untypical. This insight I owe to Professor John Schnorrenberg's unpublished paper, "George Herbert, Poet and Churchman," delivered to the Philological Club of the University of North Carolina at Chapel Hill in January, 1966. On the other hand, Herbert's view has many supporters in the Restoration Church.

[9] In our own day Professor Mascall ties the centrality of devotion in the Church of England to the role of its liturgy: "The Church lives neither by tradition alone, nor by the Scriptures directly. The Church lives day by day by her liturgy, which is her living tradition but of which the Scriptures are both constituent and normative." (*Toward a Church Architecture*, 1962, p. 198.)

Though private prayer be a brave design
Yet publick hath more promises, more love;
And love's a weight to hearts, to eies a signe.
We are all but cold suitours; let us move
Where it is warmest. Leave thy six and seven
Pray with the most: for where most pray is heaven.

The other focus of worship was provided by the font, almost always at the west end of the church, symbolizing the entry into the Christian community through Baptism.[10] The principle on which the Gothic churches inherited by the Anglican church were organized was that of "two rooms." That is, the chancel was used as the centre for Holy Communion, the communicants receiving at the altar rail, and the nave was used as the centre for prayers and preaching and psalmody in the services of morning and evening prayer.[11] The Book of Common Prayer helped to instruct the builder engaged in additions, or alterations that the church building was primarily a place of common prayer, including sacramental devotion.

For the Roman Catholics, in England as well as elsewhere, the Sacrament of the Altar, and therefore the altar itself, was the most sacred part of the sacred space. But during the seventeenth century, as a result of the spread of the ideals of the Counter-Reformation in which the Jesuit Baroque churches of Italy, Spain, and France took the lead, the pulpit occupied an increasingly important role and position in worship. It was, however, only in the chapels of foreign embassies in London, or in those of a Catholic queen in England or of the Catholic aristocracy in the country that members of the old faith were likely to get a glimpse of the new architecture and ornaments, and the growing importance of the pulpit. From

10 Yet the font was most awkwardly placed, if it was intended that the congregation should share in the sacrament of initiation, for they had to turn round. This fact of itself must have encouraged the separation of Baptism from the regular congregational services of the Church of England, and encouraged the unfortunate practice of private Baptism, often with socially elite godparents rather than Christian sponsors.

11 The Anglican modifications of Roman Catholic fanes for worship are duly described in G.W.O. Addleshaw and Frederick Etchells, *The Architectural Setting of Anglican Worship* (1948), p. 45. On the Continent, there were three types of adaptation, including losing the nave and moving into the choir (at the cathedral of St. Pierre, Geneva), closing the choir and moving into the nave (as at Basel), and the two chamber arrangement by retaining the ancient choir-screen followed by the Church of England and also used in St. Bavo's Church, Haarlem. See André Biéler, *Architecture in Worship* (Edinburgh and London, 1965), pp. 57-60 and Donald J. Bruggink and Carl H. Droppers, *Christ and Architecture: Building Presbyterian/Reformed Churches* (Grand Rapids, Michigan, 1965), p. 86.

9

Gunpowder Plot to the Titus Oates Conspiracy, the Catholics espoused a forbidden and hidden faith and were apparently a doomed and therefore desperate minority, a people fleeing the light (*gens lucifuga*, as Cardinal Newman described them two centuries later). It must have been small consolation to them that every cathedral and practically every parish church they saw in England was a mute testimony in its cruciform shape and Gothic style to the faith of their ancestors, however much the interiors might have been simplified together with the ceremonial. England remained Gothic as far as its church buildings were concerned until the first waves of Renaissance work in Inigo Jones reached its shores and the flood tide came with Sir Christopher Wren. Some private Anglican chapels or college chapels (like those of Peterhouse, and Emmanuel College in Cambridge or Lincoln, Exeter, and Pembroke Colleges at Oxford) were the few exceptions. They, however, as we shall see later, are mixed Gothic-Renaissance creations.

The only alternative to Gothic architecture in England (Wren's classicism excepted) was the austere, scrubbed and domesticated simplicity of post-Restoration Puritan or Quaker architecture. Puritan and Quaker meeting-houses resembled the middle-class houses of the later seventeenth century, with large and long windows, allowing the unstained light to pass through them. They were, in the most literal sense of the words "house churches." Since all, as led by the Holy Spirit could preach, or rather, speak in the meeting, there was no need for a pulpit in Quaker meeting-houses and the building reflected a complete egalitarianism where all the Lord's people were prophets, both men and women. Since Sacraments, on the Quaker interpretation, were individually renewable experiences of the Holy Spirit which dispensed with the outward means such as water, bread, and wine, no altar was needed.[12] All was simplicity and the streamlining of spirituality to the Quakers, if iconoclasm to their critics. The name of the edifice, "meeting-house" (as contrasted with Roman Catholic and Anglican dedications to the Holy Trinity, St. Michael and All Angels, and the like) indicated that here was the meeting-place of God's people with their God, not in any sense a "house of God."

The Puritans, of course, used the same term for the same reason, but they emphasized the co-ordinate importance of the Word and Spirit, so that the preaching of the Word and the celebration

[12] See Robert Barclay's *Apology for the True Christian Divinity* (1678) Chaps. XII and XIII for the exposition of this viewpoint.

of the "Gospel Sacraments" (Baptism and the Lord's Supper) required in Puritan assemblies for worship a centrally placed pulpit, usually on the long wall of the rectangular-shaped church, and beneath it a Communion table centrally placed surrounded by a pew in which the elders or deacons sat, and a font (usually rather inconspicuous). Apart from these fittings, both Quaker and Puritan meeting-houses gave the same family-at-worship appearance— a study in black and white etching, rather than the coloured and multi-textured appearance of Anglican and the highly dramatic and even theatrical Baroque effect of Counter-Reformation Catholic churches on the Continent, of which their English analogues (when visible and not hidden for reasons of persecution) were restrained adaptations.

In both Catholic and Anglican churches the primacy of the altar or Communion table was to be seen, with a strongly subordinate emphasis on the pulpit, for the Mass or Holy Communion was primary in both forms of worship. In Puritan meeting-houses the primacy was given to the pulpit with its central position and high stairs, often one on each side, and a subordinate position was given to the Communion table, though not as secondary as is often supposed. In the meeting-houses of the Society of Friends (as also in the first meeting-houses of the Baptists), we see the expression of Cistercianism in Dissenting worship, and the egalitarianism[13] of benches as opposed to pews which developed from the fourth to the tenth decade of the seventeenth century to great lengths in the Church of England.[14]

3. Numinosity or Functionalism?

Already the importance of functionalism in sacred architecture has been considered. In addition, however, there is a grand general distinction to be made between Catholic-Anglican and Puritan-Quaker places of worship. This depends upon the decision of

---

[13] While the statement about the egalitarianism expressed in Quaker architecture is substantially true (and applies with equal relevance to early Baptist churches, in each case deriving, as H. L. Short suggests from their common Mennonite background in Holland), it should also be recognised that both Quakers and early Baptists had a pew respectively for "elders" and "messengers," who were lay leaders of their religious communities, and in many cases these benches were raised up a little. H. L. Short of Manchester College, Oxford, made the suggestion in an article in the *Listener*, March 17, 1955, pp. 471f., "Changing Styles in Nonconformist Architecture."

[14] Sir Christopher Wren was aesthetically averse to filling a church with pews, especially the high-backed variety, but he also desired for greater space so "that the poor may have room enough to stand and sit in the alleys, for to them equally is the Gospel preached." (See Stephen Wren, *Parentalia*, 1750, pp. 319f.)

whether to employ symbolism and ornamentation, or whether to adhere strictly to functional considerations. To begin with, recognition must be given to the fact that both Roman Catholics and Anglicans give a value to symbolism and ornamentation which the Puritans and Quakers deny for theological, cultural, and economic reasons.

Hooker speaks for the medieval view (and therefore for both Roman Catholic and Anglican viewpoints) when he argues that the Church Fathers claimed that "the house of prayer is a Court beautified with the presence of the celestial powers; that there we stand, we pray, we sound forth hymns to God, having his Angels intermixed as our associates."[15]

Hooker is also aware of the importance of atmosphere in a church, for he insists that "the very majesty and holiness of the place where God is worshipped hath in regard to us great virtue, force, and efficacy, for that it serveth as a sensible help to stir up devotion, and in that respect no doubt bettereth even our holiest and best actions in this kind."[16] A Roman Catholic could go even further and claim that the stained-glass windows and the statues were a notable teaching device; in short, the Bible and church history of the poor. It would be possible to make the same claim if Laud's views had prevailed in the Church of England, and certain Oxford and Cambridge College chapels in the 1630s have fulfilled Laud's reverential and didactic intentions by their images in windows, and wood, as by their splendid ceiling bosses. If one seeks pedagogy in glass, he has only to think of the remarkable east window in Lincoln College Chapel, Oxford, with its typological exegesis as constituting an astonishing sermon on the Old Testament anticipations of New Testament fulfillments, as seen, for example, in Adam's creation as foreshadowing the nativity of Christ the second Adam, or of Jonah's three-day stay and deliverance from the "great fish" presaging Christ's resurrection after three days in the tomb.[17]

Indeed, the differing views on church architecture and worship as between the Caroline divines (from Lancelot Andrewes to Archbishop Laud and his friends, John Cosin and Matthew Wren)

---

[15] *The Laws of Ecclesiastical Polity*, Bk. v, Chap. 25, Para. 2.

[16] *Ibid.*, Bk. v, Chap. 16, Para. 2.

[17] As another example of the astonishing veneration of the Carolines for King Charles I, even before what they considered as his "martyrdom" at the hands of the regicides, it should be observed that the east window of Lincoln College shows Christ with a Vandyke beard, bearing a clear resemblance to the royal "saint." The window is dated 1631.

and the Puritan divines (aided by the fierce parliamentarian Prynne) were the cause of a furious controversy. It is not too much to claim that this controversy helped to polarize the nation into irreconcilable factions and thus was one of the causes of the Civil War. It was, in part, a fight between the iconophiles and the iconoclasts, between a reverence that might lead to mere formality and a spontaneity that could degenerate into casualness, and an aesthetic as against an ethical test of worship.

Archbishop Laud's views were stated with the greatest clarity and vigour before the Star Chamber in a speech made on June 14, 1637, at the censure of John Bastwick, Henry Burton, and William Prynne, "concerning pretended innovations in the Church."[18] The Archbishop began by stating that he worships with his body as well as his soul, and that even if there were no holy table in the church he would still revere God on entering it as it is God's House, and even if no stone were left in Bethel, he would still worship wherever he came to pray. The misery of the present is, he asserts, that it is accounted "superstition nowadays for any man to come with more reverence into a church than a tinker and his bitch come into an ale-house." He then shrewdly pointed out that the Lords of the Garter bowed towards God's altar in their great solemnities because it is "the greatest place of God's residence upon earth." He continues with great conviction and emotion:

> I say the greatest, yea, greater than the pulpit; for there it is *Hoc est Corpus meum*, "This is My Body"; but in the pulpit it is at most but *Hoc est verbum meum*, "This is My Word." And a greater reverence no doubt is due to the Body than to the Word of Our Lord. And so, in relation answerably to the throne where His Body is usually present, than to the seat whence the Word useth to be proclaimed. And God hold it there at His Word."[19]

This vivid expression of Laud's view is indistinguishable from the Roman Catholic viewpoint and expresses a strong belief in the "Real Presence" in the Eucharist. Moreover, it is interestingly defended by images derived from the sovereign and the nobility, just as Hooker had urged the earthly court as an image of the heavenly court of the King of Kings. (By a complete contrast, it will be seen that the Puritan Fifth Monarchist, John Archer, defends

18 Laud's *Works* (Library of Anglo-Catholic Theology), VI, Pt. 1, pp. 56f.
19 *Ibid.*

the sitting posture at the service of the Lord's Supper precisely because Christ had called His disciples to be friends, not serfs of a sovereign.) A Puritan might also have argued that the Archbishop was undervaluing the transforming power of the Word of God which was also and equally evidence of His presence.

The Laudian view of the importance of the church as housing the very Body of Christ in the Eucharist was expressed in the canons issued by the Convocation of 1640, which had continued to meet by the royal warrant after the closure of the Short Parliament, one of which required the Communion table to be placed under the east window and railed to avoid profanation. It is declared that the purpose is to encourage reverence, "because experience hath shown us how irreverent the behaviour of many people is in many places, some leaning, others casting their hats, and some sitting upon, some standing and others sitting under the Communion table in time of Divine Service. . . ."[20] One of Laud's most enthusiastic disciples, Foulke Robarts, Prebendary of Norwich, even argues for the enclosure of the font with rails.[21] William Hardwick, curate of Reigate, cites St. John Chrysostom's description of a church in his own rather free translation: "The Church is no Barber's or Apothecary's Shop; it is no Westminster or Guildhall but the place of Angels, the Court of Heaven, yea, Heaven itself."[22] He urges that those who are afraid of superstition, should beware its opposite, profaneness. He then provides two vivid companion pictures of reverence and disrespect for God:

> For my part, when I come into a Church and there behold a poor sinner kneeling upon his knees, weeping with his eyes, and with a humble and lowly reverence, both petitioning and hearing his God, my charity bids me think the best, as how that these shews are not without substance, because I know no other—it being a peculiar privilege and prerogative of Almighty God to be καρδιαγνώστης, a knower, a Searcher of the heart. But again, let me see a man here sitting in his Master's

[20] Ibid.

[21] Gods Holy House and Service according to the primitive and most Christian forme thereof (1639), pp. 45-46: "And if (as in some Churches it is) the font were decently with rayles enclosed: it were (I speake under correction) more suteable to the reverence due thereunto."

[22] The Latin source which Hardwick cites (itself a translation from the Greek original) reads: Non est Ecclesia tonstrina aut unguentaria taberna aut officina forensis; sed locus Angelorum, Regia Coeli, Coelum ipsum. William Hardwick, Conformity with Piety requisite in God's Service (1638), cited in P. E. More and F. L. Cross, eds., Anglicanism, the Thought and Practice of the Church of England (2nd ed., 1957), p. 606.

house in his Master's presence, as if he were rather God Almighty's fellow than His servant, seldom uncovering his head, seldomer bending the knee, or saucily lolling on his elbows; let such a man make never so many protestations that his heart is upright to Godward, I shall never be brought to believe him.[23]

Prebendary Robarts insisted that it was an act of piety to build houses of worship for God, especially as the men of noble houses and of wealth outtopped the poor church with their "Patrons' Pyramids." Otherwise, the impiety of the affluent would be seen in the "poore Church . . . [which] standeth cringing behinde, as ashamed to be seene, so tattered without in her roofe, walls and windows: so dusty, sullied, and forlorn within, as that the stone doth answere it."[24] He maintained that many individual men in a parish each spend more on their own house than they combine to "lay out on the house of God." The same author argued that the required raising of the altar or holy table was so that it "should provoke in you a desire for that blessed food."[25] Clearly then, the splendour of God's house is an indication of the piety of those that build, furnish, or repair it, and of the impiety of those who neglect it or abuse it. Further, the fittings of the church, whether altar, font, windows, or royal arms serve a didactic or monitory purpose.[26]

One of the most learned defences of the view that Christians ought to use special places for worship and had in fact even in early days done so was the work of the great writer on eschatology in the seventeenth century, Joseph Mede, Fellow of Christ's College, Cambridge, a notable centre of Puritanism. At any rate at this stage in his life, Mede was both a believer in the sacrificial interpretation of the Eucharist, and a defender of the view of the

---

23 *Ibid.*

24 F. Robarts, *Gods Holy House and Service* (1639), p. 33. Before Laud's advent to power, the fabric of churches had been allowed to deteriorate in sad fashion. For one example of slow but steady improvement, see F. W. West, *Rude Forefathers* (1949), pp. 10-14.

25 Robarts, *op. cit.*, p. 45.

26 Robarts's didacticism is plainly to be seen in his comments on the windows and the king's arms above the chancel arch of the church: ". . . what meane those images and pictures which are in the glasse? They are not there for any matter of worship of either God, Saint or Angell; but for history and ornament" (*ibid.*, p. 46). The Royal Arms are set "to professe the subjection of every soule to the higher power. For as the written sentences upon the walls by letters, so these Scutchions by their expressions do put us in minde of that *Defender of the Faith* and of our duty to him who is *next and immediately under God* supream governor over al persons and causes as well Ecclesiasticall as Temporall in all his Majesties Realmes & Dominions" (*ibid.*, p. 46).

appropriateness of erecting churches, or, as his title implies, *Churches, that is, appropriate Places for Christian Worship both in and ever since the Apostles Times* (1638). He sets out to repudiate the view held by "most of our Reformed writers" that when in early days the church "lived under pagan and persecuting emperors Christians had no oratories, or places set apart for Divine Worship, but that they assembled here and there promiscuously and uncertainly as they pleased, or the occasion served in places of common use. . . ."[27] The very appropriate text that he uses is I Corinthians 11:22: "Have ye not houses to eat and drink in? Or despise ye the Church of God?" He demonstrates that Augustine and Basil, Chrysostom and Theodoret interpret this text the same way as he does, and learnedly traces the development of the idea of the place where the church assembles through the Fathers of the second and third centuries. He also shows the development of the church from a convenient room in a house (usually a *coenaculum* or upper room) of a disciple to a mansion donated by a wealthy Christian for his numerous fellow Christians to worship in, until finally, as the multitude of believers grew, "they built them structures of purpose, partly in the coemiteries of martyrs, partly in other publique places."[28]

It is significant how far the sense of the inherent holiness of a church had developed under the impetus of Archbishop Laud and his supporters by the end of the fourth decade of the seventeenth century, as our citations and references have shown. This can be verified further by contrast from the sermon preached by John Prideaux, only fourteen or fifteen years before, at the consecration of the Exeter College Chapel, Oxford,[29] which looks like a diminutive Sainte Chapelle. Prideaux, then Rector of Exeter, Regius Professor of Divinity, and Vice-Chancellor of the University of Oxford, argued from the text, Luke 19:46 ("My house is the house of prayer") that there was a warrant for churches and for their consecration, and provided directions for their chief uses. But it is especially interesting that he would not argue for the inherent sanctity of the building, since this was the contention of Cardinal Bellarmine in *De Cultu Sanctorum*, which he expressly repudiates and to which his printed sermon makes reference in the margin: "Not for the inherent sanctity of the place (which our Adversaries

---

[27] Mede, *op. cit.*, pp. 2-3. [28] *Ibid.*, pp. 15-16.
[29] See *A Sermon preached on the Fifth of October 1624: at the Consecration of St. Iames Chappel in Exeter College* (Oxford, 1625).

presse too far) but through the obiective Holinesse adherent to it, by Christs promises, sacred meetings, united devotion, ioynt participating of the Word and Sacraments, lively incitements through others examples."[30] Thus from Hooker to Laud there is an increase in the claims made for the churches; they are not merely convenient, or their fittings didactically valuable, or the encouragements from the example of others worshipping, or even the place where angels join with humans in worship, but they are the places of God's presence and most fully in the Body and Blood of Christ in the Eucharist centred on the elevated and enclosed altar.

The fullest confirmation of the high evaluation placed upon churches by the Caroline divines, however, is to be found in their Orders for the Consecration of Churches, from that of Jesus Chapel, Peartree, Southampton by Bishop Lancelot Andrewes in 1620 to that of Sir Ranulf Crewe's private chapel in Crewe by Bishop John Bridgman in 1635. In Andrewes's first Prayer of Consecration the purposes for which the church was erected are declared to be, "as an habitacion for thee, and a place for us to assemble and meete together in, for the observacion of thy divine worship, invocation of thy great great name, reading, preaching and hearing of Thy heavenly Word, administring thy most holy Sacraments, above all, in this place, the very gate of heaven upon earth, as Jacob named it, to do the work of heaven, to sett forth Thy most worthie praise, to laud and magnifie thy most glorious Maiestie for all Thy goodness to all men, and especially to us that are of the household of faith."[31] The second Prayer of Consecration in the same order includes the petition, "consecrate it to the invocation of thy glorious name: wherein supplications, prayers, intercessions, may be made for all men; thy sacred word may be read, preached, and heard; the holy sacraments, the laver of regeneration, the commemoracion of the precious death of Thy deer sonne, may be administered; thy praises celebrated and sounded forth, thy people blessed by putting thy name upon them." If the first prayer expresses in part the numinous aspect of worship as aided by church architecture, the second stresses more its liturgical functionalism.

The consecration of the private chapel of Sir Ranulf Crewe, the judge, by the Bishop of Chester fifteen years later demonstrates

---

30 *Ibid.*, C 3 *recto*. The marginal reference is to "*lib.* 3, *cap.* 5" of Bellarmine's book.

31 J. W. Legg, *English Orders for Consecrating Churches in the Seventeenth Century* (Henry Bradshaw Society, Vol. XLI, 1911), p. 57.

through the prayer of consecration a stronger sense of the Communion of Saints, a more vivid and fresh use of the image of the sovereign and the court (God's "Whitehall") and the king by implication the supreme governor of the Church of England, and the increasing importance of music in the worship, while it has also its intriguing commercial metaphor, which makes one wonder whether this was for the special benefit of the well-to-do Sir Ranulf. The prayer begins:

> Theise houses are the Courts of thyne Audience where thou dost sitt to heare our prayers and supplications unto thee, they are that Royall Exchange where thou and we doe meete. And as it were comerce and trade together, for thou dost bring thy graces when we bring our devotions hither. They are parte of thy heauenly Quire, for here our Cryings make an Eccho to thyne Angels singinge (for they rejoyce when we repente) when we cry Peccavi here on Earth, they answere Halleluviah aboue in heauen, O let our Musique be as sweet to thee here on the ground, as is that Angels descant in their full harmonie and heauenly Sound.[32]

It continues and concludes:

> 'Tis true, o Lord, Heauen is thy glorious Temple, thy *Whitehall*, thy dwellinge house, the Earth also is thyne, and the whole round world and all that is therein, This is thy Outhouse, thou art the good Husbandman which thy sonne speaks of, who so beautifyest those vpper roomes where thy Saintes doe lodge, as thou dost dispise theise meaner receptacles of thy Servantes. Accept therfore this slender and poore habitacion and accept it not according to ye worth of the guifte but the harte and desire of those that giue it or rather accordinge to thy wonted loue and favour to thy Children.[33]

While the spirit of the later consecration orders is clearly that of Archbishop Laud, greatly dependent on the theology, patristic knowledge, devotion, and example of Lancelot Andrewes, there is only one church that Laud is known to have consecrated, namely that of St. Catherine, Cree, on Sunday, January 16, 1630/1, when he was Bishop of London. There is no order extant for this consecration, but there is an account of it from the vitriolic pen of William Prynne. Prynne is particularly caustic in describing the

[32] J. W. Legg, *op. cit.*, p. 202.   [33] *Ibid.*

prostrations which Laud made towards the altar, as indicating his great reverence for it, however overdone the ceremonial gestures were in Prynne's rather jaundiced eyes. Prynne leaves nothing to the imagination in his description of what is to him an artificial, idolatrous, and frenetic imitation of Roman ceremonial. Thus the ensuing report is both an account of Laud's gestures of reverence and of a Puritan's intense dislike of them:

> . . . when the Bishop approached neare the Communion Table, he bowed with his nose very neare the ground some six or seven times; Then he came to one of the corners of the Table, and there bowed himselfe three times; then to the second, third and fourth corners, bowing at each corner three times; but, when he came to the side of the Table where the bread and wine was, he bowed himselfe seven times, and then, after the reading of many praiers by himselfe and his two fat chaplins (which were with him, and all this while were upon their knees by him, in their Sirplisses, Hoods, and Tippits) he himself came neare the Bread, which was cut and laid in a fine napkin, and then he gently lifted up one of the corners of the said napkin, and peeped into it till hee saw the bread (like a boy that peeped after a bird-nest in a bush) and presently clapped it downe againe, and flew backe a step or two, and bowed very low three times towards it and the Table: when he beheld the bread, then he came neare and opened the napkin againe, and bowed as before; then he laid his hand upon the gilt *Cup* which was full of wine, with a cover upon it; so soone as he pul'd the Cupp a litle neerer to him, he lett the Cupp goe, flew backe, and bowed againe three times towards it: then hee came neere againe, and lifting up the cover of the Cupp peeped into it, and seing the wine, he let fall the cover on it againe, and flew nimbly backe and bowed as before: After these and many other Apish Anticke Gesturs he himselfe received, and then gave the Sacrament to some principall men onely they devoutly kneeling neere the Table, after which more prayers being said, this Sceane and Enterlude ended.[34]

For Roman Catholic and High Anglican alike, objects could be consecrated as well as people because of their dedication to God's service. For Quakers and Puritans, however, consecrated people

---

34 *Canterburies Doome* (1646), pp. 114f.

alone were God's true temples. The difference of attitude is concisely expressed in a poem of 1664, in which the Puritan exclaims:

> I love no such triumphant Churches—
> They scatter my devotion; whilst my sight
> Is courted to observe their sumptuous cost,
> I find my heart lost in my eyes. . . .

The Churchman replies:

> But I love Churches mount up to the skies,
> For my devotion rises with their roof;
> Therein my soul doth heav'n anticipate.[35]

The Puritan objections to the sumptuous and numinous edifices of the Church of England were precisely to their sumptuousness and what we today would call their "triumphalism" the distraction of ornaments in worship ("I find my heart lost in my eyes"), and the idolatry involved in the representation of divine persons as forbidden in the Decalogue. Also, the conviction grew (*pace* Joseph Mede's claims to the contrary), especially after St. Bartholomew's Day, 1662, when Puritan ministers became Dissenters and were ejected from their livings, that the most faithful companies of Christians in the apostolic and early days of the persecuted Christian church convened in rooms and houses or in the open air in great simplicity and fervour.

Furthermore, it was a great comfort to the Dissenting divines and their secretly gathered congregations, while smarting from the five-stringed whip of the Clarendon Code, to recall that the Epistle to the Hebrews lauded the faithful who lived in caves and dens of the earth "of whom the world was not worthy."[36] In the same way they recalled that the Christ whom they tried to imitate had been buried in a borrowed grave, had lived in no settled home since Nazareth, and had warned his disciples of the danger of riches and of the subtler danger of the Pharisaism that desires its piety to be seen of men.

In short, the simplicity of Puritan architecture and fittings was a matter of choice, since the Puritans preferred an unsumptuous worship. Bernard Manning, a modern historian belonging to that tradition, has rightly pointed out that to enter into conversation

---

[35] "Philonax Lovekin" (probably a pseudonym for J. Wilson, *Andronicus* [published 1664]), and cited by E. F. Carritt, *A Calendar of British Taste, From 1600 to 1800* (1948), p. 61.

[36] Hebrews 2:38.

with the living God is so transcendent an experience and so momentous in its consequences, that it renders all human artifice merely meretricious. In his words, "To call upon the name of God, to claim the presence of the Son of God, if men truly know and mean what they are doing, is in itself an act so tremendous and so full of comfort that any sensuous heightening of the effect is not so much a painting of the lily as a varnishing of sunlight."[37]

Behind the simplicity and even iconoclasm of Puritanism, there lay a simple and profound truth known to Judaism, and Islam, as well as to St. Bernard of Clairvaux and the Cistercians, together with the Quakers: that is the great danger of idolatry. The worst feature of idolatry is that it will try to limit, to fix, and even freeze the living God by our human concepts or representations of him. It is this fear of what may be called the absolutisation of the finite, whether in art or in credal confinement, that controls this simplicity in all the cases mentioned. It is the recognition that God must be sovereign, and cannot be "boxed in," since He is the Holy Spirit who blows as invisibly, freely, unpredictably, and mysteriously as the wind, whether as zephyr or cyclone, that lies behind this tradition.

There is a further reason for Puritan simplicity, apart from the economic which will be considered later, and that is the great fear that the aesthetic will distract the people of God from the ethical. Its classical expression in the Bible is given in the monition: "For all that is in the world, the lust of the flesh, and the lust of the eyes, and the vainglory of life, is not of the Father, but of the world."[38] In Puritan worship there were no stained-glass windows to lure the eye as the light shone full upon the pages of Holy Writ and upon the faces of the people of God being sanctified by the Holy Spirit who made them His temple. This worship was an etching; while Anglican and Catholic worship were oil-paintings.

Its rationale is a profound sense of the universality and ubiquity of the Spirit of God, taught so vividly by Psalm 139, and felicitously expressed by John Rainolds, one of the translators of the King James Version of the Scriptures, and reaffirmed by George Gillespie when the Laudian-Puritan controversy was at its height in 1637: "How much more soundly do we hold with J. Rainolds, That unto us Christians no land is strange, no ground unholy; every coast in Jewry, every house is Sion; and every faithful

---

[37] *Christian Worship* (ed. Nathaniel Micklem, Oxford, 1936), p. 162.
[38] I John 2:16.

company, yea, every faithful body a Temple to serve God in . . . whereas the presence of Christ among two or three gathered together in his Name (Matthew XVIII.20) maketh any place a Church. . . ."[39] Their simplicity of architecture and fittings was a matter of conviction, but it was also a matter of economic necessity.

4. *Social Prestige as an Architectural Factor*

A fourth element will help to account for the differences between the churches or meeting-houses of seventeenth-century religious groups. This is the factor of social prestige, by which the exterior and interior of religious buildings will be a mark of the standing in society of their donors and to some extent those who worship in them. To this extent elegance and sumptuousness will mark the sanctuaries of the monarch and the nobility, and simplicity and even poverty will distinguish the buildings for worship erected by the persecuted or the underprivileged.

As might be expected on this basis, the most splendid new church buildings in England during the seventeenth century were the royal chapels of the Stuart kings or their queens, and none more splendid than the short-lived transformation of the Tudor Royal Chapel of Windsor at the request of the Roman Catholic James II by the combined talents of Hugh May, Grinling Gibbons and Verrio, respectively architect, sculptor, and painter. Evelyn, good Anglican that he was, found himself greatly impressed by such splendour.[40] From the time of James I, the Stuarts lost no opportunity by their aesthetic commissions (whether royal portraits or decoration of their audience chambers, and even of their own or their Catholic queen's chapels) or in their high-handed actions of regarding Parliaments mainly as existing to vote them monies, of asserting in the strongest way their belief in the divine right of kings. Moreover, as "supreme governors" of the Church of England, they counted on the unwavering support of the archbishops and bishops. James I at the Hampton Court Conference had informed the Puritans, who had hoped that the Presbyterians in Scotland had taught him to distrust prelates, that in fact it was their opponents he most distrusted. Succinctly, even abruptly,

---

[39] The citation is not from the 1637 but the 1660 edition of Gillespie's *Dispute Against the English Popish Ceremonies*, p. 123. It should, however, be noted that the Puritans in avoiding the visual images were not protected from the auditory images of the Scripture lessons or the illustrations in the sermons of their preachers, but these, being transitory, were less likely to have permanent features of "idolatry."

[40] *Diary*, October 18, 1685, which is cited in full in Chap. II, Sect. 4.

James insisted on the common interest of hierarchy in state and church: "no bishop, no king."

Since in Italy, France, Spain, Flanders, and Portugal, Baroque architecture and art were used for the glorification of absolute monarchy and the assertion of the claims of the post-Tridentine Church,[41] it naturally appealed to the Stuarts, and especially those who had married Roman Catholic queens,[42] and, most of all to James II who openly avowed his Catholicism, while still head of the Reformed Church of England. Its allure was increased after the sojourn of the future Charles II and James II in the brilliant court of France, and the English court of the Restoration copied the French fashions in taste, morals, and politics. Consequently, another feature of Baroque, its marriage of many arts, such as architecture, sculpture, painting, and carving, together with vocal and instrumental music, was immensely popular in secular and sacred gatherings. This was seen earlier in the century in the masques staged with many elaborate changes of scenery by Inigo Jones, England's earliest Renaissance-type architect, and in the later part of the century in the opera and stage plays, as well as in the elaborate services in royal chapels or in the London embassy chapels of Catholic countries.

These services in royal chapels and embassies were splendidly theatrical attempts to enthrall all the senses. By ingenious *trompe l'oeil* devices, the eye of the spectator would be swept up into the ceiling which pierced the dome to reveal a sky of Italianate blue,[43] as he followed the ascension of Christ or of the saints.[44] The processionals and recessionals—with the monks and priests wearing

[41] See Margaret Whinney and Oliver Millar, *English Art, 1625-1714* (Oxford, 1957), Chap. XII, especially p. 285.

[42] Queen Henrietta Maria's Chapel at Marlborough Gate, built about 1627 from Inigo Jones's design, had departed from the "Gothic survival" tradition which was Archbishop Laud's preference for English ecclesiastical architecture, by the choice of a semi-Palladian style, with three long windows at the east end divided by pilasters, the middle one being round-headed and itself surmounted by the royal coat of arms, and it had a richly panelled reredos and a barrel roof with gilded stucco bosses (*ibid.*, illustration 3). The apotheosis of Queen Catherine of Braganza, consort of Charles II, was depicted by Verrio who shows her, in a painting in the Queen's audience chamber, proceeding in a triumphal car in the clouds to the Temple of Virtue. Whinney and Millar (*ibid.*, p. 298) claim that there "can have been few more wholly Baroque iconographies in Europe than the glorification of the English Crown with which ceiling after ceiling at Windsor was concerned."

[43] Such was the ceiling painting of Verrio in the Royal Chapel of Whitehall described by Evelyn (*Diary* entry for October 18, 1685).

[44] *Il Gesù* at Rome and other distinguished Jesuit churches often depicted the triumph of St. Ignatius and the martyred Jesuits who ascended in a spiral into the empyrean of Heaven.

their dramatic habits or richly embroidered vestments, the angels on the bosses of the roof suggesting the closeness of the court of heaven to the earthly court, the many gestures of adoration and obeisance in various parts of the Mass, the perfume of the incense, and the richly encrusted golden chalice and the reliquaries, not to mention the honeyed eloquence of the preacher and in anthems and voluntaries, the contrapuntal music of the voices, organs, and instruments echoing and re-echoing—were a consort of ecstasies. All this splendour was the acme of social prestige as well as of aesthetic tribute to God, and his vicegerent the monarch. On September 21, 1662, Pepys crowded into Queen Catherine of Braganza's chapel and was greatly impressed by the elegance of the fittings, where he "saw the fine altar, ornaments, and the fryers in their habits, and the priests come in with their fine crosses and many other fine things." For social prestige fineness is all.

Nowhere did the Church of England seem more to be the *via media* than when, after the Great Fire of London, her churches in the city underwent a classical renaissance. There is neither theatricality, nor anything gaudy or tawdry in the architecture or fittings of Wren's churches. There is a decent, sober suitability, dignity, and orderliness, as well as inventiveness, in almost all of Wren's work. These "auditory" churches were built in part to meet the needs of as many worshippers as could be accommodated within sound and sight of the preacher.[45] The undramatic nature of the altars, as compared with their Roman Catholic counterparts on the Continent, and the restricted expenditure possible depending upon the coal tax which financed these churches and St. Paul's Cathedral, together with the Protestant emphasis on the pulpit which was of growing importance in Restoration Anglicanism,[46] and the fact that these churches would be used predominantly by merchants of the City of London and their wives and servants, tended to make for elegant simplicity, but of course, not for Puri-

---

[45] The younger Christopher Wren as cited in *Parentalia* (p. 318) makes it clear that for Wren a "convenient auditory" is one in which "everyone should hear the Service and both hear and see the Preacher." Thus the altar was not, as in the Counter-Reformation continental churches the focal point of the entire design, emphasized by plan, lighting, and decoration. But the altar itself had to be against the east wall, safeguarded from profanation by rails, and sufficiently unhidden (as had been the case in apse or chancel in Gothic type churches) to be visible to all who would participate in the Holy Communion.

[46] One cannot fail to notice the importance of the pulpit in this period in the frequent references to sermons by the Presbyterian sympathiser Pepys and the loyal Anglican Evelyn in their diaries. Another indication of its importance would be the variety of pulpits designed by Wren, and their impressive sounding-boards.

tan austerity. It is also significant that Wren designed many galleries, for which there were medieval precedents, not forgetting their prevalence in the churches of both Huguenots in France[47] and Jesuits in northern Europe,[48] two communities which emphasized preaching strongly.

The open, well-lit interiors of Wren's churches have a functional simplicity, and an absence of ostentation which would please not only the government but, one supposes, also the city merchants, who were not admirers of extravagance. On the other hand, the fittings, while not usually elaborate, were often panels that were richly carved, especially in the later decades of the century. These panels were sometimes framed by pilasters and sometimes bore, especially in St. Stephen's, Coleman Street, delicately carved flowers and fruit. Grinling Gibbons, at his richest, is to be found in the marvellously varied cherubs and festoons of the choir stalls of St. Paul's Cathedral. But these fittings were the exception. The general impression was of quiet good taste such as pleased the bourgeoisie.

Puritan (strictly Nonconformist) meeting-houses built during the last decade of the seventeenth century were also examples of unostentatious good taste, especially those built in London and the larger provincial towns such as Ipswich and Norwich, Bury, St. Edmunds, and Taunton. The earlier Puritan chapels of the century were of two kinds. Either they were simplifications of Anglican churches in the Commonwealth period, or they were built during a short lull in the sixteen-year period of persecution which lasted from 1662 to 1688, and then they were often only private houses or cottages or public rooms used for Puritan worship.[49] In any case, they are domestic architecture for the

47 Salomon de Brosse built the Huguenot Temple at Charenton in 1623, which Wren must certainly have visited when he was in Paris. It is illustrated in Margaret Whinney's *Christopher Wren* (1971), p. 32.

48 One might give as an example the Jesuit Church in Antwerp built between 1625-1631, and burnt in 1718. (Whinney and Millar, *English Art, 1625-1714*, p. 156.)

49 King Charles II published a Declaration of Indulgence in 1671/2 allowing non-Anglican places of worship to be used. Twenty-five hundred licences were issued during this shortlived lull in the persecution, but it is doubtful if even a handful of new Puritan sanctuaries was built. It is far more probable that private houses were more openly equipped for worship or that even public halls were used. It is in the final decade that, under the toleration encouraged by William III, 2418 buildings were registered for public worship by Presbyterians, Independents, and Baptists, besides scores of Quaker meetings. It is in this final decade that the typical Puritan meeting-houses emerge. See the list of surviving chapels from this time in Martin S. Briggs, *Puritan Architecture and Its Future* (1946), p. 23.

gathering of the families of God, never houses of God. While they do not express any sense of social prestige, still less do they symbolize social servility. They express a quiet confidence in the promises of God and an integrity of outlook that is as uncomplex as a white wall.

The same lack of triumphalism, save the triumph of simplicity, would have been found in the fittings of Anglican churches where there were Puritan incumbents. One such church, complete with its Puritan fittings, survives from the seventeenth century, almost untouched by the restorer's hand. This is Langley Chapel, near Acton Burnell between Bridgnorth and Shrewsbury. This chapel has avoided any Augustan or Victorian change of its interior, partly through the disappearance of the neighbouring hall and the depopulation of the village, and the virtual disuse of the chapel since the beginning of the nineteenth century.

It is a simple rectangular one-room building, with a three-light east window and two doors on the southern wall. It is filled with Jacobean pews. It has a pulpit on the south side and opposite this is a box-pew containing a reading-desk, all constructed of unpolished oak cut in the simplest designs. Its liturgical arrangements, however, are most intriguing and worthy of detailed consideration.[50]

There is no structural separation of the chancel from the nave, but a distinction is made by a slight raising of the level of the chancel floor. The simple Communion table (measuring 41½ inches long by 25¼ inches wide by 34 inches high) is surrounded on the north and east sides by a bench, and may originally have had a further bench on the west side of the holy table. The north bench is 44½ inches distant from the table and the east bench is only 29 inches distant. The most interesting feature of all is the kneelers or footrests attached to and below the seats of the benches. These are usually described as kneelers, since this is the almost invariable Anglican posture for prayer and the reception of Holy Communion. On examining them, however, this writer thinks it

---

[50] The date 1601 appears in the roof timbers, but the pews are almost certainly a decade or two later. Information on the history of this chapel will be found in the *Victoria County History of Shropshire*, Vol. 8 (1968), p. 145 and there is a photograph of the interior opposite p. 144. My own drawing appears as illustration no. 7 of the present volume.

I wish to thank the Reverend D. W. Gould, the Rector of Acton Burnell, for his great kindness in arranging for me to visit Langley Chapel and for answering various queries.

highly probable that they are footrests not kneelers. My first reason is that they are almost impossibly uncomfortable to serve as kneelers, though some might argue that this very masochism might identify them as Puritan for this reason. In fact, however, the declivity from the back to the front of the lower rest being 3¼ inches meant that the knees would slip off the rest while the foot could remain comfortably on it. Furthermore, it is only 22 inches from the front of the seat to the nearest point of the kneeler or footrest, diagonally, which is uncomfortable for kneeling but convenient for sitting. Finally, it should be remembered that the Puritans (along with John Knox who is reputed to be responsible for the last-minute inclusion of the "black rubric" in the 1552 Prayer Book) objected most strongly to receiving the Communion kneeling, for they considered this a "noxious ceremony" countenancing idolatry. Why, then, should Anglican Puritans erect kneelers when footrests for those who were invited guests at Christ's Table seemed the most appropriate gesture at what they called The Lord's Supper? Whether my theory is right or wrong, it is intriguing to see the survival of the Puritan treatment of the holy table as a table, by surrounding it on two if not three sides with benches and not as an altar. One kneels before an altar, but one sits at a table.

In any case, the single-room chapel, the plain unstained windows, and unpolished oak furnishings, the functional benches and uncomplicated holy table, speak of the simplicity of Anglican as well as of Nonconformist Puritanism in our period. Neither sought the good opinion of the great, but only to fear God and to worship Him in the ways commanded in his ordinances in Holy Scripture. To the holders of such convictions social and political prestige and all its external trappings, however impressive, were only an impudent irrelevance in the eyes of God.

5. The Economic Factor in Building

It is obvious that social prestige in architecture is dependent upon having the finance to support it, when it is desired. But it is still true, social and political prestige apart, that economy will have a considerable impact on architecture and fittings. For example, it costs much less to build in brick than stone, to leave a wall white-washed or painted in monochrome than to panel it, to erect a simple pulpit or choir stall without the elaborate festoons of fruit and flowers and cherubs that are the distinctive mark of Grinling Gibbons' work or to have a flat ceiling rather than a barrel-vaulted one with golden bosses or to use plain rather than stained windows.

The old Catholic aristocracy paid dearly for the recusancy of its members. One has only to contrast the splendour of the Baroque Catholic chapels in Europe in noblemen's houses, with the disguised domesticity of their English counterparts, where perhaps the most distinctive feature of their architecture were "priests' holes" where the hunted celebrants of Mass might hide once the *poursuivants* came close. If this was the case for the Roman Catholics, it was equally so for the Nonconformists during the reigns of Charles II and James II, when they, too, met in private cottages or in the open air, and designed pulpits that closed like cupboards. In the case of the former and latter, it was necessity that drove them to simplicity; but had theirs not been a forbidden faith there is little question that the wealthier Catholics, at least, would have erected ornate and splendid chapels for the celebration of the mysteries.

The greatest architect of the age was also limited by financial considerations. Sir Christopher Wren's fifty-two churches in London were built to replace the eighty-seven churches destroyed or damaged by the Fire of London.[51] The fittings were to be paid for by the individual parishes and the more richly fitted ones often indicated the wealth of one of the City companies that financed them, or the affluence of a particular Croesus in the neighbourhood. The fabric of all the churches was, however, to be paid for out of the tax on "sea coal"; that is, from a tax paid on all the coal that entered London. This is one reason why the spires of churches were often added fifteen or twenty years after the rest of the buildings had been completed.[52] It also accounted for his use of galleries as a means of greatly adding to the size of the congregation without adding proportionately to the cost of the building. A further evidence of the economic element was the fact that Wren used the same medieval foundations wherever possible, and since these had often been cheek by jowl with houses and shops (rapidly rebuilt by their owners) he had often only a front façade to provide. This financial factor, in his case at least, was not always a disadvantage. On the contrary, it made him use his considerable

[51] St. Clement Dane's, St. James's, Piccadilly, and St. Anne's Soho, were also Wren's work, but these were erected to the west of the city proper.
[52] Margaret Whinney, *Wren* (1971), p. 67.

ingenuity in varying his single-room church plans, and encouraged the inventiveness employed in his splendid and varied steeples.[53] This twofold preoccupation of Wren's mind, functional and economic, can be seen in his memorandum written after 1708 in which he gave advice on how the newer churches to the west of the city of London should be built: "in our reformed Religion, it should seem vain to make a Parish church larger than all who are present can both see and hear. The Romanists, indeed, may build larger Churches, it is enough if they hear the murmur of the Mass, and see the Elevation of the Host, but ours are to be fitted for Auditories."[54] His uncle Bishop Matthew Wren would have loved to extol the mystery of religion in rich architecture and splendid ceremonial. Wren was typical of his age in preferring explanation to mystification, the simple to the symbolical, and the functional to the fantastic.

The complex of five factors—the nature of the religious community, the foci of worship, numinosity or functionalism, social and political prestige, and the degree of financial support—is involved to a greater or lesser degree in all the religious buildings erected during the seventeenth century.

Moreover, all testify to the differing definitions of the church which each tradition holds and transmits to the future. For the Anglican the church is the house of God's presence, both convenient and symbolical, where the English people of God gather for prayer, preaching and Holy Communion. For the Roman Catholic it is the sacred place where God re-enacts the daily miracle of Transubstantiation in the presence of the people, the angels, and the saints. For the Puritans it is the place where the covenanted holy community ("visible saints") are gathered to hear the oracles of God expounded and the Lord's Supper shared. For the Quakers, who regard dedicated personalities as the only true temples of the Holy Spirit, who illumines them with inner light and garrisons them with interior peace, only the simplest and least distracting of buildings is suitable for silent worship.

Roman Catholics and Anglicans are aware of the numinous element in architecture, while Puritans and Quakers stress the functional and pragmatic considerations. Roman Catholics and Angli-

53 *Ibid.*, pp. 47, 66. They evidently impressed Canaletto for in 1746 he painted several views of the Thames, and in each of them showed the steeples like the masts of great stranded stone ships, piercing an unusually Italian skyscape.
54 Cited from the *Parentalia* by the younger Christopher Wren in Margaret Whinney's *Wren*, p. 48.

cans emphasize the historical continuity of the Christian faith and the hierarchy in the style and symbolism of their sanctuaries, while Puritans and Quakers concentrate on the contemporaneity of divine providence and the direction of the Holy Spirit. Roman Catholic churches or chapels (whenever permitted) and new Anglican churches are impressive, while Puritan and Quaker meeting-houses are expressive. The danger of Roman Catholic churches or chapels (especially on the Continent) during this Baroque era is theatricality and idolatry. The danger of Laudian Anglican churches or their fittings is that beauty may prove a substitute for ethical duty. The danger for Puritan and Quaker meeting-houses is that colour-blindness and poverty of the imagination may be confused with simplicity and restraint, and the *tabula Domini* with a *tabula rasa*.

CHAPTER II

CHURCH ARCHITECTURE: ACHIEVEMENTS

F ROM THEORETICAL and theological considerations we turn
to the actual achievements in English religious architecture
during the seventeenth century, from Inigo Jones to Christopher Wren. This will involve a survey of the Anglican, Roman
Catholic, Puritan, and Quaker churches or meeting-houses, and
their fittings and plate. Inevitably, however, it will be only a selection of distinguished church architecture or of typical meeting-
houses, especially from 1660 onwards.

It has been argued that there is no denominationally or even
distinctively religious architecture in this age,[1] no more than there
is an Anglican mathematics or a dissenting geometry and that an
age builds in a certain style without distinguishing except functionally between sacred and secular buildings. Even further, it is
maintained that a "style" is seen to exist not by contemporaries,
who merely build, but only by successive and troubled ages which
are in the throes of a new and contrasting form of building. Such
a view could be maintained by showing, for example, the likeness
between Wren's London churches of the unpretentious kind and
the simple meeting-houses built in 1688[2] and in the next genera-

---

[1] This point has been forcibly put by an architect, Ronald F. Jones, in *Nonconformist Church Architecture* (1914), pp. 8-11.

[2] A. L. Drummond, *The Church Architecture of Protestantism* (1934), pp.
36-37, claims: "Wren was the creator of the modern Anglo-Saxon Protestant
church." So far so good. Then he immediately continues: "The effect of the late
Puritan supremacy in moulding the English attitude to public worship and
church building could not be undone. Wren recognised the change by designing
places of worship that were primarily meeting-houses; his aim was to ensure
seeing and hearing." R. F. Jones, see footnote 1 immediately above, takes the
same view, but neither of them does justice to Wren's preference for rectangular
over square ground plans, nor to the fact that Wren's altars are in the east of
his churches while meeting-house Communion tables are in the centre. Finally,
they ignore the further fact that Wren's pulpits though similar in shape are not
located on the south walls of his edifices but against pillars and on the north.
These differences are fundamental. See also H. Lismer Short's interesting suggestion that the distinctive interior arrangements of the meeting-houses derive
from Calvinist precedent in Geneva, Holland, and Scotland, in the adaptation of
medieval fanes, and that the transmission of these ideas was either by Marian
exiles or university students going to Dutch or Scottish universities in the seventeenth century. ("The Architecture of the Old Meeting Houses," *Transactions
of the Unitarian Historical Society*, Vol. 8, No. 3, 1944, pp. 98-112.)

tion, or even by demonstrating the similarities between Wren's ecclesiastical and domestic architecture.

There is, of course, considerable truth in this view. In the choice of brick rather than stone, in the use of clear rather than stained-glass windows, in the use of circular or oval windows with "cobwebbed" glass, in the porticoes, and the functional well-lit simplicity of the architecture of the period, there are parallels between sacred and secular architecture, and between a Wren church and a Dissenting meeting-house.

On the other hand, however, there are important differences between Wren's type of church architecture and a Dissenting meeting-house, as our second footnote has already demonstrated. In addition, there is a considerable difference between the sacred architecture of Inigo Jones and Wren, and also between their Italianate styles and the "Gothic survival" which Archbishop Laud favoured, and which produced some intriguing mixtures of Gothic-Renaissance chapels in Oxford and Cambridge. Furthermore, one must distinguish Wren in his early and late styles. One must also note the differences in Wren's architecture due to diverse patrons, such as James II, or the dean and canons of St. Paul's Cathedral or the state, or even when affluent guilds are providing the fittings of his churches in the City or west of the City of London.

The seventeenth century was a great period for building churches. In Elizabeth's reign by contrast only nineteen churches or chapels were built or rebuilt.[3] Between 1603 and 1662 (and Wren's most important and prolific commissions are executed after this time) at least a hundred and thirty-three churches are known to have been newly erected or entirely rebuilt on an old site, and nearly four hundred were significantly remodelled.[4]

It is of particular interest to note that these churches were built in three distinct and one mixed style of architecture. There is the "Gothic survival"[5] style so much favoured by Laud as emphasising

[3] See John M. Schnorrenberg's "Anglican Architecture, 1558-1662: Its Theological Implications and Its Relation to the Continental Background" (Princeton University Ph.D., 1964, Department of Art and Archaeology), p. 46.

[4] Ibid., p. 51.

[5] Eric Mercer (English Art, 1553-1625, Oxford, p. 85) had argued that there were three reasons for the continuance of Gothic church architecture in England: one was to advertise by the familiar exterior the functions of the building as a church; another was to give the building an archaic air (which would link with the Laudian motive of creating a sense of continuity through the centuries); and the third was to emphasise a particular feature of the church by its Gothic form contrasting with the classical details of the ornamentation. Marcus Whiffen (Stuart and Georgian Churches, 1947, p. 9) argues that Gothic was still the nat-

the continuity of Anglicanism with the medieval Church which preceded it and the constructional techniques which had never been lost. There is, by contrast, the "Italianate" style so greatly favoured by Charles I and exemplified in the works of Inigo Jones. In Wren's work we find an "English Palladianism," which is a more domesticated Italianate style than that of Inigo Jones. The "mixed" style may be Gothic mingled with Flemish mannerism[6] (as in the Jacobean and Caroline strapwork, diamonds, obelisks, and curlicues that abound in the interior ornamentation and detail of this period). This can be seen, for example, in St. John's Church, Leeds. Or, it can be Gothic mixed with Italian details (such as cherubs, framed paintings used as a reredos, festoons of fruit and flowers), some of which are found in part in the chapels of Trinity College and Lincoln College, Oxford, or in Peterhouse Chapel in Cambridge.

1. Anglican Architecture

The most famous architect in England before Wren was, of course, Inigo Jones, whose court masques familiarised England with Italian *mises-en-scène*. His most famous ecclesiastical architecture includes St. Catherine Cree,[7] St. Paul's Covent Garden, the new portico of St. Paul's Cathedral, and the Marlborough Chapel.

St. Catherine Cree, built in 1628, combines Gothic elements with classical. It resembles Lincoln's Inn Chapel, since both are Gothic buildings that have Italian arcades surmounted by shouldered Gothic windows. St. Catherine's has a Gothic plan, Gothic vaulting, and Gothic window tracery while the west doorway, however, has a classical character, but the most notable classical characteristic is, of course, the Corinthian order of the nave arcading.

The more characteristically classical work is St. Paul's Covent Garden which is indubitably the creation of Inigo Jones, and which provides a kind of miniature *piazza* setting for the church. It was the first English and ambitious attempt to use the Tuscan Order according to the rules of Vitruvius.[8] It was built between

---

ural way of building in out of the way places, and so the idea of a conscious "survival," especially country districts, may be greatly exaggerated.

6 Gerald Cobb, *The Old Churches of London* (1942), p. 8.

7 *Ibid.*, p. 7, is doubtful whether Inigo Jones built St. Catherine Cree, London. But whether or not it is an intriguing mixture of Gothic and classical elements and of the transitional character associated with the earlier work of Inigo Jones.

8 *Ibid.*

1631 and 1633. It has a rectangular simplicity, open interior, and a Tuscan portico, all features that spell a long farewell to Gothic.

About 1627 Inigo Jones was commissioned to build the Queen's Chapel in Marlborough Gate by King Charles I for the use of his Catholic Queen, Henrietta Maria. The vaulted and bossed roof provides a gilded ceiling that overarches the three long windows divided by pilasters, with the double-width central window with a superimposed lunette window. Below the windows is a richly panelled reredos stretching the width of the sanctuary and converging on a framed painting, in front of which is the altar. The whole effect is of restrained Baroque, with clear lighting and a single room or chamber, rather than the Gothic standard cruciform. The decoration is restricted to the panelled and embossed roof and the royal arms above the lunette of the central window. It is all the more effective because it is modest rather than heavily ornamented, as contrasted with later royal chapels in the century.[9]

The most widely seen work of Inigo Jones was the western front of St. Paul's Cathedral, which accorded with the taste of Charles I rather than that of his Bishop of London, as Laud was at the time it was projected. It was begun in 1633 and it put a classical face on the Gothic body of the old St. Paul's. In fact the restoration of the cathedral was to occupy Jones for a decade. Jones built a great portico sixty-six feet high, with a Corinthian Order of fourteen columns, while huge scrolls filled in the side angles between the high nave and the low aisles. Above the entablature there was a balustraded parapet instead of a pediment. It had pedestals set at intervals that were to receive the statues of the benefactors of the cathedral. The purpose of this portico was to be used as a public ambulatory to avoid the cathedral's interior being similarly employed, a concern very much in the forefront of Laud's mind who could not endure the desecration of edifices built for the worship of God. But if the proposer of the portico was Laud, the style was that of the bishop's royal master, and Charles I paid for it as a memorial to his father, King James I.[10]

[9] Its interior as restored, is the fourth illustration in Margaret Whinney and Oliver Millar, *English Art, 1625-1714* (Oxford, 1957).

[10] Doreen Yarwood, *The Architecture of England* (1963), pp. 191ff. The subsequent history of St. Paul's during the Commonwealth period was deplorable. The scaffolding set up to support the vaulting and tower was cut down and sold, so that much of the vault collapsed. The building was entirely secularised, the nave being used as stables and the portico as a cover for stalls and shops, while the undercroft of the chapter-house became a wine-cellar. The Great Fire of 1666 was an apocalyptic ending to the sorry state of the old Gothic St. Paul's, which rose Phoenix-like from its ashes, in Wren's new masterpiece.

2. The Impact of Laud

It was unquestionably Laud, a subject for distant admiration rather than close affection because of his great energy and rigour, with the unswerving support of Charles I, who left the greatest impact on Anglican architecture in the first half of the century, as did Wren in the second half. Laud had inherited the triple tradition of Bishop Lancelot Andrewes,[11] a concern to main spiritual continuity between the doctrine and discipline of the church of the first five centuries and the Church of England, a profound concern for reverence in worship, including a particularly high evaluation of the chief Sacrament, and a respect for the divine right of kings that his Puritan enemies could only consider as subservient if not servile. In these convictions Laud was supported by such a prelate as Matthew Wren, uncle of the great architect. It is this conservatism of outlook in aesthetics, combined with determination in execution that explains what must be called "Gothic survival" in the church architecture of the period.[12] For Laud, since his consecration as Bishop of Bath and Wells, on his way to the sees of London and Canterbury, not forgetting his earlier years as President of St. John's College, Oxford (1611-1621) which prepared him for the role of Chancellor of the University of Oxford (1630-1641), dominated Anglican aesthetic taste. It is clear that he had little sympathy with the Italianate fashions of Inigo Jones. Even in the semi-Baroque splendour of the Canterbury Quadrangle of St. John's, it seems as if medievalism is attempting to suppress the future. For if both open ends of the quadrangle have loggia, the façades that surmount them are medieval in shape as are the ornaments. And it is quite typical that his loggia spandrils are filled with busts of the theological and cardinal virtues and of the seven liberal arts, with half-length angels on the central arch. This was an iconographical programme "common in the ecclesiastical art of the middle ages, but it is probably unique in the secular art of the seventeenth."[13]

11 But Bishop Lancelot Andrewes was a great preacher and a man of wit, while Laud was afraid of the latitude preaching allowed and lacked the psychological insight which produced humour.

12 See Sir Alfred Clapham's article, "The Survival of Gothic in 17th century England," *Architects' Journal*, CVI, Supplement (1942), 44; also the unpublished doctoral dissertation of John M. Schnorrenberg, *op. cit.*, pp. 51ff.

13 Mary Whinney and Oliver Millar, *English Art, 1625-1714* (Oxford, 1957), p. 55. The authors point out that the only concession made to contemporary taste are the larger than life bronze figures of Charles I and his Queen Henrietta Maria by Le Sueur, the King's sculptor. These were placed in the niches above the entrances.

If his secular buildings are Gothic in inspiration and iconography, how much more will be the sacred architecture he sponsored or otherwise influenced? The impact of Laud can be seen in the vigorous chapel building programme at Oxford, and, to a lesser degree, at Cambridge. A harlequin floor of black and white marble was laid in Magdalen College Chapel and there was a partial remaking of the stalls. The decoration showed a curious mingling of classical swags and pediments with Gothic style tracery and finials. More decisively Laudian was the decision of Accepted Frewen,[14] President of the College, in 1631 to substitute an altar for the Communion table, the first similar transformation since the Reformation. Despite his Puritan Christian name, the offence was made even ranker to the Puritans by the later addition of a crucifix, and the provision of painted hangings featuring scenes from the life of Christ, while from the roof there was suspended a corona of lights. By 1635, as was noted in Laud's diary, the work had been completely finished and it included the surviving brass eagle lectern and eight statues provided by the Christmas brothers.[15]

Even Lincoln College Chapel, Oxford, which was the gift of Laud's inveterate enemy, Bishop Williams, and which was consecrated in 1631, is at least as Gothic in plan and treatment as it is neo-classical. It has traceried Gothic windows and a wooden and canted roof, with small ribs that divide it into panels, even though the bosses in the panels are gilded and include cherubs and swags. The splendid east window, almost unquestionably the work of Bernard Van Linge, has a thoroughly medieval iconography, since it consists of Old Testament anticipations and the New Testament fulfilment of events central in the life of Christ and is a typical example of Patristic typological exegesis. In conception it is thoroughly medieval,[16] if not earlier, but in execution the Vandyke

---

[14] Later to be Archbishop of York.

[15] Whinney and Millar, op. cit., p. 55.

[16] This astonishing window deserves detailed consideration for its iconography which suggests that Bishop Williams was trying to outdo Bishop Laud at his own game. Moving from left to right, and upper light to lower light, we have the following series of themes. First, the Nativity of the Second Adam, Christ, and below it the birth of the First Adam in Paradise (both expounding I Cor. 15:45). Next comes the Baptism of Christ (Matthew 3:16) and below the dramatic drowning of the kings and soldiers presumably of Egypt (I Cor. 10:2). The third upper light depicts the institution of the Communion (Matthew 26:26-30) and the light below depicts a lamb resembling a child and illustrates Exodus 12:3. The fourth upper light shows the Crucifixion and Christ surrounded by his Mother and the Magdalen (Colossians 2:4) with its anticipation in the serpent raised by Moses in the wilderness in the light below (John 39). The fifth upper

beards of Christ and the prophets bear a distinct contemporary resemblance to royal tonsorial fashions. The arrangement of the figures is dramatic, and the colours are as fresh as they are subtle.[17] But the shape of the chapel is medieval not modern, and so is its fenestral iconography.[18]

Another Laud-inspired addition to Oxford was the new porch added to the Church of St. Mary the Virgin in 1637. As William Prynne described it, on the deposition of Sir Nathaniel Brent, it was "standing in the very heart of the University towards the street [High Street], to which Church all the University resorted."[19] It was peculiarly offensive to Presbyterian Prynne because "in front of which porch was a statue of the *Virgin Mary* cut in stone with the Picture of a child in her armes, commonly taken to be the Picture of Christ." He might have been even more displeased if he had known that the twisted columns supporting the pediment were smaller reminders, if not replicas, of the Solomonic pillars (reputedly remaining from the Constantinian basilica) of St. Peter's in Rome, which Bernini had used ten years before to construct his impressive balddachino over the High Altar.[20] The donor of St. Mary's portico was Laud's chaplain, Dr. Morgan Owen.

The College Chapel in Cambridge most clearly associated with the Laudian movement was that of Peterhouse during the Mastership of Dr. Matthew Wren, Laud's protégé. Almost all of it was built between 1628 and 1632, except for the east and west facings which were added at the charge of Dr. John Cosin, Wren's successor as Master.[21] Here again there was a mixture of Gothic and neo-classical styles. The outside combined a Jacobean frieze with

---

light illustrates the Resurrection (Acts 2:24) and below is Jonah and the great fish in which he was incarcerated for three days (Matthew 12:24). The sixth and final light (upper) depicts the Ascension (Acts 1:9) and below it is shown the burning chariot of Elijah ascending into heaven (2 Kings 2:6). In each case the inscription from the Bible is given in Latin, emphasising medievalism.

17 Van Linge, a native of Emden, created the East window of Oxford's Wadham College Chapel and of Lincoln's Inn Chapel in London (1623-1624) and was associated with Christ Church Cathedral in Oxford when this was refurnished by Dean Duppa (between 1629 and 1638). The pictorial window in the N. aisle showing a sulking Jonah beneath the gourd, with Nineveh in the background is the work of Abraham Van Linge, his brother or his son. See C. Woodforde, *English Stained and Painted Glass* (1954), pp. 42ff.

18 For details and photographs, see the report of the Royal Commission on Historical Monuments, *City of Oxford* (1939), pp. 64, 67 and plates 121-26.

19 See *Canterburies Doome* (1646), p. 71.

20 The four bronze twisted columns were not unveiled until June 29, 1627 and the *balddachino* was inaugurated exactly six years later. See Rudolph Wittkower, *Gian Lorenzo Bernini, Roman Baroque Sculptor* (2nd edn., 1966), pp. 189-90.

21 Whinney and Millar, *op. cit.*, p. 57.

THE CONTEXT OF WORSHIP

perpendicular tracery in the window. Inside there were statues of the four evangelists, the patron saint, and figures of angels and cherubim. Prynne gives us the report of a Mr. Wallis, a rather jaundiced observer, on the interior: ". . . in *Peter house* Chappel there was a glorious new *Altar* set up, & mounted on steps, to which the Master, Fellowes, Schollers bowed & were enjoyned to bow by Dr. *Cosens* the Master, who set it up; that there were Basons, Candlesticks, Tapers standing on it, and a great Crucifix hanging over it."[22] Even more sinister was the note made by the iconoclast William Dowsing, describing his work of destruction at Peterhouse, just before Christmas in 1643: ". . . we pulled down 2: mighty great Angells, with wings and divers other Angells, & the 4: Evangelists, & Peter, with his Keies, over the Chappell Dore, & about a hundred Chirubims & Angells, & divers superstitious Letters in gold: & at the upper end of the Chancell these words were written as followeth. Hic lucus [locus] est Domus Dei, nil aliud, et Portae Coeli."[23]

It is noteworthy that the fondness for cherubim and angels in the decoration of churches in the high-church tradition is more than a fancy.[24] It is rather the attempt on the part of sensitive Anglicans to visualise the heavenly context in which the liturgy is celebrated. It gives the worshippers the visual complement to the priest's vocal affirmation "therefore with angels, and archangels, and the whole company of heaven," to which the people's response is the *Sanctus*. The latter is, of course, an exact echo of the words in which the prophet Isaiah expressed the adoration of God after realising the divine presence behind the six-winged cherubim in the temple. This sense of the invisible host of saints surrounding the heavenly throne described in the Seventh Chapter of the Book

---

[22] Prynne, *op. cit.*, pp. 73-74.

[23] *The Cambridge Journal of William Dowsing*, transcribed by A. C. Moule and reprinted from the *History Teachers' Miscellany* (1926), p. 5.

[24] Cosin had a notable penchant for angelology. When he was a Prebendary of Durham, Canon Peter Smart had criticised him for his introduction into Durham Cathedral of "popish baits and allurments of glorious pictures and Babylonish vestures." Cosin was also charged with setting up many images about the choir, "some of the angells, in long scarlet gowns, greene petticotes golden wings and gilded beards." Instead of the prescribed wooden altar, he had substituted "a double table very sumptuous of stone . . . upon 6 stone pillars, curiously polished, and fastened to the ground, having upon every black pillar 3 cherubim—faces as white as snow." Smart thought the high Gothic font-cover (still extant) and which he claimed cost £140 both "fantastical" and "capricious." (See Rawlinson Mss. A. 441f. 28; also *The Correspondence of John Cosin*, D.D., Surtees Society, 1869, Vol. I, p. 161.)

of Revelation, has persisted in Roman Catholicism through its sanctoral cycle in the liturgy, with special days remembering the saints and invoking their aid. Furthermore, Rome as the mother of saints has added to their number by the careful process of canonisation through the centuries, thus recognising post-Biblical eminent imitators of God. Moreover, most Roman Catholic churches have images of the saints in windows and statues.

The Anglican Communion has managed to retain the sense of the Communion of saints (the New Testament saints[25] rather than the saints of ecclesiastical tradition), through its more restricted sanctoral cycle in the Book of Common Prayer, which had the advantage of stressing the Christological feasts and fasts. This verbal remembrance of the examples of the saints was reinforced, as we have noted, by the Laudian tradition through stained-glass windows, and, even occasionally, by statues, as at Peterhouse. It is significant that the Puritans (although they had their own martyrologists from Foxe to Adam Clarke) restricted the term "saints," according to St. Paul's example in his epistles, to those in whom the Holy Spirit was indwelling, namely, the "elect," who ultimately were known only to God, though one might presume that men and women living according to the Divine ordinances were "visible saints." Far from depicting the historic saints in their places of worship, the Puritans even destroyed those represented in the national church as a fitting recompense (in their view) for the idolatry of breaking the Second Commandment.

All in all, the university chapels (especially Peterhouse in the Puritan stronghold, Cambridge) were a bold and beautiful tribute to the new respect for reverence, the sense of the primacy of the Eucharist over preaching, and the sheer aesthetic sensibilities of the upholders of the Laudian tradition. At least one contemporary felt that they rivalled the royal chapels and the cathedrals; George Garrard chaplain to the Earl of Northumberland, summed up the situation thus: "the Churches or Chapels of all the Colleges are much more beautified, extraordinary cost bestowed upon them; scarce any Cathedral Churches nor Windsor nor Canterbury, nay

---

[25] One consequence of the restriction of the number and the role of the saints in Anglican worship was the paucity of opportunity for sculptors, who had in large measure to confine themselves to secular work. By contrast, the many side altars in Roman Catholic churches on the Continent provided great scope for sculptors of the saints in the ecclesiastical tradition of the west. Bernini, for example, would have been exceedingly hampered in England, and his famous St. Teresa unthinkable.

nor Paul's Choir exceeds them, most of them new-glazed; richer glass for figures and painting I have not seen, which they had most from beyond the seas."[26]

Other interesting examples of mixed Gothic and Baroque churches are to be found outside London and the ancient university cities. One of the earliest, dating from 1634, is St. John's, Leeds. Its distance from the centre probably helps to account for the fact that it is more Gothic than Baroque. In fact, it is essentially "Gothic survival." It was founded, furnished, and endowed by John Harrison, a merchant and a native of the town, whose generosity equalled his wealth.[27] It is an oblong building, divided by an arcade that runs along its length. It has twin roofs. Its exterior is in the austere late perpendicular style, but its interior, emerging relatively unspoiled from the restorer's hands, presents in its screens and pews a splendid display of Caroline decoration with carved strapwork and scrolls.

At about the same time St. Mary's, Leighton Bromsgrove (only about four miles away from the remarkable "Arminian monastery" of Little Gidding), was being built by the joint efforts of the brothers Nicholas and John Ferrar, and of the Prebendary, the poet George Herbert. John Ferrar wrote to his brother on the progress of the rebuilding of the ruined parish church in July 1632: "We have 18 Masons and Labrores at worke at Layton Church and we shall have this weeke 10 Carpenters. God prosper the worke and send mony in. Amen."[28] Apparently the plea was answered because the nave was finished that year and the neighbouring Duke of Lennox paid the cost of the rustic tower added later. The outline of the thirteenth century chancel was retained, and much of the stone was re-used. The existing church, despoiled of its original white plaster inscribed with golden texts, looks barer and starker than it was. It still retains, however, its famous canopied reading pew and canopied pulpit of identical pattern and height, thus fulfilling

[26] *Calendar of State Papers, Domestic* (1636-1637), p. 113. A late example of a College Chapel at Oxford is Brasenose (1656-1659). Like the previous examples considered, it mingles Gothic and Classical elements in its design, which incidentally is the work of a master mason, John Jackson. There is geometrical tracery in the windows, yet they have entablature above them, and at the top there is a crocketted, finialled gable. The side windows, with their pointed arches, yet have pilasters of the Corinthian order at their sides. (See Doreen Yarwood, *The Architecture of England*, 1963, p. 194.)

[27] Marcus Whiffen, *Stuart and Georgian Churches* (1947), pp. 12-13.

[28] Cited in *ibid.*, p. 12 from *The Ferrar Papers* (ed. B. Blackstone, Cambridge, 1938).

Herbert's demand that prayer and preaching should be equally esteemed.[29]

Other examples of provincial church architecture combining a Gothic shape with classical details include: Staunton Harold church, Leicestershire, built between 1653 and 1663; Compton Wynyates in Staffordshire erected in 1663.[30] Newent church in Gloucestershire, however, was classic in shape as well as in details. The change to the classical style was, of course, immensely accelerated by the Great Fire[31] of London in 1666 and the renowned examples of the work of Sir Christopher Wren in the City churches and St. Paul's Cathedral from 1670 onwards. The influence was so great that it deserves the collective noun of a "Wrenaissance."

3. The "Wrenaissance"

Wren dominated the church building of the seventeenth century in England, and for a variety of reasons. For one thing he built more churches than anyone else. For another, they were almost all concentrated in London where they were more easily visible than elsewhere, where they could easily impress the rising generation of architects and potential clients as well. They were, moreover, almost all built about the same time, largely because the Great Fire of London destroyed or damaged eighty-seven churches and made a vast scheme for rapid and economical building essential, and Wren had the energy, ingenuity, and brilliance to prove himself to be the man for this gigantic task. Moreover, his designs, whether he was building a small church like St. Mary Abchurch or a vast one like St. Paul's Cathedral, were marked by versatility in the use of often cramped sites and variety in planning both the interiors and the superb steeples of his churches.[32] He changed the entire skyscape of London. The Venetian painter Canaletto

---

29 Izaak Walton's *Life of Herbert* (World's Classics edn., 1927), p. 278. Walton thought the church a "costly mosaick."

30 Whiffen, *op. cit.*, p. 18.

31 The two largest town churches in the provinces in the late seventeenth century owe their origin to fires. All Saints Church, Northampton, was burnt to a cinder in the autumn of 1675 and nineteen years later the same fate befell St. Mary's, Warwick. The new nave of All Saints was opened in 1680 and the striking Ionic colonnade on the west front was added in 1701. It bore above it a statue of Charles I to commemorate his gift of a thousand tons of lumber from his woods for the rebuilding of the church. In 1704 the cupola was added. The plan for the nave is a square within a square—a total departure from the Gothic. St. Mary's, Warwick, a fascinating church was not even begun in our period. (For the latter, see Marcus Whiffen, *Stuart and Georgian Architecture*, pp. 18ff.)

32 Whiffen, *op. cit.*, p. 14 and Cobb, *op. cit.*, p. 9.

was obviously fascinated by the "masts" of the churches as he viewed them from the Thames-side in 1746, for he painted several views in which the masts of the ships in the river make a point that is counterpointed by the slender spires of Wren's churches as they contrast with the great rounded bulk of St. Paul's.

One is impressed by the energy and planning devoted to his great task and the speed with which he accomplished it. To say that he had to start from the ground up is an understatement, because his first task was to clear away the clutter left by the holocaust of the great fire, the melted ruins and slag and charred wood. John Evelyn reported on September 3, 1666: "I left it [the City of London] this afternoone burning, a resemblance of Sodome or the last day . . . the ruines resembling the picture of *Troy*: *London* is no more." The following day he described the enlarged fire moving to the west: "the stones of Paules flew like grenados, the Lead melting down the streetes in a streame, and the very pavements of them glowing with fiery rednesse, so as nor horse nor man was able to tread on them." Of the eighty-seven churches destroyed or seriously damaged, it was decided to rebuild fifty-two in the City and three other churches in the west beyond the City limits—St. Clement Dane's, St. James's, Piccadilly, and St. Anne's, Soho. Sixteen new churches were started in 1670, four more in 1671, and another fifteen before the end of the decade, so within ten years of commencing the Herculean effort, thirty-five churches were being or had been built under Wren's direction and responsibility.[33]

What was distinctive about these churches of Wren's? Primarily, it was the coming-of-age of classical architecture for English churches. For the long delay there was a variety of reasons. Though King Charles I and Inigo Jones were in favour of it, Archbishop Laud fought strongly against it. The unsettled religious and political climate discouraged any buildings other than those that were absolutely necessary: it was the Fire of 1666 that was the necessary urgency. Up to this time England had been well supplied with a host of medieval churches which needed repairing rather than supplanting.[34]

But Wren did much more than provide an impressive panorama of neo-classical architecture, both sacred and secular.[35] He

[33] Margaret Whinney, *Wren* (1971), p. 45.
[34] Whiffen, *op. cit.*, pp. 14ff.
[35] His great secular buildings included: the Sheldonian Theatre, Oxford; the

knew the values of elegance and impressiveness, but his primary approach was strictly functional. That is, he asked the fundamental question: what is this church to be used for? As he was building Anglican churches there was no question that a central Communion table at the east end would be essential, but he did not feel the need to provide an apse or high steps or a balddachino to dramatise the altar. It was enough to provide a table and to ward off sacrilegious persons with a simple set of balustraded rails, and occasionally a simple reredos. What did, however, receive special treatment with Wren was the pulpit, with its sounding-board. For this was the era in which the sermon was ceasing to be a political weapon as it had been with the Puritans during Commonwealth days and by some of their inveterate foes among Anglican prelates in the last years of Laud's archiepiscopate, and was now becoming the means of reasoned discourse. Wren saw that a Protestant church, such as the Reformed Church of England appeared to him to be, needed an "auditory" where each member of the congregation could hear the exposition of God's Word and see it visibly re-enacted in the celebration of Holy Communion. He could, of course, have found and, in fact, probably saw, Jesuit churches in France during his important visit there from the summer of 1665 to the spring of 1666 (when he met Bernini and almost certainly also Mansart) where great emphasis was given to the pulpit and to Counter-Reformation preaching, but these "auditories" gave an even greater prominence to the altar.[36] Wren's churches were single-room churches that banished the Gothic distinction between chancel and nave, suppressed side chapels, and eliminated chancel screens to grant maximum audibility and visibility.

Another novelty in Wren's churches was the use of galleries. This was for both functional and economic reasons. They were included in his designs in order to gain the largest number of people in the space who could both see and hear the leader of worship in comfort. Moreover, Wren's synthetic mind probably added these to the typical neo-classical Catholic contemporary churches by seeing the possibilities in the great French Huguenot Temple in Charenton, with its three tiers of galleries.[37]

Library of Trinity College, Cambridge; Chelsea Hospital; the enlargement of Kensington, Hampton Court and Whitehall Palaces; and, supremely, the Royal Hospital, Greenwich.

36 Whinney, *op. cit.*, pp. 48-49.

37 *Ibid.*, pp. 32, 53 and illustration 22 opposite p. 33 in Margaret Whinney's *Wren*.

The evidence for affirming that Wren had a functional and rather Protestant conception of the nature of his churches is derived from an important memorandum which he prepared for a Commission, on which he served, which had been appointed as the result of an Act of Parliament passed in 1708 to build new churches to the east and west of the old City of London boundaries. It is an expression of his mature views gained after long experience as a builder of churches. He advocated the building of large churches, "but still, in our reformed Religion, it should seem vain to make a Parish church larger than that all who are present can both hear and see." At this point Protestant pride rides high, as he continues, "The Romanists, indeed, may build larger churches, it is enough if they hear the murmur of the Mass, and see the Elevation of the Host, but ours are to be fitted for Auditories. I can hardly think it practicable to make a single Room so capacious with Pews and Galleries, as to hold above 2000 persons, and all to hear the service and both to hear distinctly, and see the Preacher."[38] Margaret Whinney makes the very apt comment, particularly so for the Restoration era of experimentation and enlightenment, "Exposition rather than the mysteries of religion was the major concern of the Anglican Church."[39] She confirms this judgment by pointing out that the building was planned so that the altar would not be the main focal point, but that the seats of the clergy reading the service, the lectern, and supremely the pulpit must be so placed that all could see and hear.

A third novel characteristic in Wren's church architecture was the use of cupolas, which had not been seen in England even in Inigo Jones's day. The most impressive examples were, of course, to be found in St. Paul's Cathedral, with its vast central dome dominating the seventeenth-century skyline. The most miniature examples are the tops of the spires of some of his churches, such as St. Magnus Martyr and St. Benet, Paul's Wharf, and the most regal, St. Paul's Cathedral excepted, is St. Stephen, Wallbrook.

---

[38] Stephen Wren, *Parentalia* (1750), pp. 317ff. A. L. Drummond in *The Church Architecture of Protestantism* (1934), p. 36f., has argued that Wren conceived his churches essentially as meeting-houses, and that this functional Protestantism was derived in large measure from the late Puritan attitude predominant in the Commonwealth and Protectorate, with a streamlining encouraged by the development of the scientific spirit which wished to do away equally with clutter and mystery, and was fascinated with optics. There may, in fact, be a debt to Puritanism, but there are also many other influences, such as Vitruvius and Michelangelo, quite apart from such Baroque masters as Bernini, Mansart and Lemercier, and the Huguenot architect, Salomon de Brosse.

[39] Whinney, *op. cit.*, p. 48.

What distinguishes Wren's cupolas from those on the Continent, however, is the austerity of their decoration and lack of colouring. Least of all do they resemble *coup d'oeil* paintings that seem to transform the interior of the dome into cerulean blue in which phalanxes of saints are flying, as in the leading Jesuit churches of Europe at this time. Wren's work has an aesthetic simplicity, with reserve, probity, and lack of theatricality.

Wren's greatest resourcefulness, however, is seen in the variety of his interiors, often planned on sites of irregular shape[40] presenting considerable challenges, and in the profusion of differing steeple designs. It is part of Wren's genius that in adopting the neo-classical style of building, he recognised that this style had forgone the aspirational quality of the great verticals in the Gothic spires, and he invented classical spires to provide this missing element in classical architecture. It should also be noted that Wren's steeples all rise from the ground, and not merely from the roofs of his churches: they are therefore significant and distinctive elements of his architecture, and never extras "tacked on" even though he often had to wait for further money before he could finish them. As Wren's steeples provide the soaring and mystical element missing in classical architecture, his single-room churches with minimal chancels and absence of screens, and stained-glass windows, allow the light to pour in great floods into his buildings, banishing "storied windows, richly dight, casting a dim religious light." Both literally and metaphorically this was the ecclesiastical architecture of the Enlightenment.

Wren's church exteriors are much less interesting than his interiors, with the single important exception of the steeples. The reason for this is that many of the burned domestic and commercial buildings huddled close to the medieval churches in the old City of London were rebuilt before the churches were, and hence few churches presented any significant façade to the street. This was a disadvantage if impressiveness were being sought, but an advantage if speed and economy were the targets. So many of the exteriors are plain brick walls with stone dressings. Wren was able to use the foundations of medieval churches, and on often cramped sites, produce a variety of solutions to similar problems, so inventive was his mind. Not least resourceful was his brilliance in modi-

40 The varieties of site led to varieties of interiors determined by those sites; many were rectangular, some irregular (St. Stephen, Coleman Street), coffin-shaped (St. Olave, Old Jewry), and even angular oval (St. Benet, Fink).

fying the ceilings of his interiors. One is impressed by the great variety in Wren's earlier city interiors, granted that he had committed himself in favour of an aisled and galleried type of church for the "Reformed" Church of England. It is significant that there are plans for plain rectangles with or without a single aisle. There are plans for a cross in a square with intersecting vaults or domes above. There are plans for domes on squares and domes on polygons.[41]

Another way of looking at Wren's interior plans is to divide them into two main groups, the one consisting of large oblong churches and the other of small square churches.[42] One example of the large, oblong church is St. Bride's, Fleet Street (begun in 1670), the nave and aisles of which were divided by arcades, supported by large doubled columns established on high bases. Galleries were arranged above the aisles. The nave had a large barrel vault that was plastered, and was lighted by oval clerestory windows. St. James's, Piccadilly (1682) is another example of a long oblong church that Wren himself regarded as one of his greatest successes, for he recommended its plan as being commodious, economical, convenient, and beautiful in his memorandum prepared about 1710, already referred to. A gallery, supported on square wooden piers, runs round three sides of the interior. At the level of the gallery small columns of the Corinthian order carry the barrel-vaulted roof, and each bay has a small barrel at right-angles to the main vaulting of the nave. St. James's Church has fine fittings; the carved reredos and font were the work of Grinling Gibbons. The gilded plasterwork of the ceiling, with its bosses and gilding, was richly finished.[43]

But the most triumphant solution of a difficult site problem was the planning of St. Stephen, Walbrook,[44] the most brilliant of the smaller square type of church to be built (1672-1679). The site is squat, but the plan suggests spaciousness within, so accomplished is its design. Yet the dimensions of the building do not exceed 82 by 60 feet.[45] How is this effect achieved? Although the shape of the site was oblong, he made one bay at the west into a miniature nave, thus enabling him to bring the central space into

[41] Gerald Cobb, *The Old Churches of London* (1942), p. 10.
[42] Whinney, *op. cit.*, p. 52.
[43] A church of very similar design but with even richer plastering and gilding on the ceiling, moreover one containing Wren's only apse, was St. Clement Dane's, begun in 1680.
[44] See illustration in the section following p. 30 of this book.
[45] A. L. Drummond, *op. cit.*, p. 36.

a square. In brief, the plan is a cross-in-square with a large central dome. What is particularly ingenious is the refusal to use the usual plan of bringing the square into a circle by erecting a dome on pendentives above the four arches made by the ends of the vaults. Instead of this, Wren arranged for the dome to rest upon eight equal arches carried on twelve columns.[46] The four corners have flat ceilings, and Wren inserted windows into the flat ceilings to give a maximum of light. Small sections of groined vaults cover the space between the windows, and the latter help to support the dome. The complex roof, held up by sixteen columns, with plain shafts, which contrasted with the rough and richly textured plaster-work above, is striking. Each type of ceiling is combined here: flat, groined, domical, and pendentive. Similarly, the arrangement of the columns suggests a Greek cross, a circle, and a polygon, in its complexity. It is intriguing to see how John Wesley regarded this church, as reported in his *Journal* entry for December 4, 1758: "I was desired to step into the little church behind the Mansion House, commonly called St. Stephen's, Walbrook. It is nothing grand, but neat and elegant beyond expression, so that I do not wonder at the speech of the famous Italian architect who met Lord Burlington in Italy, 'My Lord, go back and see St. Stephen's in London. We have not so fine a piece of architecture in Rome.' " Other domical churches built by Wren are St. Mary, Abchurch, and St. Mildred, Bread Street.

Wren's resourcefulness in his interiors was even exceeded in his steeples. Some were in stone, and others were of lead. While the main work of building the churches was completed by 1685, many of the steeples were added fifteen or twenty years later. By that time London had recovered its prosperity, and Wren's maturity coincided with the greater opulence that was available. So splendid was the effect of Wren's spires on the architectural silhouette of London that it almost looked "as if the shipping on the river had somehow spread itself over the lands." These heaven-pointing spears formed "a train to St. Paul's, stretching from the East up to the Cathedral, as it looked towards the setting sun, with Christ Church, St. Martin and St. Bride as forerunners."[47]

---

[46] Whinney, *op. cit.*, pp. 64ff.

[47] Cobb (*op. cit.*, p. 56) offers a most elaborate classification of the varieties of Wren's steeples. One group is of plain towers with pierced parapet. Another is a series of towers with parapets enriched with urns, pineapples, obelisks. A third includes towers with bell-cages or turrets (lead covered). A fourth group is of towers with bell-cages or lanterns on domes, pyramids or steps. A fifth series is distinguished by elaborations of the bell-turret. A sixth group consists of

St. Mary-le-Bow is exceptional both in that it was finished at the same time as the church in 1680, and soared to the height of 225 feet. Since the true Londoner is defined as one born within the sound of Bow bells, it was a particularly important commission, rendered the more difficult by the juxtaposition of high buildings at Cheapside. Not only is the belfry emphasised by coupled Ionic pilasters at each corner, but there is an elegant arcade immediately above it which marks the transition from square to rounded shape, and the cylindrical core is surrounded by a colonnade, with another balustrade above it. The next higher story is a group of twelve inverted brackets, Wren's version of "bows," and the next higher story reverts to the square shape with small Corinthian columns. This leads to a high pyramid or obelisk, bearing a weathervane in the form of a dragon. Never before had a classical steeple of many stories been seen in England, nor would Wren have visited one in France. Its origin is Italian.[48] No other steeple of Wren's exploits so many ideas in different stories.

St. Bride's, Fleet Street[49] is about 10 feet higher than Bow steeple. It has a more unified design, with four octagonal diminishing stories and an octagonal pyramid at the top. Inside is an open stone staircase.

Christ Church, Newgate Street (1704), also has a single idea, that of a group of five diminishing squares, the middle story consisting of a free-standing Ionic colonnade of great elegance, through which the sky can be seen, and which contrasts perfectly with the solid belfry square with pilasters, two stories below.

There are more Baroque variations in steeple design. One of them is St. Vedast, Foster Lane (1694-1697), for above the rectangular belfry the stories are concave, convex, and concave again.

---

towers with built-up spires in stone, and a seventh with towers having true spires. The eighth group is of towers with octagonal trumpet-shaped spires of lead. Group nine is of towers with built-up spires mainly concave in outline. The tenth group consists of a single tower with lantern, dome and spire (St. Magnus Martyr). There are churches with Gothic stone towers forming the eleventh and twelfth groups, the former being distinguished by pinnacles and the latter has a single example (St. Dunstan's-in-the-East) of a tower with a spire on arches. This over-elaboration of categories does at least illustrate Wren's fecundity of invention. *Ibid.*, p. 41 for the steeple of St. Mary-le-Bow.

[48] Margaret Whinney (*op. cit.*, p. 72) states that the best known example is Antonio de Sangallo's model for St. Peter's, which had twin western towers of this type, showing a transition from two lower square stories to two higher round ones. The idea of multi-storied classical steeples first appeared in print, however, in Alberti's *De re aedificatoria.*

[49] This is reproduced in Horton Davies, *Worship and Theology in England* (1961), III, following p. 38.

This example is reminiscent of Borromini's more dramatic S. Ivo della Sapienza in Rome, but the pilasters are more reticent in their projection than Borromini's. Other startling steeples are St. Michael, Paternoster Royal (completed in 1713) which has columns projecting from an octagonal core, with superimposed vases, and St. James, Garlickhythe (1714-1717) which is similar except for paired columns on four of the eight faces. The most splendid of all are the western towers of St. Paul's Cathedral.

Unusual steeples include St. Magnus Martyr (completed 1705) which moves from the square belfry stage into an octagon carrying a small lead cupola with leaden lantern and small spire above. Here the borrowing seems to have come from the Jesuit church at Antwerp,[50] dedicated to St. Charles Borromeo. Another unique steeple is that of St. Martin, Ludgate, where the top story of the stone tower is octagonal, on which there is an ogee dome in lead, with a balcony below the lantern, all culminating in a very slender obelisk and ball. Here as in all Wren's work is God's plenty for variety and ingenuity.

4. St. Paul's Cathedral

His crowning ecclesiastical work was, however, St. Paul's Cathedral. Even here, however, he was far from getting his own favourite design approved, but had to settle for a compromise between his wishes and those of the dean and canons of the Cathedral.

Wren's own wish was to provide an entirely novel design in England—in the shape of a four equal-armed Greek cross, with an extension to the west. The latter, according to the Great Model plan as Wren's preferred design is known, ended in a vestibule entered by a large Corinthian portico which was to be covered with a small dome. The four arms of the cross were linked with concave walls and over the centre of the church was a dome supported by eight piers allowing complete circulation around their bases. It would have been a vast cathedral for the base of the dome would have been 120 feet, only 17 feet smaller than St. Peter's and 8 feet wider than the dome finally erected.

Wren's design was a brilliant amalgam from several sources, but united by its fine proportions and the lucid subordination of the parts to the whole. The dome's drum borrows from Bramante and the ribbed section above from Michelangelo. The Corinthian portico was taken over from Inigo Jones, while the domed vestibule

50 Whinney, op. cit., pp. 77-78.

probably came from Sangallo's design for St. Peter's. The arrangement of the dome over eight piers, instead of the conventional four, was almost certainly derived from a design of Mansart's. In Wren's Great Model plan, however, the hints of borrowings are fused into a grand and noble unity.[51]

The plan, however, fell foul of the conservatism of the dean and chapter of St. Paul's. The clergy hardly considered any church a true church unless it were built according to the Latin cross plan, and they were particularly concerned to emphasize their continuity with the great church of the medieval centuries. Furthermore, they had two practical considerations in mind in opting for a two-room design instead of the vastly impressive single room that Wren was offering them. For one thing they envisaged a cathedral as providing a choir for regular daily services and a nave when larger congregations were expected, on Sundays, festivals, and state occasions. In addition, it would mean that their plan could be achieved in two separate parts, for the choir could be finished first and the nave extended as further funds became available. The Great Model plan did not have a separate choir, and all that remained of such was the area between the eastern apse and the beginning of the dome. Furthermore, it was not possible to build the cathedral in instalments. As soon as the eastern end should be completed, all eight piers would have to be erected to provide a roof for the cathedral.

Wren had no alternative but to accept a compromise, despite the impropriety of building a Renaissance church on a medieval cruciform plan.[52] His second design is known as the Warrant design, and dates from May 14, 1675, seven years after the commencement of planning for the Great Model. The Royal Warrant indicates that Wren was allowed by King Charles II "the liberty in the prosecution of his work, to make variations, rather ornamental than essential, as from time to time he should see proper."[53] The Warrant design was that of a Latin cross, with a choir of three bays and a nave of five bays. The east was to have an extra demi-bay and an apse. Each transept of three bays was to be entered through an inset porch, with a large projecting portico at the west of the nave. There was a dome carried on eight piers at the crossing. This plan would have allowed the choir to be built

[51] *Ibid.*, pp. 89-90.
[52] See the criticisms of Drummond, *op. cit.*, p. 36.
[53] The Royal Warrant with its designs attached is to be found in the Library of All Souls College, Oxford.

separately and used before the rest of the church was started. The most striking feature of the exterior of the Warrant design was the termination of the dome by a tall spire of six diminishing stories, similar to what he was eventually to build at St. Bride's, Fleet Street.

Yet there are considerable differences between the executed plan and the Warrant design. Wren must obviously have used the latitude allowed him by the Royal Warrant to the utmost and extending from ornamentals even to essentials. One great difference was apparent early. This was that the walls were to be taken to the height of two stories,[54] instead of merely to aisle height as shown in the Warrant design. This gave an immediate effect of grandeur and spaciousness. Furthermore, the walls had a new elegance in the execution, for the single strips of Inigo Jones were replaced by double pilasters. Among other important modifications of the Warrant plan was the reduction of the nave from five bays to three. Further, at the west end of the nave a larger bay was to be added, and this was to be covered with a small dome and on each side of it were to be chapels. Other changes were the additions of two semicircular porticos which replace the flat colonnades on the transept fronts. The great drum of the dome is a variation upon Bramante's design, but with a brilliant addition providing a solid interval between the columns at every fourth intercolumniation to prevent the contrast between the open columns in the western towers being too great.[55] The dome itself is a work of surpassing beauty as well as of technical brilliance, and it is topped by a large stone lantern, reminiscent of the west towers, and thus stressing the unity and interrelationship of the entire building. The cross at the top of the lantern is 365 feet above the ground.[56] The interior radiates with light, and would have done so even more in Wren's own day, when the windows had plain, not Victorian stained glass. The great central space makes the overwhelming impact he intended and irresistibly draws the eyes upwards.[57]

[54] Yet the impression these walls give that the aisles are raised to the height of two stories is a trick, for the upper part of each wall is false since the windows of the choir are set several feet behind it. Behind the false walls are stepped flying buttresses over the aisle roofs to help to support the dome.

[55] Whinney, op. cit., p. 105.

[56] Wren rightly rejected the six diminishing stories of the Warrant design's spire surmounting the dome. Also his complex western towers were greatly improved in the executed design. The latter also included small windows low in the walls for lighting the crypt, and the modification of the Warrant design.

[57] The impact of the central space would be greater in Wren's day because he closed the east vista from under the dome by a screen with the great organ above it. Thus he stressed the centralized planning of his Cathedral.

The greatest seventeenth-century church in England had been thirty-five years in building. The foundation stone was laid on the southeastern corner of the building on June 21, 1675, and the work was finished in 1710, when the final accounts were made up. This masterpiece had cost £738,845 5s. 2½d.[58] and the exhilarating exhaustion of its architect. It was the first cathedral England had built since the Reformation and it was in the new style.

St. Paul's is the finest example of the splendid fittings of Wren's churches. They set the standard for Restoration England and were its particular pride. The sculptural possibilities of the exterior of St. Paul's were fully utilized in a way that was not possible for the churches on their hemmed in and cramped sites, and the woodcarving of the interior and the wrought-iron were of the very highest standard.

Grinling Gibbons[59] carved the twenty-six delicate and different stone panels beneath the great round-headed windows, with their exquisite flowers, foliage, fruit, and cherubs. Jonathan Maine carved similar panels on the exterior of the west chapels. The transept fronts were also richly ornamented with their chains of fruit and flowers hanging down the sides of the central windows. Moreover, each of the pediments above has carvings set in the curved lunettes. The carving on the south transept front exhibits a phoenix rising from the ashes, a symbol alike of Christ's resurrection and of the re-emergence of the Cathedral. This is the noble work of Caius Gabriel Cibber. Gibbons's less distinguished work on the north transept front displays the royal arms flanked by two unconvincing angels. The dean's door is embellished by the elegant carvings of William Kempster, with coiling scrolls, life-like cherubs' heads, and delicate wreaths and fronds as good as Gibbons when the latter is in top form.

The wood-carving of the choir stalls and the screen behind them exhibits Grinling Gibbons at his superb best. He also carved the rich and complicated organ case. Both works have brilliantly devised scrolls, fruit, flowers and heads of cherubs or full length angels.

The ironwork of St. Paul's is splendid, especially the wrought-

[58] Whinney, *op. cit.*, pp. 97, 105.

[59] Gibbons is not well represented in London, with the exceptions of St. Paul's and his reredoses at St. James, Piccadilly and St. Mary Abchurch. Horace Walpole caught the essence of his art in the statement that he "gave to wood the loose and airy lightness of flowers, and chained them together in a fine disorder natural to each species." *Anecdotes of Painting*, II (edn. 1859), p. 552.

iron gates that are the work of Jean Tijou the Huguenot in 1698. These gates are at the east end of the choir and are a series of complex and interwoven variations on acanthus leaves. They make an exceedingly effective contrast between the gilded and plain iron-work of the gates creating a rich effect.

The dominant Protestantism[60] in the City of London, reinforced by the defection of James II to Roman Catholicism, forbade the use of paintings behind the altars or on the walls or cupolas, as well as the sculpture of saints required for the Baroque Catholic churches on the Continent. Thus Wren was prevented from imitating the most striking effects of Baroque architecture and the collaboration of the architect with painters and figure sculptors. He made up for this restriction at least in part, by encouraging the production of outstanding wood-carving, and occasionally also of high relief in plaster, and, sometimes, of wrought-iron work. Even here, however, economy as well as a dislike of flashy exuberance and theatricality restrained Wren.

The most impressive examples of fittings and furnishings in Wren's churches deserve at least a fleeting tribute. Generally, the Communion tables were simply carved. The notable exception was that of St. Stephen, Coleman Street, which was supported by four eagles and a straddling cherub.[61] Altar rails were usually of the balustrade shape. They were of richly carved and twisted wood at St. Stephen's, Coleman Street, and at St. Mary-at-Hill. Occasionally they were of wrought-iron, as at St. Mary, Woolnoth. In one single case, at All Hallows, Barking, they were of brass.[62]

Pulpits, in conformity with Wren's conception of the importance of "auditories" in which the age shared, were particularly imposing in both position and decoration. St. Mildred, Bread Street, had a polygonal sounding-board. St. James, Garlickhythe had twisted railed-in steps leading to the pulpit, and there were carved swags on the pulpit sides. The carving in St. Stephen, Walbrook, was even more elaborate, for it boasted cherubs, sea-shells, and swags on the sounding-board and enrichments on the sides of the pulpit. Full and detailed carving also marked the pulpit of St. Edmund the King, Lombard Street.[63]

---

[60] Resurgent national Protestantism on the part of both Anglicans and Nonconformists was expressed in great affirmations of loyalty to William and Mary and in gratitude for the re-establishment of the Protestant succession to the throne. This spilled over into architecture and ecclesiastical fittings, in part in the determination to avoid the theatricality and multi-coloured effects of Baroque Catholicism.

[61] Whinney and Millar, *op. cit.*, p. 162.

[62] Cobb, *op. cit.*, p. 74.   [63] *Ibid.*, p. 75.

Richly carved reredoses could be found at St. Stephen, Walbrook, St. Mary-le-Bow, and a most elaborate one at St. Martin, Ludgate. Gibbons carved his only reredos in the old City of London at St. Mary Abchurch, but he provided a splendid reredos for the west end church of St. James, Piccadilly, depicting a pelican feeding her young from the flesh of her own breast, an apt, if medieval, symbol of the Eucharist.[64]

Carved font covers of unusual elegance included those of St. Giles, Cripplegate (an octagonal dome surmounted by a dove), St. Margaret, Lothbury (eight heads of cherubs topped by a flaming torch), and St. Swithin, Cannon Street (a domed cover with a crown above).[65]

Organ cases, too, offered carvers great opportunities. A simple one of great dignity was to be found in St. Margaret Pattens, with which should be contrasted the impressively detailed carving of the organ case at St. Lawrence Jewry.[66]

Other opportunities for the skilled carver were the sword rests for the Lord Mayor on his Sunday pilgrimages to the various City churches, stave-heads for beadles (often bearing the figure of the patron saint of the particular church), specially enriched pews for the churchwardens, the royal arms, tablets for memorials or lists of bequests to the poor, alms boxes, lecterns, and, particularly, enriched doors.

The plasterwork was, of course, largely limited to the ceilings of the churches, with vaulting, crossvaulting, and coffering. The high relief was most impressive, as previously indicated, in St. Stephen, Walbrook, and in St. Mary-le-Bow, Cheapside. Wren's earlier plasterwork tended to be exuberant, but his later work in the same medium, though still luxurious, was more controlled in design. He well understood the importance of contrasted textures and surfaces, both in the use of brick and stone for his exteriors, and in the use of contrasted high relief and flat plaster, together with wood and ironwork in the interiors. All over England and New England he was paid the supreme tribute of imitation.

After dining him, his friend John Evelyn noted in his Diary for May 5, 1681, that Sir Christopher Wren was actually engaged in building fifty churches at that time, leading him to conclude that "a wonderful genius had this incomparable person." Yet his

---

[64] *Ibid.*, and Whinney and Millar, *op. cit.*, p. 162.
[65] Cobb, *op. cit.*, p. 75.   [66] *Ibid.*

splendid achievements are not without their critics, nor without flaw or blemish.

The first criticism is that his churches are not traditionally Christian either in shape or in the emblems used in their decoration. They are accused of supplanting Christian symbolism with Erastian and pagan decoration.[67] Wren unquestionably gave the lead in England on a wide scale in introducing a medley of urns, swags, scrolls, fruit, flowers, foliage, cherubs—later to be followed by willows, skulls, hour-glasses and such macabre symbols—into churches, though they were relatively commonplace features of Baroque decoration on the Continent at this time. Here the contrast with the surviving medievalism of Archbishop Laud and his party was strong, except, of course, for the Erastianism[68] displayed in the royal arms which Laud had approved as a vigorous supporter of the divine right of kings. In brief, Wren was not traditional enough in the shape of his buildings (as his struggle with the dean and chapter of St. Paul's demonstrates) or his symbolism.

The opposite criticism, that he is not contemporary enough in exploiting all the possibilities of drama inherent in Baroque architecture and art has also been made. Such a criticism contrasts the intellectual clarity, love of proportion, reserve, simplicity, restricted palette, and coldness of Wren's churches with the emotional excitement, geometrical strainings,[69] surprises, complexities and variegated colours of contemporary southern Baroque churches of the same period. The visual brilliance of the ceiling of Il Gesù combining painting and sculpture, the tension in the concave surfaces of Borromini's S. Carlo alle Quatro Fontane, and Bernini's moving statue of Saint Teresa in the jewelled casket of the Cornaro Chapel, as well as his towering and serpentine balddachino over the high altar of St. Peter's and his Cathedra Petri supported on four bish-

---

[67] A. L. Drummond, *op. cit.*, p. 37, expresses this viewpoint with stridency.

[68] An example of rampant Erastianism is the gateway of All Hallows, Lombard Street. As for accusations of paganism, the amorous cupids or cherubs seem more often to be devotees of Venus than angelic servants of God. The Puritans, who are sometimes blamed for this unchristian symbolism (see J. D. Sedding, *Art and Handicraft*, 1893, pp. 36-37), were iconoclasts and neither Erastians nor pagans. Moreover, with the arrival of the Restoration of the monarchy Puritanism was defeated, but Catholic tradition was not restored either doctrinally or symbolically in decoration.

[69] Here I refer to some frenetic features of Baroque architecture or sculpture, such as the alternation of juxtaposed concave and convex shapes, the columns that twist in agony, the ovals that seem to have been created by elongating circles, not to mention the eternally agitated draperies of the marble statues as if they had been carved in the cave of the four winds. (See H. W. Janson, *History of Art* [1962], pp. 410f.)

ops and surmounted by the dove of infallible truth that disappears in a blaze of golden glory—these rightly have their ardent admirers. Baroque architecture, like the angelic dart that pierced the heart of Saint Teresa, transfixes the emotions. Such admirers[70] will find Wren's architecture practically colourless (except for the contrast of gold and white in some plastered ceilings or black and gold in very rare wrought-iron, and the very common contrast between brown wood and white walls), and his geometrical harmonies of design will seem coldly intellectual. They may find his work too reserved, and even occasionally insipid. But the grandeur and glitter that these critics seek were alien to the taste and temper of England and to the reasoned and pragmatic faith of those who would worship in the fanes he built.

If Wren's work in its vastness and fertile variety is not itself the fullest refutation of both sets of critics, then it may be counted to his credit that he rebuilt all the churches of a city and its Cathedral, on restricted finances, on hemmed in and awkward sites, and that he had only spent six months out of England visiting France (but never setting foot in Italy), and that perforce much of the details of the work had to be left to less gifted subordinates. The wonder is not that he occasionally repeated an idea, though never exactly, or that occasionally his invention flagged, but rather that he accomplished a gigantic task so well and gave to Anglicanism churches splendidly equipped for the reasoned exposition of Christian faith and duty, expressing such rational pragmatism in the well-lit clarity and good proportions of his sacred buildings.

5. Roman Catholic Chapels and Churches

The history of Roman Catholic church architecture in seventeenth-century England is largely limited to royal chapels built for the three Stuart queens and the last of the Stuart kings, James II. Catholicism was a forbidden faith until James II's open avowal of it, such services as were held even in aristocratic houses forbade the use of any but a disguised chapel.[71] A fugacious worship had

---

[70] Margaret Whinney and Oliver Millar, *op. cit.*, pp. 155-56 relate this viewpoint without concurring in it.

[71] Even a chapel over the border in Wales, at Abergavenny, which informers about the Popish Plot in 1679 said was fully equipped for Catholic worship, when rediscovered in 1907 turned out to be no more than a long attic on the ceiling of which were the remains of a painting of the Adoration of the Magi, and there was a Jesuit emblem above one of the windows. (See *The Catholic Record Society*, Vol. xviii, pp. 98-235.) For stirring accounts of the maintenance of Catholic worship in noble houses in recusant times, see Godfrey Anstruther,

to make do with ordinary tables and movable altar stones, pewter chalices, and equipment that could be easily dismantled. High Mass was unthinkable, and Low Mass had to be muttered in a murmur so as not to be overheard by disloyal servants who would report such gatherings to the authorities.[72] Private citizens however noble could not run the risk of building chapels for Catholic worship. The only time in the entire century when it was possible to build Catholic churches or chapels openly was during the brief reign of James II.

The first English chapel to be built without a trace of Gothic in its form or details was prepared originally in 1623 for the probable use of the Infanta of Spain whom Charles was then courting as Prince of Wales. This match was, however, never made and eventually Inigo Jones's Marlborough House Chapel, part of the complex of buildings of St. James's Palace, was fitted out for the use of Henrietta Maria, who eventually became the Queen of Charles I. It was thought impolitic to give it an ornate Baroque façade for England was officially a Protestant nation. Nonetheless, its restrained classicism of style distinguished it from its Gothic neighbours. It had a large "Venetian" window of Palladian style at the east end. Its ceiling was richly coffered. Behind the altar was elegant panelling and a painting, and there were, it is said, large statues of prophets in the arched niches of the sidewalls.[73] Here the social elite of London's Catholics attended Mass as they might in the embassy chapels of the Catholic powers, even though it was a royal and theoretically a private chapel.

Queen Henrietta Maria, however, wanted a more impressive chapel in the capital than that of Marlborough House and one designed solely for her. Again Inigo Jones was chosen as architect for the Somerset House Chapel. Externally it was restrained, if not undistinguished except for its great length of 100 feet, with two short transepts for the altars of the private chaplains of the Queen. The interior was resplendent in its glory. The nave was in the fashionable shape of a double cube. A gallery at the west end afforded seclusion for the Queen and her attendants. The arches were round-headed or pedimented and the ceiling was coffered and

---

O. P., *Vaux of Harrowden, A Recusant Family* (Newport, Monmouthshire, 1953) and R. J. Stonor, O.S.B., *Stonor: a Catholic Sanctuary in the Chilterns* (Newport, Monmouthshire, 2nd edn., 1952).

[72] Bryan Little, *Catholic Churches since 1623* (1966), p. 23.

[73] *Ibid.*, p. 21.

brilliant with its contrast of gold and white. The screen was a masterpiece of carving, with its fluted Doric columns, herms, and crests.[74]

Queen Henrietta Maria's French Baroque taste was more fully exemplified in her Chapel at Oatlands, where she had engaged her fellow-countryman, Simon Vouet, to paint a ceiling depicting the Blessings of Faith and Love—what sinister suspicion led her to exclude Hope from the trio?—under the union of lilies and roses, symbolizing her marriage.[75]

The Civil War's ravage and the iconoclasm of the Commonwealth led to the sacking of both the Marlborough House and the Somerset House Chapels. With the Restoration of the monarch, Charles II's Queen, Catherine of Braganza, chose first to use the refitted Chapel in St. James's Palace and then the refurnished Chapel of Somerset House.

It was only at the end of the reign of Charles II and particularly in that of his successor (James II) that Roman Catholic worship in all its Counter-Reformation vigour and confidence sought for its appropriate architectural expression. Here at last was the chance that the advocates of the divine right of kings (and therefore of absolute monarchy) and of Catholic supremacy had been waiting for—to build, paint, and sculpt in the new Baroque style as was being done with such dramatic splendour in France, Italy, and Flanders.

Charles II had commissioned May as architect, Gibbons as sculptor, and Verrio as painter to transform the Tudor private chapel at Windsor Castle by creating a coruscatingly brilliant interior. On the ceiling was a tempestuous fresco of the Ascension, and the north wall exhibited a series of scenes of the miracles of Christ. There was also an elaborate colonnade and an open sky. This was the most theatrical chapel to have been built in England up to this time.[76]

Breathtaking as the new Windsor Royal Chapel was, even it could not match the almost Mariolatrous iconography of the new Royal Chapel built by the command of James II at his Palace of Whitehall by Sir Christopher Wren. The exterior was unassuming in its brick and stone, but the interior was stunning, from the

[74] *Ibid.*, p. 22.
[75] Whinney and Millar, *op. cit.*, p. 287.
[76] *Ibid.*, pp. 299-300. See also G. Webb, "Baroque Art" in *Proceedings of the British Academy*, XXXIII (1947) for an analysis of the fittings and architecture of this Royal Chapel.

towering altarpiece by Gennari to the superb ceiling painting of the Assumption of the Blessed Virgin into a heaven crowded with Verrio's figures, not forgetting the four marble statues by Gibbons. Its impact is unforgettably conveyed by Evelyn:

> I went to heare the music of the Italians in the New Chapel now first opened publickly at Whitehall for the Popish service. Nothing can be finer than the magnificent marblework and architecture at the end, where are four statues representing St. John, St. Peter, St. Paul, and the Church, in white marble, the work of Mr. Gibbons, with all the carving and pillars of exquisite art and great cost. The Altar-piece is the Salutation; the volta in fresca, the Assumption of the Blessed Virgin according to their tradition, with our Saviour and a world of figures painted by Verrio.[77]

A few far less dramatic churches were built for Catholic worship under the protection afforded by James II's Declaration of Indulgence of 1687. Of two erected in London, one was run by the Franciscans and it was in the west end. Two others were staffed by Jesuits, a modest one in Wigan, and a more spacious one in Newcastle-upon-Tyne. The new church on which the fullest information is available was built for Birmingham Catholics under the leadership of Father Leo Randolph.[78]

It was partly financed by the donation of 180 tons of lumber from the king's forest in Staffordshire. It was in the form of a Latin cross, but the transepts were only large enough to accommodate side chapels each 15 feet square. The nave was 80 feet by 33 feet and the sanctuary was 15 feet long by 23 feet wide, thus providing an overall length of 95 feet. The nave had no pillars to obscure the people's view of the high altar. The chief altarpiece framed by two Corinthian pillars, showed the Risen Christ appearing to Mary Magdalene. The side altars had reredoses formed by two Corinthian pillars each. One had a painting of the Virgin and the other of St. Francis. Yet, despite their Baroque elements, these churches for reasons of economy, temperament, and taste, "were closer in spirit to Wren than to the Fontanas or Borromini."[79]

77 *Diary*, entry for October 18, 1685.
78 See Oscott Mss., Introduction to Register Book of St. Peter's, Birmingham, printed in *Warwickshire Parish Registers* (1904). The information is also summarized in Little, *op. cit.*, p. 25.
79 Little, *op. cit.*

6. Puritan and Quaker Meeting-Houses

The contrast between Catholic and Puritan churches could hardly be more sharp, though the furtive conditions in which both groups met in penal days were much alike. But the Catholics loved the drama and colour forbidden to Recusants, while the Puritans feared both as distractions to divine obedience and human duty.

After the Restoration the Puritans found the religious and political atmosphere unpropitious for the development of an appropriate type of church architecture. When they had been tolerated by or dominant in the religious establishment (from 1644 to 1660), there were numerous Anglican churches available for their use. In fact, they even divided some of the cathedrals for multi-congregational use. Exeter Cathedral choir, to take a notable example, was used by the Presbyterians (as "East St. Peter's"), and the nave by the Independents (as "West St. Peter's") during the interregnum.[80]

After St. Bartholomew's Day, 1662, the Nonconformists (as Puritans then refusing to accept the Restoration Settlement of Religion became known), being forbidden to worship according to their conscience were forced to gather secretly in houses and warehouses. Occasional and fitful Acts of Indulgence and the growing Protestantism of the Church of England (partly in reaction to James II's open avowal of Roman Catholicism) led the Nonconformists to hope for inclusion (or "Comprehension" in the noun of that day) in the Church of England. This tended to make the heirs of the Puritan and Calvinist tradition content with makeshift arrangements for worship. The consequence was that when it was finally realised that the hope of reunion was a delusion, the Nonconformists had become habituated to these simple and functional domestic buildings. Furthermore, when the time came for them to think of erecting their own meeting-houses in 1688 and afterwards, so many were needed (and all to be supplied at the voluntary charge of the Dissenters), that economy became a further reason for simplicity and even austerity. Thus the typical impression made by a late seventeenth-century meeting-house is that of a square with a double row of windows looking like a rather squat and wholly staid domestic building, utterly lacking any sense of the numinous. As Drummond points out, if the rectangular plan

---

[80] See John Stoughton, *Religion in England* . . . (1884), Vol. II, p. 366, and W. J. Harte, *Devonshire Association Transactions* (1937), pp. 44ff. Wells and Worcester Cathedrals were also used for Puritan services.

had been more often employed than the square, it would not have been necessary for the spacious meeting-houses to have the roofs designed in two parallel ridges with several obtrusive interior supports.[81]

The Puritan tradition was, of course, exceedingly suspicious of ostentation in general (after all, the God of all the earth could outdo man in grandeur, so why enter into competition with Him whose Son's Incarnation was in the stable of an inn?), and of colour in particular. This was to result in two distinguishing characteristics. The first was an emphasis on form, which is often lost in flashy splendour or intricacies of detail, and this expressed clarity, simplicity, and dignity. The second was a preference for sobriety in colour, which meant white or grey, with the brown of the woodwork as a contrast. There was, generally, good workmanship but little elegance. Nor would one find a contrast of textures, aspiration in steeples or towers, the curving delight of cupolas, the ingenuity and complexity of Gibbons's carved cornucopias or, least of all, the eye-deceiving skyscapes of Verrio.

There were some intriguing foreshadowings of the fully developed Independent and Presbyterian meeting-houses. Such anticipations could be found either in the sacred buildings of other radical religious groups, or in the occasional rare and now surviving Puritan chapels on the estates of the Puritan gentry. The former group were houses for worship built by the Baptists or the Quakers, who never had any hope of inclusion in any religious establishment, not even Cromwell's. For both groups, therefore, there was no reason for postponing their simple architectural needs. The buildings of the early Baptists and Quakers were very similar in style, as might be expected. They may well share a common ancestry in the stricter group of Dutch Mennonites—the Waterlanders.[82] Each religious group insisted on the importance of possessing rather than merely professing a Christian faith, as well as on the significance of the "inner light" or the indwelling of the Holy Spirit in the individual. Both groups revalued the Sacraments, and both insisted on the democratic rights of all men (and women, too, in the case of the Quakers) to testify publicly of their religious experience. Neither

---

[81] *The Church Architecture of Protestantism* (Edinburgh, 1934), p. 42. Wren, using a rectangle on many occasions, employed his piers to support roofs and even galleries, but far less obtrusively than in the square meeting-houses.

[82] See Bernard Picart, *Cérémonies et Coûtumes Religieuses de tous les Peuples du Monde* (Amsterdam, 1736), tome IV, p. 200, and H. L. Short's article in *The Listener*, "Changing Styles of Nonconformist Architecture," issue of March 17, pp. 471ff.

group had an ordained ministry. The latter is reflected strikingly in the absence of any pulpit in the earliest Quaker and Baptist[83] churches—a very marked difference from the dominating two or three decker pulpits of the Puritan meeting-houses. Instead of a pulpit there is a long bench, usually raised slightly above floor level, in front of which there was often a low panelled wall.[84] On such a bench the Quaker elders or the Baptist messengers sat facing the rest of the congregation as *primi inter pares*, just—to adapt Orwell's phrase—slightly more equal than others. As each could and did testify to the Spirit within, there was no need for an elevated place from which a single leader could address the assembled congregation.[85]

These simpler anticipations of the developed Puritan meeting-house had "the quality of a well-scoured farmhouse kitchen."[86] Their similarity is easily discernible if one compares the Jordans Quaker meeting-house (1688) in Buckinghamshire with Cote Baptist Chapel (1657) in Oxfordshire. The floors would be of stone or tiles, the open seats or forms of oak, the walls white-washed, the windows of clear glass, and wainscoting on the lower part of the walls when it could be afforded. The only distinguishing mark would be the raised seat for elders or messengers. The impression is that of simplicity, sincerity, and austerity; and appropriately so, since the early Baptists and Quakers were the Cistercians of English Nonconformity.

There are also a few early Dissenting buildings, belonging to neither Baptists nor Quakers, which may also be forerunners of the fully developed Nonconformist meeting-houses. One of these is a thatched cottage at Horningsham,[87] Wiltshire, which is

---

[83] There is a pulpit in the seventeenth-century Particular Baptist Chapel at Tewkesbury, Worcestershire, but its exact age is difficult to determine. The interior of the chapel is illustrated in Davies, *op. cit.*, III, p. 38.

[84] Short, *op. cit.*, pp. 471f.

[85] One would expect a simple Communion table to differentiate early Baptist from Quaker meeting-houses. Since, however, one early group of English Baptists (led by Helwys the apostle of religious toleration) was deeply influenced by the Mennonites in Holland where the English had fled as refugees, and since the Mennonites of the Waterland group held the Lord's Supper only once each year, they might have copied them in this respect. If this were so, then it would be a simple matter to bring a table into the meeting-house annually. The Calvinistic or Particular Baptists, it should be emphasised, were, with the single exception of Believers' Baptism which they practised, very close to the Independents in the matter of worship, and celebrated the Lord's Supper frequently and also ordained their ministers towards the end of the century and used pulpits for their preaching.

[86] John Betjeman, *First and Last Loves* (1952), pp. 90f.

[87] Martin S. Briggs, *Puritan Architecture and Its Future* (1946), p. 14.

claimed to have been built in 1566 by Sir John Thynne for the Scots (and Presbyterian masons) who were imported for building his palatial residence at nearby Longleat. Although it has for centuries been used by Independents (later known as Congregationalists), this represents a transplanted Scottish kirk rather than an indigenous Independent chapel. There are also other chapels of the utmost simplicity for which early dates are claimed. One is the "Ancient Chapel of Toxteth" near Liverpool, supposed to have been built in 1618, but which was extensively reconstructed in 1773. There is also an ancient Independent chapel at Walpole[88] in Suffolk, built about 1647. This is certainly a likelier date than the Toxteth Chapel. Its exterior is indistinguishable from that of two twin-storied semi-detached cottages; its interior, however, has the high pulpit on one long wall, the central Communion table, and the three galleries facing the pulpit, which were probably added considerably later. Indeed, the presence of galleries and the high pulpit necessitated by them suggests that the two cottages were used in penal days for worship and that when Toleration arrived, the interiors were remodelled. In this case, then Walpole would represent an important transition between the cottage church and the meeting-house. Another claimant to distinction as a pioneering church is St. Mary's Independent Chapel, Broadstairs,[89] Kent. It is claimed that this was first equipped for worship in 1601 by the local Puritan family of the Culmers. It has been carefully restored. The existence of these and other ancient Puritan chapels,[90] and the unhampered development of Puritan architecture in New England,[91] provided the prototypes of developed Dissenting meeting-houses.

When Charles II authorised the Declaration of Indulgence in 1671/2, permitting the use of non-Anglican places of worship, over 2,500 licenses were applied for within ten months. It is very probable, however, that most of the meetings for worship were held in private houses or in public rooms. The habitual use of temporary buildings, the simplicity and functionalism of the prototypes considered, the self-supporting character or Dissenting reli-

[88] *Ibid.*, p. 17.   [89] *Ibid.*, p. 19.
[90] Another family chapel was that erected in 1647 at Bramhope by the Puritan Robert Dynely of the adjacent Hall near Ottley, Yorkshire. It has belated Gothic details, but is still a building of great simplicity.
[91] Where wood usually replaced stone, with frequent ingenuity and great elegance, and Puritan worship could be celebrated openly a generation before the establishment of the Commonwealth in England, and two generations before the Glorious Revolution of 1688.

gious communities, the urgently rapid need for many buildings simultaneously as well as for great economy in building them, and the consistently Calvinist character of the worship of Dissent—all helped to determine the shape of the fully fledged meeting-houses of the late seventeenth century. Final permission to build was granted only in 1689, after twenty-seven years of persecution, only fitfully eased by occasional Indulgences.

From that year of great relief for Nonconformity, 1689, to the end of the century, a total of 2,418 buildings was registered for public worship by Presbyterians, Independents, and Baptists, besides many Quaker meeting-houses. From that era there survive, in whole or in part, a considerable number of Dissenting meeting-houses.[92]

It would be difficult, even if profitable, to describe all these meeting-houses in detail, since they are all built very much in the same unostentatious manner. At the risk of creating a stereotype, an attempt will be made to describe a typical larger meeting-house of the period, of which those at Norwich (the Old Meeting built in 1693), Ipswich (Friar Street built in 1700), and Taunton (Mary Street built in 1721) are representative.

Their model, as has been cogently argued by Principal H. L. Short of Manchester College, Oxford, would be no new-fangled adaptation of Wren's Anglicanism—for the Anglicans were their persecutors in this period—but what they tried to do in the parish churches when they had power, namely to follow Calvin and the manner of the best Reformed churches in Europe.[93] They would now renounce all relics of pre-Reformation times in their meeting-

[92] The following list of surviving meeting-houses was made by the architect, Martin Briggs near the end of the Second World War in 1946, in op. cit., p. 23. Dampier Street, Bridgewater, Somerset, is dated 1688, and Brook Street, Knutsford and King Edward Street, Macclesfield, both in Cheshire, from 1689. Box Lane, Boxmoor, Hertfordshire, was built in 1690, and St. Saviourgate, York, in 1692. Norwich Old Meeting, a distinguished meeting-house, was built in 1693, as was Dean Row, Stockport, Cheshire; and in the next year Elder Row, Chesterfield, Derbyshire, was erected. Waterside, Newbury, Berkshire and Dagger Lane, Hull, Yorkshire, date from 1697; and in 1699 the Presbyterian (now Unitarian) Chapel, Gloucester, the Watergate Chapel, Lewes, Sussex, and Doddridge Chapel, Northampton, as well as Upper Chapel, Sheffield, were all built. Another splendid chapel, Friar Street, Ipswich was built in 1700, also Tottlebank Chapel, near Ulverstone, in the Lake District. Later meeting-houses were: Rook Lane, Frome, Somerset (1707); Great Meeting, Leicester (1708); Churchgate Street, Bury St. Edmunds (1711); Chinley (1711); High Street, Portsmouth (1714); the famous Cross Street, Manchester (1715); and the elegant Mary Street, Taunton, Somerset (1721); and Crediton (1721).

[93] See "The Architecture of the Old Meeting Houses," Transactions of the Unitarian Historical Society, Vol. 8, No. 3 (1944), pp. 98-112.

houses, eliminating towers and spires, transepts, apses, or chancels. Most distinctive would be their arrangement of the pulpit against a long wall (north or south), with a centrally placed Communion table, with the minister presiding like a father at a meal of the family—Calvin's eucharistic arrangement at St. Pierre in Geneva and copied in the great Nieuwe Kerk in Amsterdam, familiar to most religious radicals exiled from England in Holland's hospitable and tolerant land. The pews would face the Communion table from three sides, and the holy table itself would be railed or surrounded by a Communion pew which was often occupied by the poor on non-sacramental Sundays. It was curiously conservative that they built their churches with a main east-west axis, for the absence of an altar at the east end made such orientation quite unnecessary. Equally curious was their placement of the pulpit on a south wall, flanked by round-headed clear windows through which the morning sun shone with brilliance to cause those in pews facing the pulpit extreme discomfort. The only architectural distinction that can be made between the two sets of Calvinists, the Presbyterians and the Independents concerns the fittings for the Lord's Supper. It seems that the Independents preferred a small Communion table from which the minister took the consecrated elements to the people sitting in their pews, while the Presbyterians favoured a long table at which all the church members sat, passing the bread and wine that had been blessed to each other. Galleries were provided in many meeting-houses, and there was good precedent for this in the great three stories of galleries in the Huguenot Temple at Charenton, near Paris. Galleries in meeting-houses were either single—that is, over the door and opposite the pulpit—or, on the three sides not occupied by the pulpit. These were, as in the case of Wren's churches, clearly auditory, designed for the hearing of God's Word, but also particularly designed around a central Communion table.

Their exteriors were built of good brick (Churchgate Street, Bury St. Edmunds had notable brickwork), with hipped roofs, and were covered with tiles but lacked gables. Doorways were decorated with the usual classical columns or pilasters common to the middle-class dwellings of the times. They were well-proportioned, but rarely ornate. The windows had either flat or semi-circular tops and were divided into small panes with good leadwork. The chapels at Bury St. Edmunds and Friar Street, Ipswich, as well as St. Mary's, Taunton, also had elegant oval windows. Walls were white-washed and the polished dark brown wood of the pews contrasted well with them. Similarly, a simple beauty was discovered in the contrast between the open rails or balustrading on the pulpit stairs and the solid panels of the pulpit itself, surmounted by a sturdy canopy or sounding-board. Occasionally there would be carving on the pulpit, and even, though rarely, on the gallery fronts. St. Mary's meeting-house in Taunton has exquisitely carved square Corinthian piers supporting the roof, and superbly finished brass chandeliers, consisting of stems with four spheres from which radiate S-branches and candleholders, all surmounted by a dove.[94]

The most vivid and yet accurate pen-picture of the Dissenting meeting-house is the work of the historian, Stoughton. "Your attention," he writes, "would be attracted to the pulpit, either a good large platform enclosed by wainscot sides, with a carved projection in front supporting a bookboard, or a deep narrow box . . . surmounted by a heavy sounding-board." After referring to the possibility that this canopy might bear a carved dove with an olivebranch in its mouth—the proof that God keeps His covenant promises with His people as with Noah—Stoughton continues: "Occasionally a desk for the precentor, and in front was almost always placed a table-pew . . . a large square or oblong enclosure, containing a seat running all round, with the Communion-table in the middle." It would have on it a Bible and less frequently that token of faithful Protestantism, Foxe's *Book of Martyrs*, or even a volume of sermons.[95] The poor would occupy a "table pew" except when Holy Communion was being celebrated, when they would give place to the Minister and deacons. The font would often be brought into the meeting-house and placed in a ring at the side of the pulpit. "The principal pews," writes Stoughton, "were spacious like parlours; and those appropriated to rich men[96] resembled such as were appropriated in a country church to the squire of the parish. They were lined with green baize and were often concealed behind thick curtains, whilst on the door, in a few distinguished instances, was carved either a monogram or a family crest. Two or three large brass chandeliers were in numerous cases suspended

94 Illustrated in Davies, *op. cit.*, III, following p. 38.

95 The latter was there presumably in case a visiting minister failed to arrive as preacher, and so, in a pinch, a sermon might be read to the congregation, a practice that would have horrified a first generation Puritan leader like Thomas Cartwright.

96 See the castigation of erecting pews in meeting-houses as essentially undemocratic offered by Clement E. Pike in "Pews and Benches" in *Transactions of the Unitarian Historical Society*, Vol. 2 (1919-1922), pp. 131ff.

from the ceiling by a chain, and with a few candles they gave a winter's afternoon just enough light to make darkness visible."[97]

Stoughton's description, especially in his closing sentences, seems to fit the 1730s rather than the 1690s, for the Dissenters were not at ease in Zion in the very first decade after persecution ended. The earliest meeting-houses and even later ones in country settings were not so much indicators of rising social status as they were of simplicity, sincerity, and a costing spirituality.

These meeting-houses were the perfect architectural expression in their secluded back streets of a different conception of the church than that of the nation on its knees to which Wren's aspiring towers and spires bore witness. This was rather a retiring religion for men and women who saw the church as gathered from the world (not one to attract worldlings with an imposing site or an attractively seductive interior). These were not public buildings for all and sundry to attend: they were the quiet trysting-places of the visible church of Christ meeting there. This Calvinism which had been at its zenith so eager for a public reorganisation of the state for the sake of the saints, now insisted on a separation of the "saints" from the world.

[97] *Religion in England*, Vol. v, pp. 447-48.

CHAPTER III

SPIRITUALITY: PREPARATION
FOR PUBLIC WORSHIP

EXCEPT FOR the most isolationist of mystics, spirituality in private or family devotions, is the preparation for liturgy or public worship. It is in the "closet" of the layman, or in the cell of the monk or nun, or about the family table which serves as the domestic altar, that the interior struggle with doubt and temptation goes on and where the true sources and motives of the Christian life are to be found. No one knew this better or expressed it with greater power than John Donne in the eightieth of his *LXXX Sermons*:

> I thrust myselfe down in my Chamber, and I call in, and invite God, and his Angels thither, and when they are there, I neglect God and his Angels, for the noise of a Flie, for the ratling of a Coach, for the whining of a doore; I talke on, in the same posture of praying; Eyes lifted up; knees bowed downe; as though I prayed to God; and if God, or his Angels should ask me, when I thought last of God in that prayer, I cannot tell: Sometimes I finde that I had forgot what I was about, but when I began to forget it, I cannot tell. A memory of yesterdays pleasures, a feare of tomorrows dangers, a straw under my knee, a noise in mine eare, a light in mine eye, an anything, a nothing, a fancy, a Chimera in my braine, troubles me in my prayer. So certainly is there nothing, nothing in spirituall things, perfect in this world.

It is in the privacy of spirituality that the soul,[1] in Eliot's phrase, "swinging between Heavengate and Hellgate" re-enacts the drama of the interior Civil War. It is in the devotional life that the pattern of the religious life is known, the true icon or false idol is served in the imagination, and the springs of affection and motivation are discovered to the eye of faith. Here, when the final capture of the errant soul by Christ is acknowledged, argument ends

[1] For the first half of the century on this topic Helen C. White's *English Devotional Literature* (Madison, Wisconsin, 1931) is unequalled, needing to be supplemented only by Louis L. Martz's *The Poetry of Meditation* (New Haven, Connecticut, 1954), and by Gordon S. Wakefield's *Puritan Devotion* (1957).

in adoration. Then the private preparation is completed by corporate participation in worship. For worship that is unprepared by devout souls and praying households is largely an antique and meaningless mimicry. In the seventeenth century, however, Catholic, Anglican, and Puritan found private and public prayers the celestial journey of the heart in pilgrimage, Herbert's "reversed thunder" and "Christ-side-piercing spear." They believed that they were heard and answered.

The spirituality of the Catholic Counter-Reformation of the sixteenth century had been the most brilliant since the fourteenth century. Some of the influence of the new methods would be felt not only by the English Catholic exiles in the Low Countries and France, but also by the Anglican high-church divines and the meditative or metaphysical poets of the seventeenth century. The Papal approval of St. Ignatius Loyola's impressive *Spiritual Exercises*[2] in 1548 marked the high point of recognition, and there followed a flood of books of spiritual direction. Among the most influential were Friar Luis de Granada's *Book of Prayer and Meditation* (1554),[3] Lorenzo Scupoli's *The Spiritual Combat*,[4] which was equalled in European popularity only by the late medieval *Imitation of Christ*, and Gaspar Loarte's *Instructions and Advertisements, How to Meditate the Misteries of the Rosarie* and *The Exercise of the Christian Life* (both of which probably appeared in 1579).[5] Shortly after the turn of the century there was published the important *Introduction to the Devout Life* by St. François de Sales (1609).[6] During the *siglo d'oro* or golden sixteenth

[2] H. Watrigant, "La genèse des Exercises de Saint Ignace de Loyola," *Études*, Vol. 71 (1897), pp. 506-29; Vol. 72, pp. 195-216; Vol. 73, 199-228, shows that behind Loyola there were important methods of meditation in the Low Countries, including Mauburnus's *Rosetum exercitiorum spiritualium et sacrarum meditationum* (1494), meditations on the life of Christ by the Pseudo-Bonaventure and Ludolph the Carthusian, the exercises of Abbot Garcia de Cisneros of Montserrat, in the chapel of which Loyola had exchanged the life of a soldier for the defender of the Virgin Mother and the church, and the interior self-examination counselled by the *Imitatio Christi* and its imitators.

[3] See Helen C. White, *op. cit.*, pp. 104-109, and Maria Hagedorn, *Reformation und Spanische Andachtliteratur* (Leipzig, 1934), who both claim that Luis de Granada was far and away the most popular spiritual writer read in England at the start of the seventeenth century.

[4] This work, attributed to Scupoli, is, in fact, probably the work of a group of Theatines, according to Pierre Pourrat, *Christian Spirituality*, tr. W. H. Mitchell and S. P. Jacques, 3 Vols. (1922-1927, Paris), III, pp. 239-40.

[5] The former work of Loarte is important also because it stimulated the composing of the *Christian Directory* by the Jesuit, Robert Persons, which, in the Protestant adaptation of Bunny, converted Richard Baxter and was again adapted for Anglican purposes in 1700 by Dean Stanhope of Canterbury.

[6] This treatise was so attractive in its appeal that it superseded even Fray

century in Spain St. Teresa of Avila and her friend St. John of the Cross scaled the topmost of ecstatic heights of union with God, but before they had lived in the desolate abandonment of the dark night of the soul.[7]

English Protestantism of the sixteenth century had nothing to show worthy of comparison with these Roman Catholic maps of mysticism, probably because Anglicans and Puritans were at the foundational and very often acutely controversial stage of developing their theology and ecclesiology, quite apart from the Pelagianism the Calvinists among them detected in Catholic mystical methods.

The seventeenth century, however, exhibits a greater maturation of spirituality in both Anglicans and Puritans and leads to the production of several classics of the spiritual life. Three of them are by Anglicans. These are the *Preces Privatae* of Bishop Lancelot Andrewes, and Bishop Jeremy Taylor's companion volumes, *Holy Living* and *Holy Dying*. A fourth is a Puritan classic, Richard Baxter's *The Saint's Everlasting Rest*. (An English Benedictine also produced a classic in Augustine Baker's *Sancta Sophia*.) Setting these masterpieces aside, however, the level of serious cultivation of the spiritual life by the wayfaring Christian had perceptibly risen in quality and quantity.

1. General Characteristics

The first impression that is made by the devotional books so prolifically produced in this period is their strenuous and persistent earnestness, their deep and occasionally desperate seriousness. They are prepared with the complete concentration and effort of those who wrote them and tested them out in their experience. This was unquestionably the fruit of the conviction that all human affairs are constantly directed by God, so that each moment and every event is providentially determined. It lies behind their spirituality as it lies behind the belief in special providences that explains the official days of thanksgiving and humiliation. Even a Puritan tinged with Arminianism (instead of the characteristic Calvinism) exhibits this high seriousness, as in the case of Richard Baxter. His

---

Luis de Granada's spiritual handbook, as Helen C. White shows, *op. cit.*, pp. 111-13.

[7] See E. Allison Peers, *Studies of the Spanish Mystics*, 2 Vols. (1927-1930); Alois Mager, O.S.B., *Mystik als seelische Wirklichkeit* (Salzburg, 1945), pp. 144-203; Louis Oechslin, O.P., *L'Intuition mystique de sainte Thérèse* (Paris, 1946); and Jean Baruzi, *Saint Jean de la Croix et le problème de l'expérience* (Paris, 1924).

conclusion to his masterpiece of spirituality can speak for the age, as well as for himself in its monumental and moving concern:

> Thus, Reader, I have given thee my best advice, for the attaining and maintaining a heavenly Conversation. The manner is imperfect, and too much mine own; but for the main matter, I dare say, I received it from God. From him I deliver it thee, and this charge I lay upon thee, That thou entertain and practise it. If thou canst not do it methodically and fully, yet do it as thou canst; onely, be sure thou do it seriously and frequently . . . Be acquainted with this work, and thou wilt be (in some remote sort) acquainted with God: Thy joys will be spiritual, and prevalent, and lasting, according to the nature of their blessed Object; thou wilt have comfort in life, and comfort in death; When thou hast neither wealth nor health, nor the pleasure of this world, yet wilt thou have comfort: Comfort without the presence, or help of any Friend, without a Minister, without a Book, when all means are denied thee, or taken from thee, yet maist thou have vigorous, reall Comfort. Thy Graces will be mighty, and active, and victorious; and the daily joy which is thus fetcht from Heaven, will be thy strength. Thou wilt be as one that standeth on the top of an exceeding high Mountain; he looks down on the world as if it were quite below him: How small do the Fields, and Woods, and Countreys seem to him? . . . The greatest Princes will seem below thee but as Grasshoppers; and the busie, contentious, covetous world, but as a heap of Ants. Mens threatenings will be no terrour to thee; nor the honours of this world any strong enticement: Temptations will be more harmless, as having lost their strength; and Afflictions less grievous, as having lost their sting; and every Mercy will be better known and relished.
>
> Reader, it is, under God, in thine own choice now, whether thou wilt live this blessed life or not; and whether all this pains which I have taken for thee shall prosper or be lost.[8]

This sense of the providential governance of the world by God which gives Baxter and his contemporaries such a solemn temper

---

[8] *The Saint's Everlasting Rest*, Pt. IV, pp. 295-98 (3rd edn., 1652); *Works* (ed. W. Orme, 1830), XXXIII, p. 406f. This devotional classic was written by Baxter during a period of apparently irrecoverable illness. It first appeared in 1650 and reached a third edition in two years, continuing to be read by all parties in the church with undiminished popularity to the end of the century.

in their writings also has three other consequences. It generates deep fervour, in the first place. Here, again, Baxter warrants quotation, when his theme is perseverance in the life of contemplation:

> Keep it close to the business till thou have obtained thine end. Stir not away, if it may be, till thy love do flame, till thy joy be raised, or till thy desire or other graces be lively acted. Call in assistance also from God; mix ejaculations with thy cogitations and soliloquies; till having seriously pleaded the case with thy heart, and reverently pleaded the case with God thou hast pleaded thyself from a clod to a flame, from a forgetful sinner to a mindful lover; from a lover of the world to a thirster after God, from a fearful coward to a resolved Christian, from an unfruitful sadness to a joyful life.[9]

Its second result is to give time a profounder significance, and in this respect it may be contrasted with the medieval, neo-Platonic and timeless *visio Dei*. Robert Bolton in *Some Generall Directions for a Comfortable Walking with God* (1625) exemplifies this typical Puritan attitude: "Wee must bee countable for time at the dreadfull Barre of that last Tribunall, as we must be exactly answerable even for wandring vaine imaginations, idle words, and every the very least errour of our whole life . . . so must we also give up a strict account for the expence of every moment of time."[10]

The third consequence will manifest a sense of strain in this spirituality. It may take the form of making the Christian feel, at least sometimes, that he is walking the giddying path on the edge of a precipice, with the engulfing whirlpool of the frenzied enthusiasts below, and nearer the indifferent but jagged rocks of the uncaring and worldly, and wondering why the way to salvation is so inordinately narrow. This strain is demonstrated in the diatribes (even in devotions) against the enemies of God or of one's own theological position. Michael Sparke whose prayers scintillate with joy and charity begins a "Morning Prayer" with adoration of the Immortal God, yet ends it scabrously with the following petition: "We beseech thee, remember the groaning griefs of all thy Churches, in all parts. Root out, O dig up, destroy, and root out all that be not planted by thy hand, all Quakers, Shakers, Ranters, and Seekers, such as look not after thy Laws, or that live not

---

[9] *Op. cit.*, Pt. IV, p. 205.   [10] *Op. cit.*, pp. 165-66.

according to thine Ordinances, but according to their own list, and wickednesse of theire wills."[11]

Another characteristic of the books of devotion of this age is their sheer practicality. They do not fly in the spacecraft of the great Carmelites to reach mystical ardour and ecstasy; their Piper cubs of small planes get them airborne with difficulty for the most part; but even then they always remain in direct radio contact with the earth, and the directions they give are always clear.

The Protestant conviction that God is to be served not *per vocationem* (through a special world-renouncing calling) but *in vocatione* (in one's daily, secular calling) is partly responsible for this practical emphasis. This activism on the part of holders of a predestinarian faith seems curiously contradictory, as does the emphasis on good works by those who maintain that justification is by faith and not by good works. But the spiritual life was the way of making one's election sure, and devotional exercises were not the causes but the consequences of a salvation already assured. The Anglicans and Puritans alike believed in an intramundane holiness—in fight, not flight from the world. Robert Bolton claimed "An honest Calling is a Schoole of Christianity."[12] Moreover, attendance at this school was not voluntary, but compulsory. Not only so, but it was as necessary for the ennobled as the lowly. Arthur Dent in his phenomenally popular and persuasive manual, *The Plaine Man's Path-way to Heaven* (1601) permits his simple man to wonder, "But may it not be allowed unto Lordes, Gentlemen and Gentlewomen, and other great ones, to live idly, sith they have wherewith to maintaine it?" The levelling of society before God is clearly affirmed in the answer of Theologus (obviously a Puritan Teacher): "God alloweth none to live Idlely: but all both great and small, are to be imployed one way or another: either for the benefite of the Churche, or Commonwealth: or for the good government of their own households: or for the good of Townes and Parishes, and those amongst whom they doe converse: or for the succour and reliefe of the poore: or for the furtherance of the Gospell, and the maintenance of the Ministerie: or for one good use or another."[13]

---

[11] *The Crums of Comfort to Groans of the Spirit, The Second Part* (1652), sigs. B10-B10 verso.
[12] *Some Generall Directions for a Comfortable Walking with God* (1625), p. 49.
[13] *Op. cit.*, pp. 191-92. This work, according to the early part of *Grace Abound-*

Moreover, this service of God in daily business and diurnal duty counterbalances the other-worldliness of seventeenth-century Christianity seen, for example, in the nostalgia of the religious English Catholic exiles in their monasteries and nunneries in France and the Low Countries, or in the Anglican "Arminian Nunnery" of Little Gidding, where the Ferrar family and friends offered unceasing adoration and praise to God through the day and the night. The this-worldly emphasis of service to God was not exclusively Anglican or Puritan. This was a central concern of St. François de Sales whose *Introduction to the Devout Life* was directed at lay folk living in the world, not at the religious who had adopted the counsels of perfection. A translation of this work issued from Rouen in 1614 for the English exiles (and also presumably for crypto-Catholics in England) makes this clear in the Preface: "Those who have treated of devotion before me have allmost all attended onelie to the instruction of persons alltogether retired from worldly conversation. . . . But my intention is particularly and principally to instruct such as live in citties and townes, busied with the affaires of their household, or forced by their place and calling to follow their princes court, such as by the obligation of their estate are bound to take a common course of life, in outward shew, and exteriour proceedings. . . ."[14] What had begun with Luther as an expression of the priesthood of all believers, had, within a century, been adopted in part by the Counter-Reformation. One might say that for Catholics the degree of holiness possible for the religious was still *summa cum laude*, but good men and women could now aspire to an honours degree—a *cum laude*—instead of merely taking the pass degree.

The high Anglican and Puritan recognition that one's daily duties could be the expression of a spiritual calling gave the common task a deep meaning, since it was work for the glory of God and the benefit of mankind. It had occasionally, however, the unfortunate consequence of assuming that material prosperity is the reward of the godly, and worse, their right and due. Michael Sparke's prayer for Monday morning petitions God thus: "Grant

---

ing, together with Bishop Bayly's phenomenally popular *Practice of Piety*, made up the totality of the dowry of Bunyan's wife, and may well have given Bunyan the idea for *Pilgrim's Progress*.

[14] *An Introduction to the Devout Life composed in Frenche by the R. Father in God Francis Sales, Bishop of Geneva, and translated into English by I. Y.* [Yakesley] (3rd edn., 1614), pp. 10-11.

we may deale uprightly & let the carriage of our Affairs be (O Lord) so pleasing unto thee, that they may draw downe thy blessings upon us; and keep us we pray this weeke following, thriving in our estates, and religious in our carriage, alwaies meditating of good for thy glory, for the Church and Commonwealth's good, so that whatsoever we lay our hands unto, thou wilt bend our hearts to do the same, so it be to thy praise and glory."[15] Hedged about as the revealing phrase "thriving in our estates" is by protestations of seeking God first, it nevertheless expresses a sense of cupboard love, of Christianity as its own reward with ten per cent profit. This was one of the dangers of the doctrine of election that it slipped easily into a concept of divine favouritism, which the prophet Amos had warned against in the eighth century B.C.

The same divine favouritism is expressed in many partisan prayers in this period for both Cavaliers and Roundheads were sure that God was on their side, the former because of their conviction of the divine right of kings,[16] the latter because of their assurance that God would honour his "visible saints." Sparke begins his "Heavenly Meditation" in celestial serenity, but he crashes to earth in his pedantic partisanship as he informs God, "It is manifest & plaine (O Lord) that *Papists* depend more upon Pharisaicall working then upon Christian believing; and it is as true that the loose Libereine [Libertine] careth little either for faith or fruits, and both these are flat enemies against the Crosse of thy deare Sonne, our alone Saviour Christ Jesus. . . ." He ends with the smug assurance, "Farre bee it from mee (deare Father) to be ensnared by either of these."[17]

Perhaps the most significant characteristic that these books of devotion share in this contentious time, when theologians were using the resources of logic, scholarship, and rhetoric for dogmatic defences of their own positions or vituperative denunciations of the views of their opponents, and at a time when extreme enthusiasm was viewed with dislike by Laudians and Puritans alike, is a recognition of the importance of the feelings in religion, or "heart work" as it was called. Increasingly there develops a deepened appreciation of the love of Christ and a responsive affection elicited by that boundless love. Moreover, what is even more remarkable

---

15 *Crums of Comfort* (edn. of 1628), sigs. D3-D3 verso.
16 Some partisan prayers offered by supporters of the Cavaliers in desperation are cited in Chap. VI on "Calendary Conflict."
17 *Crums of Comfort* (1628), sigs. H7-H7 verso; also cited by Helen C. White, *op. cit.*, pp. 229-30.

and little appreciated is the fact that it is shared by high Anglican, Roman Catholic, and Puritan alike.

At least since the time of St. Bernard of Clairvaux, Catholic piety has made much of the humanity of Jesus, as did St. Francis of Assisi—to whom the custom of having a Christmas crib at the festival of the Incarnation is due.[18] So it was not unexpected that St. Ignatius Loyola should encourage retreat masters to get the retreatants to use all their senses, especially sight and scent, to assist Jesus of Nazareth to walk out of the pages of the New Testament into their imaginations. Nor was it surprising that the cult of the Sacred Heart should be inaugurated in the Roman Catholic church in the seventeenth century, with St. John Eudes in 1646 instituting the feast of the Holy Heart of Mary and in 1672 the feast of the Sacred Heart of Jesus, only a year before St. Marguerite-Marie Alacoque received her first revelations at Paray-le-Monial. It was a feature of the sermons of Bishop Lancelot Andrewes that they enabled his hearers in court or cathedral to visualise the Christ-child with vividness and love, but without sentimentality, and Donne's dramatic gifts were used to make the Sacred Humanity relevant to his congregation. What is perhaps less to be expected, because it is insufficiently appreciated, is that several Puritan writers should concentrate on the humanity of the Saviour, among them Preston, Rous, Sterry, and Thomas Goodwin.

John Preston had as an appendage to his *Five Sermons on the Divine Love* in the edition of 1640, which is entitled, *The Soliloquy of a Devout Soul to Christ, Panting after the Love of the Lord Jesus*.[19] One passage shows that Preston wishes not merely for a historical knowledge of Christ, but more deeply for Jesus at his heart's centre. His soul muses:

> . . . If I look to Mount Tabor, I see thee in glory, and I cannot but love thee for that. If I look to the garden, I see thee lying on the cold ground sweating drops of bloud for me, and I cannot but love thee for that. If I look to Golgotha, I see thee nailed to the Cross, and thy heart broached that I may drinke thy bloud and live, and I cannot but love thee for that. If I looke to Mount Olivet I see thee ascending farre above all

[18] A Giotto fresco in the Church at Assisi depicts St. Francis adoring the Christ Child in a Christmas crib.

[19] John Preston, *A Heavenly Treatise of the Divine Love of Christ* (1640), pp. 89ff.

heavens, and I cannot but love thee for that also. Indeed in Tabor thou hadst visible glory but it soon vanished; in the garden and Golgotha thou hadst little visible beauty why I should desire thee; and in Olivet thou wast quite carried out of my sight. If then thou liest for me nowhere else what hope have I to love thee, Oh thou to be beloved of all? Art not thou in the tents of the shepherds? Dost thou not walke in the midst of the golden candlesticks? Dost thou not dwell in the hearts of men by faith? Oh let me see thee here below in the Church and in myselfe.

Francis Rous, a Presbyterian layman who became an Independent, and had been both Provost of Eton and Speaker of the House of Commons, composed a manual on *The Mysticall Marriage* (1635) between Christ and the soul. This, to be sure, will be consummated in eternity, but there is a solemn betrothal here and now between Christ and the trusting soul.[20] The way is by ethical conformity of the human will to Christ's, since in his invasion of the soul, "the more spiritual he doth make her; yea the more he doth melt a soule in himselfe; the more he doth turne her into his will, and the more doth he increase his own image in her; and we know that his image is righteousness and true holiness."[21] The closeness of Catholic and Puritan spirituality has been said to be fully confirmed[22] by another Puritan, Thomas Goodwin, the Independent who was Cromwell's chaplain and President of Magdalen College, Oxford, and author of a work said to anticipate the Roman Catholic Cult of the Sacred Heart, namely, *The Heart of Christ in Heaven towards Sinners on Earth* (1652). This, however, as we shall see later in this chapter, has differences from the Catholic cultus as significant as the affinities with it.

Two more excerpts from devotional books, one Puritan and the other Anglican, will suffice to establish the remarkable concurrence of streams of spirituality concentrating on transformations effected by the divine love. The Platonist Puritan to be cited is

20 *Op. cit.*, p. 43. The sub-title is: *or Experimental Discourses of the Heavenly Marriage between a Soul and her Saviour.*

21 *Ibid.*, pp. 255-56.

22 For example, the Oratorian historian of spirituality, Louis Bouyer writes: "A Number of Cromwell's chaplains figured among the eminent representatives of this vehement mystical feeling for Christ, and, surprising as it may seem, they were closer to many aspects of the Jesuits and Visitandines of the period than were the traditional Anglicans—at least as far as we can discover." (*Orthodox Spirituality and Protestant and Anglican Spirituality*, tr. in 1969 by Barbara Wall, from the French original published in Paris in 1965, p. 134.)

Peter Sterry whose book, *The Rise, Race and Royalty of the Kingdom of God in the Soul of Man* was published in 1683, eleven years after the death of this chaplain of Cromwell's. Sterry sees the divine love as "the most universal and importunate beggar" knocking at the door of every soul, not only at the soul of the elect. The divine love is experienced as joyful celebration, holy laughter: "Abide in the Father's love by spiritual joy. Joy is love flaming. One saith, that laughter is the dance of the spirits, their freest motion in the harmony, and that the light of the heavens is the laughter of angels. Spiritual joy is the laughter of Divine Love, of the Eternal Spirit, which is love, in our spirits."[23]

Philip Traherne writing *The Soul's Communion with her Saviour* in 1685 is an Anglican in the succession of Lancelot Andrewes, but his emotion is expressed with less reserve. Meditation on the nativity of Christ results in a paean of praise:

O Thou *Light of the World*, who was born in the Night, an Emblem of that dark and disconsolat Estate where into We by Transgression fell: Thou art *the Sun of Righteousness, by whose Rising upon the Earth the Peepl that walked in Darkness hav seen a great light, and upon them that dwell in the Land of the Shadow of Death hath the Light shined.* Thy glorious Appearing hath dispersed the Cloud of thy Father's Wrath, under which the whol Creation groaned, together with those unwholsom Mists of Sin, Error, and Ignorance wherin Mankind was lost and benighted: Thou hast dissolved the Everlasting Chains of Darkness which were justly prepared to bind us in Hell and Despair, and once more restored us a Day of Hope to rejoice in the Light of thy Countenance for ever.[24]

Finally, these devotional manuals or guides to spirituality, however much they differ in the methods they inculcate or in their theological emphases, all express a robust conviction of the reality of God, of the finality of Christ's revelation of his love, of the interior transformation wrought by the Holy Spirit, and the substantiality of heaven and the comparative shadowiness of earth. For the last time in modern European history we have a sense that theology

---

[23] *Op. cit.*, p. 390. See V. da Sola Pinto, *Peter Sterry, Platonist and Puritan* for a biographical and critical introduction to an anthology of his voluminous writings.

[24] *Op. cit.*, pp. 36-37. One is reminded by this passage of the *risus Paschalis* of the Easter Liturgy and of Paul Claudel's *le grand rire divin de l'univers*.

is in the main current of life, not an irrelevant deviation from the most serious business of living. Later piety will often seem artificial, strained, sentimental, apologetic. In the seventeenth century it is robust, and it is significant that in different decades both Puritan and Anglican piety were the expressions of those who suffered for their faith, while throughout the period the English Catholics were Recusants, leading—except when the sun of royal patronage shone—a crepuscular and clandestine life in England and a nostalgic life in Continental religious houses. The choicer souls in each of these groups had earned the promise of the last Dominical Beatitude.[25] This gave their spirituality a profound sincerity, marked by sacrifice. As Helen White has so aptly expressed it: "Here is no thin diagram of a possibility but the full round of the dominant view of the world."[26] Whether with the aid of a Catholic crucifix, an Anglican cross, or a Puritan mental image of the suffering Redeemer, this piety was so Christocentric and so cosmic that one could say of it, in a way unintended by Marlowe, "See, see, where Christ's blood streams in the firmament."[27]

2. Roman Catholic Spirituality

It is peculiarly difficult to trace Roman Catholic spirituality among the English of the seventeenth century because it is so scattered, so multiform, and necessarily so clandestine. But there is no question at all of its influence on the Recusants, whether in exile or at home, and even on Protestants. It was profound and pervasive in its old or its new forms, in its medieval or Counter-Reformation methods.

The older forms of spirituality continued to fascinate with all the tenacity of a great tradition, confirmed by the experiences of the religious orders. St. Augustine of Hippo persisted in popularity among Protestants as well as Catholics. A Catholic translation of his *Confessions* attributed to Sir Tobie Mathew, to whom we also owe a translation of the Benedictine Rule, appeared in 1620, while in 1631 there was published another translation of the same work by William Watts. There was also published a number of treatises on the Christian life attributed to him.

Only a little less popular than St. Augustine was St. Bernard of Clairvaux. In 1616 William Crashaw, the indefatigable Puritan father of Richard, the metaphysical poet and Catholic convert, extracted and translated from the Bernardine collection of devo-

25 Matthew 5:10-12.   26 *Op. cit.*, p. 236.   27 *Faustus*, I, l. 1432.

tional works, *The Complaint or Dialogue, Betwixt the Soul and the Bodie of a damned man.* Another work, *Saint Bernard His Meditations: or Sighes, Sobbes and Teares, upon our Saviours Passion* . . . translated and edited by "W.P.," a Cambridge graduate, appearing first in c. 1610 ran to four editions. Three other treatises of St. Bernard, bound together, appeared in 1613; they were the *Golden Treatise, Joy in Tribulation,* and *the forme of an honest life.* In 1631 an anthology of St. Bernard's devotional meditations appeared in Douai with the mellifluous title, *A Hive of Sacred Honie-Combes containing most Sweet and Heavenly Counsel.* . . .

The third most popular survival of medieval devotions, which has always had its Protestant as well as Catholic admirers, was, of course, Thomas à Kempis's *Imitation of Christ* (the title perhaps better translated by the earlier Catholic versions as "The Following of Christ"). It had first appeared in Latin between 1470 and 1475. By the seventeenth century more than 280 Latin editions of the *Imitatio Christi* had appeared on the European Continent.[28] The first English translation was that of William Atkinson printed by Wynkyn de Worde in 1502, but the most popular in England was that of Thomas Rogers the sixth translator, which came out in 1580 and ran through fourteen editions in the next sixty years. Rogers, a Protestant, not only omitted the fourth book of the *Imitation,* that on the Eucharist, but substituted for it another treatise of à Kempis, providing his own translation of the *Soliloquium Animae* under the punning title of *The sole-talke of the Soule.* . . . The fishiest part of the whole proceeding, however, was his bland assumption that a better (i.e., Protestantly) instructed Thomas à Kempis would have taken this very decision. This is corroborated to the translator's satisfaction by the following words in his "Address to the Christian Reader," assuring him that à Kempis's prayer for correction "God hath heard, and discovered those things for thy benefit, and testification besides howe Kempisius, the Auctor, howsoever living in a Popish time, was yet in hart no Papist, but would like well of that which is doon, as I trust thou wilt, whose edifieing, and spirituall comforting, I have onlie aimed at."[29]

While they are not properly either devotional manuals or collections of prayers, yet the rules of the founders of medieval orders

[28] White, *op. cit.,* p. 81.
[29] *The Imitation of Christ* (tr. Thomas Rogers, London, 1592), sig. A4 verso. Cited Helen White, *op. cit.,* p. 85.

aim at the culture and discipline of the spiritual life, and so they are ancillaries to devotion.[30] The Rules of both St. Benedict and St. Francis of Assisi were Englished and translated. The former appeared in Ghent in 1632 and parts two through four comprise "Statutes compyled for the better observation of the holy rule for the use of the English Benedictine nuns at Brussels." *The rule and testament of the seraphical father S. Francis* was published in Douai in the Richard Mason translation in 1635, while eleven years earlier there had appeared in Brussels a translation by Arthur Bell of *The rule of the religious of the third order of Saint Francis . . . living together in communitie and cloyster.*

In estimating the impact of the older forms of devotion of Catholicism the continuance of the primers should not be forgotten. They were exceedingly popular in the sixteenth century,[31] and in many homes they must have been retained in the seventeenth century, however dog-eared or even tattered.

The new methods of spirituality encouraged by the renewal of the spiritual life in the Roman Catholic Church through the Council of Trent and by the founding of the Jesuits and the reform of the Carmelites and Franciscans (all of which took place in the sixteenth century) had a profound impact on seventeenth-century English devotional life. Far and away the most popular Spanish author in translation was Luis de Granada,[32] Provincial of the Dominican Order in Portugal. His *Libro de la Oracion y Meditacion* written in 1561 was translated and published in Paris in 1582 by Richard Hopkins, an exile Recusant. The edition of 1599 is an anonymous adaptation for Anglican purposes, and with it is bound up an additional work, Granada's *An Excellent Treatise of Consideration and Prayer.* In 1598 the same author's *Guia de Pecadores* was digested and translated by Francis Meres as *The Sinners Guide.* As early as 1586, however, there had appeared a most influential volume of Fray Luis de Granada, Englished as *A Memoriall of a Christian Life* "from the beginning of his conversion until the end of his conversion." This reached a fourth edition in 1625. It contained seven treatises of which the fourth is of special interest. It comprises "two principal Rules of a Christian life," the first for beginners and the second for experts. The former are described

---

[30] There should also be noted the publication in Paris in 1636 of *S. Austin's Rule . . . together with the Constitutions of the English Canonesse regulars of our B. Ladyes of Sion in Paris.* Tr. and ed. Miles Pinkney.

[31] See Davies, *op. cit.*, I, pp. 409-15.

[32] See E. Allison Peers, *Studies in the Spanish Mystics* (1927), I, pp. 33-76.

in the table of contents as "such Christians as beginne newlie to serve God, and have a desire to be saved." The latter are described as "all professed Religious persons in Monasteries, and for such other Christians as are not contented with the doinge of all such things as they know to be of necessitie for their Salvation, but will endeavour to wade further and profit more and more in the Way of vertues." It is important to recognise, however, that the spiritual method outlined by the Dominican friar was an adaptation for daily morning and evening use of the important *Spiritual Exercises* of St. Ignatius Loyola, designed to be performed in a month of spiritual intensity.

The impact of Ignatian spirituality was very strong in England because of the intrepidity of the Jesuits in the English Mission and the impact of their martyrdoms. One of their number, Robert Persons, wrote the highly popular *Christian Directory*[33] (originally called *The First Booke of the Christian Exercise appertayning to resolution* in 1582) which reached the seventh approved and authorised edition in 1633 under the imprint of the English College at St. Omer. It was also successful in the Protestant bowdlerisation by Bunny in 1584, which went through nine impressions in sixteen years. It was the Bunny version that converted that exemplary Puritan, Richard Baxter.[34] In Rouen in 1630 there appeared leaflets for those making St. Ignatius's *Spiritual Exercises*. Furthermore, Tomas Villacastin's *A Manuall of devout Meditations and Exercises, instructing how to pray mentally* was another adaptation of the Ignatian *Exercises*. It was translated by Fr. Henry More and was published at St. Omer in 1618, and two further editions were called for in 1623 and 1624. Finally, as another index of widespread Jesuit influence in spirituality, there was Michael Lancicius's biography, *The glory of the B. father S. Ignatius of Loyola, founder of the Society of Jesus*, first published in Ghent in 1628 and reissued in 1633.

---

[33] Persons owed much to the work of a Jesuit predecessor, Gaspar Loarte, two treatises of which were translated into English. The first was *Instructions and Advertisements, How to Meditate the Misteries of the Rosarie* which appeared ca. 1579, and the other, *The Exercise of a Christian Life* (1579) which resembled Luis de Granada's most popular work, and had reached four more editions by 1634. For the origin of the use of the rosary as a means of recollection see Herbert Thurston's article "Genuflections and Aves, a study in Rosary Origins" in *The Month*, Vol. 127 (1916), pp. 546-59, a reference among others I owe to the kindness of Dr. D. M. Rogers of the Bodleian Library, Oxford, an authority on English Recusant history.

[34] *Reliquiae Baxterianae* (ed. M. Sylvester, 1696), p. 3.

The extraordinary success of the Jesuit spirituality was owed to certain intrinsic qualities, not forgetting its timeliness.[35] St. Ignatius knew that the clue to the changing of the will is to be found in the imagination and his was an imagistic, pictorial spirituality, not an abstract or negative one. "Composition of place" is the technique for capturing all the senses for Christ. In the second place, he knew that the inveterate complacency and lukewarmness of the unredeemed or only partly redeemed human must be shaken loose by fear and self-analysis. Finally, he was able to enlist the resolution of his retreatants by a modern Crusade in which courage, loyalty, devotion, and manliness were all elicited. Its impact is powerfully envisaged in English literature in the poems of Southwell, Donne, and Gerard Manley Hopkins and in the Ignatian-shaped blank in James Joyce's *Portrait of the Artist as a Young Man* and *Ulysses*.

An important, though less popular, writer of devotional treatises was a Franciscan friar, St. Peter of Alcantara, who wrote a *Treatise on Prayer and Meditation* (c. 1558). This opens with a definition of devotion which derives from St. Thomas Aquinas, continues with an exhortation on the needs and advantages of meditation from the pseudo-Bonaventure, and ends with a similar one from St. Laurence Justinian, the Augustinian, thus combining the precise theology of the Schoolmen with the ardour of the mystics,[36] and making the transition from older to newer spiritual methods easier. His *Golden Treatise of Mental Prayer* was published in translation in Brussels in 1632 and the *Pax Animae* (attributed to him though almost certainly the work of another Spanish Franciscan, Juan de Bonilla) appeared in translation in Paris in 1665.

The most striking omission, while Spanish mystical treatises are under consideration, is of any of the great works of either St.

---

35 Of its timeliness, Professor David Knowles, O.S.B., has written: "in the Catholic camp . . . the need for a firm and explicit grasp of doctrine, and for an active, apostolic, sacramental, apologetic reply to opponents brought about a new model of the devout life which concentrated attention upon the war against vice and ignorance, and developed the technique of spiritual exercises, regular retreats, set meditations, and methodical direction." (*The English Mystical Tradition*, 1961, p. 152.)

36 The forerunner as author of this type of meditative treatise combining theological acuity with mystical ardour is Jean Gerson, Chancellor of the University of Paris in the early fifteenth century, with his *On the Mountain of Contemplation*. It may be of interest to note that the future Anglican Bishop Joseph Hall in *The Arte of Divine Meditation* (1606) lists the masters of meditation as follows: Origen, Augustine, Bernard, Hugh of St. Victor, Bonaventure, Gerson (Chap. 16).

Teresa of Avila or St. John of the Cross. There is, however, as a partial counterpart for this tragic loss a translation of her autobiography by "W. M. of the Society of Jesus" which is entitled, *The lyf of the Mother Teresa of Jesus foundresse of the Monasteries of descalced or bare-footed Carmelite nunnes and fryers . . . Written by her self. . . .* Such a mountain-top view, Alpine in its chill austerity and bitter climbing through the dark nights and dazzling days, seemed perhaps impossible of attainment by English temperaments. Richard Crashaw, the Baroque poet and convert to Catholicism, however, was deeply influenced by her Christological ardours.

The most influential French writer of devotional works translated into English was St. François de Sales, the Bishop of Geneva. His impact was felt early in the century, but its fullest force was reserved for the Restoration of the monarchy in 1660 when the light ladies who returned to England with Charles II brought their French devotional books with them. It was the triumph (and failure) of St. François de Sales that he succeeded in recommending the practise of piety to the world of fashion, for this could rouse an aesthetic interest without any ethical transformation. The first English translation of *The Introduction to a Devout Life* was published in Douai in 1613 hardly five years after its original had appeared in Paris. Another edition of this translation was published in Paris in 1637, while a new edition bore the imprint of the English priests at Tournai in 1648. Thomas Carre, English exile and Recusant, published his translation of de Sales's *Of the Love of God* in 1630. It was from the eighteenth French edition of the work. It is questionable whether this actually crossed the English Channel, as also was the case of the *Delicious Entertainments of the Soule* (also by de Sales) which had been translated by "a Dame of our Ladies of Comfort" and published in Douai in 1632.

The Ignatian spirituality is a pugnacious, even bellicose one, while the Salesian devotion seems more reconciliatory. The Salesian spirit relies much less on the "terrors of the Lord"—the concentration on sin, death, hell and judgment—inculcated as a deliberate unsettlement and divine disturbance of a complacent soul by the Ignatian spirituality. It focuses rather on the love, mercy, and goodness of God, and more on the attracting power of the love of Christ than on what must be expelled by that power. As Louis L.

Martz has rightly seen,[37] for St. François de Sales all meditation and self-analysis must be performed *tout bellement et doucement*. Its typical expression is found in the following citation from John Yakesley's translation of *An Introduction to a Devoute Life* (3rd edn., Rouen, 1614): "When thou desirest earnestly to be freed from any evil, or to obtaine any good; the first thing thou must doe, is to repose thy mind, and quiet thy thoughts and affects from over-hastie poursuite of thy desire; and then faire and softly beginne to pourchase thy wishe, taking by order, one after another, the meanes which thou judgest convenient to the attaining thereof."[38] Such a spirituality must have proved increasingly attractive in the century which had known the Thirty Years War in Europe[39] and the Civil War in England.

So far it seems as if English Catholic spirituality is limited to the translation of medieval and modern European works of devotion with the Spanish influence predominating. This is largely the case, but not wholly so. During our period there are some minor indigenous treatises on the devotional life,[40] some important collections of prayers in English, one Catholic metaphysical poet of distinction (Crashaw), and one original masterpiece worthy of comparison with the fourteenth century English mystics. The selections of prayers continue the tradition and structure, if not the larger part of the contents of the primers.

A very useful and popular collection of prayers for the use of Catholics (one of a number of such) was printed first in 1583 and published most probably in Rouen.[41] Its full title was, *A Manuall of prayers newly gathered out of many and famous divers authors as well auncient as of the tyme present*. Its history is an index of the difficulties Recusants faced in publishing and disseminating copies to the faithful. It was compiled and translated by George Flinton. Another edition appeared in Rouen in 1589. Three

---

[37] *Op. cit.*, p. 149. [38] *Op. cit.*, p. 479.

[39] In our days a play which has poignantly revealed the upheavals of the Thirty Years War is Berthold Brecht's *Mother Courage*.

[40] The reference is to Benet Fitch and Gertrude More. The former (alias Canfield) besides producing a translation of his fellow friar and Capuchin's Constantin Barbanson's the *Anatomie of the Soule*, wrote the treatise, *Of the threefold will of God*, referred to approvingly by Augustine Baker, O.S.B., in his distinguished work, *Sancta Sophia*, I, pp. 86-87. The latter, Dame Gertrude More, published in 1657 in Paris *The Holy Practises of a Divine Lover: Sainctly Idiot's Devotions*. One is bound to guess that Sir Thomas More would have provided a very retired nook in *Utopia* for his great-granddaughter to meditate in, quite alone and utterly undisturbed.

[41] Helen C. White, *op. cit.*, p. 128.

further editions were secretly printed in England; one probably in 1593 and the two others certainly in 1595 and 1596. One other appeared in 1599 falsely claiming to be issued at Calice [Calais], but was in fact secretly printed in England. Further secret editions appeared in England between 1599 and 1604, and another definitely in 1604. There then appeared in Douai an expanded version of the work, retitled, *A Manual of prayers now newly corrected and also more augmented and enlarged.* This ran to eighteen further editions.[42] The enlarged edition of 1604 deserves a digest, both because of its inherent interest, and also because its wide popularity makes it a normative manual of English Recusant piety for at least the first half of the seventeenth century.

Chapter I consists of daily prayers, to be said at morning, noon, and night, with an exercise to be used in meditating on the Passion of Christ with aspirations and meditations on his holy wounds. The second chapter contains prayers to be said before, during, and after Mass. For example, at the elevation of the Chalice, the recommended meditation reads: "Al haile, most precious & blessed blood, flowing out of the side of my Lord and Saviour Jesus Christ, wasting away the spottes both of the old and new offences: cleanse, sanctifie, and keep my soule, I beseech thee to everlasting life."[43] There follow brief directions with prayers before and after sacramental Confession. Chapter III contains prayers for Sunday, with praises and thanksgivings directed to the Holy Trinity. Chapter IV has Monday prayers in commemoration of departed souls. Chapter V invokes saints and angels in Tuesday prayers. Wednesday prayers (Chapter VI) are for "our troubles and necessities, both spiritual and temporal." Thursday prayers (Chapter VII) deal with repentance for sins. The Friday prayers, not unnaturally, focus on the "Passion of our Saviour" (Chapter VIII), while the prayers of Chapter IX for Saturday are directed to "our Blessed Ladie." Chapter X (the last) comprises "Advertisements, with prayers and suffrages for the sick." An appendix contains the Jesus Psalter. The whole comprises 275 pages.

It is methodical, simple to follow, comprehensive, and fervent. It must have warmed the hearts of the faithful in testing times,

---

[42] These editions are fully documented in A. F. Allison and D. M. Rogers, *A Catalogue of Catholic Books in English printed abroad or secretly in England, 1558-1640* (Bognor Regis, 1956).

[43] *Op. cit.*, p. 50. It is noteworthy that the meditations are not based on the text of the Liturgy or on the text of Scripture. Strictly, they are extra-liturgical meditations.

and kept them loyal to the old religion, while instructing the young, and, given to both groups of Catholics the stability of tradition. It was a typical collection of prayers for the Catholic household of faith.[44]

Richard Crashaw (1603-1649), the single Catholic among the metaphysical poets, was the son of a distinguished Puritan and preacher to the Temple, and moved from the high churchmanship of a fellowship at Peterhouse, the most Laudian of Cambridge colleges to the highest of high Catholicism, a canonry at Loreto, where he died. The ardour and austerity of Catholic religion in its most Baroque forms attracted him by its captivity of the senses for spirituality. This lover of painting and music, demonstrated this in poetry that is rich with vivid word-painting and richly musical in its cadences. His spirituality is Baroque in the brilliance of its tortured sensibility, its vivid portrayal of the religous emotions of awe, ecstasy, and pity, but it easily degenerates into sentimentality or mere theatrical posturing.

The distinctiveness of his spirituality, without its extravagances, can be sensed if we compare two poems on the Nativity, Crashaw's "Sung as by the Shepherds" and Milton's great Ode. Milton ends where Crashaw begins, in visualising the scene of the Nativity, for Milton's interest is in the Redemption wrought by the power of Christ, while Crashaw's is on the Incarnation and its expression of God's love:

> See, see, how soon his new-bloom'd CHEEK
> Twixt mother's breasts is gone to bed
> Sweet choise, said we! no way but so
> Not to ly cold, yet sleep in snow.

Christ's is paradoxically a gentle Kingship that rules by affection:

> To thee, dread Lamb! whose love must keep
> The shepheards, more then they the sheep.
> To THEE, meek Majesty! soft KING
> Of simple GRACES & sweet LOVES
> Each of us his lamb will bring
> Each his pair of sylver Doves;
> Till burnt at last in fire of Thy fair eyes,
> Our selves become our own best SACRIFICE.

[44] In many ways it resembled the parallel Protestant collections of prayers such as *A Booke of Christian Prayers* (1581 and many later editions), which had originally been issued by John Daye in 1569 under another title.

Milton's theme is Redemption, announcing at the very beginning:

> This is the Month, and this happy morn
> Wherein the Son of Heav'ns eternal King,
> Of wedded Maid and Virgin Mother born,
> Our great Redemption from above did bring. . . .

The emphasis in Catholic meditation and meditative poetry is on the paradoxical gentleness of omnipotence in the Nativity of Christ, with the tribute of love responding to his love; the emphasis in Puritan poetical spirituality is on the role of Christ in power, not on his tenderness. Catholicism glories in the sacred humanity, Puritanism in the divine powers of God as man. This generalization is, however, subject to partial revision as more is learned of the mystical tendencies of some Puritan writers such as Rous, Thomas Goodwin, and Sterry.

For the man or woman who wished to advance further in spirituality, there was one masterpiece, originally prepared for a group of English Benedictine nuns in exile by their director, Father Augustine Baker, O.S.B.[45] Born in Abergavenny, South Wales, in 1575, he was educated at Christ's Hospital, Broadgates Hall (now Pembroke College), Oxford, and trained as a lawyer at Clifford's Inn and the Middle Temple. He was admitted as a Benedictine novice in 1603. After difficult, even desperate times and failures, he was reconverted in 1608, the thirty-second year of his life. There followed twelve years of tepid spiritual life after which he was reconverted again. In 1624 he was appointed to Cambrai, as auxiliary confessor to the Benedictine dames which Crisacre More, grandson of Sir Thomas More, had established for his daughter and her seven companions. Somewhere between 1620 and 1624 he gained his most faithful disciple, Serenus Cressy, the chaplain to Lady Falkland.

During the following nine years he was prolific, producing about forty treatises on spirituality, of which roughly twenty-five were original, and the rest collections from the writings of others. Four years at Douai followed, and he died in 1641 while on the English Mission in which he had been engaged for about three years. He died aged sixty-five, presumably happiest in the recollection of the

---

[45] See *Memorials of Father Baker* (ed. R. H. Connolly and Justin McCann, Catholic Record Society, XXXIII, 1933) and [Augustine Baker], *Sancta Sophia, or Directions for the Prayer of Contemplation . . . Extracted out of more than Forty Treatises written by . . . Augustin Baker and Methodically digested by . . . Serenus Cressy* (Douai, 1657).

instruction he had given in the spiritual life, for there duty and delight were combined.

His many treatises, existing only in manuscript form, were arranged most systematically by his pupil and brother in the Benedictine Order, Fr. Serenus Cressy, thus providing an encyclopedic and well-ordered account of the stages in the spiritual life. This collection, known as the *Sancta Sophia* (or *Holy Wisdom*) is distinguished by its exhaustive treatment, and by the extraordinary richness of its citations from the devotional masters and mystics of the Christian past. He recalls the Greek and Latin Fathers of the ancient church who wrote on spirituality, such as Gregory of Nyssa, Gregory Nazianzen, and Gregory the Great. He cites medieval writers such as St. Bernard, St. Francis of Assisi, and St. Catherine of Siena and the late medieval masters such as Tauler, Suso, Ruysbroeck, and Harphius, as well as the English mystics of the fourteenth century such as Walter Hilton, Richard Rolle, and the author of *The Cloud of Unknowing.* Among the moderns he is fondest of St. Teresa of Avila and St. John of the Cross, as well as the French writers, de Blois, Barbanson, and St. François de Sales, and a host of minor figures as well. His candour, moderation, common-sense, and practicality, together with a tendency towards angularity, are among his more obvious characteristics.

It is an unusual genre of devotional book, half formal treatise on ascetical theology and half personal instruction taught with urgency. The *Sancta Sophia* is over five hundred pages in length, and thus difficult to summarize. Its teaching emphasizes three means of interior enlightenment: the spiritual director, spiritual reading, and divine inspirations. It then focuses on mortification of the passions, and the cultivation of solitude and silence, as well as of the virtues of charity, patience, and humility. A lengthy chapter deals with various scruples. The final two hundred and twenty pages deal with prayer and its distractions, the three stages in meditation, acts of the will and "aspirations." It ends with an outline of the mystical life.

It is a highly impressive book, but not without errors. It is intended for those engaged in the religious life, and particularly for the "monastic contemplative life." According to Professor David Knowles, himself a Benedictine monk, it is at its best on such topics as mortification, divine inspiration (the belief that when a person can find no compelling guidance, he will be given light to see and strength to act, provided he offers his prayer in faith and goodwill), and the necessity and stages of mental prayer.[46] The same historian and critic asserts that "some of his spiritual writings, though unquestionably orthodox, are on important points confused, and at variance with what would seem to be the accepted doctrine of the great masters."[47] Fr. David Knowles makes the precise charges that he is mistaken in assuming that all would-be mystics are capable of attaining to the unitive experience, and also that his thinking is confused on active and passive contemplation, and even doubts whether Baker himself had any experience of the mystical life. So, he concludes, this prolix and melancholy book, may suffice to guide some for a very great part of their lives, but that Fr. Baker cannot communicate what he does not possess (*Nemo dat quod non habet*) and therefore will be unable to show a true contemplative the way to the summit. He may even mislead him into thinking that what is merely a foothill is the massif of Mount Carmel.[48]

On the other hand, this is a learned and creative work and one unique in English Catholic spirituality. For parallels one must look back to the English mystical writers of the fourteenth century.

One wonders how these clandestinely printed volumes of devotion ever reached the Recusants in England, for whom many copies were intended. Evidence of such secret activities is, by its very nature, difficult to discover. The successes are silent: the failures are discovered and usually punished by the law. Two lists of books of a Roman Catholic nature seized by the searchers (seventeenth-century equivalents of customs men) at Newcastle-upon-Tyne are known.[49] The first consignment was almost certainly, because of the many copies of practically every book, intended for a distributor of illegal books, especially as they were in English or Latin and no other European language. The second consignment discovered was with equal probability intended for a priest, and might well have been a travelling priest's library, for it included a little missal for travelling priests[50] and theological and devotional works

---

[46] *The English Mystical Tradition* (1961), pp. 178-81.
[47] *Ibid.*, p. 160.　　　　　　　　　[48] *Ibid.*, p. 187.
[49] Respectively to be found in *Calendar of State Papers: Domestic: Charles I*, xxiv, No. 23, iii, Newcastle-upon-Tyne, "Popish Bookes taken in a Dutch Shippe the 1 of Apr. 1626" and *Calendar of State Papers: Domestic: Charles I*, xxvi, No. 16, vi, Newcastle-upon-Tyne, "A Catalogue of the Popish Bookes and Reliques of Popery seized on by the Searchers Men in searching of a Shipp in this Porte the last day of Aprile 1626."
[50] *Missale Parvum pro Sacerdotibus itinerantibus.*

in Hebrew, Greek, Italian, and French, as well as the customary English and Latin.

The names of Catholic devotional books are of special interest here, presumably because the first list included commonly used books, and the second list mentioned those of special professional interest to a priest in the English Mission. The first consignment seized on April 1, 1626, included one copy of the *Breviarium Romanum*, for a member of a religious order presumably, while there were twenty-five copies of the *Jesus Psalter*, and several copies of Luis de la Puente's *Meditations upon the Mysteries of our holy Fayth, with the practise of mentall prayer*, Thomas à Kempis's *The Following of Christ*, and of Persons's *A Christian Directory*. One can, therefore, infer that the devotional life of the less educated of Catholics centred on the Rosary,[51] the stations of the Cross (though these would be difficult to hide in a hurry), and the *Jesus Psalter*[52] with its 150 petitions, with fifteen decades for the fifteen chief petitions, and further divided into three series according to the three states of the mystical life—purgation, illumination, and union.

The second consignment may indicate the kind of treatises a priest on the English mission in the first year of the reign of Charles I would be reading. They would include Bellarmine's *The Art of Dying Well*, R[obert] S[outhwell's] *An Epistle of Comfort* (1593), Diego de Estella's *The Contempt of the World*, *St. Peters Complainte* and *Mary Magdalens Tears*, an unnamed work of

51 See Luca Pinelli, *The Virgin Maries Life*, tr. "R. G." and printed at Rouen in 1604, which was combined with *The Society of the Rosarie* in a St. Omer edition of 1624. Other similar books were: Alexis de Solo, *An Admirable Method to Love, Serve and Honour the B. Virgin Mary* (tr. "R.F.," Rouen, 1639); Thomas Worthington, *The Rosarie of our Ladie* (Antwerp, 1600); Sabin Chambers, *The Garden of our B. Lady. Or a devout manner, how to serve her in her Rosary* ([St. Omer], 1619); *The Society of the Rosary*, newly augmented ([St. Omer, possibly], ca. 1600). While there are many ways of meditating on the Rosary, the most important form is the official Dominican Rosary, comprising 150 "Aves," divided into fifteen "decades" which are subdivided for purposes of meditation into three parts of five decades each: meditation on the five joyful, the five dolorous, and the five glorious mysteries. These are, respectively, the Annunciation, Visitation, Nativity, and Finding of Christ in the Temple; Gethsemane, the Whipping of Christ, the Crown of Thorns, the Carrying of the Cross, the Crucifixion, the Resurrection, Ascension, Coming of the Holy Ghost, Assumption of the Virgin, and Coronation of the Virgin. (See Martz, *op. cit.*, pp. 101-102.) Legend is added to Scripture in these devotions, especially in the two concluding Marian mysteries. The popular piety of the laity was a combination of the Rosary and the Stations of the Cross.

52 This was attributed to Richard Whytford, a member of the Brigittine order. An edition of 1575 bore the title, *Certaine devout and Godly Petitions, commonly called Iesus Psalter*.

91

Dionysius the Areopagite and another unnamed of St. Bonaventure, as well as two of Tauler's works, namely, the *De Vita et Passione Salvatoris* and *Pious Meditations upon the Beads*.[53]

John Gee's *The Foot out of the Snare* (1624) is evidence for a long catalogue of books that have been sold "by the priests and their agents" during the previous two years. He mentions a priest who has rooms full of illicit religious books for sale near the Savoy, and refers to a wealthy vintner who stores them in a church, and tells how booksellers pay copyists of banned books and get four times the regular price for them. An easier way to get such volumes, though this required wealth, was to pick them up while travelling on the Continent.[54]

However these books of spirituality were obtained, they helped to keep the embers of the devotional life of the English Catholics glowing. More, they even passed on the fire to converts like Richard Crashaw from a strong Puritan family, and gained readers in adapted versions among both high Anglicans and supposedly low Puritans, as will be seen. So well trained were some lay Catholics that they retained their contemplative zeal in the unlikeliest situation—amid the corruption and worldly ambition of the court. One such was Sir Oliver Manners, the king's carver, who had been converted by Father John Gerard the Jesuit. The latter writes of his spiritual son: "You might see him in the court of the Presence Chamber, as it is called, when it was crowded with courtiers and famous ladies, turning aside to a window and reading a chapter of Thomas à Kempis's *Imitation of Christ*."[55]

3. *The Spirituality of the Caroline Divines*

A case can be made for combining the Caroline divines and the Puritan divines in a common spirituality termed "Anglican" for the piety of their laity was very much alike.[56] This, however, would not do justice to the historical antagonism between the two tradi-

[53] The first five items in this list are by Jesuits, which heightens the probability that this travelling library was destined for a Jesuit father, whose taste in spirituality was discriminating.

[54] Helen C. White, *op. cit.*, pp. 178-82.

[55] *John Gerard. The Autobiography of an Elizabethan* (tr. Philip Caraman, intro. Graham Greene, 1951), p. 367.

[56] A. Tindal Hart, *The Man in the Pew 1558-1660* (1966) writes of the typical Anglican holy household that "in addition to its regular round of worship and prayer, its Bible study and the reading of countless books of devotion, of which perhaps the favourites were Foxe's *Book of Martyrs*, Lewis Bayly's *Practice of Piety*, Jeremy Taylor's *Holy Living* and *Holy Dying*, and *The Whole Duty of Man*, it inculcated habits of personal discipline and social benevolence" (p. 189).

tions which finally issued in a permanent rupture in 1662 when the Puritans left the Church of England, if they had not already left for New England, and their new name was Dissenters or Nonconformists.

The growing fissure in the Church of England was, indeed, widened by the production of one of these Caroline books of devotion, namely, the anonymously published, *A Collection of Private Devotions in the practise of the Antient Church, called, The Hours of Prayers.* . . . . This was the work of John Cosin, subsequently Master of Peterhouse, Dean of Durham, and, in Restoration days, a reviser of the Book of Common Prayer and Bishop of Durham. It helped to cost his two major critics, William Prynne and Henry Burton, the one a fearless Presbyterian lawyer and the other an intrepid London Puritan divine, the cropping of their ears, and it led eventually to Cosin's going into exile after the downfall of his patron, Archbishop Laud and the death of his King, Charles I, who is rumoured to have instigated Cosin to prepare this very volume.

This notable but controversial volume is not a masterpiece of spirituality, as are most of the others we shall consider in detail. While a significant supplement to prayer, public or private, it is also an important pointer to the rapid growth of the high-church movement in the Church of England in the early years of the reign of the first Charles. Its sub-title, as if expecting opposition and trying to disarm it in advance, included, after "Hours of Praiers," the clause, "as they were much after this manner published by Autoritie of Queen ELISA, 1560," and, as a further sop, "TAKEN out of the Holy Scriptures, the Antient Fathers, and the Divine Service of our own Church."

The first edition of 1627 was followed by a second in 1655 and the ninth in 1693. Its Baroque frontispiece contained the Jesuit monogram, IHS surrounded by flames, suggestive of a monstrance, and was calculated to please royal, Catholic, and European taste, but to alienate democratic, Puritan, and English sensibilities. William Prynne in his punning title, *A Brief Survay and Censure of Mr. Cozens His Couzening Devotions*, bluntly asserted: "That booke, whose frontispiece, title, frame and method, stile, and phrases, yea, and doctrine too, is altogether Popish; must needes be meerely Popish, both in forme and matter."[57]

The contents of Cosin's book proved even more heinous in the

[57] *Op. cit.*, p. 38.

eyes of his Puritan critics. The preface reflects a strong and sarcastic anti-Puritan bias, with its scathing reference to "extemporall effusions of irksome and indigested praiers which they use to make, that herein are subject to no good order or form of words, but pray both what and how and when they list."[58] It claims that the first purpose of the book is to use the anciently approved forms of prayer of Christ's Church rather than the rude dictates which are framed by private spirits." Its second aim is to tell the world that England has neither set up a new faith nor a new church, neither has it "abandoned All the *Antient Forms of Piety and Devotion*," nor "taken away all the *Religious Exercises and Praiers of our Forefathers*," nor "despised all the old *Ceremonies*," nor have English Churchmen "cast behind us the Blessed Sacrament of Christ's Catholic Church."[59] The third value claimed for this book of devotions is that it will provide a means of private prayer for those prevented from attending public prayers who desire to practise religion. Finally, it was prepared "that those who perhaps are but coldly this way yet affected, might by others example bee stirr'd up to the like heavenly duty of performing their *Daily* and Christian Devotions, as beeing a work of all others most acceptable to his divine Majestie."[60]

This work is a return to the royal Tudor primers. Though Cosin claims his authority and example is Elizabeth's primer of 1560, this is itself largely dependent on the Reformed Catholic primer of Henry VIII of 1545. It could be legitimately argued that this is equally a briefer Breviary, with instruction on the Christian life, since it restores the prayers for the seven traditional hours of the day.[61]

This *horarium* provides practical instruction on prayer, forms of prayer, the Calendar, the Creed, the Lord's Prayer, the Deca-

---

[58] *Op. cit.* (edition of 1655, which is used throughout), sig. A5; the Bodleian Library copy in Oxford (shelfmark Douce C 111) is particularly interesting for its pertinent notes in the bibliographer's handwriting.

[59] *Ibid.*, sig. A6.   [60] *Ibid.*, sigs. A7-A7 verso.

[61] In fact, H. Boone Porter in an article, "Cosin's Hours of Prayer: a Liturgical Review" (*Theology*, 56, 1953, pp. 54-58) claims that the *Devotions*, since their first appearance in 1627, have been the classical English order of the Canonical Hours. Next to the various versions of the Prayer Book itself, they have been the most important Anglican liturgical compilation of the Reformation." Boone Porter further observes that "most of the classical Anglican writers urge at least a partial observation of the hours" by example or recommendation in their devotional treatises. This group and their works are: Andrewes's *Preces Privatae*, Laud's *Private Devotions*, Sherlock's *Practical Christian*, and the *Whole Duty of Man*.

logue, the Seven Sacraments (while insisting that Baptism and the Lord's Supper are "the two principal and true Sacraments"), and it lists the Spiritual Works of Mercy, and the Corporal Works of Mercy. It also contains abbreviated forms of the seven canonical hours of prayer, collects for the major festivals, the Seven Penitential Psalms, prayers before and after receiving the "Blessed Sacrament" and prayers to be used at Confession and Absolution, as well as forms for the sick and dying. Inevitably, also, prayers for the king and queen were included.

Cosin's ecclesiastical fidelity consists in keeping the Morning and Evening Offices close to those of the Prayer Book, while his originality is displayed in making Terce as an Office of the Holy Ghost and Sext and Nones as Offices of the Passion more consistently and relevantly so than in the Latin versions.

There are two major theories current as to the origin of this book. Evelyn the diarist reports a story he claimed to have confirmed from the lips of Cosin himself. This was that Charles I had commissioned the book, using Bishop White of Carlisle as his intermediary, and that the royal reason for the commission was because his Queen had remarked on the absence in the Church of England of any book of prayers to be used at regular intervals during the day like the Hours of Prayer in the church of Rome.[62] The other theory is the explanation offered by Jeremy Collier that the book was written at the request of the Countess of Denbigh (sister of Charles's favourite, the Duke of Buckingham), to offset her attraction to the Roman church.[63] The second theory is advanced three generations later than the event and *prima facie* is less likely to be true than the first. On the other hand, it is curious that if King Charles was its instigator there was no reference to this patronage in a dedication or preface, unless the King used Cosin as his stalking-horse to see how far he and Laud could move in a Catholic direction without seriously alienating a large number of his subjects. Perhaps the simplest explanation is that offered by C. J. Stranks[64] and partly suggested by the second edition, because it combines the first and second theories. Cosin says in the second edition that he compiled it for a friend's private use, without any

---

[62] *The Diary of John Evelyn* (ed. E. S. de Beer, Oxford, 1955), III, pp. 45-46. For another reference to this Roman Catholic taunt, see Sir Edwin Sandys, *Europae Speculum* (1673), pp. 87-88.

[63] *An Ecclesiastical History of Great Britain* (1708), p. 742.

[64] C. J. Stranks, *Anglican Devotion* (1961), p. 67.

intention of making it public, but that the friend had two hundred copies printed for his friends to avoid manuscript copying. Cosin was a collector of prayers and liturgies, and it is quite possible that he made printed copies available for both the King and the Countess.

How Catholic (as contrasted with Protestant) was Cosin's *Devotions?* Prynne felt that Cosin was cozening or cheating the English church and people. The author's sole aim, wrote Prynne, was "to introduce and usher Poperie into our Church" and he had tried to make Queen Elizabeth "the Patroness of this his Poperie" and to delude the simple people into believing she countenanced Popery.[65] He found four parallels to Cosin's work: The *Horas de Nuestra Senora* (Paris, 1556), the *Horae beatissimae Virginis Mariae secundum usum Saru* [Sarum, or Salisbury], Laurence Kellam's *Manuell of Praiers* (Douai, 1624), and *Our Ladies Primer in Latine and English* (Antwerp, 1604). He effectively demonstrated the Roman Catholic character of Cosin's sources by printing the *Devotions* and the supposed sources in parallel columns.

Cosin's other published Puritan critic was Henry Burton, the Rector of St. Matthew's Church, Friday Street, London. His work was *A Tryall of Private Devotion, or a Diall for the Houres of Prayer* (1628). His prefatory epistle deplores the inroads Arminianism and Popery have made into the Church of England in the previous seven years, observing that the most convenient and visible way of determining the degree of true religion is to visit any town or village on the Lord's Day to discover if it is treated as a holy day or only as a holiday. "That's the true touchstone of a truely religious man," since "The seventh day sanctifieth our six. . . ."[66] He contends that Cosin's book is turning the Church of England back to Roman Catholicism by reintroducing the seven Sacraments,[67] in referring to marriage as an "unnecessary avocation,"[68] by stating that the Sacraments are of the church's and not of Christ's appointment, by urging the restoration of the seven canonical hours and over-turning Queen Elizabeth's reduction of them to Matins and Evensong.[69] The crowning insult is the publication of the Jesuit emblem and symbol, IHS.[70] Burton

---

[65] *A Briefe Survay and Censure of Mr Cozens His Couzening Devotions* (1628), p. 3.

[66] *Ibid.,* sig. G2. [67] *Ibid.,* sigs. H2-H2 verso.

[68] *Ibid.,* sig. E4 verso. [69] *Ibid.,* sig. C4 verso.

[70] *Ibid.,* sig. C1 verso.

seems to be less choleric than the irascibly erudite and fulminating Prynne. He also marshalls his information more carefully. But he, too, can be vividly amusing in the satirical vein, as when he is protesting what he calls "Lent-relenting" and the eagerness with which the priest on Easter Day withdraws the veil which has obscured the images in the church, with the result that the worshippers "down they fall on their Maribones, beating their breasts more eagerly now than ever, as imputing it to their sinnes, that they have been so long withheld from their prettie-pettie gods."[71]

The founder of the Anglo-Catholic tradition in theology was Hooker, while in patristic scholarship, preaching, spirituality and the exalted role of a truly pastoral bishop, it was Lancelot Andrewes, although he can only be called a Caroline divine by a hair's breadth, since he died a year after Charles I came to the throne. His chief contribution to spirituality (apart from the dignity and beauty of the ceremonial with which he celebrated at the service of Holy Communion in the Prayer Book)[72] was his *Preces Privatae*, which did not appear in a complete edition until 1675, though a tolerable edition from the Greek text was translated and issued by Drake in 1648, twenty-two years after his death,[73] and twenty-one years after the first edition of Cosin's *Devotions*.

The *Private Prayers* (to translate the title) were found in manuscript after Andrewes's death, and it was said that the pages were frayed and worn away by the constant pressure of his fingers and the stains made by his copious tears. They are the index to the mind and heart of a distinguished scholar (the Pentateuch and some of the historical books of the Authorized or King James Version of the Scriptures are part of his lasting memorial), a cultivated mind, a tender spirit, and a saintly man. There are echoes in the *Preces* of his knowledge of the Greek and Latin Fathers, the medieval Schoolmen and the mystics, the great pagan classical authors such as Sophocles, Euripides, Aristophanes, Virgil, Seneca and Horace, as well as of the moderns like Erasmus. He also had an unrivalled knowledge of the ancient liturgies and other forms of prayer, and even of Knox's *Book of Common Order*, and made

71 *Ibid.*, sig. I1.

72 See the illustration of the altar arrangements and furnishings in his chapel at Winchester in P. A. Welsby, *Lancelot Andrewes* (1958).

73 Parts of the *Preces* appeared in *Institutiones Piae* (1630) prepared by his secretary, Henry Isaacson. The best modern edition, with critical introduction, is that of F. E. Brightman, published in 1903.

use of the Roman Missal and Breviary of his day, as well as of the English Prayer Book and primers.

In structure the *Preces* are a superb example of the old type of devotional book, the manual of prayers for every day, which stretches back through Protestant primers to their Catholic medieval examples. They are written like prose poems, with broken lines, deliberately so as to suggest the rhythms and pauses of contemplative meditation. They are usually in Greek or Hebrew, but occasionally in Latin. Their concision means that they are a series of direction posts on the map of prayer, but not walking-talking guides to the terrain. In these succinct prayers there is neither garrulity nor sentimentality, but catholicity and homely practicality. The joins of this mosaic of heterogeneous sources are forgotten, so well do the individual phrases fit together. Louis Bouyer reminds us that Cardinal Newman kept these prayers of Andrewes on his *prie-dieu* where he offered his thanksgiving after Mass, and says of them: "Never has the image of a bee going from flower to flower to gather a honey of fragrant simplicity been so apt."[74]

Andrewes has four types of devotions in his *Preces Privatae*: prayers of penance; meditations on the mystery of faith (which was always a paradox that transcended reason for Andrewes who yet believed with St. Anselm of Canterbury that faith is the clue to understanding);[75] prayers of intercession for all kinds and conditions of people with a deeply practical knowledge of their needs; and throughout an inexhaustible fountain of praise for God as creator, sustainer, and redeemer of the world.

One example of these "golden zig-zag prayers," as the Abbé Brémond called them, must be given to show their skeletal structure, concise directions, and richness of allusion, yet all are articulated into an objective whole, concentrating on love to God and charity to mankind and excluding the man who is on his knees writing them or praying them. This is the concluding "Praise" of the first day's prayers:

> Let us lift up our hearts unto the Lord, as it is very meet, right, and our bounden duty, that we should *in* all, and *for* all Things, *at* all *Times*, *in* all *Places*, by all *Means*, ever, every where, every way,

[74] *Orthodox Spirituality and Protestant and Anglican Spirituality* (Paris, 1963, tr. Barbara Wall, 1969), p. 111.

[75] Anselm's famous definition of the relationship of faith and intelligence was *credo ut intelligam* (I believe in order to comprehend).

Make mention of Thee,
Confess to Thee,
Bless Thee,
Praise Thee,
Sing laud to Thee,
Give Thanks to Thee,
    Creator,
    Nourisher,
    Preserver,
    Governor,
The   Physitian,   of all
    Benefactor,
    Perfector,
    Lord & Father,
    King & God
The   Fountain of Life and Immortality
    Treasury of eternal good things:
      Whom
The   Heavens, and the Heavens of Heavens,
    Angels, and all the Celestial Powers sing praise unto;
Uncessantly crying one to another,
    (and we, base and unworthy we, with them under their feet)
    Holy, Holy, Holy,
Lord God of Hosts,
    Heaven and Earth is full of the Majesty of Thy Glory,
    Blessed be the Glory of the Lord from His place.
    Divinity,
    Incomprehensibleness,
For His   Sublimity,
    Dominion,
    Almightiness,
    Eternity,
    Praevision and Providence
        my God, my
    Strength and Stay,
    Refuge & Deliverer,
    Helper & Defender,
    Horn of salvation,
        and my Lifter up.[76]

[76] *A Manual of the Private Devotions and Meditations of the Right Reverend Father in God, Lancelot Andrewes* (tr. and ed. R. Drake, 1648), pp. 86-89.

This superb prayer begins with the Preface in the Prayer of Consecration in the Book of Common Prayer, then moves from duty to thanksgiving for the divine roles by which God helps men, and then into the Heaven of Heavens where the *Tersanctus* of the cherubim and the saints surrounding the throne of God allows unworthy humans to join in the chorus of adoration of God's transcendent attributes, and, by mentioning his prevision and providence prepares for the return to earth, sustained by the comfort of his stabilising, liberating, aiding, saving, and encouraging divine presence. The whole prayer is like Jacob's ladder, in that the petitions or ascriptions are like angels ascending to heaven and returning down the ladder to earth carrying the blessed booty of grace.

Helen C. White has caught the distinctive character of the spirituality of Andrewes, which, in her view resembles that of the *Imitatio Christi* and which she described as a savouring or long brooding over things first thought of by others and meditated on so thoroughly that they have become one's own, and an even deeper quality, that "intimately as they seem to spring from the heart of the writer, they have a certain austerity, a certain objective impersonality, as if in the presence of its God the soul sheds its idiosyncrasy and laying down all shadow of temperament and whim, finds in what is least personal, the fullest expression of its innermost being."[77] What is most distinctive in Andrewes, apart from his rich reading and meditation, is a profound concern for the unity of the Church of Christ throughout the world and a charity sympathetic enough to envision the plight of the world's poor in their various callings, all *sub specie aeternitatis*. His heritage was nobly possessed by Donne, Herbert, Ferrar, Jeremy Taylor, and others.

It is difficult, at the outset, to imagine a spirit and temper more unlike Andrewes than John Donne, author of *Devotions upon Emergent Occasions*, apart from their common erudition and metaphysical style of preaching. For if Andrewes was classical and objective, Donne was romantic and subjective. One cannot imagine Andrewes for all his capacity to dazzle the court with the wordplay of his sermons, ever preaching like Donne in his winding-sheet, drawing attention to the man as much as to his message. It is true, at least for moderns, that they go to Andrewes for what he writes, but to Donne because of his manner of writing. Andrewes, like the last medievalist, submits to the divine gover-

[77] Helen C. White, *op. cit.*, p. 249.

nance with joy; Donne, like Jacob, fights with God's angel to the very break of day. He would, like his own poem suggests, be the kind of pilgrim who rides westward on Good Friday. Andrewes was a Puritan (at least on the Sabbatarian issue) before he became a high Anglican, but there never was, so far as is known, a time when he was not a Christian. Donne had been a moral prodigal and a sceptic, knowing the new philosophy that puts all in doubt. Andrewes offers a Johannine spirituality, Donne is a doubting Thomas who must fight for faith and struggle against sensuality. Andrewes is lost in God in his spirituality; Donne is lost in admiring Donne trying to be lost in God. Brilliant in his psychological penetration and wide-ranging imagination that garners from a wide direct experience, as well as from unusually exotic sources of knowledge derived from reading, Donne yet incurs a suspicion of the impure motive, of the exhibitionist.[78] His rhetoric exceeds even that of Andrewes in its sustained power and daring, but his *Devotions* seem too contrived to suit the poor in spirit. They were printed immediately after they were written; those of Andrewes were *Privatae*: the difference is significant.

It began as a kind of spiritual diary kept during a serious illness, but it tells one much more about the ways of Donne than the ways of God and it has more literary and psychological interest than spiritual. Individual prayers capture the passionate longing for God found in some of the sermons and the divine poems, but it is perhaps in the latter his finest spirituality is to be found.

> There is his searing honesty:
> > I durst not view heaven yesterday; and to day
> > In prayers and flattering speeches I court God:
> > Tomorrow I quake with the true feare of his rod.[79]

There is his passionate and paradoxical cry for God to conquer him:

> Batter my heart, three-person'd God . . .
> > . . . for I
> Except you enthrall mee, never shall be free,
> Nor ever chast, except you ravish mee.[80]

There is the hope that the civil war between spirit and sense, that was forever waging in himself would be overcome in death, at once

78 T. S. Eliot, *For Lancelot Andrewes* (1928), p. 20.
79 *Holy Sonnets*, No. 19.
80 *The Divine Poems* (ed. Helen Gardner, Oxford, 1952), p. 11.

despair to the natural man and deliverance to the spiritual, where the divine love would prove stronger than death:

I joy, that in these straits I see my West;
    For though theire currants yeeld return to none,
What shall my West hurt me? As West and East
    In all flatt Maps (and I am one) are one,
So death doth teach the Resurrection. . . .

We thinke that Paradise and Calvarie
    Christs Crosse, and Adam's tree, stood in one place;
Look Lord, and find both Adams built in me;
    As the first Adams sweat surrounds my face,
May the last Adams blood my soule embrace.

    So, in his purple wrapp'd receive me Lord,
        By these his thrones give me his other Crowne;
    And as to others Soules I preach'd thy Word,
        Be this my Text, my Sermon to mine owne,
        Therefore that he may raise the Lord throwes down.[81]

The influence of the Ignatian spirituality on this former Catholic is exceedingly strong, and it may account in part for Donne's hard gaze at the many forms of death that terrify him in order to attain to the resolution that will keep him safe with Christ and search for the stratagems to humiliate pride, as well as the severe self-analysis that make him realize his chief temptations are fear and intellectual arrogance.[82]

George Herbert (1593-1633), according to Louis L. Martz, shows greater affinity to the Salesian than the Ignatian spirituality and temper.[83] Earlier in his life than Donne he gave up the dazzle of the court and the intellectual attractions of Cambridge, where he was public orator of the university, to become an exemplary country parson, though he came of aristocratic lineage and his elder brother Lord Herbert of Cherbury was the first English Deist and his beautiful and devout mother Lady Magdalen, Sir Philip Sidney's sister, had been celebrated by Donne in the immortal couplet:

[81] *Ibid.*, p. 30.
[82] See Louis L. Martz, *The Poetry of Meditation*, pp. 38, 43-56, 106, 219-20, where it is claimed that there is strong Jesuit influence upon Donne's religious poetry. Martz's brilliant thesis is that Jesuit methods of meditation influenced Donne, the Salesian method, Herbert, and the Augustinian (via Bonaventura) Vaughan and Traherne.
[83] *Ibid.*, pp. 58, 154-59, 299, 318.

No Spring, nor Summer hath such grace,
As I have seen in one Autumnal face.[84]

Herbert[85] is widely regarded as the model country priest of the
Church of England of his century, a high Anglican counterpart to
the Puritan pastor, Richard Baxter. His life retold eulogistically
by Izaak Walton, his own admirable handbook on the ministry,
*A Priest to the Temple, or the Country Parson, His Character and
Rule of Holy Life*, and, supremely, his sacred poems, all create the
image. In fact, however, he had been a priest only two years as
Rector of Bemerton, near to Salisbury, when he died. This hardly
gave him time to warrant the encomiums poured upon him as a
pastor, but it was time enough to provide us with a glimpse that
was exemplary in its holiness, though we have no devotional treatise written by him.

In *A Priest to the Temple*, he insists on two basic spiritual
requirements, "because the two highest points of life wherein a
Christian is most seen are patience and mortification—patience in
regard of afflictions, mortifications in regard to lusts and affections— . . ."[86] He expects the country parson not only to be an
expert on agriculture, as well as in the Scriptures in which he will
find "precepts for life, doctrines for knowledge, examples for illustration, and promises for comfort."[87] He also assumes that he will
be familiar with the Fathers and the Schoolmen, and that he will
make a commonplace book of divinity. He is perceptive in pointing
out that the parson will fail as an interpreter of the Scriptures
unless he lives a holy life and calls in the aid of prayer.

Such was the theory, but what of Herbert's practice? According
to Walton, Herbert's devotion to God both public and private
matched the theory. He read divine service in full from the Book
of Common Prayer twice each Sunday, preaching in the morning
and catechising in the afternoon, and celebrating Holy Communion about six times each year. More impressive still was his daily
practice of reading Matins and Evensong at the canonical times
with his whole family, namely, at 10:00 A.M. and 4:00 P.M.[88]
Walton adds the touch that canonises Herbert: "and some of the

84 Donne's ninth elegy, "The Autumnal."
85 See an early edition, *The English Works of George Herbert*, 3 Vols. (ed.
G. H. Palmer, Boston and New York, 1905), and *The Works of George Herbert*
(ed. F. E. Hutchinson, 2nd edn., Oxford, 1945).
86 *Works* (ed. Palmer, 1905), I, p. 213.
87 *Ibid.*, I, pp. 215-17.
88 Izaak Walton, *The Life of George Herbert* (ed. George Saintsbury, World's
Classics edn.), pp. 301-302.

meaner sort of his parish did so love and reverence Mr. Herbert that they would let their plough rest when Mr. Herbert's Saints'-Bell rung to prayers, that they might also offer their devotions to God with him."[89] Nor, according to the same authority, did he neglect his private prayers, "nor those prayers that he thought himself bound to perform with his family, which was always a set form, and not long. And he did always conclude them with that Collect which the Church hath appointed for the day or week."[90]

It is in his poetry above all that Herbert's spirituality soars. *The Temple*, a series of sacred poems carefully interrelated, includes one poem at least that says more about devotion and its potentialities than many pedestrian treatises. It deserves full citation:

> Prayer the Churches banquet, Angels age,
>   Gods breath in man returning to his birth,
>   The soul in paraphrase, heart in pilgrimage,
> The Christian plummet sounding heav'n and earth;
> Engine against th'Almightie, sinners towre,
>   Reversed thunder, Christ-side-piercing spear,
>   The six-daies world transposing in an houre,
>
> A kinde of tune, which all things heare and fear;
> Softnesse, and peace, and joy, and love, and blisse,
>   Exalted Manna, gladnesse of the best,
>   Heaven in ordinarie, man well drest,
> The milkie way, the bird of Paradise,
>   Church-bels beyond the starres heard, the souls bloud,
>   The land of spices; something understood.[91]

Such paradoxes as "reversed thunder" Luther or Kierkegaard would have appreciated, and such ecstasy straining the language to its limits to express the ineffable the mystics would appreciate. But Herbert knew that the deepest unity is reached in uniting with the suffering Redeemer, and this he expressed with characteristic simplicity and sincerity in the eucharistic poem, "The Banquet":

> But as pomanders and wood,
>   Still are good,
>   Yet being bruis'd are better sented,

[89] *Ibid.*   [90] *Ibid.*
[91] *Works* (ed. Hutchinson, 1945), p. 51.

God, to show how farre His love
Could improve
Here, as broken, is presented.[92]

Metaphysical poets other than Donne and Herbert made their contribution to spirituality, either directly like Traherne in his *Centuries of Meditations* (1653), which had little impact in its own time and was only rediscovered in 1895, and like Vaughan in his *Mount of Olives*, or indirectly in their poems which depicted the splendour of God and the love of Christ irradiating all things, save where the shadow of sin obscured. Space forces compression and omission of all these religious poems to concentrate on treatises of devotion that were either masterpieces or had profound popular impact, or to describe unusual experiments in spirituality such as Little Gidding, the creation of Nicholas Ferrar.[93]

This consecrated spirit was a deacon of the Church of England who never became a priest, but had been a high executive of the Virginia Company and travelled widely in Germany, France, Italy, and Spain. In his travels he had found little help from the rather Quietistical Catholic circles he frequented, so he returned greatly enamoured of the piety of the Church of England. At Little Gidding, near Huntingdon and fairly near to Cambridge, he established a community of about thirty persons who shared his family monasticism. Its memory has been kept green in a Victorian novel, *John Inglesant* by J. H. Shorthouse, and in the final one of T. S. Eliot's *Four Quartets*.

The community, centred on his family and that of his brother-in-law, to which neighbouring friends came from time to time, lived a life of prayer and work according to a strict rule. At the beginning of every hour, from 6:00 A.M. to 8:00 P.M., there was an office lasting for about a quarter of an hour, in which several groups in the community took their turn. This office comprised a hymn and portions from the Psalms and Gospels, so that the entire Psalter was recited each day and the Gospels once a month. Furthermore, two or more members kept a vigil from 9:00 P.M. to 1:00 A.M. while reciting the Psalter once more. Charles I visited the community in 1633 and called it his "little Arminian Nunnery."

92 *Ibid.*, p. 181.
93 See B. Blackstone, *The Ferrar Papers* (1938), which includes a critical ed. of a contemporary life written by Nicholas's brother, John Ferrar; also A. L. Maycock, *Nicholas Ferrar of Little Gidding* (1938), and the D.N.B. life by M. Creighton, XVIII (1889), pp. 377-80, and the *Oxford Dictionary of the Christian Church* (ed. F. L. Cross, reprint of 1963), pp. 500b-501a.

The community was chiefly engaged in the adoration of God, but its members also visited the sick and the poor of the village and taught the children the Psalms. Such recreations as they had included gardening, manuscript illumination, and exquisite book-binding. The British Museum has an example of this in the cover for a harmony of the Gospels, and the Page liturgical collection at the Huntington Library in California has a prayer book of Little Gidding decorated by the community which is reproduced in the illustrations of the present volume.

Mary Collett of the community, inaccurately described in *John Inglesant* as having a love affair, consecrated herself to Christ as a virgin. The austerities of the founder, Ferrar, were also genuine. He kept the late watch in the chapel in his manor house two or three times a week and slept only four hours on other nights, and was sparing in eating and drinking. His piety was modelled upon the Bible and in a filial conformity with the canons of the Church of England. He died in 1637, but the community was not disbanded until 1646, after being the subject of several Puritan criticisms. One of these, printed in 1646, shows how its author was offended by what he thought to be the "idolatry" of the chapel, but he could not—fortunately for another age—forget it, so he wrote:

> I observed the Chapel in general to be fairly and spaciously adorned with herbs and flowers, natural and artificial, and upon every pillar along both sides of the chapel . . . tapers (I mean great Virgin-wax candles on every pillar). The half-pace [a semi-step dividing nave and east end?] was all covered with tapestry, and upon that half-pace stood the Altar-like Table, with a rich carpet hanging very large on the half-pace, and some plate, as a chalice and candlesticks . . . a laver and cover all of brass, cut and carved with imagery work . . . and the cover had a cross erected on it. . . .[94]

Here for twenty-one years could be found the Caroline Anglican holiness of beauty, the fit context for the beauty of holiness.

No Caroline divine has exhibited more beauty in his style than Jeremy Taylor (1613-1667) whose loyalty to the Church of England during the days of the Commonwealth and Protectorate were

[94] *The Arminian Nunnery, or, A Brief Description and Relation of the late Erected Monasticall Place called the Arminian Nunnery at Little Gidding in Huntingdonshire* (1641), pp. 7-8.

honoured by his consecration soon after the Restoration to the Irish see of Down and Connor, to which Dromore was joined later, the cathedral of which he built and was buried in. His *Holy Living* (1650) and *Holy Dying* (1651) are both masterpieces and yet representative of Anglican devotional writing at this time at its best. Taylor was erudite, quarrying from obscure and exotic as well as traditional mines, a distinguished casuist, a splendid preacher, a stylist of magnificence, a man combining sympathy and imagination with practicality, all directed by a pastoral heart. In the beginning of *Holy Living*, he complained that as a consequence of the Civil War religion was "painted upon banners, and thrust out of churches." He considered even more serious the fact that God was worshipped, "not as he is, the Father of our Lord Jesus Christ, and afflicted Prince, the King of Sufferings; nor as the God of peace; . . . but . . . rather as the Lord of hosts, which title He was pleased to lay aside when the Kingdom of the Gospel was preached by the Prince of Peace."[95] So distressed was the state of the Church of England in 1650, with the use of the Prayer Book forbidden, and many of the bishops silenced, that Taylor felt it to be his duty to encourage Anglicans in faith and hope. Under the onslaughts of successful Calvinism it seemed that some of them doubted whether they were saved, ironically the very problem that over-scrupulous Puritan spirits had felt some forty years earlier about their election. Taylor in one pithy paragraph enumerates twelve signs of "grace and predestination" to prove that those who have them as certainly belong to God and are His sons as certainly as they are His creatures.[96]

Holy Living is a combination of a guide to prayer, a collection of prayers, a book of meditations, and a book of general directions for living the good life, all in one literary parcel. "I thought," he wrote in the introduction as he recalled the difficulty of being loyal to the dispossessed Church of England, "I had reasons enough inviting me to draw into one body those advices which the several necessities of many men must use at some time or another and many of them daily: that by a collection of holy precepts they might less feel the want of personal and attending guides, and that the rules for conduct of souls might be committed to a book which they might always have; since they could not always have a prophet

[95] *The Rule and Exercises of Holy Living* (ed. A. R. Waller, 1901), p. 1.
[96] *Ibid.*, p. 3.

at their needs, nor be suffered to go up to the house of the Lord to inquire of the appointed oracle."[97]

The book has an introduction followed by four chapters. The introduction affirms that there are three instruments or helps to a holy life: "care of our time," "purity of intention," and "the practise of the presence of God." The first chapter is concerned with the right use of time, the next with the duties the soul owes to itself, the third with duties owed to others imposed by Christian justice, and the last chapter with the duties we owe to God.

It is this last and longest section that is chiefly concerned with spirituality. The primary demand is for faith, through which we believe in God's self-revelation, which motivates us to pray and enact good works, and which is also the basis of hope in God's bounty for time and for eternity. Of these the chief blessing is love, for this is to receive God himself, and it evokes the response of human love in return. But this does not, and should not in Taylor's view, lead to supernatural and ecstatic visions or trances. He insisted upon the quietness of the Divine approach: "It is sweet, even, and full of tranquility; having in it no violences or transportations, but going on in a course of holy actions and duties which are proportionable to our condition and present state."[98]

Bible reading and fasting are recommended as aids for the development of the soul. The Word of God is the foundation of Christian doctrine and duty. A soul thus nourished upon the Scriptures and prayer must serve its neighbour with superabounding charity.

Holy Dying was written for Lady Carbery, Taylor's patroness in Golden Grove, Carmarthenshire, but she died before it was completed, and at her funeral he preached the greatest panegyric of its kind in the English language.[99] His wife, to whom he had been long and happily married, died about the same time. His accustomed spirit of joyful acceptance of all that God sends is still there, but the trumpet is muted, and the shining confidence is framed in clouds. This was no academic exercise in trying to console the sick and dying and those who minister to them: this intensely sympathetic divine was describing and prescribing for his own pain.

He begins by warning against postponing repentance, the beginning of the godly life, until sickness starts, because then

---

[97] *Ibid.*, pp. 1-2.   [98] *Ibid.*, p. 158.   [99] See Chap. IV, Sect. 4.

there are lacking both mental clarity and physical vigour. He is highly critical of the church of Rome's emphasis on extreme unction, because it was often used "when the man is half dead, when he can exercise no act of understanding."

This briefer companion volume keeps to the essentials in trying to persuade the healthy that sickness and death are subjects for immediate consideration, and not to be postponed. So the opening chapter by reflection, and the second chapter by the use of religious exercises, stresses the brevity of human life and its unexpected termination. The third chapter treats the special temptations induced or increased by sickness, while the fourth deals with the special graces elicited in those who count on God's continuing goodness, turning sickness into a school of virtue. The last chapter expounds the duties of a priest ministering to the sick and closes with a moving account of the duties of relatives to the dying.

One citation from this curiously erudite and richly wrought tapestry must suffice for the many passages deserving citation. It tells magnificently of the equalising brevity of human life in the long span of the historical centuries:

A man may read a sermon, the best and most passionate that ever may be preached, if he shall but enter into the sepulchres of kings. In the same Escurial where the Spanish princes live in greatness and power, and decree war or peace, they have wisely placed a cemetery where their ashes and their glory shall sleep till time shall be no more; and where our kings have been crowned, their ancestors lay interred, and they must walk over their grandsire's head to take his crown. There is an acre sown with royal seed, the copy of the greatest change from rich to naked, from ceiled roofs to arched coffins, from living like gods to die like men. There is enough to cool the flames of lust, to abate the heights of pride, to appease the itch of covetous desires, to sully and dash out the dissembling colours of a lustful, artificial, and imaginary beauty. There the warlike and the peaceful, the fortunate and the miserable, the beloved and the despised princes mingle their dust, and pay down their symbol of mortality, and tell all the world that when we die our ashes shall be equal to kings, and our accounts easier, and our pains or our crowns shall be less.[100]

[100] *The Rule and Exercises of Holy Dying* (ed. A. R. Waller, 1901), pp. 28-29.

This book, of the *ars moriendi* genre, was so obviously a twin of its immediate predecessor that it was soon bound up with it, and *Holy Living* and *Holy Dying* were thought of as a single book. It has had an incalculable influence on English life and even played a part in starting two of England's later great religious movements, Methodism and Tractarianism.[101] John Wesley read it while a young man at Oxford and, as a result, began to doubt if he was saved; he also attributed to it his keeping a journal.[102] Also, John Keble, whose sermon on "National Apostasy" from the pulpit of St. Mary's Church is generally accepted as marking the beginning of the Oxford Movement in 1833, studied Taylor's companion volumes sixteen years earlier, evaluating them as an epoch in his religious life.[103]

What are Jeremy Taylor's leading characteristics? First, he expresses great tenderness of devotion, but no ecstasy, no delight in tears for their own sake, no posturing. He also exhibits that sobriety and moderation which the Caroline divines thought should mark the Christian life. Taylor recaptures the spirit of medieval devotion, as in the following "Act of Desire" in a Communion meditation: "O now come Lord Jesus, come quickly; my heart is desirous of thy presence and thirsty of thy grace, and would fain entertain thee, not as a guest but as an inhabitant, as the Lord of all my faculties. Enter in and take possession, and dwell with me for ever; that I also may dwell in the heart of my dearest Lord, which was opened for me with a spear and love."[104]

Taylor, like the metaphysical poets and other Caroline divines, sees through a transparent world to its Creator, or, to change the metaphor, views all creatures as ladders leading up to God. "Let everything you see," he writes, "represent to your spirit the presence, the excellence and the power of God; for so shall your actions be done more frequently with an actual eye to God's presence by your often seeing him in the glass of the Creation."[105] Also, let the human creation prove worthy of its Creator: "Let us remember that God is in us, and that we are in Him: we are His workman-

---

[101] Stranks, *op. cit.*, p. 93; also see R. Southey's *Life of Wesley* (1848), I, p. 3. I am indebted to Canon C. J. Stranks's book for this reference and for the two immediately following.

[102] See *The Journal of John Wesley*, 8 Vols. (ed. Nehemiah Curnock, 1909), I, p. 42.

[103] See J. T. Coleridge, *Memoir of John Keble* (Oxford, 1870), p. 68.

[104] *The Rule and Exercises of Holy Living* (ed. A. R. Waller, 1901), II, p. 186.

[105] *Ibid.*, I, p. 45.

ship, let us not deface it; we are in His presence, let us not pollute it by unholy and impure actions."[106]

Taylor is, also, the humanist as well as the Christian in his concern to educate people out of their follies, inconsistencies, and absurdities; in his use of illustrations to bring the truth home to them (he is a master of sustained metaphors, vivid word-painting and of simpler similes); in his use of pre-Christian classical authors; and, above all, in his rational desire to remove obscurity and paradox. All his writing is reminiscent of *l'Humanisme Dévot*, Abbé Brémond's term for the French spirituality of the seventeenth century in his monumental *Histoire du Sentiment Religieux en France*.

A closing citation from *Holy Living* on contentment will reveal Taylor's human qualities of sympathy and helpfulness that make this book break through the moulds of his religion and century in a deep understanding of the perennial human condition:

> We are in the world like men playing at tables; the chance is not in our power, but to play it is; and when it is fallen we must manage it as we can; and let nothing trouble us but when we do a base action, or speak like a fool, or think wickedly: these things God hath put into our powers; but concerning those things which are wholly in the choice of another, they cannot fall under our deliberations, and therefore neither are they fit for our passions. My fear may make me miserable, but it cannot prevent what another hath in his power and purpose: and prosperities can only be enjoyed by them who fear not at all to lose them; since the amazement and passion concerning the future takes off all the pleasure of the present possession, therefore if thou hast lost thy hand, do not also lose thy constancy: and if thou must die a little sooner, yet do not die impatiently. For no chance is evil to him that is content, and to a man nothing is miserable unless it be unreasonable. No man can make another man to be his slave unless he hath first enslaved himself to life and death, to pleasure or pain, to hope or fear: command these passions, and you are freer than the Parthian kings.[107]

All other writings on spirituality among high-church divines in this century are necessarily anticlimactic after Jeremy Taylor, and will therefore receive the briefest treatment.

---

[106] *Ibid.*, I, p. 46.   [107] *Ibid.*, I, pp. 147-48.

4. *Popular Anglican Spirituality and Liturgical Devotions*

The two most popular devotional guides in the seventeenth century were *The Practice of Piety, Directing a Christian how to walk with God*, the earliest recorded edition of which appeared in 1612, and *The Whole Duty of Man* published in 1657. Both were anonymous, but the former was soon claimed to be the work of Lewis Bayly, Bishop of Bangor in North Wales.[108] The author of *The Whole Duty of Man* is still veiled in obscurity, though he was a royalist, a loyal churchman in the days when Anglicanism was in the shadows, and probably a clergyman. Intriguingly enough all three of the names put forward as putative authors were at one time or another canons of Christ Church, Oxford: the theologian Dr. William Hammond, Dr. John Fell (Dean of Christ Church in November 1660 to which was added the office of Bishop of Oxford in 1676), and Dr. Richard Allestree (Regius Professor of Divinity at Oxford from 1663 to 1679), the most probable author.[109]

Both books were widely influential, Bayly's for four of the first five decades and Allestree's for the last five decades of the century. Bayly's was influential when Calvinism was the dominant theology, Allestree's when Arminianism was on the eve of its victory and through the era of rationalistic moralism. Though it would be inaccurate to call any bishop a Puritan, as has been done in the case of Bayly, he seems to have followed Calvin in everything except church order, and therefore his work was eagerly purchased and used in Puritan circles,[110] although dedicated to Prince Charles, afterwards Charles I. It reached its twenty-fifth edition by 1630, its fifty-ninth in 1735, and was last republished in 1848.[111] Allestree's book reached its twenty-eighth edition by 1790. While it appealed to all classes, its tone was definitely high church. Its orthodoxy, rationality, sobriety, practicality and prudence made it particularly suitable as a guide to eighteenth-century

[108] A chaplain to Prince Henry, his Puritan views brought royal disfavour, so he apparently trimmed his sails, and was appointed chaplain to James I in 1616, and later in the same year Bishop of Bangor in North Wales. The best account of him and his devotional handbook is J. E. Bailey, "Bishop Lewis Bayly and his *Practice of Piety*" in *The Manchester Quarterly*, II (1883), pp. 221-39. His contentiousness made many enemies for him, not to mention a yawning gap between profession and practice. See H. R. Trevor-Roper, *Archbishop Laud* (1940), p. 188.

[109] See Paul Elmen, "Richard Allestree and *The Whole Duty of Man* in *The Library*" (5th series), VI, pp. 19-27.

[110] See Gordon S. Wakefield, *Puritan Devotion* (1957), p. 4.

[111] It was translated into French in 1625, Welsh in 1630 (the year before Bishop Bayly's death), German in 1629, Polish in 1647, and into a North American Indian dialect in 1665 at Cambridge, Massachusetts.

piety when it was even more popular than in the seventeenth century.

Bayly in the epistle which prefaces *The Practice of Piety* provides both incentives to piety and dissuasives from its disuse: "For as Moses his face, by often talking with God, shined in the eyes of the *People,* so by frequent praying (which is our talking to God) and hearing the Word (which is God speaking unto us), we shall be changed from glory to glorie, by the Spirit of the Lord, to the Image of the Lord."[112] Piety "hath the promise of this life and that which shall never end. But without Pietie, there is no internall comfort to be found in Conscience nor externall peace to be looked for in the World, nor any eternall happiness to be hoped for in Heaven."[113]

His work combines meditations and prayers, together with the noncontroversial elements of the Protestant conception of Christian practice. The nature of God, the misery of an unreconciled, and the blessedness in life and death of a man reconciled to God in Christ, take up the first 103 pages. The next 234 pages are concerned with seven obstacles to piety, reading the Bible beneficially once a year, and prayers for the morning and evening. Meditations and prayers for a godly householder, family prayers, graces before and after meals, a lengthy discourse on the Sabbath day, and prayers for the Sabbath occupy the next 163 pages. Fasting, giving alms, feasting, meditations on receiving Holy Communion together with a confession of sin and a soliloquy before and a prayer after reception take up the next 115 pages. Then there follows a large miscellaneous collection of directions, meditations, and prayers, for the beginning of sickness, when making one's will, "comfortable thoughts against despair," consolation for one about to die, "the last speech of a godly man dying," and a controversial set of meditations on martyrdom, attempting to prove that the martyrs of Popery cannot be found. This book of almost 800 pages ends with a colloquy between Christ and the soul about the efficacy of his Passion, and the soul's soliloquy addressed to Christ her Saviour.

Bayly provided the model for Puritan and "low church"[114] devo-

---

112 *Op. cit.* (11th edn. of 1619), sig. A5 verso.

113 *Ibid.*, sigs. A6-A6 verso.

114 This term is anachronistic but it points to an important fact: namely, that there was a Puritan Anglicanism, that is, Puritanism *within* the Church of England until 1645, when Parliament and the Westminster Assembly of Divines established Puritanism in its Presbyterian and Independent forms as the officially

tion, by his recommendation that Bible study was as necessary as prayer and meditation. One chapter of the Bible was to be read before leaving the bedroom, another at noon, and a third at night. If this method was kept up regularly, and the part of the Psalter appointed for the day in the Book of Common Prayer, then the whole Bible would be read through once a year, six chapters excepted which could be added for December. The result of Bible reading should be a heart sorrowing for sin, and a resolve (assisted by divine grace) to amend. An hour should be given to private prayer, according to Bayly, and the same time to household prayer. Christians are then ready to do their daily work fortified by the promises of God and the directions of the Word of God. The product of such a work of piety would be perhaps excessively conscious of human sin, original and actual, but would never dare to be trivial with God, and it would seem to mould men and women of gravity and dignity, as well as intrepidity. Fearing God, they were unafraid of men. Bayly shows us the profound respect for the Bible as the guide in all aspects of living, an insistence on morality, a sense of individual responsibility before God, and the unremitting effort to justify justification by faith and make one's election sure, which was at the heart of Protestantism in its Calvinist manifestation, and especially in Puritanism.

The whole style and temper of *The Whole Duty of Man* is as different as the time in which it was written. That was a time when men were exhausted with religious controversy, and doubtful whether any reconciliation could come from the bitter factions of the supporters of either the King and the bishops, or of the Protector and his Puritan divines, some of whom were as disaffected as Richard Baxter in the final days of the Protectorate. The book, suitably written for the changing climate of theological opinion, avoided the disputatious points of theology and concentrated on morality. Its title came from the final words of the Book of Ecclesiastes, where the penetrating sceptic's thrusts are sidestepped by the impatient statement that the essence of religion is "Fear God, and keep his commandments: for this is the whole duty of man."

The full title is also a summary of the contents: *The Whole*

---

supported religion of England. From 1662 onwards the Puritan tradition in religion and worship continued *outside* the Church of England as Nonconformity or Dissent. The other alternative term, the "Puritan wing" is an importation from nineteenth century French politics, and this is an anachronism and an anatopism also, but it suggests something of the dynamic and shifting nature of Puritanism.

Duty of Man, laid down in a plain and familiar way for the use of all, but especially the meanest reader; divided into seventeen chapters, one whereof being read every Lord's Day, the whole may be read over thrice in the year; necessary for all families. With private devotions for several occasions. Here was an attempt on the part of a high churchman to write a book on devotion which would reach the middle and working classes, which Bayly and the Puritan writers had particularly aimed at with their plain English. Hence its determination to make this plain in the title, despite being open to the charge of snobbery in assuring "the meanest reader" that he would understand it. The book's opening paragraph makes its purpose clear: "The only intent of this ensuing treatise, is to be a short and plain direction to the very meanest readers, to behave themselves so in this world, that they may be happy for ever in the next."[115] The emphasis was to be on behaviour, less on belief, especially any speculative matters such as election and predestination. Furthermore, enlightened self-interest is the sensible man's guide here to get to the hereafter. Duty is all, and delight and imagination and vision are completely excluded from consideration. We are offered orthodoxy with blinkers, respectability without rapture, but the thrill of adventure and the daring of faith with the aid of grace are almost entirely absent.

For all the limitations of the book it has its strengths, particularly in its instruction on the two Sacraments and the due preparation for them. There is an abundance of clear and commonsense advice. And if the instruction on prayer lacks the lyricism of Herbert, there were times when the author of *The Whole Duty of Man* could express affection in his prayers and even a longing for eternity and the company of the saints, but not in this volume. In another volume, *The Whole Duty of Prayer*,[116] there is a fine extended "aspiration" which concludes: "Lord, let the hope and expectation of this eternal rest and felicity sweeten all my labours, and ease my torments, let it mitigate my afflictions, and comfort my spirits, that I faint not in my journey, nor be depressed under my burden, and hold on cheerfully and valiantly, till I arrive at the Land of Promise, and there receive the Lot of mine inheritance with the Saints in Light for evermore."[117] If there is more of Sto-

115 *Op. cit.* (quarto ed. of 1684), sig. A1.
116 The full title is: *The Whole Duty of Prayer containing devotions for every day of the week, and for several occasions ordinary and extraordinary; By the author of The Whole Duty of Man. Necessary for all Families.* All references are to this edition of 1692.
117 *Op. cit.* (1692), p. 47.

icism than of St. Bernard's mysticism here, at least the spirit of calculation is muted.

A new type of Anglican devotion appeared just prior to and during the Restoration of the monarchy. The latter led to the restoration of the Book of Common Prayer which had been proscribed by Parliament since 1645, though its defenders had secretly used it in apocopated services or had combined liturgical and non-liturgical elements in worship as a disguise.

In 1660, however, the Prayer Book became the symbol alike of Anglican loyalty and of the overthrow of Puritanism and its despised *Directory of Public Worship*, and of the rejection of all informal and extemporaneous worship which was soon equated with anarchy or rebellion. A generation had grown up which was ignorant of the Book of Common Prayer, and so there was a need for liturgical information and devotional discipline. The new books combined to make devotions more liturgical, and less supplementary to or independent of the Book of Common Prayer.

One of the very best of these was Anthony Sparrow's *A Rationale upon the Book of Common Prayer*, the first known copy of which is dated 1657. The preface defends the Prayer Book from the contradictory charges of being "old Roman dotage" (the Puritan criticism) and "schismatically new" (the Roman Catholic criticism). Its answer was that it is primitive and reasonable, neither anachronistically irrelevant nor superstitious. "As for those that love it and suffer for the loss of it, this will show them reasons, why they should suffer on, and love it still more and more."

This work is a commentary on every part of the Prayer Book in the order in which its contents appear. It demonstrates an impressive knowledge of Scripture, the Fathers, and especially of the liturgical customs of the non-Papal Catholicism of the eastern churches. Sparrow is very fond of St. John Chrysostom, among the eastern Fathers, and of St. Augustine among the western Fathers.

His concise comments are often not merely liturgically informative, but devotionally full of insight. The versicle of salutation: "The Lord be with you" is a text for a good example of Sparrow's commentary. After remarking on its Biblical origin and its use in ancient liturgies, he explains that it means, in effect: "The Lord be with you, to lift up your hearts, and raise your devotions to his service. The Lord be with you, to reward you hereafter with eternal life." The response: "And with thy spirit," is explained as meaning virtually, "thou [the priest] art about to offer up prayers and spiritual sacrifices for us, therefore we pray likewise for thee, that He without whom nothing is good and acceptable may be with thy spirit while thou art exercised in these spiritual services, which must be performed with the Spirit, according to St. Paul I Cor. 14.14." The summary is most pithy: "Thus the priest prays and wishes well to the people, and they pray and wish well to the priest."[118]

Among several partly didactic, partly devotional commentaries on the Prayer Book,[119] the most complete are those of Thomas Comber[120] (1645-1699), who became Dean of Durham in 1691. Between 1672 and 1677 he published a series of four studies of the Prayer Book, dealing with Matins and Evensong (1672), Holy Communion (1674), the Litany and Occasional Prayers (1675), and the Occasional Offices (1677). His largest work, however, was entitled, *A Companion to the Temple; Or, a help to Devotion in the use of the Common Prayer, Divided into Four Parts* (1684). Its primary aim was to reconcile Dissenters to the Church of England services, for Comber was opposed to James II's attempt to fill Anglican benefices with Roman Catholics, and he warmly welcomed the arrival of William and Mary.

His work was prolix, thorough, accurate, and deadly dull, except when he forgot to be devotional and turned controversial. The triple advantages of this type of book which was to have many successors in the eighteenth and particularly in the nineteenth centuries,[121] were that it fostered an informed appreciation of the Prayer Book, cultivated loyalty to the Church of England, and promoted liturgical devotion as contrasted with idiosyncratic devotions that were extra-liturgical.

5. *Puritans and the Devotional Life*

In considering Puritan piety, we shall not analyse such "guides to godliness"[122] as the one Downame wrote with that very title in

---

118 *Op. cit.*, p. 62.

119 As examples, H. L'Estrange, *The Alliance of Divine Offices* (1659) and T. Elborow, *An Exposition of the Book of Common Prayer* (1663).

120 See ed. C. E. Whiting, *The Autobiography and Letters of Thomas Comber* (Surtees Society, CLVI-CLVII, 1941-1942).

121 See R.C.D. Jasper, *Prayer Book Revision in England, 1800-1900* (1954) and William Seth Adams, "William Palmer of Worcester, 1803-1885, The Only Learned Man among Them" (Princeton University, Ph.D., 1973). It is an account of him as liturgiologist, theologian and Tractarian.

122 This title for Puritan devotional treatises and collections of prayers has been popularized by Gordon S. Wakefield, *op. cit.*, pp. 6 and 85, but it also happens

1622, nor his more famous *The Christian's Warfare* (1609), nor even Arthur Dent's highly popular *A Plain Man's Pathway to Heaven* (1601), because this has been done elsewhere,[123] and because the difference between non-high-church Anglican spirituality and Puritan devotions is negligible. This will enable us to concentrate on two masterpieces of the way to godliness, both produced by men who had never been to a university, who, like George Fox, the founder of Quakerism, were experts in the experimental knowledge of God. One was Richard Baxter, who declined the bishopric of Hereford at the Restoration, and was the leader of the Presbyterian delegation who were considering a possible ecumenical revision of the Book of Common Prayer at the Savoy Conference, with a representative group of Anglicans, and who is the author of *The Saints' Everlasting Rest*. The other is the immortal tinker and allegorist, John Bunyan, whose superb imagination extracted from his experience in the Civil Wars and from his understanding of God gained in fair weather and more often foul, created the prose epic of Puritanism, *The Pilgrim's Progress*.

Richard Baxter (1615-1691) wrote his classic devotional work, *The Saints' Everlasting Rest* at Rouse Lench when recovering from a most serious illness. It was an instantaneous success and was reprinted nine times in the decade following its first publication in 1650. It is a treatise of a familiar type in Anglicanism, namely the persuasive to a good life; but within Puritanism, as Louis L. Martz has argued,[124] it is most unusual in that it employed the Catholic techniques of meditation using the Ignatian "composition"—employing the senses usually regarded as inimical by Protestants to true spirituality, to enable the soul to concentrate more fully on Christ in his sufferings and redemption or on the joys of heaven, and the interior soliloquy as a way of preaching to

---

to be the title of a devotional treatise of Downame's, *A Guide to Godliness, or a Treatise of a Christian Life* (1622).

[123] One reason is that they do not differ greatly from the Anglican works of the period such as Bishop Bayly's, Dent's and Downame's, but also because some of the earlier works of the period have already been treated in Davies, *op. cit.*, I, pp. 317, 320, 322f., 417, 432.

[124] Louis L. Martz claims: "Baxter deliberately sets out to recover for the Puritans some of these devotional practices which had fallen away as a result of Calvinist thinking. This is perfectly clear from his constant marginal references to St. Bernard, Gerson, Cardinal Nicholas of Cusa, the Jesuit Nieremberg, and . . . Bishop Hall who was himself engaged in this kind of devotional recovery." (*Op. cit.*, p. 168; see also pp. 169-75.) This statement is correct, but it does not do justice to some of the Puritan predecessors of Baxter, such as John Preston or Francis Rous, who also had meditations on the sacred humanity of Christ.

one's self. At the same time he shares the desperate Puritan desire
for assurance that he is one of the elect. Both Catholic techniques
and Protestant concerns are mated in this volume.

The Saints' Everlasting Rest is, in fact, his calm assurance of
salvation, his conviction that he belongs to the elect. Yet, as it is
perfectly clear from Baxter's wide experience as a minister in
Kidderminster and as an army chaplain, there were very many
apparently God-fearing Christians who had no such assurance, but
only a turbulence produced by anxiety and fear. "Why do they
lack the calmness of the sense of assurance?" says Baxter. He finds
two answers to his question. The first is that many Christians seem
to have a false idea of grace—that one must just sit and wait for
it, without making any preparation for it. The other is that many
feel, knowing that many are called but few are chosen, that their
chances seem infinitesimally small. The only remedy that Baxter
proposes is a very practical one. That is, "to ply his duty, and exercise his Graces, till he finde his Doubts and Discomforts vanish."[125]

Baxter is addressing himself to Puritanism's central problem:
how one may know for sure whether God has chosen him as a
brand to be plucked from the burning? It was as acute a problem
at the start of the century as at its mid-point. Dent had consoled
many bruised and tender consciences by providing them with
"eight signes of salvation." These all-important marks were: "A
love of the children of God, a delight in his word, often and frequent prayer, zeale of God's glorie, deniall of our selves, patient
bearing of the crosse with profit and comfort, faithfulnesse in our
calling, and just, honest, faithful, and conscionable dealing in all
our actions amongst men."[126]

The fourth part of Baxter's treatise is concerned with meditation, moving from intellectual issues to exciting the heart's affections in order to free the will for conformity to God. His defence
of this is most interesting: "As the Papists have wronged the Merits of Christ by their ascribing too much to our own works, so it is
almost incredible how much they [Protestants] on the other
extream, have wronged the safety and consolation of men's souls
by telling them that their own endeavours are only for Obedience
and Gratitude, but are not so much as Conditions of their Salva-

---

125 *Op. cit.* (4th edn., 1653), Pt. III, p. 168.
126 *A Plain Man's Pathway to Heaven*, pp. 31-32. See also on this important
point of Puritan casuistry, M. M. Knappen, *op. cit.*, pp. 348, 393-95; William Haller, *op. cit.*, pp. 88-91; and Max Weber, *The Protestant Ethic and the Spirit of
Capitalism* (trans. Talcott Parsons, 1930), pp. 98-128.

tion, or Means of their increased Sanctification or Consolation."
He continues: "had they bestowed but that time in exercising holy
Affections, and in serious thoughts of the promised Happiness,
which they have spent in enquiring only after Signs, I am confident, according to the ordinary workings of God, they would have
been better provided with both Assurance and with Joys."[127]

He provides several "meditations" that are vivid word-paintings,
and "compositions" of the Ignatian type. One,[128] a lengthy meditation on the suffering Saviour, is fairly commonplace, though not
lacking in genuine fervour. Another, worthy of citation, is part of
his canvas of the Eternal City:

> Thus take thy *heart* into the *Land of Promise*; shew it the
> pleasant hills, and fruitful valleys; Shew it the clusters of
> Grapes which thou hast gathered; & by those convince it that
> it is a pleasant Land, flowing with better then milk and
> honey; enter the gates of the *Holy City*; walk through the
> streets of the *New Jerusalem*, walk about *Sion*, go round
> about her, tell the Towers thereof, mark well her bulwarks;
> consider her places; that thou mayest tell it to thy Soul . . .
> What sayest thou now to all this? This is thy Rest, O my Soul,
> and this must be the place of thy Everlasting habitation.[129]

This work was one of the most popular companions to the Bible
England had ever seen. It appealed to the unlettered and the let-
tered alike, because of its clarity, simplicity, practicality, and its
willingness to break new ground. For this highly original man any
label is a libel. No wonder he preferred to be called a "meer
Catholick."

John Bunyan's masterpiece also appealed to the simple and
the cultured alike and has now been translated into more than a
hundred languages. Bunyan[130] (1622-1688) followed his father's

---

[127] *Saints' Everlasting Rest*, Pt. IV, p. 5. He (Baxter) tells us that Bishop
Joseph Hall of Exeter and Norwich, who was suspended by Archbishop Laud in
1641, had taken the same step as himself, in using a method derived from Roman
Catholic spirituality, as this was documented in Hall's *Arte of Meditation* (1606).
This was itself derived from Jean Mompaer's famous *Rosetum* which was the
principal source of Abbot Garcia de Cisneros's treatise which indirectly assisted
St. Ignatius Loyola's composition of *Spiritual Exercises*. These, in Bunny's Anglican adaptation, had converted Baxter to Christianity. Hence Baxter knew the
value of such methods from experience.

[128] *Op. cit.*, Pt. IV, pp. 191-96.   [129] *Ibid.*, Pt. IV, pp. 205-206.

[130] See Henri Talon's magisterial *John Bunyan, the Man and His Works* (1931).
For a modern edition, see ed. R. Sharrock, *Pilgrim's Progress* (Oxford, 2nd edn.,
1950). There is also a combined edn. of *The Pilgrim's Progress, Grace Abounding,
and a Relation of his Imprisonment* (Oxford, 1925) by Edmund Venables.

trade as a brazier (he is loosely termed a "tinker"), fought on the parliamentary side in the Civil War, and about 1649 married a poor woman whose dowry comprised Bishop Bayly's *Practice of Piety* and Arthur Dent's *A Plain Man's Pathway to Heaven*. The Bible, Foxe's martyrology, and the two devotional treatises mentioned, appear to have constituted all his reading. Most of the years between 1660 and 1672 he spent in Bedford prison for refusing to be silent as an unlicensed preacher of the Gospel in Independent and Baptist circles. *Grace Abounding to the Chief of Sinners* (1666), his spiritual autobiography, shows that he had been in anxiety about his salvation for seven years, and that was written in durance vile, while his greatest work, *Pilgrim's Progress*, was also written during a second period of imprisonment in 1676 and printed about two years later.

This work shows life as an almost unending spiritual warfare, and salvation as the Gospel pearl of great price worth losing the whole world to gain. It depicts vividly, spiritually, and simply, and with the greatest sincerity, earnestness, and intensity, Christian's journey from the City of Destruction to the Heavenly City, through the Slough of Despond, up the daunting Hill of Difficulty, through Vanity Fair, and the Valley of the Shadow of Death, each symbolizing the pitfalls on the way to salvation. Christian's companions or persons he encounters are also vividly imagined, as helpful like Evangelist or Greatheart, or as hindrances like Mr. Worldly-Wiseman, Mr. Legality, or Mr. Facing-both-Ways. The theme has been compressed into a popular hymn, "He who would valiant be . . ." which is a modification of the heartening lines sung by the pilgrims on the way to the Enchanted Ground.

Despite the criticism of Fr. Louis Bouyer, the French Oratorian, that this is a "tedious and boring book," which has contributed much "to Puritanism's reputation as being the quintessence of boredom,"[131] it has been a perennial favourite with the English-speaking people, to say nothing of being in C. H. Firth's phrase "the prose epic of Puritanism."

It represents the values inculcated by Puritan religion, especially the doctrine of the perseverance of the saints, which was the Puritan counterpart of the Catholic pursuit of perfection. It stresses the constant need of grace to face the hardships of life. It exposes the glittering and insubstantial nature of temptations. It emphasizes the strenuous loneliness and singularity of the Christian life,

[131] *Op. cit.*, p. 160.

and its Calvinism is clearly revealed in the overwhelming sense of divine providence and guidance and in the acknowledgment that the gate leading to everlasting life is narrow. Yet for all its gravity, the joy of the elect pilgrims can be seen when their solemn countenances break into psalmody and praise.

What can be said generally about the nature of Puritan spirituality? Almost all commentators emphasize its dark view of human nature, its depressing pessimism, its constant self-scrutiny. But Puritans themselves would have argued that this was realism, and it was the glory of Christ that he delivered men and women from the scum and foulness of original and actual sin. Nor was this peculiarly Puritan, for it was shared alike by John Donne in his sermons and by St. Ignatius Loyola in the first part of his *Exercises* to shake the soul out of its complacency. In all fairness, however, it cannot be denied that some gentle souls have been unnecessarily frightened by being "dangled over the pit" by Calvinism. There was the notable case of Mistress Katherin Brettergh, an admirable woman, and the sister of John Bruen[132] of Bruenstapleford himself a godly man. Her long illness and her supposed temptation by Satan were a bitter and prolonged testing of her election, so much so that they occupy pages 11 to 37 of the 38 page pamphlet entitled, *A Brief Discourse of the Christian Life and Death of Mistris Katherin Brettergh . . . who departed this world the last of May, 1601* (published 1612). When she knew she was going to die, she was terrified by the thought that she would be damned. Although her minister tried to console her, and even after a Puritan posse of parsons was called in to fortify her without effect, her despair disintegrated just prior to her death, and for five hours she praised God without ceasing, being assured that she was an elect soul. "And after this, shee fell into a short slumber, and awaking said, Oh come kisse me with the kisse of thy mouth for thy love is better than wine! Oh, how sweet the kisses of my Saviour bee."[133] This echo of the Song of Songs is at once the indication of the passion of Puritan devotion, and, in this case, the desperation inflicted by such a prolonged interior scrutiny of motives and actions.

With equal certainty one can affirm that the home is the chief locus of Puritan piety, as the monastery or the convent is of Catholic piety. The flowers of Puritan piety flourished best in rich domes-

---

[132] Described in Davies, *op. cit.*, I, pp. 428-32.
[133] *Op. cit.*, p. 33.

tic loam. William Perkins calls the family "a little church,"[134] while William Gouge referred to it as "a seminary of the Church and Commonwealth, a beehive in which is the stock."[135] Baxter made the same point in the following words: "A Christian family . . . is a church . . . a society of Christians combined for the better worshipping and serving God."[136]

This home-bred holiness was nurtured by the parents, themselves taught by the Scriptures, their minister's example and exposition of the sacred oracles, as well as by stirring books such as Foxe's Book of Martyrs or guides to the good life like Bishop Bayly's or Downame's or Dent's, or later, Baxter's or Bunyan's. Richard Baxter's comprehensive and influential *Christian Directory* (1673) devotes considerable space to family worship. This should be held twice each weekday, as Scripture, experience and reason all recommend. The latter dictates: "1. That it is seasonable every morning to give God thanks for the rest of the night past. 2. And to beg directions, protection and provisions and blessing for the following day. 3. And that the evening is a fit season to give God thanks for the mercies of the day, and to confess the sins of the day, and ask forgiveness, and to pray for rest and protection in the night."[137] On the Lord's Day the head of the household has specially important duties. These begin with holding family prayers as a solemn preparation for the services of the day. Then the father leads his family to church for the public service. "After dinner," instructs Baxter, "call your families together, and sing a Psalm of Praise, and by examination or repetition or both, cause them to remember what was publickly taught them."[138] After the afternoon church service, the father is again instructed to "call your families together and first crave God's assistance and acceptance: and then sing a Psalm of Praise: and then repeat the Sermon which you have heard; or if there was none, read out of some lively profitable book; and then pray and praise God: and with all the holy seriousness and joy which is suitable to the work and the day."[139] The father's work is not yet done, for after supper he has to examine the children and servants on what they have learned about the life of a Christian during that day. The day's duties end with family prayers and praises. It was in Puritanism that the principle of the priesthood of all believers was carried out

134 *Works* (1605), p. 865.
135 *Workes* (1627), II, p. 10.
136 *Works* (ed. Orme, 1830), IV, p. 75.
137 *Op. cit.*, Vol. II, Pt. III, p. 507.
138 *Ibid.*, p. 572.
139 *Ibid.*, p. 573.

to its logical conclusion, with the father of the household acting as priest at the family table.

Private or "closet prayers" were also an important part of the Puritan spiritual regimen. This is most vividly shown in the short and exemplary life of John, Lord Harrington as recorded by Richard Stockton, Milton's childhood rector at All Hallows, Bread Street, London.[140] We are informed that "he usually rose every morning about four or five of the clock, not willingly sleeping above his six hours. As soon as he was thoroughly awake, he endeavoured religiously to set his heart in order and to prepare it for goodness all the day after, offering the first fruits of the day and of his thoughts unto God."[141] He next read a chapter of Scripture, then went to prayers with his servants in his chamber and this lasted the better part of an hour. "After this he read some divine treatise to increase his knowledge in spiritual things, and this for the greater part of an hour. He had of latter times read over in this course Calvin's *Institutions*, and he was at the time of his sickness reading the works of a reverend man now living, one Master Rogers."[142] Then he led the family devotions and returned to his closet, and "after his own private prayer disposed himself to some serious study, if some special business interrupted not his course, for the space of three or four hours."[143] After dinner, if not detained by other business, he again withdrew to his closet and there meditated "upon some sermons, which he had lately heard, for which use he retained some five or six in his mind. . . . He did ordinarily meditate and call to mind four or five in a day" even when he was travelling.[144]

Another characteristic of Puritan spirituality was a very careful self-scrutiny and scrupulous spiritual auditing. Here again John, Lord Harrington's example, is of value. Stockton's account states that "which is markable above many other things," Lord Harrington, after prayers with his servants, in the evening, "withdrew himself, and there in a book which he kept for the account of his life

---

[140] In *The Church's Lamentation for the Loss of the Godly* (1614), pp. 63-88, which has been republished in ed. Everett H. Emerson, *English Puritanism from John Hooper to John Milton* (Durham, North Carolina, 1968), pp. 189-98.

[141] *Ibid.*, pp. 194-95.

[142] *Ibid.*, p. 195. The "Master Rogers" referred to is almost certainly Richard Rogers, author of the popular *Seven Treatises . . . leading and guiding to true happiness both in this life and in the life to come* (1603). His diary is reproduced in ed. M. M. Knappen, *Two Elizabethan Puritan Diaries by Richard Rogers and Samuel Ward* (1930), and on pp. 7-8 diary keeping is discussed.

[143] *Ibid.*   [144] *Ibid.*, pp. 195-96.

he set down what he had done all that day; how he had either
offended or done good, and how he was tempted and withstood
them, and according to his account he humbled himself."[145] He also
scrutinized his spiritual accounts for the whole week on Saturday
evening "to call himself to a strict account how he had spent the
whole week, that, according as he found his estate, he might better fit himself to sanctify the Sabbath following."[146] Stockton also
reports that a great friend of Lord Harrington's told him that he
did on the last Saturday of the month a monthly spiritual audit
also, to see, in a good month or week, "how he had added and got
more grace and strength of piety."[147] Here was one, indeed, who
could say, with John Milton, though Harrington did not reach
his twenty-third birthday, "All is if I have grace to use it so, as ever
in my great Task-Master's eye."[148]

Puritan spirituality was Bible-centred, and therefore exceedingly
suspicious in general of traditional Catholic methods of spirituality,
though there were significant exceptions.[149] The suspicion has
already been met in its most vitriolic form in the diatribes of
Prynne and Burton against Cosin's *Devotions*. Baxter approved of
mental prayer, but was critical of the inconvenient, time-wasting
and health-endangering austerity of the night office.[150] The Puritans also ridiculed those who considered that continence and the
virgin life were superior to the married life, and affirmed that it
was the continent who achieved the greatest mystical heights. It
seemed inconsistent to them to consider virginity an excellent calling and yet to call holy matrimony a Sacrament, for this was to set
one Sacrament against another (holy orders against matrimony).[151]

The Bible-centred character of Puritan spirituality involved several other significant consequences. One was that the emphasis on
the sole mediatorship of Christ excluded any possibility of invocation of the saints. Another consequence was that there was no
unmediated union with God, least of all any absorption into God,

[145] *Ibid.*, p. 196. [146] *Ibid.*, p. 197.
[147] *Ibid.* [148] Milton's *Sonnet* II.
[149] It is interesting that Ambrose Isaac, Richard Baxter, and William Gouge,
all Puritans, approve of mental prayer, but Owen does not; but it is typical that
Gouge should justify the practice by Biblical precedents in Moses, Nehemiah, and
Hannah (*Workes*, 1627, I, p. 208).
[150] *Works* (ed. Orme, 1830), IV, p. 239: "unless men did irrationally place the
service of God in praying this hour rather than another, they might see how
improvidently and sinfully they lose their time in twice dressing and undressing,
and in the intervals of their sleep, when they might spare all that time by sitting
up the longer or rising the earlier for the same employment."
[151] W. Gouge, *Workes*, II, p. 72.

apart from Christ. Moreover, that union was attainable proleptically here and now, and was not the final stage and ultimate prize of a concentrated spiritual regimen over the years. To maintain that respect for and appreciation of the Bible, Bible study was necessary (and many godly Puritans read several chapters of Holy Scripture every Sunday and also sometimes every day). Equally needed was an ear attentive to the minister's exposition of it in his Sabbath sermons. Further, there was the responsibility, if the head of a household with children and servants or a master with apprentices under him, to see that all understood and repeated the main lessons inculcated in the sermons. Such Biblical exposition could be idiosyncratic, but it was kept in check to a considerable degree in Puritanism by a ministry learned in the Biblical languages, trained in logic and rhetoric, by discussion of the spiritual life in the fellowship of the church, and the reading of reliable guides of godliness.

Another characteristic of Puritan spirituality is that it relies on experience. The fact that every father of a household could be his own priest to the family and did not need a clergyman as confessor and spiritual guide gave a welcome independence to the strong but led to anxiety on the part of the unsure, as in the case of Mistress Brettergh who was sorely tried by Satan. But it was in the daily experience of the providence of God as either blessing or threatening, that the Puritan saw the confirmation of His ways revealed in Scripture. So quite apart from the national days of thanksgiving and humiliation (to be considered in Chapter VI), Puritanism instituted private days of fasting and humiliation and private days of thanksgiving. These customs outlived the demise of the Commonwealth and the Protectorate. Oliver Heywood, a Presbyterian divine in the West Riding of Yorkshire, enters into his diary for October 7, 1679: "My wife and I rode to little Horton, we kept a solemn day of thanksgiving at Mr. Sharps for his wife delivered of a daughter a month before."[152] The following March 5, Heywood writes: "we had a solemne day of thanksgiving for my wives and sons recovery, my son Eliezer begun, Mr. Dawson, John proceeded, I concluded with preaching, prayer, we feasted 50 persons and upwards, blessed be God."[153] Heywood also reports days of fasting and humiliation that were kept by Puritan families, for the recov-

---

[152] *Diaries*, I and II (ed. J. Horsfall Turner, Brighouse, 1882), III (Bingley, 1883), II, p. 207.
[153] *Ibid.*, II, p. 110.

ery of sick persons, or in days of persecution. Our Northowram divine notes that on December 2, 1679, "I rode to Wyke, kept a solemne fast at Joshua Kersheys, he being in a consumption, God helped me in discoursing extempore on Jer. 17.13.14 and praying, it was a good day blessed be God."[154] Family feasts and fasts were far more common than might be imagined. In 1690 Heywood participated in 40 fasts and 17 days of thanksgiving; in 1691 he officiated at 37 fasts and 11 days of thanksgiving; in 1692 he was at 50 fasts and 14 days of thanksgiving; while in 1693 he presided at 35 fasts and 12 days of thanksgiving.[155]

Perhaps the most striking example of the relevance of prayer in daily life is that of Oliver Cromwell, who in the midst of his military and political duties, insisted on finding time to commend himself to God and to find in the events of the time the signs of divine approval or displeasure. The letters of this Puritan leader abound in advice to others to seek the will of God in prayer.[156] There was a celebrated occasion, when Cromwell and the other Roundhead generals were convinced that through their temporizing with the king and their consequent lack of popular support, they had earned God's disapproval, Cromwell called a special meeting of the army leaders. Its purpose was, in the words of Adjutant Allan: "To go solemnly to search out our own iniquities, and humble our souls before the Lord in the sense of the same; which, we were persuaded had provoked the Lord against us, to bring such sad perplexities upon us that day."[157] The whole day was then spent in prayer and the examination of their consciences. On the second day, following the exposition of Scripture and further prayers, Cromwell addressed them, urging them to make "a thorough consideration of our actions as an Army, and of our ways particularly as private Christians: to see if any iniquity could be found in them; and what it was, that if possible we might find it out, and so remove the cause of such sad rebukes as were upon us (by *reason* of our iniquities, as we judged) at that time."[158]

It is not commonly recognized that the Puritans, although they ridiculed Catholics for their belief in the invocation of the saints,

---

154 *Ibid.*
155 *Ibid.*, III, pp. 247, 254, 262, 264.
156 *The Letters and Speeches of Oliver Cromwell* (ed. Thomas Carlyle, 1845), I, pp. 121, 167. He received similar letters, as one from Major-General Harrison which is cited in ed. Nathaniel Micklem, *Christian Worship* (Oxford, 1936), p. 185.
157 *Ibid.*, I, p. 264.   158 *Ibid.*, p. 265.

had their own saints. This is to go considerably beyond the statement of Gordon S. Wakefield that "the people of God in the wilderness, patriarchs and prophets, were the companions of the Puritan's way. He lived with them as intimates, as the Catholic with his saints."[159] The frequency with which Foxe's Book of Martyrs was reprinted and referred to as approved devotional reading is one pointer to their admiration for the English Protestant Martyrs in Queen Mary's reign. Yet another is the popularity of the sale of funeral sermons extolling the virtues of the godly deceased, their trials and temptations, and their exemplary public and private devotions. One among hundreds is the memoir of John, Lord Harrington, while another, also already referred to, is that of Mistress Katherin Brettergh. One interesting example is *A Pattern of Pietie, Or, the Religious life and death of that Grave and gracious Matron, Mrs. Jane RATCLIFFE, Widow and Citizen of Chester. Of whom the discourse is framed and applied so as the commemoration of the dead may best serve to the edification of the living, whether men or women, whereof part was Preached, and the whole written* (1640). Its author was John Ley, Vicar of Great Budworth and Prebendary of Chester Cathedral. The work is in part a defence of the national Church which he says has been calumniated by the Papists and Brownists "for want of holiness in those that are members of it."[160] He is exceedingly critical of the Roman Catholic conception of sainthood because of their extreme austerities, and instances a report that St. Anthony of Padua is said to have kicked his mother as a child and to have cut off his foot "for the wickednesse of the fact" and St. Catherine of Siena is commended by Catholics "for licking and sucking the sores of such as were leaprous and cankered."[161] The piety of Mrs. Ratcliffe is particularly admired and defined as "the affections of the heart as they tend towards God."[162] Moreover, five tests of her piety are given. These include: her frequent and fervent communion with God in private; her zealous and affectionate discourse of Him; her love for things that had nearest reference to Him; her estrangement from communion with the world for his sake, especially in reference to sensual delights, worldly profit, and from the desire of life itself; and, finally, her "conscionable and constant endeavour to keepe all

[159] *Puritan Devotion*, p. 27.
[160] *Op. cit.*, the heading of Chap. 27. This is the work of one who is more Anglican than Puritan, but the latter element is there.
[161] *Ibid.*, p. 193. [162] *Ibid.*, p. 57.

Gods Commandements."[163] The final proof that the Puritans had their own saints, as eminent imitators of God worthy of emulation is the publication of Samuel Clarke, *A Collection of the Lives of Ten Eminent Divines* (1661), a distinctively Puritan hagiography.

All in all, Puritan spirituality is impressive by its intramundane simplicity, sincerity, relevance, and the large numbers of otherwise ordinary people who tried to live up to the high demands of the elect. It was a foul weather as well as a fair weather piety, for it gained in strength during the days of persecution following 1662. It was a secular piety exercised in the calling and duties of every day, and demanded ethical fight, not flight. It was, above all, vertebral piety.

6. *Concluding Contrasts*

Since it is the glory of the Church of England to be the *via media*, combining both Catholic and Protestant elements, its spirituality does not lend itself conceptually to the polarity and contrast that there is between Roman Catholic and Puritan spirituality. Since the opening section of this chapter stressed the common interconfessional factors in spirituality, the concluding section, avoiding the perils suggested by Ronald Knox's "Re-union All Round," will emphasize the distinctions that give these pieties shape, definition, and recognition, without denying any significant common characteristics. Some similarities will be seen to hide important differences.

To take an example of the latter, one might note the remarkable way that the Puritans, for whom all honouring of saints was a form of idolatry and therefore dishonouring of the Creator, seemed to have taken a leaf out of Catholic hagiographies in writing the lives of their own saints. This is true, however, only at a superficial level, because the Catholic saints are invoked for their aid whereas the Puritan saints are not. The Catholic saints are almost demigods; the Puritan saints are human.

Yet again, it has been argued by E. I. Watkin in his fascinating volume, *Poets and Mystics*,[164] that the Puritan Thomas Goodwin's *The Heart of Christ in Heaven towards Sinners on Earth*[165] is an

---

[163] *Ibid.*, p. 58.

[164] *Op. cit.* (1953), pp. 56ff. The point is also accepted by Fr. Louis Bouyer, *op. cit.*, p. 67, and was earlier remarked upon by the Abbé Henri Brémond in his magisterial *Histoire littéraire du sentiment religieux en France*, 11 vols. (Paris 1915-1932), III, p. 641.

[165] This appeared in 1652.

astonishing anticipation of the Roman Catholic cult of the Sacred Heart, as envisioned by St. John Eudes and St. Marguerite-Marie Alacoque. There are parallels, indeed: the emphasis on the affections in an age of controversy where the intellect has divided too much, the permanent disposition of Christ as loving towards sinners, and its Biblical basis in his Farewell Discourses in the Fourth Gospel. But the differences are equally significant. For the Catholic the mystical union sought in the prayer of love is one in which Neo-Platonism and Christian practice have amalgamated, and the mystic's aim is to be absorbed in the infinite God, at the end of a long process of which the prior steps are purgation and illumination. For the Puritan, however, conformity of wills is sought, not a loss of identity. Furthermore, the sense of the love of God is not a rapture at the end of a long and strenuous spiritual regimen, it is felt at the beginning of the way. Thirdly, for the Puritan there is a sense that sanctification offers a proleptic fruition in God, but there is always "eschatological distance" between the soul and the beloved in even the most rapturous and mystical of Puritans, like Thomas Goodwin, Francis Rous, and John Preston. Puritans have no sense of the "alone with the Alone"—it is always a mediated presence of God in their hearts, known in Christ, and shared with the people of God, who are incorporated into Christ in the Lord's Supper. So the notion of absorption, or of unmediated and immediate awareness of God is not part of Puritan experience. Even the Cornish layman, Rous, who wrote *The Mysticall Marriage* makes his mystical union an experience "intermediate between sinful historical existence and the pure life of the Godhead, but the union is mediated by Christ."[166] The precondition of the eschatologically consummated union is radical, no less than the death of the old husband, the old self. Rous, like St. John of the Cross, knows that the divine lover sometimes withdraws his consolations from the soul, and he is certain that "His [Christ's] best coming is his last coming . . . without any more going asunder."[167] These examples of the prayer of love in Puritanism are proof positive that its devotional life was not a cold, grey, cerebral piety, for it changed the affections and therefore transformed the wills of those who used it. But, again it must be said, this is not the same as Catholic mysticism. The distinction has been perceptively expressed by Gordon Wakefield in the observation: "For the Puritan, too, it may be said

[166] Wakefield, *op. cit.*, p. 103.
[167] Published 1635, the reference is to p. 56.

that there are three ways, but these are justification, sanctification, glorification. *Union with Christ is not the end but the beginning of the Christian life.*[168]

The point need not be laboured, but it also ought not to be ignored that the locus of the life of perfection for the Catholic is the monastery or the convent, whereas for the Puritan it is in the home and at one's daily work. There is, therefore, a big difference between an extra- and an intra-mundane spirituality.

The devout Catholic is able to make effective use of the senses so that art, architecture, music, and poetry combine for the instruction in and expression of spirituality. The aesthetic approach to God as the Divine Artist is natural for the Roman Catholic and the high Anglican metaphysical preachers and poets. For the Puritans, with the possible exception of Baxter and perhaps Sterry, the ethical repelled the aesthetic, and this was a moral victory but an aesthetic defeat.

Even in the language of prayer, the differences are most noticeable. Catholic prayer uses stately language to address God, whereas Donne and Herbert use conversational and even argumentative and expostulatory approaches to God (e.g., "Batter my heart . . ."). The same filial naturalness was cultivated by the Puritans and especially the Separatists (like the Brownists and Barrowists). This reflects a different conception of God and a different idea of the community of the faithful. One cannot fail to be impressed by the Roman Catholic and high Anglican fondness for referring to God as the King to whom homage and obedience are due, and to whom it is appropriate to kneel, and who must be addressed in the language suitable to the celestial court, while His Son can be called "Prince of Peace" or, more imperially, "King of Kings." The Puritans, on the other hand, are filled with awe as they approach God, but, as their fondness for citing Romans 8:15 and 16 shows, their image of Him is that of a Father who has adopted them into His family, and their speech with him is intimate, personal, natural, and simple.[169] In some cases it was crudely simple, even boorish, but these were the exception. Thus the political preferences of the parties coloured even the language of prayer, as much as at times it did the very partisan nature of the petitions offered up.

---

[168] Wakefield, *op. cit.*, p. 160. The italics are Gordon Wakefield's.
[169] John Owen in *Works* (ed. W. H. Goold, 1851), IV, p. 269 wrote: "There is no more required unto prayer either way but our crying, 'Abba, Father'—that is, the making of our requests known unto him as our father in Christ—with supplications and thanksgivings, according to our state and occasions do require."

There is also a difference between the Catholic, Anglican, and Puritan concepts of the nature of the religious community and the style of approach appropriate in prayer. For the Roman Catholic there is a sense of belonging to an international community that spans oceans and overleaps seventeen centuries. For the Anglican there is a sense of the entire nation on its knees in common prayer. For the Puritan there is the sense of the gathering of several of the families of God, His elect. A stately and liturgical style of prayer is entirely appropriate for both Roman Catholics and Anglicans, while an intimate, filial, familiar style of address fits the *ecclesiola*, the context of Puritan piety and prayer.

In one respect, however, the unity among Catholics, Anglicans, and Puritans in their spiritual treatises and in their devotional depth is astonishing—and that is when they are persecuted. This is true of the prayers and Prayer Books of the English Catholics in penal times (through most of our period, except when the sunshine of monarchical favour cheered them), as of the *Holy Living* and *Holy Dying* of Anglican Bishop-to-be Jeremy Taylor writing during the darkest days of the Church of England, as also of the Nonconformists, successors to the Puritans, under the Cross of Persecution. One of the greatest of them, Richard Baxter, came reluctantly to the conviction that suffering is the Church's true *métier*, "even when there are none but formal, nominal Christians to be the cross-makers, and though ordinarily God would have vicissitudes of summer and winter, day and night, that the Church may grow extensively in the summer of prosperity and intensively in the winter of adversity, yet usually their night is longer than their day, and that day itself has its storms and tempests."[170]

The medieval cry *Intra tua volnera absconde me* is heard echoing through the seventeenth century by all who fight the good fight and are wounded for their loyalty, and who hope to share the promise that "if we suffer with Him, we shall also reign with Him."[171]

[170] Cited from *Reliquiae Baxterianae* (ed. M. Sylvester, 1694) by Alan Simpson, *Puritanism in Old and New England* (Chicago, 1955).
[171] II Timothy 2:12.

CHAPTER IV

PREACHING: SUPPLEMENT AND
STIMULUS TO WORSHIP

ERMONS WERE perhaps never more devoutly heard nor read
with greater avidity than in the England of the seventeenth
century. The passion for preaching reached its highest peak
during the 1640s and 1650s when it seemed, to use an anachronistic analogy, that the whole of England was a Hyde Park Corner,
where every sectarian, no matter how eccentric his viewpoint,
could climb onto a pulpit and progagate his opinion. John Evelyn
wrote in his *Diary* for August 4, 1650: "I heard a sermon at the
Rolls, and in the afternoone I wander'd to divers churches, the
pulpits full of novices and novelties."

1. *Sermons in General*

During these two decades and for part of the third following
them there was the constant possibility that the daring preacher
might be fined, put into the pillory, sequestrated, ejected from his
living, or even imprisoned, as a penalty for his rashness in speaking his mind. In Archbishop Laud's case the penalty was beheading. In the case of his opponent, Hugh Peters, it had been hanging, drawing, and quartering.[1] Throughout the century religion
was a central and highly controversial issue and if print provided
the wider audience, the spoken word gained the immediate impact,
and many preachers exploited both media by expanding and publishing the spoken sermon in print.

What is equally impressive about the seventeenth-century sermon is its great variety of style. There is the moving naïveté and
apocalyptic expectancy of the Fifth Monarchy utterances of such
a man as Archer, or the Biblical fidelity, plainness, and compassionate pastoral urgency of Richard Baxter, in which he was emulated by so many Puritan "painful" (that is, painstaking) and
plain preachers. Or, at the other end of the stylistic scale, there
are the elegant, urbane, rational addresses of a Stillingfleet or a
Tillotson at the end of the century, mirroring the new scientific
spirit and natural mode of clear thinking and crystal expression

---

[1] Caroline F. Richardson, *English Preachers and Preaching, 1640-1670* (New
York, 1928), p. 48.

inspired by the Royal Society. Then, most important of all, there was the Golden Age of the English pulpit in the days of James I and Charles I. It glittered in the etymological analysis, far-fetched analogies and patristic learning of Bishop Lancelot Andrewes, as in the passionate and sceptical mind of Dean Donne, like Jacob, trying by sheer will to wrest a blessing from the angel of divine inspiration and holding the congregations of St. Paul's Cathedral spell-bound by his coruscating imagery, his shrewd observation of the ways of the world, and his theological acrobatics as he walked the tightrope between heaven and hell. Or, again, there was the brocaded style of Jeremy Taylor, raiding the classics, the Fathers, and the Scriptures, and emerging with his own tenderness and profoundly ethical concern, becoming—with the exception of his extreme sensitivity and his tendency to divagation like the meandering Towy River in his golden grove retreat in Carmarthenshire—a kind of English Bossuet.[2]

The uses to which seventeenth-century preaching was put were manifold. Normally, of course, the purpose of the sermon was to unfold divine revelation as recorded in the Old and New Testaments, with a view to instruction and correction of the mind, and the encouragement of the will in the ways of God. This purpose was fulfilled in many pulpits throughout the century with great fidelity. But there were other uses or abuses of preaching. In this highly partisan and controversial century one cannot fail to be impressed (or depressed) by the political tuning of the pulpit, whether by Cavalier parson or by Puritan preacher. Moreover, it is as useless to deprecate the servility of Bishop Lancelot Andrewes to his sovereign in the court sermons preached at Whitehall, as it is to disapprove of the way Puritan preachers in the pulpit of St. Margaret's, Westminster, excoriated and flattered Parliament[3] prior to and during the Commonwealth. Preaching was often propaganda, a political weapon during this period. Some sermons were for the demonstration of theological and patristic learning, and particularly to vindicate the claims of the Church of England to be true to the early church in its orthodoxy of doctrine and ceremonies without diminution or addition. Such apologetical or defensive sermons were preached by Hooker and Andrewes early in the

---

[2] I have in mind in particular his great funeral orations, especially the one commemorating his patroness, Lady Carbery (1650).

[3] For the most thorough and judicious analysis of these sermons see the work of my colleague, John F. Wilson, *Pulpit in Parliament* (Princeton, N.J., 1969).

century, as by Bramhall, Hammond, and Thorndike in the middle of the century, and by the irenical Stillingfleet in behalf of comprehension towards its end. Another type of sermon in which this century was prolific was casuistical preaching; that is, attending to particular ethical cases or problems that concerned the parishioners of the preachers. The Caroline divines excelled in casuistical divinity and the Anglican Puritan, Richard Baxter, was not behind them in this. After the Restoration there appeared the rational address, which was devoted to the calm and well-reasoned elaboration of a single theme. It avoided both the word-splitting exegesis of an Andrewes and the divisions and sub-divisions of the Puritan divines working on the basis of doctrine, reason, and use.[4]

This division of sermons into expository, political, apologetical, ethical and rational, is, of course, the way that a modern attempts to analyse them. Seventeenth-century men were clearly aware of the differences between "Anglo-Catholic" and Puritan sermons in topics and styles. What is, however, most interesting is the way a mid-seventeenth-century Anglican divine, writing at a time when Anglicanism was proscribed, classifies the types of preaching in his own time. This is precisely what Abraham Wright does in his *Five Sermons in Five several Styles or Waies of Preaching* (1656). This former Fellow of St. John's College, Oxford, and presumably a Laudian, cleverly insinuates his own preferences for the first two sermons of his anthology. The first is "In Bp. Andrews his Way, before the late *King* upon the first day of Lent." The second is "in Bp. Hall's Way; before the Clergie at the Author's own Ordination in Christ Church, Oxford." The third category comprises the sermons of Dr. Maine and Mr. Cartwright before the University of Oxford at St. Mary's Church. The fourth is "in the Presbyterian Way; before the *Citie at St. Pauls, London.*" And the final type is "in the Independent *Way*; never preached."[5] The earlier sermons are marked by learning, rather than the "inspirations" and "revelations" that distinguish the final sermon, with its philistine attitude towards education and its endless repetition. The Preface indicates that Wright means his work to show the importance of "humane learning," the ability to meet the needs of differing auditories, and thus "should I see an *English Clergie-man* to equal at the least the *Jesuite* or *Capuchine*, who by his exact skill in the Arts and Oratorie can command a confused Rabble (met to see an

---

[4] This triple Puritan schema will be considered fully later.
[5] Wright, *op. cit.*, all parts of the very lengthy descriptive title.

Interlude or a Mountebank) from their Sport to a Sermon, and change this *Theater* to a *Church*; having a greater power over the passions of their *Auditorie*, then the Actor hath upon the *Stage*; being able to turn even the *Player* himself into a *Monk*, and the *Mimical Jester* into a religious Votarie."[6] The book's chief present interest, however, is its recognition that the Anglican sermons whether "metaphysical" or moral are marked by the use of rhetoric and Patristic and classical lore, while the Presbyterian sermons are distinguished by the schema of reason, doctrine, and use, as well as by elaborate analysis and definitions, whereas the Independent sermon which he prints is characterized in its ultra-Calvinistic form, by an affirmation of grace which involves a refusal of all learning and natural gifts, by several cant phrases, and by a desire for spiritual states beyond those produced by the ordinances and Scripture itself. This is, in fact, a complete caricature of the kind of sermon that John Owen or Thomas Goodwin would have preached, and Wright has the honesty to admit that he invented it. Throughout the century, however, the most significant change is from the *oration* as found in the metaphysical divines like Andrewes, Adams, and Donne, to the *address* or urbane lecture, as exemplified by Tillotson, Stillingfleet, Burnet, and the Latitudinarian divines of the Restoration and afterwards, and to which oddly enough the Puritan "plain" style, the thematic concentration of the preachers at the French Court, and the scientific functionalism of the time, all contributed. Bishop Burnet signalled the change in 1692 in his *Discourse of Pastoral Care*, in which, after referring to the return to "plain Notions of simple and genuine Rhetorick," he claims:

> The impertinent way of dividing Texts is laid aside, the needless setting out of the Originals, and the vulgar Version, is worn out. The trifling Shews of Learning in many Quotations of Passages, that very few could understand, do no more flat the Auditory. [Here Bishop Andrewes must have turned in his grave] *Pert Wit* and *luscious Eloquence* have lost their Relish. So that Sermons are reduced to the plain opening of the meaning of the Text, in a few short illustrations of its Coherence with what goes before and after, and of the Parts of which it is composed; to that is joined the clear Stating of such Propositions as arise out of it, in their Nature, Truth,

6 *Ibid.*, sig. A3 verso.

and Reasonableness; by which, the Hearers may form clear Notions of the several Parts of Religion, such as are best suited to their Capacities and Apprehensions: In all which Applications are added, tending to the Reproving, Directing, Encouraging, or Comforting the Hearers, according to the several Occasions which are offered.[7]

Apart from the Whiggish smugness of the citation and the influence of Locke in the emphasis on the clarity of ideas, one can detect most clearly the difference between the older "hard-sell" technique and the newer "soft-sell" approach in preaching. Anglican preachers by metaphysical wit or *recherché* lore, and Puritan preachers by Biblical fidelity, pastoral psychological insight, and the urge to sanctification had made a determined effort to change their listeners into ardent partisans. The preachers of the new mode were much less concerned to please and delight their hearers;[8] they were more detached and less enthusiastic in outlook; less reliant upon tradition (whether Scriptural or Patristic) and more on reason and common-sense; less urgent and more urbane. After the hot, not to say fevered, intensity of the earlier decades, the cooler approach must have come as a relief. At least it offered an armistice after a prolonged theological civil war, even if it came at the cost of dissolving supernatural mystery in natural explanation, and of substituting prudence for going the sacrificial and ethical second mile.

2. *Anglican and Puritan Sermons Compared*

If sermons were of great importance[9] alike for Anglicans and Puritans, yet they were not so to an equal degree. The Puritans valued preaching more highly than the Anglicans. Hooker, as the leading Anglican apologist against the Puritans, and himself a most competent composer of sermons, derides the Puritans for implying that these are the only roads that lead to God, reminding them that conversation in the bosom of the church, "religious education," "the reading of learned men's books," "information

---

[7] *Op. cit.* (3rd edn. of 1713), pp. 192-93.

[8] Rapin in his *Réflexions sur l'Eloquence de la Chaire* (1672), so greatly admired by English imitators of the new rational style of French preaching, declared: "L'éloquence de la chaire aime la pureté, sans rechercher l'élégance: elle veut estre forte, sans se soucier d'estre agréable." (Cited in J. Fraser Mitchell, *op. cit.*, pp. 121-22.)

[9] This conviction was gleefully expressed by Vavasor Powell in his *The Bird and the Cage* (2nd edn., 1662, p. 9) when he asked: "Hath any generation since the Apostles days had such powerful preachers and plenty of preaching as this generation?"

received by conference," as well as the public or private reading of the Scriptures, all are avenues to God. In his view it is far too restrictive to tie the term "God's Word" to sermons alone, and even to sermons preached apart from a book.[10] His irony is scathing as he refers to the Puritan claims: "How Christ is by Sermons lifted up higher, and made more apparent to the eye of Faith; how the savour of the Word is made more sweet, being brayed, and more able to nourish, being divided, by Preaching, than by only Reading proposed; how Sermons are the keys of the Kingdom of Heaven, and do open the Scriptures, which being but read, remain in comparison still clasped. . . ."[11] Laud and his followers tended to depreciate sermons in order to elevate the sacraments. Archbishop Laud himself had dared to argue that the preacher only presents the Word of Christ in the sermon, while the priest represents the very Body of Christ in the chief sacrament.[12] Laud insisted that all altars should be railed: he had never thought of railing off the pulpit. He was far more likely, as Archbishop of Canterbury, to have eliminated all pulpits that he could not tune, so alert was he to the danger of deviation from theological or political orthodoxy.

The greater Puritan estimation of sermons was due to a number of causes. The greatest unquestionably was the evidence in the pages of the New Testament that preaching had effected the conversion of the godless into the godly. It was, as St. Paul indicated, "the power of God unto salvation." By it the apostles transformed a crowd on the day of Pentecost into the first Church of Christ. One had only to preach the Word faithfully and the inner testimony of the Holy Spirit in the heart of the elect would cause it to be receptive soil for that holy seed to grow and fruit. But the seriousness with which the Puritans viewed and practised preaching can be gathered from four subordinate considerations also.

It should be noted that in the Book of Common Prayer no sermon is required for the Offices of Morning or Evening Prayers, yet it would be unthinkable for any service to be held in which Puritans did not merely read but also expounded Holy Writ. Where otherwise were men to find the revelation of the living God, except in His own Word, and its confirmation in their daily experience of His providence? No diet of worship, as they might have phrased

[10] *The Laws of Ecclesiastical Politie*, Bk. v, Chap. xxi, Sect. 2.
[11] *Ibid.*, v, xxii, 12.
[12] *Works* (Library of Anglo-Catholic Theology), vi, Pt. i, pp. 56f.

it, would be complete without the "Bread of Life," for as their Master had taught them: "Man does not live by bread alone, but by every word which proceeds out of the mouth of God." The sermon was necessary even when they were celebrating the Lord's Supper which they recognised to be, with St. Augustine, the *Verbum visibile*, or visible Word of God. This insistence on the primacy and sovereignty of God's Word was their reason for rejecting officially written and prescribed homilies as a substitute for preaching, for in their mind there was no alternative to a godly divine's own responsibility to instruct, exhort, encourage, and correct his congregation from his own study of God's revelation and his personal knowledge of the needs of his flock based upon catechising them and on pastoral visitation. A further proof of the intense seriousness with which preaching was taken is found in the demand that heads of households and fathers of families (and their charges, whether children, servants, or apprentices) should memorize and cause to be rehearsed the main headings of the sermon on Sunday evenings at home. We are able to glimpse this in the *Memoirs of the Life of Colonel Hutchinson*, penned by Lucy, the devoted wife of this Cromwellian commander. "By the time I was four years old," she writes, "I read English perfectly, and having a great memory, I was carried to sermons; and while I was very young could remember them and repeat them exact. . . ."[13] It was, however, the great length of Puritan sermons which demonstrated conclusively the extraordinary pains taken in their preparation to say nothing of the godly endurance and patience required by the congregations who listened to them.

Two famous Puritan stories, not to mention the criticisms of Anglican opponents, are evidence of the prolixity of Puritan preaching.[14] The first of them concerns the demagogue Hugh Peters, that darling of the Puritan groundlings, who once preached for three hours on a fast day. When the hour-glass had twice been emptied, he took it in his hand, turned it, and said, "Come, my beloved, we will have the other glasse, and so we'll part."[15] Our second story proves that variety of matter and fluency of delivery

13 *Op. cit.* (ed. C. H. Firth, 1906), p. 15.
14 Anglicans and Quakers also erred in this respect, but not as frequently as Puritans. A great offender was the learnedly loquacious Master of Trinity, Dr. Isaac Barrow, whose sermon was once abruptly terminated by a sexton drowning him out by blowing the organ. Fox could be long-winded, for he mentions in his *Journal* (ed. N. Penney, 1924, p. 145) that while at Leominster, he "stood up and declared about three hours."
15 *Tales and Jests of Mr. Hugh Peters* (1807), Jest No. 50.

were regarded as major qualities in the estimation of a good preacher. It appears that Cromwell wished to test John Howe as a chaplain. Summoning him to his camp headquarters, he gave him a text to study on the eve of the Sabbath. The next day, immediately after the prayer preceding the sermon, Cromwell altered the text which he had commanded Howe to expound; the worthy divine preached on the changed text until the monitory sands of the first and second hour had run out. Only when he was turning the hourglass for the third hour was he called upon to desist.[16] One wonders how often congregations had to endure preaching marathons of this type.

Anglicans were not slow to criticise either the frequency or prolixity of Puritan preaching. Two examples deserve citation for their vividness and wit. Dr. Nicholas Andrews is reported by the Puritan divine John White as saying that "Peter's sword cutt off but one eare, but long sermons like long swords, cutt off both at once . . . and that the silliest creatures have longest eares, and that preaching was the worst part of God's worship, and that if he left out anything, he would leave that out."[17] Herbert Thorndike, a more distinguished and scholarly Anglican divine, believed that the fame of preaching among the Puritans could be proved to be merely a matter of physical endurance and observed: "I call the World to witness; is it not a work as much of lungs and sides, as an office of God's service, which takes up the time of their Church Assemblies?"[18] But these views of Anglicans, who had suffered in penal times, are tinged with bitterness rather than characterized by balance. They would not have been approved of by Andrewes or Donne. Indeed, Donne wished to insist on the co-ordinate importance of sermon and the chief sacrament, declaring that they are like thunder and lightning, since preaching is like the lightning in clearing the air of ignorance and the sacrament is the presence of Christ himself.[19] On another occasion, as if to forestall the criticism that he made too much of preaching, Donne reminded his hearers that Christ "preached long before He instituted the sacraments, and that the sacraments were instituted by Christ as subsidiary things, in a great part because of human

[16] E. Calamy, *Continuation of the Ejected Ministers* (1727), I, p. 250f.
[17] *The First Century of Scandalous Malignant Priests* (1643), p. 8.
[18] *The Due Way of Composing the Differences* (1660), p. 50.
[19] *The Sermons of John Donne*, 10 vols. (eds. George R. Potter and Evelyn M. Simpson, Berkeley and Los Angeles, California, 1953-1962), IV, p. 105.

infirmity who need such sensible [that is, apprehensible by the senses] aids to our understanding of divine things."[20]

Another important difference between Anglican and Puritan preaching consisted in the way in which sermons were prepared and delivered.[21] Theoretically there were four possibilities. The sermon could be read from a full manuscript. Or, it could be preached from notes or headings, as summaries or mnemonics. Or, again, it could be learned by heart and preached without manuscript. Or, finally, and most brashly, it could be preached *ex tempore*,[22] so as allegedly to be more completely the work of the Holy Spirit. (The last alternative was employed almost exclusively by the most radical sectarians and "mechanick" preachers.)

Anglican custom generally favoured the reading of the manuscript (as was clearly so in the cases of Hooker and Sanderson), or the use of notes, as in the case of Hammond or Donne, though either of the latter two could have preached sermons from memory. Izaak Walton informs us, for example, that Donne, as Dean of St. Paul's Cathedral, preached at least once a week. Moreover, "he never gave his eyes rest, till he had chosen out a new text, and that night cast his sermon into a form, and his text into divisions; and the next day betook himself to consult the Fathers, and so committed his meditations to his memory which was excellent."[23] An amusing anecdote about Dr. Robert Sanderson, former Regius Professor of Divinity at Oxford and a future bishop, informs us of that divine's practice. According to Walton, when the learned Dr. Henry Hammond tried to persuade Dr. Sanderson to trust himself to preach a short sermon without reading his manuscript so as to address a neighbouring village congregation with greater liveliness, directness, and freedom, the result was disastrous for both congregation and preacher. Hammond, who had Sanderson's sermon manuscript in his hand, saw that the latter was "so lost as to

---

20 *Op. cit.*, x, p. 69. Donne spoke as if he normally preached a sermon of an hour's length. Indeed, on one occasion he indicated that each of his four divisions lasted for a quarter of an hour. (*Op. cit.*, VI, p. 64.)

21 See the fascinating essay of John Sparrow, "John Donne and Contemporary Preachers," *Essays and Studies by Members of the English Association* (Oxford, 1931), XVI, pp. 144-78.

22 Donne anticipated this theory by arguing, in rebuttal, that the Holy Spirit would give the preacher "a care of delivering God's messages with consideration, with meditation, with preparation; and not barbarously, not suddenly, not occasionally, not extemporarily, which might derogate from the dignity of so great a service." (*Works*, XI, p. 171.)

23 *The Lives of John Donne, Sir Henry Wotton, Richard Hooker, George Herbert, and Robert Sanderson* (World's Classics edn., 1927), p. 67.

the matter, especially the method, that he also became afraid for him, for it was discoverable to many of that plain auditory." The upshot was that as they walked together back to Hammond's home, Dr. Sanderson said most eagerly, "Good Doctor, give me my sermon and know, that neither you nor any man living shall ever persuade me to preach again without books." A chagrined Dr. Hammond replied, "Good Doctor, be not angry; for if I ever persuade you to preach again without book, I will give you leave to burn all the books that I am master of."[24]

After the Civil Wars the Anglican custom changed decisively in favour of the use of notes only in the pulpit and schemes that could be retained in the memory of preacher and congregation, instead of the earlier preference for learning the manuscript by heart. This change tended to give sermons less of an oratorical and more of a conversational quality, and it was precisely the qualities of naturalness and clarity that previous sermons lacked. The only major exceptions to the changed rule on the part of post-Restoration preachers were Barrow and Tillotson.

For their part, the Puritans throughout the century encouraged the delivery of sermons carefully written out either from memory or from notes. A few among them went with notes into the pulpit, and may well have written the sermon out in full (with additions) for its publication in print.[25]

3. The Metaphysical Preachers

The two most distinguished members of this famous circle were, of course, Bishop Lancelot Andrewes and Dean John Donne, but there were others such as Bishop John King (author of the superb tribute to his dead wife, *The Exequy*), Richard Corbet, and John Hacket, and even a Puritan divine, Thomas Adams, whom some have claimed, perhaps erroneously, to be of this company. Yet even before Donne and contemporary with Andrewes there was a distinguished preacher of the same mode, Thomas Playfere.[26] So great

---

[24] Walton reports the incident in the last part of his *Lives* and it is also recorded with interesting comments in the *Works of Robert Sanderson, D.D.* (ed. William Jacobson, Oxford, 1854), VI, pp. 314-15.

[25] J. Fraser Mitchell, *English Pulpit Oratory from Andrewes to Tillotson* (1932), p. 26.

[26] Reference is made to Playfere in Davies, *op. cit.*, I, pp. 236, 245. In a sermon named "Heart's Delight" he spoke of Christ as "our heavenly Ulysses" and the cross as "the mast to which we must bind ourselves for safety." (*The Whole Sermons*, 1623, p. 8.) This reference is an incidental reminder that the metaphysical preachers used not only the Scriptures and the Greek and Latin Fathers, but the classical pagan writers also, and, in some cases, even the cabbalists.

was the attraction of the metaphysical style in preaching for the learned and witty men that were its practitioners that they were unable to give it up even when the style was no longer in the mode. Cosin, for example, continued to preach in this manner even as Bishop of Durham after the Restoration, a whole generation after its popularity had waned. And as late as 1679 Evelyn recorded: "The Bp. of Gloucester preach'd in a manner very like Bishop Andrews, full of divisions, and scholastical, and that with much quicknesse."[27]

The epithet "metaphysical" as applied to these preachers is curious to modern eyes. It cannot be metaphysics as distinguished from logic, the two traditional major divisions of philosophy, because these men were as much concerned with dividing and subdividing their texts as their Puritan opponents. Their analytical powers were striking, but so were those of the Presbyterians. Nor could the controversial term be thought to refer to their philosophical profundity. Andrewes was, indeed, a deeply devout Christian, a mine of patristic lore, and a polylingual scholar,[28] but he was no philosopher. Nor was Donne, however penetrating his psychological knowledge of the springs of human behaviour. The term "metaphysical" can then only have been used in the loosest sense to describe preachers who emphasized the paradoxical character of the Christian revelation, who used far-fetched analogies to create surprise and interest, and whose word-play was dazzling, while their erudition and culture were wide. It was, without doubt, highly intelligent preaching of the relevance of the essential dogmas of the Christian faith to the human condition. Bishop Andrewes preached seventeen different sermons which shed light on different aspects of the Incarnation of the eternal Son of God, and Donne kept on recurring to the theme of the Life Everlasting, that stage beyond his macabre meditation on death on which his sceptical spirit sought assurance. Above all, this witty, learned, ingenious word-play was the delight of the Jacobean court before whom Bishop Andrewes preached at the request of James I, as it was the

---

27 *Diary*, April 4, 1679.

28 "His admirable knowledge in the learned tongues, Latine, Greeke, Hebrew, Chaldee, Syriack, Arabick, besides other Moderne Tongues to the number of *fifteene* (as I am informed) was such & so rare, that he may well be ranked in the first place as one of the rarest linguists in Christendom." (*A Sermon preached at the funerall of the Right Honourable and Reverend Father in God Lancelot late Lord Bishop of Winchester . . . on Saturday being the XI of November A.D. MDCXXVI.*) By Iohn late L. Bishop of Ely (p. 18). These skills were used to their greatest advantage in his translation of the Pentateuch in the Authorised (or King James') version of the Scriptures.

pleasure of the polite in St. Paul's Cathedral where Donne made every sermon on occasion.

Lancelot Andrewes was pre-eminently the preacher for great occasions (festivals and fasts in the life of the church and the nation). His collected sermons are almost all classifiable in this way; 67 sermons were preached on important days in the church year, 18 on state days, and a further 10 on widely different occasions. Further subdivisions show that Andrewes preached 18 Easter Day sermons, 17 Nativity Day sermons, 15 on Whitsunday (Pentecost), 8 on Ash Wednesday, 6 general Lenten sermons, and 3 on Good Friday. State occasions on which he preached were 8 sermons on Gowrie Day, recalling the deliverance of the King from the treachery and sedition of the Earl of Gowrie, and 10 Gunpowder Plot sermons. The miscellaneous sermons vary from those preached as early as 1590 and 1591 at Whitehall, respectively on "Justification in Christ" and on "Caesar his due" to a Coronation Day sermon in 1606 and one in time of pestilence in 1609. His most enduring sermons are, naturally, those which concentrate on the great days in the Life of Christ, for he was an exceedingly devout[29] man who has enriched his meditations with those of the Fathers in east and west.

Andrewes never ceased to be astonished by the sheer generosity of divine grace in the Incarnation.[30] On the text, "Unto us a child is born," he makes the fullest use of the inherent paradox of God made man, as he develops the themes of child and son:

> All along His life you shall see these two. At His birth: a *Cratch* for the *Childe*; a *Starre* for the *Sonne*: A company of *Shepheards* viewing the *Child*; a *Quire of Angels* celebrating the *Son*. In His life: *Hungry* Himselfe, to shew the nature of the *Child*; yet *feeding five thousand*, to show the power of the *Sonne*. At His death: dying on the *Crosse*, as the Son of Adam; at the same time disposing of *Paradise*, as the *Sonne of God*.

[29] *Ibid.*, p. 21, pithily informs us that *vita ejus, vita orationis*, and that "a great part of five houres every day did he spend in prayer and devotion to God." His *Preces Privatae*, a veritable classic of Anglican devotion, was considered in our Chapter III.

[30] When expounding the Prologue of St. John's Gospel and the words, "And the Word became flesh" Andrewes says: "I add yet farther: what flesh? The flesh of an infant. What, *Verbum infans*, the Word an infant? The Word, and not able to speak a Word? How evil agreeth this! This He put up. How born, how entertained? In a stately palace, cradle of ivory, robes of estate? No; but a stable for His palace, a manger for His cradle, poor clouts for His array."

If you aske, why both these? . . . But that He was a *Childe*,
He could not have suffered. But that He was a *Sonne* He had
sunke in His *suffering*, and not gone through with it . . .
Therefore, that He might be *lyable*, He was a *Childe*; that
He might be *able*, He was the *Son*: that He might be both,
He was both.[31]

This is most impressive for its concision, perfect balance of
Christ's two natures, divine and human, splendidly exemplified in
his prose, and with a singular objectivity, and the whole ordered
with such admirable planning. It is only the rather strained contrast between "lyable" and "able" that seems distracting in its
artificiality.

One example of the witty etymological word-play of Bishop
Andrewes must suffice: It is taken from his explanation of Isaiah
7:14.

This *Immanu* is a Compounde againe: we may take it, in
sunder, into *Nobis* and *cum*: And so then have we three
pieces. 1. *El*, the mighty GOD: 2. and *Anu* wee, poore wee;
(Poore indeed, if we have all the world beside, if we have not
Him to be *with us*:) 3. And *Im*, which is *cum*, And that
cum, in the midst betwene *nobis* and *Deus*, GOD and Vs;
to couple GOD and *us*; thereby to conveigh the things of the
one to the other.[32]

T. S. Eliot has rightly insisted on the capacity of Andrewes to
derive a world from a word, "squeezing and squeezing the word
until it yields a full juice of meaning, which we should never have
supposed any word to possess."[33] His words are like firework displays in which rockets emit one jet of sparkling chrysanthemums
of fire only to be succeeded by others as beautiful. And his style,
also like fireworks in this respect, springs surprise after surprise.

What were the strengths of England's first great pulpit orator
since the Reformation? First, he wisely concentrated his attention
on the major facets of the Christ-event which are renewed in the
church year. He meditated on the extraordinary generosity of God
in order to lead his hearers to admire holiness and to attempt it.
His subjects were: the Incarnation in which God came closest to
man that he might raise man; the Crucifixion and the reconcilia-

---

31 *XCVI Sermons*, "Second Nativity Sermon" (3rd edn., 1635), p. 12.
32 *Ibid.*, "Ninth Nativity Sermon," p. 77.
33 *For Lancelot Andrewes, Essays on Style and Order* (1928), p. 25.

tion thus effected between sinful man and gracious God and the forgiveness won for man; the Resurrection and its promise of hope for the Christian; and the Pentecost with its donation of the Holy Spirit as the church's bond of solidarity and that divine empowerment that overcomes human frailty and makes holiness possible. In life he was forced to use his pen in the controversial battle between Canterbury and Rome (and, incidentally, acquitted himself well with no less an antagonist than the brilliant Jesuit, Cardinal Bellarmine), but this he avoided in the pulpit like the plague, just as he avoided such points of speculative divinity as the counsel of God in predestination, a theme which so much engaged the Puritan divines.

He it was, along with Hooker, who insisted upon the continuity of the Church of England with the church of the first five centuries. This was manifest not only in the themes of his sermons, as in the mosaic of his *Preces Privatae*, but in his extraordinary knowledge of and fondness for the Greek and Latin Fathers of the church, whom he loved to cite in the original tongues, with hints to the unlearned listener of their meanings. In the same sense that the *Patres* were Fathers of the universal church, Lancelot Andrewes was a Father of the early Anglican church, a pillar of orthodoxy and stability in doctrine, in devotion, and in the exemplary charity of his life.

His third quality is wit. This combines the most subtle wordplay, the use of surprising even startling images and comparisons, and brings before the hearer's amazed eyes the treasures of exotic knowledge drawn from the distant caves of Greece, Rome, Jerusalem, the deserts of North Africa, and from Renaissance Italy or medieval Christendom. One fact or legend may come from a medieval bestiary and the next from the speculations of the *Cabbala*.

These great gifts and qualities, combined with the exacting court audience for whom his sermons were prepared, might have led Andrewes to play to the gallery. In a word, his conceits might have made him conceited. Perhaps his most astonishing quality in his apparent objectivity—his capacity to lose himself in the grandeur of his message and the splendour of the mighty acts of God to which he drew attention. In a very self-conscious situation Andrewes makes one share his God-consciousness. Here he presents a notable contrast with Donne who may have his head in the clouds like an angel, but is a man very much with his feet on the solid earth; or, to vary the image, has one eye on God and one eye on the effect he is making. Eliot claims that Andrewes's intellect and sensibility were in complete harmony.[34] Certainly, one does not feel in reading Andrewes that he is exploiting our curiosity by sensationalism or using secular bait to entrap us for holiness. Even if, as the twentieth century has taught us to believe, all motives are mixed, one has the assurance that those of Andrewes are mixed with a high concentration of consecration.

What, then, were the defects of his preaching? Probably the over-concentration on the literary craftsmanship, admirable as the rhetoric is, leads to a sense of sheer artificiality and this creates a "credibility gap." The fact is that so much contrived eloquence overwhelms conviction. The superb etymological and syllable-by-syllable analysis of texts has another defect of its quality: the style is so jerky, so staccato in its effect, that it never allows the reader to relax even for the purposes of deeper meditation on the meaning. His distinctions are frequently over nice, requiring brackets within brackets, and this is the result of a very tortuous and often fussy exegesis. Moreover, even when the exegesis does not strain at a gnat, but sustains a relevant exposition of central themes, his applications are rarely driven home to hearer or reader.[35] This may well be related to the fact that while Andrewes had a great knowledge of the Fathers, he was no expert in human psychology; in this respect he was far inferior to John Donne. The result was that while he was admired in polite and aristocratic society for his brilliance, learning, and devotion, he had his critics in his own day and since. Some have despised what they consider his playing less to the gallery than the royal box,[36] and certainly his respect for the divine right of kings seems to tread between the verges of servility and idolatry. Others have felt that his word-play made folly of preaching. The serious Richard Baxter averred "when I read such a book as Bishop Andrews *Sermons*, or heard such kind of preaching, I felt no life in it: methought they did but play with holy things."[37] A Presbyterian Lord had made much the same observation to King James at Holyrood: "No doubt your Majesty's bishop is a learned man, but he cannot preach. He rather plays with his text than preaches on it."[38] These are over-censorious judgments

---

[34] *Ibid.*, p. 20.
[35] F. E. Hutchinson, "The English Pulpit from Fisher to Donne," *Cambridge History of English Literature*, IV, Chap. 12, p. 238.
[36] Charles Smyth, *The Art of Preaching* (1952), p. 122.
[37] *The Safe Religion* (1657), the epistle to the reader.
[38] *Op. cit.*, ed. F. E. Hutchinson, IV, p. 239. George Herbert would have been sympathetic to this viewpoint as he complained of those who practise "crumbling

and one wonders what success Baxter would have had in court or cathedral circles with his plain, urgent, pathetic Puritan style.

Though both Donne and Andrewes are classed as metaphysical preachers, they are read today for different reasons. Those who value theology will read Andrewes despite his style, while those who love Donne read him less for the theology than the style, capable of splendidly ascending climaxes, of wilting satire, of surprising paradoxes and amazing images, of macabre concentration on death, or of conscience-piercing directness, and always the vivid index of a mind that is curious and a personality that is passionate, and a memory that is served by rapacious reading. Donne seemed in his day a second St. Augustine, the voluptuous rhetorician (or poet) converted whose sermons sometimes assumed the form of the *Confessions*, a direct address and even argument with God for man's sake.

On his mother's side, Donne was descended from the courageous humanist, St. Thomas More, and was ever haunted by the Catholicism[39] that had formed him and from which he had never entirely dissociated himself. It was only at the age of forty-three that the minor diplomat and courtier took holy orders in the Church of England, that is in 1615. A year later he was appointed Reader in Divinity to Lincoln's Inn, the major professional training-centre for lawyers who admired his preaching for its brilliance and profundity. On November 19, 1621, he came to his rightful throne—the pulpit of the old Gothic St. Paul's Cathedral in London. Learned and simple, the merely curious and the sincere enquirer, the lover of learning and the collector of quips and witticisms, the godly and the godless flocked to listen to him, and knew—especially after the death of Bishop Lancelot Andrewes in 1626—that there was no finer preacher in England.

Walton, who had been his parishioner, shows us what his contemporaries admired in Donne, who preached

---

a text into small parts. . . ." (*Works of George Herbert*, ed. F. E. Hutchinson, Oxford, 1941, pp. 234f.)

[39] It is not easy to determine why Donne left his ancestral faith. It may have been the difficulty of a secular career as a Recusant in Protestant England. In his sermons, Donne quarrels with Rome ostensibly because he disapproves of her additions to fundamental primitive and patristic doctrines, as also of her rather theatrical ceremonialism, calling her a "painted Church." (Cf. *Sermons*, eds. Potter and Simpson, IV, p. 106; I, p. 246.) Correlatively, he admires the Church of England because she distinguishes between essentials and non-essentials (*Sermons*, II, pp. 203f.).

the Word so, as shewed his own heart was possest with those
very thoughts and joys that he laboured to distill into others:
A Preacher in earnest; weeping sometimes for his Auditory,
sometimes with them: always preaching to himself, like an
Angel from a cloud, but in none; carrying some, as St. Paul
was, to Heaven in holy raptures, and inticing others by a
sacred Art and Courtship to amend their lives; here picturing
a vice so as to make it ugly to those who practised it; and a
vertue so as to make it be beloved even by those that lov'd it
not; and all this with a most particular grace and an unexpressible addition to comeliness.[40]

He well knew the purpose of a sermon was to proclaim the saving
power of God in the lives of men:

There is no salvation but by faith, nor faith but by hearing,
nor hearing but by preaching; and they that thinke meanliest
of the Keyes of the Church, and speak faintliest of the Absolution of the Church, will yet allow, That those Keyes lock,
and unlock in Preaching; That Absolution is conferred, or
withheld in Preaching, That the proposing of the promises of
the Gospel in Preaching, is that binding and loosing on earth,
which bindes and looses in heaven.[41]

In fact, his interesting choice of images to describe the preacher,
is an indication of the variety of the duties and privileges of his
divine calling. "Not only," writes William Mueller, using Donne's
terms, "is the preacher a husband to his congregation: he is an
archer, a watchman, a trumpeter, a harmonious charmer; he pos-
sesses the most desirable qualities of a lion, an ox, an eagle, and a
man; he is an earthquake, a son of thunder, the fall of waters, the
roaring of a lion."[42]

What are the strengths of this famous and engaging preacher?
He offers, in the first place, an incisive meditation on the scriptural
texts that he is expounding, coloured by patristic, medieval and
contemporary commentaries, but above all by his own rich experience of the world. If Andrewes makes his single predominant

---

40 *The Lives of John Donne* (World's Classics edn., 1927), p. 49.
41 *Sermons* (ed. Potter and Simpson), VII, p. 320.
42 William R. Mueller, *John Donne: Preacher* (Princeton, N.J., 1962), p. 43.
This is an admirable study of Donne's theology and his rhetorical style.

theme the Incarnation (also a theme to which the paradoxical Donne is also attracted), Donne makes his *leitmotiv* the transition from death to resurrection, thus making the human tragedy end triumphantly as the divine comedy. But, and this is distinctively Donne's contribution, he faces the horror of death and dissolution to the full and in the most macabre detail, before he gives the reassurance that God will collect and resoul the scattered parts of bodies at the General Resurrection. Donne gives us the horrific nightmare of "this death of corruption and putrifaction, of vermiculation and incineration, of dissolution and dispersion" before he confidently affirms in faith that "God knowes in which Boxe of his Cabinet all this seed Pearle lies, in what corner of the World every graine of every mans duste sleeps, shall recollect that dust, and then recompact that man, and that is the accomplishment of all."[43] That is his distinctive treatment of a central Christian theme, but far from his only theme. He is concerned with the entire theme of man's fall and redemption, and particularly in his treatment of the church, he is not afraid to be a bold defender of the Church of England as the *via media* between the accretions of Rome and the nakedness of Geneva. In fact, part of his magnetism is the sense he gives that he has fought through scepticism to conviction in almost every article of Christian belief. J. Fraser Mitchell describes him as a "Tamerlane confined to a pulpit, or Faustus desiring all knowledge and vivid for sensual enjoyment, but held spellbound by the eyes of the Crucified."[44] It is because, like Augustine of Hippo before him and Francis Thompson after him, he gives the impression of having tried all other ways of life until in exhaustion he reaches Christian discipleship, that his invitations to Christian morality are psychologically insinuating and so persuasive. For him as truly as for St. Augustine, *Cor nostrum inquietum donec requiescat in Te.* Yet to stress this *taedium Christianum*, inevitable in a man who becomes a priest in middle age after a profligate youth, is entirely to forget Donne's abounding sense of the joy the devout life brings, with its conviction of the providence and protection of God. Donne found in Him the constant Love that he failed to discover in his earthly amours. God was all in all to him eventually as he implies in one passage where he speaks of God as our Father, potter, minter, sculptor, tailor, steward, physician, neighbour, Samaritan, gardener, architect, builder, sentinel, and

[43] *LXXX Sermons* (1640), p. 212.   [44] *Op. cit.*, p. 181.

shepherd.[45] In short, his themes were the central topics of the Christian faith and life.

Another admirable quality in his preaching was his use of striking, often esoteric, and always vivid images, which gives his prose a poetical and even dramatic quality. These images come from many walks of life or ways of observation. There are commercial, agricultural, geographical, geometrical, and marine images, and Donne is especially effective in using anatomical analogies, as we might expect from the love poems. Such is the pictorial pliability of Donne's mind that, as Mueller observes, he can use the same image of the fishing net in two different senses in two sermons: once, as when Jesus first called His fishermen disciples, as obstacles in the way of following Him, and, second, as a metaphor for the Gospel itself which catches men as a net catches fish.[46] Moreover, it is very often in the use of an apt or striking image that his considerable wit is seen. "The Devel is no recusant," he observed; "he will come to church, and he will lay his snares there."[47] How vividly he contrasts Roman Catholicism with Presbyterianism, Rome with Geneva when he says—arguing that true religion is not to be found "either in a painted Church, on one side, or in a *naked Church* on another; a Church in a *Dropsie*, overflowne with *Ceremonies*, or a Church in a *Consumption*, for want of such Ceremonies, as the primitive Church found usefull and beneficiall for the advancing of the glory of God, and the devotion of the Congregation." Donne had a most vivid artist's eye, but even this was, as M. M. Mahood[48] pointed out, almost certainly assisted by the use of emblem books, a common feature of this time. In variety and richness and originality of imagery Donne was more than a match for Andrewes.

In another respect also Donne is better than Andrewes in the pulpit. This is the way he related his teaching to the practical needs of his congregation. His preaching has about it a sanctified worldliness. His concern was not merely to move his hearers, but to move them to Christian action. He will not, for example, allow them to plead their humours or temperaments (as we might today excuse

45 *Sermons* (eds. Potter and Simpson), IX, pp. 131-32.
46 Mueller, *op. cit.*, p. 121.
47 F. E. Hutchinson, "The English Pulpit from Fisher to Donne," p. 241.
48 *Poetry and Humanism* (1950), p. 147. George Herbert made extensive use of emblem books for his poems, as most preachers did of commonplace books for suitable citations. There were also compilations of illustrations for sacred or secular use, as Robert Cawdrey's *A Treasure or Store-House of Similies* (1600).

our conduct or our complexes, our heredity or our early environment): "Let no man therefore think to present his complexion to
God for an excuse, and say, My choler with which my constitution
abounded, and which I could not remedy, inclined me to wrath,
and so, to bloud; my Melancholy enclined me to Sadnesses and so
to Desperation, as though thy sins were medecinall sins, sins to
vent humours."[49] Donne knew that the minister must preach "for
the saving of soules, and not for the sharpning of wits."[50]

Andrewes deliberately rejected controversial divinity from his
sermons, while Donne accepted it as having a subordinate place in
the pulpit. He seemed to be doubtful about using the double-edged
weapon of irony, but when he did, it was used to devastating effect
as a form of ridicule. Consider, for example, how he makes bovril
out of Papal bulls and claims of infallibility by sheer ridicule; he
has just observed that the Roman Catholic church has imprisoned
the Holy Spirit in the bosom of the Pope: "And so the Holy Ghost
is no longer a Dove, a Dove in the Ark, a Dove with an Olivebranch, a Messenger of Peace, but now the Holy Ghost is in a Bull,
in Buls worse than *Phalaris* his Bull, Buls of Excommunication,
Buls of Rebellion, and Deposition, and Assassinates of Christian
Princes."[51] It may have been conducive to excitement, it was not
to the spirit of devotion appropriate to worship.

Donne's most characteristic quality, his passionate subjectivity,
has been acclaimed by some and disapproved by others. In a
particularly harsh judgment, T. S. Eliot, who greatly preferred
the reserve, objectivity, and "relevant intensity" of Andrewes,[52]
described Donne as shadowed "by the impure motive," which
added to his "facile success." Even worse, and in what one can
only regard as a most unfortunate personal comparison with a
stunter and exploiter in religion,[53] Eliot refers to Donne as "a little
of the religious spell-binder, the Reverend Billy Sunday of his time,
the flesh-creeper, the sorcerer of emotional orgy. . . ."[54] One may
recognize that Donne was conscious of the various technical devices

[49] *LXXX Sermons* (1640), p. 390.
[50] *Sermons* (eds. Potter and Simpson), VIII, p. 42.
[51] *Ibid.*, VIII, p. 265.
[52] Mueller has countered this by claiming for Donne "existential intensity"
in *op. cit.*, p. 246.
[53] One must contrast the dedication and modesty of D. L. Moody, for example,
in order to understand the reprehensible self-advertising and "scalping" activities
of Billy Sunday, who was a shrewd ignoramus. This makes the comparison of
the learned and consecrated Donne with Sunday so inept, a mere caricature unworthy of T. S. Eliot's usual perceptive and balanced judgments.
[54] *For Lancelot Andrewes*, p. 20.

necessary for keeping his congregation awake, without charging him with entirely spurious motives. Furthermore, it could be argued that it was the lessons bitterly learned from his experience that made him so appropriate a preacher to Renaissance minds and hearts in court and law court. He was, indeed, a "personality" and a "character" but there is nothing but regret in one of the most famous passages of an autobiographical nature, which seems so moving in its sincerity, even if couched in majestic cadences:

> Let me wither and weare out mine age in a discomfortable, in an unwholesome, in a penurious prison, and so to pay my debts with my bones, and recompence the wastfulnesse of my youth with the beggery of mine age; Let me wither in a spittle under sharpe, and foule, and infamous diseases, and so to recompence the wantonnesse of my youth, with that loath-someness in mine age; yet if God with-draw not his spirituall blessings, his Grace, his Patience, If I can call my Suffering his Doing, my passion his Action, All this that is temporall, is but a caterpillar got into one corner of my garden, but a mill-dew fallen upon one acre of my Corne; The body of all, the substance of all is safe, so long as the Soule is sage.[55]

Donne's gift was his capacity to identify with his auditory, to make their fears of death his, their hopes of amendment because of remorse his, and their longing for eternal life beyond the muta-bility of the age and the daily decrepitude his, and to do this, while reminding them of the power and promises and provisions of the living God. Andrewes may hide himself in his doctrine, but he is incapable of the direct and passionate address and therefore of the persuasion of Donne.

Homer nods and Donne had his faults. There is an obscurity in many of his sermons unsuitable for one whose main aim is edification.[56] It may take the form of esoteric lore,[57] or even of a coinage of new words often of a quinquepedalian length.[58]

---

55 *Sermons* (eds. Potter and Simpson), VII, p. 56. For another passage of this kind, see II, p. 300.

56 In *ibid.*, VII, p. 95, Donne declared: "a sermon intends *Exhortation* prin-cipally and *Edification*, and a holy stirring of the religious affections, and then *matters of Doctrine*, and points of *Divinity*. . . ."

57 See Mary P. Ramsey, *Les Doctrines Médiévales chez Donne* (Oxford, 1917), which shows his fondness for Tertullian, Aquinas and especially Augustine. H.J.C. Grierson in *Poetical Works*, II, pp. 223-24, shows his fascination with Rabbinical and Cabbalistic writings, even in the original Hebrew.

58 Some five-syllabled examples are the following: *contesseration, exhaeredation, immarcessible, pre-increpation, repullulation, re-efformation.*

Despite his splendid eloquence, much of his homiletical writing is dated, by its far-fetched allegorical interpretation which cannot stand up to historical criticism, not to mention the extraordinary importance on his view of the church's relation to the sovereign and the nation, inappropriate in the modern democratic and secular context of culture.

His sermon structure was more often conceived than kept. He sometimes breaks the form to great effect; more often his meandering leads to a loss of concentration and therefore of effectiveness.

Despite the need to keep the attention of both the intelligentsia and the groundlings, he sometimes degenerated into melodrama, and his final shroud sermon, though most Baroque and contemporary, is in fact to be described as Pelagian posturing, however good its motive to preach unforgettably.[59] But all in all his like has not been seen, nor will be. He was the unique glory of the English, not merely the Jacobean, pulpit.

4. The "Senecan" Preachers

From the beginning of the century until the Restoration there was a flourishing group of preachers, who used rhetorical devices without what they would consider to be the extravagances, conceits, witty word-play, esoteric knowledge, and over-fragmented exegesis of the metaphysical divines. Their pithier and more compact oratory and its powerfully ethical content, as well as their citations from classical moralists, has earned them the name of "Senecan,"[60] though this is as unsatisfactory a designation as "metaphysical" for the other group. The new group comprised such Calvinist Anglicans as the witty Puritan Thomas Adams, or the gifted Bishop Joseph Hall who held the sees of Exeter and Norwich in succession, and perhaps midway between the metaphysicals and the Senecans was the superb stylist, Bishop Jeremy Taylor, whose Patristic lore and ornate imagery link him with the former, and his moral teaching with the latter.

Thomas Adams is particularly interesting because he belonged to the Puritan wing of the Anglican church and was like Hall in being a Calvinist not an Arminian like the Laudian Metaphysicals,

---

[59] A modern secular equivalent would be the famous picture of Salvador Dali, very much alive and advertising, lying in an open, silk-lined coffin, with lilies about his head. A religious equivalent would be the annual circus service in Birmingham, England, in which the elephants are led round to the congregation with yoghurt cartons in their trunks for offertory basins!

[60] J. Fraser Mitchell, op. cit., pp. 352f.

as also in making a great use of "characters," that is, descriptions of types of persons who have been carefully observed, and which are used for minatory purposes. Here are two examples of Adams's "characters" in order to drive home moral lessons. First the usurer wracked with anxiety: "And though the usurer struffe his pillow with nothing but his bonds and mortgages, softer and sweeter in his opinion then downe or feathers; yet his head will not leave aking."[61] The second is the old man, possessed by his possessions: "No man is so old but still he thinks he may live another year; and therefore lightly the older, the more covetous; and *Quo minus viae restat, eo plus viatici quaeritur*: the less journey men have, the more provision they make."[62]

Adams struck like a poniard to the conscience of his bearers. One of his most ingenious images is that of a clock's pendulum swinging from presumption to despair:

> The Conscience is like the poyse of a clocke: the poyse being downe all motion ceaseth, the wheels stirre not: wound up, all is set on going. Whiles Conscience is downe, there is no noyse or moving in the heart; all is quiet; but when it is wound up by the Iustice of God, it sets all the wheels on working: tongue to confess, eyes to weepe, hands to wring, breast to be beaten, heart to ake, voyce to crie; and that where Mercy steps not in, a fatall crie, to the hilles, *Fall on us, and hide us.*[63]

For its brilliance and sustained power it is worthy of a Donne. His command of language is also reminiscent of Donne, as in the following "character" of the epicure, in which we are given his *credo*:

> I beleeue that sweet wine and strong drinkes; the best blood of the grape, or sweate of the corne is fittest for the belly. I beleeue that midnight revels, perfumed chambers, soft beds, close curtaines, and a Dalilah in mine arms, are very comfortable. I beleeue that glistring silkes, and sparkling jewels, a purse full of golden charmes, a house neatly decked, Gardens, Orchards, Fishponds, Parkes, Warrens, and whatsoeuer may yeeld pleasurable stuffing to the corpse, is a very heauen upon earth. I beleeue that to sleepe till dinner, and play till supper, and quaffe till midnight, and to dally

---

[61] *Works* (folio ed. of 1630), p. 634.
[62] *Ibid.*, p. 684.
[63] *Ibid.*, p. 757.

till morning; except there be some intermission to toss some paynted papers, or to whirle about squared bones . . . this is the most absolute and perfect end of man's life.[64]

The success of Adams was due to such vivid characterization, to his use of the classics such as Juvenal, Horace, Martial, Seneca, Ovid, and Aesop as well as a collation of the most intriguing sections of the Scriptures, to his employment of allegories, to his relentless pursuit of the consciences of his hearers, to his use of brilliant titles for his sermons,[65] and to his capacity to sustain attention.

Joseph Hall (1574-1656) resembled Donne in his wit and in having been a man of letters before he became a divine, and won fame in 1608 for naturalising in England the Theophrastan character. Like Donne, and his nearer contemporaries, such as Ussher[66] and Burton, Hall brought back cargo from the further shores of learning, and embedded Latin and Greek citations in his sermons. But the style is natural, and pithily aphoristic. The rhetoric is there, but less obtrusive than in the metaphysicals, and it points to the type of writing that came to be admired by the Restoration writers and preachers. His qualities are exemplified in the following citation from a sermon preached on the unpromising text of Deuteronomy 33:8: "And of Levi he said, Let thy Thummim and thine Urim be with thy holy One." Bishop Hall described Moses nearing the end of his life as he prepared to ascend Mount Nebo to die:

> *Moses* will do his best for God's people; being not satisfied with his own happinesse, unlesse his charge may prosper; nor content to have been their convoy all his life except he might direct the way at his death also. 'Tis a clear sun-set that commends the day, and the chief grace of the Theater is a good com off: wherefore our Prophet reserves his best Scene for the last Act, and in the evening of his life shines most gloriously; breaking forth upon the Tribes with a double ray of counsel and blessing.[67]

[64] *Ibid.*, pp. 498-99.

[65] As examples, "Mysticall Bedlam" and "The Devills Blanket."

[66] Ussher, who became Primate of the Anglican church in Ireland, was the author of an interesting book on church order recommending a conciliar rather than a monarchical episcopate, and this "reduced episcopacy," supposedly primitive, appealed greatly to Baxter and others who disliked Independency and feared prelacy. His sermons are dull, impersonal, argumentative, and plain to the point of nudity. He was a Calvinist like Adams and Hall.

[67] Cited from Abraham Wright's *Five Sermons in Five Several Styles or Waies*

There is an easy natural flow of the diction, perfect balance of the clauses, vivid images drawn from the stage and from nature, and an affectionately drawn portrait of the faithful father in God, Moses. Like most Calvinist divines he was a most loyal and exact expositor of Holy Writ, but also much livelier than most of the others.

Bishop Sanderson also belongs to the Senecan school of divines, partly because of the naturalness of style, the use of Patristic and classical learning, a great moral concern expressed through the study of particular cases (casuistry), though unlike those we have already considered he was no Calvinist. One of the best examples of his pellucid prose is his introduction to the revised Book of Common Prayer of 1662. His style of writing and preaching is adequately described by Walton, as follows: "there was in his sermons no improper rhetoric, nor such perplexed divisions as may be said to be like too much light, that so dazzles the eyes, that the sight becomes less perfect; but there was therein no want of useful matter, nor waste of words; and yet such clear distinctions as dispelled all confused notions, and made his hearers depart both wiser, and more confirmed in virtuous resolutions."[68]

The greatest homiletician of the non-metaphysical Anglican divines was unquestionably Bishop Jeremy Taylor (1613-1667). His writing is aesthetic in style and ethical in concern. His allusions to the classics and the Fathers are the references of a well-stored mind, rather than that of a well-conned commonplace book. He has the gift of mingling Christian and pagan writers in the most natural fashion, as when he claims that the Christian hope of eternal life "will make a satyr chast, and a Silenus to be sober, and Dives to be charitable, and Simon Magus to despise reputation, and Saul to turn from a Persecutor to an Apostle."[69] No writer of sermons has been so continuously read in English than Jeremy Taylor. His spirit appealed particularly to John Keble, two centuries later, who wrote that Taylor was "so gentle in heart, and so high in mind, so fervent in zeal, and so charitable in judgment. . . ."[70]

His major collection of sermons is entitled, *Eniautos, or A*

---

of Preaching (1656), pp. 23-24. It was preached at Wright's own ordination at Christ Church, Oxford by Bishop Hall and is the second sermon included in his anthology.

[68] Walton, *op. cit.*, p. 397.
[69] "Of Growth in Sinne," Sermon XVI from *XXVII Sermons* (1651).
[70] J. T. Coleridge, *Memoir of John Keble* (1869), p. 108.

Course of Sermons for all the Sundays of the Year, fitted to the great necessities and for supplying the wants of preaching in many parts of this nation (1651). It is in two parts, the first containing twenty-seven sermons is known as "The Summer Half," and the other with twenty-five sermons is known as "The Winter Half." It is curious that there is little apparent reference to the Christian year and therefore to the life of Christ, though that subject had been elaborated theologically and devotionally before in *The Great Exemplar.* The subjects of this particular collection of sermons include prayer, godly fear, flesh and spirit, the house of feasting, the marriage ring, Christian simplicity, mercy, sin, the righteous cause oppressed, and Taylor's pet-aversion, death-bed repentance.

It has been assumed that these polished sermons cannot have been preached in this printed form, but that the originals were simpler and less learned. On the other hand, Taylor's auditory in Lord and Lady Carbery's retreat at Golden Grove in South Wales, would not be country yokels, but the aristocrats and their friends, neighbouring clergy, and servants on the estate.[71] Moreover, it was conventional for Anglican divines of the day to include Greek and Latin citations in their sermons. No one could better illustrate C. J. Stranks' contention that while Puritan sermons were plain, "the Anglicans coveted that same love of beauty which made them embellish their churches and their ritual into the enrichment of their sermons"[72] than Jeremy Taylor.

Taylor is adept at the art of a striking beginning to a sermon. One, on original sin, begins thus: "It is not necessary that a commonwealth should give pensions to orators to dissuade men from running into houses infected with the plague . . ."[73] In the beginning of "The House of Feasting" Taylor begins by citing the proverb, "Let us eat, drink, and be merry, for to-morrow we die" and comments: "This is the epicure's proverb, begun upon a weak mistake, started by chance from the discourses of drink, and thought witty by the undiscerning company; but . . . when it comes to be examined by the consultations of the morning and the sober hours of the day, it seems the most witless and the most unreasonable in the world."[74]

---

[71] C. J. Stranks, *The Life and Writings of Jeremy Taylor* (1952), pp. 118-19.
[72] *Ibid.*, p. 119.
[73] *Works*, IV, p. 356. The first sermon in a series on "The Descending and Entailed Curse cut off."
[74] *Works*, IV, p. 180.

It is, however, his images that are Taylor's chief glory and delight. The majority of them are taken from Nature in its varied seasons, its flora and fauna, dawn, and sunset. One apt example is the description of cold prayers which are like "the buds of roses which a cool wind hath nip'd into death."[75] His most quoted passages are those which are elongated similes or metaphors, as "For so I have seen a lark . . ."[76] or "But so I have seen a rose. . . ."[77] Yet it is almost always the microcosm in nature which he admires—the miniature rather than the masterful.

His jokes are very gentle gibes, as when he pokes fun at the celibate, who "like the fly in the heart of an apple dwells in perpetual sweetness but sits alone, and is confined and dies in singularity."[78] Even in his funeral oration for Bramhall, he takes a sly dig at Papal infallibility (which should be compared with the roistering mood of Donne gibing at the same claim). Taylor observes that when St. Peter came back and informed the disciples that Christ was risen, because "he was not yet got into the Chair of the Catholic Church they did not think him infallible and so they believed him not at all."[79]

His learning is, of course, immense, even rapacious. C. J. Stranks has calculated that in his collected works there are citations or references to over 1300 different authors. The list is headed by Augustine with 684, followed by Chrysostom with 286, then Cicero with 216, Seneca with 190, and Juvenal with 116.[80] His vast reading included medieval legends, chronicles, casuistry, controversy, secular and sacred histories, the Fathers in east and west, the Scholastic theologians, the Rabbinical lore, Roman Catholic books of devotion and martyrologies, apart from the classical moralists and orators. While he is usually associated with the Laudian group, they were far from subscribing to his virtualist view of the Holy Communion, and it should not be forgotten that this most tolerant of divines[81] and author of *The Liberty of Prophesying* (1647) had an early link with Chillingworth and was a

---

[75] *XXV Sermons*, Sermon V, "The Return of Prayers."

[76] *Ibid.* This image for the soul fastened itself on the retina of posterity. It was used in Baxter's *The Saints' Everlasting Rest* and by Henry Smith's "A Caveat for Christians" in *Sermons and other Treatises* (1675).

[77] *Holy Dying*, cited by J. Fraser Mitchell, *op. cit.*, p. 250.

[78] *Works*, IV, p. 278.   [79] *Works*, VIII, p. 398.   [80] *Op. cit.*, p. 129n.

[81] Taylor claimed that the best ways of uprooting error are "by preaching and disputation (so that neither of them breed disturbance), by charity and sweetness, by holiness of life, assiduity of exhortation, by the work of God and prayer." (*Liberty of Prophesying, Works*, V, p. 354.)

close friend of Henry More, the Cambridge Platonist.[82] Perhaps one should expect this of a divine who enjoyed reading Plato and Descartes, as Taylor did.

His qualities as a preacher are many. His sermons were as graceful in their delivery as in their craftsmanship. He stirred up the holy affections by his proclamation of the God of Nature and of Grace, and distilled a love for the continuity of the Anglican church with the early centuries in its doctrine and ceremonies. He knew that the genuineness of Christianity was to be found in a consecrated life, and so he helped others along the path that led to the beauty of holiness. He taught that theological roots must bear ethical fruits. In the beauty of his images, in the wide range of his learning, in the charity and joyfulness of his spirit, and in the loyalty to his church, he set an excellent example in difficult days.

His three weaknesses as a preacher were related. His style sometimes failed of its effect because it was too ornate, too contrived, and because his well constructed sentences were too long and moved at so leisurely a pace that they lost the attention of his congregation. Second, all that literary lore gives his written sermons at least a grievously impersonal and remote air. Finally, because his had been a sheltered life, even in penal days, his experience of life was restricted to university, court, and other polite society, and this prevented him from being in the best sense a popular preacher. The Civil War had interrupted his start as a parish priest, and so he had no message for the shop or the cottage, but only for those who lived in the Hall.[83] It is in this respect that the Puritans have the advantage over him in observation, directness of approach, and psychological insight. But these are charges that could with equal justice be made against many high churchmen of his day. His most valuable legacy in an age of fevered and embattled partisanship was the demand for tolerance and an insistence that only the essentials, not speculative matters, were worthy of loyalty. In a plea that links him with the Great Tew Circle of his own time and with the pragmatism of the post-Restoration preachers, but expressed in his own incomparable prose, he addresses the future:

How many volumes have been writ about angels, about immaculate conception, about original sin, when all that is

[82] *The Autobiography of Richard Baxter* (ed. J. M. Lloyd Thomas, Everyman edn.), p. 177.

[83] This point is most effectively made by C. J. Stranks, *op. cit.*, p. 280.

solid reason or clear revelation in all these three articles may be reasonably enough comprised in forty lines? And in these trifles and impertinences men are curiously busy, while they neglect those glorious precepts of Christianity and holy life which are the glories of our religion, and would enable us to a happy eternity.[84]

5. Puritan Preaching

No one who is looking for a "ghost in marble" style (such was Coleridge's brilliant description of Taylor's), should read Puritan sermons. By a self-denying ordinance the Puritan preacher, especially in the days of the Commonwealth, hid his literary lore and his rhetoric so that he might transmit the light of the Gospel more transparently. His was, by choice, a plain and unadorned style for another reason: it was understood by the simple people. We look in vain, therefore, for the Patristic learning[85] of the Laudian school, because it seemed to Puritan divines out of place in the pulpit though very much in place in the study or in controversial writings with Roman Catholics. We shall find images, not as extensive set pieces in Taylor, but as brief illustrative devices to clarify the meaning rather than to adorn. We shall find occasional flashes of humour and aphorisms and proverbs. We shall also discover denunciation. Above all there will be directness of approach and application, and the sermon will have a precise structure, while throughout it will be clear that the preacher's task is to expound the oracles of God. If the Puritan preacher does not regard himself as under the divine orders of the Word, he is impudently overreaching himself. Hence these sermons will often seem no more than a mosaic of Biblical texts, but they come to the congregation with the authority of God Himself. That is why faithful Scriptural exegesis is the prime requirement of Puritan preaching, and, close after it, a sense of urgency, perfectly captured in Richard Baxter's couplet:

---

84 *Works*, V, p. 359.

85 For the Puritan disapproval of citing from the Fathers in sermons, see Perkins, *Works* (1631), II, p. 664, and Richard Baxter's *Works* (1707), IV, p. 428. For the Puritan preference for the plain style, see the preface to Bunyan's *Grace Abounding*, where he observes that he might "have stepped into a style much higher than this. . . . But I dare not. God did not play in convincing of me, the devil did not play in tempting of me, neither did I play when I sunk as into a bottomless pit, when the pangs of hell caught hold of me; wherefore I will not play in my relating of them, but be plain and simple, and lay the thing down as it was."

> I preach'd as never like to preach again
> And as a dying man to dying men.

Its third great quality was its practical character: to tell the hearers not only what they should think (where Andrewes and Donne had excelled), how they should feel (Taylor's forte), but also exactly what they should do.

Preaching was primarily then for revelation of the divine love and will and for the conversion of the soul. William Bradshaw spoke for all Puritans in the statement: "They hould that the highest and supreame office and authoritie of the Pastor, is to preach the gospell solemnly and publickly to the Congregation, by interpreting the written word of God, and applying the same by exhortation and reproof. They hould that this was the greatest worke that Christ & his Apostles did." The compilers of the Parliamentary *Directory*, three decades later, make the high claim again: "Preaching of the Word, being the power of God unto salvation, and one of the greatest and most excellent works belonging to the ministry of the Gospel, should be so performed that the workman need not be ashamed, but may save himself and those that hear him."[86] For the Puritan, who never forgot the vast and yawning chasm that separated puny and sinful man on earth from the almighty and holy God in highest heaven, it was infinitely more important that God should descend in revelation and redemption than that man should ascend in prayer and praise. Perhaps the finest definition of the awesome responsibility of preaching was penned by Baxter: "It is no small matter to stand up in the face of a congregation, and deliver a message of salvation or damnation, as from the living God, in the name of our Redeemer. It is not easy matter to speak so plain, that the ignorant may understand us; and so seriously that the deadest hearts may feel us; and so convincingly, that contradicting cavillers may be silenced."[87] With such a view of the august significance of preaching, the Puritan preacher mounted the meeting-house stairs to the pulpit as if he were a modern Moses of the New Dispensation ascending Mount Sinai as the friend of God.

The preacher was not in the pulpit as a scholar to impress with his learning, nor as a wit to tickle the fancy of men about town or court, nor to gain tributes to his eloquence. On the contrary, he

[86] *Reliquiae Liturgicae*, ed. Peter Hall, III, *Directory*, p. 35.
[87] *The Reformed Pastor* (London, edn. of 1860), p. 128.

was the man of God, the prophet who denounced the people for their sins without fear or favour, the preacher who unfolded the "mystery" of the Gospel, revealing the whole plan of salvation, under compulsion to bring men to the parting of the ways that lead to salvation or damnation. What might be labelled "enthusiasm" by his critics, as if it were mere emotional energy, was in reality the expression of his sense of urgency. By his proclamation of the Gospel he was, under Christ, binding or loosing the souls of his congregation. Thus, in the words of Thomas Goodwin, Commonwealth President of Magdalen College, Oxford, preaching produced "experimental, saving, applying knowledge." It was equally far removed from didacticism as from subjectivism. In teaching, the Puritan preacher imparted not human knowledge which might make him and his charges proud but divine knowledge which humbled the recipients. If he referred to his own experience, it was only by way of illustrating what God had done for the undeserving in His mercy. The preaching of the Word of God, as the Puritan interpreted his task, was neither a moral homily nor a philosophical disquisition, but the authoritative declaration of the will of the blessed God from the written Word and twin Covenants or Testaments of God.

A Puritan type of sermon had already been specially constructed that would be a faithful exposition of Scripture, that would go plainly and directly and urgently to the doctrines as a straight arrow to its target, and that would apply the doctrines for the use of the hearers with the utmost daily relevance. The lineaments of it are found in Perkins's *Arte of Prophesying* (1607), which enjoyed a magisterial reputation among the Puritans. Its conclusions may be given in the author's own summary:

1. To reade the Text distinctly out of the Canonicall Scriptures.
2. To give the sense and understanding of it being read, by the Scripture it selfe.
3. To collect a few and profitable points of doctrine out of the naturall sense.
4. To apply (if he have the gift) the doctrines rightly collected, to the life and manners of men in a simple and plaine speech.[88]

[88] *Works* (1631), II, p. 673. Perkins, while insisting that "humane wisdom" should be concealed because the preacher is declaring the divine, not the human

Such functional clarity was evidence of the impact of Ramus in the Cambridge University whence this preaching advice came. It is significant that Ramus wrote important textbooks in logic as well as in rhetoric, both of which had seminal influences on English education. This scheme advocated by Perkins, and the vogue for the rest of the century and beyond first for Puritans and then for Dissenters, was simplified even further in the triple schema— by which all Puritan sermon-structures are identified—of "Doctrine, Reason, and Use." It is interesting that, although he does not use the terms, yet John Wilkins (1614-1672), a founder of the Royal Society, and future Bishop of Chester, uses the concepts in his frequently reprinted, *Ecclesiastes: or a Discourse concerning the Gift of Preaching*, which had reached its eighth edition by 1704. Wilkins says that the chief parts of a sermon are: Explication (which corresponds to Doctrine), Confirmation (which corresponds to Reason), and Application (which corresponds to Use).[89]

The Parliamentary *Directory* made official the Puritan sermon-structure in the following instructions to the preacher according to the triple schema: "In raising doctrines from the text, his care ought to be, First, that the matter be the truth of God. Secondly, that it be a truth contained in, or grounded on, that text that the hearers may discern how God teacheth it from thence. Thirdly, that he chiefly insist upon those doctrines which are principally intended, and make most for the edification of his hearers."[90] Clearly, the first aim of the sermon was evangelical instruction. Such doctrines then have to be explained to the congregation and their contraries refuted. Thus the second division of the sermon was a logical defence of the assumptions of the first section. Then the *Directory* urges: "The arguments or reasons are to be solid; and, as much as may be, convincing. The illustrations, of what kind soever, ought to be full of light, and such as may convey the truth into the hearer's heart with spiritual delight."[91] The third section of the sermon was intended to drive home the practical

---

message, yet is adamant in denying that he means by this that barbarism should be brought into the pulpit: "hee must understand that the Minister may, yea and must privately use at his libertie the arts, Philosophy, and variety of reading, whilest he is in framing his sermon: but he ought in publike to conceale all these from the people, and not to make the least ostentation." (*Ibid.*, p. 670.)

[89] *Ecclesiastes* (8th edn., 1704), pp. 6-9.

[90] *Reliquiae Liturgicae*, ed. Peter Hall, III, *Directory*, p. 37.

[91] *Ibid.*

advantages of belief in the particular doctrine being expounded. It usually concluded with admonitions and encouragements. Thus, doctrine, reason, and use might be regarded as the declaration, the explanation and confirmation, and the application of the Christian faith. The first two sections should convince the reason, while the last section warmed the heart into acceptance of the doctrine.

Plain the Puritan sermon might be, but it was purposefully streamlined. It proceeded from informing the mind and stirring up the affections—there was a considerable element of Christ-mysticism in Puritanism as Chapter III has shown—to effect the transformation of the will. The structure of the Puritan sermon was the perfect instrument for its purpose.

Where then, since historical lore and rhetoric were forbidden, was there room for ingenuity? First, in the careful exposition of texts and contexts, and the collation of doctrines from the remoter parts of the Old Testament, not forgetting those who were living exemplars of them. Secondly, ingenuity was needed in applying these lessons to the condition of the congregation, and, as we shall see in the case of Richard Baxter, was likely to be more effective when the pastor regularly visited the people in their homes. Thirdly, there was room for intelligence in the determining of the spiritual condition of the preacher's patients and in prescribing for their soul's healing, their psychiatry. Puritan preachers were particularly gifted in this regard.[92] Fourthly, there was the deep well of human experience and observation and reading to draw upon in the search for analogies, similes, metaphors, any and all kinds of illustrations to bring home the lessons to the preacher's charges. A fifth place for ingenuity was provided by the often excessively lengthy series of Puritan sermons on the same theme or on a book or even a chapter of a book of the Bible. Anthony Burgess preached, for example, 145 sermons on John 17, which he published in 1656 and Manton preached 190 sermons on Psalm 119; while George Trosse spent several years preaching a Marathon series on the attributes of God. One congregation, however, became so exhausted by their minister preaching for four months on Joseph's coat of many colours that they called him "Eternal Bragge."

It would be the gravest error to attribute the Puritan plain style to dullness of mind, ignorance of rhetoric, or servility of

92 See Davies, op. cit., I, pp. 319-24, for Puritan sermons that are studies in the psychology of religion.

spirit. Baxter, a man of broad culture and critical mind, said: "The plainest words are the profitablest Oratory in the weightiest matters. Fineness is for ornament, and delicacy for delight; but they answer not *Necessity*."[93] The great demand for self-discipline imposed by the Puritan plain style is admirably exemplified in John Cotton, who after being convinced of the truth of Puritanism gave up his erudite and ornate style of preaching for one much simpler. It is recorded in Cotton Mather's *Magnalia Christi Americana*, along with the plain sermon on repentance which Cotton preached and caused the conversion of Preston. Here is the record of the incident:

> Some time after this Change upon the Soul of Mr. *Cotton*, it came his turn again to preach at St. *Maries*; and because *he* was to preach, an High Expectation was raised throughout the *whole University*, that they should have a Sermon, flourishing indeed, with all the *Learning* of the *whole University*. Many difficulties had Mr. *Cotton* in his own mind now, what Course to steer. On the one side he considered, That if he should preach with a Scriptural and Christian *Plainness*, he should not only wound his own *Fame* exceedingly, but also tempt Carnal Men to revive an Old Cavil, *That Religion made Scholars turn Dunces*, whereby the Name of God might suffer not a little. On the other side, he considered, That it was his Duty to preach with such a Plainness, as became the Oracles of God, which are intended for the Conduct of Men in the *Paths of Life*, and not for Theatrical Ostentations and Entertainments, and the Lord needed not any *Sin* of ours to maintain his own Glory. Hereupon Mr. *Cotton* resolved, that he would preach a plain Sermon. . . ."[94]

That this simplicity in other Puritan divines was deliberate, is amply proven. One more example must suffice. Arthur Dent, in the Preface to his *Sermon of Repentance* of 1637, apologizes for not having produced it in a high-flown style: "Let no man therefore be offended that I have not strained my selfe to flie an high pitch, to fome [foam] out the froth of mans wisedome, and to make a great show of learning, by blowing the bladder of vanity, till it burst with swelling; but it is not my use: I seek especially the

---

[93] Cited in F. J. Powicke, *A Life of the Reverend Richard Baxter* (1924), p. 282.
[94] This comes from the introduction to the reprinted Repentance sermon in *Magnalia*, in a section entitled, "Cottonus Redivivus."

salvation of the simple and ignorant: and therefore stoope down to their reach and capacity."[95]

One of the most popular Caroline Puritan preachers was John Preston (1587-1628), a favourite of Charles I's favourite, Buckingham. He had been Preacher at Lincoln's Inn and Chaplain to the King. After his death, there was published a tri-partite volume of sermons, entitled, *The Golden Sceptre held forth to the Humble, with the Churches Dignitie by her Marriage, and the Churches Dutie in her Carriage* (1638). The first part comprised sermons delivered in Cambridge in 1625 for the weekly Fasts, and the other two consisted of two series of sermons preached at Lincoln's Inn. What is particularly interesting about this volume is the table of contents because it so clearly marks the structure of the Puritan sermon and illustrates it in skeletal form:

Doct[rine]	1. God afflicts his owne people.	3.
Reas[on]	1. Because he loves them.	4.
	2. That his name be not blasphemed.	*Ibid.*
	3. He will be sanctified in those that draw neare him.	*Ibid.*
	4. He walks among them.	5.
Vse.	1. To feare the Lord.	6.
	2. Want of feare provoketh God.	13.
	3. Gods severity to wicked men.	18.
	4. Not think strange that God afflicts his.	19.
Doct.	2. God pities his people in affliction.	20.
Reas.	1. He is slow to afflict.	21.
	2. He sustains them in affliction.	*Ibid.*
	3. He brings them through affliction.	25.
Vse.	1. Not to be Discouraged in affliction.	32.
	2. To come to God when we have offended him.	35.
	3. To lead us to repentance.	37.
	4. To choose the Lord for our God.	41.
	5. To confirme us in that choice.	45.

To give flesh to one "Use," the last one on our list, Preston's historical and contemporary application must also be cited: "God hath been mercifull to it [the church] in all ages, and is so still; so he saith, *I have been her habitation*, that is a house for the

95 *Op. cit.*, A3 recto and verso.

Church to dwell safely in . . . looke on the Church when it was in the worst condition, take the Church of God, even when it seemed to be cut off, as in that great massacre in *France*, yet then was the Lord an habitation to it, a company was kept alive, that grew greater than the former. So the Church in Queen *Marie's* time, he suffered the storme to overtake them a little, but it was soone blowen over, he was an habitation to keepe off the storme from destroying them, and so he hath been, and will be to *Bohemia*, and the *Palatinate*, but so he hath beene found to be to our Church above all the rest, for our Nation hath been like *Gideon's Fleece*, when all about us have been wet and wallowed in blood, we have been dry. . . ."[96] There was the strength of steel in Puritanism because it was prepared for affliction, and it did so in the conviction that it was called upon to suffer for Christ's sake, because its members were the elect. Preston's next passage shows that the great strength of Puritanism lay in the conviction of being an elect people, in the bond of God's covenant with his people, "so that it seems—there is a certaine match between them, a mutuall agreement and relation, as there is betweene a husband and a wife, a father and a sonne; so if thou beest one who is married to Christ, and hee hath changed thy heart, and begotten thee anew by his Word, and art dedicated to his service as his temple; then art thou called by his Name."[97]

Another sermon, preached almost fifty years after Preston's, will serve as an indication of the weaknesses of this mode of preaching. This was preached in London in October 1682—during a lull in persecution of the Dissenters—at a morning exercise of the Nonconformist ministers in London. Such an "exercise" was rather like the "prophesyings" of Elizabethan Puritanism, ultimately derived from Zwingli's Zurich. The subject is: "Whether it be expedient and how the Congregation may say *Amen* in publick Worship." The text is Nehemiah 8:6: "And Ezra blessed the Lord, the great God, and all the People answered, Amen, Amen." It is virtually a sermon on the single word, *Amen*. The Doctrine taught is "That it is a lawful and laudable practice for people at the conclusion of publick prayer or praysing God to pronounce an *Amen*." Then follows a series of definitions of *Amen*: 1. "*Amen*

---

[96] *Op. cit.*, pp. 46-47. This was a Puritan historical commonplace apparently, because the same instances in almost the same words are used by Thomas Jackson, Prebend and Lecturer in Canterbury Cathedral in his book of sermons, *The Raging Tempest stilled* (1623), p. 127.

[97] *The Golden Sceptre held forth to the Humble* (1638), p. 48.

Substantive" (God himself); 2. *"Amen* Affirmative" (verily); 3. *"Amen* Optative"; and 4. "Double *Amen.*" This is succeeded by a statement of the Uses of the Doctrine: first, "it is connatural to Prayer and Praise"; secondly, it has the authority of both testaments; thirdly, *"Amens* after Prayer and Praise, is the mans consent, judgment and approbation of what is offered unto God"; fourthly, "This vocal *Amen* is the . . . summ of all our petitions and praises to God"; fifthly, "it involves a strong faith"; sixthly, it is "an assurance that God will accept our Praises and Answer our Prayers"; lastly, "this unanimous *Amen* of Faith strikes terror into the enemies of the Church, whether Devils or men."[98] And such prolixity, one fears, produces torpor in the friends of the church! It has ingenuity in discovering seven different uses for the doctrine, but the definitions of *Amen* are exceedingly pedantic, and the entire sermon is wanting in proportion. This is Puritan prolixity, pedantry, and poverty of the imagination at its worst. For the best Puritan sermons one must look to the wit of Thomas Adams, the warmth of Richard Sibbes, the spiritual insight of John Downame, the clear analysis and strong contemporary applications of Preston, and the spirituality linked with scholarship of John Owen, Thomas Goodwin, Richard Baxter, Matthew Henry, John Howe, and William Bates.

It may well be, of course, that Puritan sermons seem much duller than they were only because we are reading them rather than listening to them. Not only was the tone of the Puritan preacher urgent, but often his gestures were vehement. This was one ground of Anglican ridicule of Puritan preaching. One such critic writes: "How often have you seen a Preacher heat himself beyond the need of any vestments? Throwing off his Cloak, nay and his Gloves too, as great impediments to the holy performance, squeeking and roaring beyond the example of any Lunatick? Sometimes speaking in a tolerable tone, and presently again crying out as if under some immediate distraction?" The result is that the Puritan congregation "have gaped upon him, and when he hath finished, given him this honourable Encomium, Well, hee's a rare man, a man mighty zealous for the Lord, a powerful preacher, and one that hath taken abundance of pains that day. . . ."[99]

[98] Sermon XXI in *A Continuation of Morning Exercise Sermons,* ed. Samuel Annesley, John Wesley's grandfather on the distaff side (1683).
[99] *A Free and Impartial Inquiry into the causes of that very great Esteem and Honour that the Nonconforming Preachers are generally in with their followers* (1673), pp. 118f.

The popularity of Puritan preaching cannot be accounted for alone in terms of the accumulation of factors already considered, such as fidelity in scriptural exposition, the plain style intelligible to the simplest, the urgent sincerity of the minister, or even the political daring of some preachers[100] and especially during the apocalyptic excitement associated with the impending reign of the saints—though the latter is an important factor. There is one essential missing element: it is the pastor's intimate knowledge of his people obtained by regular visitation of them. Possibly because the Anglican parish priest adopted other priorities, perhaps through disinclination, probably because many priests had too vast parishes for anything except sick visitation, the fact remains that it is not the Laudian clergy, but the Puritan ministers who made a conscience of spiritual as opposed to social visitation on a regular basis, going from house to house. This is true whether we take as our example Richard Baxter, the Anglican Puritan,[101] at Kidderminster in Worcestershire during the Commonwealth and Protectorate, or Oliver Heywood in Northowram in Yorkshire in Restoration penal times for Presbyterians. In an earlier day George Herbert was a true pastor of his flock, but he seems to have been the exception that proved the Laudian rule.

Baxter's parish at Kidderminster was a market town with about twenty villages, consisting of about three to four thousand souls, or eight hundred families, and about eighteen hundred were of age to be communicants. Most went to church to hear him preach because the law required it, but there would be only about six hundred souls serious about religion. The town had a bad reputation from its drunkards who raged weekly before the minister's

---

[100] Some idea of the political excitement may be obtained from the following probably biassed and exaggerated report on the controversial Hugh Peters, who, "having shaken hands with his Text and raised himself upright in his Pulpit, with his Hand laid across his Breast, thus roars out, O Joab, Joab, *thou faithful Counsellor to David; I love thee* Joab, whom weepest thou for? David! *a Boy, a bloody Cavalier, a Prince Rupert, a plundering Cavalier. Come forth* David, *speak kindly* to thy Servants . . . Come to thy Parliament, King Charles, wilt not come? I swear unto thee by the Lord, it will be the worst thing hath befallen thee from thy youth until now." (From *What has been, maybe again, or an instance of London's Loyalty in 1640, &c* . . . [Anon], 1710, p. 7.)

[101] Baxter was sick of ecclesiastical party labels, which he thought were more often libels. At the end of his life he wrote: "You could not (except a Catholic Christian) have trulier called me, than an Episcopal-Presbyterian-Independent." (*A Third Defence of the Cause of Peace*, 1681, Pt. 1, p. 110, cited in Geoffrey F. Nuttall's learned and vivid *Richard Baxter* [1965], p. 84.) For Baxter as visitor, see A. S. Langley, "Richard Baxter—Director of Souls," *The Baptist Quarterly*, Vol. 3 (1926-1927), pp. 71-80.

door.[102] In estimating the change that had come over the town through his long and faithful ministry there, Baxter is honest enough to admit that the Civil War took off the most notorious enemies of godliness. A real change had taken place: "When I came hither first, there was about one Family in a Street that worshipped God and called his Name," but "when I came away there was not past one Family in the Side of a Street that did not do so." "On the Lord's Day there was no disorder to be seen in the Streets, but you might hear an hundred Families singing Psalms and repeating Sermons, as you passed through the Streets."[103] By his love for these people, by his regular catechising of them and visiting them in their homes, by his detailed and individual knowledge of each of them, and by his earnest preaching based upon such pastoral insight, he was, under God, the agent for the transformation of the carpet-weaving town. The congregation responded so well to his evident concern for them that "we were fain to build five Galleries"[104] in the church. One who knew him in his old age, and indeed, edited the *Reliquiae Baxterianae*, Matthew Sylvester, said of his speaking what may well have characterized his preaching, that "He had a moving πάθος [pathos] and useful Acrimony in his words; neither did his Expressions want their Emphatical Accent, as the Matter did require. And when he spake of weighty Soul-Concerns, you might find his very Spirit Drench'd therein."[105] To all who met him, with the exception of Judge Jeffreys, his spirituality was transparent. As Edmund Calamy said, near the time of Baxter's death, "He talked in the pulpit with great freedom about another world, like one that had been there, and was come as a sort of express from thence to make a report concerning[106] it." That one might expect of the author of both the devotional classic, *The Saints' Everlasting Rest* and the celebrated manual on the pastoral ministry, *The Reformed Pastor*, and he set an enduring example for Puritan ministers as George Herbert did for Anglican priests.

The frequency of the demand for sermons is perhaps the best indication of the value in which preaching was held by the Puritans. Baxter tells us: "I preached before the Wars twice each

---

102 Nuttall, *op. cit.*, pp. 46-47.
103 *Reliquiae Baxterianae* (ed. M. Sylvester, 1696), I, Pt. 1, Sect. 137, Para. 15.
104 *Ibid.*, I, Pt. 1, Sect. 136.
105 Cited by G. F. Nuttall, *op. cit.*, p. 49.
106 E. Calamy, *Historical Account of my own life* (ed. J. T. Rutt, 1829), I, pp. 220f.

Lord's Day; but after the War but once, and once every Thursday, besides occasional sermons."[107] This was, however, far from exhausting his duties. He spent two entire days of each week catechising families. He also met a group every Thursday evening at his home "and there one of them repeated the Sermon, and afterwards they proposed what Doubts any of them had about the Sermon, or any other Case of Conscience."[108] One other night each week was given over to teaching his young people to pray. Also he met with his fellow ministers for discipline and disputation once a month and presided over the monthly meeting for parish discipline. On national days of humiliation also he preached to his congregation. His ardour and seriousness were indefatigable.

An equally significant series of testimonies is given to the importance of preaching by the northern divine, Oliver Heywood. Reviewing his work in 1689, when he had reached the age of sixty, he claims: "I doe find that I had travelled 1358 miles, preacht 131 times in weekdays, kept 34 fasts, 8 days of thanksgiving, baptized 21 children &c."[109] He records in the following year that he has preached 135 times on weekdays, as well as twice each Lord's Day. Even in his seventieth year, despite asthma and needing two men to carry him to Northowram chapel in a chair, he asserts "yet was enabled when I got into the pulpit to preach audibly—baptized 8 children, kept 8 conferences, preacht on week-days 23 times, writ 7 treatises, 4 short for Warly-people, 104 letters, observed 14 fasts, 3 days of thanksgiving, 2 books printed viz. the two worlds and Christs intercession—my dear Lord was with me all along."[110] On an average this Puritan pastor preached five times a week; no itinerant, he was minister to the Dissenting community at Northowram near Halifax. He was also an author of some note. To have preached so often in the midst of a busy life, is itself an enthusiastic testimony to the high opinion in which preaching was held by the sons of the Puritans.

But even they fell behind the Puritans of the 1640s. The peak of the Puritan appreciation of preaching was surely reached when the clergymen of the Westminster Assembly spent the larger part of the day on Monday, October 16, 1643, preaching and praying, with psalms for relaxation. The occasion was a solemn fast day. Lightfoot relates how the time went:

---

[107] *Reliquiae Baxterianae*, p. 83.   [108] *Ibid.*
[109] *The Reverend Oliver Heywood, B.A., 1630-1702: His Autobiography, Diaries, Anecdote and Event Books* (ed. J. Horsfall Turner, Bingley, 1883), III, p. 238.
[110] *Ibid.*, p. 285.

First Mr. *Wilson* gave a picked psalm, or selected verses
of several psalms, agreeing to the time and occasion. Then
Dr. *Burgess* prayed about an hour: after he had done, Mr.
Whittacre preached ypon Isa. xxxvii. 3, 'This day is a day of
trouble,' &c. Then, having had another chosen psalm, Mr.
Goodwin prayed; and after he had done, Mr. *Palmer* preached
upon Psal. xxv. 12. After whose sermon we had another
psalm, and Dr. *Stanton* prayed about an hour; and with
another psalm and a prayer of the prolocutor [Dr. Twisse],
and a collection for the maimed soldiers . . . we adjourned till
tomorrow morning.[111]

These learned Puritan preachers were in their and our own sense
of the term "painful" preachers; they took pains and they gave
pain to all but the most diligent and devoted of their persuasion.

For all their qualities, Puritan or Dissenting sermons had their
faults. It was all very well to insist that true art hides the artifice
of rhetoric and avoids the ornate style; this is morally good but
literarily dull. Without question, the Anglican preachers, whether
metaphysical or Senecan, produced sermons that must have been
more interesting to hear as they certainly are to read.

The first charge against a great deal of the apolitical preaching
of the Puritans, is that it was dull. A combination of prolixity,
pedantry, and an atomistic splitting up of the text into divisions
and subdivisions after the manner of the more scholastic of the
Calvinists like John Owen and Thomas Goodwin, combined with
intensity in delivery, guaranteed exhaustion except for the most
obdurate or masochistic listeners. Anglicans could be prolix and
pedantic, as indeed the famous Isaac Barrow was,[112] but he avoided
dullness by his superb flights of rhetoric. Puritans prevented divagation but also delight through banning most rhetorical aids. The
stories of John Howe's preaching test by Cromwell and of Peters'
"second glass" are reminders of the long-windedness of Puritan
preachers.

Every preaching style of a theological party soon develops its
own jargon. The Puritans were no exception. Both Robert South
and Simon Patrick hugely enjoy themselves by poking fun at the
Puritan sermon structure, delivery and jargon, which took the form

[111] Ed. J. R. Pitman, *The Whole Works of the Rev. John Lightfoot, D.D.,*
13 Vols. (1825); Vol. XIII contains "The Journal of the Proceedings of the Assembly of Divines, from January 1, 1643 to December 31, 1644," see *ad loc.*
[112] Caroline F. Richardson, *English Preachers and Preaching, 1640-1670* (New
York, 1928), p. 2.

of "Covenant" talk, based upon their recognition of the covenant-relationship between God and his elect, and therefore a fondness for legal and marital metaphors.

South in his brilliant sermon of 1660, *The Scribe instructed to the Kingdom of Heaven* had wittily excoriated the pedantry of Andrewes, after which he gave the Puritan divines in general, and John Owen in particular, a drubbing. The entire passage begins with urbanity, proceeds by exaggeration, and ends with blasphemy.

I hope it will not prove offensive to the Auditory, if, to release it (could I be so happy) from suffering by such Stuff in the future, I venture upon some short Description of it; and it is briefly thus. First of all they seize upon some Text, from whence they draw something (which they call a *Doctrine*), and well may it be said to be *drawn* from the Words; forasmuch as it seldom naturally flows, or *results* from them. In the next place, being thus provided, they branch it into several Heads; perhaps, twenty, or thirty, or upwards. Whereupon, for the Prosecution of these, they repair to some *trusty Concordance*, which never fails them, and by the Help of that, they range six or seven Scriptures under each Head; which Scriptures they prosecute one by one, first amplifying and enlarging upon one, for some considerable time, till they have spoiled it; and then that being done, they pass to another, which in its turn suffers accordingly. And these impertinent, and unpremeditated Enlargements they look upon as *the Motions and Breathings of the Spirit*, and therefore much beyond those *carnal Ordinances of Sense and Reason*, supported by Industry and Study; and this they call *a saving Way* of Preaching, as it must be confessed to be a way to save much Labour, and nothing else that I know of. . . . But to pass from these Indecencies to others, as little to be allowed in this sort of Men, can any tolerable Reason be given for those strange new Postures used by some in the Delivery of the Word? Such as *shutting the Eyes, distorting the Face, and speaking through the Nose*, which I think cannot so properly be called *Preaching*, as *Toning of a Sermon*. Nor do I see, why the *Word* may not be altogether as effectual for *the Conversion of Souls*, delivered by one, who has the Manners to look his Auditory in the Face, using his own Countenance, and his own native Voice, without straining it to a lamentable and doleful *Whine* (never serving to any Purpose, but where some religious Cheat is to be carried on). . . . For none surely will imagine, *that these Men's speaking, as never Man spoke before*, can pass for any Imitation of Him. . . .[113]

So well had the criticisms of Puritan preaching been received by the Cavalier congregation that South returned to the attack a year later, in the sermon, *False Foundations Removed*: "Some you shall have amusing their Consciences," so he tells his Oxford congregation, "with a Set of fantastical new-coin'd Phrases, such as *Laying hold on Christ, getting into Christ, and rolling themselves upon Christ*, and the like; by which if they mean any Thing else but obeying the Precepts of Christ, and a rational Hope of Salvation thereupon (which, it is certain that generally they do not mean), it is all but a *Jargon* of empty, senseless Metaphors; and though many venture their Souls upon them, despising *good Works* and *strict Living* as meer *Morality*, and perhaps as *Popery*, yet being thoroughly look'd into and examined, after all their Noise, they are really nothing but *Words* and *Wind*."[114] The jargon was there, but the doctrine of justification by faith is far too superficially dismissed as mere antinomianism by South, and this is a charge that misses the intensely serious Puritans among the Westminster divines, and may only hit some of the "mechanick preachers" of the time.

These Puritan clichés are amusingly satirised by Simon Patrick also. In *A Friendly Debate between a Conformist and a Non-Conformist* (1668), we are informed that "one man comes to tell them of the *streamings* of Christ's *Blood freely* to Sinners: another bids them *put themselves upon the stream of Free grace*, without having any foot on their own bottom." [The latter was a contortion presumably of which even the most agile Puritan was incapable.] "A third tells them how they must *apply Promises*, absolute Promises. A fourth tells them there is a special Mystery in looking at the *Testamentalness* of Christ's *Sufferings*. . . ."[115] This has the authentic character of exact reporting, especially the awkwardness in the term "*Testamentalness*." Patrick, in a work of a year later, *A Continuation of the Friendly Debate*, castigates the fad for a "Covenant" phrase, however indelicate its associations: "When a Preacher, for instance, from that text, *David served his Genera-*

---

[113] Robert South, *Works* (Oxford, 1823), III, pp. 34-37.
[114] *Ibid.*, II, p. 346. [115] *Op. cit.*, pp. 25-26.

tion by the will of God, raised this impertinent Observation; *That it is our duty to mind Generation-work*; instantly all Pulpits sounded with this Doctrine of *Generation-work*. That was the phrase in those days: In so much that you should hear both Minister and people bewailing it in their prayers, that they had not minded *Generation-work* more. Which made some good innocent souls, that were not acquainted with the secret, blush when they first heard it, and wonder what they meant."[116]

Puritan preaching, however, survived the artillery of abuse. The sincerity of its preachers during the penal days of the Clarendon Code was without question, and the style dropped its splintering divisions. In the work of the Presbyterian divine, William Bates (1625-1699) there is, besides plainness a pleasing fluidity, and a selection and development of topics that is, in this respect, like Tillotson. One citation from his work must suffice as an index of the whole. It is typical in its rationalism, its concentration on Creation rather than on Grace, and on natural rather than revealed theology, as well as in its urbane approach to an intelligent congregation. Its subject is the first man and his reflections upon God:

And as by contemplating the other works of God, so especially by reflecting upon himself, *Adam* had a clear sight of the Divine *Attributes*, which concurr'd in his Creation. Whether he considered the lowest part, the Body, 'twas formed of the Earth, the most artificial and beautiful piece of the *visible* world. The contrivance of the parts was with that proportion and exactness, as most conduc'd to Comeliness and Service. Its stature was erect and raised, becoming the Lord of the Creatures, and an observer of the Heavens. A divine Beauty and Majesty was shed upon it. And this was no vanishing *ray*, soon eclips'd by a Disease, and extinguish't by Death, but shin'd in the countenance without any declination. The *Tongue* was Man's peculiar glory, being the interpreter of the mind and capable to Dignifie all the affections of the Soul. In short, the Body was so fram'd as to make a visible discovery of the Prerogatives of his Creation. And when he reflected upon his Soul, that animated his dust, its excellent endowment, wherein it is comparable to the Angels, the capacity of enjoying God himself for ever, he had an internal

[116] *Op. cit.*, p. 81. See also John Eachard, *Grounds and Occasions of the Contempt of the Clergy* (1671).

and most clear testimony of the glorious perfections of the Creator. For Man, who alone admires the works of God, is the most admirable of all.[117]

If, with the Restoration, composers of sermons were to drop pedantry of all kinds, avoid the more elaborate forms of rhetoric as artifice, and cultivate plainness of style and lucidity in exposition, and attempt to be as practical as possible, some portion at least of the change is to be attributed to Puritanism for these were the strengths of its manly and direct preaching.

6. Restoration Preachers

The plain and functional style of Puritan preaching was only one factor helping to account for the change of style of preaching in Restoration days. Another cause was the influence of the preachers at the French court, such as Massillon, Bossuet, and Bourdaloue, whom many Englishmen had heard during the years that the remnants of the English court sought refuge in France. This constellation of French preachers were exemplars of a sacred oratory of a Ciceronian kind, in which their Scriptural quotations and ethical exhortations were adopted to illustrate a topic and adorn a theme rather than to apply the comfort and criticism of the Gospel. Divorced from the liturgical context (not being expositions of the lessons of the day), and honoured by the presence of the great, whether king or nobility, they praised the dead in their *oraisons funèbres* and maybe flattered the living by easing their consciences in their Lenten sermons. It is rarely that these French sermons reach the height of the prophetic, however sublime their rhetoric and their meditations on mutability. They not infrequently breathe the desiccated air of moralism and despite protestations to the contrary, that practical deism of the remoteness of God[118] which marks the enlightenment. Charles II, in particular, wished to encourage this kind of preaching which found the perfect context in the most baroque and absolutist of courts.

An equally significant but wholly English influence was that of the Royal Society, and the immediate need for the exact, clear, and denotative language suitable for describing experiments in natural science. Thomas Sprat, himself a Bishop of Rochester as well as

---

117 *Harmony of the Divine Attributes* (1674), Discourse I, pp. 7-8.

118 John Howe epitomised Deism perfectly in its exaggerated doctrine of the Divine transcendence, by asserting that its *credo* was: "There shall be a God; provided He do not interfere."

the author of *The History of the Royal-Society of London, For the Improving of Natural Knowledge* (1667), remarked that the fellows had adopted "a close, naked, natural way of speaking, positive expressions, clear senses, a native easiness, bringing all things as near the Mathematical plainness as they can, and preferring the language of Artizans, Countrymen, and Merchants, before that of Wits and Scholars."[119]

There was also, it must not be forgotten, a change of spirit in the nation and in Europe, which demanded a change of style. Thoughtful people were tired of extravagance, of unprovable speculations, of notions that were merely fantastic, of enthusiastic extremes, and sought—especially in religion—for a faith and way of living that were rational, practicable, and useful. Pope, in his *Essay on Man*, was to give perfect expression to these deliberately limited objectives and values in life:

> For modes of faith let graceless zealots fight,
> His can't be in the wrong whose life is in the right.
> In Faith and Hope the world will disagree
> But all mankind's concern is Charity.
> All must be false that thwart this one great end,
> And all of God that bless mankind or mend.[120]

The new pulpit style did not easily or rapidly convert those who admired the ornate eloquence of Jeremy Taylor, and who imitated him poorly in what John Eachard called "high-tossing and swaggering preaching,"[121] in strained similitudes and far-fetched metaphors, aiming at ingenuity rather than simplicity and relevance, and discussing remote theological matters rather than down-to-earth concerns. This criticism in turn evoked James Arderne's *Directions Concerning the Matter and Stile of Sermons* (1671),[122] which is an excellent summary of what the Dean of Chester admired in the contemporary pulpit and its shining lights of whom Tillotson was the most stellar.

Arderne recommended the young deacon whom he is instructing in homiletics to select plain and practical parts of the Scrip-

---

[119] *Op. cit.*, Pt. II, Sect. xx. [120] *Op. cit.*, Bk. III.

[121] John Eachard's *The Grounds and Occasions of the Contempt of the Clergy* (1670) reduced the causes of unpopularity to two: poverty and ignorance, and regarded inept preaching as due to ignorance.

[122] This work has been re-issued under the editorship of John Mackay as No. 13 of the Luttrell Reprints (Oxford, 1952). Subsequent references are to the pagination of this reprint.

ture to expound and apply, and "not to chuse obscure passages, or sublime controversies, or nice speculations to be propounded to any in publick, much less to the uncapable multitude."[123] The practical doctrines to use as sermon topics are: "the Attributes of God's Holiness, Justice, Soveraignty, All-Sufficiency, Faithfullness, Mercie, Infinite Knowledge, and the rest of the Divine perfections: furthermore from the dictates of Nature, and testimony of Conscience, and loveliness of Vertue, and deformitie of Vice, from the obligation of a created being, and edification of others, and vanity of the World, and the hazard of miscarriage."[124]

The structure the Dean recommends to the neophyte is the old Puritan one rephrased by Wilkins, which Arderne calls in his triple analysis "Proposition, Confirmation and Inference."[125]

Reason is to be satisfied by relevant arguments, as we have seen, but the emotions require other persuasives. The motivation which Arderne proposes are appeals to reputation, equity, piety, gratitude, safety, prudence, delight, "demonstrating that Religion is a way of pleasantness, and that Mortification it self brings joy as its fruit to those who make it their exercise."[126]

The diction should avoid the dangerous extremes of either "high flights enthusiastick and giddy" or "by a groveling stoop to clownish phrases"[127] both of which are unsuitable to the practical seriousness of the subject-matter. The gestures, too, are to be grave and decorous "free from apish postures and distorted looks."[128] The pronunciation is to be clear and manly, with a slight inflexion in the voice to avoid dulness. In all things moderation is recommended, as befits the exemplars of the Anglican middle way, which is intended to be sensible, practical, prudential, and useful. These are all valuable ends for preaching, but are not by any means the only aims and qualities that count.

Furthermore, there was a new theology, of which the Great Tew Group and their friends were the forerunners, aided in part by the Cambridge Platonists, the theology of the Latitudinarian movement. Its teachings were characterized by plainness and directness, and it was believed that the essential content of the Christian Faith was summed up in the Fatherhood of God and the duty of benevolence in man. These divines were fully persuaded of the divine beneficence of the Creator and argued that the chief duty of men

123 Op. cit., p. 3.   124 Ibid., pp. 13-14.
125 Ibid., p. 9.   126 Ibid., p. 15.
127 Ibid., p. 16.   128 Ibid., p. 30.

was to imitate the divine charity by good works. Religion thought of in these terms required no abstention from innocent social life. On the contrary, it required involvement rather than renunciation, and regarded this involvement in the earthly kingdom as the best preparation for the heavenly city. Inevitably, in the popular mind there was the convenient notion that religion supplies an extra bonus in a course of moderation and virtue.

The dominance of theology up to 1660 was succeeded by the increasing dominance of the natural sciences, and its impact was to be found not only in the style, but also in the content of preaching. Within this period both the telescope and the microscope were invented, the one enabling the vastness of the universe to become recognized more fully, and the other showing the marvellous "contrivance of the parts . . . with that proportion and exactness" of which, as we have seen, Bates had spoken, as if Adam's self-reflection was that of a rather junior Fellow of the Royal Society. Now it became the fashion to think of God in his work of Creation, rather than in the paradoxical and mysterious communication of Himself in Grace. While there are two admirable preachers in the satirical South and eloquent and erudite Isaac Barrow, the man most suited to express the new style was a former Presbyterian turned Anglican, John Tillotson (1630-1694), who was to become Archbishop of Canterbury.

Robert South (1634-1716) is more important as a barometer, perhaps, than as a bringer of light and rain to the parched territory of the sermon. He served his function chiefly as warning the Anglican church of stormy weather, of what to avoid in the pulpit. While his wit can be brilliant, it can also be scurrilous. As in his famous 1660 sermon he had warned against the pedantry and over-subtle etymological divisions of texts in Andrewes and the Biblical battery of the Puritans, so in 1668 he had attacked the luscious if not over-ripe metaphors of Jeremy Taylor, and pleaded for plainness, naturalness, and familiarity in language used in the pulpit. It is enough to say that South seemed more of a pulpit journalist than a theologian in the pulpit; he could even degenerate into being an Anglican Hugh Peters, as when, on a notorious occasion, he described Cromwell as an impoverished and dirtily dressed impostor, who killed one king and banished another, who "wanted nothing of the state of a King but the changing of his hat into a crown."[129] W. Fraser Mitchell says justly of him, "all that a great

[129] *Works*, Vol. I, Sermon VIII, p. 213-14.

180

technician could do, he did; but it remained for the finer and more sympathetic personality of Tillotson to invest with charm a manner excellently calculated to impress, but at times too truculently employed to convince or persuade."[130]

Isaac Barrow (1630-1677) was a greater scholar and a more eloquent preacher than South. He was a considerable mathematician and theologian, who drank deep of the Pierian spring, for his favourite authors were Sophocles, Demosthenes, and Aristotle, as well as St. John Chrysostom. He succeeded best with a learned auditory, for his sermons, which issued from the "loads of learned lumber in his head," were said to be of three hours' duration, making it impossible for an ordinary congregation to endure them. There is a legend that his sermon preached in Easter Week 1671 at the Spital "On the Duty and Reward of Bounty to the Poor" took three and a half hours to deliver (and that this was an apocopated version), the Court of Aldermen desired the preacher to print his sermon with whatever further material he had prepared to deliver at that time.[131] The original folio edition of his works allotted thirty-nine pages to this sermon, so there may be some exaggeration in the story. His subjects were treated in too great detail and at too great length, but they were nothing if not thorough. He had some superbly sustained passages of oratory, dazzling but required great endurance from his auditory.

Far less spectacular in eloquence than Barrow or the South of the pyrotechnic denunciations, but far more influential in becoming the new exemplar of preaching for a century to come, was John Tillotson. The latter had a style that combined the seriousness of the Puritans, the rationalism of the Cambridge Platonists, the arrangement of his homiletical material as discourses on certain themes as exemplified by the French preachers, and a warm pragmatism that was all his own.

By his parentage as his training (at Clare Hall, Cambridge where his tutor was Clarkson, and in his fondness for the sermons of Thomas Hill, the Parliamentary Master of Trinity), Tillotson had been strongly influenced by Puritanism and hardly less so by the Cambridge Platonists. His rational amiability in personality as in sermons took him to the deanery of St. Paul's Cathedral, where he would happily have remained for the rest of his life, but for a summons to Canterbury, the primatial see, which he held for only

---

130 *Op. cit.*, p. 321.
131 Henry Wace, *The Classic Preachers of the Church* (1877), p. 29f.

three years. It is from the vantage point of the present day exceedingly difficult to understand his renown. In brilliance he would have been eclipsed by the French sacred orators of his day. There seems to be little stimulus in either his lucid and candid style, or in his rational moralism. One can only suppose that his success comes from his correct anticipation of the prevailing religious and homiletical taste of the century succeeding his own. He was an Augustan ahead of his century: in that sense alone could he be said to be a prophetic preacher. Nor was he a liturgical preacher: he does not preach upon the lessons of the day, nor are there anything except the most occasional references to the Christian year in his sermons. His great strength lay in a transparent arrangement of his subject matter, with stated theme, and simple, logical development, often in three parts. This essay-type sermon of which he was the most cultivated English exponent was notable also for the lucidity and naturalness of the style, the balance of the cadences, the classical simplicity of the illustrations, and the quiet amiability of the personality of this candid preacher which tepidly warms his discourses.

He can only be fully appreciated if entire sermons of his are read, where the effect is slowly and surely created of admiration for his sound reasoning and pellucid explanation of the advantages of belief in and service to God and men. Perhaps the dominant impression is that of the reasonableness of a moral life, in which both the moralists of antiquity and Christ, the great teacher of Christianity, concur. His appeal is to the best morality of all times and in the natural theology which is presupposed in the writings of Cicero, Juvenal, Seneca, Plutarch, Epictetus, and Plato. His style is lofty and luminous, and he proposes for his hearers a simple, relevant and practical piety which will issue in the fruits of goodness and kindness. Its spirit can be easily grasped in the following citation from Sermon CLII:

> I would by no means encourage men to be over censorious to others, there is too much of that Spirit already in the World: but it is not amiss that Men should be strict and severe towards themselves. And I would to God Men would bring themselves to the test, and examine the truth and sincerity of their Religion not by the Leaves of an outward profession, but by the Fruits it produceth in their lives. Every man that will take the pains to look into himself, and to

observe his own actions, may by comparing the temper of his mind, and the general course of his life and practice with the Rules and Precepts of Religion, easily discern what power and efficacy Religion hath in him. A man may as easily know himself, and make as sure a judgment of his state and condition toward God this way, *as a tree is known by its fruit.* Therefore let us not flatter ourselves: for if we indulge any lust, or irregular passion in our Souls, and do not endeavour to mortify and subdue it; if we allow in ourselves with an opinion of our Godliness and whatever the *shew* and *appearance* we may make of Religion, we are certainly destitute of the *power* of it.[132]

Even a slight acquaintance with this passage enables one to realise that it creates an impression of conversational naturalness, candid manliness, good common-sense, and a concern for the hearer or reader that is far from a merely polite interest, in a desire that he may find integrity through unity of profession and practice in the pragmatic Dominical proof of virtue.

Even more famous is Tillotson's sermon on the text, *His Commandments are not grievous.* He began with the aim of showing "that the laws of God are reasonable, suited to our nature, and advantageous to our interest; that we are not destitute of sufficient power and ability for the performance of them; and that we have the greatest encouragements to this purpose." How are Divine commandments advantageous to our interest? "Two things make any course of life easy; present pleasure and the assurance of future reward. Religion gives part of its reward in hand, the present comfort and satisfaction of having done our duty; and for the rest it offers us the best security that heaven can give. Now these two must needs make our duty very easy; a considerable reward on hand, and not only the hopes but the assurance of a far greater recompense thereafter."[133] After analysing this sermon, Norman Sykes justly observes: "It was plain that every means had been adopted to temper the demands of Christianity to the infirmities of unregenerate human nature, and to promise the consolations of religion to the weakest of its professors."[134] Here is an unequalled

---

[132] Tillotson, *Two Hundred Sermons and Discourses*, II, p. 336; cited by W. Fraser Mitchell, *op. cit.*, p. 339.

[133] *Ibid.*, Vol. I, Sermon VI, pp. 152-73.

[134] *Church and State in England in the XVIII Century* (Cambridge, 1934), p. 262.

combination of eudaemonism, utilitarianism and Pelagianism, masquerading as authentic Christianity. It was left to the men of latitude to conceive of a contradiction, Christian discipleship without the taking up of a cross.

No other age would surely have presumed to give Jesus Christ a testimonial of good character, or so deftly to remove the "scandal of the Cross" from the record. Here is Tillotson's transformation of Jesus into a gentleman with a tie-wig who is the very soul of moderation in all things: "The Virtues of his Life are pure, without any Mixture of Infirmity and Imperfection. He has Humility without Meanness of Spirit; Innocency without Weakness; Wisdom without Cunning; and Constancy and Resolution in that which was good without Stiffness of Conceit, and Peremptoriness of Humour: In a word, his Virtues are shining without Vanity, Heroical without anything of Transport, and very extraordinary without being in the least extravagant."[135] One can only offer the comment of Dr. Samuel Johnson when he heard of women preachers: "Sir, a woman's preaching is like a dog walking on his hinder legs. It is not done well; but you are surprised to find it done at all."[136] However admirable the new Tillotsonian style is, and however popular (the counting of noses does not make it right or wrong), its content reduced Christianity to rationalism and moralism, the former diluting faith and the latter abandoning grace. For all their word-splitting pedantry and scraps of classical and Patristic learning, the metaphysical divines were expounding the adamantine orthodoxy of the Fathers. For all their forcing of texts into the Procrustean bed of a triple scheme of reason, doctrine, and use, the Puritan preachers were faithful exegetes of the faith of the New Testament in the Holy Trinity, and not any convenient reduction of it. As a result, the homiletical journey through the century has taken us down the precipitous slopes of an anticlimax: from the twin peaks of Donne and Andrewes, through the plains of Jeremy Taylor and the greater Puritan divines like Baxter, to the foothills of Tillotson, until we reach the muddy margins of the lake below, where his imitators paddle. Their ancestors breathed a rarer air. It is in the high mountain air of adoration that oracles and oratories best flourish and in which sermons are indeed the supplement of and stimulus to worship.

[135] Tillotson, *op. cit.*, Vol. II, Sermon CXXXVII, "The Life of Jesus Christ consider'd as our Example," pp. 241f.

[136] Boswell's *Life of Johnson* (L. F. Powell's revision of G. B. Hill's edn., Vol. I, p. 463).

PART TWO
CULTIC CONTROVERSIES

CHAPTER V

STYLE IN WORSHIP: PRESTIGIOUS OR PLAIN?

ONE OF the most acute controversies between the Anglicans and Puritans of the seventeenth century was concerned with the most appropriate style in which to approach God—in prayer, in gesture, and in vesture. Was it fitting, the Anglicans asked, to approach the most high God, Creator and Sovereign Ruler of the Universe, with casual and unpremeditated prayers, when one would not address an earthly monarch without careful preparation, appropriate etiquette, and elegant diction? For these reasons divine worship was appropriately expressed in a liturgy in which dignity, formality, and order were the leading characteristics. Similarly, it was asked, could one act as God's representative to the people, His ambassador, as it were, without using the appropriate ceremonies and gestures, such as bowing and kneeling, the sign of the Cross, and other forms of reverence and respect? And, finally, inquired the Anglican, could one be God's servant-priest without the fitting livery, or vestments that indicated the high dignity of the office of serving the King of Kings and Lord of Lords? The Anglican answer was to judge the Divine Majesty as desiring and demanding forms of address, gesture and ceremonial, as well as vesture, appropriate to the greatest potentate; to offer less seemed to them to slight Almighty God.

By contrast, the Puritan argued that Christ had taught men that it was not servility but sonship that was to characterize the new relationship with God for his disciples. Had not Christ himself insisted that he called his own "not servants, but friends," and had He not forbidden his disciples to exercise lordship as the rulers of the Gentiles did? Moreover, had not Christ given his disciples an acted parable of the new dispensation by performing the humblest duty of washing his disciples' feet at the Last Supper? All this made it superfluous to try and flatter the God who saw through human pretensions and who desired to be loved as adopted sons love their father, and who wished to be approached in the filial manner—that is, naturally and spontaneously in free prayer. He also desired the disciples of His Son to be marked by the simplicity

187

(not the pomp) of the Gospel, a sincere and natural (not artificial and contrived) ceremonial, and, above all, by a simple, unostentatious vesture.

Perhaps the easiest way to illustrate the difference between the Anglican and Puritan styles of worship is to contrast the views on ceremonial held by Archbishop John Bramhall of Armagh with those of an anonymous Puritan writing in 1640 who was a contemporary of the Archbishop. Bramhall enthusiastically eulogizes ceremonial. "Ceremonies," he affirms, "are advancements of order, decency, modesty, and gravity in the service of God; expressions of those heavenly desires and dispositions which we ought to bring along with us to God's house; adjuments of attention and devotion, furtherances of edification, visible instructors, helps of memory, exercises of faith, the shell that preserves the kernel of religion from contempt; the leaves that defend the blossoms and the fruit."[1]

For the Puritan, however, ceremonies suffocate rather than stimulate religion. They are, by contrast, thought to be the shell not the kernel of religion, its shadow not its substance. Prebendary Peter Smart of Durham attacked excessive ceremonial in an anti-Laudian outburst of a sermon which cost him four years in gaol. He asked in the course of it, ironically, whether religion consisted in "altar-decking, cope-wearing, organ-playing, piping and singing, crossing of cushions and kissing of clouts, oft starting up and squatting down, nodding of heads, and whirling about till their noses stand eastward, setting basins on the altar, candlesticks and crucifixes, burning wax candles in excessive numbers when and where there is no use of light; and what is worst of all, gilding of angels and garnishing of images, and setting them aloft. . . ." He answered his own question: "if, I say, religion consists in these and such like superstitious vanities, ceremonial fooleries, apish toys, and popish trinkets, we had never more religion than now."[2]

The Anglican viewpoint was one that preferred a prestigious, the Puritan a plain style in worship. And on this basic difference between the Anglican desire for splendour and the Puritan desire for simplicity, much of the seventeenth-century controversy on worship turned. We shall follow it as it is expressed in prayers, gestures, and vestments.

In the matter of prayer, the issue was argued as offering a sim-

---

[1] Cited from Bramhall in *Hierurgia Anglicana* (ed. Vernon Staley, 1902), I, p. viii.

[2] Smart's Sermon of 1628, pp. 23-24, also cited in ed. Staley, *op. cit.*, I, p. 187.

ple choice between set forms or spontaneity. That is, a liturgy or license for the minister to conceive his own prayers in his own words.

By the mid-seventeenth century liturgical prayers and spontaneous prayers became the symbols and party-badges respectively of the Anglican Cavaliers and the Puritan Roundheads of the Civil War era and later. The importance of the debate is not measured by the heat that it engendered, but by the significant issues it raised. It has more than a historical interest in a day like our own when the Roman Catholic church is engaged creatively in the revision of the liturgy, and when the proponents of the "underground church" argue vociferously for the introduction of spontaneous and even silent prayer into the liturgy.

1. *The Puritan Critique of Liturgical Prayer*

The Book of Common Prayer of the Church of England, an amalgam of Catholic and Protestant traditions of worship, is the only surviving vernacular liturgy of the Reformation period to have remained in continuous use for over four centuries. Moreover, it has also been welcomed by the various provinces of the Anglican Communion in the British Commonwealth of nations and in the United States of America. It is furthermore unique as a Prayer Book which combines the priest's part with that of the people. In these circumstances it may excite surprise that it should have been subjected to such a sustained barrage of criticism from the Puritans, who included in their number both Presbyterians and Independents, as well as those that a later age would denominate "low churchmen" or "evangelicals."

The Presbyterian opposition, in particular, calls for explanation precisely because the original Calvinist tradition favoured a set liturgy, such as Calvin's *La Forme des Prières Ecclesiastiques* (Geneva, 1542), which contained not only a set order of items of worship, but set prayers as well, though it also allowed the minister to frame the prayer for illumination before the sermon in his own words. The change within British Presbyterianism from what the Scottish church knew as *John Knox's Genevan Service Book* to the acceptance of a manual of worship consisting only of general directions and topics for prayers, such as *A Directory of the Public Worship of God in the Three Kingdoms* (1644) requires an explanation. The summary answer is that the Independents (later to be known as Congregationalists) in the Westminster Assembly

189

of Divines persuaded the Presbyterian majority to accept this compromise, partly on the strength of their Biblically based arguments, and partly because the Independent support was strongest in Cromwell's Ironsides. The Independents, however, were using arguments that had been provided by the Separatists and proto-Puritans of Queen Elizabeth's days.

A second occasion for surprise might be that one could find in the Bible any precedents for spontaneous prayer. John Robinson, the pastor of the Pilgrim Fathers in Leyden before they set sail for North America, freely admitted that the Psalms and the Aaronic blessing in Numbers were admirable Old Testament forms for praise and prayer, but he held that these were not binding on members of the new dispensation. If one affirmed that the Lord's Prayer was clearly intended to be repeated, Robinson was ready with two answers. The first was that St. Paul had insisted that only the pastor's voice was to be heard in public prayer to which the people were to give their concurrence by the single word, *Amen* (I Cor. 14:14, 16). His second reply was that the use of set prayers was a "quenching of the Holy Spirit" and a denial of the necessary dependence upon the Holy Spirit, for, according to Romans 8:26: "the Spirit helps our infirmities for we know not what to pray for as we ought." Robinson's ironical comment on this verse, assuming the Anglican reply was: "Yes, Paul by your leave, right well; for we have in our prayer-book what we ought to pray, word for word, whether the Spirit be present or not."[3]

Other Puritans would argue that the introduction to the Lord's Prayer in St. Matthew's Gospel ("After this manner pray . . .") could best be interpreted as offering a model on which to compose their own prayers rather than a set prayer. Yet others argued that the longer and shorter forms in the Gospels of Luke and Matthew were proof that the words were not sacrosanct and not to be repeated literally. The Anglicans, of course, regularly used the Lord's Prayer in worship, while the left-wing Puritans and Separatists did not. The Presbyterians in the Westminster Assembly prevailed upon the Independents to use it, but their own practice in the latter part of the century veered between the Anglican and Puritan views.

On the larger issue of whether a liturgy was desirable or not, both groups of theological contestants argued their own interpreta-

[3] John Robinson's *Works*, 3 Vols. (ed. Robert Ashton, 1852), III, pp. 21f.

190

tion of Christian antiquity. The Laudian Anglicans contended that the early church had used liturgies in such centres as Rome, Jerusalem, Alexandria, and elsewhere. The Puritans, however, insisted that this was chiefly a product of fourth-century dominance of the church by the state and a departure from the relative freedom of the earliest church. The Puritans, using Robinson again as a representative, cited Tertullian's *Adversus Gentes*: "We pray, saith he, without any to prompt us, because we pray from the heart."[4] This *de pectore, sine monitore* citation became a commonplace of the Puritan apologetic. But in this logomachy we have not penetrated to the heart of the Puritan position. The enemies of the Puritans might accuse them of having a dervish's notion of prayer, but they were affirming the sovereign freedom of the Creator Spirit whose invisible power is known in the stormy wind and tempest, whom liturgists and liturgiologists try to trap and tame in a net of words. They were so afraid of the dullness of repetition, and the staleness that is bred by indifference. They had learned in the love of Christ to speak to God as a Father, and it seemed to the Puritans as if the Anglicans wanted to approach Him only in a chill and distant court etiquette. Others might affirm God's majesty; they were amazed at His mercy. Anglicans might approach God with the words, "Your Majesty"; they would only say, "Abba, Father."

Barrow, a proto-Puritan, expressed the positive value of spontaneous prayer in the following definition. "Prayer," he wrote, "I take to be the confident demanding which faith maketh, thorow [through] the Holy Ghost, according to the will of God for their present wants, estate, etc."[5] Such spontaneous prayer was characterized by assurance, simplicity, naturalness, intimacy, and a moving directness in the approach to God. Its great abuse in practice was a tendency towards prolixity, diffuseness, disorder, and a chain reaction of clichés.

There were, in fact, five chief arguments advanced by the Puritans against liturgical prayers (or "stinted forms" as they called them). First, there was the insistence that the constant use of set forms of prayer deprived both minister and people of the desire to devise prayers for themselves. As a result, Dr. John Owen, the Puritan Vice-Chancellor of Oxford University in the days of the Cromwellian Protectorate, averred: "we daily see men napkining

---

4 *Ibid.*
5 *A Brief Discoverie of the False Church* (Dordrecht, 1590/1), pp. 64-65.

their talents until they are taken from them."[6] The point was expressed even more roundly by the anonymous author of *The Anatomie of the Service Book* (1641) in his sarcastic questions: "What, we pray you, is the procreant and conservant cause of dumbe dogges that cannot barke [Anglican clergymen]; idle shepheards, saying Sir Johns; mere Surplice and Service-Book men, such as cannot do so much as a Porter in his frocke; for he doth Service, and the Priest onely sayes service; is it not the Service Book?" The Puritan clergy anticipating their ejection from the Anglican church in 1662 affirmed the year before: "We cannot believe that it is lawfull for us at all times, by submitting ourselves to a Form of Prayer, to smother the Gift of Prayer, given (we hope) to some of us, or to cool the heat and fervency of our hearts in Prayer, or the Affections of them that hear us."[7] In short, for a minister or church member to remain satisfied with set prayers instead of his own, is like a man who, using crutches when he is lame, refuses to give them up when his legs are healthy again.

A second criticism of liturgical prayers was that they could not meet the varying needs of different congregations and occasions. While the Book of Common Prayer was comprehensive in its appeal, it lacked the particularity and immediate relevance of spontaneous prayer. Isaac Watts, a son of the Puritan tradition and the father of English hymnody, wrote in his admirable *Guide to Prayer* (1716) that it was impossible to produce forms of prayer perfectly adapted for all occasions, since "we have new sins to be confessed, new temptations and sorrows to be represented, new wants to be supplied." Moreover, he added that "every change of providence in the affairs of a nation, a family, or a person, requires suitable petitions and acknowledgments. And all these can never be well provided for in any prescribed composition." He further maintained that the weakness of set prayers is that they are so general in character that they do not warm the souls of those participating in worship.[8]

The third argument the Puritans advanced against a liturgy was that it was an abridgement of Christian liberty in that its prescription persuaded the people that it was an absolute necessity, thus equating a human composition with divine revelation, and

---

[6] *Works* (ed. W. H. Goold, Edinburgh, 1862), xv, p. 52.
[7] *A Sober and Temperate Discourse concerning the Interest of Words in Prayer* by H.D.M.A. (1661), p. 96.
[8] *Works* (ed. Russell), iv, pp. 92-97.

192

leading to uncharitable censures on the churches that did not use a liturgy. Representative spokesmen for this standpoint were John Owen and that ecumenical spirit in an age of impassioned partisanship, Richard Baxter.[9]

A fourth Puritan criticism of liturgical prayers was that their constant use led to hypocrisy, mere lip-service. The result was that worshippers were often tempted to use unsuitable forms and expressions of prayer simply because they were at hand.

The fifth and final argument was one which was only too bitterly true in Restoration England when the approximately two thousand ministers who had found it impossible to affirm that the Book of Common Prayer was in all things conformable to the Word of God were deprived of their livings in universities and parishes. John Owen spoke for all the ejected Nonconformist ministers of 1662 when he accused the imposers of liturgies of bringing "fire and faggot into the Christian religion." He had been anticipated by the anonymous author of *The Anatomie of the Service Book* (1641) who declared that "the Hierarchie and the Service-Booke are resembled already to Mother and Child, so may they be to two twins, begotten and born of Pride and Superstition, nursed and brought up in the lap of Covetousnesse. . . ."[10]

Apart from these criticisms of liturgical prayer, the Puritans had a very rich understanding of the potentialities of Scriptural prayer.[11] They were familiar with the Bible—in the strictest sense they *were* Bible men and women. The Bible was the most thumbed volume in their homes, regularly used each morning and evening in family prayer. There was little other popular reading material to compete with it or to distract them from its message. The young had heard it read by their parents and had themselves learned passages of it by heart. They had heard their elders discuss it and argue over the interpretations of various parts of the Bible as they touched on the great issues of the day. This was the language that Christian people were most accustomed to hear, so it provided the natural diction, rich in associations, for the approach to God.

9 For fuller treatment of these themes, see John Owen, *A Discourse concerning Liturgies and their Imposition* (1662) and *A Discourse of the Holy Spirit in Prayer* (1662); also Richard Baxter, *Five Disputations of Church Government and Worship* (1659) and *A Christian Directory* (1673).

10 *Op. cit.*, p. 61.

11 See A. G. Matthews, *Mr. Pepys and Nonconformity* (1954), pp. 115-20 for an illuminating exposition of Puritan Scriptural prayer from which I have borrowed.

Not only so, but the Scriptural prayers of the Puritan ministers and fathers of households at home were deeply emotional and affecting. However austere the outward mien of the Puritan, he unbent in his religious duties, for he expected "meltings," "enlargements," and "quickenings" when he approached God in prayer. These were the tokens of the Spirit bearing witness within his spirit, and the Holy Spirit inspired him with love, joy, and peace. What fitter words to approach God in than a selection from His Word? The language of Scripture had an incantatory power of communication, creating the moods of adoration, penitence, or aspiration. Admirers of the prayers in the Book of Common Prayer often forget that they are, in fact, admirable mosaics of Holy Scripture.

Furthermore, Scriptural prayer—that great ideal of the Puritans—gained the ready concurrence of those called to join in it. For prayer to have the effectual and fervent spirit appropriate to evangelical supplication, it must be the result of whole-hearted consent. On these three grounds, Scriptural prayer moved by the Spirit, was the simple but august Puritan alternative to liturgical prayer.

2. *The Anglican Critique of Spontaneous Prayer*

The Anglicans, who had a profound knowledge of and respect for the *traditio quinquesaecularis* of the early and undivided church, were not silent under these Puritan provocations. They gave as good as they got. Their representative spokesmen included such distinguished Bishops as Dr. Jeremy Taylor, the English Chrysostom, and Dr. William Beveridge, as well as Dr. Henry Hammond, Patristic scholar and apologist, but not a bishop.

Four major arguments were used against spontaneous or extemporary prayers. First, it was argued, that they might be less the product of the Holy Spirit than of mental laziness. Secondly, it was urged that the glib tongues that utter such prayers tend to ostentation rather than edification. Thirdly, it was denied that any spontaneous prayer was able to gain the full assent of any congregation since no time was allowed for its testing. Finally, it was claimed that the Puritan assumption that all ministers are able to express themselves as felicitously as fluently in divine worship is sheer folly.

Bishop Jeremy Taylor's most extensive critique of extemporary prayer and apologia for liturgical prayer is his *An Apology for*

194

Authorized and Set Forms of Liturgies against the presence of the Spirit (London, 1649).

His answer to those who urge the superiority of spontaneous prayer is to present them with a question: "Whether it is better to pray to God with consideration or without? Whether it is the wiser man of the two, he who thinks and deliberates what to say, or he who utters his mind as fast as it comes?" He also insists that the gifts of the Holy Spirit to the church "are improvements and helps of our natural faculties, of our art and industry, not extraordinary, miraculous, and immediate infusions of habits and gifts." He denies that the desire for variety in prayer is necessarily good, claiming that this is reminiscent of the children of Israel during the Exodus who "cry out that *Manna* will not nourish them, but prefer the *onions of Egypt* before the *food of Angels*," hence it is important to transform the men rather than to change the liturgical arrangements of the church.[12]

Taylor makes a further charge against spontaneous prayers, namely, that they are so variable and contradictory, depending on the viewpoint of the sectarians who offer them, that no man can in conscience "say *Amen* to their prayers that preach and pray Contradictories."[13] He also accuses the Puritans of inconsistency in approving written sermons while disapproving written prayers. He rebuts the charge that set prayers limit the Holy Spirit by reminding the Puritans that their Westminster *Directory* makes the same error by prescribing the matter if not the words to be used in public prayers. Most serious of all—to Taylor's mind—is his conviction that the absence of a liturgy officially approved means that there is no instrument for the expression of the union of Christians in belief, behaviour, and worship. The result is that in many places "Heresie and Blasphemy, and Impertinency, and illiterate Rudenesses" are "put into the Devotion of the most solemne Dayes, and the most publick Meetings, . . . and that there are diverse parts of the Lyturgie; for which no provision at all is made in the Directory; and the administration of the Sacrament let so loosely, that if there be anything essentiall in the Formes of Sacraments, the Sacrament may become ineffectual for want of due Words, and due Administration. . . ."[14] In short, private men are not to be entrusted to represent the people before God in public,

---

[12] *Op. cit.*, pp. 4, 8, 41. [13] *Ibid.*, p. 70.
[14] *Reliquiae Liturgicae* (ed. Peter Hall, Bath, 1847), III, p. 90.

"for the people in *such Solemnities*, in matters of *so great Concernment*, where the *Honour of God, the benefit of the People, the interest of Kingdomes*, and the *Salvation of Soules* are as much concerned as they are in the publick Prayers of a whole national Church."[15]

Beveridge, who declined the see of Bath and Wells in 1691 only to accept St. Asaph in 1704, had the distinction of preaching the best known defence of the Prayer Book in a frequently reprinted sermon. It was entitled, *A Sermon on the Excellency and Usefulness of the Book of Common Prayer* (1682). In it Beveridge argued for an authorized liturgy on the following grounds: the Pauline demand for decency, order, and edification in the worship of the church at Corinth; the custom of the earliest provincial churches of Christendom; Our Lord's own prescription of the Lord's Prayer; and the value of repetition for true learning. The latter pragmatic point is strongly stressed because a set form of prayers will so imprint on the mind of the worshippers what they must think and do as Christians "that it will be no easy matter to obliterate or rase them out; but, do what we can, they will still occur on all occasions; which cannot but be much for our Christian edification." Further, he argues that one can be ductile to a known prayer, but that an entirely new prayer requires a critical challenge and not the obedience of faith. In sum, the Book of Common Prayer contains the prayers of the entire national church, "which are common to the ministers and people, to ourselves, and to all the members of the same Church, so that we have all the devout and pious souls that are in it concurring and joining with us in them; which cannot, surely, but be for the edifying not only of ourselves in particular, but of the Church in general, than any private prayer can be."[16]

The most devastating Anglican critique of Puritan prayers is that contained in the anonymous *Eikon Basilike, The Portraiture of His Sacred Majesty in His Solitudes and Sufferings* (1648), which may owe something to the "martyred" King Charles I, but probably owes more to John Gauden. Free prayers are accused of every possible spiritual and rhetorical fault, for they are charged with "affectations, emptiness, flatness, levity, obscurity, vain and ridiculous repetitions, senseless and often blasphemous expressions (all these burdened with a most tedious and intolerable length)"

---

[15] *Ibid.*
[16] Beveridge's *Works*, 12 Vols. (ed. J. Bliss, 1843-1848), VI, pp. 370-73.

which "do sufficiently convince all men but those who glory in that Pharisaic way." The objections are possible, but not compossible. On the other hand, the advantages of a set and authorized liturgy are succinctly stated. They include: soundness of doctrine (while avoiding heresy); comprehensiveness (instead of the favourite themes and limited experience of the prayers of private persons); order (instead of wanderings around the universe such as characterize some long pastoral prayers); gravity (instead of accidental levity); and, finally, unity (instead of sectarianism).

It is not to be assumed, however, that because the Anglicans stated their viewpoint with such vigour and clarity, the Puritans were left without any answer to the Anglican critique. On the contrary, the Puritans answered the Anglicans point by point.

One of the most vivid and idiomatic rejoinders is that of the anonymous author of *The Anatomie of the Service Book* who replies in particular to the Anglican arguments against the removal of the Book of Common Prayer when anti-Laudian opposition to it as an engine of tyranny was at its height in 1641. If the antiquity of the Prayer Book is urged against its removal, our Puritan author replies: "Antiquity without truth is no better than a custome of errour, *Et nullum tempus occurrit Deo*, there is no prescription to the King of Kings."[17] If it be urged that the Prayer Book was approved and used by many of the godly, our Puritan responds: that we can see further than those of the early reforming days and we ought to do more in the way of reform ourselves. If the claim is made that the Prayer Book has much that is good in it, our Puritan retorts, "so do the Alcoran, the Talmud, and the Apocrypha, but they are not therefore to be included in Christian worship."[18] If the Anglican maintains that it is better to revise than to rescind the Book of Common Prayer, the Puritan avers that no State has ever prospered in cleaning "the Pope's leprous stuffe" and that God's method is to command the pulling down of idolatry.[19] Finally, when the Anglican insists that the Prayer Book was legally established by an Act of Parliament introduced by the King, the Puritan answers with a wickedly apposite anecdote. When a Scottish nobleman was asked if it were legal to base prelacy on an Act of Parliament, he replied: "It never went well with them since their Churchmen laboured more to be versed in the Acts of Parliament than in the Acts of the Apostles."[20] The obduracy

[17] *Ibid.*, p. 69.
[19] *Ibid.*, pp. 70-71.
[18] *Ibid.*, p. 70.
[20] *Ibid.*, p. 71.

of the Puritan opposition to the Liturgy and the conviction of the superiority of conceived prayer inspired by the Holy Spirit and saturated by Scripture, was ultimately due to the belief that God had so ordered it in His Word—and neither King nor Parliament had any authority in the celestial court.

In the same year John Cotton stated the point plainly: "Wee conceive it also to be unlawful to bring in ordinarily any other Bookes into the publique worship of God, in the Church, besides the Book of God. . . ."[21] This was his reason for rejecting both Prayer Book and Homilies. Another Independent minister, Jeremiah Burroughes, was to insist that only that type of worship which had warrant in the divine Word was acceptable to God. Here he trumpeted the basic Puritan liturgical contention: "That in God's worship there must be nothing tendered up to God but what hee hath commanded: Whatsoever we meddle with in the worship of God, it must be out of the Word of God."[22]

3. Prayers as Reflections of Ecclesiastical Concepts

The two notions of prayer, liturgical and spontaneous, reflect two different concepts of the church and its relation to the state. The Anglicans held a national and parochial view of the church, while the Puritans thought of the Christian community as "gathered" out of the world and comprising committed Christians. While at the outset Puritanism worked for a national establishment of religion, the ejection of the Puritan divines of all persuasions from the national church in 1662 and the failure to include them in 1689, led the Nonconformists, whether Presbyterian or Independent, to adopt the Congregational conception of the church. The earliest definition of a "gathered church" was that of Robert Browne, which stated: "The Church planted or gathered is a company of Christians or believers, which, by a willing covenant made with their God, are under the government of God or Christ, and

---

21 John Cotton, *A Modest and Cleare Answer to Mr Balls Discourse of set formes of Prayer. Set forth in a most Seasonable Time when this Kingdome is now in Consultation about Matters of that Nature, and many godly long after the Resolution in that Point* (1642), p. 5.

22 *Gospel-Worship or the Right Manner of Sanctifying the Name of God in generall* (1648), p. 8. Exactly the same point is emphatically made by John Barnard in *A Short View of the Prelatical Church of England* (1641, reprinted 1661), p. 21: "That nothing be allowed in God's service which cannot be proved by some *warrant* out of Gods word; for the Scriptures are a perfect Rule for any thing necessary, either in substance or circumstances, in and about the holy word of God."

keep his laws in one holy communion. . . ."[23] Here is a repudiation of all inherited, nominal, birthright ideas of Christianity in the emphatic demand that the true Church of Christ shall consist only of the redeemed who, by an act of will as expressed in a covenant they have signed, have recognised God's calling of them and gathering of them out of the world for salvation. This was the concern for intensity in religion which stressed holiness above Catholicity, charity, and unity.

Such a concept of the nature of the church will demand prayers that presuppose the warmth, intimacy, spontaneity, and even informality of a gathering of friendly families, well known to each other. It also presupposes a minister who is the under-shepherd of his little flock, who has baptized their children, catechized them, married them, and admitted them to the fellowship of the holy table, and in his visitations "rejoiced with them that do rejoice, and wept with those that weep." It also assumes that the free and spontaneous and spirit-directed prayers of their minister will not scruple, if need be, to speak of their peculiar circumstances, even mentioning them by name in the petitions. There is little place for formality or uniformity in such a view of the church or of prayer appropriate to it. Its distinguishing marks are, therefore, freedom, particularity, flexibility, and the intimacy of fellowship—all expressed in sincere and spontaneous prayers. Such prayers in the mouth of a devout, learned and fluent pastor could seem the re-enactment of a miniature Pentecost, but it was too much to expect for every Christian community and every minister without such gifts.

The Anglicans still held the medieval view, restated with vigour by their leading apologist Hooker, that church and state are essentially co-extensive bodies, and that as a child is born a member of the English nation so he should be baptized as a member of the Church of England. Thus for the Anglicans the prayers of the local church are a reflection of the prayers of the entire national church. It is clear that for a type of worship which is to be comprehensive enough to include the entire nation, saints and sinners alike, beginners and mature Christians, which is to stress continuity with the church of the centuries, and which is to maintain unity by imposing uniformity of devotion, doctrine, and discipline, the Book of Common Prayer is the admirable medium and instrument.

[23] *A Booke which sheweth the Life and Manners of all True Christians* (Middelburg, 1582), C3 recto.

In our ecumenical days these two conceptions of the nature of the church are seen to be complementary, not competitive, as viewed in the seventeenth-century perspective. Our age can see that liturgical prayers may be enlivened by the inclusion of more personal, contemporary, and newly created prayers (not unlike the spontaneous prayers of the Puritans, but carefully composed). Thus the uniformity, comprehensiveness, order, dignity, and tradition that characterize liturgical prayer, with the corresponding defect of impersonality, may be combined with the flexibility, contemporaneity, and spontaneity of free prayers which, without a liturgical framework, may become diffuse and amorphous, and leave no more trace than footprints in the sand overwhelmed by the incoming sea. This was a possible compromise undiscerned by the seventeenth-century controversialists.

4. Ceremonies

Another hotly contested issue in worship was the question of the appropriateness or inappropriateness of elaborate or simple ceremonial and gesture in worship, not to mention setting. Once again, the Anglicans were cast in the role of defending dignity and splendour in ceremonial, while the Puritans were the protagonists of simplicity and plainness.

If in prayer the Puritan tended to equate the formal with the insincere, in ceremonial and furnishings he tended to equate spirituality with immateriality and the lack of sensuousness. The Anglican, by contrast, appreciated the senses as the conduits of communication. The Puritan seemed to think of a congregation at worship exclusively in terms of discarnate spirits, and even when considering the sacraments regarded them as divine accommodations to human necessity. The Puritan asserted the ethic only to banish the aesthetic. While valuing the doctrine of redemption, he ignored the doctrines of creation and incarnation which give a status to the senses as the avenues of divine communication to the psycho-physical personality of man; instead he depreciated them as earthly allurements and distractions.

It was not, however, insensitivity to the aesthetic dimensions of life, which resulted in the nakedness of Puritan ceremonial and furnishings. It was rather the conviction that this was the will of God in His Word. To worship God in ways other than He had commanded was the height of arrogance and disobedience.

It seemed to the Puritan theologians who discussed the matter in some detail that the Second Commandment which forbade the making of "graven images" demanded the removal from churches of all representations of the Divine Majesty in stained-glass windows or carvings in wood or stone. An interesting pamphlet of this century, entitled *The Blindness of the Unhappy Jews*, stated that there were three current interpretations of the Second Commandment. One prohibits the secular as well as the sacred use of images, and this is the attitude of Moslems. A second view holds that images may be used in secular life, but not in sacred life. A third view maintains that images may be used in churches provided they are not worshipped. The second view is the Puritan, and the third is the Anglican position. The author himself took the second position, arguing that images waste money that should be spent on the poor who are God's true images, that they give false impression of God, and that they are expressly forbidden in the Bible.

Perkins, the Nestor of Puritan theologians, discussed images in his important work, *A Reformed Catholike* (1603). He approved the civil use of images in buildings and on coins, and the historical employment of them in sacred or profane books used in private. He even allowed that images might denote the presence of God as in the case of the brazen serpent erected by Moses or the cherubim placed over the mercy-seat in the Temple, but only because they were positively required by God. The true images of the New Testament, said Perkins, are the doctrine and preaching of the Gospel, "hence it follows that the preaching of the Word is as a most excellent picture in which Christ with his benefits are lively represented unto us."[24] In conclusion, he insisted that images in divine worship were forbidden as idols, as strictly as Israel's golden calf ever was.

Thus the celebrated iconoclasm of William Dowsing, the Parliamentary visitor to the churches of Cambridgeshire and Suffolk in 1643 and 1644, becomes a less puzzling phenomenon than it otherwise might seem to be. He was no aesthetically deficient barbarian pulverising images in stained glass or stone. He was simply the Puritan government's agency for removing traces of superstition and idolatry.

Furthermore, while representations of the Virgin Mary or of other saints were not vetoed by Holy Scripture, they were pro-

[24] *Works* (1605), p. 705.

hibited by the Puritans as a potential danger to the "weaker brethren." They were the monuments of an older religion, "the badges of Anti-Christ," and their very existence might revive the abuses they brought to memory. But more than this, they were often agents in promoting abuses. For they bore testimony to the medieval prayers offered to the Virgin and the saints. The apostle Paul's injunction to "avoid the appearance of evil" was at the root of iconoclasm such as Dowsing's.

Simplicity seemed more in keeping with the religion of the Christ who had declared that "foxes have holes, the birds of the air have nests, but the Son of Man has nowhere to lay his head," and who, in death, was laid in a borrowed sepulchre. The relative bareness of the chapels of the Dissenters (with a similar ceremonial), when the danger of a resurgence of abuses had passed, was mainly the result of economic necessity. The impoverished Nonconformists were unable to afford lavish ecclesiastical edifices, even if they had wished to erect them.

It is also worth recalling that the Puritans never valued their meeting-houses in the way the Anglicans esteemed their churches. If the clergy of the establishment thought of the church as an edifice, the Puritans meant by the same concept the *sancta plebs*, the people of God indwelt by the Holy Spirit.

The differing attitudes towards edifices of worship can be seen in a comparison of the views of Richard Hooker, the chief Anglican apologist, and of George Gillespie, a Scottish Presbyterian divine, who was the youngest member of the Westminster Assembly. For Hooker the church is a sacred building, with hallowed associations and symbols that lead the worshipper to thankfulness and aspiration; for Gillespie the sanctity rests in the "saints," under the inspiration of God's Holy Spirit. Hooker writes: "the very Majesty and holiness of the place where God is worshipped, *hath in regard of us*, great virtue, force and efficacy, for that it serveth as a sensible help to stir up devotion; and, *in that respect*, no doubt, *bettereth* even our holiest and best actions in this kind."[25] Gillespie, on the contrary, writes:

> How much more soundly do we hold with J. Rainolds,
> That unto us Christians no land is strange, no ground unholy;
> every coast is Jewry, every house Sion; and every faithful
> company, yea every faithful body a Temple to serve God

[25] *Ecclesiastical Polity*, Bk. v, Chap. xvi, Sect. 2.

in . . . whereas the presence of Christ among two or three gathered together in his Name (Matthew XVIII. 20) maketh any place a Church, even as the presence of a King with his attendants maketh any place a Court.[26]

Hooker's conviction led to the creation of churches which would aim at being houses of God, honouring His presence, and reminders to the people that they were also the gates of heaven. Gillespie's view led to the erection of meeting-houses as simple, functional, and utilitarian as possible.

There was a deep sense in which ceremonial and elaborate furnishings were superfluous for the Puritans. They needed no such stimulants for the imagination: their imagery was mental, elicited by the Bible. As Shakespeare relied on few artificial aids as spurs to the imagination, substituting the transcendental imagery of his verse for the fictitious help of artificial scenery, the Puritans rejected the ecclesiastical "scenery" of the medieval church for the symbolism and imagery of the Bible. For them the four Gospels and the Book of the Apocalypse provided a more vivid background to faith than human manufactures in glass, wood, or stone could do. This conviction of theirs has been admirably expressed by a twentieth-century historian of Dissent, Bernard L. Manning: "To call on the name of God, to claim the presence of the Son of God, if men truly know and mean what they are doing, is in itself an act so tremendous and so full of comfort that any sensuous or artistic heightening of the effect is not so much a painting of the lily as a varnishing of sunlight."[27]

That metaphor "varnishing" is exactly the term used by John Owen, the Atlas of Independency, to express his utter disgust at the fussy, meretricious, mock-Catholic ceremonial propagated by the Laudians, a conviction that he shared with Peter Smart, Cosin's enemy in Durham Cathedral. Preaching before Parliament in 1646, Owen explained why he had to leave the Queens' College, Oxford, in 1637, because of his abhorrence of the Laudian ceremonies in the chapel: "Now such were the innovations of the late hierarchists. In worship, their paintings, crossings, crucifixes, bowings, cringings, altars, tapers, wafers, organs, anthems, litany, rails, images, copes, vestments, what were they but Roman varnish,

---

26 *Dispute against the English Popish Ceremonies obtruded upon the Church of Scotland*, originally issued in 1637, this citation is from the reprint of 1660, p. 123.

27 *Christian Worship* (ed. N. Micklem, Oxford, 1936), p. 162.

an Italian dress for our devotion, to draw on conformity to that enemy of the Lord Jesus?"[28] It was not that the Puritans disliked art; it was simply that they loved religion more.

Another telling Puritan criticism of Anglican ceremonialism was directed against its fussy distraction in worship. This was well expressed by "G.F." the author of *The Liturgical Considerator Considered* (a reply to Gauden's tract on the liturgy) which appeared in a second edition in 1661. He argues in "The Epistle to the Reader" that the desires of the church ought to be expressed "seriously and composedly," asserting that this demands that the worshipper must be "sequestered from all other acts and businesse, set and intent with all seriousness," to mention those desires before God "in a fixed posture of body and mind." It is essential for this purpose, he contends, that there be no "unnecessary variation of place, or gesture, from Desk to Table, now kneeling, anon standing, and therefore transient salutations, affectionate friendly Christian wishes, quickening versicles, desultory short options, by leaps and starts" and these "cannot square with the more serious and composed frame of solemn prayer."

Humphrey Smith made the same point with greater vividness and vigour. He considers the rubrics in the Prayer Book that require the minister to change his voice, his posture, and his place, make him appear ridiculous. As to the posture, Smith asserts, "besides the *windings, turnings, and cringings*, his face must be sometimes towards the People, and sometimes his back."[29]

The Anglican viewpoint had many capable exponents besides Hooker. One of the most distinguished of them was Bishop Lancelot Andrewes, whose main concern was to inculcate reverence in worship through its appropriate ceremonial expression. Worship, he said, ought not to be an "uncovered and bare-faced religion." We would not dare to come before the meanest prince as we do before the King of Kings. Ceremonial, so Andrewes teaches, is based upon the threefold foundation of the nature of man and his

---

[28] *Works* (ed. W. H. Goold, Edinburgh, 1850-53), VIII, p. 28. It was evidently the Laudian ceremonies which stuck in the throats of the Puritans for John Barnard in his *Short View of the Prelatical Church of England* (1641, reprinted 1661), in his Sect. VII *Of The Prelatical Service* (p. 20) criticises the "long wearisome Liturgie" taken from three Romish books, the unedifying singing and piping on organs, and "superstitious crynging to the name *Jesus* towards the Altar, towords the East," and he particularly objects to "a formal observation of Habits, Surplesses, Hoods, Copes, variety of gestures, and ceremonious devotions devised by men."

[29] *Forty-Four Queries . . . propounded to all the Clergymen of the Liturgie* (1662), p. 29.

activities, as soul and body and as having worldly goods. Man must worship with each of these instruments. The result is "if all our worship be inward only, with our hearts and not our hats as some fondly imagine [a palpable hit at the Puritans!], we give him but one of three."[30] Naturally, Andrewes rejects sitting at worship, wittily explaining that God will not have humans worship Him like elephants, as if they had no joints in their knees. He recognises that ceremonies can be unnecessarily multiplied, so he advises that they be few, necessary, for edification, for good order, and for decency.[31]

Andrewes, as we saw in an earlier chapter, gave beauty a coronation in his private chapel at Winchester, and Archbishop Laud always regarded these furnishings and the ceremonial as an Anglican ideal, which he promoted with his zeal and considerable powers. This advancement of ceremonial and ornaments found its best expression theologically and liturgically in the Consecration of Churches, services that became a new feature of Anglicanism in the seventeenth century.[32]

The new Canons of 1604 made official the Anglican conviction that the chief purpose of ceremonial was to provide opportunities for paying homage to God and encouraging reverence in divine worship. This is quite explicit in Canon XVIII on the reverence and attention that are to be used within the church in time of divine service. It begins by insisting that reverence is according to the apostle's rule, "Let all things be done decently and according to order." Kneeling is prescribed for the General Confession, the Litany, and other prayers, and standing for the Creed. It is further enjoined, "and likewise when . . . the Lord IESVS shall bee mentioned, due and lowly reverence shall be done by all persons present as it hath been accustomed: testifying by these outward ceremonies and gestures, their inward humilitie, Christian resolution, and due acknowledgement that the Lord Jesus Christ, the true and eternall Sonne of God, is the only Saviour of the World. . . ."

One of the most important Anglican treatises of the period on worship is Herbert Thorndike's *Of Religious Assemblies and the Publick Service of God: A Discourse according to Apostolic Rule*

---

30 *Sermons*, I, p. 162, cited by P. A. Welsby, *Lancelot Andrewes, 1555-1626* (1958), p. 126.

31 *Sermons*, II, pp. 334f., cited by Welsby, *op. cit.*, p. 127.

32 See J. Wickham Legg, *English Orders for Consecrating Churches in the Seventeenth Century* (Henry Bradshaw Society, XLI, 1911), and my citations from them in Chap. I, Sect. 3, *supra*.

and Practice (Cambridge, 1642). This has been curiously ignored by later interpreters. Apart from being a learned defence of liturgies from Patristic sources, and a supporter of the view that prayers are more important than sermons, it provides a most interesting discussion of the function of ceremonies. Thorndike sees their primary function, whether military, political, or religious, as making the common people respect the functions performed by their leaders, a clearly hierarchical conception of the nature of society, both religious and secular. He writes: "The circumstances and ceremonies of Public Service is indeed a kind of Discipline and Paedagogie, whereby men subject to sense are guided in the exercise of godliness."[33] He goes on to describe ceremonial as "the apparell of Religion at the heart which some think, like the Sunne, most beautiful when it is most naked," except that men do not consist of minds without bodies. But "as long as our bodily senses are managed to our souls advantage, the heat within will starve without this apparell without."

Thorndike insists that the external forms of worship help even those minds which are least in tune "to corroborate their reverence and devotion at the Service of God, by their exercise of it," while the thoughtful persons present will be greatly impressed "by the example of the world practising the Service of God in an orderly and reverent form."[34] He cites Augustine to the effect that the primary purpose of special gestures in prayers is "not used so much to lay the mind open to God to whom the most invisible inclinations of the heart are best known, as to stirre up a man's own mind to pray with more humble and fervent groans."[35] Thorndike clearly approves Augustine's conviction that "the affection of the heart antecedent to the doing of these [gestures], by the doing of them gathers strength." The use of special garments in Divine worship, according to Thorndike, is to make the service seem more solemn. They procure "inward reverence to that work which it maketh outwardly solemn, to represent to our own apprehensions, and to convey it to other mens, the due respect and esteem which it ought to bear in our hearts."[36]

One cannot avoid noticing the careful attention paid to human psychology by Anglican apologists for worship whether it be Hooker pleading for collects as arrow-like prayers requiring a short time span, or Thorndike showing how reverent gestures

---

[33] *Op. cit.*, p. 299.
[35] *Ibid.*, p. 306.
[34] *Ibid.*, p. 298.
[36] *Ibid.*, p. 305.

beget reverence on the part of even the half-attentive. Puritan writers on worship seem to ignore the human dimensions in asserting the divine demands.

Returning to the hierarchical aspect of ceremonial, so prominent in Thorndike, these considerations carry considerably less force in a society as unhierarchical as that of the twentieth century, which is increasingly suspicious of outward forms, and finds greater sympathy with the spontaneity, sincerity, and informality of Puritanism than with the conjoint hierarchical union of church and state in seventeenth-century Anglicanism. Nonetheless, the Anglican concern for a splendid style in worship has great affinity with the medieval religious tradition, the Tudor love of pageantry, which has never died in English life, an appreciation of the doctrines of creation and incarnation, and a deeper understanding of human psychology: Puritanism with its colour-blind iconoclasm had few links with tradition or taste. Moreover, the Anglican view offered a stimulus to creativity to the painter, glazier, and carver, whereas the Puritan merely domesticated these imaginative activities so that they produced works for the council chamber or the home, but not for the house of God.

The Puritans had special reasons of long standing for taking exception to both the gestures and vestures of the established church. From their perspective, the most controversial gestures were those required by the Prayer Book at the two major sacraments, Baptism and the Lord's Supper. They took particular exception to the requirement of kneeling as the only permitted posture for the reception of Communion.

The Anglican viewpoint is finely expressed by George Herbert. Reverent himself, he insists that the country parson administers Communion to none except the reverent. While the Holy Supper is a feast, yet man's unpreparedness for such a privilege requires kneeling. Hence, "he that comes to the Sacrament, hath the confidence of a Guest, and he that kneels confesseth himself an unworthy one, and therefore differs from other Feasters. . . ." This is an excellent exposition of the Anglican posture, but it is followed by an intriguing denunciation: "but hee that sits or lies puts up to an Apostle: Contentiousnesse in a feast of charity is more scandall than any posture."[37] What has elicited Herbert's vehement accusa-

---

[37] *Herberts Remains, or Sundry Pieces of that Sweet Singer of the Temple*, Mr. George Herbert, *sometime Orator of the University of Cambridge* (1652), pp. 92-93.

tion of presumption in the sitting gesture? At this time it was the Independents and the Fifth Monarchists (apart from the few remaining Separatists) who used this gesture at Communion. It was, however, rightly interpreted by Anglicans as an exceedingly revolutionary and democratic gesture.

Since the time of Knox's inclusion of the "black rubric" without Parliamentary permission in the Second Prayer Book of 1552, there had been strong Calvinist objections to kneeling at the Supper, for this implied acceptance of the Roman Catholic doctrine of Transubstantiation and hence seemed to be countenancing the adoration of the elements. It was one of the three *nocent* ceremonies objected to in all the long line of Puritan critiques of the Book of Common Prayer.

In the course of the seventeenth century, however, there developed a strong positive Puritan case for sitting as the appropriate Communion gesture. It was, of course, nearer the posture of Christ and His apostles at the Last Supper. However, in connection with the growing importance of the sanctification of the Sabbath Day for the Puritans, there was an increasing recognition that this commemorated God resting after the six days of Creation, and looked forward to the future eschatological rest of the people of God. Sitting symbolized such rest perfectly, and where was this most fittingly displayed, than at the Communion table?

The revolutionary implications of the sitting posture at the Communion table were first expounded by John Archer, Independent minister and flaming Fifth Monarchist, in his radical volume, *The Personal Reigne of Christ upon Earth, in a treatise wherein is fully and largely laid open and proved, That Jesus Christ, together with the Saints, shall visibly possesse a Monarchicall State and Kingdome in this World* (1642). The Fifth Monarchy would be Christ's (following on the kingdoms of the Assyrians, Persians, Greeks and Romans). In this treatise Archer stresses the importance of Christ *sitting down* with His disciples (Luke 22:14) at the Last Supper. He claims the sitting posture has a double significance. The first is that as Christ had served the disciples with bread and wine, they should not strive who should be the greatest. Thus, this was an exemplary act of humility on Christ's part. But the second meaning was one full of consolation for the future and for the immediate future, too, since "by his admitting them to sit and eate of that his Supper and Table, he did show and seale to them the fellowship which they should have in his Kingdome."[38] Yet this was not a foretaste of a future heaven that Archer was talking about. Quite the contrary, Archer affirms that it is a sign and seal "of our Rayning with Christ in his Kingdome in this World."[39] Here then was the supremely religious democratic symbol, a token of the equality of the saints and their sharing in the Christocratic rule shortly to be established in England as the consummation of the divine purpose through all the ages. There, with a vengeance, was the promised end of hierarchy in both state and church!

The other ceremony to which the Puritans took such great exception was the signation of the Cross in Baptism. It was objected to first as the making of an additional sacramental sign for which there was no authority in the New Testament. Query 95 of *A Survey of the Booke of Common Prayer* pertinently asks: "Whether the childe be not received againe by and with Crossing, and so may seeme to be a Sacrament as well as Baptism for that cause . . . as if regeneration were by baptisme and incorporation by crossing?"[40]

It was also scrupled as a Roman Catholic custom borrowed by the Prayer Book, and as seeming to glorify the power of the priest administering Baptism. The Anglicans, however, if Herbert may be taken as their representative spokesman, gloried in the signation with the Cross. The country parson, says Herbert, "willingly and cheerfully crosseth the Child, and thinketh the Ceremony not only innocent but reverend."[41]

Nevertheless, the Canon XXX cautiously safeguards the Crossing from misinterpretation, insisting that the church has ever taught that the sign of the Cross is not a substantial part of the Sacrament, and the infant is received as a member of Christ's flock by virtue of Baptism itself and before the signation with the Cross.

Controversy over the signation led to some ugly squabbling in parish churches in our period. On April 8, 1642, in Radwinter church at the Baptism of one Richard Clark's daughter, Alice, one of the congregation, John Traps, confronted the curate "by coming up close and standing in a daring manner by him, told him that he should not have her out of the godmother's arms, nor

[38] *Op. cit.,* p. 17. [39] *Ibid.*
[40] Frere and Douglas, *Puritan Manifestoes* (1907), p. 90.
[41] *Herberts Remains,* pp. 89-90.

sign her with the sign of the cross; and to that end flung the cloth over the face of the child, keeping his hand upon it, and saying, 'It is the mark of the Beast.'" About the same time Thomas Newcomen, Rector of Holy Trinity, Colchester, finding himself forced by threats to give up making the sign of the cross in Baptism, used to parody the Prayer Book words of admission and say: "We do not receive this child into the congregation of Christ's flock, neither do we signe it with the signe of the crosse, in token that it shall hereafter be ashamed to confesse the faith of Christ crucified."[42] So objectionable was this custom of crossing to Puritan ministers, that if it were required of them, they sometimes used an ingenious escape, by not touching the infant's forehead with their fingers, but only making a pretence of doing so.[43] It is not surprising to learn that public Baptism went out of fashion during the Commonwealth and Protectorate, so that Josselin wrote in his diary for October 5, 1656: "Sacrament of Baptisme administered this day in publique, which was not for a long time before in Colne," and children were entered into the Register as "borne" not "baptized."[44]

The Puritans had similar scruples against using the ring in Marriage, the third of the *nocent* ceremonies. They argued that there was no warrant for the use of the ring in the Bible, whereas its requirement in the Prayer Book service of Holy Matrimony was to make it an additional sacramental sign. Besides, one Robert Johnson of Northampton rightly asked, whether the Anglicans were consistent: "Wee would knowe why you do reiect *hallowed beades*, and yet receyve *hallowed Ringes*?"[45]

We have seen that ceremonial and gestures are accepted by Anglicans as suited to the mixed spiritual-sensuous nature of man, as reminders of the homage due to the King of Kings, as pedagogical incentives to adoration, confession, or aspiration, and as means of encouraging the common people to respect their leaders in civil, and religious life. For tne Puritans, who are already feeling the iron hand in the soft lawn sleeves of the Laudian prelacy about their throats, the hierarchical argument is a dissuasive from prestigious ceremonial. But chiefly, they will accept the minimum of

[42] A. Tindal Hart, *The Man in the Pew, 1558-1660* (1960), p. 136.

[43] Ronald A. Marchant, *The Puritans and the Church Courts in the Diocese of York, 1540-1652* (1960), p. 103.

[44] *The Diary of the Rev. Ralph Josselin 1616-1683* (ed. E. Hockcliffe, Camden Society, 3rd series, 1908), xv, *ad loc.*

[45] *A Parte of a Register*, Ms., *circa* 1590, in the Dr. Williams's Library, Gordon Square, London, p. 104.

ceremony and gestures since these are the externals of religion, and only when these are dictated by God's Word. Furthermore, Puritans think that simplicity and sincerity are closely allied, as pomp and pretence are.

5. *Vestments*

We have already noticed the hierarchical element in the Anglican interest in ceremony: it is also present in the Anglican preference for distinctive vestments for the celebrants of divine worship. It can be seen in the Canons of 1604 which require those administering Communion on principal festivals in cathedral and collegiate churches to wear copes, while surplices and hoods are to be worn in such churches when there is no Communion (Canon XXIII), and students in the Oxford and Cambridge Colleges are to wear surplices in time of worship (Canon XXV). It was believed, as Thorndike maintained, that if the leaders in worship dressed solemnly, this would encourage the worshippers to believe in the great importance of honouring God in worship.

The Puritans cherished a long tradition of criticising the Anglican vestments and the fact that Archbishop Laud "dressed up" rather than "down" made them less likely to change their minds on this issue. They were especially critical of the surplice and the cope. In the early seventeenth century, when Susan Cook of Little Baddow, Essex, a Puritan stronghold, was charged with "laying her linen in the church to dry," she replied insolently that "she might lay her rags there as well as the surplice."[46] Archbishop Parker's *Advertisements* of 1566 had already sparked the Vestiarian Controversy in the Church of England and the rigour with which the policy was enforced had caused some notable "Genevans" such as William Whittingham, Dean of Durham, to lose their livings.

The Puritans rested the case against distinctive vestments on the following grounds. First and foremost, the insistence upon a particular vesture was an infringement of Christian liberty; the church which had been freed by Christ from the bondage of the law was now attempting to infringe the crown rights of Christ the Redeemer by introducing new sartorial burdens on the conscience.[47] This was especially foolish when the Anglicans them-

---

[46] A. Tindal Hart, *The Man in the Pew*, p. 175.
[47] Cf. *A Parte of a Register*, p. 41: "if it be abolished and *Christ* bee come in steede, then a great injurie is done to Christ for manie causes. The one is,

selves admitted that such matters were *adiaphora*, or in the realm of indifferent things. Secondly, the vestments were disliked because of their association with Roman Catholicism, and so were thought of as "badges of Anti-Christ," upholding the priesthood of the clergy and denying the priesthood of all believers. (Again, we observe the democratic and anti-hierarchical emphases in Puritan apologetic.) Thirdly, these vestments were symbols of pomp and grandeur, ill-befitting the humility with which all men should approach God, and contrary to the simplicity of the first disciples and apostles of Christ, they should be done away with, even if indifferent, for the sake of the weaker brethren.[48]

Anglicans desiring to retain the vestments argued that this national Church of England was autonomous and need not abolish vestments because other national Reformed churches did so.[49] Its teachings were evangelical and this minimized any danger accruing from the retention of traditional vestments. Furthermore, these vestments were not forbidden in Scripture. Indeed, they were decent and becoming, and the early church had favoured the use of distinctive vestments for those who discharged a public function. The surplice was to be retained for the sake of a uniform decency.

Our brief survey of the controversial difference in styles of worship between Anglicans and Puritans is reaching the end. It is clear that there was a radical dichotomy of viewpoint held on each side with equal definiteness and certainty, if not with obstinacy. The Anglicans believe in the holiness of beauty, and in the order, dignity, uniformity, and decent splendour of a liturgy, ceremonial, and ornaments that glorify God by giving Him man's best artistic creations and which thereby impress the ordinary people with the extraordinary. Ceremonial and gesture solemnise worship and lead the people to make the appropriate gesture of kneeling, for example, so that they may feel the contrition and sorrow that the liturgical action symbolizes. The acts of homage, such as bowing

---

that those ceremonies which Christ by his passion did abolishe, should in contempt of him and his passion be taken agayne."

[48] *Ibid.*, pp. 43f.: "for foure causes ought the surplisse, the coape, the Tippet, and other popish ceremonies to be taken away and removed out of God his Church. 1. First, that Christ may more clearly shine and appear in his Gospell, without the darkness of mans devyces. 2. Secondly, that papistrie may appeare more to be hated and detested. 3. Thirdlie, that the offence of the weake may be taken away. 4. Fourthlie, that contention amongst brethren might cease."

[49] A point developed by Hooker in the *Ecclesiastical Polity*, Bk. v, Chap. xxix.

(what the Puritans call "cringing") and kneeling, are the religious equivalents of the civil courtesies, and if appropriate in an earthly court, they are thought to be even more so in the presence chamber of the King of Kings, which is what Anglicans claim the church is.

By contrast, the Puritan believes that God sees through all the posturing to the hearts of His worshippers, and prefers to be worshipped, not as King of Kings and Lord of Lords, but as "the God and Father of our Lord Jesus Christ" and "Our Father." He requires filial familiarity, not servile fear from His worshippers, and greatly prefers simplicity and sincerity to splendour and theatricality.

It sometimes seems as though the contending parties prayed to a different God—the Anglicans to a majestically transcendent Deity, and the Puritans to a familiarly immanent God. It is almost to be expected, therefore, that a Puritan should make this very accusation against the Anglicans, that they seemed to him to worship, like the Athenians, an "Unknown God." He felt that his opponents had framed this Deity according to their own rich fancy as "some carnall man, whose senses are delighted with such service; as his ears with organs, his eyes with goodly images, curious wrought copes, rich palls, fair gilded plate; his smell with sweet incense, his Majesty with sitting upon your stately high altar as upon his throne, and to keep his residence in your goodly cathedral as in his Royal Court."[50]

Equally, the Anglican might well have retorted to the Puritan, that he worshipped a colour-blind Creator, and an Eternal Son who had never become incarnate but was always the speaking Word, and a Holy Spirit who had inspired prophets and preachers, but never artists, and that the Puritan himself was an insensate and discarnate spirit, not a man.[51]

Each of the controversial parties saw the truth, but not the whole truth. They were right in what they affirmed, wrong in their dogmatic denials. Each saw in a mirror darkly, blinded by their prejudice and blinkered by their obduracy, mistaking the segments of truth which they apprehended for the whole circle. A later age

---

[50] *Reply to a Relation of the Conference* (1640), pp. 102, 104, cited in *Hierurgia Anglicana* (ed. Vernon Staley, 1902), I, pp. 194-95.

[51] The same charge might with perhaps greater accuracy have been made against the members of the Society of Friends who carried the principle of immateriality so far as to eliminate sermons and sacraments and sacerdotalism, but that is another story told in Chapter XIV on "Radical Worship."

may see that spontaneity can add a personal element to the liturgy otherwise missing, and that the potency and promises of Anglican ceremonialism and vestments needed the Puritan warnings that have come full circle in our age which has finally turned its back on triumphalism.

CHAPTER VI

CALENDARY CONFLICT:
HOLY DAYS OR HOLIDAYS?

ONTROVERSY over the sacred calendars of Catholics, Anglicans, and Puritans was woven into the fabric of the common life of our period. It is referred to casually in the thirty-eighth of R. Chamberlain's collection of *Conceits, Clinches, Flashes and Whimsies newly studied* (1639). This reads: "One said to another that his face was like a popish almanack all holydayes because it was full of pimples." On the same analogy the Anglican's complexion was clearer, while the Puritan's face was unspotted except for a Sabbatarian blush every seventh day.

The seventeenth-century people of God shared in the political ups and downs of the events of their own exciting century, and in the return of the natural seasons, but they also lived in sacred time, marked by their Christian calendars. That is, as members of churches, they were communities of memory and hope, celebrating the Christ-event, retrospectively and prospectively. However they differed in the emphasis they placed on the tenses of time in their calendary conflict; Catholics, Anglicans, and Puritans alike were conscious of living in "the fulness of time"—in the interval between the first and second Advents of Christ. Thus for them all the Incarnation was the hinge of history, dividing the recorded past into before and after Christ, the old and the new covenants, prophecy and fulfilment. As Christians they gratefully believed that they had been delivered from time's tyranny as sheer meaningless duration and boredom, because Christ had come to demonstrate beyond guessing the nature of God, and the origin and end of human destiny. Thus each minute of each day was lived with the backdrop of an eternal destiny which gave significance to the strivings of each human soul, and the further assurance from the Gospel itself that the humble in time might be exalted in eternity in the divine reversal of human evaluations, so that the first shall be last and the last shall be first.

Furthermore, by their celebration of sacred feasts and fasts (in which all three religious groups participated, though differently), any tendency to the humdrum and dully repetitive was overcome

215

by the exuberant joy of thanksgiving or the rueful sadness of penitence. Perhaps more important still was a consolation rarer in our own secular age, but one which was theirs in great measure. This was the conviction that as Christ had conquered sin and suffering, so also he had taken away the worst horror of time—the threat of extinction. For these Christians saw the Resurrection of Christ as the death of death, even though paradoxically their shorter spans of life and the frequency of women dying in childbirth, and the many tombstones of infants and children meant that they had seen death and were more familiar with it than our own age which trains undertakers to cosmeticise the dead. It is important to recognize this unity in recalling the saga of God's acts in Christ accomplished and to come which characterized Catholics, Anglicans, and Puritans, because it could so easily be forgotten in their more typical relations as adversaries during this embattled century of religious wars.

Indeed, as will only be too obvious, calendary conflict is a vivid mark of distinction between the three groups.[1] Differing sacred calendars are vivid symbols of the religious differences between Anglicans and Puritans, and the attempt to enforce a particular way of celebrating sacred time, whether by the king and the bishops or the Puritans and Parliament, is an attempt at a form of social control.

The Anglican calendar is of course much closer to that of the Roman Catholic church than to Puritanism's system of calculating sacred time. Both churches, Roman and English, keep the Christian year as a cyclical remembrance and renewal of the most important events in the birth, life, passion, resurrection and ascension of Christ and the coming of the Holy Spirit, except for the Roman Catholic extension of the Marian feasts and its considerably fuller cycle of commemoration of the saints. The most radical difference is to be found between the annual Anglican and Roman celebration of the Christological calendar (with a particular emphasis on Lent) and the iconoclastic reductionism of the Puritan calendar which rejected the Christian year and substituted the Sabbath as its sole regularly recurring festival. There will also be calendary differences of hardly less significance than these to be noticed, but it may prove most intriguing to discover that there were often

---

[1] This chapter owes much to the research of Professor Howard Happ whose Ph.D. at Princeton University on the theme of late Tudor and early Stuart Calendary Conflict I have had the honor of supervising.

political, economic, and social factors almost as important as the clinching theological reasons that were advanced for the differing calendars.

The three distinctive ways of marking sacred time will be examined, by noting the history of the conflict among them (recalling that England will not have a distinctive Roman Catholic calendar, but that the remembrance of certain saints in English history will be ways of "naturalising" the international church in England, and also that in our century it is a fugitive and clandestine faith, so it will not openly enter the lists of calendar conflict). The concentration will inevitably, then, be on the conflict between the religious calendars of the Cavaliers and of their opponents the Roundheads. Of the proponents of both calendars a series of questions will be asked.

Do feasts or fasts predominate? Such a question will reveal whether there is a prevailing sense of joy which can degenerate into laxity, or a dominant sense of religious intensity which can deteriorate into gloom and vindictiveness, and the confusion between being the elect and the élite. Sir Toby Belch's question of the Puritan Malvolio: "Dost thou think because thou art virtuous, there shall be no more cakes and ale?" is an illustration of calendar conflict.[2] It was the reversal of roles in the masques and merriment that ended on the twelfth night after Christmas and in maypoles on May Day, and the indiscretions at the Whitsun and harvest ales that the Puritans disliked because of their encouragement of beery buffoonery, bawdiness, idleness, and profanity. The same occasions were regarded by Royalist Anglicans as occasions of relatively harmless fun and games, providing intervals of jollity in the otherwise uneventful lives of the "lower orders." In fact, both King James I and King Charles I issued their *Book of Sports*[3] as a counterblast to the Puritan Sabbatarianism, which seemed to them to turn smiles into snarls.

Another question will be: Is the predominant tense of the festivals past, present, or future? The point of such a question is that if the religious stance is conservative it will be mainly retrospective, but if intense it may be contemporary as recognising the continuing revelation of God as holy in days of judgment and loving

---

2 *Twelfth Night*, act II, scene iii.

3 James issued the *Book of Sports* in 1618, after recommending its provisions to the magistrates of Lancashire the year before. Charles, his son, reissued it in 1633.

in days of thanksgiving for deliverance. Or, again, if the religious stance is radical it may well stress the apocalyptic and imminent future as the most important tense in its calendar as well as being a fantasy of the future to compensate for present dissatisfaction.

A third question will demand whether the festivals relate to cosmic, national, ecclesiastical party, or private history? The presumed value of the answers to such a question will be that they will indicate whether God is conceived as universal deity or as a tribal totem, or a combination of both.

Moreover, in all cases, the religious values presumed to be in each competitive calendar will be investigated for possible political, social, and economic components, whether acknowledged or not. These latent or overt factors will help to explain the ferocity with which the calendars were attacked or defended. Nor should it be forgotten what a large part of the time of the men and women of the seventeenth century was taken up in festivals and fasts. Davenant in the middle year of the century attested to this in the preface of his play, *Gondibert*: Divines . . . are Tetrarchs of Time, of which they command the fourth Division, for to no less the Sabbaths and Daies of Saints amount, and during these daies of spiritual triumph Pulpits are Thrones, and the People oblig'd to open their Eares. . . ."

1. *The Roman Catholic Calendar*

Consideration of the Roman Catholic calendar will be brief because it did not differ significantly in England as the faithful moved from the sixteenth to the seventeenth century, though it became increasingly difficult for the Recusants to celebrate their festivals with the pomp and circumstance thought appropriate in countries such as France or Spain where Counter-Reformation Catholicism prevailed. In England, especially after the discovery of the Gunpowder Plot, late in 1605, supposedly aimed at both king and both Houses of Parliament, the patriotism of all Catholics was suspect and their priests led a hunted life as fugitives, except when protected as court chaplains of Catholic queens. To practise Roman Catholicism was forbidden, and Recusants were fined for their unwillingness to attend service according to the Book of Common Prayer. However, simply and secretly, except in royal or embassy chapels or in the houses of the nobility distant from London, the Catholic year was maintained as it had been

218

with little change from the pre-Reformation days, according to the Use of Sarum.

Nonetheless, it is crucial to consider its essential character, not only because of its historic importance and influence as the calendar of the largest church in Christendom, but also as a standard with which the Anglican calendar can be compared and the Puritan calendar contrasted.

Essentially it is marked by three leading characteristics. It is cyclical, Christological and sanctoral. That is, each year it recalls the same major events in the life of Christ, his Virgin Mother, and also the saints and martyrs who bridge the centuries between Biblical times and the seventeenth century, many of them being contemporaneous with Christ, but many also belonging to the medieval "ages of faith." Precisely because the calendar is cyclical, repeating itself each year, it is strongly retrospective in character, and inevitably so because Christianity is a historical religion affirming that "God has visited and redeemed his people." The proof of that redemption is found not only in that divine revelation contained in the Scriptures of the Old and New Testaments, but also in the facts of the Incarnation, and its consequence, the church, created to be the salvific community, and in its holiest representatives, the apostles, saints, and martyrs, who show that grace can make the ordinary extraordinary. These were all helped by the Christian year and its sacred festivals—each of which is a separate segment of the circle of the Incarnation encouraging profounder focus and concentration on the meaning of each—to meditate and mould their lives on the example of Christ, God as man.

The Roman calendar also wisely makes provision for "naturalising" (strictly speaking, supernaturalising) the international faith in each of the nations to which it has brought the Gospel by remembering the contributions of its holy men and women. Thus England's Catholics rejoice that Alcuin of York, the great Benedictine scholar and adviser of Charlemagne, was an Englishman and Hilda, the great Abbess of Whitby, was an English woman, and that, although he was brought up in the Anglo-Norman abbey of Bec, that Italian expatriate, St. Anselm the innovative philosopher-theologian was England's chief religious adviser as Archbishop of Canterbury. But the saints are not restricted to the company of monks and nuns: kings such as St. Louis of France and lay women such as the martyrs in the Roman arena, Perpetua and Felicitas, span the social chasm and consecrate different secular callings. Thus there was variety in sainthood.

Our age mistakenly regards the saints as misanthropes and despisers of this world, concentrating on what they have given up. The saints themselves, however, counted the world well lost for the love of Christ and his company of the blessed, and they stressed rather what they had gained—a rich increase in the theological virtues, faith, hope, and charity. However painful the resurgence of temptations, they were striving for the prize of eternal life, and heaven seemed only a little higher than the gilded *flèche* atop the roof of the cathedral. The medieval saints had a holy hilarity, and earth resembled heaven in this respect at least that it was a place of festivity. Whatever criticisms may be brought against the medieval church, it certainly encouraged in its feasts, "the capacity for genuine revelry and joyous celebration" because it related men and women to the "parade of cosmic history, or to the great stories of man's spiritual quest." Not only so, but even a calendar so rooted in the past, still encouraged fantasy, the dream of the future establishment of the Kingdom and City of God. Such joyful occasions put work in its proper subordinate place, for like contemplation and loving, festivity was seen to be an end in itself, not a means to an end unlike modern ideas of relaxation which are only frenetic "times-off" from work, unrelated to the history of the cosmos and incapable of effecting a social transformation. The sanctoral calendar, as well as the Christological cycle, provided such opportunities for festival and, more rarely, for the fasting that alternated with the feasting.[4]

In the northern hemisphere there was a particular fitness in the celebration of the most joyful mystery of the Incarnation during the darkest and coldest days of the year, when spirit and body would otherwise be numb. Equally apt was the general coincidence of the festival of Christ's Resurrection at Easter with the spring of the year, and the freshest green of ferns is ready coiled. As the coldness of winter was warmed by the festivities that lasted twelve

---

[4] Harvey Cox has written most imaginatively of the resources of festivals, both retrospective and prospective, in *The Feast of Fools* (Cambridge, Mass., 1969). His own summary of his major thesis is the following: "Festival occasions enlarge enormously the scope and intensity of man's relation to the past. They elevate his sense of personal worth by making him part of an epic. Fantasy offers an endless range of future permutations. It inevitably escalates man's sense of his powers and possibilities. Therefore, the cultivation of celebration and imagination is crucial to religion and to man himself, if the Biblical estimate of his status ("a little lower than the angels") has any validity" (p. 18).

days, so the austerities of Lent were concluded by the good cheer and roast beef of Easter Day. The Roman Catholic calendar was intimately related to the natural seasons, at least in the northern hemisphere. That suggests how entirely appropriate it was for those who lived by tilling the land.

It also suggests that with the growth of a desire for rationalising manufacture in the cities and towns, there would be an objection on the part at least of the manufacturers and their ambitious apprentices that the Roman Catholic calendar, and even its Anglican modification, would be an excessively interrupted calendar, offering too many holy days and holidays, encouraging indolence, and increasing the danger of social turbulence and the difficulty of maintaining public order when hundreds of single young apprentices, sailors, carriers and others were at a loose end day after day.[5] What had been instituted in part as safety valves by the authorities, and which served their old function in the rustic environment, became potential sources of danger in the enlarging cities of the seventeenth century. Thus pragmatic factors, as well as purely theological considerations, played a part in the revision of the Catholic calendar by the Church of England, and its abolition by the Puritan alternative calendar.

2. Calendars as Symbols of Conflict

The political importance of the calendars, especially those of Anglicans and Puritans, is that they are the symbols of different bases of power in the state, and that the prerogative of authorising or modifying the official calendar and regulating the use of these holidays by law is hotly contested by the king and the church, on the one hand, and by the Parliament and its Puritan members, on the other. A brief recounting of the history of this conflict provides illumination on the meanings of the differing Anglican and Puritan systems of marking sacred time.

The conflict was particularly marked on the issue of how most appropriately to celebrate Sunday, which the Puritans called, on the authority of the Fourth Commandment, the Sabbath, and which the high-church Anglicans called the Lord's Day, recalling that the early church had changed the day from the Jewish Sabbath to

---

[5] In Spain the holidays took up five whole months of the year, so the charge of encouraging indolence is not unfounded. As for turbulence and violence, it is known that May Day in 1517 was to be devoted almost entirely to the intended wholesale slaughter of Frenchmen in London.

221

honour it as the day of the Lord's Resurrection. The scrupulous keeping of the Sabbath, with all the appropriate religious exercises, was the immediately visible badge of Puritan allegiance. The more relaxed spending of Sunday after attending Morning Prayer, and engaging in various games, on the authority of the royal *Book of Sports*, was the equally visible sign of the royalist, Laudian, high-church position.

The issue was raised by two incidents that involved animosity (followed by legal proceedings) between clergy in Suffolk and local gentry in Somerset. The first concerned John Rogers, chaplain to Archbishop Whitgift, who had been hurt by his rejection from a fraternal gathering of Suffolk clergy and who vented his spite on one of them, Nicholas Bownde, by attacking his recently published book, *The doctrine of the Sabbath, plainely layde forth, and sundly proved* (1595). The book was banned in 1599, and in 1600 the Lord Chief Justice Popham ordered the remaining copies of the book to be burned. Immediately the book became a *succès de scandale*, its price doubled, and its teachings were enthusiastically adopted by all opponents of the religious and civil settlements.[6]

In the second case two gentlemen of Somerset who took opposed views of the propriety of holding a church ale forced the issue into court. Sir Robert Philips and John, Lord Paulett, were the persons involved whose disagreement in a case in the quarter sessions made it necessary for the matter to be referred to the Assizes, at which Mr. Justice Richardson gave his judgment. Archbishop Laud, fearing that an ecclesiastical matter such as a church ale having come under the authority of the civil courts might be a wedge for the further diminution of churchly authority, overruled Richardson, severely reprimanded him before the council, and had him demoted to the Essex Circuits, and two years later he died. Twenty-one justices of the peace were alienated by Laud after he and Bishop Pierce of Bath and Wells had collected statements favouring church ales from sufficient clergymen in the diocese to offset the petitions of the justice for the abolition of church ales. This incident gave Laud the opportunity to persuade Charles I to republish James I's *Book of Sports*, which contradicted the tenaciously

---

[6] See Wilfrid Barnett Whitaker, *Sunday in Tudor and Stuart Times* (1933), p. 64, and Patrick Collinson, "The Beginning of English Sabbatarianism," in C. W. Dugmore and Charles Duggan, eds., *Studies in Church History* (1964), I, pp. 219-220.

maintained Puritan viewpoint on the keeping of Sundays, and to order it to be read from every pulpit in the land.[7]

The issue became a matter of greater political than religious significance, and the promoters respectively of the relaxed and serious spending of Sunday were engaged in a struggle to see who was to hold the reins of power. From the time of Elizabeth onwards, bills had emerged from Parliament proposing the reform of the Sabbath. Each one had been consistently rejected by the crown, particularly by James, for it was increasingly clear that Parliament wished to increase its power and lessen that of the crown and church.[8] In 1621 Parliament had tried to overrule James's imposition of the *Book of Sports*, for it viewed this as the crown's attempt to determine the religion and morals of the kingdom, and to mock Puritan intensity in religion with the excuse that the traditional customs, however abhorrent to Puritan bluenoses, must be maintained. With the increasing influence of the Puritan clergy and justices of the peace, it was evident that power would meet countervailing power.[9] Christopher Hill has observed that the Somerset church ale's case made it abundantly clear that the church preferred the common man to disport himself at the tavern rather than be edified by attending a Puritan religious lecture.[10]

The latter policy was clarified when the crown, strongly backed by the church, issued in 1629 a Proclamation, which forbade the giving of lectures on Sunday afternoons, which was one of the main media for the transmission of Puritan influence. These lectureships constituted a network of Puritan religious power operating independently of the centrally controlled ecclesiastical system. The right to them was purchased by merchants sympathetic to Puritan ideals and opposed to the increase of royal and ecclesiastical prerogatives.[11]

Thus the Sabbatarian controversy is only one, though dramatic, way of showing how the calendar conflict reflects the political struggle for power reaching its zenith in the third and fourth decades of the century. It is therefore time to consider the distinctives

[7] See Thomas G. Barnes, "County Politics and a Puritan Cause Célèbre: Somerset Church Ales, 1633," in *Transactions of the Royal Historical Society* (1959), pp. 112-18.

[8] See Christopher Hill, *Society and Puritanism in Pre-Revolutionary England* (2nd edn., New York, 1967), pp. 160-61.

[9] *Ibid.*, pp. 194-95.   [10] *Ibid.*

[11] See S. R. Gardiner, *The Personal Government of Charles I, 1628-1637* (1877), pp. 163f.

of first the Anglican and then of the Puritan calendar in much greater detail.

3. The Anglican Calendar

The Protestantism of the Anglican calendar is seen in its dominant Christological cycle (omitting the exclusively Marian feasts), and its reduction of the sanctoral cycle to the saints of the New Testament who, with the exception of Paul, were eye-witnesses to the Resurrection of Christ. Its Catholicism is seen (if it is contrasted with Calvinistic Protestantism) in its retention of a cyclical calendar at all, in its focus on Lent as a period of special spiritual discipline, and in its devotion to the Incarnation and the festival of Christ's nativity, which is so deep and tender a trait of Caroline sermons and spirituality. Apart from the rich ecumenical potentiality of this partly Protestantized Catholicism, it shares the retrospective look and the cosmic concentration of Roman Catholicism.

Its second major characteristic is its royalism, peculiar to a national church whose head was at once sovereign of the nation and its ecclesiastical leader. This sense of the divine right of kings was exaggerated by the high-church divines (beginning with Lancelot Andrewes whose almost fawning subservience to his king is his least likeable attribute), with the effect of alienating all those who like the Puritans objected to Stuart absolutism with its minimum of Parliamentary devolution. It reached its zenith in the virtual apotheosis of King Charles I as martyr of the Anglican church, who indeed loved the national church and went to his death as one calmly resigning this world for the next. This, of course, emphasized the retrospective nature of the Anglican calendar, though admittedly, its commemorations of royal accessions or deliverances were of events of fairly recent history.

A third characteristic is shared, though not to the same degree or with the same intensity, with Puritanism; namely the provision of officially appointed fast days of humiliation or thanksgiving to mark some national emergency or deliverance, the former to be days of repentance and the latter days of thanksgiving. These were recommended in the Book of Homilies.[12]

---

[12] The Second [Elizabethan] Book of Homilies (1571), has the sixteenth homily "On Fasting" and a twentieth homily "Of the Time and Place of Prayer." For the mode of and authority for public fasting, reference is made to Leviticus, Chaps. 16 and 23, and the fast is to be on the 10th day of the 7th month, while Zechariah (Chap. 8:19) says there are to be three more fasts in the year. The ends of the fast, according to the homily, are: "to chastise the flesh" and tame it for the

The reduction of the many saints' days in the Roman Catholic calendar had the effect of making the major events in the life of Christ stand out with greater significance. The sanctoral foothills in the Roman Catholic calendar took away some of the solitary grandeur of the peaks of the Christological cycle. Furthermore, though the red-letter days were fewer, those retained were all holidays, and the black-letter days kept ceased to be holidays. The fasts called for national emergency were few, and so the ecclesiastical festivals predominated over the fasts in numbers and mood. The result was that, apart from Roman Catholics, and others who were tenacious of all the older mores in a day of rapid social change, and the less industrious apprentices, the Anglican calendar was fairly popular because it was more joyful and merry than the one it replaced. The sense of jollity in the Anglican calendar is expressed incidentally by that vivid recorder of London life, the dramatist Dekker. Firke, an apprentice cobbler, speaks for all the gentle craft when he hails the prospect of Shrove Tuesday, with its promise of venison pasties, fritters and pancakes, chickens and oranges, custard tarts, and the headiest of ale, crying: "Every Shrove Tuesday is our year of jubilee. And when the pancake bell rings, we are as free as my Lord Mayor. We may shut up our shops and make holiday."[13]

THE CHRISTOLOGICAL CYCLE

The Anglican emphasis on the Christological cycle was, of course, the inheritance from Cranmer, as also the celebration of the days of the Biblical saints.[14] In the days of the Puritan overthrow of the Anglican calendar, it is interesting to read John Doughty's reasons for defending the chief Anglican festivals. He claims that the saints whose days are retained are at least historical, not legendary, and that being Christological and apostolical in

---

Spirit; to encourage the spirit to be "more earnest and fervent to prayer" and as a sign before God of our inward contrition. The twentieth homily, stresses the importance of Sabbath keeping, since God worked for six days and rested the seventh, so must his obedient people, and give themselves "wholly to heavenly exercises of God's true religion and service" commanded by God and even exemplified by Him through the paradigm of the Creation of the world.

13 Thomas Dekker, *The Shoemaker's Holiday*, Act v, Scene 2, ll. 220-23. Shrove Tuesday is, of course, the day before Ash Wednesday, the beginning of the season of Lent. The play reflects life in 1599. This reference I owe to Marie-Hélène Davies, my wife, as also the opening citation of this chapter.

14 It should be noted that there was an unofficial celebration of the red-letter days of the English Protestant martyrs marked by Foxe.

character, they are not merely traditional, but foundational. "I mean," he writes, "not such *Dayes* the Papists celebrate, for the most part *dedicated* to Saints that ne'er were *men* or had a *being*; Again, to them whose names it is to be feared may sooner be found written in the *Rubrick*, than in *Heaven* . . . I understand *dayes* of *solemnity* instituted on *good grounds* in honour of *Christ* himself in the first place, in *memoriall* of those *speciall Saints*, the *Apostles, Evangelists etc.*"[15]

Since the Puritans argued that the only festival for which there was an explicit Biblical warrant was the Sabbath, on the basis of their belief that what the Scriptures did not command they impugned, the Anglicans were forced to defend their retention of the major feasts of the Christian year on grounds beside church tradition. It is interesting, for example, that Bishop Lancelot Andrewes, who had been a strict Sabbatarian in his earlier days in Cambridge, takes the highest ground by defending Lent on the example of the forty days of fasting undergone by Christ in the wilderness. Lent is to inculcate repentance as a fruit of fasting and penance, "for Repentance is the agonie, the bloodie sweat, the Cross of every Christian; whereby he dies into sin, and is crucified with his Saviour. Each circumstance then of Christ's Passion, each bloodie Scene in this Tragedie must be re-enacted on our own bodies. . . ."[16] The Christological cycle was clearly to encourage the *imitatio Christi*. Bishop Thomas Ken of Winchester appeals on the same firm foundation. The purpose of Lent is for the Christian to be identified with Christ in his sorrows and Resurrection. Hence, "a devout soul . . . fastens himself to the Cross on Ash Wednesday, and hangs crucified by contrition all the Lent long" so that he may sympathise with all the anguish and desertion "which God Incarnate endured when He bled upon the Cross for the sins of world; that being purified of repentance and made comformable to Christ crucified, he may offer up a pure oblation at Easter and feel the power and the joys and triumph of Saviour's Resurrection."[17]

As there had been controversy over the Sabbath, so the celebration of Christmas became a fighting issue between Anglican and

---

[15] I. D. Phil-Iren-Alethius, *Velitationes Polemicae or Polemicall short Discussions of certain particular and select Questions* (1651), pp. 202-203.

[16] See his sermon on "Holy Days" reprinted by Abraham Wright, *Five Sermons in five several Styles; or Waies of Preaching* (1656), pp. 19-20.

[17] *A Sermon Preached at the King's Chapel at Whitehall in the Year, 1685.* (*Prose Works*, ed. W. Benham, pp. 85f.)

Puritan contestants. Christmas in successive years falls one day later in the week, whereas Easter and Whitsun are both Sundays; thus the Anglican and Puritan controversy over Easter and Whitsun was not so acute for the Puritans celebrated the Sabbath while the Anglicans celebrated the pivotal events of the Christian saga. Christmas falling irregularly and only about once every seven years on a Sabbath raised the theological issues most acutely, though the arguments advanced for its celebration or negation apply equally well to the other Christological events.

On the positive side, the Anglicans increasingly affirm the psychological argument that one cannot celebrate everything on one day, and the need for continuity with the primitive church, as well as urging the claims of reason. Nor are they above using the *tu quoque* charge against the Puritans that while the authority of Scripture is claimed for the Sabbath alone as a red-letter day, the Puritans inconsistently observe the fifth of November as Gunpowder Plot Day for which there could not be any specific divine mandate. These abstractions will take on life in the vivid arguments of the Anglican defenders of the Christological cycle.

Dr. Henry Hammond writing in 1644 marshalls his Patristic learning[18] to support the argument for the claim that Christmas is authorised on the basis of "the practice of the Primitive Universal Christian Church." He concludes, with typical carefulness, that Christmas "appears to be at the least an ecclesiastical institution, very early received over all the West and the far greatest part of Christendom, and within four hundred years universally solemnized."[19]

Even more interesting is Bishop Joseph Hall's apologia, *A Letter for the Observation of the Feast of Christ's Nativity*, because he is a Calvinist answering the objection of Calvinist Puritans. Hall begins by arguing that if this nativity was "the best tidings of the greatest joy that ever was or ever could be possibly incident to mankind," its celebration should be correspondingly joyous. His critic is assumed to reply that a set anniversary day is needless, because "every day we should, with equal thankfulness, remember this inestimable benefit of the Incarnation of the Son of God."

Hall cleverly uses the Puritan argument of the Sabbath as the

---

18 The authorities he cites are the *Apostolical Constitutions*, Origen, and Cyprian.
19 Henry Hammond, *A Practical Catechism*, Chap. II, Sect. 12 (ed. Library of Anglo-Catholic Theology, 1847-1850, pp. 193-96). The first edition appeared anonymously in 1644, the second with the author's name in 1646, and the twelfth in 1683.

high peak of the week, but turns it against the Puritans by reminding them that the creation and the deliverance from Egypt should be daily recalled, but that God ordained one special day of the week "for the more special recognition of these marvellous works." Special days, he then argues, are a remedy for human forgetfulness. Otherwise, one might well say, why keep a single day of remembrance, let it be the work of the whole year. Hence it is for concentration and focus that special days were authorized by the primitive church "no doubt, by the direction of the Holy Ghost."

He then deals with a second criticism: that we are probably ignorant of the exact day of the nativity of Christ, that it may possibly not even have been in the month of December and that "it is purposely not revealed, that it might not be kept." In reply, Hall admits to some uncertainty, but considers the objection irrelevant, since what matters is "that it hath pleased the Church for many hundred years to ordain this day for the commemoration of that transcendental blessing." Further, if God had intended to keep that day a secret to avoid a celebration of it, where is this prohibition revealed? Also, "why did not the same God with equal caution conceal the day of the Passion, Resurrection, Ascension of our Blessed Saviour, and of the Descent of the Holy Ghost?"

To the third objection that there is "Popery and Superstition" in keeping that day, Bishop Hall replies that this is to slander God's saints in primitive times and the Fathers of the church.

The fourth and final Puritan criticism asserted that the seventh day is enjoined for rest, but that otherwise Christians are forbidden to observe days and times as part of the pedagogy of the old dispensation. Hall's rebuttal says that first, this is *permissive* rather than *preceptive* and second, the requirements of the Judaic ceremonial law are no longer binding on Christians.

He ends by citing St. Gregory of Nazianzen on the proper mode of celebrating Christmas Day, which Hall accepts in the last analysis because it is "so ancient and received a custom in the Church of God."[20]

The major function of the Anglican calendar, as of the Roman Catholic calendar, was clearly to encourage the imitation of Christ by meditation through the Christian year assisted by appropriate Gospels, Epistles, and Collects in the Book of Common Prayer. It also had two subordinate purposes. One was to provide an alterna-

[20] *Works* (ed. Peter Hall, 1837), x, pp. 126-31.

tion of feasts and fasts. The other was to serve as a medium for the expression of the religio-political unity of the nation under the sovereign who was also head of the church.

The value of the alternation of the festivals and fasts, with the former more numerous, as well as the insistence upon the more relaxed spending of Sunday than the Puritans allowed, was to provide a release of emotional tension, which the Puritan Sabbath tended rather to exacerbate, especially for those not Puritans.[21] When Charles I republished his father's *Declaration on Sports* in 1633, the introduction states that James had "found his subjects debarred from lawful recreations upon Sundays after evening prayers ended, and upon Holy Days," and that he "prudently considered that if these times were taken away from them, the meaner sort who labour hard all the week should have no recreations at all to refresh their spirits." Lawful recreations are defined as "dancing, either men or women, archery for men, leaping, vaulting, or any other such harmless recreation . . . May-games, Whitsun-ales, and morris dances, and the setting up of May-poles, and other sports therewith used. . . ." Illegal sports are defined as "bear and bull-baitings, interludes, and at all times in the meaner sort of people by Law prohibited, bowling."[22] It was also assumed that there should be church ales at the patronal festivals of local parish churches.

The opportunity for sports after church on Sundays and on red-letter days were not the only accommodations to human need in the Anglican calendar. Lent, for example, represented six weeks out of fifty-two of renunciation for repentance, which focussed on Christ's temptations and victory over them for the benefit of the Christian, but this was focussed more clearly in Holy Week, and most brilliantly on the holy weekend from Good Friday to Easter Day. With this should be contrasted the rigorous spiritual regimen required by Puritanism for the Sabbath, which would have wound up the average man as intensely as a coiled spring, but seemed to serve the Puritans well.

---

21 E. Cardwell, *Documentary Annals of the Reformed Church of England*, II, pp. 188-93.

22 Michael Walzer has suggested that the Puritans found release in aggression, but this seems not to accord with the mysticism of such Puritans as Sterry and Baxter, as well as Sibbes. (See his *The Revolution of the Saints*, Cambridge, Mass., 1965, Chap. VIII.) Another possibility is that the work ethic for six days provided relief in contemplation on Sunday for a member of the elect and that this was a kind of austere adaptation of an intramundane Benedictinism.

ROYAL AND STATE SERVICES

The third component of the Anglican calendar was known as the "state services." They were intended to inculcate veneration for the king and thus social stability, with subordination and satisfaction for each man in his own station of life. Such special services included anniversaries of the accession of the sovereign to the throne (March 24 for James I and March 27 for Charles I) as well as commemorations of any signal deliverance of the king (also representing the nation). Each year Gowrie Day was observed on August 5, recalling James's deliverance while King of Scotland from the conspiracy of the Earl of Gowrie and his brother, and his further deliverance and that of his Parliament was recalled each November 5, the date of the discovery of the Gunpowder Plot.

No provision for an accession service was made in the 1559 Prayer Book, but about 1571 Dr. Cooper, Vice-Chancellor of Oxford University, began holding a "public celebrity" of Elizabeth's accession. This example was widely imitated and in 1576 and 1578 a special service order was issued by royal authority in commemoration of the Queen's "entry in to her reign."[23] No such service was bound up with the Prayer Book, but copies were kept for use on the anniversary each year, it can be presumed, since no further impressions appeared during the Queen's reign. Her successor, James I, according to Frank Streatfield,[24] seemed to be satisfied with two opportunities for the expression of the loyalty of his subjects and their commendation of him to God—that is, with the Gowrie Day and Gunpowder Day anniversaries—so that no form of accession service was issued during his reign. It was, however, revived by Charles I in 1526 and confirmed by Convocation fourteen years later. Since Charles II was legally restored on the day of his father's martyrdom, which was therefore declared to be a day of fasting, he had to choose his birthday and *de facto* day

---

[23] See *Liturgies and Occasional Forms of Prayer set forth in the Reign of Queen Elizabeth* (ed. W. K. Clay, Parker Society, Cambridge, 1851), pp. 453, 548.

[24] See his *The State Prayers and other variations in the Book of Common Prayer* (1950), p. 31; but he appears to be unaware of *Great Britaine's little Calendar or triple Diary in remembrance of three dayes, viz. the 24 of March the day of his Maiesties proclamation; the fift of August the day of Gowries Conspiracy; the fith of November the day of our deliverance from the Gunpowder treason, whereunto is annexed, a short dissuasive from Popery*, written by Samuel Garey, which is listed on pp. 6-7 of *A Catalogue of such English Bookes, as lately have bene and now are in Printing for Publication, from the ninth day of October 1618 untill Easter Terme, next ensuing.*

of accession as the occasion for a special service, on May 29, but this changed the character of the occasion. James II, however, revived the Accession Service, explaining why his brother had allowed it to fall into desuetude, and it was called "The King's Day." William III preferred to mark the day of his landing at Torbay and his consequent guaranteeing of the Protestant succession of the crown, by merely causing a few prayers to be added to the regular service for November 5.[25]

A Fourme of Prayer with Thankesgiving, to be used of all the Kings Maiesties loving suiects every yeere, the 24 of March: Being the day of his highnesse entry to this kingdom which is the Order for Morning Prayer of the English Prayer Book, modified for the anniversary of the royal succession, was reissued in 1640 with March 27 as the day of the accession of Charles I. It is interesting for its emphasis on the divine right of kings and its conception of their responsibilities to the church. The first lesson is taken from Joshua 1, and recounts the death of Moses and Joshua's appointment as the leader of the people to convey them over the river Jordan to the promised land.[26] Unquestionably England's king is viewed not merely as the secular ruler, but as God's vice-gerent. The second lesson from Romans 13 stresses the necessity for showing due respect and obedience to the powers that be. The "Prayer for the Kings Maiestie" describes James I as "Shepheard, Captain, our dread Soverreigne, and Angel sent from thee [God]. . . ."[27]

A fourme of prayer with thanksgiving, to be used every yeere the fift of August, being the day of his highnesse happy deliverance from the bloody attempt of the Earle of Gowry first appeared in 1603, but there were later editions of 1606, 1618, and 1623. In the second edition thanks are offered to God for protecting King James "from the cruell and bloody treacheries of desperate men, and especially as this day from the wicked designments of those blood-thirstie wretches the Earle Gowry, with his brother, and their desperate Confederates." Loyalty to the sovereign takes the form of the ferocious petition: "Smite his enemies upon the cheekebone, breake their teeth, frustrate their counsels, and bring to nought all their devices."[28] A later prayer again emphasizes the horror of treason and the certainty that divine justice will prove inexorable to all such desperate men who plan to kill the Lord's

---

25 See Streatfield, *ibid.*, for information, and also J. H. Blunt's *Annotated Book of Common Prayer* (1866), pp. 578ff.
26 The alternative lesson is II Chronicles 1.
27 Sig. C3.   28 Sig. E2 verso.

representative; so that they had received "the due revenge of such treasonable attempts, spilling their blood who thought to spill the blood of thine anoynted, and leaving their slaughtered carkcises a worthy spectacle of thy dreadfull judgements, and their most impious designes."[29] This was political propaganda under the guise of theological diction, though the distinction is one that might well be denied by a sovereign who was also head of the national Church in England, Scotland, Ireland, and Wales.

The supreme service of royal commemoration in this century was, of course, that of the death of King Charles I on January 30 [12. Car.II, c. 30] which was prepared in 1660 and was chiefly the work of Bishop Brian Duppa. It was issued in 1661. It was revised by Sancroft and a proclamation concerning this version was made on January 7, 1662. A third revision, the product of a joint committee of Convocation, was annexed to the Prayer Book. On the accession of James II, a version nearer Sancroft's than any other replaced it until the withdrawal of all three versions with the accession of William and Mary. It is this particular service that preserved the high-church image of Charles I as the English church's martyr.[30]

He had almost been "canonised" while living by his high-church prelates, such as Archbishop Laud and those of his school. This seems especially to be the case in certain royalist prayers when the king's situation grew desperate in the Civil War. One "Prayer for the King" printed at Oxford in 1644, petitions God: "Take, we beseech thee into thy immediate hands and Divine protection thine annointed servant the King, that no sacrilegious prophane hand may come neere to touch him. . . ."[31] The same prayer refers to the "Sonnes of Violence" who "have joyned Nation to Nation, Covenant to Covenant, Army to Army, to pull down Him whom Thou hast exalted, and to roote that Religion which thine own right hand hath planted."[32] A second prayer, printed together with the first, pleads for the preservation of the University and City of Oxford. It asks God to "Save this City, this Nursery of thy Church" and of their oppressors that He will "set thy hook into their nostrills, to turn them back or confound them, according to thy good pleasure and secret wisdome by which thou disposest all Events

---

[29] Sig. G2 verso.   [30] Streatfield, *op. cit.*, p. 33.

[31] *Two Prayers, One for the Safety of His Majesties Person; The Other For the Preservation of this University and City of Oxford to be used in all Churches and Chappells* (Oxford, 1644), p. 1.

[32] *Ibid.*, p. 2.

beyond the meanes and reach of man."[33] Perhaps if the king's court had not consisted of so many flatterers and if his prelates had warned him rather than encouraging him in the belief that the king can do no wrong just because he is the Lord's anointed, Charles might have lived to be the unifier of the nation rather than the iconic property of the high-church party of the Church of England. Would that the bench had included an episcopal Nathan to warn another David!

Other services which preserved the image of the sovereign as anointed by God and given peculiar miracle-making powers were those known as "at the healing." On these occasions the sovereign's cure of the sick by touching, popularly known as "the King's Evil,"[34] was exercised. The service had been originally prepared in Latin for King Henry VII and modified from time to time, but it was never published until the reign of Anne, when it was appended to the accession service in the Prayer Book. It persisted in editions of the Prayer Book until 1732.[35]

The Latin form for Henry VII was printed in 1686, and another smaller edition in English. The English form is found regularly as an appendix to the Accession Service of the Prayer Book in Queen Anne's time. It is intriguing to see the nature of this service from the quarto edition of 1707, especially as one recalls that it was used by the Stuart kings in their royal chapels, and that Queen Anne "touched" the infant Samuel Johnson for scrofula.

After the collect, "Prevent us, O Lord . . . ," and the Gospel [Mark 16:14ff., including as a sign of the Gospel for those that are believers," "they shall lay hands on the sick, and they shall recover"], the three-fold Kyrie, and the Our Father, there follows an important rubric. It reads: "Then shall the infirm persons, one by one, be presented to the Queen on their knees, and as the Queen is laying her Hands upon them, and putting the Gold about their Necks, the Chaplain that officiates, turning himself to Her Majesty, shall say these words following: 'God give a Blessing to this Work; And grant that *these* Sick *Persons* on whom the Queen lays Her Hands, may recover, through Jesus Christ our Lord.'"

There follow four brief versicles and responses, a prayer for "these thy servants, that they being healed of their Infirmities, may give thanks unto thee in thy holy Church, through Jesus Christ our Lord, *Amen.*" The Chaplain then says to those who

---

33 *Ibid.*
35 Streatfield, *op. cit.*, p. 42.

34 See *Macbeth.*

233

come to be healed: "The Almighty God, who is a most strong tower to all them that put their trust in him . . . be now and ever-more your defence, and make you to know and feel, that there is none other Name under heaven given to man, in whom, and through whom, you may receive health and salvation, but only the Name of our Lord Jesus Christ. *Amen*." The healing service ends with the Grace.

Although all references to the sovereign are capitalized, as well as all the possessive adjectives relative to her, yet the possessive adjectives and pronouns relative to God are in the lower case, still there is little in the service, at least by the time of Anne, to indicate that it is the Queen who has wonder-working powers. The healing is unambiguously attributed to God, through Jesus Christ, for faith, and in the Name of "holy Church." Earlier forms of the "At the Healing" were celebrated with greater Baroque pomp and circumstance with ceremonial representing absolutism. Anne was a "tamed" monarch, and the service represented a less authoritarian conception of the sovereign's rule. She was less a *"reine soleil"* than a *"reine éclairée."*

The most interesting of the royal and state commemorations is that of the discovery of the Gunpowder Plot on November 5, 1605, precisely because of its ambivalence. It began as an occasion of national thanksgiving for the delivery of King James and Parliament and the English Reformed church from the machinations of Roman Catholic plotters. As the Stuart dynasty assisted by the Caroline divines emphasized more fully the Catholic element in the Catholic-Protestant compromise of the Anglican *via media*, and Stuart kings found Roman Catholic wives, who brought their priest-chaplains to court, and celebrated the Mass with splendour, the celebration of the fifth of November became a rallying festival for Parliament and the Puritans, especially during the days of the Commonwealth and Protectorate, until it became so exclusively associated with Protestantism and anti-Catholicism that, as has been noticed, William III, summoned to share the English throne with Mary, was seen as the guarantor of the Protestant succession to the throne and the defender of the independence of the Church of England from Papal interference.[36]

Parliament had instituted an observance of November 5 [3 Jac.I, c.I] soon after the event, but that only made provision for the reading of the Act during regular Morning Prayer. A special

[36] *Ibid.*, p. 33.

form of service was drawn up by the bishops and issued by royal authority in 1606.

Two features of the service are of particular interest. One is the appositeness of the selection of II Samuel 22 as the Old Testament lesson. It is King David's song of gratitude to God for his deliverance from the hands of Saul and all his enemies. The eighth verse is reminiscent of the intended results of the Plot, "then the earth shook and trembled . . . and there went up a smoke out of his nostrils and fire out of his mouth devoured: coals were kindled by it." The divine vengeance on the rebels is characterized in verse 15: "And he sent out arrows and scattered them; lightning and discomfited them." Towards the end the chapter expresses the king's gratitude to God: "Thou hast delivered me from the strivings of my people," while the final verse sums up the providential interpretation of the saving of the Lord's anointed and of the royal house: "He [God] is the tower of salvation for his king; and sheweth mercy to his anointed, unto David, and unto his seed for ever."

The other feature of this commemoration of November 5 of interest is the fact that the second lesson in the Jacobean edition was the not entirely appropriate twenty-fourth chapter of the Acts of the Apostles, which was changed in the first Caroline edition by the king's episcopal advisers. This chapter gives an account of St. Paul's defence of his conduct and preaching before the Roman Governor, Felix. It is an admirable example of the Pauline persistence in defending the faith in Christ before Felix a Roman Governor. It was probably chosen because it contrasts an old and superseded faith (Judaism) with the new and true faith (Christianity), while expecting the expositor or reader of the passage in the English context to substitute Roman Catholicism for Judaism, and Protestantism for the Christianity of the New Testament. In a service which attempts to exalt a ruler as God's anointed who deserves the loyalty of his people it has at least one serious defect: it depicts a ruler trembling before a preacher. The politically offensive verse reads: "And as he [Paul] reasoned of righteousness, temperance, and judgment to come, Felix trembled. . . ."[37] Charles I might have needed such a preacher, a Nathan of a prophet declaring the immediately hurtful but ultimately healing truth, but assuredly he did not want one, nor to hear such commended in the lessons of the church of which he was the head. Furthermore, the conclusion of the chapter shows a ruler being unjust to, instead

37 Verse 25.

of the protector of, the greatest exponent of primitive Christianity after Christ.

It is for such reasons, it may be guessed, that the bishops who advised Charles I, substituted Matthew 27 for the inappropriate lesson in their revision of the service in 1625, which was printed by Bonham Norton and John Gill. Theologically the account of the crucifixion of Christ and of his Resurrection was much superior to the lesson from II Samuel, but politically its brief account of the repentance and suicide of the arch-traitor of the Bible, Judas Iscariot, seemed an appropriate reminder of the grim consequences of conniving at the betrayal of God's supremely anointed, great David's greater Son, Christ. Another revision, at the time of the Restoration, was the characteristically careful work of Bishop Cosin of Durham.[38]

Other occasions which brought royalty to the attention of the public in the form of requiring special prayers, but not entire services or significant parts of services, were those "for the Queen's safe deliverance" (1605),[39] or "for the safe Delivery of the Queene" (1628, 1631, 1633, and 1636).[40] But, apart from such occasional prayers and the far more important annual anniversaries previously considered, the King and the members of the royal family were regularly commended to the divine protection in the Sunday and daily services of the Prayer Book. James I told the Puritans at the Hampton Court Conference, when they urged a greater parity of ministers according to the Presbyterian pattern of Geneva, "no bishop, no king." These royalist services we have considered in detail made plain that for the Anglican church throughout the century (with the exception of the Puritans who remained within it until 1662) it was a case of "no king, no church." All these occasions served to emphasize the importance of the crown as the symbol of the union between state and church in his person, and the desirability for loyalty on the part of his subjects both as members of the nation and the national church.

Nor should the state services, not specifically of a royal character, be forgotten, for the Church of England also observed other occasions of national urgency or emergency, on which the people were called to prayers to celebrate with due gratitude days of deliverance from war, plague, or other calamity. Such were gen-

---

[38] Streatfield, *op. cit.*, p. 33.
[39] Pollard and Redgrave, *Short Title Catalogue*, No. 16535.
[40] *Ibid.*, No. 16549.

erally known as days of thanksgiving. An example is *A Short Forme of Thankesgiving to God for staying the contagious sicknesse of the Plague: to be used in Common Prayer on Sundayes, Wednesdayes and Fridayes* (1625). One prayer vividly recalls death as the leveller, thanking God for deliverance from death and preservation from "that noysome pestilence, which not long since raged in the Land, sweeping away the rich with the poore, the aged with the young, leaving whole houses desolate, and filling all places with dead bodies."[41] Another prayer in the same service indicates that the plague is being recalled that the worshippers may "learne thereby, both to fear thy dreadfull Judgements against Sinne and so by true Repentance to turne unto thee from our wicked Wayes, lest a Worse Plague fall upon us; and also to put our whole trust in thy Mercy. . . ."[42] One might have thought that a repentance introduced by fear would be hardly likely to lead to entire confidence in a God who had stricken a country with one plague, and was now beseeched not to threaten his people with a deadlier one. But this does give a clue to the doctrine of special providence, by which every event is believed to be either determined by God or permitted to happen by his will.[43]

There were also national days of fasting or humiliation in which the people were summoned to church to hear the divine judgment upon the nation and the call to repentance expressed in the special prayers of the day. Such occasions were a fast for the drought (1611) and for the floods (in 1613 as in 1666, to take only two examples), and frequent fasts for "staying the plague" (as, for

---

[41] Sig. B4. [42] Sig. C2.

[43] The kindlier form of this doctrine is found in Matthew 5:45 ("for he [God] maketh his sun to rise on the evil and the good, and sendeth rain on the just and the unjust"), while the severer aspect of it can be illustrated from a prayer I once heard a Calvinist theologian of eminence offer in a college chapel, beseeching God to "succour those that are this day appointed to die." An ugly example of this would be the "cursing prayers" offered by each side in the Civil War. They believed that if they succeeded in defeating their enemies it was because God was making the victors the instruments of chastening the vanquished; if they lost a battle it was because God was chastising them for over-confidence or some other sin. An example of the latter can be found in the following excerpt from *A Collection of Prayers and Thanksgivings used in His Majesties Chappell and in His Armies* (Oxford, 1643): "we know, o Lord, that affliction cometh not forth out of the dust, neither doth trouble spring out of the ground, but it is thou that with rebukes dost chasten man for sinne." The same prayer later pleads with God to mark "We are become a reproach to the foolish people, and Servants bear rule over us, the mean Man is risen against the Honourable, and the fire out of the Bramble devoureth the lofty Cedars . . ." (pp. 13-14), a classic and moving example of conservatism's inability to cope with revolutionary change.

example, in 1604 and 1625).[44] It is often assumed that such days of thanksgiving and humiliation, accompanied by fasting, were Puritan innovations in worship, only because they were kept by them with such frequency and at what may seem to moderns inordinate length. In fact, however, they are recommended in the Elizabethan Book of Homilies, and it is of special interest that "A fourme of the Order for the generall Fast" issued in 1563[45] offers a rationale for the custom with examples drawn from both the Old Testament and the primitive church. Under both dispensations, "the people of God hath always used generall Fastyng, both in times of common Calamities, as Warre, Famine, Pestilence, &c. and also when any wayghtie matter, touchyng the estate of the Churche or the Commonwealth was begun or intended." This practise has been much neglected but is now to be remedied. So the Queen thought it suitable "in this contagious time of sicknes and other trouble, and unquietnes, accordying to the examples of the Godly Kyng Josaphat, and the Kyng of Ninive, with others, a generall Fast should be ioyned with generall Prayer, throughout her new Realme; and to be observed of all her godly subiectes. . . ."[46] It was further ordered that each Wednesday should be the appointed day of the fast and that all persons between sixteen and sixty years of age ("sicke folkes, labourers in the harvest or other greate labourers" excepted) are to eat only one competent and moderate meal each fast day, avoiding variety of meats, spices, confections, and wines, and only what is necessary, suitable, and healthy. The rich are told to eat more simply than usual so that by diminishing the costliness of their fare they can "increase therwith theyr liberalitie and almes towards the poore." The day is to be spent "in Prayer, studye, readyinge or hearying of the Scriptures, or good exhortations, &c." By a typical royal accommodation to human necessity, it is stated that when "any dulnesse or weryness shall aryse," the time is to be occupied in other godly exercise. This is rather in the spirit of the future *Book of Sports*,

[44] Other examples are listed in Pollard and Redgrave, *Short Title Catalogue*, nos. 16557 and 16559, both occurring before 1640. Another similar type of special service was *The Commemoration of the Fire of London* of 1666, which appeared in some copies of the Prayer Book towards the end of the reign of Charles II, but was discontinued in St. Paul's Cathedral only in 1859.

[45] *A Fourme to be used in Common Prayer twyse aweke, and also an order of publique fast to be used every Wednesday in the weeke, durying the time of mortalitie*. Its shelf-mark in the Bodleian Library of the University of Oxford is: 4° P 4 Th.

[46] *Op. cit.*, Sig. Cii.

until one reads "But no parte to be spent in plays, pastymes, or ydlenesse, muche lesse in lewd, wicked or wanton behaviour."[47]

In concluding the survey of the Anglican calendar, one is impressed again with its nature as a complex entity, combining Catholic, Protestant, and royalist elements. Its dominant tense was past in both its Christological-sanctoral cycle, as in its royalist commemorations. Its political significance was immensely influential, especially when a subservient church was manipulated in the interests of royal absolutism conveniently cloaked by the doctrine of the divine right of kings and the reality that the English sovereign was ecclesiastical as well as political leader by law. The regular prayers for the king and members of his household in the services of the Prayer Book, together with such annual commemorations as accessions, Gowrie Day, and the Gunpowder Plot, not forgetting the special prayers for the safe delivery of the Queen and the safeguarding of the succession to the throne, all reminded the people of the royal privileges and responsibilities, in the sacred as well as the secular realm, and of their own duties as loyal subjects. Socially, the Anglican calendar led to the sanctification of stratification. Its Erastianism made this inevitable, and, of course, it encouraged almsgiving by the rich towards the poor and concern for apprentices by their masters, and promised to all the consolations of eternity. But for any conception of social justice whether divinely or humanly introduced one must turn to the radical Puritans, the Diggers, and Levellers, and to the Fifth Monarchists (the latter a much larger group than hitherto recognized, as John F. Wilson has shown conclusively in his *Pulpit in Parliament*). The crown used the church as a medium of social control, along with the magistrates, even when, in opposition to Puritan Sabbatarianism, it proclaimed the necessity for a more relaxing observance of Sunday to make what it called "the meaner sort of people" happier with their lot, with the blissful escape of ale, and the lenitive of sports. The more aristocratic game of bowls, as it then was, came under the royal veto, presumably because it would make the ordinary man aspire to be extraordinary, and therefore socially "above himself." So he had better stick to archery. Economically, the Anglican calendary reduction of the Roman interruptions of work caused by frequent saints' days was advantageous, but there was still considerable waste in the holidays

47 *Ibid.*, sig. Ciii.

permitted, together with the indolence and intoxication encouraged on these occasions. The work ethic of Puritanism with its insistence upon the divine prescription of six days of work and a seventh of rest, demanded more working days and provided greater theological incentives for work than the Anglican calendar, though its strenuousness rejected by the nation, tired after the blood-letting of the Civil War and the vagaries and visions of the saints, proved its own undoing. For sixteen years the Anglican calendar was rejected in favour of the Puritan calendar: after what the Royalists had referred to as the "usurpation" came to an end, it was welcomed with relief.

4. *The Puritan Calendar*

The single most notable characteristic of the Puritan calendar was its iconoclasm. Turning first to the theological considerations, it is clear that its proponents rejected the Christological cycle because they found no explicit command to keep Christmas Day or Easter Day or the rest, whereas they saw that the Sabbath alone was a Scripturally demanded day, a special seventh and sacred day. This was the pattern not only prescribed in the Decalogue, but it was the cosmic scheme. For had not God, according to the Book of Genesis, created the world in six days, and rested on the seventh? So must man labour for six days, and on the Sabbath rest (this rest also prefigured the eternal rest of the elect in eternity), he must honour God in worship and in all the exercises prescribed for edification. Hence the Sabbath was the divinely appointed sacred time Scripturally authorized, whereas the Christological cycle was only of ecclesiastical and therefore of human appointment.

The same argument *a fortiori* eliminated the saints' days. Furthermore, the Puritans used the term "saints" in the New Testament manner rather than in the traditional Roman Catholic interpretation. That is, they reserved the term not for the perfect whom the churches of the centuries in the East and West had chosen to honour as worthy of imitation and capable of interceding on behalf of their admirers, but for their fellow Christians in the process of sanctification, being made holy by the Holy Spirit. As Paul had written to "the saints that are in Rome" (meaning his fellow Christians), they restored the term to its former and most primitive usage, and so had no need for a sanctoral cycle. Once again it was Scripture they were obeying and not ecclesiastical tradition; also they believed that the claim that the saints interceded for the liv-

ing was utterly idolatrous and derogating from the sole mediatorship of Christ. In short, the Puritan believed that each Sunday or
Sabbath was the Christological cycle in summary form, that each
day should be a Lent (otherwise a temporary first-class Christianity must be equated with hypocrisy for the rest of the year), and
that each of the elect should be a "saint" by the use of the religious
exercises that kept his mind informed of God's Gospel and commands, his heart tender to God, and his resolution firm.

Puritan calendary iconoclasm is further seen in the radical disjunction its theology makes between history and nature, with history having the primacy. This had the effect of disenchanting the
Puritans with the days of celebration associated with the natural
seasons, especially important for an agricultural community. They
disliked the dancing round the Maypole on the first of May, as well
as the harvest ales, as occasions in which bawdiness and buffoonery, profanity and idleness predominated. They made a radical
distinction between holidays and holy days, the latter being Sabbatarian and dedicated to the service of God. Their dislike of idleness is as economic as it is a theological factor. Indeed, they were
inseparable, for it was God who commanded them to work for
six days and God who commanded them to rest on the seventh
day, but these arrangements because of their predictableness, their
regularity, made rational planning possible for masters of crafts
and merchants, however unpopular they were with unambitious
apprentices.[48]

It is now important to recognize the positive emphases of the
Puritan calendar, both in the "Sanctification of the Lord's Day,"

[48] For the political, social, and economic aspects of the Anglican-Puritan calendary controversy see the masterly chapter, "The Uses of Sabbatarianism" in
Christopher Hill's *Society and Puritanism in Pre-Revolutionary England* (2nd
edn., New York, 1967), esp. pp. 149-56. On the theological side, the Anglicans
prepared a massive rebuttal, in which counter-offensive the big guns were Bishop
White of Ely, Heylin the historian, Sanderson the future Bishop, and Gilbert
Ironside. Between them they make the following points: that the Puritan contention that the Sabbath was an eternal ordinance of a moral and not a ceremonial
character cannot hold because it was not observed before the time of Moses and
was often poorly observed by the Jews after the giving of the Decalogue; that the
apostles had changed the day on which the Sabbath was observed from that which
the Jews had kept; and that it was kept by the early Church as a day of festival,
whereas the Puritans keep it more like a fast. Most significant, however, is the
move on the part of Anglican apologists from Biblical and traditional grounds
to rational, psychological, and more humane considerations. The kindly Sanderson
argues that charity should urge the Puritans to judge their brethren who as
"the ruder sort" need "loud and boisterous" exercises for recreation, while
gentlemen can be made happy by walking. (*A Sovereign Antidote against Sabbatarian Errors*, 1636, p. 26. I owe this reference to Howard Happ's research.)

and in the special days of "Public Solemn Fasting" and of "Public Thanksgiving."[49]

The Lord's Day was celebrated, so the Puritans were convinced by divine command, authenticated by the Word of God, Scripture. That was the strength and stay of the Puritan claim.[50] The major exponent of the Puritan understanding of the Sabbath was Nicholas Bownde, who was indebted, as Everett H. Emerson[51] has shown, to his father-in-law, Richard Greenham, minister of Dry Drayton, author of *A Treatise of the Sabbath*, and both, as M. M. Knappen has demonstrated,[52] ironically were indebted to the early work of Lancelot Andrewes, *A Pattern of Catechistical Doctrine*.[53]

How, then, was this red-letter day (almost the only regularly celebrated one in the Puritan calendar) to be spent? Greenham exhibits the intra-mundane asceticism which was developing in Puritanism, for excepting his insistence that plays and unlawful sports should be prohibited on Sundays, he would ban all recreation of any kind. Apart from attendance upon divine worship and attentive listening to the preaching, he recommends participation in religious conferences so that this may be a means of stirring up their affections. Further, he insists that as businessmen scrutinize their accounts once each week, so should the Christian spend the eve of the Sabbath in spiritual self-accounting.[54]

The discipline of the Sabbath is described in greater detail by

[49] These terms are all taken from *A Directory for Publike Worship in the Three Kingdoms*, where they are headings of important sections of this work prepared by the Assembly of Divines at Westminster meeting in 1644 and 1645. It will be briefly referred to hereafter as the "Westminster Directory."

[50] Richard Byfield (*The Doctrine of the Sabbath Vindicated*, 1631, p. 134) explodes with Puritan horror at the thought that holy days are only matters of State (therefore of human) appointment, "then also the Feasts of Christ's Nativity, of Easter, of Witsontide, &c. are of equall authority with the Lords Day, which thing what eares can heare with patience?"

[51] See E. H. Emerson's essay in the vol. he edited, *English Puritanism from John Hooper to John Milton* (Durham, N.C., 1968), p. 147.

[52] See "The Early Puritanism of Lancelot Andrewes" in *Church History*, 2 (1933), pp. 102-103. For this and the immediately preceding reference my thanks go to Howard Happ, friend and former student.

[53] See, for an accessible modern edition, *A Pattern of Catechistical Doctrine and other Minor Works* (Oxford, 1846). Andrewes calls the day of rest, which he believes to be a moral and eternal institution, the Sabbath, insists that only light and necessary work be done, requires simplicity and frugality of fare, and emphasizes the importance of hearing preaching by "persons fit . . . such as are able to do more than read and speak" and even calls for Sabbath conferences on Scripture with teachers, social equals and servants. (*Ibid.*, pp. 162-65).

[54] *A Treatise of the Sabbath* in *Works* (1601). This circulated in Ms. form for three years before it was published in 1592. Greenham further insists that the Lord's Day includes all special days, rendering the latter otiose: "Our Easter Day, our Ascension Day, our Whitsuntide is every Lords Day." (*Works*, p. 159.)

Nicholas Bownde. Heads of households are urged to rise early themselves and to see to it that the entire family arrive in ample time to enjoy all the benefits of the public worship of God. Spiritual discipline involved careful preparation by meditation, prayer, and self-examination, to hear the sermon and prayer after the service for a love of God comformable to the knowledge of God just received. Sermon summaries were to be copied down by apprentices and children, and both were required to recapitulate the sermon's main points for the heads of households, as masters or fathers. He was critical of the general Anglican keeping of sacred days, especially of Christmas, which was marked by distractions rather than devotions. His complaint is that "when they would seeme to be most devoutly keeping the remembrance of. . . the *birth and incarnation* of *Christ* . . . they doe celebrate the feast of the *drunken god Bacchus.*"[55]

One classical picture of the Puritan seriousness in the spending of Sabbath is provided by Richard Baxter in his autobiography, testifying to it as a proof of great earnestness in religion:

> In the village where I lived the reader read the Common Prayer briefly and the rest of the day even till dark night almost, except eating-time, was spent in dancing under a may-pole and a great tree not far from my father's door, where all the men of the town did eat together. And though one of my father's own tenants was the piper, he could not restrain him or break the sport. So that we could not read the Scripture in our family without the disturbance of the tabor and pipe and noise in the street. Many times my mind was inclined to be among them, and sometimes I broke loose from conscience and joined with them; and the more I did the more I was inclined to it. But when I heard them call my father Puritan it did much to cure me and alienate me from them; for I considered that my father's exercise of reading the Scripture was better than theirs, and would surely be better thought on by all men at the last. . . .[56]

The Westminster *Directory* prescribed how the Puritan Sabbath should be spent when the Puritans came to power. It was, in

[55] Bownde, *op. cit.*, pp. 133-34.
[56] The substance of the original *Reliquiae Baxterianae* (ed. M. Sylvester, 1696) has been re-edited by J. M. Lloyd Thomas in an Everyman edn., titled, *The Autobiography of Richard Baxter* (1925), p. 6.

the first place, to be prepared for, so that "all worldly business or our ordinary callings may be so ordered, and so timely and seasonably laid aside, as they may not be impediments to the due sanctifying of the day when it comes." Secondly, the entire day was to be sanctified, both publicly and privately, with "a holy cessation, or resting all that day, from all necessary labours; and an abstaining, not only from all sports and pastimes, but also from all worldly words and thoughts." Thirdly, the diet for that day is to be so arranged "as that neither servants be unnecessarily detained" from worship, "nor any other person hindered from the sanctifying of that day." Fourthly, every person and family must prepare for the Sabbath by prayer for themselves and the divine assistance for the minister, and for a blessing of his ministry; "and by such other holy exercises as may further dispose them to a more comfortable communion with God in his public ordinances." Worship is to be so organized that the whole congregation is to be in time for the beginning and stay to the end of the service, and "with one heart solemnly join together in all parts of the public worship." The time before and after public worship is to "be spent in reading, meditation, repetition of sermons; especially by calling their families to an account of what they have heard, and catechising of them, holy conferences, singing of psalms, visiting the sick, relieving the poor, and such like duties of piety, charity, and mercy accounting the Sabbath a delight."[57]

We have seen earlier how there was an acute and complex Sabbatarian controversy between the Puritans and the high Anglicans, with important political as well as religious and economic implications. One further political aspect must be referred to, and that is the fact that the Puritan insistence upon keeping of the Sabbath strictly sometimes led to a matter of pitting the individual conscience against the social or religious hierarchy. Should an apprentice, for example, insist on the scrupulous keeping of the Sabbath in the most ascetical manner, while his master requested him to spend it, as the law of the land approved, in pleasurable activities? Or, again, who was to be the authoritative interpreter of God's will, the learned bishop, or the learned minister? To keep the Sabbath strictly was, therefore, to be a political and religious radical. To spend it in a relaxed way after attending worship was to belong

[57] All the citations in this paragraph come from the Directory's section headed "Of the Sanctification of the Lord's Day." (*Reliquiae Liturgicae*, ed. Peter Hall, Vol. III: *The Parliamentary Directory*, Bath, 1847, pp. 58-60.)

to, or be loyal to the royal and ecclesiastical establishment. In fact, the sixteenth of Archbishop Laud's *Visitation Articles* for 1635 in the diocese of Winchester is directed against Puritan tendencies in the ministry by specifically enquiring: "Hath your minister taken upon him to appoint any public or private fasts, prophecies or exercises, not approved by law or public authority, or hath used to meet in any private house or place with any person or persons, there to consult how to impeach or deprave the Book of Common Prayer, or the doctrine or discipline of the Church of England?"[58] He clearly recognized that the Puritan gauntlet had been thrown down in public challenge, for he listed the chief activities enjoined by the Puritans for use on the Sabbath, and intended as a counter-blast to the re-issue of the *Book of Sports* by Charles I, as well as being godly "exercises" in their own right.

As the antagonism between high Anglicans and Puritan Anglicans grew more bitter, Henry Burton tried to reinforce the observation of the Lord's Day by collecting a group of "divine tragedies" or striking cases of divine retribution on Sabbath-breakers for their defiance of the law of God, resulting in death or injury. Seven cases are noted of those who were involved in maypole festivities, four for participating in Whitsun and two other church ales, four cases of superfluous bell-ringing, four cases of swimming accidents, and two for skating on thin ice, and one case each for serving a *subpoena*, frequenting a brothel, keeping company with young women, scoffing at the Sabbath, and feasting in celebration of the *Book of Sports*.[59]

The Sabbath was the great, regular red-letter day of the Puritan calendar, which looked both backward to the Creation and forward to the consummation of Creation in the eternal delight and rest of God's elect in heaven. Yet, in addition, this calendar had a strongly contemporary emphasis based upon the Puritan's reading of God's special providence revealed in events. This can be documented as clearly in the diary of Oliver Cromwell, whether as general of the Ironsides or as Lord Protector of England,[60] as in the diary of Samuel Sewall, the judge who presided over the notorious

---

58 Found in P. E. More and F. L. Cross, *Anglicanism* (edn. of 1957), pp. 702-15.

59 [Henry Burton] *A Divine Tragedy Lately Enacted* (Amsterdam, 1636), passim.

60 See the three volume edition of *The Letters and Speeches of Oliver Cromwell* (ed. Thomas Carlyle, 1904), passim, and the admirable theological biography, *The Lord Protector* (1955) by Robert S. Paul.

witchcraft trial in Salem, Massachusetts. It was indeed part of the Protestant tradition in England to note special providences, from the time of Foxe the martyrologist, who had learned it from the pages of Calvin's *Institutes*. This tradition affirmed that every event was a disclosure of the mysterious divine will in judgment or mercy. This providential interpretation had been given official acceptance by the national church when it summoned the people to prayer in Elizabeth's reign. For example, two special days of prayer were proclaimed in 1565, and for each a form was prepared; one a thanksgiving "for the delivery of the Christians that are now invaded by the Turke." Although the doctrine had been inserted in the Book of Homilies, it was Puritanism that made it prominent.

What, then, was distinctive about the Puritan days of special providence? Two features seem to mark their days of humiliation and thanksgiving from the previous national special days. One is the great solemnity, intensity, and length, with which they were kept, lasting most of the day, and filled with exhortations, sermons, prayers, and psalm-singing, and with only a minimal concession to the needs of the body. The other feature is that such observance of days of special providence were also kept within Puritan family life: indeed, they were encouraged so long as they did not conflict either with the Sabbath or with nationally appointed special days when the latter were decreed by Puritanism in the seat of power.

Undergirding these observances was a strong Calvinist theology of special providence, which the increasing Arminianism of high-church Anglicans found to be too sure about "the secret counsels of God"; but it meant that the rational elements in their own theology lacked the dogmatic certainties of Puritanism, the immense assurance of the elect that can rapidly recover after disaster. ("Who can lay anything to the charge of God's elect? . . . If God be for us, who can be against us? . . . Nay, in all things we are more than conquerors through him that loved us. . . .")[61]

This conviction was first widely spread among Puritans by their favourite early writer, William Perkins in 1607. He observes: "God hath sundry times sent his iudgments among us; generally by plague and famine; and particularly on sundrie families and persons; but who regardeth them?" His answer is that contemplation on God's judgments is essential to avoid their repetition, and

---

[61] These are, of course, citations from the Epistle to the Romans 8, a favourite commonplace of Puritan theology.

for this three things are requisite. "First, we must carefully observe, marke, and remember them. . . . Secondly, . . . we must apply them to our own person in particular, so as the thought thereof may make use of Gods iudgments that light upon others by applying them to ourselves."[62]

The Westminster *Directory* supplies the official theological rationale of these days and directions for their careful observance. The days of humiliation, for example, are no exercises of faith followed by fun. They are to last the entire day, and fasting requires "total abstinence, not only from all good . . . but also from worldly labour, discourses and thoughts, and from all bodily delights and such like (although at other times lawful), rich apparel, ornaments, and such like, during the fast. . . ." Each family and person is to prepare privately apart and be early at the congregation. Further, "So large a portion of the day as conveniently may be, is to be spent in public reading and preaching of the Word, with singing of psalms, fit to quicken affections suitable to such a duty." Prayer is given the highest priority on such occasions and ministers are charged to aim at "melting" the hearts of the people (and their own), "especially with sorrow for their sins, that it may be indeed a day of deep humiliation and afflicting of the soul." A special choice of Scripture lessons and texts for preaching are to be made as will most dispose the people to repentance and lead them to reformation: "Before the close of the public duties, the minister is, in his own and the people's names, to engage his and their hearts to the Lord's, with professed purpose and resolution to reform what is amiss among them, and more particularly such sins as they have been more remarkably guilty of, and to draw near to God, and to walk more closely and faithfully with him in new obedience, than ever before."[63] Thus, the heart prepared by grace, is to be melted to end in the resolution to renew the personal, familial, congregational, and national covenant with God.

There are several striking illustrations of such day-long fasts leading from thorough group self-criticism to repentance and reso-

---

[62] *A Treatise of Man's Imagination* (Cambridge, 1607), pp. 198-200. It was published five years after the author's death.

[63] All citations are from the Westminster *Directory*'s Section, entitled "Concerning Public Solemn Fasting" (*Reliquiae Liturgicae*, ed. Peter Hall, Vol. III, *The Parliamentary Directory* [Bath, 1847], pp. 73-78). See also John F. Wilson's "The Program of Humiliation and Thanksgiving," which is Chap. iii of *Pulpit in Parliament* (Princeton, New Jersey, 1969).

lution, on the part of the Westminster Assembly of Divines and of the Puritan Army Debates at Putney.[64] Lightfoot, one of the Scottish commissioners at the Westminster Assembly, tells how the Assembly spent Monday, October 16, 1643, the occasion being a solemn fast:

> First Mr. *Wilson* gave a picked psalm, or selected verses of several psalms, agreeing to the time and occasion. Then Dr. *Burgess* prayed about an hour: after he had done, Mr. *Whittacre* preached upon Isa. xxxvii.3, "This day is a day of trouble," &c. Then, having had another chosen psalm, Mr. *Goodwin* prayed; and after he had done, Mr. *Palmer* reached upon Psal. xxv.12. After whose sermon we had another psalm, and Dr. *Stanton* prayed about an hour; and with another psalm and a prayer of the prolocutor [i.e. Dr. Twisse], and a collection for the maimed soldiers . . . we adjourned till tomorrow morning.[65]

This particular occasion lasted from 9:00 A.M. to 4:00 P.M. and the collection for maimed soldiers reached £3 15s.[66]

It would seem to be a heroic endurance test of preaching and praying only lightened by psalm-singing, and possibly unique. On the contrary, though the quality of the preaching was certainly higher in the Assembly with such a galaxy of Puritan divines than it would be at any other gathering, yet the occasion was far from being unique even at the Westminster Assembly. Parliament had sought Charles I's permission to have a fast on the last Wednesday of each month (a technical error on his part in view of the political use of such occasions that would later be made against his interests), and it became statutory by 1641. There had been a notable fast day on Monday, September 25, 1643, when the Commons and the divines took the Solemn League and Covenant, meeting in St. Margaret's Church, Westminster, which remains the parish church of the House of Commons.

When on September 9, 1644, the woeful news came of the

---

[64] For the Army Debates see *Puritanism and Liberty*, ed. with an introduction of great value by A.S.P. Woodhouse (1938).

[65] Ed. Rev. John Rogers Pitman, *The Whole Works of the Rev. John Lightfoot*, 13 Vols. (1825), XIII, containing "The Journal of the Proceedings of the Assembly of Divines," from Jan. 1, 1643 to December 31, 1644," *ad loc.* October 13, 1643. It is also cited in W. Fraser Mitchell, *English Pulpit Oratory from Andrewes to Tillotson* (1932), pp. 255-56.

[66] S. W. Carruthers, *The Everyday Work of the Westminster Assembly* (Philadelphia, 1943), p. 65.

defeat of Lord Essex's forces in the West, with Waller's Army in no position to relieve Essex because his infantry had surrendered at Lostwithiel, Burgess suggested that the Assembly should hold a fast, and they then and there discussed the causes of the divine disapproval seen in the military disaster, as it applied to their own conduct as divines.

The details of this clerical group exercise in self-criticism may be of interest. Valentine said zeal had been shown for depriving scandalous ministers, but not for rebuking scandalous people. Whitaker mentioned the breaches of the Solemn League and Covenant, such as divisions among those who professed to be religious, and falsehood. Walker mentioned neglect of justice. Gillespie said that religion was subjugated to political ends.[67] Palmer spoke of slack attendance, arriving late, leaving early, impetuosity or slowness of speech, and unhappy differences. Burgess spoke of insolence and bloodthirstiness on the part of the enemy, of the gasping condition of Ireland, of the divisions in Manchester's Army; and the deliberate fomenting of sectarianism. The analysis seems to have been comprehensive, if rambling, and it was not sparing in candour.

The other providential day in the Puritan calendar was spent more cheerfully. That was the public day of thanksgiving. Here, again, the Westminster *Directory* provides a rationale and description. Such days might be occasioned by a notable victory[68] in the field, of deliverance from some impending disaster like the plague or drought or flood. When a day of public thanksgiving is held, the minister is to "make some pithy narration of the deliverance obtained, or mercy received,[69] or of whatever hath occasioned that assembling of the congregation, that all may better understand it, or be minded of it, and more affected with it." Psalm-singing was enjoined as the fittest medium for the expression of sacred joy. The minister is to exhort the people about the signal instance of God's mercy, to read appropriate passages of Scripture, and to pick a text pertinent to the occasion. After the sermon is ended, he is also to

67 One is reminded of Milton's disaffection with the Assembly by his description of it as being riddled "with plots and packing worse than Trent."

68 An example of such is the Assembly's day of thanksgiving for the surrender of the king's forces at Worcester, in July of 1646. See S. W. Carruthers, *op. cit.*, p. 85.

69 It must be recalled that thanksgiving days could be held in families and divine mercies would include gratitude for the safe delivery of a mother in childbirth, as for the gift of children, or the recovery from a serious illness, or for spiritual mercies such as reformation of life.

pray, remembering the necessities of king, church, and state, enlarging on "former mercies and deliverances; but more expecially for that which at the present calls them together to give thanks: With humble petition for the continuance and renewing of God's wonted mercies, as need shall be, and for sanctifying grace to make a right use thereof." He is also to admonish the congregation "to beware of all excess and riot, tending to gluttony or drunkenness . . . and to take care that their mirth and rejoicing be not carnal, but spiritual, which may make God's praise to be glorious and themselves to be humble and sober." Two such gatherings of the congregation on that day are expected and at one or both "a collection is to be made for the poor . . . that their loins may bless us and rejoice the more with us." Finally, the people are to be exhorted at the end of the second meeting, "to spend the residue of that day in holy duties, and testifications of Christian love and charity one towards another, and of rejoicing more and more in the Lord; as becometh those who make the joy of their Lord their strength."[70]

One can hardly fail to be impressed not only with the seriousness and solemnity of these days of thanksgiving, and with the humility that accepted weal (and even woe on days of fasting) as a divine gift for the training of the elect, without much presumptuous expectation or overt murmuring. Considering the stereotypes of Puritanism that have been widely disseminated by the Elizabethan playwrights[71] and Lord Macaulay's *History of England*, who would have guessed that joy characterized Sabbaths and days of thanksgiving, and that so much time after worship was spent in "the testifications of Christian love and charity towards one another"?

There was only one regular annual day of thanksgiving which the Puritans celebrated, and that was the fifth of November. It became increasingly interpreted as the supremely Protestant national event, given double significance for their successors the Nonconformists, through the discovery of the conspiracy of Titus Oates, a doubtful Catholic,[72] and the joining to the celebration the arrival of William of Orange in England to safeguard the English

---

[70] All citations in the paragraph up to this point are from the section of the Westminster Directory, headed "Concerning the Observation of Public Days of Thanksgiving." (See *The Parliamentary Directory*, ed. Peter Hall, Bath, 1847, pp. 78-81.)

[71] The references are to Malvolio in *Twelfth Night* by Shakespeare, and to Zeal-of-the-Land-Busy in Jonson's *Bartholomew Fair*.

[72] The events of this time are brilliantly interpreted in the cryptogrammatic narrative poem of Dryden, *Absolam and Achitophel*.

throne for Protestantism. Nonetheless, they needed all their considerable powers of exegetical elasticity to justify this celebration from the Word of God, as Anglicans were not slow to remind them. But its political and religious value to them was immense.

Apart from the regular and special sacred times we have mentioned, there was also an unofficial Puritan calendar, to which Samuel Pepys alludes in his diary. The entry for September 3, 1662, reads: "Mr. Coventry told us how the Fanatiques and Presbyters that did intend to rise about this time, did choose this day as the most auspicious to them in their endeavours against monarchy: it being fatal twice to the King, and the day of Oliver's death. But blessed be God! all is likely to be quiet, I hope." Certainly Cromwell considered the third day of September the most fortunate of his life because it marked his victories at Dunbar and Worcester. It was also remarkable for the vast storm that occurred at the time of his death, and also it was the day on which the Fire of London in 1666 raged with the greatest fury. But the fact that it marked Cromwell's success and time of death are proof sufficient of the ambiguity of events and the great theological, apart from scientific difficulties, in interpreting their significance.

In summation, one notes the strongly contemporary thrust of the Puritan calendar, as contrasted with the retrospective emphasis of the Anglican and Roman Catholic cyclical calendars. But one ought not either to ignore the emphasis on the future inherent in the Sabbath, and more directly envisaged on that day by the radical Puritans, who, in that day of rest from manual labor, were freed to contemplate in the freest fantasy the religious *bouleversement* that would come with the establishment of God's Fifth and final Monarchy, the kingdom of the saints. Here, indeed, and imminently, God would, as already foreshadowed in the *Magnificat* throw down the mighty from their seats and raise up the humble and meek. The Puritan calendar is acknowledged to be a rigorous and intensive one: it is more rarely realised that it was an exciting series of sacred days fraught with religious and political promise. Only the future would show that the intensity was too great for the majority of human beings to bear, and that the political promises were doomed, as Milton shows so movingly in *Samson Agonistes*.

Its economic importance, because of Christopher Hill's researches, is now widely recognized. The Puritan week was the perfect medium for the Puritan conception of calling, involving strenuous work for six days and a seventh for rest and holy exercises. John Boyes expressed the Puritan work ethic admirably in the words: "Every Christian should have a sweating brow and a working braine. . . ."[73] Such working was institutionalised by the Puritan Sabbath and made the rational planning of the industrialist and merchant possible, whereas the traditional Roman or Anglican calendars were too irregular, and too frequently interrupted by holidays for economic purposes. In this respect we see that it was also of social importance, for aristocrats[74] and their dependents who lived to a large extent on the land, with the squires and yeomen farmers, and they warmed to the traditional celebrations of church and the natural seasons, while the Puritans were men of the cities, merchants and masters. Certainly the Roman Catholic and Anglican calendars were more humane then and they may in the end prove to be as religious as the Puritan calendar. But if sincerity, and intensity of devotion (rather than accommodation of religion to human needs and the recognition of the claims of the earth and of the need for a reversal) are the criteria of judgment, the Puritan calendar was a heroic failure. The Restoration showed that the moderation of the *via media* in this as in most other respects suited the majority of the English nation.

[73] "The First Sunday" from his work, *An Exposition of the Dominical Epistles and Gospels used in our English Liturgy throughout the whole yeare* (1609), p. 9.

[74] Hill's *Society and Puritanism in Pre-Revolutionary England*, points out that the Court notoriously had masques, plays, and even revels on the Lord's Day (p. 160), that the Council met on Sunday mornings regularly until the reign of Charles I (pp. 163-64), whereas Parliament refrained from meeting on Sundays except under the most urgent necessity and then apologized (pp. 164-65).

CHAPTER VII

SACRED MUSIC:
SPLENDID OR SCRIPTURAL?

O UR TITLE for this chapter is an oversimplification. There was not one issue in this controversy, but a complex of interrelated ones. Indeed, it was a temptation to head the chapter "Sacred Music: Magnificent or Minimal?" in order to point out the difference between the rich Anglican tradition of cathedral music, on the one hand, and the austere Puritan restriction of sacred music to metrical psalmody, on the other. There could hardly be a greater contrast than that of the cathedral tradition inherited from the medieval church, reaffirmed by Tallis and Byrd in Tudor days, and developed in the Italian manner in the *stile nuovo* in Restoration times, with verse anthems sung in many parts, with soloists and the full choir alternating, and with a concert of violins playing in the vocal intervals, and its opposite—the sometimes solemn but often dreary simplicity of Puritan metrical psalmody lined out in common metre.

That would have been a justified contrast, because Cavaliers and Roundheads were differentiated in part by their preferences in sacred music. That is made clear by Anthony Wood who reports that at the Restoration organs were put back into the Oxford Colleges to counteract the popular interest in preaching, praying, and psalm-singing: "And that they might draw the vulgar from the aforesaid praying and preaching which was still exercised in some churches and houses, they restored organs at Christ Church, Magdalen, New and St. John's College, together with the singing of prayers after the most antient way: to which places the resort of people (more out of novelty I suppose than devotion) was infinitely great."[1]

Nonetheless, to have retained the alternative title for this Chapter would have implied that the difference between the Puritan and Anglican attitudes to sacred music was only a matter of taste, temperament, or cultural preference, a kind of choice between "penny plain" and "tuppenny coloured."

[1] *The Life and Times of Anthony à Wood* abridged from A. Clark's edition by L. Powys (1961), p. 313; cited by Christopher Dearnley, *English Church Music, 1650-1750* (1970), p. 157.

The ultimate difference between Anglican and Puritan and Non-conformist concepts of sacred music, however, cannot be resolved or explained in this simple fashion. In the first place, as Percy Scholes has established,[2] the Puritans were not the musical kill-joys of the stereotype made fashionable by Lord Macaulay's claim that in Commonwealth days "it was a sin to touch the virginals. . . . The solemn peal of the organ was superstitious."[3] John Milton, like Spenser, an exemplar of the rich culture of Puritanism, had an organ in his home and expressed in prose as well as in *Il Penseroso* his ecstatic delight in organ music: "while the skilful *Organist* plies his grave and fancied descant, in lofty fugues, or the whole symphony with artful and unimaginable touches adorn and grace the well studied chords of some choice composer."[4] Opera, it should be remembered, was imported into Britain in Puritan times.[5] Playfair published his *English Dancing Master* (1651) at the height of the Puritan regime, and dancing was encouraged by Cromwell, celebrated by Milton in *L'Allegro*, and formed an essential part of the education of the family of one of Cromwell's army commanders, Colonel Hutchinson. Puritans privately encouraged music, dancing, and portrait painting. If they were unable to encourage the use of organs and orchestras in divine worship, it was not that they disliked art, but that they loved religion more.

It is for the latter reason that we have labelled this Chapter's controversy that of the debate between splendour (and by implication medieval and royalist tradition) and Scripture. The Anglicans followed the Lutheran view of Scripture and tradition, which argued that what was not forbidden in Scripture and had the authority of tradition behind it was permissible in the church, and which had made possible the use of the hymnody of Luther and Gerhardt and the great tradition of oratorios and the sublime organ music of Johann Sebastian Bach. The Puritans, and their successors the Nonconformists, on the other hand, demanded a Scriptural warrant for every part of worship, believing it to be a repudiation of the doctrine of original sin for man to assume he was capable of deciding what was appropriate in the service of God, and arrant impudence to legislate for himself when God had already decided for him in the Word of God in the Holy Scriptures. The inflexible Puritan motto was: *Quod non iubet, vetat.* As we shall see later, it

---

[2] *The Puritans and Music* (1934).
[3] *The History of England* (1848), Chap. I.
[4] Scholes, *op. cit.*, p. 151.   [5] *Ibid.*, p. 195.

was the conviction that metrical Psalms were the Word of God while hymns were human compositions, that restricted their praise to the paraphrases until the last decade of the century.

Furthermore, Puritans were acutely critical of cathedral music on other grounds. The complexities of polyphonic compositions, the obscurities of Latin motets and anthems, the requirements of well-trained professional choirs to perform such elaborate music— all parts of the medieval cathedral tradition of music maintained to some degree in England—sinned against two of the major Puritan doctrines, namely, the primary need for "edification" or building up in the faith (so that, according to the Pauline injunction one could sing with the understanding) and the priesthood of all believers. Complexity and obscurity defeated the aim of edification and a professional choir stole the rights of the congregation as God's elect to sing His praises.

The Puritans were not slow to make their voices heard in criticism of elaborate cathedral and church music. John Northbrooke in 1577 wrote:

> First we must take heed that in music be not put the whole sum and effect of godliness and of the worshipping of God, which among the Papists they do almost . . . think that they have fully worshipped God when they have long and much sung and piped. Further, we must take heed that in it be not put merit or remission of sins. Thirdly, that singing be not so much used and occupied in the Church that there be no time, in a manner, left to preach the Word of God and holy doctrine; whereby it cometh to pass that the people depart out of Church full of music and harmony, but yet hunger-baned and fasting as touching heavenly food and doctrine. Fourthly, that rich and large stipends be not so appointed for musicians that either very little, or, in a manner, nothing is provided for the ministers which labour in the Word of God. Fifthly, neither may that broken and quavering music be used wherewith the standers-by are so letted that they cannot understand the words, not though they would never so fain. Lastly, we must take heed that in the church nothing be sung without choice, but only those things which are contained in the holy scriptures, or which are by just reason gathered out of them, and do exactly agree with the Word of God.[6]

6 *A Treatise Wherein Dicing, Dauncing, etc. Are Reproved* (1577), reprinted by the Shakespeare Society, ed. Collier (1843), pp. 113-14.

Northbrooke does not mention the need for a professionally trained choir to perform the music, but he thinks of the cost of maintaining choristers and their choir-masters and organists. He recalls that Roman Catholic worship stinted the time allowed for preaching. He also emphasises the "broken and quavering music" which makes it difficult for the congregation to understand the words. Naturally he concludes that the primary liturgical criterion is Biblical.

Robert Browne, himself a competent lutenist and lover of music, objected to the antiphonal singing of the psalms by the two sides of a cathedral choir. It seemed to him to mock the solemnity of worship: "Their tossing to and fro of psalmes and sentences is like tenisse plaie, whereto God is called to Judg who can do best and be most gallant in his worship; as bie organs, solfaing, pricksong chanting, bussing and mumling verie roundlie on divers handes. Thus their have a shewe of religion, but in deed thei turne it to gaming, and plaie mockholidaie with the worship of God."[7]

William Prynne empties his fiercest vial of rhetoric on contemporary church music, but his main point is that this music diverts the attention from instruction in divine doctrine:

> As for the Divine Service and Common Prayer, it is so chaunted and minsed and mangled of our costly hired, curious, and nice Musitiens (not to instruct the audience withall, nor to stirre up mens mindes unto devotion, but with a whorish harmony to tickle their eares:) that it may justly seeme not to be a noyse made of men, but rather a bleating of bruite beasts; while the Coristers ney descant as it were a sort of Colts; others bellowe a tenour, as it were a company of oxen: others barke a counter-point, as it were a kennell of Dogs: others rore out a treble like a sort of Bulls: others grunt out a base as it were a number of Hogs; so that a foule evill favoured noyse is made, but as for the wordes and sentences and the very matter it selfe, is nothing understanded at all; but the authority and power of judgment is taken away from the music and from the eares utterly.[8]

It is most significant that he recognises only two values in sacred music: instruction and the creation of a devotional atmosphere in worship. It is inconceivable to him that a skilfully performed

---

[7] *True and Short Declaration* (1583), cited by P. Scholes, *op. cit.*, p. 217.
[8] Cited by Scholes, *ibid.*, p. 218.

anthem or chant might itself be an act of worship, as well as creating a desire for worship in others.

It must be acknowledged that there was, at least on the part of some Puritans, an insensitivity to subtle or profound religious music. That is the only conclusion that can be drawn from the delight of John Vicars that organ music and elaborate singing were now silenced in 1649 in Westminster Abbey, both being replaced by a daily sermon. This is sheer iconoclasm:

> the most rare and strange alteration of things in the *Cathedral Church of Westminster*. Namely, that whereas there was wont to be heard nothing almost but *Roaring*-Boyes, tooting and squeaking *Organ Pipes*, and the Cathedral catches of Morley, and I know not what trash; now the Popish Altar is quite taken away, the *bellowing organs* are demolisht and pull'd down; the *treble* or rather *trouble* and base singers, Chanters or Inchanters, driven out; and instead thereof, there is now a most blessed Orthodox Preaching Ministry, even every morning throughout the Weeke, and every Weeke throughout the whole yeare a Sermon Preached by the most learned grave and godly Ministers.[9]

The crudest and most literal kind of Puritan iconoclasm is reported by Bishop Hall in the spoiling of his cathedral of Norwich in 1643:

> Lord, what work was here, what clattering of glasses, what beating down of walls, what tearing up of monuments, what pulling down of seats, what wresting out of irons and brass from the windows and graves, what defacing of arms, what demolishing of curious stone work that had not any representation in the world but only the coat of the founder and the skill of the mason, what toting and piping upon the destroyed organ pipes, and what hideous triumph on the market day before all the country, when, in a kind of sacrilegious and profane procession, all the organ pipes, vestments, both copes and surplices, together with the leaden Cross which had been newly sawn down from over the green yard pulpit, and the service books and singing books that could be had, were carried to the fire in the marketplace, a lewd wretch walking before the train, in his scope, trailing

[9] Cited by Jocelyn Perkins, *Westminster Abbey: Its Worship and Ornaments* (1952), p. 111.

in the dirt, with a service book in his hand, imitating, in an impious scorn, the time, and usurping the words of the Litany, used formerly in the Church; near the public cross all these monuments of idolatry must be sacrificed to the fire, not without much ostentation of a zealous joy in discharging ordinance to the cost of some who professed how much they had longed to see that day. Neither was it any news, upon the Guild day, to have the Cathedral now open on all sides, to be filled with musketeers, waiting for the major's return, drinking and tobaccoing as freely as if it had turned ale-house.[10]

Such desecration caused not only the loss of historical artifacts, but, as far as music was concerned, the most serious destruction was of music libraries and part-books, and the disbanding of choirs and the loss of traditions which it had taken many years to create. Much of the music would have been in sets of handwritten part-books, comprising a series of services and anthems collected by the choir-master. Music copying was both expensive and laborious, with the result that one set only, sufficient for the choir, would exist. Unless any of the parts of these services and anthems happened to be used by other churches, the loss of a set would be permanent. Furthermore, there were few extant printed part-books and they were sold in limited editions. Their widespread destruction by the Puritans led to the entire disappearance of some works and to the survival of damaged or incomplete sets of others. The result is that John Barnard's *The First Booke of Selected Church Musick* (1641), a typical compilation, which was issued in ten separate part-books, has nowhere survived in its entirety.[11]

1. *Cathedral Music*

If such were the criticisms, whether moderate or merely negative and destructive, by the Puritans of English church music in cathedrals and peculiars, what was to be said in its defence? Actions speak louder than words. Thus the best apologia for such elaborate music will be our later consideration of the sacred music actually composed by a galaxy of luminaries in the seventeenth century, including Tompkins, Weelkes, Gibbons, Lawes, Humphrey, Blow, and Purcell. Nor should the high standards set by the Royal

[10] Cited by Kenneth R. Long, *The Music of the English Church* (1971), p. 205.
[11] The information in this paragraph was drawn from Long, *op. cit.*, pp. 206-207.

Chapel in London or in Westminster Abbey (not ignoring provincial cathedrals), especially during the reign of King Charles II, be forgotten.

The conflict between Anglican and Puritan over the nature of church music raised issues which are still acute and relevant. If the Puritan claim is made that music must be straightforward and so simple that all can join in, then the only rights recognised are those of edification and the priesthood of all believers. In rebuttal, however, the Anglicans can claim that this will mean a very limited repertory of music, and prevent the humble worshipper from ever hearing most of the sublimest religious music ever composed or performed, for the highest music is complex and elaborate and must be performed by professionals. To demand that the music sung in church must be capable of being performed by everyone, is to require music restricted in range, elementary in rhythm, easily memorised, and often obvious in the extreme. By the same token such music will be irksome and restrictive to those with more advanced musical tastes, for it seems to be the case that the more musical people are, the more their taste turns towards richly decorated or elaborate music.

Then there is a second argument in favour of cathedral type music, as against popular music. Is it essential that the whole congregation should join in all the music offered in worship? Puritans said, "Yes." The Anglicans said, "No." The latter were able to point out that, in fact, the congregation does not join in audibly in a considerable part of divine service—in the Epistle, the Gospel, other lessons, prayers, collects, and the sermon. There is no reason therefore why a considerable part of the sacred music should not be delegated to the musical experts, the organist, choir-master, and choir. Nor, indeed, can a congregation join in splendid architecture, stained-glass windows, mosaics, tapestries, intricate woodcarving or wrought ironwork, although all of these are aids to devotion, raising the minds and hearts of the worshippers from the secular world to the spiritual, and creating the atmosphere conducive to the adoration of God. Music has the same capacity in the highest degree, whether without words, as in an organ voluntary, or with words that are difficult to hear, as in a complex polyphonic motet, or are not understood, as in a Latin anthem.

Not only so, but—provided there is a secure place for hymnody—even though the congregation cannot join in vocally with the elaborate music, this does not prevent them from active participation in heart and mind.

Even more significantly it can be argued that the best cathedral music is more than a stimulus to devotion; that it is, indeed, an act of worship in and of itself providing, as in expressionist art, an inspiring and moving setting, to the words it illustrates, whether the mood be that of pathos and sadness, as at the Cross, or the mourning for our sins, or of joy and triumphant jubilation as at the Resurrection and the contemplation of the Communion of saints.

It can even be argued that, in general, the parish church could realise the dreams of the Reformers in a service that is musically "understanded of the people" while the cathedral or abbey church delegates its musical offering to be provided by the experts.[12]

It will be interesting to consider seventeenth-century justifications of cathedral music. John Barnard, writing in 1641, considered it a sufficient apologia for music that it "could civilise the rough and boystrous fancies of a Nation, that is esteem'd of many to be naturally somewhat of the sourest."[13] Presumably a dyspeptic nation could not have too much music to cure its melancholy and morose temperament. In 1720, however, Thomas Besse makes some very high-flown claims for cathedral music, including its honouring of God, the example it sets to all Reformed churches, its promotion of spiritual happiness in the members of a cathedral choir (conveniently oblivious of their occasional quarrelsomeness), its benefit to the entire nation, and its offering of worship on behalf of every parish in the diocese.[14]

Yet one could also select other authors to give an entirely different impression. Christopher Dearnley, for example, claims that at the time of the Restoration music's chief use was for the glory of God and His divine service, as well as for the solace of humanity. By the beginning of the eighteenth century, the same writer contends that its function was to refresh mankind and to supply an antidote against temptation; while in the middle of the same century its main values were to provide for entertainment and to give an inducement to charity. Not only the motives for music, but also its techniques followed a similar process of secularization.[15]

---

[12] *Ibid.*, p. 37 for comparison.
[13] From the introduction to John Barnard's *First Booke of Selected Church Musick* (1641).
[14] *A Rationale on Cathedral Worship* (1720), pp. 52-62.
[15] Dearnley, *English Church Music* (1970), pp. 15f.

But, we may ask, what was the kind of musical provision made in seventeenth-century cathedrals in England? The first point is that fully choral services are sung in cathedrals on weekdays as well as on Sundays and festivals. Furthermore, far more music is customarily sung in a cathedral than in a parish church, and it is of a generally advanced type which it would be too difficult for parish choirs to attempt. Then, again, the sung parts of the prescribed services, which remain unchanged from day to day, including the ordinary of the Holy Communion, the responses and canticles, are sung to fully composed settings, several of which are highly intricate. Moreover, the set Psalms for the day are sung in full, usually by way of antiphonal chanting, verse by verse or half-verse by half-verse. The *Te Deum* and *Benedictus* in Morning Prayer and the *Magnificat* and *Nunc Dimittis* in Evening Prayer are provided usually with anthem settings.

An anthem, furthermore, is considered almost obligatory in a cathedral after the third collect (although it was introduced as an option in 1662). The type of anthem sung in a cathedral is usually longer and more elaborate than those sung in parish churches. It is this series of weekday and Sunday musical duties in worship which maintains the cathedral tradition in England.[16]

Dearnley has pointed out with the utmost clarity and conviction that it was only when a sung Eucharist was placed at the centre of Sunday worship that there was any true incentive for composers to produce their greatest work. Previously, the Holy Communion, so far as music was concerned, was regarded as a mere appendix to Morning Prayer: indeed, it was called only the "Second Service" for most of the seventeenth century. Dearnley affirms that "A cropped little Sanctus threaded in between the Litany and Ante-Communion and matched by a bobbed Creed cannot stand comparison with the wonderful tapestry of the sixteenth century settings of the Mass adorning the Liturgy, and throwing into prominence its rich symbolism."[17] It was such a noble centre that had inspired the work of Byrd and Palestrina. Morning Prayer was a poor substitute, and it is greatly to the credit of English composers that they made good use of the devotional treasury of the Psalter and found there a variety of religious affirmations and moods on which to exercise their creative gifts.

If we consult the work of Edward Lowe, organist and choirmaster of Christ Church Cathedral, Oxford, at the Restoration, and

---

16 Long, *op. cit.*, pp. 39-40.   17 Dearnley, *op. cit.*, pp. 96-97.

of James Clifford, a minor canon of St. Paul's Cathedral, London, during the same period, we will obtain a good idea of the sacred music performed in cathedrals shortly after the Restoration.

Lowe's *Short Direction for the Performance of Cathedrall Service* (1661) shows that the task he set himself, possibly on account of the dislocation of cathedral music in Puritan days, was unambitious, to say the least. Morning Prayer began with a monotoned introduction and Responses, except that there was a four-part setting for festal use. The *Venite* followed and the Psalms for the day were sung antiphonally to one or two simple unison tunes, one for weekdays and the other for Sundays and festivals. Three four-part tunes were provided for the following canticles; namely, the *Te Deum* and *Benedictus* (or *Jubilate*) at Morning Prayer, and the *Magnificat* and *Nunc Dimittis* at Evening Prayer. Then the Apostles' Creed and Lord's Prayer were chanted in monotone. Unison responses followed and the choir sang "Amen" to each of the three succeeding collects.

Lowe's directions for the "Second Service" are hardly more inspiring. The celebrant begins the Lord's Prayer, reading it in a deep tone, and then the Decalogue in a higher tone, to which the choir responds similarly, unless they sing a setting with organ accompaniment. Prior to the Epistle the collects are read to which the choir sings "Amen." The Gospel follows, the choir singing, "Glory be to Thee, O Lord." Then the priest (or choir) says or sings the Nicene Creed, but as no music is provided, it is presumed to be a simple harmonised setting or a unison version. The account finishes inconclusively, leaving the reader to suppose that the choral part of the service ended before the Communion, or that the choir remained in position but was not used. It seems significant that mention is made of neither anthems nor Psalms.

James Clifford made good the latter deficiency in his *Divine Services and Anthems* (1663), which contained a collection of the words of anthems sung at St. Paul's Cathedral. The following year an enlarged second edition was issued. Lowe's very brief list of chanting tunes for Psalms and canticles is considerably augmented by Clifford who provides thirteen unison melodies and four harmonised chants in his preface. Also, the alternative canticles, *Benedicite* at Morning Prayer and *Cantate Domino* and *Deus misereatur* at Evening Prayer are included by Clifford. Interestingly, he informs us that an organ voluntary followed the Psalms at both Morning and Evening Prayer, and that another was played after the Litany and before the "Second, or Communion Service." As for anthems, two were sung in the morning (one after the third collect, and the other after the sermon), while in the evening there were two anthems in exactly parallel positions. St. Paul's appears to have had no psalmody at all.

It is noteworthy that neither Lowe nor Clifford refers to either a *Sanctus* or a *Gloria* being sung. One can only suppose that the earlier practice of restricting the Communion music to settings of the Creed and the Responses to the Decalogue continued after the Restoration at least for a few years. It was not long before a place (though not the correct one) was found for both of these Eucharistic hymns. The *Sanctus* became a kind of introit to the Communion Service, taking the place of the organ voluntary, while the *Gloria* acted as an anthem concluding the choral part of the service.

A complete choral Eucharist was celebrated in many churches only on "Sacrament Sundays," which were sometimes limited to four times a year. Even churches that celebrated weekly had a choral Communion only once a month.

2. *The Masters of Cathedral Music: Gibbons, Purcell, Blow*

Despite the liturgical limitations under which the English composers worked, their achievements were highly competent and, in several cases, notably those of Gibbons, Purcell, and Blow, even distinguished and brilliant. For this accomplishment—as it affects Purcell and Blow—some credit must be given to King Charles II for his encouragement and for the high standard of music set by the Chapel Royal. The Restoration led to a reaction against austerity, drabness, and propriety in both life and music; instead there was a demand for pomp and circumstance, for pleasure and mirth. The services in the Chapel Royal were musically superb, drawing the most talented composers, organists, and singers in the nation. They were attended by the famous, the fashionable, and the cultured. They were audiences rather than congregations, who were attracted by the new instrumental music, as by the excitingly brilliant solos demanding vocal pyrotechnics from their favourite singers, and sacred programme music in which words and actions were illustrated and imitated by the music—a theatrical gift in which Purcell in particular excelled. The Chapel Royal choir included thirty-three gentlemen singers, twelve children, and three organists. The men of the Chapel Royal were England's nearest equivalent to Italy's opera stars, delighted to display their vocal gymnastics in florid solos.

The most popular development encouraged by the Chapel Royal was the verse anthem with strings. The older contrapuntal and polyphonic music now gave way to an air supported by a single bass part, its brilliant effects created by contrasting the soloist with the choral ensemble, while the stringed instruments played a dramatically independent role which added cohesion, contrast, and colour. Following the example of Louis XIV, King of France with his "vingt-quatre violons du roi," Charles II gave his twenty-four violins (strictly, violins, violas, and cellos) the additional responsibility of taking part in the services of the Chapel Royal. The string band improved the interest in the verse anthems by its symphonies and *ritornelli*. Pepys heard the new combination of strings and voices on September 14, 1662. His report was: "This first day having vialls and other instruments to play a symphony between every verse of the anthem." On December 21, 1662, that other diarist of fame, John Evelyn, attended the Chapel Royal and noted: "Instead of the ancient grave and solemn wind musique accompanying the organ, was introduced a Consort of 24 Violins between every pause after the *French* fantastical light way, better suiting a Tavern or Play-house than a Church. This was the first time of change, and now we have no more heard the cornet which gave life to the organ, that instrument quite left off in which the English were so skilful." But innovative as was the use of stringed instruments, even more significant was the use of the solo song, foreshadowed in Gibbons, but used fully as recitative by Purcell.

Orlando Gibbons (1583-1623), despite his short life, was organist of the Chapel Royal and also of Westminster Abbey. Part of his genius was that, along with Byrd, he anticipated later developments in music. In his dramatic and declamatory style of composing Gibbons is seen not only as at the climax of Renaissance music but also as a forerunner of the Baroque style, "prospecting a new path which is to lead to Blow, Pelham Humfrey and Purcell."[18] His unusual theatrical quality can be heard to advantage in the full anthem, *Hosanna to the Son of David*, especially if this setting is compared with that of Thomas Weelkes. The latter makes all his voices together shout "Hosanna" twice in massive clarity, thus implying that the curious in the crowd had turned to

---

[18] *Tudor Church Music*, Vol. IV: *Orlando Gibbons* (eds. Buck, Fellowes, Ramsbotham and Townsend Warner, 1925), p. xxii.

worship the Messiah. Orlando Gibbons, in contrast, suggests all the excitement of a jostling, hurrying crowd, with their individual acclamations tossed backward and forward as they press to see Jesus, and quieted momentarily by the vision of eternal peace. Weelkes suggests united worship, but Purcell mounting excitement. Gibbons is humanistic as Purcell after him. Neither is a contemplative, preoccupied with mystical adoration, or even with dogma or liturgy. They exploit human situations and emotions, especially when these are expressed in action.

Of Gibbons's forty anthems (two-thirds are verse anthems), his *Lift up your heads and O clap your hands*, together with the previously mentioned *Hosanna* are among his most impressive works. His tenderness is finely exhibited in *Behold Thou hast made my days*, which was written for Dean Maxie of Windsor in 1618 when he knew that he was dying. It requires a counter-tenor soloist and a five-part choir. More impressive still is the anthem, *See, See, the Word Incarnate*, the lengthy text of which covers the birth, ministry, crucifixion, and resurrection of Christ, and is a *tour de force* of surging and driving music. His short Morning and Evening Services have never lost their popularity.

The other master composer was Henry Purcell (1659-1695), whose life was even shorter than that of Gibbons. Like his father and uncle he had been a chorister in the Chapel Royal under the direction of the masterful Captain Cooke. He studied under Blow, whom he followed when only twenty as organist of Westminster Abbey, and in 1687 he also became one of the three organists of the Chapel Royal.

Purcell's anthems are of three types.[19] The first group is composed in the older style and may be sung without accompaniment. Two admirable examples are: *Hear my prayer* and *Remember not, Lord, our offences*. A second category comprises those with an organ accompaniment. A third type of verse anthem was written for string accompaniment with symphonies and *ritornelli*. This class includes Purcell's most impressive work, yet most of these anthems are excluded from a cathedral repertoire because of their length, the special occasions for which they were written, the need for extraordinarily well-trained voices of great range, and because no organ can adequately substitute for strings. Yet these full ceremonial anthems with solo voices, trios, and quartets, with sections

---

19 The classification is that of Edmund Fellowes, *English Cathedral Music* (5th rev. edn. by J. A. Westrup, 1969), p. 163.

for full choir, and intervals for strings, provide Purcell with his greatest opportunities and which his talent took to the full.

The largest, most impressive, and most important of all Purcell's verse anthems is *My heart is inditing*, which was written for the coronation of James II on April 23, 1685, and required eight verse soloists, an eight-part choir, and strings—providing the latter with an overture lengthy enough to stand as a separate work. The polyphonic chorus leads into a brilliant Allelujah coda and united shouts of acclamation. It was as dramatic and colourful as the occasion for which it was composed.

Another splendidly resounding anthem of Purcell's is his *Blow up the trumpet in Sion*. His most moving anthem is *Thou knowest, Lord, the secrets of our hearts*, which was written for the funeral of Queen Mary in 1695.

A less famous anthem, *Praise the Lord, O my soul*, will be analysed to show how elaborate verse anthems had grown since the Restoration. It has a dozen separate sections. The first is an orchestral overture beginning in common time and then becoming faster. The second section has six-part verses for *Praise the Lord* (with high voices responding to the low voices, and then all together). The third section is an orchestral interlude. The fourth is another six-part verse, starting as if it repeated the second section. The fifth section is another orchestral interlude. The sixth section is a slow verse trio: *The Lord is full of compassion and mercy*. The seventh section is a tenor solo: *He hath not dealt with us*. The eighth is a *ritornello*, repeating the second section of the overtures. Section nine is a bass recitative: *For look how high the heaven is*. The tenth section is a six-part verse, *O speak good of the Lord*, with the high voices answered by the low voices, and then all together. The eleventh section is another *ritornello*, deriving from the fifth section. The twelfth and final section is the full chorus singing, *Praise thou the Lord*. Such anthems could take as long as twenty minutes to perform.

Purcell's genius is found in the variety and quality of his music (he wrote more secular than sacred music), his ability to rise to a great ceremonial occasion, his brilliance of matching accompaniment to dramatic words,[20] and the over-all inventiveness of his effects.

For more mystical or meditative music (and less theatrical bril-

[20] For examples, the music to "the singing of birds" and "the voice of the turtle" in Purcell's *My beloved spake*.

liance) one would have to turn to the compositions of John Blow (1649-1708), most of whose work was sacred music. A prodigy,[21] at nineteen he was appointed organist of Westminster Abbey, after being a chorister in the Chapel Royal of which he became Master of the Children in 1674. About three years later he also became one of the three organists of the Chapel Royal, and in 1687 he also became Master of the Children at St. Paul's Cathedral. In 1695, on Purcell's death, he succeeded his pupil, becoming again the organist of Westminster Abbey. He was easily the most experienced organist and choir-master of his century.

This prolific, but unequal, composer produced nine complete services, eleven Latin motets, and ninety-six English anthems (twenty-eight with orchestral symphonies), and several settings of canticles.

He is inevitably compared with his contemporary Purcell, and few can stand the comparison as well as he. Certainly his contribution to James II's coronation service, *God spake sometimes in visions*, is a noble parallel to Purcell's *My heart is inditing*, composed for the same occasion. Each represents the acme of English Baroque sacred music.

Blow's outstanding gift was the ability to provide settings expressive of sadness, tenderness, penitence, nobility, resolution, and desperate grief. *O Lord, I have sinned*, an anthem prepared for General Monck's funeral in 1670 is outstanding in its evocation of sympathy. He is, however, not as successful in expressing gratitude, jubilation, or contentment.

Yet he is equalled only by Byrd in his poignant and mystical empathy with Christ's sufferings as in his *My God, my God, look on me*, which plumbs the depths of the Saviour's cry of dereliction insofar as a human can, and which expresses the quintessence of pity. It is one of the most moving anthems in the English language.

Other full anthems of great power are his eight-part works, notably *God is our hope and strength* and *O Lord God of my salvation*. Their rich concentrated contrapuntal harmonies are as subtle as the iridescence on a butterfly's wing caught in a shaft of sunlight, but as powerful in thrust as a lion. His Latin anthems also are inspiring. The five-part setting of *Salvator Mundi* is gloriously sonorous. It reaches perfection in a passage of ethereal beauty, *auxiliare nobis*, pleading humanity's desperate need of God's power

[21] Three of his compositions were included in Clifford's collection of 1663, when he was only fourteen years of age.

and holiness, following the choir's singing of *qui per crucem et sanguinem redemisti nos.* At such points Blow's mysticism becomes luminous.

This necessarily sketchy account of three great composers has at least shown the extraordinary riches in sacred music available to the English cathedrals in the seventeenth century. Admittedly, we have concentrated on the Chapel Royal at Whitehall, Westminster Abbey, and St. Paul's Cathedral. But we may assume that the cathedral tradition at Salisbury was well maintained or George Herbert would not have walked twice a week from Bemerton to attend worship there. Wise, its organist and choir-master, was paid an unconscious tribute when Herbert averred that the time he spent in prayer and at cathedral music elevated his soul and was his heaven upon earth. Lichfield Cathedral choir, too, had almost as high a reputation after the Restoration.

The real musical importance of verse anthems in cathedral music, however, was the opportunity it gave for full expression to the evolving musical style of the seventeenth century. This has been defined with great clarity by Christopher Dearnley as "the departure from many-voiced music to an air supported by a single bass part, from a continuous interweaving to the clear-cut definition of sections with cadence and modulation, and from the inner intensity of polyphony to the dramatic contrasts obtainable from the juxtaposition of various combinations of solo and ensemble."[22] An exclusive dependence upon metrical psalmody's music would have been a narrow groove indeed, if not a grave.

It is difficult to understand how cultured Puritans, many of whom were music-lovers, could have jettisoned this rich tradition of sacred music unless they were convinced that the Word of God refused to countenance it.

Already we have seen that cathedral music violated by its obscurity and its complexity two strong tenets of the Reformed faith, those of edification and the priesthood of all believers. We have yet to realise the importance of the alternative, sung with such gusto by the Puritans, Scriptural paraphrases in metre and rhyme.

3. *The Attractions of Metrical Psalmody*

Superficially, to choose metrical Psalms as a musical diet in preference to verse anthems seems like selecting Shakespeare's "remainder biscuit" after the voyage in lieu of a five-course dinner.

---

[22] Dearnley, *op. cit.*, p. 41.

Yet there were attractions in this rhymed psalmody more than met the ear.

In trying to evaluate it, one must not make the mistake of considering it only as poetry. The awkward inversions of style, the doggerel to which it often descended, the largely unvarying boredom of the predictable stresses of common metre, the obvious diction and the forced rhymes, only mask the secret of its attraction, which is almost exclusively theological in character. The Puritans and many of the common folk of England who were not Puritans loved them because they were *God's own Word at one slight remove.*

Foxe's *Book of Martyrs* kept the English Bible before the imagination of the English people as a volume sanctified by the blood of the English Protestant martyrs, and reminded them that England continued an independent nation only because it had broken the thralldom of Rome after Queen Mary's death and had defeated the Catholic Spanish Armada. The Bible and the Protestant succession on the throne were intimately interrelated so that the Bible was in a peculiar sense the Book of England's destiny, quite apart from its intrinsic religious merits.[23]

This popularity of the Bible was greatly increased by the Scriptural exclusiveness of the Puritan movement from 1570 to its apex in the years following 1643, when all traditions in church and state were tested by the Biblical rule, and only Scripture was allowed in divine service as the vehicle of praise.

Furthermore, during the struggle with the Cavaliers the Roundheads, who were Puritans, adopted many metrical Psalms as their battle-songs.[24] These Old Testament thought-forms suited them admirably, with faith hammered out on the anvil of difficulty, the unyielding controversy with God's enemies, the sacred invective and vivid vituperation, and in the glare of the Psalms they saw themselves as the elect army fighting under the banner of Christ the King and Son of David against King Charles. Psalmody was the song of wrath and war.

The most renowned stories associated with the metrical Psalms are not about those revered today, such as Psalms 23 and 84; rather they concern the fighting Psalms such as Psalms 68, 74,

[23] This theme is carefully worked out in William Haller's *Foxe's Book of Martyrs and the Elect Nation* (New York, 1963).

[24] Erik Routley in *Hymns and Human Life* (1952), p. 59, writes: ". . . there was the more primitive and human fact that the Puritanism of seventeenth century England found in the Psalter just what it wanted."

and 124.[25] The most famous story of all concerns Psalm 117. Cromwell's force of 11,000 men defeated Leslie's army of 23,000 at Dunbar. The Ironsides surprised the Scottish army at five in the morning in the pale gleam of the moonlight, and Cromwell's cavalry and infantry shouted their watchword, "The Lord of Hosts." A complete rout followed as the Scottish horsemen broke and fled, crushing the undisciplined thousands of infantry behind them. The pursuit of the fugitives continued for eight miles until Cromwell halted and ordered his men to sing Psalm 117. "It was but a brief respite. Practical in his religion as in all else, Cromwell chose the shortest psalm in the book."[26]

One could well believe that the Psalms were the iron-rations of Cromwell's Ironsides, so thoroughly was their chief commander's thought and vocabulary nourished on them. R. E. Prothero rightly observed that the spirit of the Psalms governed him in supreme crises, that he cited from them at the most dramatic stages of his career, while in his public despatches and private letters, as in his speeches before Parliament, he made their phraseology entirely his own.[27]

It is exceedingly difficult for us to imagine how almost universal the use of the psalter was. Psalms were sung at the Lord Mayor's feasts at city banquets; soldiers sang them on the march or beside camp fires; ploughmen and carters whistled or sang them at their tasks; and pilgrims sought a new continent in which to gain liberty to sing only the Psalms. Far from being the songs of the sour-faced, they were sung by ladies and their lovers.

The translation of the Psalms into the vernacular is not to be attributed to Calvin, but to Clément Marot, the court poet of Francis I. He began by translating Psalm 6 into French verse in 1533; seven years later his translation of the Psalms were highly popular throughout the French court, and by 1554, the year of Marot's death, he had fifty metrical Psalms to his name. The enthusiasm for the rhymed Psalms is finely depicted by Prothero, who writes:

> When Marot's Psalms first appeared they were sung to popular tunes alike by Roman Catholics and Calvinists. No one delighted in the *sanctes chansonettes* more passionately than the Dauphin. He sang them himself. . . . To win his favour the gentlemen of the court begged him to choose for

[25] See R. E. Prothero (Lord Ernle), *The Psalms in Human Life* (1903), pp. 194-95 and 134, for stories about the 68th and 124th metrical psalms.
[26] *Ibid.*, p. 194.   [27] *Ibid.*, p. 189.

. each a Psalm. Courtiers adopted their special Psalms, just as they adopted their particular arms, mottoes, and liveries.[28]

It was to Calvin's credit that he moved these metrical Psalms from their secular milieu into the worship of the French Reformed church in Strasbourg. While they were as yet unpublished, he introduced twelve of them into his first psalter, the *Aucun Pseaumes et Cantiques mys en Chant* (1539). These were popularised in English translation by William Whittingham, a refugee in Geneva from the Marian persecution and future Dean of Durham, in the Anglo-Genevan Psalter of 1556. Their popularity was assured when they were matched with popular, catchy tunes known as "Genevan jigs," though the Genevan tunes of Bourgeois were joyously solemn.

Proponents of the metrical Psalms encouraged Psalm-singing in the hope that they would drive out bawdy ballads. The preface to the 1562 edition of the Old Version states that it was intended "to be used of all sorts of people privately for their solace and comfort: laying apart all ungodly songs and ballads which tend only to the nourishing of vice and corrupting of youth." Nor was the devil to have all the best tunes!

The relevance of the metrical Psalms to seventeenth-century Puritanism may perhaps best be appreciated if we consider, following Sir John Hawkins's suggestion,[29] the treatise which they prefixed to their earliest impressions of the metrical Psalms and which was attributed to St. Athanasius. The following citations from it should indicate how apt it seemed to the circumstances of the fighting and God-fearing Roundheads:

> If thou seest that evill men lay snares for thee, and therefore desirest God's eares to heare thy praiers, sing the 5 psalme.
>
> If thine enemies cluster against thee, and go about with their bloody hand to destroy thee, go not thou about by man's helpe to revenge it, for al men's judgments are not trustie, but require God to be judge, for he alone is judge, and say the 26, 35, 43 psalmes.
>
> If they press more fiercelie on thee, although they be in numbers like an armed hoast, fear them not which thus reject

---

[28] *Ibid.*, p. 51.
[29] In his *General History of Music* (1776), Chap. CXVI.

thee, as though thou wert not annointed and elect by God, but sing the 27 psalme.

If they yet be so impudent that they lay in wait against thee, so that it is not lawful for thee to have any vocation by them, regard them not, but sing to God the 48 psalme.

If thou hast suffered false accusation before the King, and seeest the Divel to triumph therat, go aside and say the 50 psalme.

The Psalms were the creeds and battle-songs of the Puritans. In them they found a supernatural sanction for their conduct and comfort in perplexity and danger. Through them *Vox Dei* became *vox populi*, which was both solace and a spiritual danger.

One might readily assume that because of their closeness to sacred Scripture all Christians in this century would have welcomed metrical psalmody, whatever their reservations about verse anthems and orchestral interludes. Yet, despite all the attractions of the metrical Psalms, there were others, even among the dissenting religious groups, who utterly refused to use them, and for a variety of reasons.

The General Baptists, in this true to the tradition of their pioneer, John Smyth,[30] in rejecting all set forms in worship as a quenching of the Spirit, also rejected metrical psalmody. On this view the only acceptable spiritual songs in divine worship were charismatic solos. Thomas Grantham, their leader, certainly held this as his conviction. In his *Christianismus Primitivus* (1678) he rejected "musical singing with a multitude of voices in rhyme and metre," while approving that "such persons as God has gifted to tell forth his mighty acts . . . should have liberty and convenient opportunity to celebrate the high praises of God one by one in the churches of God, and that with such words as the nature of the matter and present occasion requires. . . ."[31] The controversy was still acute in 1689, for the General Assembly decided after thorough discussion that year that "it was not deemed any way safe for the churches to admit such carnal formalities [as metrical psalms sung in unison] . . . the singing of one was the same as the

---

[30] See John Smyth, *The Differences of the Churches of the Separation* (1605), p. v: "singinging [sic] a psalme is a parte of spirituall worship therefore it is unlawfull to have the booke before the eye in time of singinge a psalme."

[31] Cited by Spencer Curwen, *Studies in Music and Worship*, 5 Vols. (1880-1885), I, p. 95.

singing of the whole, as the prayers of the one are the prayers of the whole congregation."[32]

A closely related group, the Seventh Day Baptists, held similar views. Francis Bampfield, formerly a Prebendary of Exeter, became a Sabbatarian pastor. He claimed to have had a vision of Christ which "raised him into a higher way of Latter-Day-Glory-hymnifying, than his former way of singing by Mens Forms, read out of a Book, could reach unto."[33]

So strong was the conviction that all set forms, whether of prayers like the Book of Common Prayer, or of sermons like the Anglican Books of Homilies, or of praise like the metrical Psalms, were contrary to the ineluctable leading of the Spirit, that the early Independents in the Westminster Assembly scrupled a metrical psalter. Baillie, one of the Church of Scotland Commissioners and a hammer of sectaries, reports the views of Philip Nye, the leader of the small Independent group: "Mr. Nye spoke much against a tie to any Psalter and somewhat against the singing of paraphrases, as of preaching homilies; we *understand* will mightily oppose it; for the Psalter is a great part of our conformity which we cannot let pass until our church be well advised with it."[34] It was, however, a scruple which the Independents quickly overcame, and metrical psalmody in New England, according to the report of John Cotton, was one of their most valued ordinances: "Before Sermon, and many times after, wee sing a Psalme."[35]

Another argument against metrical psalmody used by the stricter sects was its unsuitability for a mixed or promiscuous congregation. The Psalms were the songs of God's covenanted people, the elect, and they were misused if sung by the unregenerate. The children of Israel had lamented in their Babylonian Captivity, "How shall we sing the Lord's song in a strange land?" True Christians were similarly putting themselves into the captivity of the ungodly by singing Scriptural songs with them.

Yet another negative criticism of the metrical Psalms and a powerful one was that God's Word was changed in meaning, however slight, when it was put through the straitjacket of rhyme and

---

[32] *Minutes of the General Assembly of the General Baptists, 1654-1728* (ed. W. T. Whitley, 1909), p. 27.

[33] *A name, an after-one; or* "Ονομα καινου, *a name, a new one, in the latter-day glory* (1681), p. 4.

[34] Benjamin Hanbury, *Nonconformist Memorials*, 3 Vols. (1839-1844), II, p. 225.

[35] *The Way of the Churches of Christ in New England* (1645), p. 66.

metre. Even when the non-Biblical words were little more than conjunctions, and were italicized to draw attention to the least departure from Holy Scripture, the fact remained that the words of the Word of God were no longer inalterably sacrosanct.

The argument of guilt by association was also used. The Roman Catholics by their antiphonal recitation of the Latin Psalms in their Daily Office in monasteries, the Anglicans by the chanting of prose Psalms in their cathedrals and their responsive recitation in parish churches,[36] both used and misused psalmody in worship. Therefore the sectarians avoided contamination by refusing to use them in worship.

During the days of persecution for the heirs of the Puritans, when they worshipped in secret conventicles, it became dangerous to sing Psalms as they might disclose their whereabouts to informers trying to trap them with the Conventicle Act. The latter held Nonconformists were forbidden to hold meetings at which more than five persons were present. At a conventicle gathered in St. Thomas's parish, Southwark, it was recorded: "1692. April 1st. We met at Mr. Russell's in Ironmonger Lane, where Mr. Lambert of Deadman's Place, Southwark, administered to us the ordinance of the Lord's Supper, and we sang a psalm in a low voice."[37] The view that it was dangerous to sing Psalms in penal times can, however, be questioned. If the conventiclers in Southwark sang in a low voice not to give the alarm, the Broadmead Baptists in Bristol sang Psalms to imply that they were a convivial group rather than a congregation at worship. It was prearranged that when intruders came in "we were singing, that they could not find anyone preaching, but all singing."[38]

A summary of these objections to metrical psalmody is provided by that arch-conservative Baptist author, Isaac Marlow, in his ominously entitled book, *Prelimiting Forms of praising God,*

[36] It should be noted, however, that while in the Prayer Book there was substituted a vernacular prose translation for the Vulgate Psalms, an extra-liturgical custom developed whereby a metrical psalm was sung before and after the prescribed order of worship. This appears to have obtained temporary official sanction early in Elizabeth's reign, and may have been due to the influence of the returning Marian exiles. The Elizabethan Injunctions to the clergy in 1559 directed: "For the comforting of such as delight in music, it may be permitted that at the beginning or end of Common Prayer, either at Morning or Evening, there may be sung a hymn or such like song to the praise of Almighty God, in the best melody and music that may be devised, having respect that the sentence of the hymn be understood and perceived."

[37] Spencer Curwen, *op. cit.,* I, p. 84.

[38] *Broadmead Records* (ed. E. B. Underhill, 1847), p. 226.

Vocally sung by all the Church together, Proved to be no Gospel-Ordinance (1691). He uses five main arguments to make his case. The first assumes that the essence of singing is the praise of God, but this is not necessarily "tunable." Secondly, women are prohibited from speaking in the assembly (I Corinthians 14:34-35), therefore promiscuous singing must be rejected. Thirdly, singing in the primitive church is no precedent for contemporary singing, since the former was made possible by the dispensation of an extraordinary gift limited to that era. Fourthly, unison singing demands precomposed forms, and these are as unwarrantable in singing as in praying. Fifthly and finally, there is no New Testament ground for believers to unite with unbelievers in singing God's praise.

Thus acute scrupulosity prevented many from using the songs of Sion, whether for Biblical, ecclesiological, or psychological reasons or excuses. The consequence was that it became necessary for defenders of the metrical psalms to provide dissuasives from such attitudes.

The apologists for metrical psalmody asked first: What is more suitable for God's praise than God's own Word? Indeed, not to use the Psalms and to prefer human compositions is an insult to the Divine Majesty as well as a denial of original sin. As David had been inspired by the Holy Ghost to compose his Psalms, we can rest assured of their acceptance with God. Furthermore, there is psalmody and hymnody in the New Testament and therefore for the people of the New Covenant.

In favour of metrical psalmody it was also argued that its simplicity in common metre made it accessible to God's people in the way that anthems were not. Hence William Whittingham issued the first Sternhold and Hopkins metrical Psalter with music in Geneva, along with *The Forme of Prayers . . . used in the English congregation at Geneva; and approved by the famous and godly learned man, John Calvyn* (1556). The preface denounces elaborate or obscure church music, and, by implication defends the metrical psalter it introduces:

> But as there is no gift of God so precious or excellent that
> Satan hath not after a sort drawn to himself and corrupt[ed]:
> so hath he most impudently abused this notable gift of sing-
> ing, chiefly by the papists, his ministers, in disfiguring it,
> partly by strange language that cannot edify, and partly by a

275

curious wanton sort, hiring men to tickle the ears and flatter the fantasies, not esteeming it as a gift approved by the Word of God, profitable for the church, and confirmed by all antiquity. . . .

In conformity with this view the tunes were unharmonised and the underlay was carefully syllabic.

It was also argued that the putting of the Psalms into metre and rhyme made them much more easily memorised by the common people. This was particularly important when many folk were still illiterate. But there was the objection that metre and rhyme significantly altered the wording of the Psalms. This was countered by the ingenious but valid argument that the originals were Hebrew poetry and that it is better translation to turn them into poetry than to leave them as prose.

As for the arguments that Marlow had prepared, that a pre-composed form invalidated worship, that Paul commanded women to silence in worship, and that God's praise ought not to be sung by a congregation including the unregenerate, it is significant that Benjamin Keach, pioneer Baptist hymnodist, disposed of them rapidly.[39] He saw no more reason to exclude a precomposed metrical Psalm than a precomposed sermon, and was convinced that he had the assistance of the Holy Spirit in each. If the silence of women in worship were to be absolute, how could they then give an account of their conversion before the church and be admitted to membership? He cites two passages in I Corinthians 14, where the apostle speaks of unbelievers entering the church, and argues that praise as well as preaching can instruct such in the ways of God.

Ultimately, the powerful Genevan tradition of metrical psalmody overcame any initial scruples on the part of the Puritan Independents. The Presbyterian Puritans were never in any doubt as to their value. It was not long before the Puritans were known as "the Psalm-roaring Saints." The duty of Psalm-singing was canonised in the Westminster *Directory* for both public and private worship. It encouraged psalmody strongly as unison singing and so apt for congregations, contrasted with the elaboration of anthems to be sung only by expert musicians, and it was recommended as Scriptural and non-traditional. The *Directory* urged: "It is the duty of

[39] In *The Breach Repair'd in God's Worship* (1691), a landmark in the history of English hymnody.

276

Christians to praise God publickly by singing of psalms together
in the congregation, and privately in the family. In singing of
psalms the voice is to be tunably and gravely ordered, but the chief
care must be to sing with understanding and with grace in the
heart, making melody unto the Lord."[40]

4. *The Metrical Versions and Their Tunes*

Many interesting poetical versions of the Psalms were published
during the seventeenth century but almost all, Milton's excepted,
were because of obscure language or metrical subtlety unsuitable
for common praise. Partial translations of the Psalms were written
by George Herbert (1632), John Donne (1633), Phineas Fletcher
(1633), and Richard Crashaw (1634). Bishop Hall translated the
first ten with an easy naturalness (1607), and Lord Bacon translated a few (1625). A version, with considerable poetical grace,
set to the music of Henry Lawes, was that of George Sandys
(1636), son of an Archbishop of York.

John Milton translated Psalms 80 to 88 in 1648 directly from
the Hebrew. There could be no finer illustration of Puritanism's
concern to preserve the exact meaning of the oracles of God than
this, for the Hebrew words are printed in the margin, and every
word not in the original is printed in italics. In addition to exactness, these versions have the sonority and syntactical subtlety that
were Milton's gifts. Three of his paraphrases are the exception in
outliving the generation for which they were written. They comprise: his work as a fifteen-year-old, "Let us with a gladsome mind"
(Psalm 136) written in 1623; "How lovely are thy dwellings fair"
(Psalm 84) and "The Lord will come and not be slow" (a paraphrase of selections from Psalms 82, 85, and 86), both published
in 1648.

Other distinctively Puritan versions were the complete and rival
metrical psalmodies of Rous and Barton, and the important Scottish Psalter (1650). The last mentioned provided the justly celebrated version of Psalm 23, "The Lord's my shepherd." Francis
Rous's Psalter of 1641 was an attempt to meet the request of the
Committee of Peers in their Report on Religion of 1640 that "the
meeter in the Psalms should be corrected and allowed of publicly."
Thus it was an attempt to improve on Sternhold and Hopkins, the
"Old Version." A second edition was ordered to be printed by the

[40] *Reliquiae Liturgicae*: Vol. III: *The Parliamentary Directory* (ed. Peter Hall,
Bath, 1847), p. 81.

House of Commons in 1643. The Westminster *Directory* (1644) required that each literate person should have a Psalm book and Rous's third edition was ordered to be printed by the Westminster Assembly of Divines, of which Rous was a lay member. He was also a Member of Parliament and Speaker of the House of Commons. The Scottish Commissioners, however, suspected him of heterodoxy and thought him too much in Cromwell's pocket to approve of his version, while they wanted their own version. The House of Lords preferred the version of Rous's rival, William Barton, minister of St. Martin's, Leicester, who had produced first and second editions of his Psalter in 1644 and 1645. The Lords submitted his revised edition of 1646 to the Westminster Assembly but it was rejected by them. The Assembly equally refused to sanction exclusively the choice of the Commons, namely Rous's version. Sternhold and Hopkins inevitably continued to reign supreme, its popularity untouched by the post-Restoration attempts at metrical psalmody made by Richard Baxter, Sir John Denham, and John Patrick.

The popularity of the Old Version was quite remarkable.[41] It lasted for 147 years. Sternhold's Psalter was first published in 1549. Sternhold and Hopkins was first published with music, as we have seen, in 1556 in Geneva by William Whittingham, which encouraged a great sale for it among Puritan households. By 1561 the Old Version became the standard English metrical Psalter. The rapid proliferation of editions underlined its popularity. Between 1560 and 1579 there were at least 20 editions; between 1580 and 1600 the number had grown to 45 editions; between 1600 and 1620 it had increased to 65 editions; and between 1620 and 1640 over 100 appeared.

It was abundantly clear that Psalm-singing with the aid of the easily memorised stanzas of Sternhold and Hopkins was regarded as the most divine part of divine service. Heylin reported that "the reading of psalms with the first and second lessons being heard in many places with a covered head, but all men sitting bare-headed when the psalm was sung."[42]

The poor quality of the poetry makes it extremely difficult to account for the popularity of Sternhold and Hopkins. Certainly there was little variety in metre or tune. Of the 150 Psalms 134

---

[41] Peter Le Huray, *Music and the Reformation in England, 1549-1660* (1967), p. 376.

[42] Cited by John Julian, *A Dictionary of Hymnology* (rev. edn., 1925), p. 864b.

were in common metre, which has a predictable jog-trot about it. The tunes were generally dull and only 47 of the Psalms had a tune of their own. The contorted, labouring, halting, and dreary monotony of the verses fully justified Fuller's criticism of them that "their piety was better than their poetry; they had drank more of Jordan than of Helicon."[43] Probably the inherent weakness of this and other versions in the same century was, as Baxter said in the preface to his own version, due to the fact that "the ear desireth greater melody than strict versions will allow."[44] Exact fidelity to the original ruled out almost all hymnody in this period; it also practically destroyed the freedom desirable within the bonds of metrical psalmody to permit poetry to be written rather than mere verse. For the illiterate or those with a poor memory these religious jingles filled a useful function, and this must be the most important single factor accounting for their success among the commonalty.

Some attempts, however, were made to provide a greater variety of tunes, but most were too elaborate to be accepted by the majority of people. Robert Tailour prepared complicated five-part settings in the contrapuntal style of Tudor anthems in 1615, and John Cosin had composed a five-part harmonised metrical psalter in 1585. It was, however, Thomas Ravenscroft with his *Whole Booke of Psalmes* (1621) with harmonised settings, who successfully provided additional new, simple, and therefore acceptable tunes.

The dreariness of metrical psalmody was compounded by the practice of "lining-out." That is, each line of the words of a metrical Psalm was first read or intoned by the minister, precentor, or clerk, then in turn taken up and sung by the congregation.[45] This meant each Psalm took twice as long and, since it was thought to be reverent by proceeding at a funereal pace, the psalmody must sometimes have seemed as tiring as an unending road. The disadvantage of the lining-out system was that the congregation concentrated so fully on what was going to be sung that they forgot what they had sung; also the sense often spilled over from one line

---

[43] Thomas Fuller, *The Church History of Britain* (1655), Vol. IV, p. 73.

[44] Julian, *op. cit.*, p. 919a.

[45] The *Directory* prescribed lining-out as a hopefully interim measure in 1645: "That the whole congregation may join herein, every one that can read is to have a Psalm-book; and all others not disabled by age or otherwise, are to be exhorted to learn to read. But for the present, where many of the congregation cannot read, it is convenient that the Minister, or some other fit person appointed by him and the other ruling officers, do read the Psalm line by line, before the singing thereof." (*Reliquiae Liturgicae*, ed. Peter Hall, III, p. 81.)

to the next. Furthermore, the clerk in the local parish church might have a defective sense of pitch and pace and rhythm. One suspects that the clerk who had served Buxted parish church for forty-three years received an obituary that might have been only too suitable for many others of his calling, "whose melody warbled forth as though he had been thumped in the back by a stone."[46]

In these circumstances it was to Ravenscroft's credit that he tried to introduce some variety in the singing of the psalter. His intriguing preface shows that his aim was to pick tunes appropriate to the character of each Psalm. He recommended singers to adopt the following rules:

1. "That psalms of tribulation should be sung with a low voice and long measure"—these included Psalms 6, 32, 38, 51, 102, 130, and 143.

2. "That psalms of thanksgiving be sung with a voice indifferent, neither too loud, nor too soft, and with a measure neither too swift nor too slow."

3. "That psalms of rejoicing be sung with a loud voice [and] a swift and jocund measure"—these included Psalms 33, 34, 47, 95, 96, 98, 99, 108, 113, 117, 135, 136, 145, 147, 148, and 150.[47]

The only other radical attempt to enliven the tunes of the Old Version was as desperate as it was disastrous. William Slatyer's *Psalmes or Songs of Sion turned into the language and set to the tunes of a strange land* (1635) was far too secular for those who admired sacred music, since he chose as settings for his Psalms the popular tunes of the day, such as "Goe from my window" for Psalms 8 and 11, and "Susan," "Sweet Robin," and "The Queen of Love" for others.[48] It was too much to hope that boudoir ballad tunes might be used to sing the praises of Calvin's august God.

In some quarters, however, Psalm-singing was not at all popular. Strictly speaking, it was illegal to mingle metrical psalmody with the Anglican liturgy in the seventeenth century, whatever Elizabethan Injunctions might have permitted. Its Genevan origins, its development into a Puritan badge of loyalty, and its intrusion into the Prayer Book services, produced frowns from the ecclesiastical hierarchy, such as Laud, Wren, and Cosin. Since,

---

[46] Dearnley, *op. cit.*, p. 146.
[47] Peter Le Huray, *op. cit.*, pp. 382-83.
[48] *Ibid.*, pp. 383-84.

nonetheless, metrical psalmody had come to stay, it became necessary even for high churchmen to accommodate to it. In fact, while the Puritans and evangelical Anglicans preferred metrical psalmody sung to common metre tunes in unison, the high-church party preferred elaborate harmonised tunes such as Tailour's anthem-like settings, John Cosin's five-part settings, as well as the harmonised musicianship of Ravenscroft.[49]

Just beyond our period, in 1696, the monopoly of the Old Version came to an end, and it was replaced by Tate and Brady's *A New Version of the Psalms of David, Fitted to the Tunes used in Churches*. It appeared under the best auspices. It was sanctioned by the sovereign and recommended by the Archbishop of Canterbury and Compton, the Bishop of London. Its authors clearly wished it to be regarded as a substitute for the Sternhold and Hopkins psalter which had become increasingly disenchanting to the musical public.

It is not a distinguished publication, but it is smoother verse than the Old Version. Some of Sternhold and Hopkins was ruggedly robust and characterful in comparison with the frequent insipidity of Tate and Brady. On a few rare occasions the New Version rose to the occasion. Among those would have to be included their versions of Psalm 33 ("Through all the changing scenes of life"), Psalm 42 ("As pants the hart"), Psalm 51 ("Have mercy, Lord, on me"), and Psalm 84 ("Oh God of hosts, the mighty Lord") which have continued to appear in hymnbooks even in the twentieth century.

5. *The Reluctant Birth of Hymnody*

The more one studies the limitations of metrical psalmody, the sorrier one is that Protestant England did not follow the example of the Protestants of Luther's Germany in encouraging the writing and singing of hymns as freer transcripts of Christian faith and experience, without the bibliolatrous restrictions of metrical psalmody. In this matter, at least, the influence of Luther would have been better than the impact of Calvin.[50]

The reluctance of the English people to turn to hymnody can be explained by the very same factors that made psalmody so very popular. Such would include the power of the Bible in English which was regarded as the well-spring of national Reformation

---

[49] K. R. Long, *op. cit.*, pp. 209-10.
[50] See Charles Stanley Phillips, *Hymnody Past and Present* (1937), pp. 123-24.

and individual renovation of life; the fact that so much of the Bible consisted of songs and the rapturous praises of holy men and women; and, above all, the conviction that in using only the words of the Word of God men believed themselves to be secure from human error.

Despite the dominance of metrical psalmody in the seventeenth century, there were some notable exceptions to the rule. These were chiefly of two types. One was a handful of hymns written for private devotion. Such could be the free compositions of devout minds for the reading or singing of the few so inclined. One example would be Cosin's fine translation of *Veni Creator*, beginning, "Come, Holy Ghost, our souls inspire" which was to be found in his *Collection of Private Devotions* (1627), which eventually found a place in the Prayer Book of 1662. In 1623 the poet George Wither made a valiant attempt to produce and publish the first hymnbook of the Church of England entitled *Hymns and Songs of the Church*, with seven tunes contributed by Orlando Gibbons. His preface tells how he was invited by clergymen to collect and transmute into lyrical poetry the many hymns dispersed throughout the canonical Scriptures. To these he added "such parcels of Holy Writ, Creeds, and Songs" as he thought wise. Its importance is that it extended the material available for religious songs, for these included festal days, Holy Communion, and providential events in the life of the nation. He attributes its unpopularity to the attempt of the Stationers' Company to quash it, but the banality of some of its stanzas[51] might prove a complementary, if not an alternative explanation.

A second group of hymns consists of sacred poems that were written without any intention of their being used in public or private worship, but which later ages discovered as potential hymns. John Wesley,[52] for example, discovered George Herbert's and edited them unsparingly, but four of them are now popular hymns: "Let all the world in every corner sing"; "The God of love my shepherd is"; "Teach me my God and King" and "King of Glory."

---

[51] The following stanza from Song 13 is an example of his rendering of the First Canticle of the Song of Solomon:

> Oh, my love, how comely now,
> And how beautiful art thou!
> Thou of dove-like eyes a pair
> Shining hast within thy hair,
> And thy looks like kidlings be
> Which from Gilead hill we see.

[52] See Erik Routley, *Hymns and Human Life* (1952), p. 58.

Such modern editors as the Anglican Percy Dearmer[53] and the Free churchman Garrett Horder have also found hymns in the divine poems of the metaphysical poets, including Donne, Traherne, and Vaughan, and a recent edition of the Roman Catholic *Westminster Hymnal* includes hymns by Richard Crashaw.

Other notable hymns of the seventeenth century are Dean Samuel Crossman's "Jerusalem on high" and the delicate "My song is love unknown"; also Richard Baxter's noble hymn of faith as obedience and trust "Lord it belongs not to my care" and his seraphic song on the Communion of saints, "He wants not friends who hath thy love." During the last two decades of the century the saintly and prophetic Bishop Thomas Ken produced those masterpieces of devotion, his Morning Hymn ("Awake my soul and with the sun") and his Evening Hymn ("Glory to thee my God this night"). Both hymns end with the rhymed doxology, now famous throughout the English-speaking world, beginning, "Praise God from whom all blessings flow." It is a fitting monument to the piety and sensitive consciences of the Non-Juring divines.

The majority of these hymn-writers were clergy of the Church of England,[54] with the exception of the Roman Catholic priest, Crashaw. But what of the contribution of the Baptists or the Independents to hymnody? As we have seen, the General Baptists refused to use metrical psalmody, and therefore *a fortiori* hymnody. The Independents were, like the Presbyterians, deeply committed to metrical psalmody, and their pioneer hymnodist Isaac Watts only began to write in the last decade of the century while in his teens.[55] It was a Calvinistic or Particular Baptist minister, Benjamin Keach, who inaugurated Free church hymnody and in doing so demonstrated astonishing tact and patience in combatting entrenched religious prejudice against change, which the conservatives regarded as lusting after the garlic and onions of Egypt.

Apparently in 1673, Benjamin Keach, as minister of Horsleydown Baptist church in Southwark, persuaded his congregation to sing a hymn at the close of the celebration of the Lord's Supper in imitation of Christ and his disciples at the end of the Last Supper.

---

[53] For Dearmer's contributions to Anglican worship, see Davies, *op. cit.*, V, pp. 284f., and 110f.

[54] Yet they were very much in advance of their church, for the Church of England did not officially authorise hymns in worship until 1821. (See Routley, *op. cit.*, p. 8.)

[55] His first hymn was written to answer his father's challenge to prove he could compose something better than the current metrical psalmody. It was "Behold the glories of the Lamb," which was produced ca. 1695.

Later he extended the practice to days of thanksgivings and Baptisms, and, finally, to the regular Lord's Day worship. Writing directly to his own congregation in the preface to his *The Breach Repair'd in God's Worship* (1691) we can see what a patient gradualist he had been:

> 'Tis no small grief to me to see (since the Church in such a solemn manner agreed to sing the praises of God on the Lord's Day) to find some of you so offended; I am perswaded 'tis for want of Consideration, for you have no new thing brought in among you. Hath not the Church sung at breaking of bread always for 16 or 18 yeares last past, and could not nor would it omit it in the time of the late Persecution? . . . And have we not for this 12 or 14 years sung in *mixt Assemblies on Days of Thanksgiving*, and never any offended at it, as ever I heard?[56]

Keach composed his own hymns[57] and it is only fair to say that Baptists would rather their seventeenth-century contribution to hymnody was represented by John Bunyan's song, "Who would true valour see"[58] than by any composition of Keach's. His importance is solely that of a pioneer who points the way to the future, from Old Testament paraphrase to Christian hymnody. It will be the grand aim of Watts to cross Jordan to the promised land by the only possible path. As Watts put it himself: "In all places I have kept my grand design in view; and that is to teach my author [David] to speak like a Christian."[59]

Now that the end of the seventeenth century has been reached, it is possible to make out the various slow stages by which hym-

---

[56] *Op. cit.*, p. ix.

[57] A fairly typical example of Keach's pathetic doggerel is on the theme of repentance from his *Spiritual Melody* (1691), containing almost 300 hymns:

> Repentance like a bucket is
> To pump the water out;
> For leaky is our ship, alas,
> Which makes us look about. (p. 254)

The judgment of a twentieth century fellow Baptist, citing Blake's couplet, may stand for the quality of Keach's verse:

> The languid strings do scarcely move,
> The sound is forced, the notes are few.

(Adam A. Reed, "Benjamin Keach, 1640," *The Baptist Quarterly*, N. S., Vol. 10, 1940-1941, pp. 76f.)

[58] Written for Mr. Valiant-for-Truth in *Pilgrim's Progress*.

[59] *The Psalms of David imitated in the language of the New Testament and applied to the Christian State and Worship* (1719), in Burder's edn. of Watts' *Works* (1810), Vol. IV, p. 119.

nody was finally reached. They were five in all. First, there were translations of the Psalms into vernacular prose, which were recited or antiphonally chanted in the Book of Common Prayer. Next there came metrical psalmody. Thirdly, metrical versions were made of passages of the New Testament.[60] Then there was the combination and omission of different parts of New Testament paraphrases. Fifthly and finally, there was reached the hymnody of Christian faith and experience which blossomed gloriously in the early eighteenth century in Isaac Watts and in the middle eighteenth century in Charles Wesley.

Perhaps the most unpredictable issue and itself an ironic comment on the entire controversy examined in this chapter between tradition and Scripture, between intricate verse anthem and unison singing of metrical psalmody, and between high Anglican and Puritan protagonists, is that it was the heirs of the fiercest defenders of metrical psalmody who first introduced modern hymnody to their initially unwilling churches in England.

[60] Julian, *op. cit.*, pp. 345a-46b.

CHAPTER VIII

THE CHIEF SACRAMENT:
MEANS OF GRACE OR MNEMONIC?

AMONG THE major cultic controversies of the century, in addition to spirit versus form, and magnificence versus simplicity in decor and also in praise, there was another debate. This was: how is the chief Sacrament to be evaluated? To reduce the complexity to a manageable issue—was the Sacrament, as most Catholics and Anglicans believed, a means of grace, or, as many Puritans affirmed, was it mainly a mnemonic? That is, did the sacraments act as channels of grace that fortified the Christian soul (as bread and wine strengthen the body), or were they merely vivid reminders of the Cross and Resurrection of Jesus Christ and the benefits these events had brought to the faithful in the assurance of forgiveness and the promise of eternal life?

If the former or high view of the sacraments as channels of grace and healing is held, this high view will be described as a doctrine of Transubstantiation by Catholics, as the "real presence" by high Anglicans of the Andrewes-Laud-Cosin school of divines (often accompanied with an unwillingness to define the modality of the presence), and as "dynamic receptionism" by those Puritans or their successors who maintain with Calvin that the Holy Spirit "seals" to believers the benefits of Christ's Cross and Resurrection. The lower doctrine is often described as "Memorialism" (and often attributed to Zwingli, whether with truth is another matter).[1] If the lower view of the Sacraments is held, then their function is to be teaching aids and tender reminders of the Passion, Death, and Resurrection of Christ, so that the costliness of these events is represented vividly to the conscience and compassion of the believer. This doctrine often degenerates (though it need not) into a touching tribute to a heroic leader who died for the cause and is the supreme martyr of Christianity. (Some Communion services of the Dissenters have at times been so restricted to the commemoration of the Passion and sacrificial death of Christ, without any suggestion of the liberation and joy of the Resurrection and Ascension, that they gave precisely the impression of a defeated martyrdom.

[1] For the fullest recent treatment see F. Schmidt-Klausing, *Zwingli als Liturgiker* (Göttingen, 1952).

The Free churches have occasionally forgotten that the Resurrection lies between the Last Supper and the First Eucharist.) The lower view of the chief sacrament frequently stresses that attendance at the Lord's Supper is a badge of the membership of the church, a kind of Christian loyalty test.

The two different theories of sacramental presence in fact lead to two very different practical sets of results. The higher view makes the altar central; the lower view gives precedence to the pulpit. The higher view appropriately demands greater splendour in the decoration and fittings of the church, for the altar becomes the throne of the presence of Christ and turns the church into the dwelling place of a king (a *basilica*, quite literally), a palace. Furthermore, the same view regards the Sacrament as virtually the extension of the Incarnation, and thus the hallowing of the five human senses, including the impressiveness of the eye-gate to the soul. This appropriately expresses the splendour of the Lord of glory. The lower view restricts the Sacrament to a didactic *aide-memoire* and reduces it to a mere abstraction, a mental construct, and such a view operates with less distraction in a plain, scrubbed meeting-house.

The high view of the Sacrament leads it to be celebrated frequently; the low view of the Sacrament is satisfied with a quarterly celebration such as Zwingli's in Zurich or those of the Scottish church.

This high view of the Sacrament expects it to be celebrated with pomp and circumstance in the ceremonial—marking out the altar by a sacred canopy or ciborium and raising it on steps above the sanctuary floor, veiling it in part by a balustrade or a wrought-iron screen, or beautifying it by frontals changing their colours with the liturgical seasons. The high-church view expects the Sacrament to be approached with deep obeisance—in crossings, genuflexions, kneelings, and prostrations. The low view of the Sacrament leads to its celebration with domestic simplicity, on a simple Communion table covered with a white cloth, and the gestures are simply standing or sitting about the table.

Finally, a high view of the Sacrament carries with it a high evaluation of the priesthood (often associating it with celibacy), a legitimation of it in the apostolical succession, and dressing up of the minister in special Eucharistic vestments such as the chasuble, alb, and cope. Such a high view of the priesthood and the Sacrament is often associated with a profound loyalty to the traditions of belief and practice of the church of the Fathers of the first centuries. The lower view of the Sacrament, on the other hand, is content to regard the presiding minister as first a prophet expounding the divine Word and only subordinately a dispenser of the sacraments. He is not a man of a higher status than other men; he shares the same standing but has merely a different office.

It will be seen that a difference in the interpretation of the Sacraments, and especially of the Eucharist, leads to very different conceptions of the essential task of the Christian church, the locus of authority in religion, and in the understanding of the relative importance of ethics and aesthetics. We shall see if the writings of the contentious seventeenth century bear out the implications of this theoretical analysis.

1. *The Roman Catholic View of the Sacrament*

As a persecuted community the Roman Catholic church in England had few opportunities for publishing defences of its sacramental doctrine. As a result it relied upon such famous catechetical expositions as those of Cardinal Bellarmine or of St. Peter Canisius,[2] or on the treatises written by English exiles in the Low Countries, such as those written by two Jesuits, John Heigham and Henry FitzSimon.[3]

Father Heigham's treatise, as we might expect, insists that in the Mass the bread and wine are converted into the physical body and blood of Christ. His theory of consecration is that it is Christ, the Second Person of the Holy Trinity, who "imparted the virtue of his holie benediction upon the bread and converted the substance thereof into that of his pretious bodie." This was, in fact, a renewal of Christ's action at the creation of the world, "when He ordayned the multiplication and increase of His creatures, every one according to his kind."[4] Heigham supports these assertions by the reminder that "never do we reade that He blessed the bread, but that there insued some notable Miracle, as in the multiplication of the five loaves and two fishes, whereof the fragments were twelve baskets after the refection of five thousand souls."[5]

Father FitzSimon's exposition is a characteristic example of a

---

[2] Editions of English translations of his catechism appeared in Douai in 1578 or 1579, Paris 1588, England between 1592 and 1596, St. Omer 1622, with a third edition in 1639.

[3] Each treatise is expounded more fully in Chap. XIII, Para. 5 *infra*.

[4] *A Devout Exposition of the Holie Masse* (Douai, 2nd edn., 1622), p. 252.

[5] *Ibid.*, p. 253.

common theological genre in this country, namely, controversial divinity, aimed at convincing Protestants of the inherent reasonableness of Catholic Eucharistic doctrine. FitzSimon insists strongly that the Roman Catholic doctrine of the real corporal presence of Christ in the Mass is that of the primitive Church in its representatives such as Cyprian, Ambrose, Augustine, John of Damascus, and Cyril of Jerusalem. Answering the Protestant objection that Christ's body is now since the Ascension in heaven and cannot be on the altar, he replies: "I aunswer with St. Damascen abouve alleaged that the assumpted bodie of Christ discendeth not from heaven, but that (without discension) the bread and wyne by the omnipotencie of his woord is transubstantiated or converted into his bodie and bloud."[6]

What, then, are the benefits of the Mass? Citing Bede, FitzSimon states them negatively: "The priest not lawfully hindred, omitting to celebrate, in as much as he may, depriveth the holy Trinitie of prayse and glorie; the Angels of ioye; the sinners of pardon; the iust of healp and grace; them in purgatorie of refreshment; the Church of spiritual assistance; & himselfe of medicine and remedie."[7] Manifestly, the benefits include the forgiveness of sins and eternal life, and the "medicine and remedy" of grace strengthens the soul against temptations.

Another Jesuit, John Floyd, wrote in 1624 *A Plea for the Reall-Presence*, which he defines as "to wit, the Reall Presence, or the change of bread and wine into the body and blood of Christ."[8] He summarizes the Patristic argument for a literal interpretation of Christ's words: "This is my body" and this he contrasts with the Protestant metaphorical interpretation:

> And this is the argument . . . used by the Fathers who prove the Reall Presence, because Christ being God can do it, to wit, can convert the substance of bread and wine into the substance of his body and blood. For if this literal sense be possible unto God, then it is neyther wicked nor absurd, then to be received as the true sense; if to be received as the true sense, then also to be received as an article of fayth, being the true litteral sense of Gods Wordd. Cōcerning the substāce of a most mayne mystery of Religion & consequently

---

[6] *The Iustification and Exposition of the Divine Sacrifice of the Masse* (1611, republished Menston, Yorkshire, 1972), p. 342.
[7] *Ibid.*, p. 69.　　　　　[8] *Op. cit.*, p. 20.

the Protestant Metaphor that destroyes this litteral sense is an accursed Heresy.[9]

Such was the instruction given by the priests as to the meaning and benefits of the Mass to the faithful, but what did the laity, in fact, believe? We can only take one glimpse at the edge of a curtain covering the stage of a vast auditorium. This is provided on a blank leaf of an Antwerp missal which once belonged to Mary, daughter of Sir Peter Middleton of Ilkley, Yorkshire. The inscription reads: "The faythfull go to Masse they ought / to ioyne with the Priest and offer up the / Body and Blood of Christ / First For the giving supreme worship/and honour to God./ Secondly in thankes /giving for all his blessed benefits./ Thirdly new graces/ and blessings and even in Remembraunce of Christes passion."[10]

The essentially medieval interpretation of the benefits of the Mass provided even in Counter-Reformation theology can be seen in the inclusion in FitzSimon's treatise of a translation of the *Anima Christi* as if it were part and parcel of a seventeenth-century Eucharistic prayer, with its pleas for purification and forgiveness, for a permanent union with Christ, and for assurance of eternal life with all the saints.[11]

The point need not be laboured, but neither should it be ignored that the treatises of both Heigham and FitzSimon not only indicate in their full titles their interest in rites and ceremonies as much as doctrines, but they actually devote considerable attention to the symbolism of ornaments and vestments and gestures, as entirely appropriate to the high mystery and miracle of the Mass.[12]

Not only did Catholics hold a high view of the Mass, they also deplored Protestants accepting what they could only regard as a doctrine of the "real absence." FitzSimon has his imaginary Protestant interlocutor saying: "At least we can not be persuaded to believe the real presence of Christ." To this FitzSimon replies: "I know and lament to know it to be true of Calvinists and Zwinglians. . . ."[13]

The later period, during and after the Restoration sees the publication of treatises that do not materially add to our appreciation of the Catholic understanding of the Mass. In 1674 Robert Fuller

9 *Ibid.*, pp. 43-44.
10 Ampleforth Abbey MS 704, cited Hugh Aveling, *The Catholic Recusants of the West Riding of Yorkshire, 1558-1790* (Leeds, 1963), p. 250.
11 *Op. cit.*, p. 118.
12 See Heigham, *op. cit.* (edn. of 1614), pp. 7-8, 27-50, 52-59, 171, 217-18, and 399.
13 *Op. cit.*, p. 343.

published anonymously his *Missale Romanum Vindicatum, or the Mass Vindicated from D. Daniel Brevent's calumnious and scandalous Tract.* Its leading idea is that the miracles claimed for the Mass do not seem improbable once one has accepted the central miracle of the real presence. Two more intriguing essays on the Mass were published in 1687 in Oxford by Abraham Woodhead, a convert while in Anglican orders, entitled *Two Discourses concerning the Adoration of our B. Saviour in the H. Eucharist.* The first affirmed that while Anglicans denied a crudely carnal doctrine of Transubstantiation such as was affirmed by Paschasius Radbertus, they nevertheless accepted a Berengarian doctrine of the real presence, such as the author himself held. Woodhead also insisted that while Anglicans rejected the view that Christ's natural body was in the Eucharist because it could not be in two places at once, yet any doctrine of a real presence is open to the identical objection. His second treatise dealt more fully with the same positions.

In summary, it can be said of the Roman Catholic view that it held to a real conversion of the bread and wine into the body and blood of Christ, while maintaining the appearance of bread and wine, that this sacrifice was acceptable to God for the remission of the sins of the living, for the refreshment of the souls in purgatory, for the strengthening of souls against temptation, and was the medicine of immortality. This set of convictions sustained and was sustained by the splendid *mise-en-scène* of the Mass in its ceremonial, ornaments, and vestments.

2. The Anglican View of the Sacrament

At the very outset we find that however impressed the high Anglican divines in the Andrewes-Laud-Cosin tradition are with the doctrine of the real presence as a primitive doctrine of the early undivided church, they have a serious quarrel with Roman doctrine and practice. These differences are reported with telling simplicity by a chaplain of Charles I, John Pocklington in his *Altare Christianum, or, the Dead Vicar's Plea* (1637). He cites Casaubon to the effect that "the things which the King's Majesty and our Church condemn are the celebration of the Eucharist without Communicants, the selling of private Masses, making a game of the simplicity of ignorant people, and causing them to pay more than once or twice for fetching of Soules out of Purgatory, by vertue of the Sacrifices of their Masses."[14]

14 *Op. cit.,* p. 109.

The high-church divines of the Church of England rejected both Transubstantiation and Consubstantiation.[15] John Bramhall, Bishop of Derry and afterwards Archbishop of Armagh at the Restoration, rejected the Roman doctrine as contrary to common sense, asking: "Surely you cannot think that Christ did actually sacrifice Himself at His Last Supper (for then He had redeemed the World at His Last Supper; then His subsequent Sacrifice on the Cross had been superfluous); nor that the priest doth now more than Christ did then?"[16] Herbert Thorndike uses a different argument, but the ground is the same: Transubstantiation is rejected because "the substance of the elements is not distinguishable by common sense from their accidents."[17]

Even in the controversial Canons of 1640 that Laud introduced as Archbishop of Canterbury, requiring the Communion table to be railed in and that worshippers should do reverence and obeisance towards it on entering or leaving the church, he is careful to distinguish Anglican from Roman concepts of Christ's presence: "The reviving of this ancient and laudable custom we heartily recommend to the serious consideration of all good people, not with any intention to exhibit any religious worship to the communion table . . . or to perform the said gesture upon any opinion of a corporal presence of the body of Jesus Christ on the holy table, or in mystical elements, but only for the advancement of God's Majesty. . . ."[18]

The second affirmation made by all Anglican divines, both high and low, was that the Sacrament was to be received in faith by the communicants. Thus they denied the *ex opere operato* Roman doctrine. Archbishop Laud[19] was as insistent upon the requirement of faith for true reception as his most convinced Puritan antagonist. In this respect he was following Richard Hooker in rejecting both Transubstantiation and Consubstantiation, and in affirming Hooker's third alternative interpretation of the mode of Christ's presence in the Sacrament. Hooker had phrased it thus: "This hallowed

[15] See Chap. 8 of Lancelot Andrewes's *Responsio ad Apologiam Cardinalis Bellarmini*, parts of which are translated in Darwell Stone's *A History of the Doctrine of the Holy Eucharist*, II, pp. 264-66; also William Laud's *Works*, 7 Vols. (ed. W. Scott, J. Bliss, Library of Anglo-Catholic Theology, Oxford, 1847-1860), II, pp. 339-41 and III, p. 355.

[16] *Works*, 5 Vols. (ed. A. W. Haddan, Library of Anglo-Catholic Theology, Oxford, 1842-1845), I, p. 54. See also Bishop Jeremy Taylor's *Works*, 10 Vols. (ed. C. P. Eden, 1847-1854), II, pp. 637ff.

[17] *Works*, 6 Vols. (ed. A. W. Haddan, Library of Anglo-Catholic Theology, Oxford, 1844-1854), IV, p. 26.

[18] E. Cardwell, *Synodalia*, 2 Vols. (Oxford, 1842), I, p. 406.

[19] Laud, *Works*, 5 Vols. (Library of Anglo-Catholic Theology, Oxford), II, pp. 370-71.

food, through concurrence of divine power, is in verity and truth unto faithful believers instrumentally a cause of that mysterious participation whereby, as I make Myself wholly theirs so I give them in hand an actual possession of all such saving grace as My sacrificed Body can yield, and as their souls do presently need, this is to them and in them *My Body.*"[20]

Hooker did not so describe it, but later theologians have applied the term "dynamic receptionism" to this doctrine, as implying both the objective reality of divine power and the subjective necessity for faith.

Another important element in the statement of Hooker, which was to be repeated throughout the century, was the stress on mystery. This has both strength and weakness. The strength was the recognition that in dealing with God, the ground of all being, humans are always dealing with mystery, with what transcends their understanding or God would not be God, and that Job's profound attempt to grapple with the concept resulted in the humble confession "these are but the outskirts of Thy ways." The weakness was that in the name of piety it was always possible to be theologically vague about the modality of the presence and therefore at a dialectical disadvantage in apologetical writings during this controversial century.

Bramhall, while insisting that "a real true presence" is confessed by every genuine son of the Church of England, typically adds that Christ did not say, "This is my body after this or that manner, *neque con, neque sub, neque trans.*" He concludes that we should not presume to analyse mysteries. Assuredly, the presence of Christ was sacramental and efficacious, but "whether it be in the soul only, or in the Host also, and if in the Host, whether by consubstantiation, or transubstantiation; whether by production, or adduction, or conservation, or assumption, or by whatsoever other way bold and blind men dare conjecture—we determine not."[21]

Bishop Cosin takes a similar stand partly because he believes that precise definitions of the mystery of Christ's presence were scholastical and Jesuitical departures from the primitive church's attitude, partly because he saw no point in arguing about God's omnipotence "whether it can do this or that, presuming to measure an infinite power by our poor ability. . . ."[22] On the other hand,

---

20 *Laws of Ecclesiastical Polity*, Bk. v, Chap. LXVII, Sect. 12; *Works*, 3 Vols. (ed. J. Keble, Oxford, 1836), II, pp. 359ff.

21 *Works*, I, p. 22.

22 *Works*, 5 Vols. (ed. G. Ornsby, Library of Anglo-Catholic Theology, Ox-

Cosin denied absolutely that it was necessary in affirming God's omnipotence to accept Transubstantiation as the consequence. On the contrary, he held that this was to deny the use of the ordinance as the Lord intended it, since it destroys the accidents and thus confuses the sign with the substance—the bread with the Body.

James Ussher, the future Archbishop of Armagh, preaching before the House of Commons in 1620, lamented that the Holy Sacrament ordained by Christ to be a bond of unity had become the occasion of "endless strifes and implacable contentions."[23] Rejecting the Aristotelian metaphysics of substance and accidents, he declared that the real presence must be left an inexplicable mystery.[24]

Granting the painful inadequacy of theological probings into the divine mystery, can anything further be said about the presence of Christ in the Sacrament which is neither "bold" nor "blind"? A seventeenth-century versifier (he was hardly a poet even though a president-designate of Harvard), Nathaniel Eaton expressed the difficulties inherent in being too precise in defining a presence in the Sacrament:

> . . . yet it is confest
> That when the holy Elements are blest
> By the Priest's powerful lips, though nothing there
> To outward sense but bread and wine appear,
> Yet doth there under those dark forms reside
> The Body of the Son of Man that died.
> This, what bold tongue soever doth deny
> Gives in effect even Christ Himself the lie.
> Yet this, whoe'er too grossly doth maintain
> Pulls his ascended Lord from Heaven again.
> A middle course 'twixt these two rocks to steer,
> Is that becomes the Christian Mariner;
> So to believe the Ascension as to grant
> His Real Presence in the Sacrament;
> Yet so His Real Presence there to own
> As not to make void His Ascension.[25]

---

ford, 1843-1855), IV, which includes the *Historia Transubstantiationis Papalis* which was written in 1656 and published posthumously in 1675.

[23] *Works*, 17 Vols. (eds. C. R. Elrington-J. H. Todd, Dublin and London, 1847-1864), II, pp. 246ff.

[24] P. E. More and F. L. Cross, *Anglicanism, The Thought and Practice of the Church of England illustrated from the Religious Literature of the Seventeenth Century* (1935), p. xxxvi.

[25] Cited *ibid.*, p. 467.

The problem was that the Apostles' Creed itself reminded the faithful that Christ's natural body was "dead and buried," and that his glorified body was located "at the right hand of God the Father Almighty." How, then, could Christ's body be present on the altar? On the other hand, if it was insisted that it is Christ's Spirit that is present in the hearts or souls of believers (which is indeed possible for a Spirit not bound in space or time), in what sense is it present sacramentally in any way different from its presence, for example, in the preaching of the Word? Furthermore, Christ said of the bread, "This is my Body" and not, "This is my Spirit." Equally, it is exceedingly difficult to explain a "mystical presence" of Christ in, with or under the elements in such a way as neither abolishes nor diminishes the physical elements.[26]

The author who has written most clearly on the befogging issue (and whose clarity, according to C. W. Dugmore,[27] almost certainly caused his Golden Grove neighbour, Jeremy Taylor, to drop a high view of the presence for a more moderate view) was William Nicholson, the Bishop of Gloucester at the Restoration. His views are contained in the *Plain but Full Exposition of the Church of England*, which first appeared in 1654 and in a later edition in 1663. He interpreted Christ's presence at the Lord's Supper in four ways:

1. Divinely, as God, and so He is present in all places. *Whither shall I flee from Thy presence? I, the Lord, fill heaven and earth.*
2. Spiritually, and so He is present in the hearts of true believers. *Christ dwells in our hearts by faith.*
3. Sacramentally, and so He is present in the Sacrament because He hath ordained the Sacrament to represent and communciate Christ's death unto us. The cup of blessing which we bless, is it not the communion of Christ, etc.?
4. Corporally, so present in Judaea in the days of His flesh.[28]

The same clarity and cogency are exhibited in Nicholson's analyses of the "real presence." He demonstrates that there are three meanings for the term "real" in this context. The first is real as opposed to pretended, imaginary, or fanciful; the second is real as opposed to figurative, barely representative, or metaphorical;

---

[26] Cf. C. W. Dugmore, *Eucharistic Doctrine in England from Hooker to Waterland* (1948), pp. 89-90.
[27] *Ibid.*, pp. 93-94.
[28] *Works* (2nd edn., reprint in Library of Anglo-Catholic Theology, Oxford, 1844), pp. 176-77.

and the third is "opposed to that which is spiritual, and imports as much as corporal or bodily."[29] The third meaning he rejects with reference to Christ's real presence in the Sacrament. He concludes that Christ is present in the Eucharist "divinely after a special manner, spiritually in the heart of the communicants, sacramentally or relatively in the elements, and this presence of His is real in the two former acceptions of real, but not in the last, for He is truly and effectually there present, though not corporally, bodily, casually, locally."[30] This account does not, of course, clear up all difficulties. How Christ can be sacramentally present in the elements, though not corporately, is difficult to comprehend; it would be easier if the presence were stated to be in the action as a whole, rather than in the elements.

In fact, there appear to be two positions and only two, which are to be expounded with great clarity and understanding. The one is Transubstantiation which affirms too much, and the other is Zwinglian Memorialism which affirms too little, and the Church of England desired a third mediating position, very difficult to explain. Transubstantiation was not acceptable to Anglican divines because as Eutychianism was a Christological heresy of the fourth century that denied the human nature of Christ by its overwhelming affirmation of Christ's godhead and divinity, so Transubstantiation denied the continued existence of the bread and wine except in appearance and destroyed, so to speak, its human or material substance. For Bishop Lancelot Andrewes this was Eucharistic Docetism. He had warned Cardinal Bellarmine: "There is that kind of union between the visible Sacrament and the invisible reality (*rem*) of the Sacrament which there is between the Manhood and Godhead of Christ, where unless you want to smack of Eutyches, the Manhood is not transubstantiated into the Godhead. . . ."[31]

The Zwinglian reductionism was also unacceptable to the Anglican divines because it affirmed that the Spirit of Christ represents without transmitting the benefits achieved by the Body of Christ sacrificed on the Cross, but is in no way a special Eucharistic presence, only a general presence of Christ with His own as believers.

Bishop Cosin asserts that the Roman Catholics misrepresent Anglican doctrine by affirming that they are only interested in transmitting the sign, and not the reality signified by the sign. On the contrary, says Cosin, there are represented and offered Christ's

---

[29] *Ibid.*, p. 179.   [30] *Ibid.*
[31] *Responsio ad Apologiam Cardinalis Bellarmini*, Chap. 8.

"very Body which was crucified and His blood which was shed for us" so that "our souls may receive and possess Christ as truly and certainly as the material signs are by us seen and received." Cosin affirms a doctrine of dynamic receptionism, but he desires even more: "We do not say that in the Lord's Supper we receive only the benefits of Christ's Death and Passion, but we join the ground with its fruits, that is, Christ, with those advantages we derive from Him, affirming with Paul, that *the bread which we break* is κοινωνία, and the cup which we blesse the communion of His Blood—of that very substance which He took of the Blessed Virgin and afterwards carried into Heaven."[32]

There are, however, several clear landmarks in the cloudiness of the Anglican doctrine of the Eucharist. One is the insistence that while there is no change in the substance of the elements, there is a change in the use to which the bread and wine are put. William Nicholson, for instance (as also Bishop Cosin)[33] emphasizes this: "That which is more material to know is the change of these, which is wholly sacramental, not in substance, but in use. For they remain bread and wine, such as before in nature: but consecrate and set apart to represent our Saviour's passion. . . ."[34]

Another clear feature of Anglican exposition is the declaration that the chief Sacrament "seals" the benefits of Christ's act of atonement on the Cross to believers. A strong statement of this viewpoint (which inevitably recalls Calvin's Eucharistic theology) is offered by Archbishop Ussher. He holds that the Lord's Supper is not merely commemorative (the Zwinglian assertion), but also communicative; not a bare sign but an exhibitive sign of grace; in short, a seal as well as a sign of the Covenant of Grace.[35] The link between the Body of Christ in Heaven and the church on earth is the Holy Spirit. Ussher continues his exposition:

> If any do further enquire how it is possible that any such union should be, seeing the Body of Christ is in Heaven and we are upon earth, I answer . . . it being altogether spiritual and supernatural, no local presence, no physical or mathematical continuity or contiguity is any way requisite thereunto. It is sufficient for a real union in this kind that Christ

---

[32] *Works*, IV, Chap. IV, Sects. 2, 5.

[33] Cosin writes: "We own the union betwixt the Body and the Blood of Christ and the elements, whose use and office are changed from what it was before." *Op. cit.*, Vol. IV, Chap. iv, Sect. 5.

[34] *Op. cit.*, pp. 176-77.   [35] *Works*, II, p. 429.

and we, though never so far distant in pleace each from the other, be knit together by those spiritual ligatures which are intimated unto us in the words alleged out of the Sixth of *John*; *to wit*, the quickening Spirit descending downwards from the Head to be in us a fountain of supernatural life; and a lively faith wrought by the same Spirit, ascending from us upward to lay fast hold upon Him, Who having by Himself purged our sins, sitteth on the right Hand of the Majesty on High.[36]

Bishop William Nicholson also affirms that the purpose of the Communion is not only "to represent our Saviour's passion" but also to "exhibit and seal to a worthy receiver the benefits of that passion."[37]

The high Anglican divines, however closely they approximated to Calvin in some respects in their doctrine of dynamic receptionism, yet were not content to assert that the Holy Spirit united the glorified Body of Christ in heaven with the believers on earth, and communicated the benefits of Christ's Passion. They wanted to affirm even more.

Hence, there is another important element in their Eucharistic doctrine. This is the inclusion of a doctrine of sacrifice carefully formulated to avoid any idea of a repetition of the uniquely efficacious Sacrifice of the Cross, and deriving its Scriptural basis from the Epistle to the Hebrews. Essentially, the claim is that Christ eternally offers His sacrifice to God the Father for the sins of men, and that the church on earth represents that sacrifice by which Christ intercedes for the church which is also His Body. The doctrine is most comprehensively stated by Archbishop Bramhall and by Herbert Thorndike. Bramhall avers: "We do readily acknowledge an Eucharistical Sacrifice of prayers and praises: we profess a commemoration of the Sacrifice of the Cross; and in the language of Holy Church, things commemorated are related as if they were then acted. . . . We acknowledge a representation of that Sacrifice to God the Father: we maintain an application of its Virtue: so here is a commemorative, impetrative, applicative Sacrifice."[38] Henry Thorndike also defines the term "sacrifice" with great caution. He acknowledges that there is an oblation of the elements immediately prior to their consecration.[39] Furthermore, he asserts

---

[36] *Ibid.*
[38] *Works*, I, pp. 54-55.
[37] *Op. cit.*, p. 177.
[39] *Works*, I, p. 860 and IV, p. 106.

that the Eucharist is "nothing else but the representation here upon earth of the offering of the Sacrifice of Christ upon the Cross to the Father in the highest heavens to obtain the benefits of His Passion for us."[40] His conclusion is: "it cannot be denied that the Sacrament of the Eucharist, inasmuch as it is the same Sacrifice of Christ upon the Cross (as that which representeth is truly said to be the thing which it representeth) is also both propitiatory and impetratory by virtue of the consecration of it, whereby it becometh the Sacrifice of Christ upon the Cross."[41] The earlier Jeremy Taylor accepted a similar view, declaring:

> . . . as Christ is a priest in heaven for ever, and yet does not Sacrifice Himself afresh, nor yet without a Sacrifice could he be a priest; but by a daily ministration and intercession representeth His Sacrifice to God, and offers Himself as sacrificed; so He does upon earth by the ministry of His servants; He is offered to God, that is, He is by prayers and the Sacrament represented or offered up to God, as Sacrificed.[42]

There the doctrine must be left with whatever residual difficulties. The only later addition came from the Non-Jurors, who believed they had made their Eucharistic doctrine more objective, on the pattern of the Eastern Orthodox churches, by the invocation or *epiklesis* of the Holy Spirit to effect the conversion of the elements into the Body and Blood of Christ. It was a doctrine approximating to Transubstantiation, except that the agent in the transformation was not the Second, but the Third Person of the Trinity. Bishop George Bull held a doctrine not greatly differing from that of the Non-Jurors, except that it posited Christ rather than the Holy Spirit as the agent in the Sacrament. Bull explained its working thus: "by or upon the sacerdotal benediction, or a divine virtue from Christ descends upon the elements, and accompanies them to all faithful communicants, and that therefore they are said to be and are the Body and Blood of Christ; the same divinity which is hypostatically united to the Body of Christ in heaven, being virtually united to the elements of Bread and Wine upon earth."[43] Even so, considerable difficulties remain as pointed out by C. W. Dugmore.[44]

---

[40] *Works*, IV, p. 108.   [41] *Ibid.*, IV, p. 117.
[42] *Works*, II, p. 643.
[43] *The Corruptions of the Church of Rome* (1705) in *Works*, 6 Vols. (ed. E. Burton, Oxford, 1827), II, p. 255.
[44] *Op. cit.*, pp. 154-55. C. W. Dugmore points out that even the Non-Jurors

The Latitudinarians, as might be expected, preferred a less mystical and more functional and practical doctrine of Holy Communion. Their leading representative was John Tillotson (1630-1694) who became Archibishop of Canterbury. Although the *Oxford Dictionary of the Christian Church* claims[45] that his Eucharistic doctrine was Zwinglian, it was in actual fact Calvinist. It is stated in a posthumously published sermon, entitled, *A Discourse to His Servants Concerning Receiving the Sacrament.* This refers to it as "the most solemn institution of our Christian religion" and urges its frequent reception, otherwise Christ is treated with contempt. The memorial aspect is stressed, but the doctrine is more than mere Memorialism, since "it does not only represent this exceeding love of our Saviour in giving His Body to be broken, and His Blood to be shed for us, but it likewise seals to us all those blessings and benefits which are procured for us by His death and passion, the pardon of sins, and power against sin." He adds that "the benefit also of it is great, because hereby we are confirmed in goodness, and our resolutions of better obedience are strengthened, and the grace of God's Holy Spirit to enable us to do His will is thereby conveyed to us."[46]

Probably the best term for describing the Anglican doctrine of the real presence is "instrumental symbolism." The adjective indicates that there is a real communication of grace effected, and the noun emphasizes the significance of the symbolism. The latter includes the concepts of sacrifice and banquet, and it may well be that the confusion in interpretation is caused by trying to elaborate incompatible analogies drawn from different realms of discourse. For example, if the symbol of sacrifice is chosen, the altar is appropriate, but if that of a banquet, a table is more appropriate. A table-altar seems a contradiction in terms. John Pocklington saw this clearly when he wrote: "For the use of an altar is to sacrifice upon, and the use of a table is to eate upon."[47] It is possible, however, to speak meaningfully of a "table-altar" if it is recognized that a sacrificial meal is eaten thereon, giving equal significance to the adjective "sacrificial" and to the noun "meal."

---

left many ambiguities, such as how Christ is united sacramentally with the elements or what is intended by a "material sacrifice" of a "spiritual body" and why a material one is better than a spiritual one, to say nothing of the mind-boggling idea that at the Last Supper Christ offered both His natural and His sacramental body, and how they are related.

[45] *Op. cit.*, ed. F. L. Cross, p. 1359a.
[46] *Works* (ed. T. Birch, 1820), x, p. 211, cited Dugmore, *op. cit.*, p. 153.
[47] *Altare Christianum or the Dead Vicars Plea* (1637), p. 141.

It was argued at the outset that the higher the conception of the Eucharist, the richer would be its setting in the ornaments of the church, as in its ceremonial, and the more frequent would be its celebration. How far are these indications found in the Church of England in the seventeenth century?

In the matter of frequency of celebration alone, the pragmatic indication would be that there was a low doctrine of Holy Communion. But the infrequency can, in fact, be explained on other grounds, including the disruption caused by the Civil Wars and the official proscription of the Prayer Book for fifteen years. Indeed, this would itself lead to a depreciation of the chief Sacrament, except among the few high Anglican "conventicles" of the kind at which Jeremy Taylor presided and which John Evelyn attended in London. It is significant and more typical, however, that Ralph Josselin, recording his administration of Holy Communion in his parish at Earl's Colne on Easter Day, 1665, observed that "twelve of us received the Sacrament of the Lord's Supper publicly for which I bless God; I believe its 22 or 23 years since received on that day and occasion."[48] It is clear that the habit of regular attendance at the Sacrament had been lost for an entire generation. As late as 1679 a preacher in the University pulpit at St. Mary's, Oxford, complained of the disuse of the Sacrament in Commonwealth days: "Those intruders who called themselves the University of *Oxon.* from the bloudy and fateful year of 1648 to the King's happy Restoration, did not think fit so much as once to celebrate the Communion together in this Church, and a public Sacrament was not seen in several College Chapels during the same space of time."[49] The impression given is not entirely correct, however. It is credibly reported by his biographer that John Owen, no friend to the Prayer Book, the Independent Dean of Christ Church, Oxford, allowed about three hundred Anglicans to celebrate divine service according to the Church of England in the lodgings of the physician Willis in the Canterbury Quadrangle of the College and

---

[48] *Diary of Ralph Josselin, 1616-1683* (ed. E. Hockliffe, Camden Society, 3rd Series, 1908), Vol. IV, p. 146.

[49] Thomas Smith, *A Sermon about Frequent Communion, Preached before the University of Oxford, August the 17th, 1679* (1685), p. 33. Dr. Thomas Comber, future Dean of Durham, similarly observed: "If we consider how terribly this Sacrament was represented and how generally it was layd aside in the late times, we might wonder how Monthly Communions should be so well attended on by the people as they are." (*The Remains of Denis Granville*, Surtees Society, 1865, Vol. XLVII, p. 86, cited by J. Wickham Legg, *English Church Life* (1914), p. 21. However, it will be pointed out that the Puritans, even if they did not celebrate the Sacrament in the high Anglican way, celebrated frequently and valued their own Lord's Suppers.

later in Merton College Chapel "to which place admitting none but their confidants, prayers and surplices were used on all Lord's Days, Holy Days and their Vigils, as also the Sacrament according to the Church of England administered."[50]

The infrequency may be exaggerated by jeremiads, and it is notable that the Rector of Clayworth reported in 1676 to the Archbishop of York that 200 of 236 persons of age to communicate in his parish did so on Easter Day of that year.[51] The rehabituating of people to regular attendance at Holy Communion after two decades of absenteeism was an uphill task for the clergy, but they succeeded tolerably well. In any case, a lower estimate of Communion was inevitable at the end of the century, partly as a result of the unmystical pragmatic emphasis of the Latitudinarian divines, and even more because of the deistic diatribes against priestcraft and superstition.

Consequently our question now becomes: is there any evidence of symbolism in the decoration of the altar or of the church plate, or any ceremonialism that would imply a high doctrine of the Eucharist?

Pepys can be taken as a witness from ceremonial of a very high doctrine of the Eucharist during the Restoration. He was at Whitehall Chapel on Easter Day, 1666, and recorded: "I staid till the King went down to receive the Sacrament, and stood in his closett, with a great many others and there saw him receive it, which I never did see the manner of before. But I do see very little difference between the degree of the ceremonies used by our people . . . and that in the Roman Church. . . ."[52] A convinced Protestant critic of Anglican ceremonies during these years writes of the way to treat clergymen who admire high ceremonialism:

> Consequently handle him *as if he really were* a Popish Priest; his *Cope*, his *Hood*, his *Surplice*, his *Cringing Worship*, his *Altar* with *Candles* on it (most Nonsensically *unlighted* too) his *Bag-Pipes* or *Organs*, and in some places *Viols* and *Violins*, singing Men and *singing* Boyd &c. are *so very like*

[50] V.H.H. Green, *Religion at Oxford and Cambridge* (1964), p. 147.

[51] Eds. Harry Gill and E. L. Guilford, *The Rector's Book, Clayworth, Notts.* (Nottingham, 1910), p. 18. It should be noted also that Simon Patrick at Covent Garden and William Beveridge at St. Peter's, Cornhill, introduced weekly Communion. This was, of course, exceptional, but it shows that conscientious clergy made much of the Sacrament (Florence Higham, *Catholic and Reformed, a study of the Anglican Church, 1559-1662*, 1962, p. 332).

[52] See also Pepys's *Diary* entries for July 29, 1660, April 22 and October 18, 1666, for further comparisons between Anglican and Roman ceremonial.

Popery, (and all but the Vestments illegal) that I protest when I came in 1660, first from beyond Sea to *Pauls*, and *White-Hall*, I could scarce think my self to be in *England*, but in *Spain* or *Portugal* again, I saw so little difference, but that their *Service* was in *Latine* and ours in *English*.[53]

What evidence does the decoration or symbolism of altars provide for the evaluation of Eucharistic doctrine? There are two very impressive altars built and carved in important London churches at All Hallows, Lombard Street, and at St. James's, Piccadilly, both significantly employing the medieval symbol of the self-wounding pelican feeding her young with her own flesh. This, it will be noted, is a symbol that combines the element of sacrifice with that of eating, and this betokens a high Eucharistic doctrine. Evelyn records a visit to see the new altar at St. James's, Piccadilly:

> I went to see the new church at St. James's, elegantly built; the altar was especially adorn'd, the white marble inclosure curiously and richly carved, the flowers and garlands about the walls by Mr. Gibbons in wood; a pelican with young at her breast, just over the altar in the carv'd compartment and border, invironing the purple velvet fring'd with I.H.S. richly embroidered, and most noble plate were given by Sir R. Geere, to the value (as was said) of £200. There was no altar anywhere in England, nor has there been any abroad, more handsomely adorn'd.[54]

The following is a description of the altar at All Hallows, Lombard Street a few years after its construction:

> The Altar-piece is the most spacious and best carved that I have thus far met with: It is of right Wainscot, and consists of 4 Columns with their Entablature, all finely Cut with 5 Pediments of the *Corinthian* Order; viz. a Circular, and above it a Triangular, belonging to the two N[orth] Columns, and to the two S[outhward]; the Inter-Columns are the Commandments done in Gold Letters on Black, and the Lord's Prayer and Creed is done in Black upon Gold. And in the middle bet[ween] the Arching parts of the Frames for the Commandments, is a Pelican feeding her Young with her own Blood

53 Edmund Hickeringill, *The Ceremony Monger* (1689), p. 18, cited Legg, *op. cit.*, p. 43.
54 *Diary*, entry for December 7, 1684.

(an Emblem of our Saviour); and above the Cornish, over the Commandments, is a Glory finely painted and adorned, with an Enrichment of Carving, as Flowers, Fruit, &c. above all which is a large triangular Pediment and seven Candlesticks, representing the Seven Golden Candlesticks we read of in the Revelations; which Altar-piece, I am credibly assured, cost no less than £186. The Communion-Table is finely finnier'd, under is the Holy Lamb on a Chalice, and at each of the four feet of the Table is a Dove.[55]

These two altars, at least, manifest that the Eucharist was still thought to be highly important even in two of Wren's most distinguished churches, and "auditory" churches at that, constructed primarily for those who had come to hear preaching.[56]

It is also worth considering what evidence is provided by the Communion plate[57] of the period for the contemporary estimation of the Eucharist. Here, again, we are likelier to learn of the evaluations of the Eucharist by wealthy patrons and donors, than those of the average Anglican communicants. Without question it was Bishop Lancelot Andrewes who contributed most to the development of Communion plate in England in the seventeenth century by his example and enthusiasm, as well as his knowledge of ecclesiastical history. In enriching ritual "he became a patron of all the crafts which could contribute to the embellishment of churches."[58] However austere he was in private life, as a bishop he spent lavishly on furnishing his private chapel. His influence endured for fifty years after his death and it can be traced in the style and symbolism of English Communion plate.[59] Thanks to the accurate observation of the hawk-eyed and critical William Prynne, a prelate-baiter, who discovered in Archbishop Laud's private papers several documents relating to a richly furnished chapel (it was Andrewes's which Prynne mistook for Laud's) we have a full account of Andrewes's preferences in the matter of Communion plate.[60] These include some experiments which were not copied by

[55] *A New View of London* (1708), I, p. 109.

[56] For altar frontals, candlesticks, crosses, religious pictures during the latter part of our period, see Legg, *op. cit.*, pp. 125-39.

[57] The two best recent studies are Charles Oman's *English Church Plate, 1597-1830* (1957) and James Gilchrist's *Anglican Church Plate* (1967).

[58] Oman, *op. cit.*, p. 145.

[59] See Thomas Fuller, *Church History of Britain* (1655) reissued 1868, Box XI, III, p. 391.

[60] See original plan of altar and furnishings in British Museum Harleian Ms.

others, such as a "tun" with a cradle for sacramental wine, or a "tricanale" with triple spouts for the water to be added to the wine. All the pieces on the altar were of gilt, and they included a chalice and cover, two patens, an alms basin, a ewer and basin (for ablutions), two candlesticks, a censer, and a canister for wafers, with the exotic additions already mentioned. The innovative Elizabethan chalices and covers do not continue to be produced because as a result of Puritan influence bread is preferred to wafers, and bread is too bulky to be kept on the chalice covers which also did duty as patens.

Andrewes's disciple, Bishop John Cosin, had seen the splendour of Baroque church ornaments in Paris when he was chaplain to the Anglican retinue of the exiled Queen Henrietta Maria. He was determined to return with some ecclesiastical splendour to England at the Restoration when he became Bishop of Durham. He converted the medieval great hall at Auckland into the largest bishop's chapel in England, and equipped it magnificently. His silver Communion plate included a chalice and cover, a French chalice with English cover, two patens, two candlesticks, an altar dish, and a Bible and Prayer Book, both mounted in silver. (This, it should be noted, is in contrast to a normal set of episcopal plate which comprised only a chalice, a standing paten, and an alms basin.)[61]

It is most significant that the style of chalices that prevailed among high-church divines (others merely purchased chalices that looked like the secular drinking cups of the period) was Gothic revival, and that this can be traced to Andrewes and was supported by Laud. The earliest example is a chalice of St. John's College, Oxford, dated prior to 1620, probably a gift to the College while Laud was its President. It bears the typical image of the Good Shepherd who sacrificed His life for His sheep, one that was reintroduced by Andrewes into England. The very earliest example associated with Andrewes is of 1620, for it was made for the church of St. Mary Extra, Southampton, out of the funds collected on the day of its consecration by Bishop Andrewes. It is practically identical with one made by the same "R. B." almost twenty years later for the chapel at Staunton Harold. The influence of this type of chalice was great since there are extant 71 chalices of Gothic revival style made between 1620 and 1704.[62] Chalices for the

---

3795 f. 23 reproduced in William Prynne's *Canterburies Doome* (1646), p. 122. See also Laud's *Works*, IV, p. 251.

[61] Oman, *op. cit.*, p. 186. [62] *Ibid.*, pp. 203ff.

Communion of the sick were first made in the last years of the reign of Charles II, and they, too, indicate a high estimate of Holy Communion.

Returning to iconography, it became a distinguishing mark of the high-church tradition to have engraved religious subjects on chalices, patens, and flagons, and the custom died out almost completely after the Revolution of 1688, when so many high-church divines left the Church of England as Non-Jurors. Almost all (with the single exception of the sacrifice of Isaac engraved on a chalice and paten of St. Botolph's, Aldgate in 1635) depicted subjects from the New Testament. Since the representation of a Crucifix was felt to be too obviously Roman Catholic a device, it is surprising to learn that there were three chalices engraved with this emblem, at Melbury Sampford Church, Dorset (1607), Weston St. Mary's church, Lincolnshire (1611), and on both chalice and paten at Kingerby, Lincolnshire (1637). Moreover, three Warwickshire churches were the recipients of covered patens inside which were engraved the Crucifix accompanied with the Instruments of the Passion. These were the gifts of Lady Dudley to Ashow, Kenilworth, and Leek churches. Other New Testament themes used to decorate chalices were: the Flight into Egypt, the Temptation of Christ, and the Last Supper.

Easily the most popular image to be inscribed on chalices was that of the Good Shepherd, which had been a common theme in the Catacombs[63] and in early Christian art, but relatively neglected by the Middle Ages. Its revival in the seventeenth century is uniquely Anglican for which there is no European parallel. The first reference to this theme (which combines the tender compassion and protection of Christ with His sacrificial death, and was illustrated by His parable) is found in an account of Bishop Andrewes's chapel, where it is recorded that there is "a Chalice having on the outside of the bowl Christ with the lost sheep on His shoulders."[64] Andrewes, as an erudite Patristic scholar, must have known that Tertullian in the De Pudicitia had made reference to "that Shepherd will play the patron whom you depict on your chalice."[65] The Bishop also gives an account of the Good Shepherd

[63] Eric Newton and William Neill, 2000 Years of Christian Art (1966), pp. 30-31; see also Walter Lowrie, Art in the Early Church (New York, 1947), pp. 7, 11f., 42f., 50, 74.

[64] Andrewes, Minor Works (1841), II, p. 29.

[65] The Latin of the citation from Chap. X reads: "cui ille si forte patrocinabitur pastor, quam in calice depingis."

in a sermon written but not delivered on Easter Day, 1625, which shows that he was struck by this image: "You may see Him in the parable coming with His lost sheep on His shoulders. That one sheep is the image of us all. So careful He was, as He laid him on His own neck, to be sure; which is the true portraiture or representation of His ἀναγογή."[66]

The only other image on the Communion plate which is associated with Andrewes is the Star of the Wise Men which directed them to the Nativity of the Incarnate Son of God. According to Andrewes, this was "not only *Stella gentium* but *Stella majorum*, the great men's, the wise men's Star" and "in the old Ritual of the Church we find on the cover of the Canister wherein was the Sacrament of His Body, there was a Star engraven to show that now the Star leads up to His Body there."[67] Here, again, there is quite unmistakably a high doctrine of the Sacrament since the very Body of Christ is on the altar. The significant fact is that there were over seventy Gothic revival chalices made as a result of the inspiration and influence of Andrewes, and continued by Laud. As we have noted, the other chalices of the period are merely imitations of the secular wine cups of their time.[68]

A lower evaluation of the Eucharist, indeed a deliberate lowering of it, is probably the explanation of both Treen ware and of beaker-shaped Communion ware of the seventeenth century, alleged to be used in Puritan celebrations of the Lord's Supper. The earliest Treen ware cup,[69] dated about 1620, comes from Vowchurch in Herefordshire. This wooden cup is oviform on a baluster stem, rising from a circular base. The simple incised decoration consists of three birds each enclosed in a circle. Other wooden cups of this type were decorated with the royal arms of James I and with armorial beasts. It is very significant that it was Ulrich Zwingli who introduced sycamore cups into the Lord's Supper in Zurich in 1525.[70] The lengthy inscriptions carved on these Treen ware chalices suggest Puritan didacticism, with distinctive Puritan tenets such as election. One reads: "Drink well and welcome you that Christians be, you that have sure faith and sound repentance

66 *Works*, III, pp. 89-90.
67 *Works*, I, p. 247, cited by Oman, *op. cit.*, p. 227.
68 James Gilchrist, *Anglican Church Plate* (1967), p. 73.
69 *Ibid.*, reproduced in Plate 41.
70 See *Liturgies of the Western Church* (ed. Bard Thompson, Cleveland and New York, 1961), p. 151. Zwingli's rubric reads: "The plates and cups are of wood that pomp may not come back again."

from every evil. Christ has made you free and from that last most heavy fearful sentence which driveth such into eternal fire as on the earth has every evil." This sounds as if it were part of a typical Calvinist fencing of the holy table. Another reads: "The Blood of Christ to them is drinke indeed, indeed, His Word and Spirit their soules but lively feede with joy and peace." A third inscription reads: "Behold what drink the Lord of life doth give now in this life, the assurance of salvation to his elect who holy do live, for unto them there is no condemnation."[71]

Another distinctively Calvinist custom in the Reformed churches of Europe was the use of beakers. Such a set was naturally used by the Dutch church meeting at Norwich in the seventeenth century, and is now in the custody of the Castle Museum in Norwich. There are also early seventeenth-century beakers in three neighbouring churches in the mid-Suffolk area.[72] Two other beakers[73] used in two Nottinghamshire Halls, those of Walesby and Walkeringham, also come from the beginning of the century, and it is known that Walesby was notorious as a Puritan parish. There is, at least, a very strong probability that extreme Puritans used both wooden cups and beaker-shaped metal cups to resemble less and less a Catholic or high Anglican chalice and more and more a simple cottage repast, using vessels that were entirely appropriate for placement on a simple table.

Thus both high and low views of the Eucharist or Lord's Supper had their fitting ceremonial, ornaments, and chalices or beakers. Until the advent of the Latitudinarians the Church of England had a high view of the real presence of Christ in the Eucharist. The judgment of J. Wickham Legg must therefore stand that although Archbishop Laud and King Charles had died for their then unacceptable convictions, their ecclesiology had gained a complete triumph at the Restoration. He writes:

> The aim of the Puritan was to have a moveable Communion table on tressels [trestles] brought out of the vestry for the Communion service, and set down in some vacant place in the church, the long sides facing north and south, while no rails protected it. After 1660 this struggle with the Puritan is over; the place of the Holy Table is determined to be in the place of the medieval altar, with one of its long sides against the east wall; it is covered with a decent carpet of silk;

[71] Gilchrist, *op. cit.*, p. 66.   [72] *Ibid.*, p. 67.
[73] Sidney Jeavons, *The Church Plate of Nottinghamshire* (1965).

there are often two candles upon it; and it is fenced with rails, at which the people no longer hesitate to communicate kneeling.[74]

The conclusion is inescapable that the Anglican high-church tradition always regarded the Holy Communion as a means of grace, but there is at least the possibility that some of the Puritans, in imitation of Zwingli, thought of it as a vivid sermon, an *aide-memoire*, a mere mnemonic. The examination of the latter charge is our next task.

3. *The Puritan View of the Lord's Supper*

A scurrilous but witty enemy of the Puritans declared that their creed was: "I believe in *John Calvin*, the Father of our Religion, the Disposer of Heaven and Earth, and in *Owen, Baxter*, and *Jenkins* his deare Sons our Lords, who were conceived of the Spirit of Fanaticism, born of Schism and Faction, suffered under the *Act of Uniformity*."[75] Their spiritual father was, indeed, John Calvin and nowhere were the paternal features of their doctrine more apparent than in their doctrine of the Lord's Supper. It will be a convenient beginning, therefore, to attempt to summarize the chief points of Calvin's Eucharistic doctrine from his *Institutes*.

It is sometimes alleged that Calvin regarded the Lord's Supper as merely offering Christ to the eye, as He was offered to the ear in preaching. On this view, the chief Sacrament would be merely a personal greetings telegram from God. Calvin can, indeed, be cited to this effect.[76] If this were all his teaching, or the brunt of it, then it could be argued that the Lord's Supper is a reminder of Christ's sacrifice, a particularly moving mnemonic. But this is to do Calvin considerably less than justice. Not only so, but in this statement he is chiefly concerned to deny that the Sacrament has any inherent efficacy of itself, and the correlative positive assertions are that objectively it is the Holy Spirit who conveys the grace in the sacraments,[77] and that subjectively they are received by faith;[78] but no Sacrament, according to Calvin is effective *ex opere operato*.

---

[74] *Op. cit.*, p. 119.

[75] "The Presbyterian Pater-Noster" (1681), a broadsheet now in the Bodleian Library, Oxford.

[76] "Let us abide by this conclusion, that the office of the Sacraments is precisely the same as that of the word of God, which is to offer and present Christ to us, and in him the treasures of his heavenly grace . . . The Sacraments . . . fulfil to us on the part of God the same office as messengers of joyful intelligence. . . ." *Institutes*, Bk. IV, Chap. XIV, Sect. 17.

[77] *Ibid.*   [78] *Ibid.*

His essential teaching, according to his own digest of it, includes three components: the signification, the substance, and the virtue, or effect. The signification consists of the promises of God interwoven with the sign (in the case of the Supper, to be the Christian's food and nourishment). The substance is Christ's sacrificial Death and Resurrection. The effect is "redemption, righteousness, sanctification, eternal life, and all the other benefits which Christ confers upon us. . . ."[79]

When it comes to defining or explaining the mode of Christ's presence in the Lord's Supper, Calvin's logic forsakes him as he stands in grateful awe before a mystery:

> If anyone inquire of me respecting the manner, I shall not be ashamed to acknowledge that it is a mystery too sublime for me to be able to express, or even to comprehend; and, to be still more explicit, I rather experience it than understand it. Here, therefore, without any controversy, I embrace the truth of God, on which I can safely rely. He pronounces his flesh to be the food and his blood the drink of my soul.[80]

Calvin may not be able to explain the mystery, but he is ready to reject what he considers to be erroneous attempts at explanation put forward by the Roman Catholic and Lutheran theorists. He considers both to be "exceedingly deceived," because they "cannot conceive of any presence of the flesh of Christ, except it be attached to the bread. For on principle they leave nothing to the secret operation of the Spirit which unites us to Christ. They suppose Christ not to be present unless he descends to us; as though we cannot equally enjoy his presence if he elevates us to himself."[81]

He here adumbrates the conviction that it is necessary to recognize that Christ's glorified body is now at the right hand of God the Father in heaven, and is not to be imprisoned in the bread (as the Roman Catholics affirm), nor should he be "deprived of his corporeal dimensions" by representing His Body as being in different places at once or given "an immensity diffused through heaven and earth" (as the Lutherans teach by their view of the ubiquity

---

[79] *Ibid.*, Chap. XVIII, Sect. 11.   [80] *Ibid.*, Sect. 32.

[81] *Ibid.*, Sect. 31. This concept of spiritual elevation is expressed in Calvin's Strassburg and Genevan Order of worship for the Lord's Supper in the conclusion of the Exhortation in words which are a kind of shadowy *Sursum corda*: "let us lift up our spirits and hearts on high where Jesus Christ is in the glory of the Father whence we expect him at our redemption. . . ." *Liturgies of the Western Church* (ed. Bard Thompson, p. 207.)

of Christ's human nature).[82] Nor, again, will Calvin accept the Zwinglian view that the Sacrament represents the benefits of Christ's Death and Resurrection, but does not present them. This would be to make the Sacrament a bare sign (*signum nudum*) not a seal (*sigillum*) of God's covenant of grace, a confirmation of His promises through Christ to the church.

Furthermore, Calvin insists that the reality of Christ's human nature is received in the Sacrament, for its efficacy is "not only to afford our minds an undoubted confidence of eternal life, but also to give us an assurance of the resurrection and immortality of our bodies. For they are vivified by his immortal flesh."[83]

The Sacrament is, therefore, for Calvin, "an external sign by which the Lord seals on our consciences His promises of goodwill towards us in order to sustain the weakness of our faith, and we in turn testify our piety towards Him, both before Himself and before angels as well as men."[84]

All these strong affirmations and equally vigorous denials will become familiar to us in Calvin's Puritan disciples. Like him they will see a Sacrament as a seal of the Gospel, the authentication of God's grace, just as the seal of the sender stamped on the back of the envelope guaranteed the genuineness of the communication, or the seal on a royal proclamation assured those who read it of the King's own will in the matter. The Sacrament of the Lord's Supper was like an amnesty to rebels. This is exactly how John Preston, Puritan divine and also Chaplain to King Charles, illustrated its meaning in a sermon: "You know, a Pirate, as long as a proclamation of rebellion is out against him, will not come in, but a pardon being promised, and advancement annexed to it, that, if anything, will bring him in: the theefe runnes away as long as he is pursued with Hue and Crie, but the promise of the pardon makes him returne back. . . ."[85]

There are hints of this in Calvin, but for its fuller elaboration—and this was the distinctive emphasis of later Puritanism—we must turn to the covenant or federal theologians, who are in a succession from William Perkins to his disciple William Ames, to Ames's disciple John Cotton who spread the doctrine in New Eng-

---

82 Bk. IV, Chap. XVII, Sect. 19.
83 Bk. IV, Chap. XVII, Sect. 32. The concluding phrase of the citation might have been penned by St. Athanasius.
84 Bk. IV, Chap. XIV, Sect. 1.
85 *The Cuppe of Blessing. Delivered in three Sermons upon I Cor. 10.16* (1633), p. 43.

land, and Ames's pupil in Franeker, Johannes Cocceius, whose *Summa Doctrinae de Foedere et Testamento Dei* (1648) was the most extensive treatise on the theme. The influence of covenant theology was profound in Dort, in the Westminster Assembly, and throughout New England.[86]

The best known exposition of the covenant theology in English was that by William Ames known as the *Marrow of Theology*.[87] To understand what a "seal of the covenant" is, the favourite Puritan description of the two Gospel sacraments, we must first understand the nature of the divine covenants as Ames expounds them.

For Ames God is essentially a promiser who also performs, irrespective of man's action or inaction, fidelity, or infidelity. Also it is this action of God as one who makes a covenant of grace or renews such a covenant (as contrasted with the transactionalism of a covenant of works) that is central for his theology. The New Covenant is unconditional on God's part, whereas the Old Covenant was dependent upon man's obedience. This covenant of grace is the saving promise of a God whose initiating love made him declare: "I will be their God and they shall be my people" (Jeremiah 31:33 and Hebrews 8:10). This concept and fact of covenant links both testaments (or covenants), beginning with the promise in Genesis 3 that Christ, or the seed of Eve, would overcome man's alienation from God and death. This covenant found renewed expression in the lives of many Old Testament figures, chief among them being Abraham, the father of the faithful who was told: "I will establish my covenant between me and you, and your descendants after you throughout their generations for an everlasting covenant and to your descendants after you" (Genesis 17:7). The covenant reached its climax in the New Testament with God's offering of Himself in the Life, Death, and Resurrection of Jesus Christ; and this was clearly seen as an unconditional covenant of grace in St. Paul's Epistle to the Romans, for "When we were yet sinners, Christ died for us" (Romans 5:8).

The Old Covenant was marked by external ritual and ceremonial, the New by interior spiritual obedience. The Old was characterized by fear, the New by love. The Old risked a bondage

[86] See Perry Miller, *Errand in the Wilderness* (Cambridge, Mass., 1956), and J. G. Møller, "The Beginnings of Puritan Covenant Theology," *Journal of Ecclesiastical History*, XIV (1963), p. 53.

[87] Citations will be taken from the excellently edited modern translation of the third Latin edition by John D. Eusden, entitled, *The Marrow of Theology* (Boston and Philadelphia, 1968).

to works, the New affirms liberation in faith. The Old was limited to the Jews, the New is for all people. The Old was oppressive, the New is inviting.[88]

So important was this conception of the covenant that for many Puritans covenants replaced creeds, as engagements of the heart and will, as contrasted with creeds as merely offering the assent of the top of the mind.[89] Personal covenants were made as solemn undertakings to serve God. Group covenants were subscribed by new members of Puritan church fellowships, and these vows were renewed on days of humiliation or thanksgiving. Marriages were rightly seen as enduring covenants. Moreover, the chief politico-religious engagement of the Puritans was naturally termed "The Solemn League and Covenant." It is in this richly theological and social context that the definition of a Sacrament as a "seal of the covenant" was made and it carried with it the absolute verification and authentication of the divine love, God's continuing providential concern, and His gracious care for the unworthy—a deeply devotional idea which had removed some of the harshness and austerity from the Calvinism of double predestination—that *decretum horribile*, as Calvin himself recognized.

William Ames writes of the sacraments with clear Ramist definitions. Arguing that a holy sign is either a bare sign or a seal, he makes much of the fact that a seal "not only represents, but presents something by sealing," and that "a sign sealing the Covenant of God is called a Sacrament, Rom. 4.11."[90] In consequence, "a Sacrament of the New Covenant, therefore, is a divine institution in which the blessings of the New Covenant are represented, presented, and applied through signs perceptible to the senses." Further, the "special application of God's favour and grace which arise from true faith is very much furthered and confirmed by the Sacraments."[91] The primary purpose or end of a Sacrament is, for Ames, "to seal the Covenant. And this occurs not on God's part only, but secondarily on ours, for not only are the grace and promises of God sealed to us, but also our thankfulness and obedience to him."[92]

Moving from sacraments in general to the Lord's Supper, Ames described the latter as "the Sacrament of nourishment and growth

---

[88] *Ibid.*, Introduction, pp. 53-54 to which I am indebted.
[89] See Champlin Burrage, *The Church Covenant Idea* (Philadelphia, 1904).
[90] *The Marrow of Theology* (ed. Eusden), p. 197.
[91] *Ibid.*   [92] *Ibid.*, p. 198.

for the faithful in Christ." His argument against Transubstantiation is an extraordinary reminder how abhorrent the eating of flesh
and the drinking of blood are to human nature.[93] The spiritual
nourishment in this Sacrament does not require a change of substance, but only of the application and use of the bread and wine,
and that Christ be spiritually present with those who receive Him
in faith.[94]

So far is Ames from accepting a literal interpretation of the
crux, "This is my Body," that he finds a threefold figure in it! There
is a primary metaphor (bread used for Body); then there is a part
for the whole (Body is used for the Body-soul); and, finally, Christ
is a shorthand term for all the benefits the Christian derives from
Him.[95]

Ames is clearly in the tradition of Calvin, but the logical rigour
of his definitions, the consecutive march of his propositions like
soldiers, and the general take-it or leave-it attitude, indicate that
we are in a different atmosphere. In it Calvin's sense of awe, humble recognition of mystery, and sheer gratitude, have disappeared.
Yet this understanding of the chief Sacrament was immensely popular because admirably clear for inclusion in the catechisms that
proliferated in this century. Part of its popularity was also due to
its removal of some of the divine arbitrariness inherent in earlier
Calvinism's disposal of the reprobate.[96] Perkins defines a Sacrament as an external sign which exhibits and seals to the faithful
man Christ's saving grace.[97] The Westminster Confession of 1647
(and it is echoed by the Independent Savoy Declaration of 1658)
defines sacraments as "Holy signs and seals of the covenant of
grace, immediately instituted by God, to represent Christ and his
benefits and to confirm our interest in him; . . ."[98] The Westminster
Shorter Catechism defines a Sacrament in words that echo Ames
to perfection: "A Sacrament is a holy ordinance instituted by
Christ; wherein by sensible signs, Christ and the benefits of the
new covenant are represented, sealed, and applied to believers."[99]

The Puritans are as eager as the high-church Anglicans to re-

---

[93] *Ibid.*, p. 212.   [94] *Ibid.*   [95] *Ibid.*, p. 213.
[96] For the softening of reprobation in Ames, see Eusden's intro. to *The Marrow
of Theology*, pp. 29-30.
[97] *Works*, I, p. 72. Perkins's doctrine of the Lord's Supper is considered briefly
in Davies, *op. cit.*, I, p. 283.
[98] Chapter 27. See Philip Schaff, *The Creeds of the Evangelical Protestant
Churches* (1877), p. 660. The marginal Biblical references to "covenant of grace"
are Romans 4:11 and Genesis 17:7 and 10.
[99] Question 71; Schaff, *op. cit.*, p. 696.

pudiate Transubstantiation as the mode of Christ's presence in the Lord's Supper. Thomas Cartwright, for example, has six arguments against the Roman doctrine. One is that if it is accepted, "at the first institution there must be two Christs, one that giveth, another that is given." The second is that it eliminates the sign, bread and wine, and hence eliminates a Sacrament. Thirdly, for Christ to be physically present on each altar there would have to be an ubiquity of his human nature, which is contrary to the nature of a body. Fourthly, the apostles and evangelists call the elements bread and wine *after* the consecration. Fifthly, all other miracles have been apparent to the senses, so this one would be the greatest miracle in the world as it is utterly invisible. Finally, if this were true doctrine, then the wicked as well as the godly would receive Christ in the Sacrament, and even "(which is horrible to consider) mice and rats may eate the true bodie of Christ and drinke his blood."[100]

Thomas Gataker's short treatise, *A Discussion of the Papist Doctrine of Transubstantiation* (1624) covers similar ground. It ends: "Whence I conclude that since this *Corporall presence*, such as the *Church of Rome* maintaineth, hath no warrant from *Gods word*, as their own *Cardinal* [Bellarmine] confesseth; and is besides contrary to *Scripture*, to *nature*, to *sight*, to *sense*, to *reason*, to *religion*, we have little *reason* to receive it, as a *truth of Christ*, or a *principle of Christianitie*."[101] The body of the treatise also claims that the doctrine is contrary to the Church Fathers and to Reformation ancestors as well.

Edward Reynolds finds Consubstantiation, or, at least, the teaching of the ubiquity of Christ's human nature which is its Lutheran underpinning, equally unacceptable as a way of explaining Christ's presence in the Lord's Supper. His major objection is to an inherent contradiction in this view, namely, that "in a finite nature there should be room enough for an infinite attribute";[102] for it is not the nature of a body to have ubiquity, but only of God the Spirit. His own view of the mode of Christ's sacramental presence is one of "energy and power." It is a "Sacramentall, Relative, Mysticall Presence." He supplies an analogy for understanding it, thus: "The King is in his Court or Presence chamber only *locally and*

---

100 *A Treatise of the Christian Religion, Or, The Whole Bodie and Substance of Divinitie* (1616), p. 228. It was published thirteen years after Cartwright's death.

101 *Op. cit.*, p. 33.

102 *Meditation on the Holy Sacrament* (1638), p. 91.

physically [as Christ's human nature is a carnal, physical, and local presence in heaven], but *representatively* he is wherever his Chancellor or subordinate Judges are, in as much as whatsoever they in a legall and judiciall course doe determine is accompted by him as his own personall act."[103] His analogy has one unfortunate flaw—that as the chancellor acts for the king in his absence, so the priest or minister acts for Christ in His absence also.

Elsewhere in this work Reynolds does make two important points: that Christ is in the action of the Lord's Supper, and it is the *whole* Christ who is present. Thus, while Christ cannot be said to be present in, with, or under the elements, as if the sacraments were automatically efficacious (which would be to deny the energising power of the Holy Spirit and the necessity for the elect to receive by faith), yet He is present in the action. Thus "the Sacrament, however by consecration it be separated from a common unto a divine life, yet is never properly to bee called the Body of Christ till Taken and Eaten, by means of which Actions (if they be Actions of Faith) that holy Bread and Wine does as really convey whole Christ with the vital influences that proceed from him unto the soule, as hand doth them unto the mouth, or the mouth unto the stomach."[104]

The Sacrament was not valued less by the magisterial Puritan divines of the Commonwealth, such as Thomas Goodwin or Richard Baxter. In fact, in two places in his writings, Goodwin, the Independent President of Magdalen College, Oxford, seems to value the Lord's Supper more than preaching. In one place, he writes:

Many things in a sermon thou understandest not, and haply not many sermons; or if thou doest, yet findest not thy portion in them; but here [in the Lord's Supper] to be sure thou mayest. If sermons, some are for comfort, some to inform, some to excite; but here in the Sacrament is all thou canst expect. Christ is here light, and wisdom, and comfort, and all to thee. He is here an eye to the blind, a foot to the lame; yea, everything to everyone.[105]

[103] *Ibid.*, p. 94.

[104] *Ibid.*, p. 88. Cf. the parallel with Hooker's *Ecclesiastical Polity*, Bk. v. Chap. XVII, Sect. 12.

[105] *The Government of the Churches of Christ* in *Works* (ed. J. Miller, 1861), XI, p. 408.

Goodwin also believes that the Lord's Supper admits the Christian to the closest intimacy with Christ, and that Christ speaks more directly in His own words and actions than through the second-hand utterance of a preacher in a sermon. Also the Sacrament is more immediately impressive than the Word. The Word preached is of Christ, but it is nowhere called Christ, but the bread is Christ, of which the Lord says, "This is my Body." The Word preached is like the moon, variable; but the Christ of the Communion is constant, like the sun.[106]

One consistent theory of the Eucharistic presence runs constantly throughout Puritanism, whether Presbyterian or Independent. The presence of Christ is mystical and spiritual, not carnal or local, and it represents, presents, and applies to the believers the benefits of the covenant of grace, which it seals and authenticates to their faith by the power of the Holy Spirit. In the words of Matthew Henry, these benefits are: "Christ and a Pardon, Christ and Peace, Christ and Grace, Christ and Heaven."[107]

So much for the theory: what of the practice? Are these teachings we have considered really expressed in the Puritan rites? We cannot, of course, know the answers in detail, but we can examine three representative celebrations of the Lord's Supper, one Independent, and the other two Presbyterian. They are, respectively, John Cotton's account of Independent worship in New England, the Westminster or Parliamentary *Directory*'s[108] Communion Order, and Richard Baxter's *The Reformed Liturgy*[109] (sometimes called *The Savoy Liturgy* because it was prepared for the Savoy Conference of the Presbyterians and the Anglicans at the Restoration).

John Cotton had the unusual privilege in New England of showing Old England what the powerful new form of Puritanism, Independency, was like in practice, while this was an unknown quantity in England. His reputation in Boston, England, was so great before he emigrated that he was nominated a member of the Westminster Assembly though he had left for the shores of the New World, and consequently *The Way of the Churches of Christ in New England* (1645) was read with considerable excitement by Cromwell's supporters in England, and with some trepidation by

---

106 *Of Gospel Holiness* in *Works*, VII, pp. 313-15.
107 *The Communicant's Companion* (1704), p. 27.
108 Analysed in the first section of Chapter XI entitled, "Puritan Service Books."
109 Analysed in Chap. XI, Sect. 3.

orthodox Presbyterian divines such as Robert Baillie and Thomas "Gangraena" Edwards. Cotton writes:

> Ceremonies wee use none, but are careful to administer all things according to the primitive institutions. . . . The Lord's Supper we administer for the time, *once a moneth at least*, and for the *gesture*, to the people *sitting*; according as Christ administered it to his Disciples *sitting*, (*Mat.* 26. 20. 26) who also made a Symbolicall use of it to teach the Church their majoritie over their Ministers in some cases, and their judiciall authoritye, as co-sessors with him at the last Judgement, (*Luke* 22. 27 to 30.) which maketh us to looke at kneeling at the Lords Supper, not only as adoration devised by man, but also as a violation by man of the institution of Christ, diminishing part of the Counsell of God, and of the honour and comfort of the Church held forth in it.
>
> In time of *solemnization* of the Supper, the Minister having taken, blessed, and broken the bread, and commanded all the people to take and eate it, as the body of Christ broken for them, he taketh it himselfe, and giveth it to all that sit at Table with him, and from the Table it is reached by the Deacons to the people sitting in the next seats about them, the Minister sitting in his place at the Table.
>
> After they have all partaked in the bread, he taketh the cup in like manner, and *giveth thanks a new*, (blesseth it) according to the example of Christ in the Evangelist, who described the institution *Mat.* 26. 27. *Mark* 14.23. *Luke* 22.17. All of them in such a way as setteth forth the Elements, not blessed *together*, but either of them *apart*; the bread first by it selfe, and afterwards the wine by it selfe; for what reason the Lord himselfe best knoweth, and wee cannot be ignorant, that a received solemne blessing, expressly performed by himselfe, doth apparently call upon the whole assembly to look againe for a supernatural and speciall blessing in the same Element also as well as in the former for which the Lord will be againe sought to do it for us.[110]

The double prayer of blessing or thanksgiving is a distinctive custom of the Independents, almost certainly inherited from the Brownists. It was done in order exactly to reproduce Christ's

[110] *The Way of the Churches of Christ in New England* (1645), pp. 68-69.

318

actions at the Last Supper. While not strictly necessary, as Cotton implies ("for what reason the Lord himselfe best knoweth"), it was a token of total obedience to the very letter of the Scripture as God's orders. It was also a singular proof of their belief in the real presence, for in it they looked for "a supernaturall and speciall blessing." Nothing could be simpler; yet it was profound because faith expected an epiphany in the Eucharist.

The *Directory* is a series of rubrics with suggested prayers and exhortations for all the ordinances of worship, which carries the approval of the English and Scottish Presbyterians and of the English Independents; it is an important, normative, and representative liturgical document.

Does it have a high or a low doctrine of the Lord's Supper? We may note to begin with that it states "the Sacrament is frequently to be observed."[111] Next it should be noticed that the holy table is to be "fenced" or guarded against unworthy receivers who will bring dishonour to the ordinance.[112] In the third place, also to prevent attendance at the Lord's Supper becoming a mere formality, there should be self-scrutiny and instruction on the Sacrament on either the previous Sunday or during the preceding week "that . . . all may come better prepared to that heavenly feast."[113] Fourthly, the Prayer of Consecration gives God thanks "for all means of grace, the Word and Sacraments, and for this Sacrament in particular, by which Christ and all his benefits are applied and sealed up unto us"; it also includes an *epiklesis*, beseeching God "to vouchsafe his gracious presence, and the effectual working of his Spirit in us, and so to sanctify these elements of bread and wine, and to bless his own ordinance that we may receive by faith the body and blood of Jesus Christ crucified for us."[114] Finally, the Post-Communion Prayer of Thanksgiving again mentions the energising power of the Holy Spirit as it pleads "for the gracious assistance of his good Spirit whereby they [the communicants] may be enabled to walk in the strength of that grace, as becometh those who have received so great pledges of salvation."[115] On all these grounds, it must be adjudged a consistently high doctrine of the real spiritual presence of Christ in the action mediated by the Holy Spirit, and a true means of grace.

---

[111] *Reliquiae Liturgicae*, III: *The Parliamentary Directory* (ed. Peter Hall, Bath, 1847), p. 52.

[112] *Ibid.* [113] *Ibid.*

[114] *Ibid.*, p. 56. [115] *Ibid.*, p. 58.

What of the doctrine in Baxter's *The Reformed Liturgy*? We need do little more than recall the judgment of the late Regius Professor of Divinity in the University of Cambridge, E. C. Ratcliff. That eminent liturgiologist observed that Baxter's Eucharistic doctrine was "markedly higher than the doctrine expressed or implied in the Communion Office of the Prayer Book of 1552 or 1559" and that it was "nearer to the historic Western tradition. . . ."[116] From such a careful scholar and an Anglican priest that is a high evaluation. The Communion service itself bears out his assessment. Baxter's *The Reformation of the Liturgy* was intended to be, as its name implies, a more Biblically grounded alternative to the Prayer Book acceptable to the English Presbyterians, though it was entirely Baxter's own and not the composition of a committee. It has value, therefore, as a representative conservative Puritan production by a very distinguished pastor and writer.

Baxter had many gifts, but concision was not among them. Hence, his definitions are lengthy, but they are essential data for the evaluation of his sacramental doctrine. His introduction defines the Lord's Supper as having a commemorative and representational significance, so that the consecrated bread and wine are given "to signify and solemnize the renewal of his holy covenant with them and the giving of himself unto them, to expiate their sins by his sacrifice, and to sanctify them further by his Spirit, and confirm their right to everlasting life."[117] The Prayer of Consecration has an explicit *epiklesis*.[118] The sense of divine pardon as a benefit received from Christ is conveyed in the phrase, "Behold the sacrificed Lamb of God that takes away the sins of the world!"[119] Christ is begged "to feed us with the bread of life."[120] The virtue and efficacy of the Sacrament is attributed definitely to the Holy Spirit, not only, of course, in the *epiklesis*, but in the prayer immediately following the libation, which begins, "Most Holy Spirit," and which continues, "Sanctify and quicken us that we may relish the spiritual food and feed on it to our nourishment and growth in grace."[121] A Post-Communion Exhortation emphasizes the concept of the celestial banquet, as Baxter reminds the communicants

---

[116] *From Uniformity to Unity* (ed. G. F. Nuttall and O. C. Chadwick, 1962), p. 123.

[117] *Reliquiae Liturgicae*, IV: *The Savoy Liturgy* (ed. Peter Hall, Bath, 1847), p. 57.

[118] *Ibid.*, p. 68.

[119] *Ibid.*, p. 61.

[120] *Ibid.*, p. 67.

[121] *Ibid.*, p. 71.

that "we have feasted with the Son of God at his table upon his flesh and blood, in preparation for that feast of endless glory."[122] In short, in Baxter's own summary words, this is a "renewed covenant of pardon, grace, and glory."[123] It wipes out the past, gives strength or grace for the present, and prepares for the life beyond death. What more could the Sacrament do? Further, which is most unusual for Puritanism for whom the saints are visible, Baxter does not forget the Communion of saints and the church triumphant in heaven. Unquestionably he expresses a high doctrine of the Lord's Supper.

It is particularly fortunate that we have a manuscript letter of Baxter's written in March, 1657, in which he described how he celebrated the Lord's Supper at Kidderminster:

> A long table being spread, I first open the nature and use of the ordinance, and the qualification and present duty of the communicants; and then the deacons (3 or 4 grave, pious men chosen and appointed to that office) do set the bread and wine on the table; and in prayer we beseech the Lord to accept of those his own creatures now dedicated and set apart for his service, as sanctified to represent the body and blood of his Son; and after confession of sin, and thanksgiving for redemption, with commemoration of the sufferings of Christ therein, and ransom thereby, we beg the pardon of sin, and the acceptance of our persons and thanksgivings now offered up to God again, and his grace to help our faith, repentance, love, etc. and renewal of our covenant with him, etc. And so after words of institution etc. I break the bread and deliver it in Christ's general terms to all present, first partaking myself, and so by the cup: which is moved down to the end of the table by the people and deacons (who fill the cup when it is emptied); and immediately after it, each one layeth down his alms for the poor, and so arise, and the next table ful succeedeth to the last: after which I first proceed to some words of exhortation, and then of praise and prayer, and sing a psalm, and so conclude with the blessing.[124]

This description does not allow Baxter to develop his Eucharistic thought as thoroughly as in *The Reformed Liturgy*, but it is sig-

---

[122] *Ibid.*   [123] *Ibid.*, p. 77.
[124] Dr. Williams's Library: Baxter Ms. 3: 156; cited by G. F. Nuttall, *Richard Baxter* (1965), p. 53.

nificant that the role of the Holy Spirit is implicit in the sanctification of the elements, the covenant is mentioned, and, above all, the petition for "his grace to help our faith, repentance, love" means that the Lord's Supper is clearly conceived as a means of grace.

If we apply the tests of frequency of celebration, high ceremonial, and emblems on chalices, to determine whether the Eucharistic doctrine is high or low, the results will, to say the least, be ambiguous for Puritanism. On frequency the score will be high for the Independents and low for the Presbyterians. If a monthly Communion became the norm for Independents, they had followed Calvin[125] at the beginning by requiring a weekly celebration. *The Apologeticall Narration* prepared by the Independent Brethren for the Westminster Assembly stated that they celebrated the Lord's Supper every Lord's Day,[126] and John Owen's Catechism said that Communion is to be administered "every first day of the week, or at least as often as opportunity and conveniency be obtained."[127] But it soon became the custom, as John Cotton records,[128] for Independents to have the chief Sacrament "once a moneth at least." It is not safe, however, to argue that an infrequent celebration means a low evaluation of the Lord's Supper for, although the Presbyterian Church of Scotland, had a quarterly and sometimes a twice-yearly celebration, it was often attended by vast gatherings[129] that were prepared for by Communion discourses at several week-night services. It seemed only that Presbyterians gathered in larger numbers on fewer occasions for the Lord's Supper, apparently on the principle that familiarity breeds contempt.

The appropriate Puritan gestures (whether Presbyterian or Independent) for receiving the elements were standing or sitting, and certainly not kneeling. The latter was associated with Transubstantiation and had been a "noxious ceremony" objected to by the earliest Scottish Presbyterians like John Knox, who had caused the "Black Rubric" to be inserted in the 1552 Prayer Book to explain that kneeling carried no idolatrous innuendo. What had begun as a protest against kneeling, developed, as far as sitting is concerned, into a symbol in its own right, defended either as a

[125] *Institutes*, Bk. IV, Chap. XVII, Sect. 43: "very frequently, and at least once a week."

[126] P. 8.

[127] William Orme, *Memoirs of the Life, Writings and Religious Connexions of John Owen, D.D.* (1820), p. 308.

[128] *Op. cit.*, p. 68.

[129] William D. Maxwell, *A History of Worship in the Church of Scotland* (1955), pp. 141f.

proleptic sign of the rest of the eternal banquet which Christ will give to His faithful, or as an indication that Christ invites his "saints" to share His theocratic rule. But this is, of course, a very simple ceremony which could be interpreted as carrying no disrespect for the Eucharist, but equally as conveying no unusual respect to the elements either.

Then as we saw earlier, the domestication of the Eucharist in Puritanism by the use of simple Treen ware, or of functional beakers, such as might be used for family meals in cottages, would probably be consonant with a low, Memorialist interpretation of the Communion. This hypothesis is reinforced by the fact that Zwingli, the father of Memorialism, introduced wooden chalices and patens into the Lord's Supper in Zurich.

4. The Subsequent History of Communions

Although there was continuing controversy over the Eucharist in the seventeenth century concerning the mode of Christ's presence and its ornamental and ceremonial adjuncts, particularly in the days when Laud was Archbishop of Canterbury, it would be exceedingly difficult to distinguish Anglican from Puritan sacramental doctrine.

So the question remains: Which ecclesial community, Anglicans or Nonconformists, preserved the higher doctrine and the greater appreciation of the Holy Communion? The answer, even allowing for a certain lowering of the Anglican estimation of the chief Sacrament in Latitudinarian and deistic days, must be in favour of the Anglicans.[130] As Howard Hageman has shown in *Pulpit and Table*,[131] in a memorable chapter entitled, "Tale of Two Cities," there is a perpetual danger in Reformed churchmanship for a high Genevan evaluation of the Lord's Supper to deteriorate into a low Zurich diminishing of its value, as Calvin's theory and practice is replaced by Zwingli's. The Zwinglian interpretation is much less complex, therefore easier to understand than Calvin's, and to defend. This is to regard Communion as a sign of the Christian community's loyalty, and as a vivid illustration of Christ's love for His people; in a word it is a powerful mnemonic. Puritanism allowing its ministers with freedom to be inspired by the Holy Spirit in interpreting the Word of God, or equally to be inspired by the *Zeitgeist*, was unprotected in its Communion doctrine. The Church

---

[130] See G. J. Cuming, *A History of Anglican Liturgy* (1969), p. 114.
[131] Published in Richmond, Va. and London (1962).

of England was protected by having a set Order of Holy Communion, whereas the Puritans had only a set of rubrics.

It is unquestionably true that there were in seventeenth-century England several factors working towards a depreciation of the Holy Communion, and these were less easily resisted in Puritanism than in Anglicanism. A dualistic depreciation of the body and the senses (with a consequent diminishing of the value of sacraments) was a characteristic trend of the middle and later part of our period. It was to be found to some small extent even in Calvin[132] himself who stressed that the sacramental signs are God's accommodation to our weak nature needing sensible tokens. It was found in increasing strength among the so-called spiritual Puritans like William Dell, John Saltmarsh, and William Erbury, who, like Joachim of Fiore, proclaimed the coming dispensation of the Spirit and the end of institutions. This emphasis on dematerialisation was found in an extreme form in many of the new Commonwealth sects, such as the Seekers, Ranters,[133] and Muggletonians, and even the Socinians[134] would minimise the importance of Communion. The most important group who opposed the sacraments as unspiritual were, of course, the Quakers[135] whose insistence on the Inner Light equated outward forms with the outer darkness. The cumulative impact of all these protests against externality and hypocrisy in religion was seriously to diminish the general estimation in which the sacraments were held.

Another factor, having the same effect, as Stephen Mayor[136] has acutely observed, was the paradoxical fact that the Puritan insistence on preserving at all costs the purity and integrity of the Lord's Supper, actually endangered it. It was thought wiser to have no Lord's Supper than to have it celebrated by an unpreaching minister; and better to forgo it than to admit a "mixed multitude" of unworthy communicants along with the "visible saints." The logical absurdity of the position was evident in the attitude of a certain A. Pinchbeck who in 1654 went to become Rector of

---

[132] *Institutes*, Bk. IV, Chap. XIV, Sect. 3, to take but one notable example.

[133] See A. L. Morton, *The World of the Ranters* (1970), which also deals with the Joachite ideas of the Seekers (pp. 126-30; 155-57).

[134] H. J. McLachlan, *Socinianism in Seventeenth Century England* (1951), pp. 317f.

[135] On this topic see Hugh Barbour, *The Quakers in Puritan England* (New Haven, Conn., 1964), p. 164f.; W. C. Braithwaite, *The Beginnings of Quakerism* (Cambridge, 2nd edn., 1955), pp. 137f.; and Elbert Russell, *The History of Quakerism* (1942), pp. 49f. This is also considered in the second part of Chapter XIV, "Radical Worship: the Baptists and Quakers."

[136] *The Lord's Supper in Early English Dissent* (1972).

Masbury in Essex and who refused to celebrate the Lord's Supper because in his judgment there was no true church there.[137]

Another powerful dissuasive from attending Holy Communion must have been the increasing emphasis on sin and unworthiness, especially in Presbyterian and Independent circles, and the consequent enlargement of the catalogue of sins listed in the monitory "fencing of the Table," and the whole system of ecclesiastical espionage and tale-bearing leading eventually to excommunication. The sense of liberation and joy in the earliest celebration of the Sacrament in the apostolic church, which Puritanism claimed to repristinate, had obviously been lost.

In these circumstances the Lord's Supper could all too easily degenerate into memorialism and a mnemonic. From this fate the set Order of Holy Communion of the Book of Common Prayer, the round of the festivals of the Christian year, the high-church veneration for the Fathers, and its rich sacramental tradition, delivered the Church of England, for which the Holy Communion had never ceased to be a valued means of grace. For the Puritans, largely also because of their high evaluation of preaching, the Communion, unless carefully safeguarded, might slip into being only a sermon illustration.

[137] Geoffrey F. Nuttall, *Visible Saints* (Oxford, 1957), pp. 134f.

PART THREE
THE HISTORY AND
FORMS OF WORSHIP

CHAPTER IX

THE ANGLICAN PRAYER BOOK
ADMIRED AND REJECTED:
1603-1659

THE MOST fascinating feature of the history of the Book of Common Prayer in the seventeenth century is the differing image it presents at different times to both friends and foes. It exhibits at least seven different faces (occasionally masks) to its supporters and critics.

1. Changing Images of the Prayer Book

Its dominant image under the Stuarts is that of its admirers by whom it is viewed as an excellent medium for the expression of the spirit of the English church and people before God. It is moderate. That is, it avoids the extremes of Popery and Presbytery, neither superstitiously nor anachronistically backward-looking, nor enamoured of innovation for its own sake. It is rational. That is, it avoids the mystical ecstasies of the Carmelites on the right, and the artificial hothouse warmth of the chaotic sermons and prayers of the sectaries on the left. This is a well-ordered worship of great dignity and decency. It is Scriptural in contents and in giving the Scripture a large place in the lectionary and in the prayers and sermons, but it also follows the doctrine and usages of the primitive church. It is a book alike for priest and people, intended for edification rather than the maintenance of mysteries, so it is in the vernacular tongue and it allows for the responses of the people in prayers, as well as in the psalmody. It is neither sacerdotally authoritarian, nor popularly indiscriminate. On this view, it is an admirable and entirely apt instrument of the Anglican *Via Media*, midway between Roman Catholicism and extreme Protestantism. This, we may suppose, was the view of the majority of the clergy and of the majority of the English people, thinking or unthinking, since it was revived at the Restoration, reviewed, and left not greatly changed.

Other faces presented by the Prayer Book were seen with equal vividness perhaps, but not over as long a time. The Crown and the hierarchy in church and state saw the Prayer Book as a very convenient expression (and engine) of political-religious conformity. Such is the unmistakable impression left by the partly negative response of King James I and the wholly negative response of the bishops to Puritan demands for changes in worship and church government at the Hampton Court Conference of 1604,[1] summed up in the angry rebuttal, "No Bishop, No King." After this James maintained the connexion between the divine right of kings and the apostolical succession, harrying the Puritans. The same impression is left by the high-church veneration of the unfortunate King Charles as "King and Martyr" of the Anglican church and Prayer Book.[2] The leaders in church and state found the Prayer Book a convenient way of cultivating the virtues of humility and acceptance of one's position in society as God-given, as well as of inculcating honour for the king by the daily prayers for his majesty and the members of the royal household included in the Prayer Book. And as long as the occasional service or parts of services commemorated the horror of treason on Gowrie Day and on the Anniversary of the Gunpowder Plot, social and religious revolution

[1] The Hampton Court Conference, over which James I presided, was convened to consider the demands of the Puritan Millenary Petition of 1603, supposedly backed by a thousand Puritan ministers, asking for changes in the Prayer Book, and deploring the profanation of the Sabbath. Its Puritan leader, a former Dean of Lincoln, now President of Corpus Christi College, Oxford, was Dr. John Rainolds, and the leaders among the Bishops were Richard Bancroft, Archbishop of Canterbury, and Bilson of Winchester. It was an abortive meeting for the Puritans, except for Rainolds's suggestion that a new translation of the Scriptures be undertaken, to which Bancroft reluctantly agreed, and which was to be the Authorized Version of the Bible (known also as the "King James Version") published in 1611. Bancroft saw the need for greater uniformity in worship and for discipline among Anglican clergy and to that end largely composed and saw through Convocation the Canons of 1604. Early in the new century orthodox Anglicans and Puritan Anglicans were preparing their strategies and flexing their theological muscles. See Mark H. Curtis, "The Hampton Court Conference and its aftermath," *History*, Vol. XLVI, No. 156 (Feb. 1961), pp. 1-16.

[2] Charles I, however arbitrary his rule and his character, was even in defeat unwilling to concede to his Puritan adversaries any agreement to give up episcopacy, and his inflexibility at this point made many consider him a martyr to the cause of the Church of England. In the days before his death he showed great courage, devotion to God and dignity; in Marvell's words about his execution,

> He nothing common did or mean
> Upon that memorable scene
> . . . .
> But bowed his comely head
> Down as upon a bed.

On the day of his death there appeared a hagiographical work, the *Eikon Basilike* [Image of a King], which many attributed to the King himself, but is generally thought to be the work of John Gauden, later to be Bishop of Exeter. The anniversary of the day of his execution, January 30, was kept as a day of national fasting and humiliation from 1662 to 1859.

seemed only a very distant possibility. Thus the Prayer Book fortified the joint rule of sceptre and mitre.

In the penal days for Anglicanism, so often referred to as the "Interregnum" (to avoid recognition of the legitimacy of the Commonwealth or Protectorate), the Prayer Book had become the symbol of a secret, exciting, and prohibited worship (like the Mass for the English Recusants), and, even more significantly, the symbol of loyalty to a suffering church. Even in palmier days, it was never to lose this profound respect; as if it was necessary for it to have been prohibited for it to be fully appreciated.

Yet another face was presented by the Prayer Book at the Restoration. To the Parliament of Charles II, bent on restoring English life to what it was like before the "Great Rebellion," the Prayer Book was the very image of conservatism, of the unchanging island in a sea of turbulence. So much was this the case that even the most well considered and liturgically researched suggestions for revision proposed by two bishops in particular whose loyalty to the Church of England had been proven in exile and imprisonment, were rejected because they *were* changes. The Prayer Book became almost sacrosanct.

Yet to experts in worship the Prayer Book was respected but not idolised; it was improvable. For the liturgiologists, Bishops Wren (who had been imprisoned for eighteen years in the Tower of London) and Cosin (who had gone into exile in France with the residue of the English court), the Prayer Book was an important symbol of loyalty, but it was not sacrosanct. In fact, it needed bettering in several respects, notably in the Office for Holy Communion, which is what they had hoped to do with it in their "Advices" and "Proposals." To Richard Baxter, the leader of the moderate Puritans (or Presbyterians) at the Savoy Conference of 1661, convened to try and arrange a revision of the Prayer Book to make it acceptable to both Anglicans and Puritans, it was also improvable, as some of its phraseology could be more Scriptural, and certain ceremonies offensive to tender Puritan consciences might be made permissive or even dropped altogether.

Perhaps, however, more interesting is the fact that the Prayer Book was seen by him as an *eirenicon*, an ecumenical and uniting formulary. It is interesting because this is exactly how a later Anglican, Dean Thomas Comber (1645-1699), who was a strong supporter of the "Glorious Revolution" of William and Mary, saw the Prayer Book as "so comprehensive, so exact, and so inoffensive a Composure; which is so *judiciously contrived* that the wisest may exercise at once their knowledge and devotion; and yet so plain, that the most ignorant may pray with understanding. . . ."[3]

To the generality of Puritans the Prayer Book presented three masks rather than faces. The earlier Puritans of Elizabethan and Jacobean times saw it not so much as the instrument or channel of the *Via Media* as the exhibition of a cowardly compromise, a Mr. Facing-Bothways, a Laodicean unwillingness to go all the way towards a thoroughly Scriptural and Reformed liturgy, such as was used in Geneva or Zurich or Strasbourg, or Scotland[4] before 1637 when the so-called Laudian liturgy was imposed. Certainly this was the view of the Presbyterians who were far from objecting to liturgical forms. The more radical Independents viewed the Prayer Book as an idol, a creation of men which was prescribed for the people's worship, and which led to a quenching of the Holy Spirit in prayer, encouraged laziness in the clergy, and was flatly contradicted by the Epistle to the Romans 8:26, 27.[5]

Eventually all Puritans, moderate or radical, came to see the Prayer Book as the repressive instrument of despotic absolutism, the symbol of the retention of "the rags of Popery" and therefore of disloyalty to the Reformation, the sinister emblem of compromise and unreliability. By that time its fate was sealed. Parliament, as advised by the Westminster Assembly of Divines, issued the *Directory for the Public Worship of God* to replace the Prayer Book. This ordinance was passed by both Houses of Parliament on January 4, 1645, and penalties for using the Prayer Book or failing to use the Directory were imposed on August 26, 1645.

The theme of the ensuing pages will be the changing fate of the Book of Common Prayer, admired and then despised and rejected, and eventually restored. The arguments advanced by its Anglican defenders and its Puritan detractors will be considered only incidentally.[6] The successive changes proposed and accepted, the alternatives, such as the *Scottish Prayer Book of 1637* (mis-

[3] *A Discourse Concerning the daily frequenting the Common Prayer* (1687), p. 13.

[4] See W. D. Maxwell, *John Knox's Genevan Service Book, 1556* (Edinburgh, 1931).

[5] John Owen, Puritan Dean of Christ Church, Oxford and Vice-Chancellor of Oxford University, wrote a treatise, *A Discourse of the Work of the Holy Spirit in Prayer* which is an extended sermon on this text (see particularly *Works*, IV, 55, and *A Discourse concerning Liturgies and their Imposition* [1662] which is a formidable critique of all liturgies).

[6] These have been discussed in detail in Chap. v.

called the "Laudian liturgy"), and the interesting but entirely unofficial adaptations of the Anglican liturgy used by the future Bishops Robert Sanderson and Jeremy Taylor during the Commonwealth and Protectorate will be considered. All these are part and parcel of the history of the Anglican liturgy in our period. But more astonishing even than the protean images of the liturgy itself will be the discovery that in the most changing century of recent English history, the Prayer Book itself remained almost unaltered, apparently immune from savage attacks of time and revolution.

2. The Early Stuart Settlement of Worship: 1603-1645

The Jacobean settlement of worship comprised two components: the Hampton Court Conference and the Canons of 1604.

The demands of the Puritans at the Conference, following on their Millenary Petition presented so hopefully to the monarch of a fully Reformed church in Scotland now arriving in England to take up the English throne in 1603, provided a convenient summary of their critique of the Prayer Book. The Millenary Petition, while avoiding the thorny question of episcopacy to which James was known to be attached, made several requests, among which were the following: "That the cross in Baptism, Interrogatories administered to infants, Confirmations[7] as superstitious, may be taken away; Baptism not to be ministered by women, and so explained,[8] the Cap and Surplice not urged; that examination may go before Communion; that it be administered with a Sermon, that divers terms of priests and absolution, and some other used, with the ring in marriage, and such like in the book, may be corrected; the longsomeness of service abridged; church songs and music moderated to better edification; that the Lord's Day be not profaned; the rest upon holidays not so strictly urged; that there may be an uniformity of doctrine prescribed; no popish opinion to be any more taught or defended; no ministers charged to teach their people to bow at the name of Jesus; that the canonical Scriptures only be read in the Church."[9]

The matter was referred to the Conference convened at Hamp-

---

[7] Confirmation was seldom administered by the Elizabethan bishops, many of whom had vast dioceses, some of which had been kept vacant for long years by the Crown. See E. C. Ratcliff, *The Booke of Common Prayer of the Churche of England: its Making and Revisions, 1549-1661* (1949, Alcuin Club Collections XXXVII), p. 18.

[8] Provision for such was made in the new Canon 55.

[9] E. Cardwell, *A History of Conferences and other Proceedings* (Oxford, 1841).

ton Court in January, 1604. The established church was represented by eight bishops, seven deans, and two doctors of divinity. The Puritans were limited to four spokesmen. The agenda, by royal request, was also limited to consideration of six major criticisms made by the Puritans. These were: the general Absolution, the Confirmation of children, private Baptism administered by women, the inordinate brevity of the Prayer Book Catechism and the too great length of Dean Nowell's Catechism (sometimes used as an alternative), the inaccuracy of existing translations of the Bible, certain inaccuracies in the Prayer Book, the inclusion of the Apocrypha in the lectionary, and other various minor matters.

After three days of discussion, the following conclusions were reached. The title of the Absolution was clarified by the addition of the words "of pronouncing the remission of sins," while to Confirmation was to be added "catechising or examination of the children's faith." It was also agreed that private Baptism was to be "by the ministers and curates," and that a "uniform short and plain catechisme be made," as also a translation of the entire Bible without marginal notes,[10] which was to be required for all the churches in England for use during divine service. Lessons from the Apocrypha repugnant to canonical Scripture would "be removed and not read." The words in the Marriage service were to be made clearer. The signation of the cross in Baptism was retained as being merely significative and not a "sign effective."[11]

Such were the agreements, whereas the changes actually made as authorized in a letter from the Archbishop of Canterbury and the bishops of London and Chichester, and enforced by a proclamation prefixed to the Prayer Book, were more favourable to the established church than to its critics.[12]

The really important changes were the exclusion of Baptism performed by women or laymen, and the enlargement of the catechism by two sections on Baptism and Holy Communion, the new material being substantially based on the two catechisms of Nowell. Four lessons from the Apocrypha were replaced by lessons from the Old Testament. And, of course, the Authorized Version of the

[10] A palpable hit at the Genevan version of the Bible, with its tendentious marginal notes, and much beloved by the Puritans.

[11] The point here is that the established church representatives were denying that the signing with the cross was any sacrament, but only had symbolical or pedagogical value.

[12] G. J. Cuming's admirable *A History of the Anglican Liturgy* (1969), to which this chapter owes much, carefully notes the slight differences between the agreement and the execution on pp. 138ff.

Bible was put in hand and published in 1611.[13] The most significant difference between the agreement and the execution of it was that no change was in fact made in the wording of the service of Matrimony.

The Puritans were still dissatisfied since the ring in Marriage and the crossing in Baptism (two of the three originally "noxious ceremonies") were retained and the surplice would be uniformly enjoined in the canons. There was to be an examination of intending communicants before the reception of Holy Communion, which was considered a profanation of that ordinance and an act of disobedience to the implicit injunction given by St. Paul in I Corinthians 11:27-29. They had less reason to grumble about the other additions made. These included a prayer for the royal family at Mattins and Evensong, together with a suffrage for them in the Litany. One may suppose that the provision of six prayers of thanksgiving "for diverse benefits" was very much to their liking, for Dr. Reynolds and others had complained of this lack of prayers for specific benefits in the Prayer Book. According to G. J. Cuming,[14] while this suggestion is not reported at the Hampton Court Conference, yet it may have come from Dean Overall of St. Paul's who was a member of the Conference, and he might have told it to John Cosin[15] who became his chaplain.

The Puritans were presumably glad that the discovery of the Gunpowder Plot of Guy Fawkes and the Roman Catholic conspirators with him to blow up both Houses of Parliament and destroy the King, Lords, and Commons, led to a renewed protest of Protestantism, and that this was annually commemorated on November 5 in a special service[16] added by royal proclamation to the Book of Common Prayer in 1605, which continued until 1859, thirty years after religious toleration had been granted to Roman Catholics in England. Gowrie Day, an annual thanksgiving for the deliverance of James as ruler of Scotland from an attempted assassination by the Earl of Gowrie and his brother, was of less interest, and it lapsed at James's death.

Puritan liturgical dissatisfaction was expressed in a more rigor-

---

[13] The most significant difference between the agreement and the execution was that no change in wording in the service of Matrimony was made, although promised.

[14] *Op. cit.*, p. 138.

[15] John Cosin, *Works*, 5 Vols. (Library of Anglo-Catholic Theology, 1843-1855), v, pp. 455-56.

[16] This service, as also the Gowrie Day commemoration, is considered in Chap. VI, "Calendar Conflict: Holy Days and Holidays."

ous form than hitherto in 1606 in *A Survey of the Book of Common Prayer*, which compared the Prayer Books of 1549, 1552, and the Canons of 1604, in order to point out in meticulous detail the inconsistencies between them, as well as their reduplications, and which argued for the substitution of *The Book of Common Order*, the Scottish Reformed Service Book, for the Book of Common Prayer, which would thus guarantee a unity of worship in England and Scotland.

The changes in worship in the reigns of the early Stuarts were due in part to differences between Anglicans and "Genevans" (as old as the Cox-Knox "Troubles of Frankfort" of 1554) which widened in this period as the gap between the Catholic and Puritan trends became an abyss. It was accentuated by the Canons of 1604 and the development of the so-called Laudian tradition of high churchmanship. This is perhaps more adequately described as the Hooker-Andrewes-Laud tradition of which Hooker was the theologian, Andrewes the liturgiologist-preacher-bishop, and Laud the fervent disciple and chief executant as Bishop of London (1628) and Archbishop of Canterbury (1633-1645).

The canons, so far as they applied to worship, established a new norm. The Common Prayer was to be said on all holy days and their eves, as appointed by the Prayer Book (Canon 13). As regards Baptism, godparents must have received Holy Communion (Canon 29), and an explanation of its meaning is included in this service. The wearing of the surplice is re-enforced (Canon 58). The furniture of every parish church is to include a stone font (Canon 87), a decent Communion table covered ordinarily with a silk carpet, but at the time of Communion with a fair linen cloth, and the table is to be placed conveniently for hearing and for communicating. Also, the Decalogue is to be inscribed on the east wall, with other chosen sentences (Canon 82). Further requirements are: a pulpit (Canon 83), an alms-chest (Canon 84), a Bible and Prayer Book (Canon 80), and a table for the prohibited degrees of marriage (Canon 99).

The lengthy morning service of the Church of England consisted of Mattins, the Litany, and the Ante-Communion with sermon, except when the Communion completed the whole. It was generally celebrated with order and dignity, as required by the canons, with greater or lesser attention to the enrichment of vestments and ceremonial, and with a shorter or longer sermon, depending on whether the rector of the parish were inclined to Laudianism or to Puritanism.

3. The Laudian Tradition

If, as we have suggested, the Puritans were flexing their theological muscles early in the century, the high-church or Catholic Anglicans of the Hooker-Andrewes-Laud tradition were also preparing their liturgical strategy at this time.

This tradition found its earliest expression in the enrichment of the altar and its furnishings and of the ceremonial. Bishop Lancelot Andrewes at Winchester[17] provides the outstanding early example in his private chapel, but cathedrals and chapels of the nobility were also richly ornamented. Laud, who became Dean of Gloucester in 1616, had a row with his diocesan because of moving the altar to the east end and for embellishing it, while Matthew Wren, the former chaplain of Andrewes, made glorious the Chapel of Peterhouse, Cambridge, while Master of the College. The favour that all three received at court raises the interesting question as to whether the ecclesiastical enrichment led or followed the heightened court ceremonial and elaborately artificial dress correlative to developing absolutism in the monarchy, and of which the future Sun King in France is Europe's most notable example. It is a subject worth exploring in detail, though not here, because of the link between Baroque art and architecture with absolutism and the Counter-Reformation in Europe. It would be surprising if high Anglicanism did not follow the European pattern, especially as the king was the supreme governor of the Church of England, and the Catholic wing of the church (as the Non-Jurors were to prove) accepted the divine right of kings and the bishops among them believed in the indissolubility of promises of fealty even when the particular king (like James II) broke his promise to maintain the Protestant faith of the Church of England.

Bishop Andrewes, as mentioned, set the example for the adornment of the altar. Apart from the altar coverings of silk that lapped lavishly over the corners, the two lighted candlesticks, and the finely carved altar rails, there was the higher ceremonial, the censing, together with the "mixed chalice," symbolizing the blood and water that flowed from the body of Christ on the Cross. Copes and Prayer Books were brilliantly ornamented. The very ceremonies

---

17 See Chap. II, "Church Architecture: Achievements," above.

that the Puritans objected to were made more elaborate. Infants were not only signed with the cross in Baptism, but they were carried up to the altar.[18] Kneeling at the altar for the reception of Communion became only one of a series of genuflexions and bowings.

On the other hand, despite the common charges to the contrary, there was little inclination on Laud's part[19] to tamper with the text of the Prayer Book to make it conform to his higher doctrine. Dean Overall of St. Paul's, however, was willing to imply a higher Eucharistic doctrine than Cranmer's by using the Prayer of Oblation (as in the Prayer Book of 1549) after he had consecrated, since he believed the Sacrament was "the true public sacrifice of the Church." Andrewes, too, was an innovator. He distinguished between the contiguous words "alms and oblations" by insisting that the congregation should bring their oblations to the altar rails after the Creed, during which the celebrant read a newly devised set of Sentences in which the idea of offering was dominant. The people were to stay in the chancel until the end of the *Gloria in Excelsis,* and only then were they to return to their seats, placing their alms in the poor chest, while the priest read the Prayer Book Sentences.[20]

When he became Archbishop of Canterbury in 1633, Laud's liturgical concern was concentrated on placing the altar against the east wall of the church, fencing it with rails, and requiring the communicants to come forward to the altar to receive the sacred elements. Furthermore, he required the Ante-Communion to be read at the altar, not in the reading pew. But the custom went against the Protestantism of the population which had been long accustomed to drinking a heady cocktail of English patriotism with a dash of anti-Catholic bitters, shaken by the vivid words and images of Foxe's Book of Martyrs. The Communion table now looked like an altar against the east wall, not like a table at all. Furthermore, the gesture of kneeling for Communion (which the Puritans had always disliked since the time of Edward VI as implying a belief in Transubstantiation) was not only reintroduced, but

---

[18] Cardwell, *op. cit.,* p. 234.

[19] In fact, when the charges against him as Archbishop were investigated, Laud was shown to have made two very small and insignificant verbal changes in prayers. (Cf. Cardwell, *ibid.,* p. 234).

[20] See Andrewes, *Works,* 11 Vols. (Library of Anglo-Catholic Theology, eds. J. P. Wilson and J. Bliss, 1841-1854), vol. entitled *Minor Works,* pp. 153, 158, and ed. Vernon Staley, *Hierurgia Anglicana,* 3 Vols. (1902), II, pp. 99-104.

became one gesture in increased genuflexions and bowings at the name of Jesus, which the Puritans had deprecated at the Hampton Court Conference.

It was of little use for Laud or any of his supporters to insist that the fencing of the Communion table was done to prevent persons profaning it, or that the Communion offered Christ's flesh to the communicant while the pulpit only offered Christ's Word, or that the most splendid furnishings and the most courtly etiquette were suitable for the audience chamber of the King of Kings. Far from avoiding any compromise with the national and religious enemy, Roman Catholicism, Laudianism seemed to embrace it by imitation. Laud was a man of devotion, discipline, erudition, and sympathy for the poor, as well as a loyal royalist and churchman, but he had no psychological understanding of the independence and invincible stubbornness of those who, with equal conviction, felt themselves as Puritans and patriots to be the defenders of the Reformed Church of England. What was tragic in this era of religious intolerance was that what was secondary in importance in doctrine or worship assumed major importance as the line between Catholic and Puritan Anglicans hardened.

What were the ideals of Laud and his followers? It is clear, to begin with, that there were now one major and two minor foci in the worship of the Church of England, as represented by the furnishings. The dominant focus was, of course, the raised and fenced in altar at the centre of the east end (with the subordinate foci of the pulpit at the side and the stone font at the front of the church). Clearly, the sacraments were being given precedence over the Word, splendid preachers as there were in the Andrewes-Laud tradition, including Andrewes himself and Jeremy Taylor.[21] The typical Laudian sanctuary had an altar on which was placed a silk or velvet carpet, the rails surrounding it were finely carved, and the floor of the sanctuary was usually paved with black and white marble squares. The roof was often embossed with emblems of church and state (mitres, crowns, angels), of which Lincoln College Chapel, Oxford, is one admirable Laudian-inspired example. The stained glass here, too, though of exceptional quality was not necessarily exceptional in its typological interpretation or choice of themes, emphasising as it did the Old Testament anticipations of the New Testament sacraments and the sacrifice of Christ.[22]

21 See Chap. IV on Preaching.
22 See detailed analysis of this window in Chap. II, footnote 16.

Two further developments of the Laudian tradition, or partly such, were to come, both of which aroused the fiercest Puritan opposition. The first, considered in detail elsewhere,[23] was John Cosin's *Collection of Private Devotions* (1627), commissioned by Charles I as a book of private prayers for the ladies of his court, like the brief offices of the French ladies-in-waiting but "with regard to the ancient forms before Popery."[24] This may well have been a trial liturgical balloon, testing whether the country was ready for a revision of the Prayer Book in a more Catholic direction. It is significant that its author was at the time the corrector of the text of the Prayer Book at the king's printers. Moreover, it is equally significant that in the *Devotions*, the Mattins of the Prayer Book service is extended by the inclusion of Terce, Sext and None, while Evensong combines Vespers and Compline as was originally the case. Most important of all, a prayer to be said privately during the Act of Consecration at the Holy Communion borrows from the canon of the First Prayer Book of Edward VI, the most Catholic of the editions. Not only so, but the same is the basis of a "Prayer and Thanksgiving for the whole estate of Christ's Catholic Church, with a Commemoration of the Saints before us."[25]

4. *The Scottish Prayer Book of 1637*[26]

The second clue to the Laudian liturgical direction is to be found in events in Scotland. James I had sought to interest the Scottish bishops in a new service book, and Charles I revived the project. The future Bishop of Ross, John Maxwell, brought to England in 1629 a draft service that had been drawn up ten years before. In 1634 he revisited England with several proposals contained in a Prayer Book known as the "Haddington Book" because it was fairly recently discovered in the library of the Earl of Haddington. This was, in fact, more a revision of the English Prayer Book than an independent book prepared for Scottish use. The only details of present interest are that the Authorized Version of the Bible was used for lessons and there was much freedom allowed in the

---

[23] See Chap. III on Spirituality.

[24] So John Evelyn reported in his *Diary*, October 12, 1651.

[25] The preceding paragraph owes much to G. J. Cuming's analysis, *op. cit.*, pp. 142-43.

[26] *The Scottish Liturgy of 1637* (ed. G. Donaldson) will be found in *The Making of the Scottish Prayer Book of 1637* (Edinburgh, 1937), pp. 95-247. It has an excellent historical and critical introduction to the text.

observance of saints' days. Donaldson's conclusion on the changes in the book is that they "seem to reflect the views of a small-minded and sacerdotally inclined layman rather than a churchman interested in doctrine and in other larger issues."[27]

In 1635 Maxwell again came south with a full manuscript which received royal approval, and printing began prematurely in the autumn of that year. Prematurely, because James Wedderburn, Dean of the Chapel Royal and soon to be consecrated Bishop of Dunblane, proposed other changes aimed at restoring the Communion Service to the 1549 model. After Archbishop Laud and his chief helper, Bishop Wren of Norwich, had considered these changes, the King approved this new version in 1636, and Laud entered it into another Prayer Book (the Christ Church Book).[28] It was printed in 1637.

Its introduction into Scotland, where it was widely if erroneously known as "Laud's liturgy," led to rioting and it was immediately dropped. Imprudently, it had never been submitted to the General Assembly of the Scottish church. However, because of its later influence on revisions of the Anglican liturgy in Britain and overseas, and for its expression of Laudian liturgical ideals, it merits more than a passing mention.

For our purposes the chief interest is to discover during the negotiations for the Scottish liturgy what Laud's views were on the various proposals submitted for his consideration. Of the first seven proposals put forward in Wedderburn's "Notes" the most important changes either approved or suggested by the Archbishop were: that in addition to the new Scottish Offertory Sentences, numbers 2, 4, 6-10, and 13-15 from the English Prayer Book should be retained. On his own initiative Laud volunteered the proposal that in the Communion Office the rubric preceding each prayer or action should explain these activities by a brief description of them. The order of the prayers in the Communion Office was to be radically altered on the Scottish initiative. Laud approved the transference of the Prayer of Oblation, the Lord's Prayer, and the Prayer of Humble Access, to a new position between the Consecration and the Administration. He rejected, however, the proposed change of position for the Invitation, Confession, Absolu-

---

27 *Ibid.*, p. 47.
28 So-called because it was borrowed from the Norwich City Library in 1719 at Archbishop Wake's request and is now preserved among his papers in the library of Christ Church, Oxford.

tion, Comfortable Words, Prefaces and Sanctus, which would have almost restored the 1549 Communion Office in toto. Laud approved of Wedderburn's suggestion that a rubric should be inserted directing the manual acts during Consecration.[29]

The clearest evidence of Laud's approval of a high doctrine of Eucharistic sacrifice is found, not only in the changed position of the Prayer of Oblation and the additional Offertory Sentences, but even more strikingly in his approval of Wedderburn's suggestion that the second Sentence of the Words of Administration in the Communion Order should be dropped.[30] Furthermore, Laud put forward an awkwardly phrased rubric in response to seeking his opinion on whether it was desirable to have a rubric directing the celebrant to use the eastward position during the Consecration.

Other changes of interest in the Scottish liturgy are the short invocation of the Holy Spirit on the water in the font which is added to the "flood" prayer, together with a blessing of the water immediately before Baptism (which seems superfluous in view of the previous addition). In the Churching of Women, Psalm 27 is added as an alternative, and Ash Wednesday is made the focal point of the Service of Commination.

The Scottish Prayer Book of 1637 was interesting generally for its series of explicit rubrics, its reordering of the Communion Office with a partial return to the structure of Edward VI's First Prayer Book, the use of the *epiklesis* (or, invocation of the Holy Spirit at the Consecration), the thanksgiving for the saints in the prayer for the church, the use of the Authorized Version Bible for the lectionary (including the Psalms), and changes introduced into the calendar for the Scottish saints.[31] Its influence was to be profound on the present Scottish liturgy of the Episcopal church in Scotland, on the 1662 revision of the English Prayer Book, and on the Communion Offices of the Protestant Episcopal church in

[29] The items hitherto listed in Wedderburn's proposals with Laud's additions are referred to in a letter from Laud to Wedderburn, April 20, 1636. Cf. Laud's *Works*, 7 Vols. (eds. W. Scott, J. Bliss, Library of Anglo-Catholic Theology, 1847-1860), VI, pp. 457-58.

[30] Laud (*Works*, III, pp. 356-57) stated that the words "Take, eat," etc. "may seem to relish somewhat of the Zwinglian tenet, that the Sacrament is a bare sign taken in remembrance of Christ's passion." Cuming, *op. cit.*, p. 144, mistakenly attributes them to Wedderburn. Laud also observed that the second sentence in the administration was not found in the 1549 Book.

[31] Donaldson, while insisting that it is highly ironical that the Scottish liturgy should go by the name of the man who pressed so hard for the introduction to Scotland of the English liturgy (*op. cit.*, p. 79), yet acknowledges that it is likely "that many of the changes made in the book of 1637 found their way into the programme of the Laudian party." (*Ibid.*, p. 81.)

the United States of America and of the Church of the Province of South Africa.[32]

The injudiciousness which had marked the imposition of a Catholic-tending liturgy on the Scottish Reformed church, fine fruit as it was of Caroline Anglican research into the liturgies of the primitive church, also characterized Archbishop Laud's attempts' to provide new canons and a pontifical for the Church of England. The religious differences in the church grew so acerbic and profound, and the storm cloud of the coming Civil War so threatening, that the House of Lords appointed a committee of lay peers and divines of moderate opinions and conciliatory attitudes to try to find the basis for a settlement. Archbishops Williams of York and Ussher of Ireland, Bishop Wren, and Dr. Robert Sanderson, represented the established church. Their *Proceedings*[33] provide some clues to the more unpopular Laudian practices and some moderate criticisms of the Prayer Book from a Puritan standpoint. Twenty-one "Innovations in Discipline" are criticized and six of them deal with the furnishings of the church, while eight others are concerned with posture and movement. Hardly any deal with textual changes in the Prayer Book. The real gravamen of the Committee's criticism is in its indication that the source of the Laudian deviation is "putting-to the Liturgy printed *secundo tertio Edwardi sexti*, which the Parliament hath reformed and set aside."[34]

In September, 1641, the House of Commons passed a series of resolutions on "divers innovations in or about the worship of God" which provide a convenient summary of the Laudian "innovations." These resolutions ordered:

> That the churchwardens of every parish church and chapel . . . do forthwith remove the communion table from the east end . . . ; and that they take away the rails, and level the chancels; . . . That all crucifixes, scandalous pictures of any one or more persons of the Trinity, and all the images of the Virgin Mary, shall be taken away and abolished; and that all tapers, candlesticks and basins be removed from the communion table: That all corporal bowing at the name of

---

[32] Ratcliff, *op. cit.*, p. 19. See also Peter B. Hinchliff, *The South African Liturgy* (Cape Town, 1959), and M. H. Shepherd, Jr., *The Oxford American Prayer Book Commentary* (New York, 1950). The present Communion Services of the three churches referred to will be found in *The Liturgy in English* (ed. B. J. Wigan, 2nd edn., 1964) on pp. 38-51 (Scottish), 52-61 (American), and 73-81 (South African).

[33] See Cardwell, *op. cit.*, pp. 273ff. for an account of the conclusions.

[34] Cardwell, *ibid.*

Jesus or towards the east end of the church, . . . or towards the communion table be henceforth forborne. . . . That the Lord's Day shall be duly observed and sanctified.[35]

5. *The Prayer Book Proscribed and Defended*

When the Puritans came into the ascendant, they had no desire to retain the Prayer Book, though the Presbyterians—the vast majority of the Westminster Assembly of Divines—did not object to a national liturgy as such, and would have preferred one using John Knox's *Genevan Service Book*[36] as its model. Of course, they disapproved of the Book of Common Prayer because of its association with political absolutism and because of certain customs and phrases in it which had none or only a dubious Biblical warrant. The Independents were unalterably opposed to liturgies in any shape and form as a quenching of the inspiration of the Holy Spirit. Between them, the Presbyterians and the Independents in the Westminster Assembly ousted the Prayer Book as the national formulary for prayer. The Long Parliament declared the Prayer Book illegal on January 3, 1645, and exactly a week later Archbishop Laud went to his execution on Tower Hill. Wren went into imprisonment for a long period, and Cosin fled to France as the chaplain to the English members of the court of Henrietta Maria, the widowed Queen of Charles I. Thus was the Laudian tradition eclipsed. The verdict of John W. Packer seems justified: "The Laudians during the Interregnum did little to allay these stresses [between the Papistical and Presbyterian parties] either by their staunch advocacy of the Book of Common Prayer or by their refusal to compromise over the outward expression of their worship. Once again it can be argued that this very refusal to compromise gave strength to the restored church, but it made a comprehensive church further away than ever."[37]

In place of the Book of Common Prayer, the *Directory of Public Worship* of 1645, the product of the Westminster Assembly of Divines appointed by Parliament, was decreed as the new national formulary of ordinances and prayers in worship.[38]

---

[35] *Journals of the House of Commons*, II, p. 279; printed in S. R. Gardiner, *The Constitutional Documents of the Puritan Revolution* (1889), pp. 197-98.

[36] See William D. Maxwell, *The Liturgical Portions of the Genevan Service Book* (2nd edn., 1965).

[37] *The Transformation of Anglicanism 1643-1660, with special reference to Henry Hammond* (Manchester, 1970), p. 131.

[38] This will be considered in detail in Chap. XI. The king's reply to the Parliamentary Ordinance came in the following November 13, *A Proclamation com-*

In these stormy days for the Church of England there were two possible strategies for Anglicans who wished to remain loyal. The one was literary counterattack. That is, the use of the considerable literary and historical talents of the Caroline divines was brought to bear in criticizing the Parliamentary *Directory*, and in defending the use of set liturgies from primitive precedent, and on rational and functional grounds. The other strategy was evasion of the law, by gathering clandestinely to worship according to the Book of Common Prayer, or an abbreviation of it, and even for the secret ordaining of priests and deacons of the Church of England.

Criticisms of the *Directory* came fast and furious. Perhaps the most learned was the work of Dr. Henry Hammond, *The View of the New Directory and a Vindication of the Antient Liturgy of the Church of England* which came out in 1645. Hammond begins his criticisms by noting what is missing in the *Directory*. His list includes: no liturgy or set forms only directions as to content, no uniformity in worship, no outward or bodily worship, no responsive role for the people, no divisions of the prayers into collects but one long prayer, and no ceremonies of kneeling at Communion, Cross in Baptism, or ring in Marriage. He also notes, in comparison with the Prayer Book, that the Absolution, the Hymns (Introit, Te Deum, etc.), the Doxology, the Creeds, the Lord's Prayer, the Prayer for the King, "the observation of divers Feasts commemorative, not only of Christ, but of Saints departed" with their appropriate lections and collects, the reading of the Commandments, the order of the Offertory, are all set aside in the services of Mattins and Holy Communion. Further, he observes the entire disuse of many Prayer Book occasional services, such as private Baptism, a prescribed form of Catechism,[39] Confirmation, a Solemn Burial

---

manding the use of the Book of Common Prayer according to Law, notwithstanding the pretended Ordinances for the New Directory. Thomas Fuller, in *The Church History of Britain* (1655, edn. 1837), III, pp. 481-83 shows how fierce the intellectual war between proponents and opponents of the liturgy was in 1645, and supplies "Breviates of the Arguments" on both sides. There were nine in all. The negative arguments can be listed most briefly: (1) The English liturgy has offended many godly; (2) and many of the Reformed churches abroad; (3) Calvin disliked it as he indicated in a letter to Lord Protector Somerset; (4) the liturgy confines the Holy Spirit in prayer and its absence encourages the gift of extemporary prayer; (5) it complies with the Papists in a great part; (6) it makes an idle and unedifying ministry; (7) it is tediously long for the people; (8) it imposes many burdensome ceremonies; and (9) many faithful ministers have been disbarred from their office and their families ruined by imposing the liturgy.

39 This omission was soon to be rectified in the Assembly's Shorter Catechism with its inspired Augustinian opening, "Man's chief end is to glorify God and to

Service, thanksgiving after child-birth, the Communion of the sick, the service containing the Commination, and the observation of Lent and the Rogation.[40]

On the positive side, Hammond is convinced that the liturgies of St. James, St. Basil and St. John Chrysostom prove that the early church used set liturgical forms. Ceremonial gestures (or "bodily worship" as he calls them) are authorized by the precedent of Scriptures and early liturgies. He favours uniformity of liturgy rather than the unpredictability of "leaving all to the chance of men's wills."[41] He claims that the English liturgy gives the people a large part in worship by responses in the prayers, as in the hymns, and in encouraging them to read the alternate verses in the Psalms, while the Litany gives them a very large part to say. He replies to the common charge of the unnecessary repetition of the Lord's Prayer in one service, that "one of the gravest and most reverend men of the [Westminster] Assembly, being asked his opinion about the use of the *Lord's Prayer*, to have answer'd to this purpose, God forbid that I should ever be upon my knees in Prayer, and rise up without adding Christs form to my imperfect petitions."[42]

Hammond rebuts several criticisms of the Prayer Book. The small provision made for preaching is denied by affirming the importance of catechetical teaching on the basics of faith. The entire second chapter answers the charge that the Prayer Book is largely compiled from the Roman Catholic service books. He counters: "The truth is notorious, that our *Reformers* retained not any part of the *Popish Service*, *reformed* their *Breviary* and *Processional*, and *Mass-book*; as they did their *Doctrine*, retained nothing but what the *Papists* had received from purer *Antiquity*, and was as clear from the true charge of *Popery* as any period in either Prayer or Sermon in the *Directory*."[43] His shrewdest thrust at the worship forms of the Assembly of Divines comes when he accuses them of contradicting their own argument by publishing "a Book just now come to my hands, called, *A Supply of Prayer for the Ships that want Ministers to pray with them agreeable to the Directory established by Parliament, published by Authority*."[44]

---

enjoy him for ever." (See P. Schaff, *The Creeds of Christendom* [New York, 4th edn., 1877, III, p. 676].)

[40] *The Workes of the Reverend and Learned Henry Hammond, D.D.*, 4 Vols. (ed. William Fulham, 1674-1684), I, pp. 135-36.

[41] *Ibid.*, I, p. 145. [42] *Ibid.*, I, p. 150.

[43] *Ibid.*, I, p. 169. [44] *Ibid.*, I, p. 180.

Hammond thoroughly enjoys himself in trouncing the Puritans for their inconsistencies, demonstrating that since it is a set form there can be no objection to such, especially as it is officially authorized, and that some obviously find extemporary prayer difficult, and, finally, since these are taken from the *Directory*, a Puritan minister need make no others and so can remain as lazy as his supposed Anglican brother is alleged to be. His ironical conclusion is that the *Directory* should be licensed for a trial period, and its use would lead to its own effective confutation and the restoration of the liturgy.[45]

A telling, if incidental criticism of the *Directory* and encomium for the Prayer Book was the unique and anonymously published, *Eikon Basilike, The Portraiture of His Sacred Majesty in His Solitudes and Sufferings*, which was attributed to John Gauden,[46] but which may well have been inspired and even partly written by Charles I. This argues against the Westminster Assembly as authors of the *Directory*, "That these men (I say) should so suddenly change the Liturgy into a Directory, as if the Spirit needed help for invention, though not for expressions; or as if matter prescribed did not as much stint and obstruct the Spirit as if it were clothed in, and confined to, fit words—so slight and easy is that legerdemain which will serve to delude the vulgar." The author considers that the ostentatious vanity and the frenetic search for variety in prayer are worse than the coldness attributed to set prayers. Moreover, he avers that if constant forms of prayer flatten the spirit of prayer, unpremeditated and confused variety serve as well to distract the spirit of devotion. His catalogue of the sins of free prayers charges extemporaneity with "affectations, emptiness, impertinency, rudeness, confusions, flatness,[47] levity, obscurity, vain and ridiculous repetitions, the senseless and often blasphemous

---

[45] *Ibid.*, p. 182. J. W. Packer, *op. cit.*, p. 135, reminds us that the king and leading bishops considered the idea of permitting the *Directory* for a trial period. Charles I wrote asking Bishops Juxon of London and Duppa of Salisbury for their advice. On October 14, 1646, they replied that Charles should permit the use of the *Directory*, suggesting a "temporary toleration." (See Bodleian Library's Tanner Ms. 59. II. 560 [transcript].) Charles agreed to their suggestion in November 1648, but events had moved too far by then.

[46] A former member of the Assembly of Divines, John Gauden, was consecrated Bishop of Exeter in 1660 and translated to Worcester (not to Winchester as he had hoped) in 1662. *Eikon Basilike* appeared in 1649, provoking John Milton's *Eikonoklastes* in reply. For the authorship see Christopher Wordsworth, *Who wrote* ΕΙΚΩΝ ΒΑΣΙΛΙΚΗ? (1824), and H. J. Todd, *Bishop Gauden, author of* Εικών Βασιλική (1829).

[47] This seems a highly improbable charge, unless extemporary prayers among ministers of an extremely restricted vocabulary became repetitious and predictable.

347

expressions (all these burthened with a most tedious and intolerable length)" which "do sufficiently convince all men but those who glory in that Pharisaic way." The advantages of a liturgy are soundness of doctrine, comprehensiveness, order, and gravity.[48]

If Hammond's was the most learned defence of the Prayer Book and critique of the liturgy, Jeremy Taylor's *An Apology for Authorised and Set Forms of Liturgies against the Presence of the Spirit. 1. For ex tempore Prayer, 2. Formes of Private Composition* (1649) was the better argued and expressed apologia. Taylor asserts that extemporary prayer can be the fruit of laziness (insisting that it is better to pray to God with consideration than without),[49] or even the product of ostentation rather than edification. He denies that the favourite Puritan citation—"the Spirit helpeth our infirmities"—is to be interpreted as a miraculous and immediate infusion of the Holy Spirit rather than the gift of the improvement of the natural faculties. "The summe is this: . . . this spirit of prayer . . . is to be acquired to humane industry, by learning of the Scriptures, by reading, by conference, and by whatsoever else faculties are improved and habits enlarged."[50] Otherwise, it is to ask for the multiplication of unnecessary miracles. Taylor also asks whether the man who prays *ex tempore* with God's Spirit is deprived of it if he writes the same prayer down, "Or, is the Spirit departed from him, upon the sight of a Pen and Inkhorne?"[51]

The desire for variety is not worthy, and like the Israelites on the way to the Promised Land, they are tired of the Manna of the Book of Common Prayer, preferring *"the onions of Egypt to the food of angels."*[52] It is the men not the Prayer Book which should be mended.

Scripture, says Taylor, abounds in precedents for set forms. Moses composed a set form of prayer and a song or hymn for the children of Israel, and David composed many for the service of the Tabernacle, which Solomon and the holy kings of Judah continued in the worship in the Temple. Hezekiah's reform required the priests and levites to use the words of David and Asaph in their praises. Since all Scripture is left for our learning, this must include the forms of prayer incorporated in Scripture. *A fortiori*, Christ's disciples begged for and were given a form of prayer, which is binding on his disciples of the future, "as a Breviary of Prayer,

---

[48] This paragraph summarizes pp. 96-100 of *Eikon Basilike* (1649).
[49] *Op. cit.*, p. 4.
[50] *Ibid.*, p. 21.
[51] *Ibid.*
[52] *Ibid.*, p. 41.

as a rule of their devotions, as a repository of their needes, and as a direct addresse to God."[53] The clinching consideration is this: "Now it is considerable that no man ever had the fulnesse of the Spirit, but onely the holy Jesus, and therefore it is also certain, that no man had the spirit of prayer like to him, and then, if we pray his prayer devoutly . . . do we not pray in the Spirit of Christ?"[54]

Liturgies, so Taylor insists, are symbols of union, the "ligament" of the ecclesial society, so that by a *reductio ad absurdum* this may "teach us a little to guesse . . . into how many innumerable atomes, and minutes of Churches those Christians must needes be scattered, who alter their Formes according to the number of persons, and the number of their meetings, every company having a new Forme of Prayer at every convention."[55] Further, how can members of the congregation approve by their *Amen* contradictory doctrines prayed over by contentious sectarians?[56] By contrast, public forms of prayer have great advantages "to convey an article of faith into the most secret retirement of the Spirit, and to establish it with a most firme perswasion, and indeare it to us with the greatest affection."[57] To the Puritan charge that this is to restrain the Spirit, Taylor replies that the *Directory* prescribes the matter but not the words, yet when the Spirit prescribes the Words (as in Holy Scripture), there can still be considerable liberty of meaning and interpretation.[58] The Puritans further ask why should not prayers be as unrestrained as sermons? Taylor answers that the minister offers prayers on behalf of the people and therefore they ought to know beforehand, so that if they do not like the message they may refuse to communicate. Further, he argues that liberty is more fitting in sermons than prayers, because discourses have to be adapted to the capacities of the audience, their prejudices must be removed, and they are to be "surprised that way they lie most open," and "discourses and arguments *ad hominem* . . . may more move them than the most polite and accurate that do not comply and wind about their fancies and affections."[59] Yet this technique in preaching is inapplicable in the approach to God in prayer.

---

53 *Ibid.*, p. 48.   54 *Ibid.*, p. 49.
55 *Ibid.*, p. 69.
56 *Ibid.*, pp. 70-71. Taylor refers to the habit of Independents, Presbyterian and Baptist ministers to "pray over" the points of their sermon in a concluding prayer.
57 *Ibid.*, p. 72.   58 *Ibid.*, p. 79.
59 *Ibid.*, pp. 82-83.

Taylor is scathing in his criticism of Puritan long prayers. "They *make Prayers* and they *make them long*, by this meanes they receive double advantages, for they get reputation to their ability and to their piety."[60] The more eminent Puritan divines, he charges, make their prayers longer.

His final peroration is a most moving plea for the return to the liturgy of the Church of England:

> He that considers the universall difformity of Publick Worship, and the no means of Union, no Symbol of Publick Communion being publickly consigned; that all Heresies may, with the same authority, be brought into our Prayers, and offered to God in behalf of the people, with the same authority, that any truth may, all the particular manner of our Prayers being left to the choice of all men, of all perswasions, and then observes that actually, there are in many places, Heresie, and Blasphemy, and Impertinency, and illiterate Rudenesses, put into the Devotion of the most solemne Dayes, and the most Publick Meetings; and then lastly, that there are diverse parts of Lyturgie, for which no provision at all is made in the Directory; and the very administration of the Sacraments let so loosely, that if there be anything essentiall in the Formes of Sacraments, the Sacrament may become ineffectual for want of due Words, and due Administration; I say, he that considers all these things . . . will finde that *particular men* are not fit to be intrusted to offer *in Publike* with their *private Spirit, to God*, for the people, in *such Solemnities*, in matters *of so great concernment*, where the *Honour of God*, the *benefit of the People*, the *interest of Kingdomes*, the *being of a Church*, the *unity of Mindes*, the *conformity of Practise*, the *truth of Perswasion*, and the *Salvation of Souls* are so much concerned as they are in the Publick Prayers of a whole national Church. An unlearned man is not to be trusted, and a wise man dare not trust himselfe; he that is *ignorant* cannot; he that is *knowing* will not.[61]

There were, of course, other pre-Restoration defences of the Prayer Book, notably Anthony Sparrow's *Rationale or Practical Exposition of the Book of Common Prayer* of which the earliest extant edition dates from 1657. Its main purpose was to demon-

[60] *Ibid.*, p. 90.   [61] *Ibid.*, pp. 91-92.

strate that the services of the Church of England were neither "old superstitious Roman dotage" nor "schismatically new." This important book, which continued to be reprinted frequently and was reissued by Newman in 1839, provided an explanation of the origins, purposes, and meanings of the different parts of the Book of Common Prayer, as, for example, the Collects, the Holy Days, the Communion Service, and of chancels, altars, and the fashion of churches. It provided no new arguments for the Prayer Book or against the *Directory*, but it promoted a love and appreciation for the Prayer Book through its historical lore and inspired rationality. One example of his writing, on the doctrinal value of the celebration of the Christian year, must do duty for the rest. It commences:

> And this visible as well as audible Preaching of Christian Doctrine by these Solemnities and Readings in such an admirable Order, is so apt to infuse by Degrees all necessary Christian Knowledge into us, and the Use of it to the Ignorant is so great, *that it may well be feared* (as a Reverend Person hath forewarned) that *When the Festivals and Solemnities for the Birth of Christ and his other famous Passages of Life, and Death, and Resurrection, and Ascension, and Mission of the Holy Ghost, and the Lessons, Gospels, and Collects, and Sermons upon them, be turned out of the Church, together with the Creeds also, it will not be in the power of weekly Sermons on some Heads of Religion to keep up the Knowledge of Christ in Men's Hearts, &c.*[62]

The Prayer Book commentary is a new devotional and historical genre in theology in England, though its medieval ancestry is suggested in the title which recalls Bishop William Durandus of Mende's *Rationale divinorum officiorum*.[63] It was quickly followed by the work of a loyal Anglican layman, Hamon L'Estrange's *The Alliance of Divine Offices exhibiting all the Liturgies of the Church of England since the Reformation* (1659), which includes annotations upon each of the liturgies, "vindicating" as the sub-title indicates, "the Book of Common Prayer from the main objections of its *Adversaries*, Explicating many parcels hitherto not clearly understood, shewing the conformity it beareth with the *Primitive*

---

[62] *Op. cit.* (edn. of 1722), pp. 79-80.
[63] He was consecrated Bishop of Mende in 1285 and incidentally produced a model Pontifical.

practice and giving a faire prospect into the usages of the *Ancient Church.*" A very learned book, with a command of the Greek and Latin sources of liturgiology, it has not the spiritual insight of Sparrow's *Rationale*, yet it helped to keep alive an admiration for the Prayer Book which would openly flourish at the Restoration. Reprinted in 1690 and 1699, it laid the foundation for a serious historical investigation of the development of liturgies, which was to come to fruition in the work of the Victorian Sir William Palmer's *Origines Liturgicae* (1832) and in Dom Gregory Dix's *The Shape of the Liturgy* (1945).

Hammond, Jeremy Taylor, Sparrow, and L'Estrange, in their different ways both by their criticisms of the *Directory*, explicit or implicit, as by their reminder of the values of the proscribed Anglican liturgy, and of its maintenance of a tradition of the primitive church, kept alight the lamps of nostalgia and of hope in the Anglican darkness. Others adopted a more daring strategy, that of arranging and attending clandestine services according to the Prayer Book. Jeremy Taylor alone among the famous divines tried both strategies.

6. *Clandestine Anglican Worship*[64]

The celebration of clandestine Anglican worship must be considered from two viewpoints, that of the loyal lay member of the

---

[64] The Common Prayer services were more frequent during the Protectorate than is commonly supposed. In 1653 it was reported that "conventicles for Common Prayer are frequent and much desired in London." (*Calendar of the Clarendon State Papers*, ed. O. Ogle *et alii*, II, p. 234; also R. H. Bosher, *The Making of the Restoration Settlement*, New York, 1951, p. 11.) In both London and in the country, services according to the Prayer Book were being read by clergymen who, although ejected from their parishes, were kept as chaplains or tutors in various households, or by visiting clergymen, such as John Evelyn's Mr. Owen who preached in his library at Says Court and afterwards administered the Communion on October 25, 1653. Thus disregard for the law was relatively easy until the end of 1655, when a royalist attempt at a rising forced sterner compliance, requiring that on the third offence royalists who kept clergymen to preach in public or private (except to their own families) or to keep any school, or administer the sacraments, or solemnise marriages, or "use the Book of Common Prayer or the forms of prayer therein contained" would be punished by imprisonment or banishment. (See W. K. Jordan, *The Development of Religious Toleration in England* [1938], III, pp. 194f., and *From Uniformity to Unity, 1662-1962* [eds. G. F. Nuttall and Owen Chadwick, 1962], pp. 96-97.) Even under the stricter enforcement of the law, Drs. Wild, Gunning and Taylor continued to convene secret episcopalian services. Indeed, in 1657 the Council advised the Lord Protector Cromwell to send for the two latter "and require an account of the frequent meetings of multitudes of people held with them, and cause the ordinance for taking away the Book of Common Prayer to be enforced." (*Calendar of State Papers, Domestic, 1657-1658*, p. 159.)

Church of England, and that of the clergy who directed worship and celebrated the sacraments, though forbidden to do so. Our faithful and articulate Anglican lay observer will be the diarist, John Evelyn (1620-1706), whereas our clergy will be two future bishops, Robert Sanderson (1587-1663) and Jeremy Taylor (1613-1667), both of whom have left texts of their modifications of or substitutes for the Prayer Book Services.

Evelyn's *Diary* mirrors the increasing difficulty of gathering for Anglican worship during the days of the Protectorate. It seems that on festival days, in 1654, he either attended worship conducted by an "orthodox sequestered divine" in London or obtained the services of one of them in his own house. On Advent Sunday, December 3, 1654, he writes: "There being no office at the church, but extemporie prayers after the Presbyterian way, for now all formes were prohibited, and most of the preachers were usurpers, I seldome went to Church upon solemn feasts, but either went to London, where some of the orthodox sequestered Divines did privately use the Common Prayer, administer sacraments, &c. or else I procur'd one to officiate in my house, wherefore on the 10th, Dr. Richard Owen, the sequester'd minister of Eltham, preach'd to my family in my library, and gave us the holy communion." On Christmas Day of that year, he remarks: "No public offices in churches, but penalties on observers, so I was constrain'd to celebrate it at home."

On March 18, 1655, he went to London "on purpose to heare that excellent preacher Dr. Jeremy Taylor on Matt. 14:17. shewing what were the conditions of obtaining eternal life: also concerning abatements for unavoidable infirmities, how cast on the accompts of the Crosse." On the thirty-first of the same month he visited Dr. Jeremy Taylor, "using him thenceforward as my ghostly father."

It seems that the authorities had been fairly lenient up to this point, but a new severity is recorded by Evelyn on December 14, 1655. He had gone up to London to hear Dr. Wild, the future Bishop of Derry, preach. This was "the funeral sermon of Preaching, this being the last day, after which Cromwell's proclamation was to take place, that none of the Church of England should dare either to preach or administer Sacraments, teach schoole, &c. on paine of imprisonment or exile." Evelyn viewed this as the most dismal day in the life of the Church of England since the Reformation, and one that comforted both Papist and Presbyter. "Myself, wife, and some of our family receiv'd the Communion; God make me thankfull, who hath hitherto provided for us the food of our soules as well as bodies!"

The same Dr. Wild, a former chaplain of Archbishop Laud, convened a regular secret Anglican gathering for worship in Fleet Street, London. Here Evelyn went on August 3, 1656, "to receive the B. Sacrament, the first time the Church of England was reduced to a chamber and conventicle, so sharp was the persecution." They had "a greate meeting of zealous Christians, who were generally much more devout and religious than in our greatest prosperity." On Christmas Day of the same year he again received the Holy Communion at Dr. Wild's lodgings, "where I rejoiced to find so full an assembly of devout and sober Christians."

The following year, 1658, Evelyn was more circumspect in participation in clandestine worship, until on Christmas Day he and his wife were caught attending a service according to the Prayer Book at Exeter Chapel on the Strand, where Dr. Peter Gunning (1614-1684), the future Bishop of Chichester and of Ely, was directing worship. The account conveys the excitement of the occasion.

> Sermon ended, as he [Gunning] was giving us the Holy Sacrament, the chapell was surrounded with souldiers, and all the communicants and assembly surpriz'd and kept prisoners by them, some in the house, others carried away. It fell to my share to be confin'd to a roome in the house . . . In the afternoone came Col. Whaly, Goffe and others, from White-Hall to examine us one by one; some they committed to the Marshall, some to prison. When I came before them they tooke my name and abode, examin'd me why, contrarie to an ordinance made that none should any longer observe the superstitious time of the Nativity (so esteem'd by them), I durst offend, and particularly be at Common Prayers, which they told me was but the masse in English, and particularly pray for Charles Steuart, for which we had no Scripture. I told them we did not pray for Cha. Stewart, but for all Christian Kings, Princes, and Governors. They replied, in so doing we praid for the K. of Spaine too, who was their enemie and a Papist, with other frivolous and insnaring questions and

354

much threatening; and finding no colour to detaine me, they dismiss'd me with much pitty of my ignorance. These were men of high flight and above ordinances, and spake spiteful things of our Lord's Nativity. As we went up to receive the Sacrament the miscreants held their muskets against us as if they would have shot us at the altar, yet suffering us to finish the office of Communion, as perhaps not having instructions what to do in case they found us in that action. So I got home, late the next day, blessed be God.

The two documents which show how Robert Sanderson and Jeremy Taylor adapted the Prayer Book for secret Anglican gatherings for worship during the Commonwealth and Protectorate are of great liturgical interest. Sanderson's document is known as, *A Liturgy in Times of Rebellion;*[65] while Taylor's liturgical compilations are found in *A Collection of Offices.*[66] The former is strictly an adaptation, while the latter is either a radical reconstruction of the Prayer Book services or, more probably, an alternative to the Prayer Book, the wording and order of which it occasionally echoes.

Sanderson, having gained the favour of Laud, was made a royal chaplain in 1631 and became Regius Professor of Divinity at Oxford in 1642. However, he had to leave his chair for an obscure living in Boothby Pagnell in Lincolnshire in Commonwealth days. Izaak Walton tells us that Sanderson had hoped for privacy there, but that he was disappointed since the nation was filled with "Covenanters, Confusion, Committeemen, and Soldiers," who were defacing monuments, smashing stained-glass windows, and seeking revenge, power, or profit. A group of such soldiers "would appear and visibly oppose him in the Church when he read the Prayers, some of them pretending to advise him how God was to be served more acceptably, which he not approving, but continuing to observe order and decent behaviour in reading the Church Service, they forced his Book from him, and tore it, expecting extemporary prayers."[67] Walton then asserts that about 1650 Sanderson

---

[65] It can be found in *Fragmentary Illustrations of the History of the Book of Common Prayer* (ed. W. K. Jacobson, 1874), pp. 1-40.

[66] This was edited by R. Heber in Taylor's *Works*, 15 Vols. (1822), xv, pp. 237-389. The Communion Service alone is in *Anglican Liturgies of the Seventeenth and Eighteenth Centuries* (ed. W. J. Grisbrooke, 1958), pp. 183-99.

[67] Walton's *Life of Sanderson* is included in Vol. vi of William Jacobson's edition of Sanderson's *Works*; the reference is to pp. 311-12. Such interruptions of

was advised by a Parliament man of influence who befriended him "not to be strict in reading all the Book of Common Prayer, but to make some little variation, especially if the Soldiers came to watch him; for if he did, it might not be in the power of him and his friends to secure him from taking the Covenant or sequestration. For which reasons he did vary somewhat from the strict rules of the Rubric." Such is Walton's apologia for Sanderson's variations from the Prayer Book.

He was not alone in this practice of "following the Prayer Book outline, abbreviating freely, and varying a phrase here and there."[68] R. Nelson's *Life of Dr. George Bull*[69] alleges that Bull, the future Bishop of St. Davids and apologist of the Church of England, followed Sanderson's example, using it as justification for his own practice of composing his public devotions from the Book of Common Prayer when the times made it impractical or imprudent to use the liturgy constantly and regularly. Edward Rainbow, Restoration Bishop of Carlisle, when ejected from the Mastership of Magdalene College, Cambridge, selected prayers from the Prayer Book and "so gradually brought the ignorant people to affect the Common Prayers, a little transformed and altered, who disliked the Common Prayer Book itself, they knew not why."[70] Sanderson was deeply exercised at what was his duty as an Anglican clergyman who yet had to be a law-abiding citizen under the Commonwealth and Protectorate. Hence he presented his problem as a casuist in *The Case of the Liturgy Stated in the Late Times*.[71] His

divine service as the one Sanderson experienced at Mattins were fairly common. For example the autobiography of Sir John Bramston (published 1845) on p. 75 records: "At Chelmsford at a special Commission of Oyer and Terminer for trial of some Soldiers who had broken into the Church at Easterford-Kelvedon, burnt the rails about the Communion table, stolen the Surplice and Church Plate, or some of it." See also *ibid.*, p. 95, where Bramston records that it was his practice to frequent "St. Gregory's, Dr. Mossam's, Dr. Wild's, Dr. Gunning's or some other Congregation where the orthodox clergy preached and administered the Sacraments; but the Soldiers disturbing the Congregations it was not convenient for my father to be there." For a similar disturbance, but while at Communion, and at the hands of Baptists rather than the military, see Bishop Gilbert Burnet's *The Life and Death of Sir Matthew Hale* (1682) referred to by Jacobson, *op. cit.*, Vol. VI, p. 313, and reprinted in C. Wordsworth's *Ecclesiastical Biography*, 6 Vols. (2nd edn., 1818), VI, pp. 1-106.

[68] G. J. Cuming, *The Anglican Liturgy*, p. 147.
[69] Published 1713, p. 43.
[70] Jonathan Banks, *Life of Edward Rainbow*, p. 48, referred in Jacobson, *op. cit.*, VI, p. 312.
[71] Printed in Sanderson's *Works* (ed. Jacobson), V, pp. 37-57. It was prepared about 1652.

conclusion was that it was his duty "to forbear the use of the Common Prayer Book, so far as might satisfy the letter of the ordinance, rather than forsake [his] station."[72] He did not use the Prayer Book slavishly or word for word, partly because the book was taken from him and he had a memory like a sieve, partly also because he was now forced to abbreviate, and to change a phrase here and there, while following the outline of the Prayer Book, its order of items, and its spirit. His own description states that, since the threatening soldiers who had interrupted Mattins did not stay for Communion, he used the Prayer Book Office for Communion in full, but that after their departure, "I took the liberty to use either the whole Liturgy, or but some part of it, omitting sometimes more, sometimes less, upon occasion, as I judged it more expedient in reference to the Auditory, especially if any Soldiers or other unknown persons happened to be present. But all the while, the substance of what I omitted I contrived into my Prayer before Sermon, the phrase and order only varied; which yet I endeavoured to temper in such sort, as that any person of ordinary capacity might easily perceive what my meaning was; and yet the Words left as little liable to exception or cavil as might be."[73]

Such was Sanderson's practice before receiving a warning from a man of influence with Cromwell's regime. He then resolved on further changes which continued as his custom until a happy change of affairs would restore to him "the liberty of using the old way again."[74]

His Sunday morning service followed Mattins as far as the first lesson, where there ensued a choice of Psalms and a thanksgiving made up of Psalms and church collects "which I did the rather because some have noted the want of such a Form as the only thing wherein our Liturgy seemed to be defective."[75] The second lesson then was read, and a Prayer before the Sermon consisting of several collects "new modelled into the language of the Common Prayer."[76]

Sanderson provided his own version of the General Confession, which may be compared with the Prayer Book version, by setting them out in parallel columns:

[72] The Prayer Book was declared illegal by Parliament on January 3, 1645.
[73] Op. cit., V, pp. 39-40.   [74] Ibid., p. 39.
[75] Ibid., p. 42.   [76] Ibid., p. 41.

Prayer Book Version:

Almighty and most merciful Father, We have erred and strayed from thy ways like lost sheep. We have followed too much the devices and desires of our own hearts. We have offended against thy holy laws. We have left undone the things which we ought to have done. And we have done those things which we ought not to have done. And there is no health in us. But thou, O Lord, have mercy upon us, miserable offenders. Spare thou them, O God, which confess their faults. Restore thou them that are penitent, according to thy promises declared unto mankind in Christ Jesus our Lord. And grant, O most merciful Father, for his sake, that we may hereafter lead a godly, righteous, and sober life, to the glory of thy holy name. Amen.

Sanderson's Version:

O almighty God and most merciful Father, we thy unworthy servants do with shame and sorrow confess, that we have all our life long gone astray out of thy ways like lost sheep and that, by following too much the vain devices and desires of our own hearts, we have grievously offended against thy holy laws, both in thought, word, and deed. We have many times left undone those good duties which we might and ought to have done; and we have many times done those evils, when we might have avoided them, which we ought not to have done. We confess, O Lord, that there is no health at all in us, nor help in any creature to relieve us. But all our hope is in thy mercy, whose justice we have by our sins so far provoked. Have mercy upon us, therefore O Lord, have mercy upon us miserable offenders, spare us, good Lord, which confess our faults, that we perish not; but according to thy gracious promises declared unto mankind in Christ Jesus our Lord, restore us, upon our true repentance, to thy

grace and favour. And
grant, O most merciful
Father, for his sake, that
we henceforth study to serve
and please thee, by leading
a godly, righteous, and
sober life, to the glory of
thy holy Name, and the
eternal comfort of our own
souls, through Jesus Christ
our Lord. Amen.[77]

Sanderson's version of the General Confession expands the
Prayer Book's 133 words to 235, clarifies some of the obscurer
wording, but at the cost of concision, crispness of diction, definiteness of statement, and loss of cadence. Even Jeremy Taylor, as
will be seen, master rhetorician and wordsmith as he was, could
not improve on the brevity, clarity, and felicity of Cranmer's diction. Cranmer's English, except where time has obscured the meaning of an occasional word, is best left untouched, because so very
rarely is it bettered.

Sanderson's Order for Holy Communion begins at the Exhortation, follows the order of the Prayer Book, but it omits the Comfortable Words,[78] while it inserts the Collect, "Prevent us, O Lord"
before the Blessing.

The Orders for the Churching of Women (thanksgiving after
child-birth), Baptism,[79] and Matrimony, follow the Prayer Book
closely, while that of Burial is modified, so that the service begins
with Sentences at the church gate, then moves into the church, and
ends at the graveside. The usual Prayer Book service went from
the church stile to the graveside and ended in the church, which,
while not the logical order of succession, might well be a psychological order of advantage to the mourners whose last associations
would be with the community of living Christians rather than with
the community of the dead awaiting the trumpet of the Day of
Judgement. Sanderson's Burial Service adds two Psalms (39 and

[77] *Ibid.*   [78] *Ibid.*, pp. 40-41.

[79] He rather abbreviates than omits (as Cuming erroneously states, *op. cit.*,
p. 147) the Prayer of Thanksgiving (see *Fragmentary Illustrations of the History
of the Liturgy*, ed. W. K. Jacobson, Oxford, 1874, p. 27). Cuming also asserts
that Sanderson omits Evensong, when, in fact, Sanderson compares his "forenoon"
and "afternoon" practices at worship in Sanderson's *Works*, ed. Jacobson, v,
p. 41.

90) and concludes with the Grace. His exhortations have the lucidity in explanation that presages the admirable introduction that Bishop Sanderson will write for the revised Prayer Book of 1662.[80]

Jeremy Taylor was employed during the dark days of the Commonwealth and Protectorate (dark, that is, for Anglicans) as a private chaplain to the Earl of Carbery at Golden Grove in Carmarthenshire, South Wales, where he went in 1645 and where he remained for the most part until 1658. Here his leisure was put to good use in composing his two famous devotional treatises (*Holy Living* and *Holy Dying*),[81] his major work on casuistry (*Ductor Dubitantium*), and the liturgical compilation now to be considered. This is, to give it its full title, *A Collection of Offices, or Forms of Prayer in Cases Ordinary and Extraordinary; Taken out of the Scriptures and the ancient Liturgies of several Churches, especially the Greek, Together with A Large Preface in Vindication of the Liturgy of the Church of England.*

It was published in 1658, and there may well have been an earlier edition or editions.[82] It was written for Anglican use when the Prayer Book was proscribed. There is, however, a built-in contradiction in the volume, for while its preface vindicates the Prayer Book, the *Collection of Offices* makes use of "the devotions of the Greek Church with some mixture of the *Mozarabick* and *Aethiopick* Liturgies"[83] and we are led to believe, at least implicitly, that these are better than the Prayer Book. In favour of this volume, however, it can be said to have acquainted the Church of England clergy and thoughtful laity with the solemn splendour, the high reverence, and the radiance of the Resurrection that coruscates in

[80] It is, however, worth noting that Sanderson introduces into the service of Baptism a phrase which would delight the Puritans, namely, "the Covenant of Grace," but which would be abhorrent to Anglicans recalling the "Solemn League and Covenant" which led to the overthrow of the king and the liturgy.

[81] These are considered in Chap. III above.

[82] According to a letter written on January 14, 1656-1657, Evelyn pleads with the Lieutenant of the Tower of London on behalf of Dr. Jeremy Taylor, presumably a prisoner or about to be "of whom I understand you have conceived some displeasure for the mistake of his Printer." A footnote by William Bray the editor of *Memoirs of John Evelyn* (including the *Diary* and a selection of letters, 1818 first edition), declares that Jeremy Taylor had been committed to the Tower for setting the picture of Christ praying before his *Collection of Offices* contrary to a new Act concerning "scandalous Pictures" as this was called. I have, however, been unable to confirm this footnote. If true, however, it would indicate that there was an earlier edition of *A Collection of Offices* than 1658, which may well have been withdrawn.

[83] From the vindicatory Preface (W. Jardine Grisbrooke, *Anglican Liturgies*, p. 20).

these early eastern liturgies. In his preface Taylor argues that these devotions, since they are taken from ancient liturgies and the fountains of Scripture "and therefore for the material part have great warrant and great authority: and therefore *if they be used with submission to Authority*, it is hop'd they may doe good. . . ."[84]

The importance of this *Collection of Offices* is rather to be found as a quarry from which lapidary devotions can be hewed, than as any alternative to the Anglican liturgy, though its influence was probably profound. Taylor's prose is too swelling (occasionally even flatulent), too consciously rhetorical, and too slow in making its points, for regular liturgical use. Moreover, its Communion Office differed too much from the Prayer Book Eucharist in structure and order, as well as in diction (except for the Words of Administration) for it to be an acceptable substitute or alternative.

Some of his borrowings were most imaginative. Such were the substitution of the Beatitudes for the Decalogue, the two private preparatory prayers taken from the liturgy of St. John Chrysostom and from the Greek Church's Office of Preparation for the Eucharist, and also the "Denunciation" adapted from the anthem sung at the Great Entrance in the liturgy of St. James.

Taylor's prayers are written to reflect doctrine. As W. Jardine Grisbrooke demonstrates,[85] they admirably mirror and express the Eucharistic Sacrifice through which Christ the Great High Priest presents to the Father his perfect Sacrifice in which the worshippers (and their offerings) are incorporated as his Body. The richness of this concept and act can be illustrated from the prayer that begins, "O Lord God our Creator," in its petition: "grant that, with a holy fear and a pure Conscience, we may finish this Service, present a holy Sacrifice holily unto thee, that thou maist receive it in Heaven, and smell a sweet Odor in the union of the eternal Sacrifice, which our blessed Lord perpetually offers. . . ."[86] The same doctrine is also found in the post-Communion prayers, as in "Receive, O Eternal God, this Sacrifice for and in behalf of all Christian people whom thou hast redeemed with the Blood of thy Son and purchased as thine own inheritance. . . ."[87]

The *epiklesis* (or invocation of the Holy Spirit) which was in the first English Prayer Book of 1549 and missing thereafter (except in the Scottish liturgy of 1637 and in subsequent litur-

[84] *Ibid.*
[86] *Ibid.*, p. 187.
[85] *Ibid.*, p. 25.
[87] *Ibid.*, p. 197.

gies of the Scottish Episcopal church) returns in Taylor's Holy Communion Rite. Above all in this Collection one is infected by his enthusiastic admiration for the Biblical depth and fidelity, and the vividly conceived personal and corporate piety of the primitive and powerful liturgies he has raided like an absolute monarch claiming the divine right of the King of Kings.

Our chapter ends with the Prayer Book still prohibited and the *Directory* still prescribed. We began with the Prayer Book aloft and end with it humbled but secretly read and followed as far as may be. Already the defences of the Prayer Book such as Hammond's, L'Estrange's and Taylor's, with the increasing knowledge and love of the primitive liturgies which they show, promise that phoenix-like the Book of Common Prayer will rise again from its own ashes. The stratagems of Taylor and Sanderson were desperate, but it was in the deepest darkness just before the dawn. Such were the metaphors and images in which loyal Anglicans saw these crepuscular years of the Commonwealth and Protectorate just prior to the Restoration of the Monarchy, the church, and the liturgy in 1660. Loyalty to the Prayer Book reached its zenith in that year, based on its new status as the channel of devotion of a suffering church.

CHAPTER X

THE PRAYER BOOK RESTORED
AND REVISED: 1660-1689

EVELYN PUT the capitalised heading of "ANNUS MIRA-BILIS" over his first diary entry on January 1, 1660. On May 29 his joy knew no bounds. "This day," he wrote, "his Majestie Charles II came to London after a sad and long exile and calamitous suffering both of the King and Church, being 17 yeares. This was also his birth-day, and with a triumph of above 20,000 horse and foote, brandishing their swords and shouting with inexpressible joy; the wayes strew'd with flowers, the bells ringing, the streetes hung with tapistry, fountaines running with wine." Evelyn "stood in the Strand and beheld it and bless'd God." His next entry in the diary for June 4 records that he went home, hoping to meet the English Ambassador to France, Sir Robert Browne, who, in fact, returned a few days later after an exile of nineteen years, "during all which time he kept up in his chapell the Liturgie and Offices of the Church of England, to his no small honour, and in a time when it was so low, and as many thought utterly lost, that in various controversies both with Papists and Sectaries our Divines us'd to argue for the visibility of the Church, from his chapell and congregation."

Although the new King had promised on April 4, 1660, in the Declaration of Breda "a liberty to tender consciences," and owed his return to his throne partly to General Monk and his Presbyterian supporters, and was to ask for the Savoy Conference to be convened in the hope of making it possible for the Presbyterians to be included in a wider national church, the Cavaliers in Parliament—to say nothing of the old or new members of the bench of bishops and the clergy now repossessed of their livings—were determined to restore the Prayer Book which now wore the halo of a persecuted and therefore doubly sacred book. Loyalty to the Prayer Book was sealed in the blood of King Charles the Martyr, his Archbishop, William Laud, and the thousands of Cavaliers who had died in the defence of their King and church. A triple cord bound together the restored King, church, and liturgy. So firm was the conviction that the liturgy must be retained, that

363

Parliament could only be restrained with difficulty from insisting that the Prayer Book as mildly revised in 1604 should be restored,[1] and would be alarmed to hear that the revision in which the Convocation would be engaged in 1661 resulted in over six hundred changes and would have to be reassured that these were merely alterations of wording, not of substance. Clearly the abolition of the Prayer Book in the abhorred days of the Commonwealth and Protectorate, and the risks that faithful Anglican priests had taken to maintain its worship, and the defences of it from Thorndike's very learned *Of Religious Assemblies, and the Publick Service of God* (1642)[2] up to Sparrow's *Rationale* (1655) and L'Estrange's *Alliance of Divine Offices* (1659) had created a great loyalty to the Prayer Book on the part of many who previously took its existence for granted. A new anxiety and even protectiveness about the liturgy was to be seen on the part of some of the bishops in their writings and in the Savoy Conference.

The outstanding exemplar of this attitude was John Gauden who was, as we have seen, the supposed author of *Eikon Basilike*. In 1661, now rewarded for his fidelity to Charles I by being appointed to the see of Exeter by Charles II, he wrote a timely treatise, *Considerations touching the Liturgy of the Church of England* (1661) while the revision of the Prayer Book was still under consideration. Right at the outset he makes it plain that the King's indulgent declaration at Breda "was not to show any *disaffection* or *disesteem* in *His Majesty* toward the ancient and excellent Liturgy of the Church of *England*, which was His companion and comfort in all His distresses, and which still is the daily rule

---

[1] On May 26, 1660, the House of Commons received the Sacrament according to the use of the 1604 Prayer Book, excepting three or four members who were suspended from sitting because of their refusal. Entirely disregarding the King's promise to consider revising the Prayer Book to accommodate the scruples of Presbyterian ministers, the Commons began measures for confirming the liturgy of the Church of England as it stood on June 25.

[2] The sub-title was characteristic of the best Caroline theology, namely, "A Discourse according to Apostolicall Rule and Practice." It was published by Cambridge University. Thorndike provided an erudite attempt to show that the Offices of the Church of England were in direct line with the development of worship in the synagogue, the nascent church of the New Testament, in accord with the descriptions of worship given by such early Fathers as Justin Martyr, Tertullian, and Irenaeus, and like the offices of the liturgies of the Apostolical constitutions, and of those of the early Roman Rite, as well as of St. James, St. Mark, and St. John Chrysostom. Incidentally, it reinterprets and confutes some of the Scriptural and Patristic proof-texts of the Puritan apologists. It has not received the attention it warrants probably because it requires close reading. It was not reprinted in the six volume edition of Thorndike's *Works* prepared for the Library of Anglo-Catholic Theology (1844-1854).

and measure of His Majesties publique Devotions; as it hath been of His *Royal Fathers* of blessed memory, and all His *Princely Progenitors* since the Reformation."[3] He continues with criticisms of Puritan prayers for their "rudeness, weaknesse and familiarity of some Ministers devotions"[4] which are bound only by their own fancies. The positive benefits of a prescribed liturgy, as he sees them are five. Such conduces much "to the more *solemne, complete, august,* and *reverent* worship of the Divine Majesty in Christian Congregations." It is, secondly, an admirable means "to preserve the truth of Christian and Reformed *Doctrine* by the consonancy of *publicke Devotions.*" It is also a necessity for the expression of harmony and communion on the national level as well as on the parochial, for all Christians. Fourthly, a liturgical form benefits and comforts the well-bred and judicious type of Christian, but is also a measure that will guarantee security and "*composure* of their spirits in the Worship of God." Finally, "But above all, a constant and compleat Liturgy mightily conduceth to the *edification* and *salvation* as well as unanimity and peace of the *meaner sort of people. . . .*"[5] This warning of itself would serve notice on the Puritans of every stripe that not much should be hoped from either the Declaration of Breda or the Savoy Conference.

1. The Savoy Conference of 1661

From the standpoint of the Presbyterian ministers (now the dominant Puritan group) events built up to a disappointing and frustrating anti-climax. While the King was preparing to return to England, he granted these ministers an interview at Breda. They, counting on his favour, and at his suggestion, drew up "The first Address and Proposals of the Ministers" which included four prefatory demands they considered necessary before they could be happy in a wider Church of England. They asked that the various congregations may have "liberty for edification and mutual provoking to godliness"; that each congregation may also have "a learned, orthodox, and godly pastor residing amongst them"; "that none may be admitted to the Lord's Supper, till they completely understand the principles of the Christian religion and do personally and publickly own their baptismal covenant, by a credible profession

---

[3] *Op. cit.,* p. 1.   [4] *Ibid.,* p. 6.
[5] *Ibid.,* p. 7. These snobbish words were presumably meant for the Independents and Baptists who practised extemporary prayer, the members and supporters of Cromwell's Ironsides, and who often included in their midst "mechanick preachers" like the immortal Bunyan.

of faith and obedience . . . and that unto such only confirmation (if continued in the church) may be administered"; and "that an effectual course be taken for the sanctification of the Lord's day, appropriating the same to holy exercises both in public and private without unnecessary divertisements."[6] The rest of the proposals dealt with liturgy in general and ceremonies in particular. In principle the ministers approved of a liturgy "provided that it be for the matter agreeable unto the word of God, and fitly suited to the several ordinances, and necessities of the church; neither too tedious in the whole, nor composed of too short prayers, unmeet repetitions or responsals: not to be dissonant from the liturgies of other reformed churches; nor too rigourously imposed; nor the minister so confined thereunto, but that he may also make use of those gifts of prayer and exhortation, which Christ hath given him for the service and edification of the church."[7]

The ensuing paragraph contained the genesis of the idea of a comprehensive Scriptural liturgy to be agreed upon by a conference of Anglican and Dissenting divines. It reads:

> that for the settling of the church in unity and peace, some learned, godly and moderate divines of both persuasions, indifferently chosen, may be employed to compile such a form as is before described, as much as may be in Scripture words; or at least to revise and effectually reform the old, together with an addition or insertion of some other varying forms in Scripture phrase, to be used at the minister's choice; of which variety and liberty there be instances in the Book of Common Prayer.[8]

The tactful reference in the final sentence needs to be pointed out, so rare is the phenomenon. It is followed by the more typical intractableness in utterly rejecting all ceremonies for which no Scriptural warrant can be found, such as kneeling at the Lord's Supper, the crossing of the child at Baptism, the use of the surplice, the erection of altars, and desires the abolition of "such holy days as are but of human institution." The only ceremony they were prepared to retain which other Puritans had rejected was the use of the ring in marriage. This they wished to leave optional.

The Presbyterians were making only minimal concessions, such as the ring just mentioned, the acceptance of a liturgy (although

---

[6] *Puritan Documents* (ed. and intro., Peter Bayne, 1862), pp. 14ff.
[7] *Ibid.*, p. 17.　　　　　　　　　　[8] *Ibid.*, p. 18.

Scripturally not traditionally determined, excluding all responses and practically every ceremony and wanting to aggregate the collects into a longer prayer, and allowing many alternatives for the minister), and a willingness to accept a synodal as contrasted with prelatical or monarchical episcopate.[9] Their church order looked more Genevan than English, and the Prayer Book they had in mind seemed more like a cross between John Knox's Genevan Service Book and the Parliamentary *Directory*, since it bore little resemblance to the Book of Common Prayer.

When the Savoy Conference was eventually authorized by the King on March 25, 1661, it was to prove the Anglican representatives at least as obdurate as the Presbyterian divines. Not even the bishops were masters in their own house for although the Conference was called for a liturgical purpose, it "was managed by politicians rather than by liturgical scholars."[10] Clarendon's men, former Oxford dons and members of the Great Tew Circle of which Lord Falkland was the centre, and Latitudinarians[11] like the Lord Chancellor Clarendon himself, were Gilbert Sheldon, Bishop of London, and George Morley, Bishop of Worcester. The liturgists on the Anglican side were Laudians, Bishops Cosin and Wren, but the Latitudinarians won. The terms of the Commission reflect the intentions of those in power. The Commissioners are authorized "to advise upon and review the said Book of Common Prayer, comparing the same with the most ancient liturgies which have been used in the Church, in the primitive and purest times." While provision is made for changes, it is carefully limited to permit the Commissioners "to make such reasonable and necessary alterations, corrections, and amendments therein, as . . . shall be agreed upon to be needful or expedient for the giving satisfaction to tender consciences, and the restoring and continuance of peace and unity." Not only so, but there is a further restriction, namely, that of "avoiding, as much as may be, all unnecessary alterations of the forms and liturgy wherewith the people are already acquainted, and have so long received in the Church of England."[12] The Con-

---

[9] They had in mind Archbishop James Ussher's "reduced episcopacy." His former chaplain, Nicholas Bernard, had issued it in 1656 after the Archbishop's death under the title, *The Reduction of Episcopacy unto the form of Synodical Government received in the Ancient Church.*

[10] G. J. Cuming, *A History of Anglican Liturgy* (1969), p. 153.

[11] According to B.H.G. Wormald's biography, *Clarendon* (Cambridge, 1951), p. 240, he took the view that ceremonial was "not in itself of that important value to be either entered on with that resolution, or to be carried on with such passion."

[12] *Documents relating to the settlement of the Church of England by the Act of Uniformity of 1662* (ed. G. Gould, 1862), p. 109.

ference began on April 15, 1661, and met during the ensuing four months, ending on July 21, 1661.

What was the composition of the Commission? Anglicans and Puritans each had twelve representatives, selected for their moderation. The nominal leader of the bishops was Accepted Frewen, Archbishop of York, but because of the latter's advanced years the actual leader was Sheldon of London. During the Interregnum Sheldon had approved of modifications of the Prayer Book to permit it to be used without contravening the law, as had Robert Sanderson, Bishop of Lincoln, another member of the Commission. John Gauden, a convert from Puritanism, and Bishop of Exeter, was now a convinced apologist for both episcopacy and liturgy. Morley, Bishop of Worcester, and Cosin, Bishop of Durham (the most learned in liturgical lore), had been chaplains on the Continent during the Civil War and Protectorate.

Two Presbyterian ministers had been given the responsibility of selecting the Presbyterian members of the Commission. One was Edward Reynolds, the first Puritan Vice-Chancellor of Oxford University as Dean of Christ Church, who had been ejected from office because he could not accept the Engagement of 1649 (which was to prepare for a republic), and who had conformed at the Restoration and accepted appointment as Bishop of Norwich before the Savoy Conference was summoned, but was still attached to a synodical conception of his office. The other was Edmund Calamy, a Cambridge man, a strict Calvinist, a monarchist but against bishops. Other Presbyterian Commissioners were John Wallis, the Saville Professor of Geometry at Oxford, and Matthew Newcomen, a London minister, as Calamy was. The most notable member on the Presbyterian side was, however, the superb pastor, preacher, and prolific writer on spirituality, controversial divinity, and casuistry, Richard Baxter. No one on either side worked harder or contributed more to the Conference than he. Cosin knew most about worship on the Anglican side, Baxter knew most about worship on the Presbyterian side; both would eventually be disappointed for different reasons.

Sheldon's opening move was to state that the bishops were satisfied with the Book of Common Prayer as it was, and that as the Conference had been called at the behest of the Presbyterians, it was their responsibility to present both exceptions and alternatives. This policy put the onus for change on the Presbyterians and meant that the Anglican strategy would be to criticize the criticisms. It did have one unfortunate effect for the Anglicans: it meant that the Laudian hope of amending the Prayer Book in the direction of the 1549 Book of Common Prayer or even to bring it closer to the Scottish liturgy of 1637 was doomed, as Cosin must have realized though it did not prevent him (with the aid of Bishop Wren not of the Commission) from making his own liturgical revisions.[13]

Baxter reported that, "When we were withdrawn, it pleased our Brethren presently to divide the undertaken work: The drawing up of *Exceptions against the Common-Prayer*, they undertook themselves, and were to meet from day to day for that end: The drawing up of Additions or new Forms they imposed on *me alone*, because I had been guilty of that Design from the beginning, and of engaging them in that piece of Service (and some of them thought it would prove odious to the Independents and others who are against a Liturgy as such)."[14]

The Presbyterian Brethren produced a solid document of *Exceptions*, of which eighteen were general in character and seventy-eight particular. These are an admirable summary of the historic Puritan objections to the liturgy, as these had been advanced since the Elizabethan days of Cartwright, Travers, and Field, and renewed in the Hampton Court Conference and in the preface to the Parliamentary *Directory*.[15] The criticisms are of three kinds: major principles, weaknesses in wording, and ceremonies and customs.

It is proposed that the Prayer Book should be doctrinally acceptable to all Protestants; that the gift of conceived prayer should be allowed as a supplementation of the liturgy; that all readings from the Apocrypha will be eliminated (thus excluding the *Benedicite* and Offertory sentences from the Book of Tobit); that the practice of having godparents at Baptism, defunct since 1645, should not be revived; that since Baptism and Holy Communion are *the* two Sacraments, lax wording suggestive of Confirmation and Matrimony as Sacraments should be amended; the presumption that all worshippers are regenerate is a false one and this presupposition in the Baptismal and Burial Services should be removed; and, final-

---

13 Their preliminary studies for Prayer Book revision will be considered immediately after the present section of the chapter.

14 *Reliquiae Baxterianae* (ed. M. Sylvester, 1696), I, Pt. II, Sect. 175.

15 John Wesley was to review these "Exceptions" before preparing his adaptation of the Prayer Book for the use of Methodists in North America. See Davies, *op. cit.*, III, p. 190.

ly, a stricter control of admission to Baptism and Communion should be applied to maintain discipline and the purity of the church.

In matters of wording, there is a strong objection raised against any responses of the people in prayers, since their duty is to listen reverently and, on the Pauline prescription, merely to say, "Amen." This, of course, would radically alter the Litany. "Minister" is to be substituted for "priest" and "Lord's Day" for "Sunday." No parts of the Old Testament or of the Acts of the Apostles are to be called "Epistles." The Collects need revision. The new translation of the Scriptures should be used for all lections from Scripture, and a truer version of the metrical Psalms should be made. Such obsolete words as "prevent," "depart," and "worship" should be amended.

The "noxious ceremonies," as might have been confidently predicted, reappear in the criticisms of customs and usages: kneeling for Communion, the surplice, the sign of the Cross in Baptism, and the ring in Matrimony. Neither is Lent to be kept, nor are Saints' Days. Unnecessary movement in services is to be avoided as distracting. On rainy days the entire burial service should be said in church. As Cuming points out,[16] this provoked the witty rejoinder from the bishops, "being not pretended to be for the ease of tender consciences, but of tender heads, [this] may be helped by a cap better than a rubric."

The criticisms were too thorough-going and radical to be acceptable, and they went far beyond the rather limited terms of the warrant for the Commission. Not surprisingly, therefore, even their most sensible proposals were given a curt rebuttal by the bishops. In fact, only seventeen of the ninety-six exceptions were conceded, three of them of a general and fourteen of a particular nature. The most significant was to require the Authorized Version of the Bible for all readings, which, of course, changed neither the structure nor the doctrine of the Prayer Book. Some agreement was found in the desire to avoid archaisms. But over-all Anglican obduracy overcame Presbyterian persistence.

The meagre concessions on unimportant points clearly disappointed the ministers, for in their "Rejoinder" they complain: "we find ourselves disappointed . . . as may appear both by the paucity of the concessions and the inconsiderableness of them, they

16 *A History of Anglican Liturgy,* p. 156.

being for the most part verbal and literal, rather than real and substantial."[17] They realized that the cause of comprehension in a wider national church was lost, for they take their farewell in terms that are more critical of the Prayer Book than even their detailed criticisms of it: "Prayer and humility are, indeed, the necessary means of peace; but if you will let us pray for peace in no words but are in the Common Prayer book, their brevity and unaptness, and the customariness, that will take off the edge of fervour with human nature, will not give leave (or help sufficient) to our souls to work towards God, upon this subject, with that enlargedness, copiousness, and freedom as is necessary to true fervour. A brief, transient touch and away, is not enough to warm the heart aright; and cold prayers are likely to have a cold return. . . ."[18] Here the main thrust of the Puritan tradition was finely expressed.

Their rejoinder was at its reasonable best, however, in its criticism of an exclusive dependence upon liturgical prayer, without the admixture of any extemporary prayers on the part of individual ministers. "Yet must we," the Presbyterian ministers insist, "before God and men, protest against this opium you would here prescribe or wish for, as that which plainly tendeth to cure the disease by the extinguishing of life, and to unite us all in a dead religion."[19] It is sincerity, they claim, rather than "comeliness of expression" by which prayers must be judged, and they cannot be wholly confined to a liturgy "that pretends to help the tongue" while it "hurts the heart." They saw themselves as moderates to the last: "We would avoid both the extreme that would have no forms, and the contrary extreme that would have nothing but forms."[20]

Richard Baxter's *The Reformation of the Liturgy*,[21] sometimes also known as *The Savoy Liturgy*, received equally short shrift from the bishops. The work was entirely his own composition, the work of a fortnight but, of course, using his experience in Kidderminster over many years. He wrote: "I could not have time to make use of any Book, save the Bible and my Concordance."[22] This astonishing achievement included a Lord's Day Service, Orders for Communion, Baptism, Matrimony, and Burial, with Forms for Catechising, the Visitation of the Sick (including Communion), for Extraordinary Days of Humiliation and Thanksgiving and

17 Bayne, *Puritan Documents*, p. 201. 18 *Ibid.*, p. 213.
19 *Ibid.*, p. 230.   20 *Ibid.*, p. 247.
21 This work will be considered in detail in Chapter XI "Puritan Service Books."
22 Sylvester, *op. cit.*, I, Pt. II, Sect. 172.

Anniversary Festivals, for Prayers and Thanksgiving for Particular Members of the Church, and for Pastoral Discipline (including Public Confession, Absolution, and Exclusion from the Holy Communion of the Church). An Appendix included A Larger Litany, or General Prayer and The Church's Praise for our Redemption both of which were to be used at discretion.[23] The surprise is the high doctrine of the Eucharist (though this was also a characteristic of the *Directory*'s Order for the Lord's Supper with its *epiklesis*), contained in "The Sacrament of the Body and Blood of Christ."[24] Though we have only the author's word for it, it was apparently well received by the rest of the Presbyterian ministers. Baxter writes: ". . . they past it at last in the same Words I had written it, save only that they put out a few lines in the Administration of the Lord's Supper, where the word *Offering* was used; and they put out a Page of Reasons for Infant Baptism, which I had annexed unto that Office, thinking it too long: and Dr. *Wallis* was desired to draw up the Prayer for the King, which is his Work (being somewhat altered by us). And we agreed to put before it a short Address to the Bishops, professing our readiness in Debates to yield to the shortning of anything that may be found amiss."[25]

Baxter's fondest hope must have been that his *Reformation of the Liturgy*, with its marginal Biblical references as proof that it was entirely according to the Word of God, would be accepted as an alternative to the Book of Common Prayer, an alternative particularly congenial to those of the Puritan persuasion. But this would have created a permanent dichotomy within the Church of England, and perpetuated not eased, the strife between orthodox and Puritan Anglicans. Bishop Gilbert Burnet of Salisbury (1643-1715), himself a former Presbyterian minister in the church of Scotland and former Professor of Divinity in the University of Glasgow, wrote that Baxter had convinced his colleagues that they

[23] For a text of *The Reformation of the Liturgy* by Richard Baxter, see *Reliquiae Liturgicae*, IV, *The Savoy Liturgy* (ed. Peter Hall, Bath, 1847), or *The Practical Works of the Rev. Richard Baxter* (ed. W. Orme, 1830), XV, pp. 450-527. The latter edition, however, excludes the prefatory Address to the Bishops.

[24] Baxter defines the Lord's Supper as "an holy Sacrament instituted by Christ, wherein bread and wine, being first by consecration made sacramentally, or representatively, the body and blood of Christ, are used by breaking and pouring out to represent and commemorate Christ's body and blood upon the cross once offered up to God for sin; and are given in the name of Christ unto the Church to signify and solemnize the renewal of his holy covenant with them, and the giving of himself unto them, to expiate their sins by his sacrifice, and sanctify them further by his Spirit, and confirm their right unto everlasting life." (ed. Peter Hall, *op. cit.*, p. 57.)

[25] Sylvester, *op. cit.*, I, Pt. II, Sect. 182.

should "offer everything which they thought might conduce to the good or peace of the Church, without considering what was like to be obtained, or what effect their demanding so much might have, in irritating the minds of those who were then the superior body in strength and number."[26] Baxter was proven to be no more a politician than Cosin would be and both traditions they represented were eventually rejected.

A series of events in the late spring and summer of 1661 made it appear that revision of the Prayer Book in a Laudian or a Puritan direction would be exceedingly unpopular. The Parliament consisting predominantly of Cavaliers who had lost lands and been mulcted by fines under the Puritan regime, and many of whom had been tutored by ejected Anglican clergymen in their youth, were in no mood to accommodate even the most conservative of Puritans, the Presbyterians. The House of Commons determined to burn publicly the Solemn League and Covenant on May 17. Nine days later the members of Parliament received the Sacrament according to the rite of the Jacobean Prayer Book. On June 18 the bishops were restored to the House of Lords. In entire disregard of the Savoy Conference, then meeting, the House of Commons commenced measures "for confirming the Liturgy of the Church of England." The aim was to pass a new Act of Uniformity, with the Prayer Book of 1604 annexed. This proposal was forwarded to the House of Lords on July 10, and there it stayed until January 1662. It was only the King and his government, together with a strong feeling in convocation that some rubrical and literary clarification was needed, with the need for a few additional services, that overcame the reluctance of the Commons which had been confirmed by the failure of the Savoy Conference to produce agreement.

2. The Durham Book

Two bishops, however, were preparing to make the best of the opportunity that might be given to the Church of England to revise its liturgy. One of them, Bishop Wren of Ely, had eighteen years in the Tower of London in which to think about improving the Prayer Book[27] and was seventy-six years of age in 1661, the

---

[26] *History of My Own Time*, 2 Vols. (1723-1724), Vol. I, p. 320.

[27] Wren when incarcerated considered that "Never could there have been an opportunity so offenceless on the Church's part for amending the Book of Common Prayer as now, when it hath been so long disused that not one of five hundred is so perfect in it as to observe alterations." (G. J. Cuming, *The Durham Book*,

embodiment of the Laudian tradition. The other, John Cosin, had succeeded Wren as Master of Peterhouse, Cambridge, had gone into exile in 1643, and was also a trusted Laudian; in 1660 he had been consecrated Bishop of Durham at the age of sixty-six. Wren's work is contained in a manuscript which he himself terms "Advices" and so can conveniently be called by that name.[28] Cosin probably saw the "Advices" shortly after he returned to England in 1660 and then prepared his own proposals which are contained in a paper with the heading, *Particulars to be considered, explained, and corrected in the Book of Common Prayer.*[29] This probability is based on the facts that the similarity of title, the specifying of reasons for each proposed change, and the over-riding concern for accuracy in detail, also characterize Wren's work.

It may also be conjectured that Cosin and Wren on learning that the King was proposing a conference such as the Savoy, combined their proposals for revision in the volume entitled the *Durham Book*, a Prayer Book dated 1619, in which Cosin had written in the changes and additions put forward by Wren and himself, together with much other material, the larger part of which was now added by Cosin himself. In preparing the *Durham Book*, it was obvious that a major source was Wedderburn's Scottish liturgy of 1637 which influenced the Order for Holy Communion. This can be seen in the introducing of a thanksgiving for the departed, rearranging the canon, restoring the *epiklesis* and the commemoration of the Passion, Resurrection and Ascension of Christ, which is "now represented" to God the Father. There is no reference to Christ's death, without the addition "and sacrifice." "Christ's Church militant here upon earth" is changed to "Christ's Catholic Church." Andrewes's Offertory Sentences reappear and the alms are first to be presented upon the holy table, and afterwards the elements. There are both epistoller and gospeller, in addition to the celebrant. The Creed and *Sanctus* may be sung, but the *Agnus Dei* is required to be sung as also the added Post-Communion Sentences. The 1549 Prayer Book was used, but Wedderburn was given the preference.

1961, pp. 287-88.) Cuming, *ibid.*, p. xv, writes of Cosin that "yet, he remains with Wren, the most copious contributor to the Prayer Book since Archbishop Cranmer."

[28] The text can be found in Cuming, *ibid.*, and in *Fragmentary Illustrations of the History of the Book of Common Prayer* (ed. W. K. Jacobson, 1874), pp. 43-109.

[29] Cuming, *A History of the Anglican Liturgy*, p. 150.

Other sources for the *Durham Book* are the Prayer Book itself. Several proposals are modifications of materials from other parts of the book, while others involved the changing of rubrics into phrases and sentences. The Canons of 1604 and even the Elizabethan *Injunctions* and *Advertisements* are occasionally consulted for rubrics. Cosin's *Devotions* is the source of some small changes. G. J. Cuming[30] emphasizes the caution with which they approached debatable matters, for they never refer to the Scottish liturgy associated with Laud, nor do they mention the requirement of Laud that the people should come up to the altar rails to receive Communion, for the words "Draw near" are diluted to read "Draw near with a true heart in full assurance of faith." But of the Laudian character of their proposed revision there is no question. This is evident not only in the changes borrowed from Wedderburn (which were approved by Laud as Archbishop of Canterbury), but also in the blessing of the water in Baptism, as in the emphasis on bodily gestures for the honouring of God in the Catechism, both objectionable to the Puritans.

Cosin, as we have seen, had been a member of the commission of the Savoy Conference, which ended July 25, 1661. He then returned to his diocese of Durham, and his chaplain, William Sancroft, took charge of the *Durham Book*. First, he added the concessions made at the Savoy Conference. Then he revised the book in thoroughgoing detail, with the result that the rubrics were clarified in about eighty cases, and the printed text was restored in sixty-six cases. Many of these revisions were mere minutiae, and about a dozen of them came from Wren's materials, little, if any, from Cosin's. Next follows new material of importance, including an Ember Collect composed by Cosin. Also the Presbyterians' request that the Sentences from Tobit be rejected as apocryphal material not in the canon of Scripture, was acceded to and entered, and their other request that the sick man receiving Communion shall be absolved, not as a matter of course, but "if he shall humbly and heartily desire it."

Hitherto, the *Durham Book* had been a private, unofficial attempt by two liturgically learned Laudian bishops to suggest Prayer Book revisions. About the beginning of September, 1661, the contents were to be considered by authority in the person of Sheldon, Bishop of London and ecclesiastical adviser to the government, for Sheldon and Wren wrote an urgent letter to Cosin, bid-

30 *Ibid.*, p. 153.

ding him return with all speed to London by the beginning of November, as he, in fact, did.[31]

The *Durham Book* was not yet complete. Cosin started to correct The Ordering of Deacons in a Prayer Book of 1634 because there was no Ordinal in the *Durham Book*, and Sancroft completed the work by writing in Wren's proposals for the improvement of the text. He then copied the contents of the *Durham Book* into the new book, which is known as *The Fair Copy*.[32] This included twenty additional rubrical improvements, twenty-eight more rejections of alterations, and there is a new and conservative edition of the Canon, besides the *Durham Book* version of the Canon, which is written out fully on a separate sheet, and which retains the old Canon intact, while allowing the *Durham Book* rubrics and Words of Administration. A laconic note added by Sancroft adds that both versions of the Canon are "left to censure." His final note in the *Durham Book* completes the account: "My lords the bishops at Ely House ordered all in the old method."[33] It is sufficient explanation as to why he then gives the outline of an order corresponding exactly to the new Canon of 1662.

Both the ceremonial and the doctrine of the *Durham Book* were higher than the Prayer Book of 1662, and on this double count were probably rejected. While rails about the Communion table were too bitter a memory and therefore too controversial an issue to raise again, yet the holy table is to stand in the upper part of the chancel, and there are to be both epistoller and gospeller at the Holy Communion, and the collection and the elements are to be presented at the altar by the celebrant. Wafers may be used, and the manual acts of fraction and libation are stressed. Though this was considerably less than the young Cosin would have liked, it was more than Convocation (or Parliament behind Convocation) would tolerate. The same was the case with the doctrine. In the bidding of the prayer for the church, the phrase "militant here upon earth" was omitted, leaving one to assume that the bidding was for the church militant and triumphant, and that was made explicit in the restoration at the end of the prayer of the thanksgiving for

---

[31] Cosin, *Correspondence* (Surtees Society Publication LV, Vol. II, p. 31, cited by Cuming, *A History of the Anglican Liturgy*, p. 159. The entire revisionary studies of Wren and Cosin have been described at length in Cuming's *Durham Book* and are very clearly and conveniently summarized in his *A History of the Anglican Liturgy*, both of which have proved invaluable for this section of this chapter.

[32] The text of the "Fair Copy" is to be found in Cuming's *Durham Book*.

[33] *Ibid.*, p. 180.

the dead. Convocation rejected a petition for their well-being "at the day of the generall Resurrection." Cosin also makes much of the Communion as a sacrifice, though insisting that Christ's sacrifice is unrepeatable and unique, and places the Prayer of Oblation immediately after the Prayer of Consecration. The *epiklesis*, based on the 1549 Prayer Book and the 1637 Scottish liturgy, affirming a transformation effected by the Holy Spirit, wisely avoids the subjective term "that they may be unto us." Finally, it should be noted that Cosin insisted that the Body and Blood of Christ were "sacramentally and really" but not "sensibly" present in the Sacrament. This view was strengthened by the inclusion of the 1549 phrase "these holy mysteries" and of the *Agnus Dei*, both of which were later rejected by convocation, presumably as seeming too Romanist.

If we compare the experiences of Baxter and Cosin as frustrated liturgists, each has a different but dubious consolation. Cosin's is one for the distant future, for the South African alternative form of 1929, the American Episcopal church rite of 1935, and the proposed Indian rite of *The Holy Eucharist* of 1951, all followed the Cosin proposals in general outline and intention.[34] Baxter's was a more immediate consolation, though it is doubtful that Cosin ever told him of it, namely, that in a few important respects Cosin accepted Baxter's proposals for bettering the Book of Common Prayer. The latter is the interesting conclusion of E. C. Ratcliff.[35] Baxter had criticised the Prayer Book Consecratory Prayer thus: "It is a disorder . . . to begin in a Prayer and to end in a Narrative" and urged that "The Consecration Commemoration . . . are not distinctly enough performed."[36] This first requirement was met in the *epiklesis* of the Scottish liturgy, and the second in Cosin's alternative Prayer of Consecration in which the Institution Narrative is followed by the Prayer of Oblation (a "Memoriall") containing a commemoration of the Passion, Resurrection, and Ascension of Christ. Not only so, but in the Savoy liturgy of Baxter the action in the Holy Communion Service is said to be a representation of Christ's death, and it is linked with his heavenly Intercession.[37]

[34] *Ibid.*, p. xxvi.

[35] "The Savoy Conference and the Book of Common Prayer," being Chap. 2 of *From Uniformity to Unity* (eds. Geoffrey F. Nuttall and Owen Chadwick, 1962), p. 134.

[36] *Reliquiae Baxterianae*, ed. M. Sylvester, I, Pt. II, Sect. 174.

[37] This "explication" of the Sacrament, at the beginning of Baxter's "Order of Celebrating the Sacrament of the Body and Blood of Christ" includes the following statement (*Reliquiae Liturgicae*, IV, *The Savoy Liturgy*, ed. Peter Hall, Bath, 1847, pp. 56-57): "And when Christ was ready to leave the world, and to

The point is that the English and Scottish Consecration prayers make no reference to either of these points, yet Cosin changed part of the Prayer of Consecration to read "by the Merits & Death of thy Sonne Jesus Christ, now represented unto thee, & through faith in his Bloud, who maketh intercession for us at thy right Hand. . . ." Cosin's Prayers of Consecration were never submitted to Convocation for the consideration of the two Houses. As we shall see, conservatism, moderation, and pragmatism, were the dominating characteristics of the revision, especially conservatism.

3. The Prayer Book of 1662

The clue to the character of the revision accomplished by Convocation in 1661 and authorized by King and Parliament in 1662 is to be found in the Preface, which was the work of Bishop Robert Sanderson of Lincoln. He wrote:

> That most of the Alterations were made, either first, for the better direction of them that are to officiate in any part of Divine Service, which is chiefly done in the Kalendars and Rubricks; Or secondly, for the more proper expressing of some words or phrases of ancient usage in terms more suitable to the language of the present times . . . ; or thirdly, for a more perfect rendering of such portions of holy Scripture, as are inserted into the Liturgy; which, in the Epistles and Gospels especially, and in sundry other places are now ordered to be read according to the last Translation.

The primary concern was to restore rather than to revise the Prayer Book, but to revise only where directions or language could be made clearer. As for the additions made, they were necessities. So Sanderson wrote of them:

> . . . it was thought convenient that some Prayers and Thanksgivings, fitted to special occasions, should be added in their due places; particularly for those at sea, together

---

give up himself a sacrifice for us, and *intercede* and exercise the fulness of his kingly power as the Church's Head, and by his grace to draw men to himself, and prepare them for his glory; he did himself institute the Sacrament of his body and blood at his last supper, to be a continued *representation* and remembrance of his death . . ." (I have italicized the key concepts). See also *ibid.*, pp. 61, 64, and especially p. 70 with its petition, "we beseech thee, by thine intercession with the Father, through the sacrifice of thy body and blood, give us the pardon of our sins, and thy quickening Spirit . . ." and p. 73 (an alternative prayer of Consecration), "and through his sacrifice and intercession give us pardon of our sins."

with an Office for the Baptism of such as are of riper years; which . . . by the growth of Anabaptism,[38] through the licentiousness of the late times crept in amongst us, is now become necessary, and may be always useful to the Baptizing of Natives in our Plantations, and others converted to the Faith.

The work of revision was not only politically restricted, but also it was rushed.[39] The Convocation of Canterbury was convened on May 8, 1661. Before it adjourned on July 31, it had completed three tasks. One was the preparation of a form of prayer with thanksgiving for the anniversary of the King's birth and Restoration on May 29. A second was the provision of a form of prayer commemorating the death of King Charles I, the anniversary of which was January 29. A third achievement was the completion of an Office for the Baptism of adults. But as yet nothing was done about a revision of the 1604 Prayer Book.

The latter responsibility was committed to Convocation when it was reconvened on November 21, 1661. The upper House appointed eight bishops to act in the name of all in the work of revision, and to maintain revision between the full sessions of Convocation. These Bishops were Cosin of Durham, Wren of Ely, Skinner of Oxford, Warner of Rochester, Henchman of Salisbury, Morley of Worcester, Sanderson of Lincoln, and Nicholson of Gloucester. It is this group (at least the six excluding Cosin and Wren) which must ultimately be held responsible for suppressing the proposals in the *Durham Book*, and it is not difficult to see how this could have been done. In the group Sheldon's strong supporters were Morley, Sanderson, Henchman, and Nicholson, while Skinner and Warner were under a cloud and needed the sunshine of Sheldon's approval. In any case, the Laudian proposals of Cosin and Wren would have been unlikely to win any support from the Latitudinarian bishops who wished to placate the Presbyterians, or from the House of Commons which was satisfied with the Prayer Book of 1604.

The debates, held in the full session of both Houses, and lasting from 8:00 A.M. to 10:00 A.M., enabled the committee to devote the rest of the day to revision. The whole work was accomplished

38 A left-handed compliment to Tombes the learned Baptist who became Master of the Temple, and others, who had spread the tenets of their fellow believers, and the "licentiousness of the times" is an unintended tribute to the toleration of the Lord Protector, Cromwell.

39 J. Parker, *An Introduction to the History of the Successive Revisions of The Book of Common Prayer* (Oxford, 1879), pp. cccix, cccx.

in twenty-two days. The work was finished on December 18, 1661. This was copied out and subscribed to by both Houses of the Convocation of Canterbury and by the upper House and the proxies of the lower House of York on December 20 and sent to the King. This rapidity (necessarily involving some superficiality of supervision) was made possible, partly by the political pressure and partly also because Cosin and Wren had done the preliminary work of clarifying archaisms in diction and obscurities in rubrics in great detail. Furthermore, the additional forms had been prepared by the previous session of Convocation and only needed pruning, while experts dealt with such technical items as the table of moveable feasts. Although many of the most far-reaching proposals of the loyal Laudian bishops were not accepted, yet the bulk of the revisions in detail in the 1662 Prayer Book were clearly derived from the improvements in wording and rubrics set forth in the *Fair Copy* combining part of the *Advices* of Wren and part of the *Particulars* of Cosin, with additional material.[40] As the work went on, a full manuscript text was prepared by several scribes. This was finally signed by the proctors in Convocation and annexed to the Act of Uniformity. It kept a number of readings which were later rejected. Some, it is conjectured,[41] derived from a source otherwise unknown, and others were innovations arising in the committee. Four can plainly be attributed to Sanderson, while Wren secured the inclusion of several suggestions in his *Advices* which had not been incorporated in the *Durham Book*, and Cosin managed to get several suggestions accepted which had been left out of the *Fair Copy*. The three most prominent men on the committee were Sanderson, Cosin, and Wren. Only one other bishop, not on the committee, Reynolds of Norwich contributed significantly to the 1662 Prayer Book, since he is the author of the admirable General Thanksgiving, excellent in its comprehensiveness as in its concise and balanced phrasing,[42] and even the Prayer for All Conditions of Men has been attributed to him.[43] It is a singular irony

---

[40] Cuming, *A History of Anglican Liturgy*, p. 159.

[41] *Ibid.*, p. 160. See also F. E. Brightman, *The English Rite*, 2 Vols. (1915, 1922), I, pp. cc-cci.

[42] Consider these phrases as basis for the evaluation: "humble and hearty thanks"; "our creation, preservation, and all the blessings of this life"; and "for the means of grace and for the hope of glory."

[43] Another attribution is to Dr. Peter Gunning, Master of St. John's College, Cambridge, and afterwards Bishop of Chichester (1670-1674) and of Ely (1675-1684), an active participant in the Savoy Conference. Although it is a misuse of prayer, he may have directed the petition "that all who profess and call themselves Christians, may be led into the way of truth, and hold the faith in unity

of history that a proponent of the view that a minister should supplement the liturgy with prayers of his own composition, should have contributed so much to the prescribed Anglican liturgy of 1662, and as a prelate who disbelieved in the monarchical episcopate.

What were the important changes made in the conservative revision of 1662? Sanderson's Preface was prefixed to it, and the original preface of 1549 became an ensuing chapter "Concerning the Service of the Church." Higher language indicated the more elevated status of the threefold ministry of the church. For example, the Absolution at Morning and Evening Prayer was to be pronounced by the "Priest" instead of the "Minister." Also, "bishops, priests, and deacons" was substituted for "bishops, pastors, and ministers of the Church." In several cases "church" replaces "congregation." It is possible that each of these verbal changes, as also the clear denial of parity of ministers in the new Ordinal, was aimed at the Presbyterians who had preferred the older terms.

The changed language is also a clue to the increasing reverence with which worship was celebrated. One important example was seen in the terminological changes used in the rubrics for the Holy Communion. "Consecrated bread and wine" were substituted for the former "bread and wine" and instructions were given for "reverently" replacing the consecrated elements on the altar after Communion, for covering them with a linen cloth, and consuming them immediately after the blessing, instead of the priest taking them home for consumption at the table. The fraction in Communion was restored also. Furthermore, the idea of "offering" was restored in requiring the priest to offer the alms at the altar instead of putting them in a box, with the added petition for the acceptance of "our alms and oblations" at the beginning of the intercessions immediately ensuing.

---

of spirit, in the bond of peace, and in righteousness of life" as an arrow against the Puritans. It may originally have been written for the chapel of St. John's College as a substitute for the Litany in Evening Prayer, and its prefatory petitions for the king and clergy, were eliminated by the 1662 revisers in view of the alternative provision made for them. (See Massey H. Shepherd, Jr., *The Oxford American Prayer Book Commentary*, New York, 1950, pp. 18-19.) On the other hand, G. J. Cuming in "The Prayer Book in Convocation, November, 1661" in *The Journal of Ecclesisastical History*, VIII (1957), pp. 182-92, and in "Two Fragments of a Lost Liturgy," *Studies in Church History* (Leiden, 1966), III, pp. 247-53, argues that Reynolds composed both the General Thanksgiving and the Prayer for All Conditions, but that both were thoroughly revised by Sanderson.

There were also changes which the Presbyterians could well have approved, and might have been caused by their protests backed by Sanderson. The *Benedicite* disappeared, along with plainsong. In the Office of the Communion of the Sick, the invalid is to make a confession only if moved to do so, not by requirement, while newly married couples are recommended to make their Communion the same day, but not obliged to do so. Their criticism of the disorderliness of the Collects had been taken with the utmost seriousness, with the result that several of them were given clearer direction by a Scriptural quotation or a more memorable incisive phrase, and the hands of Cosin and Sanderson can be detected in this tidying up. The four "nocent" ceremonies were retained, but there was a reference to Canon 30 as an explanation for the signing of the Cross in Baptism and the Declaration on Kneeling was restored, probably as late as the Privy Council meeting of February 24, 1662, long after the book had been signed, on December 21, 1661. The Prayer Book was annexed to the Act of Uniformity. It received the royal assent on May 19, 1662, and was to come into use no later than St. Bartholomew's Day, August 24, 1662, which also marks the beginning of orthodox Dissent from the Church of England on the part of all the Puritan ministers who could not conscientiously affirm that the same Prayer Book was in all things conformable to the Word of God. A liturgical formulary which had initially intended to unite the nation, despite critics, was now the instrument of acute religious division.

The most significant changes of all, however, have yet to be considered. Among them the chief was the improvement in the Ordinal. There was an amplification (and ensuing clarification) of the formulae for ordination and for consecration to the episcopate. The formula of ordination to the priesthood pronounced by the bishop in 1552 as also in 1559 was "receiue the holy ghost: whose sinnes thou doest forgiue, etc." It was changed in 1662 to read, "Receive the Holy Ghost, *for the Office and work of a Priest, in the Church of God, now committed unto thee by the imposition of our hands.* Whose sins thou dost forgive, etc." Similarly at the consecration of a bishop the presiding Archbishop in 1552 and 1559 pronounced the formula, "Take the holy ghost, and remember that thou stirre vp the grace of God, which is in thee by the imposition of hands. For God, etc." In 1662 this was changed to: "Receive the holy Ghost, *for the office and work of Bishop in the Church of God, now committed unto thee by the Imposition of our hands, in*

382

the Name of the Father, and of the Son, and of the holy Ghost. Amen. And remember that thou stir vp the grace of God, which is *given* thee by *this* Imposition of *our* hands, For God, etc." These amplifications of the ordination and consecration formulae was due, at least in part, to the criticism of the validity of Anglican orders made by a Roman Catholic controversialist, who had drawn attention in particular to a defect in the ordination formula. This Peter Talbot, S.J., wrote in *A Treatise of the Nature of Catholick Faith and Heresie* (Rouen, 1657): "The intention of the Ordainer expressed by generall words, indifferent and appliable to all, or divers degrees of holy Orders, is not sufficient to make one a Priest, or a Bishop. As for example, *Receive the holy Ghost,* these words being indifferent to priesthood and Episcopacy, and used in both Ordinations, are not sufficiently expressive of either in particular . . . In the words of forme, whereby Protestants ordaine Bishops, there is not one word expressing Episcopall power, and authority."[44]

The new services, the work of the summer session of Convocation in 1661, were also important. The forms for the return of the King and the martyrdom of Charles I were allocated to two committees on 16 May, and the first had been completed in time to be used on May 29. It was on the same lines as the form of thanksgiving for the delivery from the Gunpowder Plot and was probably Wren's work, and he certainly introduced it into Convocation on May 18. The service commemorating the martyrdom of Charles I probably originated from prayers issued for the Cavalier army in the 1640s, supposedly collated by Bishop Duppa of Winchester, revised by Sancroft and published for use on January 30, 1661. Its excessive and idolatrous glorification of King Charles I amounting almost to an apotheosis, rendered it generally unacceptable, and the last version of it was printed on January 7, 1662.[45]

On May 18, 1661, another committee was appointed to prepare a form of Baptism for adults. The adaptation of the existing form

[44] *Op. cit.*, p. 22. The point (with a confirmatory citation from Talbot) is made by Ratcliff, *op. cit.*, p. 137.

[45] It finally read as follows: "Blessed Lord, in whose sight the death of thy Saints is precious, We magnify Thy Name for that abundant grace bestowed on our late martyred Sovereign, by which he was enabled so cheerfully to follow the steps of his Blessed Master and Saviour, in a constant meek suffering of all barbarous indignities, and at last resisting unto blood; and even then, according to the same pattern, praying for his murderers. Let his memory, O Lord, be ever blessed among us, that we may follow the example of his patience and charity. And grant that our land may be freed from the vengeance of his blood, and thy mercy glorified in the forgiveness of our sins. And all for Jesus Christ his Sake. *Amen.*"

for public Baptism was a simple matter, and it is attributed to Lloyd, the Bishop of St. Asaph.

It is to Sanderson's selection and editing that the 1662 Prayer Book owes the new "Forms of Prayer to be used at sea," which are a choice of prayers and Psalms rather than complete forms.[46]

Among alterations made, there are small but significant changes in the Services for Baptism, Confirmation, and Burial, with a very important modification in Ordination. In Baptism, the number of godparents is specified, and the promises are made in the child's name, which was previously the case only in private Baptism; also the petition for the sanctification of the water is borrowed from the Scottish liturgy of 1637. The dislocation in the Order for Confirmation is removed, an explanatory Preface is prefixed, and the Lord's Prayer is placed so that it follows immediately on the laying-on of hands, and thus, in this respect, corresponds with the order of the other occasional offices. In the Ordinal, in addition to the major changes already considered, Cosin's translation of the *Veni, Creator Spiritus* replaces the older version. In the Burial Service the order is changed to correspond with Sanderson's practice during the Interregnum.

Other additions included the provision of Proper Psalms for Ash Wednesday and Good Friday. A Collect, Epistle, and Gospel were provided for the Sixth Sunday after Epiphany, together with an Epistle for the Purification, an additional Easter anthem, and a Collect for the eve of Easter (originating from the Scottish liturgy but improved). The section with the heading Prayers was amplified by the inclusion of a second prayer "in time of dearth" (restored from the 1552 Prayer Book and omitted in 1559), two Ember prayers (one of Cosin's composition and the other from the Scottish liturgy), a revision of the Prayer for Parliament, and Wren's thanksgiving "for restoring public peace at home." In the Visitation of the Sick there are four additional prayers in an appendix, which bear the imprint of Sanderson. But the most important prayers to be added, which, because of their use at Morning and Evening Prayer for two centuries have become classics of devotion, deserve detailed consideration.

These are, of course, "A Prayer for all Conditions of Men" and "A General Thanksgiving." Their structure is similar in both prayers in that God is approached as Creator, Preserver and Redeemer, and the benefits of redemption in Christ are sought. In "A Prayer

---

[46] Izaak Walton's *Life of Dr. Robert Sanderson* (1678), p. 15.

for all Conditions," these are the way of truth, the unity of spirit, the bond of peace, and righteousness. In "A General Thanksgiving," they are the means of grace and the hope of glory. It is worth observing that in the "Prayer for all Conditions of Men" the missionary note first appears in the Prayer Book ("Thy saving health unto all nations"), and may well reflect the expansion of English colonization in the seventeenth century. The second petition[47] of the same prayer mirrors the bitter divisions in the Christian Church in Britain, and the Thirty Years War made it equally applicable in Europe. The third petition for the afflicted or distressed begs for divine comfort and finishes strongly with the words, "giving them patience under their sufferings, and a happy issue out of all their afflictions."

Earlier (footnote 43) it was pointed out that while it is agreed that Edward Reynolds, Bishop of Norwich at the Restoration, wrote "A General Thanksgiving," yet it is disputed whether he wrote "A Prayer for all Conditions of Men," or whether Dr. Peter Gunning did so. On grounds of both style and content, even when allowance is made for the editorial hand of another such as the apparently omnipresent Bishop Sanderson, I find it difficult to credit these two prayers to the same author. "A Prayer for all Conditions" is characterized by a compulsion to use alternating pairs of alternative words, presumably so that there are two chances of understanding. Thus we have "all sorts and conditions," "guided and governed," "profess and call themselves," "afflicted or distressed," and "comfort and relieve." In "A General Thanksgiving," there are only two such pairs of alternatives, namely, "goodness and loving-kindness," and the second word is not necessarily the same in meaning as the first. The second couplet is "holiness and righteousness." "A Prayer for all Conditions" has a slower rhythm and a longer line of phrases before stops, while "A General Thanksgiving" is more staccato and the diction is more concise, yet it has a regularity and balance that is most felicitous for it reads like poetry. It is also evident that the former has many more direct Scriptural citations,[48] is, in fact, a mosaic of them, while the latter is fully theological but rarely[49] echoes directly Scripture. Unques-

[47] "More especially we pray for thy holy Church universal, that it may be so guided and governed by thy good Spirit, that all who profess and call themselves Christians may be led into the way of truth, and hold the faith in unity of spirit, in the bond of peace, and in righteousness of life."

[48] Notably, Psalm 67:2; John 16:3; Psalm 25:9; and Ephesians 4:3.

[49] The exceptions are "hope of glory" (from Colossians 1:27) and a fainter echo from Luke 1:75.

tionably, however, they, together with the revised Ordinal, justify the work of revision which otherwise was meagre in results, clarification excepted. And even clarification is only a poor second best to creative innovation. Although "A General Thanksgiving" is listed among the occasional prayers, it soon gained for itself an essential place in the Anglican liturgy, for thanksgiving is at the very heart of worship.

4. An Evaluation of the Revision of 1662

What can be said by way of evaluating the 1662 Prayer Book? The usual adjectives apply, and Sanderson in his Preface indicates that "Our general aim was not to gratify this or that party in any of their unreasonable demands; but to do that . . . which . . . might most tend to the preservation of peace and unity in the Church." There was to be no rocking of the ark of the Church of England, whether by Laudian pushing or by Presbyterian pulling, though their combined efforts had at least taken the Prayer Book out of the harbour of 1604. Cuming rightly observes that "Sheldon had a more accurate sense of the nation's religious temper than either Cosin or Baxter."[50] This is a conservative, middle-of-the-way, safe, prudential, logical, lucid, moderate, and modest revision. Perhaps the best that can be said of it, excepting its additions, or possibly in part because of them, is that it has lasted practically unchanged until 1928, when significant alternatives to it were proposed, and in that period of 266 years (and nine generations) it has moulded the moderate, sober, and dignified devotions of the moderate, sober, and dignified English people; and has provided liturgical living space to the general satisfaction, barring some vehement disputes, of the three different parties of the Church of England, high, low, and broad.

In recent years, however, its liturgical fare is felt to be too lacking in vitamins, as well as in variety, to satisfy the needs of modern man.[51] Nor has it been able to keep up with the generally higher

---

[50] A History of Anglican Liturgy, p. 167.

[51] See, for example, W. Jardine Grisbrooke, "The 1662 Book of Common Prayer: its History and Character" in Studia Liturgica (Rotterdam), I, No. 3, Sept. 1962, with its conclusion (p. 166): "—despite its virtues and its beauty, neither of which should be underestimated—it is, as the attempted revision of 1927-8 and the all but universal practice of making considerable unauthorised alterations in the services both prove, sadly inadequate as a vehicle for the worship of twentieth century congregations." The words of the late Professor E. C. Ratcliff should also be noted: "If the Anglican Churches are alive and healthy, they cannot be content with an ossified form of worship derived from sixteenth and seventeenth century England, and marked by the time and circumstances of

and more advanced trend of Anglican worship since the impact of the Tractarian Movement of the nineteenth century.

There are two indicators of the unsatisfactory nature of the liturgical provisions of the Prayer Book of 1662, quite apart from the contemporary frustrations experienced by Cosin and Wren on the one hand, and Baxter and his Presbyterian associates on the other. One indicator of dissatisfaction is the many changes proposed within the Church of England for the improvement of the 1662 Book of Common Prayer, especially in the nineteenth and twentieth centuries.[52] The other indicator is the improvements and changes introduced into other liturgies in the Anglican Communion which were unrestricted by any subservience to the state, which had the effect of hampering revision in England because of the need for the Parliamentary approval of liturgical change.[53]

Using both sources of information, it will be found that it is in five major areas that improvements are felt to be necessary. First, there is great need for supplementation. Forms of worship are required for patronal festivals and harvest festivals, as also for the institution or induction of a minister to a parish or to other types of clerical responsibility (such as a chaplaincy), and for a late evening service.

Secondly, the enrichment of existing services (and the provision for greater variety) is needed. This is evident particularly in Holy Week, which, apart from a daily Eucharist, is not treated as the culmination and climax of the long preparation of Lent, with different lections, collects, and prayers for each successive day. There is also a paucity of significant ceremonies hallowed by traditional usage at this time. These could include: palm processions on Palm Sunday, the washing of altars on Maundy Thursday; the veneration of the Cross and subsequent burial of it at the Easter Sepulchre on Good Friday, reaching a climax in the Easter Vigil and the Midnight Mass of the Resurrection. None of these customs find

---

its production. Life and worship and Liturgy must move in step." (*The Anglican Tradition* by Meredith Dewey, E. C. Ratcliff, and Norman Sykes [being Sermons delivered in Chichester Cathedral on three Sunday mornings in July, 1958], p. 26.)

[52] R.C.D. Jasper documents the dissatisfactions with the rite in the nineteenth century in his *Prayer Book Revision in England, 1800-1900* (1954). See, for example, a perceptive criticism cited on pp. 85-89.

[53] This point is interestingly documented in J. Gordon Davies's article (itself a most useful modern critique), "The 1662 Book of Common Prayer: its virtues and vices" in *Studia Liturgica*, I, No. 3, Sept. 1962, pp. 167-74. Its virtues are claimed to be: an orderly and logical arrangement; dignity and clarity of style; a strong Biblical basis in lections and in the thought and imagery of the prayers; and some provision for lay participation.

any place in the Prayer Book of 1662 and could not have done, without invoking charges of "Popery."[54]

A third need is for calendric implementation. There is little point in replacing the seventeenth century State Services[55] with modern equivalents. There is, however, a great need for commemorations of the eminent imitators of God in Britain and in the wider reaches of the Anglican Communion who, by their exemplary holiness, Christian service to humanity, or defence and exposition of the Christian faith as theologians and teachers, deserve remembrance for they bridge time and space for their Incarnate Lord, demonstrating His relevance and contemporaneity to each generation. There is no argument, of course, for diminishing the primacy and centrality of the Christological cycle in the calendar; but there is a need to expand the Sanctoral cycle beyond the saints of the first century A.D. Not to do so, despite the grave problems of selection, is to imply that God has left Himself without witness for the past nineteen hundred years.

A fourth area for improvement, especially in the light of the emphasis of the modern liturgical movement[56] on the corporate responsibility of the people of God in worship (for "liturgy" means the work of the people), is the provision of new forms of worship allowing and encouraging a greater amount of participation on the part of the people, a need, incidentally, which was even less well met in Puritan worship. It was to meet this need that hymns were composed for and sung by the congregation, though there is no rubric in 1662 to allow for this practice. The Prayer Book of 1662, apart from a few versicles and responses, is almost as priest-ridden,[57] as Puritan worship, and is a ministerial monologue.

Fifthly, the unhurried Sunday of the seventeenth century has been replaced by a rushed week (and often weekend) in which there is no time for the leisurely model of service in 1662, which envisaged in succession, Mattins, Litany, and Holy Communion. That is why in many modern parishes it has been replaced by the Parish Communion, which includes a brief sermon.

[54] This catalogue of desirable enrichments is that of ibid., p. 172.

[55] These services were discussed earlier in Chap. VI, "Calendar Conflict: Holy Days or Holidays."

[56] See Chaps. I and XIII of Davies, op. cit., v.

[57] J. Gordon Davies, op. cit., p. 173, calculates that if the Communion Service is taken, with the third exhortation and the proper for the first Sunday in Advent, "we find that the congregation has some seven hundred words to say and the celebrant over 3500," excluding notices, banns, and sermon. He advises Litanies and an offertory procession as remedies.

Finally, as was the case with Cosin and Wren, so with many modern Anglicans there is a serious dissatisfaction with the Communion Service. When it is celebrated as part of the Parish Communion, there is an abbreviation of the Service of the Word, for there is usually no lesson from the Old Testament and the sermon becomes a sermonette.[58] Furthermore, there is an excessive priestly domination of the Office. Not least there is criticism because the structure of the Eucharist is seriously obscured because the Intercessions (now a part of the Prayer for the Church) should precede the Offertory. In addition, it seems wrong that the medieval Communion devotions should be interposed between the Offertory and the Prayer of Consecration. Moreover, the final Blessing is otiose, since the communicants are already united with Christ through the Holy Communion.

The preceding critique, it might be objected, employs several anachronisms adducing criticisms which were not made in its own day. This is not denied; but the point of the critique was to demonstrate that a more thoroughgoing revision in a higher direction might have made the Prayer Book a more adequate medium for seventeenth-century as for modern worship. It is surely not without significance that Baxter's *Savoy Liturgy*, together with the proposals of Wren and Cosin, included a prayer for the invocation of the Holy Spirit to consecrate the elements that they might sacramentally become the "Body and Blood of Christ."[59] The Prayer Book of 1662 had not advanced theologically beyond the Eucharistic doctrine of Cranmer in 1552, and that had been left behind by both the Laudians and the Presbyterians.

5. *The Ceremonial and Furnishings of the Restoration Church*

Before describing and evaluating further revisions, it might be well to consider how effectively the 1662 Prayer Book rubrics were implemented, and what the nature of Anglican worship was in fact, not merely in theory, in the aftermath of the Restoration. It is interesting that J. Wickham Legg thought that disregard for

[58] See the criticisms of A. M. Ramsey (later Archbishop of Canterbury, then Bishop of Durham) in *Durham Essays and Addresses* (1956), p. 20, and of E. L. Mascall, *Corpus Christi, Essays on the Church and the Eucharist* (1953), p. 78.

[59] E. C. Ratcliff has written that Baxter's Eucharistic doctrine is "more advanced than Laud's" and that his conception of the liturgical action of the Lord's Supper "is nearer the historic western tradition than the conception which Cranmer embodied in the Communion Service of the Prayer Book of 1522." (*Op. cit.*, p. 123.)

rubrics was a characteristic of the Anglican worship of the seventeenth century.[60] In making this charge, he doubts whether the priest placed on the holy table, after the presentation of the alms, so much bread and wine as he shall think sufficient. He very much doubted whether the curate, after the recitation of the Nicene Creed, did in fact declare to the people which fasting days of the following week were to be observed. The rubric at the end of the Holy Communion Service directed that in cathedral and collegiate churches that "they shall all receive Communion with the Priest every Sunday at the least": Legg thinks this was more honoured in the breach than in the observance. As for the requirement in the same liturgical context for the wearing of the cope at the Eucharist, this was not even insisted on in Durham where copes were provided. More seriously, attendance at Holy Communion was lamentably infrequent, except in a time of national anxiety.[61]

These charges are further substantiated by a lengthy letter sent by a young legal student in January 1683,[62] complaining of neglect in saying the daily service. He claims that "wee have yet as many severall wayes of Worshipp, as wee have Ministers, and every one that I could yet Discover, offends in some thing that is clearly contrary to Law. . . ." The excisions include: Exhortations, the *Benedictus*, the *Jubilate* (or substitution of a metrical Psalm), intrusion of part of Sick Visitation Office into public worship, prefacing the Creed with an idiosyncratic statement, telescoping first and second services, cutting off the Lord's Prayer and Nicene Creed, the Prayer for the Church Militant and the final Benediction, or the substitution of an invented Benediction. Other liberties include making the Churching of Women and Baptism into private services, which should be public. Other defects are: the reading of the Communion Service at the desk instead of at the altar; many churches have a weekly service (if that) instead of a daily one; children are often catechised only in Lent instead of throughout the entire year; conducting sacraments without a surplice and sometimes even without a gown. Particular indignation is reserved for those who break their canonical oath by "Venting a Prayer

[60] *English Church Life from the Restoration to the Tractarian Movement* . . . (1914), pp. 359-60.

[61] Evelyn's *Diary* records that on October 7, 1688, when people were afraid that Roman Catholicism might be brought back as the religion of the State, and Dr. Tenison preached at St. Martin's-in-the-Fields, "After which neere 1000 devout persons partook of the communion."

[62] The source is Bodleian Library Ms Rawlinson D. 851 (198 f.). It has also been printed as Appendix to Chap. IV of Legg, *op. cit.*, pp. 111ff.

(and sometimes I have had an impertinent one) of Private Composure."[63]

Another feature of Anglican worship in the period after 1660 was the ceremonial victory won by the Laudians. Whatever might be said of Anglican Eucharistic doctrine after the Restoration, unquestionably a higher ceremonial was maintained. One who loathes high ceremonial writes of how to treat a clergyman inordinately fond of it: "consequently handle him *as if he* really were a Popish Priest; his *Cope*, his *Hood*, his *Surplice*, his *Cringing Worship*, his *Altar* with *Candles* on it (most Nonsensically *unlighted* too), his *Bag-Pipes* or *Organs*, and in some places *Viols* and *Violins*, singing Men and *singing* Boys &c. are all *so very like* Popery (and all but the Vestments illegal) that I protest when I came in 1660, first from beyond Sea to *Pauls*, and *White-Hall*, I could scarce think my self to be in *England*, but in *Spain* or *Portugal* again, I saw so little difference, but that their *Service* was in *Latin* and ours in *English*."[64]

After the Restoration candlesticks were again placed on the altars. For example, Dr. Sancroft, Dean of York in 1664, presented a pair which had been made two years before.[65] Sancroft had also been begged by William Fuller, the Bishop of Lincoln, to procure him a splendid altar frontal for his cathedral, "one pane thereof to be Cloth of Gold, the other I thinke Damaske, of a sky colour; if it be not too Gawdy. Our Cathedrall hath a purple one of cloth paned with crimson Damaske: Mine I intend for solemne Dayes."[66]

Chancel screens were again built, which must have added an important element of mystery in a century becoming increasingly rationalistic and Latitudinarianly pragmatic.

Organs, which the Puritans liked for private and secular purposes but considered a distraction in church services, returned to the churches at the Restoration. Pepys observes on July 15, 1661: "Then to King's College chappell [Cambridge], where I found the scholars in their surplices at the service with the organs, which is a strange sight to what it used to be in my time to be here." It soon became the custom in Charles II's reign to play an organ voluntary after the Psalms.

<hr>

[63] *Ibid.*, pp. 112-14.
[64] Edmund Hickeringill, *The Ceremony Monger* (1689), p. 18. See also Pepys's *Diary* entries April 15, 1666, April 22, 1666, and October 16, 1666; also for July 29, 1660.
[65] T. M. Fallow and H. B. McCall, *Yorkshire Church Plate* (Leeds, 1912), p. 4, cited Legg, *op. cit.*, p. 139.
[66] Bodleian Library, Tanner Ms. 44 (f. 66).

There was a return to celebrating the church year with its different seasons. Pepys writes in his *Diary* for December 23, 1660, that his pew was decked with rosemary and bays. This custom of "sticking of Churches" with boughs at Christmas gave them a festive look, but, according to the *Spectator*[67] one church was "overdeckt" and looked more like a greenhouse than a place of worship; the pulpit was so swathed in holly and ivy, that "a light fellow in our Pew took occasion to say, that the Congregation heard the Word out of a Bush, like *Moses*."

Crosses and religious pictures after the Restoration are commonly used in the furnishings of churches. These are recommended by Dr. Thomas Tenison (1636-1715), afterwards Archbishop of Canterbury, who argues that devotional pictures are "helps to excite memory and passion" and to deny this is to "impute less to a Crucifix than to the Tomb of our friend, or a thread on our finger."[68]

Gestures which had been recommended by the Laudians as ways of expressing reverence were commonly seen again. Such was bowing at the sacred name of Jesus, and the signation of the Cross at Baptism. There is incidental reference to such customs in a fragment of a discussion by "Prejudice" (standing for Puritanism) and "Reason" (standing for Anglicanism):

Prejudice: "Have I not seen your Gravest Divines among you, at their entrance into the Church, cast their Eyes upon the Glass Windows, bow towards the Altars, worship the Pictur'd Saints, and make Leggs to the Brazen Candlesticks?" *Reason*: "All this is said upon the account of Bowing towards the Altar."[69]

In all these ways the dignity and beauty of worship, and the importance of reverence was stressed in post-Restoration Anglicanism, despite the fact that the rubrics were often laxly interpreted. In matters of ceremonial, it is clear that the Puritans have been utterly routed in the Church of England by the Laudians and their successors.

6. *Further Attempts at Revision or Supplementation*

This century seems to prove—in matters of liturgy at least—that those who will not learn the lessons of history must suffer for

---

[67] No. 282, Wed., Jan. 23, 1711-1712.
[68] *A Discourse of Idolatry* (1678), p. 279.
[69] *A Dialogue between Mr. Prejudice . . . and Mr. Reason, a Student in the University* (1682), p. 7.

their ignorance. There would be, once again, an unsuccessful attempt to move the Church of England towards comprehension in the hope of including the Presbyterians by meeting some of their criticisms of the Prayer Book. It did not work in 1661. Nor would it work in 1688 and 1689, although the external threat posed by the proselytising Roman Catholicism of the sovereign, King James II, was a strong inducement to present a united Protestant front.

Once again there would also be an attempt to supplement the latest Prayer Book with the usages of the 1549 Book or of the Scottish liturgy of 1637, believing that both were more faithful to the liturgies of the primitive church. This was, again, a maintaining of the Laudian tradition (as in the cases of Cosin and Wren), except that this time it would be the work of a single liturgical enthusiast, the lawyer turned Anglican priest, Edward Stephens. His supplement to the liturgy was published in 1696. Its character is clearly indicated in its title, *The Liturgy of the Ancients, as near as well may be, in English Forms.*[70] It was an heroic effort at making the Prayer Book read like a "primitive liturgy."

Both the corporate revision and the individual work of Stephens require to be set in their historical context of the Revolution of 1688. James II's Declaration of Indulgence in 1688 was a shrewd move. It appeared to offer the Nonconformists a breathing-space from persecution, and to promise the removal of their civic disabilities, while it was actually aimed at giving the Roman Catholic fellow-believers with the King a more favoured position. This was the final move that, starting with the "Popish Plot" of 1678-1681 in which Titus Oates had inflamed public opinion to believe that Charles II's younger brother James was involved in a plot to supplant him and to establish Catholicism as the religion of England, reached its culmination in this Declaration, and sealed the suspicions of Protestants. James had no alternative but to flee England, and William and Mary were enthroned as guarantors of the Protestant succession to the throne of England, and as supporters of the Anglican establishment. In 1691, however, the Non-Jurors (or those bishops and clergy who refused to swear the Oath of Allegiance to William and Mary because by so doing they would break their previous oath to James II and his successors) were deprived of their offices in the Church of England. The Non-Jurors (or Non-

[70] The text is to be found in W. Jardine Grisbrooke, *Anglican Liturgies of the Seventeenth and Eighteenth Centuries* (Alcuin Club Collections, No. XL, 1958), pp. 203-19.

Swearers) numbered about four hundred clergy, a few laymen, and some leading bishops. They included Archbishop Sancroft, and Bishops Ken of Bath and Wells, Turner of Ely, White of Peterborough, Lloyd of Norwich, Frampton of Gloucester, Lake of Chichester, and Thomas of Worcester. The last two died before the sentence of deprivation could be carried out, and Cartwright, Bishop of Chester, followed James II to France. Their guiding principles had included the conviction of the divine right of kings and, as its consequence, the duty of passive obedience. They also had a high view of the church as a divine society and were deeply interested in primitive and historic liturgies and in the devotional life.[71]

The difference between those bishops who were willing to swear allegiance to William and Mary and those who were Non-Jurors was deep and tragic. On the one hand, several Latitudinarian or broad-church bishops backed the "Revolution" and were eager to unite the Protestant forces in a more comprehensive Church of England, expressing its faith and worship in a Prayer Book responsive by permissive rubrics to the customs objected to by the heirs of the Puritans. They were supported by high-church bishops, such as Compton of London. The Non-Juring bishops, however, and those clergy that supported them were far more interested in remoulding the Prayer Book according to the pattern of the liturgies of the ancient and primitive church, than in accommodating it to the oversensitive consciences of the Presbyterians. In the end, they would mostly refuse to worship according to the Prayer Book of 1662 and took the step of either supplementing the Prayer Book, or even of creating their own liturgies in 1718 and 1734.

7. The Rites of Edward Stephens

These go far beyond the boundaries of our period, but at least we can examine the rites produced by the Non-Juror Edward Stephens, one consisting of "such enlargements of the Church Service as I thought most agreeable to the ancient Form" for private celebrations, another an expansion of it, and the third and most important, a form for public worship. This consisted of confining "ourselves to the Church Forms only supplying what I thought defective therein, as well I could, out of other parts of our Liturgy."[72] The

---

[71] See George Every, *The High Church Party, 1688-1718* (1956), p. 61. See also J. H. Overton, *The Nonjurors* (1902), and J.W.C. Wand, *The High Church Schism* (1951).

[72] Grisbrooke, *op. cit.*, p. 46.

rite designed for public use was published in 1696 as, *The Liturgy of the Ancients Represented, As near as well may be, In English Forms. With a Preface concerning the Restitution of the most Solemn Part of the Christian Worship in the Holy Eucharist, to its Integrity, and just Frequency of Celebration.* It warrants careful consideration.

Stephens denounced the 1552 Prayer Book as a defective liturgy because it spiritualised the concept of sacrifice and eliminated the *epiklesis*, and weakened disastrously the sense of the communion of saints, as well as omitting prayers for the dead. Furthermore, lawyer Stephens found it impossible to have a daily Eucharist in any London Anglican church, but decided with a group of fellow enthusiasts, to meet each day at 5 A.M. for Communion, to follow the example of the early Christians, to avoid offending any, especially Anglicans, and this practice continued for two and a half years.

The following description is taken from a letter by Stephens to Archbishop Tillotson:

When we had continued it near a year, the person who did officiate being like to be called from us, that it might not fail, I took orders myself; and as soon as we obtained the favour of the Bishop of Gloucester to have the use of his Church at Cripplegate (which was as unexpected as the other), we without delay removed our meeting thither, the very next day, out of respect to the Church; as we had before, for the same reason, continued it in private under a tacit connivance, rather than make use of the late Act for Toleration. And we have now had it in public near three quarters of a year without intermission. While we had it in private, we used such enlargements of the Church Service as I thought most agreeable to the ancient Form: but when we came into Church we forebore most of that, and confined ourselves to the Church Forms, only supplying what I thought defective therein, as well as I could, out of other parts of our Liturgy. This I did before ever I had seen the book made by our Bishops, and published at Edinburgh, for the use of the Church of Scotland, in 1627, which I believe to be the best of any modern form whatever, and, therefore, when this lately came into my hand, it was no little satisfaction to me to find that I had so completely concurred in judgement with such eminent persons, and had so great authority to allege for what I did, besides what I had before. . . .[73]

Stephens's public liturgy, *The Liturgy of the Ancients . . . in English Forms*, shows a detailed knowledge of English liturgies and, apart from its tendency to long-windedness, a craftsman's ability to join parts of liturgies together in a unified composition. He makes use of the Prayer Book of 1549, as of the Scottish liturgy of 1637. The liturgy of the catechumens is overloaded with anthems (the first half of both the *Venite* and of the *Benedictus*, together with *Gloria in Excelsis* and *Deus misereatur*) and there are seven collects (if the Collect of the Day is included). The Office of the Faithful begins with *Christ our Pascal Lamb* as invitatory anthem (borrowed from 1549), followed by Invitation, Confession, Absolution and Comfortable Words (all as in 1549 order). The Offertory follows, the *Sursum Corda*, a Preface derived chiefly from the General Thanksgiving, the *Sanctus*, with "The Worship of the Lamb" from the book of Revelation, which is taken from the lectionary. There follows the Prayer for the whole State of Christ's Church Militant here on earth, based chiefly on 1637, with optional and more specific commemoration of the saints and the departed, added in a footnote. The Prayer of Consecration's opening paragraph conflates 1549, 1637, and 1662, and there is one change in wording which is later followed in the eighteenth century Scottish rites. Instead of "his *one* Oblation of himself once offered" Stephens reads "his *own* Oblation of himself once offered." The Invocation or *epiklesis* precedes the Institution Narrative (as in 1549 and 1637) is a slight expansion of the 1637 form: "Hear us, O merciful Father, we most humbly beseech thee, and of thy abundant Goodness vouchsafe to bless and sanctifie with thy Word and holy Spirit these thy Gifts and Creatures of Bread and wine, that they may be unto us the Body and Blood of thy most dearly beloved Son, our Saviour Jesus Christ. . . ."[74] The Memorial, or Prayer of Oblation, follows 1637 almost word for word, except that there is a clause from 1549 in a footnote, "And command these our Supplications and Prayers to be, by the Ministry of thy Holy Angels, brought up into thy Holy Tabernacle, before the sight of thy Divine Majesty." On the conclusion of the canon, there ensues an intercessory Litany ending with the Lord's Prayer, and this is taken from the Prayer Book Litany. There then follow the

[73] *Ibid.*, p. 39.　　　　　[74] *Ibid.*, p. 214.

Prayer of Humble Access, the Communion, the Prayer of Thanksgiving, the *Gloria in Excelsis*, and the Blessing.

Stephens compiled two other rites, one having only the liturgy of the faithful,[75] and supposedly based on "ancient forms" which, of course, meant Book VIII of the *Apostolic Constitutions*, and another being a revised form of the rite, entitled, *A Compleat Form of Liturgy, or Divine Service, According to the Usage of the Most Ancient Christians*.[76] Stephens is better as a reviser than as an innovator or translator, but he deserves credit for breaking through English liturgical insularity, and marks the way forward from Laud and 1662 to a consideration of eastern liturgies as models instead of the examples of the "incorrigible Cranmerians."

It is interesting to note that while the Non-Juring bishops and clergy found it impossible to read the new state prayers, laity sympathetic to their convictions found several ways of avoiding compliance. Various modes of salving their conscience were adopted. Some refused to say, "Amen," at the end of the prayers. Others took Prayer Books to church printed before the Revolution containing the old prayers and the old names. Yet others showed their dislike of the new prayers by refusing to kneel when they were said. Some others took snuff at the appropriate moment and sneezed their disapprobation! That was a ruse not available for Non-Juring clergy.[77]

The true greatness of the Non-Jurors can be seen in the saintly life of the greatest of them, Thomas Ken, like them a man of principle and honour, but more conciliatory than most. The lasting contribution of the Non-Jurors to the Anglican liturgy will be found in the further development of the liturgy of the Scottish Episcopal church in the eighteenth century and in its impact on the American Episcopal liturgy. Their devotional spirit is nowhere better summed up than in the piety of Thomas Ken.

Brought up virtually as a ward of Izaak Walton (for he had married Ken's half sister), he was a thorough Wykehamist. A scholar of Winchester School, a scholar and fellow of New College, Oxford, and chaplain to Bishop Morley of Winchester from 1665, he became a fellow of Winchester. He then drew up for the School a *Manual of Prayers for the Use of the Scholars of Winchester College* in 1674 to counteract the rather unstructured Puritan influence which he remembered there as a boy. This related

---

75 This text will be found *ibid.*, pp. 223-30.
76 This text will be found, *ibid.*, pp. 233-45.
77 Wand, *op. cit.*, p. 12.

prayer to the daily life and was remarkable for its Eucharistic reference. At about the same time it is conjectured that he composed his famous Morning, Evening, and Midnight Hymns which are included in an appendix to the third edition of his Manual in 1695. Perhaps the most famous is the Evening Hymn,[78] which begins: "Glory to thee my God this night/ For all the blessings of the Light." The sincere and simple directness of the devotion and its profound dependence upon God is perfectly expressed in the verse:

> Teach me to live that I may dread
> The Grave as little as my Bed;
> Teach me to die, that so I may
> Triumphing rise at the last day.

The Hymn ends with the adoring gratitude of a Doxology which is known throughout the English-speaking world:

> Praise God from whom all blessings flow,
> Praise him all creatures here below,
> Praise him above y'Angelick host[79]
> Praise Father, Son, and Holy Ghost.

His conviction of the divine right of kings and of the duty of passive obedience did not prevent him from enacting the role of the prophet Nathan to King David. While seconded as chaplain to Princess Mary at The Hague, he remonstrated against a case of court immorality and was immediately dismissed. Yet a similarly motivated refusal of his Winchester residence to accommodate Nell Gwynne at Charles II's bidding, earned him soon afterwards the Bishopric of Bath and Wells. A faithful preacher to high and low, Charles II said he would "go and hear Ken tell him his faults." One could ring a coin on his integrity. Macaulay's verdict on his character was that it approached "as near as human infirmity permits to the ideal perfection of Christian virtue."[80]

8. The Attempted Revision of 1689

The final attempt in this century to revise the Prayer Book was begun by William Sancroft, Archbishop of Canterbury, with the

---

[78] For Ken's work as a hymnwriter, see John Julian's *Dictionary of Hymnology* 2nd edn., 1925), pp. 616b–622a.

[79] This is the original third line as printed in 1688 in the Second Book of Henry Playford's *Sacra Harmonia* (1688) which gave it wide publicity. The revised text of 1709 reads: "Praise him above ye heavenly host" which is close to the modern rendering.

[80] Cited Julian, *op. cit.*, p. 617a.

purpose of relaxing some of the ceremonies by providing permissive rubrics and by making some verbal changes that would make the Prayer Book more acceptable to Presbyterians supporting a Protestant monarchy in a wider Church of England.

Such a revision was proposed in the last clause of the Comprehension Bill, which called for the establishment of a commission of thirty representative Anglican divines to prepare the business. This included ten bishops, seven deans, four archdeacons, one head of a university college and two divinity professors, and six London clergy, five of whom later became bishops. The Latitudinarians in the commission naturally predominated, including such bishops as Burnet of Salisbury, Stillingfleet of Worcester, Stratford of Chester, and Humphreys of Bangor, and clergy such as Tillotson (Dean of St. Paul's) and Tenison (then the popular vicar of St. Martin-in-the-Fields) both of whom were future Archbishops of Canterbury. The most prominent Latitudinarians in the revisions were Burnet, Stillingfleet, Tenison, and Tillotson, together with the orientalist Kidder. The middle position was held by Compton, Bishop of London, Dean John Sharp (later Archbishop of York), and Simon Patrick, Bishop of Chichester, who had been a Presbyterian minister. Among the ten high churchmen in the commission (the highest of high churchmen being the Non-Jurors), the most influential was Archdeacon Beveridge, later to become Bishop of St. Asaph.

In trying to produce acceptable recommendations, the commission faced two ultimately insuperable obstacles. One was the difficulty of trying to satisfy the largely contrary desires of Non-Jurors and Nonconformists; the other was trying to gain the approval of Convocation, especially as about half of the high churchmen boycotted the proceedings of Convocation. Because of this double failure the recommendations were never completed and embodied in a detailed report.[81] They can be reconstructed, however, from two sources. One is an interleaved Prayer Book in the Lambeth Palace Library, and the other is a private journal kept by Dr. John Williams, later to become Bishop of Chichester.[82]

---

[81] Every, *op. cit.*, p. 47.

[82] A very rough idea of the work of revision was provided in E. Calamy's *Abridgment of Mr. Baxter's History of his Life and Times.* When the Prayer Book was discussed in Parliament in 1854, a motion for papers was carried in the House of Commons, and *marginalia* and journal were collated by William Henry Black of the Public Records Office. His copy was printed as a *Parliamentary Paper* and formed the basis of John Taylor's edition of *The Revised Liturgy of 1689* (Dublin, 1855). See Every, *ibid.*

Although the attempted revision was a failure, it is interesting to consider the liturgical views of the majority of influential broad churchmen, together with the views of some cooperative high churchmen. The reconstruction must, however, be partly conjectural.

The preparatory work for the revision was divided and begun in July of 1688. Archbishop William Sancroft seems to have been responsible for overseeing the revision of prayers, thanksgivings, the catechism, and the Orders for Baptism and Confirmation. Simon Patrick was in charge of the revision of the collects, and Macaulay said acidly of this, "whether he was or was not qualified to make the collects better, no man that ever lived was more competent to make them longer."[83] The Daily Office and the Communion Service were to be revised by a committee including Dean John Sharp and John Moore.[84]

The arrival of William of Orange in England created a new situation, precipitating the whole question of the validity of oaths of allegiance. The seven Non-Juring bishops (who believed that their original oaths of fealty to James II could not be set aside for William's benefit without them perjuring themselves and who might have been able to support him as regent but not as monarch) were sequestered for six months in the Tower of London, while one fled to France, and two died before their homage would be required. The official commission of thirty divines was not able to begin its work until October 1689. It had Sancroft's work before it as a basis and also "a complete list of all the exceptions that ever had been made to the Prayer Book, either by Puritans before the Civil War, or by Nonconformists afterwards." The latter was the compilation of Thomas Tenison. Furthermore, Richard Kidder had prepared a translation of the Psalms.

Among the proposals for revision in 1689 there were several important ones of a high-church source and character. One was to add the Beatitudes as an alternative to the Decalogue in the Communion Service, a repetition of Jeremy Taylor's proposal in his *Collection of Offices*, but with a different response from his. The Confirmation Service was expanded to include a renewal of Baptismal vows, an idea borrowed from the *Durham Book*. Sancroft wrote "A Prayer for Repentance" and another as preparation for

[83] *History of England* (1856), III, p. 476.
[84] Every, *op. cit.*, pp. 23-24.

400

receiving Communion. He may also have originated the emphasis on Ember Weeks and provided the Proper for Rogation Sunday. The influence of the high church may also be found in a Proper Preface for Good Friday, in the Prayer of Humble Access, and in the rubric recommending "that all ministers exhort their people to communicate frequently" as well as in the reference in the catechism to "the sacrifice" of Christ's Body and Blood.

On the other hand, twenty of the "Exceptions" made by the Presbyterian ministers at the Savoy Conference have been accepted, though these are chiefly verbal changes. The four noxious ceremonies are retained, but they need not be used. Any minister having scruples about using the surplice or signing with the cross in Baptism can obtain from his bishop a dispensation and the bishop can appoint a curate who does not share the minister's scruples to act in his stead. Parishioners, after raising the matter with their parish priest, need not kneel at the altar for the reception of the consecrated elements, but may receive them "in some convenient place or pew." A rubric asserts that the marriage ring is a civil pledge and ceremony and not a religious ceremony. The too easy assumption of regeneration in Baptism and the Burial Office is acknowledged and modified accordingly. The priest says to the sick man: "I pronounce thee absolved" and no longer, "I absolve thee." Godparents are optional in Baptism. Black-letter saints' days disappear from the calendar. Sentences from the Apocrypha deriving from Tobit and used at the Offertory, as well as the *Benedicite*, disappear. Psalms 8 and 134 are substituted for the *Magnificat* and the *Nunc Dimittis*. Dissenting ministers are even allowed conditional ordination, while the deacon's formula would be sufficient for the admission of continental Protestant ministers.[85] A small but important change was made in the Prayer of Humble Access. Instead of the petition "that our sinful bodies may be made clean by his body and our souls washed through his most precious blood," there was substituted "that our souls and bodies may be washed and cleansed by the sacrifice of his most precious Body and Blood." The emphasis on sacrifice would seem to be a high-church change in Eucharistic doctrine, but unquestionably the rest of the sentence was altered to meet Nonconformist criticism.[86]

[85] *Ibid.*, p. 45.
[86] According to William Clagett's *An Answer to the Dissenters Objections against the Common Prayers and some other parts of Divine-Service prescribed*

A third group of alterations would have been equally acceptable to both high churchmen and broad churchmen. Such were: the joining of the Litany and the Holy Communion and the revised order of the latter is interesting. The prayer "We humbly beseech thee" was followed immediately by the Collect for Purity, and the usually ensuing Collect for the King was left out. The Creed was followed by the General Thanksgiving, the Prayer of St. Chrysostom, the grace, the notices, the "singing Psalm," and the sermon. All these were to be said from the reading-pew. On "Sacrament Sundays" the Communion Service followed its regular course. As for Confirmation, it is directed that an exhortation is to be read on the previous Sunday; the Doxology is added to the Lord's Prayer, and a prayer and a second exhortation are interposed before the Blessing. In the Burial a sensible substitution of a lesson from I Thessalonians is allowed "in colder or later seasons."

The attempted improvement of the collects initiated by Bishop Simon Patrick was overseen by Stillingfleet, Burnet, and Tillotson. Their major amelioration consists of adding quotations from the Epistle or Gospel of the day, as had been attempted by the revisers of 1662. Bishop Burnet also tried to remodel the formula for Ordination, following the findings of Jean Marin, and was seconded by Tillotson. If approved, which it was not, it would have read:

> Pour down, O Father of lights, the holy Ghost upon thy servant, for the office and work of a priest in the Church of God, now committed unto thee by the imposition of our hands, that whose sins he does forgive they may be forgiven, and whose sins he doth retain they may be retained, and that he may be a faithful dispenser of God's holy word and sacraments, to the edification of his Church, and to the glory of his holy name through Jesus Christ, to whom with the Holy Ghost be all honour and glory world without end, Amen.[87]

Burnet also wished to omit the Athanasian Creed as too Western in viewpoint. While he failed to carry his point, this Creed was hence-

---

in the Liturgie of the Church of England (1683), p. 34, the Dissenters urged that in the unrevised petition "a greater efficacy in cleansing is attributed to Christ's body than Christ's blood." Clagett also says that the Dissenters objected to the individual reception of Communion, saying "it should be done in companies, as Take ye, Eate ye, all of this." (Ibid.)

[87] Parliamentary Paper (1854), p. 87, cited in Every, op. cit., p. 55.

forth used in public worship only five instead of thirteen Sundays of the year.

The failure of this revision of 1688 and 1689 meant that the Presbyterians and Independents who had shared persecution together were now practically driven into each other's arms, and the Independent view of the Anglican liturgy as an engine of compulsion rather than an instrument of union prevailed in Dissent, together with a concept of "conceived prayer" as always superior to "stinted forms." Eighteenth-century attempts at Prayer Book revision still aimed at comprehension, not of the Presbyterians, but of their successors, the Unitarians.[88]

9. A Conclusion

The century had begun with the Hampton Court Conference and the attempt of the Puritans to have some of their criticisms of the Book of Common Prayer accepted, but with little success. The Presbyterian ministers had also hoped for accommodation in worship at the Savoy Conference in 1661, but with the same dismal result. The last attempt at Prayer Book revision had been undertaken in 1689, with the professed purpose of making it less difficult for Nonconformists to accept. This too failed miserably.

Similarly, just as the two Laudian Bishops, Cosin and Wren, had proposals for revising the Prayer Book in 1661 and 1662 that would have emulated the first and most conservative Prayer Book of 1549 and the Scottish liturgy of 1637, so would Edward Stephens, a Non-Juror, argue against all later forms of the Anglican liturgy from 1552 to 1662, that they were Cranmerian treason against the historic western and Catholic rite. The "primitive" supplementation of the Book of Common Prayer by the additions of Stephens were not accepted by others, and as the Non-Jurors went out of the Church of England, their eighteenth-century alternative rites were also failures.

Indeed, the ding-dong battle between the high churchmen, on the one hand, and the Puritans, Presbyterians, or Nonconformists, on the other hand, can only lead to the inevitable conclusion that the Dissenting demand for a liturgy conformable in all things to Scripture and the Laudian and Non-Juror request for a liturgy conformable to the liturgies of the primitive church were utterly

[88] See Davies, *op. cit.*, III, Chap. IV, "Unitarian Worship: The Liturgy of Rationalism."

incompatible. In the *art nouveau* period at the beginning of the present century it was common to see juxtaposed outside a theatre or on its proscenium arch two masks: one laughing and the other crying. The saddest fact about liturgical revision in the seventeenth century is that it was begun each time, with the actors wearing the smiling mask of comedy, and it ended in practically every case with them wearing the mask of irritation, if not of tragedy.

CHAPTER XI

PURITAN SERVICE BOOKS

HE IDEA is widely prevalent in English-speaking countries
that Presbyterians and Congregationalists[1] have almost
always over three centuries practised free or extemporary
prayers and disdained a set liturgy or even the use of a manual by
their ministers. This erroneous view would have surprised their
seventeenth century predecessors. The English Presbyterians
would certainly have preferred a set liturgy for which there was
a Scriptural authority for each of the ordinances. This would have
been in line with Calvin's *La Forme des Prières* of Geneva (1542)
based upon Calvin's adaptation of Bucer's Strassburg liturgy in
1540. This was, in fact, Englished and used, with but a few insignificant alterations by the congregation of English exiles over which
Knox and Whittingham presided in Geneva. It was published in
1556 as *The Forme of Prayers and Ministration of the Sacraments,
etc., used in the English Congregation at Geneva: and approved
by the famous and godly learned man, Iohn Calvyn.* It was alike
the parent of the Scottish Book of Common Order and of four editions of an English Puritan Prayer Book,[2] which should—for the
sake of accuracy—be called Presbyterian or Reformed Prayer
Books. Further editions of the Waldegrave *A Booke of the Forme
of Common Prayers etc.,* published in 1584/5 appeared in Middleburgh in 1586, 1587, and 1602.[3] The Presbyterians, however
much they might have smarted from the imposition of a high-
church Anglican Scottish liturgy upon the Church of Scotland in
1637, had no objection in principle to a liturgy or set order and
prescribed words in worship; but the vociferous and persistent
caucus of the Independents, led by the learned and pertinacious
Thomas Goodwin, and the sense that the many Independents of
New Model Army of the Roundheads were ever drawing nearer
to the Westminster Assembly, pressured the Presbyterians into the
compromise of accepting a directory. The natural development of

[1] In 1972 the English Congregationalists and Presbyterians were united in one
denomination, the United Reformed Church.

[2] It is Peter Hall, the editor of *A Booke of the Form of Common Prayers* who
calls the Waldegrave edition of c. 1584 a *Puritan Liturgy* in his republishing of it
in *Fragmenta Liturgica* (Bath, 1848), Vol. III.

[3] See the *British Museum Catalogue*, Vol. L, 50, pp. 711-12 for their exact
titles. See Horton Davies, *Worship of the English Puritans* (1948), pp. 122-37, for
an analysis of the Waldegrave and Middleburgh service books.

Presbyterian worship was towards a prescribed form of prayers, with alternatives, and the occasional opportunity for extemporary prayers. It is significant that, once the Presbyterians had cut loose from their association with the Independents, as at the Savoy Conference of 1661, their leader Richard Baxter, with the concurrence of the brethren, composed a Biblical liturgy.

Furthermore, the Independents, who were anxious that the ministers should not lose the gift of extemporary prayer at the prompting of the Holy Spirit, were glad to join in the production of a directory which would have provided the structure, the theology, and the order of various ordinances, regular and occasional, with sample prayers but without dictating their very wording. Thus the *Directory* of 1644 produced jointly by Presbyterians and Independents was a compromise, exacting too little for the Presbyterians and too much for the Independents.

Yet the *Directory*'s importance is considerable and twofold. In the first place it demonstrates the kind of worship that the coalition of Puritans thought suitable for the entire three kingdoms when they came to power, after almost a century of being in the minority. Secondly, and of even greater importance, it formed the Free Church tradition of worship for almost three hundred years in Britain, the British Commonwealth, and the United States of America. This tradition would come to include the Baptists and Methodists, as well as the Presbyterians and Independents (or Congregationalists); in short, all who can be called a part of the Puritan-Pietist tradition. It should be made clear, however, that many ministers, even a generation after the *Directory*'s issue, might not own a copy of the work, yet the *Directory* had set the style of their long prayers (as opposed to brief collects), with their heavy emphasis on actual as well as original sin, the retrospective rather than prospective look in the Lord's Supper, the austere simplicity of the ceremonial and furnishings, the sermon as the high point and climax of the service, and its characteristic Calvinism as expressed in its Biblical obedience to the revealed will of God as the only legitimate authority, its perennial didacticism, and its congregational character.

1. *The Parliamentary or Westminster Directory*[4]

On March 13, 1644, it was ordered "by the Lords and Commons in Parliament assembled, that this *Directory*, and ordinance

---

[4] This has been reprinted in *Reliquiae Liturgicae*, III, *The Parliamentary Directory* (ed. Peter Hall, Bath, 1847), and by the Scottish Church Service Society,

concerning it, be forthwith printed and published. . . ." It was the official manual of worship for the English, Welsh, and Scottish people for sixteen years. Indeed, it continued in use among the Scots long after the Prayer Book was restored in England and Wales in 1662.

The Westminster Assembly, to which Parliament had delegated the responsibility for advising on the religious settlement produced a form of church government, confessions of faith (the Shorter and Longer Catechisms), and a *Directory for the Publick Worship of God in the Three Kingdoms.* The Assembly was chosen by Parliament on a county basis of representation, but the members also included ten peers, twenty members of the House of Commons, and commissioners of the Church of Scotland, in consequence of the taking of the Solemn League and Covenant. Some moderate Episcopal clergy were invited, but declined. Hence the business of the Assembly was almost exclusively in the hands of the Presbyterian divines, with only a handful of Independent "Brethren" who presented an *Apologeticall Narration* for their minority standpoint.[5]

It appears that originally all that was contemplated was a revision of the Book of Common Prayer, excising from it all those ceremonies or statements that conflicted with the Biblical mandate. This opinion is confirmed by a declaration of Parliament on April 9, 1642, to the effect "that they intend a due and necessary reformation and liturgy of the church, and to take away nothing in the one or the other but what shall be evil and justly offensive, or last unnecessary and burdensome."[6]

Even at the end of the deliberations, there were still two viewpoints. One believed in the need for a revised liturgy; the other argued for a manual or directory. This is confirmed by Robert Baillie, Principal of Glasgow University and a Scottish commissioner, in his letter of November 21, 1644, referring to the Assembly's approval of the hotly disputed Preface, "and in this piece we expected most difficulty; one party purposing by the preface to turn the Directory to a straight Liturgie; the other to make it so loose

---

The Westminster Directory (ed. Thomas Leishman, Edinburgh and London, 1901).

[5] See a recent republication edited by Robert S. Paul, *An Apologeticall Narration* (Boston and Philadelphia, 1963).

[6] *The Book of Common Order* (eds. G. W. Sprott and J. Leishman, Edinburgh, 1868), p. 261.

and free, that it should serve for little use: but God helped us to get both these rocks echewed. . . ."[7]

The rough draft of the *Directory* was prepared by a small subcommittee consisting of Marshall (Chairman), Palmer, Goodwin, Young, Herle, and the Scottish commissioners. The composition of this subcommittee, which included only one Independent, Goodwin, helped to account for the Scottish character of the *Directory*, which bears a close structural resemblance to the Scottish Book of Common Order, a near relative of John Knox's *Genevan Service Book*, while Goodwin's presence is presumably responsible for the several alternatives supplied and the variations from the Genevan Book.

The Preface clearly indicates the aims of the compilers. It began with a generous tribute to their "wise and pious ancestors" who produced the Book of Common Prayer which had repressed the vanity, error, superstition, and idolatry of medieval Catholic worship, and had provided a service in the vernacular tongue. Nonetheless, experience showed that the liturgy used in the Church of England has proved offensive to the godly at home and the Reformed churches abroad. "For (not to speak of urging the reading of all the prayers, which very greatly increased the burden of it), the many unprofitable and burdensome ceremonies contained in it have occasioned much mischief, as well as disquieting the consciences of many godly ministers and people who could not yield to them; . . ."[8] Meanwhile, "prelates and their faction have laboured to raise the estimation of it to such a height, as if there were no other worship, or way of worship of God amongst us, but only the Service Book; to the great hindrance of the preaching of the word, and, in some places (especially of late), to the justling of it out, as unnecessary or (at best) as far inferior to the reading of Common Prayer, which was made no better than an idol by many ignorant and superstitious people."[9] Even Roman Catholics, it is claimed, boasted that it complied with much of their service. Furthermore, "the Liturgy hath been a great means, as, on the one hand, to make and increase an idle and unedifying ministry, which contented it self with set forms made to their hands by others, without putting forth themselves to exercise the gift of prayer, with which our Lord Jesus Christ pleaseth to furnish all his servants whom he calls to that office; so, on the other side . . . it hath been . . .

---

[7] *The Letters and Journals of Robert Baillie*, 3 Vols. (ed. David Laing, Edinburgh, 1841), II, p. 240.

[8] *Reliquiae Liturgicae*, ed. Peter Hall, III, p. 14.   [9] *Ibid.*, p. 16.

a matter of endless strife and contention in the Church, and a snare to many godly and faithful ministers who have been persecuted and silenced upon occasion. . . ."[10]

The compilers believed that Providence was now calling them to a further reformation, as was made evident in the need to satisfy their own consciences, to be more comfortable to other Reformed churches, and to make public testimony of efforts at uniformity in worship as promised in the Solemn League and Covenant. All these considerations demanded a new collection of orders of worship such as the *Directory* provides.

On the positive side, they have kept three aims consistently in mind. First and foremost, "our care hath been to hold forth such things as are of Divine institution in every ordinance: and other things we have endeavoured to set forth according to the rules of Christian prudence, agreeable to the general rules of the word of God."[11] The second aim was uniformity in worship in the three kingdoms: "our meaning therein being only that, the general heads, the sense and scope of the prayers, and other parts of public worship, being common to all, there may be a consent of all the Churches in those things that contain the substance of the service and worship of God. . . ."[12] The third aim is to provide such general help for ministers as not to create a total dependence upon set forms, "and the ministers may be hereby directed in their administrations, to keep like soundness in doctrine and prayer; and may, if need be, have some help and furniture, and yet not so as they become hereby slothful and negligent in stirring up the gifts of Christ in them; but that each by taking heed to himself and the flock of God committed to him, and by wise observing the ways of Divine Providence may be careful to furnish his heart and tongue with further or other materials of prayer and exhortation, and shall be needful upon all occasions."[13]

It is clear, then, that the *Directory* hoped to combine in a way never previously achieved, the advantages of a Prayer Book without its attendant disadvantages. It was to be Scripturally authenticated in every ordinance, comprehensive, and orderly. But it was not to obtain these benefits at the cost of suppressing the creativity of the minister's own wording of the prayers. It would, in brief, try to match order and liberty, form and the spirit, unity and variety, hitherto deemed incompatible and certainly estranged.

The most distinctive changes introduced were supposed improve-

---

[10] *Ibid.*   [11] *Ibid.*, p. 18.   [12] *Ibid.*
[13] *Ibid.*, pp. 18-19.

ments on the Book of Common Prayer, and they were the common-place reform proposals of Puritan liturgical apologetics. In the lections the Apocrypha writings were to be rejected; private Baptism and godparents were to be discontinued; and the sign of the Cross and the ring in Marriage, together with the administration of the Communion to the sick, were to be abolished. The Communion table was to be moved away from the east wall (where Laud had wanted it) back into the body of the church, and sitting or standing were alternative postures for the reception of the Lord's Supper, both being preferred to the Anglican kneeling gesture. All saints' days were eliminated from the calendar, as were distinctive liturgical vestments. No service was appointed for the Burial of the Dead, and none for the Churching of Women. No creed was recited, nor was the Decalogue recited by the people in worship. All these innovations had been contended for since the first years of Elizabeth's reign, while in some instances the criticisms went back to John Hooper, the iconoclastic Edwardian Bishop of Gloucester and Worcester.

While there was substantial agreement in the Puritan coalition on the *delenda*, there was considerable disagreement on the *agenda*.[14] This is mirrored in part by the different degrees of constraint or permissiveness expressed in the tenses and moods of the rubrics. As Leishman rightly observes: "The obligation to a practice is not the same when it is called *necessary, requisite, expedient, convenient,* or *sufficient*; or when in one place the minister *is to,* or *shall*, or, in another, *may* do such and such things."[15]

The close structural resemblance of the Lord's Day service in the *Directory* can be seen by comparing it with *A Booke of the Forme of Common Prayers* in the table below.

This Lord's Day service begins with the minister's "solemn calling on them [the congregation] to the worshipping of the great name of God" in a prayer that bows before the sovereign mystery of God, and affirms the "vileness and unworthiness" of the worshippers, confesses human inability, and begs for divine assistance, pardon, and for help in meditating on the Word of God. It was common Presbyterian usage to provide a separate prayer for illumination before the sermon; here the petition for illumination is part

---

[14] Thomas Edwards, *Gangraena* (1646), Pt. I, p. 31, observed that some sectaries held "that a Directory or Order to help in the way of worship is a breach of the second commandment." This was probably true of the Brownists, Barrowists, and their successors, among whom were the early Independents.

[15] *The Book of Common Order*, eds. Sprott and Leishman, p. 238.

A Booke of the Forme of Common Prayers	A Directory for the Publick Worship of God (1644)
(Reader's Service: Chapters of Scripture)	
Scripture Sentences	Call to Worship
Confession of Sins	Prayer of Approach: Adoration Supplication Illumination
Metrical Psalm	Metrical Psalm
Prayer for Illumination and Lord's Prayer	Old Testament Lection (one chapter)
(Scripture Reading) Text	(Metrical Psalm) New Testament Lection (one chapter)
	Prayer of Confession and Intercession
SERMON	SERMON
Prayer of Intercession for Whole State of Christ's Church	General Prayer and Lord's Prayer (if no Communion is to follow)
Apostles' Creed, Decalogue, and Lord's Prayer (said by minister)	
Metrical Psalm	Metrical Psalm
Blessing (Aaronic or Apostolic)	Blessing (Aaronic or Apostolic)

of the general opening prayer, and the change was requested by the Independents who claimed the authority of I Timothy 2:1 for starting with a comprehensive prayer.

Lections are confined to the canonical Testaments, excluding the Apocrypha. Also in contradistinction from the Book of Common Prayer, it was judged convenient to read at least one whole chapter from each Testament in preference to the shreds known derisively as "pistling" and "gospelling" by the Puritans. An interspersed commentary on Scripture during its reading was forbidden because too distracting. Exposition was permitted only when the whole

411

chapter had been read. This qualified permission was also a concession to the Independents.[16] After the lections and following the Psalm, a larger confession of sin was to be made. The ideal was for the minister "to get his own and his hearers' hearts to be rightly affected with their sins, that they may all mourn in sense thereof before the Lord, and hunger and thirst after the grace of God in Jesus Christ."[17] The generalisations of the Prayer of Confession in the Anglican liturgy should be contrasted with the particularisations of the confession in the *Directory*. The same prayer then moves from Confession and Petition to Intercession. There is Intercession for the propagation of the Gospel to all nations, the conversion of the Jews, for all distressed Christians, and for the Reformed churches. The prayer intercedes on behalf of the king, for the conversion of the queen, for ministers, universities, schools, religious seminaries, for the particular city and congregation, for the civil government, for those in distress, for seasonable weather and the averting of the judgments of God in famine, pestilence, or sword. It concludes with the dedication of pastor and people to the Christian life. It is not regarded as necessary for the minister to include all these groups of people in one Prayer of Intercession. Some can be deferred until the prayer after the sermon. The inclusion of all these petitions in one prayer was yet another concession to the Independents, for Baillie calls the long prayer "a new fancy of the Independents, grounded on no solid reason, and contrair to all the practice of the Church, old or late, who divided their prayers in more small parts, and did not have any one of a disproportionable length."[18] Then followed the climax of the Sermon, the obedient listening to the oracle of God.

The directions "Of the Preaching of the Word" presuppose not only a conscientious but a learned ministry, conversant with Hebrew and Greek and "in such arts and sciences as are handmaids unto divinity." The spiritual qualifications are not less needed. The minister must "know and believe in the Scriptures above the common sort of believers." The sermon is to be constructed on the model of doctrine, reason, and use.[19] That is, the preacher is to begin with an exposition of a text or passage of Scripture, then to provide the reasons why the doctrine is to be held, and, finally, he

---

16 Robert Baillie, *A Dissuasive from the Errours of the Time* (1646), p. 118.
17 *Reliquiae Liturgicae*, ed. Peter Hall, III, p. 25.
18 Baillie, *A Dissuasive* . . . , pp. 118f., cited in *The Book of Common Order*, eds. Sprott and Leishman, p. 332.
19 See the careful analysis of these concepts and their exemplification in Chapter IV above.

is to apply the doctrine to the daily exigencies of life, demonstrating the practical advantages to be derived from believing it. The following adverbs indicate how the minister is to preach: "painfully" (that is, taking great pains), "plainly," "faithfully," "wisely," "gravely," "with loving affection," and "as taught by God." No directions are given on the controverted issue of whether sermons should be read or not. It is known that sermons were not usually read in Scotland, but the practice was not unknown in England. According to Baillie, Nye the Independent was unpopular with an Edinburgh congregation because he had read a large part of his sermon.[20]

The sermon ended, a prayer of thanksgiving followed. This included an acknowledgement of the benefits brought by the Gospel, "as, namely, election, vocation, adoption, justification, sanctification, and hope of glory." The advice is also offered "to turn the chief and most useful heads of the sermon into some few petitions." This points to one of the weaknesses of Puritan prayer. It was excessively edifying, missing no opportunity to preach, even in the prayer following a long and strenuous sermon. Adoration is expelled by exhortation or dehortation. The prayer concludes with a petition for forgiveness, as well it might. The Lord's Prayer is recommended not only as "a pattern of prayer" (the Independent view), but also "as itself a most comprehensive prayer" (the Presbyterian view). It is to be assumed, therefore, that the prayer after the sermon concluded with the Lord's Prayer, though this is allowed, not prescribed. The spontaneity of extemporary prayer is guaranteed for the minister at the administration of the Lord's Supper and on days of thanksgiving and humiliation. The service of the Lord's Day ends with a Psalm and a blessing.

The order for the celebration of the Lord's Supper occupied eighteen out of the seventy-five sittings of the committee. Each point was keenly contested, particularly when the Scots or Independent party felt that its own principle was at stake. Baillie referred, on June 7, 1644, to "the Independents, our great retarders."[21] In a letter written a few days later, he gives a lively impression of the intense controversy between the parties, from his own Presbyterian standpoint: "This day before noone we gott sundrie propositions of our Directory for the sacrament of the Lord's Supper past, but in the afternoone we could not move one inch.

20 See *The Book of Common Order*, eds. Sprott and Leishman, p. 338.
21 *Letters and Journals of Robert Baillie*, II, p. 191.

The unhappie Independents would mangle that sacrament. No catechising nor preparation before; no thanksgiving after; no sacramentall doctrine or chapters, in the day of celebration; no coming up to any table; but a carrying of the element to all in their seats athort the church: yet all this, with God's help we have carried over their bellies to our practise. But exhortations at tables yet we stick at: they would have no words spoken at all. Nye would be at covering the head at the receiving. We must dispute every inch of our ground; . . ."[22] The point at issue which kept them arguing the longest, that was over three weeks, was the method of communicating. Here, again, Baillie gives a vivid account of it on July 12, 1644: "The Independents and others keeped us three long weeks upon one point alone, the communicating at a table. By this we came to debate; the diverse coming up of companies successively to a table; the consecrating of the bread and wine severallie; the giving of the bread to all the congregation, and then the wine to all, and so twice coming to the table, first for bread and then for the wine; the mutual distribution, the table-exhortations, and a world of such questions, which to most of them were new and strange things." The conclusion arrived at after being "overtoyed with debate" is a most significant one: "we were forced to leave all these things, and take us to generall expressions, which, by a benigne exposition, would infer our church-practises, which the most promised to follow, so much the more as we did not necessitate them by the Assembly's express determinations."[23] A rubric in the *Directory* simply states that the Communion table is to be "conveniently placed that the communicants may orderly sit about it, or at it."[24] This allowed the Independent and Presbyterian alternatives: the Independents received the consecrated elements sitting, which were brought to them in their seats "athwart the church" (in Baillie's phrase Anglicised), and the Presbyterians sat at a table or series of tables placed end-to-end. Neither group would approve the Laudian custom of requiring the communicants to kneel at the Communion rail about the altar to receive the Sacrament. Thus the Presbyterians were insistent that the communicants should "sit at" the table, while the Independents stuck to their point that the communicants should "sit about" the table. The Scottish Presbyterians believed that only by sitting at the table they could symbolize the great evangelical truth that they were guests at

[22] *Ibid.*, p. 195.   [23] *Ibid.*, p. 204.
[24] *Reliquiae Liturgicae*, ed. Peter Hall, II, p. 54.

Christ's table and that the Lord invited his modern disciples with the reminder "I have called you friends." The Independents did not object to the doctrine, indeed one of the most radical of them, the Fifth Monarchist Archer, argued that the seated posture at the Communion table was the proof of spiritual and political republicanism,[25] and the equality of the saints, whereas kneeling implied a monarchist posture; and they sat rather than knelt though at a distance from the table. But the Independents objected to the need for several successive companies at the table and thus the destruction of the temporal unity. The Independents might receive the elements separately, but presumably they ate the bread simultaneously, and drank the wine at the same time together. The debate seemed to resolve itself into a preference for unity of place for the Presbyterians, and temporal unity for the Independents.

The Scots differed from the Independents in two other ways. They had a single consecration prayer, whereas the Independents imitating the details of the Last Supper, had two prayers of consecration, one over each element. These two graces were rejected in the *Directory*. On the other hand, the Presbyterians thought they were imitating the order of the Last Supper more exactly in requiring their ministers to communicate first, with the rest of the communicants distributing the elements from hand-to-hand. The minister was to say, "According to the holy institution, command, and example of our blessed Saviour Jesus Christ, I take this bread; and, having given thanks, I break it, and give it to you. Take ye eat ye. This is the body of Christ, which is broken for you. Do this in remembrance of him."[26]

The all-important question of the desirable frequency of attendance at Communion was not decided at the Assembly. It was left to the discretion of each minister and office-bearers of every local congregation to arrange. The Scottish Presbyterians favoured a quarterly Communion, the Independents one monthly or even weekly. But the relative rarity of the ordinance does not argue for its depreciation in value. On the contrary, two rubrics in the *Directory* show how highly it was regarded. One directs that, when the Sacrament cannot conveniently be celebrated at frequent intervals,

---

25 See John Archer's *The Personal Reigne of Christ upon Earth* (1642), p. 17.
26 *Reliquiae Liturgicae*, ed. Peter Hall, III, p. 57. In taking the cup the minister is to say, "*According to the institution, command and example of our Lord Jesus Christ, I take this cup and give it to you.* (Here he giveth it to the communicants.) *This cup is the New Testament in the blood of Christ, which is shed for the remission of the sins of many; drink ye all of it.*"

then either on the preceding Sunday or on a day of the preceding week, "something concerning that ordinance, and due preparation thereunto, and participation thereof, be taught; that, by the diligent use of all means sanctified by God to that end, both in public and in private, all may come better prepared to that heavenly feast."[27] The second rubric is a reminder that "the ignorant and scandalous" are not fit to receive this Sacrament of the Lord's Supper.[28] Furthermore, the table is "fenced" by a lengthy exhortation forbidding "all such as are ignorant, scandalous, profane, or that live in any sin or offence against their knowledge or conscience, that they presume not to come to that holy table."[29]

The structure of the Communion Service is as follows:

1. Exhortation
2. Fencing of the Table
3. Words of Institution and Exhortation
4. Eucharistic Prayer
5. Fraction
6. Delivery
7. Minister communicates himself, the officers, and then the congregation
8. Exhortation to a worthy life
9. Post-Communion Prayer
10. Metrical Psalm
11. Blessing

If the rite is prolix and didactic, it is also comprehensive. Perhaps its most striking characteristic is the emphasis given to the Words of Institution detached from the Eucharistic prayer and the high-lighting of the prophetic symbolism of the Fraction and Libation also detached from the Eucharistic Prayer. The latter has the advantage that the eyes of the congregation will not be closed in prayer (as is supposed to be the case when the Fraction and Libation take place during the Catholic and Anglican Prayers of Consecration). The Reformed services are sparing in the use of symbolism, but it gives to these *sigilla Verbi*, or dramatic demonstrations of the Gospel, their true value for eye-gate. Another significant emphasis is that on the holiness which should characterize God's elect, as indicated in both the "fencing" or the table and in the post-Communion Prayer.

27 *Ibid.*, II, p. 52. 28 *Ibid.*
29 *Ibid.*, p. 53.

The Eucharistic Prayer itself is also comprehensive, lacking only a thanksgiving for Creation. Although it is relatively short it contains the following parts: a Prayer of Access; a Thanksgiving for all benefits, especially Redemption; an *Anamnesis* (or Memorial of the Passion of Christ); and an *Epiklesis* (or Invocation of the transforming Holy Spirit). The rubric preceding the prayer reads: "Let the prayer, thanksgiving, or blessing of the bread and wine, be to this effect," and the prayer itself follows immediately:

With humble and hearty acknowledgment of the greatness of our misery (from which neither man nor angel was able to deliver us), and of our great unworthiness of the least of all God's mercies; to give thanks to God for all his benefits, and especially for the great benefit of our redemption, the love of God the Father, the sufferings and merits of the Lord Jesus Christ, the Son of God, by which we are delivered; and for all means of grace, the word and Sacraments, and for this Sacrament in particular, by which Christ and all his benefits are applied and sealed up unto us; which, notwithstanding the denial of them unto others, are in great mercy continued unto us, after so much and long abuse of them all.

To profess that there is no other name under heaven by which we can be saved, but the name of Jesus Christ; by whom alone we receive liberty and life, have access to the throne of grace, are admitted to eat and drink at his own table, are sealed up by his Spirit to an assurance of happiness and everlasting life.

Earnestly to pray to God, the Father of all mercies, and God of all consolation, to vouchsafe his gracious presence, and the effectual working of his Spirit in us; and so to sanctify these elements both of bread and wine, that we may receive by faith the body and blood of Jesus Christ crucified for us, and so (to) feed upon him that he may be one with us, and we with him, that he may live in us, and we in him and to him, who hath loved us, and given himself for us.[30]

Having considered the Lord's Day Service and the Lord's Supper, it is time to look at the *Directory*'s provisions for Baptism, Marriage, and Burial. Baptism is described in true Calvinist fashion as "a seal of the covenant of grace";[31] yet any notion of its immediate and inherent efficacy is denied in the assertion "the

---

[30] *Ibid.*, pp. 55-56. [31] *Ibid.*, p. 46.

inward grace and virtue of baptism is not tied to that very moment of time wherein it is administered."[32] Baptism, according to the prefatory rubrics, is to be administered by the minister, not a private person, in the presence of the congregation and not in a private place, and "in the face of the congregation, where the people may most conveniently see and hear; and not in the places where fonts in the time of Popery were unfitly and superstitiously placed."[33] No godparents are allowed, since God's promises are to parents and their seed, and so the father is to present the child to the minister, or in the father's necessary absence, some Christian friend. The minister begins the Sacrament by instruction to the congregation on its meaning, and exhorts the parent "to bring up the child in the knowledge of the grounds of the Christian religion, and in the nurture and admonition of the Lord: and to let him know the danger of God's wrath to himself and child if he be negligent; requiring his solemn promise for the performance of his duty."[34] A prayer follows "joined with the word of institution, for sanctifying the water to this spiritual use." The name of the child is then demanded, and the minister then baptizes the child by name using the Trinitarian formula: *I Baptize thee in the name of the Father, of the Son, and of the Holy Ghost*.[35] The manner of baptizing is "to be by pouring or sprinkling of the water on the face of the child, without adding any other ceremony" (a deliberate exclusion of signing with the Cross).[36] The final act of the Sacrament with its touching reminder of heavy infant mortality in those days includes a petition that God "would receive the infant now baptized, and solemnly entered into the household of faith, into his fatherly tuition and defence . . . that if he shall be taken out of this life in his infancy, the Lord, who is rich in mercy, would be pleased to receive him up into glory," or otherwse that he may be upheld by divine power and grace "that by faith he may prevail against the devil, the world, and the flesh, till in the end he obtain a full and final victory. . . ."[37]

There was a long dispute between Independents and Scottish Presbyterians before the order for the Solemnization of Marriage was completed. Goodwin and his fellow Independents held Marriage to be a civil contract in which the minister acted only as the delegate of the magistrate. The Presbyterians, however, repre-

---

[32] *Ibid.*, p. 47.
[34] *Ibid.*, pp. 48-49.
[36] *Ibid.*

[33] *Ibid.*, p. 45.
[35] *Ibid.*, p. 50.
[37] *Ibid.*, p. 51.

sented by Rutherford, distinguished between marriage, the essence of which is consent, and solemnization which is concerned with the making of vows.[38] Also, the Presbyterians argued that since Marriage is commanded by God it is therefore worthy of religious solemnization. The Presbyterians gained their point.

The Service of Marriage consists of the following parts: a prayer of confession with a petition for the divine blessing on the couple; and an exhortation, Biblically grounded, reminding them of their duties to God and to one another. Then the man and woman in turn promise fidelity to one another; the minister pronounces them man and wife, and concludes with a prayer of blessing. The entire Service is modelled on a covenant relationship, as between God and humanity in Christ, so between man and wife, and a relationship freely entered into.[39] The mutuality of the relationship is stressed in the exhortation with its reference both to "the conjugal duties which in all faithfulness they are to perform each to the other"[40] and the spiritual duties, "praying much with and for one another, watching over and provoking each other to love and good works, and to live together as the heirs of the grace of life."[41] The same emphasis is found in the vow which the wife makes: *I N. do take thee N. to be my married husband, and I do, in the presence of God, and before this congregation, promise and covenant to be a loving and faithful wife unto thee, until God shall separate us by death.* The husband's vow is identical except for the substitution of "wife" for "husband" and the addition of "and obedient" after "loving and faithful."[42] The service lacks the aesthetic richness of the Anglican setting and the lovely rhetorical cadences of the promises which go back to the medieval Sarum Service, but there is still a simple, solemn strength about the *Directory*'s Service, with its sense of Marriage as an earthly image of the engagement between Christ and His church.

As we have now come to expect, the Scottish commissioners and the Independents argued fiercely about their different understandings of the significance of the Burial of the Dead. Baillie

38 Sprott and Leishman, *op. cit.*, p. 356.
39 A rubric directs that "Parents ought not to force their children to marry without their free consent, nor deny their own consent without just cause." (*Reliquiae Liturgicae*, ed. Peter Hall, III, p. 61). For the Puritan understanding of love and marriage, see James T. Johnson, *A society ordained by God; English Puritan marriage doctrine in the first half of the seventeenth century* (Nashville, 1970).
40 *Reliquiae Liturgicae*, ed. Peter Hall, III, p. 63.
41 *Ibid.*, III, pp. 63-64.   42 *Ibid.*, p. 64.

reported in a letter of December 6, 1644, that they had "after many sharp debates" and "with much difficultie past a proposition for abolishing their ceremonies at buriall: but our difference about funerall sermons seems irreconcileable." He asserts that in England the custom is to preach funeral sermons "to serve the humours only of rich people for a reward" and that it is often "a good part of the ministers livelyhood."[43] The Scottish church refused to have funeral sermons at all.

The *Directory* tries to take the middle way between the Presbyterians and the Independents. It excoriates superstitious customs such as praying to or by the corpse and refuses to permit praying, reading, or singing on the way to or at the grave. But it is judged convenient "that the Christian friends which accompany the dead body to the place appointed for public burial, do apply themselves to meditations and conferences suitable to the occasion: and that the minister, as upon other occasions, so at this time, if he be present, may put them in remembrance of their duty."

The *Directory* also gives help for the right way to sanctify the Lord's Day, how to make the visitation of the sick an improving occasion for them, how to observe days of solemn thanksgiving and humiliation, and of "Singing of Psalms."[44]

There appears to have been great difficulty in getting the people to accept the fact that the *Directory* was replacing the Book of Common Prayer early in 1645, not surprisingly since it had been in use almost continuously since 1549. For this reason Parliament produced an Ordinance on August 23, 1645, "for the more effectual putting into execution the Directory for Public Worship" within all the parish churches and chapels in England and Wales and for disseminating copies of it. The penalty for using the Book of Common Prayer in any public place of worship or in any private place or family in England, Wales or Berwick-on-Tweed, was a fine of five pounds for the first offence, ten pounds for the second offence, and a whole year's imprisonment for the third offence. Any minister refusing to use it is to be fined forty shillings on each occasion, and any person depraving the *Directory* is to be fined an appropriate sum, not less than five pounds and not more than fifty pounds. All copies of the Book of Common Prayer are to be

[43] *Letters and Journals of Robert Baillie*, II, p. 245.

[44] The Puritan observance of Sabbaths and solemn days of thanksgiving or humiliation is considered in detail in Chapter VI, "Calendary Conflicts: Holy Days or Holidays?"

removed by churchwardens or constables and disposed of as Parliament shall direct.[45]

2. *Critiques of the* Directory[46]

Just as the Puritans had not scrupled for the best part of a century to offer detailed critiques of the successive editions of the Book of Common Prayer, when the tables were turned the Episcopalian clergy were not slow to criticise the *Directory*. But former Anglicans were by no means the only critics of the *Directory*, for the Quakers were among the most iconoclastic writers about this service book.

Two representative examples of Anglican criticism are the brief diatribe of Judge David Jenkins and the learned and lengthy critique of Dr. Henry Hammond, one of the most erudite apologists of the century.

Jenkins's title is *A Scourge for the Directorie and the Revolting Synod, which hath sitten this 5 Yeares, more for foure shillings a Day then for Conscience sake* (1647). The length of the title compensates for the brevity and occasional scurrility of the treatment. Judge Jenkins argues that many who had approved of the Book of Common Prayer as Protestants suddenly find that it is described as an idol by the writers of the preface to the *Directory*. Further, since some country folk are very unlikely to have the means to employ a preacher, they will henceforth receive little or no religious instruction, whereas a reader of the Prayer Book would have assured them of some regular instruction in the knowledge of God's laws. To tell such folk of praying by the Spirit, "you may as well tell them a tale of the Man in the Moone."[47] Moreover, Jenkins believes that many of the Reformation fathers who had a hand in compiling the Prayer Book were indued with God's Spirit.

He then provides a description of the state of worship in England three years after the imposition of the *Directory*. Although

---

[45] The Ordinance is reprinted in *Reliquiae Liturgicae*, ed. Peter Hall, III, pp. 83-88.

[46] A common criticism, one not entirely fair, is that of Walter Lowrie the Kierkegaard scholar and American Episcopalian who wrote of the *Directory* that "it is the only liturgy consisting of nothing but rubrics." (*Action in the Liturgy*, New York, 1953, p. 220), a judgment that ignores the sample prayers and liturgical formulae. James Hastings Nichols better characterizes the *Directory* as "not a service book to be placed in the hands of all literate worshippers, but a manual for the discretionary use of ministers." (*Corporate Worship in the Reformed Church*, Philadelphia, 1968, p. 99.)

[47] *Op. cit.*, p. 1.

the account is biassed, the picture of the disorder is probably not entirely exaggerated:

> O lamentable! what times do we live in? When the Church is without true discipline, Gods Lawes quite taken from us, no Lords Prayer, no Creed, no Common Prayer allowed, but *Master Presbyter* to do as his fickle braine serves him, the Sacrament of the Lords Supper not administered once in halfe a yeare, and when it is delivered wonderfull out of order it is, the Sacraments of Baptisme celebrated as any would have it that is in fee with Master Parson; the dead body buryed with five or 6 words at the most; no decency in the Churches, no manners nor order, forgetting that God is the God of Order.[48]

He is even more critical of the Independents (whom he calls the *"New-New-England* brood"[49] or "Nondependants") than the Presbyterians, for he condemns their extemporary prayers as no more than "these puddles and light-headed fooleries" and their ranting sermons preached by *"Ananias* the Button-maker, *Flash* the Cobler, Nondependants" which he claims are mere "tongue-sermons" that harm poor souls and especially poor women more than many Presbyterian sermons do good in half a year.[50] The entire pamphlet is an appeal to return from the chaos induced by the *Directory* to the uniformity, reverence and ordered dignity of the Prayer Book.

Henry Hammond's work is entitled, *A View of the New Directory and a Vindication of the Ancient Liturgy of the Church of England; In Answer to the Reasons pretended in the Ordinance and Preface for the abolishing the one, and establishing the other.* The first edition appeared in 1645 (and was 112 pages long), and the third edition in 1646. It will be possible to give only the most rapid summary of a book which combines much Patristic lore with a good deal of common sense.

After denying the legality of the abolition of the Book of Common Prayer, he provides several grounds to establish the lawfulness of a liturgy or form of worship. These include the precedents set by God's holy men in the Old Testament, Jewish practice since the time of Ezra, the practice and precept of Christ, the practice of John the Baptist, the apostles and the eastern church (the liturgies of Saints James, Basil and Chrysostom), the practice of the universal church since that time to this, the judgment and

---

[48] *Ibid.*, p. 2. [49] *Ibid.*, p. 4. [50] *Ibid.*, pp. 4-5.

practice of the Reformed churches in other kingdoms, the example of heathens such as Plato who took up the practice, and the "irrational concludings" of the anti-liturgical groups.[51]

It is in the latter section that he provides two very telling rational arguments against the compilers of the *Directory*. The first is that "while they in opposition to set Formes require the Minister to conceive a Prayer for the congregation, they observe not, that the whole congregation is by that means as much stinted and bound to a set Forme, to wit of those words which the Minister conceives as if he read them out of a Book."[52] He also makes much, in the second place, of the inconsistency of presuming to prescribe the matter while refusing to prescribe the words of the prayers in the *Directory*. Is not the "prescription of the matter" a stinting of the Spirit as well as the form of words?[53]

As for extemporary prayers, Hammond considers them to have often been occasions of scandal to the faithful by their indiscretions, and he thinks their fascination is superficial, namely, "to the itching eare, exercise and pleasure to the licentious tongue, and the vanity of the reputation of being able to performe that office so fluently. . . ."[54]

He concentrates his chief fire on the omissions of the *Directory*. By avoiding a set form it sacrifices uniformity, and an active vocal role for the people through eliminating responses. It removes the correspondence between external bodily gestures and the inward spirit and rejects time-honoured ceremonies, while it omits the concision of collects for a long prayer, contrary to Jewish and ancient ecclesiastical practice.

After considering these general omissions, he concentrates on particular omissions. To deny any absolution at Communion, sick bed, or death, is "barbarous inhumanity."[55] The *Directory* seems to be indifferent to music and prescribes metrical psalmody only after the sermon and on special days of thanksgiving or humiliation.[56] It rejects the three larger creeds, including the Apostles' Creed.[57] It is lacking in any sense of the Communion of saints, the mutual charity of the church triumphant in heaven with the church militant on earth, which the Prayer Book's emphasis on the "Scripture-Saints" with their days and "propers" ensures.[58] As to the often criticised repetition of the Lord's Prayer, Hammond explains it as

---

51 *Op. cit.*, pp. 12-18. 52 *Ibid.*, p. 18. 53 *Ibid.*, pp. 18-19.
54 *Ibid.*, p. 19. 55 *Ibid.*, p. 20. 56 *Ibid.*, p. 31.
57 *Ibid.*, p. 35. 58 *Ibid.*, pp. 39-40.

due to the fact that they appear in different parts of the liturgy (as, for example, the Litany), which could be separate. Also he adds pointedly, "I remember to have heard one of the gravest and most reverend men of the [Westminster] Assembly, being asked his opinion about the use of the *Lord's Prayer*, to have answer'd to this purpose, *God forbid that I should ever be upon my knees in Prayer, and rise up without adding Christs forme to my imperfect petitions.*"[59]

He particularly excoriates the absence of any order for Confirmation, the miserable provisions for burial in the *Directory* and asserts the need of the living for Lessons and Prayers as "laudable Christian civilities" at a time when events make human hearts malleable through mourning.[60] He laments the absence of any thanksgiving after child-birth by which the *Directory* is effectively setting up "Schools of *ingratitude* in the Church."[61]

Hammond's art is to prove his points with historical learning and then to show the practical superiority of the Book of Common Prayer over the *Directory*. He particularly delights in demonstrating the inconsistencies of the compilers of the *Directory*. He does not fail, towards the end of his book,[62] to note that all the arguments in favour of extemporary prayer (to spread the gift of prayer, to stop idle men in the ministry, etc.) are contradicted by the issuance of *A Supply of Prayer for the Ships that want Ministers to pray with them agreeable to the Directory established by Parliament, published by authority.*

The Quaker criticism of the *Directory* can be represented by Francis Howgill who wrote *Mistery Babylon the Mother of Harlots discovered . . . in answer to a Book tituled the Directory for the publick Worship of God* (1659). It was not an appeal to historical precedent like Hammond's, nor to the practical effect of using the *Directory* rather than a uniform liturgy like the Prayer Book. Rather it accuses the proponents of a spiritual or Spirit-inspired worship, such as the Independents, of not going far enough in that direction. Ironically, he suggests that if any man says the Spirit instructs each person, then he is told this is an illusion and he needs "Hebrew, Greek, and Latin, and the original of which you should expound the Scripture."[63] If he claims Christ is his teacher he is declared a heretic for despising the ministry and ordinances of the Reformed churches, natural learning, the ancient fathers, and worst

---

59 *Ibid.*, pp. 35-36.   60 *Ibid.*, pp. 50-51.   61 *Ibid.*, p. 53.
62 *Ibid.*, p. 101.   63 *Op. cit.*, p. 7.

of all, such would "make void all our arts and parts."[64] It will be heresy and blasphemy if any man in fact claims that Christ has made him free of sin in this life. If any one call the church or chapel an "Idols temple," Scriptures will be brought to prove that God commanded a temple to be built in Jerusalem and how the Jews used synagogues.[65] Further, if any one were to say that the Spirit should move or inspire any one "before any Teacher, Minister, or Believer ought to pray" then a "multitude of Scriptural arguments and precedents will be brought to prove him wrong."[66]

With supreme irony he describes the Puritan method of praying:

> And reverend Brethrens, let us all agree not to be idle but diligent, read the Scriptures, and pack them up together, a deal of exhortations, reprehensions, admonitions, and prophecies, and read some old Authors, as *Ireneus, Ambros, Cyprian, Ierom, Bazel, Austin, Origen, Damazin,* and its not amisse we take in *Luthar* and *Calvin, Memno* [Menno Simons], *Beza* . . . and so by much reading & meditation our actions will be shetted up and Quikened, and those words which we read often will lodge in our memory, so that we shall be able to pray half an houre *ex tempore,* or an hour and a halfe upon a Fast-day . . . without tautologies, or reiterations. . . .[67]

He then proceeds to make observations on the *Directory* chiefly with the intention of showing the superiority of the understanding of worship and prayer that the Society of Friends has. He does, however, point to one contradiction. He asks why it is that the *Directory* has so much to say about Baptism effecting regeneration and yet there is also emphasis on the need to confess sins. This he calls sheer hypocrisy![68] He can see no point in requiring prayer and the words of institution to sanctify water to its spiritual use in Baptism, since God the Word originally instituted the water and hallowed it, so why does it need sanctifying again?

Again, Howgill cannot see any reason for requiring the Communion Service after the morning sermon, when it was instituted in the evening to be a Supper; nor since the wine was already hallowed by God's creation does it need to be made holy again for the Communion.[69] He is also critical of singing in worship, accusing the Puritans of turning David's crying in the Psalms into a song.[70]

64 *Ibid.*
65 *Ibid.*, p. 8.
66 *Ibid.*, pp. 9-10.
67 *Ibid.*, p. 10.
68 *Ibid.*, p. 24.
69 *Ibid.*, p. 30.
70 *Ibid.*, p. 35.

It is clear that Howgill accepts neither tradition and Scripture, as the Anglicans, nor Scripture alone as the Puritans, but the interior guidance of the Holy Spirit as the criterion of worship. Hence he uses the *Directory* as a means of proving the superiority of Quaker spirituality, its dispensing with forms and its immateriality.

Whatever the criticisms, valid or invalid, of the *Directory*, it shaped Reformed and Free church worship for the better part of three hundred years in English-speaking countries, and even had an impact on Non-Calvinistic Methodism[71] for two hundred years. Thus, as the Anglican Communion throughout the world owes an incalculable debt to the successive revisions of the Book of Common Prayer for the forming of its spirituality, so do English-speaking Presbyterians, Congregationalists, Baptists, and Methodists, to the *Directory*.

3. *Baxter's* The Reformation of the Liturgy (*1661*)[72]

The *Directory* had been in use for only sixteen years when the Restoration of the monarchy naturally led to the desire for the restoration of the Prayer Book, but a conference was held at the Savoy to see whether the Presbyterians might not be included in a more comprehensive Church of England, if some changes were made in the Prayer Book or some alternative orders were provided which Presbyterians would not scruple. While the other Presbyterian commissioners prepared their list of Exceptions to the Prayer Book, Baxter busied himself with producing the alternative Scriptural Orders of Service. The *Reformed Liturgy* was entirely Baxter's own work, the product of an intense fortnight, in which "I could not have time to make use of any Book, save the Bible and my Concordance."[73] His colleagues refused, at first, to allow him

[71] Methodist worship is, of course, an amalgam of the Free church Lord's Day Service, with the Anglican Order for Holy Communion, and the superb hymns of Charles and John Wesley. It is interesting that Wesley's adaptation of Prayer Book for American use took note of the Presbyterian criticisms of the Savoy Conference as related in a breviate of Baxter's life (the *Reliquiae Baxterianae*, ed. M. Sylvester), by Calamy.

[72] The text of *The Reformation of the Liturgy*, or *The Reformed Liturgy*, or the *Savoy Liturgy*, can be found in *Reliquiae Liturgicae*, IV, *The Savoy Liturgy* (ed. Peter Hall, Bath, 1847), and, excluding the prefatory "Address to the Bishops," in *The Practical Works of the Rev. Richard Baxter* (ed. W. Orme), XV, pp. 450-527. The Hall text will be used for references and citations. The previous Chapter, "The Prayer Book Restored and Revised" dealt with the purpose, development and results of the Savoy Conference between the Anglican and Presbyterian representatives who convened in 1661, but not in detail with Baxter's Scriptural alternative liturgy.

[73] *Reliquiae Baxterianae*, ed. M. Sylvester, Vol. II, Pt. II, Sect. 172.

to specify rubrics or directions but only prayers, since they thought the terms of the Conference forbade it.[74] The final revision by his Presbyterian colleagues left Baxter's work largely unchanged, as he was delighted to report.[75]

It is a remarkable work to have been accomplished in two weeks. Baxter's work, so F. J. Powicke suggested, is accounted for "by the fact that he was but writing out and supplementing what he had practised in Kidderminster."[76] Geoffrey F. Nuttall, however, would qualify this judgment: "Of the order of service this may be true, in whole or in part; but in so far as *The Reformed Liturgy* is, as the name indicates, a reforming of the 'liturgy' of the Book of Common Prayer, it is incorrect."[77] Nuttall then cites the following passage in which Baxter writes of his practice at Kidderminster: "As to the report of my using a form, the truth is, I never used one publicly or privately since I was 17 or 18 years of age; except the Lord's Prayer, which I use most Lord's Days once; . . . and except that I used much of the public liturgy in the congregation the first year and half of my ministry. And I find myself of late disposed in secret to end with the Lord's Prayer, as having a perfect method and satisfactory comprehensiveness of all that I had omitted."[78] In the light of this evidence, it would be nearer the truth to observe that Baxter was not using any forms that he had employed during his Kidderminster ministry, but was relying on his experience in conceived prayer. Even as late as 1684 Baxter prayed without a form because he found it difficult to remember forms.[79]

The following are the contents of the *Reformed Liturgy*:

1. The Ordinary Public Worship of the Lord's Day.
2. The Order of celebrating the Sacrament of the Body and Blood of Christ.
3. The celebration of the Sacrament of Baptism.
4. Of Catechising, and the Approbation of those that are admitted to the Lord's Supper.

[74] *Ibid.*, Vol. II, Pt. II, Sect. 175.   [75] *Ibid.*, Sect. 182.
[76] *The Life of the Reverend Richard Baxter* (1924), II, p. 95.
[77] *Richard Baxter* (1965), p. 50.
[78] Dr. Williams's Library, London, Ms 5:9, cited by Nuttall, *op. cit.*, p. 50.
[79] *Catholick Communion Defended against both Extreams* (1684), p. 20. Many forms of Baxter's own writing are scattered throughout his works, which were intended as "a help subordinate to the Spirits help, to those that have it but in part; as Spectacles to dark Sights, and Sermon Notes to weak Memories . . . I can truly say, that Forms are oft a help to me." (*Ibid.*, p. 19.)

5. Of the celebration of Matrimony.
6. The Visitation of the Sick, and their Communion.
7. The Order for solemnizing the Burial of the Dead.
8. Of Extraordinary Days of Humiliation, and Thanksgiving; and Anniversary Festivals.
9. Of Prayer and Thanksgiving for particular Members of the Church.
10. Of Pastoral Discipline, Public Confession, Absolution, and Exclusion from the Holy Communion of the Church.

In addition, there is an Appendix containing:

11. A Larger Litany, or General Prayer: to be used at discretion.
12. The Church's Praise for our Redemption; to be used at discretion.

While 12 as a Scriptural mosaic of praise of Christ is wholly new, much of the rest comprises alternative provisions to those of the Prayer Book. This is especially true of 1, 2, 3, 5, and 11. Nine has a Prayer Book parallel in the "Churching" of Women, but it has an additional prayer for women drawing near the time of child-birth, and a thanksgiving for those that are restored from dangerous sickness. Eleven consists only of general directions and 7 is the same, except that suitable Scripture lessons are suggested. Four is the Presbyterian equivalent for Confirmation, without a bishop, and 10 is the traditional Puritan process of discipline. Eight provides an alternative to the Prayer Book observance of feasts and fasts.

If the structure of the service for the Lord's Day is examined, it will be seen that the order bears a close resemblance to the *Directory*. The *Directory* has an order consisting of nine items only: a Prayer; readings from the Old and New Testaments in succession; a Psalm; the Prayer before the Sermon; the Sermon; Intercessory Prayer, and Lord's Prayer; a Psalm; and the Blessing. The *Reformed Liturgy* has seventeen items:

1. A Prayer of Approach (with shorter alternative).
2. The Apostles' or Nicene or occasionally the Athanasian Creed read by the Minister.
3. The Decalogue.
4. Scripture Sentences moving to Penitence and Confession.

5. Confession of Sin and Prayer for Pardon and Sanctification ending with the Lord's Prayer (shorter alternative provided).
6. Sentences of Scripture declarative of Absolution and for comforting the penitent.
7. Sentences of Scripture declarative of the conditions of salvation.
8. Psalm 95 or 100 or 84, followed by "the Psalms in order for the day."
9. A chapter of the Old Testament.
10. A Psalm or Te Deum.
11. A chapter of the New Testament.
12. The Prayer for the King and Magistrates.
13. Psalm 67, or 98, or other Psalm, or Benedictus, or Magnificat.
14. An extemporary Prayer for the Church and the theme for the Sermon.
15. Sermon "upon some text of Holy Scripture."
16. Prayer "for a blessing on the word of instruction" and of Intercessions for causes not mentioned in 14 above. [A set form of "General Prayer" is provided, or the "Larger Litany" may be used at this point.]
17. Blessing.

The dominating characteristic of this order is, of course, its Biblicism. Two years before the composition of this liturgy, Baxter had conceived of a liturgy entirely composed of Scriptural materials. He wrote: "The safest way of composing a stinted Liturgie, is to take it all, or as much as may be, for words as well as matter out of the Holy Scriptures."[80] His grounds for such a conviction are three: the infallibility of Scripture; its ecumenical advantages; and "there is no other words that may be preferred before the words of God, or stand in competition with them."[81]

A second outstanding quality is its flexibility. It contained shorter alternatives to all the longer prayers, which the 1662 Book of Common Prayer did not. Moreover, it was intended itself to provide some alternatives to the Prayer Book Orders of Service.

The needs of the congregation were very much in mind when Baxter framed the Lord's Day Service. Their part in the worship is more than doubled, for they are allotted five Psalms (compared

---

[80] *Five Disputations of Church Government and Worship* (1659), p. 378.
[81] *Ibid.*, p. 379.

with the *Directory*'s two), while similar prayer-material was divided into five sections in the Reformed liturgy as compared with four in the *Directory*. The proof of Baxter's psychological insight is seen in the separation of the two Scripture lessons by a Psalm, to make concentration easier.

E. C. Ratcliff has commented on the logical character of the service,[82] to which one only needs to add its completeness. It fittingly began with a prayer for the divine acceptance of the worship. It followed by a profession of obedience to God in both mind and will, in the Creed and Decalogue respectively. By a natural transition the worshipper confessed his transgressions of the Holy Law. This was made all the more relevant by the use of sentences inciting to penitence and faith. The worshipper rightly begged forgiveness through the merits of his Saviour and as a token of reliance upon Christ recited the Lord's Prayer. The minister then read sentences declarative of God's absolution and strengthening of the sinner, with a Scriptural exhortation to a godly life. This was fittingly confirmed by the congregation which now joined in a Psalm of praise. This preparation had made the people ready to receive the Word of God or divine oracle, which was now both read and preached to them. After they had said "Amen" to intercessory prayers, and sung another Psalm, they were dismissed by a blessing. Thus the service ranged over all the Christian moods of prayer: from Adoration and Confession to Petition, and from Intercession to Consecration. It included the Christian duties of belief and conduct, and particularly in the prevalence of praise the warming of the religious affections. It is worth recalling that Baxter wrote: "For myself I confess that Harmony and Melody are the pleasure and elevation of my soul, and have made a Psalm of Praise in the Holy Assembly the chief delightful Exercise of my Religion and my life."[83]

When "the Sacrament of the Body and Blood of Christ" was to be administered, the celebration was to follow the service just outlined. The minister was to begin with an "explication of the nature, use, and benefits of this Sacrament" at his discretion, using either his own words or the form provided, and an exhortation which movingly depicted the Passion of Christ in the Sacrament.[84] There

---

[82] *From Uniformity to Unity, 1662-1962* (eds. G. F. Nuttall and Owen Chadwick, 1962), p. 121.

[83] *Poetical Fragments* (1683), Epistle to the Reader.

[84] *Reliquiae Liturgicae*, ed. Peter Hall, IV, pp. 60-62. Two excerpts from this exhortation will show how direct and moving Baxter's appeals were: "You were

followed a Prayer of Confession and a Petition for Pardon. Then the elements were received by the minister if they had not previously been placed on the table. A Prayer of Consecration followed: "Almighty God, thou art the Creator and the Lord of all things. Thou art the Sovereign Majesty whom we have offended. Thou art our loving and most merciful Father, who hast given thy Son to reconcile us to thyself: who hath ratified the new testament and covenant of grace with his most precious blood; and hath instituted this holy Sacrament to be celebrated in remembrance of him till his coming. Sanctify these thy creatures of bread and wine, which, according to thy institution and command, we set apart to this holy use, that they may be sacramentally the body and blood of thy Son Jesus Christ. Amen."[85] Either before or after this prayer, the Pauline warrant or Words of Institution were read, followed by the declaration that "this bread and wine, being set apart, and consecrated to this holy use by God's appointment, are now no common bread and wine, but sacramentally the body and blood of Christ."[86] There was next a prayer addressing Christ directly pleading his Atonement, and through his Intercession and sacrifice, asking for the gifts of pardon, sanctification through the Holy Spirit, and reconciliation with the Father, and "nourish us as thy members to eternal life."[87]

The consecrated bread was broken in the sight of the people with these words: "The Body of Christ was broken for us, and offered once for all to sanctify us: behold the sacrificed Lamb of God, that taketh away the sins of the world." The Libation was made in front of the congregation with the words: "We were redeemed with the precious blood of Christ, as of a Lamb without blemish and without spot."[88] There followed a prayer for sanctifi-

---

lost and in the way to be lost for ever, when, by the greatest miracle of condescending love, he sought and saved you. You were dead in sin, condemned by the law, the slaves of Satan; there wanted nothing but the executing stroke of justice to have sent you into endless misery; when our Redeemer pitied you in your blood, and shed his own to heal and wash you. He suffered that was offended, that the offended might not suffer. He cried out on the cross, 'My God, my God, why hast thou Forsaken me,' that we, who had deserved it, might not be everlasting forsaken. He died that we might live . . . See here Christ dying in his holy representation! Behold the sacrificed Lamb of God, that taketh away the sins of the world! It is his will to be thus frequently crucified before our eyes. O how should we be covered with shame, and loathe ourselves, that have procured the death of Christ by sin, and sinned against it! And how should we all be filled with joy, that have such mysteries of mercy opened, and so great salvation freely offered to us! O hate sin! O, love this Saviour!"

85 Ibid., p. 65.   86 Ibid., p. 69.   87 Ibid., pp. 69-70.
88 Ibid., p. 70.

cation and the administration of the elements with the minister receiving first after saying: "Take ye, eat ye; this is the body of Christ, which is broken for you. Do this, in remembrance of him." The cup was delivered with the words: "This cup is the New Testament in Christ's blood, [or Christ's blood of the New Testament,] which is shed for you for the remission of sins. Drink ye all of it, in remembrance of him."[89] It was left to the minister's discretion whether to consecrate the bread and wine together, or separately and severally. "And if the Minister choose to pray but once at the consecration, commemoration, and delivery, let him pray as followeth, or to this sense." A further rubric, following a slightly longer Prayer of Consecration, showed the discretionary latitude Baxter allowed the celebrant: "Let it be left to the Minister's discretion, whether to deliver the bread and wine to the people, at the table, only in general, each one taking it and applying it to themselves; or to deliver it in general to as many people as are in each particular form; or to put it into every person's hand. . . . And let none of the people be forced to sit, stand, or kneel in the act of receiving, whose judgment is against it."[90] Then followed a splendid Prayer of Adoration and Thanksgiving ending with a petition that God's redeemed people "present themselves a living sacrifice to be acceptable through Christ useful for thine honour."[91] The Communion Service ended with part of a hymn in metre or Psalm 23, 100, 103, 116, and the Blessing: "Now the God of peace. . . ."

The flexibility of the rubrics for this Communion Service makes one curious to know how Baxter celebrated the Eucharist in Kidderminster. This is, in fact, known from a letter he wrote in March 1657:

A long table being spread, I first open the nature and use of the ordinance, and the qualification and present duty of the communicants; and then the deacons (3 or 4 grave, pious men chosen and appointed to that office) do set the bread and wine on the table; and in prayer we beseech the Lord to accept of those his own creatures now dedicated and set apart for his service, as sanctified to represent the body and blood of his Son, and after confession of sin, and thanksgiving for redemption, with commemoration of the sufferings of Christ therein, and ransom thereby, we beg the pardon of sin, and

[89] *Ibid.*, p. 72. [90] *Ibid.* [91] *Ibid.*, pp. 74-77.

the acceptance of our persons and thanksgivings now offered up to God again, and his grace to help our faith, repentance, love, etc. and renewal of our covenant with him, etc. And so after words of institution etc. I break the bread and deliver it in Christ's general terms to all present, first partaking myself, and so by the cup; which is moved down to the end of the table by the people and deacons (who fill the cup when it is emptied); and immediately after it, each one layeth down his alms for the poor, and so arise, and the next tableful succeedeth to the last after which I first proceed to some words of exhortation, and then of praise and prayer, and sing a psalm, and so conclude with the blessing.[92]

Baxter's Eucharistic doctrine is a high one, as not only the *epiklesis* implies, but also the combination of a strong emphasis on sacrifice with the recognition that Christ intercedes with the Father for his Body, the church, through that once offered but ever-efficacious offering of himself upon the Cross for the world's ransom. While the exhortations are too many, too long, and too didactic, yet the language is always serious and dignified, and the element of adoration is far stronger than is usual in Presbyterian liturgies of this period, where it is all too often remembered that God's people are *miseri et abiecti*, and forgotten that the ransomed should also be *laeti triumphantes*.

Since Baxter's *The Reformation of the Liturgy* failed to win the approval of the Savoy Conference as a whole as an alternative to the Book of Common Prayer—itself too ambitious a hope for the work of a single liturgist—it has received little attention either at its own time or subsequently, with the exception of the evaluation of it prepared by the late distinguished liturgiologist, and Regius Professor of Divinity at Cambridge University, Edward C. Ratcliff. Although he considered that this genre of composition, in which a deft and dignified mosaic of Biblical citations was created, unlikely to appeal today, and he noted the lack of a prayer of thanksgiving corresponding to the Preface of the Consecration Prayer of the Roman Catholic Mass and the Anglican Communion Order, yet he concluded: "This failure apart, Baxter's conception of the liturgical action of the Lord's Supper is nearer to the historic western tradition than the conception which Cranmer embodied in the Com-

---

92 Dr. Williams's Library, Ms. 3:156, cited by G. F. Nutall, *Richard Baxter*, p. 53. Nuttall asserts that the posture for receiving Communion at Kidderminster was sitting, as can be determined from a sermon of 1657, *op. cit.*, p. 55.

munion Service of the Prayer Book of 1552."[93] That was high praise.

The Reformed Liturgy was a landmark in the history of English worship. While the *Westminster Directory* was a compromise between Presbyterians and Independents, the Reformed liturgy represents the liturgical convictions of one party, the English Presbyterians, and was drawn up by one man, rather than a committee. It is a homogeneous production. It is also valuable as an indication of how the *Directory* might have turned out, had the Independents not pressed their views on the Presbyterians, though there was not complete agreement between Scottish and English Presbyterians in the Westminster Assembly. It is, unquestionably, a clear indication that, even while the particular liturgy of the Church of England—the Book of Common Prayer—was severely criticized, the Presbyterians had no objection to a liturgy on a Biblical basis, provided it were not to be imposed with no regard to tender consciences. Moreover, it presented, with the Presbyterian critique of the Prayer Book, both the denials and the affirmations of the moderate Puritans on the subject of public worship.

The rejection of *The Reformed Liturgy* by the Anglican representatives at the Savoy Conference, while politically, ecclesiastically, and liturgically understandable, had one unforeseen and disastrous consequence. It turned the moderate Puritans (the Presbyterians) after their inability to take an oath required of them before Bartholomew's Day in 1662 affirming that the Book of Common Prayer was in all things conformable to the Word of God, into permanent Dissenters in England, and they, like the Independents, thereafter became the enemies of liturgy because they had suffered deprivation of their ministerial office for one unacceptable liturgy. Henceforth the liturgical Presbyterians became proponents of free prayer, the very party which had given the Book of Common Prayer in 1662, through Edward Reynolds, one of its glories, the General Thanksgiving.

---

[93] *From Uniformity to Unity, 1662-1962*, eds. G. F. Nuttall and Owen Chadwick, p. 123. Ratcliff also observed that Baxter might have assumed that the element of thanksgiving was sufficiently stressed in the regular Sunday Ante-Communion part of the Service, and it is interesting that this element is there in the description Baxter gives of his service at Kidderminster in the letter of March 1657. See footnote 92.

CHAPTER XII

NONCONFORMIST WORSHIP: PRESBYTERIAN AND INDEPENDENT, 1662-1690

PURITANISM becomes Nonconformity when it is excluded from the Church of England in 1662. It is a significant fact of religious life in the seventeenth century that every denomination of British Christianity underwent persecution at one period or another. The Roman Catholics lived under penal laws for the entire period, apart from three years of the unhappy reign of James II, and his encouragement of Catholicism cost him his throne. The Anglicans suffered obloquy and displacement from 1644 to 1660. The Nonconformists, the heirs of the Puritans, suffered under the five-stringed whip of the Clarendon Code and even when that was ended from 1662 to 1688.

The Presbyterians had much to hope for at the Restoration: the Declaration of Charles II at Breda to their ministers, the Savoy Conference to enable Anglicans and Presbyterians to consider widening the liturgical formulary to include the Presbyterians in the establishment, and the offer of bishoprics to three Presbyterians, all made this abundantly clear. The Independents, most of whom had been firm supporters of Cromwell and had received patronage from him, had almost nothing to hope for at the hands of the King and his advisers. In the event, neither Presbyterians nor Independents gained anything, and lost—if they were ministers or tutors at the universities—their livings and livelihoods.

From each minister intending to stay in the Church of England there was demanded a declaration to be made in front of the congregation before the feast of St. Bartholomew in 1662 of his "unfeigned assent and consent to every thing contained and prescribed in . . . the book of common prayer" and to "the form and order of making, ordaining, and consecrating of bishops, priests, and deacons."[1] There was also to be an abjuration of the solemn league and covenant, and the requirement that all not episcopally ordained should seek episcopal ordination. The penalty for refusal was deprivation of all the spiritual offices held. Thus ministers of

[1] Cited by Daniel Neal, *History of the Puritans*, 5 Vols. (edn., 1822), IV, p. 335.

435

the Puritan tradition, both Presbyterian and Independent, were being required to renounce their serious criticism of both prelacy and the Book of Common Prayer as conditions of remaining within the Church of England. It strained their consciences to the uttermost, and in the end almost two thousand ministers found they could not in decency comply.

The consequences, as we shall see, were formidable. The Presbyterians and the Independents were driven together as comrades in suffering, and so loathed was the Book of Common Prayer as an engine of oppression that the Presbyterians who had believed in Scriptural liturgies joined the Independents in the exclusive use of free prayers, and it is impossible to judge what the effect on the national church was through the withdrawal of such a learned, conscientious, and compassionate group of deeply spiritual ministers from their community. A persecuted and convinced congeries of conventicles of Nonconformists found its personal religion and its familial piety deepened through testing in the crucible of persecution, and the best devotional books of the Nonconformists, by authors such as Alleine, were written during this period "under the Cross."

The concern of this chapter will be to try and experience along the pulse and in the anxious and hurried beating of the heart what it was to worship secretly as a Nonconformist. We shall attempt to understand the difficulties of ministers with consciences, but also with pastoral responsibilities, expected to sign the declaration of conformity, the sufferings they underwent as a result of noncompliance by way of deprivation, imprisonment, and change of occupation in many cases. We shall also consider the different stratagems of Nonconformist conventicles employed to avoid discovery, or, if found, the methods by which they sought to escape the long arm of the law and its informers. Finally, consideration will be given to the effects of persecution on personal religion and corporate worship. This, by contrast, will prepare us for the great relief of the toleration of Dissent under William and Mary in the "Revolution" of 1688, and the "Heads of Agreement" for a happy union between the Presbyterians and Independents, the forerunner of the recent formation of the United Reformed Church in England in 1972 from the union of the Congregational Church of England and Wales and the Presbyterian Church of England. Such unity in Dissent was an unintended result of the Earl of Clarendon's and

Archbishop Sheldon's policy of "thorough" towards the heirs of the Puritans.

1. Black Bartholomew's Day and After

Some of the Nonconformist ministers left their livings in the Church of England before August 24, as did Richard Baxter, in order to let all the ministers in England know their resolution beforehand. Many ministers in London preached their farewell sermon on August 17, the Sunday before St. Bartholomew's Day, including such leaders as Thomas Manton, Edmund Calamy the elder, Matthew Mead, and William Bates.

Pepys made a point of hearing the farewell discourses of Dr. Bates at the church of St. Dunstan's-in-the-West. His diary entry for August 17, 1662, records his eagerness to be present at what he hoped would be a dramatic and highly emotional occasion. In fact, he seems to have been disappointed that Dr. Bates made no allusion to the situation at the morning service. Nonetheless, Pepys returned for the afternoon service, for which he had to stand in the crowded gallery, and there he heard a brief and moderate statement at the very end of the service. Bates spoke to this effect: "I do believe that many of you do expect that I should say something to you in reference to the time, this being the last time that possibly I may appear here. You know it is not my manner to speak anything in the pulpit that is extraneous to my text and business; yet this I shall say, that it is not my opinion, fashion, or humour, that keeps me from complying with what is required of us; but something, after much discourse, prayer and study, yet remains unsatisfied and commands me herein. Wherefore if it is my unhappiness not to receive such an illuminacion as should direct me to do otherwise, I know no reason why men should not pardon me in this world, as I am confident God will pardon me for it in the next." Madam Turner, with whom Pepys had lunch between the services that day and who was a regular attender at Parson Herring's services, presumably gave Pepys the information which he passed on. Herring apparently offered his apologia, not in a sermon, but as a postscript to a lesson from the Acts of the Apostles which recounted how Annas and Sapphira had kept their private possessions from the common treasury of the apostolic church. Herring is then reported as saying: "This is the case of England at present. God he bids us to preach, and men bid us not to preach; and if we do, we are to be imprisoned and further punished. All I can say to it is, that I beg your prayers, and the prayers of all good Christians for us."

These two accounts are sufficient to indicate the torments of conscience posed by the King and the established church to its ministers of Puritan persuasion who could not, in the light of their known convictions, accept an unreformed Prayer Book as fully in accordance with the Word of God (their liturgical criterion), especially as a century of Puritan scrutiny of the Book of Common Prayer made them acutely aware of its defects. Yet, equally, how could they leave their flocks to the hirelings who would succeed them? The astute could only conclude that the Act of Uniformity was a ruse to rid the established church of all dissenters by driving them into open Nonconformity.

It is worth comparing the reasons for Nonconformity adduced by the Presbyterian divine, John Howe, with those of the Independent minister, John Owen. Howe's inability to conform was based on three grounds: he could not submit to re-ordination without denying the fruits of the Holy Spirit in his previous ministry nor to the absolute enforcement of ceremonies not warranted by the Word of God, and he found the Anglican church unable or unwilling to exercise a strong Scriptural discipline for the maintenance of the purity of its church members.[2] Owen confined himself, in the main, to an attack on the imposition of the liturgy. This leads, he believes, to three disastrous results: the atrophy of spiritual gifts and to "men napkining their talents" in free prayer; the uniformity of a liturgy makes impossible the application of grace to the varying needs of different congregations; it abridges the liberty of the followers of Christ in unnecessary matters. Moreover, in the past such impositions have "brought fire and faggot in their train."[3]

Some supporters of the ministers made a less dignified and more threatening protest on their behalf on St. Bartholomew's Day. Pepys is again our informant. He states that "there has been a disturbance in a Church at Friday Street, a great many young people knotting together and crying out 'Porridge!' often and seditiously in the Church, and they took the Common Prayer Book, they say, away; and, some say, did tear it; but it is a thing which appears to me very ominous. I pray God avert it."

[2] *Works*, ed. Hewlett, I, p. xviii.   [3] *Works*, ed. Goold, xv, pp. 52ff.

438

Apparently "porridge" was the nickname given by Dissenters to the Prayer Book at this time. A contemporary play, *The City Heiress*, includes the following conversation. Sir Anthony says to Sir Timothy, "You come to Church, too." Sir Timothy replies: "Ah! needs must when the devil drives. I go to save my bacon, as they say, once a month, and that, too, after the porridge is served up."[4] The implication is that the real meat of the service is the sermon, the porridge only a preliminary that can be dispensed with.

Almost two thousand of the most conscientious ministers in England refused to comply with the new and stringent terms of conformity and lost their livelihoods. Some were men of considerable standing (two had refused bishoprics) and all, according to the testimony of John Locke, were "worthy, learned, pious, orthodox divines."[5] The roll of honour of these men of conscience is an impressive one for it includes: Bates, Gilpin, Manton, Jacomb, John Owen, Thomas Goodwin, Burgess, Annesley (John Wesley's maternal grandfather), Baxter, Calamy, Caryl, Charnock, Gouge, Gale, Cradock, Mead, Howe, Favel, and Philip Henry among the most famous. A few eminent men of Puritan persuasion complied, including Bishops Reynolds and Wilkins.

Of the 1,603 ejected about whom there is available detailed information, A. G. Matthews has established that 1,285 had received university education. Of this number 733 had been educated at Cambridge, 513 at Oxford, 20 at the Scottish universities, 12 at Harvard, and 2 at Trinity College, Dublin; 11 heads of colleges and halls, 39 resident fellows, 3 non-resident fellows, and 3 college chaplains were removed from Oxford in 1660, while 3 heads of colleges and 4 fellows were ejected from the same university in 1662. In Cambridge 5 heads of colleges, 18 fellows, and 2 college chaplains were removed in 1660, and 1 head and 14 fellows two years later. The headmaster and 5 fellows of Eton suffered the same fate in 1660. In all, 149 divines holding academic positions were ejected at or soon after the Restoration.[6] While many of these would place their wisdom and expertise at the services of the new Dissenting academies and there write a new

---

4 Footnote in the Everyman edn. of Pepys's *Diary*, I, p. 282, which also observes that a contemporary pamphlet entitled, *A Vindication of the Book of Common Prayer against the contumelious Slanders of the Fanatic Party* terming it *Porridge*, is cited in Sir Walter Scott's novel, *Woodstock* (edn., 1822), I, p. 22.

5 Neal, *op. cit.*, IV, p. 335.

6 For a full and accurate account of the careers of ejected ministers, see A. G. Matthews's *Calamy Revised* (Oxford, 1948).

chapter of modern English education, they were a grievous loss to religion and sound learning.

Some younger divinity students changed their vocations to law or medicine. Other ministers were not as young or as fortunate. Some few became private chaplains in noble houses. Others officiated as prison or hospital chaplains. Many became tutors or schoolmasters. Some became noted physicians or lawyers. Many had to turn to unaccustomed and rougher work.

Daniel Neal, the historian of Puritanism, reports the pathetic shifts to which some ministers had to resort. One ploughed for six days and preached on the seventh. Another was reduced to cutting tobacco for a living. Others survived on the charity of the congregations which they served and which gathered in secret. John Goodwin became the proprietor of an eating house. Many for their persistence in leading conventicles were gaoled.

False reports stated that the Nonconformist ministers were living high off the hog. Indeed, Baxter reported that the Bishop of Chichester, Dr. Gunning, had repeated the *canard* to him. Baxter told him that "he was a stranger to the men he talked of" and added: "I had but a few days before had letters of a worthy minister who, with his wife and six children, had many years had seldom other food than brown rye-bread and water, and was then turned out of his house, and had none to go to. And of another that was fain to spin for his living. And abundance I know that have families, and nothing or next to nothing of their own, and live in exceeding want on the poor drops of charity which they stoop to receive from a few mean people."[7]

What the experience meant to a conscientious and wholly consecrated Nonconformist minister can be visualised more readily in the life of a single person than in terms of generalities or statistics. The man chosen is Joseph Alleine, the Presbyterian divine whose short life ended at thirty-nine, a former scholar and tutor of Corpus Christi College, Oxford, whose writings on covenant theology and personal religion were the basis of John Wesley's innovative annual service of the renewal of the covenant. A minister in Taunton, Alleine refused to be silenced on Bartholomew's Day, 1662, and, indeed, preached with undue frequency and redoubled seriousness and urgency knowing that he would soon be stopped. His wife wrote: "I know that he hath preached four-

[7] *The Autobiography of Richard Baxter* (ed. J. M. Lloyd Thomas, Everyman edn.), p. 223.

teen times in eight days, and ten often, and six or seven in these months, at home and abroad, besides the frequent converse with souls."[8]

He received the warrant on a Saturday evening after supper in May 1663 (this was in time to prevent him preaching the next day). He immediately repaired to the justice's house, where he was charged with breaking the Act of Uniformity by his preaching. This he denied, on the grounds that he had preached neither in any church nor in any chapel, nor place of public worship, but only in his own family, with such friends as cared to join with them. He was then accused of being present at a riotous assembly, but he replied that the meeting was wholly peaceful, without threats or weapons, the only business being preaching and prayer. He was ridiculed and called a rogue and, while forbidden to preach the next day, a warrant was made out for him to go to gaol on Monday morning. He returned home at 2:00 A.M. Sunday, slept briefly and prayed during much of the night. Throughout the day friends visited him, and he advised ministers to continue to fulfil the divine commandment to preach the Gospel by breaking the human law, and the people to encourage them by their attendance. Companies of the godly from neighbouring towns came to converse with him during the day.

His wife writes of the cheerfulness of his spirits that day: "full of Admirations of the Mercys of God, and encouraging all that came to be bold and venture for the Gospel, and their Souls." He told them he did not in the least repent of his actions; on the contrary, he "accounted himself happy under that promise Christ makes to his in the 5th of Matthew, that he should be doubly and trebly blessed now he was to suffer."[9]

This faithful pastor felt it his duty to exhort his flock before leaving them for prison, so he appointed them to meet him about 1:00 A.M. on Monday, and to "young and old, many Hundreds, he preached and Prayed with them about three hours," however inconvenient the time was. This, incidentally, is a remarkable tribute to the closeness of pastor and people in Nonconformity in these penal days.

In the common gaol at Ilchester, he found six other ministers committed on the same charges as himself and fifty Quakers. Soon

8 *The Life and Death of Mr. Joseph Alleine, Late Teacher of the Church at Taunton, in Somersetshire, Assistant to Mr. Newton* (1672), p. 53.
9 *Ibid.*, p. 55.

after, ten more ministers joined them in the same suffocating room. Alleine was four months in this stinking prison before he was brought to the Sessions at Taunton on July 14, 1663, but the evidence was so slender that he was not asked to testify, and so he was returned to the old prison. On August 24, he was again indicted at the Assizes, found guilty by the petty jury, and sentenced by the judge to pay a hundred marks and to lie in prison till final judgment should be made. He then spent a whole year further in gaol, except for three days. Once he was freed from gaol, his attempt to fulfil his ordination vow to preach the Gospel was made even more difficult because the Five Mile Act had been passed. His was now a wholly itinerant existence dependent utterly on the hospitality given him in the houses of supporters at which he preached. But his marvellous courage never failed, and he would say, joyfully, echoing the old Elizabethan Puritan and nonagenarian, John Dod, that he had a hundred houses for one he had parted with.[10] His faith was invincible, and it bred true courage.

Two examples of the latter can be seen in his letters. One of them urging constancy of commitment in a person of rank and title, scoffs at fair-weather friends of Christ, but argues that stormy days are the true test of discipleship. "Verily," he concludes, "it is a greater Honour to you to be vilified for Christ, than to be dignified with the highest Titles that the greatest on earth can confer: and to be call'd *Puritan*, or *Phanatique*, for the bold and constant owning of Christianity. . . ."[11] A second letter is written to a conforming divine. Beginning ominously, "Dear Friend, . . . I hear you have Parsonages," it continues by reminding him of the souls for which he is responsible before God, and ends by urging him "and it let it be seen, however others aim at the Fleece, you aim at the Flock; and that you have indeed *curam animarum*."[12]

We have not read of the way that this man of conscience conducted worship, but we have two interesting testimonies of his mode of public prayer which is the heart of worship. A former student reported his reaction to Alleine's prayers when the latter was chaplain at Corpus Christi College, Oxford, as follows: "We were not used to a great deal of Noise, vain Tautologies, crude Effusions, unintelligible Sense, or mysterious Nonsense, instead of

---

[10] *Ibid.*, p. 65.

[11] *Christian Letters full of spirituall Instructions, tending to the Promotion of the Power of Godliness, both in Persons and Families* (1672), by Joseph Alleine, pp. 140-41.

[12] *Ibid.*, p. 156.

Prayer. His Spirit was serious, his gesture reverent, his words few, but premeditated and well weighed. Pithy, solid, and to the full expressive of his as truly humble, as earnest desires. He loathed the Sauciness which went by the name of holy Boldness, and drew near to God, not as if he had been going to play with his mate, but as became a creature overaw'd with the Majesty of his great Creator."[13] His colleague, the senior minister at Taunton, George Newton, spoke in the funeral sermon of his great fervency in praying and preaching: "He was infinitely and insatiably greedy of the conversion of souls, wherein he had no small success, in the time of his ministry; And, to this end, he poured out his very heart in Prayer, and in Preaching. *He imparted not the Gospel only, but his own Soul.* His supplications, and his exhortations, many times were so affectionate, so full of holy zeal, life and vigor, that they quite overcame his hearers. He melted over them, so that they thawed, and mollified, and sometimes dissolved the hardest hearts. But while he melted thus, was wasted and consumed himself."[14] Clearly, here was a candle of the Lord who burnt himself out at both ends, weakened by imprisonment, exhausted by itinerating and pleading God's cause with the greater urgency because of the threat of renewed imprisonment. And there were hundreds like him.

Perhaps the most convincing proof of the sincerity of the Nonconformist ministers came during the Plague of 1665. It is best described by Baxter:

> And when the plague grew hot most of the conformist ministers fled, and left their flocks in the time of their extremity, whereupon divers Nonconformists, pitying the dying and distressed people that had none to call the impenitent to repentance, nor to help men to prepare for another world, nor to comfort them in their terrors, when about ten thousand died in a week, resolved that no obedience to the laws of any mortal men whosoever could justify them for neglecting of men's souls and bodies in such extremities, no more than they can justify parents for famishing their children to death. And that when Christ shall say, "Inasmuch as ye did it not to one of these, ye did it not to me," it will be a poor excuse to say, "Lord, I was forbidden by the law."[15]

13 *The Life and Death of Mr. Joseph Alleine*, p. 23.
14 *Ibid.*, p. 37.
15 *The Autobiography of Richard Baxter*, ed. Thomas, p. 196.

To the Anglicans of this period, such ministers were outlaws, and the meetings at which they presided for worship were drab conventicles; but for the Nonconformists themselves they were miniature Pentecosts.[16]

2. Covert Conventicles

Apart from short intervals of toleration, which the Nonconformists were suspicious of, because they usually meant a toleration of Roman Catholicism, we shall have to hunt the Nonconformists in their worship in barns, forests, fields, simple houses in the back alleys of towns, and anywhere except in churches. Their meetings are as difficult to track down as those of the Catholics in the same period and for the same reason: they were forbidden, and exposure cost their leaders and members imprisonment and heavy fines. But in both cases, the reward of attendance at such secret gatherings for worship was an experience of intense seriousness, sincerity, the courage of faith, and the sense of belonging to God's tried and trusty elect.

What was it like to be a harried congregation? George Trosse, minister, arrested in 1685 at an Exeter conventicle is the reporter:

We were discover'd by a malignant Neighbour, who went and inform'd against us to the Magistrates, who were then at Feast with the Mayor of the City. Three Magistrates, with Constables, and some of the baser and ruder Sort, came to find us out and seize us. After they had search'd an house or two, at length they discover'd our little Meeting, and found about Twenty People, of whom Three were Aged Ministers [Trosse himself was 54 at this time], and I the Youngest of them. They gave us hard Language, and treated us as if we had been the worst of Malefactors. The Ministers were committed to the care of the Constables, to be by them sentenc'd to be sent to Gaol, unless we would take the Oath . . . [the Oxford Oath] . . . We refus'd that Oath . . . Then, they reply'd, "You must go to Prison." I pleaded, That the Act did not extend to me, because the Law expressly says: "That he must either be a Non-conformist turn'd out for Nonconformity, or one

---

[16] Conformist or Nonconformist, one can readily echo the compassionate comments of Pepys: "While we were talking came by several poor creatures carried by, by constables, for being at a conventicle. . . . I would to God they would either conform, or be more wise, and not be catch'd." (*Diary* entry for August 7, 1664.)

convicted of keeping Conventicles." Now I was obnoxious on neither of these Accounts for I never had a Benefice to be turn'd out of, neither was ever legally convicted of keeping Conventicles. But . . . yet they committed me to Prison, without any law to warrant what they did.[17]

Trosse's experience was a relatively pleasant one in gaol, compared with Alleine's, for he had well-placed friends outside. Four other ministers shared with him the liberty of walking in the common hall and garden, and the victuals that were sent daily to them in prison, because "fourteen wealthy Friends by turns sent us Dinner every day."[18]

The interruptions of worship were not always as relatively dignified as that one. On May 29, 1670, when the authorities were searching for the meeting-place of Thomas Watson's conventicle, they could not find him or his congregation but "they brake down his pulpit and the seats, and nailed up the doors, so no meeting there."[19] On the same day other representatives of the law repaired to Mr. Thomas Doolittle's London meeting, but found only his substitute, an old gentleman, but the officers were not able to get at him to apprehend him, so the report goes, "the hearers closing fast together, they called to him to leave off and come down; to which he replied he would, so soon as he had done, but had a way of conveyance, so that he was not to be seen afterwards."[20] The "way of conveyance" may well have been a secret trap-door by which the preacher escaped through the basement.

The Nonconformists in self-defence had to provide such "escape-hatches" for their preachers and themselves. Thomas Vincent, who held Nonconformist services in a Southwark secret conventicle, had a series of ingenious devices for escaping the constables and informers. On February 12, 1682, a posse consisting of leading magistrates, and all the constables, churchwardens, and overseers of the four Southwark parishes, as well as all the officers of a regiment, tried to entrap Mr. Vincent and his congregation, but found no one there. "However," the official report continues, "we went round the place and find that almost every seat adjoining the sides of the conventicle has a door like the sally port of a fireship to escape by,

[17] G. Trosse, *Life* (1714), p. 93, cited in Allen Brockett, *Nonconformity in Exeter, 1650-1875* (Manchester, 1962), p. 46.
[18] Brockett, *op. cit.*, p. 47.
[19] *Calendar of State Papers, Domestic*, 1670, p. 240.
[20] *Ibid.*

and in each door a small peep-hole, like taverns' and alehouses' doors, to ken the person before they let them in."[21]

Some of the Nonconformist worshippers proved more than equal in physical fitness to their disturbers. Such were the hardy seamen of the vicinity of Great Yarmouth on November 4, 1674. The report to the government indignantly records: "They were so rude, as I am credibly informed, meeting at one Brewster's, near Wrentham, about twelve miles hence, that, two informers coming to the house and inquiring at the door what company they had within, they within, hearing them inquire, came running out, crying, 'Thieves,' and fell upon them, knocking them down, then drew them through a foul hog sty, and from thence through a pool. One of the two is since dead by their rash handling."[22] One can spill only crocodile tears for the misfortunes of informers on men and women of conscience.

There are so tantalisingly few reports of the nature of secret Nonconformist worship, that it is good to know the informer of Great Yarmouth sent a description to headquarters, which in its brevity still leaves much to the imagination.

> Their discipline at their meeting is: their teacher first goes up into the pulpit and there prays extempore. When he has spent himself he sits down, and then they sing a psalm, which is of their own making. When done, he stands up and preaches. They never read a chapter in the Old or New Testament, nor so much as a verse, except it be for a proof in their teaching. Their meeting-house continues yet shut. If these people designed no more than their own liberty, what occasion had they to build so large a house, which is 50 foot one way and 60 the other, with a gallery quite round it close to the pulpit, with six seats in it, one behind the other, and all accommodation possible for the reception of people below. I acquainted you that there was not above 100 men that were members. I since understand by one of them that they are not above 60.[23]

There are two possible answers to the amazement of the informant that so commodious a house is used for those relatively few Nonconformists who only want liberty to worship God in their own way. One is that it might well have been constructed in the lull in

[21] *Ibid.*, 1682, pp. 75-76.   [22] *Ibid.*, 1674, Nov. 4, pp. 396-97.
[23] *Ibid.*

persecution in 1670 for a permanent meeting-house, as the extensive gallery would seem to indicate. The other answer would be to point out that house-meetings varied very greatly in size, and could stretch the capacity of a private house. In and about Exeter, for example, there were meetings involving 90 persons at Thomas Boyland's house on July 3, 1681; 157 at John Hopping's house on February 6, 1686; and 144 at John Guswell's house on March 6, 1687. All of these were cases dealt with under the Conventicle Act of 1670.[24]

Persecution was sporadic, varying in intensity from place to place and from year to year. The Clarendon Code did not merely pass the Act of Uniformity of 1662 to dispossess ministers: on the contrary, other acts followed which harried both ministers and people in the desperate attempt to stamp out Nonconformity. The Conventicle Act of 1664 made illegal the gathering of five or more persons over the age of sixteen under the colour of religion. A fine of £5 was imposed for the first breach of the law, while for the third breach the penalty was transportation to a colonial plantation other than Virginia or New England. In 1665 there followed the act for restraining Nonconformists from inhabiting corporations, commonly called the Five Mile Act. It forbade all preachers and teachers who refused the oaths to come within five miles of any corporate town. Such persons and any who refused to attend worship at a parish church, were prohibited from teaching, under a penalty of £40, whether as schoolmasters or private tutors.

Despite the stringency of the laws and their execution, here and there they were evaded by ingenious stratagems. The combined congregation of Baptists and Presbyterians meeting at Broadmead, Bristol, hit on the device of singing Psalms; immediately they were warned of the approach of informers. Their plans were carefully laid:

> And when we had notice that the informers or officers were coming, we caused the minister or brother that preached, to forbear and sit down. Then we drew back the curtain, laying the whole room open, that they might see us all. And so all the people began to sing a psalm, that, at the beginning of the meeting we did always name the psalm that we would sing, if the informers or the Mayor or his officers come in. Thus still when they came in we were singing, that they could

24 Brockett, *op. cit.*, pp. 45-46.

not find anyone preaching, but all singing. And, at our meeting, we ordered it so, that none read the psalm after the first line, but everyone brought their bible, and so read for themselves; that they might not lay hold of anyone for preaching, or as much as reading the psalm, and so imprison any more for that, as they had our ministers.[25]

Another congregation, meeting in St. Thomas's, Southwark, almost whispered the Psalms to avoid attracting attention. A report of this conventicle states: "1692. April 1st. We met at Mr. Russell's in Ironmonger Lane, where Mr. Lambert of Deadman's Place, Southwark, administered to us the ordinance of the Lord's Supper, and we sang a psalm in a low voice."[26]

When persecution became intense, however, the Nonconformists invented (necessity being their mother) some ingenious ways of defeating the constables and their informers. Some made use of architectural conveniences. Weeks' congregation of Presbyterians in Bristol divided their meeting-room by a wooden partition, so that their minister could escape behind it into another part of the house.[27] A less ambitious ruse, but equally successful, was to hang a curtain across the room so that a stranger entering could not see the preacher, while he, wearing a cloak over his dark preaching gown was able to make his escape in the confusion of interruption. The congregation of Independents ministered to by Mr. Thompson of Bristol had two lofts above their usual meeting-room; while the preacher stood in the middle loft he could be heard above and below. The door at the foot of the stairs was kept free from strangers, and if constables or others broke it down, the minister could escape from the second storey to an adjacent house.[28] Sometimes a trap-door was employed which opened onto a lower chamber; this was probably the means of escape used by Mr. Doolittle's elderly substitute who conveniently "disappeared" in the midst of the congregation. Sometimes a hatchway on the stairs could be closed at a moment's notice, and the preacher who had used the lower part as a pulpit, could escape to the upper floor and get away to a neighbouring house.[29] Thomas Jolly, of the Northern coun-

---

[25] *Broadmead Records* (ed. E. B. Underhill, 1857), p. 226.
[26] Spencer Curwen, *Studies in Music and Worship*, 5 Vols. (1880-1885), I, p. 84.
[27] C. E. Whiting, *Studies in English Puritanism from the Restoration to the Revolution, 1660-1688* (Cambridge, 1931), p. 372.
[28] *Ibid.*
[29] G. R. Cragg, *Puritanism in the Period of the Great Persecution* (Cambridge, 1957), pp. 41-42.

ties, stood outside a door whose top half was set on hinges, so that the room could be immediately hidden from any intruder ascending the stairs, and he preached to an audience within the room itself.[30]

Simpler devices were also successful in aiding concealment. The door of a room used for worship was often hidden by moving a great cupboard against the entrance. Sometimes a table was spread with food, so that, in an emergency, a religious gathering might be made to look like a festive occasion.[31]

When the situation grew desperate, more stringent measures were taken by Nonconformist congregations. We may be sure that the Baptists of Broadmead, Bristol, were not alone in taking to a cave on Durdham Down, or in Kingswood, or other retired places, as they did in 1682 and 1683. In April of 1685 they gathered at four in the morning, while in December of the same year they held their worship meeting in thick snow in the middle of the woods.[32] Dissenters in the South Midlands used to meet near Olney at a place known as Three Counties Point, where Northamptonshire, Buckinghamshire, and Bedfordshire adjoined. If attacked from any side, it was an easy matter to escape over the border into another county.[33]

When persecution was at its fiercest, worship was held at the dead of night, in the open air, in the woods or orchards, caves or dens of the earth, in shops or barns. It was a return to the church of the catacombs. The toponomy of England in such place-names as Gospel Beech, or Gospel Oak, testifies to the resourcefulness of proscribed conventiclers in the seventeenth century.

3. Effects of Persecution on Worship and Religion

The first effect of persecution on Nonconformist worship was to make its apologists even more inflexible in the defence of free prayer than they had ever been, and the powerful influence of John

---

[30] Henry W. Clark, *History of English Nonconformity*, 2 Vols. (1911), II, pp. 67-69.

[31] *Ibid.*

[32] *Broadmead Records* (ed. Underhill), p. 268. Dissenters in the West Riding of Yorkshire used to meet in a cave on the Rawdon estate of John Hardacre; it was sheltered by a "lean-to" roof. Occasionally the Presbyterian divine, Oliver Heywood, preached there, with watchers posted on the heights of the Buckstone Rock above (*Baptist Quarterly*, III, p. 179). It is interesting that the Nonconformists at Andover in Hampshire met in a dell four miles from the town, or occasionally in a private house at night, where they barred all doors and windows, and even put the candle out to prevent even a gleam of light from attracting informers. (J. S. Pearsall, *The Rise of Congregationalism at Andover*, 1844, p. 94.)

[33] C. E. Whiting, *op. cit.*, p. 60.

Owen was pushing entirely in this direction. It will be recalled that the Presbyterians in Scotland had the Book of Common Order (sometimes known as John Knox's *Genevan Service Book*), and that the English Presbyterians at the Savoy had no objection to a liturgy as such, as long as it observed the Scriptural demands. In the common crucible of suffering under the Clarendon Code, the Presbyterians came to the Independent viewpoint on spontaneous prayer, probably very largely because the Book of Common Prayer became for both groups the very symbol of tyranny and the requirement of which had caused them to lose their livings in the Church of England. On the other hand, however, it is clear that there was much preparation for prayer in the minister's study; there was a discipline of the devotional life,[34] that prevented any slipshod or superficial spontaneity in this intimate and free approach to God. Just as persecution had endeared the Book of Common Prayer to its Anglican clergy, so did the practice of free prayer in penal days become as cherished in the minds and hearts of Presbyterians as it had always been in those of the Independents.

In other ways, of course, Nonconformist worship in the time of what Gerald Cragg calls "The Great Persecution" had learned a great flexibility. This was inevitable when one considers the hours at which they had gathered in conventicles in times of emergency, or the very places in which they had met, varying from private houses to caves cut out of solid rock. Inevitably also, Nonconformists disliked even more than before, all false dignity, pomposity, externality, and formality in worship. The values they esteemed are the values of the church as a resistance movement of the Spirit: the courage of faith, the costliness and risk of devotion, utter sincerity and total absence of pretence, the sense of God's elect being an anvil which wears out the hammers of persecution, intense loyalty, and the close family feeling of those who share danger. It would take two hundred years before the heirs of the Puritans could even conceive of the possibility that a liturgy had anything to commend it, because the one liturgy the Nonconformists knew—the Book of Common Prayer—had become an idol, lifted to the same height as the Bible in being made obligatory, and a tyrant as well. Indeed, the anti-liturgical spirit took the extreme form of recommending the disuse of the Lord's Prayer. Philip Nye, the Independent minister, expounded this iconoclastic viewpoint in *Beams*

---

[34] Cragg, *op. cit.*, p. 200. See also Thomas Manton, *Complete Works*, 12 Vols. (1870-1873), I, p. 33.

of Former Light; Discovering how Evil it is to impose Doubtful and Disputable Forms or Practices upon Ministers (1660), while the learned Baptist, Vavasour Powell, propagated the same conviction in *The Common Prayer Book no Divine Service*.

Thus there is even more than in the past a concern for interiority in worship: no psychological concessions are made, and theological imperatives continue to rule absolutely. We find this typically in John Wilson's *Cultus Evangelicus*—the sub-title stresses the dominant values—*Or, a brief Discourse concerning the Spirituality and Simplicity of New Testament Worship* (1667). The author interprets worshipping in spirit to mean "that we must not worship Him only with the *body* or *outward* man, as heathens and hypocrites used to do, but with the *soul* or *inner* man, which is that He in all holy addresses mainly looks after."[35] The divine acceptance of such spiritual worship can be counted on, says Wilson, because it is grounded on the will of God, suits the nature of God as Spirit, proceeds from the inner man and is "a Celestial *Spark*, a *beam* of light, darted from God out of Heaven," and because "until we worship Him in *Spirit* we worship Him in vain."[36] It is very significant as representative of the Nonconformist view of worship in this period, that Wilson's contrasts are between spiritual, on the one hand, and carnal, corporeal, external, on the other hand, while he also contrasts truth to what is figurative, ritualistic, and ceremonial.

Another characteristic of this worship, which was true of Puritan worship, but is even more true of Nonconformist worship, is the closeness of the bond between minister and people, which owes nothing to any hierarchical respect but everything to shared friendship in danger. We saw how close Joseph Alleine was to his people, who, when he was to go to prison for his faith, had them coming in hundreds for his farewell messages to them, and when he was homeless, vied to have him and his wife as guests in their own homes. One senses in this worship in conventicles a rare and extraordinary spirit of *camaraderie*.

In this time also we are made aware of the heightened importance of serious Biblically based preaching, dealing with the plight of man and the succour of God. The pleading characteristic becomes even more prominent in this period, and there is a deep emotional charge as of electricity in the urgency with which the messages are delivered and the desperate seriousness with which

---

[35] *Op. cit.*, pp. 16-17.   [36] *Ibid.*, p. 33.

they are received. Nonconformist preachers, as G. R. Cragg reminds us, "did not preach in order to parade their learning or to express their personal convictions; they were messengers and heralds, sent by the Most High to proclaim to his people his demand for repentance and his assurance of pardon."[37] Most vividly the preacher made his listeners aware of the dangers of sin, most passionately he discoursed on the dissuasives from sin, and most eloquently he urged the divine encouragements for those who would be diligent. Bunyan probably reflects the preaching of the period as well as his own practice, when, in *The Holy War*, he speaks of the preacher who was practical and cogent in applying the message to the souls of the hearers: "he was very pertinent in the application, insomuch that he made poor Mansoul tremble. For this sermon . . . wrought upon the hearts of the men of Mansoul; yea, it greatly helped to keep awake those that were aroused by the preaching that went before."[38] The Nonconformist divines not only moved their hearers to tears, but themselves also. Their emotional involvement was extraordinarily deep. Oliver Heywood, no frail flower of femininity, but a robust and virile man, writes in his diary: "I found extraordinary enlargement in prayer and praise and oh! what floods of tears were poured forth!"[39] Thomas Jolly, another Northern divine, noted that his eyesight had deteriorated after preaching for many years, and he attributed it to weeping in the pulpit, for he had never failed to drench two handkerchiefs during every service he had conducted.[40]

Perhaps the most notable impact persecution had on worship was due to its influence on personal religion. Put briefly, it excluded the hypocrites from worship, and retained only the faithful remnant. Insincerity could not bear the searching test of suffering for the sake of Christ. In these penal years, and not merely at the end of history in the Great Assize, God was separating the sheep from the goats. Those who suffered were confirmed in the truths for which they made sacrifice. They were pruned by persecution to realise how meretricious the allure of the world was and how deceitful; they sought to produce in themselves and in others for whom they were responsible, the fruits of life everlasting and the harvest of the Holy Spirit. Faith was streamlined, stripped down to essen-

[37] *Op. cit.*, p. 201. [38] *Works* (ed. Offor), III, p. 329.
[39] Oliver Heywood, *Autobiography, Diaries, Anecdote and Event Books*, 4 Vols. (ed. J. Horsfall Turner, Brighouse and Bingley, 1882-1885), I, p. 113.
[40] *The Note-Book of the Revd. Thomas Jolly, 1671-1693* (Chetham Society, Manchester, 1895), p. 57.

tials, patience became more enduring, love was more other-directed, and hope was the silver lining of the storm clouds that promised a heavenly compensation for the earthly difficulties. It was consolation to remind themselves that in God's eternal kingdom the last would be first and the first last.[41] Baxter in a prolonged self-analysis during the time of persecution, claims: "The tenor of the Gospel predictions, precepts, promises and threatenings are fitted to a people in a suffering state. And the graces of God in a believer are mostly suited to a state of suffering. Christians must imitate Christ, and suffer with Him before they reign with Him; and His kingdom was not of this world."[42] John Howe writes in a similar strain: "Every sincere Christian is in affection and preparation of his mind a martyr. He that loves not Christ better than his own life, cannot be His disciple."[43]

There are two proofs of the deepening of personal religion during this period. One of them is the number and quality of the devotional treatises written under the cross of suffering. Baxter's *Now or Never*, Joseph Alleine's *Call to the Unconverted*, John Howe's *The Living Temple*, John Owen's *A Discourse of the Holy Spirit in Prayer*, and Bunyan's *Grace Abounding to the Chief of Sinners* are the by-products of persecution. This was also the time when John Milton, the great poet of Puritanism, overcame his blindness and political disappointment in the composition of *Paradise Lost* and *Samson Agonistes*. These are plummets sounding the uttermost depths of Nonconformist religious experience.

The second proof is that this is the period when Nonconformist family worship was at its deepest. At night, especially on Sunday nights, the members of the family were collected together. The children, servants, and apprentices were questioned on the sermons they had heard that day. Psalms were sung. The head of the family offered a simple spontaneous prayer and often read a sermon by an approved Puritan divine. It was these simple but profound conversations with the living God that made the Sunday conventicles gathered for worship such profoundly significant encounters with a covenant-keeping God.

Another consequence of 1662 and after was the creation of a new phenomenon in English life, the Nonconformist conscience. As

---

[41] See Charnock, *Works* (Edinburgh, 1864), I, p. 111. Oliver Heywood, *Whole Works* (Idle, 1837), II, p. 122, and Baxter, *An Apology for the Nonconformists' Ministry* (1681), p. 196.

[42] *The Autobiography of Richard Baxter* (ed. Thomas), p. 122.

[43] Cited in R. F. Horton, *John Howe* (1894).

David Ogg has written, "As nowhere else men acquired the habit of thinking for themselves." And the insistence upon uniformity served only to strengthen disagreement, so that to Clarendon may be attributed "some responsibility for the entrenchment in our national life of the one native institution which no foreigner can hope to copy—the nonconformist conscience."[44] Perhaps we can also trace to the Nonconformist love of liberty born in this period the fact that radical movements were never anti-clerical in England. What is unquestionable, however, is that the Nonconformist conscience led to a sturdy questioning, an ethical sensitivity which often manifested itself as a concern for the rights of others and especially of minorities in religion. It became a powerful force in the nation's life, reaching its apex in the nineteenth century. Its chief outward characteristics were a fear of God but of no man, and an integrity that could not be bought. All this would be expressed in the searing honesty of the prayers of the Nonconformists in ensuing centuries, whether in the form of intellectual honesty as in the Unitarians who sprang from the Presbyterians, or in the moral forms in the confessions and petitions of the Independents and Presbyterians. Certainly it was manifested in the Nonconformist sermons which refused to curry favour with congregations.

Another effect—a very sad one—of the persecution of the Clarendon Code was to create a religious and cultural divide between the "church" and the "chapel" outlooks.[45] The former controlling admission and the granting of degrees in the ancient universities, prevented any Nonconformists who could not accept the Thirty-Nine Articles from entering Oxford or Cambridge for two centuries, forcing them to establish their own Dissenting academies[46] in which modern languages, history (which began as the history of liberty), geography, and the natural sciences were taught with greater superiority than in the ancient universities. Moreover, in these institutions the students learned the art of self-government. This division had the serious disadvantage of giving the Anglicans an innate sense of social superiority, and of puttng the Nonconformists constantly on the defensive. It had two very bad effects on

[44] *England in the Reign of Charles II*, 2 Vols. (Oxford, 1955), I, p. 218.

[45] See G. N. Clark, *The Later Stuarts* (Oxford, 1934), p. 23: "It became one of the dividing lines in party politics, in the press, and in everything else, even in economic life."

[46] See J. W. Ashley Smith, *The Birth of Modern Education: the contribution of the Dissenting Academies, 1660-1800* (1954).

religion itself. One was that in the continuing conflict between church and chapel, the bystander was apt to forget how much in doctrine and practice the disputants held in common. The other was that this quarrel in the same English household of faith was an appalling advertisement for the Christ who, on the eve of His Atonement on the Cross had prayed that all His disciples might be one, even as He and the Father were One, that the world might believe. This bitterness, and the exclusion of the Nonconformists from both national and local government, as from becoming officers in the armed forces, gave them a chip on the shoulder which prevented them from developing to the full the grace of *agape*, the love which forgets all hurts in serving others for Christ's sake.

Perhaps the marvel is that the Independents and Presbyterians survived this period with such firm convictions as to the nature of true Christian worship being simple, sincere, and spiritual, and that they passed on that heritage to the English-speaking countries of the world where their adherents greatly outstripped in size the small remnants of both denominations in Britain.

The most immediately impressive result of persecution (apart from the deepening of the spiritual life) was the growing comradeship of Presbyterian and Independent ministers in this period. Before this time the Independents had considered the Presbyterians legalistic and rather stuffily bourgeois with their strong merchant support, whereas they retaliated by considering the Independents too sectarian, radical, and even wild. The common suffering bred a common respect that led to serious plans for a union between the two groups, of which John Howe was the leading architect.

4. *The Revolution of 1688 and Its Aftermath*

One of the first effects of the "Glorious Revolution" of 1688 was to guarantee toleration for the Nonconformists. They immediately made plans for either temporary or permanent meeting-houses. Between 1688 and 1690, 796 temporary and 143 permanent Nonconformist chapels were erected, while between 1691 and 1700 another 1,247 temporary meeting-houses were erected and 32 permanent ones.[47]

As we have indicated already, the Presbyterians and Independents also planned to unite. The famous *Heads of Agreement*, proposals for the effective practical cooperation of both denomina-

[47] Duncan Coomer, *English Dissent* (1947), p. 61.

tional groups gained the assent of over a hundred ministers in the City of London, and the scheme spread immediately to the provinces. Party-cries were dropped, the beating of the denominational drum was silenced, and the cooperating ministers worked together happily from 1690 to 1694 as the "United Brethren." This promising union involved concessions on both sides, of course. Presbyterianism accepted that local congregations would desire a larger part in government, while Independents recognised the advisory authority of neighbouring churches. The union disintegrated after only four years because of a doctrinal feud, in which certain Independents out-Calvinised the Presbyterians. Closer cooperation between the denominations who had suffered persecution was to bear fruit in the next century in the formation in 1732 of the body known as "The Dissenting Deputies," whose task was to defend Nonconformist civil rights and which was granted the privilege of direct access to the sovereign. The tragedy is that John Howe's ecumenical spirit was rendered ineffectual by internecine dogmatisms. His view was that "without all controversy the main inlet of all the distractions, confusions, and divisions of the Christian world hath been by adding other conditions of Church communion than Christ hath done."[48]

What was Nonconformist worship like in the warmer and more genial climate of toleration? Fortunately, this question can be answered with greater particularity than usual because of the assiduity with which a visiting minister of the Episcopal church of Scotland, the Rev. Robert Kirk, attended churches, chapels, and even a synagogue during 1689 and 1690, recording his observations in detail.[49] It is important to know his prejudices before citing his reports. He is very critical of the vagueness of Dissenting sermons, as of their repetitiousness, both faults of extemporaneity. He greatly prefers the practicality, preciseness, and learning of Anglican sermons. His favourite Anglican preacher is Stillingfleet, as his favourite Dissenting preacher is Baxter, and he admires both because they are for widening the boundaries of the Church of England.

Of the Dissenters whom he heard, he liked the Presbyterians best, and the Quakers worst. He first heard Richard Baxter in a

[48] *Works*, v, p. 226.

[49] The Ms. of Robert Kirk's small commonplace book is in the Library of Edinburgh University. A catena of the most interesting observations will be found in Donald Maclean's *London at Worship* (The Presbyterian Historical Society of England, Manchester, 1928), from which references will be made.

hall near Charterhouse Hospital on November 10, 1689, taking as his text, "Blessed are the peacemakers." Of the service we are told: "His clerk first sung a Psalm reading the line. Then the reader read 3 Ps[alms], Isaiah 5 and Matt. 22 after he had given an extempore prayer. Then the minister, reading the papers of the sick and troubled in mind and intending a journey, he prayed and preached a sermon on popery." The report continues: "Mr. Baxter prayed in general for the King and Royal Family and Parliament; for Jacobites, Grecians, and Armenians enlightening in further knowledge; for Christians distressed with burning, dislodging and oppression of merciless enemies. The congregation all kneeled or stood up at prayer."[50] Two clarifications may be made of this report. The first is that psalmody was made so much duller by the clerk reading out every line of every metrical Psalm in advance. The second is the interesting custom by which church members sought the minister's petitions for themselves or intercessions for others by writing them down and having them conveyed to him on slips of paper put into a slotted stick. It was typical of Baxter, even in a time of toleration, to remember distressed Christians across the world.

A second visit to hear Baxter gives us further information on that notable divine. One prayer of his sounded the ecumenical note. In Kirk's words: "that all ministers might have a sound mind and a quiet disposition, and for a reconciling all differences, that party nor sect be never heard any more among Protestants." Baxter repeated the Lord's Prayer and at the last blessing said, "Blessed of God are all who consider, believe, love, and obey this word."[51]

Presbyterian ministers, however, did not pray alike. Baxter used the Lord's Prayer, but Dr. William Bates did not. Nor did Bates have any reading of Scripture. "He prayed not for King or Queen nor Church; he reflected on none. . . . He, as all regular clergy, had all intercession and thanksgiving in his first prayer, where he began by beseeching that we might approach God with a filial freedom."[52]

The third Presbyterian minister he went to hear was the animated Daniel Burgess. This minister's prayer was an exceedingly independent one, for "he prayed that the Church and ministry of England might be freed of Lords over God's heritage, and that they may no more have ministers who do not preach, nor ministers that are not of truth sound. Before the blessing he said it was fit-

50 Maclean, op. cit., p. 16. 51 Ibid., pp. 16-17.
52 Ibid., p. 17.

ting every man challenged himself quickly that he has been doing service all his life and yet knows not his master. He had many additions to the usual blessing." Mr. Kirk liked a dependable liturgy, not extemporaneous effusions in prayer or sermon. His next comment indicates his bewilderment: "Not any two Presbyterians do I find keep one way." His summation is interesting: "Mr. Baxter reads the Scriptures and preaches; Dr. Bates only has one sermon and two prayers; Mr. Burgess lectures, preaches, sings the 'Doxology,' and in his bold way speaks diminutively of the King, saying before God, 'a king and chimney sweeper are all one and death values them so, too.' "[53]

Kirk visited the meeting-house of only one Independent minister, that of George Cokayne. The congregation of about two hundred were rather crushed and Kirk noted with some disdain that "few persons of good rank were present, only two coaches or so attended the doors." There was no Psalm sung before or after the sermon. The people stood for prayer, listened to the sermon with their hats on, but took them off for prayer. There was no blessing at the end of the service, and no church at home or abroad was prayed for. But Kirk preserves one gem which is so touching in its vivid directness that it is almost an apologia of itself for spontaneous prayer. Kirk writes: "He did plead vehemently with God for a young man at the grave's mouth, the only hope and visible standing of his father's family, saying: 'Lord, 'tis rare to find a good man, more a good young man. Thou sparedst 10,000ds. of debauched youths, may not this one not dry but tender and fruitful branch escape the blast of Thy displeasure. Save his soul. Spare his body. Sanctify all to the parents seeing Thou dost it; not theirs nor ours, but Thy will be done.' "[54]

The spirit of Puritanism clearly had been resurrected in Nonconformity. The bold confidence in approaching and beseeching God, the intensity of the sincerity, the pleading pastoral concern, and above all, the final willingness to accept God's will as Christ had done in the Garden of Gethsemane in almost identical words, prove that free prayer could reach the greatest heights, and scale the walls of heaven itself.

[53] *Ibid.*, pp. 17-18.   [54] *Ibid.*, p. 21.

CHAPTER XIII

ROMAN CATHOLIC WORSHIP

I N THIS turbulent century of upsets, the Anglicans were in the saddle for the whole period except for the seventeen years when the Puritans exchanged places; the Roman Catholics, on the other hand, were never in the saddle as an established church. It was their singular misfortune, as a great international Christian community—with the exception of five years in the sixteenth and three years in the seventeenth century—to live in the shadow of persecution from 1534 to 1829. The clouds lifted for them in our period only for the three fitful and disastrous years of the reign of their champion, James II.

The contrast between Catholicism on the European Continent and Catholicism in England must have been heart-rending for the Recusants; as heart-rending as the lot of the Presbyterians in Scotland or Switzerland compared with their English fate after 1662, or that of the Independents in New England compared with their destiny in old England after 1662. There was only one difference: the Roman Catholics seemed to pin their hopes on political changes that were doomed to disappointment. Indeed, their lot was made the harder precisely because of the hotheads of their number involved in plots and conspiracies.

The era was punctuated by the rumours and the realities of Catholic plots and their expected explosions. The reign of James I had hardly begun when there were two plots on his life by Catholics. The first, the Bye plot, was a harebrained scheme of a secular priest, William Watson and his associates, to kidnap the King and force him to obey their instructions. Hard on its heels followed the more threatening Gunpowder Plot to overthrow King and both Houses of Parliament in November 1605, which was agreed to by the four main conspirators, Catesby, Winter, Percy and Fawkes, in the Spring of 1604 and who were discovered tunnelling towards the cellars beneath Parliament. The "Popish Plot" associated with Titus Oates renewed the general fear of the Catholics from 1678 to 1681. The result of these conspiracies was that they sent dense clouds of smoky suspicion in their train never to be dissipated during this century. The Gunpowder Plot, in particular, caused the Catholics irreparable harm, because the State Service of November 5 reminded the nation annually of the treasonable proclivities of Roman Catholics, as enemies of the royal family, Parliament, and the Church of England. Even the children as they prepared the image of Guy Fawkes to be burned on their bonfire, and as they begged "a penny for the guy" to spend on fireworks, were indoctrinated with the notion that Catholicism was a cruel, sinister, violent and unreliable faith. This was a formidable shadow under which they had to live. All the more was this so when the lot of Catholics in France or Spain seemed to be a life of basking in the approval of a *roi soleil*.

What a contrast there is between the theatrical Baroque worship on the continent of Europe and the furtive celebration of the Mass in barns or upper rooms in England. When one recalls the effulgence of the brilliant European monstrances, shining like miniature meteors, the domes of such churches as the *Gesù* in Rome with the spiral of Jesuit martyrs climbing to heaven, or the mystical ravishment of St. Teresa of Avila in Bernini's statue, or the imitation of the royal courts in the etiquette of Baroque worship and its splendid appurtenances, one sees the English parallel with the church of the catacombs before the advent of the first triumphalism of Constantine. Both are secretive communities running risks by merely being Recusants and refusing the official worship dictated by the state; both also by their daring are producing martyrs whose blood is the seed of the church.

Has the impact of persecution, because it was sporadic, been exaggerated? Certainly, it was minimal in the reign of Charles I, whose Queen Henrietta Maria was a Catholic. Well-to-do Catholics could then afford to have their own chaplains and be unmolested, but the poor found it difficult to interest priests in their plight. Father Thomas Greene, the ageing Archdeacon of Essex, proposed that rich families should raise funds to pay priests to minister to the poor, but warned: "A poor man's priest must be apostolical in spirit, zealous for souls and fond of hard work, and no lover of his back or belly, and diligent to instruct."[1] Yet there were such apostolical men. One of them was Father Henry Morse whose work was chiefly among the plague-stricken poor in the city of London, and who was forced to spend nine years in three prisons. The context of his prayers and the consolation of the Mass and the *viaticum* must be imagined to contrast it with the absolutist splendour of

[1] Cited by Martin Havran, *The Catholics in Caroline England* (Palo Alto, California, 1962), p. 78.

continental Catholicism: "In March 1637 he was incarcerated with 47 criminals awaiting death on the gallows. Their stench made him ill . . . as did their habit of slobbering their food like starving animals. Morse managed to obtain quarters in a third-storey room which proved somewhat better than the common wards below. The room had bars on the window as thick as a man's wrist, and stone walls on which the prisoners had scribbled scriptural texts, verses, and obscenities. The only furnishings were board beds, a table, and chairs black with age and rot. The jailer sold sleeping holes in the walls at high rates, advertising them free of vermin, and he charged exorbitant rates for an hour of fresh air in the prison yard."[2]

Nor was all comfortable in ancient country houses, especially immediately after the unhappy year 1605. For a companion picture one should turn to a description of Harrowden Hall when the hunt for Father Garnet, the Provincial of the Jesuits, was in full cry, and he was finally "earthed" in January of 1605-1606. Sir Henry Bromiley, the local justice who was instructed by the Privy Council to carry out the search, reported that eleven secret corners were found in which priests could hide. On the eighth day of the search Henry Garnet and his Jesuit co-priest, Oldcorn, emerged like wan ghosts from the hiding-place behind the chimney. The report mentions that "marmalade and other sweetmeats were found there lying by them, but their better maintenance had been by a quill or reed through a little hole in the chimney that backed another chimney into the gentlewoman's chamber, and by that passage cawdles, broths, and warm drinks had been conveyed in unto them." Bromiley continues his malodorous report: "Now in regard the place was so close those customs of nature which of necessity must be done, and in so long time of continuance, was exceedingly offensive to the men themselves, and did much annoy them that made entrance in upon them, to whom they confessed they had not been able to hold out one whole day longer, but either they must have squealed or perished in the place."[3] Such was the price of loyalty to Roman Catholicism, magnificently paid by the Society of Jesus. As Godfrey Anstruther[4] points out, the most eloquent testimony to the growing fear and hatred of Popery and the costliness of recusancy is found in the Recusant Rolls of Northamptonshire, an area where Puritanism was strong and from which Browne of

---

2 Philip Caraman, *Henry Morse: Priest of the Plague* (1957), pp. 125-28.
3 Godfrey Anstruther, O.P., *Vaux of Harrowden, A Recusant Family* (Newport, Monmouthshire, 1953), p. 336.
4 *Ibid.*

Brownist fame hailed. These were the lists of Roman Catholics convicted for non-attendance at the Protestant services, and fined £20 a month. Before the Gunpowder Plot the number in the country never exceeded twelve; by 1608 it had risen to 182, and this level was fairly well maintained until 1620. Since few were wealthy enough to pay such fines for a long period, they had the option of parting with two-thirds of their property as the price for prolonged recusancy. Such fines became a lucrative source of royal income, since the receipts for 1612 amounted to £371,000. Many faithful Catholics suffered imprisonment for their loyalty to the old religion, for we know that when James I was persuaded by the Spanish ambassador in 1622 to liberate those incarcerated for the Catholic faith, 40,000 were set free.[5]

Cromwell's regime was equally concerned to get the full value of the Recusants' fines. The death-penalty for priests or people found participating at Mass continued, parents were forbidden to instruct their own children in Catholicism, and Catholics were disfranchised and refused entry to such professions as the army or the law.

1. Catholic Life and Worship

The effect of these conditions of life was profound on their worship. In the first place, as it was illegal in England it was quite secret or at least unobtrusive. Moreover, this was at a time when the effect of the Counter-Reformation had been to emphasise the distinctive tenets of the faith and the characteristic elements of the cultus, such as the dramatic miracle of the Mass, the intercession of the saints vividly represented in statues or stained-glass, and the pre-eminence of the Blessed Virgin as first among the faithful and the Mother of God the Son. Continental Catholic worship was religion on parade; English Catholic worship was religion in hiding.

In the second place, the quality of Catholic devotion was inevitably strained, self-conscious, and sometimes strident. It was cultivated most successfully in the monasteries and convents of the English exiles in the Low Countries in the seventeenth century. As might be expected, these English "colonies of heaven" were more English than England itself, and the standard of religious life that they trained for left the laity trailing a long way behind in the

[5] Robert Julian Stonor, O.S.B., *Stonor, A Catholic Sanctuary in the Chilterns from the Fifth Century till today* (Newport, Monmouthshire, 2nd edn., 1952), p. 271.

race, and gasping. These monasteries, convents and seminaries "never regarded themselves as forming anything else but little bits of Great Britain" and were animated by "an extraordinary spirit of fervour."[6] While concentrating on the contemplative life, they often poured out commentaries on the spiritual life, expositions of the Mass, catechisms and the like, and mediated to England the rich developments of seventeenth-century French, Italian and especially Spanish mysticism and spirituality.[7] Though they were not wealthy, the worship in these religious houses would approximate that of the Continent in its Baroque expressions, though, one would suppose, with some English reserve.

In the third place, Catholic worship was inevitably marked in England by a longing for the good old days, a retrospective glance over the shoulder, not least because the Andrewes-Laud tradition of the high church in Anglicanism seemed to be taking a few leaves out of the missal and breviary, if not out of the pontifical. Even this worship must have seemed pale beside the Sarum Rite in the first third of the sixteenth century or Counter-Reformation celebrations of Mass on festivals in European cathedrals or abbeys. We can only guess how these thoughts were sparked by the sight of a precious relic, or a richly embroidered vestment, or a chalice with begemmed knop. The Benedictine Chapel of the Rosary in London which opened about 1652-1654 had among its treasures "a most glorious and wonderfully exquisite relic of the Crown of Thorns of our Saviour, kept in Catholic times in the most flourishing monastery of Glastonbury, the burying place of the noble Decurio S. Joseph of Arimathea, who had the blessing of entombing our Lord" and also "a curious piece of the most Holy Cross, which came from the most renowned and worthy John Fecknam, last Abbot of the Royal Abbey of Westminster. . . ."[8] The superlatives in the citation are themselves a clue to the exaggerated praise of the past seen through rose-tinted spectacles.

The Jesuits, too, retained some vestiges of ancient splendour in their liturgical treasures. Father Gerard's autobiography refers to their "vestments and altar furniture" as being "both plentiful and costly." Their festal vestments were embroidered with gold and pearl. Lamps hung from silver chains above the altar which bore six massive candlesticks besides some others at the side for the

---

[6] *Ibid.*, p. 300. [7] See Chapter III above for details.
[8] Dom Hugh Connolly, "The Benedictine Chapel of the Rosary in London" in *Downside Review*, Vol. LII (N.S., Vol. XXXIII), pp. 320-29.

elevation of the Host. It also had a pure silver Crucifix. Father Gerard was rightly proud of a gold Crucifix a foot high, "on the top of which was represented a pelican, while at the right arm of the Cross was an eagle, with expanded wings, carrying on its back its young ones, who were attempting to fly: on the left arm a phoenix expiring in flames, that it might leave an offspring after it; and at the foot was a hen with her chickens gathering them under her wings."[9] The subtlety of the modelling was matched by the appropriateness of the fourfold symbolism of the self-wounding pelican representing Christ who by his sacrificial death is the food of the soul; the eagle is emblematic of the persistence of faith; while the fabled phoenix dying to be reborn represents Christ and His incorporating His faithful in the sacraments to share eternal life; the hen and her chickens are reminders of Christ weeping over Jerusalem which knew not the day of her visitation and founding the New Israel whom He protects and for whom He intercedes. Such superb artistry spoke to the wondering eye, whereas perhaps a sermon might only have led to a wandering ear. Above all, such images evoked the grandeur of a diminishing Catholicism in England.

In the fourth place, there was a fairly easy way to adapt medieval practice to seventeenth-century need on the part of the Catholic gentry. It was the use of the private house-chapel and chaplain in times of persecution for the family, servants, and nearby tenantry, forming a type of "peculiar" apart from the parish church. There would be a family liturgy of morning and evening prayers based on the divine Office and supplied by a Primer or Persons' *Christian Directory* which were also used privately. In the Primer there would also be much incidental religious instruction. On this view, according to Hugh Aveling, a learned Benedictine, "the households of the gentry would have been already provided by long tradition and way of life with forms admirably suited to maintain Catholic life in small *enclaves* amidst a hostile environment and with priests in short supply."[10] He also suggests that the compromise arrangement used by the Tyrwhit family at Thornton in Lincolnshire in the 1590s became fairly common. This was to employ an Anglican

[9] John Gerard, *The Autobiography of Fr. John Gerard, S.J.* (edn., 1881), p. 383.

[10] Hugh Aveling, O.S.B., *The Catholic Recusants of the West Riding of Yorkshire, 1558-1790* (Leeds, 1963: Proceedings of the Leeds Philosophical and Literary Society, Literary and Historical Section, Vol. x, Pt. vi, pp. 191-306), pp. 246-47.

chaplain who said prayers for the conformist members of the household (including the church-Papist head) in the hall of the house. Meanwhile, the recusant members of the family and servants went off to Twigmore, one of the "citadels" of Father Holtby, S.J., to Mass and the other sacraments.[11] If a priest were in residence, then the Recusants would hear Mass in a secret upstairs room of the house.

On the other hand, when after 1660 the secular authorities were more lenient to Catholics, the gentry with a resident priest or frequent visiting priests, began to set aside a suite of rooms on the first floor as chapel, a priest's room for conferences and confessions, and a sacristy. In the West Riding of Yorkshire, this occurred in the country houses at Carlton and Quosque in 1667, at Barnbow in 1661, and at Broughton by the 1680s.[12]

In the fifth place, there was a very surprising development for a religion as hierarchical as Catholicism and which exalted the priesthood as highly as it did. It was the growth in days of persecution of a lay spirituality in which either the master of the house (as we have just seen) became a substitute for the priest-chaplain and led in prayers, or there was a desire on the part of groups of women to live informally together to promote the religious life. Evidence for the latter development is found in a document from the Stonyhurst Anglia Mss, dated October 30, 1604, titled, "An instruction and direction for the spiritual helpe of such Inglish gentelwomen as desyre to lead a more retired and recollected life then the ordinarie in Ingland doth yeald."[13] This was similar to what was going on in Italy and Spain at this time. Informal groups of women friends might live together. There was no need for habits, and vows might be taken for a time or permanently, one, two or three of them, as the individual felt able to make the promises. Some, as might be expected, took the further step of entering a religious order. This is how the Benedictine community at Brussels was founded from groups of English exiles under the leadership of Lady Mary Percy. Similarly, the creative Mary Ward organised her Institute of Women, first known as the "Daughters of St. Agnes." They took only private vows and wore no distinctive habits in order to fulfil their active life as teachers of English girls; it was such a success that they numbered over sixty by 1616 and

11 *Ibid.*, p. 248.   12 *Ibid.*, p. 249.
13 Cited by Hugh Aveling, *Northern Catholics; The Catholic Recusants of the North Riding of Yorkshire, 1558-1790* (1966), p. 254.

by 1629 they were to be found in Italy, Germany, and Austria. This lay initiative was remarkably akin to that shown by their opposite numbers, the Puritans, who wanted every household to be a little church, while the Catholics desired every household to be a little monastery. This was a remarkable flourishing of the Counter-Reformation spirit and spirituality.[14]

2. *High Baroque Worship and Ornaments*

The unrestrained Baroque ceremonial of Catholic worship was to be found only in the London chapels of the ambassadors of Catholic countries, or in the chapels of the Stuart Catholic queens, namely, Henrietta Maria, consort of Charles I, or of Catherine of Braganza, consort of Charles II, or, grandiosely, in the chapel of King James II, open in his avowal of Catholicism. These were the great exceptions, but they are important as showing what ordinary Catholic worship lacked and would love to have, had the law and the funds permitted such opulence.

Queen Henrietta Maria's Chapel at Somerset House was completed in 1635, being the work of Inigo Jones, the Surveyor-General and himself a Catholic. Its exterior did not call the Anglican world to notice that this was the fane of a prohibited faith. But the structure and decoration of the interior proclaimed the splendour of Catholicism without any false modesty. The dome was forty feet high, suspended over the altar. The latter was raised on three broad tiers of steps and was separated from the rest of the nave by balustrades. On each side of a columned arch were niches in which there were statues of prophets or saints. Rich tapestries, silver-gilt chandeliers, and many costly vases made this a mirror of contemporary French court ceremonial in worship, although probably a little subdued for English purposes.

The Chapel of the Queen in Somerset House was served by French Capuchins, that Counter-Reformation renewal of the Franciscan Order which returned from relaxation and mitigation to the strong and simple love of the impoverished which had characterized their founder, *Il Poverello*. They laboured tirelessly among London's poor,[15] however splendid their Royal Chapel. Every Saturday the friars recited the Litany of the Blessed Virgin and held the Benediction of the Blessed Sacrament, blessing the congrega-

---

[14] *Ibid.*, and Hugh Aveling, *Post-Reformation Catholicism in East Yorkshire* (York, 1960), p. 36.

[15] James Lee-Milne, *The Age of Inigo Jones* (1953), pp. 86-89.

tion with the Sacrament reserved and exposed in the monstrance.[16] It was an extra-liturgical devotion of great popularity in the sixteenth and seventeenth century, especially among Catholic fraternities. The Capuchins would bring Communion to Catholics on sick beds or in prison, and were humbler than their Oratorian predecessors as the chaplains of the Queen.

Queen Catherine of Braganza, the consort of Charles II, had a Royal Chapel at St. James, which was served by the English Benedictines, one of whom, Father John Huddleston, preserved the life of the future King Charles II on his flight from Worcester fight in 1651 and reconciled him on his deathbed to the Catholic church. Pepys, who seemed more inclined to Presbyterianism than to Catholicism, was impelled by curiosity—seeing the Queen's coach pass by on a Sunday morning—and so, he wrote in his *Diary* for September 16, 1661, "I crowded after her, and I got up to the room where her closet is; and there stood and saw the fine altar, ornaments, and the fryers in their habits, and the priests come in with their fine crosses and many other fine things. . . . By and by, after Masse was done, a fryer with his cowl did rise up and preach a sermon in Portugese, which I not understanding, did go away, and to the King's chapel, but that was done."[17]

John Evelyn, that sturdy Anglican diarist, was more critical of Roman Catholicism at worship. Of one experience, he wrote: "I went to see the fopperies of the Papists at Somerset House and York House, where now the French Ambassador had caus'd to be represented our Blessed Saviour at the Paschal Supper with his Disciples, in figures and puppets made as big as the life, of waxwork, curiously clad and sitting round a large table, the roome nobly hung, and shining with innumerable lamps and candles: this was expos'd to all the world, all the City came to see it, such liberty had the Roman Catholics at this time obtain'd."[18]

In Evelyn's too negative judgment there are implied some of the chief criticisms that could be made of Baroque worship. Waxwork suggests something of its artificiality; "big as life" its theatricality, and the place of this chapel, in a palace, the absolutist monarchs who were its chief supporters. For all the splendour of

16 *Ibid.*, p. 147. For the history of the devotion of the Benediction of the Blessed Sacrament, see the articles of Herbert Thurston, S.J., in *The Month*, Vol. XCVII (1901), pp. 587-97; Vol. XCVIII (1901), pp. 58-69, 186-93, 264-76, and Vol. CVI (1905), pp. 394-404.

17 Pepys's *Diary* (Everyman edn., 1906), I, pp. 288-89.

18 Entry for April 4, 1672.

these Royal Chapels, however, and despite the fact that they were meant to serve as the throne room of the King of Kings, Christ, they were not in the least typical of seventeenth-century English Catholic worship. The secret worship of Recusants in barns, or attics, or in remote country houses, where fines mulcted their owners and exposed them to greater risks of imprisonment, was very different, with an improvised altar and confessional, and the candlesticks, kneelers, and vestments hurriedly extracted from a cupboard, all to be rapidly dismantled as soon as a *poursuivant* was glimpsed riding in the distance.

3. *Simpler Celebrations of the Mass*

We must penetrate beyond the furtiveness, the makeshift character, and the probable shabbiness of the appurtenances of such worship, to recognise the astounding loyalty and great risks undertaken to attend or celebrate such worship and the deep sincerity that characterized it. Reports of such clandestine gatherings, where they are to be had at all, are few and short.

There is one vivid description, though all too brief, of a mission centre in the East Riding of Yorkshire in the 1620s at Osgodby Hall, the home of the Recusant family of the Babthorpes. It was frequented by many guests and visitors, and it lodged never less than two priests, and occasionally three or four. One chaplain was appointed to look after the souls of the family and household and another looked after the neighbouring Catholics. The mission centre is described thus:

> Our house I might rather count as a religious house than otherwise, for though there lived together in it three knights and their ladies with their families, yet we had all our servants Catholic. On the Sundays, we locked the doors and all came to Mass, had our sermons, catechisms and spiritual lessons every Sunday and holiday. On the work days we had for the most part two Masses, and of them the one for the servants at six o'clock in the morning at which the gentlemen, every one without fail and the ladies if they were not sick, would even, in the midst of winter, of their own accord be present; and the other we had at eight o'clock for those who were absent from the first. In the afternoon, at four o'clock, we had Evensong, and after that, Matins, at which all the knights and ladies, except extraordinary occasions did hinder them,

468

would be present, and stay at their prayers all the time the priests were at Evensong and Matins. The most of them daily used some meditation and mental prayer, and all, at the least every fourteen days and great feasts, did confess and communicate; and after supper, every night at nine o'clock, we had all together litanies, and so immediately to bed.[19]

Particularly in the early part of the century the Mass must have been celebrated with only the bare essentials. A manuscript book of the period which provides the missioners with advice for difficult cases of conscience observes that in cases of deep necessity the priest may use an unconsecrated table, an unblessed tin chalice, omit some of the under-vestments, use a single unblessed cloth on the altar and one oil light. Nor is a Crucifix absolutely necessary, however desirable. If the priest can remember the Mass, he need not use a missal. He may have the help of women in serving Mass, and can say Mass in necessity at any time after midnight and until an hour after midday. For a grave reason he can even say three or four Masses a day.[20]

With the distractions of the Civil War and the greater leniency of the Restoration of the monarchy after 1660, the Masses became less streamlined. At this time more permanent house chapels were furnished, and more elaborately. The Yorke family in the West Riding of Yorkshire imported fittings from abroad in the 1650s or 1660s. Their receipted bill for the order shows that they had purchased taffeta for frontals, sets of vestments, six candlesticks, Crucifixes, several holy pictures, several thuribles and an incense boat.

For most Catholics who were not gentry, Mass was celebrated simply, possibly even shabbily, but with great dignity, as can be seen from a longer account of clandestine worship—a generation after our period closes, but still in the "penal days" for English Roman Catholics. The account is of a Mass celebrated by Bishop Challoner in the 1740s to which Mr. and Mrs. Marlow Sidney, a newly married couple, came to be received into the church. Mrs. Sidney recalls the occasion many years later for the benefit of her granddaughter:

19 Hugh Aveling, *Post-Reformation Catholicism in East Yorkshire*, p. 33 citing Henry Foley, *Records of the English Province of the Society of Jesus* (1877-83).
20 Aveling, *The Catholic Recusants of the West Riding of Yorkshire, 1558-1790*, pp. 250-51.

We started from our lodgings at five in the morning to be present for the first time at a Catholic religious service, or at "Prayers" as it was generally called, for the word "Mass" was scarcely ever used in conversation. We arrived at a public house in some back street near the house at which Mr. Horne resided. I felt rather frightened, seeing some very rough-looking poor people as we passed through the entrance, though all was very quiet. These people I was told, were Irish workmen, who, with a few women, were assembled on that Sunday morning to hear "Prayers" when they could be admitted. We hurried past them; but I could not help clinging to Marlow, having a sort of undefined fear of what was going to happen, for I had no inclination to laugh then. We mounted higher and higher, escorted by a young man whom Marlow had seen at the priest's house, who had come forward at once to conduct us. When we arrived at the top, the door of the garret was unlocked, and as we entered we saw at the furthest end what seemed a high table, or a long chest of drawers with the back turned towards us. A piece of carpet was spread before it by the young man, who, after he had placed a few chairs and cushions in order, pointed us to our seats. In a few minutes, the door opened, and the Venerable Dr. Challoner, accompanied by Mr. Horne and another priest, entered the garret, the door of which was secured inside by the assistant, who then proceeded to unlock some drawers behind what I found was to be used as an altar, and take out vestments and other things requisite for the Church service. Water was brought to the Bishop, and from his hands we received our conditional Baptism, which had been fully explained to us. We then, one after the other, entered a sort of closet with the door open, and kneeling, received Absolution, having previously made our confession to Mr. Horne. After returning to our seats, the Bishop put on a vestment and a mitre, and gave us a short and excellent exhortation. We then knelt before him, and he administered to us the Sacrament of Confirmation . . . Soon afterwards we heard the door-key turn, and several rough foot-steps entered the garret; then some gentle taps, and words were exchanged between a powerful-looking Irishman, who kept his post close to it, and those outside, which were pass-words of admission. The key was again turned each time anyone entered, and just before the Bishop vested himself to say Mass, bolts were drawn also, and no one else could pass into the garret. In the meanwhile, the young man in attendance had prepared all that was required for Mass, taken from behind what was used as the altar, which was covered with a linen cloth. A crucifix and two lighted candles were placed on it, and in the front was suspended a piece of satin damask, in the centre of which was a cross in gold lace. The ceremonies of the Mass had been explained to me by Marlow, who seemed to follow the Latin prayers as if he had been used to them all his life. We received the Holy Communion when notice was given to us, both the priests holding before us a linen cloth.

When all was over, and I was praying to God to increase my faith, I heard the door-key turn once more, and all the rough foot-steps leaving the garret. The Bishop having unvested, remained kneeling before us while the people departed. The two priests, assisted by the young man in attendance, replaced the vestments, candlesticks and all that was used at the Mass, behind the altar, locking all up carefully, and leaving the garret an ordinary one in appearance, as before. Mr. Horne then requested us to follow him to the house where he was staying and breakfast with the Bishop. After breakfast we asked his blessing and took our leave; and so ended, that to us, most important morning on which we had received five sacraments of the Catholic Church. During the remainder of our stay in London we heard Mass every Sunday, either in the same garret, or at one of the ambassadors' chapels. Mass was rarely said on weekdays for a congregation.[21]

This report is valuable for its length and its detailed descriptions. It shows us that Catholic worship drew both middle-class and working class to the same service, and the authenticity of the description is proven by the presence of the "bouncer" as comfortable, it would seem, guarding the door at a celebration of the Mass as he would be beside a tavern door. The sense of secrecy and arcaneness for the neophytes, the improvisation of furniture, the simplicity of the ornaments, the dignity and reverence of the service, and the fidelity of the congregation, are most moving

21 E. H. Burton, *The Life and Times of Bishop Challoner* (1691-1781), 2 Vols. (1909), I, pp. 139-41, also cited in Michael Richards, *The Liturgy in England* (1966), pp. 8-10.

in their combined impact. These were the attractions of an unthe-atrical worship in the Baroque Age. Sincerity makes a scenario superfluous.

The paucity of evidence from penal days makes the temptation to generalise difficult to resist, dangerous though it is. Yet it is not even known how public or private the worship of the Recusants had to be during the different decades of this century, except in the first decade when persecution was fierce and during the eighth decade when it was almost non-existent. Lest we should imagine heroics where compliance was possible, it should be recalled that there was a great gulf between theory and practice in persecution; there were vagaries in royal policy, exceptions were made for rela-tives, officials were often venial and occasionally humane, and a good lawyer could exploit the complexities of the legal system.[22]

What was the strength of Catholicism in this dark century? The most reliable source of information for the country comes from a report of Gregoris Panzani, Papal envoy to the English court from 1634-1637, *Breve raguaglio di alcuni abusi introdotti nella Chiesa anglicana, delle Cause di esse el modo estirparli dal quale si rac-cogli il miserissimo stato de Catholici in Inghilterra suiche savanno senza Vescovi.*[23] Panzani estimates that there are about 600 priests of whom only 100 are in first-class positions. The latter are lodged by approximately one-fifth of the peerage (24 lords out of 130) or by perhaps 75 of the lesser nobility or gentlemen. Many of them are concentrated in London which harbours too many hopeful priests in search of generous patrons. In many of the remoter parts of England, many Catholics die without receiving the sacraments. The religious orders take in more postulants than they can afford to maintain.

Two-thirds of the priests were secular, and about one-third were members of orders. In 1632 there were 164 Jesuit fathers,[24] and a year later there were 63 Benedictine priests[25] in the English congregation.

Panzani's report casts some light in the liturgical darkness of the period in its recounting of abuses, caused in part by the com-petitiveness of the priesthood. For example, we learn that some

---

[22] Aveling, *Post-Reformation Catholics in East Yorkshire*, p. 38.

[23] Archives of the Sacred Congregation for the Propagation of the Faith, Rome, *Anglia*, I, pp. 99-143. It is summarised by Philip Hughes, *Rome and the Counter-Reformation in England* (1942), pp. 409-12.

[24] *Records of the English Province of the Society of Jesus* (ed. Henry Foley, 1875-1883), I, pp. lxxiii-lxv, cited by Philip Hughes, *op. cit.*, p. 336.

[25] *Catholic Record Society*, Vol. xxxiii (1933), p. 265.

ROMAN CATHOLIC

priests, in order to maintain their dependence on more than one
family, did not hesitate to celebrate two or three Masses on the
same Sunday. A list of twenty priests is given with their irregulari-
ties in worship. Some of them allow children to be baptized in the
parish church. Others admit parents to the sacraments who permit
their children to attend heretical services. Others make an alteration
in a will a condition of granting Absolution to the dying. Three,
it is alleged, are married and continue to act as priests, and one of
them is a bigamist. It is a melancholy record of desperation and
an indication of the great difficulties in "the most pitiable state of
the Catholic in England."

But if these are the black threads in the tapestry, there is also
the crimson of martyrdom. As Philip Hughes reminds us,[26] the
very same years exhibit such saintly Jesuits as Edmund Arrow-
smith and Henry More, Benedictines as holy as John Roberts and
Ambrose Barlow, seraphic Franciscans such as Henry Heath and
Arthur Bell, and heroic seculars such as William Ward and John
Southworth. Each of these prepared for the crown of the martyrs
by lives of consecration and danger, and made the sensitive worshippers to whom they administered the sacraments aware of the
sanctoral succession which transforms a squalid conventicle into a
Pentecostal palace of the Holy Spirit. It was, in these penal years
that Father Augustine Baker, the Benedictine monk, was preparing his masterpiece of devotional theology *Sancta Sophia, or, Holy
Wisdom.*[27]

The mention of Father Baker's name is sufficient to recall the
importance of the Benedictine ideal maintained steadily during
these years. Father Baker himself thought the period· had exaggerated the importance of the role of the spiritual director, and he
modestly conceived of himself as only "God's usher." Furthermore,
he claimed an important place for affective prayer as a stage in
prayer distinct from meditation and distinct also from the extraordinarily difficult forced acts of the will.[28] A tribute to his teaching is
the spiritual life of the Benedictine nun, Dame Gertrude More,[29]

[26] Hughes, *op. cit.*, p. 429.
[27] It appeared posthumously in 2 Vols. in 1657. See *Memorials of Father Augustine Baker and other Documents relating to the English Benedictines*, ed. J.
McCann and [R.] H. Connolly (*Catholic Record Society*, Vol. XXXIII, 1933), pp.
1-154. His spirituality is discussed in the chapter of that title in this present
volume.
[28] See David Mathew, *Catholicism in England* (1936), p. 273.
[29] See Augustine Baker's *The Inner Life of Dame Gertrude More* (ed. Benedict
Weld-Blundell, 1911), and H. Lane Fox, *The Holy Practices of a Divine Lover*
(1909).

a woman of wit and spirit, and of austere dedication, who was a worthy descendant of St. Thomas More. A postulant at the English Benedictine congregation at Cambrai in 1623, her distress caused by scruples and fierce temptations was removed under the direction of Fr. Baker, and her reputation for sanctity caused her to be made abbess at twenty-three. She died four years later, but not without bequeathing to the future her *Confessiones Amantis* which defend her way of prayer and contain "affective meditations of considerable beauty."[30]

Such spirituality is the austere and visible tip of the shining iceberg, the vast and invisible depths of which are submerged, and strong. These depths were the English religious communities abroad. If Elizabethan Catholicism was "red martyrdom" (with its prodigal effusion of martyrs' blood), then Jacobean and Caroline Catholicism was marked by "white martyrdom" (the efflorescence of spirituality in the monasteries and convents of the English abroad). At the beginning of the reign of Charles I an English Catholic travelling on the Continent could have visited a community of Augustinian Canonesses at St. Ursula's in Louvain with a group of twenty-two English nuns, and an English daughter-house would be founded in the same city three years later (St. Monica's). He would also have found English houses of Poor Clares at Gravelines, Franciscans and Benedictines at Brussels, and Carmelites at Antwerp.[31] These communities were sustained by the Mass and the Daily Office. Their life was vigorous. They abounded in vocations, and by their examples of a life dedicated to holiness encouraged members of their own natural families in England to emulate their holiness. By 1642 there were some seventeen completely English convents belonging to eight different orders, besides an unknown number of English nuns or postulants in foreign communities.

There were also over forty religious communities for men, eventually six seminaries for the theological training of priests, and a few secular colleges in the Low Countries in the middle decades of the seventeenth century. The tide of Counter-Reformation spiritual life was running high. One striking example of it comes from the West Riding of Yorkshire, where from an adult Catholic community of only 1,500 there was produced among the men, 33 Benedictines, 6 Carthusians, 5 Franciscans, 1 Dominican, and 35

[30] *The Oxford Dictionary of the Christian Church*, ed. F. L. Cross, p. 923b.
[31] Mathew, *op. cit.*, p. 72.

Jesuits, 80 in all.[32] Among these sacred refuges of the English pride of place must be given to Douai because it was in that great seminary founded by Cardinal Allen that many of the martyrs and missionaries were trained. There, too, was the principal school for the sons of English Recusants, and there, also, British Benedictine monks gathered themselves together into a community again. This was a power-house of devotion, discipline, and learning, as well as of publishing.

4. Baptisms, Marriages, and Burials

It was to be expected that the first service book for the use of post-Reformation English Catholics would be published at Douai in 1604. Its title was: *Sacra Institutio Baptizandi, Matrimonium Celebrandi, Infirmos Ungendi, Mortuos Sepelandi, ac alii nonnulli ritus ecclesiastici juxta usum insignis Ecclesiae Sarisburiensis* and it was republished in 1610 (Old Style), but with another title, namely, *Manuale Sacerdotum, hoc est Ritus administrandi Sacramenta Baptismi*. This title served as a reminder that it was substantially a re-arrangement of portions of the old Sarum *Manuale*. It provides us with a picture of the celebration of Baptism and of Marriage before the introduction of the official *Rituale Romanum*, identified with Pope Paul V, which appeared in 1614.

In Baptism, the rubrics of the Sarum *Manuale* made it crystal clear that infants were invariably baptized, apart from rare exception, by immersion. The priest was to stand at the western side of the font, take the child (presumably nude) from the godmother and holding it by the sides, with the infant's face away from him,[33] he dipped it into the water three times, the infant's head always pointing to the east, and thus in the direction of the altar. The priest first plunged the child into the water, right side downwards so its face was toward the north, saying, *N. ego baptizo te in nomine Patris*, next he immersed it, face downwards, so its face was towards the south, saying, *et Filii*, and lastly face downwards, saying, *et Spiritus Sancti, Amen*. Priests in penal times must have found it difficult to employ Baptism by immersion requiring the use of a capacious font. Yet the rubrics were retained because this

---

[32] Aveling, *The Catholic Recusants of the West Riding of Yorkshire*, p. 237.
[33] Herbert Thurston, S.J., "English Ritualia, Old and New" in *The Month*, Vol. CXXVI, No. 613 (July 1915), pp. 61-62. The Latin reads: "Deinde accipiat sacerdos infantem per latera, in manibus suis . . . et mergat eum semel versa facie ad quilonem et capite versus orientem, etc."

was a hallowed English tradition, but the *Rituale Romanum* which displaced the Sarum *Manuale* and its derivatives assumed that infusion would replace immersion as the mode of Baptism.

The first edition of the *Rituale Romanum* of 1614, which the English *Ordo Baptizandi* of 1626 and subsequent editions follows exactly, provides the following directions: "Then the god-father, or the god-mother, or the two together (if it be a case in which there are both) holding the child, the priest takes baptismal water from a vessel or ewer and pours some of it over the head of the infant in the form of a cross, and pronouncing the words at the same time, says once, distinctively and attentively, *N. ego baptizo te*, etc."

Although the Council of Trent required that there should be only one sponsor, whether godmother or godfather, or at the most both, the Douai *Manuale* consistently speaks of *patrini* and *matrinae* in the plural, but places a limit at three persons. There are two brief addresses to the godparents (one printed in English) which are both taken from the earlier Sarum books.

The supposed benefits of the Sacrament of Baptism are listed in the celebrated *Short Catechisme of Cardinall Bellarmine illustrated with Images* and Englished in 1614. The distinguished Jesuit theologian asks: "What effect doth Baptisme work?" and the answer he provides reads: "It maketh a man become the Child of God and heire of Paradise; it blotteth out all sinnes and filleth the soul with grace and spirituall gifts."[34]

Recusants faced great difficulties in arranging for Catholic Baptism for their children. This is evident from the problems of missioners when their charges pleaded the case for exceptions. The theory is, of course, that Catholic children are not to be baptized by Anglican clergymen. In practice, however, permission was given for Catholics under the tutelage of Anglican relatives on whom they depended financially to have their children baptized at Anglican fonts. They were also allowed to have them first secretly baptized by a Catholic priest and then proceed to an Anglican Baptism. Moreover, they were even permitted to bribe the Anglican clergyman to enter the names of their children in the parish register that he may give it out falsely that he has baptized them.[35] These equivocations dishonour the persecutors as much as they do the victims.

[34] *Ibid.*, p. 73.
[35] Hugh Aveling, *The Catholic Recusants of the West Riding of Yorkshire*, pp. 250-51.

The most important revision of the Douai *Manuale* was that of 1626, which incorporated the changes brought about in the *Rituale Romanum* of twelve years before. The most important change in the Marriage Service was the substitution of a simple Roman form of consent for the complex medieval promises of bride and groom. The bride's promise to obey her husband, though still retained as late as 1662 in the Anglican Prayer Book, was abolished in the Roman order.[36]

It has been seen that in cases of great difficulty a certain latitude was allowed for Baptism by Anglican clergy. No such leniency was permitted in the case of Marriage by Anglican clergy, for that was always regarded as apostasy from Catholicism. Recusants, therefore, had to be married before a Catholic priest and witnesses, if a priest could be found. According to the medieval canon law, which was still valid in this matter, a clandestine marriage, whether by the two parties alone or before witnesses, was regarded as valid by the Roman Catholic church and if a priest could not be found, it was also lawful. All Catholic couples in penal times were in danger of being delated to Anglican ecclesiastical courts for contracting secret marriages and the priest who had married them would also be endangered.[37]

Extreme Unction, or the Viaticum, continued to be a highly important Sacrament. It could not be received in the Baroque setting, with which the rite was dignified in France, as for example, in Picart's illustration. The latter shows the dying man supported beneath a canopied bed, while the elegant priest bends gracefully over to offer him the Host. In the foreground are members of the family devoutly kneeling, the men with tricorned hats held carefully in the crook of their left arm and shoulder and hands piously clasped, while the women meekly kneel with upward pointed hands, and the several bewigged priests are crossing themselves. A richly carved side table bears a Crucifix and two long candlesticks, and in the columned doorway partly hidden by rich hangings, men bearing torches can be seen.[38] It is clearly an important social as well as religious occasion.

For the English Recusants the receiving of the Viaticum was not a social, but only a religious event of importance. The Jesuit,

---

36 Thurston, *op. cit.*, p. 73.
37 Aveling, *The Catholic Recusants of the West Riding of Yorkshire*, p. 251.
38 Bernard Picart, *Les Cérémonies et Coutûmes Religieuses de tous les peuples du monde* (Amsterdam, 1723), II, pp. 74-76, with appropriate accompanying illustration.

Father John Gerard, has left an account of the great efficacy this Sacrament was believed to possess at this time. The person receiving the Viaticum was the married sister of his host, the latter being Sir Philip Wodehouse of Kimberley who had been knighted for his services under the Earl of Essex in the Cadiz voyage. Father Gerard writes:

I must not omit mentioning an instance of the wonderful efficacy of the Sacraments as shown in the case of the married sister of my host. She had married a man of high rank, and being favourably inclined to the Church, she had been well prepared by her brother, that it cost me but little to labour to make her a child of the Catholic Church. After her conversion she endured much from her husband when he found that she refused to join in heretical worship, but her patience withstood and overcame all. It happened on one occasion that she was so exhausted after a difficult and dangerous labour, that her life was despaired of. A clever physician was at once brought from Cambridge, who on seeing her said that he could indeed give her medicine, but that he could give no hopes of her recovery, and having prescribed some remedies, he left. I was at that time on a visit to the house, having come, as was my wont, with her brother [a notable Recusant]. The master of the house was glad to see us, although he knew well we were Catholics, and used in fact to dispute with me on religious subjects. I had nearly convinced his understanding and judgment, but the will was rooted to the earth, "for he had great possessions." But being anxious for his wife whom he dearly loved, he allowed his brother to persuade him, as there was no longer any hope for her present life, to allow her all freedom to prepare for the life to come. With his permission, we promised to bring in an old Priest on the following night: for these Priests who were ordained before Elizabeth's reign were not exposed to such dangers and penalties as the others. We therefore made use of his ministry, in order that this lady might receive all the rites of the Church. Having made her confession and been anointed, she received the Holy Viaticum; and behold in an hour's time she so far recovered as to be wholly out of danger; the disease and its cause had vanished, and she had only to recover her strength. The husband, seeing his wife thus snatched from the jaws of death, wished to know the reason. We told him it was one of the effects of the holy sacrament of Extreme Unction, that it restored bodily health when Divine Wisdom foresaw that it was expedient for the good of the soul. This was the cause of his conversion; for admiring the power and efficiency of the Sacraments of the true Church, he allowed himself to be persuaded to seek in that Church the health of his own soul.[39]

Shortly after receiving Extreme Unction the recipient usually died. Burials created great difficulties for English Catholics. The law demanded an Anglican Burial Service, and Recusants being usually excommunicated by Anglicans were denied burial in Anglican churches and graveyards, and these were the only legal burying places. The only way out of this difficulty was to arrange for the secret burial of a Recusant by his or her relations at night, and this was not uncommon. In 1677 Robert Sherburne of Stonyhurst was accused of burying the corpse of a Romish priest in Mitton parish church without asking the vicar to officiate. In the more lenient 1630s there was a practice of the relatives of a dead Recusant obtaining a formal permission for ecclesiastical burial by the device of assuring the authorities that the Recusant had regretted his defection from Anglicanism when at the point of death.[40] Panzani reported that such Catholic relatives as had to accept an Anglican burial for the deceased member of their family used to bless a little earth and throw it on the corpse in the coffin, thus "Catholicising" the Anglican ceremony.[41] Apparently, some also were able to purchase immunity from excommunication as the price for a genuinely Catholic burial. It is a sad and seamy story.

In 1721, when the practice of Catholicism was less dangerous, it is intriguing to read that Elizabeth Dunbar, wife of Charles Fairfax, caught the smallpox, died, and "Prayers" (a Requiem Mass) were said for her in the Bath chapel at her burial and on the anniversary, while "the persons that said prayers for Lady Dunbar in all the chapels were forty"—the traditional number of Masses.[42]

[39] Augustus Jessop, *One Generation of a Norfolk House* (1879), pp. 206-207; the same incident can be found in a different translation from the Latin original on pp. 19-20 of *John Gerard, the Autobiography of an Elizabethan* (1951), trans. Philip Caraman.

[40] Aveling, *The Catholic Recusants of the West Riding of Yorkshire*, p. 252.

[41] Cited by G. Anstruther, *Vaux of Harrowden, A Recusant Family* (Newport, Monmouthshire, 1953), p. 453.

[42] Aveling, "The Catholic Recusancy of the Yorkshire Fairfaxes," in *Recusant History*, No. 6 (1961-1962), p. 18.

5. *The Meaning of the Mass*

Hitherto we have been concerned to discover how the Recusants worshipped in the seventeenth century; now it is of greater interest to ask how the chief means of grace, the Blessed Sacrament of the Altar, was interpreted, and how communicants were taught to regard it and to prepare to receive Communion. At different times in the history of the Christian church different facets of its many meanings have been stressed. Indeed, it is not the least of the merits of Dom Gregory Dix's remarkable book, *The Shape of the Liturgy*, that it shows that while the central actions of the liturgy in east and west have remained the same, yet their interpretation has varied from time to time. Sometimes it is the memorial aspect which is stressed; at other times it is a proleptic anticipation of the Eucharistic banquet in eternity. Sometimes it is the concept of a mystery that prevails; at other times the idea of sacrifice dominates the rite. Sometimes thanksgiving and blessing are the main concerns; at other times it is communion with God.

In the seventeenth century (as in the Counter-Reformation of the sixteenth) in sheer contrast with the emphasis on *beneficium* and thanksgiving in Luther, as in contradistinction from the memorial emphasis in Zwingli and in Calvin (though the latter's emphasis on the dynamic power of the Holy Spirit led the way to an *epiklesis* in certain Calvinian rites), the primary, if not the exclusive, Catholic emphasis was on *sacrifice*.[43] This is made plain in the expositions written by English priests during our period or translated from foreign originals by them.

Two of the most notable interpretations of the Mass are the work of Jesuits John Heigham of Douai and Henry FitzSimon of Dublin. Heigham's is called *A Devout Exposition of the Holie Masse with an ample Declaration of all the Rites and Ceremonies belonging to the same* (Douai, 1614, with an expanded second edition in 1622). His reasons for writing the exposition, apart from the general need for it, are: "the incomparable dignitie and most excellent sublimitie of this divine and dreadfull sacrifice"; the great honour and reverence which devout Catholics have always

---

[43] The missals used by missionary priests in England in the first three decades of the seventeenth century were: (1) *Missae aliquot pro sacerdotibus itinerantibus in Anglia, Ex Missale Romano reformata* (1615 [St. Omer, English College Press]); (2) *Missale parvum pro sacerdotibus in Anglia itinerantibus, Ordo etiam baptizandi & rituale . . . extractus* (1623) which was issued in two parts, and (3) *Missale parvum pro sacerdotibus in Anglia, Scotia, & Ibernia itinerantibus* issued in three parts in 1626, the third part, without a title, containing three supplementary Masses.

paid to this Sacrament; and, a true Counter-Reformation motive and motif, "the deep, mortall and cankred mallice of wicked heretics, their most execrable blasphemies in contempt of this divine sacrifice. . . ."[44]

The Mass is declared to be the most excellent of all Sacraments because of "the great and superabundant grace which it containeth," and to be both "a Sacrament and a Sacrifice," which is "the most noble, divine, and most worthy that ever was offered nor can there possibly be a greater, it being no other then the onlie, true, and eternall Sonne of God."[45] The superlatives, typical of the Baroque decking out of the Sacrament, cloy. Heigham insists that the vestments of the priest celebrating, the richness and variety of the ornaments, the magnificence of churches and altars, the plenitude of lights, and the splendour of the ceremonies have as their main aim to declare the greatness, sanctity, and power of the Sacrifice of the Mass. To emphasize this point he likens it to a man who, on entering a great palace, and observing the arras and tapestry hanging on its walls, presumes that the owner must be a personage of nobility and wealth, for poor people could never own such a splendid house. So it is in attending Mass, for wise and virtuous men would not be at such expense unless they believed that this work was the greatest to which any man can devote his attention in the world.[46] The Baroque piety, with its strong sacerdotal emphasis, reaches its apex in the claim that the priestly dignity in offering Christ as a sacrifice excels that of the Blessed Virgin, for she "once onlie, corporallie conceived the Sonne of God," whereas "Priests as his instruments are dailie the cause that the selfsame Sonne of God . . . is trulie and reallie present in the Blessed Sacrament."[47] The end of the Mass is "chieflie to honour God, by and with soe divine a Sacrifice." The Mass is also offered for the preservation of the universal church, and the propagation of the Catholic religion, and for the Pope's Holiness; also for bishops, pastors and religious persons; for peace and concord among Christian princes; for parents, friends, and benefactors; for thanksgiving to God for all his benefits; and for our temporal substance; "and generally for all manner of necessities either of soul or body."[48] Perhaps most striking, because the image is partly used unconsciously, is the constant likening of the setting of worship to an

44 *Ibid.*, p. 3.   45 *Op. cit.*, p. 6.
46 *Ibid.*, pp. 7-8.   47 *Ibid.*, p. 11.
48 *Ibid.*, p. 17.

earthly royal court, and worship itself is viewed as court etiquette in the presence of the King of Kings. The monarchical image conveys both the absolute obedience due to God, and the impressiveness that should characterize worship. The first fruit of the Mass, says Heigham, is "that a man is admitted into the inward familiarity of our Lord Jesus Christ, and to be neare his person, as his secretarie or chamberlaine, where he both heareth and seeth so manie devine secrets: which places and roomes in the courts of earthlie Princes, are so much sought after even by the greatest Lords and Nobles of this world, and are so highly esteemed that oftentimes they are content to serve their whole life for them without anie recompense at all in the end: whereas our Lord Jesus Christ (the King of Heaven and earth, doth never unles he be forsaken) forsake him who hath done him service, nor leaveth him without reward and recompense."[49]

If splendour indicates the "real presence" of the Divine King, bareness implies the real absence. The churches of heretics are so "utterlie destitute of all hangings, and other costlie ornamentes, yea so emptie and quite disfurnished, that to enter into them is much like as to enter into some emptie grange or barne, after all the corne, hay and strawe, is carried out of it." Some heretics travelling into Catholic countries overseas have been converted to Catholicism by the magnificence of the ornaments of their churches. They, seeing the "ornamentes, riches, and beautifull ceremonies of the Catholike Church do so greatlie wonder and admire thereat that when they do depart, they find themselves so marvelouslie delighted and comforted thereby, as if they had bin for the time in some earthlie Paradise. Yea, to some this hath bin a chief motive of their change & conversion to the Catholike faith."[50]

The second and augmented edition of Heigham's work appeared in 1622, and it is significant that its theory of Consecration expressly links the Transubstantiation of the bread and wine into the Body and Blood of Christ, with his creative power as the Second Person of the Holy Trinity. "After the giving of thankes," writes Heigham, "he imparted the virtu of his holie benediction upon the bread, and converted the substance thereof in to that of his pretious bodie. The same likewise he did at the creation of the world, when he ordayned the increase and multiplication of his creatures, everie one accordinge to his kind. Never do we reade that he blessed the bread, but that there insued some notable miracle, as in the multiplication of the five loaves and the two fishes, whereof the fragments were twelve baskets, after the refection of five thousand soules."[51]

The other interpretation of the Mass by a Jesuit, is Henry Fitz-Simon's *The Justification and Exposition of the Divine Sacrifice of the Masse and of al Rites and Ceremonies* appeared in 1611. It was divided into two books. The first dealt with controversies, difficulties, and devotions of the Mass; the second with a vindication and detailed exposition of the action and symbolism of the Mass. What is perhaps most remarkable is the repeated double emphasis on the Mass as the presence of the King of Kings and the rich ornaments appropriate for such a celebration. The book differs from Heigham's only in being directed against the Puritans now growing increasingly powerful as an opposition to the religious establishment. The image of the sovereign majesty of God on his throne and his monarchical presence appears in widely scattered passages of a lengthy book. "I have seen," writes FitzSimon, "the ushers exact a fine in the chamber of presence, if any weare not bare headed befor the cloth of Estate, in which the only images of lions and dragons are figured: yea, and the very cushions wherupon the Deputie of Irland was to sit at time of sermon, to be borne in al wether by gentlemen bare headed; & passers by for honour therto to discover their heads. . . . I therfor can not conceave, why we Catholiks may be iudiciously reprehended for our wonted devotion toward the expresse resemblance of Christ, or his Saincts, when we passe to, or befor them."[52] The image of the throne is applied to the Virgin, by citing a Mariological passage from the liturgy of St. James with its stiff Latinity in the translation into English: "To the ô ful of grace, doth every Creature gratulat, both the troups of Angels, and al mankinde, which art the sanctifyed temple, the spiritual paradise, the glorie of virgins, from whom our God assumpted flesh, and became a childe, who was befor al time. He made thy wombe a throne, and thy bellie more broad, and ample, then the very heavens."[53]

FitzSimon, too, contrasts the richness and glory of Catholic Churches with the nakedness of heretical churches, accusing the "late reformers" of being happy to criticise the splendour of Catholic churches only because they have purloined them to make a brave show at a banquetting table and "to adorne his wives beddchamber with curtins and cushins."[54] With admirable rhetoric he

---

[51] *Ibid.* (2nd edn.), p. 252.　　[52] *Op. cit.* (1st edn.), pp. 124-25.
[53] *Ibid.*, p. 217.　　[54] *Ibid.*, p. 16.

demands whether "the naked Churches, the glasseles patent windowes, the ruinous roofs, the razed monuments, the rotten lofts,
and unpaved flooers belonging to God, compared to their own
hauty habitations, delightsome prospects, sumptuous galeries, silke
tapistrie, cupboards plate, and all desirable commodities, demon-
strat, that their studie is turned from the ould to the new, from
God to the bellie, from devotion to dissolution, from charity to
carnality?"[55]

The expositions of both Heigham and FitzSimon, while showing
the new Jesuit emphasis on worship as an offering to the greater
glory of God, and obeisance to the King of Kings, so vividly re-
imagined in the *Spiritual Exercises* annually undergone by every
member of the Society, and emphasize the importance of Catholic
honouring of the Mass to make reparation for heretical insults
against it, also make use of the medieval allegorical explanation
of the actions and ornaments and appurtenances of the Mass.[56]

The point of the retention of the allegorical interpretation of the
actions of the Mass may be made from another Jesuit treatise, that
of the Frenchman, Nicolas Caussin, translated by T. H. [Sir
Thomas Hawkins] and printed at Paris in 1626. This insists that
one must concentrate on the signification of all the parts of the
Mass: "as at the Confession to represent yourselfe Man, banished
from Paradise, miserable, supplyant, confessing, deploring his
sinne. At the Introite, the enflamed desires of all nature, expecting
the *Messias*. At the *Hymne* of angels, Glory be to God on high, the
Nativity. At the prayers, thanksgiving for such a benefit. At the
Epistle, the preaching of the precursor, *S. Iohn*. At the Ghospell,
truth preached by the Saviour of the World, and so of the rest."
As if this were not already enough, it is stated that the Mass must
be divided into "certayne parcels" and thus "represent to your selfe
five great things in the Mystery of the Masse from which you
ought to dream of so many fruits; These five things are, Representation, Prayse, Sacrifice, Instruction, Nourishment."[57]

It was, of course, never forgotten by Catholics that the Mass
was primarily a sacrifice for the living and the dead; the common-
est term for it was the one Henry FitzSimon uses—a "propitiatory
sacrifice"—which he defines as "a reconciliation of God offended, a
defacing of the obligation to suffre punishment; the universal doc-

[55] *Ibid.*

[56] Heigham, *op. cit.*, pp. 3, 16, 28-34, 52-59, 207; and FitzSimon, *op. cit.*,
pp. 167, 187, 343.

[57] *Op. cit.*, p. 399.

trin of the Church."[58] There was also a very strong subordinate stress on the miracle and mystery of the Mass. Nowhere is this more strongly exhibited than in FitzSimon's defence of the use of Latin in the rite, primarily because this preserves the mystery of the Mass. It is alleged (quite wrongly in fact) that Jesus did not use the vernacular language when he cried out, *Eli, Eli, Lama Sabachthani.* It is further urged that the mysteries of divinity, philosophy, science, and physic, are concealed and not conveyed to the common people. Nor should the highest mysteries of religion be subjugated to the understanding of common folk. For "as *panis absconditus suavior*, the secret bread is sweeter, so the hidden mysteries are in greater respect and veneration."[59] Augustine is cited to show that it is not quickness of understanding but simplicity of believing that makes the common sort more secure, and it is argued that the safeguarding of altars with rails is a symbolic proof that the Mass was never applied to the vulgar understanding.[60] While the "elitism" of Latinity must have appealed to the sacerdotalists, and while it was argued that Latin provided uniformity in worship (among the intellectuals), and an invariability in the rite and therefore less danger of misinterpretation, it was curiously forgotten that the over-emphasis on mystery and transcendence can easily result in maintaining the divine "Otherness" at the cost of human nescience. One has the disturbing conviction that the acceptance of the vernacular tongue could not be argued on its own grounds because it would be thought to be a concession to Protestantism, just as that any emphasis on the joint participation of the people of God would have been seen as an anti-sacerdotal move. Catholics and Protestants were locked into their assailable but impregnable fortresses of faith and practice in this period. (It has taken four centuries to erode them.)

6. Popular Devotions

It is often forgotten that the remarkable renewal of Counter-Reformation spirituality seen most strikingly in the Spanish saints and writers on spirituality[61] such as St. Ignatius Loyola, Luis of Granada, and Sts. Teresa of Avila and John of the Cross, had a powerful if indirect impact on England through the exiles and missionary priests who followed the new methods of devotion, or

---

58 *Ibid.*, pp. 87-88.   59 *Ibid.*, pp. 90-91.   60 *Ibid.*, p. 91.
61 Catholic spirituality in England is treated in more detail in Chap. III, entitled, "Spirituality: Preparation for Public Worship."

who translated them into English and sent copies of these works to their relations and friends at home. While the works of the Carmelites were only for the advanced mystics, and had little effect on the day-to-day life of lay Catholics, this was emphatically not the case with Ignatian or Salesian spirituality, nor was it true of devotions of the Rosary or the cult of the Sacred Heart.

The Jesuits were the most significant missionary priests in England in our period, and they had a powerful impact on thoughtful laymen and women. In particular, the *Exercitia Spiritualia* was a form of meditation that aimed at total transformation of the inner man and which led at its conclusion into mysticism for the many. This book of instructions on how to make a successful retreat and lead to a firm resolution to be Christ's soldier, activated the intellect, the senses, and the imagination, with the aim of influencing the will to make the firm decision to order one's life according to the purpose of God and to "think with the Church." The book breathes the spirit of the new age, since it is intimately concerned with human psychology: so much so that visualization of the Christ of the Gospels and meditation on him is encouraged, not as an end in itself, but rather as a spur to the individual who uses these "Exercises" as a generous service of God *ad majorem Dei gloriam*—the motto of the Society of Jesus founded by St. Ignatius. The Exercises end with a section called "Contemplation for Obtaining Love" which is a description of the mystical life.[62] The educational work of the Jesuits ensured that many young men of ability committed their lives to Christ, and as priests of the Society they expressed its profound sense of obedience, its vitality, and its vividness in the brilliant and entrancing worship they conducted, as brilliant as the sermons they preached or the monstrances with effulgent rays in which they exposed the Host.

Another exceedingly popular writer on spirituality was Luis of Granada, the Dominican, whose *Libro de la Oracion* (1553)[63] provided a detailed method of prayer simpler to follow than the Ignatian. This stressed the value of the preparation of the heart in devotion, and provided fourteen meditations on the Passion and the Last Things. His influence was great on St. Francis of Sales whose

[62] The substance of this paragraph is derived in part from Hilda Graeff's *The Story of Mysticism* (1966), pp. 232f.

[63] His influence is recognized in John Gee's *The Foot out of the Snare* (1624) in a list of Catholic books for sale in England and surreptitiously published, including "Granadoes *Memoriall*, Granadoes *Compendium*, and Granadoes *Meditatións*, translated" (sig. S3).

Introduction to the Devout Life[64] (1608) removed piety from the cloister to the home and the street.

Of course, the most popular Catholic devotion was that of the Rosary,[65] which commended itself by its simplicity, its mnemonic devices, and its convenience, especially when the liturgy had to be celebrated secretly and sporadically. The Mysteries of the Rosary direct attention to fifteen subjects of meditation, divided into three groups of five. The "Joyful Mysteries" are: the Annunciation, the Visitation, the Nativity of Christ, the Presentation of Christ in the Temple, and finding the Child Jesus there. The five "Sorrowful Mysteries" recall the Agony of Christ in Gethsemane, the Scourging, the Crowning with Thorns, the Carrying of the Cross, and the Crucifixion. The "Glorious Mysteries" are the Resurrection, the Ascension, the Descent of the Holy Spirit at Pentecost, the Assumption of the Virgin into Heaven, and her Coronation, providing— apart from the two final extra-Biblical events—an admirable summary of the Christ epic or events in the New Testament.

The importance of the Rosary in the seventeenth century is witnessed to by the establishment by the English Benedictines of a Chapel of the Rosary, which was probably housed in the London home of the Earl of Cardigan, the Prefect or protector of the sodality. The first Dean was Father Anselm Crowder, who was greatly devoted to the Blessed Virgin and in her honour he obtained a privilege from Pope Innocent X for an altar of Our Blessed Lady of Power. The Chapel was frequented by those who could no longer attend the Chapel Royal at Somerset House which was forbidden to Catholics during the Commonwealth and Protectorate. The opulently devout presented the chapel with important relics including one of the thorns from Christ's Crown of Thorns, and a piece of the true Cross. Dom Hugh Connolly reported[66] having seen a booklet of thirty-one pages (no longer extant) entitled, *The Method of Saying the Rosary of Our Blessed Lady, As it was ordered by Pope Pius the Fifth, of the Holy Order of Preachers, And as it is said in her Majesties Chappel at St. James* (1669). The royal sponsor

[64] Gee, *op. cit.* (sig. 82), also lists this work of de Sales translated by York, a London Jesuit.

[65] Gee, *ibid.*, also lists four books on the Rosary: *The Rosary of Our Lady; Meditations upon the Rosary; An Exposition of the Rosary;* and *The Mysteries of the Rosary.* See also Herbert Thurston, S.J., "Genuflexions and Aves, a study in Rosary Origins," in *The Month,* Vol. 127 (1916), pp. 546-59; also an earlier part of the same article in same Vol., pp. 441-52.

[66] "The Benedictine Chapel of the Rosary in London," in *The Downside Review,* Vol. LII (1934), pp. 320-29.

of this devotion was Catherine of Braganza, Queen of Charles II. The second Dean of the Rosary Chapel was Father Thomas Vincent Sadler who died in the monastery of Dieulouard (where he may have sought refuge during the time of the Titus Oates plot). The inventory of the effects in his custody specified as belonging to the Rosary Altar at Cardigan House in London, include the following objects of silver: statues of SS. Benedict and Joseph, a large Cross and Crucifix, six candlesticks, a lamp, two large flower pots, various important relics, together with a chalice, vestments, and "a wooden statue of our Bl. Lady & Savr., which usually was dressed in silken clothes when set upon the Altar."[67] From these hints we can visualize the splendour of the Altar of Our Lady of Power and the riches of those who supported the Benedictines.

The last new devotion of the century was that of the Sacred Heart, one that would be more directly related to the Blessed Sacrament, and aimed at the reparation of the insults against the love of Christ caused by the coldness of Catholics or the blasphemies of heretics. This was the vision vouchsafed to a Visitandine nun, St. Margaret Mary Alacoque (1647-1691) belonging to an Order of which the co-founder was St. Francis of Sales. This visionary and devout nun was directed by the Jesuit Père de la Colombière at Paray-le-Monial. It was too late in the century to have a profound impact on English spirituality in our period. It is, however, significant in having a link with England, in that St. Margaret-Mary's director was a chaplain to the Duchess of York, later the Queen and Consort of James II. De la Colombière[68] it was who preached and popularized the cult of the Sacred Heart of Jesus.

The danger of sentimentality was inherent in this cult, but far more important was its correlation with the liturgy and the Sacrament of Sacrifice. It was not a pious extra, nor a devotion for the elite. On the contrary, it encouraged Mass for the masses. Its very sentimentality can be defended in part as a challenge to the rationalistic inroads of deism which would otherwise have blighted the blossoms of devotion with the frosts of reductionism.

One can say, in conclusion, that while a secret worship lacked splendour, the clandestine character of Roman Catholic worship in England for most of our period saved it from the obvious defects

[67] *The Downside Review*, Vol. LII (1934), p. 590.

[68] This information I owe to Dr. D. M. Rogers, authority on English Recusant history, of the Bodleian Library, Oxford, in an interview of August 25, 1971.

of the Baroque, such as artificiality, theatricality, and too close an association with monarchical absolutism. At the same time, it is clear also that public worship was sustained by the private spirituality of the religious, especially by the ardour shown by the new orders of the Counter-Reformation.

CHAPTER XIV

RADICAL WORSHIP:
THE BAPTISTS AND QUAKERS

IT MUST seem curious to the present-day members of these two highly respectable religious denominations to find their ancestors labelled, if not libelled, as "radicals." Yet this was their reputation in the seventeenth century, which accounts for an early Quaker historian, Gough, observing that next to the Quakers the Baptists were the most hated and persecuted sect.[1] The more orthodox found it convenient to confuse the Baptists with the Anabaptists, and to recall that they had in 1534 established a New Jerusalem in Muenster in Westphalia, defended by the sword, and desecrated by imitating the immorality of the patriarchs. It was even harder to forget the eccentricities of their contemporary, Nayler the Quaker, who so over-emphasised the possession of the inner light that he ordered his enthusiastic companions to throw branches of trees before him as he made his triumphal entry into Bristol. In brief, the first Baptists and Quakers (ignoring the learning of Tombes or the education and social position of Penn) were considered to be part and parcel of the gallimaufry of Commonwealth Antinomian sectarians, represented by the Diggers, Levellers, Fifth Monarchists, the Family of Love, the Ranters, the Seekers, and even the Muggletonians the only article of whose creed was said to be:

> I do believe in God alone
> Likewise in Reeve and Muggleton.

A more exhaustive study might have discovered some intriguing characteristics in these sects with reference to their worship. Of all the groups omitted in this chapter, however, it would have been most tempting to include the Fifth Monarchists because they developed some very interesting characteristics in worship, and may well have anticipated the Quakers in interrupting the worship of other more staid groups. They envisioned radical changes in worship when the millennium would arrive. Both ministry and church would disappear, as Christ would be present in person. All ordi-

---

[1] *History of the People called Quakers*, I, p. 52 n., cited Supplement V, p. 141 of Daniel Neal's *History of the Puritans* (edn. of 1822).

490

nances would also be swept away, and even faith would be unnecessary at the advent of the truth. The saints would pay their homage to Christ in prayers and praises only.[2]

Until that time, however, their worship would not materially differ from that of the Independents and Baptists from whose ranks the Fifth Monarchists had largely been recruited. They held their services in a variety of locales, including churches, cellars, warehouses, taverns, and in the open air.[3] Like the earliest Separatists, they refused all set prayers, including even the Lord's Prayer, and rejected organs and choirs as sensuous and carnal concessions. They did, however, accept Psalms and hymns as being Scriptural. Their highly emotional services consisted almost entirely of extemporary prayers and prolix sermons, the latter sometimes lasting five or six hours and being frequently interrupted by the comments or criticisms of the congregation. One critic observed later, a little snobbishly, that the Fifth Monarchist "so hates a Gentleman, as he can't endure God shud be serv'd like one."[4] Their most distinctive contribution to worship, as we have noted elsewhere, sprang from their egalitarianism, and took the form of insisting upon the sitting posture for receiving the elements at the Lord's Supper.

It is not likely, however, that a detailed and exhaustive study of other sectarians would have yielded much novelty. This is partly because many such as the Diggers and Levellers were more concerned with social reform than spiritual reformation, and other sectarians were absorbed into long surviving denominations, such as the Seekers and Ranters in the Quakers. It seemed the wiser path to follow, therefore, to pursue the original contributions made to worship in the Free church tradition in English-speaking lands by the Baptists and the Quakers. Both Particular (or Calvinist) and General Baptists have affirmed believers' Baptisms (while denying the validity of infant Baptism), and the General Baptists have added colour to worship by practising foot-washing as an ordinance inculcating humility, and anointing the sick with oil, and they have anticipated the Methodists of England in the celebration of love-

---

2 See H. Danvers, *Theopolis* (1672), pp. 172-75; J. Archer, *The Personall Reigne of Christ* (1642), pp. 17, 27; and T. Edwards, *Gangraena* (1646), I, p. 23. For an erudite study of radical ideas during the English Revolution see Christopher Hill, *The World Turned Upside Down* (1972).

3 G. Lyon Turner, *Original Records of Early Nonconformity* (1911-1914), I, pp. 144, 155; T. Crosby, *The History of the English Baptists* (1738-1740), I, p. 377.

4 R. Flecknoe, *Enigmatical Characters* (1665), p. 28, cited by B. S. Capp, *The Fifth Monarchy Men* (1972), an admirably researched account of the movement.

feasts. The Quakers have been second to none in their insistence upon interiority in worship, taking the negative form of eliminating the Seven Sacraments of Catholicism and Eastern Orthodoxy, as well as singing, and the positive form of silent waiting upon the God who speaks to the soul in quietude. These contributions to worship have at least the significance of survival value, and they had—when they originated—the shock values of innovation and iconoclasm.

1. Parallels between Baptists and Quakers

Though there are significant differences between them in worship as in the style of religious life (notably in that the Scriptures are final authority for the Baptists and the Holy Spirit for the Quakers), yet they have many striking similarities.

It is significant that both religious Communions gained their greatest accessions during the days of the Puritan Commonwealth and Protectorate and can, from one point of view, be regarded as part of the great spiritual intensification characteristic of that time of unexampled religious seriousness on the part of the masses united with great liberty for experimentation.

Both Baptists and Quakers in England had been brought up on Foxe's Book of Martyrs,[5] and this had taught them that true discipleship was marked with suffering. A staunch Christian, like a staunch soldier, was known by his wounds. The faithful of God were prepared even for martyrdom, if necessary. John Bunyan, the Baptist, as well as George Fox the founder of the Quakers, had proved their integrity of faith by long periods of imprisonment during the Restoration. They were both cheered and consoled by the concept so concisely expressed in the title of William Penn's classic of Quaker practice, No Cross, No Crown (1669). The calm and serene courage with which the Quakers in particular faced persecution was simply astonishing. Drums might be beaten to stop the meetings of other Dissenters at worship, but could do nothing against the silence of the Friends. The driving of coaches into their midst could part them, but utterly failed to disperse them. Violence could clap them in prison, but not make them lose their composure. Indeed, when a justice had, in a fit of choler, thrown the benches out of a meeting-house, he found that the Quakers had quietly taken

[5] William Haller, Foxe's Book of Martyrs and the Elect Nation (1963).

492

possession of them, for as one of them observed, "since they belong to us, we might as well sit on them."[6]

Both groups shared the total dependence upon divine providence that was the hall-mark of Calvinism. However much the General Baptists and the Society of Friends dissented from the doctrines of election and predestination, they acknowledged the sovereignty of the divine government of the universe, and God's care for every individual who put his trust in Him.

A third parallel between Baptists and Quakers is found in their dream of making every city and country a community of the righteous. Here, again, both had borrowed from Calvin's theocracy; and Geneva, the Commonwealth of England, and the "Holy Experiment" of Pennsylvania, were three versions of the same vision of the *sancta plebs Dei*.

The Baptists and Quakers in their form of church government, as in their worship, demonstrated a profoundly democratic faith. They believed in the common man's religious capacity to become uncommon. The following parody of the preaching of a Baptist lay preacher by a Presbyterian could have been directed with equal fairness at some of the early Quaker witnesses:

> Gainst Schooles and learning, he exclaim'd amain,
> Tongues, Science, Logick, Rhetorick, all are vain,
> And wisdom much unfitting for a Preacher,
> Because the Spirit is the only Teacher.
> For Christ chose not the Rabines of the Jewes,
> No Doctors, Scribes or Pharisees did chuse,
> The poore unlearned simple Fisherman. . . .[7]

Another common characteristic of Baptists and Quakers was a strong abhorrence of any merely formal or nominal membership of a Christian community, and their insistence on "gathering" the Christian community from the world at large. For the Baptists this was symbolized by the profession of faith on the part of the believers who then were submerged in the water of a river, as if drowning the old Adam, and re-emerged as totally consecrated to Christ. The Society of Friends also required from its members outward tokens of their inward change of heart, such as a refusal to bear

---

[6] Joseph Besse, *A Collection of the Sufferings of the People called Quakers*, 2 Vols. (1753), I, p. 412.

[7] John Taylor, *A Swarme of Sectaries*, cited in William York Tindall, *John Bunyan, Mechanick Preacher* (New York, 1934), pp. 72-73.

arms or to take oaths, or to doff hats in subservience to authority, but chiefly, of course, in the endurance of sufferings for the proclamation of the truth. Fox had insisted strongly on the contrast between "professors" and "possessors" of the Holy Spirit. The Baptists were also as greatly concerned with sincerity and integrity in their spiritual fellowships.

Yet, as Troeltsch so rightly insisted, this is an intramundane asceticism that William Penn clearly recognized: "The Christian convent and monastery are within, where the soul is encloistered from sin; and this religious house the true followers of Christ carry about with them; who exempt not themselves from the conversation of the world, though they keep themselves from the evil of the world in their conversation . . . True godliness don't turn men out of the world, but enables them to live better in it and excites their endeavours to mend it."[8] This was an ethics of fight, not flight, of transformation, not evasion.

Not only the Puritans, but also the Baptists and Quakers expected genuine, if undramatic, conversion of life on the part of their religious societies. All called for what the Puritans termed "visible sainthood" by reliance upon the sanctifying power of the Holy Spirit.

Not surprisingly, then, the worship of the Baptists and Quakers shared common features. Both groups were iconoclasts, rejecting infant Baptism. Both groups considered forms as a hindering and hampering of the Spirit of God. Smyth, the Se-Baptist, took this conviction to the extreme: he insisted upon translating the Scriptures himself from the original tongues, and refused to allow a Bible in the hand of the preacher, or a Psalm book in the hand of the solitary singer of God's praise, for, as he explained it, "the worship of the new testament properly so-called is spirituall proceeding from the hart."[9] Both spiritual communities sought the supreme liturgical virtues of simplicity, freedom, spontaneity, and intimacy, avoiding pomp, coercion, formality, and distant superiority.

Each of the religious groups bears the marks of the Puritanism which it inherited and from which it partly dissents. It has even been suggested recently by a Quaker historian, Hugh Barbour,[10] that Quaker worship itself evolved by stages from the Puritan

---

[8] William Penn, *The Witness of William Penn* (eds. F. B. Tolles and E. G. Alderfer, New York, 1957), p. 48.
[9] *The Differences of the Churches of the Separation* (1605), p. v.
[10] *The Quakers in Puritan England* (New Haven, Conn., 1964), p. 8.

Bible-study sessions of "prophesyings" which were the weekday gatherings of pastors and laymen meeting to expound and discuss Scripture as God's marching orders to his covenanted people.

The closest similarity of Baptists and Quakers is found in their earliest meeting-houses. It is most significant that in these scrubbed domestic dwellings a bench for seniors and elders has replaced the Anglican altar, and even the central pulpit and Communion table of the Puritan meeting-house.

Radical Puritanism might well prove to be, however, the matrix from which Quakerism was formed. The ancestors of the Quakers have often been sought in the mystics and spiritual reformers of the left-wing Continental Reformation, but they might more easily be found among the so-called Spiritual Puritans among whom were those charismatic chaplains of Cromwell who depended on the Holy Spirit's direct guidance in worship and conduct.[11] They included John Saltmarsh, William Dell, Peter Sterry, and Walter Cradock. These anticipated Fox in their condemnation of worship attained through human gifts and which exhibited only the outward form of godliness without the inner reality. This demand for a Spirit-endowed, utterly sincere, interior, and heart-deep worship is already over half-way towards Quakerism. It stops short only by retaining the "ordinances"—preaching and the two Gospel sacraments, with the primacy of the Scriptures to which the Spirit bears witness. The Baptists stand on the thin Puritan line of demarcation from the Quakers.

If the outline of iconoclasm may be regarded, only for diagrammatic purposes, as a declivity, with Roman Catholicism at the top of the hill and Quakerism at the bottom, then the Baptists are on the foothill. To limit the process of reductionism and stripping the Christian religion to what are believed to be its essentials in England, it began with the lopping off of the Pope, the liturgy in Latin, images, and five of the sacraments, thus forming the Church of England. The Presbyterians subtracted the rule of bishops and established the parity of ministers, assisted by lay elders. The Independents, like the Presbyterians, exalted preaching and celebrated the sacraments of Baptism and Holy Communion, while decentralising church government even further to the extent of local autonomy. The Baptists followed the Independents, but eliminated Paedobaptism in favour of believers' Baptism by submersion, and

11 See Geoffrey F. Nuttall, *The Holy Spirit in Puritan Faith and Experience* (Oxford, 1946).

made church membership depend upon conversion and the gift of the Spirit. Finally, the Quakers completed the process of interiorisation by eliminating all the sacraments, claiming that they had the experience of sanctification without the ritual that had usually accompanied it,[12] and doing away with a professional ministry. In the latter respect many Baptist congregations had led the way by having laymen with spiritual gifts, but without formal theological training, minister to them. Both Baptists and Quakers emphasised the importance of charismatic "leadings" of the Spirit in prayer and in witness. If the Spirit was identified by the Cambridge Platonists as reason operative in the soul of man, and by Cromwell with God's providential ordering of history, the radical Puritans, Baptists, and Quakers interpreted it as a sudden insight, or the recollection of a singularly relevant Biblical verse.

Thus Baptists and Quakers were united in the intensity of their Christian commitment, their willingness to suffer for the faith, their total dependence upon divine providence, their theocratic concern, their democratic belief in the possibilities of ordinary folk, their abhorrence of a merely nominal membership of the church, their intramundane asceticism, and their emphasis on conversion of life. In worship, they were iconoclasts, stripping ritual and ceremonial away to the bare essentials, rejecting liturgies and all set forms, and seeking the virtues of simplicity, freedom, spontaneity, and intimacy in their approach to God, and recognising the need for dependence upon the leading of the Holy Spirit. The same characteristics are reflected in their simple meeting-houses, which are as unsacerdotal and unecclesiastical as it is possible to be.

So far we have considered the ideas and practices they had in common, but were there any historical links between them such as will prove or make highly probable direct dependence of the Society of Friends on the Baptists? The following considerations will bear out the close links between these two religious communities.[13]

It was, says W. C. Braithwaite, the Quaker historian, "a 'shattered' Baptist Society" at Mansfield in 1648 which first supplied George Fox with congenial fellowship and under his guidance it became the earliest congregation of the Religious Society

---

[12] Howard H. Brinton, *Friends for 300 Years* (New York, 1953), pp. 12-13 shows this process illustrated from the journal of John Gratton, a very searching Quaker.

[13] See Sir William Collins, "The General Baptists and the Friends" in *Transactions of the Baptist Historical Society*, Vol. v (1916-1917), pp. 65-73.

of Friends.[14] The very concept of the "inner light" had been expounded by the General Baptist minister, Henry Denne, in his *Drag-net* published in 1646 before Fox had begun his public witness.

Furthermore, it is most probable that the General Baptists mediated to the early Quakers those concepts and practices which were common to the Mennonites of Holland and the Quakers, and it is known that Fox and Barclay were in contact with the Collegiants, Dutch Baptists, several of whom were the first converts of Quakerism. The Mennonites, it should be recalled, were averse to war, refused to take oaths, and would not limit salvation to the elect. They were, moreover, the first Protestants to practise silent prayer in public worship.[15] They rejected creeds, sacerdotalism, and forms of worship. They believed in guidance through the inner light and in immediate conversion.[16] The very same attitudes characterized John Smyth and the first group of Baptists who had sought refuge in Holland and brought these convictions back to England. These "spiritualising" tendencies are made explicit in the following citation from the statement of faith made by the remnant of Smyth's church in their *Propositions and Conclusions* of 1612: "That the new creature which is begotten of God, needeth not the outward scriptures, creatures, or ordinances of the Church to support or help them . . . seeing he hath three witnesses in himself, the Father, the Word, and the Holy Ghost: which are better than all scriptures or creatures whatsoever" (Proposition 61). Proposition 73 of the same Confession of Faith states "That the outward baptism and supper do not confer, and convey grace and regeneration to the participants or communicants: but as the word preached, they serve only to support and stir up the repentance and faith of the communicants till Christ come, till the day dawn, and the day-star arise in our hearts."

The fact that proves the closeness of the Baptists and Quakers, however, is that three or four of the most ardent apostles of Quakerism in northwest England, namely, Francis Howgill, Thomas Taylor, John Wilkinson, and John Audland had been Baptist ministers in that area, and in some instances they had brought their congregations with them into the Religious Society of Friends.

---

[14] *The Beginnings of Quakerism* (2nd edn., Cambridge, 1955), p. 12.
[15] Robert Barclay, *The Inner Life of the Religious Societies of the Commonwealth* (3rd edn., 1879), p. 86. Some even rejected the sacraments. See reference in footnote 13 above, pp. 67-68.
[16] *Ibid.*, p. 73.

Our conclusion must be that while the Presbyterian and Independent Puritans were included in Cromwell's state church, the Arminian Baptists, Mennonites, and Quakers were pioneering a more charismatic type of Christian life and worship.[17]

Nonetheless there were differences between the Baptists and Quaker contributions to the worship of the English Free churches, and to these distinctives we now turn.

2. *Four Types of Baptists*[18]

There have been four types of Baptists on the English scene. The earliest to emerge were closely linked to the Dutch Anabaptists, and since 1608 when they can be traced in England leaving for Holland have been distinguished for their Arminianism. They are known by the designation of General Baptists. "General," because they refused to restrict salvation to the elect with the Calvinists. They did not associate with the Particular or Calvinistic Baptists who eventually came greatly to outnumber them. They did, however, as has been indicated, contribute some distinctive and interesting ordinances to English worship. Their leaders were John Smyth, Henry Denne, Thomas Grantham, and Joseph Wright. They were strongest in Lincolnshire, Northamptonshire, Buckinghamshire, Kent, Sussex, and London. From 1642 they practised Baptism by total immersion, thinking it as important as restricting it to believers and making redemption generally available.[19] They claimed to have twenty thousand adherents by 1661.

A second important group can be designated Calvinistic Baptists, but with open membership. They evolved from the Calvinist Separatists and were occasionally led by former clergymen of the national church, such as the learned John Tombes and Henry Jessey. They would not refuse admission to their membership to true believers who differed from them only in practising the rite of infant Baptism, and so they formed open membership churches. In practise they were autonomous religious communities of Independents and Baptists, and they were particularly strong in Bed-

---

[17] Henry W. Clark, *History of English Nonconformity*, 2 Vols. (1911-1913), I, pp. 374-75.

[18] Information on the four divisions of Baptists was derived from an anonymous article, "Baptist Literature till 1688" in *Transactions of the Baptist Historical Society*, I, pp. 114-20, probably written by W. T. Whitley, the denominational historian, and editor of the *Transactions* at the time.

[19] C. E. Whiting, *Studies in English Puritanism from the Restoration to the Revolution, 1660-1688* (1931), p. 83.

fordshire. John Bunyan[20] was the most distinguished minister of this ecumenical group. Eventually most of these local churches became Baptist or Independent.

The third group of Baptists were convinced that the fourth commandment retained its original force, and so they became known as Seventh Day Baptists. These have now practically died out, and were never strong, but they included in their number Joseph Stennett the elder, "the earliest English Baptist hymnwriter whose hymns are now in common use,"[21] and which were composed for use at the Lord's Supper.

The great majority of Baptist churches, however, belong to a fourth classification, namely, the closed Communion Particular Baptists. They derive from a split in the English Independents whom they resemble theologically and in church polity. In 1633 the first congregation under Spilsbury formally separated from the London Independent congregation meeting at Blackfriars and built a meeting-house at Broad Street near Coal Harbour.[22] This body has the distinction of first bringing hymns into English worship as distinct from metrical psalmody in the person of Benjamin Keach who in 1673, in imitation of Christ and His Apostles, composed a hymn to be sung at the close of the Lord's Supper.[23] The other leaders of the Particular Baptists included William Kiffin and Hanserd Knollys. It is estimated that at the end of the Commonwealth period there were in England 115 General Baptist congregations, and 131 Particular Baptist congregations.[24]

3. The Worship of the General Baptists

As we have seen, the first group of English General Baptists under the leadership of Smyth and Helwys had contacts with the Mennonites, and like them they baptized believers by the mode of sprinkling. It was the Dutch Collegiants who first practised immersion in 1620,[25] but Helwys and his company had left Holland long before then. What a Baptism by sprinkling was like may be pictured from the vivid account of Mennonite Baptism in Holland described by Bernard Picart in 1736.

20 See *The Baptist Quarterly*, Vol. III, No. 7 (July 1927), p. 316.
21 John Julian, *A Dictionary of Hymnology* (2nd edn., 1907), p. 1091a.
22 *Transactions of the Baptist Historical Society*, Vol. I, p. 180.
23 Julian, *op. cit.*, p. 111a.
24 *Transactions of the Baptist Historical Society*, Vol. II, p. 236.
25 Supplement to *Transactions of the Baptist Historical Society*, Vol. II, No. 3 (1910-1911), article by Gould, "The Origins of the Modern Baptist Denomination."

The ceremony of Baptism takes place after the sermon. Those who are to be baptised approach the minister (or teacher) who descends from his pulpit for this purpose. Then addressing them, he asks whether they desire to be baptised, to which they reply by an inclination of the body signifying approval. Then they kneel and the minister prays, like them, on his knees. The prayer concluded, the lector or leader of praise in the church approaches with a basin full of water, following the minister as he passes from one to another of these neophytes who continue kneeling. While pouring water on the top of the head of each, the minister says these words, "N.N., I baptise you with water; may Our Lord Jesus Christ baptise you with the Holy Spirit." After all are baptised, the same minister causes each to rise one after another, offers them Christian congratulations, and, on their entering into the Church of the faithful, salutes them with the kiss of peace.[26]

The Christological orthodoxy of the Mennonites may be suspected because they do not use the customary Trinitarian baptismal formula, but there can be no doubt as to the sincerity or warmth of the ceremony.

The sacraments for the General Baptists seem to have had an almost exclusively didactic value. The remnant of Smyth's Arminian Baptist congregation in Holland affirmed in 1612 in the seventy-fourth of their *Propositions and Conclusions* "that the sacraments have the same use that the word hath; that they are a visible word, and that they teach to the eye of them that understand as the word teacheth the ears of them that have ears to hear (Proverbs 10:12) and therefore as the word pertaineth not to infants, no more to the sacraments."[27]

The regular service of the General Baptists was very like the "prophesyings" which Zwingli had begun in the Reformed Minister at Zurich as an important pedagogical device. It is comprehensively described in the Smyth-Helwys Church at Amsterdam in 1608: "The order of the worshippe and government of oure church

---

[26] My translation of Picart, *Cérémonies et Coûtumes Religieuses de tous les peuples du monde* (Amsterdam, 1736), IV, pp. 207-208. It should be noted that Robert Barclay (*op. cit.*, p. 73) asserts "we may conclude that the first Arminian Baptist Churches in England were really Mennonite." The Arminian Baptist churches in England agreed to refer their differences to the decision of the Dutch Mennonite church, and in 1626 there were churches in London, Lincoln, Sarum, Coventry, and Tiverton corresponding with the Waterlander Mennonites of Amsterdam.

[27] W. L. Lumpkin, *Baptist Confessions of Faith* (Philadelphia, 1959), p. 138.

is 1. we begynne with a prayer, after reade some one or two chapters of the bible gyve the sence thereof, and confer upon the same, that done we lay aside oure bookes, and after a solemne prayer made by the 1. speaker, he propoundeth some text out of the Scripture, and prophecieth owt of the same, by the space of one hower, or three Quarters of an hower. After him standeth up a 2. speaker and prophecieth owt of the said text the like time and space, some tyme more some tyme lesse. After him the 3. the 4. the 5.&c as the tyme will geve leave, Then the 1. speaker concludeth with prayer as he began wth prayer, wth an exhortation to contribute to the poore, wch collection being made is also concluded wth prayer. This morning exercise begynes at eight of the clock and continueth unto twelve of the clocke the like unto 5. or 6. of the Clocke. last of all the execution of the government of the church is handled."[28] What is, however, surprising is that, while "prophesying" was a device for weekday instruction of the pastors in Zurich and in Elizabethan England for training Puritan preachers, it is now the regular mode of instructing the entire congregation in the hands of the General Baptists. Even more striking is that it was used *twice* every Sunday and could have taken up as many as eight hours of the day. Two other features of this description are worthy of note. One is the importance of the offertory for the poor, prefaced by an exhortation, and concluded with a dedicatory prayer. The other novel characteristic of this Sunday service is the pneumatic emphasis on the importance of laying aside of books (even of the Bible) for the entire dependence upon the leading of the Holy Spirit.[29] Furthermore, this spiritual worship disapproved of unison singing of the Psalms, but encouraged an individual when inspired by the Spirit to do so. Edward Draper in *Gospel-Glory proclaimed before the Sonnes of Men* affirms in the most positive terms that "To singe Psalmes in the Gospel is a speciall gift given to some particular member in the church, whereby he doth blesse, praise, or magnifie the Lord through the mighty operation of the spirit." Ephesians 5:18 and 19 are given as the Biblical sanction,

---

[28] Letter of the Bromheedes to Sir William Hammerton, Harleian Ms. 360 fol. 71 *recto* in the British Museum.

[29] Helwys, Smyth's successor as minister of this congregation, in a letter of September 20, 1608 (cited Champlin Burrage, *The Early English Dissenters in the light of recent Research*, Cambridge, 1912, II, p. 166) explains that "we suppose yt will prove the truth that All bookes even the originalles themselves must be layed aside in the tyme of spirituall worshipp, yet still retayninge the readinge & interpretinge of the Scriptures in the Churche for the preparing to worship, Iudging of doctrine, deciding of Controversies as the grounde of or faithe & of or whole profession."

and the manner is suggested as requiring "to be performed I say, by one alone, at one time to the edification one of another and therefore it is an ordinance flowing from a cheerfulle heart. . . ."[30] Under the influence of the Mennonites, the English General Baptists were already half way on the road to the Quakerism of the future.

There appear to be no early accounts of General Baptist celebrations of the Lord's Supper. For this reason it will not be amiss to assume that this was like the Communion of the Waterlander Mennonites, a description of which is supplied, about a century later, by Bernard Picart.

The Supper is also in the same way administered after the sermon. The minister takes from one of the three baskets on the Communion-table, loaves which he breaks and distributes first to his colleagues, while saying these words, *Do this in memory of Our Saviour Jesus Christ.* After this distribution, two of his colleagues joining with him, and all three followed by three deacons, each of which holds a basket, they go from row to row communicating all the faithful in the congregation. But when the communication of the bread is complete, the minister who has been the preacher of the day, returns alone to the Communion-table; the others retire with the three deacons. Two things are worthy of remark in this ceremony: one, that the minister who is in front of the table asks in a loud voice whether all have been communicated, and supposing one of the faithful has not received communion, he must rise and make a sign, in which case the minister will come back to him and communicate him. The other point is, that the communicants do not eat the bread immediately after receiving it. They wait until the minister returns to the table, where, after a short prayer and communicating himself, he invites the faithful to communicate, to participate like him in the same Communion. Before partaking, they hold the bread in their hands, or fold it in a handkerchief, or simply place it in their pocket. The wine is distributed to the same faithful, after it has been blessed or consecrated by the minister, who partakes first himself with his colleagues; immediately afterwards some deacons go to present it from one of the faithful to another, until the entire congregation shall have

30 *Op. cit.* (edn. of 1649), p. 163.

communicated. A prayer and the singing of a psalm, mark for them, as for other Protestants, the conclusion of this religious act.[31]

This very simple service is no more than a memorial of the great sacrificial love of Christ, and a means of unity among the faithful gathered to honour His memory. It does not convey grace. A Midland Association of General Baptists produced a Confession of Faith in 1651, largely to distinguish themselves from the Quakers who were then making inroads on them. Article 53 makes the Memorialist interpretation of the Lord's Supper very clear: "That Jesus Christ took Bread, and the juice of the Vine, and brake, and gave to his Disciples, to eat and drink with thanksgiving; which practice is left upon record as a memorial of his suffering, to continue in the Church until he come again."[32]

The most that can be said for the General Baptist interpretation of the Lord's Supper is that it stirs up faith, so that the worshipper can mount up on wings of faith to God and there receive His spiritual gifts. Thus, John Smyth taught in *A Short Confession* of 1610 that "the whole dealing in the outward visible supper setteth before ye eye witnesseth and signifieth, y^t Christes holy body was broken uppon ye crosse & his holy blood spilt for ye remission of our synnes: That he being glorifyed in his heavenly being, is the alive-making bread meate & drinck of our soules: it setteth before our eyes Christes office & ministery in glory & majesty by houlding his spirituall supper with ye believing soule, feeding & meating ye soule with spirituall food: it teacheth us by y^t outward handling to mount upwards with ye hart in holy prayer to begg at Christes hands ye true signified good: and it admonisheth us of thankfullnes to god, & of unity & love of one another."[33] The Sacrament is already becoming a materialistic superfluity, an extra that can be dispensed with, as long as the experience it channels is obtainable elsewhere.

It is interesting that the five General Baptist churches which in 1626 wrote to the Waterlanders seeking their advice on several points, were unable to commit themselves to weekly celebrations of the Lord's Supper. Hans Ries, the leader of the Waterlanders

---

[31] Picart, *op. cit.*, IV, p. 208, my translation.

[32] *The Faith and Practice of Thirty Congregations gathered according to the Primitive Pattern*, reprinted in W. L. Lumpkin, *op. cit.*, p. 183.

[33] John Smyth, *Works*, ed. W. T. Whitley, II, p. 196; see also Lumpkin, *op. cit.*, p. 110.

to whom was brought the letter of the churches in London, Salisbury, Coventry, Lincoln, and Tiverton, asked the two representatives who accompanied it, several questions. To one of them the two General Baptists replied that "there was not a full minister at each of the five churches, and that made it impossible to observe the Lord's Supper at each on each Lord's Day."[34] It would appear that celebration at these churches was dependent upon the visit of a travelling "episcopus." At the same time the spiritualising or dematerialising tendencies would seem to make the Sacrament less important and lead one to expect infrequent celebration.

Perhaps the most innovative practice of at least some, if not all of the General Baptists, was to precede the ordinance of the Lord's Supper with a love-feast.[35] This common meal was eaten according to the Pauline precedent of the "cup after supper" (I Corinthians 11:25) and may well have taken place in the evening on Sundays. The Church Record of the Warboys congregation has this entry for the year 1655: "The order of love-feast agreed upon, to be before the Lord's Supper; because the ancient churches did practise it, and for unity with other churches near to us."[36]

Another ordinance which appears to have been used exclusively by the Baptists, and particularly by the General Baptists, was that of feet-washing. The warrant for it was the practise of Christ prior to the Last Supper in washing the feet of His disciples to inculcate humility in them, as recorded in the Fourth Gospel. It was not, however, obligatory since it was not included in Hebrews 6. The Assembly of General Baptists left the practice optional, but were fully aware that it had been urged in Lincolnshire by Robert Wright in 1653, and in Kent by William Jeffrey in 1659.[37]

A very full contemporary account of the General Baptist marriage service exists, probably because it was required by the civil authorities. The reporter is Thomas Grantham, the leader of the entire group of churches. "The parties to be married, being qualified for that state of life, according to the law of God, and the law of the land, as to the degrees, &c. therein limited, they call together a competent number of their relations and friends; and having

---

[34] W. T. Whitley, *A History of British Baptists* (1923), pp. 51f.

[35] Robert Barclay, *The Inner Life of the Religious Societies of the Commonwealth* (3rd edn., 1879), pp. 374-75.

[36] *Fenstanton, Warboys, and Hexham Records* (ed. by E. B. Underhill, 1854), p. 272.

[37] "Original Sin, Feet washing and the New Connexion," *Transactions of the Baptist Historical Society*, Vol. I, No. 2 (1908-1909), pp. 129ff.

usually some of our ministry present with them, the parties concerned declare their contract formerly made between themselves, and the advice of their friends, if occasion require it; and then, taking each other by the hand, declare, That they from that day forward during their natural lives together, do enter into the state of marriage, using the words of marriage in the service book [Book of Common Prayer], acknowledging the words to be very fit for that purpose. And then a writing is signed by the parties married to keep in memory the contract and covenant of their marriage." Grantham then gives specimens of the writings, with signatures of the witnesses, and concludes, "after these things, some suitable counsel or instruction is given to the parties, and then prayer is made to God for his blessing on the parties married, &c."[38] Marriage was sanctioned only if the contracting parties were of the same faith, for if this rule were broken it usually led immediately to excommunication. Smyth's *Short Confession of Faith* of 1610 states categorically, "We permit none of our communion to marry godless, unbelieving, fleshly persons out of the church; but we censure such (as other sinners) according to the disposition and desert of the cause."[39]

All these ordinances of the General Baptists seem, if rather uncommon, yet hardly revolutionary. Moreover, they were practised in the quietude of the meeting-houses, so that it seems difficult to account for the persecution to which the Baptists were subject in the seventeenth century. One factor, however, has been omitted, and that is that the most striking difference between the General Baptists and the rest of Christendom—their Baptism of believers at first by sprinkling or pouring, but later by immersion in rivers and ponds—was a *public* act of iconoclasm, a challenge to both Anglican and Puritan practice.

The most notable, even notorious act of public immersion in the century was performed by a member of a family noted for courting opprobrium, Samuel, father of Titus Oates, and a "messenger" of the General Baptists. According to the polemicist, Thomas Edwards, the author of *Gangraena* (1646), in the cold weather of March of the previous year he had baptized an Ann Martin

---

[38] "Marriages before 1754," *Transactions of the Baptist Historical Society*, Vol. I, No. 2 (1908-1909), pp. 122-23. It should be noted that Grantham originally published this information in "Of the Manner of Marriages among the Baptized Believers" from which John Rippon who published a *Baptist Annual Register* from 1790-1802 took it and included it in the third volume, p. 452.

[39] *Op. cit.*, Lumpkin, p. 112.

who died a fortnight after the event to the great scandal of the neighbourhood.[40] In consequence, a famous ballad circulated, ridiculing this event all over England. Its title was *The Anabaptist out of order, Or, [T]he Relation of Samuel Oates, who lately Seduced divers people in the County of Essex, where he rebaptiz'd thirty-nine and drowned the fortieth for which offence he now lies imprisoned at Colchester, till his tryall.*[41]

The ballad suggests that the scandal was not so much believers' Baptism, as the nudity of the females that he baptized. The chorus asks:

> Shall Maidens then before young men,
> Their garments to be striping?
> No; Separatists take heed of this
> There's danger in your diping.

The implication is that charismatic religion is all too convenient, requiring neither theological learning nor discipline:

> Both Besse and Nan with this young man,
>   Desire to be acquainted;
> Which to the River after ran,
>   Thinking they should be Sainted;
> For why, quoth they, if that he pray,
>   According to the Spirit;
> All faults shall all be washt away,
>   He is so full of merit.

His sincerity is impugned, as a trickster:

> Thus thirty-nine being over past,
>   As he hath them deluded;
> The fortieth coming at the last,
>   With whom he then concluded;
> His Argument he made so strong,
>   Where on her hope she grounded,
> At last he held her in so long,
>   That she poore heart was drownded.

As verse this is sorry doggerel, but it is potent propaganda. It helped to bring the Baptists into general contempt in England.

[40] *Op. cit.*, pp. 121-22.
[41] The ballad is reprinted in full in *Cavalier and Puritan* (ed. Hyder E. Rollins, New York, 1923).

Even so generous a proponent of comprehension as Richard Baxter is violently opposed to Believers' Baptism and by immersion. This attitude was in part caused by the way that Baptist leaders would goad parish ministers into debate, and Baxter had an unpleasant encounter with the most learned exponent of the Baptist viewpoint of the age, one John Tombes in 1650. In a whole series of arguments, Baxter's sixth is against their manner of Baptism "by dipping over head in a river, or other cold water." He ludicrously claims it is a breach of the Sixth Commandment, forbidding murder. He thinks covetous landlords can get rid of their tenants and make them die rapidly by encouraging them to become Baptists, and that this should appeal to grasping physicians. Dipping will increase catarrhs, apoplexies, palsies, cephalalgies phthises, dysenteries, colics, convulsions, and so forth. "In a word, it is good for nothing but to dispatch men out of the world that are burdensome, and to ranken churchyards. . . ."[42] His seventh argument against outdoor Baptism, apart from the danger to the minister's health, is its immodesty. He asks: "Would not vain young men come to a baptising to see the nakedness of maids, and make a mere jest and sport of it?" It is plain that the General Baptists had shocked the sensibilities of the English and would pay the penalty of ridicule and persecution.

4. The Worship of the Particular Baptists

The Particular Baptists, as Calvinists, were not as far outside the pale of orthodox churchmanship as their Arminian brethren, the General Baptists. In fact, Baptism apart, it would be difficult to distinguish their worship from that of the Independents, for the latter were Calvinists in doctrine, demanded Scriptural warrants for all their ordinances, believed in extemporaneous prayer, and insisted upon the local autonomy of each gathered church. For this reason their worship will be treated with a brevity which is no index of its importance, because in the long run the Particular Baptists had an honourable history and impact in England and the New World across the Atlantic, while the General Baptists eventually withered away.

Their chief difference from the two major Puritan bodies (Presbyterians and Independents) was the restriction of Baptism to

---

[42] Baxter's *Plain Scripture Proof*, pp. 134-37, cited Neal's *History of the Puritans* (1822), Supplement to Vol. V, pp. 148-49.

believers and the method of immersion. It was the church of Baptists which had seceded from Henry Jacob's Independent congregation at Southwark which first practised Baptism by immersion in 1641, and by 1642 its pastor, Henry Jessey, accepted immersion as the only legitimate mode of Baptism, though he was for the time being prepared to administer it to infants. In 1645 Jessey was himself immersed by Hansert Knollys and he introduced believers' Baptism by immersion into his own church.[43]

The first Baptist statement of faith pronouncing in favour of immersion was the famous *London Confession* of 1644, representing the convictions of the seven Particular Baptist Churches in London. Article 40 of this document begins: "The way and manner of the dispensing of this Ordinance the Scripture holds out to be dipping or plunging the whole body under water." It continues by explaining the Sacrament as signifying "first, the washing of the whole soule in the blood of Christ: Secondly, that interest the Saints have in the death, buriall, and resurrection; thirdly, together with a confirmation of our faith, that as certainly as the body is buried under water, and riseth againe, so certainly shall the bodies of the Saints be raised by the power of Christ, in the day of the resurrection, to reigne with Christ."[44]

A marginal note in the Confession meets the kinds of criticisms of adult Baptism current at this time, by insisting that *Baptizo*, the word, signifies to dip under water "yet so as with convenient garments both upon the administrator and subject with all modestie." The editions of 1651 and 1652 add: "which is also our practice, as many eye witnesses can testifie."[45]

The fullest statement of the teaching of the Particular Baptists on the Lord's Supper is contained in their *Second London Confession* of 1677 which was confirmed by the First General Assembly of the Particular Baptists with representatives of 107 Churches meeting from September 3 to 12, 1689. This long section warrants a summary. It begins by affirming that the Lord's Supper was instituted by Christ for the perpetual remembrance of Christ's death, confirmation of the believers' faith in its benefits, their spiritual nourishment, and their deeper engagement in the duties they owe to Christ, and as a bond and pledge of their union with Christ and with each other. It is denied that Christ is offered up to God

---

[43] *Transactions of the Baptist Historical Society*, Vol. I, p. 238.
[44] Lumpkin, *op. cit.*, p. 167.   [45] *Ibid.*

the Father, or that any sacrifice is made; rather this is a memorial of Christ's efficacious sacrifice made upon the Cross the "alone propitiation for all the sins of the elect." Transubstantiation is totally rejected, and the denial of the cup to the people and the elevation or adoration of the elements are repudiated.

The mode of celebration is as follows: "The Lord Jesus Christ hath in this Ordinance, appointed his Ministers to Pray, and bless the Elements of Bread and Wine, and thereby to set them apart from a common to an holy use, and to take and break the Bread; to take the Cup, and (they communicating also themselves) to give both to the Communicants."[46]

According to the same Confession, the elements are to be received "inwardly by faith, really and indeed, yet not carnally and corporally" but "spiritually" and with them all the benefits of Christ's death.

The greatest contribution made by the Particular Baptists to the worship of this century is, however, in the realm of praise, and only after a gruelling controversy between the pioneer, Benjamin Keach, and his congregation at Horsleydown, and his literary antagonist, Isaac Marlow. Keach, a leading minister of the Particular Baptists, made the daring transition from metrical psalmody to genuine hymns of Christian experience. Although the Continental Anabaptists were well known for their hymnody, the English Baptists were slow to compose or adopt hymns. This may have been due to their desire in times of persecution not to betray their secret conventicles by singing. Possibly, also, they were out of sympathy with the formal music and praise of the established church, with its organs, choirs, and anthems. Furthermore, there were subtle distinctions current among the Baptists in general about allowable or disapproved forms of praise which threatened to disrupt the unity of the local churches, and such divisions ought not to be encouraged to develop further. For example, some persons approved the singing of psalmody (as Scriptural), and even approved the metrical paraphrases of Psalms, but rejected hymns of modern composition as merely human productions. Yet others objected to hymns being sung in a "mixed" congregation of church members and non-members, especially when the latter stayed to observe though not to communicate at the Lord's Supper. Such difficulties were tolerated for years with exemplary patience by

46 *Ibid.*, p. 292.

Benjamin Keach, who composed hymns which deservedly fell into a rapid oblivion for their literary crudity which was only compensated for in part by their religious sincerity.[47]

In 1675 in *War with the Devil*, Keach had published a small collection of hymns and spiritual songs. His *magnum opus*, however, appeared in 1691. This was *The Breach Repaired in God's Worship: Or, Singing of Psalms, Hymns and Spiritual Songs, proved to be an Holy Ordinance of Jesus Christ*, which recounts the tale of his fiery combat. He argued that there was no more reason against compiling sacred hymns to be sung out of the Word of Christ, than there is to object to pre-composed sermons. He then provided hymns for public worship in the same year, in which there appeared *Spiritual Melody containing near Three Hundred Sacred Hymns*. This is the first Baptist hymnal worthy of the name to appear in the English language.

One does not know whether to admire more Keach's persistence or his prudent gradualism during fourteen years. He first gained the consent of his flock to sing a hymn at the end of the Sacrament of the Lord's Supper, and only two members opposed him. After six years of this practice, it was agreed to extend it to days of public thanksgiving, and this lasted for fourteen years. Then it was decided to sing hymns every Sunday, with the exception of about six persons who absented themselves out of several hundreds. Keach even tried to meet their scruples of conscience, by arranging that the single hymn in each service should be sung at the conclusion of the prayer after the sermon, when the dissidents could quietly and conveniently leave.[48]

The spread and defence of Baptist principles was widely disseminated by the verse of Bunyan, particularly his great "Pilgrim hymn" ("Who would true valous see, let him come hither"), and the hymns of Keach. There would be an even more impressive flowering of Free church praise in the next century in the hymnody of Isaac Watts and Charles Wesley, which would be as skilled technically as Marot's *chansonettes* (metrical Psalms) were for the French, no less Scriptural in context, but suffused with the incandescence of Christian experience, perhaps less solemn, but certainly more joyful.

[47] J. C. Foster, "Early Baptist Writers of Verse," *Transactions of the Baptist Historical Society*, Vol. III, No. 2, p. 108.
[48] Crosby, *History of the English Baptists*, 4 Vols. (1738-1740), II, pp. 373-75.

5. Quaker Worship: Its Characteristic

Because Quaker worship is so extremely undramatic, so deliberately inward, and so profoundly simple, it h[...] wise to me to use as many contemporary citations as po[...] enable non-Quakers to try to enter into its silent worship o[...] ing, accepting and experiencing the uniting and tendering d[...] spirit or "Inner Light" communicating God's power and love.

This is the most radical type of worship to have taken firm root in the Commonwealth and Protectorate. Its classical description is provided by its leading theologian, Robert Barclay: "All true and acceptable worship to God is offered in the inward and immediate moving and drawing of His own Spirit, which is neither limited to places, times, or persons: for though we be to worship always, in that we are to fear before him; yet as to the outward signification thereof in prayers, praises, and preaching, we ought not to do it when and where we will, but when and where we are moved thereunto by the secret inspiration of the Spirit in our hearts. . . ."[49]

This definition emphasises two important aspects of Quaker worship. The first is its spirituality and inwardness. It is the Spirit of God alone that must inspire, direct, and control worship for, as the Fourth Gospel insists, the Spirit is sovereign in its absolute freedom and cannot be trapped: "The wind blows where it wills, and you hear the sound of it, but you do not know whence it comes or whither it goes, so is everyone born of the Spirit."[50] The freedom of the Holy Spirit was proclaimed by the Quakers as fervently as any Puritan, with its correlate of the futility and presumption of trying to direct it. One awaits, one cannot command the Spirit of God which is "not limited to places, times, or persons."

A second characteristic is emphasis on the inwardness of true worship. This was, if not the most distinctive characteristic of Quaker worship, yet an emphasis carried by the Quakers to great extremes. All mere convention and custom, all formality and externalism, and all forms of worship lead to hypocrisy and pretence, according to the Quaker conviction, and are utterly to be refused. For them insincerity is the major sin against God and the Friends. Barclay's definition of worship makes this its second point:

> All other worship then, both praises, prayers, and preaching,
> which man sets about in his own will, and at his own appoint-

49 *Apology for the True Christian Divinity* (1678), Chap. XI.
50 John 3:8.

511

begin and end at his pleasure, do or
lf sees meet; whether they be pre-
or prayers conceived extemporarily,
l faculty of the mind; they are all
hip, and abominable idolatry in
to be denied, rejected and sepa-
spiritual arising.[51]

clasm, there was a desperate and
knowledge of the living God not in
powerment. George Fox, Quakerism's founder,
ine exemplar of this unwearied quest to be a "possessor"
not a "professor") of the inward knowledge of God. He wrote of
how this seeker became a finder and of the joy that it brought him:
"When all my hopes in them and all men were gone, so that I had
nothing outwardly to help me, nor could I tell what to do; then O!
then I heard a voice which said, 'There is one, even Christ Jesus
who can speak to thy condition'; and when I heard it my heart did
leap for joy. When God doth work, who shall hinder it? and this I
knew experimentally. My desires after the Lord grew stronger, and
zeal in the pure knowledge of God and of Christ alone, without the
help of any man, book, or writing."[52] Now such a rejection of all
outside assistance, whether advice from persons or aid from books,
seems like arrogant Philistinism, at first blush. This judgment,
however, overlooks the crucial fact that Fox was exhausted after
testing out almost every variety of faith that England had to offer
in the time of its most prolific sectarianism, and that he found much
outward protestation and little inward integrity. The result was
that he was driven to direct experiment in mysticism after rejecting
all the traditions. This experience of direct communication with
God even meant bypassing the Scriptures, except as checks on an
independent experience of God, an attitude most offensive to most
Puritans. Yet the over-riding aim was to attain that union with
God that the Scriptures witnessed to. Margaret Fell (whose home
at Swarthmore Hall became the early northern headquarters of
the Religious Society of Friends) was attracted to Fox precisely
because he knew what experimental religion was at first hand. She
testified that the Ulverstone congregation had been questioned by
Fox thus: "You will say, Christ saith this, and the apostles say this,

51 Barclay, op. cit., Chap. XI.
52 Journal (ed. N. Penney, 1902), pp. 11-12.

but what canst thou say? Art thou a Child of Light, and hast walked in the Light, and what thou speakest is it inwardly from God, etc.?" Her own comment was: "This opened me so it cut me to the heart, and then I saw clearly we were all wrong, So I sat me down in my pew again, and cried bitterly: and I cried in my spirit to the Lord, 'We are all thieves, we are all thieves, we have taken the scriptures in words, and know nothing of them in ourselves.' "[53] This was, in short, an experience of moving behind the words to the Word of God. It was vividly expressed by Isaac Pennington, thus: "The scriptures are words, whose chief end and service is to bring men to the Word."[54]

If simplicity (or inwardness) and spirituality are two primary marks of Quaker worship, so also are silence and unity. William Britten, formerly a Baptist pastor, wrote in 1660 an interesting pamphlet on silent worship, entitled, "Silent Meeting, A Wonder to the World." It gives an invaluable analysis of silence as a help to self-criticism and solid spiritual judgment, whereas when speech is permitted there is almost always the tendency to reply in immediate self-justification. Silence for Britten is golden, especially for objective meditation on existential issues. He writes: "He is not a true minister of Jesus Christ but [he] who is led forth by His Spirit; and such we rejoice to hear declaring the things of God. Otherwise, upon meeting, we sit silent in the tongue, yet having a heart full of praises, where we worship God in Spirit and truth, Who makes our bodies temples for the same Spirit, not speaking of hearsay and human arts, but lay all that down, when earthy thoughts, earthy deeds and earthy works are all laid aside and the temple within us is ready, the light of Christ shining in it, and the Lord with a further manifestation of His love enters it by His eternal power, whereupon we can truly say that the Lord's presence is amongst us, feeding His flock and making us feel the power of an endless life."[55]

Important as silent worship was, it should however be made clear that there was no absolute requirement of silence. Isaac Pennington makes this point: "In absolutely silent meetings (wherein there is a resolution not to speak) we know not, but we wait on the Lord, either to feel Him in words or in silence of spirit without words, as he pleaseth. And that which we aim at, and are instructed

53 *Journal* (Bicentenary edn. of 1891), II, p. 512.
54 Isaac Pennington, *Works* (3rd edn., 1784), IV, p. 57.
55 Cited by W. C. Braithwaite, *op. cit.*, p. 510.

by the Spirit of the Lord as to silent meetings, is that the flesh in every one be kept silent, and that there be no building up [edification] but in the Spirit and power of the Lord."[56]

The other remarkable characteristic of the first Quaker meetings was their striking unity, a unity created in the silence of waiting upon God and sealed in their sufferings for their religion. Just in passing, it might be recalled that in ten and one-half years of witnessing as a Quaker, Isaac Pennington spent four and three-quarter years in prison, and that when William Williams, a Cambridgeshire Quaker, who was a poor man with a large family of small children was imprisoned in 1662, when his wife appealed to a justice, he told her "to fry her children for steaks, and eat them, if she wanted food."[57] That was the cost of Quaker witness!

The sense of unity developed in Quaker worship is most movingly described by Robert Barclay: "As iron sharpeneth iron, the seeing of the faces of one of another, when both are inwardly gathered into the life, giveth occasion for the life secretly to rise and pass from vessel to vessel. And as many candles lighted and put into one place to greatly augment the light and make it more to shine forth, so when many are gathered together into the same life, there is more of the glory of God and his power appears, to the refreshment of each individual, for that he partakes not only of the Light and life raised in himself, but in all the rest."[58]

A fine modern account of the experience of silent group mysticism in the Society of Friends is given by the novelist, Christopher Isherwood, in *The World in the Evening* (1954). Since the locale of the experience is the contemporary bustling metropolis of Philadelphia, the description's evocation of an ancient peace is all the more significant. The context of the experience is the white walls of the meeting-house, the hard and plain old benches, and the elders seated on the low facing gallery, as part of a community of inclined heads in prayer and contemplation. This is the experience: "Nevertheless, the Silence in its odd way, was coming to life. Was steadily filling up the bare white room, like water rising in a tank. [N. B. Isherwood employs the very same image as Barclay.] Every one of us contributed to it, simply by being present. Togetherness grew and tightly enclosed us, until it seemed that we must all be breath-

---

[56] Pennington, *Works* (3rd edn., 1784), IV, p. 59, cited in *Isaac Pennington, The Hidden Life. A Series of Extracts from the Writings of Isaac Pennington* (ed. Robert Davis, 1951), p. 31.
[57] C. E. Whiting, *op. cit.*, pp. 205f.
[58] Barclay, *Apology for the True Christian Divinity* (1678), p. 383.

ing in unison, and keeping time with our heart-beats. It was massively alive, and somehow, unimaginably ancient, like the togetherness of Man in the primitive caves."[59]

The recognition that true unity is the fruit of reconciliation has been central in Quaker belief and practice and is, of course, exemplified in the witness for peace so characteristic of the Friends. Their conviction is that unity is achieved in the sphere of the inner light. This light is "the Word of Life, the Word of Peace, the Word of Reconciliation which makes of twain one new man, and if ye do abide there, there is no division but unity in the life. . . ." The consequence is "Therefore in the Light wait where the Unity is, where the Peace is, where the Oneness with the Father and the Son is, where there is no Rent nor Division."[60] One cannot understand the emphasis on reconciliation unless one appreciates the historical circumstances, with the bitter divisions caused in English society by the Civil War. Reconciliation was England's most pressing need, as spiritual interiority was religion's primary current demand, both of which were met by Quakerism.

Thus the leading characteristics of Quaker worship are its simplicity and inwardness, its spirituality, its silent character, and its healing understanding of reconciliation and unity between God and men. The rigour with which these characteristics of worship were maintained led to some fascinating practical consequences, often innovative and iconoclastic.

6. Consequences for Quaker Life

The most striking simplification of Quaker worship and religious life was the disavowal and rejection of all set forms of prayer and of the sacraments. For this iconoclasm there are at least four reasons, the first and last of which are specially influential. The first and the most frequent reason given was the belief that no external rite can guarantee internal sincerity. The second is that the Quakers were profoundly aware of the many manifestations of God's providence and power in the world, and that, believing in such a sacramental universe, they refused to restrict the sacraments to seven, like Roman Catholics and Eastern Orthodox, or to two, like the Protestant churches. Thirdly, they refused to celebrate sacraments because in other religious groups these had been dependent on a specially ordained priesthood or ministry, and this was to deny the priesthood of all believers. This was an emphasis in line with

---

[59] *Op. cit.*, p. 51.   [60] *Epistle* 115 of 1656.

their thoroughgoing democratic insistence on the right of prophetesses as well as prophets to be the publishers of truth. A fourth
and significant reason against set prayers and sacraments was the
conviction that God was not transcendent and remote, but immanent and near. This view was admirably expounded by Jacob
Bauthumley in 1650: "And truly, I find by experience, the grand
reason why I have, and many others do now use set times of prayer,
and run to formal duties, and other outward and low services of
God: the reason hath been and is because men look upon God as
being without [i.e. outside] them and remote from them at a great
distance, as if He were locally in Heaven, and sitting there only,
and would not let down any blessing or good things, but by such
and such a way and means."[61]

The Quaker claim was that they experienced mystical union
with God and that this was not channelled through the sacraments,
but was independent of them, rendering them unnecessary. The
Quakers questioned by Bernard Picart before 1736 insisted that
"the true Baptism of Christ was the ablution of the soul, which
alone saves men."[62] He states also that their opinion of Holy Communion was not less scandalous to orthodox Christians, since they
declared that the only Communion they knew was that of hearts.[63]
Barclay, the Quaker apologist, claimed that Quakers knew the
experiences which the sacraments were supposed to convey. Baptism, so he held, was "a pure and spiritual thing, to wit, the Baptism of the Spirit and fire, by which we are buried with him, that
being washed and purged from our sins, we may walk in newness
of life."[64] One cannot help feeling that Barclay has, in this way,
reduced sacraments to the status of mere metaphors. Similarly, he
asserts that "the Communion of the Body and Blood of Christ is
inward and spiritual . . . by which the inward man is daily nourished in the hearts of those in whom Christ dwells."[65]

The positive side of this iconoclasm was that it made the Quakers practise the art of meditation more thoroughly, and enabled
them to listen openly and attentively to the various messages God
delivered through male and female human agency. Furthermore,
religion was—in the absence of sacraments—a delight rather than
a prescribed set of rules.

[61] *The Light and Dark Side of God*, p. 4.
[62] *Op. cit.*, IV, p. 135 in my translation.
[63] *Ibid.*   [64] Barclay, *Apology*, Chap. XII.
[65] *Ibid.*, Chap. XIII.

Too much must not be made of the importance of silent worship. Certainly this was not invented by Quakers, since their contemporaries, the Trappists, practised it even more rigorously, and they had been anticipated by the Mennonites in their gatherings for public worship. Nor is it entirely true to characterize most seventeenth-century Quaker meetings as silent, for more time was spent in listening to speeches than was spent in quietness, where statistics are available. The nineteenth-century historian of Quakerism and allied religious groups, who also is named Robert Barclay, claims after the careful perusal of minutes of Quaker meetings for worship in London "that silence to any large extent was the exception rather than the rule."[66]

The Quaker conviction that the truth will vindicate itself in a free and open encounter (a belief shared by Milton in the *Areopagitica* and memorably expressed), can be seen in their frequent interruption of services held in the "steeple-houses" and challenging of the ministers to debate with them. This conviction was most dramatically exhibited in the large-scale testimony and apologetical gatherings they convened in London. Early in 1655 part of a vast old house in Aldersgate Street (an address to be associated in less than a century with another popular movement in religion, Methodism) was taken by the Quakers as a meeting-place. It was called the Bull and Mouth Meeting, so named for the inn sign that adorned another part of the old mansion. In this "new hired great tavern chapel" (as the critics of the Quakers termed it), a thousand people could stand up. What transpired there under the leadership of Edward Burrough is recalled by William Crouch:

I have beheld him filled with power by the Spirit of the Lord . . . when the room hath been filled with people, many of whom have been in uproars, contending one with another, some exclaiming against the Quakers, accusing and charging them with heresy, blasphemy, sedition, and what not . . . others vehemently endeavouring to vindicate them and speaking of them more favourably. In the midst of all which noise and contention, this servant of the Lord hath stood upon a bench, with his Bible in his hand . . . speaking to the people with great authority from the words of John vii.12; "And there was much murmuring among the people concerning

66 R. Barclay, *The Inner Life of the Religious Societies of the Commonwealth* (3rd edn., 1879), p. 401.

Him": to wit, Jesus, "for some said, He is a good man: others say, Nay; but He deceiveth the people." And so suitable to the present debate amongst them, that the whole multitude was overcome thereby, and became exceedingly calm and attentive, and departed peacably, and with seeming satisfaction.[67]

Such meetings were held "to thresh among the world" to winnow and win future Quakers from the chaff of the masses, a work in which Burrough and Howgill were especially proficient.

Perhaps the most dramatic manifestation of early Quakerism was in its appropriation of prophetic symbolism by its prophets and prophetesses on the precedents provided by the Old Testament prophets. Individual Quakers, chiefly men, would go naked as a sign of the way God was uncovering sins. As early as 1652 George Fox writes approvingly of this custom to the people of Ulverstone: "the Lord made one go naked among you, a figure of thy nakedness, and of your nakedness, and as a sign amongst you before your destruction cometh, that you might see that you were naked and not covered with the truth."[68] William Simpson frequently offered this type of testimony. Fox also mentions that Simpson "went three years naked and in sackcloth in the days of Oliver and his Parliament, as a sign to them and to the priests showing how God would strip them of their power, and that they should be naked as he was, and stripped of their benefices."[69] Such dramatic gestures would seem merely extravagant eccentricities on the part of those who believed themselves to be merely publicity-mongers for a new sect; but were entirely appropriate acts for those conceiving themselves to be prophets of a new dispensation of the Spirit, as the Quakers did. Moreover, the Quakers knew these "signs" were often a cause of their sufferings, yet they felt it essential to continue the witness made by such signs. In a document addressed to the King and both Houses of Parliament in 1664 concerning the sufferings of over six hundred Quakers in prison, they include this among the reasons for their ill-treatment: "because we speak in the Synagogues and Temples, or Steeple-houses, as we are commanded and moved of the Lord, and sometimes moved to go as signes amongst them, which was the practise of the prophets

[67] *Posthuma Christiana* (edn. of 1712), p. 26.
[68] *Journal* (Bicentenary edn.), I, p. 153.
[69] *The First Publishers of Truth* (ed. N. Penney, 1907), p. 365.

of old and the apostles in primitive times."[70] The most unfortunate example of a sign that embarrassed the Quakers was Nayler's quasi-messianic entry into the city of Bristol, which was intended to be a demonstration of the divine immanence and of the inner light shining through Nayler, yet was interpreted as a claim that Nayler thought himself to be the light of the world. It is a short step from the inner light to the outer darkness.

The most impressive witness of the Quakers, however, was their ability to irradiate the whole of their life from day to day with their religious convictions. Fox saw the correlation between the convincing power of Quakerism and the integrity of the ethics of its members. He paid it a handsome tribute in the *Journal*:

At the first convincement when Friends could not put off their hats to people, nor say you to a particular, but thee and thou; and could not bow, nor use the world's salutations nor fashions nor customs—and many Friends being tradesmen of several sorts—they lost their custom at the first, for the people could not trade with them nor trust them. And for a time people that were tradesmen could hardly get money enough to buy bread, but afterwards, when people came to see Friends' honesty and truthfulness and yea and nay at a word in their dealing, and their lives and conversations did preach and reach to the witness of God in all people, and they knew and saw that they would not cozen and cheat them for conscience' sake towards God:—and that at last they might send any child and be as well used as themselves at any of their shops, so then the things altered so that the inquiry was where was a draper or shopkeeper or tailor or shoemaker or any other tradesman that was a Quaker: then that was all the cry, insomuch that Friends had double the trade beyond any of their neighbours: and if there was any trading they had it, insomuch that the cry was of all the professors and others, If we let these people alone they will take the trading of the nation out of our hands. . . And this was from the years 1652 to 1656 and since.[71]

The historian must be impressed by the boldness and originality of the witness of the early Quakers, the costliness of their suffer-

70 [To the?] *King and both Houses of Parliament, Being a Declaration of the present Suffering and imprisonment of above 600 of the people of God in scorn called Quakers, who now suffer in England for Conscience Sake* (1664), p. 5.
71 *Journal*, I, p. 185.

ings for the truth, their close correlation of profession and practice, and their obedience to the voice of the Holy Spirit, even when it contradicted the values of the age, questioned society's hypocritical courtesies and titles, condemned war in the age of the Thirty Years War, and demanded of its publishers of truth that they give up the comforts of home life to accept itinerating and even imprisonment. The spiritual power-house and dynamo of all these activities was the Quaker meeting convened for worship which was charged with the energy of the enabling spirit.

7. Developments in Quaker Worship

A movement so dynamic in its origins, coming into being in a time of political and religious revolution, was bound to change. And change it did.

At the very beginning there was not only much speech in the silent meeting, but even singing to the Lord. Fox and Hubberthorne wrote in 1658: "Those who are moved to sing with understanding, making melody to the Lord in their hearts we own; if it be in meeter we own it."[72] Psalms, even metrical Psalms, were permitted as solos and almost certainly not as conjoint exercises, since it was not until 1690 that congregational singing was approved by the Baptists. Furthermore, the Quakers suspected those who sang words or recited prayers they did not believe. They ridiculed those who were "singing David's Psalms with Saul's Spirit, in such Meeter. . . as Q. Elizabeth's Fiddlers have moulded them into, and . . . as some Priest, Clark or Saxton saves them lineatim."[73] Yet Thomas and Elizabeth Holme ministered movingly to the Quakers by their singing.[74]

Also at the very beginning, it seems that the Friends kept love-feasts. Fox's earliest tract make references to such, affirming "we have the Lord's Supper" or "the Table and Supper of the Lord we own" with the accompanying denial that the mode in which it was celebrated by others was according to the practice either of the Sacrament itself or the common meal that preceded it in the apostolic church which bore relation to it.[75] It is likelier that this was a love-feast than the Lord's Supper, precisely because the former was not imbued with the sacerdotalism of a sacrament. The

---

[72] *Truth's Defence against the Serpent*, p. 21.
[73] Samuel Fisher, *The Testimony of Truth Exalted* (1679), p. 92.
[74] The *Cambridge Journal of Fox*, I, p. 245.
[75] R. Barclay, *The Inner Life* (3rd edn., 1879), pp. 374-75.

increasing iconoclasm of the Society of Friends led to the abolition of this ordinance, whether Communion or love-feast.

A third development was the provision of a simple Marriage Service for Friends entering into matrimony. This simple exchanging of vows owed much to the Puritan simplification of the Anglican service as provided in the Westminster or Parliamentary *Directory*. The couple repeated their mutual vows of fidelity in the silent meeting convened for this purpose, then signed a certificate which was read aloud and also signed by the Friends present after the meeting concluded.[76]

Inevitably as the Society's numbers increased, and as persecution diminished, and a new haven was established for the expression of a gentler theocracy of the Friends in Pennsylvania, the more dramatic public witnessing of the Quakers, whether in "threshing Meetings" or in prophetical signs, or in challenges in the local parish churches, lessened. During the years of persecution the Friends had turned inward at their meetings for worship, instead of attacking their detractors or competitors as in the exciting polemics of earlier days. The serenity, security, and compassion of the silent meetings grew as the outward lot of Quakers worsened in days of "durance vile" and duress. This was the permanent legacy of Quakerism, which seems only more relevant in our cacophonous age.

[76] Ruth C. Burtt, "The Quaker Marriage Declaration," *Journal of the Friends Historical Society*, Vol. 46 (1954), pp. 53-59.

CHAPTER XV

CONCLUDING SURVEY
AND CRITIQUE

HITHERTO OUR exclusive interest has been to try to understand by the way of empathy the most varied rites and ceremonies whether complexly grandiose or severely simple. Our concluding concern will be to survey the developments in worship of the entire century and to attempt to evaluate them.

1. New Developments

The seventeenth century produced some fascinating new developments in worship. The English people were offered a choice of no less than four alternative modes of public prayer. The oldest and the most familiar was the use of a liturgy. The Roman Catholics used a venerable international liturgy in Latin. The Anglicans used a national liturgy in the English vernacular, which combined Catholic traditions and Reformed insights. In its revised form of 1662 their Prayer Book contained two superb new prayers, the General Thanksgiving and the General Confession. The second type of public prayer was the substitute for the Book of Common Prayer, the *Westminster Directory* of 1644, which provided an order of worship and proposed themes for prayers without prescribing their wording, thus combining fixity and freedom. It was almost certainly the first and only time that a manual of worship rather than a liturgy has been devised for the Christian worship of three kingdoms. The third type of public prayer was "conceived" prayer, either free or extemporary, the former giving the minister the right to prepare a prayer of his own composition and take it with him into the pulpit, and the latter an immediate and spontaneous creation under the inspiration of the Holy Spirit. The fourth and last option was taken by very few: it was the most radical of all types of public prayer, the silent unitive prayer of the Religious Society of Friends.

A second very significant development (with much greater promise for the eighteenth century in the gifted pens of Isaac Watts and Charles Wesley) was the transition made from prose psalm to metrical Psalm and eventually to hymnody. This provided the lyrical element so badly needed in worship, which without the element of adoration dries up in a dreary didacticism; but there were few oases in this seventeenth-century desert of hymnody. The efflorescence of the cacti of metrical psalmody among the Puritans and of the more luxuriant orchids of verse anthems in cathedrals and abbeys was another feature of the period.

A third characteristic, particularly strong in the Church of England, was a high evaluation of the doctrine and act of the Incarnation, and of its consequence, the continuing presence of Christ in the Eucharist, and the conviction that this was the church member's greatest privilege. (The Puritans, by contrast, felt the presence of Christ more potently in the audible than the visible World.) This sense of the "real presence" gave Anglicanism a great impetus to high ceremonial, to symbolical ornaments, and to the recognition that the sanctuary was the presence chamber of the King of Kings, and the altar was Christ's throne. Not until the advent of the Oxford and Cambridge[1] Movements of the mid-nineteenth century would the Church of England again have as splendid and beautiful a setting for the liturgy. This was the legacy of Hooker, Andrewes, and Laud and their trustees were Bishops Cosin and Wren.

A fourth feature of the age was the high level (abating some controversial cantankerousness) of the defences offered for the different types and styles of worship. The chief Anglican liturgical apologists were Henry Hammond and Herbert Thorndike, Bishops Jeremy Taylor and William Beveridge, and Archbishop Bramhall. The stalwart Puritan defenders of their type of worship were Perkins, Owen, and Richard Baxter. The single outstanding Quaker apologist was Barclay. These men penetrated to the core of the matter in their descriptions and defences of their own type of worship, but were generally myopic (with the probable exception of Baxter) in their views of other liturgical styles than their own. It is in this century that a new and important genre of ecclesiastical writing was born, namely, the Prayer Book commentary. It provided an analysis of the contents of the Anglican liturgy with historical notes in a devotional spirit. It aimed to enable loyal Anglicans to offer worship as "their reasonable service." The deep antagonisms of the ecclesiastical parties often produced an "either/or" demand where an unpolarised experience might have preferred

1 See James F. White, *The Cambridge Movement: The Ecclesiologists and the Gothic Revival* (Cambridge, 1962).

"both/and" as more comprehensive and wiser. The century did, however, see sharply stated alternatives argued with conviction, historical lore, and enthusiasm.

Nor should it be forgotten in the confusion of controversy about the cultus that this was the golden age of English preaching. Dean Donne and Bishop Lancelot Andrewes were spectacular practitioners of the brilliant and daring art of metaphysical preaching. Bishop Jeremy Taylor dazzled his congregation with his ornate oratory, as freighted with golden metaphors and figures of speech as a captured Spanish galleon with ingots. Richard Baxter exemplified the plain, direct, yet emotionally charged, Puritan style seeking for a verdict from his congregation, and Tillotson preached modest, rational, pragmatic sermons as a Latitudinarian should. Here, indeed, was God's plenty in quality, quantity, and variety.

A minor but significant change was the recognition on the part of John Archer, the revolutionary Independent minister, that sitting at the Communion table was not the careless gesture that a later age might dub "the Congregational crouch," but a profoundly democratic and radical protest. It declared that the seventeenth-century disciples of Christ need not kneel in subservience to him as to an earthly king, as Roman Catholics and Anglicans did. It recognised that Christ had called the "visible saints" his friends and that they were to share in the political Christocracy to be established in this world.

In major ways the seventeenth-century developments in worship were to have effects that would last for centuries to come. Presbyterianism, which had hitherto followed Calvin and Knox in preferring a Biblically based liturgy and a set form of worship, now used a *Directory* or manual. This became the pattern of worship for all those in the Puritan-Pietist tradition for three centuries in England and New England, in the British Commonwealth of nations and in the United States. Free prayer would become characteristic of the worship of not only Independents and Baptists, but also of Presbyterians and Methodists. Even Lutherans, who began with liturgies, would go through a period of having free prayers and finally reappropriate liturgical forms.

Similarly, the long-range influence of the Caroline divines was great on the Anglican Communion throughout the English-speaking world. They established the characteristic ethos of Anglican worship: a reverence for the Sacrament of Holy Communion as an incentive to holiness, a dignified and beautiful ceremonial and setting for the liturgy as the expression of the holiness of beauty, and a conviction (with the Church of the Fathers) that the Incarnation (and its annual remembrance in the calendar of the Christian year) is the lever for the raising of humanity to the service of God and neighbour. The great Anglican monastic recovery in the nineteenth century is foreshadowed in the seventeenth century at Little Gidding, where the family of the Ferrars and their friends offered a round of praise and prayers to God through the day and the night.

Furthermore, the Quaker emphasis on the group waiting for the guidance of the inner light in silence has become not less, but more relevant with the passage of the frenetic years, and the arrival of our own cacophonic age, and is now providing extraordinary experimental opportunities for Quakers and Buddhist and Hindu contemplatives to meet in colloquia in depth.[2]

2. The Strengths and Weaknesses of Liturgical Worship

The necessity for Roman Catholics, except those in the highest places, to practise a cryptic cultus in our period, while their European co-religionists were worshipping in a setting of Baroque theatrical magnificence, forced their ceremonial and ornaments to approximate those of the Anglican liturgy. It is therefore appropriate to consider them together, despite their differences, because they both are strongly committed to liturgical worship.

It will probably be generally conceded that a cultus fulfils three major functions. First, it provides an ordered rite that enables a religious community to worship God together. Secondly, its structure and contents are designed to consecrate (and hopefully transform) the whole of life as an offering to God. Thirdly, its ritual and ceremonial provide an outward visible and audible expression for the inner devotion of the personality.

The first function—that of providing a structure for the common corporate expression of divine worship—is the chief benefit of a liturgy. It is a historical fact that no liturgy has ever united a larger group of Christians than the Roman Catholic liturgy, whether in its simple and early Roman form, in its medieval allegorical form, in its post-Tridentine rubrical uniformity, or in its modern, vernacular, alternative forms since Vatican II.[3] It has unified the devotions of countless millions in the Mass, as of count-

---

2 See Douglas V. Steere, *On Being Present Where You Are* (Pendle Hill Pamphlet No. 151, Pendle Hill, Pennsylvania, 1967), pp. 20-27.

3 See Hermanus A. P. Schmidt, *Introductio in Liturgiam Occidentalem* (Rome, Freiburg, Barcelona, 1960), passim.

less thousands of the religious in the Breviary and the Daily Office. Unquestionably, its venerable age and widespread tradition strengthened the loyalty of persecuted Roman Catholics in seventeenth-century England.

Similarly, the Anglican Book of Common Prayer proved an admirably suitable medium for expressing religious unity, though it was not comprehensive enough to include either the seventeenth-century Puritans after 1662 or the Methodists after 1795. It was unique in being both a priest's book and a people's book of worship in the vernacular, and in combining Catholic tradition with Reformation insight. We have, however, seen that the underside of the uniformity it claimed to provide was that it developed into an engine of "soul control" bringing persecution in its train.[4]

Furthermore, it is only fair to recognise that both the Roman and Anglican liturgies are considerably more flexible than the mystical liturgies (for example) of the Eastern Orthodox churches. Their lections, their collects, and their prefaces in the Eucharistic Prayer of Consecration, change according to the Christian year. (Puritan worship can hardly be accused of invariability; its weaknesses are casualness and anarchy.)

If a second function of corporate worship is to consecrate and transform the whole of life, then much will depend on how prominently the concept of sacrifice is kept before the worshippers, or how strongly the emphasis on sanctification is maintained. On both scores it would be impossible to fault the Roman rite. If the worship of Eastern Orthodoxy can be characterized as the rehearsal of a mystery drama, and Puritan worship as listening to the oracles of God, Roman worship is unquestionably the representation of Christ's sacrifice. Furthermore, Rome is rightly known as the mother of saints, and the sanctoral round in the Roman Catholic calendar is its remembrance. At the very heart of the Mass there is sacrifice, primarily Christ's own eternally efficacious sacrifice offered to God the Father for the reconciliation of the world, and subordinately, the sacrifice of the people of God united to Christ.[5] It is this central sacrifice that provides the Mass with its great

---

[4] There is an extended consideration of this charge in Davies, *op. cit.*, I, pp. 219f.

[5] The sacrificial language of the Mass may be illustrated from the following citations from its prayers: in the Offertory the terms *oblatio*, *sacrificium*, *hostia* and *calix salutaris* are used; and the great prayer, *Te igitur* pleads that God will accept and bless *haec dona, haec munera, haec sancta sacrificia illabata, quae tibi offerimus pro ecclesia tua sancta catholica.*

objectivity in its transcendent reference, its independence of psychological moods. It is the awesome sense of Christ's corporal presence on the altar that makes the event renewed at Mass so numinous, so important, so life-changing.

Has the Anglican liturgy proved able to transform life? (This question has already been answered positively in our chapter on spirituality.) But *how* was this done? Clearly, Anglican worship had a strong sense of the "real presence" of the sacrificial Christ in its services of Holy Communion, though Anglican theologians of the seventeenth century insisted that this was a spiritual, not a corporal, presence. It cannot be claimed that the sense of sacrifice is as dominant as in the Roman Mass, but it is there and it is too frequently expressed to be ignored. The actual term "sacrifice" is rather carefully kept for the original sacrifice of Christ upon his Cross to avoid any possibility of misinterpreting this as the renewal of this unique act. The Prayer of Consecration most cautiously stresses that Christ made at the Cross "his one oblation of himself *once offered*." The term sacrifice is also used for the congregation's responsive "sacrifice of praise" (and a post-Communion Prayer of Thanksgiving affirms that "we offer and present unto thee, O Lord, ourselves to be a reasonable, holy, and living sacrifice to thee").

On the other hand, the Church of England's Eucharistic rite is conceived primarily as a commemoration of a sacrifice and a spiritual banquet. At the heart of the Prayer of Consecration is the reminder that Christ made "a full, perfect, and sufficient sacrifice for the sins of the whole world, and did institute and in his holy Gospel command us to continue a perpetual memory of that his precious death until his coming again." Nonetheless, along with the images of "holy mysteries" and spiritual banquet, that of sacrifice is unquestionably important. And, although the sanctoral cycle is diminished, compared with the Roman calendar, the sense of spiritual transformation or sanctification is to be found in the exhortation that in warning against unworthy reception is, in effect, a "fencing" of the table. The same emphasis is also present in both alternative post-Communion prayers, the second of which asks God "so assist us with thy grace that we may continue in that holy fellowship, and do all such good works as thou hast prepared for us to walk in."

The third function of a cultus, namely, to provide an outward form for the expression of inner devotion, is admirably fulfilled by both Roman and Anglican liturgies in their ceremonial and words. Both take the Incarnation seriously and recognise the importance of that divine accommodation to the mixed psycho-physical nature of man. They both supply in processions, in varied gestures of reverence, in the use of "eye-gate" as well as "ear-gate," in arrow-like prayers that catch the attention and in responses, and in architectural symbolism and music, aids to assist worshippers. Moreover, the very forms of worship themselves inculcate the appropriate response to the living God whose mercy is as his majesty. (By contrast, Puritan worship made fewer concessions to human psychology and to the five senses. It almost eliminated ceremonial, and in the intensity of concentration required for its long prayers and longer sermons strained the attention of the elect.) Above all, it cannot be too strongly stressed that the Catholic and Anglican traditions of worship recognised the importance of the concept of an offering being made by the congregation as Christ's flock. Here, again, the contrast with the Puritan and later Free church tradition is glaring. In the course of time, as the Baptist exponent of worship, Stephen Winward reminds us, in the Free church tradition "getting a blessing" came to replace "making an offering" to the depreciation of worship.[6] Here at once is the greatest strength of the Catholic and Anglican tradition, and the greatest weakness of Nonconformist worship. Puritans and their successors seem to be unaware that habitually performed acts not only evoke the appropriate emotions, but even strengthen them. So even if one does not feel a sense of gratitude to God at the beginning of worship, it may be created by the experience of worship.[7] Worship is not only expressive as the devotees of sincerity insist, it is also (which the same coterie ignores) instrumental in creating emotions that ought to be felt.

Puritanism was far from doing justice to the strengths of Roman Catholic and Anglican worship—their uniformity (universality in

[6] See *The Reformation of our Worship* (1964), p. 3. Winward suggests the following cluster of reasons for the absence of the idea of offering in the Puritan and Free church tradition of worship: since Christ has made the perfect offering no other is needed; a prophetic criticism of Israel's cultus is misinterpreted to mean the prophets were against all sacrifices; there is a false pitting of prophet against priest; the strong and exclusive Puritan stress on the downward or revelational movement from God to man led to the exclusion of the upward response or the offering of man to God.

François Mauriac, the Catholic novelist, in *La Pharisienne*, makes his priest comment on the fact that a tragedy of Calvinism is that human acts of sacrifice seem to count for nothing, for they cannot add anything to Christ's complete and perfect sacrifice.

[7] Baron Von Hügel in his *Selected Letters* criticizes the Puritan viewpoint in the following citation: "What a curious psychology which allows me to kiss my child because I love it, but strictly forbids me to kiss it in order to love it."

528

the case of the Mass), transcendental reference and objectivity, the responsive element in the prayers, the variety in the Christological and sanctoral cycle, and the multi-medial aesthetic approach. In the Puritan criticisms of the superstition, formalism, impersonality, and rigidity of the Roman and Anglican rites, the Puritans ignored the large Biblical element in the lections, as in the actual wording of the prayers (especially strong in Anglican prayers which are often Biblical mosaics, and the Book of Common Prayer rejected legendary sanctoral material), and the strong Christological focus. The Puritans were unreasonably iconoclastic in their attitude towards the Book of Common Prayer because of its "guilt by association" in the retention of certain noxious ceremonies also used by Roman Catholics, and failed utterly to do justice to the centrality of Christ in lections, collects, and calendar.

For all this, the gravamen of the Puritan objection is the recognition that a liturgy can become exceedingly formal, mechanical, and artificial. It can project an idea of God as a remote and utterly transcendent sovereign "King of Kings and Lord of Lords" and not "the God and Father of our Lord Jesus Christ." Its spirit can be exceedingly sober, dignified, even stuffy. It can be singularly lacking in adoration and joy. Familiarity can breed contempt or indifference for its repetitiousness. Above all, the incantatory magic of the words of the Prayer Book and the medieval beauty of the setting may transform worship into a reverie rather than prepare the Christian for a re-entry into life transformed into a deeper commitment to serve God and humanity. Puritan worship may be a cold shower and bracing, but Anglican worship is likelier to be a soothing and possibly enervating bath.

3. The Strengths and Weaknesses of Puritan Worship

Had the criticisms of liturgical worship which we have just listed been entirely without substance, Puritans would not have gone to the enormous effort of creating an alternative cultus, least of all one which offered so few incentives to the natural man and was about as colourful as an etching.

What were the strengths of Puritan worship? Its greatest strength was its bracing Biblical authority. The Word of God, the authority of God's own appointing in Scripture, is its sanction, whether for the primacy of preaching as an exposition of the oracles of the living God (prepared for by a prayer for the illumination of the Holy Spirit), or for every other "ordinance" (as it was characteristically called, being a mandate from the Mediator). The lections are entire chapters of Scripture; no apocopated "pistling" or "gospelling" for them. Baptism and the Lord's Supper are prefaced as ordinances by reading their Biblical warrants and the formulae for the act of Baptism as for the reception of the consecrated elements in the Lord's Supper are directly from the New Testament. The curious Independent double Consecration, successively, of bread and wine, is justified not by reason, or custom, but only by fidelity to the New Testament narrative of its institution. The same submission to Scripture accounts for the unusual Independent order of having prayers of intercession and petition before prayers of confession, because it is thus given as the order in I Timothy. The songs were not human compositions, but the divinely inspired Psalms of David made into English poetry by translation into rhyme and metre. To worship God as he had commanded, rather than to be determined by reason, custom, beauty, convenience, or human psychology, was the commanding and demanding authority of Puritan worship, and it made vertebral Christians, supported by such a conviction into spiritual Ironsides. Their daily private and family prayers made the Puritans approach the worship of each Lord's Day with the expectation of a miniature Pentecost.

A second characteristic of Puritan worship was its utter simplicity and sincerity. This unostentatious and modest form of worship found its appropriate domestic setting in meeting-houses, scrubbed and whitewashed (not in ecclesiastical palaces or throne-rooms). It rejected all "storied windows richly dight, casting a dim religious light" to allow the sun to shine through unstained windows as the natural illumination of the Creator. The Puritans refused to

> let the pealing organ blow
> To the full-voiced quire below
> In service high and anthems clear . . .[8]

in favour of the pedestrian metres of the Psalms so that all could memorize them and sing them in unison. Their meeting-houses were, in fact, large homes, made spiritually so by the invisible presence of their Heavenly Father, whom they approached with a natural respect, and in the unaffected simplicity and spontaneity of free prayer that resembled a conversation. This simplicity did

8 Milton's *Il Penseroso*, ll. 15-55.

not mean that they lacked all sense of the numinous. On the contrary, their sense of holiness in approaching God was so strong that they could do without any theatrical or adventitious aids which would make tawdry the splendour of the Creator's covenant mercies to his own. What could be more numinous than to hear the voice that thundered at Sinai or whispered the promises beside Galilee?

A third characteristic of Puritan worship was its interiority (which was, of course, carried to the furthest extreme by the Quakers). Negatively, it was an attempt to prevent all formalism and hypocrisy by recognising that the Spirit of God searches the heart and can unmask all pretences and disguises. Negatively also it is expressed as iconoclasm in the rejection of ecclesiastical vestments, of all ceremonial except the divinely donated signs of the Gospel sacraments, of set prayers, and set sermons (such as the homilies), and set creeds. Positively, it was an affirmation of the dominating role of the Holy Spirit in untrammelled freedom and sovereignty— and here again the Quakers carried this conviction to its logical conclusion, insisting that the Spirit must not be imprisoned in times, places, or sacraments.[9]

The gradual Puritan depreciation of the sacraments through infrequency and a memorialist doctrine, and the Quaker rejection of all sacraments was a serious defect. It left both Puritans and Quakers naked to the arrows of subjectivism, for once the august authority of the inerrant Scripture was lost, they were stripped of their defences. Indeed, the Quakers had already chosen the inner spirit over the exterior Word of God as their authority.

In the radical Puritan sects such as the Fifth Monarchists or the Seekers, the dependence upon the Holy Spirit uncontrolled by Scripture led to charismatic worship in which spontaneous witnessing and singing produced ecstasy. Within central Puritanism, however, the Holy Spirit generated illumination more obviously than warmth, although even here the Christ mysticism of Thomas Goodwin, Preston, Rous, and Sterry must not be forgotten. The point is that Scripture and the Spirit were conjoint authorities in

---

[9] Douglas V. Steere expresses the Quaker conviction in *The Hardest Journey* (The West Coast Quaker Lecture of 1968, published in the *Whittier College Bulletin*, Whittier, California, p. 4): "For Friends who know no outward Sacraments, this tendering action of the Holy Spirit is the baptism; it is the communion; it is the hallower of all facets of life. It is the revealer of injustice and the dissolver of men's dikes of reservation to the costly correction of those wrongs; it is the great magnet to draw men here and now from their enmities, their violence, their wars—into the peaceable Kingdom. . . ."

Puritanism, while in Quakerism the Spirit had precedence over Scripture which was used only for the confirmation of experience.

In the fourth place, in both Puritanism and Quakerism there was a profound concern for sanctification and integrity of life. Externally, this was visible in the Puritan fencing of the Communion table against all scandalous persons who dishonoured the holy community, in the "holy discipline" which cut off the dead limbs on the trunk of the church by excommunication, and, upon public repentance, re-grafted them. It is also evidenced in the deep concern of both Puritans and Quakers to live as children of the light, eagerly listening to God's Word as heard from the pulpit or in the heart, and (at least in the case of the Puritans) keeping a ledger book of the soul recording one's covenant promises to God and one's melancholy failures and resolutions to improve. The same procedure on a local, regional, or national scale was seen in the Puritan recognition of God's providence in criticism or in comfort, respectively in days of humiliation and days of thanksgiving. Puritans occasionally looked grim in their tenseness and censoriousness. They were never trivial with God and they were hard on themselves. They allowed neither the favour nor the flattery of men to divert them from offering to God the supreme homage of the obedience of faith issuing in sanctification.

The worship of the Puritans certainly strained after sanctification, for they wished to establish the rule of God in all the affairs of life. As a medium for the expression of unity, however, it was not as successful as a liturgy. If the Roman Catholics and the Anglicans stressed Catholicity and Apostolicity in the hope of attaining unity, the Puritans counted all else well lost for the sake of holiness. The conception of the "gathered church" necessarily meant separation from the world, and the Puritans considered compromise too great a price to pay for unity.

Nor was Puritan worship able to minister to the mixed spiritual-physical nature of man. Its worshippers were expected to live as angels, as bodiless spirits, using their ears, but neglecting the senses of touch, of scent, of taste, and above all, of sight. Its prolix prayers and marathon preaching left congregations edified and often even elated, but also exhausted. Catholics and Anglicans acknowledged with St. Thomas Aquinas that *natura non tollit sed perfecit naturam*, that grace does not trample on but raises nature. The Puritans seemed to think that heaven and earth, grace and nature, form and spirit, structure and freedom were antithetical and not complementary. Gerard Manley Hopkins, the Jesuit poet, knew the delights and dangers of beauty as well as any Puritan, but he recognised that it was a gift from the Creator. His poem, "To what serves Mortal Beauty?" is both the statement of the problem and the answer. He admits that beauty is

> —dangerous; does set danc-
> ing blood—the O-seal-that-so- feature, flung prouder form
> Than Purcell tune lets treat to? See: it does this: keeps warm
> Men's wits to the things that are; What good means

And "how meet beauty?" His answer is,

> Merely meet it; own,
> Home at heart, heaven's sweet gift; then leave, let that alone.
> Yea, wish that though, wish all, God's better beauty, grace.[10]

Moreover, Puritan worship had another defect arising from its concentration—over-didacticism. It was forgotten that symbols may teach more powerfully, if quietly, than scolding sermons, and that "where reason fails with all her powers, there faith prevails and love adores." There seemed to be, at least before 1662, so much argumentation and controversy in Puritan preaching, and so much frenetic experimentation in prayer, that it must have been difficult to attain to the serenity of contemplation or even to the lower levels of contentment, which Roman Catholics and Anglicans found in their familiar forms. The nemesis of didacticism was reported by Increase Mather, the New England Puritan divine, who was unconscionably fond of jeremiads, in the words: "We may here take notice that the nature of man is woefully corrupted and depraved, else they would not be so apt to sleep when the precious Truths of God are dispensed in his Name, Yea, and men are more apt to sleep then, than at another time. Some woful Creatures have been so wicked as to profess they have gone to hear Sermons on purpose, that they might sleep, finding themselves at such times much disposed that way."[11]

While Puritan worship was admirable in its concentration on the divine revelation in the audible and visible Word (in preaching and the Gospel sacraments), as the means for transforming the

---

10 *Poems of Gerard Manley Hopkins* (2nd edn., with critical intro. by Charles Williams, 1930, p. 60).
11 Perry Miller and T. H. Johnson, *The Puritans* (New York, 1938), p. 374.

human will, it left much to be desired as a medium for common worship. It had few responses for the people who became (except for the metrical Psalms they sang) attuned to the tyranny of the single ministerial voice. As we have seen, it had virtually no place for the offering by the people of their weekly work and witness. It lacked the radiant joy of discipleship, and expressed rather the desperate seriousness of duty. Puritanism is a resistance movement, and its worship provided the iron-rations. It was not a religion or a form of worship that would flourish, except in times of danger.

4. Complementarity

In the last analysis, Catholic styles of worship (whether Roman or Anglican) provide order, unity, dignity, historical continuity and popular participation, and they resemble the etiquette of a court and are appropriate for large traditional assemblies. The Puritan and Quaker styles of worship are rather an informal domestic gathering of Christian households of faith valuing sincerity, simplicity, spontaneity, and friendliness, as well as humility. Roman Catholics and Anglicans run the risk of formalism and hypocrisy; Puritans and Quakers run the risks of anarchy and subjectivity, especially when Scripture no longer speaks with unchallenged authority as it did in the middle seventeenth century before the advent of deism. Possibly even more significant for an age of increasing secularity is the fact that Puritan and Quaker modes of worship with their flexibility, experimental nature, and simplicity are able to operate in turbulent and uncertain times as expressions of a spiritual resistance movement. This may be their distinctive contribution to the history of worship.

In normal times, however, worshippers need a form of cultus which transmits the great tradition in the way that liturgies do, provided they also leave room for the contemporary expression of devotion. A genuine sense of the creativity of variety in worship might result in a lessened desire for competitiveness and a greater longing for complementarity. Just as one might hope for the inclusion of many present denominations as "religious orders" under the overarching aegis of One Holy, Catholic and Apostolic church, so one also might wish to see the creation of a liturgy comprehensive enough to include a place for free prayer and for silent prayer. Such a view was beyond the gaze of even so ecumenical a theologian and pastor as that self-styled "meer Catholick," Richard

Baxter. It may even be beyond the possibility of general acceptance in the late twentieth century.

It is worth recalling that those members whom we in this age would have elected to the *communio sanctorum*, Lancelot Andrewes, John Donne, Jeremy Taylor, Augustine Baker, the Benedictine, George Fox, the Baptist, John Bunyan, and the Puritan, Richard Baxter, would have found it impossible to worship together, for Roman Catholics, Anglicans, Puritans, Baptists, and Quakers unchurched one another at the least provocation. It may be, therefore, more realistic to recognise that pluralism in worship is likely to remain with us for many years. It might even have the advantage of giving a wider set of options to the people of God and lead to greater creativity in the attempt to produce a worthier worship.

BIBLIOGRAPHY

1. Liturgical Texts
2. Manuscripts
3. Periodicals and Publications
4. Sources in English Literature
5. Books

1. SELECTED LITURGICAL TEXTS

(Arranged Chronologically by Denomination)

ANGLICAN

Grisbrooke, W. Jardine. *Anglican Liturgies of the Seventeenth and Eighteenth Centuries.* Alcuin Club Collections, No. XL, 1958. This contains the so-called Laudian or Scottish Liturgy of 1637, the major liturgies of the Non-Jurors, and the liturgical compilation of Jeremy Taylor, *A Collection of Offices,* but in each case it is limited to the Order for Holy Communion. The latter is also to be found in Jeremy Taylor's *Works,* Ed. R. Heber. 15 Vols. 1822. XV, pp. 237-389.

Sanderson's *A Liturgy in Time of Rebellion,* an adaptation of the Prayer Book rite, can be found in *Fragmentary Illustrations of the History of the Book of Common Prayer.* Ed. W. K. Jacobson. 1874. Pp. 1-40.

Cuming, G. J., *The Durham Book, Being the First Draft of the Revision of the Book of Common Prayer in 1661.* Oxford, 1961.

The Book of Common Prayer. 1662.

Legg, J. Wickham, ed. *English Orders for Consecrating Churches in the Seventeenth Century.* Henry Bradshaw Society, Vol. XLI, 1911.

PURITAN AND REFORMED

John Knox's Genevan Service Book, 1556. Ed. William D. Maxwell. Edinburgh, 1931.

The Book of Common Order. Eds. G. W. Sprott and J. Leishman. Edinburgh, 1868.

A Booke of the Forme of Common Prayers, Administration of the Sacraments, &c. agreable to Gods Worde, and the Use of the Reformed Churches. Published in 1584 and 1586, respectively, as the Waldegrave and Middelburg Puritan liturgies; reprinted, *Fragmenta Liturgica.* Ed. Peter Hall. Vol. 1. Bath, 1848; and *Reliquiae Liturgicae.* Vol. 1. Bath, 1847.

The Parliamentary Directory, originally entitled, *A Directory for Publique Worship in the Three Kingdoms* (1644), issued by the dominantly Presbyterian Westminster Assembly of Divines. *Reliquiae Liturgicae,* reprinted; ed. Peter Hall. Vol. III. Bath, 1847. Also *The Westminster Directory.* Ed. T. Leishman. Edinburgh and London, 1901.

A Supply of Prayer for the Ships that want Ministers to pray with them agreeable to the Directory established by Parliament, published by authority. 1645.

Richard Baxter's *The Reformation of the Liturgy* (1661), sometimes known as the *Reformed Liturgy* or the *Savoy Liturgy* (the latter because it was prepared with the approval of the Presbyterian ministers for submission to the Anglicans, both parties meeting in the Savoy, an attempt at a possible comprehensive liturgy in 1661). *Reliquiae Liturgicae.* Ed. Peter Hall. Vol. IV. Bath, 1847.

BIBLIOGRAPHY

ROMAN CATHOLIC

Sacra Institutio Baptizandi, Matrimonium Celebrandi, Infirmos Ungendi, Mortuos Sepelandi, ac alii nonnulli ritus ecclesiastici juxta usum insignis Ecclesiae Sarisburiensis. Douai, 1604.
Missae aliquot pro sacerdotibus itinerantibus in Anglia, Ex Missale Romano reformata. St. Omer, English College Press. 1615.
Missale parvum pro sacerdotibus in Anglia itinerantibus, Ordo etiam baptizandi & rituale . . . extractus. 1623.
Missale parvum pro sacerdotibus in Anglia, Scotia, & Ibernia itinerantibus. 1626.

2. MANUSCRIPTS

In the Ampleforth Abbey Library: Inscription on blank leaf of an Antwerp Missal owned by the Middleton family.
In the Bodleian Library, Oxford: Rawlinson Ms. A. 441. f. 28; Rawlinson Ms. D. 85. f. 198; Tanner Ms. 59. II. 560 (transcript).
In the Dr. Williams's Library, London: Baxter Ms. 360. f. 71; Harleian Ms. 3795. f. 23.
In the Dr. Williams's Library, London: Baxter Ms. 3. 156; Baxter Ms. 5. 9; A Parte of a Register.
In the Edinburgh University Library: Ms. of Robert Kirk's Commonplace Book.

3. PERIODICALS AND PUBLICATIONS

DENOMINATIONAL

ANGLICAN
Theology

BAPTIST
The Baptist Quarterly
Transactions of the Baptist Historical Society

CONGREGATIONALIST (INDEPENDENT)
The Congregational Quarterly
Transactions of the Congregational Historical Society

QUAKER (FRIENDS)
Journal of the Friends' Historical Society

ROMAN CATHOLICS
The Downside Review (Benedictine Abbey of Downside, near Bath, England)
The Month (London)
Recusant History
Worship (The Benedictine Abbey and University, St. John's, Collegeville, Minnesota, U.S.A.)

540

UNITARIAN
Transactions of the Unitarian Historical History

INTERDENOMINATIONAL
Church History (published by the American Society of Church History, Chicago)
Journal of Ecclesiastical History (London)
Journal of Theological Studies (Oxford)
Studia Liturgica (Rotterdam, Holland)

SECULAR
Devonshire Association Transactions
History
The Library
The Listener
The Manchester Quarterly
Proceedings of the British Academy
Transactions of the Royal Historical Society

4. SOURCES IN ENGLISH LITERATURE

Since this is the Golden Century of the English Pulpit, considerable use was made of the sermons of Lancelot Andrewes, John Donne, and Jeremy Taylor, distinguished as literature as well as sacred oratory. It so happens that the greatest poets of the seventeenth century were also men of religion. The poetry they wrote is therefore invaluable as an index of their spirituality. For this reason much use was made of the sacred poetry of John Donne, George Herbert, Richard Crashaw, Henry Vaughan, and Thomas Traherne, and occasional use of John Milton's poetry and prose. Dekker, Davenant, Herrick, Marvell, and Dryden were also cited but only incidentally. Reference was also made to Bunyan's *Pilgrim's Progress* as well as to his autobiography, *Grace Abounding*.

Invaluable contributions to the period were made by those vivid and distinguished diarists, Samuel Pepys and John Evelyn, and by a minor figure, Ralph Josselin.

The *Lives* of leading Caroline divines by Izaak Walton were also important.

From other periods use was made of an Addison essay from the *Spectator*, Sir Walter Scott's novel, *Woodstock*, and Gerard Manley Hopkins's poems.

5. BOOKS

(Except where otherwise indicated, all books were published in London)

Adams, Thomas. *Works*. Folio edn., 1630.
Adams, William Seth. "William Palmer of Worcester, 1803-1885, the only learned man among them." Ph.D. Princeton University, 1973.

Addison, W. *The English Country Parson.* 1948.

Addleshaw, G.W.O. *The High Church Tradition: A Study in the Liturgical Thought of the Seventeenth Century.* Alcuin Club, 1963.

Addleshaw, G.W.O. and Frederick Etchells. *The Architectural Setting of Anglican Worship.* 1948.

A Kempis, Thomas. *Imitation of Christ.* Tr. Thomas Rogers, 1580.

————. *The sole-talke of the Soule.* . . . A trans. of *Soliloquium Animae* by Thomas Rogers, 1580.

Alexander, H. G. *Religion in England, 1558-1662.* 1968.

Alleine, Joseph. *Christian Letters full of Spirituall Instructions, tending to the Promotion of the Power of Godliness, both in Persons and Families.* 1672.

Alleine, Theodosia. *The Life and Death of Mr. Joseph Alleine, Late Teacher of the Church at Taunton, in Somersetshire, Assistant to Mr. Newton.* 1672.

Allison, A. F. and D. M. Rogers. *A Catalogue of Catholic Books in English printed abroad or secretly in England 1558-1640.* Bognor Regis, 1956.

Allison, C. F. *The Rise of Moralism; The Proclamation of the Gospel from Hooker to Baxter.* New York, 1966.

Ames, William. *The Marrow of Theology.* Tr. and intro. by J. D. Eusden. Boston and Philadelphia, 1968.

Andrewes, Lancelot. *A Manual of the Private Devotions and Meditations of the Right Reverend Father in God, Lancelot Andrewes.* Tr. R. Drake, 1648.

————. *Ninety-Six Sermons.* 5 Vols. Oxford, 1841-1843.

————. *A Pattern of Catechistical Doctrine and other Minor Works.* Oxford, 1843.

————. *Preces Privatae.* Ed. F. E. Brightman. 1903.

————. *Works.* Eds. J. P. Wilson and J. Bliss in Library of Anglo-Catholic Theology. 11 Vols. Oxford, 1841-1854.

Andrews, Nicholas. *The First Century of Scandalous Malignant Priests.* 1643.

Annesley, Samuel, ed. *A Continuation of Morning Exercise Sermons.* 1683.

[Anon.]. *The Arminian Nunnery, or, A Brief Description and Relation of the late Erected Monasticall Place called the Arminian Nunnery at Little Gidding in Huntingdonshire.* 1641.

————. *A Collection of Prayers and Thanksgivings used in His Majesties Chappell and in His Armies.* Oxford, 1643.

————. *A Dialogue between Mr. Prejudice . . . and Mr. Reason, a Student in the University.* 1682.

————. *Eikon Basilike, the Portraiture of His Sacred Majesty in His Solitudes and Sufferings.* 1648.

————. *A Free and Impartial Inquiry into the causes of that very great Esteem and Honour that the Nonconforming Preachers are generally in with their followers.* 1673.

————. *From What has been, may be again, or an instance of London's Loyalty in 1640, Etc.* 1710.

542

————. *A Manuall of prayers newly gathered out of many and famous divers authors as well aūcient as of the tyme present.* [Rouen], 1583.

————. *A New View of London.* 2 Vols. 1708.

————. *The Presbyterian Pater Noster.* A broadsheet of 1681.

————. *A Survey of the Book of Common Prayer.* 1606.

————. *Two Prayers, One for the Safety of His Majesties Person; The Other For the Preservation of this University and City of Oxford to be used in all Churches and Chappels.* Oxford, 1644.

————. *The Whole Duty of Man, laid down in a plain and familiar way for the use of all, but especially the meanest reader; divided into seventeen chapters, one whereof being read every Lord's Day, the whole may be read over thrice in the year; necessary for all families. With private devotions for several occasions.* 1692.

————. *The Whole Duty of Prayer containing devotions for every day of the week, and for several occasions ordinary and extraordinary.* . . . 1692.

Anstruther, Godfrey. *Vaux of Harrowden, A Recusant Family.* Newport, Monmouthshire, 1953.

Archer, John. *The Personal Reigne of Christ upon Earth, in a treatise wherein is fully and largely laid open and proved, that Jesus Christ, together with the Saints, shall visibly possesse a Monarchicall State and Kingdome in this World.* 1642.

Arderne, James. *Directions Concerning the Matter and Stile of Sermons.* 1671. Reissued, ed. John Mackay. Oxford, 1952.

Aubrey, John. *Brief Lives.* Ed. Andrew Clark. 1898.

[Augustine, Saint, of Hippo]. *S. Austin's Rule . . . together with the Constitutions of the English Canonesse regulars of our B. Ladyes of Sion in Paris.* Ed. and Tr. Miles Pinkney. 1636.

Aveling, Hugh. *The Catholic Recusants of the West Riding of Yorkshire, 1558-1790.* Leeds, 1963.

Babbage, Stuart Barton. *Puritanism and Richard Bancroft.* 1962.

[Baillie, Robert]. *A Dissuasive from the Errours of the Time.* . . . 1646.

————. *The Letters and Journals of Robert Baillie.* Ed. David Laing. 3 Vols. Edinburgh, 1841.

[Baker, Augustine]. *Augustine Baker's The Inner Life of Dame Gertrude More.* Ed. Benedict Weld. Blundell, 1911.

————. *Memorials of Father Augustine Baker and other Documents relating to the English Benedictines.* Eds. J. McCann and [R.] H. Connolly. Catholic Record Society. Vol. 33. 1933.

————. *Sancta Sophia, or Directions for the Prayer of Contemplation . . . Extracted out of more than Forty Treatises written by Augustine Baker. And Methodically digested by . . . Serenus Cressy.* Douai, 1657.

Ball, Frank E. "A Liturgical Colloquy: An Examination of the Savoy Conference, 1661." B. Litt. Oxford University, 1958.

Bampfield, Francis. *A name, an after-one, or* Ὄνομα καινοῦ, *a name, a new one, in the latter-day glory.* 1681.

BIBLIOGRAPHY

Barbour, Hugh. *The Quakers in Puritan England*. New Haven, Conn., 1964.

Barclay, Alexander. *The Protestant Doctrine of the Lord's Supper*. 1927.

Barclay, Robert. *The Inner Life of the Religious Societies of the Commonwealth*. 3rd edn., 1879.

Barclay, Robert [Quaker apologist]. *Apology for the True Christian Divinity*. 1678.

Barnard, John. *A Short View of the Prelatical Church of England*. 1641. Reissued 1661.

————. *First Booke of Selected Church Musick*. . . . 1641.

Barrow, Isaac. *Works*. Ed. J. Tillotson. 4 Vols. 1683-1687.

Barrowe, Henry. *A Brief Discoverie of the False Church*. Dordrecht, 1590-1591.

Barry, A., ed. *Masters of English Theology*. 1877.

Baruzi, Jean. *Saint Jean de la Croix et le problème de l'expérience*. Paris, 1924.

Bates, William. *Harmony of the Divine Attributes*. 1674.

Bauthumley, Jacob. *The Light and Dark Side of God*. 1650.

Baxter, Richard. *An Apology for the Nonconformists' Ministry*. 1681.

[Baxter, R.]. *Autobiography of Richard Baxter*. Ed. J. M. Lloyd Thomas. Everyman Library, 1931.

Baxter, R. *Call to the Unconverted*. 1658.

————. *Catholic Communion Defended against both Extreams*. 1684.

————. *A Christian Directory, a Summe of Practical Theologie and Cases of Conscience*. 1673.

————. *Five Disputations of Church Government and Worship*. 1659.

————. *Now or Never*. 1671.

————. *Poetical Fragments*. 1683.

[Baxter, R.]. *The Practical Works of the Rev. Richard Baxter*. Ed. William Orme. 23 Vols. 1830.

Baxter, R. *The Reformed Pastor*. Edn. of 1860.

[Baxter, R.]. *Reliquiae Baxterianae*. Ed. M. Sylvester. 1696.

————. *The Safe Religion*. 1657.

Baxter, R. *The Saints Everlasting Rest*. 3rd edn., 1652.

————. *A Third Defence of the Cause of Peace*. 1681.

[Bayly, Lewis]. *The Practice of Piety, Directing a Christian how to walk with God*. 1612.

Bayne, Peter, ed. *Puritan Documents*. . . . 1862.

Bede, John. *The Right and Prerogative of Kings, Against Cardinal Bellarmine and other Jesuits*. 1612.

Bellarmine, Robert. *An ample declaration of the Christian Doctrine*. English trans., 1604.

————. *Short Catechisme of Cardinall Bellarmine illustrated with Images*. 1614.

Benson, Louis F. *The English Hymn: Its Development & Use in Worship*. New York, 1915. Reprinted Richmond, Va., 1962.

[Bernard, John]. *The Anatomie of the Service Book*. 1641.

544

BIBLIOGRAPHY

Bernard, St. of Clairvaux. *The Golden Treatise, Joy in Tribulation, and the forme of an honest life.* 1613.

——. *A Hive of Sacred Honie—Combes Containing most Sweet and Heavenly Counsel.* [Douai], 1631.

[Bernard, St. of Clairvaux]. *St. Bernard His Meditations: or Sighes, Sobbes and Teares, upon our Saviour's Passion. . . .* Ed. and Tr. "W.P.," ca. 1610.

Besse, Joseph. *A Collection of the Sufferings of the People called Quakers.* 2 Vols. 1753.

Besse, Thomas. *A Rationale on Cathedral Worship.* 1720.

Bethell, Samuel L. *The Cultural Revolution of the Seventeenth Century.* 1951.

Betjeman, John. *First and Last Loves.* 1952.

Beveridge, William. *A Sermon on the Excellency and Usefulness of the Book of Common Prayer.* 1682.

[Beveridge, William]. *Works.* Ed. J. Bliss. 12 Vols. 1843-1848.

Biéler, André. *Architecture in Worship.* Edinburgh and London, 1965.

Blackstone, B. *The Ferrar Papers.* 1938.

Blanfield, R. *A History of Renaissance Architecture in England, 1500-1800.* 2 Vols. 1897.

Blunt, J. H. *Annotated Book of Common Prayer.* 1866.

Bolton, Robert. *Certain Devout Prayers of Mr. Bolton. . . .* 1638.

——. *Some Generall Directions for a Comfortable Walking With God.* 1625.

Bosher, R. S. *The Making of the Restoration Settlement.* New York, 1951.

Bourne, E.C.E. *The Anglicanism of William Laud.* 1947.

Bouyer, Louis. *Orthodox Spirituality and Anglican Spirituality.* Tr. Barbara Wall. 1969.

Bownde, Nicholas. *The doctrine of the Sabbath, plainely layde forth, and sundly proved.* 1595.

Boyes, John. *An Exposition of the Dominical Epistles and Gospels used in our English Liturgy throughout the whole yeare.* 1609.

Boyle, Robert. *The Excellency of Theology Compared with Natural Philosophy.* 1673.

Braithwaite, W. C. *The Beginnings of Quakerism.* 2nd edn. Cambridge, 1955.

——. *The Second Period of Quakerism.* Ed. H. J. Cadbury. 2nd edn. Cambridge, 1961.

Bramhall, John. *Works.* Ed. A. W. Haddam in Library of Anglo-Catholic Theology. 5 Vols. Oxford, 1842-1845.

Brémond, Henri. *Histoire littéraire du Sentiment Religieux en France.* 11 Vols. Paris, 1915-1932.

Briggs, Martin S. *Puritan Architecture and its Future.* 1946.

——. *Wren the Incomparable.* 1953.

Brightman, F. E. *The English Rite, a Synopsis of the Sources and Revisions of the Book of Common Prayer.* 2 Vols. 1915.

Brinton, Howard H. *Creative Worship.* Swarthmore Lecture. 1931.

Brinton, Howard H. *Friends for 300 Years*. New York, 1953.

Brockett, Allen. *Nonconformity in Exeter, 1650-1875*. Manchester, 1962.

Browne, Robert. *A Booke which sheweth the life and manners of all true Christians*. Middelburg, 1582.

——. *A True and Short Declaration*. . . . 1583.

——. *The Writings of Robert Harrison and Robert Browne*. Eds. A. Peel and L. H. Carlson. 1953.

Bruggink, J. and Carl H. Droppers. *Christ and Architecture: Building Presbyterian/Reformed Churches*. Grand Rapids, Mich., 1965.

Buck, Fellowes, Ramsbotham and Warner, eds. *Tudor Church Music:* Vol. IV: *Orlando Gibbons*. 1925.

Bukofzer, Manfred. *Music in the Baroque Era, from Monteverdi to Bach*. New York, 1947.

Bull, George. *The Corruptions of the Church of Rome*. 1705.

——. *Works*. Ed. E. Burton. 6 Vols. Oxford, 1827.

Bunyan, John. *Grace Abounding to the Chief of Sinners*. 1666.

——. *The Holy War*. 1682.

——. *Pilgrim's Progress*. 1678.

——. *The Whole Works*. Ed. George Offor. 3 Vols. Glasgow, 1862.

Burnet, Gilbert. *Discourse of Pastoral Care*. 1692.

——. *History of My Own Time*. 2 Vols. 1723-1724. Republished. 6 Vols. Oxford, 1833.

——. *The Life and Death of Sir Matthew Hale*. 1682.

Burrage, Champlin. *The Church Covenant Idea*. Philadelphia, 1904.

——. *The early English Dissenters in the light of recent research, 1550-1641*. 2 Vols. Cambridge, 1912.

Burroughes, Jeremiah. *Gospel-Worship or the Right Manner of Sanctifying the name of God in generall*. 1648.

Burton, E. H. *The Life and Times of Bishop Challoner*. 2 Vols. 1909.

[Burton, Henry]. *A Divine Tragedy Lately Enacted*. Amsterdam, 1636.

——. *A Tryall of Private Devotion, or a Diall for the Houres of Prayer*. 1628.

Bury, A. *The Constant Communicant, a Diatribe proving that Constancy in Receiving the Lord's Supper is the Indispensable Duty*. Oxford, 1681.

Byfield, Richard. *The Doctrine of the Sabbath Vindicated*. 1631.

Calamy, Edmund. *Continuation of the Ejected Ministers*. 2 Vols. 1727.

——. *Historical Account of my Own Life*. Ed. J. T. Rutt. 2 Vols. 1829.

Calder, I. M. *Activities of the Puritan Faction of the Church of England, 1625-1633*. 1957.

Capp, B. S. *The Fifth Monarchy Men*. 1972.

Caraman, Philip. *Henry Morse: Priest of the Plague*. 1957.

Cardwell, E. *Documentary Annals of the Reformed Church of England, 1546-1716*. 2 Vols. Oxford, 1844.

——. *A History of Conferences and other Proceedings*. Oxford, 1841.

————. *Synodalia.* 2 Vols. Oxford, 1842.

Carpenter, E. *The Life and Times of Thomas Tenison, Archbishop of Canterbury.* 1948.

Carpenter, S. C. *The Church in England, 597-1688.* 1954.

Carritt, E. F. *A Calendar of British Taste, From 1600 to 1800.* 1948.

Carruthers, S. W. *The Everyday Work of the Westminster Assembly.* Philadelphia, 1943.

Carter, T. T. *Nicholas Ferrar, his Household and his Friends.* 1892.

Cartwright, Thomas. *A Treatise of the Christian Religion, Or, The Whole Bodie and Substance of Divinitie.* 1616.

Cary, Lucius (Lord Falkland). *The Discourse; The Answer; and The Reply.* Published in one vol. 1651.

Cawdrey, Robert. *A Treasurie or Store-House of Similies.* 1600.

Chamberlain, R. *Conceits, Clinches, Flashes and Whimsies newly studied.* 1639.

Chambers, Sabine. *The Garden of our B. Lady. Or a devout manner, how to serve her in her Rosary.* [St. Omer?], 1619.

Charnock, S. *Complete Works.* 5 Vols. Edinburgh, 1864-1866.

Chillingworth, William. *The Religion of Protestants, a Safe Way of Salvation.* 1637.

Chute, Marchette. *Two Gentle Men: The Lives of George Herbert and Robert Herrick.* New York, 1959.

Clagett, William. *An Answer to the Dissenters Objections against the Common Prayers and some other parts of Divine-Service prescribed in the Liturgie of the Church of England.* 1683.

Clarendon, Earl of. (See Hyde, E., 1st Earl of Clarendon.)

Clark, George N. *The Later Stuarts, 1660-1714.* Oxford, 1934. 2nd edn., 1955.

————. *The Seventeenth Century.* Oxford, 1929. 2nd edn., 1947.

Clark, Henry W. *History of English Nonconformity.* 2 Vols. 1911.

Clarke, Samuel. *A Collection of the Lives of Ten Eminent Divines.* 1661.

Clay, W. K., ed. *Liturgies and Occasional Forms of Prayer set forth in the Reign of Queen Elizabeth.* Cambridge: Parker Society, 1851.

Clifford, James. *Divine Services and Anthems.* 1663.

Cobb, Gerald. *The Old Churches of London.* 1942.

Cocceius, Johannes. *Summa doctrinae de Foedere et Testamento Dei.* 1648.

Cocks, H. F. Lovell. *The Religious Life of Oliver Cromwell.* 1960.

Coleridge, J. T. *Memoir of John Keble.* Oxford, 1870.

Collier, Jeremy. *An Ecclesiastical History of Great Britain.* 1708.

Collinson, Patrick. *The Elizabethan Puritan Movement.* Berkeley, Calif., 1967.

[Comber, Thomas]. *The Autobiography and Letters of Thomas Comber.* Ed. C. E. Whiting. Vols. CLVI-CLVII. Surtees Society, 1941-1942.

Comber, Thomas. *A Companion to the Altar.* 4th edn., 1685.

————. *A Companion to the Temple.* 7 Vols. 1672. Reissued Oxford, 1841.

Comber, Thomas. *A Discourse Concerning the daily frequenting the Common Prayer.* 1687.

Connolly, R. H. and Justin McCann, eds. *Memorials of Father Baker.* Vol. XXXIII. Catholic Record Society, 1933.

Coomer, Duncan. *English Dissent.* 1947.

[Cosin, John]. *A Collection of Private Devotions in the practise of the Antient Church, called, The Hours of Prayers.* 1627. Reissued; ed. P. G. Stanwood, Oxford, 1967.

————. *The Correspondence of John Cosin, Lord Bishop of Durham.* Vols. LII and LV. Surtees Society, 1869, 1872.

————. *Historia Transubstantiationis Papalis.* 1675.

————. *Works.* Ed. G. Ornsby. 5 Vols. Library of Anglo-Catholic Theology, Oxford, 1843-1855.

Cotton, John. *The Keyes of the Kingdome of Heaven.* 1644.

————. *A Modest and Cleare Answer to Mr. Balls Discourse of set formes of Prayer.* 1642.

————. *The Way of the Churches of Christ in New England.* 1645.

Cox, Harvey. *The Feast of Fools.* Cambridge, Mass., 1969.

Cragg, Gerald R. *The Church and the Age of Reason, 1648-1789.* 1960.

————. *From Puritanism to the Age of Reason.* Cambridge, 1950.

————. *Puritanism in the Period of the Great Persecution.* Cambridge, 1957.

Crashaw, Richard. *Poems* in *Complete Works.* Ed. A. B. Grosart. 2 Vols. 1872-1873.

Crashaw, William. *The Complaint or Dialogue Betwixt the Soul and the Bodie of a damned man.* 1632.

[Cromwell, Oliver]. *The Letters and Speeches of Oliver Cromwell.* Ed. Thomas Carlyle. 2 Vols. 1845.

Crosby, T. *The History of the English Baptists.* 4 Vols. 1738-1740.

Cross, F. L., ed. *The Oxford Dictionary of the Christian Church.* Corrected impression of 1963.

Crouch, William. *Posthuma Christiana.* Edn. of 1712.

Cudworth, Ralph. *The Works of Ralph Cudworth.* Ed. T. Birch. 4 Vols. Oxford, 1829.

Cuming, G. J., ed. *The Durham Book, Being the First Draft of the Revision of the Book of Common Prayer in 1661.* Oxford, 1961.

————. *A History of Anglican Liturgy.* 1969.

Curnock, Nehemiah, ed. *The Journal of John Wesley.* 8 Vols. 1909.

Curwen, Spencer. *Studies in Music and Worship.* 5 Vols. 1880-1885.

Danvers, H. *Theopolis.* 1672.

Davenant, William. *Gondibert.* 1650.

Davies, Godfrey. *The Early Stuarts, 1603-1660.* 2nd edn. Oxford, 1959.

Davies, Horton. *The Worship of the English Puritans.* 1948.

————. *From Cranmer to Hooker, 1534-1603, From Watts and Wesley to Maurice, 1690-1850, From Newman to Martineau, 1850-*

BIBLIOGRAPHY

1900, The Ecumenical Century, 1900-1965. Worship and Theology in England. Vols. 1, 3-5. Princeton, 1961-1970.
Davies, J. Gordon, ed. *A Dictionary of Liturgy and Worship.* 1972.
Dearnley, Christopher. *English Church Music 1650-1750 in Royal Chapel, Cathedral and Parish Church.* 1970.
Dekker, Thomas. *The Shoemaker's Holiday.* 1599.
Denne, Henry. *The drag-net of the Kingdome of Heaven.* Republished as Part III of *Anti-Christ unmasked* in three treatises, 1646.
Dent, Arthur. *The Plaine Man's Path-way to Heaven.* 1601.
―――. *Sermon of Repentance.* 1637.
Dewey, Meredith, Ratcliff, and Sykes. *The Anglican Tradition.* Sermons delivered in Chichester Cathedral, July 1958.
Dexter, H. M. *The Congregationalism of the Last Three Hundred Years.* 1880.
Dix, Gregory. *The Shape of the Liturgy.* 1945.
Dod, John. *A briefe dialogue concerning preparation for the Lord's Supper.* 1627.
Donaldson, Gordon. *The Making of the Scottish Prayer Book of 1637.* Edinburgh, 1954.
Donne, John. *The Divine Poems.* Ed. Helen Gardner. 1952.
―――. *The Sermons of John Donne.* Eds. George R. Potter and Evelyn M. Simpson. 10 Vols. Berkeley and Los Angeles, Calif., 1953-1962.
[Doughty, John]. Phil-Iren-Alethius, I. D., pseud. *Velitationes Polemicae or Polemicall short Discussions of certain particular and select Questions.* 1651.
Dowden, Edward. *Puritan and Anglican: Studies in Literature.* 1900.
Downame, John. *The Christian Warfare.* 1604.
―――. *Guide to Godliness.* 1622.
[Dowsing, William]. *The Journal of William Dowsing.* Ed. A. C. Moule. Cambridge, 1926.
―――. *Journal of William Dowsing.* Ed. E. H. Evelyn White. 1885.
Drummond, A. L. *The Church Architecture of Protestantism.* Edinburgh, 1934.
Drysdale, A. H. *History of the Presbyterians in England, their Rise, Decline and Revival.* 1889.
Dugmore, C. W. *Eucharistic Doctrine in England from Hooker to Waterland.* 1942.
―――― and Charles Duggan, eds. *Studies in Church History.* Vol. I. 1964.
Duppa, Bryan. *Private Formes of Prayer.* 1645.

Eachard, John. *Grounds and Occasions of the Contempt of the Clergy.* 1671.
Edwards, Thomas. *Gangraena.* 1646.
Elborow, T. *An Exposition of the Book of Common Prayer.* 1663.
Eliot, T. S. *For Lancelot Andrewes, Essays on Style and Order.* 1928.
Emerson, Everett H., ed. *English Puritanism from John Hooper to John Milton.* Durham, N.C., 1968.

549

Eusden, John D., ed. *The Marrow of Theology, William Ames, 1576-1663.* Boston and Philadelphia, 1968.

Evelyn, John. *Devotionarie Book.* Intro. W. H. Frere. 1936.

———. *Diary.* Ed. E. S. de Beer. 6 Vols. Oxford, 1955.

Evennett, H. O. *The Spirit of the Counter-Reformation.* 1963.

Every, George. *The High Church Party, 1688-1718.* 1956.

Fallow, T. M. and H. B. McCall. *Yorkshire Church Plate.* Leeds, 1912.

Farnworth, Richard. *Christian Religious Meetings.* 1664.

Fellowes, E. H. *English Cathedral Music.* 5th edn. Ed. J. A. Westrup. 1969.

Field, Richard. *Of the Church.* 1606. Reissued in 4 Vols. 1847-1852.

Firth, Charles H. *The Last Days of the Protectorate.* 2 Vols. 1909.

Fisher, Samuel. *The Testimony of Truth Exalted.* 1679.

FitzSimon, Henry. *The Iustification and Exposition of the Divine Sacrifice of the Masse and of al Rites and Ceremonies.* 1611. Reprinted Menstone, Yorkshire, 1972.

Flecknoe, R. *Enigmatical Characters.* 1665.

[Flinton, George]. *A Manuall of prayers newly gathered out of many and famous divers authors as well auncient as of the tyme present.* [Rouen ?], 1583.

Floyd, John. *A Plea for the Reall-Presence.* 1624.

Foley, Henry. *Records of the English Province of the Society of Jesus.* 7 Vols. in 8. 1875-1883.

Fox, George. *Journal.* Ed. N. Penney. 1902.

———. *The journal of George Fox.* Revised; ed. J. L. Nickalls. Cambridge, 1952.

Fox, George and Hubberthorne, Richard. *Truths Defence against the Serpent.* 1658.

Francis, St., of Assisi. *The rule and testament of the seraphical father S. Francis.* Tr. Richard Mason. Douai, 1635.

———. *The rule of the religious of the third order of Saint Francis . . . living together in communitie and cloyster.* Tr. Arthur Bell. Brussels, 1624.

Frankel, P. *Gothic Architecture: Literary sources and interpretations through eight centuries.* Princeton, N.J., 1960.

Frere, W. H. and C. E. Douglas. *Puritan Manifestoes.* 1907. Ed. N. Sykes. 2nd edn., 1954.

Frost, Maurice. *English and Scottish Psalm and Hymn Tunes c. 1543-1677.* 1953.

———. *Historical Companion to Hymns Ancient and Modern.* Rev. edn. of Frere's "Historical Edition," 1962.

[Fuller, Robert]. *Missale Romanum Vindicatum, or the Mass Vindicated from D. Daniel Brevent's calumnious and scandalous Tract.* 1674.

Fuller, Thomas. *The Church History of Britain.* Ed. J. S. Brewer. 6 Vols. Oxford, 1845.

———. *The Worthies of England.* Ed. J. Freeman. 1952.

Fürst, V. *The Architecture of Sir Christopher Wren.* 1956.

BIBLIOGRAPHY

Gardiner, S. R. *The Constitutional Documents of the Puritan Revolution.* 1889.
————. *The Personal Government of Charles I, 1628-1637.* 1877.
Garey, Samuel. *Great Britaine's litle Calendar or triple Diary in remembrance of three dayes, viz. the 24 of March the day of his Maiesties proclamation, The fift of August the day of Gowries Conspiracy; The fift of November the day of our deliverance from the Gun powder treason, whereunto is annexed, a short dissuasive from Popery.* 1618.
Gataker, Thomas. *A Discussion of the Papist Doctrine of Transubstantiation.* 1624.
Gauden, J. *Considerations touching the Liturgy of the Church of England.* 1661.
————. *Ecclesiae Anglicanae Suspiria, the Tears, Sighs, Complaints and Prayers of the Church of England, setting forth her former Constitution compared with her Present Condition.* 1659.
Gee, H. and W. J. Hardy. *Documents Illustrative of English Church History.* 1914.
Gee, John. *The Foot out of the Snare.* . . . 1624.
George, Katherine and Charles. *The Protestant Mind of the English Reformation.* Princeton, N.J., 1961.
[Gerard, John]. *The Autobiography of John Gerard, S.J.* Edn. 1881. Tr. Philip Caraman of edn. of 1951.
Geree, John. *The Character of an old English Puritane or Nonconformist.* 1646.
G. F. *The Liturgical Considerator Considered.* 1661.
[Gibbons, Orlando]. *Tudor Church Music, vol. IV: Orlando Gibbons.* Eds. P. C. Buck, E. H. Fellowes, A. Ramsbotham, and T. Warner. 1925.
Gilchrist, James. *Anglican Church Plate.* 1967.
Gill, Harry and E. L. Guilford. *The Rector's Book, Clayworth, Notts.* Nottingham, 1910.
Gillespie, George. *Dispute Against the English Popish Ceremonies.* 1660.
Glanvill, Joseph. *Essays on several important subjects in Philosophy and Religion.* 1676.
————. *Philosophia Pia.* 1671.
Goodwin, Thomas. *The Heart of Christ in Heaven towards Sinners on Earth.* 1651.
————. *Works.* Ed. J. Miller. 12 Vols. 1861-1866.
Gosse, Edmund. *The Life and Letters of John Donne.* 2 Vols. 1899.
Gotch, J. A. *Early Renaissance Architecture in England.* 2nd edn., 1914.
————. *Inigo Jones.* 1928.
Gouge, William. *Workes.* 1627.
Gough, John. *History of the people called Quakers.* 4 Vols. Dublin, 1789-1790.
Gould, G., ed. *Documents relating to the Settlement of the Church of England by the Act of Uniformity of 1662.* 1862.
Graeff, Hilda. *The Story of Mysticism.* 1966.

Granada, Luis de. *Libro de la Oracion.* 1553.

————. *A Memoriall of a Christian Life.* 1586.

————. *The Sinners Guide.* Tr. F. Meres. 1598.

Grantham, Thomas. *Christianismus Primitivus.* 1678.

[Granville, Denis]. *The Remains of Denis Granville.* Surtees Society. Vol. XLVII. 1865.

Greaves, Richard L. *John Bunyan.* Grand Rapids, Mich., 1969.

Green, V.H.H. *Religion at Oxford and Cambridge.* 1964.

Greenham, Richard. *A Treatise of the Sabbath.* 1592.

————. *Works.* 1601.

Grisbrooke, W. Jardine. *Anglican Liturgies of the Seventeenth and Eighteenth Centuries.* Alcuin Club Collections. No. XL. 1958.

[Grove, George]. *Grove's Dictionary of Music and Musicians.* Ed. E. Blom. 9 Vols. 5th edn., 1954.

Guilday, Peter. *The English Catholic refugees on the Continent, 1558-1795.* Vol. I: *The English Colleges and Convents in the Low Countries.* 1914.

Hagedorn, Maria. *Reformation und Spanische Andachsliteratur.* Leipzig, 1934.

Hageman, Howard. *Pulpit and Table.* London and Richmond, Va., 1962.

[Hales, John]. *The Golden Remains of the Ever Memorable Mr John Hales.* Ed. John Pearson. 1659.

Hall, Joseph. *The Arte of Divine Meditation.* 1606.

————. *Works.* Ed. Peter Hall. 1837.

Hall, Peter, ed. *Fragmenta Liturgica.* Vol. I: *Puritan.* Bath, 1847.

————, ed. *Reliquiae Liturgicae.* Vol. I: *Middleburgh*; Vol. III: *Directory* [Westminster]; Vol. IV: *Savoy* [Baxter's]. All published in Bath, 1848.

Haller, William. *Foxe's Book of Martyrs and the Elect Nation.* New York, 1963.

————. *Liberty and Reformation in the Puritan Revolution.* New York, 1955.

————. *The Rise of Puritanism, 1570-1643.* New York, 1938.

[Hammond, Henry]. *The Miscellaneous Theological Works of Henry Hammond.* Ed. N. Pocock in the Library of Anglo-Catholic Theology. 3 Vols. in 4. Oxford, 1847-1850.

————. *A Practical Catechism.* 1644, 1646, etc.

————. *A View of the New Directory and a Vindication of the Antient Liturgy of the Church of England.* 1645.

————. *Works.* Ed. William Fulman. 4 Vols. 1684-1689.

Hanbury, Benjamin. *Nonconformist Memorials.* 3 Vols. 1839-1844.

Happ, Howard. "Calendary Conflicts in Renaissance England." Ph.D., Princeton University, 1974.

Hardwick, William. *Gods Holy House and Service according to the primitive and most Christian forme thereof.* 1639.

Harley, John. *Music in Purcell's London.* 1968.

[Harrison, William]. *A Brief Discourse of the Christian Life and Death of Mistris Katherin Brettergh . . . who departed this world the last of May, 1601.* 1612.

Hart, A. Tindal. *The Country Clergy in Elizabethan and Stuart Times, 1558-1660.* 1958.

————. *The Man in the Pew, 1558-1660.* 1966.

Havran, Martin J. *The Catholics in Caroline England.* Palo Alto, Calif., 1962.

H.D.M.A. *A Sober and Temperate Discourse concerning the Interest of Words in Prayer.* 1661.

Heber, R., ed. *The Whole Works of Bishop Jeremy Taylor.* 15 Vols. 1822.

Henry, Matthew. *The Communicant's Companion.* 1704.

[Henry, Philip]. *Diaries and Letters of Philip Henry, M.A.* Ed. M. H. Lee. 1882.

Henson, H. Hensley. *Studies in English Religion in the XVII Century.* 1903.

[Herbert, George]. *The English Works of George Herbert.* Ed. G. H. Palmer. 3 Vols. Boston and New York, 1905.

————. *Herbert's Remains.* 1652.

————. *The Works of George Herbert.* Ed. F. E. Hutchinson. 2nd edn. Oxford, 1945.

Hetherington, W. M. *History of the Westminster Assembly of Divines.* 1843.

Heylyn, Peter. *Cyprianus Anglicus; History of the Life and Death of that most Reverend and Renowned Prelate William* [Laud]. 1668.

————. *Aerius Redivivus, or, the History of the Presbyterians.* 1670.

————. *Ecclesia Restaurata, the History of the Reformation of the Church of England.* 1661.

[Heywood, Oliver]. *The Reverend Oliver Heywood, His Autobiography, Diaries, Anecdote and Event Books.* Vols. I and II: Brighouse, 1882. Vol. III: Bingley, 1883.

————. *Works.* 2 Vols. Idle, Yorkshire, 1837.

Hickeringill, Edmund. *The Ceremony Monger.* 1689.

Higham, Florence. *Catholic and Reformed: a study of the Anglican Church, 1559-1662.* 1962.

————. *Lancelot Andrewes.* 1952.

Higham, John. *A Devout Exposition of the Holie Masse with an ample Declaration of all the Rites and Ceremonies belonging to the same.* Douai, 1614; enlarged edn., 1622.

Hill, Christopher. *The Century of Revolution, 1603-1714.* 1962.

————. *Economic Problems of the Church from Archbishop Whitgift to the Long Parliament.* Oxford, 1956.

————, ed. *The English Revolution; Three Essays.* New edn., 1949.

————. *Intellectual Origins of the English Revolution.* Oxford, 1965.

————. *Puritanism and Revolution; Studies in Interpretation.* 1958.

————. *The World Turned Upside Down.* 1972.

Hinchliff, Peter B. *The South African Liturgy.* Cape Town, 1959.

Holden, William P. *Anti-Puritan Satire, 1572-1642.* New Haven, Conn., 1954.

[Homilies]. *The* [Second] *Book of Homilies.* 1571.

Hooker, Richard. *The Ecclesiastical Polity and other Works of Richard Hooker.* Ed. Benjamin Hanbury. 3 Vols. 1830.

Horton, R. F. *John Howe.* 1894.

Howe, John. *The Living Temple.* Intro. T. Chalmers. 2nd edn. Glasgow, 1839.

————. *Works.* Ed. J. Hunt. 8 Vols. 1810-1822.

Howell, W. S. *Logic and Rhetoric in England, 1500-1700.* Princeton, N.J., 1956.

Howgill, Francis. *Mistery Babylon the Mother of Harlots discovered . . . in answer to a Book tituled the Directory for the Publick Worship of God.* 1659.

Hügel, Baron Friedrich Von. *Selected Letters, 1896-1924.* Ed. Bernard Holland. 1927.

Hughes, H. T. *The Piety of Jeremy Taylor.* 1960.

Hughes, Philip. *Rome and the Counter-Reformation in England.* 1944.

Hutchinson, F. E., ed. *The Works of George Herbert.* Oxford, 1941.

Hutchinson, Lucy. *Memoirs of the Life of Colonel Hutchinson.* Ed. C. H. Firth. 1906.

Hyde, A. G. *George Herbert and His Times.* 1906.

Hyde, E. 1st Earl of Clarendon. *Calendar of the Clarendon State Papers.* Ed. O. Ogle. 1872.

————. *History of the Great Rebellion.* 6 Vols. Oxford, 1807.

————. *Life and Continuation.* 2 Vols. Oxford, 1857.

I. D. Phil-Iren-Alethius. *Velitationes Polemicae or Polemicall short Discussions of certain particular and select Questions.* 1651.

Isaacson, Henry, ed. *Institutiones Piae.* 1630.

Isherwood, Christopher. *The World in the Evening.* 1954.

Jackson, Thomas. *The Raging Tempest stilled.* 1623.

Jacobson, W. K. *Fragmentary Illustrations of the History of the Book of Common Prayer.* 1874.

James I, King. *The Book of Sports.* 1618. Reissued by Charles I in 1633.

Janson, H. W. *History of Art.* New York, 1962.

Jasper, Ronald C. D. *Prayer Book Revision in England, 1800-1900.* 1954.

Jeavons, Sidney. *The Church Plate of Nottinghamshire.* 1965.

Jenkins, David. *A Scourge for the Directorie and the Revolting Synod which hath sitten this 5 Yeares, more for foure shillings a Day then for Conscience sake.* 1647.

Jessop, Augustus. *One Generation of a Norfolk House.* 1879.

[Jolly, Thomas]. *The Note-Book of the Revd. Thomas Jolly, 1671-1693.* Manchester: Chetham Society, 1895.

Jones, Richard Foster. *The Seventeenth Century: Studies in the History of English Thought and Literature from Bacon to Pope.* Palo Alto, Calif., 1951.

BIBLIOGRAPHY

Jones, Ronald F. *Nonconformist Church Architecture.* 1914.
Jones, Rufus M. *Spiritual Reformers in the Sixteenth and Seventeenth Centuries.* 1914.
————. *Studies in Mystical Religion.* 1909.
Jordan, Wilbur K. *The Development of Religious Toleration in England.* 4 Vols. 1932-1940.
[Josselin, Ralph]. *The Diary of the Rev. Ralph Josselin, 1616-1683.* Ed. E. Hockcliffe. 3rd series, Vol. xv. Camden Society, 1908.
Julian, John. *A Dictionary of Hymnology.* 1925.

Kaufmann, E. *Architecture in the Age of Reason; Baroque and Post-Baroque in England, Italy, and France.* 1955.
Kaufmann, U. Milo. *The Pilgrim's Progress and Traditions in Puritan Meditation.* New Haven, Conn., 1966.
Keach, Benjamin. *The Breach Repair'd in God's Worship.* 1691.
————. *The Spiritual Melody containing near Three Hundred Sacred Hymns.* 1691.
————. *War with the Devil.* 1675.
Kellam, Laurence. *Manuell of Praiers.* Douai, 1624.
[Ken, Thomas]. *Prose Works.* Ed. J. T. Round. 1838.
Ken, Thomas. *A Sermon Preached at the King's Chapel at Whitehall in the year, 1685.*
King, Henry. *An Exposition upon the Lords Prayer.* 1628.
Kinloch, T. F. *The Life and Works of Joseph Hall.* 1951.
Knappen, M. M. *Tudor Puritanism; A Chapter in the History of Idealism.* Chicago, 1939.
————, ed. *Two Elizabethan Puritan Diaries by Richard Rogers and Samuel Ward.* 1930.
Knowles, David, O.S.B. *The English Mystical Tradition.* 1961.

Lancicius, Michael. *The glory of the B. father S. Ignatius of Loyola, founder of the Society of Jesus.* Ghent, 1628.
[Laud, William]. *The Works of the Most Reverend Father in God, William Laud, D.D., Sometime Lord Archbishop of Canterbury.* Eds. W. Scott and J. Bliss. 7 Vols. in 9. Oxford, 1847-1860.
Lees-Milne, James. *The Age of Inigo Jones.* 1953.
Legg, J. Wickham. *English Church Life from the Restoration to the Tractarian Movement considered in some of its neglected or forgotten features.* 1914.
————. *English Orders for Consecrating Churches in the Seventeenth Century.* Henry Bradshaw Society. Vol. xli. 1911.
Le Huray, Peter. *Music and the Reformation in England, 1549-1660.* 1967.
L'Estrange, Hamon. *The Alliance of Divine Offices exhibiting all the Liturgies of the Church of England since the Reformation.* 1659. Reprinted Library of Anglo-Catholic Theology. Oxford, 1846.
Ley, John. *A Patterne of Pietie, Or, the Religious life and death of that Grave and Gracious Matron, Mrs. Jane Ratcliffe, Widow and Citizen of Chester.* 1640.

Leys, M.D.R. *The Catholics in England: 1559-1829, a Social History.* 1961.

Lichtenstein, Aharon. *Henry More, the Rational Theology of a Cambridge Platonist.* Cambridge, Mass., 1962.

[Lightfoot, John]. *Works.* Ed. J. R. Pitman. 13 Vols. 1825. Vol. XIII contains "The Journal of the Proceedings of the Assembly of Divines" from January 1, 1643 to December 31, 1644.

Little, Bryan. *Catholic Churches since 1623.* 1966.

Loarte, Gaspar. *The Exercise of a Christian Life.* 1579.

———. *Instructions and Advertisements, How to meditate the Misteries of the Rosarie.* Ca. 1579.

Long, Kenneth. *The Music of the English Church.* 1971.

"Lovekin, Philonax" [pseudonym for J. Wilson]. *Andronicus.* 1646.

Lowe, Edward. *Short Directions for the Performance of Cathedrall Service.* 1661.

Lowrie, Walter. *Action in the Liturgy.* New York, 1953.

———. *Art in the Early Church.* New York, 1947.

Lumpkin, William L. *Baptist Confessions of Faith.* Philadelphia, 1959.

Macaulay, Thomas Babington. *A History of England.* 1848.

Maclean, Donald. *London at Worship.* Presbyterian Historical Society of England. Manchester, 1928.

Maclure, Millar. *The St. Paul's Cross Sermons, 1534-1642.* Toronto, 1958.

Mager, Alois. *Mystik als seelische Wirklichkeit.* Salzburg, 1945.

Mahood, M. M. *Poetry and Humanism.* 1950.

Manton, Thomas. *The Complete Works.* 12 Vols. 1870-1873.

Marchant, Ronald A. *The Puritans and the Church Courts in the Diocese of York, 1560-1642.* 1960.

Marlow, Isaac. *Prelimiting Forms of praising God, Vocally Sung by all the Church together, Proved to be no Gospel-Ordinance.* 1691.

Martin, Hugh. *Puritanism and Richard Baxter.* 1954.

Martz, Louis L. *The Poetry of Meditation.* New Haven, Conn., 1954.

Marvell, Andrew. *The Poems and Letters of Andrew Marvell.* Ed. H. M. Margoliouth. 2 Vols. Oxford, 1927.

Mascall, E. L. *Corpus Christi, Essays on the Church and the Eucharist.* 1953.

———. *Toward A Church Architecture.* 1962.

Mather, Cotton. *Magnalia Christi Americana.* 1702.

Matthews, A. G. *Calamy Revised.* 1934.

———. *Mr. Pepys and Nonconformity.* 1954.

———, ed. *The Savoy Declaration of Faith and Order, 1658.* 1959.

———. *Walker Revised.* 1948.

Maxwell, William D. *A History of Worship in the Church of Scotland.* 1955.

———. *John Knox's Genevan Service Book.* Edinburgh, 1931. 2nd edn., 1965.

Maycock, A. L. *Nicholas Ferrar of Little Gidding.* 1938.

Mayor, Stephen. *The Lord's Supper in Early English Dissent.* 1972.

BIBLIOGRAPHY

McAdoo, H. R. *The Spirit of Anglicanism*. 1965.
McLachlan, H. J. *Socinianism in XVII Century England*. 1951.
McMillan, William. *The Worship of the Scottish Reformed Church, 1550-1638*. 1931.
Mede, Joseph. *Churches, that is, appropriate Places for Christian Worship both in and ever since the Apostles Times*. 1638.
Mercer, Eric. *English Art, 1553-1625*. Oxford, 1962.
Meres, Francis. *The Sinners Guide*. 1598.
Micklem, Nathaniel, ed. *Christian Worship*. Oxford, 1936.
Miller, Perry. *Errand into the Wilderness*. Cambridge, Mass., 1956.
————. *The New England Mind: From Colony to Province*. Boston, 1960.
————. *The New England Mind: The Seventeenth Century*. Boston, 1961.
————. *Orthodoxy in Massachusetts, 1630-1650*. Boston, 1959.
———— and T. H. Johnson. *The Puritans*. New York, 1938.
Milton, John. *Prose Works*. Yale edn. New Haven, Conn., 1953.
————. *Works*. Columbia edn. 13 Vols. New York, 1931-1938.
Mitchell, A. F. and John Struthers, eds. *Minutes of the Westminster Assembly of Divines . . . Nov. 1644 to March 1649*. Edinburgh and London, 1874.
Mitchell, W. Fraser. *English Pulpit Oratory from Andrewes to Tillotson*. 1932.
Montagu, Henry. *Appello Caesarem*. 1625.
[More, Gertrude]. *Augustine Baker's The Inner Life of Dame Gertrude More*. Ed. Benedict Weld-Blundell. 1911.
————. *The Holy Practises of a Divine Lover*. Paris, 1657.
More, Henry. *Philosophical Poems*. Ed. G. Bullough. Manchester, 1931.
More, P. E. and F. L. Cross, eds. *Anglicanism, the Thought and Practice of the Church of England*. 1935. 2nd edn., 1957.
Morgan, Edmund S. *Visible Saints, the History of a Puritan Idea*. New York, 1963.
Morgan, Irvonwy. *The Nonconformity of Richard Baxter*. 1946.
Morris, John. *The troubles of our Catholic forefathers*. 3 Vols. 1872-1877.
Morton, A. L. *The World of the Ranters*. 1970.
Mueller, William R. *John Donne: Preacher*. Princeton, N.J., 1962.

Neal, Daniel. *The History of the Puritans*. 5 Vols. 1822.
Nelson, R. *Life of Dr. George Bull*. 1713.
New, John F. H. *Anglican and Puritan, The Bases of Their Opposition, 1558-1640*. Palo Alto, Calif., 1964.
Newcome, Henry. *The Autobiography of Henry Newcome*. 2 Vols. Chetham Society, 1852.
————. *The Diary of the Revd. Henry Newcome*. Chetham Society, 1849.
Newton, Eric and William Neill. *2000 Years of Christian Art*. 1966.

Nichols, J. H. *Corporate Worship in the Reformed Church*. Philadelphia, 1968.

──────. *A History of Christianity, 1650-1950*. New York, 1956.

Nicholson, William. *Plain but Full Exposition of the Church of England*. 1654.

──────. *Works*. 2nd edn., reprint in Library of Anglo-Catholic Theology. Oxford, 1844.

Northbrooke, John. *A Treatise Wherein Dicing, Dauncing, etc. Are Reproved*. 1577. Reprinted by the Shakespeare Society, ed. Collier, 1843.

Notestein, Wallace. *English Folk; a Book of Characters*. New York, 1938.

Nuttall, G. F. *The Holy Spirit in Puritan Faith and Experience*. Oxford, 1946.

──────. *Richard Baxter*. 1965.

──────. *Visible Saints; the Congregational Way, 1640-1660*. Oxford, 1957.

──────. *The Welsh Saints, 1640-1660*. Cardiff, 1957.

────── and Owen Chadwick, eds. *From Uniformity to Unity, 1662-1962*. 1962.

Nye, Philip. *Beams of Former Light; Discovering how Evil it is to impose Doubtful and Disputable Forms or Practices upon Ministers*. 1660.

Oechslin, Louis, O.P. *L'Intuition mystique de sainte Thérèse*. Paris, 1946.

Ogg, David. *England in the Reign of Charles II*. 2 Vols. Oxford, 1955.

Oman, Charles. *English Church Plate, 1597-1830*. 1957.

Orme, William. *Life and Times of Richard Baxter, with a Critical Examination of his Writings*. 1830.

──────. *Memoirs of the Life, Writings and Religious Connexions of John Owen, D.D.* 1820.

Osmond, Percy. *A Life of John Cosin*. 1913.

Overton, J. H. *Life in the English Church (1660-1714)*. 1885.

──────. *The Non-jurors, their Lives, Principles and Writings*. 1902.

Owen, John. *A Brief Instruction in Worship*. 1667.

──────. *A Discourse concerning Liturgies and their Imposition*. 1662.

──────. *A Discourse of The Holy Spirit in Prayer*. 1662.

──────. *Eschol, or Rules of Direction*. 1648.

──────. *An Inquiry into the Origin, Order, and Communion of Evangelical Churches*. 1681.

──────. *Works*. Ed. W. H. Goold. 16 Vols. Edinburgh, 1850-1853.

Packer, John William. *The Transformation of Anglicanism 1643-1660, with special reference to Henry Hammond*. Manchester, 1969.

Page, William. *A Treatise of Justification of Bowing at the Name of Jesus*. 1631.

Palmer, William. *Origines Liturgicae*. 1832.

BIBLIOGRAPHY

Parker, J. *An Introduction to the History of the Successive Revisions of the Book of Common Prayer.* Oxford, 1879.
Passmore, J. A. *Ralph Cudworth.* Cambridge, 1951.
Patrick, Simon. *A brief account of the New Sect of Latitude Men.* 1662.
————. *A Continuation of the Friendly Debate.* 1669.
————. *A Friendly Debate between a Conformist and a Non-Conformist.* 1668.
Paul, Robert S., ed. *An Apologeticall Narration.* Boston and Philadelphia, 1963.
————. *The Lord Protector, Religion and Politics in the Life of Oliver Cromwell.* 1955.
Pearsall, J. S. *The Rise of Congregationalism at Andover.* 1844.
Peaston, A. Elliott. *The Prayer Book Tradition in the Free Churches.* 1964.
Peers, E. Allison. *Studies of the Spanish Mystics.* 2 Vols. 1927-1930.
[Penn, William]. *The Witness of William Penn.* Eds. F. B. Tolles and E. G. Alderfer. New York, 1957.
[Pennington, Isaac]. *The Hidden Life; A Series of Extracts from the Writings of Isaac Pennington.* Ed. Robert Davis. 1951.
————. *Works.* 4 Vols. 3rd edn., 1784.
Percival, A. P., ed. *The Original Services for the State Holidays.* 1838.
Perkins, Jocelyn. *Westminster Abbey: Its Worship and Ornaments.* 1952.
Perkins, William. *Arte of Prophesying.* Cambridge, 1607.
————. *A Reformed Catholike.* 1603.
————. *A Treatise of Mans Imaginations.* Cambridge, 1607.
————. *Works.* Edn. of 1631.
Persons, Robert, S.J. *The First Booke of the Christian Exercise appertayning to resolution.* 1592.
Peter, Saint, of Alcantara. *Golden Treatise of Mental Prayer.* A translation, Brussels, 1632.
————. *Treatise on Prayer and Meditation.* Ca. 1558.
[Peters, Hugh]. *Tales and Jests of Mr. Hugh Peters.* 1807.
Pettit, Norman. *The Heart Prepared: Grace and Conversion in Puritan Spiritual Life.* New Haven, Conn., 1966.
Phillips, C. S. *Hymnody Past and Present.* 1937.
Phillips, John. *The Reformation of Images . . . 1535-1660.* Berkeley, Calif., 1973.
Picart, Bernard. *Cérémonies et Coutumes Religieuses de tous les Peuples du Monde.* 4 Vols. Amsterdam, 1736.
Pinto, V. da Sola. *Peter Sterry Platonist and Puritan.* Cambridge, 1934.
Playfere, Thomas. *The Whole Sermons of that Eloquent Divine of Famous Memory: Thomas Playfere, Doctor of Divinitie.* 1623.
Playford, Henry. *Harmonia Sacra.* 1688.
Playford, John. *English Dancing Master.* 1650.
Pocklington, John. *Altare Christianum or the Dead Vicars Plea.* 1637.
Pope, Alexander. *An Essay on Man.* 1733-1734.
————. *Works.* Ed. W. Elwin and W. J. Courthope. 1871-1889.

BIBLIOGRAPHY

Potter, G. R. and E. M. Simpson, eds. *The Sermons of John Donne.* 10 Vols. Berkeley and Los Angeles, Calif., 1953-1962.

Pourrat, Pierre. *Christian Spirituality.* Tr. W. H. Mitchell and S. P. Jacques. 3 Vols. Paris, 1922-1927.

Powell, Vavasor. *The Bird and the Cage.* 2nd edn., 1662.

———. *Common Prayer Book no Divine Service.* 1660.

Powicke, F. J. *The Cambridge Platonists.* 1926.

———. *The life of the Reverend Richard Baxter.* 2 Vols. 1924.

Preston, John. *The Cuppe of Blessing.* 3 sermons. 1633.

———. *Five Sermons on the Divine Love.* 1640.

———. *The Golden Sceptre held forth to the Humble, with the Churches Dignitie by her Marriage, and the Churches Dutie in her Carriage.* 1638.

———. *A Heavenly Treatise of the Divine Love of Christ.* 1640.

———. *The Soliloquy of a Devout Soul to Christ, Panting after the Love of the Lord Jesus.* 1640.

Prideaux, John. *A Sermon preached on the 5 Oct. 1624 on the Consecration of St. James Chappell at Exceter Colledge.* 1624.

Prothero, R. E. [Lord Ernle]. *The Psalms in Human Life.* 1903.

Prynne, William. *A Brief Survay and Censure of Mr. Cozens His Couzening Devotions. . . . 1628.*

———. *Canterburies Doome.* 1646.

[Quakers, The]. *The First Publishers of Truth.* Ed. N. Penney. 1907.

———. [*To the?*] *King and both Houses of Parliament, Being a Declaration of the present Suffering and imprisonment of above 600 of the people of God in scorn called Quakers, who now suffer in England for Conscience Sake.* 1664.

Ramsey, Arthur Michael. *Durham Essays and Addresses.* 1956.

Ramsey, Mary P. *Les Doctrines Mediévales chez Donne. . . .* Oxford, 1917.

Rapin. *Reflexions sur l'Eloquence de la Chaire.* Paris, 1672.

Ratcliff, E. C. *The Booke of Common Prayer of the Churche of England: its Making and Revisions, 1549-1661.* Alcuin Club Collections. 1949.

Ravenscroft, Thomas. *Whole Book of Psalmes.* 1621.

Reynolds, Edward. *Meditations on the Holy Sacrament of the Lord's Last Supper.* 1638.

Rice, H.A.L. *Thomas Ken: Bishop and Non-Juror.* 1965.

Richards, Michael. *The Liturgy in England.* 1966.

Richardson, Caroline F. *English Preachers and Preaching, 1640-1670.* New York, 1928.

Risbrooke, W. Jardine. *Anglican Liturgies of the Seventeenth and Eighteenth Centuries.* Alcuin Club. 1958.

Robarts, Foulke. *Gods Holy House and Service according to the primitive and most Christian forme thereof.* 1639.

[Robinson, John]. *The Works of John Robinson.* Ed. J. Ashton. 3 Vols. 1852.

Rogers, Richard. *Seven Treatises . . . leading and guiding to true happiness both in this life and in the life to come.* 1603.

Rollins, Hyder E., ed. *Cavalier and Puritan.* New York, 1923.

Rous, Francis. *The Mysticall Marriage.* 1635.

Routley, Erik R. *Hymns and Human Life.* 1952.

————. *The Music of Christian Hymnody.* 1957.

[Royal Commission on Historical Monuments Report]. *City of Oxford.* 1939.

Rugoff, Milton Allan. *Donne's Imagery: A Study in Creative Sources.* New York, 1939.

Russell, Elbert. *The History of Quakerism.* New York, 1942.

Sales, St. Francis de. *An Introduction to the Devout Life. . . .* Tr. T. Y. [Yakesley]. 3rd edn. [Rouen], 1614.

————. *Delicious Entertainments of the Soule. . . .* Douai, 1632.

————. *Of the Love of God.* Tr. Thomas Carre. 1630.

Sanderson, Robert. *The Case of the Liturgy Stated in the Late Times.* Ca. 1652.

————. *A Sovereign Antidote against Sabbatarian Errors.* 1636.

————. *Works.* Ed. W. Jacobson. 6 Vols. Oxford, 1859.

Sandys, Edwin. *Europae Speculum.* 1673.

Schaff, Philip. *The Creeds of the Evangelical Protestant Churches.* New York, 1877.

Schenk, W. *The Concern for Social Justice in the Puritan Revolution.* 1948.

Schmidt, Hermanus A. P. *Introductio in Liturgiam Occidentalem.* Rome, Freiburg, Barcelona, 1960.

Schmidt-Klausing, F. *Zwingli als Liturgiker.* Göttingen, 1952.

Schnorrenburg, John M. "Anglican Architecture, 1558-1662: Its Theological Implications and Its Relation to the Continental Background." Ph.D., Princeton University, 1964.

Scholes, Percy A. *The Oxford Companion to Music.* 3rd edn., 1941.

————. *The Puritans and Music.* 1934. Reissued 1970.

Seaver, Paul S. *The Puritan Lectureships: the Politics of Religious Dissent, 1560-1662.* Palo Alto, Calif., 1970.

Sedding, J. D. *Art and Handicraft.* 1893.

Sekler, E. F. *Wren and his Place in European Architecture.* 1956.

Sewel, William. *History of the Rise, Increase, and Progress of the Christian People called Quakers.* 1722.

Sharrock, Roger. *John Bunyan.* 1954.

Shaw, William A. *A History of the English Church during the Civil Wars and under the Commonwealth, 1640-1660.* 2 Vols. 1900.

Shepherd, Massey H., Jr. *The Oxford American Prayer Book Commentary.* New York, 1950.

Simpson, Alan. *Puritanism in Old and New England.* Chicago, 1955.

Skipton, H.P.K. *The Life and Times of Nicholas Ferrar.* 1907.

Slatyer, William. *Psalmes or Songs of Sion turned into the language and set to the tunes of a strange land.* 1635.

Smith, Henry. *Sermons and other Treatises.* 1675.

BIBLIOGRAPHY

Smith, John. *Select Discourses*. Ed. John Worthington. 1660.
Smith, J. W. Ashley. *The Birth of Modern Education: the Contribution of the Dissenting Academies, 1660-1800*. 1954.
Smith, Thomas. *A Sermon about Frequent Communion, Preached before the University of Oxford, August the 17th, 1679*. 1685.
Smyth, Charles. *The Art of Preaching*. . . . 1952.
Smyth, John. *The Differences of the Churches of the Separation*. 1605.
————. *Works*. Ed. W. T. Whitley. 2 Vols. Cambridge, 1915.
South, Robert. *False Foundations removed*. 1661.
————. *The Scribe instructed to the Kingdom of Heaven*. 1660.
————. *Works*. 7 Vols. Oxford, 1823.
Southey, Robert. *The Life of Wesley and the Rise and Progress of Methodism*. 1846.
Sparke, Michael. *The Crums of Comfort to Groans of the Spirit*. 1652.
Sparrow, A. *Rationale or Practical Exposition of the Book of Common Prayer*. 1657. Reissued by J. H. Newman. Oxford, 1839.
Sprat, Thomas. *The History of the Royal-Society of London, For the Improving of Natural Knowledge*. 1667.
Sprott, G. W. and J. Leishman, eds. *The Book of Common Order*. Edinburgh, 1868.
Staley, Vernon. *Hierurgia Anglicana, Documents and Extracts Illustrative of the Ceremonies of the Anglican Church after the Reformation*. 3 Vols. New edn., 1903.
Stearns, Raymond P. *Congregationalism in the Dutch Netherlands*. Chicago, 1940.
Steere, Douglas V. *The Hardest Journey*. Whittier College Bulletin, Whittier, Calif., 1968.
————. *On Being Present Where You Are*. Pendle Hill Pamphlet. No. 151. Pendle Hill, Pa., 1967.
Stephens, Edward. *The Liturgy of the Ancients Represented, As near as well may be, In English Forms*. . . . 1696.
Stephens, W.R.W. and W. Hunt. *History of the English Church*. 9 Vols. 1901-1910.
Sterry, Peter. *The Rise, Race, and Royalty of the Kingdom of God in the Soul of Man*. 1683.
Stillingfleet, Edward. *Origines Sacrae*. 1662.
————. *The Unreasonableness of Separation*. 1680.
Stinton, George. *A Sermon . . . in the time of Pestilence . . . Nov. 27, 1636*. 1637.
Stock, Richard. *The Church's Lamentation for the Loss of the Godly*. 1614.
Stone, Darwell. *History of the Doctrine of the Holy Eucharist*. 2 Vols. 1909.
Stone, Lawrence. *The Causes of the English Revolution, 1529-1642*. London and New York, 1972.
————. *The Crisis of the Aristocracy, 1558-1641*. Oxford, 1965.
Stonor, R. J. *Stonor: a Catholic Sanctuary in the Chilterns*. Newport, Monmouthshire. 2nd edn., 1952.
Stoughton, John. *History of Religion in England*. 5 Vols. 1867-1874.

BIBLIOGRAPHY

———. *Religion in England from 1800 to 1850.* 2 Vols. 1884.
Stranks, C. J. *Anglican Devotion.* 1961.
———. *The Life and Writings of Jeremy Taylor.* 1952.
Streatfield, Frank. *The State Prayers and Other Variations in the Book of Common Prayer.* 1950.
Summers, Joseph H. *George Herbert: His Religion and Art.* 1954.
Summerson, John. *Architecture in Britain, 1530 to 1830.* Harmondsworth and Baltimore, 1954.
Sutherland, James. *English Literature of the Late Seventeenth Century.* Oxford History of English Literature, Vol. V. Oxford, 1969.
Sykes, Norman. *Church and State in England in the XVIII Century.* Cambridge, 1934.
———. *The Church of England and Non-Episcopal Churches in the Sixteenth & Seventeenth Centuries.* 1948.
———. *Old Priest and New Presbyter.* 1956.

Talbot, Peter. *A Treatise of the Nature of Catholick Faith and Heresie.* Rouen, 1657.
Talon, Henri. *John Bunyan: The Man and his Work.* (English trans. of *John Bunyan, l'Homme et l'Oeuvre,* by Barbara Wall, 1951.)
Tate and Brady. *A New Version of the Psalms of David, Fitted to the Tunes used in Churches.* 1696.
Tatham, G. B. *The Puritans in Power, The English Church from 1640 to 1660.* Cambridge, 1913.
Taylor, Jeremy. *An Apology for Authorised and Set Forms of Liturgies against the Presence of the Spirit. 1. For ex Tempore Prayer, 2. Formes of Private Composition.* 1649.
———. *A Collection of Offices, or Forms of Prayer in Cases Ordinary and Extraordinary; Taken out of the Scriptures and the ancient Liturgies of Several Churches, especially the Greek, Together with A Large Preface in Vindication of the Liturgy of the Church of England.* 1658.
———. *Eniautos, or A Course of Sermons for all the Sundays of the Year, fitted to the great necessities and for Supplying the wants of preaching in many parts of this nation.* 1651.
———. *The Liberty of Prophesying.* 1647.
———. *The Rule and Exercises of Holy Living.* Ed. A. R. Waller. 1901.
———. *XXVII Sermons.* 1651.
———. *The Whole Works of The Right Rev. Jeremy Taylor, D.D., Lord Bishop of Down, Connor and Dromore.* Ed. Reginald Heber, revised by Charles Page. 10 Vols. 1847-1852.
Taylor, John. *A Swarme of Sectaries.* 1641.
Taylor, John, ed. *The Revised Liturgy of 1689.* Dublin, 1855.
Tenison, Thomas. *A Discourse of Idolatry.* 1678.
Teresa, Saint, of Avila. *The lyf of the Mother Teresa of Jesus foundresse of the Monasteries of descalced or bare-footed Carmelite nunnes and fryers.* Tr. "W.M. of the Society of Jesus." Antwerp, 1611.
Terry, Richard R. *Calvin's First Psalter* [1539]. Facsimile edn., 1932.

563

BIBLIOGRAPHY

Thompson, Bard, ed. *Liturgies of the Western Church.* Cleveland and New York, 1961.

Thorndike, Herbert. *The Due Way of Composing Differences.* 1660.

————. *of Religious Assemblies and the Publick Service of God: A Discourse according to Apostolic Rule and Practice.* Cambridge, 1642.

————. *Works.* Ed. A. W. Haddan in Library of Anglo-Catholic Theology. 6 Vols. bound in 9. Oxford, 1844-1854.

[Tillotson, John]. *The Golden Book of Tillotson.* Ed. James Moffatt. 1926.

————. *Sermons.* Ed. R. Barker. 14 Vols. 1695-1704.

————. *Works.* Ed. T. Birch. 10 Vols. 1820.

Tindall, William York. *John Bunyan Mechanick Preacher.* New York, 1934.

Todd, H. J. *Bishop Gauden, Author of εἰκὼν βασιλική.* 1829.

Traherne, Philip. *The Soul's Communion with her Saviour.* 1685.

Traherne, Thomas. *Centuries of Meditations.* 1653.

Trevelyan, G. M. *England under the Stuarts.* 1933.

Trevor-Roper, Hugh R. *Archbishop Laud, 1573-1645.* 2nd edn., 1962.

Tulloch, John. *Rational Theology and Christian Philosophy in England in the Seventeenth Century.* 2 Vols. 1872.

Turner, G. Lyon. *Original Records of Early Nonconformity.* 3 Vols. 1911-1914.

Underhill, E. B., ed. *Broadmead Records.* 1847.

————, ed. *Fenstanton, Warboys and Hexham Records.* 1847.

Underwood, A. C. *A History of the English Baptists.* 1947.

Usher, Roland G. *The Reconstruction of the English Church.* 2 Vols. New York, 1910.

Ussher, James. *The Reduction of Episcopacy unto the form of Synodical Government received in the Ancient Church.* 1656.

————. *Works.* Eds. C. R. Elrington and J. H. Todd. 17 Vols. Dublin and London, 1847-1864.

Vann, Richard T. *The Social Development of English Quakerism, 1655-1755.* Cambridge, Mass., 1969.

Victoria County History of Somerset. Vol. 8. 1968.

Villacastin, Tomás. *A Manuall of devout Meditations and Exercises, instructing how to pray mentally.* Tr. H. More. St. Omer, 1618.

Wace, Henry. *The Classic Preachers of the Church.* 1877.

Wakefield, Gordon S. *Puritan Devotion, its place in the development of Christian Piety.* 1958.

Walker, Williston. *The Creeds and Platforms of Congregationalism.* New York, 1893.

Wallace, Ronald S. *Calvin's Doctrine of the Word and Sacraments.* Edinburgh, 1953.

Walton, Isaak. *The Lives of John Donne, Sir Henry Wotton, Richard Hooker, George Herbert and Robert Sanderson.* World's Classics edn., 1927.

Walzer, Michael L. *The Revolution of the Saints: A Study in the Origin of Radical Politics.* Cambridge, Mass., 1965.

Wand, J.W.C. *The High Church Schism.* 1951.

Warner, John. *A brief discourse of right worship.* 1684.

Warwickshire Parish Registers. 1904.

Waterhouse, Ellis. *Painting in Britain, 1530-1790.* Harmondsworth and Baltimore, 1953.

Waterland, D. *Works.* Ed. W. Van Mildert. 6 Vols. 2nd edn., Oxford, 1843.

Watkin, E. I. *Poets and Mystics.* 1953.

Watkins, Owen C. *The Puritan Experience; Studies in Spiritual Autobiography.* New York, 1972.

Watts, Isaac. *Guide to Prayer.* 1716.

————. *The Psalms of David imitated in the language of the New Testament and applied to the Christian State and Worship.* 1719.

————. *Works.* Ed. G. Burder. 6 Vols. 1810-1811.

Weber, Max. *The Protestant Ethic and the Spirit of Capitalism.* Tr. Talcott Parsons. 1930.

Wedgwood, C. Y. *The King's Peace, 1637-1641.* 1955.

Welsby, Paul A. *George Abbot: The Unwanted Archbishop.* 1962.

————. *Lancelot Andrewes, 1555-1626.* 1958.

[Wesley, John]. *The Journal of John Wesley.* Ed. Nehemiah Curnock. 8 Vols. 1909.

West, F. W. *Rude Forefathers.* 1949.

Whiffen, Marcus. *Stuart and Georgian Churches.* 1947.

Whinney, Margaret. *Christopher Wren.* 1971.

———— and Oliver Millar. *English Art, 1625-1714.* 1957.

Whitaker, Wilfrid Barnett. *Sunday in Tudor and Stuart Times.* 1933.

White, Helen. *English Devotional Literature, 1600-1640.* Madison, Wisc., 1931.

White, James F. *The Cambridge Movement: The Ecclesiologists and the Gothic Revival.* Cambridge, 1962.

White, John. *The First Century of Scandalous, Malignant Priests.* 1643.

Whitelock, Bulstrode. *Memorials of the English Affairs; or An Historical Account of what passed from the Beginning of The Reign of King Charles the First, to King Charles the Second His Happy Restauration.* Edn. of 1682.

Whiting, C. E. *Studies in English Puritanism from the Restoration to the Revolution, 1660-88.* Cambridge, 1931.

Whitley, W. T. *A History of the British Baptists.* 1923.

————, ed. *Minutes of the General Assembly of the General Baptists, 1654-1728.* 1909.

[Whittingham, William]. *The Forme of Prayers ... used in the English Congregation at Geneva; and approved by the famous and godly learned man, John Calvyn.* 1556.

Whyte, Alexander. *The Spiritual Life; The Teaching of Thomas Goodwin as received and reissued.* Edinburgh, 1917.

[Whytford, Richard]. *Certaine devout and Godly Petitions, commonly called Iesus Psalter.* 1575.

Wigan, B. J., ed. *The Liturgy in English.* 2nd edn., 1964.

Wilkins, John. *Discourse concerning the Gift of Prayer.* 1649.

――――. *Ecclesiastes; or a Discourse concerning the Gift of Preaching.* 1646.

――――. *On the Principles and Duties of Natural Religion.* Edn. of 1675.

――――. *Sermons.* 1682.

Willey, Basil. *The Seventeenth Century Background.* 1934.

Williams, Peter. *The European Organ, 1450-1850.* 1966.

Wilson, John. *Cultus Evangelicus, Or, a brief Discourse concerning the Spirituality and Simplicity of New Testament Worship.* 1667.

Wilson, John F. *Pulpit in Parliament.* Princeton, N.J., 1969.

Winward, Stephen. *The Reformation of our Worship.* 1964.

Wither, George. *Hymns and Songs of the Church.* 1623.

Wittkower, Rudolph. *Gian Lorenzo Bernini, Roman Baroque Sculptor.* 2nd edn., 1966.

[Wood, Anthony A.]. *The Life and Times of Anthony à Wood.* Abridged from A. Clark's edn. by L. Powys, 1961.

Wood, Thomas. *English Casuistical Divinity during the Seventeenth Century.* 1952.

――――, ed. *Five Pastorals: Selections from the Caroline Divines.* 1961.

Woodfill, Walter. *Musicians in English Society from Elizabeth to Charles I.* Princeton, N.J., 1953.

Woodforde, Christopher. *English Stained and Painted Glass.* Oxford, 1954.

Woodhead, Abraham. *Two Discourses concerning the Adoration of our B. Saviour in the H. Eucharist.* Oxford, 1687.

Woodhouse, A.S.P. *Puritanism and Liberty.* 1938.

Wordsworth, Christopher. *Ecclesiastical Biography.* 6 Vols. 2nd edn., 1818.

――――. *Who wrote* ΕΙΚΩΝ ΒΑΣΙΛΙΚΗ? 1824.

Wormald, B.H.G. *Clarendon.* Cambridge, 1951.

Worthington, Thomas. *The Rosarie of our Ladie.* Antwerp, 1600.

Wren, Stephen. *Parentalia, or Memoirs of the Family of the Wrens.* 1750.

Wright, Abraham. *Five Several Sermons in Five several Styles or Waies of Preaching.* 1656.

Yarwood, Doreen. *The Architecture of England.* 1963.

Yule, George. *The Independents in the Civil War.* Cambridge, 1958.

Zimmerman, Franklin B. *Henry Purcell, 1659-1695: His Life and Times.* 1967.

INDEX

I. Index of Persons

II. Index of Places (and Churches)

III. Index of Topics

577

II. INDEX OF PLACES (AND CHURCHES)

(Churches are assumed to be Anglican unless otherwise identified.)

INDEX

Lent, 144, 221, 224, 226, 229, 346, 370, 387, 390
Lessons, see Epistles and Gospels
Levellers, the, 239, 490f
Libation, 376, 416, 431
"Lining out," 279, 456
Litany, Anglican, 117, 203, 205, 258, 261, 263, 335f, 346, 372, 381n, 388, 396, 402, 424, 428f
of the Blessed Virgin, 466, 469
Liturgical colours, 287
Liturgies, Ancient, xvii, 94, 97, 346, 360f, 364n, 367, 393f, 403f, 422f
Liturgy, Anglican, see Book of Common Prayer
Liturgy of the Ancients, 393-397
Lord's Day, see also Sabbath, 96, 171, 208, 221, 241f, 284, 322, 344, 366, 370f, 417, 420, 423, 530
Lord's Prayer, 6n, 94, 190, 233, 262, 303f, 341, 345f, 348, 390, 396, 402, 413, 422, 424, 426, 428f, 436, 450, 457, 491
Lord's Supper, the
Baptist celebrations of, 499, 509
Baptist doctrine of, 508f
Calvinist and Puritan doctrines of, 286, 297, 300, 309-323, 530f
Independent celebrations of, 283, 314, 318, 322f, 391, 406, 413-417, 530f
Presbyterian celebrations of, 322, 406
Zwinglian doctrine of, xxi, 290, 296, 300, 307, 310, 323, 342n, (see also Memorialism)
Love feasts, 491, 504, 520
Lunette window, 34
Lutes, 256
Lutheranism and Lutherans, 292, 310f, 315, 480, 524
Lyrical element in worship, 524

Magi, the, 56n
Magnificat, the, 261, 401, 429
Manual of worship, 524
Mariolatry, 58
Mark, Liturgy of St., 364n
Marriages, 125, 210, 313, 334, 359, 371, 382, 417f, 428, 477f, 504f, 521
Martyrs, 219, 224, 225n, 232, 286, 330, 363, 383, 460, 474f
Martyrologies, 66, 128f, 159, 246, 269, 338, 347, 492
Mass, the, 460, 462, 465f, 470f, 472
as a dramatic miracle, 462, 482f
as a mystery, 485
as a sacrifice, 98, 291, 480f, 484f, 526f
criticized by Anglicans, 291f, 315

criticized by the Reformers, 289f, 310f
Expositions of its meaning, 288-291, 480-485, 526f
High, 466-468
Low, 468-473
private, 291
Requiem, 479
Matrimony, Holy, see Marriage
Mattins (Morning Prayer), 138, 222, 231, 234, 261, 274n, 335f, 340, 345, 357, 381, 384, 388, 469
Maundy Thursday, 387
Maypoles and May Day, xx, 217, 229, 241, 243, 245
Meeting-houses, xix, xxii, 7, 10f, 25, 32, 60-67, 287, 446f, 455f, 492, 495, 514, 531
Memorialism, doctrine of, 286, 296, 480, 503
Mennonites, 11n, 61, 497f, 499f, 502
their Communion Service, 502f
Mercy
corporal works of, 95
spiritual works of, 95
Messengers, 62, 505
Methodism, 369n, 406, 426, 439f, 491, 517, 524, 526
Midnight Mass, 387
Ministers, 66, 170, 192, 288, 318, 347, 365-373, 401, 409, 457, 490, 495
deprived, 434f
Missal, the, 98, 290, 346, 463, 469, 480n
Mitre, 470
Monasteries, 462f, 474f, 487, 494, 525
Monstrances, 460, 467, 486
Morris dances, xx
Morning Prayer, see Mattins
Mosaics, 259
Moslems, 201
Motets, 255, 259, 267
Muggletonians, 324, 490
Music, religious or sacred, VII, 18, 23, 333, 528
Mysticism, 129f, 265, 329, 460, 463, 486, 531

Nave, 8, 9n, 26, 43, 50, 51, 59
Nonconformist Conscience, 453f
Nonconformity, 8, 20, 28, 60, 62, 132, 202, 250, 254, 382, 393, 399, 437-444
reasons for, 430f
stratagems of, 436, 444-449
worship of, XII, xxi
Non-Jurors, the, 8, 283, 299, 306, 337, 393f, 399f, 403
Numinosity in architecture, 4, 11-22, 29

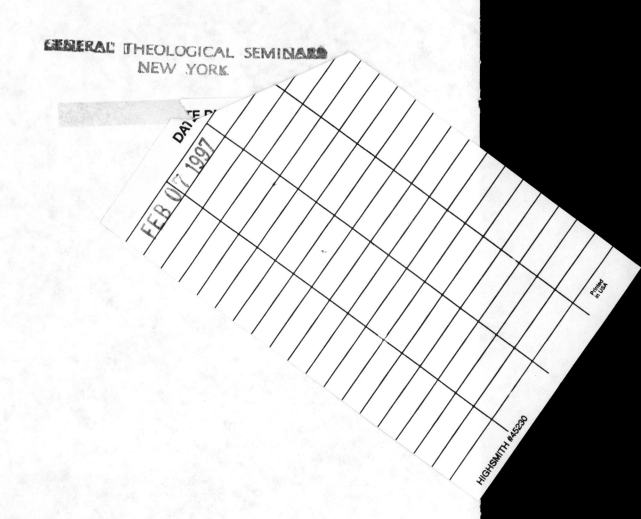